KW-054-010

THE BRITISH YEAR BOOK OF INTERNATIONAL LAW

341 BR I

UNIVERSITY OF WOLVERHAMPTON
NOT FOR LOAN

WITHDRAWN

Keep for Historical
Purposes
JB 16.1.16

WP 1146085 7

THE
BRITISH YEAR BOOK OF INTERNATIONAL LAW
1991

SIXTY-SECOND YEAR OF ISSUE

WITHDRAWN
UNIVERSITY OF WOLVERHAMPTON LIBRARY
Acc No. 146085
CLASS 341 BRI
CONTROL
DATE 26.11.92
SITE AL

OXFORD
AT THE CLARENDON PRESS
1992

Oxford University Press, Walton Street, Oxford OX2 6DP

Oxford New York Toronto
Delhi Bombay Calcutta Madras Karachi
Kuala Lumpur Singapore Hong Kong Tokyo
Nairobi Dar es Salaam Cape Town
Melbourne Auckland Madrid

and associated companies in
Berlin Ibadan

Oxford is a trade mark of Oxford University Press

© *Unless otherwise stated, Oxford University Press 1992*

All rights reserved. No part of this publication may be reproduced, stored in a retrieval system, or transmitted, in any form or by any means, electronic, mechanical, photocopying, recording, or otherwise, without the prior permission of Oxford University Press

The British Year Book of International Law is an annual publication, starting with Volume 52 (1981). Orders for subscriptions or for individual volumes can be placed through a bookseller or subscription agent. In case of difficulty please write to the Retail Services Dept., Oxford University Press Distribution Services, Saxon Way West, Corby, Northants NN18 9ES, UK

British Library Cataloguing in Publication Data

The British year book of international law.
1991; sixty-second year of international law
1. International law—Periodicals
341'.05 JX1
ISBN 0-19-825445-8

Computerset by
Promenade Graphics Ltd., Cheltenham, Glos.

Printed in Great Britain
on acid-free paper
by Biddles Ltd.
Guildford and King's Lynn

Editors
PROFESSOR IAN BROWNLIE
PROFESSOR D. W. BOWETT
Assistant Editor: MRS C. A. HOPKINS
Book Review Editor: PROFESSOR J. G. MERRILLS

Editorial Committee
JUDGE SIR ROBERT JENNINGS (Chairman)
SIR MAURICE BATHURST
P. B. CARTER
J. G. COLLIER
LAWRENCE COLLINS
PROFESSOR JAMES CRAWFORD
SIR VINCENT EVANS
LADY FOX
CHRISTOPHER GREENWOOD
PROFESSOR D. J. HARRIS
PROFESSOR ROSALYN HIGGINS
E. LAUTERPACHT
PROFESSOR I. C. MACGIBBON
DR P. M. NORTH
PROFESSOR MALCOLM SHAW
PROFESSOR K. R. SIMMONDS
SIR IAN SINCLAIR
HUGH THIRLWAY
SIR FRANCIS VALLAT
SIR ARTHUR WATTS
PROFESSOR GILLIAN WHITE
LORD WILBERFORCE
DR DERRICK WYATT

Editorial Communications should be addressed as follows:

Articles and Notes:
PROFESSOR IAN BROWNLIE
All Souls College, Oxford, OX1 4AL.

Books for Review:
PROFESSOR J. G. MERRILLS
University of Sheffield Faculty of Law,
Crookesmoor Building, Conduit Road,
Sheffield, S10 1FL.

The Editors and members of the Editorial Committee do not make themselves in any way responsible for the views expressed by contributors, whether the contributions are signed or not.

The British Year Book of International Law is indexed in *Current Law Index*, published by Information Access Company.

CONTENTS

THE LAW AND PROCEDURE OF THE INTERNATIONAL COURT OF JUSTICE 1960–1989*

PART THREE

By HUGH THIRLWAY‡

II. Treaty Interpretation and Other Treaty Points

* © Hugh Thirlway, 1992.

‡ Principal Legal Secretary, International Court of Justice.

Introduction

The present article, the third in the series designed to continue the studies of the work of the Court by Sir Gerald Fitzmaurice, will cover a somewhat wider chronological period than its two predecessors. Since, as explained in the first article,[1] the last cycle of articles planned by Sir Gerald was never completed, it is necessary to refer to points discussed in decisions dating from the period to which that cycle was addressed, 1954–1959, where Sir Gerald had not found the opportunity to discuss those decisions from the particular angle presently under consideration.

For practical reasons, the present author has reversed the order of two major sections of Fitzmaurice's plan. In the 1947–1951 and 1951–1954 cycles, 'Particular Topics of International Law' followed 'Sources of Law' and preceded 'Treaty Interpretation and Certain Other Treaty Points'; the third cycle, 1954–1959, was broken off after 'Sources of Law'. To some extent this latter period is covered in Fitzmaurice's articles on 'Hersch Lauterpacht—The Scholar as Judge',[2] but inevitably these concentrate on the views of Lauterpacht in his opinions, rather than on the judgments to which they were appended. In the present series, 'Treaty Interpretation and Certain Other Treaty Points' is being taken before the wider, and probably more lengthy, section on particular topics of international law; it forms

[1] This *Year Book*, 60 (1989), p. 5.

[2] This *Year Book*, 37 (1961), pp. 1–71; 38 (1962), pp. 1–83; 39 (1963), pp. 133–88; *Collected Edition*, II, pp. 634–842.

a pendant to Fitzmaurice's two articles on the subject,[3] and covers the period 1954–1989.

As a result of limitations on the author's time resulting from the increased workload of the International Court—in itself a development to be welcomed[4]—it has not been possible to cover all aspects of treaty law in the present article; that topic will be concluded in the article to appear in the next *Year Book*.

A further special aspect of the present article, being addressed to treaty interpretation, is that it spans a period during which the Vienna Convention on the Law of Treaties was concluded and came into force. At the public sitting of the Court on 23 May 1969, Sir Humphrey Waldock, appearing as counsel for Spain in the *Barcelona Traction* case, referred to the conclusion of the work of the Vienna Conference, an event which would, he believed,

> be a matter of personal satisfaction not only to a number of counsel taking part in your proceedings but also to several Members of the Court who, at different stages of work, have made their own valuable contribution to the task of codification[5]

—a category which certainly included Sir Gerald Fitzmaurice, author of five reports on the subject for the International Law Commission.[6]

Although the Convention was not designed to be codifying in the strict sense, and did not come into force until 1980, its influence, as a convenient statement of principles and rules applicable to treaties, was felt from the date of its adoption,[7] and the Court could not remain immune to that influence. In a number of recent decisions, the Court stated a principle of the law of treaties in the terms in which it was defined in the Convention, adding that the relevant provisions in the Convention 'may in many respects be considered as a codification of existing customary law on the subject',[8] or words to that effect.

As a result of the adoption of the Vienna Convention it is now appropriate for a commentator on the Court's decisions to see the Court's handling of treaty questions, and its dicta on the law of treaties, against a background

[3] This *Year Book*, 28 (1951), pp. 1–28; 33 (1957), pp. 203–93; *Collected Edition*, I, pp. 42–69, 337–427.

[4] See Highet, 'The Peace Palace Heats Up: The World Court in Business Again?', *American Journal of International Law*, 4 (1991), pp. 646–54.

[5] *Barcelona Traction*, *Pleadings*, vol. 9, p. 103.

[6] *International Law Commission Yearbook*, 1956, vol. 2; 1957, vol. 2; 1958, vol. 2; 1959, vol. 2; 1960, vol. 2. The tribute by Sir Humphrey Waldock may have rung somewhat hollow to Sir Gerald, since, as his successor as ILC Rapporteur, Waldock departed substantially from Fitzmaurice's approach, and the Convention as finally adopted, while owing much to Fitzmaurice's research, was inspired as to form by Waldock's concepts.

[7] Cf. Jennings, 'Gerald Gray Fitzmaurice', this *Year Book*, 55 (1984), p. 59.

[8] *Namibia* case, *ICJ Reports*, 1971, p. 47, para. 94; see also *Fisheries Jurisdiction*, *ICJ Reports*, 1973, p. 18, para. 36, and p. 63, para. 36; *Aegean Sea*, *ICJ Reports*, 1978, p. 39, para. 95; *Interpretation of the Agreement of 25 March 1951 between the WHO and Egypt*, *ICJ Reports*, 1980, pp. 94–5, para. 47; *Frontier Dispute*, *ICJ Reports*, 1986, p. 563, para. 17; *Border and Transborder Armed Actions*, *ICJ Reports*, 1988, p. 85, para. 35; *Arbitral Award of 31 July 1989*, *ICJ Reports*, 1991, p. 70, para. 48. Cf. the previous article in this series, this *Year Book*, 81 (1990), pp. 88–93.

of the intellectual construction constituted by the Vienna Convention and—since the Court has yet to reject a rule stated in the Convention as incorrect or inapplicable outside the strict terms of reference of the Convention—as confirmatory of it. In the particular context of the present articles, it is however enlightening to refer such dicta also to the analyses offered by Fitzmaurice in his 1951 and 1957 articles, and in particular to the principles of interpretation of treaties which he there enunciated.

As a matter of presentation, in the present article it has seemed appropriate to follow Fitzmaurice's plan, if for no other reason, because

> other systems of organization might commend themselves, but do not appear to present advantages outweighing the convenience of relating the treatment of a particular point in this series to Sir Gerald's handling of the same point . . .[9]

In that structure the section on treaty law was divided into Division A: Interpretation of Treaties, and Division B: Substantive Points of Treaty Law. This system has been retained; but it appeared desirable to deal at the outset with certain questions raised in recent decisions concerning the very nature and existence of a treaty, rather than reserving them for inclusion in Division B, and a preliminary division has therefore been added.

Preliminary: When is a Treaty not a Treaty?

In his second article concerning treaties,[10] Fitzmaurice touched briefly, in the light of the *Anglo-Iranian Oil Co.* decision, on the question of what is meant by or included in the term 'treaty' or 'treaties and conventions'. This is a question which has arisen more than once in the period now under study. In the last article he wrote in the series he also discussed at some length the 'Basic nature of a legal (treaty) obligation; the essentials of "treaty character" ' in the light of the judicial opinions of Judge Sir Hersch Lauterpacht.[11]

If we decline to essay any general answer to the question, What is a treaty?, we do so in good company.[12] There is much to be said for the light-hearted definition quoted by Reuter: 'On a pu dire, par boutade, du traité international qu'il était un acte juridique qui n'était assujeti à aucune forme et qui portait sur un objet quelconque'.[13] The Vienna Convention of course contains a definition in Article 2, paragraph 1(*a*), which however is only valid 'for the purposes of the present Convention'; and most definitions have had to be made for the purposes of a particular text.

[9] This *Year Book*, 60 (1989), pp. 6–7.

[10] This *Year Book*, 33 (1957), p. 248; *Collected Edition*, I, p. 382.

[11] 'Hersch Lauterpacht: The Scholar as Judge (III)', this *Year Book*, 39 (1963), pp. 168 ff.; *Collected Edition*, I, pp. 822 ff.

[12] Cf. Jennings, 'General Course on Principles of International Law', *Recueil des cours*, 121 (1967–II), p. 529; Widdows, 'What is an Agreement in International Law?', this *Year Book*, 50 (1979), p. 118; O'Connell, *International Law*, vol. 1, p. 205: 'There is no general touchstone for determining what is a treaty. Everything depends upon analysis of the instrument in question.'

[13] 'Traités et transactions: réflexions sur l'identification de certains engagements conventionnels', *Le Droit international à l'heure de sa codification* (*Mélanges Ago*), vol. 1, p. 402.

In order to have some point of reference, we may however quote the first paragraph of Fitzmaurice's own all-embracing definition, given in his First Report on the Law of Treaties for the ILC:

For the purposes of the application of the present Code, a treaty is an international agreement embodied in a single formal instrument (whatever its name, title or designation) made between entities both or all of which are subjects of international law possessed of international personality and treaty-making capacity, and intended to create rights and obligations, or to establish relationships, governed by international law.[14]

So far as the Court is concerned, it is not so much the question 'What is a treaty?' which is likely to require judicial response as the problem whether a particular instrument or transaction is a treaty. Even then, the question will necessarily be whether it is a treaty for the purposes, or within the meaning, of some text which employs the word 'treaty' or 'convention'.

This has been the case as regards Article 36 of the Court's Statute, whereby 'The jurisdiction of the Court comprises . . . all matters specially provided for . . . in treaties and conventions in force',[15] and Article 37, ensuring continuation of the jurisdiction of the Permanent Court where provided for in 'a treaty or convention in force'.

1. *Ex consensu advenit vinculum: the* South West Africa *cases*

In the *South West Africa* cases, one of the jurisdictional objections raised by South Africa to the proceedings instituted by Ethiopia and Liberia was that the Mandate for South West Africa was no longer a 'treaty or convention in force' within the meaning of Article 37 of the Statute. Though this objection was to be rejected by the Court, it was, in view of the disappearance of the League of Nations, by no means unarguable. In the course of the proceedings, however, and as a consequence of a question put by Judge Sir Percy Spender,[16] the South African submissions were amended so as to contend also that the Mandate had *never been* a 'treaty or convention in force'.[17] This was not a view put forward with any great enthusiasm by South Africa,[18] and it may well be that South African counsel had adverted to what, in the present writer's opinion, is a fatal flaw in this contention—to be explained below. It was however taken up by Sir Percy Spender and Sir Gerald Fitzmaurice in their joint dissenting opinion,[19] and was also discussed at some length, before being rejected, by the majority of the Court.

[14] *ILC Yearbook*, 1956, vol. 2, p. 107.

[15] It was this provision which fell to be interpreted in the *Anglo-Iranian Oil Co.* case, which decision prompted Fitzmaurice's comments on the question of the nature of a treaty: loc. cit. above (n. 10).

[16] *Pleadings*, vol. 7, pp. 326–8.

[17] *Pleadings*, vol. 7, p. 382.

[18] See de Villiers at *Pleadings*, vol. 7, p. 376.

[19] Whether Fitzmaurice continued subsequently to hold the view that the Mandate was not a treaty is unclear; his lengthy dissenting opinion in the *Namibia* case does not refer to the point, but his argument on the alleged acceptance by South Africa of UN supervision as a 'novation' implies the existence of a *consensual* bond between a mandatory and the League: see *ICJ Reports*, 1971, p. 253, para. 52.

There was agreement between the majority and the two authors of the joint dissenting opinion that the name given to an instrument is not determinative of the question whether or not it is a treaty: 'Terminology is not a determinant factor as to the character of an international agreement or undertaking'.[20]

In simplified terms, the Spender/Fitzmaurice argument relies, first, on an emphasis on the institutional aspect of the mandates as something effected by a decision of the League Council, rather than as an agreement reached in each instance between the Principal Allied and Associated Powers and the mandatory State; and secondly, on an analysis of the succession of individual stages by which the Mandate for South West Africa came into existence, each of which in isolation can plausibly be represented as not in itself constituting an agreement which could be defined as a 'treaty or convention'.

The judgment of the Court, however, puts together what the joint dissenting opinion dismantles, and has no difficulty in finding that the Mandate, as made up of the whole corpus of acts and instruments, 'in fact and in law, is an international agreement having the character of a treaty or convention'.[21] A key sentence in the judgment has been quoted in truncated form in later texts,[22] but should be set out in full to show the care with which the Court added together all the successive stages of the mandate-creation process:

> It incorporates a definite agreement consisting in the conferment and acceptance of a Mandate for South West Africa, a provisional or tentative agreement on the terms of this Mandate between the Principal Allied and Associated Powers to be proposed to the Council of the League of Nations and a formal confirmation agreement on the terms therein explicitly defined by the Council and agreed to between the Mandatory and the Council representing the League and its Members. It is an instrument having the character of a treaty or convention and embodying international engagements for the Mandatory as defined by the Council and accepted by the Mandatory.[23]

The authors of the joint dissent emphasize the status of the Mandate—identified with the Council Resolution of 17 December 1920—as 'a quasi-legislative act of the League Council, carried out in the exercise of a power given to it by the Covenant';[24] the majority judgment emphasizes the consensual aspect—the fact that the Mandate 'incorporates' agreement.[25] The

[20] *ICJ Reports*, 1962, p. 331: cf. joint dissenting opinion, *ICJ Reports*, 1971, pp. 474–5.

[21] *ICJ Reports*, 1962, p. 330.

[22] e.g., in the *Namibia* opinion, *ICJ Reports*, 1971, p. 46, para. 94.

[23] *ICJ Reports*, 1962, p. 331, para. 3.

[24] Ibid., p. 490.

[25] The joint dissenting opinion is perhaps less than fair when it accuses the Court of propagating the 'fallacy' of identifying 'the idea of an international agreement with any act or instrument embodying, or giving rise to, international obligations, or which contains or involves an international "engagement" ' (*ICJ Reports*, 1962, p. 476).

true position is perhaps that expressed later by Fitzmaurice himself in his dissenting opinion in the *Namibia* case: 'a régime like that of the mandates system seems to have a foot in both the institutional and the contractual field'.[26] While argument in the *South West Africa* cases was addressed primarily to the interpretation of a particular text, namely Article 37 of the ICJ Statute, it omitted examination of an important element for the interpretation of that text, and one which, it is suggested, confirms the Court's view as against that of the two dissenting Judges.

It was the conclusion of Judges Spender and Fitzmaurice that

> the conditions requisite to give the Court jurisdiction under Articles 36 and 37 of its Statute are not fulfilled, inasmuch as the Mandate was the act of the League Council and is not and never was a 'treaty or convention' (or other form of international agreement); . . . [27]

It is however surely indisputable that the terms 'treaties or conventions in force' in Articles 36 and 37 of the ICJ Statute must be taken to be identical in meaning to the same terms in the PCIJ Statute. But it follows that, if the Spender/Fitzmaurice view is correct, the Permanent Court would have had no jurisdiction to entertain an application submitted on the basis of Article 7 (the jurisdictional clause) of the Mandate, as not being a matter 'specially provided for in a treaty or convention in force'. This would have been the case even in respect of a dispute whereby a member of the League sought to protect its own rights—the situation for which, in the view of Spender and Fitzmaurice, Article 7 was designed. In other words, Article 7 of the Mandate would have been, from the outset, a dead letter. This however is clearly an untenable conclusion.

The position surely is that, despite all the indications expounded by Spender and Fitzmaurice pointing to the non-conventional character of the Mandate, it must have been intended to have sufficient of the character of a 'treaty or convention' for it, or at least for Article 7, to fall within the category of 'treaties and conventions in force' in Article 36 of the PCIJ Statute. An alternative way of putting the point is to observe that Article 36 of the PCIJ Statute must be read as sufficiently wide to cover a virtually contemporary instrument—the Mandate—Article 7 of which was devised to operate under Article 36. If this is right, the exact degree of 'treaty-ness' of the Mandate is immaterial: if it is a treaty for Article 36 of the PCIJ Statute, then it must be a treaty for Article 37 of the ICJ Statute. (Whether the Mandate was still a treaty 'in force' at the relevant moment for Article 37 to operate is of course another question.)

In fact, the argument could be reversed. If an instrument contains a compromissory clause conferring jurisdiction on the Court, this must surely be indicative of an intention that that instrument is intended to be a

[26] *ICJ Reports*, 1971, p. 267, para. 69.
[27] *ICJ Reports*, 1962, p. 503.

treaty so as to link up with Article 36, paragraph 1, of the Statute of the Court;[28] and, more broadly, the jurisdiction of the Court being dependent on consent, such an instrument must be consensual in nature at least to the extent of the compromissory clause.[29] The Court did not however employ this argument in the *South West Africa* judgment of 1962.

It thus seems that Judges Spender and Fitzmaurice, by arguing in their dissenting opinion that Article 7 of the Mandate protected the individual rights of League members, but that the Mandate was never a treaty, were in effect sawing off the branch they were sitting on. This confirms the conclusion that to discuss the Mandate in terms of the general principles relating to the identification of treaties is a vain exercise. The Mandates as an institution were *sui generis*: they must have entailed a sufficient degree of legal obligation resulting from voluntary acceptance to make them enforceable, and not mere empty gestures, but they do not need to be forced into the definition of a 'treaty' which is inappropriate to them. Little is therefore to be learned from the Court's handling of them which is of general applicability in the field of treaty law, other than the basic point that it is agreement of the parties which makes a treaty.

2. *The intent to create legal obligations: the* Nicaragua *v.* United States *and* Aegean Sea Continental Shelf *cases*

(1) *The* condicio si volam: *the* Nicaragua *v.* United States *case*

In his study of 'Hersch Lauterpacht—The Scholar as Judge', Fitzmaurice drew attention, in the context of treaty law, to the view of Lauterpacht that it is an

> essential aspect and requirement of what constitutes a treaty (or analogous) obligation . . . that the instrument . . . should purport to, and should create legal rights and obligations, and that the parties should, by it, enter into understandings of a legal character, which a court having jurisdiction in the matter could appraise, interpret and give effect to.[30]

One of the two contexts in which this view directed Lauterpacht's thinking was that of the significance, for the possibility of revocation of the Mandate for South West Africa, of the unanimity voting rule in the Council of

[28] Unless of course the instrument is to be read as a special agreement 'referring' a case to the Court directly—in which case there can hardly be any question of its treaty nature—, or as a unilateral acceptance of jurisdiction, when the consent of the declarant State is evident, and the intention to create legal effects will generally be so also (but see section 2, below).

[29] A point made by Judges Spender and Fitzmaurice themselves: *ICJ Reports*, 1962, p. 478.

[30] This *Year Book*, 39 (1963), pp. 167–8; *Collected Edition*, I, pp. 822–3. Cf. Barberis, 'Le Concept de "traité international" et ses limites', *Annuaire français de droit international*, 1984, p. 239 at pp. 251 ff., who gives an interesting example of provisions (in the Bonn Convention on the Conservation of Migratory Species) of pseudo-treaty provisions—provisions with no definable legal content.

the League of Nations;[31] this aspect will not however be discussed here. The other context is one which has presented itself in more recent case law of the Court, and therefore requires comment here.

The problem of determining whether there was an intention to create legal relations of course arises not only with regard to treaties but also in the case of unilateral acts, which, though not treaties, may raise analogous problems, in particular as regards their interpretation.[32] The class of unilateral acts which has most frequently required the attention of the Court is that of declarations of acceptance of jurisdiction under Article 36, paragraph 2, of the Statute. It appears to be generally accepted that treaty-law,[33] or at least rules for the interpretation of treaties, can be applied to declarations of this kind, on the basis that, as Fitzmaurice put it, 'although these declarations are unilateral *in form*, they give rise to a 'treaty situation . . . '.[34] These declarations can of course be taken *a priori* to be intended to create legal relations: that is their whole *raison d'être*.[35] A State which makes such a declaration can only be intending to subject itself to the regime of the Optional Clause.

Lauterpacht applied his theory as to the requirement of an intention to create legal relations to the question of the validity of an acceptance of the Court's jurisdiction under the Optional Clause containing what is known as the 'automatic' or 'Connally' reservation.[36] In two lengthy and fully reasoned opinions, in the *Certain Norwegian Loans* and *Interhandel* cases, Lauterpacht explained his thesis that this reservation is invalid, both as contrary to the Court's Statute and as contrary to the essential requirement of a legal instrument as defined in the quotation above; that the reservation is not severable from the declaration, and therefore the declaration as a whole is invalid; and that where such a reservation is invoked as jurisdictional basis, the only course open to the Court is to hold that 'there is not before it an instrument by reference to which it can assume jurisdiction in relation to any aspect of the dispute'.[37] He accordingly dissented from the

[31] See Lauterpacht's separate opinion in the *South-West Africa (Voting Procedure)* case.

[32] In the *Anglo-Iranian Oil Co.* case, the Court however emphasized the need to bear in mind that a unilateral act expresses the will of only one State: *ICJ Reports*, 1952, p. 105.

[33] *Contra*, Judge Schwebel in the *Nicaragua* v. *United States* case, *ICJ Reports*, 1984, p. 620, para. 99.

[34] This *Year Book*, 34 (1958), p. 76; *Collected Edition*, II, p. 503. See also Crawford, 'The Legal Effect of Automatic Reservations to the Jurisdiction of the International Court', this *Year Book*, 50 (1979), p. 76, who raises the separate, and interesting, question whether reservations to Optional Clause declarations are subject to the treaty-law rules governing reservations to treaties.

[35] It was in respect of such a declaration that the Court in the preliminary objection phase of the *Right of Passage* case stated as a 'rule of interpretation' that 'a text emanating from a Government must be interpreted as producing and as intended to produce effects in accordance with existing law and not in violation of it' (*ICJ Reports*, 1957, p. 142); see further pp. 60 ff. below.

[36] The reservation excluding 'disputes with regard to matters which are essentially within the domestic jurisdiction of' the declarant State 'as determined by' the declarant State.

[37] *Interhandel, ICJ Reports*, 1959, p. 119. The view that if the reservation is invalid, the whole declaration fails, is probably indisputable: in this sense Crawford, loc. cit. above (n. 34), at p. 68.

view of the majority in *Interhandel* that it was open to the Court to put on one side the question of the effect of the automatic reservation, and deal with other preliminary objections, one of which, in the view of the Court, disposed of the case. For him, the declaration containing the reservation was an absolute nullity, which could not give rise to any legal effects whatever.

Lauterpacht's view was not shared by the majority of the Court either in the *Norwegian Loans* case or in the *Interhandel* case. In the former case, the Court upheld the Norwegian preliminary objection based on the presence of the automatic reservation in the declaration of the applicant (France); it stated expressly that it

> does not consider that it should examine whether the French reservation is consistent with a legal obligation and is consistent with Article 36, paragraph 6, of the Statute . . . ,[38]

but it did indicate that it was not prejudging that question.[39] In the *Interhandel* case, however, the Court decided the case on the basis of an objection of non-exhaustion of local remedies, and stated that 'Having regard to the decision of the Court' on this objection, the objection based on the automatic reservation 'is without object at the present stage of the proceedings'.[40]

Lauterpacht had to meet the objection that in an earlier case *(US Nationals in Morocco)* proceedings had been brought against the United States on the basis of its Optional Clause declaration, which contained the automatic reservation, and the Court had accepted jurisdiction without any comment on the validity or otherwise of that declaration. In that case, the United States did not seek to rely on the automatic reservation, and Lauterpacht considered that 'There was, therefore, no direct occasion for the Court to embark upon an examination of the validity of that reservation and of the Acceptance as a whole'.[41] In his view,

> the jurisdiction of the Court was in fact exercised not on the basis of the Optional Clause but on the principle of *forum prorogatum*, i.e., on what was actually a voluntary submission independent of the source of jurisdiction originally invoked by the applicant party.[42]

Whether or not this is a correct legal analysis of the jurisdictional situation in the *US Nationals* case,[43] the same cannot be said of the decision on jurisdiction in the *Nicaragua* v. *United States* case in 1984. The jurisdic-

[38] *Norwegian Loans, ICJ Reports*, 1957, p. 26.
[39] Ibid., p. 27.
[40] *Interhandel, ICJ Reports*, 1959, p. 26.
[41] *Norwegian Loans, ICJ Reports*, 1957, p. 59.
[42] Ibid., p. 60.
[43] The question will be discussed further in a later article on questions of jurisdiction and competence.

tional basis invoked by Nicaragua was the United States declaration under the Optional Clause, with its automatic reservation. The United States in no way consented to jurisdiction: it raised a number of objections, all of which accepted by implication that the declaration was in itself a valid instrument, capable of conferring jurisdiction. In its counter-memorial on jurisdiction,[44] it stated however that it had determined not to invoke the automatic reservation. The Court found that it had jurisdiction, not on a basis of *forum prorogatum*, but specifically on the ground that 'the present Application is not excluded from the scope of the acceptance by the United States of America of the compulsory jurisdiction [i.e., the Optional Clause jurisdiction] of the Court' and that 'the two Declarations [that of Nicaragua and that of the United States] do afford a basis for jurisdiction of the Court'.[45] Judge Schwebel, in his dissenting opinion, referred to the Lauterpacht thesis of absolute invalidity of the United States declaration, and recalled that in a pre-judicial capacity he had himself expressed agreement with it; he was not however disposed to find that on that basis the Court lacked jurisdiction.[46]

What is of interest for present purposes is however not the strict jurisdictional point, but the philosophy as to the essential nature of a treaty or other obligation which underlies it, and this philosophy is, at that level of abstraction, best expounded by Fitzmaurice in the article referred to above. The question for consideration is: by rejecting Lauterpacht's view as to the essential validity of a declaration containing the automatic reservation, is the Court to be taken to have rejected also its jurisprudential underpinnings in the thinking of Lauterpacht and Fitzmaurice?

An acceptance of jurisdiction under the Optional Clause (and indeed under a treaty) is normally creative of obligation; but what precisely is that obligation? As the present writer has endeavoured to show elsewhere,[47] it is simply the obligation to accept as binding the Court's resolution of any dispute falling within the terms of the acceptance. A connection is required between the individual dispute, Article 36 of the Statute, and Article 94 of the Charter requiring compliance with a judgment of the Court. The automatic reservation enables the declarant State, as it were, to 'switch off' that connection, already established by the nature of the dispute and the fact of seisin of the Court.

The Court's decision in the *Nicaragua* v. *United States* case establishes that the existence of this power to 'switch off' the obligation does not mean that the obligation does not exist so long as no switching-off has occurred. It also signifies that once the power to switch off has been renounced, as it

[44] Quoted in *ICJ Reports*, 1984, p. 422, para. 67.

[45] Ibid., p. 441, para. 110.

[46] Ibid., pp. 601–2, paras. 64–5.

[47] ' "Normative Surrender" and the "Duty" to Appear before the International Court of Justice: A Reply', *Michigan Journal of International Law*, 11 (1990), p. 912 at pp. 919 ff.

was in that case, the obligation is irreversibly established; and that renunciation may be tacit, by conduct.[48]

This approach is perfectly reconcilable with the basic philosophy which is, it is suggested, shared by the Court and Judge Lauterpacht; that as the Digest puts it, *sub hac conditione: si volam, nulla fit obligatio*.[49] Contrary to the view expressed by Fitzmaurice, in his gloss on Lauterpacht's opinion, the declaration falls into the category—from which Fitzmaurice insisted it was distinguishable—

> where the fulfilment or otherwise of a condition governing the existence or continuance of an obligation depends upon the action of one of the parties, which it is free to take or not as it pleases, so that in that sense that party can itself determine the existence or continuance of the obligation,[50]

a category of agreements which Fitzmaurice regarded as 'perfectly valid'. The case of the automatic reservation was, in his view, distinguishable because in the case of the valid conditional obligation,

> it would in no way lie with [the party concerned] to determine such things as whether the action in question had in fact been taken or not; whether it was of the required nature; or whether it sufficed to bring about the results provided for in the treaty,[50]

all these being 'for a court of competent jurisdiction to decide'. But it is open to the Court to decide that the 'switching-off' process has been effected (*Norwegian Loans*) or that it has not (*US Nationals in Morocco, Nicaragua* v. *United States*). What is of course open to criticism, and provoked Lauterpacht to adopt his 'absolute invalidity' theory, is that the 'switching-off' takes the form of a determination which would, in the absence of the automatic reservation, be left in the hands of the Court.[51]

We may conclude that an apparent treaty or other instrument which did not involve the acceptance of any legal obligation at all would not be regarded as a treaty or act having legal effects; but that the acceptance of

[48] This was what occurred in the *US Nationals in Morocco* case. It might be questioned whether this view is compatible with the dictum of the Court in the *Right of Passage* case that 'It is a rule of law generally accepted, as well as one acted upon in the past by the Court, that once the Court has been validly seised of a dispute, unilateral action by the respondent State in terminating its declaration, in whole or in part, cannot divest the Court of jurisdiction' (*ICJ Reports*, 1957, p. 142). However, this refers only to action in terminating a declaration, not action under a power reserved in the declaration itself; and while India was arguing in that case that the Portuguese Third Condition could be read as capable of acting retrospectively and such operation would be contrary to the Statute, all the Court decided was that the Condition could not be interpreted as intended to act retrospectively. See below, pp. 96 ff.

[49] Quoted by Judge de Castro in his separate opinion in the *Namibia* case, *ICJ Reports*, 1971, p. 214.

[50] This *Year Book*, 39 (1963), p. 172; *Collected Edition*, II, p. 826.

[51] This is also the view taken by Crawford, writing well before the *Nicaragua* v. *USA* case: 'The Legal Effect of Automatic Reservations to the Jurisdiction of the International Court', this *Year Book*, 50 (1979), p. 63; he observes that 'the Court's power under Article 36, paragraph 6 [of the Statute] does exist' in these circumstances, although it is 'of rather a nominal character': loc. cit., p. 75. Crawford rejects Lauterpacht's thesis for additional reasons which are not material to the point now under discussion, but which will be considered in a later article devoted to matters of jurisdiction of the Court.

jurisdiction subject to the automatic reservation does not, *pace* Lauterpacht and, it seems, Fitzmaurice, fall into that category.

(2) *What is an agreement? The* Aegean Sea Continental Shelf *case*

In the *Aegean Sea* case, Greece offered as an alternative basis of jurisdiction (the primary base asserted being the 1928 General Act for the Pacific Settlement of International Disputes) a joint communiqué issued in Brussels on 31 May 1975 at the conclusion of a meeting held between the Prime Ministers of the two countries. This communiqué contained the following sentence:

> They [the Prime Ministers] decided that those problems [specified earlier] should be resolved peacefully by means of negotiations and as regards the continental shelf of the Aegean Sea by the International Court at The Hague.[52]

In its application, Greece claimed that by this communiqué the two Governments 'jointly and severally accepted the jurisdiction of the Court in the present matter, pursuant to Article 36(1) of the Statute of the Court'.[53]

A point which was never entirely cleared up in the course of the proceedings, or not in specific terms, was the precise status attributed by Greece to the joint communiqué in terms of Article 36, paragraph 1, of the Statute. That text defines the Court's jurisdiction as comprising 'all cases which the parties refer to it and all matters specifically provided for . . . in treaties and conventions in force'. According to the commonly accepted interpretation, the reference to 'treaties and conventions in force' is to treaties containing a compromissory clause, protocols for dispute settlement, or treaties for the pacific settlement of disputes, while 'all cases which the parties refer to it' refers to cases brought by 'the notification of the special agreement', in the terms of Article 40, paragraph 1, of the Statute or, it seems, cases in which there is *forum prorogatum*. Into which category did the joint communiqué fall, according to the interpretation given to it by the Government of Greece?[54]

The Statute (Article 40, para. 1) makes a corresponding distinction between two methods of seising the Court: either notification of a special agreement by which the parties 'refer' a case to the Court; or application, citing a basis of jurisdiction (treaty or Optional Clause declaration); but there may be cases in which the distinction is not so clear-cut.[55] In the *Aegean Sea* case, the form of institution of proceedings was dictated by the primary basis of jurisdiction asserted by Greece, the 1928 General Act, so

[52] *ICJ Reports*, 1978, pp. 39–40, para. 97.

[53] Ibid., p. 39, para. 94.

[54] The point was specifically raised by Turkey: *Pleadings*, p. 610.

[55] Cf. the recent *Territorial Dispute* case between Chad and Libya, in which, virtually simultaneously, one party notified the Court of a treaty on the basis that it was a special agreement, and the other filed an application citing the treaty as the basis of jurisdiction. Cases of *forum prorogatum* must by definition have been commenced by application, which may or may not have cited an alleged basis of jurisdiction; but they must be taken to have been 'referred' to the Court by the parties, with the qualification that this 'referral' took place in two successive stages.

that it did not for this purpose have to opt for one solution or the other in order to commence proceedings on the basis of the joint communiqué. On a less formal or procedural level, Greece did however contend that the communiqué enabled the parties to resort to the Court either by special agreement or by application,[56] with the implication that it was a treaty.

Turkey's challenge to the Greek claims of jurisdiction on this basis took the form of a denial that the communiqué was 'an agreement under international law';[57] the Court was therefore initially not called upon specifically to interpret the words 'treaties and conventions in force' in Article 36, paragraph 1, of the Statute, but to say whether the communiqué was or was not an 'agreement', a term at least as wide as 'treaty', and perhaps wider.

The Court's approach to the problem was as follows:

> On the question of form, the Court need only observe that it knows of no rule of international law which might preclude a joint communiqué from constituting an international agreement to submit a dispute to arbitration or judicial settlement (cf. Arts. 2, 3 and 11 of the Vienna Convention on the Law of Treaties). Accordingly, whether the Brussels Communiqué of 31 May 1975 does or does not constitute such an agreement essentially depends on the nature of the act or transaction to which the Communiqué gives expression; and it does not settle the question simply to refer to the form—a communiqué—in which that act or transaction is embodied. On the contrary, in determining what was indeed the nature of the act or transaction embodied in the Brussels Communiqué, the Court must have regard above all to its actual terms and to the particular circumstances in which it was drawn up.[58]

The distinction here made between the 'act or transaction', and the communiqué which gives it expression or embodies it, the communiqué 'constituting' the agreement, is unusual: the question examined in doctrine has been rather whether the term 'treaty' applies to the agreement of the parties, as an 'act or transaction', or to the instrument containing, embodying or evidencing it.[59] The question which determined the decision of the Court was however not whether or not the communiqué was an agreement, but whether it was 'such' an agreement, i.e., an agreement to submit a dispute to arbitration or judicial settlement. The Greek claim to the existence of jurisdiction was rejected, not because the communiqué was not an agreement, but because 'it was not intended to, and did not, constitute an

[56] *ICJ Reports*, 1978, p. 40, para. 98.

[57] Ibid., para. 99; *Pleadings*, p. 72. In argument, Greece raised the question of the international validity of an oral agreement, on the basis that the communiqué was merely the evidence of an oral agreement: *Pleadings*, pp. 267, 471–3, but the Court did not deal directly with the point. On this aspect, see Widdows, 'On the Form and Distinctive Nature of International Agreements', *Australian Year Book of International Law*, 7 (1976–7), p. 114.

[58] *ICJ Reports*, 1978, p. 39, para. 95.

[59] Cf. Basdevant, *Recueil des cours*, 15 (1926–V), p. 539; Fitzmaurice, 'First Report on the Law of Treaties', *ILC Yearbook*, 1965, vol. 2, p. 119, para. 24; Widdows, this *Year Book*, 50 (1979), p. 118. Presumably the Court had in mind the argument that the communiqué was evidence of an oral agreement: see n. 57 above.

immediate commitment . . . to accept unconditionally the unilateral submission of the present dispute to the Court'.[60]

Although the Court does not say so, it appears to have proceeded on the assumption that the communiqué was an agreement, to conclude that it was not an agreement of the kind claimed by Greece. The only comment on the classification of the communiqué as an agreement is the first sentence of the passage quoted above, which treats the matter entirely as one of form.

Turkey's contention was primarily that the communiqué was not an international treaty because it contained nothing binding: 'En définitive, le communiqué, dont les termes sont tout à fait généraux, ne renferme aucune norme conventionnelle: il n'énonce aucune règle de conduite et ne traduit aucun engagement réciproque.'[61] It also argued, however, but 'en passant', that a communiqué could never be an international agreement, because governments do not and would not enter into obligations in that way:

> Il sied de relever en passant que, si on acceptait de regarder le communiqué comme un accord international, pourvu de portée juridique, on remettrait en cause les principes essentiels qui gouvernent la formation et l'expression des volontés concordantes des Etats en droit international. Ce serait une nouveauté sans exemple et qui ferait naître les plus grands dangers. Elle risquerait de détourner à jamais les membres des gouvernements de publier des communiqués conjoints. Cette conséquence compliquerait inutilement leurs relations avec la presse et les empêcherait de communiquer normalement avec l'opinion publique.[62]

This too, however, is a question of the choice of form. Essentially, the argument is that there must be an intention on the part of the parties to an international agreement 'to create a relation between themselves operating within the sphere of international law', in the words of McNair;[63] an intention to 'modifier la situation juridique existant'.[64] For Turkey, the choice of a communiqué is in itself sufficient to negative the idea of such an intention. The Court, in the passage quoted above, was unwilling to go so far; nor was it necessary for it to do so for the decision of the case. If the communiqué committed the parties to anything, it was not to acceptance of jurisdiction on a basis of unilateral seisin; it was therefore not necessary to decide what it did commit the parties to, or whether it committed them to anything at all.[65]

[60] *ICJ Reports*, 1978, p. 44, para. 109.

[61] *Pleadings*, p. 610, para. 59.

[62] Ibid., para. 60.

[63] *The Law of Treaties*, p. 4. As Widdows observes, in words which might have referred to the *Aegean Sea* case, unless this means 'a relationship constituted by binding obligations *inter se*, the term appears unduly vague and might cover, for example, a joint communiqué where two Foreign Ministers speak in political terms of their aspirations for future relations, an instrument not normally considered a treaty': this *Year Book*, 50 (1979), p. 121.

[64] Barberis, 'Le Concept de "traité international" et ses limites', *Annuaire français de droit international*, 1984, p. 256, who suggests that a treaty may also be directed to defining certain legal concepts.

[65] Note the careful reservation of the position in the final paragraph of the Court's reasoning: *ICJ Reports*, 1978, p. 44, para. 108.

Division A: Treaty Interpretation

'If there's no meaning in it', said the King, 'that saves a world of trouble, you know, as we needn't try to find any'.

Lewis Carroll, *Alice in Wonderland*, Chap. XII.

Chapter I:

Introductory

In his articles in this *Year Book* on the subject of 'Treaty Interpretation and Other Treaty Points', Sir Gerald Fitzmaurice postulated six major principles of treaty interpretation which he discerned in the decisions of the Court in this field.[66] These were:[67]

1. Principle of Actuality (or Textuality)
2. Principle of Natural and Ordinary Meaning
3. Principle of Integration and, subject to these first three:
4. Principle of Effectiveness
5. Principle of Subsequent Practice
6. Principle of Contemporaneity.

Fitzmaurice grouped his analysis of the Court's jurisprudence concerning interpretation of treaties mainly under these headings, coupled with a catch-all supplementary heading of 'Ancillary and other interpretative findings' during the period reviewed.[68]

While the articulation of the provisions on the subject in the Vienna Convention on the Law of Treaties (Arts. 31 to 33) is different, based as it was on the drafts prepared by Sir Humphrey Waldock, Fitzmaurice's successor as Rapporteur of the International Law Commission, the effective legal relationship between the various rules, canons or principles is for the most part not a rigid structure[69] and can be as satisfactorily portrayed against the background of Fitzmaurice's system as in that of the Convention.

It is hardly surprising that many of the rules as to treaty interpretation recognized in Articles 31 to 33 of the Vienna Convention on the Law of Treaties can be found in the jurisprudence of the Court during the period under consideration. Since the Convention was adopted, the Court has referred to it as a convenient restatement of existing rules; and it was

[66] Fitzmaurice also took into account the work of the Institut de droit international on the subject culminating in the resolution adopted at Granada in 1956, when Fitzmaurice was Rapporteur (*vice* Sir Hersch Lauterpacht).

[67] This *Year Book*, 33 (1957), pp. 211–12.

[68] Ibid., pp. 227 ff.

[69] Cf. O'Connell, *International Law*, vol. 1, pp. 252–3.

largely from the decisions of the Court (and of its predecessor) prior to the drafting of the Convention that the rules adopted in it were derived.[70]

The Court has necessarily had to develop what is referred to in the *Temple* case as 'its normal canons of interpretation', to be found in 'the established jurisprudence of the Court',[71] and each of these which can be identified in decisions in the period under study will be examined below. What the Court has not had the opportunity of doing was to organize these canons into an articulated system, and it was of course this that the successive ILC Rapporteurs were able to contribute. In its decisions, the Court frequently refers to a specific principle of interpretation, but does not set out any sort of structural system for the hierarchy or interaction of those principles.[72]

1. *Good Faith in the Interpretation of Treaties*

One further preliminary remark is necessary: no reference will be found in the discussion below to the requirement stated at the outset of Article 31 of the Vienna Convention that 'A treaty shall be interpreted in good faith . . . '.[73] The simple and sufficient reason for this is that the Court has not, during the period under consideration, had to examine the significance of this requirement, whether under the Vienna Convention or in the general law of treaties.[74] It is also to be observed that what may be in question is the good faith of the parties; an interpretation by the Court in which the Court itself was animated by something other than good faith is not to be thought of. As Yasseen observes,

> Il s'agit certes de la bonne foi qui devrait animer les parties au traité et c'est cette bonne foi qui devrait orienter l'interprétation, même si l'interprétation n'est pas faite par les parties elles-mêmes, mais par un tiers.[75]

It is however difficult to conceive circumstances in which the Court would find it necessary to reject an interpretation advanced by a party on the sole ground that it was not made in good faith. Such interpretation would almost certainly offend at the same time against some specific canon

[70] See n. 8, above. In the view of Sinclair, 'There is no doubt that Articles 31 to 33 of the [Vienna] Convention constitute a general expression of the principles of customary international law relating to treaty interpretation': *The Vienna Convention on the Law of Treaties* (2nd edn., 1984), p. 153.

[71] *ICJ Reports*, 1961, p. 32. The text to be interpreted was in fact not a treaty but a declaration under the Optional Clause; cf. p. 9, above.

[72] Individual judges have come nearer to doing so in their opinions: see for example Judge de Castro in the *Namibia* case, *ICJ Reports*, 1971, pp. 182 ff.; Sir Percy Spender, on interpretation of the Charter, in the *Certain Expenses* case, *ICJ Reports*, 1962, pp. 184 ff. That such a pattern of rules is desirable, at least in the form of the Vienna Convention, is not universally accepted: cf. O'Connell, *International Law*, vol. 1, p. 253.

[73] On this, see the authoritative study of Rosenne, *Developments in the Law of Treaties 1945–1986*, chapter 3.

[74] On the Court's jurisprudence on good faith in general, see the first article in this series: this *Year Book*, 60 (1989), pp. 7 ff.

[75] 'L'Interprétation des traités d'après la Convention de Vienne sur le droit des traités, *Recueil des cours*, 151 (1976–III), p. 21.

of interpretation; and the Court will be slow to accuse a State in its judgment of bad faith.[76]

2. *The Court's General Attitude to Treaty Interpretation*

The present study should be read against the background of, in particular, those sections[77] of Fitzmaurice's articles in which he analyses the main schools of thought in regard to treaty interpretation: the 'intention of the parties' approach, the 'textual' or 'ordinary meaning of the words' approach, and the 'teleological' or 'aims and objects' approach. Whichever of the schools of thought one may oneself favour, it must be recognized that, even after the passage of over thirty years, and the labours of the ILC leading to the adoption of the Vienna Convention, Fitzmaurice's study cannot be bettered as a survey, and to some extent a reconciliation, of the possible philosophies of interpretation.[78]

Any attempt to update that analysis would be presumptuous and unnecessary. Nor, though for slightly different reasons, will the present writer endeavour to distil into a few propositions the Court's current and recent attitude to the principles of treaty interpretation, as Fitzmaurice was able to do. One consideration militating against such an endeavour is the difficulty of discerning a consistent approach in the decisions given, over so long a period as thirty-five years (1954 to 1989), by a Court of steadily changing composition, in a wide variety of cases.

It may however be helpful to reproduce here Fitzmaurice's distillation of the Court's approach in its decisions up to 1951, which was maintained, in his view, during the period 1951–1954, and to add a few comments on this summary in the light of the subsequent jurisprudence.

(*a*) the Court, without denying the validity or relevance of the intentions of the parties, or refusing in certain circumstances to inquire into these, has not normally approached the task of interpretation from that point of view, but has, rather, favoured an approach based primarily on an elucidation of the text, following in this respect the practice of the former Permanent Court of International Justice;

(*b*) in elucidating texts, the Court has proceeded mainly on the basis of the principle of the 'natural and ordinary meaning' of terms 'in the context in which they occur': only if 'the words in their natural and ordinary meaning are ambiguous or lead to an unreasonable result' can the Court, 'by resort to other methods of interpretation, seek to ascertain what the parties really did mean when they used these words';

(*c*) so far as it may be possible to do so without departing from the natural and ordinary meaning, or doing violence to the actual terms of the treaty, or reading into it terms that are not there, the Court has been ready, through the principle of

[76] Cf. the award in the arbitration of the *Guinea/Guinea Bissau Maritime Frontier Delimitation*, *Revue générale de droit international public*, 89 (1985), p. 508, para. 46.

[77] This *Year Book*, 28 (1951), pp. 1–10; 33 (1957), pp. 204–10; *Collected Edition*, I, pp. 42–51 and 338–44.

[78] Cf. the remarks of Sir Robert Jennings, 'Gerald Gray Fitzmaurice', this *Year Book*, 55 (1984) pp. 25–6.

effectiveness, to have regard to the apparent objects and purposes of the treaty, in interpreting its terms;

(*d*) by means of the principle of subsequent practice the Court has in effect opened the door to a predominantly teleological element of interpretation in so far as the practice of the parties in applying and operating the treaty may be evidence of what its real object and intention is, and hence a guide to the true meaning of its terms.[79]

Paragraph (a). The balance between the 'textual' and the 'intention of the parties' approaches as defined here has undoubtedly swung the other way; at least in the case of multilateral treaties, it has been the 'intention' or object of the treaty which has been taken as starting point, either explicitly (*Aerial Incident (Israel* v. *Bulgaria), Namibia*) or implicitly (*ICAO Appeal*).

Paragraph (b). This statement remains valid as far as it goes; the Court has however been much more reluctant to be convinced that the words used have a 'natural and ordinary meaning' which can be accepted as the proper treaty interpretation (*Aegean Sea Continental Shelf*), so that its enquiry need be pressed no further; it has been much more ready than formerly to resort to other means of interpretation—particularly *travaux préparatoires*—, not only where the textual interpretation is doubtful or unsatisfactory, but also to confirm an interpretation already arrived at on a textual basis. The latter approach is of course specifically authorized, if not emphasized, by the Vienna Convention.

Paragraph (c). Reference to objects and purposes of a treaty no longer takes place solely through the application of the principle of effectiveness; it may for example be resorted to through reference to the 'intention' of the treaty rather than that of the parties (*Guardianship of Infants*), or even constitute the starting point of the discussion (*Israel* v. *Bulgaria*). The principle of effectiveness however remains valid, both in the form of interpreting texts so as to give effect to all terms thereof, and in the form of interpreting a treaty so as to avoid its ineffectiveness as an instrument. This distinction between effective meaning of every part of a text and effectiveness of the treaty to achieve its ends, between 'effet utile' and 'efficacité', has been made clearer.

Paragraph (d). The principle of subsequent practice has continued to be a useful tool of interpretation, but its use has proved to be less closely linked with teleological considerations than Fitzmaurice apparently foresaw. The doctrine of 'emergent purpose' as revealed in subsequent practice has come to the fore less than might have been expected, perhaps because the same end can be achieved by a treaty interpretation attributing an intention that the treaty rules are to move with the times (intertemporal *renvoi*).

[79] This *Year Book*, 33 (1957), pp. 209–10; *Collected Edition*, I, pp. 343–4.

Chapter II:

Fitzmaurice's Principles in the Case Law of the Court, 1954–1989

1. *Principle of Actuality (or Textuality)*

Shylock: Is it so nominated in the bond?
Portia: It is not so expressed; but what of that? . . .
Shylock: I cannot find it; 'tis not in the bond.

Shakespeare, *The Merchant of Venice*, Act. IV, Sc. 1.

This principle is stated by Fitzmaurice as follows: 'Treaties are to be interpreted primarily as they stand, and on the basis of their actual texts',[80] that is to say 'prima facie, without reference to extraneous factors'.[81]

Thus at the preliminary objection stage of the *Right of Passage* case the Court, in order to ascertain whether a condition in an acceptance of jurisdiction under the Optional Clause rendered the acceptance invalid, found that it 'must determine the meaning and the effect of the Third Condition by reference to its actual wording and applicable principles of law'.[82] In the same case Judge *ad hoc* Chagla observed that

> No canon of construction is more firmly established than the one which lays down that the intention of a party to an instrument must be gathered from the instrument itself and not from what the party says its intention was.[83]

The rule was also affirmed in the judgment on the preliminary objections in the *Temple of Preah Vihear* case, in the *a contrario* form of an indication of one of the circumstances in which recourse to elements outside the text is permissible: when the text would lead to 'something unreasonable or absurd',[84] namely when it contains an internal contradiction. The text being interpreted was Thailand's declaration of acceptance of jurisdiction under the Optional Clause.

> If, however, there should appear to be a contradiction between [specified provisions of the Declaration]—then, according to a long-established jurisprudence, the Court becomes entitled to go outside the terms of the Declaration in order to resolve this contradiction and, *inter alia*, can have regard to other relevant circumstances; and when these circumstances are considered, there cannot remain any doubt as to what meaning and effect should be attributed to Thailand's Declaration.[85]

The statement of the principle by Judge Sir Percy Spender in his separate opinion in the *Certain Expenses* case also bears quoting, particularly his realistic assessment of its practical usefulness:

[80] This *Year Book*, 33 (1957), p. 211; *Collected Edition*, I, p. 345.
[81] This *Year Book*, 33 (1957), p. 212; *Collected Edition*, I, p. 346.
[82] *ICJ Reports*, 1957, p. 142.
[83] Ibid., p. 167.
[84] See *Polish Postal Service in Danzig, PCIJ*, Series B, No. 11, p. 39.
[85] *ICJ Reports*, 1961, pp. 33–4.

> The cardinal rule of interpretation that this Court and its predecessor has stated should be applied is that words are to be read, if they may so be read, in their ordinary and natural sense. If so read they make sense, that is the end of the matter. If, however, so read they are ambiguous or lead to an unreasonable result, then and then only must the Court, by resort to other methods of interpretation, seek to ascertain what the parties really meant when they used the words under consideration . . .
>
> This injunction is sometimes a counsel of perfection. The ordinary and natural sense of words may at times be a matter of considerable difficulty to determine. What is their ordinary and natural sense to one may not be so to another.[86]

He also emphasized that

> Despite current tendencies to the contrary the first task of the Court is to look, not at the *travaux préparatoires* or the practice which hitherto has been followed within the Organization, but at the terms of the Charter itself.[87]

It will be convenient to consider further the application of this principle along with that of Principle II.

2. *Principle of Natural and Ordinary Meaning*

> Malvolio (*reading*): Why this is evident to any formal capacity;
> there is no obstruction in this . . .
>
> Shakespeare, *Twelfth Night*, Act. II, Sc. 5.

(1) *The principle stated and applied*

Fitzmaurice's statement of this principle is the following:

> Subject to Principle VI below [the Principle of Contemporaneity], where applicable, particular words and phrases are to be given their normal, natural, and unstrained meanings in the context in which they occur. This meaning can only be displaced by direct evidence that the terms used are to be understood in another sense than the natural and ordinary one, or if such an interpretation would lead to an unreasonable or absurd result. Only if the language employed is fundamentally obscure or ambiguous may recourse be had to extraneous means of interpretation, such as consideration of the surrounding circumstances, or *travaux préparatoires*.[88]

(a) *The 'natural and ordinary' meaning*

This is in effect what the Court in the *Temple of Preah Vihear* case designated the 'first' of its named canons of interpretation, namely:

[86] *ICJ Reports*, 1962, p. 184.
[87] Ibid., p. 185.
[88] This *Year Book*, 33 (1957), p. 212; *Collected Edition*, I, p. 345.

that words are to be interpreted according to their natural and ordinary meaning in the context in which they occur.[89]

Curiously, however, the argument introduced by these words in the *Temple* judgment is not in fact an application of the canon of interpretation stated. The Court interpreted what, on the face of it, was a renewal of an acceptance of the jurisdiction of the Permanent Court as capable of having

> no other sense or meaning than as an acceptance of the compulsory jurisdiction of the present Court, for there was no other Court to which it can have related.[90]

This is not so much taking words in 'their natural and ordinary meaning' as interpreting them, in the light of extraneous circumstances, so as to avoid an absurd result—an equally valid, but different, canon of interpretation.

In the *Right of Passage* case the Court held that, 'construed in their ordinary sense', the words 'with effect from the moment of such notification' did not mean that such notification was to have retroactive effect.[91]

In the *Aegean Sea Continental Shelf* case, the Court had to determine whether a reservation in the instrument of accession by Greece to the 1928 General Act for the Pacific Settlement of International Disputes applied to the dispute brought before the Court. The relevant text, in the original French, was:

> Sont exclus des procédures décrites par l'Acte général, sans en excepter celle de conciliation viseé à son chapitre I:
>
> (*a*) . . .
>
> (*b*) les différends portant sur des questions que le droit international laisse à la compétence exclusive des Etats et, notamment, les différends ayant trait au statut territorial de la Grèce, y compris ceux relatifs à ses droits de souveraineté sur ses ports et ses voies de communication.

The issue to which a large part of the judgment was addressed was the significance of the words 'et, notamment,'; in the contention of Greece, these words meant that disputes relating to territorial status were a sub-class of the class of disputes over questions which by international law are solely within the domestic jurisdiction of States, and that accordingly disputes relating to territorial status which did not fall within that category were not excluded from the acceptance of jurisdiction.

> In support of this interpretation of the words 'et, notamment,' the Greek Government invokes the authority of Robert's *Dictionnaire alphabétique et analogique de la langue française (Vol. IV) which explains* 'notamment' as meaning 'd'une manière qui mérite d'être notée' (in a way which deserves to be noted), and adds in brackets: 'sert le plus souvent à attirer l'attention sur un ou plusieurs objets

89 *ICJ Reports*, 1961, p. 32.
90 Ibid.
91 *ICJ Reports*, 1957, p. 142.

particuliers faisant partie d'un ensemble précédemment désigné ou sous-entendu' (most often used to draw attention to one or more particular objects forming part of a previously designated or understood whole) . . . The Greek Government also cites similar examples of this use of '*et, notamment*' given in the *Dictionnaire de l'Académie française* and in Littré, *Dictionnaire de la langue française*. On the basis of this linguistic evidence, it maintains that the natural, ordinary and current meaning of this expression absolutely precludes the Greek reservation from being read as covering disputes regarding territorial status in addition to, and quite separately from, disputes regarding matters of domestic jurisdiction.[92]

The Court did not accept this contention, which it referred to as the 'grammatical argument'; it did not however hold that the Greek interpretation led to an 'unreasonable or absurd result', but merely that it 'leads to a result which is somewhat surprising',[93] inasmuch as disputes relating to 'territorial status' and 'domestic jurisdiction' are different concepts. This in itself would not, on established principles, appear to be sufficient to displace the 'natural, ordinary and current meaning' of the words. Nevertheless, the Court took the view that

only if the grammatical arguments were compelling and decisive would the Court be convinced that such is the effect which ought to be given to the words '*et, notamment*,' in reservation (*b*).[94]

The Court relied on, first, the presence of the commas in the phrase 'et, notamment,' and secondly, the possibility, recognized by Robert's *Dictionnaire*, of other uses of 'notamment', to conclude that there was the 'possibility' that the phrase in question was intended to specify 'an autonomous category of disputes', those relating to territorial status.[95] This also would not in itself suffice to justify abandoning the ordinary meaning of the phrase; but the Court seems to have considered that it had thrown sufficient doubt on the matter to justify reference to other 'considerations of a substantive character'.[96]

These considerations were: the structure of the article of the General Act itself concerning reservations; the terms of Greece's declaration (2 years after its accession to the General Act) under the Optional Clause; the contemporary political background; and the *travaux préparatoires*. While arguments derived from these considerations added up to a formidable case against Greece's contentions,[97] the striking feature of the decision for present purposes is that if the starting point for an interpretation of the Greek reservation had been the criterion of the 'natural and ordinary meaning' of

[92] *ICJ Reports*, 1978, pp. 21–2, para. 51.
[93] Ibid., p. 22, para. 52.
[94] Ibid.
[95] Ibid., pp. 22–3, paras. 53–4.
[96] Ibid., p. 23, para. 55.
[97] It should perhaps be recalled that Turkey was not appearing in the case, so that these arguments were in effect marshalled by the Court itself.

the words used—if the 'textual' approach had been allowed to prevail—, none of these considerations would have entered the picture at all.[98]

Just how wide a disagreement there may be about the 'natural and ordinary meaning' of even a single word is apparent from the 1980 advisory opinion on the *Interpretation of the Agreement of 25 March 1951 between the WHO and Egypt*. The key sentence in that agreement was the simple opening sentence of Section 37: 'The present agreement may be revised at the request of either party'. What however was meant by 'revised'? As the Court explained,

> According to one view the word 'revise' can cover only modifications of particular provisions of the Agreement and cannot cover a termination or denunciation of the Agreement, such as would be involved in the removal of the seat of the Office from Egypt; and this is the meaning given to the word 'revise' in law dictionaries.[99]
>
> . . .
>
> Opponents of the view just described insist, however, that the word 'revise' may also have the wider meaning of 'review' and cover a general or total revision of an agreement, including its termination. According to them, the word has not infrequently been used with that meaning in treaties and was so used in the 1951 Agreement.[100]

In the circumstances, it is hardly surprising that the Court made no attempt to define what was the 'natural and ordinary meaning' of the word 'revise' in this context. For reasons discussed more fully elsewhere,[101] it was able to avoid the need to give an interpretation of Section 37 at all.

The criterion of 'natural and ordinary meaning' had been expressly employed in the 1955 advisory opinion on *South West Africa, Voting Procedure*,[102] in order to interpret, not a treaty, but the Court's own previous pronouncement in the *South West Africa* advisory opinion of 1950.[103] The same criterion was employed in the advisory opinion on *Constitution of the*

[98] In this sense, Johnson, 'The International Court of Justice Declines Jurisdiction Again (the Aegean Sea Continental Shelf case)', *Australian Year Book of International Law*, 7 (1976–7), p. 309 at p. 328. Too much weight should not, it is suggested, be attached to the decision as a rejection *in principle* of the textual approach. The Court did at least begin with the text, not the 'object and purpose' of it; and in its judgment the Court made no secret of the fact that it was anxious not to have to rule on the status of the General Act if this could be avoided by finding another insufficiency in the Greek case on jurisdiction: cf. Merrills, 'The International Court of Justice and the General Act of 1928', *Cambridge Law Journal*, 39 (1980), pp. 137, 166.

For doubts as to the soundness of the Court's use of 'reciprocity' to enforce the Greek reservation against Greece, see the present writer's 'Reciprocity in the Jurisdiction of the International Court', *Netherlands Yearbook of International Law*, 15 (1984), p. 97, at pp. 130–3.

[99] *ICJ Reports*, 1980, p. 91, para. 40.

[100] Ibid., para. 41.

[101] Pp. 70–1, below; see also the previous article in this series, this *Year Book*, 61 (1990), pp. 37–40.

[102] *ICJ Reports*, 1955, p. 72.

[103] *ICJ Reports*, 1950, p. 138. The application of this criterion to the Court's own decisions does not seem inappropriate; but if the 'natural and ordinary meaning' were not discernible, or ambiguous, what would be the next step? Recourse to *travaux préparatiores* would presumably be excluded by the principle of secrecy of the deliberations. In the case concerning the application for revision and interpretation of the judgment in the *Tunisia/Libya* case, the Court explained the meaning of a disputed expression in its first judgment simply by reference to other passages in the judgment (reliance on context): *ICJ Reports*, 1985, pp. 222–5, paras. 54–9.

Maritime Safety Committee of IMCO in 1960, where the Court had to interpret the expression 'the largest ship-owning nations' in the Convention establishing IMCO; and the Court at the same time explained how other methods of construction may only be referred to if this 'first canon' does not resolve the difficulty.

> The words of Article 28(*a*) must be read in their natural and ordinary meaning, in the sense which they would normally have in their context. It is only if, when this is done, the words of the Article are ambiguous in any way that resort need be had to other methods of construction.[104]

This is of course a restatement of the well-known dictum of the Permanent Court that 'there is no occasion to have regard to preparatory work if the text of a convention is sufficiently clear in itself';[105] and like that dictum, the statement in the *IMCO* case has to be taken with a pinch of salt. It is well known that expressions like 'sufficiently clear' are open-ended; there will be, in almost all cases, room for disagreement whether a text is 'sufficiently clear';[106] and it may be recourse to supplementary methods of interpretation like *travaux préparatoires* that will make it possible to reach a conclusion as to what the 'sufficiently clear' meaning of the text is.[107] Perhaps the only case in which no recourse to supplementary means of interpretation is necessary is when there is no disagreement between those concerned—as was the case as regards the meaning of one text in the *IMCO* case[108]—when no question of interpretation arises for decision at all!

It is thus characteristic of the difficulty of interpreting any text by the application of a single rule of interpretation that the Court in the *IMCO* case was forced to have recourse to other considerations: first, the rule that the whole of the text must be presumed to have some significance, so that an interpretation which would render part of it redundant is to be rejected;[109] and secondly the 'principle underlying' the text—i.e., the object and purpose of the treaty.[110] In a succeeding section of the judgment,[111] the *travaux préparatoires* too are pressed into service.

Similarly, in the *Fisheries Jurisdiction* cases the Court concluded in its 1973 judgment on jurisdiction that

[104] *ICJ Reports*, 1960, pp. 159–60, referring to *Competence of the General Assembly for the Admission of a State to the United Nations, ICJ Reports*, 1950, p. 8.

[105] *SS Lotus, PCIJ*, Series A, No. 10, p. 16.

[106] Sinclair (*The Vienna Convention on the Law of Treaties* (2nd edn., 1984), p. 116) points out that 'the famous principle laid down by Vattel—"La première maxime générale sur l'interprétation est qu'il n'est pas permis d'interpréter ce qui n'a pas besoin d'interprétation"—is a *petitio principii*'. (The quotation is from Vattel's *Le Droit des Gens, ou principes de la loi naturelle* (1785), book II, chap. xvii, section 263.)

[107] Cf. Anzilotti, *PCIJ*, Series A/B, No. 50, p. 383; de Castro, *ICJ Reports*, 1971, p. 183; and the separate opinion of Fitzmaurice in the *Certain Expenses of the United Nations* case: 'Were it not for the records of the San Francisco Conference for the drafting of the Charter (to which I shall refer later) the correct interpretation of Article 17, paragraph 2, would be that . . . ' etc. (*ICJ Reports*, 1962, p. 208.)

[108] *ICJ Reports*, 1960, p. 167: 'A general opinion, shared by the Court, is that . . . '.

[109] Ibid., p. 160: see section 4(1), below, p. 44.

[110] Ibid., pp. 160–1: see section 3, below, pp. 37–44.

[111] Ibid., pp. 161–5.

Since, on the face of it, the dispute thus brought to the Court upon the Application of the United Kingdom falls exactly within the terms of this clause, the Court would normally apply the principle it reaffirmed in its 1950 Advisory Opinion concerning the *Competence of the General Assembly for the Admission of a State to the United Nations*, according to which there is no occasion to resort to preparatory work if the text of a convention is sufficiently clear in itself;[112]

yet it still proceeded to 'undertake a brief review of the negotiations that led up to' the 1961 Exchange of Notes. The justification given for this was, however, 'the peculiar circumstances of the present proceedings', namely the absence of Iceland from the proceedings and the consequent duty of the Court, under Article 53 of the Statute, to 'satisfy itself that it has jurisdiction'.[113] There is of course a certain logical awkwardness here: if the Court was satisfied of jurisdiction on the face of the text, there was no need to go further; if it was not, it had to go further in any event. Does a treaty interpretation have to be more solid than usual, iron-bound and copper-bottomed, if it has to be made under Article 53? And what would have been the position if the, theoretically uncalled for, examination of the *travaux préparatoires* had pointed to an interpretation different from that regarded as evident on the face of the text?

When examining the words which were used in a treaty, the Court has felt entitled also to take into account the absence of words which might have been used, but were not.[114] This may be regarded either as a form of treatment of the 'natural and ordinary meaning' of the words which are present, or a sort of 'negative context'; at all events it is dictated by common sense and logic.

Thus in the *Right of Passage* case the Court said:

Article 17 of the Treaty is relied upon by Portugal as constituting a transfer of sovereignty. From an examination of the various texts of that article placed before it, the Court is unable to conclude that the language employed therein was intended to transfer sovereignty over the villages to the Portuguese. There are several instances on the record of treaties concluded by the Marathas which show that, where a transfer of sovereignty was intended, appropriate and adequate expressions like cession 'in perpetuity' or 'in perpetual sovereignty' were used.[115]

Similarly, at the jurisdictional stage of the *Nicaragua* v. *United States* case, the Court declined to interpret Article 36, paragraph 5, of the Statute, as urged by the United States, as if it contained the word 'binding' before 'Declarations';[116] and on this basis held that a declaration of acceptance of the jurisdiction of the PCIJ was saved by that provision even if it had not

[112] *ICJ Reports*, 1973, pp. 9–10, para. 17.
[113] Ibid., pp. 7–8, para. 12.
[114] Or a different form of drafting which could have been employed but was not: cf. *Aegean Sea*, *ICJ Reports*, 1978, p. 23, para. 56, and, more recently, *Arbitral Award of 31 July 1989*, *ICJ Reports*, 1991, pp. 70–1, para. 51.
[115] *ICJ Reports*, 1960, p. 38. Cf. also the argument of the United States in the *ELSI* case on the question of the rule of exhaustion of local remedies, discussed at pp. 64–5 below.
[116] *ICJ Reports*, 1984, p. 406, para. 30.

previously had any binding force. In its 1986 judgment in the same case, when examining the 'multilateral treaty reservation' in the United States acceptance of jurisdiction, it noted that the reservation

> does not require . . . that a State party to the relevant treaty be 'adversely' or 'prejudicially' affected by the decision, even though this is clearly the case primarily in view.[117]

(b) *Use of terms in a special sense*

> *The Chairman* felt it his imperative duty to demand of the honourable gentleman, whether he had used the expression which had just escaped him in a common sense.
>
> *Mr. Blotton* had no hesitation in saying that he had not—he had used the word in its Pickwickian sense.
>
> Charles Dickens, *The Pickwick Papers*, Chap. I.

The rule that terms are to be understood in their 'natural and ordinary meaning' may be displaced by evidence that a particular term was used deliberately with a particular, unusual meaning. This is enunciated also in Article 31, paragraph 4, of the Vienna Convention: 'A special meaning shall be given to a term if it is established that the parties so intended.' It is however for the party claiming that a term was intended to have a special meaning to prove that this was so, failing which the natural and ordinary meaning will be taken to have been intended.[118]

This rule was re-stated and applied, during the period under review, in the advisory opinion in the *Western Sahara* case:

> Implicit in Morocco's claim that these treaties signify international recognition of the exercise of its sovereignty in Western Sahara is the proposition that phrases such as 'the coasts of Wad Noun', 'to the South of Wad Noun' or 'Wad Noun and beyond' are apt to comprise Western Sahara. This proposition it advances on the basis that 'Wad Noun' was a term used with two meanings: one narrow and restricted to the Wad Noun itself, the other wider and covering not only the Wad Noun but the Dra'a and the Sakiet El Hamra. This wider meaning, it indicates, was the only one with which the term was used in Moroccan documents and treaties . . .
>
> It is for Morocco to demonstrate convincingly the use of the term with that special meaning (cf. *Legal Status of Eastern Greenland, PCIJ*, Series A/B, No. 53, p. 49) and this demonstration, in the view of the Court, is lacking.[119]

Special problems arise if the term to be interpreted is one which has, or may have, a legal connotation. In the *Aegean Sea* case, the Court was called upon to interpret the expression 'territorial status' in the 1931 accession by Greece to the 1928 General Act for the Pacific Settlement of International Disputes. It was contended by Greece, by reference to the political history of the period, that expressions of this kind

117 *ICJ Reports*, 1986, p. 37, para. 53.
118 *Legal Status of Eastern Greenland, PCIJ*, Series A/B, No. 53, p. 49.
119 *ICJ Reports*, 1975, pp. 52–3, para. 116.

are to be given a restrictive interpretation limited to the maintenance of the status quo established by treaties, normally as a result of post-war settlement.[120]

This contention partakes to some extent of a reliance on the intertemporal law principle, or Fitzmaurice's principle of contemporaneity; but it is also, and perhaps rather, an assertion of a special meaning for a term. To argue that 'territorial status' in 1931 had a certain meaning in international law generally (e.g., that it did not and could not cover the question of the continental shelf, as Greece also argued) is an intertemporal law argument. To demonstrate that 'territorial status', while it had a particular meaning in 1931 law, was used with a specific, more limited meaning because of historical circumstances, is not so much an intertemporal law point as an indication of a special meaning. It is when the term in question is a legal one that there is a risk of confusing these two hypotheses.

In the *Elettronica Sicula* case, the United States claimed that certain action by the Italian authorities in relation to the Elettronica Sicula company was a breach of a treaty provision prohibiting 'arbitrary or discriminatory measures'. The United States argued in effect that the measures complained of had been set aside on appeal in Italy on grounds which amounted to a finding that they had been 'arbitrary'; on this basis it contended that the measures were 'precisely the sort of arbitrary action which was prohibited' by the treaty.

The Chamber of the Court seised of the case however dealt with the point in terms which suggest that it saw the question not so much as one of interpretation of a treaty as one of determining what, in *general* international law, could be classified as arbitrary action. It dealt first with the argument based on municipal law:

Yet it must be borne in mind that the fact that an act of a public authority may have been unlawful in municipal law does not necessarily mean that that act was unlawful in international law, as a breach of treaty or otherwise. A finding of the local courts that an act was unlawful may well be relevant to an argument that it was also arbitrary; but by itself, and without more, unlawfulness cannot be said to amount to arbitrariness. It would be absurd if measures later quashed by higher authority or a superior court could, for that reason, be said to have been arbitrary in the sense of international law. To identify arbitrariness with mere unlawfulness would be to deprive it of any useful meaning in its own right. Nor does it follow from a finding by a municipal court that an act was unjustified, or unreasonable, or arbitrary, that that act is necessarily to be classed as arbitrary in international law, though the qualification given to the impugned act by a municipal authority may be a valuable indication.[121]

It then gave its own definition of what is 'arbitrary':

Arbitrariness is not so much something opposed to a rule of law, as something opposed to the rule of law. This idea was expressed by the Court in the *Asylum*

[120] Quoted in *ICJ Reports*, 1978, p. 30, para. 72.
[121] *ICJ Reports*, 1989, p. 74, para. 124.

case, when it spoke of 'arbitrary' action being 'substituted for the rule of law' (*Asylum, Judgment, I.C.J. Reports 1950*, p. 284). It is a wilful disregard of due process of law, an act which shocks, or at least surprises, a sense of juridical propriety. Nothing in the decision of the Prefect, or in the judgment of the Court of Appeal of Palermo, conveys any indication that the requisition order of the Mayor was to be regarded in that light.[122]

The Chamber's approach seems at first sight to be from the standpoint of general concepts, or even 'general principles of law', rather than directed to ascertaining the intention of the parties. It may however be justified on the basis that the 'natural and ordinary meaning' in a treaty of a term like 'arbitrary' must be taken to be the meaning attached to it in the context of general international law, though this logical link in the argument is implicit, not stated. Thus the contention of the United States, that 'arbitrary' in the Treaty meant whatever would be classified as arbitrary by a domestic court of one of the parties, amounted to a contention that the word was being used in a special sense; but the United States did not discharge the burden of showing that this was so.

(c) *The context of the words to be interpreted*

The reference in the 1961 dictum in the *Temple* case, quoted above, to the meaning of the words to be interpreted 'in the context in which they appear' is in no way superfluous: on the contrary, it is possible for reference to the context to override what would be the 'natural and ordinary meaning' of the words out of that context—for example in the dictionary. This is illustrated by the decision in the *Maritime Safety Committee (IMCO)* case in 1960. The text to be interpreted—Article 28*(a)* of the IMCO Convention—provided that

> The Maritime Safety Committee shall consist of fourteen Members elected by the Assembly from the Members, governments of those nations having an important interest in maritime safety, of which not less than eight shall be the largest ship-owning nations. . . .[123]

It was argued that one or more of the 'largest ship-owning nations' (however they were defined) could none the less be excluded from the Committee, in the exercise of the Assembly's discretion, *inter alia* because of the use of the word 'elected', a word which entailed 'a notion of choice which was said to imply an individual judgment on each member to be elected and a free appraisal as to the qualification of that member'.[124] The Court's view was expressed as follows:

> The contention assumes a meaning to be accorded to the word 'elected' and then applies that meaning to Article 28*(a)* and interprets its provisions accordingly. In

[122] Ibid., p. 76, para. 128.
[123] *ICJ Reports*, 1960, p. 154.
[124] Ibid., p. 158.

so doing it places in a subordinate position the specific provision of the Article in relation to the eight 'largest ship-owning nations'.

The meaning of the word 'elected' in the Article cannot be determined in isolation by recourse to its usual or common meaning and attaching that meaning to the word where used in the Article. The word obtains its meaning from the context in which it is used. If the context requires a meaning which connotes a wide choice, it must be construed accordingly, just as it must be given a restrictive meaning if the context in which it is used so requires.[125]

The hierarchy, or sequence, of considerations involved in the interpretation of a treaty text, according to the principles under discussion, will normally be: first, the words to be interpreted, in their natural and ordinary meaning; secondly, their 'context'—the significance of which will now be examined; and subsequently, if necessary, such subsidiary means of interpretation as *travaux préparatoires*, subsequent practice, etc.

In this respect the sequence of criteria applied by the Court in the case of the *Aerial Incident (Israel* v. *Bulgaria)* is anomalous. The Court considered first the text of Article 36, paragraph 5, of the Statute against its historical background, then the *travaux préparatoires* of the San Francisco Conference, and then added the following paragraph:

Finally, if any doubt remained, the Court, in order to interpret Article 36, paragraph 5, should consider it in its context and bearing in mind the general scheme of the Charter and the Statute which founds the jurisdiction of the Court on the consent of States. It should, as it said in the case of the *Monetary Gold Removed from Rome in 1943*, be careful not to 'run counter to a well-established principle of international law embodied in the Court's Statute, namely, that the Court can only exercise jurisdiction over a State with its consent'. (*ICJ Reports*, 1954, p. 32.)[126]

This is of course a wide conception of the 'context' of a provision in a treaty, though no wider, as we shall see, than that employed in other decisions. The 'context' contemplated by the criterion under discussion obviously means, first of all, the text immediately surrounding the words to be interpreted; this was presumably what was meant in the *Right of Passage* case where the Court, discussing an authorization in an eighteenth-century treaty by the Maratha rulers to the Portuguese to put down rebellion in certain villages, referred to 'the context in which this authorization occurs', in order to define its scope.[127] The context must also clearly refer to, at least, the whole of the treaty or instrument to be interpreted.[128] Thus in its judgment in the case of *Border and Transborder Armed Actions*, the Court relied, for its interpretation of Article XXXI of the Pact of Bogotá, on the operation in relation to that article of a number of other provisions of the

[125] Ibid.

[126] *ICJ Reports*, 1959, p. 142.

[127] *ICJ Reports*, 1960, p. 38.

[128] Cf. the award in the *Young Loans* arbitration, 59 ILR 495 at p. 530. Article 31, paragraph 2, of the Vienna Convention reminds us that the preamble and any annexes to a treaty are included in the 'context'.

Pact.[129] In the *Certain Expenses* case, Judge Winiarski (dissenting), quoting Roman law and Vattel, stressed the need when interpreting a provision of the Charter to look at all its other provisions.[130]

May however the reference in the 1961 dictum to the 'context' have a wider meaning?[131] Article 31, paragraph 2, of the Vienna Convention includes in the category of context other agreements between the parties 'in connection with the conclusion of the treaty' and 'any instrument' made by a party or parties in that connection accepted as such by the other parties. This does not however cover all possibilities.

A clear case in which it was appropriate to include a unilateral instrument as part of the context was the decision at the jurisdictional stage of the *Fisheries Jurisdiction* cases. The compromissory clause which had there to be interpreted read as follows:

> The Icelandic Government will continue to work for the implementation of the Althing Resolution of May 5, 1959, regarding the extension of fisheries jurisdiction around Iceland, but shall give to the United Kingdom Government six months' notice of such extension, and, in case of a dispute in relation to such extension, the matter shall, at the request of either party, be referred to the International Court of Justice.[132]

The Court declared in this respect that

> The meaning of the expression 'extension of fisheries jurisdiction' in the compromissory clause must be sought in the context of this Althing resolution and of the complete text of the 1961 Exchange of Notes . . .[133]

Where the text to be interpreted specifically refers to another document, from which the expression to be interpreted is taken, it is evident that that other document should form part of the 'context' for interpretation purposes.[134] The case falls within, or is analogous to, the category discerned by Fitzmaurice of cases where a number of instruments are part of a single complex or whole.[135] On the other hand, to introduce evidence as to the circumstances in which a treaty was concluded, or other contemporaneous documents not specifically referred to, while possibly permissible in some circumstances as aids to interpretation, could not reasonably be justified as part of the 'context' of the words to be interpreted.

A still wider 'context' was however invoked in the 1962 judgment in the

[129] *ICJ Reports*, 1988, pp. 84–5, para. 35.

[130] *ICJ Reports*, 1962, p. 229.

[131] Reuter regards it as indisputable that a term must be interpreted 'en replaçant l'élément à interpréter dans son "environnement" juridique': 'Traités et transactions: réflexions sur l'identification de certains engagements conventionnels', *Le Droit international à l'heure de sa codification (Mélanges Ago)*, vol. 1, p. 400.

[132] *ICJ Reports*, 1973, p. 8, para. 13.

[133] Ibid., para. 14.

[134] This is one way in which reference to other treaties may be appropriate, but since such reference may be justified in other ways, the question is dealt with separately below (pp. 66 ff.)

[135] This *Year Book*, 28 (1951), pp. 11–2; 33 (1957), pp. 218–19; *Collected Edition*, I, pp. 53–4, 352–3.

South West Africa cases. Referring to the rule of interpretation which relies on 'the natural and ordinary meaning of the words employed' (without reference to their context), the Court stated:

> Where such a method of interpretation results in a meaning incompatible with the spirit, purpose and context of the clause or instrument in which the words are contained, no reliance can be validly placed on it.[136]

It was apparent from the immediately following paragraphs of the judgment that the 'context' which the Court had in mind was not merely the full text of the Mandate for German South West Africa, nor even that text coupled with the League of Nations Covenant, but the whole 'Mandates System'.

A wide view of the context of a treaty was also taken in the advisory opinion in the *Western Sahara* case. Morocco had invoked, as evidencing international recognition by Great Britain that Moroccan territory reached as far south as Cape Bojador, an Anglo-Moroccan Agreement of 13 March 1895 concerning a trading station set up by a Mr Donald Mackenzie. The Court observed that

> The difficulty with this interpretation of the 1895 treaty is that it is at variance with the facts as shown in the diplomatic correspondence surrounding the transaction concerning the Mackenzie trading-station. Numerous documents relating to this transaction and presented to the Court show that the position repeatedly taken by Great Britain was that Cape Juby was outside Moroccan territory, which in its view did not extend beyond the Dra'a. In the light of this material the provisions of the 1895 treaty invoked by Morocco appear to the Court to represent an agreement by Great Britain not to question in future any pretensions of the Sultan to the lands between the Dra'a and Cape Bojador, and not a recognition by Great Britain of previously existing Moroccan sovereignty over those lands. In short, what those provisions yielded to the Sultan was acceptance by Great Britain not of his existing sovereignty but of his interest in that area.[137]

It is curious that the Court gives no reason for proceeding to look at the diplomatic correspondence—for example, that the text of the treaty was ambiguous, or that the Moroccan interpretation led to an absurdity. The justification for the Court's approach is perhaps that the question was not really one of interpretation, despite the Court's use of the term, of the 1895 Agreement. The question was not so much what the *text* of the treaty *meant*, as what the *conclusion* of the treaty *signified*, in terms of recognition of Morocco's territorial claims.[138] The intention of the parties was limited to the transaction effected by the Agreement (re-purchase by the Sultan of the trading station); although Morocco relied on certain wording in the treaty, it was more the fact of its conclusion that mattered. The distinction

136 *ICJ Reports*, 1962, p. 336.

137 *ICJ Reports*, 1975, p. 54, para. 120.

138 It is for this reason that the Court stated that the 'question of how far any of these arguments may or may not be opposable to any of the States concerned does not arise': *ICJ Reports*, 1975, p. 56, para. 126.

is however not as clear-cut as it might have been, and under the heading of practice in the field of treaty interpretation, the Court's action must be noted as something of an anomaly.

(2) Recourse to travaux préparatoires

(a) *Justification for such recourse: ambiguity or confirmation*

Both the structure of principles of interpretation advanced by Fitzmaurice, and Article 32 of the Vienna Convention, classify recourse to *travaux préparatoires* as a 'supplementary means of interpretation'.[139] For Fitzmaurice, the principal justification for recourse to *travaux préparatoires* was the situation in which 'the text is ambiguous, and does not yield any single clear and unequivocal meaning, taken in its natural and ordinary sense'.[140] He adopted the same approach in his judicial capacity in his separate opinion in the *Certain Expenses* case. After examining the text of Article 17, paragraph 2, of the Charter, he found that it was insufficiently clear in itself, and continued:

> It follows, in my opinion, that there is a sufficient element of ambiguity about the exact intention and effect of Article 17, paragraph 2, to make its interpretation on the basis of the rule of the 'natural and ordinary meaning' alone, unsatisfactory. In these circumstances it is permissible to have recourse to the preparatory work of the San Francisco Conference.[141]

It is true that, in theory, if the text is clear enough as it stands, there is no need to refer to supplementary means;[142] but where those supplementary means confirm the interpretation suggested by the text itself, there is no harm in noting the fact as a reinforcement of the conclusion stated. This is a course particularly attractive to the Court, which, partly as a result of its collegiate character, often prefers to give several parallel reasons for its decisions where one would do.

This approach is recognized by Article 32 of the Vienna Convention, which permits of recourse to supplementary means of interpretation not only to determine the meaning of a text which is ambiguous or leads to absurd results, but also 'to confirm the meaning resulting from the application of article 31', i.e., of the general rule of interpretation. This latter possibility was at one time little used by the Court: in the two *Admissions* cases, it declined to refer to the *travaux préparatoires* at all;[143] but in the

[139] An amendment to the draft, proposed at the Conference by the United States, would have placed reference to *travaux préparatoires* on the same plane as all other means of interpretation, but this amendment was overwhelmingly rejected in the Plenary; see Yasseen, 'L'Interprétation des traités d'après la Convention de Vienne sur le droit des traités', *Recueil des cours*, 151 (1976–III), p. 87.

[140] This *Year Book*, 32 (1955–6), pp. 109–10; *Collected Edition*, I, pp. 349–50.

[141] *ICJ Reports*, 1962, p. 209.

[142] But note the risk of *petitio principii* in the maxim *in claris non fit interpretatio*: p. 25, above.

[143] *ICJ Reports*, 1948, p. 63; *ICJ Reports*, 1950, p. 8. See Fitzmaurice's discussion of these cases in this *Year Book*, 28 (1951), pp. 10–11; *Collected Edition*, I, pp. 51–2.

US Nationals in Morocco case extraneous material was referred to to confirm an interpretation based on the text.[144] It is of course true that a tribunal which has arrived at an interpretation of a treaty on the basis of the 'natural and ordinary meaning' of the words cannot know in advance that examination of the *travaux préparatoires* will confirm that interpretation. If it does not, the tribunal will presumably stick to its textual interpretation and say nothing more about the matter; it may be that this is what happened in the *Admissions* cases.[145]

(i) *Ambiguity*

Gloucester: I moralize two meanings in one word.

Shakespeare, *Richard III*, Act III, Sc. 1.

In its advisory opinion in the *WHO* case,[146] the Court was faced with the clearest possible example of an ambiguity justifying recourse to *travaux préparatoires*, since

> The differences regarding the application of Section 37 of the Agreement to a transfer of the Regional Office from Egypt have turned on the meaning of the word 'revise' in the first sentence and on the interpretation then to be given to the two following sentences of the Section,[147]

and the supporters of one of the two alternative interpretations of the word

> maintain that this is confirmed by the *travaux préparatoires* of Section 37, which are to be found in negotiations between representatives of the Swiss Government and the ILO concerning the latter's headquarters agreement with Switzerland.[148]

The Court however recast the question put to it for advisory opinion, and based its opinion on 'general legal rules and principles' imposing 'mutual obligations incumbent upon Egypt and the Organization to co-operate in good faith', which obligations were 'the very basis of the legal relations between the Organization and Egypt *under general international law*'.[149] It therefore avoided any need to interpret Article 37 as such, and *a fortiori* had no occasion to consider the *travaux préparatoires*.

Three Members of the Court (Judges Gros, Ago and El Erian) in separate opinions found Section 37 applicable to the question to be decided, and

[144] See Fitzmaurice's discussion in this *Year Book*, 33 (1957), pp. 219–20; *Collected Edition*, I, pp. 353–4.

[145] There will of course be a temptation, which must be resisted, having arrived at a provisional conclusion based on the text of the treaty, to discover that in the *travaux préparatoires* the pointers in favour of that interpretation are clearer than any indications to the contrary. The Court has not yet expressly formulated any criterion for judging *travaux préparatoires* of the kind put forward by Lord Wilberforce in *Fothergill* v. *Monarch Airlines Ltd.* and *Gatoil International Inc.* v. *Arkwright-Boston Manufacturers Mutual Insurance Co.*, that the material 'clearly and indisputably points to a definite legislative intention': [1985] AC 263.

[146] *Interpretation of the Agreement of 25 March 1951 between the WHO and Egypt, ICJ Reports*, 1980, p. 73.

[147] Ibid., p. 91, para. 40.

[148] Ibid., p. 41.

[149] Ibid., p. 95, para. 48 (emphasis added); see below, pp. 70–1.

therefore requiring interpretation. Judge Gros first based his view on the text, regarding one interpretation of the key word 'revise' as 'carrying formalism a long way'; he then returned to the *travaux préparatoires* to support the opposite interpretation.[150] Judge Ago first found that

a careful consideration of the text, such as it is, of Section 37 suffices in itself to persuade me that it is highly improbable, not to say impossible, that the parties can have intended [to produce a particular effect].[151]

He then went on, however:

Secondly, I would point out that the question which has been raised in this connection could not *in any event* be resolved without a close examination of the origins of the clause . . .[152]

Judge El Erian apparently saw no reason not to plunge at once into examination of the *travaux préparatoires*: as soon as he turned from the background of 'headquarters agreements' in general, to the 1951 Agreement itself, he began:

A careful consideration of the circumstances of its conclusion, the purposes sought to be achieved by such an instrument and an analysis of its provisions clearly reveal that the Agreement is a 'host agreement'.[153]

(ii) *Confirmation*. Reference to *travaux préparatoires* for confirmation was an approach expressly adopted in the case of the *Maritime Safety Committee (IMCO)*, where the Court, having arrived at a conclusion as to the interpretation of the words of Article 28*(a)* of the IMCO Convention taken 'in their natural and ordinary meaning, in the sense which they would normally have in their context',[154] went on to find that

The history of the Article and the debate which took place upon the drafts of the same in the United Maritime Consultative Council, which at the request of the Economic and Social Council of the United Nations drew up the text of the Convention for recommendation to Member Governments, confirm the principle [i.e., the interpretation] indicated above.[155]

In the *Fisheries Jurisdiction* cases, as already noted,[156] the Court expressly cited the principle that 'there is no occasion to resort to preparatory work if the text of a convention is sufficiently clear in itself',[157] but nevertheless employed *travaux préparatoires* to confirm its reading of the 1961 Exchange of Notes, reaching the conclusion that 'This history [of the

[150] Ibid., p. 106.
[151] Ibid., p. 159. The phrase *en tant que tel*, translated by 'such as it is', might better be rendered simply 'as such'.
[152] Ibid., p. 160 (emphasis added).
[153] Ibid., p. 172.
[154] *ICJ Reports*, 1960, p. 159.
[155] Ibid., p. 161.
[156] Above, p. 26.
[157] *ICJ Reports*, 1973, pp. 9–10, 56.

negotiations] reinforces the view that the Court has jurisdiction in this case . . .'.[158]

(b) *Modalities of reference to* travaux préparatoires

Since the *travaux préparatoires* are assumed to be capable of throwing light on the intentions of those who were responsible for the drafting of the treaty, normally the original parties, questions may arise as to their opposability to States which acceded to the treaty later, taking the treaty as they found it, but possibly without any knowledge of the processes of its drafting. It will be recalled that in one case the Permanent Court in such circumstances refused to take account of *travaux préparatoires* of the Treaty of Versailles on the ground that three of the States before the Court in that case had not participated in the conference.[159] This ruling has been disapproved both by the ILC[160] and (it seems) the Institut de droit international;[161] and it seems that the Court has not followed the PCIJ on this point.

No express statement has been made by the post-war Court on the point, and it is thought that it has not been specifically raised by any party in argument. The Court has however referred to *travaux préparatoires* of, in particular, the Charter and the Statute without referring to any distinction between States present at San Francisco and States not so present.

A striking example of this is the decision in the *Aerial Incident (Israel* v. *Bulgaria)* case. The issue before the Court, as to the interpretation of Article 36, paragraph 5, of the Statute, arose specifically because Bulgaria was not an original member of the United Nations (nor, it may be noted in passing, was Israel); yet the Court placed considerable reliance on the published records of the San Francisco Conference.[162]

The use by the Court in the case of *Border and Transborder Armed Actions* of *travaux préparatoires* points up an interesting and important distinction made by Fitzmaurice, who suggested that

> certain documents prepared in the course of a conference, though extraneous to the text of the eventual treaty, do not rank as mere *travaux préparatoires*, but should be regarded as conference instruments;[163]

he referred to the frequent practice whereby 'texts are adopted (and only

[158] Ibid., pp. 13, 58.

[159] *Territorial Jurisdiction of the International Commission of the River Oder, PCIJ*, Series A, No. 23, pp. 41–2. The decision was to exclude even those records which had been published and were therefore available to the three States which had not participated.

[160] *ILC Yearbook*, 1966, vol. 2, p. 223, quoted in Sinclair, *The Vienna Convention on the Law of Treaties* (2nd edn., 1984), p. 143.

[161] Granada Session, *Annuaire*, 1956, p. 319: 'Il n'y a aucun motif d'exclure l'usage de travaux préparatoires, dûment consignés et publiés, à l'encontre d'Etats ayant adhéré au traité postérieurement à sa signature par les parties originaires'. This text, prepared by Lauterpacht, was omitted from the later version by Fitzmaurice (ibid., pp. 337–8), but apparently solely for reasons of simplification.

[162] *ICJ Reports*, 1959, pp. 140–2.

[163] This *Year Book*, 28 (1951), p. 12; *Collected Edition*, I, p. 53.

adopted) on the basis of a particular interpretation which it is agreed should be recorded in the minutes'.[164]

The Court in 1988 attached importance, for the purposes of interpretation of Article XXXI of the Pact of Bogotá, to the record of a discussion of a committee of the Bogotá Conference, when a suggestion for an additional article to make a particular point clear was considered to be not necessary,

> the representative of Peru went on to say, after the vote, that 'we should place on record what has been said here, to the effect that it is understood that adhesion is unconditional and that reservations are automatically removed'.[165]

This must cast some doubt on, or constitute an exception to, a principle of interpretation postulated by Fitzmaurice, in his judicial capacity, that 'Where a particular proposal has been considered but rejected, for whatever reason, it is not possible to interpret the instrument or juridical situation to which the proposal related as if the latter had in fact been adopted.'[166] It is however doubtful in any event whether this can be regarded as a general and rigid rule.[167]

3. *Principle of Integration*[168]

> 'Begin at the beginning,' the King said, very gravely, 'and go on till you come to the end; then stop'.
>
> Lewis Carroll, *Alice in Wonderland*, Chap. XII.

Fitzmaurice's original formulation of this principle was: 'Treaties are to be interpreted as a whole, and with reference to their declared or apparent objects, purposes and principles'.[169] There is some overlap between a requirement that a text to be interpreted should be read in its context (section 2 (1)*(c)*, above) and the requirement that treaties be interpreted 'as a

[164] Ibid. It has however been suggested that 'an agreement at a conference that a term was to have stipulated meaning does not give the term that meaning unless it is capable of bearing it', or unless the agreement is embodied in the definition clause of the treaty (Crawford, this *Year Book*, 51 (1980), p. 324, commenting on *Fothergill* v. *Monarch Airlines Ltd.*, [1980] 3 WLR 209, HL). As a matter of international law, however, it is suggested that Article 31, paragraph 2(*b*), of the Vienna Convention correctly states the law, and emphasizes the distinction made by Fitzmaurice, since an 'agreement relating to the treaty' does not, like *travaux préparatoires*, rank as a mere subsidiary means of interpretation.

[165] *ICJ Reports*, 1988, p. 86, para. 37.

[166] *Namibia*, dissenting opinion, *ICJ Reports*, 1971, p. 275.

[167] Apart from the *Namibia* decision itself, from which Fitzmaurice was dissenting, note the discussion in the judgment on jurisdiction in the *Nicaragua* v. *United States* case of the two successive French versions of Article 36, paragraph 5, of the Statute: *ICJ Reports*, 1984, pp. 406–7, para. 31, and the thorough survey of the drafting history given by Judge Oda, ibid., pp. 478–81.

[168] This is one of the rare occasions when the present writer would differ from Sir Gerald Fitzmaurice on a question of terminology: it is suggested that 'Principle of Integrality' would more correctly convey the idea intended.

[169] This *Year Book*, 28 (1951), p. 9; *Collected Edition*, I, p. 50.

whole'. The latter requirement is however one of obvious good sense; it is to be presumed that when the parties drafted their treaty, they saw it as a whole, and understood each specific provision in that light.[170]

Subsequently Fitzmaurice reduced his statement of principle to a simpler formula: 'Treaties are to be interpreted as a whole, and particular parts, chapters or sections also as a whole'.[171]

The amputation of the reference to 'objects, purposes and principles' is significant. Fitzmaurice was a life-long opponent of any excessively teleological method of interpreting treaties,[172] and was therefore suspicious of interpretation 'by reference to its objects, principles, and purposes', since 'this method, taken beyond a certain point, would involve tribunals in legislative instead of judicial or interpretative functions';[173] hence the inclusion in even the original formulation of the principle of the qualification 'declared or apparent' objects and purposes.[174]

There can be no doubt that in this respect the battle—though not necessarily the war—is lost. The Vienna Convention provides that a treaty is to be interpreted

> in good faith in accordance with the ordinary meaning to be given to the terms of the treaty in their context *and in the light of its objects and purpose*,[175]

and the criterion of the 'object and purpose' has found its way into the Court's decisions, sometimes explicitly, sometimes implicitly, though not necessarily in the teleological context. It is however respecting the letter, if not the spirit, of Fitzmaurice's analysis to deal with such decisions in the context of the third principle.

In the case of a bilateral treaty, the 'intention of the parties' and the 'object of the treaty', while not indistinguishable, are clearly of very similar significance. Even in the case of a multilateral convention, the transition from the one to the other may be gradual rather than abrupt.

In the case concerning the *Application of the Convention of 1902 govern-*

[170] This presumption may not always correspond to the facts in the case of conferences for the preparation of major multilateral conventions; see the comments of do Nascimento e Silva on the disadvantages of the procedures adopted at the 1986 Vienna Conference which produced the Vienna Convention on the Law of Treaties between States and International Organizations: 'The 1969 and 1986 Conventions on the Law of Treaties: A Comparison', *International Law at a Time of Perplexity (Mélanges Rosenne)*, p. 461, at pp. 465–6.

[171] This *Year Book*, 33 (1957), p. 211; *Collected Edition*, I, p. 345.

[172] For a devastating critique from his pen, of what was admittedly an extreme form of the teleological approach, see '*Vae victis* or woe to the negotiators: Your treaty or our "interpretation" of it?', *American Journal of International Law*, 65 (1971), pp. 358 ff.

[173] This *Year Book*, 28 (1951), p. 8; *Collected Edition*, I, p. 49.

[174] Cf. the progress of the draft resolution on interpretation of treaties at the Granada Session of the Institut de droit international in 1956. The draft prepared by Lauterpacht referred to the purpose of the treaty in the context of the principle of effectiveness (*Annuaire*, p. 319); Fitzmaurice's shortened version (ibid., pp. 337–8) made no reference to the object and purpose, which however was included, in response to the discussion, in the first text, as a supplementary means of interpretation (ibid., pp. 348–9).

[175] Article 31, paragraph 1 (emphasis added).

ing the Guardianship of Infants,[176] the Court was asked to hold that the imposition and maintenance of measures concerning an infant of Dutch nationality, applied under a Swedish law on the protection of children, were incompatible with the 1902 Convention. That Convention provided that the guardianship of an infant shall be governed by his national law, and that 'the administration of a guardianship extends to the person . . . of the infant' (Art. 6). The application of the Swedish measures on protective upbringing had the effect in practice of depriving the Dutch guardian of custody and control of the person of the infant.

The Court applied a test of intention, but in terms of the intention of the Convention, rather than that of the parties to it: since however the instrument cannot possess a subjective intention of its own, this may be taken to be simply an alternative form of words to express the same idea.[177] The Court considered that it had to determine

> whether, by stipulating that the guardianship of an infant is governed by the national law of the infant, the 1902 Convention *intended* to prohibit the application to a foreign infant of a law such as the Swedish Law on the protection of children.[178]

The subsequent discussion is in such terms as 'the Convention was intended to determine . . . '; 'It was intended . . . but it was not intended . . . '; 'the 1902 Convention was not intended to define'.[179]

The idea of the purpose of the Convention is already discernible in this terminology; there is at least a shift of emphasis, if not a transformation in meaning, if one moves from the question 'What did the parties intend should be conveyed by the text of this provision of their treaty?' to the question 'What did the parties intend to achieve by concluding this treaty?' A little further on the purpose of the treaty becomes an explicit criterion. The Court puts as a rhetorical question an argument advanced by one of the parties, and replies to it: 'So to interpret the Convention would be to *go beyond its purpose*'.[180]

Similarly, the Court observes that 'The 1902 Convention was *designed* to put an end to the competing claims of several laws to govern a single legal relationship'.[181]

A striking feature of the decision in the *Aerial Incident* case between Israel and Bulgaria is that the Court, having stated that what it had to

[176] A curious feature of this judgment is that the texts to be interpreted and applied are nowhere fully quoted in the judgment. They can be found in the dissenting opinion of Judge Winiarski, *ICJ Reports*, 1958, p. 133.

[177] The authentic French text of the judgment goes a long way in personifying the Convention: 'la Convention a entendu déterminer . . . Elle a voulu . . . elle n'a pas entendu établir . . . ' (*ICJ Reports*, 1958, p. 67).

[178] *ICJ Reports*, 1958, p. 67, emphasis added.

[179] Ibid., pp. 67–8.

[180] Ibid., p. 88, emphasis added.

[181] Ibid., p. 71, emphasis added. The French is more explicit: 'La Convention de 1902 a pour but . . . '.

determine was 'whether Article 36, paragraph 5, of the Statute is applicable to the Bulgarian Declaration of 1921',[182] immediately began its reasoning by stating what, in the Court's view, was the object of that provision of the Statute.[183] The authors of the joint dissenting opinion attached to that judgment (Judges Lauterpacht, Wellington Koo and Spender) considered that the Court, so far from interpreting the actual text of Article 36, paragraph 5, had added two unstated conditions to it.[184] The judgment itself justifies its view as to the effect of the provision by saying that

> Thus to restrict the application of Article 36, paragraph 5, to the States signatories of the Statute is *to take into account the purpose* for which the provision was adopted.[185]

It is ironic that the 'object and purpose' criterion, at least in those terms, was developed by the Court itself, not in the context of interpretation but as the test for the acceptability of a reservation to a multilateral convention; and that it failed to secure international acceptance in that function.[186] In the context of treaty interpretation, it has had the misfortune to have become associated with the various stages of the attempts to resolve, through the International Court, the thorny problem of South West Africa,[187] and the controversy which has surrounded those efforts and the legal arguments on the substantive questions of the status of the territory and the rights and duties of South Africa, has infected also some of the theoretical bases of the conflicting approaches.[188]

In the period now under examination, it was in effect in the *South West Africa* cases that the primary canon of interpretation relying on the 'natural and ordinary meaning of the words employed' was most drastically dislodged from its throne. Referring to the argument that the category of 'Members of the League of Nations' had become what is termed in mathematics an empty set—a class of which there are, or (in this case) are now, no members—the Court said:

> This contention is claimed to be based upon the natural and ordinary meaning of the words employed in the provision. But this rule of interpretation is not an absolute one. Where such a method of interpretation results in a meaning incompatible with the spirit, purpose and context of the clause or instrument in which the words are contained, no reliance can be validly placed on it.[189]

The reference to the 'spirit, purpose and *context*' stands where one

[182] *ICJ Reports*, 1959, p. 136.

[183] As pointed out by Leo Gross, 'Treaty Interpretation: the proper rôle of an international tribunal', *Proceedings of the American Society of International Law*, 1969, p. 133.

[184] *ICJ Reports*, 1959, p. 156.

[185] Ibid., p. 139 (emphasis added).

[186] See, e.g., ILC Report for 1951, para. 24.

[187] *Reservations to the Genocide Convention, ICJ Reports*, 1951, pp. 24 ff.

[188] This is not to say that reference to the purpose of a treaty, particularly a multilateral treaty, has not been made or suggested before: cf. Degan, 'L'Interprétation des accords en droit international', pp. 137 ff., on doctrinal and historical antecedents.

[189] *ICJ Reports*, 1962, p. 336.

would have expected a reference to an 'absurd or unreasonable' result as justifying rejection of the literal interpretation. The substitution is full of significance: it enabled the Court to refer, not merely to the individual mandate instrument itself, but to the whole mandates system, and in effect to reject the interpretation advanced as incompatible with the 'purpose' of the 'context' as thus widely defined.

The most evident and effective recourse to the idea of the 'object and purpose' of the treaty as relevant to, if not governing for, its interpretation, is of course to be found in the *Namibia* advisory opinion in 1971. The drafting however betrays some uneasiness in the handling of the interrelation of canons of interpretation.

After examining Article 22 of the League of Nations Covenant and the terms of the Mandate for German South West Africa, the Court stated its conclusion that

> the relevant provisions of the Covenant and those of the Mandate itself preclude any doubt as to the establishment of definite legal obligations [of the mandatory power] designed for the attainment of the object and purpose of the Mandate.[190]

The Court then rejected the South African argument, based on contemporary records, that 'C'-class mandates were intended to be 'little different from annexation'. In the view of the Court,

> It cannot tenably be argued that the clear meaning of the mandate institutions could be ignored by placing upon the explicit provisions embodying its principles a construction at variance with its object and purpose.[191]

It is not clear what purpose is served by the last part of this sentence; on classical canons of interpretation, if there is a 'clear meaning' to be derived from examination of 'explicit provisions', no other construction can be justified. It is possible, however, that the 'object and purpose' concept was so dominant that it was contemplated that in the opposite case—if the 'clear meaning' was at variance with the object and purpose of the treaty—the latter would prevail.[192] This is however to go a good deal further than does Article 31 of the Vienna Convention.

The Court then employs the method which, in the first of these articles, we have called 'intertemporal *renvoi*'[193] to reach the conclusion that 'the ultimate object of the sacred trust was the self-determination and independence of the peoples concerned',[194] from which it was not difficult to

[190] *ICJ Reports*, 1971, p. 30, para. 49.

[191] Ibid., p. 50.

[192] This appears to have been the view taken by Judge de Castro: 'even a clause which is reasonably clear cannot be interpreted literally if by doing so one reaches a result contrary to the purpose of the treaty': *ICJ Reports*, 1971, p. 183: see also, in a different context, the same judge's views at ibid., p. 203.

[193] This *Year Book*, 60 (1989), pp. 135–43.

[194] *ICJ Reports*, 1971, p. 31, para. 53.

deduce that the object and purpose of 'C' mandates was the same as that of 'A' and 'B' mandates.[195]

A further problem in ascertaining the intention of the parties to a multilateral instrument is how to be sure that the intention was one common to all parties, and not limited to some of them. In the *Namibia* case,

> The Government of South Africa, in its written statement, presented a detailed analysis of the intentions of some of the participants in the Paris Peace Conference, who approved a resolution which, with some alterations and additions, eventually became Article 22 of the Covenant. At the conclusion and in the light of this analysis it suggested that it was quite natural for commentators to refer to ' "C" mandates as being in their practical effect not far removed from annexation'.[196]

The Court objected to this interpretation on the grounds that 'It puts too much emphasis on the intentions of some of the parties and too little on the instrument which emerged from the negotiations'.[197]

This sentence is a very compressed argument. If it is established that a substantial number of the parties to a multilateral treaty envisaged that it should have a particular meaning, then much depends on the attitude of the other parties. If it appears that they had no definite view on the point, then the shared intention of the other group may be taken to be the intended meaning of the treaty; this was, in effect, the contention of South Africa. If however there is a strongly opposed view held by some or all of the other States, then there can be no *consensus ad idem* at all on the point. The Court's resolution of the difficulty consists of an amalgamation of the idea of the 'object and purpose of the treaty'—or in this case, of the mandates system—with the idea that the text of the treaty is what matters, not the subjective views which can be shown by the *travaux préparatoires* to have existed prior to its adoption. It is thus a remarkable recognition of the independence gained by the 'emergent purpose' from the will of the original parties.

Much of the subsequent argument in the *Namibia* advisory opinion is addressed, not to the interpretation of the Mandate as a treaty, but to questions of the mandate system, and of the events surrounding the end of the League and the creation of the United Nations. These discussions are thus not of assistance for present purposes, where it is the rules and principles applicable to interpretation *of treaties* which are under consideration.

In the judgment on the *Appeal relating to the Jurisdiction of the ICAO Council*, the expression 'the object and purpose' of the Chicago Convention does not appear; but the philosophy of the judgment is inspired much more by considerations of that kind than by concentration on the text. This emerges particularly from examination of the opinions appended to it. President Zafrulla Khan disagreed with the majority on the question whether the Convention provided for a particular case, on the ground that the Court

[195] Ibid., p. 32, para. 54.
[196] Ibid., p. 28, para. 45.
[197] Ibid.

had merely shown 'the desirability of a provision to that effect', and continued: 'However strong that desirability may be it cannot serve as a substitute for the lack of such a provision in the Convention . . . '.[198] Judge Lachs began his examination of the relevant text by observing that 'its strict verbal meaning should constitute a point of departure but cannot be conclusive',[199] thus highlighting the absence in the judgment of any reference to the 'ordinary meaning' of the words of the Convention. Similarly Judge de Castro begins with 'a reading of Article 84 without any preconceived views',[200] and Judge Jiménez de Aréchaga emphasizes the single word in the relevant provision which seemed to him to indicate the meaning of the text.[201]

In the judgment, the question whether a 'decision' of the ICAO Council in respect of which an appeal could be brought to the Court does or does not include a decision on jurisdiction is dealt with entirely in terms of principles of judicial competence, rather than as a matter either of the meaning of the term or of the intention of the parties.[202] Similarly, the question whether a 'complaint' under the Transit Agreement is appealable is dealt with in terms of the consequences of a hypothetical decision that it is not—an unavowed application of the *ut res magis valeat* rule.[203]

In the case of *Border and Transborder Armed Actions*, the Court applied the 'object and purpose' criterion in a less controversial way, in relation to the principle of effectiveness. It considered that an interpretation, advanced by Honduras, of Article XXXI of the Pact of Bogotá, which appeared to represent acceptance by the contracting States of the jurisdiction of the Court,

> would however imply that the commitment, at first sight firm and unconditional, set forth in Article XXXI would, in fact, be emptied of all content if, for any reason, the dispute were not subject to prior conciliation. Such a solution would be clearly contrary to both the object and the purpose of the Pact.[204]

If the intention of the rule *ut res magis valeat quam pereat* is to ensure effectiveness of treaties, it is appropriate, if not essential, to consider what the treaty was intended to do before considering whether a particular interpretation of its provisions would serve its ends, or defeat them.

In the *Elettronica Sicula* case, there is a passing reference to the criterion of the object of a treaty: when examining rival interpretations offered of a provision of the Treaty between the United States and Italy alleged to have been breached, the Chamber observed, almost as a parenthesis, that it 'has some sympathy with the contention of the United States, as being more in

[198] *ICJ Reports*, 1972, p. 71.
[199] Ibid., p. 76.
[200] Ibid., p. 119.
[201] Ibid., p. 144.
[202] Ibid., pp. 55–7, para. 18.
[203] Ibid., pp. 58–9, paras. 19–20.
[204] *ICJ Reports*, 1988, p. 89, para. 46.

accord with the general purpose of the FCN Treaty'.[205] This proves, however, to be an *obiter dictum*, as the relevant claim under this provision of the Treaty was dismissed on other grounds; and the Chamber gives no explanation of what was, in its perception, the 'general purpose' of the Treaty.

4. *Principle of Effectiveness*[206]

(1) *The two meanings of the principle*

In his observations on this principle, Fitzmaurice did not explicitly make the distinction (though it is clear that he was aware of it) between two incarnations of the same idea, which are regarded by some writers as two separate rules. In the terminology suggested by Berlia,[207] these are 'la règle de l'effet utile' and 'la règle de l'efficacité'. The first is the rule that all provisions of the treaty or other instrument must be supposed to have been intended to have significance and to be necessary to convey the intended meaning; that an interpretation which reduces some part of the text to the status of a pleonasm, or mere surplussage, is prima facie suspect. The second is the rule that the instrument as a whole, and each of its provisions, must be taken to have been intended to achieve some end, and that an interpretation which would make the text ineffective to achieve the object in view is, again, prima facie suspect. This latter rule is of course akin to the 'object and purpose' criterion, and has therefore, like that criterion, to be employed with discretion.[208]

Of the cases commented on by Fitzmaurice, the *Corfu Channel*[209] and the *Anglo-Iranian Oil Co.* decisions[210] are examples of the first rule; the dicta in the *Interpretation of Peace Treaties* case[211] and the *Ambatielos* case[212] are examples of the second.

The 'principle of effectiveness' may be, and has been, used to refer to both rules; the second is however also conveniently defined by the adage *ut res magis valeat quam pereat*.

Whether a treaty is to be interpreted so as to give effect to the presumed intention of the parties, or with a view to its object and purpose, it can be safely assumed that an interpretation which leads to an impossibility or absurdity must be incompatible with either criterion. It can further be assumed that the treaty, and each provision thereof, was meant to achieve something, so that an interpretation which would make it no more than an empty gesture must for that reason be regarded as of dubious validity.

[205] *ICJ Reports*, 1989, p. 79, para. 132.

[206] This principle is not as such provided for in the Vienna Convention.

[207] 'Contribution à l'interprétation des traités', *Recueil des cours*, 114 (1965–I), pp. 306 ff.

[208] Cf. Winiarski, dissenting opinion in *Certain Expenses*, *ICJ Reports*, 1962, p. 230.

[209] *ICJ Reports*, 1949, p. 24: discussed in this *Year Book*, 28 (1951), p. 19; *Collected Edition*, I, p. 60.

[210] *ICJ Reports*, 1952, p. 105: discussed in this *Year Book*, 33 (1957), p. 222.

[211] *ICJ Reports*, 1950, p. 229: discussed in this *Year Book*, 28 (1951), p. 20.

[212] *ICJ Reports*, 1952, p. 45: discussed in this *Year Book*, 33 (1957), p. 221.

(2) *Impossibility and its relationship to the principle*

In the *Guardianship of Infants* case, the Court, when interpreting the 1902 Convention on the subject, drew a distinction between two sets of circumstances in which the law of country A might fall to be applied in country B. The Convention had provided that 'The guardianship of an infant shall be governed by the natural law of the infant'; the Court concluded that the Convention

> thereby prescribed to the courts of each contracting State that they should apply a foreign law when the infant involved was a foreigner. It is perfectly conceivable that the courts of a State should in certain cases apply a foreign law.[213]

However, as regards the domain of applicability of the national law on the protection of children and otherwise,

> The measures provided for or prescribed by Swedish law are applied, at least in the first stage as was done in the present case, by an administrative organ. Such an organ can act only in accordance with its own law; it is inconceivable that the Swedish Child Welfare Board should apply Dutch law to a Dutch infant living in Sweden and equally inconceivable that the competent Dutch organ should apply Dutch law to such an infant living abroad. What a Swedish or Dutch Court can do in matters of guardianship, pursuant to the 1902 Convention namely apply a foreign law—Dutch law or Swedish law as the case may be—the authorities of those countries cannot do in the matter of protective upbringing. To extend the 1902 Convention to such a situation would lead to an impossibility. It is not permissible so to construe the Convention as to bring about such a result.[214]

While it is undoubtedly a sound maxim that *pactum non cogit ad impossibilia*,[215] it is worth observing that what the Court is really saying here is simply that the application of a foreign law by an administrative organ is such an unusual and therefore unlikely operation that an interpretation of the Convention which would require it is *a priori* unlikely; there is however nothing 'impossible' about such a process.[216]

What is meant, perhaps, is not so much that the effect of the disputed interpretation is impossible, as that that effect would be so exceptional or inconvenient that it is *improbable* as a result which could have been aimed at by the treaty. This approach to interpretation is to be found in the 1966 judgment in the *South West Africa* cases, in connection with the contention that the individual members of the League of Nations had the right of supervision and enforcement of the obligations of a mandatory:

[213] *ICJ Reports*, 1958, p. 70.

[214] Ibid.

[215] And the impossibility may be a legal one: cf. the discussion of the *Right of Passage* case, pp. 60 ff., below.

[216] In those legal systems in which personal status is subject to the law of the person's nationality, it may well happen that an administrative body has to apply a foreign law to determine, for example, capacity to marry.

> The theory that the members of the League possessed such rights, but were precluded from exercising them unless by recourse to adjudication, constitutes an essentially improbable supposition for which the relevant texts afford no warrant.[217]

If it is to be assumed that a treaty was not intended to achieve the impossible, it is also to be assumed that a treaty was not intended to achieve nothing at all. An interpretation which would result in a text being totally ineffective is therefore prima facie unacceptable.

It is unlikely that an interpretation would be offered which would render the whole of a treaty ineffective; it is more likely to be a particular sentence or clause which may be reduced to mere surplussage. In the *Maritime Safety Committee (IMCO)* case, it was argued that the reference in the disputed Article 28(*a*) to the members of the Committee being 'elected' meant that the 'eight largest ship-owning nations' had no absolute right to be elected, because election implies discretionary choice. The Court rejected this view:

> The argument based on discretion would permit the Assembly, in use only of its discretion, to decide through its vote which nations have or do not have an important interest in maritime safety and to deny membership on the Committee to any State regardless of the size of its tonnage or any other qualification. The effect of such an interpretation would be to render superfluous the greater part of Article 28(*a*) and to erect the discretion of the Assembly as the supreme rule for the constitution of the Maritime Safety Committee. This would in the opinion of the Court be incompatible with the principle underlying the Article.[218]

Interpretation on these lines of course implies a rejection of any idea of fallibility of the original parties to a treaty; while it may be taken as certain that the parties did not intend any part of their treaty to be ineffective, that does not mean that the drafting used was necessarily watertight, or that they foresaw and provided for all contingencies in such a way that no circumstances would find the treaty wanting. If therefore a particular set of circumstances had arisen or could be imagined in which a treaty provision, according to an otherwise acceptable interpretation, would be ineffective[219] or lead to improbable results, this is not necessarily a ground for rejecting that interpretation. The principle of effectiveness should be employed as an aid to assessment of likely intentions, rather than as a rigid canon of interpretation whereby the text must be deemed to be effective in all circumstances.

Somewhat less convincing therefore is a finding of this kind by the Court in the *Border and Transborder Armed Actions* case. The point at issue was the relationship between various provisions of the Pact of Bogotá concerning conciliation or adjudication of disputes; the drafting of the Pact was far

[217] *ICJ Reports*, 1966, pp. 31–2, para. 42.

[218] *ICJ Reports*, 1960, p. 160.

[219] Such a case has to be distinguished from the case in which some part or provision of a treaty is invalid as legally impermissible, in which case the whole treaty may be invalidated; cf. Lauterpacht in *Certain Norwegian Loans, ICJ Reports*, 1957, pp. 57–99, and see also Article 44 of the Vienna Convention.

from lucid in this respect. In respect of a particular interpretation advanced by Honduras, the Court considered that it

> would however imply that the commitment [to judicial settlement], at first sight firm and unconditional, set forth in Article XXXI would, in fact, be emptied of all content if, for any reason, the dispute were not subjected to prior conciliation.[220]

Examination both of the obscure texts of the articles of the Pact, and of the available *travaux préparatoires*,[221] suggests that as a matter of practical likelihood it cannot be excluded that the draftsmen simply did not foresee this result of the language they employed.

The principle of effectiveness is essentially negative in effect: it affords a means of excluding any interpretation of the text which would make it a dead letter, but does not of itself necessarily supply or point to the correct interpretation. Various intended 'effects' can be attributed to an ambiguous text, depending on the view one takes of the parties' intentions, or of the 'object and purpose' of the treaty; all the principle of the *effet utile* does is to exclude wholly ineffective results.

Sir Gerald Fitzmaurice touched on this aspect of the principle of effectiveness in his dissenting opinion in the *Namibia* case, when discussing the effect to be attributed to the provision in Article 80 of the United Nations Charter that 'nothing in this Chapter [Chapter XII] shall be construed in or of itself to alter in any manner the rights whatsoever of any States or any peoples . . . '. After setting out his own interpretation of Article 80, he observed:

> It is argued that the foregoing interpretation deprives Article 80 of all meaning, since (so it is contended) there is nothing in Chapter XII of the Charter that *could* alter or impair existing rights, etc. Even if this were the case, it would not be a valid juridical reason for reading into this provision what *on any view* is not there, namely a self-operating United Nations successorship to League functions,—the automatic conversion of an obligation of accountability to the League Council (still extant when Article 80 came into force) into an obligation towards the Assembly of the United Nations.[222]

What Fitzmaurice is saying, in effect, is that there must be a limit to the working of the criterion of the *effet utile*,[223] that an interpretation that leads to the practical ineffectiveness of a particular provision can only be rejected if there is an alternative interpretation which produces an effective result and does not offend against other canons of interpretation. The principle of

[220] *ICJ Reports*, 1988, p. 89, para. 46. It should be added that the Court nails its arguments with the concluding sentence: 'Such a solution would be clearly contrary to both the object and the purpose of the Pact'.

[221] As the Court noted in its judgment, these are incomplete: *ICJ Reports*, 1988, p. 85, para. 37.

[222] *ICJ Reports*, 1971, p. 240, para. 30.

[223] In the same year, in an extra-judicial capacity, he pointed out that 'the maxim "*ut magis*" is all too frequently misunderstood as denoting that agreements should always be given their *maximum possible* effect, whereas its real object is merely *("quam pereat")* to prevent them failing altogether'; '*Vae victis* or woe to the negotiators: Your treaty or our "interpretation" of it?', *American Journal of International Law*, 65 (1971), p. 358, at p. 373.

effectiveness, in other words, cannot be used to justify re-writing the treaty.[224]

Whether or not one agrees with Fitzmaurice's stand on the significance of Article 80, the force of his analysis on the general question must be recognized. Only an extreme teleological, non-voluntaristic philosophy would justify the opposite view.

5. *Principle of Subsequent Practice of the Parties*

Article 31, paragraph 3(*b*), of the Vienna Convention on the Law of Treaties authorizes and requires reference to, along with the context of the treaty terms,

> any subsequent practice in the application of the treaty which establishes the agreement of the parties regarding its interpretation.

It is of course no easy task to distinguish, in the activities of parties to a treaty subsequent to its conclusion, between, first, the mere implementation of a treaty in accordance with its terms, secondly, practice revelatory of a recognized interpretation of the treaty, thirdly, practice departing from the terms of a treaty so as to amount to an agreed modification of it,[225] and fourthly, practice in the areas covered by the treaty giving rise to new customary rights, independent of the treaty.[226] The draft produced by the ILC which eventually became the Vienna Convention included, alongside the article on practice as a means of interpretation of a treaty (Art. 27), an article (Art. 38), subsequently deleted, recognizing the possibility of a treaty being modified by subsequent practice amounting to an agreement between the parties.[227]

As already stated in the previous article in this series,[228] it is probably to the third or fourth category that one should assign the Court's recognition

[224] Fitzmaurice had already warned that 'the main problem with regard to the principle of effectiveness is to keep it within bounds, to prevent it from leading to judicial legislation (its natural tendency being teleological), and to preserve a due proportion between it and the textual principle': this *Year Book*, 28 (1951), p. 19; *Collected Edition*, I, p. 60; and in his joint (with Sir Percy Spender) dissenting opinion in *South West Africa* in 1962, he observed that 'the principle of interpretation directed to giving provisions their maximum effect cannot legitimately be employed in order to introduce what would amount to a revision of those provisions': *ICJ Reports*, 1962, p. 468; see also ibid., pp. 511–13.

[225] In this sense, Capotorti, 'Sul valore della prassi applicativa dei trattati secondo la convenzione di Vienna', *Le Droit international à l'heure de sa codification* (*Mélanges Ago*), vol. 1, pp. 199–200. See also Jean-Pierre Cot, 'La Conduite subséquente des parties à un traité', *Revue générale de droit international public*, 1966, pp. 632 ff.

[226] In this latter category should be placed, it is suggested, the acquisition by Portugal of sovereignty over the enclaved villages as a result of the inaction of the British and Indian Governments: *Right of Passage, ICJ Reports*, 1960, p. 39. Note the interesting point made by counsel for South Africa in the *Namibia* case, that practice modifying a treaty must be accompanied by an intention to change the situation, while practice creating customary law must be intended as a compliance with existing law: *Pleadings*, vol. 2, p. 210.

[227] The reasons for the deletion of this article at the Vienna Conference were debated before the court in the *Namibia* case: see the *Pleadings* in that case, vol. 1, p. 394; vol. 2, pp. 65, 203–7.

[228] This *Year Book*, 61 (1990), p. 77.

in its advisory opinion in the *Namibia* case of a 'general practice of [the] organization' as justifying the validity of resolutions of the United Nations Security Council adopted over the abstention of a permanent member, notwithstanding the requirement of Article 27 of the Charter that there be an affirmative vote of all five permanent members.[229]

The Court's decision in the *Right of Passage* case shows that the subsequent practice of the parties may be relevant not merely to the interpretation of a treaty, but even to its very existence and validity. India in that case had claimed that the 1779 Treaty relied on by Portugal 'was not validly entered into and never became in law a treaty binding upon the Marathas'[230] (the rulers of India at the time). The Court, in rejecting this contention, noted that, according to the evidence, 'The Marathas themselves regarded the Treaty of 1779 as valid and binding upon them, and gave effect to its provisions'.[231]

The practice referred to need not necessarily be practice in implementation of the particular provision of the treaty whose meaning is disputed. In the *Maritime Safety Committee (IMCO)* case, the question of interpretation was the meaning to be attached to the expression 'the largest ship-owning nations' in Article 28(*a*) of the IMCO Convention. The Court stated that

> There appear to be but two meanings which could demand serious consideration: either the words refer to the tonnage beneficially owned by the nationals of a State or they refer to the registered tonnage of a flag State regardless of its private or State ownership.[232]

The Court observed that other provisions of the Convention used such expressions as 'States . . . which . . . have a total tonnage . . . ' (Art. 60), or States 'having a substantial interest in providing international shipping services' (Art. 17(*c*)). It examined the practice of the Organization under these texts, and found that it revealed 'the reliance placed upon registered tonnage',[233] from which it felt able to deduce that

> it is unlikely that when [Art. 28(*a*)] was drafted and incorporated into the Convention it was contemplated that any criterion other than registered tonnage should determine which were the largest ship-owning nations.[234]

This is also an example of the practice of an organization, or more precisely, of the organs of an organization, being taken into account for the interpretation of its constitutive instrument. Similarly, in the *Certain*

[229] *ICJ Reports*, 1971, p. 22, para. 22.
[230] *ICJ Reports*, 1960, p. 37.
[231] Ibid.
[232] Ibid., p. 167.
[233] Ibid., p. 168.
[234] Ibid., p. 169.

Expenses case, the Court confirmed its finding in the *Admissions* case[235] that for the purpose of interpreting the United Nations Charter, it is legitimate to take into account practice of the General Assembly and the Security Council:

> The Court [in the *Admissions* case] sustained its interpretation of Article 4 by considering the manner in which the organs concerned 'have consistently interpreted the text' in their practice . . . [236]

The Security Council and the General Assembly are of course not 'parties' to the Charter, but they are composed of such parties.[237]

Negative practice—that is to say, the absence of action which would have been expected had a certain interpretation of a treaty been the correct one—has also been taken into account by the Court. In the *Border and Transborder Armed Actions* case between Nicaragua and Honduras, it was the contention of Honduras that Article XXXI of the Pact of Bogotá, if sufficient in itself as a title of jurisdiction justifying institution of proceedings by unilateral application (as the Court, contrary to the view of Honduras, held it was), was none the less to be read, as regards each State party, as subject to whatever reservations that State had appended to any declaration made by it under the Optional Clause of the Court's Statute. The Court's interpretation of the texts was that 'the commitment in Article XXXI can only be limited by means of reservations to the Pact itself. It is an autonomous commitment.'[238] The Court then observed:

> That interpretation, moreover, corresponds to the practice of the parties to the Pact since 1948.
>
> They have not, at any time, linked together Article XXXI and the declarations of acceptance of compulsory jurisdiction made under Article 36, paragraphs 2 and 4, of the Statute. Thus no State, when adhering to or ratifying the Pact, had deposited with the United Nations Secretary-General a declaration of acceptance of compulsory jurisdiction under the conditions laid down by the Statute. Moreover, no State party to the Pact (other than Honduras in 1986) saw any need, when renewing or amending its declaration of acceptance of compulsory jurisdiction, to notify the text to the Secretary-General of the Organization of American States, the depositary of the Pact, for transmission to the other parties.[239]

Negative practice is however a concept to be handled with care, for obvious reasons: actions may speak louder than words, but non-action is equivalent to silence, and silence is usually susceptible of many interpret-

[235] *ICJ Reports*, 1950, pp. 8–9.

[236] *ICJ Reports*, 1962, p. 157. The emphasis on the appeal to practice solely by way of confirmation of interpretation may be noted.

[237] Cf. also the separate opinion of Judge Jiménez de Aréchaga in the *ICAO Appeal* case, in which he found that the interpretation, which he regarded as correct, of the Air Transit Agreement was 'confirmed by the Rules for Settlement of Differences, adopted by the ICAO Council': *ICJ Reports*, 1972, p. 141.

[238] *ICJ Reports*, 1988, p. 85, para. 36.

[239] Ibid., p. 87, para. 40.

ations.[240] In the *Nicaragua* v. *United States* case, the Court had to consider whether Article 36, paragraph 5, of the Statute, maintaining in force PCIJ declarations, should be interpreted to give post-1946 validity to Nicaragua's declaration of acceptance of the jurisdiction of the Permanent Court, even though it had admittedly been without binding effect previously, for lack of ratification of the Protocol of Signature of the PCIJ Statute. One of the arguments it relied on was that, in face of a number of post-war publications showing Nicaragua as a State still bound by an acceptance of the PCIJ Optional Clause, neither Nicaragua itself nor any other State had queried such indication or protested against it. Some States had carried this listing over into their own official publications (though the Court did not take this further than to say that 'it would be difficult to interpret the fact of such reproduction as signifying objection to the interpretation thus given').[241] The Court concluded

> that the interpretation whereby the provisions of Article 36, paragraph 5, cover the case of Nicaragua has been confirmed by the subsequent conduct of the parties to the treaty in question, the Statute of the Court.[242]

It is suggested that for States other than Nicaragua itself, this conclusion may have been unrealistic. In effect, clerical action consistent with one interpretation of the treaty[243] was taken by the Registry of the Court and the UN Secretariat, in a field where those bodies were expected to establish lists for reference; if States then did not react, it is at least probable that they took the Registry publications at their face value, and did not enquire into what interpretation of the Statute might be implied by them.[244] Furthermore, the conduct relied on is with difficulty referable to consistency with an intention as to the interpretation of Article 36, paragraph 5, at the time of its adoption; it squares more easily with the concept of an independent acceptance of Nicaragua's position by conduct, independently of any question of treaty interpretation—and this is the alternative schema relied on by the Court.

It has been an essential element of the principle of the relevance of subsequent practice as developed in the jurisprudence that the practice is taken as indicative or confirmatory of what the intentions of the parties to the treaty were at the time of its conclusion.[245] The idea underlying this is well

[240] It may in fact be intended by States to leave open many interpretations, and to maintain convenient ambiguity: 'l'on ne sort de l'équivoque qu'à son détriment' (Cardinal de Berny, quoted by Buffet-Tchakaloff, 'La Compétence de la C.I.J. dans l'affaire des Actions frontalières et transfrontalières', *Revue générale de droit international public*, 1989, p. 644). This would however not seem to justify the Court in such circumstances pronouncing a *non liquet*.

[241] *ICJ Reports*, 1984, p. 410, para. 40.

[242] Ibid., p. 411, para. 42.

[243] The action was not always unambiguously referable to that interpretation: see *ICJ Reports*, 1984, p. 408, para. 36, and the observations of Judge Jennings, ibid., pp. 541–4.

[244] In this sense, Judge Oda's separate opinion, ibid., p. 488.

[245] The question is the subject of an excellent discussion in Karl, *Vertrag und spätere Praxis im Völkerrecht* (Berlin, 1983), pp. 127–39.

expressed, though in slightly different context,[246] by Fitzmaurice in his separate opinion in the *Temple* case.

It is a general principle of law, which has been applied in many contexts, that a party's attitude, state of mind or intentions at a later date can be regarded as good evidence—in relation to the same or a closely connected matter—of his attitude, state of mind or intentions at an earlier date also; provided of course that there is no direct evidence rebutting the presumption thus raised.[247]

Equally conceivable of course is a practice which establishes a working relationship between the parties which can be treated as governed by a provision of the treaty on the face of its text, but which was not in fact contemplated by the parties when they prepared the treaty. It is also possible that the meaning and effect originally attached by the parties to a particular provision proves, in practice, to be unworkable or inconvenient, or the parties change their minds, and an alternative operation of the provision is tacitly substituted;[248] such alternatives must of course be compatible with the wording of the treaty's provisions[249]—otherwise the situation would be one of modification by practice.

So long as this historical approach is adopted, it is not essential to show that the practice was common to all the parties to the treaty. At the time of conclusion of the treaty they had, by definition, a common will; and subsequent practice of some parties—even, conceivably, of only one, if not objected to—may be treated as evidence of what the will of those parties was at the time of conclusion of the treaty, and hence as evidence of the common will. It is however necessary to distinguish between the practice and the intention: the practice may be limited to some of the parties, but the intention to which it points must have been common to all; if it is clear that the intention was that of only some parties, this is insufficient.[250]

In the *Border and Transborder Armed Actions* case, a further argument on the question of interpretation described above was furnished by the existence of a reservation to the Pact of Bogotá made by the United States at the time of signature, whereby the acceptance by the United States of jurisdiction under the Pact was to be 'limited by any jurisdictional or other limi-

[246] Fitzmaurice was discussing the contention that a treaty of 1904 and subsequent conduct should be interpreted on the basis of a presumed intention of the parties to ensure stability of treaties, and this intention—rather than the actual interpretation of the text of the 1904 treaty—was, it was said, confirmed by subsequent treaties of 1925 and 1937.

[247] *ICJ Reports*, 1962, p. 61. The point has arisen before the Court of Appeal whether reference may be made, by way of *travaux préparatoires*, to the records of a conference engaged in considering amendment of a multilateral convention, in order to show what the meaning was of the *unamended* convention: *Fothergill* v. *Monarch Airlines Ltd.*, [1979] 3 WLR 491, and see the commentary of Crawford, this *Year Book*, 50 (1979), pp. 236–40.

[248] The subsequent practice thus becomes what Karl calls 'an independent factor of interpretation' (*selbständiger Auslegungsfaktor*).

[249] It was suggested by Bernhardt that the draft article prepared by the ILC be amended specifically to make this clear: 'Interpretation and Implied (Tacit) Modification of Treaties', *Zeitschrift für ausländisches öffentliches Recht und Völkerrecht*, 27 (1967), p. 491 at p. 499.

[250] See above, p. 42.

tations contained in' any Optional Clause declaration made by the United States. The Court noted that

> It is common ground between the Parties that if the Honduran interpretation of Article XXXI of the Pact be correct, this reservation would not modify the legal situation created by that Article, and therefore would not be necessary; Honduras argues however that it was not a true reservation, but merely an interpretative declaration.[251]

The Court therefore took note also of a Department of State report which made it clear that

> the United States reservation on this point was intended to achieve something which, in the opinion of the United States delegation, could not be brought about merely by applying Article XXXI.[252]

Thus the practice of one party to the treaty was indicative of the interpretation intended by all parties. It is noteworthy that the United States was not a party to the case before the Court, so that no element of admission was involved; this distinguishes the case from the situation in, for example, the advisory opinion on the *Status of South West Africa*, where admission by the South African Government confirmed a particular interpretation of the Mandate, and the Court observed:

> These declarations constitute recognition by the Union Government of the continuance of its obligations under the Mandate and not a mere indication of the future conduct of that Government. Interpretations placed upon legal instruments by the parties to them, though not conclusive as to their meaning, have considerable probative value when they contain recognition by a party of its own obligations under an instrument.[253]

Taken in isolation, the United States reservation to the Pact of Bogotá, as elucidated by the Department of State memorandum, does no more than give the view of one party, not concerned in the dispute before the Court, as to the interpretation of the multilateral treaty in question.[254] As such, its probative force is limited, amounting to less perhaps even than the 'similar treaties' relied on in the *Hostages* case.[255] It must therefore be emphasized

[251] *ICJ Reports*, 1988, p. 86, para. 38.

[252] Ibid., p. 87, para. 39.

[253] *ICJ Reports*, 1950, pp. 135–6.

[254] It is of course material that there was no objection to the United States reservation by any other party to the Pact, and this might be read as a general tacit acceptance amounting to a practice. This point was not however taken by the Court. Can a single act, even if tacitly accepted by all other parties, constitute a 'practice'? *Contra*, Capotorti, op. cit. above (n. 225), p. 208: 'per poter trarre conseguenze ulteriori (interpretative o modificative) dal comportamento delle parti, deve trattarsi di un contegno non limitato ad un singolo momento, e quindi a una singola occasione'; Sinclair, *The Vienna Convention on the Law of Treaties*, p. 137: 'A practice is a sequence of facts or acts and cannot in general be established by one isolated fact or act, or even by several individual applications'; Yasseen, 'L'Interprétation des traités d'après la Convention de Vienne sur le droit des traités', *Recueil des cours*, 151 (1976–III), p. 48.

[255] See below, p. 68.

that the Court in the *Border and Transborder Armed Actions* case only used the United States reservation as confirmatory evidence; it had already rejected the interpretation advanced by Honduras as not 'compatible with the actual terms of the Pact',[256] and had found confirmation of its reading of the text in the *travaux préparatoires*.[257]

A case in which the question whether the practice pointed to a common will of the parties or to a subsequent agreement, and the question whether such later agreement was interpretative or modificatory, gave rise to—and became embroiled in—much confusion, was the *Temple of Preah Vihear* case. To recapitulate the essential facts, the treaty in question defined the frontier between Siam and Cambodia as following a particular watershed, and entrusted the delimitation to a Boundary Commission. The map produced by the Commission showed the frontier by a line which was accepted by both parties, but which was discovered, many years later, to diverge markedly from the watershed, and to pass the 'wrong' side of the temple which was the bone of contention.

The Court, at one stage of its judgment, put the question in terms of treaty interpretation:

> The Court considers that the acceptance of the Annex I map by the Parties caused the map to enter the treaty settlement and to become an integral part of it. It cannot be said that this process involved a departure from, and even a violation of the terms of the Treaty of 1904, wherever the map line diverged from the line of the watershed, for, as the Court sees the matter, the map (whether in all respects accurate by reference to the true watershed line or not) was accepted by the Parties in 1908 and thereafter as constituting the result of the interpretation given by the two Governments to the delimitation which the Treaty itself required. In other words, the Parties at that time adopted an interpretation of the treaty settlement which caused the map line, in so far as it may have departed from the line of the watershed, to prevail over the relevant clause of the treaty.[258]

At first sight, this looks more like an agreed modification of the treaty than an agreed interpretation: it surely cannot be possible to read the word 'watershed' as meaning 'a line which the surveyors thought was the watershed but which wasn't'. The matter is also complicated by the fact that there were three successive moments in time to be considered: (i) conclusion of the treaty (frontier to be the watershed); (ii) acceptance of the map line (frontier to be the line believed erroneously to be the watershed); (iii) discovery of the true position and disagreement over the legal outcome. Further, if there was an agreement at stage (ii), it could be—and was—contended that the agreement was vitiated by common mistake.

[256] *ICJ Reports*, 1988, p. 85, para. 36.
[257] Ibid., pp. 85–6, para. 37.
[258] *ICJ Reports*, 1962, pp. 33–4.

The judgment of the Court did not however leave the question of interpretation there. It continued:

> Even if, however, the Court were called upon to deal with the matter now as one solely of ordinary treaty interpretation, it considers that the interpretation to be given would be the same, for the following reasons.[259]

Pausing there, it seems to imply that the preceding argument is one of 'ordinary treaty interpretation', but no further explanation is given.

The subsequent argument is lengthy, but may be summarized as follows. The primary object of the parties in concluding the treaty was to achieve certainty and finality in their frontier settlement; that was why they provided not only that the frontier should be the watershed, but also that it would be delimited. Thus,

> The indication of the line of the watershed in Article I of the 1904 Treaty was itself no more than an obvious and convenient way of describing a frontier line objectively, though in general terms. There is, however, no reason to think that the Parties attached any special importance to the line of the watershed as such, as compared with the overriding importance, in the interests of finality, of adhering to the map line as eventually delimited and as accepted by them. The Court, therefore, feels bound, as a matter of treaty interpretation, to pronounce in favour of the line as mapped in the disputed area.[260]

In essence, what the Court did was to read the treaty first as providing for the frontier to be delimited by a Boundary Commission, and secondly as indicating, as a desirable line for the Commission to follow, the watershed. The meaning of the obscure sentence introducing the argument, quoted above, is apparently that this is an interpretation which does *not* rest on the subsequent practice of the parties constituted by the acceptance of the map line. One weakness of the argument is thus exposed: on what basis, if not reference to subsequent practice, did the Court justify departing from the 'natural and ordinary meaning' of the words of the treaty?[261] If, on the other hand, the subsequent practice is relevant, how does it support the argument, given that when the map was accepted neither party knew that the map line was not the watershed line? Only if they had accepted the map line knowingly would this practice support the Court's interpretation.

Where however the practice tends to show the existence of agreement between the parties subsequent to the conclusion of the treaty on an interpretation compatible with the terms of the treaty, but not shown to have been the original intention, it appears that the practice must be more widespread. In terms of Article 31, paragraph 3, of the Vienna Convention, it

[259] Ibid., p. 34.
[260] Ibid., p. 35.
[261] The Court's interpretation was rejected by Judge Wellington Koo (dissenting) as 'strained and unreal', ibid., p. 98, para. 48.

appears that such an interpretative practice, to be relied on, must be equivalent to universal agreement among the parties; every party must either have participated in the practice or at least have accepted it, tacitly or otherwise.[262] The structure and language of Article 31, paragraph 3, is significant in this respect. Sub-paragraph (*a*) provides for account to be taken of 'any subsequent agreement between the parties regarding the interpretation of the treaty or the application of its provisions', and sub-paragraph 3(*b*) refers to 'any subsequent practice in the application of the treaty *which establishes the agreement of the parties* regarding its interpretation'. The text refers to the agreement as something distinct from the common intention or understanding at the time of drafting and conclusion of the treaty; and although the adjective 'subsequent' is attached to the word 'practice' and not the word 'agreement', it colours the whole phrase.

It may not be fanciful to see in this emphasis on events subsequent to the adoption of the treaty, this movement away from the historical approach, a symptom of the general trend towards treating at least major normative multilateral conventions as having a life of their own; a process exemplified both by the increased emphasis on the object and purpose of the convention over the intentions of the drafters,[263] and the appeal to the ideas of 'intertemporal *renvoi*' and 'emergent purpose'.[264]

In many situations, to distinguish between practice showing the existence of a recognized interpretation at the time of conclusion of a treaty, and practice showing a subsequent agreement as to its interpretation, may be neither necessary nor possible. In some circumstances however there is a touchstone which can be applied. Most modern multilateral conventions are open to accession by States other than those which took part in their drafting. If such a convention has in fact been acceded to by a number of such States, the question may arise whether the 'parties' whose intention is to be ascertained are solely those which took part in the preparation of the text, or can include subsequent parties. It would seem, on general principles of intertemporality, that to establish a common intention at the time of conclusion of the treaty, consideration must be limited to the intentions

[262] Cf. Yasseen, 'L'Interprétation des traités d'après la Convention de Vienne sur le droit des traités', *Recueil des cours*, 151 (1976–III), p. 52; Waldock in *ILC Yearbook*, 1966, vol. 2, p. 99, para. 18. It is said that the word 'all' before 'parties' in Article 31(3) was deliberately omitted to avoid suggesting that all parties had to have participated *actively* in the practice.

[263] Thus Yasseen has described subsequent practice of this kind as producing 'une intention commune naissante mettant en relief un nouvel objet et un nouveau but du traité': 'L'Interprétation des traités d'après la Convention de Vienne sur le droit des traités', *Recueil des cours*, 151 (1976–III), p. 49. As long ago as 1966, Jean-Pierre Cot pointed out that an interpretation which employed the conduct of the parties as indicative of anything other than their original intentions was necessarily teleological, and drew attention to the dangers of such an approach: 'La Conduite subsequente des parties à un traité', *Revue générale de droit international public*, 1966, p. 632 at pp. 647 ff.

[264] It is ironic that it was Fitzmaurice who was responsible for this elegant definition of a doctrine which he rejected as something which he considered 'cannot properly form part of the interpretative process': this *Year Book*, 33 (1957), p. 208; *Collected Edition*, I, p. 342.

of the original parties;[265] this would not be so where reliance is placed on subsequent conduct as an indication of a developed common intention.

In the *Guardianship of Infants* case Judge Winiarski (dissenting) supported his interpretation of the 1902 Convention on Guardianship of Infants with the consideration that

> The Convention was open only to States represented at the Third Conference of Private International Law and the members of this little family of nations who are bound by this Convention have, with regard to guardianship, a very old common fund of ideas and principles which was formulated in Roman law . . . [266]

On the other hand, when the Court in the *Namibia* case upheld the validity of the Security Council resolutions adopted over the abstention of a permanent member, on the basis of a 'general practice' of the United Nations, derived from 'presidential rulings and the positions taken by members of the Council',[267] it did not find it necessary to enquire whether the members who had taken part in the practice were original members of the organization or States admitted subsequently.[268]

6. *Principle of Contemporaneity*

This principle was stated by Fitzmaurice in the following terms:

> The terms of a treaty must be interpreted according to the meaning which they possessed, or which would have been attributed to them, and in the light of current linguistic usage, at the time when the treaty was originally concluded.[269]

In the light of recent decisions of the Court, and for reasons already explained in the first of this series of articles,[270] this principle might now be supplemented with the following qualification:

> Provided that, where it can be established that it was the intention of the parties that the meaning or scope of a term or expression used in the treaty should follow the development of the law, the treaty must be interpreted so as to give effect to that intention.

[265] The problem parallels that of reference to the *travaux préparatoires* of a multilateral convention where the parties to the dispute did not participate in the drafting of the Convention; see *Territorial Jurisdiction of the International Commission of the River Oder, PCIJ*, Series A, No. 23, p. 42; Berlia, 'Contribution à l'interprétation des traités', *Recueil des cours*, 114 (1965–I), p. 302; and pp. 36 ff. above.

[266] *ICJ Reports*, 1958, p. 133. The Court did 'not consider it necessary to pronounce' upon a similar contention as to the ideas of *ordre public* shared by the original parties: ibid., p. 70. Cf. the comments of Fitzmaurice on the *Asylum* case under the heading 'Local tradition as an extraneous means of interpretation', this *Year Book*, 33 (1957), p. 235; *Collected Edition*, I, p. 369.

[267] *ICJ Reports*, 1971, p. 22, para. 22.

[268] As pointed out above and in the previous article in this series (this *Year Book*, 61 (1990), p. 77), this was a case of modification of treaty by subsequent custom rather than treaty interpretation; but it is submitted that the date of admission to the organization of States participating in such an *interpretative* practice would equally be irrelevant, if only because such practice involves the reaction, or lack of reaction, of the original members.

[269] This *Year Book*, 33 (1957), p. 212; *Collected Edition*, I, p. 346.

[270] This *Year Book*, 60 (1989), pp. 135–43.

The Vienna Convention appears at first sight to contain no reference to this aspect of interpretation; but if it is permissible to look beyond the text to the *travaux préparatoires*, it becomes apparent that Article 31, paragraph 3(*c*), is directed to this issue.[271] That text requires that

> There shall be taken into account, together with the context:
>
> . . .
>
> (*c*) any relevant rules of international law applicable in the relations between the parties.

This text does not resolve the intertemporal problem, whether it is the rules of international law as they stand at the date of conclusion of the treaty which are relevant, or the rules in force at the time of the interpretation: indeed, it is not even immediately apparent that the text has anything to do with that question.[272] It is therefore doubtful whether this sub-paragraph will be of any assistance in the task of treaty interpretation.

(1) *The principle applied*

In the judicial context, the principle was well expressed by Judge de Castro in the *Aegean Sea* case:

> The meaning of words may change with time. In order to interpret any statement, to ascertain its real meaning, we must first of all concentrate on the meaning which it could have had at the time when it was made. Words have no intrinsic value in themselves. They are, or represent, sounds (*phonema*), but their semantic value depends on the time and the circumstances in which they were uttered.[273]

Not infrequently the application of the principle is so obvious and unquestioned that its place in the logic of an interpretative decision goes unremarked.[274] Thus in the *Right of Passage* case, the terms of the grant to the Portuguese relating to two Indian villages, contained in the 1779 Treaty

[271] 'It would appear from the commentary that this element in the general rule was originally designed to deal with the intertemporal aspect of interpretation. It had appeared in paragraph 1 of the text provisionally adopted by the Commission in 1964 which stated *inter alia* the ordinary meaning to be given to the terms of a treaty was to be determined "in the light of the general rules of international law *in force at the time of its conclusion*". The italicized words were intended to reflect the general principle that a judicial text must be appreciated in the light of the law contemporary with it. During the course of second reading in the Commission, some members suggested that the text as it then stood failed to deal with the problem of the effect of an evolution of the law on the interpretation of legal terms in a treaty and was therefore inadequate. For this reason, the Commission concluded that it should omit the temporal element and transfer this element of interpretation to paragraph 3 as being an element extrinsic both to the text and to the "context" as defined in paragraph 2': Sinclair, *The Vienna Convention on the Law of Treaties* (2nd edn., 1984), pp. 138–9.

[272] Thus Bernhardt, commenting on the ILC's 1966 draft, takes the text to be meant to refer to existing legal obligations of the parties: 'Interpretation and Implied (Tacit) Modification of Treaties', *Zeitschrift für ausländisches öffentliches Recht und Völkerrecht*, 27 (1967), p. 461 at p. 500.

[273] *ICJ Reports*, 1978, p. 63. The passage quoted is, however, preceded by this sentence: 'When a declaration of intention made a considerable time ago has to be construed, it will always be necessary to verify how the words should be understood at the present time.' This seems to conflict with the rest of the passage to such an extent that one is tempted to suspect a *lapsus calami*.

[274] Cf. the remarks made in the first article in this series on the application of intertemporal law: this *Year Book*, 60 (1989), p. 133, n. 471.

of Poona, were read in the light of contemporary practices as to the making of revenue grants called *jagir* or *saranjam*,[275] but the text of the judgment does not spell out that fact.[276]

It may be appropriate to refer to contemporary concepts and practices, not merely to determine the meaning of a term, but correctly to interpret the context, the significance of the treaty as a whole. In the *Western Sahara* case, among the treaties and agreements which were invoked by Morocco were certain agreements between colonial powers referring to understandings as to the 'limits of Morocco' which, it was suggested, amounted to recognition of Moroccan sovereignty in the disputed area. The Court rejected this interpretation of the agreements, noting that

> it was not their purpose either to recognize an existing sovereignty over a territory or to deny its existence . . . [but] rather to recognize or reserve for one or both parties a 'sphere of influence' *as understood in the practice of that time*.[277]

In the *Aegean Sea* case, for the purpose of interpreting the expression 'disputes relating to the territorial status of Greece' in the Greek acceptance of the jurisdiction of the Permanent Court, under the 1928 General Act, it was contended by Greece that the Court should take into account the historical context in which that declaration was made. For reasons which are set out in the Court's judgment, Greece asked the Court to draw the conclusion that

> Everything that is known of the contemporary understanding of such terms as 'territorial status', 'territorial situation' and 'territorial integrity' in the 1920s indicates that *these expressions are to be given a restrictive interpretation limited to the maintenance of the status quo established by treaties, normally as the result of post-war settlement*.[278]

The Court did not question the relevance of the historical context of a text for its interpretation, but preferred, on the facts, to follow the Greek argument only so far as this conclusion:

> In the view of the Court, the historical evidence may justifiably be said to show that in the period in question the *motive* which led States to include in treaties provisions regarding 'territorial status' was, in general, to protect themselves against possible attempts to modify territorial settlements established by the peace treaties. But it does not follow that they intended those provisions to be confined to questions connected with the revision of such settlements . . .[279]
>
> In the opinion of the Court, the historical evidence adduced by Greece does not suffice to establish that the expression 'territorial status' was used in the League of Nations period, and in particular in the General Act of 1928, in the special,

[275] *ICJ Reports*, 1960, p. 38.

[276] See the counter-memorial of India, *Pleadings*, vol. 2, p. 23, para. 56; reply of Portugal, ibid., p. 436, para. 86; Indian rejoinder, *Pleadings*, vol. 3, pp. 54–104.

[277] *ICJ Reports*, 1975, p. 50, para. 126 (emphasis added).

[278] *ICJ Reports*, 1978, p. 30, para. 72 (emphasis original).

[279] Ibid., p. 30, para. 73.

restricted, sense contended for by Greece. The evidence seems rather to confirm that the expression 'territorial status' was used in its ordinary, generic sense . . . [280]

(2) *Intertemporal* renvoi

The reader is referred to the analysis, in the first of these articles,[281] of the situation in which the parties to an international instrument may have intended to subject the legal relations not to the law prevailing at the time of conclusion of the instrument, but to such law as might from time to time thereafter become effective.[282] In that context, the application of this concept by the Court in the *Namibia* and *Aegean Sea Continental Shelf* cases was discussed.

Chapter III:

Ancillary and Other Interpretative Findings

1. *Relationship of Treaty to Existing Rules of Law*

(1) *Rules of international law*

In general, the legal obligations imposed on the parties by a treaty which they have concluded prevail over any rules of general international law by which they would otherwise be bound, subject always to considerations of *jus cogens*; but a treaty must evidently be interpreted against the background of general law.[283] It may however not always be evident what the intentions of the parties to a treaty were as regards a particular rule of law, and a question of interpretation may arise in order to determine whether that rule is abrogated (between the parties) by the treaty, incorporated in the treaty, or simply left undisturbed and unaffected.[284]

An apparently simple principle was laid down by the Court in its 1957 judgment on the preliminary objections in the *Right of Passage* case:

It is a rule of interpretation that a text emanating from a Government must, in principle, be interpreted as producing and as intended to produce effects in accordance with existing law and not in violation of it.[285]

Even setting aside the context, however, this statement prompts doubts: if the text is a treaty, or of a treaty nature, the reason why it was concluded

[280] Ibid., p. 31, para. 74.

[281] This *Year Book*, 60 (1989), pp. 135–43.

[282] See also the resolution of the Institut de droit international on 'The Intertemporal Problem in Public International Law', *Annuaire*, 56 (1975), p. 536, para. 4.

[283] Article 31, paragraph 3(*c*), provides for reference to 'any relevant rules of international law applicable in relations between the parties'; but this text is apparently intended to refer to a specific problem—that of intertemporal law. See n. 271, above.

[284] 'Treaties not infrequently assume or base themselves on the pre-existence of some fact or right. It does not follow that they thereby incorporate it as a substantive element, in such a way as to entail its perpetuation or continued duration': Fitzmaurice, this *Year Book*, 33 (1957), p. 233; *Collected Edition*, I, p. 367.

[285] *ICJ Reports*, 1957, p. 142.

may well be because it was desired to produce effects—to confer rights or impose obligations—which are not 'in accordance with existing law': that indeed may be the whole object and purpose of the instrument.[286] Does it necessarily follow that those effects must be treated as 'in violation' of general law, and a restrictive interpretation applied?

The text with which the Court was dealing was the acceptance by Portugal of the jurisdiction of the Court under the Optional Clause, and analysis of the legal situation was complicated by the operation of what is generally referred to as the principle of reciprocity.[287] That acceptance contained a 'Third Condition' whereby

> The Portuguese Government reserves the right to exclude from the scope of the present declaration, at any time during its validity, any given category or categories of disputes, by notifying the Secretary-General of the United Nations and with effect from the moment of such notification.[288]

India argued that this clause had 'retroactive effect', i.e., that it

> gives Portugal the right, by making at any time a notification to that effect, to withdraw from the jurisdiction of the Court a dispute which had been submitted to it prior to such a notification,

and this was

> incompatible with the principle and notion of the compulsory jurisdiction of the Court as established in Article 36 of the Statute and that the Third Condition is invalid inasmuch as it contemplates an effect which is contrary to the Statute.[289]

It would certainly have been an eminently reasonable rule of interpretation to say that a declaration made pursuant to a provision of the Court's Statute had to be read as intended to operate in conformity with the Statute, and not against it. The Court however went further and declared that

> It is a rule of law generally accepted, as well as one acted upon in the past by the Court, that, once the Court has been validly seised of a dispute, unilateral action by the respondent State in terminating its Declaration, in whole or in part, cannot divest the Court of jurisdiction.[290]

Thus the Court was reasoning that if the Third Condition had been meant to mean what India suggested it did, it would have been ineffective, as seeking to achieve a result which is inconsistent with the whole system of the Court's jurisdiction. Presumably even a compromissory clause in a treaty which purported to empower an eventual respondent retrospectively

[286] 'It being always open, prima facie, to any two or more States to agree, for application *inter se*, upon a rule or régime varying or departing from the rules of customary international law in the nature of *jus dispositivum*, a treaty embodying such an agreement cannot be invalid on that ground': Fitzmaurice, Article 17 of the draft Code on the Law of Treaties, *ILC Yearbook*, 1958, vol. 2, p. 27.

[287] On the disadvantages of this term, see the present writer's 'Reciprocity in the Jurisdiction of the International Court', *Netherlands Yearbook of International Law*, 15 (1984), p. 97.

[288] *ICJ Reports*, 1957, p. 141.

[289] Ibid.

[290] Ibid., p. 142.

to invalidate the seisin of the Court effected by the other party on the basis of the clause would be invalid, even though covered by the consent of the other party to the clause.

As a matter of interpretation, the Court's argument was thus in fact that Portugal could not be held to have been trying to achieve the *impossible*; the reference to 'violation' of the law is misleading because it concentrates attention on the reason for the impossibility rather than on the impossibility itself. In short, the dictum quoted above turns out to be no more than an aspect of the principle of effectiveness.[291]

A similar approach, again in relation to the Statute of the Court, is to be found in the 1985 judgment on the *Application for Revision and Interpretation of the Judgment of 24 February 1982* in the *Continental Shelf* case between Tunisia and Libya. A provision in the Special Agreement by which the case had originally been brought before the Court provided that, if agreement on delimitation was not reached within three months from the Court's judgment, 'the two Parties shall together go back to the Court and request any explanations or clarifications which would facilitate the task [of delimitation]'.[292]

The question before the Court was whether this provision overrode, or operated as a necessary preliminary to, the procedure for requests for interpretation provided for in Article 60 of the Statute of the Court. The essence of the Court's ruling on the point was:

> The effect of Article 3 of the Special Agreement, as interpreted by Libya as being *in pari materia* with Article 60 of the Statute, would be to make the right of each party to request an interpretation—a right exercisable unilaterally—subject to the prior employment of a procedure requiring the participation of both Parties. In other words, the exercise of the right of one Party to seek an interpretation under Article 60 of the Statute would be effectively blocked by the other party, if that party chose not to co-operate. Whether or not such an agreement could validly derogate—as between the parties thereto—from the Statute, it is not lightly to be presumed that a State would renounce or fetter its right under Article 60 of the Statute to request an interpretation unilaterally. Accordingly, the Court is unable to interpret the Special Agreement in that sense . . . [293]

The Court therefore did not need to base its view on the illegality, and hence impossibility, of the results of a particular interpretation: indeed, it was able to leave open whether the article, if so interpreted, would or would not be in contravention of the Statute. The relation between the article and background law was simply that a certain right existed which, on one interpretation of the article, would be abandoned or restricted; a renunciation or restriction of a right could not however be presumed, but would have to be in express terms.

A different view was taken by Judge Ruda on the point:

[291] See above, pp. 45 ff.
[292] *ICJ Reports*, 1985, p. 214, para. 41.
[293] Ibid., p. 216, para. 43.

My reading of Article 3 of the Special Agreement leads me to the conclusion that the Parties foresee a special procedure of coming to the Court, before Article 60 of the Statute could be invoked; it does not seem to be the intention of the Parties to waive their rights under the Statute, but to establish a previous procedure for coming to the Court, before they decide to ask unilaterally for an interpretation. The purpose of Article 3 is to oblige the Parties to make an effort to settle between themselves which are the points of difference, before coming to the Court; if such an effort fails, the Parties then could ask unilaterally for an interpretation under Article 60 of the Statute. Article 3 is not a bar, or a 'block'—to use the Court's terminology—, to the procedure established in Article 60 of the Statute, if one of the Parties chooses not to co-operate; it is only a procedure that the Parties should try to follow, before coming to the Court.[294]

Though he does not say so, Judge Ruda presumably thought that an interpretation whereby a party, while not waiving a statutory right, consented to 'fetter' that right (in the Court's wording[295]) by imposing on it a requirement to follow a preliminary procedure, was not so unlikely as to require to be expressly stated. It was essentially on this narrow ground that he differed from the majority of the Court.

A more difficult question arises when it is disputed whether, when concluding their treaty, the parties intended that a particular provision of *treaty law* should or should not be applied to the relationship arising out of the treaty.

In the *Namibia* advisory opinion, the Court had to deal with the contention of South Africa that

the Covenant of the League of Nations did not confer on the Council of the League power to terminate a mandate for misconduct of the mandatory and that no such power could therefore be exercised by the United Nations, since it could not derive from the League greater powers than the latter itself had.[296]

South Africa accepted that, as a matter of general law, 'unless the parties otherwise provide, an ordinary treaty may be revoked by the innocent party in the case of a material breach by the other party',[297] but argued that 'no right of reservation' on this basis could have existed if contrary to the intention of the authors of the mandates system.[298] It pointed out that there was no provision for revocation in the Covenant of the mandates themselves, and

if it had been the intention to confer a power of revocation on the League, it would have been strange not to have incorporated it in the Covenant or in the mandates themselves, especially since, as we will demonstrate, specific proposals for the inclusion of such a power in the Covenant had in fact been made . . .
had it been the intention to confer upon the League the power under consideration,

[294] Ibid., pp. 234–5, para. 13.

[295] Judge Ruda is slightly unfair in attributing the term 'block' to the Court; the word is used in a statement of *Libya's* argument, and the Court carefully uses the terms 'renounce *or fetter*' a right.

[296] *ICJ Reports*, 1971, p. 47, para. 96.

[297] *Pleadings*, vol. 2, p. 301 (Mr van Heerden).

[298] Ibid., p. 303.

that is, the power to revoke mandates, one would have expected express agreement concerning, *inter alia*, the grounds which would justify revocation, the manner in which it would have to be effected, the methods by which the future administration of the territory would have to be determined and the adjustments of the rights, financial and otherwise, of the various interested parties.[299]

The Court approached the matter from the standpoint that there is a 'general principle of law that a right of termination on account of breach must be presumed to exist in respect of all treaties' with the exception of humanitarian treaties (Vienna Convention, Art. 60, para. 5), and that

> The silence of a treaty as to the existence of such a right cannot be interpreted as implying the exclusion of a right which has its source outside of the treaty, in general international law, and is dependent on the occurrence of circumstances which are not normally envisaged when a treaty is concluded.[300]

This does not quite meet the South African argument, which was not that a right of revocation for breach must be expressly reserved in the treaty, but simply that where revocation would have complex repercussions, it was to be expected—if the parties had intended the right of reservation to be exercisable—that its modalities would be spelled out.

It is noteworthy that the Court did not go so far as to suggest that the right of revocation for breach *cannot* be excluded by agreement—which would presumably elevate the principle to the rank of *jus cogens*—but simply that exclusion must be express, and not deduced from the absence of express provision in the treaty.

A further interesting question of the relation between a treaty regime and general rules of international law arose in the *Elettronica Sicula* case. The jurisdictional basis on which the case was brought was Article XXVI of a 1948 Treaty of Friendship, Commerce and Navigation between the United States and Italy. This article was in a fairly standard form:

> Any dispute between the High Contracting Parties as to the interpretation or the application of this Treaty, which the High Contracting Parties shall not satisfactorily adjust by diplomacy, shall be submitted to the International Court of Justice, unless the High Contracting Parties shall agree to settlement by some other pacific means.[301]

Italy submitted a preliminary objection on the ground of non-exhaustion of local remedies, contested by the United States, on which the Court ruled as follows:

> The United States questioned whether the rule of the exhaustion of local remedies could apply at all to a case brought under Article XXVI of the FCN Treaty. That Article, it was pointed out, is categorical in its terms, and unqualified by any

299 Ibid., p. 305.

300 *ICJ Reports*, 1971, p. 41, para. 96. The last point is well taken as a general observation, but is somewhat inconsistent with the Court's holding that the possibility of breaches of the mandate serious enough to justify revocation *had* been foreseen.

301 *ICJ Reports*, 1989, p. 41, para. 48.

reference to the local remedies rule; and it seemed right, therefore, to conclude that the Parties to the FCN Treaty, had they intended the jurisdiction conferred upon the Court to be qualified by the local remedies rule in cases of diplomatic protection, would have used express words to that effect; as was done in an Economic Co-operation Agreement between Italy and the United States of America also concluded in 1948. The Chamber has no doubt that the parties to a treaty can therein either agree that the local remedies rule shall not apply to claims based on alleged breaches of that treaty; or confirm that it shall apply. Yet the Chamber finds itself unable to accept that an important principle of customary international law should be held to have been tacitly dispensed with, in the absence of any words making clear an intention to do so. This part of the United States response to the Italian objection must therefore be rejected.[302]

It would probably not be right to read this decision as implying that no 'important principle of customary law' can be 'tacitly dispensed with' in a treaty; if the circumstances are such that the silence of the treaty is sufficiently eloquent, any principle, not of *jus cogens*, may be taken to be waived or excluded. The relationship between the rule and the treaty in the *Elettronica Sicula* case was a special one, since the rule was not such as to apply to the day-to-day relationships of the parties under, or *dehors*, the treaty. A straightforward compromissory clause must be taken to refer to the rules of procedure and of State responsibility as they are.

(2) *Rules of the domestic law of the parties*

In his separate opinion in the *Guardianship of Infants* case, Judge Lauterpacht stated the following principle of interpretation:

In a case concerned with the interpretation of a treaty relating to a particular matter with regard to which the law and practice of both parties recognize the applicability of certain principles, due weight must be given to those principles.[303]

The principle, as so stated, seems unexceptionable; but in the application of it to a multilateral convention, difficulties arise. Lauterpacht, before applying it to the case before him, offers an example:

If the law and practice of Sweden and Holland were to recognize that the distance of twenty miles is the proper limit of territorial waters, and if these two States were to conclude a treaty laying down that their vessels shall be bound to submit to certain restrictions within their respective territorial waters, then the expression 'territorial waters' would have to be interpreted in the sense attached to it by the law and practice of those two States, namely, as extending to twenty miles.[304]

Pausing there, one would have expected that the meaning of 'their respective territorial waters' in the treaty would be the waters so denominated by the State concerned, whether or not this extent was the same as that of the territorial waters of the other party. However, Lauterpacht continues:

[302] Ibid., p. 42, para. 50.
[303] *ICJ Reports*, 1958, p. 92. Cf. also the United States' argument in the *Elettronica Sicula* case, above, p. 28.
[304] *ICJ Reports*, 1958, pp. 92–3.

By the same token, if the law of Sweden or Holland recognizes the exception of public order in the sphere of private international law, then that factor must be considered as relevant to the interpretation, as between them, of the treaty in question. It is well known, and it is admitted by both Parties, that both in Sweden and in Holland *ordre public* constitutes a valid reason for the exclusion of foreign law. Accordingly, the fact that a particular subject of private international law is covered by a convention does not, in the absence of an express prohibition to the contrary, in itself exclude the operation of *ordre public*, even if the convention is otherwise silent in the matter . . . [305]

What then is the position as between two other States, parties to the same treaty, in whose domestic law *ordre public* is not so recognized? Must the same treaty be interpreted differently as between those States? And what of a dispute between a State whose domestic law does recognize *ordre public* and one that does not?

It is suggested that Lauterpacht's principle can only operate in the case of a bilateral treaty, or in the case where all original parties to a multilateral treaty are consistent in the relevant aspect of their domestic law.

2. *Reference to Other Treaties*

One aid to interpretation—for it probably cannot work as a canon or rule of interpretation—which has been employed by the Court from time to time is reference to other treaties, particularly treaties of a similar nature, either between the same parties as the treaty which fails to be interpreted, or between one of those parties and a third State.[306] Other treaties or agreements between the same parties may of course have to be referred to as forming, with the treaty directly under consideration, a single complex transaction; the Court found that this was so, for example, in the *WHO* case.[307]

More relevant is the case in which a treaty or, as may more frequently be the case, another instrument which requires to be interpreted in accordance with treaty law, has been concluded or issued to give effect to, or pursuant to a power or entitlement resulting from, an earlier treaty. Reference to that treaty may then be justified as part of the context of the subsequent instrument.[308]

In the *Aegean Sea* case, Greece argued that the terms of its accession to

[305] Ibid., p. 93.

[306] It is possible—though the case has not arisen in the practice of the Court—that a treaty might be interpreted in the light of the interpretation given to similar treaties between parties neither of whom was before the Court, if all the treaties in question followed a common model. 'Il est bien connu que les traités bien redigés servent de modèle même pour des traités conclus par d'autres Etats': Reuter, 'Solidarité et divisibilité des engagements conventionnels', *International Law at a Time of Perplexity (Mélanges Rosenne)*, p. 623, at p. 627.

[307] *ICJ Reports*, 1980, p. 92, para. 43. On this see Reuter, 'Traités et transactions. Réflexions sur l'identification de certains engagements conventionnels', *Le Droit international à l'heure de sa codification (Mèlanges Ago)*, vol. 1, p. 399, at pp. 405 ff.

[308] See above, pp. 44 ff.

the 1928 General Act for the Pacific Settlement of International Disputes, which mentioned both disputes concerning questions which by international law are matters of domestic jurisdiction, and questions of territorial status, signified that these were not two distinct reservations, but that the one was an example, or a sub-category, of the other. The Court noted that the General Act itself 'exhaustively enumerated' the reservations which were permissible, and listed these two matters separately; and observed that

When a multilateral treaty thus provides in advance for the making only of particular, designated categories of reservations, there is clearly a high probability, if not an actual presumption, that reservations made in terms used in the treaty are intended to relate to the corresponding categories in the treaty.[309]

Being a presumption as to the intentions of the party or parties concerned, not as to what was or was not permitted by the earlier instrument (the General Act), the presumption would have to yield to evidence that the intentions of the party were in fact otherwise; Greece did not however succeed in demonstrating to the Court's satisfaction that that was so.

In the *Right of Passage* case, the question arose whether a treaty concluded in 1779 between the Maratha rulers of India and Portugal, coupled with two *sanads* (decrees) issued by the Marathas in 1783 and 1785, had or had not effected a transfer to Portugal of sovereignty over certain villages.

Article 17 of the Treaty is relied upon by Portugal as constituting a transfer of sovereignty. From an examination of the various texts of that article placed before it, the Court is unable to conclude that the language employed therein was intended to transfer sovereignty over the villages to the Portuguese. There are several instances on the record of treaties concluded by the Marathas which show that, where a transfer of sovereignty was intended, appropriate and adequate expressions like cession 'in perpetuity' or 'in perpetual sovereignty' were used. The expressions used in the two *sanads* and connected relevant documents establish, on the other hand, that what was granted to the Portuguese was only a revenue tenure called a *jagir* or *saranjam* of the value of 12,000 rupees a year. This was a very common form of grant in India and not a single instance has been brought to the notice of the Court in which such a grant has been construed as amounting to a cession of territory in sovereignty . . .

It therefore appears that the Treaty of 1779 and the *sanads* of 1783 and 1785 were intended by the Marathas to effect in favour of the Portuguese only a grant of a *jagir* or *saranjam*, and not to transfer sovereignty over the villages to them.[310]

This criterion may also be said to have been employed in the various stages of the advisory opinions and litigation concerning South West Africa, in so far as the Mandate for that territory was interpreted against the background of the other mandates, and the 'C' class mandates were not regarded as a distinct category.[311]

[309] *ICJ Reports*, 1978, p. 23, para. 55.
[310] *ICJ Reports*, 1960, p. 38.
[311] *ICJ Reports*, 1971, p. 32, para. 54.

In the case concerning *Diplomatic and Consular Staff in Tehran*, one of the bases of jurisdiction relied on by the United States was a 1955 Treaty of Amity, Economic Relations, and Consular Rights, which contained a provision that

> Any dispute between the High Contracting Parties as to the interpretation or application of the present Treaty, not satisfactorily adjusted by diplomacy, shall be submitted to the International Court of Justice, unless the High Contracting Parties agree to settlement by some other pacific means.[312]

The question of interpretation was whether this clause justified proceedings brought by unilateral application, rather than jointly. The Court ruled that

> While that Article does not provide in express terms that either party may bring a case to the Court by unilateral application, it is evident, as the United States contended in its Memorial, that this is what the parties intended. Provisions drawn in similar terms are very common in bilateral treaties of amity or of establishment, and the intention of the parties in accepting such clauses is clearly to provide for such a right of unilateral recourse to the Court, in the absence of agreement to employ some other pacific means of settlement.[313]

The statement that 'it is evident . . . that this is what the parties intended' strikes the reader as rather bold. It is however based upon—indeed a quotation from—the United States memorial, where chapter and verse are given in support.

> The text of Article XXI(2) follows the text of similar clauses in 17 of the 21 commercial treaties concluded by the United States since the Second World War, and this standard text has always been understood by the United States and its treaty partners to confer a right of unilateral resort to the Court.[314]

Reference was made to a Department of State memorandum at the time of Senate hearings on the first treaty containing such a clause, a later memorandum which listed the treaty with Iran as one of the treaties having the standard clause, and diplomatic exchanges with the Netherlands establishing that the clause in the treaty with that State was to be read as permitting unilateral seisin of the Court.[315]

Iran could however have retorted[316] that all this was *res inter alios acta*, that what mattered was the common intention of Iran and the United States at the time of the conclusion of the treaty actually under consideration. If Iran had asserted that at the relevant time it had understood the Article as providing only for *joint* application to the Court, the material produced by the United States could not have been relied on to refute that

[312] *ICJ Reports*, 1980, p. 27, para. 51.
[313] Ibid., p. 27, para. 52.
[314] *Pleadings*, p. 153.
[315] Annexes 53 and 54 to the US memorial, *Pleadings*, pp. 236–41.
[316] Iran was of course not appearing in the proceedings.

assertion. It is therefore suggested that reliance on similar treaties in these circumstances affords rather shaky support for the interpretation upheld.

What may have been in the Court's mind was the desirability of consistency in the interpretation of a standard clause employed in numerous treaties. If the Court had simultaneously been seised of a dispute under the Treaty between the United States and the Netherlands, it would have been bound to interpret the compromissory clause in that treaty as authorizing unilateral institution of proceedings. To come to the opposite conclusion on the interpretation of an identical form of words in the United States/Iran Treaty would certainly have scandalized the uninitiated and provoked an explosion of academic comment by the initiated. Yet as a matter of legal principle, the inconsistency remains theoretically possible, and might have been unavoidable; what if Iran could have set up, against the US Department of State material, passages from its own parliamentary records showing a clear and firm understanding by the Iranian Government at the time of the treaty that it authorized seisin of the Court only by joint action? Notwithstanding the identical wording used, there would have been consent by the Netherlands, and no consent by Iran, to seisin by unilateral application.[317]

The lesson is that it cannot be assumed that identical words necessarily have identical meaning. What matters is the intentions (based on the preconceptions) of those using them. The Court may therefore have been over-hasty, in its 1984 judgment in the *Nicaragua* v. *United States* case, in relying on its decision in the *Hostages* case to justify the same interpretation of a substantially identical provision in a 1956 Treaty between the United States and Nicaragua.[318] Had the treaty under consideration been concluded subsequently to the Court's decision in the *Hostages* case, it could probably have been safely assumed that the text was intended to have the same meaning, as having followed the model of the United States/Iran Treaty; not otherwise.

It might seem that a similar objection, though of less force, could be taken to the argument of Judge Oda, in his separate opinion in the *Elettronica Sicula* case, on the interpretation of the Treaty of Friendship, Commerce and Navigation between the United States and Italy. An issue in the case was whether what had been done to the ELSI company, or to its United States parent companies, amounted to a breach of Article V, paragraph 2, of that treaty, which provided that the property of nationals of either High Contracting Party 'shall not be taken within the territory' of the other; the Italian text provided that 'I beni dei cittadini . . . di ciascuna Altra Parte Contraente non saranno espropriati . . . '. The Chamber dealing with the case considered that 'Obviously there is some difference

[317] This possibility throws doubts on the suggestion (made, e.g., by d'Amato in 1969 (*Proceedings of the American Society of International Law*, p. 135)) that a glossary of treaty terms, compiled on the basis of existing treaties, could serve as a tool of treaty interpretation.

[318] *ICJ Reports*, 1984, p. 427, para. 81.

between the two versions', specifically as regards the words 'taken' and 'espropriati'.[319] Judge Oda in his separate opinion said:

In this respect, I would like to point out, as a supplementary explanation, that the verb 'take', as expressed by 'espropriare' in the Italian text, is rendered in the 1956 FCN Treaty between the Federal Republic of Germany and the United States by the German verb 'enteignen', which militates against the acceptance of an interpretation of the requisition order of the Mayor of Palermo as amounting to a 'taking' of property.[320]

However, the essential difference between Judge Oda's argument and that of the Court in the *Hostages* case is that in the latter case the interpretation based on the similar treaties was being employed against Iran, which was not the common party to the two similar treaties. In the *Elettronica Sicula* case, Judge Oda was pointing out that the United States, as a party to both the Italian and German FCN Treaties, had accepted the translation of 'taken' not only by 'espropriati' but also by 'enteignen', both of which expressions were narrower than the meaning attributed by the United States in argument to 'taken'. The objection of *res inter alios acta*, which Iran could have raised in respect of the United States/Netherlands Treaty, could not have been employed by the United States in the *Elettronica Sicula* case.

In the same case, an attempt was made by the United States to argue that the absence of any reference, in the compromissory clause relied on, to the rule of non-exhaustion of local remedies, meant that that rule was not applicable to claims under the Treaty containing the compromissory clause. In support of this argument it drew attention to an Economic Co-operation Agreement between the same parties (United States and Italy) in which it was expressly provided that the local remedies rule should apply.[321] The Chamber seems not to have been impressed by this argument.[322]

In the *WHO* case, the question originally put to the Court for advisory opinion concerned the applicability, and hence the interpretation, of a specific provision (Article 37) of the Agreement of 25 March 1951 between the WHO and Egypt, the host agreement of the WHO Regional Office in Alexandria. In the course of its opinion, the Court observed that

The Court's attention has been drawn to a considerable number of host agreements of different kinds, concluded by States with various international organizations and containing varying provisions regarding the revision, termination and denunciation of the agreements.[323]

It did not however appeal to these agreements as a means of interpreting the WHO Agreement with Egypt; it considered that they were 'not without significance in the present connection' for the following reasons:

[319] *ICJ Reports*, 1989, p. 68, para. 113.
[320] Ibid., p. 91.
[321] Ibid., p. 42, para. 50.
[322] See above, pp. 64–5.
[323] *ICJ Reports*, 1980, p. 94, para. 45.

In the first place, they confirm the recognition by international organizations and host States of the existence of mutual obligations incumbent upon them to resolve the problems attendant upon a revision, termination or denunciation of a host agreement. But they do more, since they must be presumed to reflect the views of organizations and host States as to the implications of those obligations in the contexts in which the provisions are intended to apply. In the view of the Court, therefore, they provide certain general indications of what the mutual obligations of organizations and host States to co-operate in good faith may involve in situations such as the one with which the Court is here concerned.[324]

In effect, the Court was finding the existence of a body of customary law in respect of the accommodation of international organizations on national territory, the practice creative of which was constituted by the various host agreements. The opinion might perhaps be criticized for concentrating on this body of general law to the neglect of the specific provisions of the 1951 Agreement, apparently in contradiction of the principle *generalia specialibus non derogant*.

3. *Language Problems*

When a tribunal engaged in interpreting a treaty text is directed to consider first the 'natural and ordinary meaning' of the words used, this presupposes that the members of the tribunal are equipped to determine that meaning at least to the extent of knowing the language they are written in. This may in fact not be the case. What is more, to an ever-increasing extent modern treaties tend to be drafted in more than one language, both or all texts being equally authentic.[325] The Court in the period under consideration has had to cope with both problems.

(1) *Single text in a non-official language*

In the *Continental Shelf (Tunisia/Libya)* case, the Special Agreement by which the dispute was brought to the Court was written in Arabic, and the two parties had submitted rival translations, one into English and one into French;[326] the Court included only one native Arabic speaker (Judge El-Khani). There was a dispute over the meaning of a particular provision, which affected the degree of specificity of the Court's decision on the disputed maritime delimitation. The Court was however able to resolve the difficulty without determining the linguistic point:

[324] Ibid., p. 94, para. 46.

[325] Cf. Szasz, 'Reforming the Multilateral Treaty-Making Process: An Opportunity Missed', in *International Law at a time of Perplexity (Mélanges Rosenne)*, p. 930, who refers to the political storm provoked by the moderate suggestion that not all authentic language texts be finalized before adoption of a multilateral convention. See also Rosenne, *Developments in the Law of Treaties 1945–1986*, pp. 440–3.

[326] In the case of the *Land, Island and Maritime Frontier Dispute*, commenced during the period under review but (at the time of writing) not yet concluded, the Special Agreement was in Spanish, and it was not until the oral proceedings were well advanced that the parties were able to supply an agreed translation.

The Court . . . considers the whole controversy as of minor importance, since it has in any case [i.e., whatever the Special Agreement said] to be precise as to what it decides . . .[327]

This is of course a wider problem which can arise in respect of documents other than treaties: in the *Border and Transborder Armed Actions* case, the Court found it appropriate to refer to the records, in Spanish, of the Bogotá Conference; in the *Elettronica Sicula* case, the Chamber had to refer to numerous legal and judicial texts in Italian, and in its judgment it mentioned specifically that the translation which it used and quoted was 'not always the translation supplied by one of the Parties pursuant to Article 51, paragraph 3, of the Rules of Court'.[328]

In the *Aegean Sea* case the Court was concerned to establish the significance of the words 'et, notamment', in the French instrument of accession by Greece to the 1928 General Act for the Pacific Settlement of Disputes.[329] Among the *travaux préparatoires* of this text supplied to the Court was the manuscript of the draft legislative act approving accession to the General Act, in Greek.[330] Judge *ad hoc* Stassinopoulos referred in his dissenting opinion to the Greek expression which was translated by 'et, notamment'; he pointed out that the Greek word was a comparative adverb ('more particularly'),[331] which strengthened the argument in favour of the interpretation advanced by Greece, but rejected by the Court. The judgment of the Court made no reference to this point; but in view of the wide range of considerations, over and above the 'ordinary meaning' of the words, which the Court took into account, it would seem that consideration of the original-language text would have been justifiable.

It is probable that no judge other than the judge *ad hoc* was acquainted with modern Greek;[332] it is however interesting to speculate whether, if necessary, the Court could rely on expert evidence to inform it of the 'natural and ordinary meaning' of the words of a treaty or other relevant text written in a language unfamiliar to most or all of the judges.[333]

(2) *Multilingual treaty texts*

The problem of conflicting texts in different languages of the same treaty is an increasingly familiar one,[334] and is dealt with in the Vienna Conven-

[327] *ICJ Reports*, 1982, p. 40, para. 29.

[328] *ICJ Reports*, 1989, p. 41, para. 47.

[329] See above, p. 59. Even the comma dividing these two words was prayed in aid: compare *ICJ Reports*, 1978, p. 22, para. 53, with Beaumarchais, *Le Mariage de Figaro*, Acte III, Sc. 15.

[330] *Pleadings*, p. 546, where however only the French translation is reproduced.

[331] 'εἰδικώτερον'—*ICJ Reports*, 1978, p. 77.

[332] The present writer can however give personal testimony that the remnants of a classical education proved sufficient to permit of appreciation of Judge Stassinopoulos's contentions.

[333] It appears that a problem of this kind is likely to arise in the case concerning *Maritime Delimitation and Territorial Questions between Qatar and Bahrain*.

[334] See, for example, Hardy, 'The Interpretation of Plurilingual Treaties by International Courts and Tribunals', this *Year Book*, 37 (1961), p. 72; Rosenne, 'Conceptualism and Treaty Interpretation', *International Law at the Time of its Codification (Mélanges Ago)*, vol. 1, p. 417.

tion (Article 33). In respect of the Court's own Statute, it arose in the jurisdictional stage of the *Nicaragua* v. *United States* case: Article 36, paragraph 5, of the Statute (which, it was claimed preserved or validated Nicaragua's acceptance of the jurisdiction of the Permanent Court) referred to PCIJ declarations 'which are still in force' in the English text, and in French to declarations made 'pour une durée qui n'est pas encore expirée'.

The Court's handling of the problem[335] is uneasy, and it is difficult to extract any indication of the principles to be applied; the discussion of the different treaty texts is combined with reference to the *travaux préparatoires* in a quest, not entirely successful, for an explanation of the discrepancy. Ultimately, the Court allows its perception of the 'object and purpose' of the provision (but of which text of the provision?) to prevail: the 'object and purpose' of the provisions adopted will, it is said, 'throw light upon the correct interpretation' of the paragraph in question.[336]

A striking feature of the Court's discussion—and that in the opinions of Judge Oda and Judge Schwebel—is that it referred only to the English and French texts, making no mention of the (equally authentic) Spanish, Russian and Chinese texts. Although it is not spelled out in the judgment, the justification for this is apparently that the initial drafting was effected in English and French, the other three texts being prepared on the basis of the final text in those languages.[337] All five texts were referred to by Judge Sir Robert Jennings in his separate opinion; he quoted the Vienna Convention's requirement that 'the meaning which best reconciles the texts, having regard to the object and purpose of the treaty, shall be adopted', and pointed out that

> It is not possible to reconcile this requirement with any solution which seeks to give a special meaning to the French text, which meaning cannot be collected from the Chinese, the English, the Russian and the Spanish.[338]

In the *Border and Transborder Armed Actions* case, the Court was faced with an inexplicable discrepancy between the four language texts of the Pact of Bogotá (English, French, Portuguese and Spanish). Under Article II of the Pact, disputes 'which in the opinion of the parties, cannot be settled by direct negotiations through the usual diplomatic channels' could be referred to the Court. The Portuguese and Spanish texts correspond to the English text, but the French text employed the phrase 'de l'avis *de l'une* des parties'.

The Court did not however resolve the problem posed by this textual discrepancy; it was able to find that not only Nicaragua, the applicant State, but also Honduras, was of the view that the dispute could not be settled by

335 *ICJ Reports*, 1984, pp. 406–7.

336 Ibid., p. 407, para. 32.

337 This approach is one specifically rejected at the Vienna Conference, in favour of what is now Article 33, paragraph 1, of the Convention (all authenticated texts equally authoritative).

338 *ICJ Reports*, 1984, p. 537.

diplomatic negotiations—despite Honduras' statements to the contrary. The Court explained that it would

proceed on the hypothesis that the stricter interpretation should be used, i.e., that it would be necessary to consider whether the 'opinion' of both parties was that it was not possible to settle the dispute by negotiation.[339]

By 'stricter' the Court clearly meant the interpretation which imposed the most stringent condition on the jurisdiction of the Court; but it does not appear that it meant to follow the precedent of the Permanent Court in the *Mavrommatis Palestine Concessions* case of adopting 'the more limited treaty interpretation which can be made to harmonize with both versions'.[340] The essence of its approach was that it was saying to Honduras: 'Even accepting, *arguendo*, that your interpretation is correct, on the facts the conclusion which you wish to draw does not follow.' This is a technique for side-stepping difficulties of interpretation which is, of course, only available to a third party vested with the power of decision; but it is perhaps worth noting that it involves taking as hypothesis not necessarily the 'stricter' interpretation, but the interpretation which leads on to a disputed question of fact which can be used to determine the issue.

In the *Elettronica Sicula* case, the Chamber seised of the matter had to deal with two provisions of a treaty between the United States and Italy of which the English and Italian texts did not perfectly correspond. Article V, paragraph 2, provided that property of the nationals of the other State should not be 'taken'—in Italian 'espropriati'; and Article VII dealt with ownership by nationals of the other State of 'immovable property or interests therein'—in Italian 'beni immobili o . . altri diritti reali'. On the first point, the Chamber was able to conclude that the difficulty did not have to be resolved, because on the facts 'it is simply not possible to say that the ultimate result was the consequence of the acts or omissions of the Italian authorities'.[341]

On the second point, the problem was whether the expression quoted was 'sufficiently broad to include indirect ownership of property rights held through a subsidiary that is not a United States corporation'. The Chamber said:

The argument turned to a considerable extent on the difference in meaning between the English, 'interests' and the Italian, '*diritti reali*'. 'Interest' in English no doubt has several possible meanings. But since it is in English usage a term commonly used to denote different kinds of rights in land (for example rights such as charges, or easements, and many kinds of 'future interests'), it is possible to interpret the English and Italian versions of Article VII as meaning much the same

339 *ICJ Reports*, 1988, p. 95, para. 65.

340 (1924) *PCIJ*, Series A, No. 2, p. 19. Cf. the comment of the ILC, *Yearbook*, 1966, vol. 2, p. 225; Sinclair, *The Vienna Convention on the Law of Treaties* (2nd edn., 1984), pp. 149–50.

341 *ICJ Reports*, 1989, p. 71, para. 119.

thing; especially as the clause in question is in any event limited to immovable property.[342]

The Chamber was in effect applying the rule stated in Article 22, paragraph 3, of the Vienna Convention, that 'The terms of a treaty are presumed to have the same meaning in each authentic text'.

[342] Ibid., p. 79, para. 132.

WAS THE CAPACITY TO REQUEST AN ADVISORY OPINION WIDER IN THE PERMANENT COURT OF INTERNATIONAL JUSTICE THAN IT IS IN THE INTERNATIONAL COURT OF JUSTICE?*

By STEPHEN M. SCHWEBEL[1]

In the nineteen years of active life of the Permanent Court of International Justice, 1922–1940, the Court gave twenty-seven advisory opinions. By way of contrast, the International Court of Justice, in the forty-four years 1946–1990, has given twenty advisory opinions. This is despite the fact that, prima facie, the capacity to request advisory opinions of the Court is wider under the United Nations Charter and the ICJ Statute than it was under the Covenant of the League of Nations and the PCIJ Statute. In point of fact, however, that appearance is misleading, because, in practice, the capacity to request an advisory opinion of the Permanent Court was more generously applied in important respects than is the capacity to request an advisory opinion of the International Court of Justice. It is the purpose of this paper to recall that this was so and to consider what light the PCIJ experience may shed upon the current potential of the International Court of Justice. It is appreciated, of course, that such light will not be defining, because the frequency of requests for the Court's advisory opinions depends on a number of factors, of which capacity to make a request is just one, and not the most important.

THE PROVISIONS OF THE COVENANT, THE STATUTE AND THE RULES OF COURT

Article 14 of the Covenant of the League of Nations provided:

> The Council shall formulate and submit to the Members of the League for adoption plans for the establishment of a Permanent Court of International Justice. The Court shall be competent to hear and determine any dispute of an international character which the Parties thereto submit to it. The Court may also give an advisory opinion upon any dispute or question referred to it by the Council or by the Assembly.[2]

* © HE Judge Stephen M. Schwebel, 1992.

[1] Judge of the International Court of Justice. The views expressed do not engage the responsibility of the Court.

[2] The authority of the Court, as contained in the Covenant, to render advisory opinions principally derived from drafts of the Covenant prepared by Lord Cecil, Sir Cecil Hurst and, most immediately David Hunter Miller. See David Hunter Miller, *The Drafting of the Covenant* (1928), vol. 1, pp. 52, 391–3, 406.

The Statute, as the distinguished Advisory Committee of Jurists[3] which was appointed by the Council drafted it, duly contained an article governing the Court's advisory jurisdiction. It provided that, when the Court shall give an opinion on a question of an international nature which does not refer to a dispute that may have arisen, it shall appoint a special commission of three to five members, and when it shall give an opinion on a question which forms the subject of an existing dispute, it shall do so under the same conditions as if the case had been actually submitted to it for decision.[4] That is to say, what in effect would have been a chamber would have dealt with what were termed theoretical questions, but when a 'practical case' came to the Court (which could involve the very question which had been the subject of a theoretical opinion) the full Court would sit and would not be bound by the opinion *in abstracto*. In advisory proceedings dealing with an existing dispute, the Court would deal with the case as if it were contentious; there could be *ad hoc* judges and the parties would be allowed to present arguments and proofs.

The draft Statute prepared by the Advisory Committee of Jurists was revised by the League Council in two notable and lasting respects: a provision for general compulsory jurisdiction was deleted and a provision to make English an official language (in addition to French) was added. When the draft Statute came to be considered by the first Assembly of the League of Nations, a truncated discussion in Committee ensued of the proposed provision concerning advisory opinions. In the course of it, an amendment by Argentina which would have authorized States members of the League to request advisory opinions was rejected.[5] A proposal by the International Labour Organization to give it the same right to request advisory opinions as was given to the Council and the Assembly was not seriously discussed.[6] It was unanimously recommended that the entire article proposed by the Advisory Committee of Jurists be deleted, on the ground, as M. Fromageot of France put it, that, in view of the terms of Article 14 of the Covenant, 'the Court could not refuse to give advisory opinions. It was therefore unnecessary to include a rule to the same effect in the constitution of the

[3] The Chairman of the Advisory Committee was Baron Descamps, the Rapporteur was Albert de Lapradelle, among the members were Elihu Root and Lord Phillimore, and its secretary was Dionisio Anzilotti, then Under Secretary-General of the League of Nations, subsequently Judge and President of the Court.

[4] Permanent Court of International Justice, Advisory Committee of Jurists, *Procès-Verbaux of the Proceedings of the Committee*, 16 June–24 July 1920, pp. 730–1, 732. These proposals and their rationales are recounted in Dharma Pratap, *The Advisory Jurisdiction of the International Court* (1972), pp. 6–8, and Michla Pomerance, *The Advisory Function of the International Court in the League and UN Eras* (1973), pp. 10–14. See also Kenneth James Keith, *The Extent of the Advisory Jurisdiction of the International Court of Justice* (1971), pp. 13, 22.

[5] League of Nations, *The Records of the First Assembly, Meetings of the Committees* (1920), pp. 519, 387, 401. See also League of Nations, *Documents concerning the Action Taken by the Council of the League of Nations under Article 14 of the Covenant and the Adoption by the Assembly of the Statute of the Permanent Court* (1921), pp. 68, 146, 195, 211.

[6] *Documents*, loc. cit. (previous note), pp. 74, 79, 211; *Records*, loc. cit. (previous note), pp. 401, 563.

Court.'[7] At the same time, he regretted that the Court had been given an advisory jurisdiction at all.[8] In the report recommending the deletion of the article on advisory opinions proposed by the Advisory Committee of Jurists, it was stated that the Court should give advisory opinions, whether on a dispute or a question, with the same quorum; that the distinction made by the Advisory Committee between the two categories was unclear and could give rise to practical difficulties; and that, were the Argentinian and ILO proposals to have been adopted, such provisions 'would involve a considerable extension of the duties of the members of the Court and might lead to consequences difficult to calculate in advance'.[9] The resultant report sailed through the League Assembly, and the Statute as originally adopted contained no reference to advisory opinions. This was the more surprising in view of the fact that the Covenant and the PCIJ Statute, unlike the United Nations Charter and the ICJ Statute, were not integrally bound together; the PCIJ Statute was attached to and came into force pursuant to a separate and subsequent instrument of ratification; membership of the League did not entail being party to the Court's Statute and a State could be party to the Statute without becoming a member of the League. Reliance for the Court's advisory authority upon a provision of the Covenant alone accordingly was questionable, and it gave rise to questions.

When the Court came to draft its Rules of Procedure, this singular history led Judge John Bassett Moore to submit in a comprehensive memorandum that:

> No subject connected with the organisation of the Permanent Court of International Justice has caused so much confusion and proved to be so baffling as the question whether and under what conditions the Court shall undertake to give 'advisory' opinions.
>
> This state of doubt and uncertainty may in large measure be ascribed to the nature of the proposal.[10]

Judge Moore maintained that 'to impose upon a court of justice the duty of giving advice, which those requesting it were wholly at liberty to reject, would reduce the Court to a position inferior to that of a tribunal of conciliation . . . ',[11] and he proceeded to question whether the obligation to render advisory opinions had been imposed on the Court at all. He referred in raising this challenge to the fact that the Statute contained no specific provision on the subject, and he observed that the Covenant's terms, properly interpreted, left to the Court itself 'the sole power to determine in each

[7] Ibid., p. 401.

[8] Ibid., p. 389.

[9] Ibid., p. 534.

[10] 'The Question of Advisory Opinions', Memorandum by Mr Moore, 18 February 1922, Permanent Court of International Justice, *Acts and Documents concerning the Organization of the Court*, Series D, No. 2, p. 383.

[11] Ibid., p. 383.

instance whether, and in what circumstances, and on what conditions, it would undertake to give advice'.[12] He concluded that Article 14 of the Covenant 'cannot be regarded as imposing upon the Court an obligation to render such opinions . . . ' and that 'the giving of advisory opinions . . . is not an appropriate function of a Court of Justice'.[13] He finally submitted that it was preferable that there should be no special rule concerning advisory opinions but that the Court should deal with an application for an advisory opinion 'according to what should be found to be the nature and merits of the case'.[14]

In the event, the Court did treat advisory opinions in the Rules of Court. The Rules specified that advisory opinions should be rendered by the full Court, and provided for an orderly procedure for transmission of requests, for an exact statement of the question upon which an opinion was required, accompanied by all documents likely to throw light on the question, and for notice of the request to be sent to States members of the Court and the League, as well as international organizations which were likely to be able to furnish information on the question.

Despite this uncertain beginning, the very large majority of cases brought to the Court in its earliest years turned out to be advisory. In 1927 a committee of the Court recorded:

> The Statute does not mention advisory opinions, but leaves to the Court the entire regulation of its procedure in the matter. The Court, in the exercise of this power, deliberately and advisedly assimilated its advisory procedure to its contentious procedure; and the results have abundantly justified its action. Such prestige as the Court to-day enjoys as a judicial tribunal is largely due to the amount of its advisory business and the judicial way in which it has dealt with such business. In reality, where there are in fact contending parties, the difference between contentious cases and advisory cases is only nominal. The main difference is the way in which the case comes before the Court, and even this difference may virtually disappear, as it did in the Tunisian case. So the view that advisory opinions are not binding is more theoretical than real.[15]

In that year, the Court adopted on the proposal of Judge Anzilotti a further rule providing that, on a question relating to an existing dispute between two or more States, Article 31 of the Statute (relating to the maintenance of national judges and the appointment of judges *ad hoc*) should apply.

[12] Ibid., p. 384.

[13] Ibid., p. 397.

[14] Ibid., p. 398. For further indication of Judge Moore's attitude towards the Court's advisory jurisdiction, and for an analysis of the extraordinary role which the Court's advisory jurisdiction played in the question of United States adherence to the Court's Statute, see Michla Pomerance, 'The United States and the Advisory Function of the Permanent Court of International Justice', in Dinstein and Tabory (eds.), *International Law at a Time of Perplexity, Essays in Honour of Shabtai Rosenne* (1988), pp. 567, 570–1, 575–6. See also Michael Dunne, *The United States and the World Court 1920–1935* (1988), pp. 86–121.

[15] *Fourth Annual Report of the Permanent Court of International Justice*, Series E, No. 4, p. 76.

By 1929, when revision of the Statute was undertaken, it was accepted that it should be amended to incorporate the substance of what the Rules of Court by then provided respecting advisory opinions, as well as an article providing that, in the exercise of its advisory functions, the Court should be guided by the provisions of the Statute which applied in contentious cases to the extent to which it recognized them to be applicable. The revised Statute entered into force in 1936, as did revised Rules which brought the process of assimilation of the advisory to contentious procedure as close to completion as was possible.[16]

The Capacity to Request Advisory Opinions of the PCIJ in Practice

Not only did early recourse to the Court's advisory jurisdiction exceed by far the expectations of the drafters of the Statute. A significant element of that extensive recourse proved to be the liberal practice followed by the League Council and the Court in entertaining requests for advisory opinions which in fact originated not in the League Council or Assembly but in other quarters. All requests for advisory opinions addressed to the PCIJ were transmitted by the Council; the Assembly considered but did not adopt such requests on a few occasions. But not all of the requests transmitted by the Council were, in substantial terms, requests of the Council; rather, the majority of them were actually submitted at the instance of States or of an international organization other than the League. Thus the *Fourteenth Annual Report* of the Court could as of 1938 declare:

> The twenty-eight requests for advisory opinion which the Council has submitted to the Court may be divided into two categories: those really originating with the Council itself and those – more numerous – submitted at the instigation or request of a State or international organization.
>
> The following tables give a list of the cases submitted to the Court for advisory opinion, divided into these two categories.[17]

The *Report* then lists 'Requests from the Council *proprio motu*'; under that rubric are twelve cases, listed by the name, date and 'Governments and international organizations directly interested'. These cases are described as belonging 'to the first category', i.e., cases 'really originating with the Council itself'. The table then proceeds to list the following cases which 'belong to the second category', i.e., those more numerous cases submitted

[16] See Pratap, op. cit. above (n. 4), p. 35.

[17] *Fourteenth Annual Report of the Permanent Court of International Justice*, Series E, No. 14, pp. 72–3. As early as 1925, the *First Annual Report* was similarly framed: *Annual Report of the Permanent Court of International Justice, PCIJ*, Series E, No. 1, pp. 149–50.

at the instigation or request of a State or international organization. The sixteen cases then listed are also described by name, date and 'Governments and international organizations directly interested'.[18]

As for that second category, six of the sixteen cases so instigated derived from the ILO (though it is of interest to note that the Court's *Report* lists among the international organizations interested in the case not only the ILO but various non-governmental organizations as well, both international and national, such as the International Confederation of Christian Trades Unions and the Netherlands General Confederation of Trade Unions). Thus while the ILO more than once in the history of the Permanent Court was denied the right it sought directly to request advisory opinions of the Court, in practice it, more than any international organization other than the League itself, effectively had recourse to the Court. Paradoxically, although, with the adoption of the United Nations Charter and its implementation by the United Nations General Assembly, the ILO finally won its long fight for direct access to the Court, it has made no use of that right in the years in which it has possessed it (as of this writing, forty-four).

Of the remaining ten cases described in 1938 as submitted at the instigation of States or international organizations, the other international organizations involved were the Mixed Commission for the Exchange of Greek and Turkish Populations and the Greco-Bulgarian Mixed Emigration Commission (and, arguably, the Conference of Ambassadors which represented the Principal Allied Powers).

Exchange of Greek and Turkish Populations

Greece and Turkey concluded a Convention in 1923 concerning the exchange of Greek and Turkish populations. Article 11 of the Convention provided for the establishment of a Mixed Commission composed of four members representing Greece and four members representing Turkey, respectively, and three members chosen by the Council of the League from among nationals of States which did not take part in the World War. The Mixed Commission's duties were to supervise and facilitate the emigration provided for in the Convention and to settle the methods to be followed. The principle governing emigration was, with certain exceptions, the compulsory exchange of Greek and Turkish nationals 'established' in the territory of the other.[19] The question of the meaning of that term and measures which had been taken relating to it had been raised by Greece, which

[18] Ibid., pp. 73–5.

[19] *Exchange of Greek and Turkish Populations*, advisory opinion, *PCIJ*, Series B, No. 10 (1925), p. 6.

requested the League Council to place the question on its agenda. The arrest and expulsion of some thousands of Greeks in Turkey were claimed to be at issue. Greece's action followed inconclusive consideration of the problem in the Mixed Commission. The Council, acting in the presence of the President of the Mixed Commission who addressed the Council on it, initially referred the matter back to the Mixed Commission. In so doing, the Council's Rapporteur on the question, Viscount Ishii, stated:

> Should the Members of the Commission feel, however, that there are in the Convention points of great legal difficulty, which they doubt whether they have sufficient juridical knowledge to interpret, it is always open to them to ask the two Governments signatories of the Convention to place the matter before the Court of International Justice, one of whose special duties it is to undertake the interpretation of treaties. The Council, too, would, I feel sure, be willing, should the Mixed Commission desire it, to ask the Court for an advisory opinion on such points.[20]

Following further exchanges in the Mixed Commission, the Commission unanimously agreed to request the Council of the League to seek an advisory opinion of the Court on the following question, which the Council did in these terms:

> The Council of the League of Nations, having been asked by the Mixed Commission for the Exchange of Greek and Turkish populations to obtain from the Permanent Court of International Justice an Advisory Opinion on the dispute regarding the interpretation of Article 2 of the Convention on the Exchange of Greek and Turkish populations . . . has decided to ask the Permanent Court of International Justice to give an advisory opinion on the following question:
>
> What meaning and scope should be attributed to the word 'established' in Article 2 of the Convention . . . regarding the exchange of Greek and Turkish populations, in regard to which discussions have arisen and arguments have been put forward which are contained in the documents communicated by the Mixed Commission? And what conditions must the persons who are described in Article 2 . . . under the name of 'Greek inhabitants of Constantinople' fulfil in order that they may be considered as 'established' under the terms of the Convention and exempt from compulsory exchange?[21]

In so doing, the Council invited the Mixed Commission as well as the two Governments represented thereon to furnish the Court with any documents or explanations it might require. The President of the Mixed Commission transmitted a dossier to the Court.[22] As the matter was deemed to be urgent (involving as it did the alleged arbitrary arrest and expulsion of populations), the Court met in extraordinary session to deal with it. The Court's opinion of 21 February 1925 was communicated by the League Council to the Mixed Commission with an expression of hope that it would

[20] Ibid., p. 13. For the complete text, see *League of Nations Official Journal*, 1924, pp. 1669–70.

[21] *Exchange of Greek and Turkish Populations*, advisory opinion, *PCIJ*, Series B, No. 10 (1925), p. 6.

[22] Ibid., p. 9.

facilitate the work of the Commission, which would doubtless attach to it 'the same high value and authority which the Council always gave to the opinions' of the Court.[23] The matter was thereafter dealt with by the Commission and by the governments concerned, finally by means of a convention which defined 'established persons'. The Mixed Commission ceased to exist pursuant to agreement in 1934.

Thus, while the League Council itself played more than the role of a mere conduit in requesting the Court's advisory opinion, it is clear that an international organization also played a considerable role. That international organization was neither universal nor permanent; it cannot be analogized to the ILO or to what today are termed the Specialized Agencies of the United Nations, nor even to a regional agency such as the OAS or OAU. Rather it was an evanescent international organization established by treaty and the agency of the League to resolve a passing though highly important dispute between two States.

Interpretation of the Greco-Turkish Agreement of 1 December 1926

Greece and Turkey in 1926 concluded an agreement which conferred further powers on the Mixed Commission for the Exchange of Greek and Turkish Populations. The agreement provided that any questions of principle which might arise in the Mixed Commission in connection with the new duties entrusted to it should be submitted to the President of the Greco-Turkish Arbitral Tribunal sitting at Constantinople for arbitration. That clause gave rise to differences of interpretation regarding the conditions of appeal to the arbitrator, whereupon the President of the Mixed Commission, citing the above-quoted 1924 statement of Viscount Ishii, wrote to the Secretary-General of the League recounting that the Commission had by a majority 'decided . . . to apply to the Permanent Court of International Justice . . . through the agency of the League of Nations, for an advisory opinion as to the interpretation of the article in question so far as it concerns the conditions for appeals to the arbitrator'.[24] He asked the Secretary-General to place the dispute before the Council. The Secretary-General questioned whether the item could be placed on the Council's agenda on the initiative of the Mixed Commission. The Council was advised by a committee of jurists that it could be but that, having regard to the *Eastern Carelia* precedent,[25] the Council probably would not be pre-

[23] *League of Nations Official Journal*, 1925, p. 155.

[24] *Interpretation of the Greco-Turkish Agreement of 1 December 1926 (Final Protocol, Article IV)*, advisory opinion, *PCIJ*, Series B, No. 16 (1928), p. 5.

[25] *Status of Eastern Carelia,* advisory opinion, *PCIJ*, Series B, No. 5 (1923).

pared to request the Court's opinion without Turkey's concurrence.[26] Both Turkey and Greece did agree to requesting an advisory opinion while renouncing the right to appoint judges *ad hoc*. The Council, 'Referring to the letter addressed to the Secretary-General . . . by the President of the Mixed Commission for the Exchange of Greek and Turkish Populations', thereupon requested the Court to give an advisory opinion upon the question raised in the latter's letter regarding the conditions of reference to the arbitrator contemplated by the Greco-Turkish Agreement.[27] Greece and Turkey submitted written statements to the Court and took part in oral hearings.

The Court felt bound to reformulate the question put to it. It found that, by expressing in this revised form the question contemplated by the letter

[26] The Report of the Committee of Jurists appointed by the President of the Council in order to furnish it with an opinion on the preliminary question of including on the agenda the request of the Mixed Commission for an advisory opinion from the Court is of interest in so far as it shows the then limited authority of an international organization to request an advisory opinion of the Court. It reads as follows:

'The Committee finds that the Mixed Commission's request is based upon the following passage in the report submitted to the Council by Viscount Ishii on October 31st, 1924, and approved by the Council on the same day:

"The Council, too, would, I feel sure, be willing, should the Mixed Commission desire it, to ask the Court for an advisory opinion on such points."

The Committee considers that the only preliminary objections that can be raised to the inclusion of the Mixed Commission's request in the Council's agenda are the two following:

1. Viscount Ishii's suggestions, which were approved by the Council, referred to certain special points submitted to the Council on a request from the Greek Government under Article 11 of the Covenant.

2. Viscount Ishii's report referred only to the Convention between Greece and Turkey of January 30th, 1923, whereas the request now made to the Council by the Mixed Commission concerns an agreement concluded between Greece and Turkey subsequently to the Convention and the report.

The Committee unanimously agree that the first objection is not decisive. While the origin of Viscount Ishii's report was a request made under Article 11 of the Covenant, the fact remains that the passage quoted has an entirely general signification and contemplates the future working of the Mixed Commission.

The Committee considers that the second objection is of greater importance. Some doubt arose in the Committee as to the view to be taken of this objection. On the one hand, it may be urged that the objection accurately states actual facts of the case and that the authorisation given to the Mixed Commission in regard to the application of the Convention of January 30th, 1923, cannot be interpreted as extending also to the application of the agreement of December 1st, 1926. It may, on the other hand, be observed that the Mixed Commission still exists in the form in which it was established under the Convention of 1923 and has merely acquired additional powers consonant with the object for which it was created.

It appears from the above that the Council, acting according to the spirit of the decision of 1924, might decide to place the Mixed Commission's request on its agenda; but it is equally certain that, even if it did so, the Council should respect the precedent established by the advisory opinion of the Permanent Court of International Justice dated July 23rd, 1923, on the question of Eastern Carelia between Finland and Russia. Having regard to this precedent, the Council would probably not be prepared to ask the Court's opinion without Turkey's concurrence.

In view of this circumstance, the Committee is unanimous in asking whether it might not be desirable for the President of the Council first of all to ask the two Governments concerned whether they are prepared to consent to the Council submitting to the Court the question raised by the Mixed Commission.' (*League of Nations Official Journal*, 1928, p. 404.)

[27] *Interpretation of the Greco-Turkish Agreement of 1 December 1926 (Final Protocol, Article IV)*, advisory opinion, *PCIJ*, Series B, No. 16 (1928), pp. 6–7.

of the President of the Mixed Commission to the Secretary-General, the Court was in a position to reply, while it held that it could not deal with points of dispute between interested governments which fell outside the scope of the question as the Court reformulated it to be. In the course of reaching its conclusions (which need not be set out for the purposes of the present paper), the Court made observations of interest for the international arbitral process. But what is of immediate interest is that, when the advisory opinion came before the League Council, the report placed before it re-stated the question put to the Court as reformulated by the Court and recounted the Court's unanimous answers thereto and recommended that, 'As it was at the request and for the use of the Mixed Commission that the Court was requested by the Council to give an opinion', the Council take note of the opinion and transmit it to the Mixed Commission.[28]

It will be observed that, in this case as well, the League Council exerted no control over the drafting of the question put by the Mixed Commission, which was obscurely worded; in this respect it did act as a mere conduit. However, it was prepared to act at the request of the Mixed Commission only with the concurrence of the two States whose interests were affected (one of which, Turkey, was not then a League member). As for the Court, it was not prepared to deal with differences between Greece and Turkey which fell outside the terms of the Council's question.

Greco-Bulgarian 'Communities' Case

The Greco-Bulgarian Mixed Emigration Commission was a similar body. It encountered difficulties in the interpretation of articles of the convention which established it, concerning the 'communities' whose property was subject to liquidation. The President of the Mixed Commission proposed that an advisory opinion of the Court be sought. Greece and Bulgaria agreed but the members of the Commission as a whole could not agree on the terms of the questions to be submitted; accordingly, questions drawn up by the neutral members of the Commission, and by the Greek and Bulgarian members, respectively, were transmitted by the President of the Commission to the League Council. In submitting a draft resolution for reference of the questions to the Court, the French representative, M. Briand, stated that 'Since the request is submitted by the Mixed Commission on behalf of the two Governments, and since the Council has, in the past, acceded to similar applications made by the Mixed Commission for the Exchange of Greek and Turkish Populations . . . the Council should comply with the Mixed Commission's request'.[29] The Council, 'having considered the letter addressed by the President of the Greco-Bulgarian Mixed Commission to the Secretary-General, in the name of the

[28] *League of Nations Official Journal*, 1928, p. 1487.
[29] Ibid., 1930, p. 109.

Bulgarian and Greek Governments, to submit to the Council of the League a request that an advisory opinion be obtained from the Permanent Court of International Justice, for the use of the Commission, with regard to the interpretation of those clauses of the Greco-Bulgarian Convention . . . which relate to communities',[30] requested the Court to give an advisory opinion covering the questions formulated in the annexes to the letter of the Commission's President. The Council also requested the Bulgarian and Greek Governments and the Mixed Commission to furnish the Court with the necessary documents and explanations. Greece and Bulgaria appointed judges *ad hoc* and the two Governments submitted written statements and oral arguments. The Commission submitted documentation to the Court, which put questions to the Commission's President. The Court gave its unanimous replies to the multiple questions submitted to it. When the advisory opinion came before the League Council, Briand, observing that it was 'given at the Mixed Commission's request and for the Commission's use',[31] proposed that the Council take note of it and transmit it to the Commission. It was so agreed, amidst the plaudits of the representatives of Bulgaria and Greece, it being observed that the Court's unanimous opinion included that of the national judges. The President of the Mixed Commission, addressing the Council, stated that, thanks to the Court's advice, the Mixed Commission was now in possession of an 'authoritative opinion which would be of great assistance in its work. It was to be hoped that the Commission would now be able to liquidate the question of the communities to the general satisfaction.'[32] The Commission was wound up in 1932, having successfully completed the exchange between Bulgaria and Greece of more than 150,000 persons.[33]

It will be observed that the Council, relying upon the precedent of transmitting requests for advisory opinions made by the Mixed Commission for the Exchange of Greek and Turkish Populations, transmitted the request of the Greco-Bulgarian Mixed Emigration Commission, and again did so by passing along unchanged and apparently unscrutinized the multiple questions prepared by its neutral members and its Greek and Bulgarian members.

Advisory Opinions Sought by the ILO

The process by which the International Labour Organization sought advisory opinions of the Permanent Court through the agency of the League Council will not be examined in like detail, because today the ILO has unchallenged competence directly to request an advisory opinion on a legal question arising within the scope of its activities, having been so

[30] *Greco-Bulgarian 'Communities'*, advisory opinion, *PCIJ*, Series B, No. 17 (1930), pp. 4–5.

[31] *League of Nations Official Journal*, 1930, p. 1300.

[32] Ibid., p. 1301.

[33] *League of Nations Official Journal*, 1932, pp. 469–70.

authorized by General Assembly resolution adopted pursuant to Article 96 of the Charter. Thus the capacity of the ILO and other Specialized Agencies to seek advisory opinions of the Court today is, if not wider, certainly more direct than that which the ILO enjoyed in the Permanent Court. Nevertheless some observations are in order.

The first three cases to be submitted to the Court, and the only cases before it in 1922, were three requests for advisory opinions which concerned the ILO. The first, *Designation of the Workers' Delegate for the Netherlands at the Third Session of the International Labour Conference*,[34] originated in the ILO Conference, which called upon the Governing Body to request the League Council to request an advisory opinion of the Court. Lord Balfour was the first to speak in the League Council and he expressed doubt, not about the propriety of the League Council requesting an advisory opinion at the instance of the ILO, but about a challenge to 'the undoubted discretion'[35] of a government member of the League to name a delegate. His doubt was dispelled by Albert Thomas, the ILO's Director-General, who appeared before the Council to explain that the Court's opinion would serve in the future for similar cases which might come before the Conference and that the Netherlands did not oppose the request. Lord Balfour at once agreed that there could be no further objection. The question put was precisely as posed by the ILO.[36]

The origins of the Court's proceedings in two other advisory cases were very different: *Competence of the ILO in regard to International Regulation of the Conditions of Labour of Persons Employed in Agriculture*[37] and *Competence of the ILO to Examine Proposals for the Organization and Development of the Methods of Agricultural Production*.[38] France, which questioned whether the competence of the ILO extended to agricultural labour, proposed to the League Council that the Court be requested to give an advisory opinion on the question: 'Does the competence of the International Labour Organization extend to international regulation of the conditions of labour of persons employed in agriculture?'[39] The Council had before it a letter from M. Thomas stating that it was the view of the ILO Governing Body that requests to the Court respecting the ILO should first be submitted to the Governing Body. The representative of France and some others did not find that necessary and, after a discussion in which M. Thomas suggested another rendering of the question to be put to the Court, the Council adopted that proposed by France.[40]

[34] *PCIJ*, Series B, No. 1 (1922).

[35] *League of Nations Official Journal*, 1922, p. 529.

[36] Ibid. The court held that the Workers' Delegate for the Netherlands was nominated in accordance with the provisions of the governing instrument: *PCIJ*, Series B, No. 1, p. 27.

[37] *PCIJ*, Series B, No. 2 (1922).

[38] *PCIJ*, Series B, No. 3 (1922).

[39] *PCIJ*, Series B, No. 2, p. 9.

[40] *League of Nations Official Journal*, 1922, pp. 527–8. The Court held that the competence of the ILO did extend to international regulation of the conditions of labour of persons employed in agriculture: *PCIJ*, Series B, No. 2, p. 43.

Thereafter, France proposed that a supplementary question be addressed to the Court, namely: 'Does examination of proposals for the organization and development of methods of agricultural production, and of other questions of a like character, fall within the competence of the International Labour Organization?'[41] The first speaker invited to address the Council on this proposal was Albert Thomas, who maintained that the ILO had never claimed competence in matters relating to agricultural production. He therefore failed to see why the Court should be consulted. The French representative replied that, if the ILO claimed no such competence, there was no objection to submitting a question to the Court and, in any event, the ILO might in future claim a competence as to which any question would best be resolved. M. Thomas replied:

> The International Labour Office did not concern itself with the technical problems of agriculture except in so far as these problems were bound up with problems affecting the protection of workers . . . He would like to draw the attention of the Council to the risks involved in the procedure which it was proposed to adopt. Should the Council automatically transmit every request for an opinion submitted to it? There was a danger that such a method might weaken the authority both of the Council and of the Court itself. Moreover, it might do serious harm to the International Labour Office. To refer the question to the Permanent Court would suggest that the International Labour Office had claimed a competence which, as a matter of fact, it had never claimed, and so might cause the Office once more to be unjustly suspected of desiring to extend the range of its competence.[42]

But the French representative maintained that, if France were denied recourse to the Court, other governments might be discouraged from resorting to the Court, whereas the Court's opinion would contribute to establishing a useful jurisprudence.[43] The Council unanimously agreed to put the above question to the Court.

Albert Thomas himself argued all three of ILO's cases before the Court, reportedly to great effect.[44] The cases are of high interest, arising as early in the history of the Court and of international organization as they did; as examples of a State's challenge to a claimed or perceived competence of an international organization which was submitted to the Court; as instances in which the chief administrative officer of an international organization personally argued before the Court; and as cases in which not only States and international governmental organizations, but non-governmental organizations, were heard by the Court. But only the first of the three ILO

[41] *PCIJ*, Series B, No. 3, p. 49.

[42] *League of Nations Official Journal*, 1922, p. 794.

[43] Ibid. The Court held that the functions of the ILO did not extend to the promotion of improvement in the processes to increase the amount of production, in agriculture or any other branch of industry: *PCIJ*, Series B, No. 3, pp. 59–60.

[44] The extended oral arguments of M. Thomas are reproduced in *PCIJ*, Series C, No. 1, pp. 123, 221, 309. See also p. 269. Thomas's arguments make exceptional reading, and the manner of their composition and delivery is evocatively recounted in a fascinating memoir by one of his distinguished successors: E.J. Phelan, *Yes and Albert Thomas* (1936), pp. 136–42.

cases which so early came to the Court came at the instance of an international organization not authorized itself to seek an opinion.

Three further advisory opinions were subsequently requested by the League Council at the instance of the Governing Body of the ILO: *Competence of the ILO to Regulate Incidentally the Personal Work of the Employer*,[45] *Free City of Danzig and the ILO*,[46] and *Interpretation of the Convention of 1919 concerning Employment of Women during the Night*.[47] In all three cases, the League Council requested the opinions sought by the ILO in exactly the terms sought, and with minimal discussion.[48]

Opinion Sought by the League High Commissioner in Danzig

A dispute between Poland and the Free City of Danzig in regard to treatment of Polish nationals and persons of Polish origin in Danzig was submitted to the League of Nations High Commissioner for Danzig. He, in turn, with the agreement of the parties, suggested the eminent desirability of obtaining an advisory opinion of the Court, a suggestion which was transmitted by the League Secretary-General to the Council. The Council requested the Court to give an advisory opinion.[49] Memorials were presented to the Court by Danzig and Poland and they took part in oral hearings. The opinion of the Court was accepted by the parties in settlement of the dispute.[50] For present purposes, the case is of interest as an illustration of the League Council seeking an advisory opinion at the instance of what might be described as a subsidiary organ of the League. The Council concerned itself neither with the merits of the dispute nor with the wording of the questions put to the Court.

Advisory Opinions Requested at the Instance of States

The remaining advisory opinions of the Court which were sought neither by the Council of the League on its own initiative nor at the instance of international organizations were sought on behalf of States. Among this

[45] *PCIJ*, Series B, No. 13 (1926), p. 6. For M. Thomas's argument before the Court, as well as those of representatives of non-governmental organizations, see *PCIJ*, Series C, No. 12, pp. 53, 17, 19.

[46] *PCIJ*, Series B, No. 18 (1930), p. 4. For the argument to the Court of M. Thomas, see *PCIJ*, Series C, No. 18, p. 67.

[47] *PCIJ*, Series A/B, No. 50 (1932), p. 365. In this case, Mr Phelan, then head of the Diplomatic Division of the International Labour Office, spoke for the ILO: *PCIJ*, Series C, No. 60, p. 207.

[48] *League of Nations Official Journal*, 1926, pp. 596, 857; ibid., 1930, pp. 531, 1308; ibid., 1932, p. 1169.

[49] *League of Nations Official Journal*, 1931, p. 1137; *Treatment of Polish Nationals and Other Persons of Polish Origin or Speech in the Danzig Territory, PCIJ*, Series A/B, No. 44, p. 5.

[50] *League of Nations Official Journal*, 1932, pp. 2288–9.

number were two opinions sought at the instance of the Council of Ambassadors constituted in pursuance of the Peace Treaties (however, these may alternatively be viewed as having been sought not by States but by an international body, the Conference of Ambassadors). It is striking that, although the first Assembly of the League declined to adopt a proposal which would have authorized States to request advisory opinions, in practice the League Council so often and easily agreed to act as the channel through which advisory opinions sought by States could be requested of the Court. The Court itself, however, treated this facility as one subject to the Council's authority, and it rebuffed any attempt by States to go beyond the questions which the Council had adopted.

Nationality Decrees Issued in Tunis and Morocco

As indicated above, the second and third advisory opinions requested of the Court were proposed by France through the medium of the Council. The fourth case to come before the Court, and the fourth advisory opinion to be issued by it, concerned *Nationality Decrees Issued in Tunis and Morocco*.[51] Decrees had been issued concerning the nationality of certain persons born in Tunis and in Morocco, and the British Government protested to the French Government about the application of these decrees to British nationals. The British Government proposed that the question of such application be referred to the Court or to arbitration, proposals which France did not accept. The British Government thereupon submitted the dispute to the Council of the League of Nations, pursuant to Article 15 of the Covenant. France in response invoked paragraph 8 of Article 15, which provided: 'If the dispute between the parties is claimed by one of them, and is found by the Council, to arise out of a matter which by international law is solely within the domestic jurisdiction of that party, the Council shall so report and shall make no recommendation as to its settlement.' Instead of leaving that preliminary question to the resolution of the Council, Great Britain and France agreed to submit it to the Court. The League Council accordingly adopted the following resolution:

> The Council has examined the proposals made by Lord Balfour and M. Léon Bourgeois on the subject of the following question, placed on its agenda of August 11th at the request of the Government of His Britannic Majesty:
>
> 'Dispute between France and Great Britain as to the Nationality Decrees issued in Tunis and Morocco (French zone) on November 8th, 1921, and their application to British subjects, the French Government having refused to submit the legal questions involved to arbitration.'
>
> The Council, noting that friendly conversations have taken place between the representatives of the two Governments and that they have agreed on the proposals to be made to the Council;

[51] *PCIJ*, Series B, No. 4, p. 7.

Expresses its entire adhesion to the principles contained in these proposals, and has adopted the following resolution:

(*a*) The Council decides to refer to the Permanent Court of International Justice, for its opinion, the question whether the dispute referred to above is or is not by international law solely a matter of domestic jurisdiction (Article 15, paragraph 8 of the Covenant);

(*b*) And it requests the two Governments to bring this matter before the Permanent Court of International Justice, and to arrange with the Court with regard to the date on which the question can be heard and with regard to the procedure to be followed;

(*c*) Furthermore, the Council takes note that the two Governments have agreed that, if the opinion of the Court upon the above question is that it is not solely a matter of domestic jurisdiction, the whole dispute will be referred to arbitration or to judicial settlement under conditions to be agreed between the Governments.

(*d*) The Secretary-General of the League will communicate paragraphs (*a*) and (*b*) to the Court.[52]

Just before adoption of the resolution, the representative of Italy stated that it was 'understood that this decision related simply to an arrangement between the French and British Governments, and that it did not in any way bind other Governments',[53] a statement which elicited no comment.

The British and French Governments, pursuant to agreement between them, named agents for the case, transmitted to the Court memorials and counter memorials, and engaged in oral argument before the Court, which concluded with the deposit of their respective final conclusions, as if the proceedings were contentious. Oral hearings terminated on 13 January 1923, and the Court's advisory opinion was read out in Court on 7 February 1923,[54] i.e., about three weeks later. The Court reached its well-known conclusions in favour of Great Britain, essentially on the ground that the dispute entailed the construction of international agreements, which, by international law, is not solely a matter of domestic jurisdiction. The French agent immediately announced France's acceptance of what he termed 'une décision' and proposed to submit the merits of the case to the Court.[55] The opinion was transmitted to the League Council, which took no further action in the matter. The opinion enabled the British and French Governments to reach an agreement which definitely settled the dispute and to proceed no further in the Court.[56]

[52] *PCIJ*, Series B, No. 4, pp. 7–8, and *PCIJ*, Series C, No. 2, pp. 20–1. While the foregoing version of the Council's resolution was read out in Court, and incorporated in the Court's opinion, the League's *Official Journal* contains a slightly different version: *League of Nations Official Journal*, 1922, p. 1207.

[53] *League of Nations Official Journal*, 1922, p. 1207. Of this case, the *Annual Report* stated: '. . . the Council merely transmitted the request and invited the Court to make direct arrangements with the two Governments concerned for the submission of the written documents' (*PCIJ*, Series E, No. 1, p. 150).

[54] *PCIJ*, Series C, No. 2, pp. 10, 12.

[55] *PCIJ*, Series C, No. 2, p. 13.

[56] *PCIJ*, Series C, No. 3, p. 55.

Status of Eastern Carelia

In 1922, Finland requested the League Council to deal with the dispute between Finland and the Soviet Government over the status of Eastern Carelia, particularly what Finland claimed were Soviet violations of an international agreement to accord autonomy to the Finnish-speaking population of Carelia, which had resulted in armed revolt.[57] The Council expressed its willingness to consider the question if the two Parties agreed.[58] The Soviet Government declined any intervention by the League, contending that the question of Carelian autonomy was a domestic one.[59] In 1923, Finland accordingly asked the Council to request an advisory opinion of the Court.[60] The Council voted to request the Court to give an opinion on the following question: 'Do Articles 10 and 11 of the Treaty of Peace between Finland and Russia, signed at Dorpat on October 14th, 1920, and the annexed Declaration of the Russian Delegation regarding the autonomy of Eastern Carelia, constitute engagements of an international character which place Russia under an obligation to Finland as to the carrying out of the provisions contained therein?'[61] Finland participated in the Court's proceedings, but the Soviet Government confined itself to the dispatch of a telegram from People's Commissar for Foreign Affairs Tchitcherin, which stated:

The Russian Government finds it impossible to take any part in the proceedings, without legal value either in substance or in form, which the Permanent Court intends to institute as regards the Carelian question. Whereas the Workers' Commune of Carelia is an autonomous portion of the Russian Federation without any right to independent international relations; whereas its autonomy is based on the decree of the Pan-Russian Central Executive Council, dated June 8th, 1920, which was enacted before the examination of this question by the Russo-Finnish Peace Conference at Dorpat; furthermore, whereas the Treaty of Dorpat, in connection with another matter, refers to the autonomous territory of Carelia as already existing without imposing any obligation in this respect upon Russia; whereas the Russian Delegation at Dorpat declared each time that this question was raised that it was an internal question affecting the Russian Federation; furthermore, whereas Berzine, the President of the Russian Delegation, at the meeting of October 14th, 1920, brought the fact that Carelia was autonomous to the knowledge of the Finnish Delegation solely for their information; furthermore, whereas . . . Tchitcherin . . . protested categorically against the action taken by the Finnish Government in placing the Eastern Carelian question before the League of Nations, a course which in the view of the Russian Government constituted an act

[57] *League of Nations Official Journal*, 1922, pp. 104, 165.

[58] Ibid., p. 108.

[59] *League of Nations Official Journal*, 1923, p. 660.

[60] Ibid., p. 660.

[61] *Status of Eastern Carelia*, *PCIJ*, Series B, No. 5, p. 7. The question as adopted by the Council was in substance, though not in terms, that which Finland proposed. The Finnish text is found in the *League of Nations Official Journal*, 1923, p. 661. See also the interesting Rapporteur's report and accompanying Finnish legal opinions, ibid., pp. 659, 660, 661, 663.

of hostility to the Russian Federation and an intervention in its domestic affairs; furthermore, whereas . . . the Commissary of the People for Foreign Affairs declared that the Russian Government absolutely repudiated the claim of the so-called League of Nations to intervene in the question of the internal situation of Carelia and stated that any attempt on the part of any power to apply to Russia the article of the Covenant of the League relating to disputes between one of its Members and a non-participating State would be regarded by the Russian Government as an act of hostility to the Russian State: the Russian Government categorically refuses to take any part in the examination of this question by the League of Nations or by the Permanent Court. Apart from considerations of law, according to which the question of the status of Carelia is a matter of Russian domestic jurisdiction, the Soviet Government is compelled to affirm that it cannot consider the so-called League of Nations and the Permanent Court as impartial in this matter, having regard to the fact that the majority of the Powers belonging to the League of Nations have not yet accorded the Soviet Government *de jure* recognition, and several of them refuse even to enter into *de facto* relations with it.[62]

The Court recounted the pertinent provisions of the Treaty of Dorpat and of a Declaration of the Russian Delegation on Carelian autonomy made on the day of its conclusion, which Declaration Finland claimed, and Russia denied, constituted part of the terms of the Treaty. The Court held that the question of whether the Declaration formed part of the obligations into which Russia entered, as Finland asserted, or was merely by way of information, as Russia contended, 'is, in the very nature of things, a question of fact. The question is, was such an engagement made?'[63] The Court continued:

There has been some discussion as to whether questions for an advisory opinion, if they relate to matters which form the subject of a pending dispute between nations, should be put to the Court without the consent of the parties. It is unnecessary in the present case to deal with the topic.

It follows from the above that the opinion which the Court has been requested to give bears on an actual dispute between Finland and Russia. As Russia is not a Member of the League of Nations, the case is one under Article 17 of the Covenant. According to this article, in the event of a dispute between a Member of the League and a State which is not a Member of the League, the State not a Member of the League shall be invited to accept the obligations of membership in the League for the purposes of such dispute and, if this invitation is accepted, the provisions of Articles 12 to 16 inclusive shall be applied with such modifications as may be deemed necessary by the Council. This rule, moreover, only accepts and applies a principle which is a fundamental principle of international law, namely, the principle of the independence of States. It is well established in international law that no State can, without its consent, be compelled to submit its disputes with other States either to mediation or to arbitration, or to any other kind of pacific settlement. Such consent can be given once and for all in the form of an obligation freely undertaken, but it can, on the contrary, also be given in a special case apart from any existing obligation. The first alternative applies to the Members of the

[62] *PCIJ*, Series B, No. 5, pp. 12–14.
[63] Ibid., p. 26.

League who, having accepted the Covenant, are under the obligation resulting from the provisions of this pact dealing with the pacific settlement of international disputes. As concerns States not members of the League, the situation is quite different; they are not bound by the Covenant. The submission, therefore, of a dispute between them and a Member of the League for solution according to the methods provided for in the Covenant, could take place only by virtue of their consent. Such consent, however, has never been given by Russia. On the contrary, Russia has, on several occasions, clearly declared that it accepts no intervention by the League of Nations in the dispute with Finland. The refusals which Russia had already opposed to the steps suggested by the Council have been renewed upon the receipt by it of the notification of the request for an advisory opinion. The Court therefore finds it impossible to give its opinion on a dispute of this kind.[64]

The Court added that the question of whether Finland and Russia had contracted on the terms of the Declaration as to the nature of the autonomy of Eastern Carelia was 'really one of fact',[65] and that the Court would be at great disadvantage in enquiring about the facts in the absence of Russia. The question put to the Court concerned the main point of controversy between Finland and Russia and could only be decided by an investigation into the facts underlying the case. 'Answering the question would be substantially equivalent to deciding the dispute between the parties. The Court, being a Court of Justice, cannot, even in giving advisory opinions, depart from the essential rules guiding their activity as a Court.'[66]

Recalling the *Eastern Carelia* case in some detail is merited, even if it may be seen as an example of the Council not simply acting as the conduit for a request for an advisory opinion, but rather requesting an opinion on a dispute with which a State member had earlier endeavoured to seise the Council.[67] The case is important because—at least in predominant

[64] Ibid., p. 27. Relying particularly on the first paragraph of this quotation, Keith (op. cit. above (n. 4), pp. 90–7) argues that all the Court held in *Eastern Carelia* was that the *Council* (not the Court) lacked competence in the absence of Russia's consent.

[65] *PCIJ*, Series B, No. 5, p. 28.

[66] Ibid., p. 29.

[67] See the reception in the League Council of the Court's opinion: *League of Nations Official Journal*, 1923, p. 1335. The case is among those listed by the Registry as submitted 'at the instigation or request of a State or international organization' (*PCIJ*, Series E, No. 14, pp. 72, 74).

A request for another opinion from the Court may be cited as in accord with the *Eastern Carelia* approach. The League Council requested an advisory opinion in the case of the *Expulsion of the Oecumenical Patriarch*, *PCIJ*, Series C, No. 9–11. In that case, the Prime Minister of Greece appealed to the League Council to take up a dispute between Greece and Turkey concerning the forcible expulsion from Constantinople of the Patriarch (ibid., p. 16). The Turkish Foreign Minister denied the competence of the Council to deal with the dispute, on the grounds that the status of the Patriarchate was a Turkish domestic matter and that 'the exchange of Monseigneur Constantine Araboglou is properly a matter for the Mixed Commission . . . ' (ibid., p. 19). The Council's Rapporteur recommended that the Council ask the Court to give an advisory opinion on whether the Council was empowered to deal with the dispute (ibid., p. 89). The Council requested an advisory opinion on the question: Do the objections to the competence of the Council raised by the Turkish Government . . . preclude the Council from being competent in the matter brought before it by the Greek Government . . . ?' (ibid., p. 14). The Court did not render an opinion, since the League Council withdrew the request on Greece's initiative (ibid., p. 10). But the Council's entertaining such doubts about its competence in

interpretation—it emphasizes a fundamental of States asking advisory opinions of the Court through the medium of an international organ: it must be the States concerned who so move the international organ, and not just one or some of the States concerned. If the States actually in dispute do not jointly move for an advisory opinion, or at any rate clearly manifest that they mutually desire an opinion, then, whatever the action of the international organ, it may be maintained that the Court should not give the opinion, for to do so would be to evade the basic jurisdictional contraints imposed upon the Court. The Court, in this view, is not entitled to pass upon the merits of a dispute between States without the consent of the real parties in interest. Where, as in *Eastern Carelia*, the facts are essentially at issue, there is an *a fortiori* case for the Court not to respond to the question.

But whether this predominant interpretation of the meaning of the *Eastern Carelia* case is correct, or, more, whether, if it is, it is still the law, particularly in view of the advisory opinion of the International Court of Justice in the *Peace Treaties* case,[68] is open to question.[69] It is not a question on which an answer is ventured in this article.

Question of Jaworzina

The Conference of Ambassadors of the Principal Allied Powers was entrusted in 1920 with drawing a border between Czechoslovakia and Poland. A dispute arose between those two States as to whether that authority had been exhausted or whether the border question was still open. The Governments of France, Great Britain, Italy and Japan, who were represented in the Conference of Ambassadors, brought the matter to the attention of the League Council, stating, *inter alia*, that they would have 'no objection should the Council desire to ask the opinion' of the Court on the legal question which had arisen.[70] A Rapporteur of the Council reached

response to Turkey's challenge may suggest that, particularly in the light of the *Eastern Carelia* precedent, it would have been reluctant to request the Court for an advisory opinion on the merits of the dispute between Greece and Turkey without the consent of both States.

In its advisory opinion on *German Settlers in Poland*, *PCIJ*, Series B, No. 6 (1923), pp. 6, 19, 22, the Court observed that if 'the subject matter of the controversy is not within the competency of the League, the Court would not be justified in rendering an opinion . . . '. It found that the subject-matter had been placed by the terms of the Treaty of Versailles within the competence of the League and that those terms clearly made it 'proper for the Council to exercise its power under Article 14 of the Covenant to request the advice of the Court on points of law, on the determination of which its action may depend'.

[68] *Interpretation of Peace Treaties with Bulgaria, Hungary and Romania*, *ICJ Reports*, 1950, pp. 65, 71–2.

[69] See Sir Hersch Lauterpacht, *The Development of International Law by the International Court* (1982), pp. 107–9, 248–50, 352–8; Keith, op. cit. above (n. 4), pp. 89–132; and Pomerance, op. cit. above (n. 4), pp. 287–96. Among other relevant cases are *Interpretation of Article 3, Paragraph 2, of the Treaty of Lausanne*, *PCIJ*, Series B, No. 12 (1925); *Reservations to the Convention on the Prevention and Punishment of the Crime of Genocide*, *ICJ Reports*, *1951*; and *Legal Consequences for States of the Continued Presence of South Africa in Namibia (South West Africa) notwithstanding Security Council Resolution 276 (1970)*, *ICJ Reports*, 1971.

[70] *League of Nations Official Journal*, 1923, p. 1472.

agreement with representatives of Czechoslovakia and Poland on so doing and on the terms of the question.[71] The Council thereupon agreed to request an advisory opinion of the Court on the question:

> Is the question of the delimitation of the frontier between Poland and Czechoslovakia still open, and, if so, to what extent; or should it be considered as already settled by a final decision (subject to the customary procedure of marking boundaries locally, with any modifications of detail which that procedure may entail)?[72]

In this case, the League Council acted as the conduit for requesting an opinion desired by all the States concerned. But it was not a mere conduit; it played a modest role in framing the question as well as in passing it to the Court for its opinion.

The Monastery of Saint-Naoum

As the Court stated in their advisory opinion, the question closely resembled that asked of it in the *Jaworzina* case.[73] The background of this opinion is intricate and (as others of the Permanent Court of International Justice considered in this article) is usefully summarized in a headnote found in *World Court Reports*.[74] For present purposes, what is pertinent is that the Conference of Ambassadors, acting on behalf of the Governments of the British Empire, France, Italy and Japan, remitted the question of the border between Albania and Yugoslavia at the point of the monastery of Saint-Naoum to the League Council, which decided, with the agreement of Albania and Yugoslavia,[75] to put the following request for an advisory opinion to the Court:

> Have the Principal Allied Powers, by the decision of the Conference of Ambassadors of December 6th, 1922, exhausted, in regard to the frontier between Albania and the Kingdom of the Serbs, Croats and Slovenes at the Monastery of Saint-Naoum, the mission, such as it has been recognized by the interested Parties, which is contemplated by a unanimous Resolution of the Assembly of the League of Nations of October 2nd, 1921?[76]

This appears to be a case in which the Council exerted a measure of initiative, together with that of the Conference of Ambassadors. The Conference of Ambassadors put two questions to the Council; the Council's Rapporteur concluded that the first question was 'purely legal' and 'interlocutory' and, 'in accordance with precedent', he proposed that it be referred to the Court for its advisory opinion; and this was done.[77]

[71] Ibid., p. 1474.

[72] Ibid., p. 1332, and *PCIJ*, Series B, No. 8, p. 10.

[73] *PCIJ*, Series B, No. 9, pp. 6, 15.

[74] Manley O. Hudson, *World Court Reports*, vol. I, pp. 391–2. See also *League of Nations Official Journal*, 1924, p. 1006.

[75] Ibid., p. 920.

[76] *PCIJ*, Series B, No. 9, p. 7.

[77] *League of Nations Official Journal*, 1924, p. 1006.

Jurisdiction of the European Commission of the Danube

Differences arose between Romania, on the one hand, and Great Britain, France and Italy, on the other, on the extent of the competence of the European Commission of the Danube. The British Government brought these differences to the Advisory and Technical Committee for Communications and Transit of the League of Nations, whose jurisdiction Romania challenged. As a result of discussions among the States concerned, the representatives in the European Commission of the Danube of France, Great Britain, Italy and Romania concluded an agreement (which was registered as a treaty with the League) to request the Council of the League to submit three questions to the Court for its advisory opinion.[78] When that request came before the League Council, the British representative, while not opposing its adoption, placed on record that requesting an advisory opinion of the Court,

> instead of referring the dispute for decision, must be regarded as an exceptional case, and must not be thought to constitute a precedent for similar action in the future. Nor must it be deemed to constitute an abandonment of the view that, in virtue of treaties and arrangements in force, any party to this dispute would have been entitled to bring the question to the Permanent Court of International Justice for decision . . . To abandon that contention would weaken the machinery which has been set up for the settlement of disputes as to the meaning and application of the Ports and Waterways Sections of the Treaties of Peace.[79]

In response, the representative of Romania stressed the difference between an advisory opinion and a judgment of the Court and emphasized that negotiations in progress on the dispute would continue.[80] The Council then adopted a resolution requesting the Court to give an advisory opinion on the three questions precisely as they had been drafted by the representatives of the four States concerned. The resolution also invited the four Governments to afford the Court all the assistance it might require in the consideration of those questions.[81] Those Governments filed memorials and counter-memorials and took part in oral argument.

The case is an interesting one, in that apparently there was a basis for bringing contentious proceedings but the parties nevertheless concluded a kind of special agreement, not for proceeding contentiously, but for requesting the League Council to ask for an advisory opinion. The Council did as asked.

[78] *Jurisdiction of the European Commission of the Danube*, *PCIJ*, Series B, No. 14, p. 8, and *League of Nations Official Journal*, 1927, pp. 233–4.

[79] *League of Nations Official Journal*, 1927, p. 151.

[80] Ibid., pp. 151–2.

[81] *PCIJ*, Series B, No. 14, p. 6.

Access to German Minority Schools in Upper Silesia

A last advisory opinion which is described by the Registry of the Permanent Court as sought not by the Council *proprio motu* but at the instance of States is *Access to German Minority Schools in Upper Silesia*.[82] However, as far as examination of the proceedings in the League Council,[83] as well as the Court's opinion,[84] indicates, while the question put to the Court was formulated by the Council's Rapporteur in agreement with the German and Polish Governments, it is not clear that this is an illustration of an opinion being requested at the instance of States rather than by the Council as an element of its consideration of an item with which it was dealing.

Constraints Imposed by the Court on Seeking Advisory Opinions

In its contentious proceedings over *German Interests in Polish Upper Silesia*, the Court had occasion to observe that whereas the Court may give advisory opinions at the request of the Council or Assembly of the League of Nations, 'a request of this kind directly submitted by a State will not be considered'.[85] Moreover, a request made by the Council or Assembly on behalf of States (or international organizations) will be held to the terms of the request made. Thus, in the *Interpretation of the Greco-Bulgarian Agreement of 9 December 1927*, the Council requested the Court to give an advisory opinion on two questions; however, its answering of the second question was conditional on an affirmative answer to the first question.[86] The Court held:

> As the Court has arrived at the conclusion that the answer to the first question is not in the affirmative, the second question does not arise . . .
>
> In the course of the written pleadings and also in the course of the oral arguments before the Court, the Agents and Counsel of each of the Governments concerned stated that they were anxious that the Court should give an opinion upon the second question whether the first question was answered in the affirmative or not. The Court feels unable to comply with this desire.
>
> By the terms of Article 14 of the Covenant, the right to submit a question to the advisory jurisdiction of the Court is given only to the Assembly and to the Council

[82] See *Fourteenth Annual Report of the Permanent Court of International Justice, PCIJ,* Series E, No. 14, p. 75.

[83] *League of Nations Official Journal*, 1931, pp. 228–9, 1151, 2263.

[84] *PCIJ*, Series A/B, No. 40, p. 4.

[85] *German Interests in Polish Upper Silesia (Jurisdiction), PCIJ,* Series A, No. 6, p. 21. Notice the qualification 'directly'. The Court observed that the applicant State 'could not have intended to obtain an advisory opinion, for which it was not entitled to ask' (ibid.).

[86] *PCIJ*, Series A/B, No. 45, p. 70. The questions put were:

'In the case at issue, is there a dispute between Greece and Bulgaria within the meaning of Article 8 of the Caphandaris-Molloff Agreement concluded at Geneva on December 9th, 1927?

If so, what is the nature of the pecuniary obligations arising out of this Agreement?'

of the League. The Court is therefore bound by the terms of the questions as formulated in this case by the Council. The second question is so worded as to be put to the Court conditionally upon an affirmative answer being given to the first question. To ignore this condition at the request of the Parties would be in effect to allow the two interested Governments to submit a question for the advisory opinion of the Court.[87]

Reconsideration of the Extent of Advisory Jurisdiction

It has been shown that, in the Permanent Court, while only the League Council and Assembly were authorized to request advisory opinions, in practice a large number of opinions were requested through the medium of the Council by States and international organizations. The Council retained a supervening authority, certainly in the eyes of the Court, but in most cases it actually exerted no such authority beyond being the conduit through which the request to the Court passed; that is, for the most part, the Council served as a mere conduit. It might be said that this was so because the two leading Powers of the League, Great Britain and France, were the real movers behind the requests for opinions; but while this was true in some cases, it was not true in all (as in the requests concerning disputes among Turkey, Greece and Bulgaria). When the provisions of the United Nations Charter and the Statute of the International Court of Justice relating to the Court's advisory jurisdiction came to be drafted, to what extent was account taken of this practice of the League Council and the Permanent Court?

Report of the Informal Inter-Allied Committee

The first stage of reconsideration of the Court's Statute took place in an Informal Inter-Allied Committee on the Future of the Permanent Court of International Justice (of which Gerald Fitzmaurice was the secretary), which met in London in 1943–44.

Its Report of 10 February 1944 contained these innovative passages about the scope of a projected advisory jurisdiction, which call for extended quotation:

65. Some of us were inclined to think at first that the Court's jurisdiction to give advisory opinions was anomalous and ought to be abolished, mainly on the ground that it was incompatible with the true function of a court of law, which was to hear and decide disputes. It was urged that the existence of this jurisdiction tended to encourage the use of the Court as an instrument for settling issues which were

[87] Ibid., p. 87. See also *Exchange of Greek and Turkish Populations, PCIJ*, Series B, No. 10, p. 17, where the Court indicated that it could not take cognizance of a question not asked by the Council; and, to similar effect, *Interpretation of the Greco-Turkish Agreement of 1 December 1926, PCIJ,* Series B, No. 16, p. 16.

essentially of a political rather than of a legal character and that this was undesirable. Attention was drawn to instances of this which had occurred in the past. Subsidiary objections were that the existence of this jurisdiction might promote a tendency to avoid the final settlement of disputes by seeking opinions, and might lead to general pronouncements of law by the Court not (or not sufficiently) related to a particular issue or set of facts.

66. Despite these considerations we have come to the conclusion that the jurisdiction to give advisory opinions ought to be retained and ought even to be enlarged. In the first place it is not correct to say that a jurisdiction of an 'advisory' nature is inconsistent with the proper function of a court of law. The legal systems of certain countries contain a procedure whereby certain matters can be referred to the courts for an opinion, or for a declaration of what the law is, or what the rights or status of the applicant are or would be under a given set of circumstances. The exercise of this jurisdiction by municipal courts has not, so far as we are aware, led to difficulty, and has proved of undoubted utility.

67. Secondly, it is clear that a General International Organisation, if it possesses anything in the nature of a regular Constitution, will require authoritative legal advice on points affecting the Constitution, the rights and obligations of Member States and the interpretation of the instrument setting up the Organisation. There are distinct limits to the extent to which such matters can be dealt with internally (e.g., by the legal section of the Organisation's Secretariat) or by such means as reference to an *ad hoc* committee of jurists. League experience has shown the necessity of having an authoritative standing tribunal to which, in suitable cases, questions of this kind can be referred for an opinion. On this ground alone, therefore, we think that the jurisdiction of the Court to give advisory opinions must be retained.

68. In the third place, there are reasons which make it desirable to allow two or more States, acting in concert, to obtain an advisory opinion. They are as follows:

(*a*) From an international point of view, it seems desirable to provide a procedure whereby the legal rights and position of parties can be determined or at any rate assessed, before any difference of opinion between them has ripened into an issue or definite dispute which can only be settled by actual litigation.

(*b*) It may be useful to countries to be able to ascertain their legal position without involving themselves in a judicial decision binding on them as such and requiring immediate execution.

(*c*) The faculty to ask for an advisory opinion may be very helpful to parties engaged in negotiations (e.g., for a treaty or for the settlement of some outstanding issue) where the requisite basis for negotiation does not exist until the legal rights of the parties, or the correct interpretation of some existing instrument, has been definitely ascertained.

(*d*) There may well be cases in which special relations between countries render them reluctant to appear before the Court as apparently hostile contending parties in a litigation, but where the existence of a 'friendly dispute' between them nevertheless requires some form of disposal by legal means.

(*e*) Whereas an International Organisation can to some extent meet its needs by referring questions to an *ad hoc* committee of jurists, this procedure is difficult, if not impossible, for States. Reference to some *ad hoc* tribunal is no doubt possible, but if the Court exists it is best that it should be used, and its pronouncements will carry greater weight than those of any such tribunal.

69. In the light of this conclusion, the subject of advisory opinions resolves itself mainly into two questions, whether the scope of the jurisdiction should remain as it is at present, or be enlarged; and what safeguards should be instituted to control it and to prevent its misuse. The first of these questions is, in essence, whether the faculty to request advisory opinions should be confined to the executive organs of any future General International Organisation, or should be extended to other bodies, and to individual States. The second question concerns the steps to be taken to ensure what we are all agreed are most important requirements, namely, that only questions of law should be referred for an advisory opinion, and that such questions should not be of a merely general or abstract character, but should relate to some definite issue or circumstance, and be based on an agreed and stated set of facts. Failing some such control, there is a risk that the Court may be used for making pronouncements on political issues, or in a semi-legislative capacity for making general statements or declarations of law, instead of giving advice as to what the law is in relation to a defined issue or set of facts.

70. Concerning the scope of the faculty to seek advisory opinions, we are agreed that there is no reason to confine it to the executive organs of the future General International Organisation, and that it could usefully be extended to other associations of States such as the International Labour Office, the Universal Postal Union, etc. Unless the list of such Associations is settled for this purpose, either in the Statute of the Court or from time to time by the General International Organisation, it would be for the Court itself to decide whether the body concerned had the international and inter-governmental character necessary to give it the capacity to ask the Court for an advisory opinion.

71. We are also agreed that, provided the necessary safeguards can be instituted, there would, for the reasons given in paragraph 68, be considerable advantage in permitting references on the part of two or more States acting in concert. Applications by an individual State *ex parte* could not be permitted, for, given the authoritative nature of the Court's pronouncements, *ex parte* applications would afford a means whereby the State concerned could indirectly impose a species of compulsory jurisdiction on the rest of the world. In addition, the Court must have an *agreed* basis of fact on which to give its opinion.

72. With regard to the question of how the necessary control can be secured over matters referred to the Court for an advisory opinion, so as to ensure that only questions proper to be put to the Court are heard by it, we have considered whether all applications should pass through and be required to receive the fiat of the appropriate organ of the General International Organisation. The objections to this are, first, that the nature and functions of such an Organisation are at present unsettled; secondly, that some control will require to be established over the Organisation's own applications for advisory opinions.

73. On the whole therefore it seems to us desirable to leave the necessary control to be exercised by the Court itself . . . we attach the greatest importance to the Court's jurisdiction being confined to matters which are really 'justiciable,' and this applies equally to advisory opinions. It would, accordingly, be for the Court to decline to deal with an application directed to political and not legal issues, or to require a restatement of the case so as to confine it to pure questions of law or treaty interpretation. The Court would equally refuse to consider the application if the facts were not agreed, or were inadequately stated, or if the questions put were of too general a character, not involving concrete issues in which the parties were

actively interested. In the same way the Court would refuse to allow the procedure by way of advisory opinions to be used as a means of reopening questions already judicially determined, or for pronouncing on questions of municipal law where these lay solely within the competence of domestic tribunals.

74. All these would be matters to be provided for in the Statute of the Court. In addition, it would be necessary to ensure that it was not open to two States, acting in concert, to obtain a pronouncement from the Court on a matter of interest to other States (e.g., the interpretation of a multilateral convention) where the latter had had no opportunity of intervening. We consider that this point would be adequately met by maintaining the procedure of notification by the Registrar of the Court set out in the existing Statute.

75. If such a scheme be adopted, we see no objection to allowing two or more States, acting in concert, to apply direct to the Court for an advisory opinion.[88]

Revisions Proposed by the United States to the PCIJ Statute, and the Dumbarton Oaks Proposals

No representative of the United States took part in the work of the Inter-Allied Committee. The Statute of the Permanent Court of International Justice with Revisions Proposed by the United States, August 1944, would have amended the Statute to provide that 'Questions upon which the advisory opinion of the Court is asked shall be laid before the Court by means of a written request, signed by the chairman of the executive council of the general international organization . . . '.[89] That is to say, in this initial United States conception, only the Council—which was shortly to be renamed the Security Council—would have been authorized to request advisory opinions of the Court. This regressive approach appears to have reflected the then current preoccupation of the United States with the exclusive role of the Council in the maintenance of international peace and security. Advisory opinions were viewed as adjunctive to that role.[90]

The Dumbarton Oaks Proposals for the Establishment of a General International Organization, prepared by the United States, the United Kingdom and the Soviet Union, and then by the United States, the United Kingdom and China, provided that there should be an international court of justice which should constitute the principal judicial organ of the organization, and that all members of the organization should *ipso facto* be parties to the Statute of the Court, but it did not decide whether that Statute should be that of the Permanent Court, suitably modified, or a new Statute. The Dumbarton Oaks Proposals further provided, in the Chapter on 'Arrangements for the Maintenance of International Peace and Security . . . ', and in line with the foregoing US approach, that 'Justiciable

[88] *Report of the Informal Inter-Allied Committee on the Future of the Permanent Court of International Justice* (1944), Cmd. 6531, paras. 65–74.

[89] The text is reprinted in Ruth B. Russell and Jeanette E. Muther, *A History of the United Nations Charter* (1958), pp. 1017, 1023–4.

[90] Ibid., p. 873.

disputes should normally be referred to the international court of justice. The Security Council should be empowered to refer to the court, for advice, legal questions connected with other disputes.'[91] Refinement of the bare Dumbarton Oaks proposals was left to the Washington Committee of Jurists, which convened under the chairmanship of Green H. Hackworth two weeks before the San Francisco Conference.

The Washington Committee of Jurists

When the Statute of the Permanent Court was re-examined at the session of the Washington Committee of Jurists, the United States maintained its proposal that advisory opinions should be requested only on the authority of the Security Council, 'in conformity with the Dumbarton Oaks Proposals'.[92] However, the United Kingdom made proposals which reflected the approach of the Inter-Allied Committee. It suggested:

> The jurisdiction to give advisory opinions is at present limited to those cases in which such an opinion is requested by the appropriate body of the International Organisation. There does not appear to be any sufficient ground for this limitation and it is suggested that the faculty to give advisory opinions, which has proved in the past to be of great value, should be extended to two further classes of cases. In the first place, it should be open to any recognised and properly constituted International Organisation to apply directly to the Court with a request for an advisory opinion. Secondly, it is suggested that it would also be of great value if States, *by agreement amongst themselves* (not, of course, unilaterally), were able to apply to the Court for an advisory opinion. They would thus, in many cases, obtain advice as to their legal position which would prevent an eventual dispute leading to litigation.
>
> If the foregoing suggestions concerning advisory opinions were adopted, it would of course be necessary to introduce safeguards, with a view to ensuring that the requests addressed to the Court were confined to matters of a strictly justiciable nature, and, moreover, related to actual matters of fact which had arisen between the parties concerned. To achieve this, it would be desirable to confer on the Court a right to reject any request for an advisory opinion, if the Court considered that, in the circumstances, the request was not one to which it, as a court of law, ought to accede.[93]

A number of States, including China, Guatemala, Mexico, Norway and Venezuela, proposed that the General Assembly as well as the Security Council be authorized to request advisory opinions.[94] A Chinese proposal to this effect was unanimously accepted, while, at the same time, the Committee of Jurists recognized that it was for the Charter and not the Statute

[91] *Documents of the United Nations Conference on International Organization, 1945*, vol. 14, p. 458. See also p. 455.

[92] Ibid., pp. 325, 345.

[93] Ibid., p. 319. Venezuela also proposed that States be authorized to seek advisory opinions (ibid., p. 373).

[94] Ibid., pp. 177, 445–7.

to determine what organs of the United Nations should be qualified to request an advisory opinion.[95] However, the Report of the Washington Committee of Jurists submitted to the San Francisco Conference recorded that 'The suggestion has been made to allow international organizations and, even to a certain extent, States to ask for advisory opinions. The Commission did not believe that it should adopt it.'[96]

The debate in the Committee of Jurists that led to these conclusions remains of interest. The British representative (Fitzmaurice) referred to the utility of advisory opinions as a means of avoiding actual litigation and resolving differences before they reached the stage of disputes.[97] The representative of Venezuela (Gomez-Ruiz) proposed that the right to request advisory opinions be granted directly to public international organizations and to individual States, subject to the right of the Court to decide whether it was competent in the matter.[98] He indicated that he had in mind organizations which today would be termed Specialized Agencies. The British representative seconded the Venezuelan proposal. The French representative (Basdevant) gave measured support to Venezuela's proposal, particularly in relation to the Specialized Agencies.[99] The representative of the Soviet Union (Novikov) objected to granting individual States the right to apply directly to the Court for an advisory opinion. The Court could be overloaded with minor matters. Its function was not to serve as general adviser. States could apply to the General Assembly to seek an advisory opinion, but if they were entitled directly to seek opinions of the Court, Charter procedures for dealing with international disputes might be endangered. Thus he favoured doing no more than adding the right of the General Assembly to that of the Security Council to seek advisory opinions.[100] The Australian representative (Eggleston) also maintained that the United Nations should in each case pass on whether an advisory opinion was to be asked of the Court. If the right were to be accorded to international organizations, such organizations must be permanent ones which had States as members; temporary or *ad hoc* organizations should be excluded.[101] The Venezuelan representative agreed that, if international organizations were to be accorded the authority to request advisory opinions, they should be permanent organizations of States, connected with the United Nations.[102] Judge Hudson, who was present as a representative of the Permanent Court of International Justice, declined to express a view on the policy questions involved, but observed that the Court several times had given advisory

[95] Ibid., pp. 179, 850.
[96] Ibid., p. 850.
[97] Ibid., p. 179.
[98] Ibid., p. 179. See also an earlier Belgian proposal which, in restricted circumstances, would have authorized a State to request an advisory opinion (ibid., pp. 445–6).
[99] Ibid., p. 180.
[100] Ibid., p. 181.
[101] Ibid., p. 182.
[102] Ibid., p. 182.

opinions to international organizations other than the League, such as the Danube River Commission, the Greco-Bulgarian Mixed Emigration Commission and the ILO, 'all on requests made through the League. All such requests had promptly been transmitted to the Court.'[103] The Chairman (Hackworth) observed that it was not yet known what international organizations would be created. He contrasted the orderly procedure of going through the Assembly with the confusion and crowding of dockets which might result from direct requests to the Court. There was no reason now for creating such rights. One might arise in the future, but the Committee should not look too far ahead.[104] A vote was then taken on the question whether the right to ask for advisory opinions should be extended to international organizations generally, and the proposal was disapproved by 16 votes to 4.[105] Rejection of a proposal to permit States directly to request advisory opinions appears to have been tacit.

It will be observed that this record of discussion is consistent with the conclusion that there was no intention in the Committee of Jurists to narrow the capacity to request advisory opinions from that which obtained in League days. The majority against according any international organizations, and States, the right directly to request advisory opinions was large, and a few representatives maintained that any decision which might be made to accord international organizations direct access to the Court's advisory jurisdiction should be restricted to the Specialized Agencies. But there was no disposition to debar international organizations and States from requesting the General Assembly or Security Council to request advisory opinions on their behalf, in pursuance of the precedent of the League of which the Committee was informed: via requests 'through' the Organization to be 'promptly transmitted' to the Court.

The San Francisco Conference

At the San Francisco Conference on International Organization, the United Kingdom proposed that provision be made in the Charter to empower the General Assembly and Security Council to request advisory opinions from the Court and that 'suitable provision be made to enable such international agencies as the General Assembly may authorize for the purpose to request advisory opinions on questions of a constitutional or judicial character arising within the scope of their activities'.[106] It was readily agreed to add to the Charter the provision, now Article 96, paragraph 1,

[103] Ibid., pp. 182–3.

[104] Ibid., p. 183.

[105] Ibid., p. 184.

[106] Ibid., vol. 9, p. 359. This proposal was described as designed 'to enable certain international agencies which are to be brought into relationship with the United Nations Organisation to request advisory opinions from the Court on questions relating to the interpretation of their constitutions or of conventions within their respective fields': ibid., pp. 358–9.

providing that: 'The General Assembly or the Security Council may request the International Court of Justice to give an advisory opinion on any legal question'.[107] It was likewise agreed to insert a complementary provision in the Statute (today Article 65).[108] It was also agreed to make provision for agencies authorized by the General Assembly to request advisory opinions, but this agreement was restricted to intergovernmental agencies brought into relationship with the United Nations (i.e., Specialized Agencies).[109] The United Kingdom explained that its draft to this effect was safeguarded against abuse by adding the requirement that the international agencies be ones closely connected with the United Nations. Subsequently this provision was revised to provide that other organs of the United Nations and Specialized Agencies at any time so authorized by the General Assembly may request advisory opinions of the Court on legal questions arising within the scope of their activities.[110] However, the proposal, renewed by Venezuela, that two or more States acting in agreement should be empowered to request advisory opinions of the Court failed for lack of a two-thirds majority.[111]

This drafting history at San Francisco of the Charter and the Statute is no less consonant than that of the Committee of Jurists with the maintenance of the authority of international organizations which are not Specialized Agencies, and of States, to ask the General Assembly or Security Council of the United Nations to request advisory opinions of the Court on their behalf. At San Francisco, the point was made that the General Assembly would have to authorize which agencies independently could request opinions; but nothing in the record suggests that other organizations (and States) could not request the General Assembly to transmit to the Court their requests for advisory opinions. The Charter as adopted articulated the authority of the General Assembly and Security Council to request the Court to give an advisory opinion 'on any legal question' (a broader formulation than that of the Covenant, which apparently occasioned no analytical discussion in its drafting). It represented an advance on the Covenant, in so far as it provides that other organs of the Organization and the Specialized Agencies may be authorized to request advisory opinions of the Court on legal questions arising within the scope of their activities. That advance did not fully codify and progressively develop the practice that evolved in League days, for, if it had, two further innovations would have been introduced: the right of intergovernmental organizations to be authorized to request an advisory opinion even if such organizations

[107] Ibid., vol. 13, p. 241.

[108] Ibid., p. 242, on the ground that, 'while the Statute was part of the Charter, the Charter was not a part of the Statute'. See also vol. 9, pp. 161–2, 363–4.

[109] Ibid., vol. 9, pp. 161–2, and vol. 13, p. 298.

[110] Ibid., p. 247. A Soviet proposal to require General Assembly authorization 'in each case' rather than 'at any time' was not adopted, to avoid the inconvenience and delay which going to the General Assembly in each case might occasion: ibid., vol. 13, pp. 298–9.

[111] Ibid., vol. 13, p. 235.

were not Specialized Agencies; and the right of States by agreement in a particular case to request an advisory opinion. Rosenne characterizes the restriction of Article 96, paragraph 2, of the Charter to organs and Specialized Agencies authorized by the General Assembly as 'unduly limitative' and he rightly observes that, in this respect,

> the practice of the United Nations compares unfavourably with that of the League, where, despite the formal centralization of the political control over requests in one of the two organs authorized to initiate advisory cases, several widely differing types of international organizations and organs, as well as groups of States, were in fact in a position to avail themselves of the Court's advice. It may therefore be hoped that it will be found possible to broaden the circle of public international organizations entitled to request advisory opinions, without impairing the general control of the General Assembly over those matters . . . [112]

He thus appears to recognize that, within the terms of the Charter and Statute, an evolution of practice comparable to that which existed in League days is possible.

United Nations Practice

Not only does the United Nations Charter provide for a broader capacity to request advisory opinions of the International Court of Justice than did the Covenant for requests of the Permanent Court. There are other differences between the League and the United Nations which affect their readiness, if not their authority, to request advisory opinions, some cutting one way and some the other; among them are the following. The League of Nations operated largely on the unanimity rule,[113] whereas United Nations organs operate by absolute or qualified majority vote.[114] The Covenant of the League, and the concerns of League organs, were more highly charged with considerations of international law than are those of the United Nations Charter and its organs. The League Council, at least initially, was a smaller and more homogeneous body than is the Security Council; it operated less formally and, in its early years, more congenially and effectively, than has the Security Council, and thus may have been a likelier organ to act as a conduit for requests to the Court for advisory opinions

[112] Shabtai Rosenne, *The Law and Practice of the International Court* (1965), vol. 2, p. 661.

[113] Whether, however, unanimity in the League Council (including the votes of States in dispute) was required for adoption of a request for an advisory opinion was an unsettled and vexed issue. See *Twelfth Report of the Permanent Court of International Justice, PCIJ,* Series E, No. 12, pp. 117–27; *Sixteenth Report of the Permanent Court of International Justice, PCIJ*, Series E, No. 16, pp. 63–4; *League of Nations Official Journal*, 1937, pp. 77–9; Manley O. Hudson, *The Permanent Court of International Justice, 1920–1942* (1943), pp. 488–94; and Pomerance, op. cit. above (n. 4), pp. 213–21. In practice, the League Council was generally prepared to request the Court's opinion only on the basis of a unanimous vote. There were at least two apparent exceptions to this rule: *Acquisition of Polish Nationality, PCIJ*, Series B, No. 7; and *Interpretation of Article 3, Paragraph 2, of the Treaty of Lausanne, PCIJ*, Series B, No. 12.

[114] See Rosenne, op. cit. above (n. 112), vol. 2, p. 659.

made by other international organizations and States. Moreover, unlike the League Council, the Security Council is not the executive committee of the organization at large but an organ which rather has primary responsibility for the maintenance of international peace and security. It is not clear whether the Security Council is, and would regard itself as, a suitable organ to request advisory opinions which are not directly related to that charge. Yet Chapter VI of the Charter, 'Pacific Settlement of Disputes', is a 'Security Council' chapter of the Charter, and it embraces the settlement of disputes whose continuance 'is likely to endanger the maintenance of international peace and security'. In pursuance of such settlement, and its even wider authority under Article 34 to 'investigate any dispute, or any situation which might lead to international friction or give rise to a dispute, in order to determine whether the continuance of the dispute or situation is likely to endanger the maintenance of international peace and security', the Security Council may call on the parties to settle their dispute by judicial means. It may accordingly be maintained that the Council's remit is wide enough to embrace requesting an advisory opinion on a dispute or situation which 'might lead to international friction' which is in turn requested by States or an international organization, even if the maintenance of international peace and security is not immediately at stake. That conclusion may call in aid the authority of the Security Council under Article 96, paragraph 1, to request the Court to give an advisory opinion 'on any legal question'.[115] At the same time, it may be recalled that the Security Council, in forty-five years, has asked the Court for an advisory opinion just once. The large majority of all advisory opinions have been sought by the General Assembly. While most advisory opinions requested by the League Council concerned specific disputes between States, the advisory opinions requested by the General Assembly largely have concerned questions of what may be termed international constitutional law.

Authorizing United Nations Organs to Request Advisory Opinions

In implementation of Article 96, paragraph 2, of the Charter, the General Assembly proceeded to authorize certain United Nations organs to request advisory opinions on legal questions arising within the scope of their activities. The organs so authorized are the Economic and Social Council, the Trusteeship Council, the Interim Committee of the General Assembly, and the Committee on Applications for Review of Judgments of the United Nations Administrative Tribunal. The Economic and Social

[115] It is of interest to recall that, at San Francisco, the representative of the USSR, Professor Golunsky, stated that authorizing the Security Council to give effect to decisions of the Court would accord the Council authority to deal with matters which might have nothing to do with security: *Documents of the United Nations Conference on International Organization*, vol. 17, p. 97. But see a restrictive British view of the Council's authority, ibid., vol. 9, p. 359.

Council has exercised that authority once. The Committee on Applications for Review of UNAT Judgments has exercised its authority three times. The General Assembly itself has requested the remaining advisory opinions, apart from three requested by Specialized Agencies (and the single opinion requested by the Security Council).

In connection with authorizing the Committee on Applications for Review of Judgments of the United Nations Administrative Tribunal to request advisory opinions, the question was raised whether it would be an organ entitled to request advisory opinions of the Court on legal questions arising within the scope of *its* activities, as contrasted with the legal activities of the Tribunal itself. When the first request for an advisory opinion brought by the Committee came before the Court, the Court dealt with that question in this way:

19. Article 96, paragraph 2, of the Charter, empowers the General Assembly to authorize organs of the United Nations to 'request advisory opinions of the Court on legal questions arising within the scope of their activities'. In the present instance . . . the Statute of the Administrative Tribunal expressly states that the Committee 'For the purpose of this article . . . is . . . authorised under paragraph 2 of Article 96 of the Charter to request advisory opinions of the Court'. These two provisions, prima facie, suffice to establish the competence of the Committee to request advisory opinions of the Court. The point has been raised, however, as to whether under . . . the Statute of the Administrative Tribunal the Committee has any activities of its own which enable it to be considered as requesting advisory opinions 'on legal questions arising within the scope of [its] activities'. Thus, the view has been expressed that the Committee has no other activity than to request advisory opinions, and that the 'legal questions' arise not within the scope of 'its activities' but of those of another organ, the Administrative Tribunal.

20. The functions entrusted to the Committee . . . are: to receive applications which formulate objections to judgements of the Administrative Tribunal on one or more of the grounds set out . . . and which ask the Committee to request an advisory opinion; to decide within 30 days whether or not there is a substantial basis for the application; and, if it so decides, to request an advisory opinion of the Court. The scope of the activities of the Committee which result from these functions is, admittedly, a narrow one. But the Committee's activities . . . have to be viewed in the larger context of the General Assembly's function in the regulation of staff relations of which they form a part. This is not a delegation by the General Assembly of its own power to request an advisory opinion; it is the creation of a subsidiary organ having a particular task and invested it with the power to request advisory opinions in the performance of that task. The mere fact that the Committee's activities serve a particular, limited, purpose in the General Assembly's performance of its function in the regulation of staff relations does not prevent the advisory jurisdiction of the Court from being exercised in regard to those activities; nor is there any indication in Article 96 of the Charter of any such restriction upon the General Assembly's power to authorize organs of the United Nations to request advisory opinions.

21. In fact, the primary function of the Committee is not the requesting of advisory opinions, but the examination of objections to judgements in order to decide in

each case whether there is a substantial basis for the application so as to call for a request for an advisory opinion. If it finds that there is not such a substantial basis for the application the Committee rejects the application without requesting an opinion of the Court. When it does find that there is a substantial basis for the application, the legal questions which the Committee then submits to the Court clearly arise out of the performance of this primary function of screening the applications presented to it. They are therefore questions which, in the view of the Court, arise within the scope of the Committee's own activities; for they arise not out of the judgements of the Administrative Tribunal but out of objections to those judgements raised before the Committee itself.[116]

The only bodies which may, under Article 96, paragraph 2, of the Charter be authorized by the General Assembly to request advisory opinions are 'organs of the United Nations and specialized agencies'. In the foregoing case, the Court construed 'organs' to include subsidiary as well as principal organs.[117] However, when it was contemplated that the Human Rights Committee to be constituted pursuant to the then proposed International Covenant on Civil and Political Rights should be authorized to request advisory opinions, the Secretary-General advised that, since the Committee was to be established under an instrument separate and distinct from the Charter and would be neither a principal nor a subsidiary organ of the United Nations nor a Specialized Agency, it could not itself be authorized to request advisory opinions. Nor, the Secretary-General concluded, could the Committee be given the right to request advisory opinions through the simple intermediation of another organ (as the United Kingdom had proposed):

13. After careful consideration, it is our conclusion that it is not possible under the Charter to provide that an organ shall act solely as an intermediary in transmitting to the Court legal questions which the Human Rights Committee would request. The reasons for this conclusion can be stated briefly. If an organ were to act merely as a transmitting agent, it is evident that the Human Rights Committee would, in fact, be empowered to make the requests for advisory opinions. The organ would then be only performing a purely administrative or 'ministerial' function, similar to that which the Secretary-General now performs in transmitting to the Court questions put by the General Assembly. It would, therefore, mean that a body which could not be authorized to request advisory opinions under the Charter was in fact being given that authority. This, in our view, would be contrary to Article 96.

14. We should also like to make it clear that this conclusion is not merely based on a technicality. The right to present requests for advisory opinions has been conferred by the Charter, or, in accordance with the Charter, by the General Assembly, only to [*sic*] certain organs which are expected to weigh the proposal in the light of the general interests of the United Nations as well as in regard to the particular question. During the drafting of the Charter at San Francisco, the policy

[116] *Application for Review of Judgement No. 158 of the United Nations Administrative Tribunal, ICJ Reports,* 1973, pp. 166, 172–5.

[117] Ibid., pp. 172–3.

was laid down that the right to make requests for advisory opinions should be restricted to public international organizations which are part of the United Nations or brought into relationship with it. The language of Article 96(2) was carefully drawn up to express this policy. It would be defeating the object of the provision if the authorized organs were to act merely as conduits for transmitting requests of a body which could not be authorized directly.

15. However, there seems to be no reason why an organ properly authorized to request advisory opinions may not be instructed to take into account suggestions or recommendations of another organization. As a precedent one might note that in the Covenant of the League it was considered proper for the Council to give consideration to suggestions of the ILO in regard to requests for advisory opinions concerning that organization, although it was not considered proper that the Council automatically transmit the requests of the ILO. Consequently, it would be permissible to provide in the Covenant that the proposed Human Rights Committee may recommend or suggest to a competent organ of the United Nations that that organ request the Court to give an advisory opinion on a legal question arising out of the Committee's activities. It would be clearly understood that the responsibility would remain with the authorized organ, and, therefore, that the organ would have discretion with respect to presenting the legal question and with respect to framing the language of the question. In short, the Human Rights Committee would be in a position to make suggestions but the final responsibility would be placed in a competent organ of the United Nations.[118]

In the light of the tenor of the pertinent exchanges in the Washington Committee of Jurists and at San Francisco which have been described above, the Secretary-General's conclusion is certainly a possible and even plausible one, but it goes farther than required. The drafters of the Charter and Statute were on notice of the practice of the League Council in serving as a conduit for requests of other international organizations for advisory opinions. They certainly indicated no intention and drafted no text designed to debar that practice from being pursued in the United Nations. What they did do was to provide, after some debate on the question, that only organs of the United Nations and the Specialized Agencies—i.e., international organizations as defined in Article 57 of the Charter which are brought into relationship with the United Nations—could be authorized at any time to request advisory opinions of the Court on legal questions arising within the scope of their activities. But Article 96 of the Charter does not in terms or intent preclude other international organizations from requesting that particular questions be transmitted on their behalf by the General Assembly or the Security Council to the Court. The Secretary-General indeed accepts that conclusion, provided that the role of the transmitting organ is not that of a mere conduit—i.e., provided that it is prepared to exert a measure of supervision and control over questions put.

[118] UN Doc. E/1732 of 26 June 1950, pp. 4–6 (footnotes omitted). C. Wilfred Jenks commented: '. . . the view that an organ established under an international agreement concluded under the auspices of the United Nations is not an organ of the United Nations for this purpose appears to be a somewhat narrow view which might well be reconsidered': *The Prospects of International Adjudication* (1964), p. 197.

Such a measure of supervision and control may be seen as inherent in the fact that the question cannot be directly put by the international organization immediately concerned but can be forwarded only through the medium of the General Assembly or Security Council. But in practice the General Assembly or Security Council may lawfully forgo such supervision and control, as, in practice, the League Council frequently did. Such abstinence itself would not, it is believed, invalidate the procedure. The General Assembly and Security Council may each act as conduit; either could constitute a subsidiary organ to act on its behalf; but neither could surrender ultimate responsibility for questions transmitted to the Court on behalf of other organizations or of States. The originating organization or State would not be confined, as the Secretary-General argues, to making suggestions; as in the League, the precise questions could come from the source of origin and the transmitting organ in practice could confine itself to transmitting them to the Court, provided that it retains, as it must, an ultimate authority to transmit or not to transmit, and to revise or not to revise. Of course, the fact that (as in the practice of League organs) the General Assembly and Security Council do retain a residual competence to request or not to request the advisory opinion sought, or even to amend the terms of the question to be put, may inhibit international organizations and States from having recourse to the process.

Authorizing the Specialized Agencies

The International Labour Organization, the Food and Agriculture Organization, the United Nations Educational, Scientific and Cultural Organization, the World Health Organization, the International Bank for Reconstruction and Development, the World Bank's International Finance Corporation and International Development Association, the International Monetary Fund, the International Civil Aviation Organization, the International Telecommunication Union, the World Meteorological Organization, the International Maritime Organization, the World Intellectual Property Organization, the International Fund for Agricultural Development, the United Nations Industrial Development Organization and the International Atomic Energy Agency[119] have all been authorized by the

[119] The authorizing instruments are listed in *ICJ Yearbook*, 1989–90, pp. 56–61. The IAEA is not regarded, strictly speaking, as a Specialized Agency, and the relationship agreement between it and the United Nations, unlike others, does not expressly describe it as a Specialized Agency, apparently because that agreement was not entered into by the Economic and Social Council pursuant to Article 63 of the Charter. When the General Assembly approved the authorization of the IAEA to request advisory opinions, the British representative expressed some doubt on the point. See Keith, op. cit. above (n. 4), pp. 40–1.

There are a number of other agreements which bear on the Court's advisory jurisdiction, also listed in the *Yearbooks* of the Court. For example, the Convention on the Privileges and Immunities of the United Nations provides, in Section 30:

'All differences arising out of the interpretation or application of the present convention shall be referred to the International Court of Justice unless in any case it is agreed by the parties to have

General Assembly to request advisory opinions of the Court on legal questions arising within the scope of their activities. These authorizations are largely contained in agreements between the United Nations and the various Agencies which have been approved by the General Assembly. These agreements exclude the authority to request advisory opinions on relationships of the organization in question with the United Nations or other Specialized Agencies.

There was 'some substantial initial hesitation' on the part of the United Nations about granting to the Specialized Agencies general authorization to request advisory opinions, stemming from the otherwise perspicacious Report of the Preparatory Commission of the United Nations.[120] It manifested itself in a claimed reservation by the General Assembly of a right to revoke the authorizations granted, a claim which Dr Jenks sharply criticized as legally questionable and practically unnecessary.[121] But Jenks concluded that:

> The liberal policy in regard to authorisations which has been adopted by the General Assembly should progressively and ultimately enable the Court to play a major role in the development of international institutions; a more restrictive policy would inevitably have led to the creation of a multiplicity of special tribunals and would have tended to limit severely the opportunities open to the Court to exercise a unifying influence on the development of international law, and in particular on the law relating to international institutions . . . [122]

By 1991, three Specialized Agencies had sought advisory opinions of the Court: UNESCO;[123] IMCO (IMO);[124] and WHO.[125] This paucity of requests demonstrates that frequency of recourse to the Court's advisory jurisdiction is not simply a function of the extension of the capacity to request opinions.[126]

No other international organization, such as the Organization of Ameri-

recourse to another mode of settlement. If a difference arises between the United Nations on the one hand and a Member on the other hand, a request shall be made for an advisory opinion on any legal question involved in accordance with Article 96 of the Charter and Article 65 of the Statute of the Court. The opinion given by the Court shall be accepted as decisive by the parties' (*United Nations Treaty Series*, vol. 1, p. 30).

[120] Jenks, op. cit. above (n. 118), p. 197.

[121] Ibid., pp. 197–206. See United Nations, *Repertory of Practice of United Nations Organs*, vol. 5, pp. 88–9.

[122] Jenks, op. cit. above (n. 118), p. 203.

[123] UNESCO's Executive Board requested the advisory opinion, acting within the framework of Article XII of the Statute of the Administrative Tribunal of the ILO: *Judgments of the Administrative Tribunal of the ILO upon complaints made against the UNESCO, ICJ Reports*, 1956, p. 77.

[124] *Constitution of the Maritime Safety Committee of the Inter-Governmental Maritime Consultative Organization, ICJ Reports*, 1960, p. 150.

[125] *Interpretation of the Agreement of 25 March 1951 between the WHO and Egypt, ICJ Reports*, 1980, p. 73.

[126] For speculations on why so few requests have been made, see Jenks, op. cit. above (n. 118), pp. 204–8, and H.C.L. Merillat, *Legal Advisers and International Organizations* (1966), pp. 10–12. As pointed out in the exchanges among legal advisers of international organizations reported by Merillat, there may be very good practical reasons for not requesting the Court's advisory opinion in a given case.

can States or INTELSAT, or any other of the many intergovernmental institutions in existence, has requested the General Assembly or Security Council to request an advisory opinion of the Court on its behalf. But, in view of the precedent of the League and the Permanent Court and the considerations set out in this essay, no persuasive legal reason is seen which debars that procedure. As for States requesting the General Assembly or Security Council to request opinions on their behalf, that remains an equal option. In the case concerning the *Northern Cameroons*, the Court observed that 'The Court may, of course, give advisory opinions—not at the request of a State but at the request of a duly authorized organ or agency of the United Nations'.[127] But that statement does not bear upon the ability of a State to seek an advisory opinion through the agency of the General Assembly[128] or the Security Council.

Diverse Views of States

In view of the shrunken docket of the Court in the 1960s, the General Assembly on 15 December 1970 invited States to submit their views and suggestions concerning the role of the Court to the Secretary-General who was requested to prepare a comprehensive report. That report remains an important compendium of conflicting perspectives on reviving recourse to the Court (a revival which has come about, apparently not for the most part in response to initiatives then generated—with the exception of the revision of the Rules of Court concerning chambers, which has succeeded in promoting the establishment of four *ad hoc* chambers). On the question of increasing resort to the Court's advisory jurisdiction, the United States proposed:

> Access to the advisory jurisdiction of the Court should be expanded concomitantly with access in contentious cases. Although at the present time the United Nations and its specialized agencies have the capacity to seek advisory opinions, there is a growing number of other international organizations, including regional organizations, whose activities are increasingly important to international law and yet who cannot obtain an advisory opinion from the International Court of Justice. Although the more important question is perhaps how to convince international organizations to request advisory opinions once they have that option, the essential first step is still to make that exercise possible.
>
> Accordingly, the United States favours making the advisory procedures available to more intergovernmental organizations, including regional organizations. A procedure not requiring amendment of the Statute could at the present time be

[127] Case concerning the *Northern Cameroons, Preliminary Objections, ICJ Reports*, 1963, pp. 15, 30.

[128] On the proposal that national supreme courts should be enabled to request advisory opinions of the Court on questions of international law through the agency of a committee to be established by the General Assembly, see Stephen M. Schwebel, 'Preliminary Rulings by the International Court of Justice at the Instance of National Courts', *Virginia Journal of International Law*, 28 (1988), p. 495, and the sources there cited, and Shabtai Rosenne, 'Preliminary Rulings by the International Court of Justice at the Instance of National Courts: A Reply', ibid. 29 (1989), p. 41.

> established by the General Assembly through creation of a new special committee similar to the committee used for review of decisions of the Administrative Tribunal of the United Nations. The new special committee could be given authority to request from the Court an advisory opinion on behalf of other international organizations.
>
> In addition, the new committee could be given authority to seek an advisory opinion on behalf of two or more States who voluntarily agree to submit to the advisory jurisdiction of the Court with respect to a dispute between them. This would in effect permit States which would be reluctant to submit a dispute to the binding decision of a contentious case to obtain from the Court an authoritative statement of the relative [*sic*] principles of international law.[129]

Cyprus[130] and Canada[131] expressed interest in a like approach, while a number of other States declared that they favoured international organizations in addition to Specialized Agencies, as well as States, being accorded access to the Court (some suggested amendment of the Statute to this end). Poland[132] and France[133] opposed authorizing more institutions to request advisory opinions or affording this possibility to States, while Switzerland expressed doubt about the desirability of permitting States to request advisory opinions, particularly in the case of current disputes.[134]

Conclusions

As stated above, no persuasive reason is seen for debarring international organizations which have not been authorized directly to request advisory opinions of the Court from seeking such opinions through the medium of the General Assembly or Security Council (or a standing committee of the General Assembly constituted for that purpose). Is the case for permitting States to request advisory opinions of the Court through the agency of the General Assembly or Security Council less compelling?

It may well be that, in practice, there would not be much demand among States for advisory opinions. As more than one special agreement which has been the basis of jurisdiction in a contentious case illustrates, it is possible for States as it stands to bring a case to the Court in which the Court is requested not to decide the dispute between them but to determine what are the 'principles and rules of international law'[135] which are applicable to its determination. This facility may be seen as approaching the freedom of action with which an advisory opinion leaves the States concerned; the legal principles are set forth by the Court but the disputing States may be left

[129] *Review of the Role of the International Court of Justice, Report of the Secretary-General*, UN Doc. A/8382 of 15 September 1971, pp. 92–3.

[130] Ibid., pp. 90–1.

[131] Ibid., p. 98.

[132] Ibid., p. 90.

[133] Ibid., pp. 99–100.

[134] Ibid., pp. 94–7.

[135] *North Sea Continental Shelf, ICJ Reports*, 1969, p. 6.

with the freedom to apply or not to apply them (or may not be left with that freedom: in the *North Sea Continental Shelf* cases, it was provided that the States concerned '*shall* delimit the continental shelf . . . by agreement *in pursuance of the decision requested from the International Court of Justice*').[136] Be that as it may, the possible advantages of permitting States to request advisory opinions of the Court were set out by the Informal Inter-Allied Committee in terms which remain persuasive (see paragraph 68 of its Report, quoted above).[137] Of course, the States in dispute would have jointly to request the General Assembly or Security Council to seek an opinion on their behalf; an *ex parte* request would permit a State to escape the constraints of the Court's consensual jurisdiction. Might such a facility lead to a decline in the number of contentious cases? That is possible but altogether uncertain. It is just as possible that such a facility, when used, would enable the disputing States subsequently to engage in negotiations which take account of the law of the matter as clarified by the Court's advisory opinion, and, if those negotiations do not succeed in resolving the dispute, to submit the dispute to the Court for a judgment binding upon them.

This article endeavours to interpret the relevant terms of the Charter and Statute as they stand, in the light of the precedent of the League and the Permanent Court, and in the light of the *travaux préparatoires* of the Charter and Statute which, it is significant to recall, make clear their intent to preserve the Statute of the Permanent Court to the maximum possible extent. As the Chairman of the Advisory Committee of Jurists pointed out to the San Francisco Conference, 'the basic text' of the ICJ Statute 'was essentially the same as that of the Statute of the Permanent Court of International Justice'.[138] There is, in view of this history, reason to presume that it was the intent of the drafters of the Charter and ICJ Statute to preserve not only the words of the Permanent Court's Statute, but the living law of its interpretation as that Court had formed it. The advisory jurisdiction of the Permanent Court was largely created through practice, and there is equal reason to presume that it was the intent at San Francisco to preserve that practice together with the text that underlay it, except in so far as that text was changed. A striking part of that practice was the pattern of States and international organizations seeking and receiving advisory opinions of the Court through the agency of the Council of the League.[139]

[136] Ibid., p. 6 (emphasis supplied).

[137] Above, p. 101.

[138] *Documents of the United Nations Conference on International Organization*, vol. 17, p. 99.

[139] It may be noted that the Vienna Convention on the Law of Treaties between States and International Organizations or between International Organizations provides, in Article 65, in respect of the procedure to be followed with respect to invalidity, termination, withdrawal from or suspension of the operation of a treaty, that the parties shall seek a solution through the means indicated in Article 33 of the United Nations Charter, and further provides, in Article 66, with respect to treaties conflicting with a peremptory norm of international law, that:

'(*b*) if a State is a party to the dispute to which one or more international organizations are parties, the State may, through a Member State of the United Nations if necessary, request the General

But the premiss of the present terms of the Charter and Statute is not ineluctable; in this rapidly changing world, in which the verities of the Court's jurisdiction as well as so many other matters large and small are in process of reconsideration, the question of amendment of the Charter and Statute may well arise. In such a context, various possibilities meriting study may be open: not only giving international organizations in addition to the Specialized Agencies the independent authority to request advisory opinions; not only authorizing States to request advisory opinions; but more far-reaching innovations, such as authorizing international organizations to take part in contentious proceedings, and authorizing certain entities other than States and international organizations to have direct recourse to the Court.[140]

Assembly or the Security Council or, where appropriate, the competent organ of an international organization which is a party to the dispute and is authorised in accordance with Article 96 of the Charter of the United Nations, to request an advisory opinion of the International Court of Justice in accordance with article 65 of the Statute of the Court;
(*c*) if the United Nations or an international organization that is authorized in accordance with Article 96 of the Charter of the United Nations is a party to the dispute, it may request an advisory opinion of the International Court of Justice in accordance with article 65 of the Statute of the Court;
(*d*) if an international organization other than those referred to in sub-paragraph (*c*) is a party to the dispute, it may, through a Member State of the United Nations, follow the procedure specified in sub-paragraph (*b*)'.

[140] See Elihu Lauterpacht, *Aspects of the Administration of International Justice* (1991), pp. 60–75, and Jenks, op. cit. above (n. 118), especially pp. 119–224.

NICARAGUA AND THE UNITED STATES: CONFRONTATION OVER THE JURISDICTION OF THE INTERNATIONAL COURT*

By D. W. GREIG‡

I. Introduction

The purpose of this article is to canvass and comment upon issues that were raised with regard to the jurisdiction of the International Court in the case brought by Nicaragua against the United States in respect of military and paramilitary activities on Nicaraguan territory.[1] It is not intended to deal with issues arising out of allegations by the United States that the Court was not competent to adjudicate upon matters relating to international peace and security nor concerning the legal rights of third States which were not parties to the case before the Court.

Details of the circumstances surrounding the litigation are not crucial to the disputes over the Court's jurisdiction so that only a brief summary needs to be provided. Suffice it to say that the fall of the Somoza regime in 1979 was universally welcomed. The Sandinista Government came to power in an atmosphere of goodwill. It proclaimed its support for peace and democratic ideals to the Organization of American States and received in return United States support and aid. This spirit of friendship evaporated when, in the view of the United States and some of Nicaragua's neighbours, the Nicaraguan Government attempted to export the Sandinista revolution to neighbouring countries by supporting rebel movements in those countries. The United States response was to cut off aid to Nicaragua and to promote a counter-revolution against the Sandinista Government through support of the *contras* and by more direct activities aimed against Nicaragua such as the mining of the approaches to Nicaraguan ports.

In April 1984 Nicaragua made application to the Court, requesting it to 'adjudge and declare'[2] *inter alia*

(*a*) That the United States, in recruiting, training, arming, equipping, financing, supplying and otherwise encouraging, supporting, aiding, and directing military and paramilitary actions in and against Nicaragua, has violated and is violating its express charter and treaty obligations to Nicaragua . . .

(*b*) That the United States, in breach of its obligation under general and customary

* © Professor D. W. Greig, 1992.

‡ Professor of Law, The Australian National University, Canberra.

[1] *ICJ Reports*, 1984, p. 392; *ICJ Reports*, 1986, p. 3.

[2] *ICJ Reports*, 1986, at pp. 18–19.

international law, has violated and is violating the sovereignty of Nicaragua by:

- armed attacks against Nicaragua by air, land and sea;
- incursions into Nicaraguan territorial waters;
- aerial trespass into Nicaraguan airspace;
- efforts by direct and indirect means to coerce and intimidate the Government of Nicaragua.

(*c*) That the United States, in breach of its obligation under general and customary international law, has used and is using force and the threat of force against Nicaragua

(*d*) That the United States, in breach of its obligation under general and customary international law, has intervened and is intervening in the internal affairs of Nicaragua.

(*e*) That the United States, in breach of its obligation under general and customary international law, has infringed and is infringing the freedom of the high seas and interrupting peaceful maritime commerce.

II. Background to the Jurisdictional Issues

Nicaragua's application to the Court was based upon the declaration made by that State in 1929 with regard to the jurisdiction of the Permanent Court, although subsequently, in its memorial, Nicaragua contended that the Treaty of Friendship, Commerce and Navigation 1956 between the two States provided 'a complementary foundation for the Court's jurisdiction'.[3] Below the sequence of events around which the dispute over jurisdiction revolved is outlined. However, it should be borne in mind that there is a crucial difference between the relationship of the United Nations to the present International Court and the situation that existed in the case of the League of Nations and the Permanent Court.

Under Article 93(1) of the United Nations Charter, all members of the Organization are *ipso facto* parties to the Statute. A non-member of the United Nations may become a party to the Statute upon conditions to be 'determined in each case by the General Assembly upon the recommendation of the Security Council'.[4] In addition, under Article 35(2) of the Statute, the Court is open to States not parties to the Statute in accordance with conditions to be prescribed by the Security Council.

The Statute of the Permanent Court was not integrated in the same way with the Covenant of the League of Nations, because the Statute was a later instrument. Members of the League (and States mentioned in the Annex to the Covenant) were entitled to become parties to the Protocol of Signature of the Statute of the Permanent Court of International Justice 1920. Such signatures were however expressly made subject to ratification by the terms of the Protocol.[5] Unless the signature of a State was followed by formal

[3] *ICJ Reports*, 1984, at p. 426.
[4] UN Charter, Article 93(2).
[5] *PCIJ*, Series D, No. 1, p. 5.

ratification, therefore, the signature of the Protocol remained ineffective as far as the jurisdiction of the Permanent Court was concerned.

The timetable of events may be summarized thus:[6]

24 September 1929
Nicaragua, a member of the League, signed the Protocol and made a declaration recognizing 'as compulsory unconditionally the jurisdiction of the Permanent Court'.

4 December 1934
Proposal for ratification of both instruments was approved by the Executive Power in Nicaragua.

14 February 1935
The Nicaraguan Senate decided to ratify them.

12 June 1935
The Senate's decision was published in the official *Gaceta*.

11 July 1935
A similar decision was reached by the Chamber of Deputies.

18 September 1935
This decision was also published in *La Gaceta*.

29 November 1939
The following telegram from Nicaraguan Ministry of External Relations was sent to the Secretary-General of the League:

> 'Statute and Protocol Permanent Court International Justice The Hague have already been ratified. Will send you in due course Instrument Ratification.'

But no such instrument was ever received.

6 September 1945
Nicaragua ratified the Charter and became an original member of the United Nations.

24 October 1945
The Statute of the International Court of Justice came into force, to which Nicaragua was a party by virtue of its membership of the United Nations. By Article 36(5) of the Statute:

> Declarations made under Article 36 of the Statute of the Permanent Court of International Justice and which are still in force shall be deemed, as between the parties to the present Statute, to be acceptances of the compulsory jurisdiction of the International Court of Justice for the period which they still have to run and in accordance with their terms.

26 August 1946
The United States deposited a declaration accepting the Court's jurisdic-

[6] *ICJ Reports*, 1984, at pp. 399 ff.

tion which was to 'remain in force for a period of five years and thereafter until the expiration of six months after notice may be given to terminate this declaration'. It was subject to a number of reservations excluding jurisdiction over *inter alia*:

by the Connally (automatic) reservation

(*b*) disputes with regard to matters which are essentially within the domestic jurisdiction of the United States of America as determined by the United States of America;

by the Vandenberg (multilateral treaty) reservation

(*c*) disputes arising under a multilateral treaty, unless (1) all parties to the treaty affected by the decision are also parties to the case before the Court, or (2) the United States of America specially agrees to jurisdiction.

24 May 1958
The Treaty of Friendship, Commerce and Navigation between the United States and Nicaragua came into force. Article XIX provided for freedom of commerce and navigation, and for vessels of either party to have liberty 'to come with their cargoes to all ports, places and waters of such other party open to foreign commerce and navigation'. Moreover, by Article XXIV(2):

Any dispute between the Parties as to the interpretation or application of the present Treaty, not satisfactorily adjusted by diplomacy, shall be submitted to the International Court of Justice, unless the Parties agree to settlement by some other pacific means.

6 April 1984
The United States deposited a notification with the Secretary-General of the United Nations which, with reference to the declaration of August 1946, stated:

the aforesaid declaration shall not apply to disputes with any Central American State or arising out of or related to events in Central America, any of which disputes shall be settled in such manner as the parties to them may agree.

Notwithstanding the terms of the aforesaid declaration, this proviso shall take effect immediately and shall remain in force for two years, so as to foster the continuing original dispute settlement process which seeks a negotiated solution to the interrelated political, economic and security problems of Central America.

9 April 1984
Nicaragua filed its application instituting proceedings against the United States before the International Court.[7]

The first sections of the article will concentrate on the range of issues arising from the two States' declarations accepting the compulsory jurisdiction of the Court. The approach will be to present the rival contentions of

[7] See above, p. 119.

the parties and to give the reaction of the Court. The plausibility of the Court's views will be examined, particularly in the light of the opinions expressed in the individual judgments that were recorded. A similar approach will then be adopted with regard to the Treaty of Friendship as an alternative basis of jurisdiction.

One matter that will be discussed, which was not considered by the Court, is the Connally reservation to the United States declaration. The United States did not attempt to determine that the issues before the Court were matters within the domestic jurisdiction of the United States. Nevertheless, the very reluctance of that State to rely upon the protection of the reservation does raise the question of the present status and effect of such automatic reservations.

III. The Effectiveness of Nicaragua's Declaration under the Optional Clause

(a) *The Scope of Article 36(5) of the Statute*

1. *The views of the parties*

The United States argued that, as Nicaragua had never ratified the Statute of the Permanent Court, its purported unconditional acceptance of that Court's jurisdiction was ineffective and could not be regarded as a declaration 'still in force' for the purposes of Article 36(5) of the Statute of the present Court.[8]

Nicaragua's response was that the expression 'still in force', or the French '*pour une durée qui n'est pas encore expirée*', in that provision was designed only to exclude declarations that had expired and had no relevance for a declaration which had never been perfected. Thus, the position was, as explained by the Court:[9]

> Consistently with the intention of the provision, which in Nicaragua's view was to continue the pre-existing situation as regards declarations of acceptance of compulsory jurisdiction, Nicaragua was in exactly the same situation under the new Statute as it was under the old. In either case, ratification of the Statute of the Court would perfect its Declaration of 1929. Nicaragua contends that the fact that this is the correct interpretation of the Statute is borne out by the way in which the Nicaraguan declaration was handled in the publications of the Court and of the United Nations Secretariat; by the conduct of the Parties to the present case, and of the Government of Honduras, in relation to the dispute in 1957–1960 between Honduras and Nicaragua in connection with the arbitral award made by the King of Spain in 1906, which dispute was eventually determined by the Court; by the opinions of publicists; and by the practice of the United States itself.

[8] *ICJ Reports*, 1984, at p. 400.
[9] At p. 401.

2. *The Court's judgment*

The Court pointed out that declarations under the Statute of the Permanent Court must of necessity have had a qualified existence even for a State which had not ratified the Protocol of Signature of the Statute because such a declaration could be made 'either when signing or ratifying' the Protocol 'or at a later moment' (unlike the position under the present Statute when a declaration under Article 36(2) can only be made by 'States parties to the present Statute').[10] Consequently, as Nicaragua could, at any time during the existence of the Permanent Court, have ratified the Protocol and made fully effective its declaration, 'such a declaration as that made by Nicaragua had a certain potential effect which could be maintained indefinitely. This durability of potential effect flowed from a certain characteristic of Nicaragua's declaration: being made "unconditionally", it was valid for an unlimited period.'[11] As to the bearing of Article 36(5) of the present Statute on the situation, that refrained 'from stipulating that declarations must have been made by States parties to the Statute of the Permanent Court': it was 'sufficient for them to have been made "under" (in French, "en application de") Article 36 of that Statute. . . . The chosen wording therefore does not exclude but, on the contrary, covers a declaration made in the circumstances of Nicaragua's declaration.'[12]

The crucial issue was therefore the interpretation to be placed upon the expression 'still in force' in Article 36(5) of the present Statute. In the view of the Court, the *Aerial Incident* case[13] was not directly relevant, though it did observe that, on that occasion, 'the United States took a particularly broad view of the separability of an Optional Clause declaration and its institutional foundation by concluding that an Optional Clause declaration (of a binding character) could have outlived by many years the court to which it related'.[14] In this case, the United States was advocating a narrower view, that Article 36(5) should be read as applying only to 'binding' declarations and that is what 'in force' really meant.[15] Such an interpretation was not justifiable according to the Court:[16]

According to the *travaux préparatoires* the word 'binding' was never suggested; and if it had been suggested for the English text, there is no doubt that the drafters would never have let the French text stand as finally worded. Furthermore, the Court does not consider the French text to imply that *la durée non expirée* (the unexpired period) is that of a commitment of a binding character. It may be granted that, for a period to continue to expire, it is necessary for some legal effect to have come into existence. But this effect does not necessarily have to be of a binding nature. A declaration validly made under Article 36 of the Statute of the

[10] At p. 403.
[11] At p. 404.
[12] At p. 405.
[13] *ICJ Reports*, 1959, p. 127.
[14] *ICJ Reports*, 1984, at p. 405.
[15] At p. 406.
[16] Ibid.

Permanent Court had a certain validity which could be preserved or destroyed, and it is perfectly possible to read the French text as implying only this validity.

In fact, 'the deliberate choice of the expression "*pour une durée qui n'est pas encore expirée*" seems to denote an intention to widen the scope of Article 36, paragraph 5, so as to cover declarations which have not acquired binding force.'[17]

If this was the Court's preferred view, it nevertheless had to be tested against 'the object and purpose' of Article 36(5) as far as this concept could throw light upon the correct interpretation to be placed upon the provision. In conducting this examination, the Court referred to 'the primary concern of those who drafted the Statute of the present Court' as being 'to maintain the greatest possible continuity between it and its predecessor', quoting the following passage from its judgment in the *Aerial Incident* case:[18]

the clear intention which inspired Article 36, paragraph 5, was to continue in being something which was in existence, to preserve existing acceptances, to avoid that the creation of a new Court should frustrate progress already achieved.

A declaration such as that of Nicaragua did 'constitute a certain progress towards extending to the world in general the system of compulsory judicial settlement of international disputes'. Though progress in this direction had been limited, it was 'by no means negligible'. The Court then suggested that there were 'no grounds for maintaining that those who drafted the Statute meant to go back on this progress' and place the Nicaraguan declaration 'in a category in opposition to the progress achieved by declarations having binding force'. Admittedly, 'their main aim was to safeguard these latter declarations, but the intention to wipe out the progress evidenced by a declaration such as that of Nicaragua would certainly not square well with their general concern'.[19]

This latter proposition is of course questionable. The 'main aim' was almost certainly the sole aim in the sense that it is unlikely that those who drafted Article 36(5) gave any thought to the possibility of non-activated declarations under the earlier Statute. However, there was logic in the argument that the system of devolution from the old Court to the new would suggest that ratification of the new Statute was put on a par with ratification of the old, which in the case of Nicaragua would represent 'the step from potential commitment to effective commitment'.[20] By becoming a party to the Charter and the Statute as an original member of the United Nations, Nicaragua had taken that step.

This finding was borne out by the fact that in a variety of United Nations

[17] At p. 407.
[18] *ICJ Reports*, 1959, at p. 145.
[19] *ICJ Reports*, 1984, at p. 407.
[20] At p. 408.

publications, but most notably in successive volumes of the *Yearbook* of the Court, Nicaragua had been placed on the list of States that had recognized the compulsory jurisdiction of the Court by virtue of Article 36(5) (though admittedly subject to a caveat referring to the non-ratification of the Protocol of Signature of the Statute of the Permanent Court).[21] While not assigning to 'these publications any role that would be contrary to their nature', the Court contented itself 'with noting that they attest a certain interpretation of Article 36, paragraph 5 (whereby that provision would cover the declaration of Nicaragua), and the rejection of an opposite interpretation (which would refuse to classify Nicaragua among the States covered by that Article)'.[22]

More importantly, even though Nicaragua never explicitly recognized that it was bound by the Court's compulsory jurisdiction, neither did it deny it. As the Court went on to say:[23]

> Having regard to the public and unchanging nature of the official statements concerning Nicaragua's commitment under the Optional-Clause system, the silence of its Government can only be interpreted as an acceptance of the classification thus assigned to it. It cannot be supposed that that Government could have believed that its silence could be tantamount to anything other than acquiescence. Besides, the Court would remark that if proceedings had been instituted against Nicaragua at any time in these recent years, and it had sought to deny that, by the operation of Article 36, paragraph 5, it had recognized the compulsory jurisdiction of the Court, the Court would probably have rejected that argument. But the Court's jurisdiction in regard to a particular State does not depend on whether that State is in the position of an Applicant or Respondent in the proceedings. If the Court considers that it would have decided that Nicaragua would have been bound in a case in which it was the Respondent, it must conclude that its jurisdiction is identically established in a case where Nicaragua is the Applicant.

As far as other States were concerned, 'including those which could be supposed to have the closest interest in that State's legal situation in regard to the Court's jurisdiction, they have never challenged the interpretation to which the publications of the United Nations bear witness and whereby the case of Nicaragua is covered by Article 36, paragraph 5'.[24] On the basis of these factors, the Court concluded that 'the interpretation whereby the provisions of Article 36, paragraph 5, cover the case of Nicaragua has been confirmed by the subsequent conduct of the parties to the treaty in question, the Statute of the Court'.[25]

[21] See, for example, the International Court of Justice *Yearbook*, 1946–7, p. 210 n. 1, but no such qualification was specifically referred to in the listing of Nicaragua (on p. 226) as one of the States 'which are still bound by their acceptance of the Optional Clause of the Statute of the Permanent Court of International Justice' (p. 221); and further below, p. 138.

[22] *ICJ Reports*, 1984, at p. 409.

[23] At p. 410.

[24] Ibid.

[25] At p. 411.

(b) *Tacit Consent and Article 36(2)*

1. *The views of the parties*

Nicaragua also contended that, irrespective of the formal validity of its 1929 declaration, Nicaragua's consent to be bound by the Court's compulsory jurisdiction could be based upon the whole sequence of events. This approach related to the possibility that there are no formal restrictions upon how a party's consent can be signified. As the Court explained this argument:[26]

> Nicaragua has in fact also contended that the validity of Nicaragua's recognition of the compulsory jurisdiction of the Court finds an independent basis in the conduct of the parties. The argument is that Nicaragua's conduct over a period of 38 years unequivocally constitutes consent to be bound by the compulsory jurisdiction of the Court by way of a recognition of the application of Article 36, paragraph 5, of the Statute to the Nicaraguan Declaration of 1929. Likewise the conduct of the United States over a period of 38 years unequivocally constitutes its recognition of the essential validity of the Declaration of Nicaragua of 1929 as a result of the application of Article 36, paragraph 5, of the Statute. As a consequence it was recognized by both Parties that any formal defect in Nicaragua's ratification of the Protocol of Signature of the Statute of the Permanent Court did not in any way affect the essential validity of Nicaragua's consent to the compulsory jurisdiction. The essential validity of the Nicaraguan declaration as an acceptance of the compulsory jurisdiction is confirmed by the evidence of a long series of public documents, by the general opinion of States and by the general opinion of qualified publicists.

The United States objected to the possibility that such consent could be informally given as 'flatly inconsistent with the Statute of the Court', Articles 36 and 37 of which limited the way in which consent could be manifested. The United States also referred to:[27]

> what it describes as policy considerations of fundamental importance: that compulsory jurisdiction, being a major obligation, must be based on the clearest manifestation of the State's intent to accept it; that Nicaragua's thesis introduces intolerable uncertainty into the system; and that thesis entails the risk of consenting to compulsory jurisdiction through silence, with all the harmful consequences that would ensue. The United States also disputes the significance of the publications and conduct on which Nicaragua bases this contention.

2. *The Court's judgment*

The Court's reaction, in effect, amounted to an acceptance of Nicaragua's point of view, although it suggested that jurisdiction depended upon Article 36, paragraph 2, rather than on paragraph 5. Article 36(2) reads in part:

> The States parties to the present Statute may at any time declare that they

[26] Ibid.
[27] At pp. 411–2.

recognise as compulsory *ipso facto* and without special agreement, in relation to any other State accepting the same obligation, the jurisdiction of the Court in all legal disputes.

To satisfy the requirement for a State to 'declare' its recognition of the Court's jurisdiction, presumably the 1929 declaration was in some way given new (or extended) life by the post-1946 conduct. The Court's explanation of this (meta)morphosis was, however, not entirely clear. The 'reality of Nicaragua's consent to be bound by its 1929 Declaration is . . . attested by the absence of any protest against the legal situation ascribed to it by publications of the Court, the Secretary-General of the United Nations and major States'.[28] The Court 'considers therefore that, having regard to the origin and generality of the statements to the effect that Nicaragua was bound by its 1929 Declaration, it is right to conclude that the constant acquiescence of the State in those affirmations constitutes a valid mode of manifestation of its intent to recognise the compulsory jurisdiction of the Court under Article 36, paragraph 2 of the Statute, and that accordingly Nicaragua is, vis-à-vis the United States, a State accepting "the same obligation" under that Article.'[29]

(c) *Criticisms of the Court's Approach*

1. *On the operation of Article 36(5)*

The decision that Article 36(5) operated to 'preserve', or rather to 'activate', the Nicaraguan declaration of 1929 was reached by a vote of eleven to five, though of the eleven, Judge Nagendra Singh stated in a separate opinion that the basis of jurisdiction under the Treaty of Friendship, Commerce and Navigation of 1956 'provides a clearer and a firmer ground than the jurisdiction based on the . . . Optional Clause . . . since the acceptance of the Court's jurisdiction by both . . . Nicaragua and . . . the United States presents several legal difficulties to be resolved and in respect of which there is room for differing views.'[30]

The majority's views expressed in the Court's judgment were subjected to a range of criticisms by the five judges who dissented on the issue of the effectiveness of the 1929 declaration. It does not follow, however, that, because of the weaknesses thus indicated in the judgment, the Court's decision was necessarily wrong. The dissenters' opinions are themselves open to objection in a number of respects.

It will be helpful to identify the criticisms under separate headings as follows:

(i) the *travaux* and the differences between the English and French texts (the preparatory work);

[28] At p. 412.
[29] At p. 413.
[30] At p. 444.

(ii) the significance of the expression 'still in force' and its relation to the existence of a binding obligation;
(iii) the relevance of the *Aerial Incident* case;
(iv) the general issue of the United Nations publications; and
(v) matters of treaty interpretation.

(i) *The preparatory work*. The background to the drafting of Article 36(5) was of relevance in two main respects:
(A) to explain how a difference came about between the English and French texts and what significance should be attached to it;
(B) as a guide to the intentions of the drafters of the provision.

As far as (A) was concerned, it was pointed out that both texts were equally authoritative.[31] In addition, whereas the Chinese, Russian and Spanish versions were straight translations of the English, the French was a deliberate paraphrase.[32] According to Article 33(4) of the Vienna Convention on the Law of Treaties:

> Except where a particular text prevails in accordance with paragraph 1, when a comparison of the authentic texts discloses a difference of meaning which the application of articles 31 and 32 does not remove, the meaning which best reconciles the texts, having regard to the object and purpose of the treaty, shall be adopted.

Although Judge Mosler took the position that there was no conflict and therefore no reason to have recourse to the *travaux*,[33] other members of the Court did examine the preparatory work to show that the French variation was designed, at French insistence, to make quite sure that Article 36(5) could not apply to declarations, like the French, that had lapsed by virtue of a time limitation to which they were expressly subject.[34]

As to (B), the many references to the *travaux* by individual judges were designed to establish that the intentions of those who drafted Article 36(5) were directed solely to preserving instruments creating existing *obligations* to submit to the compulsory jurisdiction of the Permanent Court for the benefit of the present Court, and not to imperfect declarations like that of Nicaragua.

The question had been raised by the United Kingdom in a document of 10 April 1945 as to whether 'existing acceptances of the "optional clause", by which a number of countries have . . . bound themselves to accept the jurisdiction of the Court as obligatory' should 'be regarded as having automatically come to an end or should some provision be made for continuing them in force'.[35] Later, on 28 May 1945, in Committee IV/1 of the San Francisco Conference, the United Kingdom representative stated that, if

[31] By Judge Ago at p. 522.
[32] See Judge Jennings at p. 537.
[33] At p. 463.
[34] Judge Oda at p. 480; Judge Ago at p. 522; Judge Jennings at pp. 537–9; Judge Schwebel at pp. 574–5.
[35] *Documents of the United Nations Conference on International Organization*, vol. 14, p. 318; quoted by Judge Oda, *ICJ Reports*, 1984, at p. 478.

'the Committee decides to retain the optional clause, it could provide for the continuing validity of existing adherence to it. Since forty members of the United Nations are bound by it, compulsory jurisdiction would to this extent be a reality.'[36]

The outcome of this examination may well have been to confirm the view, expressed by a subcommittee of the Committee of Jurists involved in drafting the Charter and Statute, that 'many nations have heretofore accepted compulsory jurisdiction under the "Optional Clause". The subcommittee believes that provision should be made at the San Francisco Conference for a special agreement for continuing these acceptances in force.'[37] Moreover, one can also accept, in the context of this issue, and in contrast to the deduction made by the majority of the Court from the *travaux*, that the alteration to the French text was not made with 'cherished feelings' for Nicaragua (to use Judge Ago's words)[38] in order to extend the Court's jurisdiction.

These various statements undoubtedly point to a specific intent to transfer existing jurisdictional links. However, this does not eliminate the more general intention of the drafters to achieve as wide a range as possible of compulsory jurisdiction for the new Court, a sentiment clearly present in the second of the pronouncements by the United Kingdom representative quoted above. While a specific intent was undoubtedly absent with regard to the position of Nicaragua, there is no reason why Article 36(5) should not inadvertently have had the effect inferred from that provision by the majority of the Court.

The arguments of the dissenters on this issue were by no means persuasive. As far as the *travaux* were concerned, a number of the observations made in the course of the San Francisco Conference were ambivalent. The Canadian representative, for example, referred to the fact that, as a result of the draft provision being considered by Committee IV/1, as soon as States became parties to the Charter and the Statute, 'the great majority of them would be automatically under the compulsory jurisdiction of the Court because of existing declarations'.[39] It was a tenable argument that the Nicaraguan declaration was 'existing' (and was treated as such by the Registry of the International Court), though its legal significance may have been open to doubt.

(ii) *Was the 1929 declaration 'still in force' for the purposes of Article 36(5)?* The judgment of the Court took the view, based in part upon its preference for a broader meaning for the French version of Article 36(5) of the new Statute, that 'still in force' related solely to the 'internal' duration of a

[36] *Documents of the United Nations Conference on International Organization*, vol. 13, p. 227; also quoted by Judge Oda, *ICJ Reports*, 1984, at p. 478.

[37] *Documents of the United Nations Conference on International Organization*, vol. 14, p. 289; quoted by Judge Jennings, *ICJ Reports*, 1984, at p. 536.

[38] At p. 522.

[39] *Documents of the United Nations Conference on International Organization*, vol. 13, p. 248; quoted by Judge Oda, *ICJ Reports*, 1984, at p. 479.

particular declaration of acceptance of the compulsory jurisdiction of the Permanent Court. The dissenters, on the other hand, argued that 'still in force' could apply only to a declaration that was in force, in the sense of binding upon the declarant State. Ratification of the Protocol of Signature of the Permanent Court was a condition precedent to the binding effect of a declaration, so that the Nicaraguan declaration was never in force to be capable of being 'still in force'.[40] On the basis of this analysis, it was not possible to qualify, as the Court had done, the declaration 'as certainly valid, but not binding' because, in Judge Mosler's opinion, this was 'a misconstruction of a legal act which was subject to a suspensive condition'.[41]

Despite the assurance with which this statement was made, it should be pointed out that it is not impossible for an agreement or other legal act to be subject to 'a suspensive condition' and yet have temporary validity and effect. In Anglo-Australian law, it is more likely today that a condition precedent will be interpreted as preventing only the operation of the principal obligation of a contract (thus enabling a court to impose a number of ancillary duties on the parties),[42] rather than preventing the operation of the contract as a whole.[43] Even under international law, a signature to an instrument, though subject to ratification, at least creates the limited obligation 'to refrain from acts which would defeat the object and purpose of a treaty', until the State concerned 'shall have made its intention clear not to become a party to the treaty'.[44]

However, as Judge Ago admitted, the real issue was not the binding nature of the 1929 declaration, which had not been contended for by the applicant, but whether Nicaragua became subject to the jurisdiction of the present Court.[45] For the dissenters on this matter, this came down to a question of whether, in order to be 'in force', the 1929 declaration had to be binding.[46]

In concluding that this binding quality had to be present, they canvassed a number of issues, but one in particular is worthy of more detailed comment. Judge Ago attempted to use as an example a comparison between the Nicaraguan position and a similar declaration (i.e. one made by a State which had not yet ratified its signature of the Protocol), though one that was subject to a time limit. He said:[47]

> let us consider the hypothesis of a declaration made by a State accepting the obligation to subject its international disputes to the jurisdiction of the Court for a

[40] See Judge Mosler at p. 462; Judge Ago at p. 519.

[41] At p. 462.

[42] For the position under Anglo-Australian law, see *Perri* v. *Coolangatta Investments Pty. Ltd.* (1982), 149 CLR 537; and Greig and Davis, *The Law of Contract* (1987), pp. 588 ff.

[43] As in the old case of *Pym* v. *Campbell* (1856), 6 E & B 370.

[44] Vienna Convention on the Law of Treaties 1969, Article 18(*a*).

[45] *ICJ Reports*, 1984, at p. 521.

[46] Judge Mosler at p. 462; Judge Oda at p. 482; Judge Ago at pp. 518–19, 524–5; Judge Jennings at pp. 536, 538.

[47] At p. 524.

given period, and the question which would then arise of determining both the *dies a quo* and the *dies ad quem* of the obligation thus entered into. I imagine it would be out of the question for the period of an obligation entered into for, say, ten years to begin to elapse before the existence of the obligation in question had been established by the determinative deposit of the instrument of ratification, and it would be difficult to imagine that it could expire until ten years had passed from that moment. The same would be true—though only for the *dies a quo*, of course—in the case of an obligation entered into for an indefinite period. Finally, in a situation like the one under present examination, where the discussion hinges on a declaration made for an indefinite period, but regarding which there has been no act of ratification capable of generating binding legal effects, I find the only admissible conclusion to be that the obligation contemplated by the declaration never began to 'elapse' for the simple reason that it never began to 'exist'.

This hypothesis is open to question. The effect to be given to the declaration depends upon the intention (stated or apparent) of the declarant. In most cases, the declaration will make clear that intention. Thus, in the case of Argentina which, in 1935, had similarly signed but not ratified the Protocol, its actual declaration was expressly made subject to ratification, and was to run for ten years from the date of deposit of the instrument of ratification.[48] It would also be clear, though implicit, in the case of a declaration, subject to ratification, which was to run for a specified period, but only with respect to facts or situations arising after such ratification, that the period specified would only begin to run from the date of ratification (as with the declaration of Belgium, signed on 25 September 1925 and ratified 10 March 1926, which was to run for 15 years;[49] and that of France, signed on 19 September 1929 and ratified on 23 April 1931, which was to run for 5 years).[50]

It would be equally clear, however, that a declaration to run for a specified period from the date thereof, or of signature, would have expired at the end of the period calculated from that date, even if it was made by a State which had signed but not ratified the Protocol at the time of the declaration, and which did so ratify some time into the five year period. Similarly, where the intention of the declarant was implicit as to the time the period was to run from, a subsequent ratification of the Protocol could not extend the specified period. For example, the declaration of Turkey was to run for a period of 5 years with respect to differences which arose subsequent to the signing 'of the present declaration'.[51] At the same time, Turkey had signed the Protocol, but it never ratified that instrument.[52] If Turkey had done so, the better interpretation of the effect of the time limitation would surely have been to bring the declaration to an end five years from the date of signing it, not five years from the date of ratification of the Protocol. It is per-

48 *PCIJ*, Series D, No. 6, 5th Addendum (1936), p. 7.
49 *PCIJ*, Series D, No. 6, p. 39.
50 Ibid., p. 45.
51 *PCIJ*, Series D, No. 6, 5th Addendum (1936), p. 8.
52 See Judge Oda, *ICJ Reports*, 1984, at p. 476.

haps conceivable that, if the ratification had taken place virtually at the end of that period (*a fortiori* after the expiry of the period), the Court, to avoid absurdity, would have interpreted the period as running from the date of ratification, notwithstanding the wording of the original declaration.

What is apparent from a consideration of these various types of declaration, and the circumstances in which ratification might have taken place, is that Judge Ago was oversimplifying the relevant issues. Even if one accepts his conclusion that 'the obligation contemplated by the declaration never began to "elapse" for the simple reason that it never began to "exist" ', there could well be circumstances in which the subsequent conduct of the declarant State indicates its intention towards an earlier declaration that differs from the inference normally arising from the instrument in question. In particular, that conduct could satisfy the Court (as in this case) that the declaration was regarded as having a provisional and limited existence.

(iii) *The* Aerial Incident *case*. The only other occasion on which the Court has had to consider the interpretation and application of Article 36(5) was in the context of the *Aerial Incident* case,[53] in which Israel sought damages from Bulgaria for the shooting down of an Israeli airliner and for the consequent loss of life. Bulgaria contested the Court's jurisdiction *inter alia* on the ground that the Bulgarian declaration of 1921 by which it had accepted the jurisdiction of the Permanent Court had ceased to be 'in force' on the dissolution of that Court in April 1946. The declaration of 1921 could not therefore be said to be in force within the meaning of Article 36(5) of the Statute when Bulgaria became a party to that instrument by reason of its admission to membership in the United Nations in 1955.

The Court upheld the Bulgarian objection on three principal grounds. First of all, it was clear from the evidence that Article 36(5) was designed to prevent the impending lapse of numerous acceptances of jurisdiction as a result of the demise of the Permanent Court. The provision could, therefore, only provide a link for parties to the new Statute. In the second place, as Article 36(5) could only apply to declarations still in force, there was no suggestion that it could maintain the existence of earlier declarations until a State had become a party to the new Statute. As to the third possibility, that Bulgaria's admission to membership had the effect of 'reactivating' its declaration of acceptance, this would mean that such admission would be subject to different legal consequences from the admission of other States, a circumstance which the Court seemed to regard as unacceptable.

On the face of it, therefore, the *Aerial Incident* case could well have been relevant. In the *Nicaragua* case, it had to be decided whether, for the purpose of Article 36(5), the Nicaraguan declaration was in force. Moreover, if the fact of becoming a party to the Statute of the present Court had the

[53] *ICJ Reports*, 1959, p. 127.

consequence of 'perfecting' that declaration, the fact of membership of the United Nations did have a unique effect as far as Nicaragua was concerned.

Despite these similarities, the *Aerial Incident* case was given no more than a passing reference in the Court's judgment in the *Nicaragua* case.[54] One reason for this reticence may have been the fact that much of what the Court said in the former case with regard to Article 36(5) was undermined by its approach to the parallel situation arising under Article 37 of the Statute in the *Barcelona Traction* case.[55] According to Article 37:

> Whenever a treaty or convention in force provides for reference of a matter to a tribunal to have been instituted by the League of Nations, or to the Permanent Court of International Justice, the matter shall, as between the parties to the present Statute, be referred to the International Court of Justice.

In the *Barcelona Traction* case, it was argued, relying upon the earlier decision, that the demise of the Permanent Court before a State, bound by a treaty of the type referred to in Article 37, had become a party to the new Statute prevented Article 37 operating on such a treaty. This argument the International Court rejected. It explained the position as follows:[56]

> Looking simply at its actual language . . . [o]nly three conditions are actually stated in the Article. They are that there should be a treaty or convention in force; that it should provide (i.e., make provision) for the reference of a 'matter' (i.e., the matter in litigation) to the Permanent Court; and that the dispute should be between States both or all of which are parties to the Statute. No condition that the Permanent Court should still be in existence at any given moment is expressed in the Article.

These criteria the Hispano-Belgian Treaty of Conciliation, Judicial Settlement and Arbitration of 1927 clearly satisfied. Nor was there any reason to displace this interpretation of Article 37 by reference to the object and purpose of that provision which 'was intended to preserve a conventional jurisdictional field from a particular threat, namely the extinction which would otherwise follow from the dissolution of the Permanent Court'.[57] The Court went on to say:[58]

> [Article 37] was not intended to create any new obligatory jurisdiction that had not existed before that dissolution. Nor, in preserving the existing conventional jurisdiction, was it intended to prevent the operation of causes of extinction other than the disappearance of the Permanent Court. In this sense but, however, in this sense only, is it correct to say that regard must be had not only to whether the treaty or convention is still in force, but also to whether the jurisdictional clause it contains is itself, equally, still in force. And precisely because it was the sole object of Article 37 to prevent extinction resulting from the particular cause which the disappearance of the Permanent Court would represent, it cannot be admitted that

[54] For which, see below, n. 63.
[55] *ICJ Reports*, 1964, p. 6.
[56] At p. 32.
[57] At p. 34.
[58] Ibid.

this extinction should in fact proceed to follow from this very event itself. Such a possibility would not only involve a contradiction in terms, but would run counter to the whole intention and purpose of the Article.

This was quite different from the position under Article 36(5):[59]

The Court . . . considers that there are differences between the two cases which require that the present one should be dealt with independently and on its merits. Not only is a different category of instrument involved—an instrument having a conventional form, not that of a unilateral declaration—but the essential requirement of being 'in force', which in the cases contemplated by Article 36, paragraph 5, bore directly on the jurisdictional clause—the unilateral declaration itself—is, in Article 37, formally related not to the clause as such, but to the instrument—the treaty or convention—containing it.

Despite this possibility of avoiding the conclusion that the two decisions are in conflict,[60] there is one principal respect in which they cannot be reconciled. The third basis for the decision in the *Aerial Incident* case[61] was the rejection of the idea that admission to the United Nations could have different consequences for different applicants. With regard to Article 37, the later Court in *Barcelona Traction* saw no difficulty in accepting this possibility:[62]

In this connection, and as regards the whole question of consent, the Court considers the case of the reactivation of a jurisdictional clause by virtue of Article 37 to be no more than a particular case of the familiar principle of consent given generally and in advance, in respect of a certain class of jurisdictional clause. . . . In consequence, States joining the United Nations or otherwise becoming parties to the Statute, at whatever date, knew in advance (or must be taken to have known) that, by reason of Article 37, one of the results of doing so would, as between themselves and other parties to the Statute, be the reactivation in relation to the present Court, of any jurisdictional clauses referring to the Permanent Court, in treaties still in force, by which they are bound.

As has already been mentioned, in the *Nicaragua* case, the Court dismissed the *Aerial Incident* decision with the observation that, 'whatever

[59] At p. 29.

[60] The authority of the *Aerial Incident* case is further weakened by the fact that the decision in *Barcelona Traction* amounted, in other respects, to an endorsement of a strong joint dissenting opinion by Judges Lauterpacht, Spender and Wellington Koo in the earlier case. The three judges had seen no difficulty in limiting the effects of the words 'in force' in relation to Article 36(5). They said (*ICJ Reports*, 1959, at pp. 164–5):

'we reach the conclusion that, having regard both to the ordinary meaning of their language and their context, the words 'which are still in force' refer to the declarations themselves, namely, to a period of time, limited or unlimited, which has not expired, regardless of any prospective or actual date of the dissolution of the Permanent Court. So long as the period of time of declarations made under Article 36 of the Statute of the Permanent Court still has to run at the time when the declarant State concerned becomes a party to the Statute of the International Court of Justice, those declarations fall within the purview of Article 36, paragraph 5, of the new Statute and "shall be deemed to be acceptances of the compulsory jurisdiction of the International Court for the period which they still have to run and in accordance with their terms".'

[61] See above, p. 133.

[62] *ICJ Reports*, 1964, at p. 36.

may be its relevance in other respects', it did not provide 'any pointers to precise conclusions on the limited point now in issue'.[63] Nevertheless there was a degree of equivocality in the Court's approach, for, in one respect, it did draw a parallel between the two cases. In the Court's view, both of them involved problems of 'separability, since the question to be decided is the extent to which an Optional-Clause declaration (without binding force) can be separated from the institutional foundation which it ought originally to have possessed, so as to be grafted onto a new institutional foundation'.[64] From such an analogy, one might have expected some conclusion to have been drawn. However, despite giving this phenomenon the pretentious title of 'separability', the Court made no use of it in its judgment and the *Aerial Incident* case was discarded as a point of reference.

On the other hand, members of the Court, who dissented from the conclusion that Nicaragua could rely upon its declaration under the Optional Clause as preserved by Article 36(5) of the Statute, did invoke the *Aerial Incident* case in support of their position. They were able to point to a number of passages from the judgment in that case in which references were made to maintaining or transferring an original or existing obligation. At one stage in its judgment in the earlier case, the Court had explained that Article 36(5) of the Statute 'governed the transfer from one Court to the other of still-existing declarations; in so doing, it maintained an existing obligation while modifying its subject-matter'.[65] After mentioning the existence of this passage, Judge Ago commented that the majority had thus 'emphasized that the provision in question was designed to transfer to the new Court the "*obligations*" which had previously existed vis-à-vis the Permanent Court, and this seems clearly to *exclude* its having been designed to extend the operation in question to declarations which, although made at a given moment, had never reached the stage of having *binding* force'.[66] The Judge went on[67] to quote the following passage from the *Aerial Incident* case:[68]

> In the case of signatory States, by an agreement between them having full legal effect, Article 36, paragraph 5, governed the transfer from one Court to the other of still-existing declarations; *in so doing, it maintained an existing obligation while modifying its subject-matter*.

In his opinion, 'the identification of "existing declaration" with "declaration

[63] *ICJ Reports*, 1984, at p. 405. The United States had already expressed its preference for the minority opinion: see the 'Observations and Submissions of the Government of the United States of America on the Preliminary Objections of the Government of the People's Republic of Bulgaria', *Aerial Incident* case (1960), *ICJ Pleadings*, p. 301 at pp. 310 ff.

[64] *ICJ Reports*, 1984, at pp. 405–6.

[65] *ICJ Reports*, 1959, at p. 138. This somewhat delphic utterance related to 'the case of signatory States' of the Statute: with regard to non-parties, the Statute 'could neither maintain nor transform their original obligation'. See also below at n. 71.

[66] *ICJ Reports*, 1984, at p. 525.

[67] Ibid.

[68] *ICJ Reports*, 1959, at p. 138 (Judge Ago's emphasis).

having *binding* legal effect" could not be more clear, and, that being so, it is difficult to imagine that the Court could at a given moment have envisaged the possibility of the *transfer* of the binding "legal effect" of a declaration which did not have one.'[69]

Judge Schwebel also relied upon the earlier judgment, pointing to a passage in which it had been said that 'the clear intention which inspired Article 36, paragraph 5, was to continue in being something which was in existence'.[70] He then went on to say:[71]

Thus the Court emphasised preservation, continuity. It excluded reviving an undertaking which has already been extinguished. How then can Article 36, paragraph 5, be interpreted to give life to an undertaking which never came into force at all?

This line of criticism of the majority in the *Nicaragua* case was not well directed, because the thrust of Nicaragua's argument was that it was the joint dissenting opinion, and not the judgment of the Court, in the *Aerial Incident* case which was of principal relevance to that State's declaration. Surprisingly, therefore, it was only Judge Schwebel who devoted much attention to the joint dissenting judgment. He was nevertheless able to select a number of passages which referred to the 'existing compulsory jurisdiction of the Court'.[72] This enabled him to play down the following passage, which did enhance Nicaragua's case:[73]

Moreover, if the interpretation contended for had been adopted by the Court in the present case, its result would be to invalidate, as from the date of the Judgment of the Court, the existing declarations of a number of States—such as Colombia, Haiti, Nicaragua and Uruguay.

His comment was that there was no reason to suppose that, in including this passage, 'the dissenters had investigated whether Nicaragua's 1929 Declaration, listed in the Court's *Yearbook*, actually had come into force'.[74]

Judge Schwebel also considered the attempt by the United States to rely upon the joint dissenting judgment in proceedings it for a while sought to pursue on behalf of its nationals killed in the same incident. In the Judge's view, the American pleadings had been directed to preserving the existing jurisdiction of the Permanent Court and not 'to expand[ing] that jurisdic-

[69] *ICJ Reports*, 1984, at pp. 525–6.

[70] *ICJ Reports*, 1959, at p. 145.

[71] *ICJ Reports*, 1984, at p. 580. See also Judge Jennings at pp. 539–40.

[72] *ICJ Reports*, 1959, at pp. 159, 160, referred to *ICJ Reports*, 1984, at p. 582.

[73] *ICJ Reports*, 1959, at p. 193.

[74] *ICJ Reports*, 1984, at p. 584. It could be said, of course, that, if the dissenters in the earlier case had read the *Yearbooks* as denoting that Nicaragua was subject to the Court's jurisdiction, less significance should be attached to the caveats than the dissenters in the present case tried to suggest (see below, p.139), and that the entry of Nicaragua in the list of States subject to the Court's jurisdiction would prima facie suggest that such was indeed the true situation. For another example of the confusion over Nicaragua's position, see Hudson, *The Permanent Court of International Justice 1920–1942* (1943), p. 696 n. 42.

tion by giving life to a declaration which had never come into force'.[75] Nor was Judge Schwebel prepared to accept that the Court in the *Barcelona Traction* case had in any sense 'overruled' the majority judgment in the *Aerial Incident* case,[76] referring to the observation of Judge Tanaka in *Barcelona Traction* that Article 37 was 'not intended to create any new obligatory jurisdiction that had not existed before', but rather to preserve 'the existing conventional jurisdiction'.[77]

The treatment of the *Aerial Incident* case by the individual judges in the *Nicaragua* case suffers from the same weakness as their discussion of the *travaux*, of reading too much into the words used. As Judge Schwebel said in his observation on the principal passage, quoted above, supporting the Nicaraguan arguments, there was no reason to suppose that any of the judges in the earlier case was choosing words because, or in the light, of Nicaragua's unique position. The same point could equally well be made of the passages referring to preserving existing obligations or jurisdiction. Rather, the crucial question was whether ratification of the Statute, containing Article 36(5), had the effect of reviving the dormant declaration of Bulgaria in the *Aerial Incident* case, or of breathing life into the declaration of Nicaragua in the later case, when the incomplete nature of that declaration stemmed from a failure to ratify the earlier Statute. The majority decision in the earlier case was not conclusively, though it was inferentially, against Nicaragua. The minority opinion in the *Aerial Incident* case, and the majority view in *Barcelona Traction*, were not by any means conclusive in favour of Nicaragua, though they were inferentially, and in varying degrees, so.[78]

(iv) *The* Yearbook *and other listings of Nicaragua as subject to the Court's jurisdiction.* Despite the existence of the caveats entered by the Registry in the various lists containing Nicaragua as subject to the compulsory jurisdiction of the International Court, the judgment in the *Nicaragua* case placed considerable reliance upon those listings. The attitude of the

[75] At p. 585. Judge Schwebel also relied, in this context, upon the substance of the following pasage from the United Kingdom memorial in the *Aerial Incident* case (*ICJ Pleadings*, p. 331):

> 'Bulgaria's acceptance of the compulsory jurisdiction of the Court is unconditional, and was made on July 29, 1921, when the instrument of Bulgaria's ratification of the Protocol of Signature of the Permanent Court of International Justice was deposited, and became effective as to the jurisdiction of the International Court of Justice by virtue of Article 93(1) of the Charter of the United Nations and Article 36(5) of the Statute of the Court on the date of Bulgaria's admission to membership of the United Nations'.

It cannot be denied that the United Kingdom (as had the United States in both its application, ibid., p. 23, and its memorial, ibid., p. 168) had based the Court's jurisdiction upon the Bulgarian acceptance having been made when Bulgaria's ratification of the Protocol was deposited. However, this was merely a recital of what had occurred and can hardly be applied for or against Nicaragua's position in the present case. Indeed, it could be argued that the use of the words 'become effective' in the second part of the above passage was more appropriate to support the Nicaraguan case that the consequence of becoming a party to the Statute could cure the defect in its earlier acceptance of the jurisdiction of the Permanent Court.

[76] *ICJ Reports*, 1984, at p. 586.

[77] *ICJ Reports*, 1964, p. 3 at p. 34.

[78] Though for the United States' view, see below, p. 276.

dissenting judges seemed to verge on one of disbelief at what they regarded as the Court's cavalier attitude. Judge Oda suggested that the approach of the majority was to 'overlook or ignore' the disclaimers;[79] or, as Judge Jennings expressed the position:[80]

For the Court, nevertheless, to attach important legal consequences to entries in the *Yearbook* is to destroy the clear effect of the disclaimer; as well as, in my view, being wrong in principle.

He then continued:[81]

But even apart from the objections of principle, the *Yearbooks* do not at all yield any certain message on the status of the Nicaraguan declaration; on the contrary they consistently—each one of them—alert the attentive reader to the existence of doubts.

Before assessing the significance of this view, it is worth considering the purpose behind the disclaimers and other similar entries in the *Yearbooks*. Nicaragua was listed amongst States subject to the compulsory jurisdiction of the present Court, originally under the heading:[82]

Communications and declarations of States which are still bound by their adherence to the Optional Clause of the Statute of the Permanent Court of International Justice.

Against the text of Nicaragua's declaration was a footnote reference which read as follows:[83]

According to a telegram dated November 29th, 1939, addressed to the League of Nations, Nicaragua had ratified the Protocol of Signature of the Statute of the Permanent Court of International Justice (December 16th, 1920), and the instrument of ratification was to follow. Notification concerning the deposit of the said instrument has not, however, been received in the Registry.

In addition, there was a second list giving the names of States, the dates of signature and ratification of their declaration, and the conditions attached thereto, under the heading:[84]

Lists of States which have recognized the compulsory jurisdiction of the International Court of Justice or which are still bound by their acceptance of the Optional Clause of the Statute of the Permanent Court of International Justice (Article 36 of the Statute of the International Court of Justice).

There Nicaragua's name appeared[85] as having accepted the jurisdiction of the Court 'unconditionally', with a footnote reference: 'For text of the declaration, see p. 210'.

[79] *ICJ Reports*, 1984, at p. 484.
[80] At p. 541.
[81] Ibid.
[82] *Yearbook*, 1946–7, p. 207.
[83] Ibid., p. 210.
[84] Ibid., p. 221.
[85] Ibid., p. 226.

In the years immediately following, the last mentioned list was retained,[86] Nicaragua's entry remaining the same, except that the footnote cross-reference was deleted.[87] However, instead of the Optional Clause list in the form contained in the first *Yearbook*, a list was included that 'gives in respect of each State which has accepted the compulsory jurisdiction of the Court, the reference to the Yearbook of the Court in which the declaration or declarations of acceptance and renewal are to be found'.[88] The reference for Nicaragua was to the 1946–1947 *Yearbook*, page 210. However, against neither entry in the *Yearbooks* after 1946–1947 was there any reference to the circumstances of Nicaragua's declaration, which could only be discovered by referring back to the 1946–1947 *Yearbook*.

This presentation of Nicaragua's position continued until the *Yearbook* for 1955–56. The reference to the entry in the 1946–47 *Yearbook* was retained, but a footnote was inserted stating: 'See footnote 1 on page 195'.[89] The footnote on that page was in effect a revised version of the caveat in the 1946–1947 *Yearbook*. The new formulation was as follows:

According to a telegram dated November 29th, 1939, addressed to the League of Nations, Nicaragua had ratified the Protocol of Signature of the Statute of the Permanent Court of International Justice (December 16th, 1920), and the instrument of ratification was to follow. It does not appear, however, that the instrument of ratification was ever received by the League of Nations.

In the 1956–57 *Yearbook*, however, a new means was adopted for setting out the various declarations under the heading: 'ACCEPTANCE OF THE COMPULSORY JURISDICTION OF THE COURT IN PURSUANCE OF ARTICLE 36 OF THE STATUTE'.[90] Apart from the specific caveat contained in the footnote to the Nicaraguan entry which was retained in the form given above,[91] there was the following general statement:[92]

The texts of declarations set out in this Chapter are reproduced for convenience of reference only. The inclusion of a declaration made by any State should not be regarded as an indication of the view entertained by the Registry or, *a fortiori*, by the Court, regarding the nature, scope or validity of the instrument in question.

It was suggested by Judge Jennings in the *Nicaragua* case[93] that the reason for deciding, after 10 years, to include such a cautionary note was

[86] See, for example, *Yearbook*, 1949–50, p. 167.
[87] Ibid., p. 173.
[88] Ibid., p. 165.
[89] *Yearbook*, 1955–6, p. 183.
[90] *Yearbook*, 1956–7, p. 207.
[91] Ibid., p. 218.
[92] Ibid., p. 207. In the *Yearbook*, 1958–9, p. 205, the wording was amended to read in the second sentence: 'The inclusion or omission of a declaration . . . '. From 1965–6 this qualification was moved to the start of the chapter on 'Texts Governing the Jurisdiction of the Court' and redrafted to read (*Yearbook*, 1965–6, p. 36): 'The inclusion or omission of any instrument . . . '.
[93] *ICJ Reports*, 1984, at p. 543.

the correspondence arising from an enquiry made to the Registrar by Manley Hudson, who was at the time advising Honduras in its dispute with Nicaragua over the boundary between the two States which had been the subject of an arbitral award by the King of Spain in 1906.[94] This view was shared by Judge Schwebel[95] who dealt at some length with that correspondence.[96] It is true that the Registrar expressed his concurrence with Hudson's view, saying in a letter to the latter:[97]

> that it would be difficult to regard Nicaragua's ratification of the Charter of the United Nations as affecting that State's acceptance of the compulsory jurisdiction. If the Declaration of September 24th, 1929, was in fact ineffective by reason of failure to ratify the Protocol of Signature, I think it is impossible to say that Nicaragua's ratification of the Charter could make it effective and therefore bring into play Article 36, paragraph 5, of the Statute of the present Court.

However, that particular communication was dated 2 September 1955, and, if it was to have any effect, it would have done so in the 1955–1956 *Yearbook*, not that for 1956–1957. And, indeed, as has already been pointed out, the footnote specifically dealing with Nicaragua's position was revived in the 1955–1956 volume. Accordingly, it is difficult to accept (as Judge Jennings did) the Schwebel thesis that the addition in the subsequent volume could also have stemmed from the same source. Moreover, the wording of the caveat ('regarding the nature, scope or validity of the instrument in question') scarcely seems appropriate for Nicaragua's situation, nor explicable on the basis of the Hudson correspondence.

The more plausible explanation is to attribute the cautionary note to events in the year ending 15 July 1957 which were covered in the 1956–1957 volume of the *Yearbook*. Viewed from this perspective, the crucial event occurred on 6 July 1957, when the Court declined jurisdiction in the *Norwegian Loans* case.[98] It held that Norway was entitled to rely upon the reservation by France that its (the latter's) declaration did 'not apply to differences relating to matters which are essentially within the national jurisdiction as understood by the Government of the French Republic'. In other words, Norway had been able to determine that the substance of the dispute fell within Norwegian national jurisdiction and this determination was binding on the parties and therefore on the Court. Because the validity of such a reservation had not been questioned by the parties, the Court had

[94] For the *Arbitral Award* case, see *ICJ Reports*, 1960, p. 192.

[95] Though with some caution, his comment being (*ICJ Reports*, 1984, at p. 592):

'It cannot be shown that the inclusion of this new proviso was stimulated by the uncertain status of Nicaragua's declaration, but it is a sensible speculation. Whatever the origins of the provision, which appears in subsequent *Yearbooks*, it serves to place the listing of Nicaragua in the *Yearbook* in its appropriate context.'

[96] At pp. 590–1.

[97] At p. 591.

[98] *ICJ Reports*, 1957, p. 9.

not been required to 'examine whether the French reservation is consistent with the undertaking of a legal obligation and is compatible with Article 36, paragraph 6, of the Statute'.[99]

More significantly, it was in this case that Judge Lauterpacht launched his attack on the validity of what he referred to as 'automatic reservations', suggesting that, because they did not give rise to a legal obligation and were in conflict with Article 36(6), such reservations, or even the declarations of which they formed part, were invalid,[100] In his separate opinion, the Judge tested the French declaration with regard to the *nature* of the obligation thus created in the following passage:[101]

> The effect of the French reservation relating to domestic jurisdiction is that the French Government has, in this respect, undertaken an obligation to the extent to which it, and it alone, considers that it has done so. This means that it has undertaken no obligation. An instrument in which a party is entitled to determine the existence of its obligation is not a valid and enforceable legal instrument of which a court of law can take cognisance. It is not a legal instrument. It is a declaration of a political principle and purpose.

The *scope* of the French declaration was considered from different points of view. In relation to the nature of the obligation created, Judge Lauterpacht asked whether it was possible to qualify the power of determination claimed by such a reservation for a declarant State by reference to 'the legal obligation to act in good faith', thus creating 'to that extent . . . a valid legal obligation and a valid legal instrument'.[102] His conclusion was that no such qualification was possible: the ' "automatic reservation" is couched in terms so comprehensive as to preclude the Court from reviewing it or interpreting it away not only by reference to any assertion of abuse of right but also in any other way'.[103]

The scope of the declaration was also examined in relation to the question of whether, if the automatic reservation was invalid, it, or part of it, could be severed from the declaration as a whole so as to leave the remainder of the instrument as a valid source of obligation.[104] On this issue, too,

[99] At pp. 26–7. For the text of Article 36(6), see n. 106, below.

[100] At pp. 43 ff. See also the *Interhandel* case, *ICJ Reports*, 1959, p. 6 at pp. 96 ff. The position with regard to such reservations is considered at greater length below, p. 181.

[101] *ICJ Reports*, 1957, at p. 48.

[102] At p. 52.

[103] At pp. 54–5.

[104] As the Judge said (at pp. 55–6):

'If the clause of the Acceptance reserving to the declaring Government the right of unilateral determination is invalid, then there are only two alternatives open to the Court: it may either treat as invalid that particular part of the reservation or it may consider the entire Acceptance to be tainted with invalidity. (There is a third possibility—which has only to be mentioned in order to be dismissed—namely, that the clause in question invalidates not the Acceptance as a whole but the particular reservation. This would mean that the entire reservation of matters of national jurisdiction would be treated as invalid while the Declaration of Acceptance as such would be treated as fully in force.)'

Judge Lauterpacht regarded the discretion retained by the reservation as conclusive: the Court 'cannot properly uphold the validity of the Acceptance as a whole and at the same time treat as non-existent any such far-reaching, articulate and deliberate limitation of its jurisdiction'.[105]

As far as the *validity* of such a reservation was concerned, the Judge's view was that, not only did it not give rise to a legal obligation by virtue of the fact that it retained for the declarant the right to determine the existence or scope of any such obligation, but also the reservation was in conflict with the Court's Statute.[106] As a consequence, the reservation, or even the whole declaration, was invalid.[107]

Nor was Judge Lauterpacht alone in raising such issues. Judge Guerrero doubted whether the reservation was consistent with the existence of a legal obligation or compatible with Article 36(6) of the Statute.[108] Judge Read made these comments:[109]

> I am unable to accept the view that the reservation should be interpreted as giving the respondent Government an arbitrary power to settle any question of jurisdiction which arises by the assertion that the Government understands that the matter is essentially within the national jurisdiction regardless of whether that assertion is true or false.
>
> Such a construction of the clause would lead to something unreasonable and absurd. It would, of course, if that interpretation is accepted, be necessary to conclude that the Declaration ran contrary to Article 36, paragraph 6, of the Statute, and was null and void.

The insertion in the 1956–1957 *Yearbook* of the reference to 'the nature, scope or validity of the instrument in question' is only explicable in the light of these statements by members of the Court. Even on a comparative basis, it is much more likely that the *Norwegian Loans* case provided the explanation of the caveat that was inserted in the 1956–57 *Yearbook* than the

[105] At p. 58.

[106] According to the Judge (at p. 45):

'If that type of reservation is valid, then the Court is not in the position to exercise the power conferred upon it—in fact, the duty imposed upon it—under paragraph 6 of Article 36 of its Statute. That paragraph provides that "in the event of a dispute as to whether the Court has jurisdiction, the matter shall be settled by a decison of the Court". The French reservation lays down that if with regard to that particular question, there is a dispute between the Parties as to whether the Court has jurisdiction, the matter shall be settled by a decision of the French Government. The French reservation is thus not only contrary to one of the most fundamental principles of international—and national—jurisprudence according to which it is within the inherent power of a tribunal to interpret the text establishing its jurisdiction. It is also contrary to a clear specific provision of the Statute of the Court as well as to the general Articles 1 and 92 of the Statute and of the Charter, respectively, which require the Court to function in accordance with its Statute.'

[107] As the Judge continued (ibid.):

'Now what is the result of the fact that a reservation or part of it is contrary to the provisions of the Statute of the Court? The result is that reservation or that part of it is invalid.'

See also at pp. 46–7.

[108] At pp. 68–70.

[109] At pp. 94–5.

concerns over Nicaragua's position which had been voiced afresh in the Hudson correspondence more than a year earlier.[110]

Overall, the reliance placed by some members of the Court on the various caveats in the *Yearbooks* is not so destructive of the majority opinion as might appear from a casual examination of circumstances. The introduction of the caveat reference to the 'nature, scope or validity' of any declaration was not designed to deal with Nicaragua's position and could hardly alter the status of its declaration. In addition, if one does apply the test of the 'attentive reader' called in aid by Judge Jennings, the doubts would not necessarily be any more substantial than those arising with regard to other declarations and their contents. Moreover, such a criterion could equally well work in the opposite direction from that indicated by Judge Jennings. It will be recalled that in the joint dissenting opinion in the *Aerial Incident* case there was a reference to Nicaragua as a State on the declaration of which Article 36(5) had operated.[111] Given the significance of that opinion, both for the United States itself when it sought to continue the proceedings it had brought arising out of the same incident, and for the Court in the approach it adopted in the *Barcelona Traction* case, it might equally be asked why the United States, as an equally attentive reader, took no action with regard to the opinion's interpretation of Nicaragua's position.

(v) *Differing approaches to treaty interpretation.*

(A) *Textual or effectiveness*. The dispute over the effect of Article 36(5) could be viewed as one of ideology over the approach to be adopted to treaty interpretation. Article 31(1) of the Vienna Convention on the Law of Treaties tends to obscure such conflicts by providing that a treaty is to be interpreted 'in accordance with the ordinary meaning to be given to the terms of the treaty in their context and in the light of its object and purpose'. In fact it is possible to see in this text support for different philosophies within a spectrum which at its most restrictive encompasses a textual approach ('the ordinary meaning' of 'the terms of the treaty'), and at the other end of the scale could include a more expansive version of the need to give effect to the object and purpose of the instrument (the principle of 'effectiveness').

The dispute over the application of Article 36(5) was subsequently portrayed by the United States as an issue that was decided adversely to that State for purely political reasons. This allegation will be returned to at the end of this paper. It does have to be admitted that, in selecting between the textual and effectiveness approaches to the interpretation of a particular

[110] Certainly Hussain, *Dissenting and Separate Opinions at the World Court* (1984), p. 155, had no hesitation in attributing the new wording in that volume to Judge Lauterpacht's influence.

[111] See above, p. 137.

text, a judge may be influenced as much by the outcome to be achieved by the adoption of one approach in preference to the other as by any intrinsic merit in the approach in question.

It does not follow that the selection between the two (or even some intermediate possibility) is inevitably based upon a preference for the politics of the United States or Nicaraguan position. It is perfectly acceptable to regard the case from the standpoint of the scope of the Court's jurisdiction, where the textual approach would represent a restrictive view, and the effectiveness approach as part of an expansive role for the Court. While in most situations the former would coincide with a sympathetic, and the latter with a less sympathetic, response to the demands of State sovereignty, this alternative would be less relevant in the present case. A reaction from the Court supporting the validity of Nicaragua's declaration could hardly be regarded as adverse to the sovereignty of Nicaragua or of the United States. Nicaragua was arguing in favour of the effectiveness of its declaration, while the United States, until the present case, had never objected to the references made to that declaration as a possible basis of jurisdiction. Restrictions were only placed upon United States sovereignty with regard to other aspects of the Court's decision (most notably, of course, in its refusal to allow the United States an untrammelled right to withdraw or amend its declaration through the Shultz letter).

One further point can be made. Article 31(1) of the Vienna Convention was something of a compromise between the rigidity of the textual approach and the open-ended nature of the effectiveness approach. Instead of allowing an interpreter the freedom to give effect to the object and purpose of a treaty (concepts that are too readily open to subjective judgment), the textual approach was given priority, but ameliorated by reference to the treaty's object and purpose. However, in concentrating upon the meaning of the terms of an instrument in the light of *its* object and purpose as the guide to the parties' intentions, the provision seems to ignore a number of possibilities. For example, a particular provision may have a specific intention behind it which is not relevant to other provisions of the treaty, nor to the treaty as a whole. More particularly, as in this case, a provision may have both a specific object and also a more general purpose. It does not follow from the fact that the specific object was perceived as the obvious (or indeed only) application of the general purpose that effect should not be given to that purpose by applying it to a situation other than the specific one which the parties had in mind. Nor would an interpreter necessarily have to go far beyond the textual approach to justify the application of the provision in such circumstances.

(B) *Control over South West Africa: a need for effectiveness?* To place the issue in context, should the approach be to apply Article 36(5) of the Statute only to the situation it was (apparently) specifically intended to deal with (existing effective jurisdictional links); or to apply it to render operative, in addition, potential links because the intention was, at a less specific level, to maximize the jurisdiction of the International Court? The majority verdict in favour of the latter approach was not very different, as the following survey indicates, from the advisory opinions given by the Court in relation to South West Africa,[112] concerning the obligations of a mandatory under the United Nations Charter.

The objects of those States which were most closely involved in the framing of Chapter XII of the Charter can only be identified at a fairly general level, although individual States may have had specific reasons for supporting general propositions about the interpretation to be placed upon this part of the Charter. For example, it cannot be doubted that Article 80(1) was designed to maintain the status quo with regard *inter alia* to the obligations of a mandatory. That provision reads:

> Except as may be agreed upon in individual trusteeship agreements, made under Articles 77, 79, and 81, placing each territory under the trusteeship system, and until such agreements have been concluded, nothing in this Chapter shall be construed in or of itself to alter in any manner the rights whatsoever of any States or any peoples or the terms of existing international instruments to which Members of the United Nations may respectively be parties.

Thus, as the United States was reported as saying of an earlier version of Article 80(1) at the San Francisco Conference:[113]

> The delegate for the United States stated that paragraph B 5 was intended as a conservatory or safeguarding clause. He was willing and desirous that the minutes of this Committee show that it is intended to mean that all rights, whatever they may be, remain exactly the same as they exist—that they are neither increased nor diminished by the adoption of this Charter. Any change is left as a matter for subsequent agreements. The clause should neither add nor detract, but safeguard all existing rights, whatever they may be.

The 'subsequent agreements' which the American delegate mentioned are those referred to as 'trusteeship agreements' in Article 77:

> 1. The trusteeship system shall apply to such territories in the following categories as may be placed thereunder by means of trusteeship agreements:
> (*a*) territories now held under mandate;
> (*b*) territories which may be detached from enemy States as a result of the Second World War; and
> (*c*) territories voluntarily placed under the system by States responsible for their administration.
>
> 2. It will be a matter for subsequent agreement as to which territories in the foregoing categories will be brought under the trusteeship system and upon what terms.

[112] *Status of South West Africa* case, *ICJ Reports*, 1950, p. 128; *Voting Procedure* case, *ICJ Reports*, 1955, p. 68; *Hearings of Petitioners* case, *ICJ Reports*, 1956, p. 23.

[113] *Documents of the United Nations Conference on International Organization*, vol. 10, p. 678.

With regard to the interpretation of this provision, most of the States represented at San Francisco seemed to be against the imposition of any obligation to transfer existing mandates to the trusteeship system, though the principal reason for adopting this stance was their objection to any process whereby the terms of trusteeship agreements might be imposed upon them.[114] Thus, an Egyptian amendment to what became Article 77(1), which would have required trusteeship to apply to 'all territories now held under mandate', was rejected.[115]

The potential for tension between the need for the agreement of the mandatory before any transfer to the trusteeship system could take place, and the intention that Article 80(1) should be of a transitional nature, was appreciated, although there was uncertainty as to how it should be dealt with.[116] However, to reinforce this understanding of the role of Article 80(1), paragraph 2 of that Article provides:

> Paragraph 1 of this Article shall not be interpreted as giving grounds for delay or postponement of the negotiation and conclusion of agreements for placing mandated and other territories under the trusteeship system as provided for in Article 77.

Even if one accepts that the intentions of a majority of States represented at San Francisco, and the object and purpose behind Article 77, were to prevent an obligation being imposed on mandatory powers to bring (all) the territories concerned under trusteeship, it does not follow that the same intentions, or understanding as to the purpose of Article 77, can be imputed to all of those States, nor to the other States which, though not represented at San Francisco, became original members of the United Nations. In debates during the first three sessions of the General Assembly, 'representatives of approximately half of the members of the United Nations expressed views on the issue. From these discussions, it appeared that approximately an equal number of Members took positions on each

[114] Hence the inclusion in the Charter of Article 79:

'The terms of trusteeship for each territory to be placed under the trusteeship system, including any alteration or amendment, shall be agreed upon by the States directly concerned, including the mandatory power in the case of territories held under mandate by a Member of the United Nations, and shall be approved as provided for in Articles 83 and 85'.

[115] The text of the amendment is given in the written statement of the United States of America submitted to the Court in the *Status of South West Africa* case, *ICJ Pleadings* (1950), p. 85 at p. 121; see also the Statement of Mr Kerno (United Nations) at a public session of the Court, ibid., p. 160 at pp. 220–2.

[116] In some respects the issue was ignored. As the written statement of the United States pointed out (at p. 122):

'The report of the Rapporteur of Committee II/4 to Commission II and the report of the Rapporteur of Commission II to the plenary session of the San Francisco Conference did not consider specifically the question whether the placing of mandated territories under the trusteeship system was to be compulsory or optional. These reports, which in part paraphrased the language of the provisions which were to become Chapter XII, contained no statements to indicate that the conversion of mandates to trust territories was to be compulsory.'

side of this issue.'[117] The point to make is that, even if the members were never sufficient to establish a two-thirds majority, there was increasing support for the view that Article 77 did establish a legal obligation upon mandatory powers. As Mr Kerno, the United Nations' spokesman before the Court, pointed out, after referring to the 'sharp division of opinion' on the matter:[118]

> While the Assembly has repeatedly recommended that the Territory of South-West Africa be placed under international trusteeship, no two-thirds majority of its Members has been found to confirm the view held by a great many members of the Fourth Committee that 'it is the *clear intention* of Chapter XII of the Charter that all territories previously held under mandate, until granted self-government or independence, shall be brought under the international Trusteeship System', and that therefore the placing of such territories under trusteeship was obligatory.

In the event, the International Court held that there was no obligation imposed upon South Africa to bring South West Africa into the trusteeship system. The various arguments in favour of the contrary view were rejected: that the use of the word 'voluntary' in category (*c*) of Article 77(1) 'shows that the placing of other territories under Trusteeship is compulsory';[119] that Article 80(2) 'imposes on mandatory States a duty to negotiate and conclude Trusteeship Agreements';[120] or at least 'to enter into negotiations with a view to concluding' such agreements;[121] that 'the Trusteeship System created by the Charter would have no more than a theoretical existence if the Mandatory Powers were not under an obligation' along these lines, for otherwise no territories might be brought within the system.;[122] The Court's reasoning on these matters was sparse indeed. The overriding factor seems to have been the inference it drew from Articles 75 and 77:[123]

> The language used in both articles is permissive ('as may be placed thereunder'). Both refer to subsequent agreements by which the territories in question may be placed under the Trusteeship System. An 'agreement' implies consent of the parties concerned, including the mandatory Power in the case of territories held under Mandate (Article 79). The parties must be free to accept or reject the terms of a contemplated agreement. No party can impose its terms on the other party. Article 77, paragraph 2, moreover, presupposes agreement not only with regard to its par-

[117] Written statement of the United States, at p. 122. The statement went on to point out (at pp. 122–3) that representatives of the following States 'maintained that mandatory Powers were under a legal obligation to place mandated territories under trusteeship: India, China, USSR, Byelorussia, Poland, Philippines, Guatemala, Uruguay, Colombia, Syria, Haiti, and Brazil'. On the other hand, representatives of 'a number of other countries expressed the view that the Charter did not impose a legal obligation upon mandatory Powers to place mandated territories under the trusteeship system of the United Nations: United Kingdom, Netherlands, United States, Cuba, Australia, Union of South Africa, Denmark, France, Greece, New Zealand, Belgium, Canada, Bolivia, and Iraq'.

[118] At p. 218.

[119] *ICJ Reports*, 1950, p. 128 at p. 139.

[120] At pp. 139–40.

[121] At p. 140.

[122] Ibid.

[123] At p. 139.

ticular terms, but also as to which territories will be brought under the Trusteeship System.

However persuasive this reasoning might be on the surface, it is not as convincing as the Court's confidence in asserting the conclusion might suggest. There was a very obvious reason why the language employed was permissive. It could not have been the intention of those responsible for formulating these provisions to require all mandates to be brought into the new system because it was recognized that some of the territories would be granted independence in their own right.[124] Indeed, this possibility was explicitly provided for in Article 78:[125]

> The trusteeship system shall not apply to territories which have become Members of the United Nations, relationship among which shall be based on respect for the principle of sovereign equality.

This plausible means of reconciling the apparently 'optional language' of some of the provisions, and the 'compromise formula'[126] of Article 80(2), seems preferable to an interpretation which ignored the obviously transitional nature of the latter.[127] Moreover, it would have been much preferable to have avoided the consequences, signs of which were already present in the discordant dealings between the United Nations and the South

[124] As the statement by Mr Kerno explained, those States believing that a transfer to the trusteeship system was compulsory with regard to mandated territories did express the view that, with regard to such territories, 'only two courses are legally permissible: either they be granted full independence or they be placed under the Trusteeship System' (*ICJ Pleadings*, at p. 218).

[125] See the comment made by the representative of the Philippines, Mr Ingles, in a statement to the Court (at p. 245), that the 'permissive' formulation in Articles 75 and 77 was only employed to cater for the fact that, in the case of category (*a*), 'not all territories held under mandate at the time the Charter came into force would necessarily have to be placed under the international Trusteeship System. This is so because of the exceptions provided in the Charter itself.' Then, having referred to Article 78, Mr Ingles said that that provision 'applied to Syria and Lebanon, which, though participants in the [San Francisco] Conference and signatories to the Charter, were still regarded by France to be technically subject to Class A Mandate of the League of Nations'.

[126] Hall, 'The Trusteeship System and the Case of South-West Africa', this *Year Book*, 24 (1947), p. 385 at p. 388:

> 'It is clear from the San Francisco records that to placate opposition to the voluntary theory the Conference deliberately accepted the compromise formula of Article 80(2) which seems to contradict the optional language of Articles 80(1), 75, and 77. It left the future to take care of this inner contradiction.'

Hall himself was of the view that Article 80(2) on its own could not render transfer compulsory. He continued by saying that 'an obligation of such importance would have to be created by clear language, not the vague phrases of Article 80(2)'. However, the gap that then arose with regard to the supervision of a mandate within the United Nations system was largely ignored with the final comment (at p. 389):

> 'The situation is anomalous, but given goodwill on both sides there is no reason why it should not be possible to serve the essential purposes of trusteeship as stated in the mandate'.

[127] As Mr Ingles observed of the apparent conflict between the provisions (*ICJ Pleadings*, at p. 247):

> 'In the light of our exposition . . . we submit that the alleged "contradiction" is more apparent than real. We take it that the function of interpretation is not to look for contradiction in isolated phrases, but rather to look at the whole instrument in order to harmonize various provisions which constitute a composite and correlated whole. We must assume that paragraph 2 of Article 80 was inserted in the Charter for a definite purpose; and therefore we should reject any interpretation which would render it without effect.'

African Government, that followed from the Court's acceptance of the views of those States which had argued for the optional nature of Article 77(1)(*a*).

There seemed little doubt that the obligations of a mandatory would not come to an end with the winding up of the League of Nations. As Article 80(1) records, nothing in Chapter XII of the Charter 'shall be construed in or of itself to alter in any manner the rights whatsoever of any States or any peoples or the terms of existing international instruments to which Members of the United Nations may respectively be parties'. In addition, in one of its final acts, the Assembly of the League of Nations passed, with a single abstention by Egypt, a resolution on mandates of 18 April 1946, which took note of 'the expressed intentions of the Members of the League now administering territories under mandate to continue to administer them for the well-being and development of the peoples concerned in accordance with the obligations contained in the respective Mandates, until other arrangements have been agreed between the United Nations and the respective mandatory Powers'.[128]

While the obligations of the mandatory towards the territory it administered could continue by virtue of the mandate agreement, notwithstanding the disappearance of the League, the situation with regard to the machinery of supervision was a different matter. The obligation to present annual reports to the League through the Permanent Mandates Commission could not be performed. Moreover, while the continuing obligations in the former category were spelt out in the League Assembly's resolution on mandates, the wording of the paragraph dealing with the United Nations' role was more circumspect. It recognized 'that, on the termination of the League's existence, its functions with respect to the mandated territories will come to an end', but noted 'that Chapters XI, XII and XIII of the Charter of the United Nations embody principles corresponding to those declared in Article 22 of the Covenant of the League'.[129]

Despite the difference between the recognition of a principle which no one would have doubted and noting a proposition amounting to the obvious, on the one hand, and the qualitatively different issue of whether the United Nations could assume the supervisory functions of the League with regard to territories under mandate, on the other, the Court described the resolution as supporting the transfer of those functions to the United

[128] Quoted by the International Court in the *Status of South West Africa* case, *ICJ Reports*, 1950, p. 128 at p. 134. In addition, South Africa made a number of statements, directed to the Secretary-General of the United Nations, in the period following the dissolution of the League referring to South Africa's continuing obligations under the mandate (quoted by the Court at p. 135). As the Court observed (at pp. 135–6):

> 'These declarations constitute recognition by the Union Government of the continuance of its obligations under the Mandate and not a mere indication of the future conduct of that Government. Interpretations placed upon legal instruments by the parties to them, though not conclusive as to their meaning, have considerable probative value when they contain recognition by a party of its own obligations under an instrument. In this case the declarations of the Union of South Africa support the conclusions already reached by the Court.'

[129] Quoted *ICJ Reports*, 1950, at p. 134.

Nations. 'This resolution', it said,[130] 'presupposes that the supervisory functions exercised by the League would be taken over by the United Nations'. Read in this way, it reinforced the Court's view of the situation, expressed as follows:[131]

> The obligation incumbent upon a mandatory State to accept international supervision and to submit reports is an important part of the Mandates System. When the authors of the Covenant created this system, they considered that the effective performance of the sacred trust of civilization by the mandatory Powers required that the administration of mandated territories should be subject to international supervision. The authors of the Charter had in mind the same necessity when they organized an International Trusteeship System. The necessity for supervision continues to exist despite the disappearance of the supervisory organ under the Mandates System. It cannot be admitted that the obligation to submit to supervision has disappeared merely because the supervisory organ has ceased to exist, when the United Nations has another international organ performing similar, though not identical, supervisory functions.

More specifically, it followed from the stipulation in Article 80(1) that nothing in Chapter XII should be construed as altering in any manner the rights of any peoples, that the right of petition granted by the Council of the League in 1923 was preserved. This was so despite the fact that the right 'was not mentioned by Article 22 of the Covenant or by the provisions of the Mandate'.[132] As the Court summarized the position:[133]

> In view of the result at which the Court has arrived with respect to the exercise of the supervisory functions by the United Nations and the obligation of the Union Government to submit to such supervision, and having regard to the fact that the dispatch and examination of petitions form a part of that supervision, the Court is of the opinion that petitions are to be transmitted by that Government to the General Assembly of the United Nations, which is legally qualified to deal with them.

The Court went on to explain that the 'degree of supervision to be exercised by the General Assembly should not . . . exceed that which applied under the Mandate System, and should conform as far as possible to the procedure followed in this respect by the Council of the League of Nations. These observations are particularly applicable to annual reports and petitions.'[134]

When it came to settling how it was to carry out this role, the General Assembly adopted the two-thirds majority formula contained in Article 18(2) in respect of 'important questions' for reaching decisions on questions relating to reports and petitions concerning South West Africa. This was challenged by South Africa on the ground that it hardly coincided with the position under the League of Nations, the Council of which had operated

130 At p. 137.
131 At p. 136.
132 At p. 137.
133 At p. 138.
134 Ibid.

on the unanimity principle. Acceptance of this argument would have deprived the Assembly of any power of supervision as Article 18 provided the only ways in which the Assembly could vote on matters before it, and unanimity was not one of them. The Court's response in the *Voting Procedure* case[135] was to adopt two propositions. The first was that the reference in the earlier advisory opinion to the 'degree of supervision to be exercised by the General Assembly' must be 'interpreted as relating to substantive matters, and not as including or relating to the system of voting followed by the Council of the League'.[136] The second was expressed by the Court as follows:[137]

> When the Court stated in its previous Opinion that in exercising its supervisory functions the General Assembly should conform 'as far as possible to the procedure followed in this respect by the Council of the League of Nations', it was indicating that in the nature of things the General Assembly, operating under an instrument different from that which governed the Council of the League of Nations, would not be able to follow precisely the same procedures as were followed by the Council. Consequently, the expression 'as far as possible' was designed to allow for adjustments and modifications necessitated by legal or practical considerations.

Such a 'modification' had clearly been necessary to enable the Assembly to comply with the voting requirements laid down in the United Nations Charter.

Because of the refusal of the South African Government 'to assist in the implementation of the Advisory Opinion of the Court and to co-operate with the United Nations concerning the submission of reports and the transmission of petitions in accordance with the procedure of the Mandates System',[138] the General Assembly's Committee on South West Africa asked the Assembly whether or not it could hold oral hearings for petitioners. As this practice had not been adopted by the Mandates Commission of the League, following objections from all the mandatory powers, the General Assembly sought the advice of the Court before proceeding with the Committee's request. In a brief opinion,[139] the Court held in favour of the institution of oral hearings. It emphasized the importance for the Committee and the General Assembly of being properly informed on such matters as were raised in petitions and how oral hearings would assist in this direction:[140]

> If as a result of the grant of oral hearings to petitioners in certain cases the Committee is put in a better position to judge the merits of petitions, this cannot be presumed to add to the burden of the Mandatory. It is in the interests of the Mandatory, as well as of the proper working of the Mandates System, that the exer-

[135] *ICJ Reports*, 1955, p. 68.
[136] At p. 74.
[137] At pp. 76–7.
[138] *Hearings of Petitioners* case, *ICJ Reports*, 1956, p. 23 at p. 26.
[139] *Hearings of Petitioners* case, *ICJ Reports*, 1956, p. 23.
[140] At p. 30.

cise of supervision by the General Assembly should be based upon material which has been tested as far as possible, rather than upon material which has not been subjected to proper scrutiny either by or on behalf of the Mandatory, or by the Committee itself.

Then the Court referred to the necessity of the situation as justifying this change in procedure:[141]

The Court notes that, under the compulsion of practical considerations arising out of the lack of co-operation by the Mandatory, the Committee on South West Africa provided by Rule XXVI of its Rules of Procedure an alternative procedure for the receipt and treatment of petitions. This Rule became necessary because the Mandatory had refused to transmit to the General Assembly petitions by the inhabitants of the Territory, thus rendering inoperative provisions in the Rules concerning petitions and directly affecting the ability of the General Assembly to exercise an effective supervision. This Rule enabled the Committee on South West Africa to receive and deal with petitions notwithstanding that they had not been transmitted by the Mandatory.

On any survey of this sequence of events, a good case can be made in support of the proposition that South Africa's membership of the United Nations and adherence to the Charter did have unforeseen consequences. There was nothing in the Charter specifically granting to the General Assembly or any other organ of the United Nations a supervisory role with regard to mandates. As Judge McNair pointed out in his separate opinion in the *Status of South West Africa* case:[142]

The first contention was that there had been an automatic succession by the United Nations to the rights and functions of the Council of the League in this respect; but this is pure inference, as the Charter contains no provision for a succession such as Article 37 of the Statute of the International Court operates in the case of the compulsory jurisdiction of the Permanent Court in regard to the Mandates. The succession of the United Nations to the administrative functions of the League of Nations in regard to the Mandates could have been expressly preserved and vested in the United Nations in a similar manner, but this was not done.

Nor was the succession argument advanced by the mandates resolution of the League to which the Court made reference. In the opinion of Judge McNair:[143]

By this Resolution the Assembly recognized that the functions of the League had come to an end; but it did not purport to transfer them, with the consent of all States interested therein, to the United Nations. I do not see how this Resolution can be construed as having created a legal obligation by the Union to make annual reports to the United Nations and to transfer to that Organization the pre-war supervision of its Mandate by the League. At the most it could impose an obligation to perform those obligations of the Mandate—and there are many—which did not involve the activity of the League.

[141] At p. 31.
[142] *ICJ Reports*, 1950, at p. 159.
[143] At p. 161.

Once it was accepted that the powers of supervision did devolve upon the United Nations, it was perhaps a small step to accept that the unanimity requirements of the League Council could not be replicated in the work of the United Nations.[144] It was a far more significant step[145] to justify the granting of oral hearings contrary to the practice of the League of Nations. In the view of the joint dissenting opinion in the *Hearings of Petitioners* case,[146] the Court had to decide the matter by reference to the 1950 opinion which had been endorsed by the General Assembly. In that case, the Court had held that South West Africa was 'still to be considered as a territory held under the Mandate' of December 1920, and it followed therefrom that the 'degree of supervision to be exercised by the General Assembly should not therefore exceed that which applied under the Mandates System'.[147] As the joint opinion pointed out, these 'words refer to the practice which was established, whether that practice remained within or went beyond the powers conferred upon the Council. The established practice is the only criterion.'[148] The opinion therefore stated:[149]

> It follows from the maintenance of the former regime that the functions of the General Assembly, in its capacity as supervising organ, are limited to those which the Council of the League of Nations in fact exercised before its disappearance. The General Assembly cannot introduce any method of supervision which the Council did not in fact establish, even if it could have done so, in accordance with the terms of the Covenant and of the Mandate. Any such new method would exceed 'the degree of supervision which applied under the Mandates System'.

(C) *The* Peace Treaties *contrast*. If there could have been any doubt in the 1950 advisory opinion that the Court was applying the principle of effectiveness to redress a gap in the arrangements made by the League on the eve of its dissolution and in the Charter by the way in which it was drafted, it is hardly possible to camouflage the operation of this principle in the *Hearings of Petitioners* case. In this respect there was a striking contrast between the Court's attitude to this situation and its opinion in the *Peace Treaties* case.[150]

In the latter case, Bulgaria, Hungary and Romania had failed to appoint

[144] For the different approach adopted by Judge Lauterpacht, see *ICJ Reports*, 1955, at pp. 90 ff.

[145] It is difficult to take seriously the statement by Judge Lauterpacht in the *Hearings of Petitioners* case, *ICJ Reports*, 1956, at p. 41, that:

> 'While I am of the view that in normal circumstances the grant of oral hearings to petitioners would result in exceeding the degree of supervision as actually applied under the Mandates System and that it would not conform with the procedure followed in this respect by the Council of the League, I believe that both the excess and the departure are of limited compass'.

The mandatories themselves certainly regarded the institution of oral hearings as unacceptable, and even the Council of the League referred to it as an 'exceptional procedure' (see Judge Lauterpacht's attempt to explain away this reference, at p. 42).

[146] Given by Vice-President Badawi, and Judges Basdevant, Hsu Mo, Armand-Ugon and Moreno Quintana.

[147] *ICJ Reports*, 1950, at p. 138.

[148] *ICJ Reports*, 1956, at p. 66.

[149] At p. 67.

[150] *Peace Treaties (Second Phase)* case, *ICJ Reports*, 1950, p. 221.

members of Commissions provided for under their respective Peace Treaties in breach of their obligations under those Treaties.[151] The idea was canvassed that, in view of the continued refusal by the three States to conform to their treaty obligations, the relevant Commissions could be established by the appointment of a member by the other party to a dispute and by the appointment of a third member by the Secretary-General of the United Nations, as he would have been entitled to do if the two members had been appointed in the normal way and had then failed to agree upon the selection of the third member. The Court refused to sanction this means for preventing the breakdown of the arbitration machinery provided for in the Peace Treaties. Even though the Commissions had the power, under the Treaties, to decide matters by majority vote, so that the concurring votes of two members were sufficient to reach a decision, tribunals of two members did not constitute the Commissions established by the Treaties. The Court placed the following limitation upon its role:[152]

> The failure of machinery for settling disputes by reason of the practical impossibility of creating the Commission provided for in the Treaties is one thing; international responsibility is another. The breach of a treaty obligation cannot be remedied by creating a commission which is not the kind of Commission contemplated by the Treaties. It is the duty of the Court to interpret the Treaties, not to revise them.
>
> The principle of interpretation expressed in the maxim: *Ut res magis valeat quam pereat*, often referred to as the rule of effectiveness, cannot justify the Court in attributing to the provisions for the settlement of disputes in the Peace Treaties a meaning which, as stated above, would be contrary to their letter and spirit.

In the *Hearings of Petitioners* case,[153] Judge Lauterpacht admitted the potential for conflict with the *Peace Treaties* case. However, he was anxious to establish that the two cases could be reconciled: they were 'dissimilar in a vital respect'.[154] As he went on to explain:[155]

> The clauses of the Peace Treaties of 1947 relating to settlement of disputes were, as shown in their wording and the protracted history of their adoption, formulated in terms which clearly revealed the absence of agreement to endow them with a full measure of effectiveness—including safeguards to be resorted to in the event of the failure of one of the parties to participate in the procedure of settlement of disputes. This was a case in which the application of the principle of effectiveness in the interpretation of treaties found, in the view of the Court, a necessary limit in the circumstances that the parties had failed—not accidentally, but by design—to render them fully effective. This is not the position in the present case when the Court is confronted with the interpretation of provisions concerning a regime in the nature of an international status of established and continuous operation;

[151] As the Court had held in the *Peace Treaties (First Phase)* case, *ICJ Reports*, 1950, p. 65.

[152] *ICJ Reports*, 1950, p. 221 at p. 229.

[153] *ICJ Reports*, 1956, at p. 58: 'The resemblance of the two cases is as striking as the apparent discrepancy between the present Opinion of the Court and that in the case of the . . . *Peace Treaties*'.

[154] Ibid.

[155] At pp. 58–9.

provisions in relation to which the Court, in the Opinion of 11 July 1950 and that of 7 June 1955 on *Voting Procedure*, affirmed in emphatic language the necessity of securing the unimpeded and effective application of the system of supervision in accordance with the fundamental provisions of the Covenant and the Charter; and with regard to which it qualified the notion of any literal and rigid continuity of the Mandates System by making it obligatory only 'so far as possible'—an expression expressly 'designed to allow for adjustments and modifications necessitated by legal or practical considerations' (I.C.J. Rep. 1955 at 77).

This being so, the present Advisory Opinion of the Court seems to be fully in accordance with its previous practice of interpreting treaties and other international instruments in a manner calculated to secure their effective operation.

There are grounds for suggesting that the distinction between the two cases is not as clear cut as Judge Lauterpacht asserted. On the one hand, the formula contained in the dispute settlement provisions of the Peace Treaties was not in any way unusual, but was a standard clause at the time.[156] If the reason why these particular provisions could not be saved by the method proposed was because of the refusal of the three countries concerned to accept an alternative version, then presumably it might have been possible to use the method of interpretation, which the Court had rejected, in situations where the formula had been adopted without discussion between, and therefore without objection by, any of the parties. In fact the clause promoted as suitable for inclusion in subsequent treaties for or dealing with the peaceful settlement of disputes was amended to avoid the gap revealed by the *Peace Treaties* case.[157]

On the other hand, the important point is that the Lauterpacht explanation ignored the very real lack of agreement as to the consequences of the dissolution of the League and as to the significance of the Charter provisions with regard to mandated territories. If it were sought to interpret the provisions of Chapter XII according to their object and purpose in order to ascertain whether or how far they were applicable to those territories, the answer would seem to have been that they were applicable temporarily, and then only to a limited extent. This is the most that can be read into Article 80, considered as a whole. Moreover, if it had come to a choice between rendering the Charter provisions effective by imposing an obligation upon a recalcitrant mandatory power to negotiate and conclude a trusteeship agreement on the alternative reading of Article 77(1), or by extending the degree of supervision exercisable by the United Nations temporally or in intensity, the former would seem to have involved the less extreme departure from the relevant texts. If there were a measure of the

[156] The approach being a modified version of the means of selection of arbitrators of the Permanent Court of Arbitration under Article 45 of the Hague Convention for the Pacific Settlement of International Disputes 1907: text in Scott (ed.), *The Hague Conventions and Declarations of 1899 and 1907* (1915), p. 59. See also the General Act for Pacific Settlement of International Disputes 1928, Articles 22 and 23: *League of Nations Treaty Series*, vol. 93, p. 343 at pp. 353–4.

[157] See the European Convention for the Peaceful Settlement of Disputes 1957, Article 21: text in *UN Treaty Series*, vol. 320, p. 243 at p. 254; Draft Code on Arbitral Procedure 1958, Article 3: text in Wetter (ed.), *The International Arbitral Process: Public and Private*, vol. 5 (1979), p. 232 at p. 234.

degree to which the principle of effectiveness might be applied, the *Hearings of Petitioners* case would be placed at, or near, the furthest end of the scale. The comparison with the *Peace Treaties* case shows that the former was on the borderline of circumstances which the International Court, at that time, regarded as subject to the principle's operation.

(D) *Analogies with the* Nicaragua *case*. To revert to the situation faced by the Court in the *Nicaragua* case,[158] there are a number of similarities with the earlier two advisory opinions. All three dealt with issues of international jurisdiction over the activities of States. In this respect, the *Nicaragua* case had the added factor in common with the *Peace Treaties* case that both concerned the ambit of competence of a judicial tribunal, rather than of a political institution. Not that Judge Lauterpacht in the *Hearings of Petitioners* case regarded this as a reason for distinguishing it from the *Peace Treaties* case. In his view, the distinctive feature of the latter was the opposition amongst some of the parties negotiating the Treaties to a more watertight formula. On this basis, the *Nicaragua* case would be more closely akin to the *Petitioners* opinion. There was no apparent objection, that can be identified from those concerned with the drafting of Article 36(5) of the Statute of the present Court, to that provision operating to vivify an unratified declaration like that made by Nicaragua under Article 36 of the former Statute.

Not that the extension of Article 36(5) to the position of Nicaragua was necessarily an appropriate circumstance for the application of the principle of effectiveness. After all, that provision had a fairly wide ambit even if it had not been extended to cover Nicaragua's declaration. The same could also be said, however, of the United Nations' authority with regard to South West Africa. Indeed, prior to the *Petitioners* case, the principle of effectiveness had already been employed, though without acknowledgment by the Court, in both the original advisory opinion of 1950 and the *Voting Procedures* case.

The only context in which the principle of effectiveness could have any relevance in the *Nicaragua* case was in relation to the object and purpose of Article 36(5) of the Statute of the International Court. Two reasons were advanced against its application. One, which has already been mentioned,[159] was that there had not been any intention of breathing life into a declaration, made with regard to the Permanent Court, that had never come into force. A second was deducible from the fact that there should have been no need to rely upon any principle of effectiveness as Nicaragua, if it had genuinely wished to be subject to the Court's jurisdiction at any time since 1929, could easily have taken the necessary steps to ratify or renew its declaration. It had not done so, it was suggested,[160] because of its

[158] *ICJ Reports*, 1984, p. 392.

[159] Above, p.129.

[160] See the accounts contained in the judgments of Judge Ago, *ICJ Reports*, 1984, at pp. 520, 528–31, and of Judge Schwebel, at pp. 596–600; and above, p. 141.

wish to avoid its boundary dispute with Honduras coming within the Court's jurisdiction, or at least being made the subject of a claim for compensation.

In contrast, the argument in favour of the extension of the Court's jurisdiction to Nicaragua by a broad interpretation of the application of Article 36(5) can at least be justified by the intention of all parties involved to preserve declarations made under the Optional Clause of the previous Statute. In the absence of any evidence of specific intent, an interpretation which extends the range of preservation would appear to be more rather than less consonant with what the parties had in mind. In this respect, at least, the decision of the Court in the *Nicaragua* case would seem to be more justifiable than the outcome in the *Hearings of Petitioners* case. As Judge Lauterpacht admitted in that case:[161]

> I have come to the conclusion that oral hearings of petitioners would—apart from the situation actually confronting the United Nations—be inconsistent with the Opinion of 11 July 1950 inasmuch as they depart from the system which obtained under the League of Nations. But, as explained, that system was predicated on the fulfilment by the Mandatory of [its] obligations in the matter of reports and petitions. As the result of the attitude now adopted by the Union of South Africa, that assumption no longer applies.

2. *Implied consent as a basis of jurisdiction*

Almost as an afterthought to its conclusion that the entries in the *Yearbooks* and other publications, and reactions, or at any rate acquiescence, thereto, constituted subsequent practice affirming its view as to the effect of Article 36(5), the International Court, in the *Nicaragua* case, went on to hold that such practice also established the necessary consent to jurisdiction being based on Article 36(2).[162] However, in its brief discussion of the issue, the Court provided no adequate explanation of why this should be so.

The Court posed the question 'whether, even if the consent of Nicaragua is real, the Court can decide that it has been given valid expression even on the hypothesis that the 1929 Declaration was without validity, and given that no other declaration has been deposited by Nicaragua since it became a party to the Statute of the International Court'.[163] By way of reply, the Court stated:[164]

> The Court . . . recognizes that, so far as the accomplishment of the formality of depositing an optional declaration is concerned, Nicaragua was placed in an exceptional position, since the international organs empowered to handle such declarations declared that the formality in question had been accomplished by Nicaragua. The Court finds that this exceptional situation cannot be without effect on the requirements obtaining as regards the formalities that are indispensable for

[161] *ICJ Reports*, 1956, p. 23 at p. 57.
[162] See above, p. 128.
[163] *ICJ Reports*, 1984, at p. 412.
[164] At pp. 412–13.

the consent of a State to its compulsory jurisdiction to have been validly given. It considers therefore that, having regard to the origin and generality of the statements to the effect that Nicaragua was bound by its 1929 Declaration, it is right to conclude that the constant acquiescence of that State in those affirmations constitutes a valid mode of manifestation of its intent to recognize the compulsory jurisdiction of the Court under Article 36, paragraph 2, of the Statute, and that accordingly Nicaragua is, vis-à-vis the United States, a State accepting 'the same obligation' under that Article.

It was on this issue that Judge Ruda joined the dissenters. Though he was prepared to accept that Article 36(5) could be employed and that the *Yearbook* entries were relevant to establishing that ruling,[165] the same conduct could not establish Nicaragua's consent to be bound by Article 36(2). In his own words:[166]

My disagreement is based on my reading of the Statute of the Court, where it is provided that the only condition necessary to make operative a declaration accepting the jurisdiction of the Court under Article 36, paragraph 2, of the Statute is, in accordance with paragraph 4 of the same Article, the deposit of the declaration with the Secretary-General of the United Nations. The consent of a State to be bound by the international obligations assumed under a treaty, should be given in accordance with the procedure laid down in the treaty. The conduct of a State is an important element in the interpretation of a convention, including the Statute, which the Court has taken into account in previous paragraphs, but it is a totally different matter to regard this conduct as constituting acceptance of the international obligations set out in a treaty, without following the procedure laid down precisely for the entry into force of these obligations.

Similarly, Judge Ago felt it necessary first to 'enter an express reservation as to the very idea that the indisputable requirement of a formal act of acceptance could admissibly be replaced—and, what is more, in so special and delicate a field as acceptance of the obligation to submit one's international disputes to the jurisdiction of the Court—by mere evidence of conduct, even if the intention revealed by this conduct is not in doubt'.[167]

There is no question that a State can become bound by an obligation in a treaty to which it is not formally a party. This possibility is referred to in the Statute of the Court itself. According to Article 38(1)(*a*), the Court is directed to apply, in a dispute submitted to it, international conventions establishing rules 'expressly recognized by the contesting States', and not just those rules in conventions to which the contesting States are parties. In other words, the obligations contained in a treaty can be accepted by means other than acceding to the treaty as a party.

In some instances, the obligations might be recognized expressly by

[165] See above, p. 126.
[166] At p. 459.
[167] At p. 527.

unilateral act.[168] However, there would seem to be no good reason why the same should not also be true of rules which a State has recognized by implication from its conduct. Thus, in the *North Sea Continental Shelf* cases,[169] Denmark and the Netherlands

> contended that the Convention, or the regime of the Convention, and in particular of Article 6, has become binding on the Federal Republic in another way,—namely because, by conduct, by public statements and proclamations, and in other ways, the Republic has unilaterally assumed the obligations of the Convention; or has manifested its acceptance of the conventional regime; or has recognized it as being generally applicable to the delimitation of continental shelf areas.

In rejecting this argument, the Court did not regard it as wrong in principle but adopted the view that 'only a very definite, very consistent course of conduct on the part of a State in the position of the Federal Republic could justify the Court in upholding' the reasoning advanced by Denmark and the Netherlands.[170] In addition, the Court went on to say, even if such a course of conduct had existed, 'that is to say if there had been a real intention to manifest acceptance or recognition of the conventional regime—then it must be asked why it was that the Federal Republic did not take the obvious step of giving expression to this readiness by simply ratifying the Convention'.[171]

It is possible to point to similar factors relating to the position of Nicaragua *vis-à-vis* Article 36(2) of the Statute. However, there is a threshold problem of deciding how far guidance might be sought in the Court's approach to treaty obligations in general when it comes to deciding upon matters concerning the Court's jurisdiction.

It could be argued that the Court's approach in the *Nicaragua* case was quite out of harmony with the caution exemplified on previous occasions towards informal consent to its jurisdiction. There is no doubt that the Court has evolved the concept of *forum prorogatum* as a means of extending its jurisdiction through giving effect to the tacit consent of States involved

[168] For an example of the recognition of the applicability of part only of the provisions of a convention, see the Israeli attitude to the Geneva Convention relative to the Protection of Civilian Persons in Time of War 1949, outlined in Shamgar, 'The Observance of International Law in the Administered Territories', *Israel Year Book of Human Rights*, 1 (1971), p. 262; and discussion thereof by various commentators, ibid., pp. 366 ff.; *Military Prosecutor* v. *Zuhadi Saleh Hussein Zohar* (1968), ibid., p. 453. The National Liberation Front in Vietnam, while not a 'party' to the 1949 Geneva Conventions, and regarding them as inapplicable, gave assurances as to the humane treatment of prisoners of war: see Petrowski, 'Law and the Conduct of the Vietnam War', in Falk (ed.), *The Vietnam War and International Law*, vol. 2 (1969), p. 439 at p. 484. Article 3 was inserted into the 1949 Conventions to deal with an 'armed conflict not of an international character' by imposing certain minimum standards of conduct as set out in that provision. By paragraph 2 of that article it is recommended that the parties to such a conflict 'bring into force, by means of special agreements, all or part of the other provisions of the present Convention'. For comment thereon, see Hooker and Savasten, 'The Geneva Conventions of 1949: Application in the Vietnamese Conflict', in Falk, op. cit., p. 417 at pp. 423–5, esp. n. 61.

[169] *ICJ Reports*, 1969, p. 3 at p. 25.

[170] Ibid.

[171] Ibid.

in litigation. As the Permanent Court observed in the *Minority Schools* case,[172] 'the submission of arguments on the merits, without making reservations in regard to the question of jurisdiction, must be regarded as an unequivocal indication of the desire of a State to obtain a decision on the merits of a suit'. However, it is clear that, for the principle to operate, there must be some act in the course of proceedings already instituted before the Court from which it is possible to imply consent, and mere inaction on receiving notice of an application would not normally be regarded as having that effect. In any case, it would be for the Court to satisfy itself 'that it has jurisdiction and must if necessary go into that matter *proprio motu*'.[173]

Forum prorogatum apart, tacit consent has played an insignificant role in the Court's jurisprudence. It received a brief mention in the *Barcelona Traction* case,[174] though only to back up the Court's application of Article 37.[175] The Court pointed out that the 'Respondent Government, in the course of diplomatic correspondence preceding the original proceedings before the Court . . . implicitly recognized the competence of the Court for the purposes of Article 17(4) of the 1927 Treaty . . . It did not demur when the Applicant stated that the International Court of Justice had been substituted for the Permanent Court in Article 17(4) of the Treaty.'[176]

Rosenne placed the following interpretation upon that segment of the Court's judgment in *Barcelona Traction*:[177]

> If a State A by its conduct induces in State B the belief, which is acted upon, that State A will accept, or will not contest, the jurisdiction if State B brings a certain issue before the Court for decision, then State A ought not to be permitted, subsequently, to contest the jurisdiction of the Court when that issue is brought before the Court for decision. In one sense, this doctrine supplies the basis for the concept of the *forum prorogatum*. It is possibly, however, wider. In the *forum prorogatum*, the conduct takes place before the eyes of the Court. The suggestion here being put forward is that the same principle may be operative from the diplomatic correspondence, before the case is brought before the Court, so that the jurisdiction will rest on an implied agreement of the parties reached before the institution of the proceedings.

This passage is open to the criticism that Rosenne seems to be confusing two distinct legal relationships, one established by estoppel, and the other arising by way of implied agreement.[178]

A similar misunderstanding is to be found in the segment of the Court's judgment dealing with the continued presence of the Nicaraguan

[172] *PCIJ*, Series A, No. 15, at p. 24.
[173] *Jurisdiction of the ICAO Council* case, *ICJ Reports*, 1972, p. 46 at p. 52.
[174] *ICJ Reports*, 1964, p. 6.
[175] Considered above, p. 134.
[176] *ICJ Reports*, 1964, at p. 36.
[177] *The Law and Practice of the International Court* (2nd rev. edn., 1985), p. 322.
[178] For the distinction under Anglo-Australian law, see Greig and Davis, *The Law of Contract* (1987), pp. 250–2.

declaration in the United Nations *Yearbook* amongst texts bestowing jurisdiction upon the International Court. Consider the following:[179]

> Having regard to the public and unchanging nature of the official statements concerning Nicaragua's commitment under the Optional-Clause system, the silence of its Government can only be interpreted as an acceptance of the classification thus assigned to it. It cannot be supposed that that Government could have believed that its silence could be tantamount to anything other than acquiescence. Besides, the Court would remark that if proceedings had been instituted against Nicaragua at any time in these recent years, and it had sought to deny that, by the operation of Article 36, paragraph 5, it had recognized the compulsory jurisdiction of the Court, the Court would probably have rejected that argument. But the Court's jurisdiction in regard to a particular State does not depend on whether that State is in the position of an Applicant or a Respondent in the proceedings. If the Court considers that it would have decided that Nicaragua would have been bound in a case in which it was the Respondent, it must conclude that its jurisdiction is identically established in a case where Nicaragua is the Applicant.

It can be seen that this passage contains a sequence of shifts *glissando*, from agreement to estoppel and back to agreement again. Initially, the Court spoke in terms of consent to the situation as proclaimed in the Court's publications: 'the silence of [Nicaragua's] Government can only be interpreted as an acceptance of the classification thus assigned to it'. Then it employed language more appropriate to estoppel, operative only against the party which is precluded from denying the situation which it led others to believe was the correct one: 'It cannot be supposed that that Government could have believed that its silence could be tantamount to anything other than acquiescence. Besides, the Court would remark that if proceedings had been instituted at any time in these recent years, and it had sought to deny that, by the operation of Article 36, paragraph 5, it had recognized the compulsory jurisdiction of the Court, the Court would probably have rejected that argument.' The gap in the Court's logic only becomes apparent in the final part of the passage when it seemed to infer, from something which the preceding passages suggested was either a matter of consent by, or estoppel against, Nicaragua, what was essentially a bilateral relationship: 'the Court's jurisdiction in regard to a particular State does not depend on whether that State is in the position of an Applicant or a Respondent in the proceedings. If the Court considers that it would have decided that Nicaragua would have been bound in a case in which it was the Respondent, it must conclude that its jurisdiction is identically established in a case where Nicaragua is the Applicant.'

If Nicaragua is the respondent State, the Court's jurisdiction is perfected by a combination of the consent of the applicant State, manifested either by a prior declaration or other title of jurisdiction, or by the application itself, and of the fact that Nicaragua is estopped from denying the existence of its declaration. If Nicaragua is the applicant State, however, its application is

[179] *ICJ Reports*, 1984, at p. 410.

simply further evidence of the existence of, or an alternative basis of jurisdiction to, its declaration. In order for the application to be regarded as admissible against the respondent State, it must be possible to point to some basis for the Court to exercise jurisdiction over that State. If the Court's jurisdiction is based upon the estoppel argument operating against the applicant, it must be possible to rely upon the same principle *vis-à-vis* the respondent State. The alternative would be to accept the startling proposition that a State which has made a declaration accepting the compulsory jurisdiction of the Court is vulnerable at the suit of any State which might have given the impression that it was subject, or was not going to object, to the exercise of jurisdiction against it by the Court.

Despite the ambiguities in, and scope for misinterpretation provided by, the above-quoted passage, analysis in the wider context of the Court's discussion may relieve some of the causes for concern. The main thrust of that discussion centred not upon estoppel in relation to the stance taken by a State on a particular matter, but upon implied consent manifested by a course of conduct. This emphasis was to be seen in the Court's conclusion that Nicaragua could validly argue that it had satisfied the requirements of Article 36(2). In its judgment,[180] the Court had referred to the fact the organs 'empowered to handle' declarations made under Article 36 had themselves stated that the necessary formalities had been 'accomplished'. It was the Court's view, therefore, that, 'having regard to the origin and generality of the statements to the effect that Nicaragua was bound by its 1929 Declaration, it is right to conclude that the constant acquiescence of that State in those affirmations constitutes a valid mode of manifestation of its intent to recognize the compulsory jurisdiction of the Court under Article 36, paragraph 2, of the Statute'.

In its submissions to the Court, Nicaragua had seen no problem in linking this *de facto* 'declaration' (the requirement specified in Article 36(2)) with the position of a specific respondent State which had formally accepted the Court's jurisdiction in accordance with that provision. However, Nicaragua had addressed the matter from the standpoint of Article 36(5). As the Court summarized Nicaragua's position:[181]

> The argument is that Nicaragua's conduct over a period of 38 years unequivocally constitutes consent to be bound by the compulsory jurisdiction of the Court by way of a recognition of the application of Article 36, paragraph 5, of the Statute to the Nicaraguan Declaration of 1929. Likewise the conduct of the United States over a period of 38 years unequivocally constitutes its recognition of the essential validity of the Declaration of Nicaragua of 1929 as a result of the application of Article 36, paragraph 5, of the Statute.

Ultimately, the Court seemed to be influenced, not by any need for specific recognition by the United States of the validity of Nicaragua's 1929

[180] At pp. 412–13. quoted above, p. 126.
[181] At p. 411. The passage is quoted in full, above, p. 127.

declaration, but by the factor referred to in a later sentence in the passage from which the above sentences are quoted:[182]

> The essential validity of the Nicaraguan declaration as an acceptance of the compulsory jurisdiction is confirmed by the evidence of a long series of public documents, by the general opinion of States and by the general opinion of qualified publicists.

As long as Nicaragua's link with the compulsory jurisdiction of the Court is seen as based upon consent, and not estoppel, the criticisms of the dissenters to the Court's judgment are not necessarily persuasive. To an extent the Court's approach shows a welcome preparedness to extend its jurisdiction and to resuscitate a version of the concept of *forum prorogatum*, though there would seem to be no reason for linking it to Article 36(2) for this purpose. It would be less acceptable to base future interpretations of the scope of the Court's judgment upon its reference to what seemed like a case of a State against which an estoppel might operate being entitled to rely upon the estoppel against other States. Serious doubts must therefore exist with regard to such a possibility. It is one thing to suggest that the consequence for Nicaragua of refraining from challenging the *Yearbook* entries was that it would be estopped from denying that it was subject to the Court's jurisdiction. It would be a totally different matter to apply the same principle to establish the Court's jurisdiction in a situation where Nicaragua was the applicant State.[183]

To rely upon an estoppel, it is the respondent State which must have misled the applicant by its conduct. The United States could only have

[182] Ibid. The United States also raised an issue of estoppel, claiming that 'even if Nicaragua is otherwise entitled to invoke against the United States the jurisdiction of the Court under Article 36, paragraphs 2 and 5, of the Statute, Nicaragua's conduct in relation to the United States over the course of many years estops Nicaragua from doing so' (at p. 413). However, having referred to the diplomatic exchanges relied upon by the United States (at pp. 413–14), the Court reiterated its view that Nicaragua's conduct evinced an intention to be bound by Article 36. As the Court summarized the circumstances (at pp. 414–15):

> 'the position of Nicaragua as to its own conduct is, as indicated above, that so far from having represented that it was not bound by the Optional Clause, on the contrary its conduct unequivocally constituted consent to be so bound.
>
> For the same reason, the Court does not need to deal at length with the contention based on estoppel. The Court has found that the conduct of Nicaragua, having regard to the very particular circumstances in which it was placed, was such as to evince its consent to be bound in such a way as to constitute a valid mode of acceptance of jurisdiction . . . It is thus evident that the Court cannot regard the information obtained by the United States in 1943, or the doubts expressed in diplomatic contacts in 1955, as sufficient to overturn that conclusion, let alone to support an estoppel. Nicaragua's contention that since 1946 it has consistently maintained that it is subject to the jurisdiction of the Court, is supported by substantial evidence. Furthermore, as the Court pointed out in the *North Sea Continental Shelf* cases (*ICJ Reports*, 1969, at p. 26), estoppel may be inferred from the conduct, declarations and the like made by a State which not only clearly and consistently evidenced acceptance by that State of a particular regime, but also had caused another State or States, in reliance on such conduct, detrimentally to change position or suffer some prejudice. The Court cannot regard Nicaragua's reliance on the optional clause as in any way contrary to good faith or equity: nor can Nicaragua be taken to come within the criterion of the *North Sea Continental Shelf* cases, and the invocation of estoppel by the United States of America cannot be said to apply to it.'

[183] Above, pp. 162–3.

been bound by the estoppel created by Nicaragua's course of conduct if it was a party to it, or if it had failed to object where the situation required a protest to be made. It can hardly be said that the United States was, with Nicaragua, party to any specific conduct suggesting that there was a common assumption, binding upon them, that Nicaragua was, *vis-à-vis* the United States, subject to the jurisdiction of the Court.[184] Alternatively, it must be possible to rely upon some independent act or omission (in this case a failure to protest where there was a duty to speak) by the United States giving rise to a further estoppel. While such a finding might have been open on the facts of the case, the Court did not appear to rely upon this possibility in its judgment.[185] Thus, the only satisfactory explanation of the Court's judgment on the matter of acceptance of the Court's jurisdiction is that the absence of protest should be interpreted solely in terms of the consent by both parties to the situation as stated in the *Yearbooks* of the Court.

IV. The Modification of the United States Declaration in the Shultz Letter

The attempt by the United States to modify its 1946 declaration, notwithstanding the fact that it was to 'remain in force for a period of five years and thereafter until the expiration of six months after notice may be given to terminate this declaration', raised a number of issues:

(a) the nature and effect of the instrument as a unilateral declaration;
(b) the principle of reciprocity;
(c) the bilateral effects of such a declaration in the context of Article 36; and
(d) the relevance of treaty rules to such an instrument.

(a) *The Declaration as a Unilateral Act*

In the *Nicaragua* case, the Court described the nature of a declaration made under Article 36 of the Statute in the following terms:[186]

> Declarations of acceptance of the compulsory jurisdiction of the Court are facultative, unilateral engagements, that States are absolutely free to make or not to make. In making the declaration a State is equally free either to do so unconditionally and without limit of time for its duration, or to qualify it with conditions or reservations. In particular, it may limit its effect to disputes arising after a certain date; or it may specify how long the declaration itself shall remain in force, or what notice (if any) will be required to terminate it. However, the unilateral nature of

[184] Similar to the estoppel by convention of Anglo-Australian municipal law: see Bower and Turner, *The Law Relating to Estoppel by Representation* (3rd edn., 1977), pp. 157 ff.

[185] Above, p. 163.

[186] *ICJ Reports*, 1984, at p. 418.

declarations does not signify that the State making the declaration is free to amend the scope and the contents of its solemn commitments as it pleases.

It then referred to its earlier pronouncement, in the *Nuclear Tests* cases,[187] that, when 'it is the intention of the State making the declaration that it should become bound according to its terms, that intention confers on the declaration the character of a legal undertaking, the State being henceforth legally required to follow a course of conduct consistent with the declaration'. As to the basis of this binding quality, the earlier judgment had explained:[188]

Just as the very rule of *pacta sunt servanda* in the law of treaties is based on good faith, so also is the binding character of an international obligation assumed by unilateral declaration. Thus interested States may take cognisance of unilateral declarations and place confidence in them, and are entitled to require that the obligation thus created be respected.

In the situation faced by the Court in the *Nicaragua* case, there was no difficulty in identifying the 'interested States'. As the Court said:[189]

the declarations, even though they are unilateral acts, establish a series of bilateral engagements with other States accepting the same obligation of compulsory jurisdiction, in which the conditions, reservations and time-limit clauses are taken into consideration. In the establishment of this network of engagements, which constitutes the Optional-Clause system, the principle of good faith plays an important role.

With regard to the nature of the links created between the various parties to this system, the Court's approach was hardly a cause for surprise. In the *Right of Passage* case,[190] the Court had used very similar language to describe the relationship of the various States which had made declarations under Article 36(2) of the Statute—not that the precise nature of the relationship was so vital in the circumstances of this case.[191] Whatever it was,[192] the important consequence was that the relationship brought the parties within the duty to act in good faith, which applied to both treaties and unilateral acts.[193]

There is perhaps more cause for surprise in the suggestion, later in the Court's judgment in the *Nicaragua* case, that 'the right of immediate termination of declarations with indefinite duration is far from established'.[194] In

[187] *ICJ Reports*, 1974, p. 253 at p. 267.

[188] At p. 268.

[189] *ICJ Reports*, 1984, at p. 418.

[190] *ICJ Reports*, 1957, p. 125.

[191] See below, pp. 176–7, 180–1.

[192] For a discussion of the significance of the distinction between a treaty and this form of agreement created by unilateral declarations, see the joint dissenting opinion of Judges Onyeama, Dillard, Jiménez de Aréchaga and Waldock in the *Nuclear Tests* cases, *ICJ Reports*, 1974, p. 253 at pp. 347 ff.

[193] See the words of the Court in the *Nuclear Tests* cases, quoted above in the text at n. 188.

[194] *ICJ Reports*, 1984, at p. 420.

making this point, the Court referred to 'the requirements of good faith' whereby unilateral declarations 'should be treated, by analogy according to the law of treaties, which requires a reasonable time for withdrawal from or termination of treaties that contain no provision regarding the duration of their validity'.[195]

In contrast, Rosenne has consistently argued that 'once a State has denounced a title of jurisdiction, and especially a declaration accepting the compulsory jurisdiction, it is politically inconceivable that another State would seek to invoke the denounced instrument as the basis for the institution of . . . proceedings'.[196] This political inconceivability was translated into legal terms by Judge Oda who, after an exhaustive survey of the forms of reservations included in declarations and the practice of States with respect to such declarations, concluded that the Court was totally wrong in suggesting that any period of notice could be required:[197]

> The above list clearly demonstrates the fact that a great number of States have made their declarations with an express statement that their declarations may be terminated or amended at any time and with immediate effect. I have also indicated a number of cases where declarations have been terminated. Thus to my mind it is quite untenable to argue that those declarations without any reference to duration (the number of which, as mentioned above, is very limited) can never be terminated or amended because of the lack of a clause concerning the period of validity of the declarations.

It followed, in his view, that, if Nicaragua was entitled to denounce without notice its declaration, then this power was also bestowed on the United States by virtue of the principle of reciprocity.[198]

Judge Jennings agreed with Judge Oda on the first point, that Nicaragua could withdraw at any time with immediate effect, because this was exactly what a number of States had done. Judge Jennings was able to point to 'no less than eleven instances of modifications made in the absence of any expressly reserved right to do so', and went on to say that in 'none of these cases was there a formal protest which questioned the right of an exclusionary modification with immediate effect and in the absence of an expressly reserved right to modify'.[199] More particularly, when in 1970 Canada introduced its legislation to establish a pollution control zone in the Arctic waters off its northern coast, it also withdrew its acceptance of the Court's jurisdiction. While the United States protested vigorously at the interference with navigation rights, it acknowledged that 'Canada's action last week excluded such disputes from its acceptance of the International Court's

[195] Ibid.

[196] Rosenne, *The Law and Practice of the International Court* (1965), vol. 1, p. 417; (2nd rev. edn., 1985), p. 417.

[197] *ICJ Reports*, 1984, at p. 510.

[198] For the issue of reciprocity, see below, p. 169.

[199] *ICJ Reports*, 1984, at p. 551.

compulsory jurisdiction'.[200] Judge Jennings concluded by saying that, because 'the unmistakable trend of recent developments' justified all States 'before seisin of the Court, to withdraw or alter their declarations of acceptance, with immediate effect', it therefore followed that 'the Shultz letter was effective to deprive the Court of jurisdiction under Article 36, paragraph 2, of the Court's Statute'.[201]

It is not altogether easy to accept how the practice of States in choosing to withdraw declarations, and in replacing them with new ones which often expressly claim a right of immediate termination, can change the nature of the United States declaration which, for nearly 40 years, had stipulated that it could only be terminated on 6 months' notice. Nor is the alternative justification given by Judge Jennings any more persuasive. In this, he relied upon the inspiration provided by Waldock's well-known article on the Optional Clause, quoting *inter alia* the following passage:[202]

> There is, in consequence, a glaring inequality in the position of a State which does and a State which does not make a declaration under the Optional Clause. The former State, for practical purposes, is continuously liable to be brought before the Court compulsorily at the suit of the latter, whereas the latter is not liable to be brought before the Court at the suit of the former unless and until it chooses to initiate proceedings before the Court as a plaintiff and makes a declaration under the Optional Clause *ad hoc* expressly for that purpose.

Judge Jennings continued by saying:[203]

> It is, therefore, at least in part in the light of what Waldock goes on to call 'this fundamental lack of reciprocity between the positions of States which do and States which do not make declarations', that the answer to the question of the legal effect of declarations should be given. It is this position of inequality and lack of reciprocity that has inevitably produced reservations by which the declarant State can withdraw or alter a declaration with immediate effect. Even so there remains inequality with those States which have chosen not to make any declaration at all. In this climate it would in my view be as impracticable as it would be inequitable to hold that a State whose declaration, like that of the United States, is expressed as subject to six months' notice, is bound by that statement of intention in respect of all comers, including those very many States which have declined to risk even a potential liability to jurisdiction; though it is of course bound once an application has been made.

Even if one were to accept this premiss, it does not support the conclusion. The vulnerability of a declarant State to a suit by a non-declarant

[200] Press Release No. 121 of 15 April 1970, text in *International Legal Materials*, 9 (1970), p. 606: quoted by Judge Jennings, *ICJ Reports*, 1984, at p. 552. It should be noted, however, that the Canadian declaration of 20 November 1929 did not specify any period of notice, but was made 'for a period of ten years and thereafter until such time as notice may be given to terminate the acceptance' (text in International Court of Justice *Yearbook*, 1956–7, p. 210). The circumstances of its termination in 1970 were not therefore analogous to the Shultz letter.

[201] *ICJ Reports*, 1984, at p. 553.

[202] 'Decline of the Optional Clause', this *Year Book*, 32 (1955–6), p. 244 at p. 280.

[203] *ICJ Reports*, 1984, at p. 548.

party to the Statute would justify the right of a declarant to withdraw or modify its declaration in contravention of the provisions of that declaration in relation to a non-declarant State. The disadvantageous position of a declarant State would not be relevant to its relations *vis-à-vis* other declarants, i.e., equally potentially disadvantaged States. Nor would it make any logical difference to this relationship that some of such States, or even a particular declarant State, had modified their or its declaration to provide protection against a non-declarant which attempted to submit to the jurisdiction and commence proceedings contemporaneously. Thus, if Nicaragua had not been (held to be) subject to the Court's jurisdiction, the making of a declaration and an application by that State on 9 April, i.e. after the Shultz letter of 6 April, would have been ineffective. The United States would have been entitled, as against Nicaragua as a non-declarant, to withdraw or modify its declaration irrespective of the fact that this action was not in keeping with the terms of the declaration.

Explained in this way, the inequality to which Waldock and Jennings referred is reconcilable with the Court's own judgment. It will be recalled that the Court was careful to explain the United States' obligations, assumed by unilateral declaration, in terms of their being owed to 'interested States'. As the Court went on to say in that part of its judgment:[204]

> The most important question relating to the effect of the 1984 notification is whether the United States was free to disregard the clause of six months' notice which, freely and by its own choice, it had appended to its 1946 Declaration. In so doing the United States entered into an obligation which is binding upon it vis-à-vis other States parties to the Optional-Clause system. Although the United States retained the right to modify the contents of the 1946 Declaration or to terminate it, a power which is inherent in any unilateral act of a State, it has, nevertheless, assumed an inescapable obligation towards other States accepting the Optional Clause, by stating formally and solemnly that any such change should take effect only after six months have elapsed as from the date of notice.

In other words, the premiss leads to the Court's conclusion, not to that advanced by Judge Jennings.

(b) *Effect of Reciprocity*

Because the system provided for in Article 36(2) of the Statute depends upon unilateral declarations in widely divergent terms, the jurisdiction of the Court only comes about to the extent that there is a common denominator between the declarations, to the extent that the two States are 'accepting the same obligation' in the words of the provision. This principle of reciprocity was expressed by the Court in the *Norwegian Loans* case[205] as requiring that 'since two unilateral declarations are involved, such jurisdic-

[204] At p. 419.
[205] *ICJ Reports*, 1957, p. 9 at p. 23.

tion is conferred upon the Court only to the extent to which the Declarations coincide in conferring it'.

The consequence of reciprocity is often expressed in the form that one State is entitled to take advantage of a reservation contained in the declaration of the other party to the proceedings. In most instances this will undoubtedly be so. If the applicant State's declaration excludes disputes arising after a specified date, the respondent is entitled to plead the reservation containing that date as limiting the Court's jurisdiction. It is less obvious how, in the *Norwegian Loans* case, Norway was entitled to take advantage of the French reservation that the declaration did not 'apply to differences relating to matters which are essentially within the national jurisdiction as understood by the Government of the French Republic' and claim that the dispute concerned matters which Norway considered within its own domestic jurisdiction.[206]

What is not permissible is an 'intertwining' of the two declarations and the limitations and reservations they contain. In the *Interhandel* case,[207] the United States' declaration of 1946 excluded from the Court's jurisdiction disputes arising prior to the date of the declaration. On 26 July 1948, the United States finally rejected the representations of the Swiss Government on behalf of the Swiss company, Interhandel. On 28 July, the Swiss Government accepted the jurisdiction of the Court without making any reservation as to time. Could the United States apply the past disputes reservation in its own declaration to the Swiss acceptance date? This suggestion was emphatically rejected by the Court in the following passage:[208]

> Reciprocity in the case of Declarations accepting the compulsory jurisdiction of the Court enables a Party to invoke a reservation to that acceptance which it has not expressed in its own Declaration but which the other Party has expressed in its Declaration. For example, Switzerland, which has not expressed in its Declaration any reservation *ratione temporis*, while the United States has accepted the compulsory jurisdiction of the Court only in respect of disputes subsequent to August 26, 1946, might, if in the position of Respondent, invoke by virtue of reciprocity against the United States the American reservation if the United States attempted to refer to the Court a dispute with Switzerland which had arisen before August 26, 1946. This is the effect of reciprocity in this connection. Reciprocity enables the State which has made the wider acceptance of the jurisdiction of the Court to rely upon the reservations to the acceptance laid down by the other Party. There the effect of reciprocity ends. It cannot justify a State, in this instance, the United States, in relying upon a restriction which the other Party, Switzerland, has not included in its own Declaration.

In the *Nicaragua* case, the United States sought to argue 'that the Nicaraguan 1929 Declaration, being of undefined duration, is liable to immediate

[206] For discussion of this issue, see Greig, *International Law* (2nd edn., 1976), pp. 649–50.
[207] *ICJ Reports*, 1959, p. 6.
[208] At p. 23.

termination, without previous notice, and that therefore Nicaragua has not accepted "the same obligation" as itself for the purposes of Article 36, paragraph 2, and consequently may not rely on the six months' notice proviso against the United States'.[209] In rejecting this contention, the Court quoted part of the above passage from the *Interhandel* judgment, but before doing so observed:[210]

> The notion of reciprocity is concerned with the scope and substance of the commitments entered into, including reservations, and not with the formal conditions of their creation, duration or extinction. It appears clearly that reciprocity cannot be invoked in order to excuse departure from the terms of a State's own declaration, whatever its scope, limitations or conditions.

The reference to duration requires comment. It must be read subject to the preceding words 'formal conditions of', which must in turn be taken as referring to some specific step such as a denunciation. Normally duration will not be a problem. Either an action will have been commenced before the duration expires, or it will not. In the latter case, the application will be ineffective; in the former, it will be valid. In the *Nottebohm* case,[211] after referring to the fact that the Guatemalan declaration of 27 January 1947 was to endure for a period of five years, the Court stated that there could be 'no doubt that an Application filed after the expiry of this period would not have the effect of legally seising the Court'.[212] Once the Court had been validly seised of a matter, however, an 'extrinsic fact such as the subsequent lapse of the Declaration, by reason of the expiry of the period or by denunciation, cannot deprive the Court of the jurisdiction already established'.[213] In other words, either an obligation to submit to the jurisdiction exists or it does not at the moment an application is made.

Where the issue is the denunciation of a declaration prior to the making of an application, the Court is faced with deciding upon the effectiveness of the former act. The Court in the *Nicaragua* case rejected the idea that reciprocity was a relevant factor in dealing with that issue:[214]

> The Court is not convinced that it would be appropriate, or possible, to try to determine whether a State against which proceedings had not yet been instituted could rely on a provision in another State's declaration to terminate or modify its obligations before the Court was seised. The United States argument attributes to the concept of reciprocity, as embodied in Article 36 of the Statute, especially in paragraphs 2 and 3, a meaning that goes beyond the way in which it has been interpreted by the Court, according to its consistent jurisprudence. That jurisprudence supports the view that a determination of the existence of the 'same obligation' requires the presence of two parties to a case, and a defined issue between them, which conditions can only be satisfied when proceedings have been instituted.

[209] *ICJ Reports*, 1984, at p. 419.
[210] Ibid.
[211] *ICJ Reports*, 1953, p. 111.
[212] At p. 121.
[213] At p. 123.
[214] *ICJ Reports*, 1984, at p. 420.

Among the dissenters, Judge Oda's view is difficult to understand. He asked whether, in the light of the reference to a declarant State recognizing as compulsory the jurisdiction of the Court 'in relation to any other State accepting the same obligation' in Article 36(2), it was 'reasonable or equitable to allow a party which, as a Respondent, is free to escape at any time from the compulsory jurisdiction of the Court to take advantage, as an Applicant, by imposing upon the other party the burden of inescapability, which it does not itself bear?'[215] The Judge then proceeded to provide this response:[216]

> The reciprocity of the obligation must exist at the date of the seisin of the case, and acceptance of the Court's jurisdiction by the Applicant and Respondent must be current at that date. I am of the view that Nicaragua is not in a position to invoke the obligation which it does not bear and the United States, as Respondent, has borne because of its previous obligation. Thus the United States is fully exempted from the Court's jurisdiction in relation to Nicaragua on the date of Nicaragua's Application.

Although this pronouncement may not be free of ambiguity, it would seem that Judge Oda was in favour of testing the application of the principle of reciprocity both at the time of the seisin of the case by the Court, and also retrospectively. The effectiveness of the Shultz letter depended upon the terms of the declaration of any State which, during the period of notice ostensibly required, actually made application to the Court against the United States.

Judge Jennings saw in this line of approach, 'espoused by the United States in its argument before the Court',[217] which he described as 'a doctrine of pre-seisin reciprocity',[218] 'a possible and practicable solution of the problem, that has considerable attraction'.[219] However, he also pointed out that the idea was 'not free from difficulty and would be something of an innovation'.[220] The critical issue was that 'what is sought to be "ascertained" at seisin—namely jurisdiction in respect of the subject-matter of the application—is quite different from what is in issue here: namely whether, or to what extent, a State can withdraw or alter its declaration, before seisin'.[221] Ultimately, the Judge's reason for rejecting the idea of a concept of pre-seisin reciprocity was that 'the practice of States—certainly the recent practice of States—has already gone beyond it'.[222] In his view there was 'ample evidence that States belonging to the Optional-Clause system have now generally the expectation that they can lawfully withdraw or alter

[215] At p. 511.
[216] Ibid.
[217] At p. 548.
[218] At p. 549.
[219] Ibid.
[220] Ibid.
[221] Ibid.
[222] At p. 550.

their declarations of acceptance at will, provided only that this is done before seisin'.[223]

(c) *Bilateral Aspects of Declarations under Article 36*

If the result of a series of unilateral acts by States making declarations under Article 36 is to create a form of quasi-treaty relationship between the States concerned, then it is arguable that a State in the position of the United States would be bound by the terms of its declaration *vis-à-vis* other declarant States.

Some support for this approach is to be found in the *Right of Passage* case.[224] Portugal, though a member of the United Nations and therefore a party to the Statute, accepted the Court's compulsory jurisdiction on 19 December 1955. Three days later it filed an application against India. The Court notified India by telegram of the application, but official notification of the existence and terms of the Portuguese declaration was not transmitted by the Secretary-General to the Indian Government until 19 January 1956. It was contended by India that the three days gap between the declaration and the application had not been sufficient time for the Secretary-General to transmit copies of the declaration to other parties to the Statute as required by Article 36(4); and that, until that step had been taken, there could be no legal relationship between Portugal and those parties. This contention the Court rejected in terms which have a bearing on the problem under discussion:[225]

> The Court considers that, by the deposit of its Declaration of Acceptance with the Secretary-General, the accepting State becomes a Party to the system of the Optional Clause in relation to the other declarant States, with all the rights and obligations deriving from Article 36. The contractual relation between the Parties and the compulsory jurisdiction of the Court resulting therefrom are established, '*ipso facto* and without special agreement', by the fact of the making of the Declaration. Accordingly, every State which makes a Declaration of Acceptance must be deemed to take into account the possibility that, under the Statute, it may at any time find itself subjected to the obligations of the Optional Clause in relation to a new Signatory as the result of the deposit by that Signatory of a Declaration of Acceptance. A State accepting the jurisdiction of the Court must expect that an Application may be filed against it before the Court by a new declarant State on the same day on which that State deposits with the Secretary-General its Declaration of Acceptance. For it is on that very day that the consensual bond, which is the basis of the Optional Clause, comes into being between the States concerned.

If a 'contractual relation', or a 'consensual bond', is created between the State making a declaration and all other parties that have made declarations accepting the Court's jurisdiction at the moment such declaration is made,

[223] Ibid. The correctness of this conclusion is of course dependent upon factors considered in the other parts of this section of the paper.

[224] *ICJ Reports*, 1957, p. 125.

[225] At p. 146.

it would seem to follow that a declarant State is bound by the terms of its declaration *vis-à-vis* those other States.

In the *Nicaragua* case, the Court adopted similar terminology, referring to the fact that 'the declarations, even though they are unilateral acts, establish a series of bilateral engagements with other States accepting the same obligation of compulsory jurisdiction, in which the conditions, reservations and time-limit clauses are taken into consideration'.[226] As has already been pointed out,[227] this pronouncement was made in the context of a discussion of the binding nature of unilateral declarations and the *Nuclear Tests* cases.[228] It is not altogether clear, therefore, what the basis was for the Court's subsequent assertion in the *Nicaragua* case that the United States, having chosen to include the six months' notice requirement in its declaration, had 'entered into an obligation which is binding upon it *vis-à-vis* other States parties to the Optional-Clause system'.[229] It could have been because of something inherent in the nature of a unilateral declaration stipulating a period of notice before withdrawal. Alternatively it might have been solely attributable to the special status of declarations made under Article 36 of the Statute.

There is no doubt that the legal relationships arising out of this system are of a 'unique character',[230] or '*sui generis*'.[231] However, it should be obvious that the emphasis is upon the word 'relationships' in the plural. Rosenne, in his analysis of the situation, seems to have run a number of different relationships together in the following passage:[232]

> This unique character of the legal bond existing between two States engaged upon litigation when both have, or may be deemed to have, accepted the compulsory jurisdiction, and the extreme difficulty of pinning down exactly what that bond is, who are the other parties to it, and when it arose (except in relation to the date of the institution of the proceedings) otherwise than in the context of a concrete case, imposes the maximum of caution before applying *en bloc* the general law of international treaties to that part of the transaction which supplies the consensual basis of the jurisdiction.

The situation has something in common with the case well known in Anglo-Australian law of *Clarke* v. *Dunraven*.[233] There could be no question that, when potential entrants to a yacht race sent signed letters to the secretary of the association which was organizing the races, they were signifying their assent to a contractual relationship with the association. However, the dispute was between two competitors whose yachts were involved in a collision. Had they bound themselves by a contract with each other to

[226] *ICJ Reports*, 1984, at p. 418.
[227] Above, p. 166.
[228] *ICJ Reports*, 1974, at p. 253.
[229] *ICJ Reports*, 1984, at p. 419.
[230] Rosenne, op. cit. above (n. 196), p. 414.
[231] *Nicaragua* case, *ICJ Reports*, 1984, at p. 546 (Judge Jennings); at p. 620 (Judge Schwebel).
[232] Op. cit. above (n. 196), p. 414.
[233] [1897] AC 59.

abide by the rules which the association had laid down for the conduct of the race? In answering this question in the affirmative, Lord Herschell had no doubt that the effect of the parties' 'entering for the race, and undertaking to be bound by these rules to the knowledge of each other' was sufficient to create a contractual relationship between them.[234]

With regard to declarations under Article 36, a nexus is created with the Court itself. In general terms, obligations are assumed towards all other declarant States (and indeed, to a more limited extent, to other States, parties to the Statute, which have not made a declaration under Article 36). More specifically, obligations are also created towards a particular State against which the State concerned makes application to the Court, or which makes application itself against the latter State. In *Clarke* v. *Dunraven*, the promise by one competitor to another was classified as 'a contractual obligation' in order to render it enforceable. In the case of declarations under Article 36, in order to render them enforceable in accordance with their terms, it was useful to refer to them as 'consensual' or 'bilateral'. In *Clarke* v. *Dunraven*, it may have been of value to consider the relationships as a series of contracts. The same may be true of relationships under Article 36 (as in the *Right of Passage* case,[235] where the Court referred to the 'consensual relations between the parties and the compulsory jurisdiction resulting therefrom'). However, it is not necessarily helpful or instructive to regard the result of such declarations as giving rise to 'treaties'.

In *Clarke* v. *Dunraven*, there was no real problem as to when the contractual relationship was created as the accident occurred at the end of the sequence of events, that is, in the course of a race. This is not dissimilar to the situation brought about as a result of an application to the Court by one of the parties to the system created by declaration under Article 36 against another such State. In the former case, it is possible to regard the contract as having come about at the time the various contestants, which had submitted entries, came under starter's order.[236] In the latter case, the extent of the obligations binding upon the applicant and respondent States could be tested from the moment the application was made.

However, with respect to both situations, it is possible to envisage circumstances in which it might be necessary to consider a relationship arising at an earlier stage. As far as Article 36 is concerned, the Nicaraguan position *vis-à-vis* the United States provides just such an example. It was necessary to rely upon the existence of a relationship predating the

[234] At p. 63.

[235] *ICJ Reports*, 1957, p. 125 at p. 146.

[236] See the views of the English Court of Appeal in the case, *sub nom*. *The Satanita*, [1895] P 248. According to one of the rules: 'Five minutes before the start . . . a gun [shall be] fired; after which the yachts in the race shall be amenable to the rules'. As Rigby LJ said (at p. 262):

> 'The contract did not arise with any one, other than the managing committee, at the moment that the yacht owner signed the document, which it was necessary to sign in order to be a competitor. But when the owner of the *Satanita* on the one hand, and the owner of the *Valkyrie* on the other, actually came forward and became competitors upon those terms. I think it would be idle to say that there was not then, and thereby, a contract between them.'

application by Nicaragua because, before that moment, the United States had purported to modify its declaration so as to exclude the application which Nicaragua was about to make. As far as the yachting illustration is concerned, if the rules had attempted to deal with pre-race accidents, there would have been no difficulty in establishing a contractual relationship to cover such circumstances. Salmond and Williams were prepared to construe a contract on the facts of the case as they actually occurred along the following lines:[237]

> The first competitor to enter must be taken to be offering, to all other persons who may subsequently enter, an undertaking to observe the rules, if they will for their part give similar undertakings. The second competitor to enter, by so doing, accepts this offer, and himself makes a similar offer to all persons who may subsequently enter; and so on.

The way in which the rules operated (in this case the time at which they began to operate, for example with regard to an incident before the vessels came under starter's orders) would depend upon the terms set out in the document to which the parties had assented. Similarly, in the case of declarations under Article 36, the way in which they operated (for example, with regard to a denunciation) would depend upon the terms set out in the declarations to which other declarants must be taken to have assented in the absence of any protest to the terms of any individual declaration.

(d) *The Relevance of Treaty Rules*

The Court has been ambivalent as to the nature of the bond created by declarations under Article 36, or by the combined effect of such declarations when an application has been made to the Court thus identifying the particular declarations between which the necessary nexus must exist to found the Court's jurisdiction. Inevitably, this attitude has been reflected in the way in which the Court has dealt with the relevance of treaty rules to the interpretation and application of unilateral declarations.

In the *Nicaragua* case, the analogy with treaty rules, as far as the declarations themselves were concerned, was drawn principally in relation to the issue of modification or withdrawal. However, the Court did equate treaties and unilateral declarations as far as the principle of good faith in international relations was concerned,[238] quoting in particular this passage from the *Nuclear Tests* cases:[239]

> One of the basic principles governing the creation and performance of legal obligations, whatever their source, is the principle of good faith. Trust and confidence are inherent in international co-operation, in particular in an age where this co-operation in many fields is becoming increasingly essential. Just as the very rule of

[237] Salmond and Williams, *Principles of the Law of Contracts* (2nd edn., 1945), p. 71.
[238] *ICJ Reports*, 1984, at p. 418; quoted above, p. 166.
[239] *ICJ Reports*, 1974, p. 253 at p. 268.

pacta sunt servanda in the law of treaties is based on good faith, so also is the binding character of an international obligation assumed by unilateral declaration.

Too much significance should not be attributed to the Court's words as far as the present discussion is concerned, because all the Court was saying was that legal obligations are dependent upon good faith, so that it mattered not whether the Optional Clause system was primarily bilateral or unilateral. In fact, of course, the Court went on to ascribe to the system aspects of both types of relationship when it said:[240]

Although the United States retained the right to modify the contents of the 1946 Declaration or to terminate it, a power which is inherent in any unilateral act of a State, it has, nevertheless, assumed an inescapable obligation towards other States accepting the Optional Clause, by stating formally and solemnly that any change should take effect only after six months have elapsed as from the date of notice.

For the Court, therefore, the principle of good faith, taken in conjunction with the bilateral nature of certain aspects of the Optional Clause system, rendered the six months' notice requirement binding *vis-à-vis* other States which had made declarations under Article 36(2). There was no need to rely upon treaty rules for this purpose, although the Court did observe, with respect to declarations of 'indefinite duration', that:[241]

It appears from the requirements of good faith that they should be treated, by analogy, according to the law of treaties, which requires a reasonable time for withdrawal from or termination of treaties that contain no provision regarding the duration of their validity.

It is not necessary to classify a relationship as arising by way of treaty to apply relevant rules of treaty law to the situation. In his first Report on the Law of Treaties, Lauterpacht asserted that it was 'clear that the totality of the declarations under the so-called optional clause of Article 36 of the Statute of the Court constitutes a treaty as between the parties making the declaration'.[242] He made this assertion despite the obvious fact that such declarations are not the outcome of a process of negotiation. Hence, it would be inappropriate, if not impossible, to apply to them rules of treaty interpretation based upon the intentions of the parties and the object and purpose for which a particular declaration was made. As the Court pointed out in the *Anglo-Iranian Oil Company* case,[243] in rejecting a rule of treaty interpretation, contended for by the United Kingdom, that a text should be interpreted, if possible, to give all words in it a meaning:[244]

the text of the Iranian Declaration is not a treaty text resulting from negotiations between two or more States. It is the result of unilateral drafting by the Government of Iran.

[240] *ICJ Reports*, 1984, at p. 419.
[241] At p. 420.
[242] *Yearbook of the International Law Commission*, 1953, vol. 2, p. 90 at p. 101.
[243] *ICJ Reports*, 1952, p. 93.
[244] At p. 105.

Nevertheless, for a time, the Commission adhered to the treaty analogy and even drafted its Articles on the Law of Treaties accordingly. Thus, Article 1(3) was once drafted as follows:[245]

> The present Code does not relate to international agreements not in written form; nor does it relate to unilateral declarations or other instruments of a unilateral character, except where these form an integral part of a group of instruments which, considered as a whole, constitute an international agreement, or have otherwise been expressed or accepted in such a way as to amount to or form part of such an agreement.

Subsequently, Waldock expressed the view that declarations under Article 36(2) 'were similar in nature to instruments of accession'.[246] At the same meeting, the Secretary of the Commission expressed his concern at their classification as unilateral declarations. He went on to say:[247]

> As a matter of theory that was perhaps possible, but such declarations could not be regarded as anything other than agreements or treaties within the meaning of the definition in Article 1, paragraph (a), of the draft. He held the view that those declarations constituted treaties themselves, though contained in separate instruments, and he thought that was also the view of many States. In fact those declarations were in practice required to be submitted to the legislature for action in accordance with the ratification process provided for in the laws and constitutions of the States.

The reference to declarations of this type was deleted from the draft Articles and in the Commentary, the amendment to the latter being proposed by Rosenne.[248] However, it seems clear enough, from the discussion in the Commission, that there was a good deal of support for the view expressed by the Secretary in the following form:[249]

> A declaration under article 36(2) of the Statute of the Court, although labelled a unilateral declaration, constituted an instrument ancillary to and an implementation of article 36. It was important to make it clear that the rules relating to such matters as the interpretation and the termination of treaties applied to declarations under article 36(2) of the Statute; otherwise much of the value of the draft articles would be lost.

Despite Rosenne's later suggestion that the deletion of the reference to declarations under Article 36(2) involved a rejection of such instruments as giving rise to a form of treaty relationship,[250] that is not the impression that is to be gained from reading the records of the International Law Commission.

Nevertheless, it has to be admitted that the issue is somewhat academic.

[245] *Yearbook of the International Law Commission*, 1959, vol. 2, p. 92; and comment thereon at p. 94.

[246] Ibid., 1962, vol. 1, p. 54.

[247] Ibid.

[248] Ibid., p. 265.

[249] At p. 56; see also Ago's comments at p. 57.

[250] See *The Law and Practice of the International Court* (2nd rev. edn., 1985), p. 410.

Under the Vienna Convention itself a treaty is defined in Article 2 as meaning, for 'the purposes of the present Convention',

> an international agreement concluded between States in written form and governed by international law, whether embodied in a single instrument or in two or more related instruments and whatever its particular designation.

If declarations do, in a number of ways, create agreements within this definition, it is also true that many of the conventional rules are inapplicable to the way in which declarations are made and operate. Nor does it really matter that the practice of States does not appear to comply with Article 56:

> 1. A treaty which contains no provision regarding its termination and which does not provide for denunciation or withdrawal is not subject to denunciation or withdrawal unless:
> (*a*) it is established that the parties intended to admit the possibility of denunciation or withdrawal; or
> (*b*) a right of denunciation or withdrawal may be implied by the nature of the treaty.
> 2. A party shall give not less than twelve months' notice of its intention to denounce or withdraw from a treaty under paragraph 1.

In the first place, the position with regard to declarations under Article 36(2) of the Statute would unquestionably fall within one or other of the exceptions in paragraph 1 of Article 56. With regard to paragraph 2, it is extremely doubtful whether that represents a requirement of universal application. It may be that withdrawal from a treaty of alliance following a change in the political complexion of the government of one of the States concerned could be justified by a plea of *rebus sic stantibus*. A more sensible approach is to regard such treaties as terminable upon reasonable notice, the period of the notice depending upon the circumstances. Nor should there be any such obstacle to, or limitation on, a State withdrawing from membership in an international organization.[251] Termination of many of the rights and duties could be immediate, though such matters as financial obligations might take a while to adjust. The practice of States also justifies the application of a different rule for declarations under Article 36(2). As Waldock concluded in his analysis of the position:[252]

> Taken as a whole, State practice under the optional clause, and especially the modern trend towards Declarations terminable upon notice, seem only to reinforce the clear conclusion to be drawn from treaties of arbitration, conciliation and judicial settlement, that these treaties are regarded as essentially of a terminable character.

And the practice in question clearly establishes a right to terminate with immediate effect in the absence of a specific requirement of notice in the declaration itself.

[251] See *Yearbook of the International Law Commission*, 1963, vol. 2, p. 69.
[252] Ibid., p. 68; quoted by Judge Schwebel in the *Nicaragua* case, *ICJ Reports*, 1984, at p. 621.

Of course, if the Article 36(2) relationships are not classifiable as constituting treaty arrangements,[253] then the same practice in any case establishes the right of termination whatever the classification that is made. In that case, other treaty rules would only operate by analogy in appropriate circumstances. As Judge Jennings pointed out:[254]

> the discussion in the oral proceedings of whether or not the legal position of declarations under the Optional Clause is, or is not, governed by the law of treaties, I found not entirely helpful and in any event inconclusive. The fact of the matter must surely be that the Optional-Clause regime is *sui generis*. Doubtless some parts of the law of treaties may be applied by useful analogy; but so may the law governing unilateral declarations; and so, most certainly, may the law deriving from the practice of States in respect of such declarations.

(e) *Summary*

The relationship between the Shultz letter and the period of notice contained in the United States declaration was not primarily a matter of interpretation. It was in part an issue of classification: where on the spectrum between a unilateral act and a bilateral (or multilateral) agreement did a declaration under Article 36(2) fall? The closer it was to a treaty relationship the more substantial the reasons for regarding the United States as bound to abide by the prescribed period of notice. The more the declaration could be regarded as unilateral in nature and consequences, the less strong those reasons might seem. Indeed the practice of States appeared to support, or at least concede, a right of unilateral termination of such declarations, although there was no clear evidence of the consequences of taking such a step in breach of the specific terms of the declaration itself.

In the latter situation the effect of taking such a step might depend, as in the case of the denunciation of a treaty, upon the acceptance of the instrument's termination by the other party or parties. In other words, this result would depend upon at least its or their acquiescence. Such an inference could not have been drawn in favour of the United States in a situation where Nicaragua made application to the Court a few days after the Shultz letter and persisted with the proceedings in reliance upon the continued effectiveness of the United States declaration. On this basis, it made little difference whether acquiescence (i.e. a failure to object within a reasonable time to the United States' modification of its declaration) was necessary, or whether, as in the Court's view, a denunciation or modification of a unilateral instrument was possible in any case on giving reasonable notice (the specified period of notice contained in the instrument itself presumably simply being one of the factors to be taken into account in assessing what constitutes such reasonable notice). Overall, the duty to act in good faith

[253] Which was very much Waldock's view in his judicial capacity in the joint dissenting opinion in the *Nuclear Tests* cases: see above, p. 166 n. 192.

[254] *ICJ Reports*, 1984, at p. 546.

constituted an aspect of treaty relations and of the creation of obligations by unilateral acts. In either case, some respect was due to the period of notice which the United States had promised to give other declarant States in the way in which it had framed its own declaration accepting the Court's jurisdiction, and by this promise at least the United States was bound.

V. The Connally (Automatic) Reservation

A curious aspect of the *Nicaragua* case was the fact that the United States did not take advantage of the reservation in its declaration containing the Connally amendment.[255] By determining that the dispute related to matters 'essentially within the domestic jurisdiction of the United States', the United States could have argued that the case was thus excluded from the ambit of its declaration.

It is probable that there were a number of factors involved in the decision on the part of the United States not to invoke this reservation. The fear may have been that the Court might have interpreted the reservation in ways which the United States would have found unacceptable. Accordingly, if it was going to make use of the reservation on future occasions, the United States would have preferred to do so in circumstances where it was likely to be regarded with greater sympathy by the Court. As far as the possible interpretations open to the Court were concerned, the issue would undoubtedly have been raised of the potential conflict between the self-judging nature of the reservation and the concept of justiciability, particularly as defined in Article 36(6) of the Statute. If the United States had sought to gain the maximum benefit by arguing that the reservation retained an unqualified discretion for the United States to decide for itself whether a case was within its domestic jurisdiction and therefore not justiciable, the reservation was in conflict with the inherent power of any judicial tribunal to determine its own jurisdiction, and more specifically with the Statute itself, Article 36(6) of which provides that the question of whether the Court has jurisdiction in a particular case is to be determined by the Court.[256]

Should the Court have decided that there was a conflict between the terms of a reservation and the Statute, it is likely that it would have regarded the reservation as void. This would have given rise to two possible alternative consequences. One would have been for the Court to hold that, because of the vital role the reservation played in relation to the declaration as a whole, the invalidity of the former vitiated the effectiveness of the latter. This ruling would have been embarrassing for the United States,

[255] Above, p. 122. The United States informed the Court that it did not intend to invoke the Connally 'proviso' at the jurisdictional stage, but stated that this was without prejudice to its rights 'under that provison in relation to any subsequent pleadings, proceedings, or cases before this Court' (*ICJ Reports*, 1984, at p. 422).

[256] See above, pp. 142–3.

particularly as, because of the alternative, though more limited, basis of jurisdiction available under the Treaty of Friendship, the United States would not have had the compensatory benefit of the Court having to discontinue the case. On the other hand, the Court could, while holding that the reservation itself was invalid, have nevertheless decided that the reservation could be severed from the declaration, leaving the remainder of the declaration in being, and therefore as constituting a valid basis of jurisdiction. There could have been a further possibility stemming from the potential conflict between the reservation and the Statute. In order to avoid declaring the reservation invalid on the ground of its conflict with the concept of justiciability and the power of the Court to determine its own jurisdiction, the Court could have limited the discretion open to a State under an automatic reservation. If the reservation was open to objective assessment by the Court (as opposed to subjective determination by the declarant State), the conflict would disappear. It is this last possibility which will be examined first.

(a) *Subjecting the Reservation to a Requirement of Good Faith*

A determination by a declarant State that the circumstances for bringing into effect an automatic reservation, contained in its declaration, had been satisfied would be reviewable by the International Court if the discretion created by such a reservation could be limited by some objectively ascertainable criterion. Thus, if the determination could be tested by the requirement that it should be made in good faith, the Court could impose its own standard on the conduct of the declarant State.

The view has been expressed, however, that there is no scope for the imposition of a duty to act in good faith upon a State making a determination in accordance with the terms of an automatic reservation. Crawford, for example, asserted that 'attempts to give content to the "obligation" of an automatic reservation by implying a duty to make a determination in good faith, or allowing the Court to set aside a manifestly unfounded determination as an *abus de droit*, are unlikely to succeed'.[257] The justification usually given is that States making such reservations intend 'to reserve the matter from judicial determination', this being 'precisely the point of making the automatic reservation'.[258] In adopting this position, Crawford was influenced by Judge Lauterpacht's assertions in the *Norwegian Loans* case:[259]

[257] 'The Legal Effect of Automatic Reservations to the Jurisdiction of the International Court', this *Year Book*, 50 (1979), p. 63 at p. 67.

[258] Crawford, loc. cit. (previous note).

[259] *ICJ Reports*, 1957, p. 9 at pp. 52–3. See also the words of Judge Spender in the *Interhandel* case, *ICJ Reports*, 1959, p. 6 at pp. 57–8; and the following statement by Judge Lauterpacht, at p. 111:

'The Court cannot arrogate to itself the competence to curtail that right of final determination by assuming the power to decide whether that right has been exercised reasonably or in good faith. To assume any such power would mean to deny to the United States of America the very right which it stipulated as a condition of its Declaration of Acceptance and which, if there were any doubt on the

The legal obligation of a Government to avail itself of its freedom of action in a manner consistent with good faith has a meaning, in terms of legal obligation, only when room is left for an impartial finding whether the duty to act in accordance with good faith has been complied with. But in the case now before the Court any such possibility has been expressly excluded. The Court has no power to give a decision on the question whether a State has acted in good faith in claiming that a dispute covers a matter which is essentially within its domestic jurisdiction. If the Court were to do so, it would be arrogating to itself a power which has been expressly denied to it. . . . [I]t is abundantly clear from the evidence which is generally available that the authors of the 'automatic reservation' have reserved for the Governments concerned the right to judge whether in invoking it in a particular case they have complied with the obligation to act in good faith. They have repeatedly declared that their own sense of international duty and propriety, public opinion within and outside their countries, and their reputation and prestige in the world would constitute a restraining factor of great potency in shaping their decision. But they have denied to the Court the power to determine the legality of that decision from the point of view of the obligation to act in good faith or otherwise. They have reserved that power to themselves.

Against this view, and in favour of a limitation being placed upon the discretion of the reserving State, may be quoted a number of opinions. In the first place, as Judge Lauterpacht admitted,[260] he had himself proclaimed the contrary position in his Report on the Law of Treaties.[261] In an attempt to escape from the shackles of the unanimity principle in relation to the need for consent to reservations to a multilateral treaty, Lauterpacht, as Special Rapporteur, had proposed that if 'two-thirds or more of the parties feel that the State making the reservation acts in good faith and in a manner which is not so unreasonable as to interfere decisively with the purpose of the treaty, then . . . that State ought not to be precluded from becoming a party to the treaty'.[262] It is clear that the Rapporteur was including relationships arising from declarations made under Article 36 of the Statute of the International Court within the scope of his survey, because he went on to say, in support of departing from the unanimity principle:[263]

It is difficult to apply to multilateral treaties the rigid requirements of the unity of the contractual relation. There is, for instance—to mention what is in effect one of the most important multilateral instruments—only a general unity and symmetry of contract in what is essentially a collective treaty of international judicial settlement resulting from the declarations of acceptance of the optional clause of article 36 of the Statute of the International Court of Justice. We find there a multiplicity of relations brought about by the interplay of reciprocity in connexion with

subject, is substantiated as rooted in an historic tradition of striking continuity. Of that tradition it is beyond the power of the Court to approve or to disapprove. This would be so even if there did not exist the additional and weighty reason that the greatest caution must guide the Court, in the matter of its jurisdiction, in attributing to a sovereign State bad faith, an abuse of a right, or unreasonableness in the fulfilment of its obligations.'

260 *Norwegian Loans* case, *ICJ Reports*, 1957, at p. 52.

261 *Yearbook of the International Law Commission*, 1953, vol. 2, p. 90.

262 At p. 126.

263 At p. 127.

reservations nowhere expressly authorized in the original instrument and never expressly accepted by the States parties to the optional clause.

With regard to the specific problem of reservations which were so extensive that they deprived the accession to the treaty of all content, the Rapporteur regarded the need to find a third of the States parties to the treaty to approve of the reservation in question as sufficient guarantee against abuse:[264]

It is in the light of such considerations that a compromise must be sought between the claims of universality and the integrity of the convention. These considerations provide the answer to the contention that half a loaf, secured by the universality of treaties, is preferable to no proof at all or to its integrity achieved at the expense of drastically reducing the number of the parties to the treaty. Half a loaf may be better than no bread. But there ought to be at least some approximation to half a loaf. Thus, for instance, if a Government in accepting a treaty were to add a reservation to the effect that it is under no obligation to apply the provisions of the treaty in cases in which they are in conflict with its law or if it were to reserve the right to determine in each disputed case the extent of its obligation, it might be held that the right to conclude a treaty is being diverted from its true purpose and that the reservation is of such a nature as to exclude the State in question from participation in the treaty. This is a conclusion which ought not to be made lightly. The danger of abuse or arbitrariness in reaching a conclusion of so serious a nature is effectively met by the provision of the present draft requiring the concurrence, for that purpose, of not less than one-third of the States accepting the obligations of the treaty concerned.

Although there is little evidence of the attitude of most States which are parties to the system of compulsory jurisdiction, the good faith limitation has received some support. Despite the fact that it was seeking to take advantage of the automatic reservation in the French declaration in the *Norwegian Loans* case, Norway advocated the imposition of such a limitation:[265]

such a reservation must be interpreted in good faith and should a government seek to rely upon it with a view to denying the jurisdiction of the Court which manifestly did not invoke a 'matter which is essentially within the national jurisdiction' it would be committing an *abus de droit* which would not prevent the Court from acting.

With regard to the United States, its position on the matter has not been uniform. In its statement of the law submitted to the Court in the *Interhandel* proceedings, the United States had referred to any determination it might make under the Connally reservation as being 'not subject to review or approval by any tribunal'.[266] However, less than two years later, the United States espoused a totally different line in the *Aerial Incident* case.

264 At p. 128.

265 For the orginal French version, see *ICJ Pleadings*, vol. 1, p. 131. The translation is taken from the separate opinion of Judge Lauterpacht in that case, *ICJ Reports*, 1957, at p. 53.

266 *ICJ Pleadings*, p. 320.

In its observations of February 1960 on the Bulgarian preliminary objections, the United States maintained that the Connally reservation 'does not permit the Government of the United States, or any other government seeking to rely on this reservation reciprocally, arbitrarily to characterize the subject matter of a suit as "essentially within the domestic jurisdiction" ';[267] the United States reservation 'does not permit the United States or any other State to make an arbitrary determination, in bad faith'.[268] Later in the same document, it was said: 'It is the view of the United States that reservation (*b*) does not confer a power to nullify the jurisdiction of this Court through arbitrary determination that a particular subject matter of dispute is essentially domestic'.[269]

Subsequently, in another *volte face*, the American Agent in the proceedings requested their discontinuance. In the course of the letter containing the request, the earlier United States position advanced in the *Interhandel* case was reaffirmed: such a 'determination is not subject to review or approval by any tribunal, and it operates to remove definitely from the jurisdiction of the Court the matter which it determines'.[270] This final assertion undoubtedly represented the more generally held United States view of the intended effect of the Connally reservation. It does not follow, however, that the Court should regard itself as bound by this aspect of American

[267] *ICJ Pleadings*, p. 305.

[268] At p. 308.

[269] At p. 324. With regard to the views it had advanced in the *Interhandel* case, the United States explained them as follows (at p. 323):

> 'When reservation (*b*) was being debated on the floor of the United States Senate in August 1946, the author of the reservation here considered made the following statement:
>
> "Several Senators have argued that by this amendment the United States would put itself in the position of corruptly and improperly claiming that a question is domestic in nature when it is not, thereby taking advantage of an international dispute and saying that since the question is domestic, we will not abide by the decision of the Court. Mr President, I have more faith in my Government than that. I do not believe the United States would adopt a subterfuge, a pretext, or a pretence in order to block the judgment of the Court on any such grounds." 92 Cong. Rec. 10695 (1946).
>
> In fact, the United States has given a practical construction to reservation (*b*) which is altogether consistent with the statement just quoted. For example, in the *Interhandel* case, the United States invoked reservation (*b*) with respect to the issue of title to shares of stock in an American corporation, while agreeing that the issue of its liability to compensate certain aliens for a taking of these shares was not essentially a matter of domestic jurisdiction. The United States considers that the practice followed by a State with respect to its own reservation is entitled to great weight in the construction of that reservation when it is invoked by another State.'

[270] At p. 677. The letter continued (ibid.):

> 'A determination under reservation (*b*) that a matter is essentially domestic constitutes an absolute bar to jurisdiction irrespective of the propriety or arbitrariness of the determination. Although the United States has adhered to the policy of not making any arbitrary determination under reservation (*b*), the pursuit of that policy does not affect the legal scope of the reservation.'

It has been suggested by Crawford (loc. cit. above (n. 257), at p. 67) that this action by the United States in some way advances the case of those arguing against the good faith limitation upon the discretion apparently claimed by the declarant State:

> 'Even if standards exist against which a determination could be assessed for *bona fides*, it seems clear that no such assessment was intended to be allowed. If confirmation is needed, it is provided by the withdrawal of the United States' argument to the contrary in the *Aerial Incident* case.'

The American communication to the Court can hardly be termed a 'confirmation': it is at best evidence supporting that writer's view, but only in so far as the terms of the withdrawal letter might reduce the effects of the argument to the contrary which the United States had at first put forward.

policy and intentions towards the Court and its jurisdiction, an issue which will be returned to later.[271] Moreover, there is no conclusive reason why one should accept so readily, as does Crawford, Lauterpacht's later view in preference to his earlier approach, or to a number of other opinions and factors suggesting that, or why, the Court might prefer to exert greater control over the scope of its own jurisdiction.

(b) *Adjudging the Reservation Invalid*

The other fear which the United States may have entertained was the possibility of the Court striking down the reservation while leaving intact the remainder of the declaration. As has already been mentioned, the Lauterpacht line was that the invalidity of the reservation stemmed from its inconsistency with the nature of a legal obligation[272] and conflict with Article 36(6) of the Statute;[273] and that, as the reservation was an essential part of the declaration, without which it would not have been ratified by the American Senate, the invalidity of the reservation destroyed the effectiveness of the declaration as a whole. It has also been pointed out that such an extreme consequence would not have greatly benefited the United States in the *Nicaragua* case. Although it would have deprived the Court of jurisdiction by virtue of Article 36, the Court would still have been able to proceed against the United States by virtue of the 1956 Treaty of Friendship.

From the American viewpoint, however, the more undesirable result would have been for the Court to have declared the reservation invalid but to have severed it from the remainder, leaving the substance of the declaration in force.[274] This doctrine is familiar in Anglo-Australian law as a means of saving from extinction a covenant in restraint of trade that is drafted unreasonably widely: 'Given that a particular promise in a contract is expressed too widely, and is consequently an unreasonable restraint on the ability of one party to trade, the covenant may be saved if some of the words therein can be deleted, so that the resulting restraint is not unreasonable.'[275]

The application of a similar approach to a declaration containing an automatic reservation was endorsed by Judge Klaestad in the *Interhandel* case. He pointed out that the American Senate had not considered the possibility that the consequence of the Connally amendment might be to render the entire declaration a nullity. It was therefore the true intention of the United

[271] See further below, pp. 191–2.

[272] For the Judge's views on automatic reservations in general with regard to this point, see the *Norwegian Loans* case, *ICJ Reports*, 1957, p. 9 at pp. 48–55, and above, p. 142.

[273] For the Judge's discussion of the question whether 'the 'automatic reservation' [is] consistent with the Statute', see *ICJ Reports*, 1957, at pp. 43–48.

[274] As for Judge Lauterpacht's answer to the question whether 'the "automatic reservation" [can] be separated from the Acceptance as such', see at pp. 55–9. For a summary of the Judge's views with regard to the United States' reservation, see the *Interhandel* case, *ICJ Reports*, 1959, p. 6 at pp. 101–2. Substantially the same conclusion was reached by Judge Spender, at pp. 55–9.

[275] Greig and Davis, *The Law of Contract* (1987), p. 1113.

States 'to issue a real and effective Declaration accepting the compulsory jurisdiction of the Court',[276] a view borne out by subsequent invitations issued by the United States to other States to file declarations of acceptance.[277] Hence, though the Court was prevented from acting on that part of the declaration which was in conflict with Article 36(6), 'this circumstance does not necessarily imply that it is impossible for the Court to give effect to other parts of the Declaration of Acceptance which are in conformity with the Statute'.[278]

Judge Lauterpacht had not been totally impervious to the possibility of severance in relation to parts of a declaration of acceptance of the Court's jurisdiction. In the *Norwegian Loans* case, he had called in aid 'general principles of law as developed in municipal law'[279] as the basis of the proposition that:[280]

> It is legitimate—perhaps obligatory—to sever an invalid condition from the rest of the instrument and to treat the latter as valid provided that having regard to the intention of the parties and the nature of the instrument the condition in question does not constitute an essential part of the instrument. . . . The same applies also to provisions and reservations relating to the jurisdiction of the Court. It would be consistent with the previous practice of the Court that it should, if only possible, uphold its jurisdiction when such a course is compatible with the intention of the parties and that it should not allow its jurisdiction to be defeated as the result of remediable defects of expression which are not of an essential character.

In this case, however, it was not open to the Court to adopt such a course:[281]

> For the principle of severance applies only to provisions and conditions which are not of the essence of the undertaking. Now an examination of the history of this particular form of the reservation of national jurisdiction shows that the unilateral right of determining whether the dispute is essentially within domestic jurisdiction has been regarded by the declaring State as one of the crucial limitations—perhaps the crucial limitation—of the obligation undertaken by the acceptance of the Optional Clause of Article 36 of the Statute.

The matter was raised again in the *Nuclear Tests* cases. By then, France had withdrawn its automatic reservation with regard to matters of 'national jurisdiction'. However, the replacement version still contained what Australia argued was a potentially subjective element in the form of a reservation excluding from the Court's jurisdiction:

> disputes arising out of a war or international hostilities, disputes arising out of a crisis affecting national security or out of any measure or action relating thereto, and disputes concerning activities connected with national defence.

[276] *ICJ Reports*, 1959, at p. 77.
[277] At p. 78.
[278] Ibid.
[279] *ICJ Reports*, 1957, at p. 56.
[280] At pp. 56–7.
[281] At p. 57.

In Australia's view, despite the apparently objective form in which it was cast, the meaning to be attached to the words 'activities connected with national defence' could 'never be ascertained independently of the views of the Government of France'.[282] As the Australian Memorial went on to explain:[283]

> It would not be for the Government of Australia nor for the Court itself to attempt to put objective content into it. This would be the task of the Government of France alone and it would be precisely because it was a task that only she could perform that the truly subjective nature of the reservation would be revealed. This might well explain why the Government of France did not develop in its Note or Annex the assertion that French tests in the Pacific constituted an activity connected with national defence, being convinced that it alone could determine whether or not it was.

On the basis that the reservation could be treated as invalid on the Lauterpacht approach, Australia argued that the effect was not to nullify the entire declaration. Unlike the earlier French declaration in issue in the *Norwegian Loans* case, or the United States declaration considered in the *Interhandel* case, the segment of the present French declaration was not 'an essential part of the instrument'.[284] This could be deduced not just from the imprecise way in which the reference to national defence was formulated, but also from the fact that these words had been added to a reservation which, from 1959 until 1966, had been limited to:

> disputes arising out of any war or international hostilities and disputes arising out of a crisis affecting the national security or out of any measure or action relating thereto.

It could not, or could not so easily, therefore be argued that France would not have submitted to the Court's jurisdiction at all without the protection of the additional limitation.

There was a measure of contrivance in this part of Australia's case on the jurisdictional issues, not least because the changes to the French declaration had been designed to deal with specific circumstances, so that it was by no means certain that France would have maintained its pre-1966 declaration. The addition of the reference to national defence 'was believed to be related to France's changed policies towards the North Atlantic Treaty Organisation, and to opposition to the projected programme of French nuclear tests in the Pacific'.[285] As events were to prove, rather than be faced

[282] *Nuclear Tests* cases, *ICJ Pleadings*, vol. 1, p. 308. Or, as the New Zealand memorial expressed the position (*ICJ Pleadings*, vol. 2, p. 194):

> 'the test of consistency with the requirements of the Statute is one of substance, not of form. The fact that a declarant State has avoided a patently subjective formulation of its reservations may, indeed, provide an indication of intention; but this interpretation must yield if the Court should find that the scope of the reservation cannot objectively be determined.'

[283] *ICJ Pleadings*, vol. 1, p. 308.

[284] Judge Lauterpacht in the *Norwegian Loans* case, *ICJ Reports*, 1957, at p. 57, quoted *Nuclear Tests* cases, *ICJ Pleadings*, vol. 1, p. 310.

[285] New Zealand memorial, ibid., vol. 2, p. 196.

with a challenge over this latter issue, France did withdraw its declaration in the aftermath of the proceedings in the *Nuclear Tests* cases.[286]

(c) *Analysis*

1. *A matter of interpretation*

Be that as it may, the Australian line of argument only casts limited light upon the question of the validity or otherwise of the American reservation and declaration. From one point of view it supported the cause of complete invalidity in that it endorsed the Lauterpacht thesis with respect to that declaration, though it proceeded to argue that the situation was distinguishable on the ground that the national defence exception was not crucial to the declaration. However, it cannot be certain whether the Australian Government fully endorsed this view of automatic reservations (after all, it had made no objections to such reservations at the time they had been made), or whether it was an *ad hoc*, and not well thought out, reaction to the exigencies of the particular case. Obviously, as with all applicant States reacting to an automatic reservation in the declaration of the respondent State, Australia wished to avoid admitting that total invalidity was a possibility, as the consequence of such a finding would have been to deprive the Court of jurisdiction under Article 36.

On the other hand, it may have been thought that there was some (perhaps psychological) advantage to be gained from denigrating the French declaration, or at least the relevant part of it. It may have seemed a preferable mode of attack rather than to argue that the reservation was valid as long as it was open to review by application of the good faith limitation upon its scope. The reason for choosing to avoid the latter approach might have been the perception that it would have been unlikely that the Court would have regarded a determination by France that the conducting of atmospheric nuclear tests was a matter of national defence as constituting an act in bad faith.

New Zealand did not feel inhibited in this way, although it adopted a more subtle approach. It contended that the application of the French reservation was a straightforward issue of interpreting the declaration as a whole, in the light of the surrounding circumstances. In the New Zealand view, those circumstances appeared 'to reinforce the evidence of a conflict of intention in the text of the French reservation, with the danger of encompassing its invalidity'.[287] In other words, invalidity was a potential end result of the process of interpretation. The New Zealand memorial explained the source of this problem as follows:[288]

[286] France notified the termination of its declarations of acceptance of the Court's compulsory jurisdiction by a letter of 2 January 1974: see International Court of Justice *Yearbook*, 1973–4, p. 49.
[287] *Nuclear Tests* cases, *ICJ Pleadings*, vol. 2, p. 197.
[288] Ibid., pp. 197–8.

This situation is, of course, the product of the tensions experienced, in great or less degree, by every State which desires to assume, and yet to limit, the reciprocal play of rights and obligations under the optional clause. In the case of France, this tension may well have been extreme, because it involved the balancing of a long record of loyalty to the Court's compulsory jurisdiction with a marked disinclination to accept restrictions upon its national freedom of action.

The resolution of this conflict was to be found in the construction of the 'actual wording' of a particular reservation.[289] In this case, there was no reason why, in the view of the New Zealand Government, 'the concept of "activities connected with national defence" can in its ordinary meaning extend to a programme of nuclear weapons testing in the atmosphere, carried out in a region of the world far removed from metropolitan France, contrary to the wishes of the Governments and peoples of that region'.[290] But if France should have claimed that such activity automatically, according to its own classification, fell within the rubric of national defence, this would have amounted to an acknowledgement of the reservation's invalidity, 'for the Court cannot administer a reservation which in effect leaves it to the declarant State to assert its own conception of its vital interests'.[291]

The New Zealand memorial thus indicated, without spelling out, an inherent weakness in the Lauterpacht view. The latter concentrated upon the forces within the United States Senate which sought to limit, to eradicate, the obligation to place American interests at risk before the Court. The countervailing factor, in the form of the executive's intention to assume, on behalf of the United States, obligations with regard to the judicial settlement of disputes, was downplayed or ignored.[292]

This tendency[293] is the more surprising because the tension between the two attitudes was even more apparent in the United States declaration than in the French declaration of 1966, which was examined by New Zealand. It was more apparent both in comparing the texts themselves and with regard

[289] Ibid., p. 198.

[290] Ibid.

[291] Ibid.

[292] This is something of a simplification as much of the impetus for submitting to the jurisdiction seems to have come from Congress: see Wilcox, 'The United States Accepts Compulsory Jurisdiction', *American Journal of International Law*, 40 (1946), p. 699, though the balance of the account may have been affected by the fact that the writer worked for the Library of Congress as Head International Relations Analyst. There was a division of opinion on the matter between the Senate and the State Department: see Briggs, 'Reservations to the Acceptance of Compulsory Jurisdiction of the International Court of Justice', *Recueil des cours*, 93 (1958–I), p. 223 at pp. 334–5.

[293] Tendency because it is not confined to Lauterpacht. It was of course a criticism of the Connally amendment made at the outset in the United States itself: see Preuss, 'The International Court of Justice, the Senate, and Matters of Domestic Jurisdiction', *American Journal of International Law*, 40 (1946), p. 720. However, it is a view which has found extraordinary support, or acceptance, amongst international lawyers from Britain: see Waldock, 'The Plea of Domestic Jurisdiction before International Legal Tribunals', this *Year Book*, 31 (1954), p. 96 at pp. 131–7: Merrills, 'The Optional Clause Today', ibid. 50 (1979), p. 87 at p. 114, describing 'the Waldock/Lauterpacht view' as having 'much to commend it'; cp. Crawford, 'The Legal Effect of Automatic Reservations to the Jurisdiction of the International Court', ibid., p. 63, esp. at pp. 83–6.

to the evidence of the *travaux* available with respect to the two instruments. Moreover, there was a more obvious problem of a potential conflict with Article 36(6) of the Statute in the case of the United States domestic jurisdiction reservation than there was *vis-à-vis* the French reservation concerning national defence.

Given these factors, it is difficult to accept the Lauterpacht approach which seemed to constitute such a departure from the normal rules of interpretation. It is true that the rules laid down in Articles 31 and 32 of the Vienna Convention on the Law of Treaties 1969 are not entirely apposite because they concern the negotiation and adoption of bilateral or multilateral instruments. In so far as that process envisages an identification of the intention of the parties,[294] there is a temptation to substitute for this, in the case of unilateral acts, the subjective intention of the declarant State.[295] To an extent, this might be justifiable in setting the limits upon a title of jurisdiction.[296] However, in relation to automatic reservations, the subjective intention was employed to override the objective manifestation of the declaration (including the reservation) in question having legal effect.

It has already been pointed out that this approach has only been possible because of a myopic view of the evidence of the declarant State's intentions, to the disregard of the factors militating in favour of the attempt to accept a juridical obligation. However, doubts as to the sustainability of the Lauterpacht view do not end there. The United States declaration was a response to the call from the San Francisco Conference to all members of the United Nations 'that as soon as possible they make declarations recognizing the obligatory jurisdiction of the International Court of Justice according to the provisions of Article 36 of the Statute'.[297] The declaration should therefore be regarded as intended to create such an obligation, though, for domestic

[294] According to Article 31(1):

> 'A treaty shall be interpreted in good faith in accordance with the ordinary meaning to be given to the terms of the treaty in their context and in the light of its object and purpose'.

This provision can reasonably be regarded as a means of implementing what McNair described as the task of treaty interpretation, namely, 'the duty of giving effect to the expressed intentions of the parties, that is, their intention as expressed in the words used by them in the light of the surrounding circumstances' (McNair, *The Law of Treaties* (1961), p. 365). McNair went on to state that 'the essential quest in the application of treaties [was] to search for the real intention of the contracting parties in using the language employed by them' (p. 386).

[295] As the International Court said in the *Anglo-Iranian Oil Company* case, *ICJ Reports*, 1952, p. 93 at p. 104:

> 'the Court cannot base itself on a purely grammatical interpretation of the text. It must seek the interpretation which is in harmony with a natural and reasonable way of reading the text, having due regard to the intention of the Government of Iran at the time when it accepted the compulsory jurisdiction of the Court.'

In this case, 'the natural and reasonable way' coincided with the apparent intentions of Iran. The above statement would have been less acceptable if the interpretation had been influenced by the subjective, and by no means apparent, intentions of Iran.

[296] As in the *Anglo-Iranian Oil Company* case, *ICJ Reports*, 1952, at pp. 106–7; *Aegean Sea* case, *ICJ Reports*, 1978, p. 3.

[297] *Documents of the United Nations Conference on International Organization*, vol. 13, p. 413.

political and constitutional reasons,[298] it was made subject to a number of reservations including the infamous Connally amendment. Even without evidence of a wish on the part of the executive to respond to the call by the San Francisco Conference, the existence of a desire to accept the Court's jurisdiction can be elicited both from the background circumstances in the San Francisco records and from the text of the United States declaration. The tension between this objective, and a countervailing wish to avoid such a commitment, is undoubtedly present, but that is not an unusual feature of declarations under Article 36.

In normal circumstances, any ambiguity created by this tension is for the Court to resolve as a matter of interpretation. One can also accept, as the starting point for this process, the assertion by Judge Lauterpacht that the 'Court is the guardian of its Statute' and that it 'is not within its power to abandon, in deference to a reservation made by a party, a function which by virtue of an express provision of its Statute is an essential safeguard of its compulsory jurisdiction'.[299] However, the course adopted by the Judge to resolve the conflict between the apparent assumption of a legal obligation on the one hand, and its apparent denial on the other, was the path of absurdity: to conclude that the attempted acceptance of legal obligations was devoid of legal effect. It is certainly the task of an interpreter to find a meaning which resolves an ambiguity, including a potential conflict between different parts of an instrument, with least violence to the text, but not if that creates an absurdity.[300]

The matter of interpretation can be approached from a different angle. The exclusive power of the Court to decide whether it has jurisdiction in a particular case is in no sense a secret: it is expressly and unequivocally set out in Article 36(6) of the Statute. It is therefore binding on parties to the Statute and they can hardly deny knowledge of it. No State can accept the jurisdiction of the Court on other terms. If it appears to have attempted to do so, it should be assumed that such was not its purpose and the declaration interpreted accordingly. As to what that interpretation might be in the present circumstances, the issue will be addressed shortly.

[298] A declaration under Article 36 was not, strictly speaking, a treaty, and various possibilities were raised as to how the matter should be dealt with under the United States Constitution: see Wilcox, 'The United States Accepts Compulsory Jurisdiction', *American Journal of International Law*, 40 (1946), p. 699 at pp. 705–7.

[299] *Interhandel* case, *ICJ Reports*, 1959, p. 6 at p. 104.

[300] As is obvious from Article 32 of the Vienna Convention on the Law of Treaties 1969, the whole purpose of interpretation is to avoid a result which is 'manifestly absurd or unreasonable.' Article 32 reads:

> 'Recourse may be had to supplementary means of interpretation, including the preparatory work of the treaty and the circumstances of its conclusion, in order to confirm the meaning resulting from the application of article 31, or to determine the meaning when the interpretation according to article 31:
> (a) leaves the meaning ambiguous or obscure; or
> (b) leads to a result which is manifestly absurd or unreasonable'.

2. *The primacy of international law over municipal law*

There are, however, further grounds for not accepting the Lauterpacht line. Whether international obligations are approached from the point of view of their creation or enforcement, it is the formal, external act which is crucial.

A number of rules or principles stem from this basic consideration. For example, international law is not usually concerned with whether the internal requirements of a State's constitutional law have been complied with.[301] Nor does it matter whether, if necessary, legislation has been passed to enable a State to comply with the obligations it has assumed by its conduct on the international plane. It is trite law that a State cannot plead the shortcomings of its municipal law as a defence to a claim for breach of its international obligations.[302] For that reason, it would make no difference in a case before an international tribunal whether, if implementing legislation were deficient in enabling the State to fulfil its obligations, the defect occurred through a misunderstanding or misinterpretation of the requirements of its international obligations. It would be a strange outcome if the United States declaration were interpreted, in a form which constituted the basis of Judge Lauterpacht's invalidity thesis, as seeking to retain for the United States a power to impose its own domestic view of the reservation upon the Court, leaving it for the Court to accept, or, if the Lauterpacht line were followed, to reject.[303]

[301] Thus by Article 46(1) of the Vienna Convention:

> 'A State may not invoke the fact that its consent to be bound by a treaty has been expressed in violation of a provision of its internal law regarding competence to conclude treaties as invalidating its consent unless that violation was manifest and concerned a rule of its internal law of fundamental importance'.

Moreover, given the informal nature of unilateral acts giving rise to international obligations, it might be almost impossible to establish a breach of a constitutional provision as a means of escaping from the undertaking given by a minister with apparent authority to deal with a particular matter: see the *Eastern Greenland* case (1933), *PCIJ*, Series A/B, No. 53, pp. 69 ff.

[302] An example of this rule is provided by Article 27 of the Vienna Convention whereby a 'party may not invoke the provisions of its internal law as justification for its failure to perform a treaty'. See also *Treatment of Polish Nationals in Danzig* (1932), *PCIJ*, Series A/B, No. 44, p. 24: 'a State cannot adduce as against another State its own Constitution with a view to evading obligations incumbent upon it under international law or treaties in force'.

[303] The link between the automatic reservation in the United States declaration and the attempt to rely upon one's own law to excuse a breach of an international obligation was referred to by Preuss, 'The International Court of Justice, the Senate and Matters of Domestic Jurisdiction', *American Journal of International Law*, 40 (1946), p. 720 at p. 734, as follows:

> 'The Connally Amendment, now a reservation to the United States Declaration, may have serious consequences in depriving the United States of judicial remedies against other states in cases in which it would otherwise have a valid legal claim. It is well known that certain Latin American countries, among others, tend to take an expansive view of the extent of their internal sovereignty, and to define as domestic matters those which fall within the jurisdiction of their courts or find a sanction in their constitutional law. The International Court of Justice, under a true system of compulsory jurisdiction, would find no difficulty in reducing these claims to their proper proportions. But the Connally Amendment offers to such states the opportunity to assert and maintain—with finality so far as settlement by judicial means is concerned—a defense which the United States has always contested: that a state may bar an international reclamation by setting up its own law or the decisions of its own courts as the final test of its international obligations.'

3. *The present status of the Lauterpacht thesis*

In the *Nicaragua* case, Judge Schwebel admitted that in 1960 he had 'agreed with Judge Lauterpacht's position' before the Senate Committee on Foreign Relations.[304] He went on:[305]

> I continue to see great force in it, while appreciating the argument that, since declarations incorporating self-judging provisions have been treated as valid, certainly by the declarants, for many years, the passage of time may have rendered Judge Lauterpacht's analysis less compelling today than it was when made.

While there is much to be said for the thrust of this view of the cumulative effect of State practice (it is at least as, if not more, compelling than the evidence in favour of a right of unilateral determination, with immediate effect, of declarations of acceptance[306]), the question has to be asked why the same factor was not regarded as influential, though perhaps not to the same degree, in the late 1950s. It was one thing to question the validity of the United States declaration in 1946 when it was made. It was a different matter a decade later. Not only had no objections been raised to this automatic reservation, but also various other States had incorporated similar self-judging reservations in their declarations.[307]

It is also worth examining why Judge Lauterpacht took the view he did of the effect of including such a reservation in a declaration accepting the compulsory jurisdiction of the Court. In a sense it was a quixotic gesture. Such practice as there was suggested a contrary view on the part of States, certainly of those which had already made declarations under Article 36. Moreover, the decision of the majority of the Court in the *Norwegian Loans*

[304] *ICJ Reports*, 1984, p. 392 at p. 601.

[305] At pp. 601–2.

[306] Above, p. 167. It could be regarded as more compelling because of the fact that the Court itself, despite opportunities for doing so, has studiously refrained from adopting the invalidity thesis.

[307] India's declaration dated 7 January 1956 (deposited on 9 January) excluded 'disputes in regard to matters which are essentially within the domestic jurisdiction of India as determined by the Government of India'.

Liberia's declaration of 20 March 1952 was not to apply 'to any dispute which the Republic of Liberia considers essentially within its domestic jurisdiction'.

Mexico's declaration of 28 October 1947 was not to 'apply to disputes arising from matters that, in the opinion of the Mexican Government, are within the domestic jurisdiction of the United States of Mexico'.

Pakistan's declaration of 23 May 1957 was not to apply to 'disputes with regard to matters which are essentially within the domestic jurisdiction of the Government of Pakistan as determined by the Government of Pakistan'.

The Sudan's declaration of 2 January 1958 was in virtually identical terms, reading 'excluding the following . . . disputes in regard to matters'.

South Africa's declaration of 13 September 1955 accepted jurisdiction over all disputes arising thereafter etc. 'other than disputes with regard to matters . . . ' in identical terms.

The United Kingdom's declaration of 18 April 1957 applied to disputes 'other than . . . disputes . . . relating to any question which, in the opinion of the Government of the United Kingdom, affects the national security of the United Kingdom or of any of its dependent territories'.

case established beyond doubt a limited effectiveness for a declaration containing an automatic reservation. The decision against the competence of the Court to hear the case was based upon the Norwegian invocation of the French reservation, not upon the fact that the French declaration was a nullity. Finally, the invalidity principle presented a stark contrast to the principle of effectiveness in extending the ambit of international jurisdiction, championed by Judge Lauterpacht, and adopted by the Court, in the *Hearings of Petitioners* case.[308] What prompted Judge Lauterpacht, therefore, to adopt such an extreme view (and in a sense restrictive view) of international jurisdiction, namely that a purported assumption of a legal obligation by a major power in a formal act was nevertheless invalid and legally ineffective?

It may have been that the Judge saw the alternative as unsatisfactory in legal and practical terms, while the invalidity approach might have seemed to offer the chance of a more satisfactory outcome in promoting the future of the compulsory jurisdiction of international disputes. From the former point of view, it could have been his assessment that, in upholding the validity of a declaration containing an automatic reservation, the Court would not have been prepared to place any, or at any rate any significant, limitations upon the power of the declarant to claim the protection of such a reservation. While it may have been true, on the other hand, that few members of the Court would have countenanced a step as drastic as declaring invalid declarations emanating from such major powers as France and the United States, Lauterpacht was not directing his message at the Court but at the two States concerned, and more particularly to those segments of the legal and political community within those States who supported the Court and its activities.

There has been a tendency to dismiss the significance of Lauterpacht's two opinions on the ground that they represented a minority view which had little influence upon the Court.[309] Though each was a *tour de force* in legal terms, the author must have realised that there was little likelihood of the Court accepting his thesis. He did, however, get his message across to the community at which he was aiming. The Institut de Droit International adopted a resolution urging States, which had included automatic reservations in their declarations, to withdraw the reservations in question.[310] A number of States were sufficiently influenced by the fact that such a reservation could well operate to their disadvantage, as was the experience of France in the *Norwegian Loans* case, and/or by the doubts raised as to the validity of such reservations in that case and the *Interhandel* case, to withdraw

[308] *ICJ Reports*, 1956, p. 32; above, pp. 152–4.

[309] See, for example, Rosenne, 'Sir Hersch Lauterpacht's Concept of the Task of the International Judge', *American Journal of International Law*, 55 (1961), p. 825 at p. 852; Hussain, *Dissenting and Separate Opinions at the World Court* (1984), p. 154, described Judge Lauterpacht as being 'in conflict with the Court on the question'.

[310] *Annuaire de L'Institut de Droit International*, 48 (1959), pp. 359–60.

their own version.[311] With regard to the United States, these factors provided the impetus for an attempt to eradicate the Connally amendment.[312] That the attempt failed cannot be attributed to the person who had, at the end of his life, made such a dramatic *cri de coeur* for the cause of compulsory jurisdiction of disputes by the International Court of Justice.

As Judge Schwebel tentatively acknowledged,[313] we are in a new era: that battle for compulsory jurisdiction has, for the moment at least, been lost. To an extent, therefore, the Court's approach to automatic reservations might seem to be academic. Nevertheless, it is worth returning to the conjecture about the consequences that would have followed if the United States had invoked the Connally amendment in the *Nicaragua* case.[314]

4. *Where does the interpretative approach lead?*

(i) *A limited effect for an automatic reservation*. It is possible to regard a declaration containing such a reservation as having a limited degree of effectiveness. The main thrust of Lauterpacht's assessment of a declaration containing an automatic reservation was that the invalidity and ineffectiveness of the declaration rendered it a nullity (i.e., void for all purposes) and therefore not cognizable by the Court. Even if this view best suited the cause he was seeking to promote, it was too extreme for most of the other members of the Court.[315] The attempt has therefore been made to limit the ineffectiveness of the declaration to its role as an instrument constituting a declaration accepting the Court's jurisdiction under Article 36(2). This would not prevent the instrument in question having jurisdictional relevance for other purposes. It could therefore have a role to play in establishing, through a sequence of acts, of which it would constitute one, the

[311] The French Declaration of 18 February 1947 was terminated and replaced on 10 July 1959.

India terminated its declaration of January 1956 by a notice of 8 February 1957. India made a new declaration on 14 September 1959 which excluded 'disputes in regard to matters which are essentially within the jurisdiction of the Republic of India'.

The Pakistan declaration of 23 May 1957 was replaced by a declaration dated 12 September 1960 which amended the reservation so that the declaration was not to apply to 'disputes relating to questions which by international law fall exclusively within the domestic jurisdiction of Pakistan'.

The United Kingdom declaration of 18 April 1957 was replaced on 26 November 1958, though exception (vi) still retained the operation of the earlier reservation with regard to 'disputes concerning any question relating to or arising out of events occurring before the date of the present Declaration'.

[312] See Whiteman, *Digest of International Law*, vol. 12 (1971), pp. 1308 ff.

[313] *Nicaragua* case, *ICJ Reports*, 1984, p. 392 at pp. 601–2.

[314] Though it reserved its position as to whether it would subsequently invoke the reservation. In a note in its counter-memorial it was stated (quoted by Judge Schwebel at p. 602):

> 'On the basis of Nicaragua's pleadings to date, the United States has determined not to invoke proviso "b" to the United States 1946 declaration (the so-called "Connally Reservation") This determination is without prejudice to the rights of the United States under that proviso in relation to any subsequent pleadings, proceedings, or cases before this Court.'

[315] The exception was Judge Spender who said in the *Interhandel* case, *ICJ Reports*, 1959, p. 6 at p. 55:

> 'In my opinion reservation (*b*) of the United States is invalid. If so, the Court is unable to give any effect to it. . . . the whole Declaration is null and void.'

Court's jurisdiction in a particular case. As Crawford described this situation:[316]

it does not follow that automatic declarations are simply void. . . . [T]here is already a model . . . for a set of 'Optional Clause' declarations which will have effect *vis-à-vis* 'genuine' declarations only when accepted as such, either *ad hoc* or generally. Examples of such acceptance would include the making of a similar reservation oneself, or a clear invocation of the reservation in an opponent's declaration. Whether acceptance could be implied from a mere non-objection is more doubtful. However this may be, the proper conclusion . . . is that automatic reservations are not void but simply non-opposable to non-consenting States.

Although this analysis is open to objections (principally as to the appropriateness of the precedent in question and as to the value of relying upon such a concept of limited effectiveness), it is not without a parallel in municipal law with regard to the making of contracts (an analogy of which has already been employed in this paper[317]). In the Australian case of *MacRobertson Miller Airline Services* v. *Commissioner of State Taxation (WA)*,[318] the High Court had to consider whether an airline ticket constituted an 'agreement or any memorandum of agreement' within the Stamp Act 1921–1971 (WA). Amongst the terms contained in tickets issued by the airline were the following:

2. The Companies reserve the right at any time to abandon any flight or, whether the scheduled flight on which the passenger or goods were booked takes place or not, to cancel any ticket or booking of any passenger or goods or to carry the passenger for portion only of any booked flight. In the event of a flight being abandoned or altered by the Companies wholly or in part or a ticket or booking being cancelled by the Companies wholly or in part, the passenger shall be entitled only to a refund of so much of the passage money as shall be proportionate to the part of his flight so cancelled or abandoned and the Companies shall not under any circumstances be under any further or other liability to the passenger for failure to carry him at the booked or scheduled time or at all.

. . .

5. The Companies are not common carriers, and reserve the right to refuse to carry any passenger, baggage or goods without assigning any reason therefor.

One member of the Court, Stephen J, employed the traditional interpretation of the issue of a ticket as constituting an offer to carry the traveller on the terms set out or referred to on the ticket, which the traveller accepted by taking and paying for the ticket without then or soon thereafter indicating

[316] 'The Legal Effect of Automatic Reservations to the Jurisdiction of the International Court', this *Year Book*, 50 (1979), p. 63 at p. 85. The model referred to was that provided for in Security Council Resolution 9(I) of 15 October 1946 whereby a State which is not a party to the Statute may lodge a declaration under Article 36(2) provided 'that such acceptance may not, without explicit agreement, be relied upon vis-à-vis States parties to the Statute which have made the declaration in conformity with Article 36, paragraph 2'. The text is given in the International Court of Justice *Yearbook*, 1946–7, p. 106 at p. 107.

[317] See above, p.174.

[318] (1975), 133 CLR 125.

his or her objection to the terms.[319] However, Barwick CJ and Jacobs J regarded the scope of the terms as inconsistent with the assumption by the airline of any obligation to carry a ticket holder on any journey.[320] A contractual arrangement would only come into existence in such circumstances if the traveller presented the ticket at the airport and performance of the carriage commenced, which would then be on the terms specified on the ticket.[321] On either interpretation of the relationship between the parties, the ticket did not satisfy the statutory description of an agreement or a memorandum of an agreement, and no duty was payable.

If the substance of this case is transposed to the arena of the jurisdiction of the International Court, there are obvious similarities, on the limited effectiveness theory, between the relationship(s) established by a declaration containing an automatic reservation and the issuing of a ticket in that form. Neither the declaration nor the ticket can be regarded as a complete nullity. The State concerned is provisionally subject to the system established by Article 36. It is therefore amenable to the Court's incidental jurisdiction, as was clear from the Court's consideration of a request by Switzerland for interim measures of protection in the *Interhandel* case,[322] notwithstanding the fact that the United States had already purported to determine that the dispute concerned a matter falling within its own domestic jurisdiction and was not therefore cognizable by the Court. Correspondingly, even if the ticket issued by the airline created no obligation for the airline to carry a purchaser of a ticket, the transaction was not devoid of effect, not least because the receipt of the fare by the airline was effective by virtue of the arrangement evidenced by the ticket, even if some further act or acts were necesssary before a contract of carriage by reference to the terms of the ticket came into existence.

(ii) Forum prorogatum *as a basis of jurisdiction*. There are obvious similarities between the process of establishing the Court's jurisdiction as described above and the principle of *forum prorogatum* as developed in the jurisprudence of the Court. In the same way as the contract of carriage in the *Airline* case was dependent upon the subsequent conduct of the parties, so too in a situation involving an automatic reservation the Court's jurisdiction would be dependent upon some further act or acts by the parties involved in a particular dispute. The declaration containing such a reservation, though sufficient in the absence of protest to bring the declarant within the system, and therefore subject to the Court's powers to take incidental measures with respect to the case, would not be enough to oblige it to accept the Court's jurisdiction. The declaration is primarily an offer

[319] At p. 137, referring to *Watkins* v. *Rymill* (1883), 10 QBD 178 at p. 188; *Nunan* v. *Southern Rly. Co.*, [1923] 2 KB 703 at p. 707; *Thompson* v. *London, Midland & Scottish Rly. Co.*, [1930] 1 KB 41 at p. 47; *Thornton* v. *Shoe Lane Parking Ltd.*, [1971] 2 QB 163 at p. 169.

[320] 133 CLR at pp. 133, 148 respectively.

[321] At pp. 133–4 *per* Barwick CJ.

[322] *ICJ Reports*, 1957, p. 105, though the request was refused on the ground that there was no immediate threat to the rights in issue in the case.

that the declarant State is prepared to decide whether to become a party to litigation of the merits of the dispute as defendant in accordance with the terms of the declaration, including the terms of the reservation; or that, if it comes to the Court as applicant, it will allow the other party to make such a decision whether to accept the role of defendant.

As in the situation just considered, the Court's jurisdiction on the merits can only be established by the subsequent conduct of one or both of the parties (in particular the decision by the defendant not to rely upon the power of unilateral determination in its own or the applicant's declaration). That this process would fall within the concept of *forum prorogatum* was certainly Waldock's view:[323]

> If declarations which contain a reservation of matters of domestic jurisdiction in the United States form are indeed invalid as declarations under the Optional Clause, they would still be of some value as a basis for establishing the jurisdiction under the principle of the *forum prorogatum*.

The writer continued:[324]

> The declaration would constitute a solemn statement of a willingness to submit to the Court matters not considered to be within domestic jurisdiction, and another State would be well justified . . . in basing a unilateral Application to the Court upon the declaration in the hope that the defendant State would accept jurisdiction. Then, if the State which had made such a declaration proceeded to defend the case without raising any objection on the score of domestic jurisdiction, the jurisdiction of the Court would be established, but on the principle of *forum prorogatum*. Similarly, if the State which had made a declaration containing such a reservation itself instituted proceedings by submitting an Application, the Application would not by itself suffice to seize the Court of the case but, if the other State proceeded to defend the case, the Court's jurisdiction would be established on the principle of *forum prorogatum*.

Crawford, on the other hand, gave three reasons for regarding *forum prorogatum* as irrelevant:[325]

1. 'if an automatic declaration is accepted by a party to the Optional Clause for the purposes of contentious proceedings the other reservations in the two declarations remain relevant. Such acceptance is not the same as accepting the Court's jurisdiction over the merits (which is what is required for a *forum prorogatum*)';
2. 'in such a case "the doctrine of successive acts", which has been developed for cases of *forum prorogatum*, will have no application'; and

[323] 'The Plea of Domestic Jurisdiction before International Legal Tribunals', this *Year Book*, 31 (1954), p. 96 at p. 133.

[324] At pp. 133–4.

[325] This *Year Book*, 50 (1979), at p. 86.

3. 'it may be proper for the Court to indicate interim measures of protection, and take other preliminary steps in the action, on the basis of an automatic declaration, steps which would not be possible simply on the basis of an anticipated *ad hoc* acceptance of jurisdiction.'

On the approach adopted in the text, and in the passage from Waldock, the first two of these considerations do not pose problems. As far as 1 is concerned, the provisional acceptance (which can take the form—and this will be the normal situation—of a failure to object to the existence of an automatic reservation) does not constitute more than one of the steps whereby jurisdiction might be established. It therefore fits in with the doctrine of successive acts referred to in 2. The problem of this approach lies in the possibility of the Court exercising its incidental jurisdiction as mentioned in 3. It is difficult to understand how the informal acceptance of the declarant State provisionally into the system carries with it the possibility of the Court exercising its incidental jurisdiction once the *forum prorogatum* principle is rendered inapplicable by an invocation by that State of its automatic reservation. While the principle of *forum prorogatum* can encompass the whole sequence of positive steps whereby the Court's jurisdiction on the merits is established, it cannot operate before that stage is reached. Hence the provisional validity concept, opening up the possibility of the exercise of the Court's incidental jurisdiction, cannot be linked to the *forum prorogatum* approach. The former, but not the latter, can hold good (as in the *Interhandel* case at the provisional measures stage) in the face of an invocation of an automatic reservation.

Not that the Crawford alternative is particularly helpful, partly at least because it is not altogether clear what hypothesis he was putting forward. He accorded a narrow meaning to acceptance of the validity of an automatic reservation, suggesting that non-objection is probably not sufficient for that purpose. Acceptance comprised either including a similar reservation in one's own declaration, or, once proceedings had commenced, invoking such a reservation in the declaration of the other party. The problem is of explaining what significance should be attached to either step.

In the *Norwegian Loans* case, it is true, the Court based the validity of the French automatic domestic jurisdiction reservation upon two factors: its invocation by Norway *and* the fact that 'France fully maintains its Declaration'. Norway was therefore entitled to the benefit of its determination that the dispute fell within Norway's domestic jurisdiction.[326] However, it is important to note the Court's explanation for this conclusion. It went on to say that, as it had 'before it a provision which both Parties to the dispute regard as constituting an expression of their common will relating to the competence of the Court', there was no reason for the Court to 'examine

[326] *ICJ Reports*, 1957, p. 9 at p. 27.

whether the French reservation is consistent with the undertaking of a legal obligation and is compatible with Article 36, paragraph 6, of the Statute'.[327] In other words, where that common will is lacking, the Court cannot rely upon this assumption as a basis for determining the effects of an automatic reservation. Thus, for example, in a situation where the parties assert different views as to consequences of the existence of an automatic reservation in the declaration of one of them, or of a determination by that party that the dispute is covered by the reservation (as in the initial stages of the proceedings initiated by the United States against Bulgaria in the *Aerial Incident* case[328]), the scope of any 'acceptance' by the parties as suggested by Crawford would be limited indeed. At most it might amount to a recognition of the potential validity of reservations in that form.

As far as Crawford's other suggestion is concerned, the mere fact that both parties to incipient litigation have declarations containing automatic reservations takes the degree of acceptance little further. In the first place, not all such reservations are in identical form, so that one relating to national security cannot necessarily be equated with recognition of one concerned with domestic jurisdiction, beyond the provisional acceptance arising in any case from non-objection by other States making declarations, in whatever form, under Article 36(2). But, more importantly, it does not necessarily follow that all parties employing the automatic version of a domestic jurisdiction reservation have the same view of its consequences. Hence, the situation may not be so different from the position of a State which takes advantage of an automatic reservation in the other party's declaration, but where the two States might assert that different consequences flow from such a situation.

While one does not have to accept Crawford's own explanation for the effects of an automatic reservation, the thrust of what he said about the principle of *forum prorogatum* in this context is undoubtedly correct. It cannot provide a justification for the indication of interim measures after one of the parties has sought to make a determination under such a reservation denying merits jurisdiction to the Court.

However, whatever the shortcomings of the *forum prorogatum* analysis, it would not have been a factor of importance in the *Nicaragua* case unless the United States had sought to invoke the reservation. If it had done so, this path to jurisdiction on the merits would have been barred. *Forum prorogatum* could only have been relied upon if the sequence of acts included an intimation by the United States of its non-invocation of the reservation.

Two additional points can be made. If the *forum prorogatum* principle had in fact been the approach selected by the Court, the United States would have had nothing to fear. The implied consent of other participants

[327] Ibid.

[328] Above, p. 185.

in the system of compulsory jurisdiction to the validity of the United States declaration and thus to the Connally reservation would have, in effect, carried with it assent to the power of determination explicit in that reservation. Only if the United States had refrained from making such a determination would an implication of jurisdiction have been possible.

Secondly, however, an additional indication that this approach is of little value is provided by the circumstances of the *Nicaragua* case. The United States neither confirmed nor denied the Court's jurisdiction in relation to the Connally reservation. It purported to leave open the possibility of subsequently invoking this reservation.[329] If indeed consent to jurisdiction along this path is established by a series of acts, it could hardly be said that the reservation of its position by the United States was sufficient to establish unequivocally the Court's jurisdiction. It would still have been possible for the United States, as indicated by the limited scope of its consent, to purport to withdraw the case from the Court. Such a possibility would seem to be even more of an infraction of the requirements of the Statute and Article 36(6) in particular.

Finally, it should be appreciated that the analogy with the *Airline* case was employed for purposes of explanation. There is one fundamental reason why it cannot be regarded as supporting the partial validity view of declarations containing automatic reservations. It is true that a ticket is prima facie treated as a contractual document. However, there is no reason why a party cannot establish that, at the moment of issue, it does not have that quality. Nor is there any reason why a party should not, by the terms of an arrangement, seek to retain a discretion as to whether or not the contract will be carried out when the time for performance arrives.

The position would be no different with regard to treaty arrangements as the parties would be free to defer to some later decision the assumption of any obligation to perform the terms set out in the particular arrangement. The same would not necessarily be the case with regard to declarations under Article 36(2) of the Statute, which must be consonant with the requirements of the Statute as a whole. This means that a State submitting a declaration is not free to retain a discretion whereby it can subsequently, after the commencement of proceedings, determine the scope of the Court's jurisdiction. Accordingly there is the strongest presumption that a State making a declaration intends to comply with the Statute and the contents of the declaration will be treated as if it were carrying out this intention. Unlike the ticket in the *Airline* case, or Crawford's view of declarations containing an automatic reservation, such declarations will be regarded as having been made with the intention by the State concerned of assuming a total

[329] See *ICJ Reports*, 1984, p. 392 at p. 422: 'the United States has informed the Court that it has determined not to invoke this proviso, but "without prejudice to the rights of the United States under that proviso in relation to any subsequent pleadings, proceedings, or cases before this Court" '.

commitment to the Court's jurisdiction subject to independent assessment by the Court itself.

(d) *Rationalization*

It is no longer possible to argue that automatic reservations are totally void. The practice of States and the caution demonstrated by the Court in its dealings with such reservations have undoubtedly bestowed upon them qualified validity. The difficulty is to conjecture what course would have been adopted had the United States invoked the Connally reservation in the *Nicaragua* case.

The United States would not have held any fear of the *forum prorogatum* approach because its very invocation of the reservation, by purporting to determine that the dispute was essentially within the United States' domestic jurisdiction, would have prevented the principle operating to bestow jurisdiction on the Court. Nor is there much value in Crawford's qualified validity notion, beyond providing an explanation of why it is possible, notwithstanding the invocation of such a reservation, for the Court to exercise its incidental jurisdiction. Jurisdiction on the merits would still be dependent upon something akin to *forum prorogatum*. At the time when the Court comes to consider whether it has such jurisdiction, it would have to decide whether the invoking State was maintaining its position in order to exclude the operation of the principle of prorogued jurisdiction.

Viewed in this light, there is little to be gained from the Crawford view. The incidental jurisdiction possibility aside, the Court would still be surrendering the ultimate power of determining the scope of its jurisdiction to a litigating State in the course of such litigation. While it is possible to contend that this is the effect of State practice and the Court's own timidity towards reservations of this type, to accept such a conclusion should surely represent only a last resort. Preserving the integrity and the intent of the provisions of the Statute should represent the cardinal objective.

There is thus much to be said for regarding the qualified acceptance implicit in State practice as attaching to the declaration itself (albeit one containing a reservation of dubious validity). From this point of view, the acquiescing State is not taking any particular stand on the status of the reservation, because that is a matter for the Court to decide. It is States themselves which have bestowed upon the Court (not upon individual States) the power to determine the scope of its jurisdiction under declarations made in accordance with Article 36. It would be for the Court, therefore, to decide between such possibilities as those of severing or reading down the offending part of the declaration on the one hand, or, on the other, of interpreting the reservation in order to reconcile it with the terms of Article 36(6) by creating an obligation which could be objectively assessed. These alternatives have the advantage that they are based upon the premiss that the declarant State intended to accept the Court's jurisdiction in a valid way and should be regarded as having achieved that objective. In so far as there might be any conflict between this aim and the terms of an automatic reservation, the intention to accept the Court's jurisdiction must prevail because a State preferring to avoid the compulsory jurisdiction of the Court would surely have made no declaration at all (the course adopted by a majority of States).

1. *Severance*

When this alternative was considered,[330] it was pointed out that Lauterpacht did not regard severance of a reservation which would otherwise render the whole declaration invalid as an inappropriate means of dealing with the situation. However, he was adamant that this possibility was not open to the Court with regard to the United States declaration because of the crucial part played by the Connally amendment in securing the approval of the Senate for the declaration. For this reason the entire declaration was invalid.

To meet these objections, three members of the Court[331] in the *Interhandel* case adopted what was, in effect, a modified version of the severance approach. According to Judge Klaestad, provided, as a matter of interpretation, a reservation is in conflict with the Statute, it cannot be applied by the Court. However, the Court can give effect to the presumed intention of the State concerned 'to issue a real and effective Declaration accepting the compulsory jurisdiction of the Court, though—it is true—with far-reaching exceptions'.[332] It followed, in Judge Klaestad's view, that:[333]

> the Court, both by its Statute and by the Charter, is prevented from acting upon that part of the Reservation which is in conflict with Article 36, paragraph 6, of the Statute, but that this circumstance does not necessarily imply that it is impossible for the Court to give effect to the other parts of the Declaration of Acceptance which are in conformity with the Statute.

As to the theoretical difference between the two approaches, it would seem that it does not matter whether it is regarded as an issue of severability or one of construction. Presumably to counter the latter classification adopted by Judge Klaestad, Judge Lauterpacht expressed the objections to severability he had advanced in the *Norwegian Loans* case in rather broader terms in the *Interhandel* case:[334]

> These reasons included the general principle of law governing the subject, namely, the principle that a condition which, having regard to the intention of the party making it, is essential to and goes to the roots of the main obligation, cannot be sep-

[330] Above, p. 187.
[331] Judge Klaestad, with whom Judge *ad hoc* Carry agreed, and Judge Armand-Ugon.
[332] *ICJ Reports*, 1959, p. 6 at p. 7.
[333] At p. 78.
[334] At pp. 116–17.

arated from it. This is not a mere refinement of private law . . . but . . . a maxim based on common sense and equity. A party cannot be held bound by an obligation divested of a condition without which that obligation would never have been undertaken.

There are defects to this line of reasoning, however it is classified. In discussing what later became Article 44 of the Vienna Convention on the Law of Treaties,[335] the International Law Commission referred to the principle of severability as follows:[336]

Acceptances of the severed clauses must not have been so linked to acceptance of the other parts that, if the severed parts disappear, the basis of the consent of the parties to the treaty as a whole also disappears.

Applied to acceptances of the Court's jurisdiction under Article 36(2), it is difficult to imagine many cases in which the 'basis of the consent' of the declarant State is not involved in a particular reservation. As has already been pointed out,[337] the Australian argument in the *Nuclear Tests* cases, based on the fact that the former French declaration had stood for seven years without the added limitation relating to national defence, was scarcely convincing. The withdrawal and replacement of the earlier declaration could hardly be described as being done for 'cosmetic purposes'. It was a deliberate act of the French Government to insert the additional exclusion.

The same criticism applies equally to Judge Lauterpacht's reformulation of his position in the *Interhandel* case to meet the approach adopted by Judge Klaestad. It is not a straightforward matter to identify with precision what is the 'intention' of a State in such matters because there might well be a conflict between different policy-making organs—in the United States, for example, the demand on the part of the Senate to insert a let-out clause contrasted with the wish of a particular administration at least to appear to support the cause of judicial settlement of disputes. In the circumstances, the question must be asked whether an enquiry should be conducted into the actual intentions of the different arms of government, especially when

[335] Article 44 reads in part:

'1. A right of a party, provided for in a treaty or arising under article 56, to denounce, withdraw from or suspend the operation of the treaty may be exercised only with respect to the whole treaty unless the treaty otherwise provides or the parties otherwise agree.

2. A ground for invalidating, terminating, withdrawing from or suspending the operation of a treaty recognized in the present Convention may be invoked only with respect to the whole treaty except as provided in the following paragraphs or in article 60.

3. If the ground relates solely to particular clauses, it may be invoked only with respect to those clauses where:

(*a*) the said clauses are separable from the remainder of the treaty with regard to their application;

(*b*) it appears from the treaty or is otherwise established that acceptance of those clauses was not an essential basis of the consent of the other party or parties to be bound by the treaty as a whole; and

(*c*) continued performance of the remainder of the treaty would not be unjust'.

[336] *Yearbook of the International Law Commission*, 1963, vol. 2, p. 212.

[337] Above, p. 188.

most attention is likely to be directed to the demands expressed in open debate. Is this not to give a distorted picture of the intentions of the United States as an entity for the purposes of international law?

Ultimately, it is for a State, through its government, to assess the extent to which it can, in accepting the Court's jurisdiction (or in maintaining a declaration previously made), at the same time reserve for itself the power to decide upon the effect of a particular limitation upon that jurisdiction. The question should not be, therefore, whether, from the public record, the reservation was a matter of greater or less significance. Rather, it should be whether a State is entitled, while expressing a commitment to the Court's compulsory jurisdiction (presumably, on any objective assessment, its overriding intention), to claim to reserve the power, after the Court is seised of a dispute, to withdraw the matter from the Court's jurisdiction. Put in that form, the answer is in the negative, but it also follows that the attempt to achieve that aim, being totally abortive, should simply be ignored. The Court cannot give effect to the reservation in question because of Article 36(6), but, as Judge Klaestad pointed out, that is no reason for dispensing with the rest of the declaration.

2. *A requirement of good faith*

The other obstacle which the United States may have perceived to a successful invocation of its automatic reservation in the *Nicaragua* case lay in what Judge Lauterpacht referred to in the *Norwegian Loans* case as the good faith limitation on its application. It was expressed in this form because of the way in which it had been presented in the Norwegian preliminary objections. It will be recalled that there it had been said:[338]

> such a reservation must be interpreted in good faith and should a government seek to rely upon it with a view to denying the jurisdiction of the Court in a case which manifestly did not involve a 'matter which is essentially within the national jurisdiction' it would be committing an *abus de droit* which would not prevent the Court from acting.

The purpose of this limitation was to give the operation of an automatic reservation an objective character and therefore to bring it within the scope of judicial review. Expressed in this form, however, it was open to objection on the ground that it might be difficult to define the circumstances in which a determination by a State that a matter is within its domestic jurisdiction has been made in bad faith. There are many matters which have at times been claimed by States as falling within their domestic jurisdiction. This point was forcibly made by Judge Lauterpacht:[339]

> Tariffs, immigration, treatment of aliens and citizens in national territory, internal

[338] Quoted *ICJ Reports*, 1957, p. 9 at pp. 53, 94; see above, p. 184.
[339] At pp. 51–2.

legislation generally—all those matters have been claimed to be essentially within the domestic jurisdiction of States. It is not necessary for me to express an opinion on the subject. However, even if that claim is admitted, those are not necessarily matters which according to international law are exclusively within the domestic jurisdiction of the State—though, as stated, they have often been described as being matters of domestic jurisdiction or essentially of domestic jurisdiction. Practically every aspect of the conduct of the State may be, *prima facie*, within that category for the reason that normally the State exercises its activity within its national territory, or, on the high seas, in relation to its ships which for some purposes are considered by States to form part of its territory. . . . For these reasons it is possible for a State to maintain, without necessarily laying itself open to an irresistible charge of bad faith, that practically every dispute concerns a matter essentially within its domestic jurisdiction. Most Judgments given by this Court and its predecessor—with the exception of those concerned with territorial disputes—have been given in relation to matters bearing on the activity of the State within its jurisdiction and related to its national legislation and administration. These are the typical occasions giving rise to State responsibility.

3. *A matter of interpretation*

In deciding upon the most appropriate approach to be adopted, a domestic jurisdiction type of automatic reservation cannot be divorced entirely from the more normal, objective version of the domestic jurisdiction exception where the matter is assessed against the standard set by international law.

Article 15(8) of the Covenant of the League of Nations excluded from the consideration of the League and its organs matters 'which by international law' were 'solely within the domestic jurisdiction' of a party to a dispute. In interpreting this provision, the Permanent Court of International Justice adopted the principle that the existence of an international obligation, whether arising by way of custom or under a treaty provision, owed to another State, was sufficient to exclude the operation of that paragraph of the Covenant.[340] The fact that even under the League,[341] and

[340] *Tunis and Morocco Nationality Decrees* case (1923), *PCIJ*, Series B, No. 4, esp. at p. 24.

[341] In the case of the League, the influence was indirect because of the express reference in Article 15(8) to the standard of international law. As the Permanent Court itself said (at p. 25):

> 'Having regard to this very wide competence possessed by the League of Nations, the Covenant contains an express reservation protecting the independence of States; this reservation is to be found in paragraph 8 of Article 15. Without this reservation, the internal affairs of a country might, directly they appeared to affect the interests of another country, be brought before the Council and form the subject of recommendations by the League of Nations. Under the terms of paragraph 8, the League's interest in being able to make such recommendations as are deemed just and proper in the circumstances with a view to the maintenance of peace must, at a given point, give way to the equally essential interest of the individual State to maintain intact its independence in matters which international law recognizes to be solely within its jurisdiction'.

However, the Court also acknowledged that the 'question whether a certain matter is or is not solely within the jurisdiction of a State is an essentially relative question; it depends upon the development of international relations' (at p. 24). And, as time was to show, an important impetus to such development took place through the activities of the League.

more so under the Charter,[342] the political authority of the organization was unavoidably going to impinge upon the rights of States had the inevitable consequence of reducing the scope of the exception. If the good faith limitation were applied to an automatic reservation of this type, the likely consequence would be seen as an issue of whether, in the light of contemporary developments and the particular circumstances of the case, the matter was to a greater or lesser extent primarily a matter of domestic concern.

Once the situation is viewed in this way, it will be apparent that the matter is principally one of interpretation, though the process of construction of the declaration in question would have to take place within the parameters set by the terms of Article 36 of the Statute. This was the position reached by Judge Read in the *Norwegian Loans* case although he in fact adopted the interpretation approach in express preference to a good faith limitation. Having first of all dismissed the applicability of notions of good faith and *abus de droit*,[343] he went on to say:[344]

> Nevertheless, I think that the basic principle underlying the position taken by Norway in this regard should be accepted. I think that the wording of the reservation to the Declaration properly construed means that the respondent State, in invoking the reservation, must establish that there is a genuine understanding, i.e. that the circumstances are such that it would be reasonably possible to reach the understanding that the dispute was essentially national. Whether the circumstances are such is not a matter for decision by a respondent Government, but by the Court. But, assuming that such circumstances existed, the conclusion reached by a respondent Government could not be reviewed by the Court.
>
> I am unable to accept the view that the reservation should be interpreted as giving the respondent Government an arbitrary power to settle any question of jurisdiction which arises by the assertion that the Government understands that the matter is essentially within the national jurisdiction regardless of whether that assertion is true or false.
>
> Such a construction of the clause would lead to something unreasonable and absurd. It would, of course, if that interpretation is accepted, be necessary to con-

[342] The equivalent provision of the Charter is Article 2(7):

'Nothing contained in the present Charter shall authorise the United Nations to intervene in matters which are essentially within the domestic jurisdiction of any State or shall require the Members to submit such matters to settlement under the present Charter; but this principle shall not prejudice the application of enforcement measures under Chapter VII'.

The most significant difference was the omission of any reference to the international law standard. Moreover, the Charter itself granted the widest competence to the organization and its organs. For example, Article 10 lays down that the 'General Assembly may discuss any questions or any matters within the scope of the present Charter' and make recommendations accordingly. As long as it does not 'intervene' in matters of domestic jurisdiction (and nothing in Article 10 appears to amount to such a degree of meddling), the General Assembly is not hampered by Article 2(7). For a discussion of the meaning of 'to intervene' in this context, see Rajan, *United Nations and Domestic Jurisdiction* (2nd edn., 1961), pp. 66 ff.

[343] *ICJ Reports*, 1957, at p. 94:

'I should be disinclined to bring notions of "good faith" and *abus de droit* into the question. Practically speaking it is, I think, impossible for an international tribunal to examine a dispute between two sovereign States on the basis of either good or bad faith or of abuse of law.'

[344] At pp. 94–5.

clude that the Declaration ran contrary to Article 36, paragraph 6, of the Statute, and was null and void.

A significant factor in applying the process of interpretation to the French reservation, invoked by Norway, was that the reservation in question referred 'to matters which are essentially within the national jurisdiction as understood by the Government of the French Republic'. In Judge Read's view, the words 'as understood' connoted 'a real understanding, and not a fictitious understanding unrelated to the facts'.[345] Applying this objective criterion to the circumstances, he suggested that, at the outset, 'when Norway invoked the reservation there can be no doubt as to the propriety of the action. At that time, it was certainly reasonably possible, considering the Application alone together with any light that had been thrown upon it by the Memorial, to reach such an understanding.'[346] However, as a result of the course taken in the written and oral proceedings, it became clear that the dispute concerned matters 'based solely on international law'. Hence, it was 'impossible to reach the conclusion that Norway could have reasonably understood that the case was essentially within the Norwegian national jurisdiction'.[347]

Total reliance upon a 'reasonable' interpretation of the particular reservation might not be a particularly satisfactory route to challenge its automatic nature. In the *Interhandel* case, Judge Spender expressed the opinion that, had Judge Read been faced with the wording employed in the United States reservation, he could not have limited it in the same way. By the Connally amendment, it was not a matter of the invoking State's *understanding* of the position, but of its *determination* that a certain state of affairs existed.[348] As Judge Read seemed to have admitted that if the reservation had been expressed in stronger terms, it would have created an arbitrary power that would have been void because of its conflict with Article 36(6),[349] it followed that had he been adjudicating in the present case he would have reached just such a conclusion. There was no possibility, in Judge Spender's view, 'for construing the United States reservation by implying into it a concept that the determination must be reasonable or that it must not be unreasonable'.[350]

4. *Synthesis*

There was undoubtedly, at the time of the *Norwegian Loans* and *Interhandel* cases, an undercurrent amongst various members of the Court in favour of the opinion either that an automatic reservation was invalid, or that it should be read down, because of its conflict with certain parts of

345 At p. 95.
346 Ibid.
347 Ibid.
348 *ICJ Reports*, 1959, at p. 58.
349 *ICJ Reports*, 1957, at p. 95.
350 *ICJ Reports*, 1959, at p. 58.

Article 36. However, as the previous survey reveals, there was no coherent view as to how the threat posed by the proliferation of automatic reservations to the Court's compulsory jurisdiction should be dealt with. Nor was there any way of divining where the sympathies of many members of the Court lay. In both cases, the Court itself avoided the question of the validity, and most of the issues relating to the effects, of automatic reservations.

The United States might have had legitimate reasons for fearing that, in 1984, the Court might, in order to assume jurisdiction over the *Nicaragua* case, have made use of these various suggestions in order to limit or eliminate the Connally reservation. Although there is no way of knowing exactly how the Court would have dealt with the matter, the various alternatives put forward in the late 1950s would undoubtedly provide a framework as to how the matter would be dealt with today.

As has already been stated, the total invalidity notion of Judges Lauterpacht and Spender would have ruled out the United States declaration altogether. The more limited jurisdiction available under the Treaty of Friendship, Commerce and Navigation 1956 apart, that would have excluded the United States from the Court and would therefore scarcely have helped the Court establish its competence with regard to the range of allegations made against the United States. Given the lack of opposition from amongst States to declarations containing automatic reservations, the rejection of such declarations *in toto* would have been a most unlikely outcome.

The apparent acquiescence by States to the use of reservations of this type would not be in conflict with the qualified validity approach espoused by Waldock or Crawford. However, both writers attached little significance to the lack of opposition from States to such reservations, beyond recognizing the need to accept a reservation's validity. Given the power bestowed upon the Court by Article 36(6) of its Statute to determine disputes as to its jurisdiction, this acquiescence must also signify that States were prepared to leave to the Court disputes arising out of the use of automatic reservations. Neither Waldock nor Crawford paid sufficient attention to the need for the Court to exercise adequate supervisory authority over the scope and consequences of such reservations and the declarations containing them.

The various other views (and indeed to a limited extent that of Judges Lauterpacht and Spender) were all based in varying degrees upon the interpretation of the reservation and the circumstances in which its invocation occurred. The principle of good faith as a means of imposing an objective standard on the employment of an automatic reservation was not espoused by members of the Court, though it was advanced both by Norway in the *Norwegian Loans* case, and by the United States, initially, in the *Aerial Incident* case. It should also be mentioned that the United States has on several occasions referred to the fact that it would not employ the opportunity presented by the existence of the automatic reservation to withdraw a case from the Court unscrupulously.[351] This framework would have provided the Court with a justification for rejecting any attempt by the United States to designate as matters within its domestic jurisdiction allegations of American involvement in the mining of the access to Nicaraguan ports, attacks on oil installations in Nicaraguan territory and the promotion of the operations conducted by the *contras* in and against Nicaragua.[352]

With regard to the gloss placed upon this approach by Judge Read, Judge Spender's interpretation of it is not necessarily the only possible view. It is true that Judge Read did place some stress on the word 'understood' in the French declaration, and expressed the opinion that he was 'unable to accept the view that the reservation should be interpreted as giving the respondent Government an arbitrary power to settle any question of jurisdiction which arises by the assertion that the Government understands that the matter is essentially within the national jurisdiction regardless of whether that assertion is true or false'.[353] However, even if a 'determination' might be regarded differently from an 'understanding' about a situation, the word that Judge Read was emphasising was the 'assertion', and the truth or falsity of that assertion. In fact, an assertion as to the existence of an understanding might be more difficult to disprove than a determination that black is white, or, as in the Nicaragua situation, that the activities conducted in or against Nicaragua were matters of domestic jurisdiction.

Ultimately, the point Judge Read was making was that an arbitrary assertion of the existence of an understanding amounted 'to something unreasonable and absurd', with consequences that were contrary to Article 36(6).[354] The result would render the declaration in question 'null and void',[355] but to adopt such a construction of the reservation would run 'directly contrary'[356] to the 'cardinal principle of interpretation', laid down by the Permanent Court in the *Polish Postal Service in Danzig* case,[357] that 'words must be interpreted in the sense which they would normally have in their context, unless such interpretation would lead to something unreason-

[351] See, for example, the letter of 30 April 1959 from the Assistant Secretary of State to the Chairman of the Senate Foreign Relations Committee giving the Department's Report on Compulsory Jurisdiction, text in Whiteman, *Digest of International Law*, vol. 12 (1971), p. 1308 at p. 1309:

> 'It was the understanding of the Senate when the automatic proviso was adopted that this reservation would never be improperly invoked and that the United States would be bound in good faith to accept the Court's jurisdiction in every case involving matters not essentially within the domestic jurisdiction of the United States. Thus, the United States as a matter of policy would expect to invoke the reservation only in those cases in which the Court itself would probably uphold a plea of domestic jurisdiction if interposed by the United States on the basis of the domestic jurisdiction reservation without the automatic proviso.'

[352] For details of which see the decision of the Court on the merits of Nicaragua's claim, *ICJ Reports*, 1986, p. 3 at pp. 45 ff.

[353] *ICJ Reports*, 1957, at p. 94.

[354] Ibid.

[355] At p. 95.

[356] Ibid.

[357] (1925), *PCIJ*, Series B, No. 11, p. 39.

able or absurd'. A determination that black was white would be equally as absurd as an assertion that one understood that black was white. Just as it would be possible 'to examine the question whether the circumstances are such that it would be reasonably possible to reach an understanding that the dispute was essentially national',[358] so it would be possible to examine a determination that a matter was essentially within domestic jurisdiction to decide whether, in the circumstances, it had been reasonably made.

Whichever way the matter of United States involvement in Nicaragua was approached in relation to invocation of the domestic jurisdiction reservation, whether it was subject to a limitation of good faith or to interpretation to avoid an absurdity, the result would surely have been the same. As a matter of interpretation the Court's role would be to avoid a result which would bring the reservation and its invocation into conflict with the Statute.[359]

However, if conflict is impossible to avoid, it does not follow that the Lauterpacht solution is the correct one. The object of Article 36(6) was to exclude any doubt on the matter of who was to have the right to determine the Court's jurisdiction. To allow a reservation in a State's declaration accepting the Court's jurisdiction to impose an alternative rule 'amounts to adding . . . an extraneous condition which it was the purpose of that Article to exclude and to disregard'.[360] This quotation relates to Article 36, though to paragraph 5, not paragraph 6. Nevertheless it was uttered in a joint dissenting opinion by three Judges, two of whom were Lauterpacht and Spender.[361] It was said in support of an expansive interpretation of the Court's jurisdiction, and could just as well be applied to the latter paragraph.

If a compatible approach to interpretation and the promotion of the Court's jurisdiction is to be found, it is not to the judgments of Judges Lauterpacht and Spender in the *Norwegian Loans* and *Interhandel* cases that one must look. The closest parallel is to be found in the approach of Judges Klaestad (with whom Judge *ad hoc* Carry agreed) and Armand-Ugon in the second of those cases. As the purpose of Article 36(6) is to remove all doubt

358 *ICJ Reports*, 1957, at p. 95.

359 If further support is required for the interpretative approach in the *Norwegian Loans* case, reference can be made to the dissenting opinion of Judge Basdevant. He placed particular significance on the way in which Norway sought to invoke the French reservation. He said, for example (at pp. 71–2):

> 'It is possible to imagine that a State invoking the reservation should intend to put it forward as categorical in character so that the opinion expressed by that State with regard to the character of the dispute would be sufficient to preclude the jurisdiction of the Court, without further consideration by the Court: it is not my intention to prejudge in any way the question of the validity of the reservation, interpreted as having such a scope. I merely observe that that State would have to manifest that that is the scope which it gives to the opinion it expresses, that its will to assume responsibility for such an attitude would have to be sufficiently apparent.'

On his assessment, Norway had not displayed that degree of assertiveness.

360 *Aerial Incident* case, *ICJ Reports*, 1959, p. 127 at p. 168.

361 The third was Judge Wellington Koo.

as to who should determine the extent of the Court's jurisdiction, any reservation, inserted in a declaration or otherwise, which attempts to achieve a contrary result, could undoubtedly be described as a 'condition which it was the purpose' of Article 36(6) 'to exclude and to disregard'. This understanding of the position was expressed by Judge Armand-Ugon as follows:[362]

no country which has announced its accession to the Optional Clause can reserve for itself the right to make its opinion prevail over the jurisdiction of the Court, once the Court has been seised of a case. From that moment the powers of the Court cannot be curtailed; they must be exercised as established by the Statute. It lies exclusively with the Court to settle any dispute about jurisdiction. No government can impose its view upon the Court in this matter. The question of the Court's jurisdiction is one which only the Court can finally settle. That intention is clearly set out in paragraph 6 of Article 36, which is binding upon all States acceding to the Statute of the Court.

It was the Judge's view therefore that:[363]

Since the reservation in regard to paragraph 6 of Article 36 contained in (b) of the American Declaration ('as determined', etc.) is obviously contrary to that paragraph, and cannot be linked to the application of any text in the Statute, the Court should regard it as unwritten and inoperative in the present case. That is to say, the respondent Government cannot rely upon it in support of its objection 4(a). The clause in question, not being provided for in any part of the Statute, should be declared without effect vis-à-vis the Court.

Taken to its logical conclusion, this view of the consequence of Article 36(6) upon an automatic reservation would be to deprive it of any effect. Whether the declarant State has grounds or not for a determination, it is still an attempt to arrogate to the State itself the right to decide whether to submit to the Court's jurisdiction after an application has been made against it. The reluctance of the United States to make such a claim to self-protection in the *Nicaragua* case may signify a belief, on a careful assessment of the legal and political factors involved, that the days when such a reservation would be regarded as 'automatic' are past. The interpretative approach, backed by the power to disregard a reservation that is in conflict with the requirements of Article 36, either diminishes, or extinguishes, the threat posed by such reservations. Indeed, to avoid such a conflict and its consequences, States which still retain this form of reservation in their declarations might feel obliged to argue a case for their legitimate use if they are ever brought before the Court. This would undoubtedly be the final step in establishing the objective character of such reservations and would constitute the clearest recognition of the Court's right of control over them.

[362] *ICJ Reports*, 1959, p. 6 at p. 92.
[363] At p. 93.

VI. The Vandenberg (Multilateral Treaty) Reservation

(a) *Background*

The origin of the Vandenberg reservation,[364] like the Connally amendment, was to be found in a 'Memorandum concerning Acceptance by the United States of the Compulsory Jurisdiction of the International Court of Justice', dated 10 July 1946, by John Foster Dulles. It took a negative view of the Court's functions and suggested only a very limited acceptance of its jurisdiction by the United States. In particular, it regarded with disfavour the possibility of the United States being involved in litigation when not all the parties to the dispute were before the Court. According to Dulles:[365]

Reciprocity: Jurisdiction should be compulsory only when all of the other parties to the dispute have previously accepted the compulsory jurisdiction of the Court.
Comment: The Court statute embodies the principle of reciprocity. It provides for compulsory jurisdiction only 'in relation to any other state accepting the same obligation' (art. 36(2)). Oftentimes, however, disputes, particularly under multilateral conventions, give rise to the same issue as against more than one other nation. Since the Court statute uses the singular 'any other state', it might be desirable to make clear that there is no compulsory obligation to submit to the Court merely because one of several parties to such dispute is similarly bound, the others not having bound themselves to become parties before the Court and, consequently, not being subject to the Charter provision (art. 94) requiring members to comply with decisions of the Court in cases to which they are a party.

In the Report of the Committee on Foreign Relations on the matter, it was said that the Dulles objections could be catered for by a reservation in the language subsequently adopted at the instigation of Senator Vandenberg, though the Committee itself did not recommend its adoption.

(b) *'Affected by the Decision'*

There were obvious difficulties with the operation of such a provision. 'At first glance', wrote one commentator, 'it might seem unworkable. Does it mean, as some have suggested, that if the Court is called upon to interpret the United Nations Charter to settle a case between two disputants under Article 36 of the Statute, it could not act unless the other 49 members of the United Nations also become parties to the dispute?'[366] As

[364] For the text of the reservation, see above, p. 122.

[365] The following extract is taken from Whiteman, op. cit. above (n. 351), pp. 1302–3.

[366] Wilcox, 'The United States Accepts Compulsory Jurisdiction', *American Journal of International Law*, 40 (1946), p. 699 at p. 715. While such an interpretation may not be possible because of the 'affected' limitation which is discussed in the text (similar phraseology is to be found in the reservations in the declarations of Malta, see International Court of Justice, *Yearbook*, 1987–8, p. 80 at p. 81; and Pakistan, ibid., p. 87 at p. 88), it would seem to be a possible interpretation of the reservations of a number of States which do not contain such a limitation: see the declarations of El Salvador, ibid.,

the writer went on to point out,[367] all turned on the interpretation placed upon the word 'affected' in the expression 'unless . . . all parties to the treaty affected by the decision are also parties to the case before the Court'. If it were interpreted to mean 'directly affected' or 'legally affected', 'it would tend to narrow the circle of States in each case to more logical and reasonable proportions'.

If the word 'affected' were given a broad interpretation to encompass any matter relating to a particular treaty, or if it were interpreted as applying to the treaty rather than to the parties,[368] the result could arguably be regarded as something akin to an automatic reservation. As Briggs said in hearings before the Senate Committee on Foreign Relations on 27 January 1960:[369]

> It seems to me what we are trying to do here—I am not quite sure what we are trying to do—but what we do say here is that we exclude from the jurisdiction of the Court certain disputes arising under a multilateral treaty unless we consent. In that case, our consent is the basis, and we are not accepting compulsory jurisdiction.

While it is undoubtedly true that the Vandenberg reservation is potentially of wide scope, it is not open to the same degree of criticism, even in the unrestricted version employed by El Salvador, India and the Philippines, as the Connally amendment. In the first place, there is no attempt in the former, as there might be in the latter, to impose the declarant's interpretation of its scope upon the Court. It is for the Court to determine which States are 'affected' by the interpretation of a particular multilateral treaty.[370] In addition, it has not the potential for covering the entire scope of the declaration. It could not apply to a dispute solely related to rules of customary international law. On the other hand, under the Connally amendment, in theory it could have been possible for the United States, whatever its protestations to the contrary,[371] to determine that almost everything fell within its domestic jurisdiction.

p. 70 at p. 72; India, ibid., p. 75 at p. 76; and the Philippines, ibid., p. 88 at p. 89. For the comment of Judge Jennings on this form of wording, see the *Nicaragua* case, *ICJ Reports*, 1984, p. 392 at p. 554:

> 'The meaning of the words, "unless all parties to the treaty . . . are also parties to the case before the Court", could hardly be plainer. The prospect of perhaps some scores of parties to a case may be bizarre; but a State is clearly entitled to make such a reservation, and the practical result is, no jurisdiction in the absence of special agreement. There can be no doubt, for example, that a State may, if it so desires, reserve against any case whatsoever involving a treaty to which it is a party.'

While the meaning of such a reservation might be so clear as to be open to no other interpretation, the question would still be, in the case of a multilateral treaty, whether the absurdity is such as to require an alternative meaning. This seems to be behind the comment of Judge Sette-Camara in the *Nicaragua* case, *ICJ Reports*, 1986, p. 3 at p. 192:

> 'It is difficult to see how the reservation could apply to universal treaties such as the Charter of the United Nations, or even treaties of a regional ambit, such as the Charter of the Organization of American States — both in cause in the Nicaraguan Application — because that would amount to bringing before the Court the entire membership of the United Nations, and the regional organization itself'.

367 *American Journal of International Law*, 40 (1946), at p. 715.

368 See the comments in the *Nicaragua* case by Judge Sette-Camara, *ICJ Reports*, 1986, at p. 193.

369 Quoted Whiteman, op. cit. above (n. 351), p. 1304.

370 See further below, p. 217.

371 See above, p. 185 n. 269.

In the *Nicaragua* case, Nicaragua alleged that the United States had been in breach of various rules of customary international law prohibiting the use of force by States. It further argued that the United States was not entitled to rely upon a plea that it had acted in pursuance of a right of collective self-defence. In defining the customary rules on the use of force and collective self-defence, Nicaragua could not avoid references to several multilateral treaties, particularly the Charter of the United Nations and the Charter of the Organization of American States. Because of this fact, it was the view of the United States that the Court could only proceed with the case if either the States affected (whoever they were) were before the Court (which they were not), or the United States 'specifically agrees to the jurisdiction' (which it had not). This objection to the Court's jurisdiction raised two specific initial issues before the Court went on to examine whether it was possible to decide the dispute in accordance with rules of customary international law alone. The first was that of identifying who were the States 'affected'; and the second that of prescribing the scope of the reservation *vis-à-vis* any States which were affected.

As far as the first question was concerned, the Court summarized the United States position as follows:[372]

> In so far as the dispute brought before the Court is thus one 'arising under' those multilateral treaties, since the United States has not specially agreed to jurisdiction here, the Court may, it is claimed, exercise jurisdiction only if all treaty parties affected by a prospective decision of the Court are also parties to the case. The United States explains the rationale of its multilateral treaty reservation as being that it protects the United States and third States from the inherently prejudicial effects of partial adjudication of complex multiparty disputes. Emphasizing that the reservation speaks only of States 'affected by' a decision, and not of States having a legal right or interest in the proceedings, the United States identifies, as States parties to the four multilateral treaties above mentioned which would be 'affected', in a legal and practical sense, by adjudication of the claims submitted to the Court, Nicaragua's three Central American neighbours, Honduras, Costa Rica and El Salvador.

The Court declined to determine the issue at the preliminary objections stage, on the ground that it raised 'matters of substance relating to the merits of the case', 'the question of what States may be "affected" by the decision on the merits' not being 'in itself a jurisdictional problem'.[373] How-

[372] *Nicaragua* case, *ICJ Reports*, 1984, p. 392 at p. 422. In addition to the two Charters referred to in the text, the other instruments were the Montevideo Convention on Rights and Duties of States 1933 and the Havana Convention on the Rights and Duties of States in the Event of Civil Strife 1928. However, as Nicaragua later, while not abandoning its claims under the last two instruments, acknowledged that 'the duties and obligations established by these conventions have been subsumed in the Organization of America States Charter', the Court decided that it would be sufficient 'to examine the position under the two Charters' (*ICJ Reports*, 1986, p. 3 at p. 34).

[373] *ICJ Reports*, 1984, at p. 425. Judge Schwebel was particularly critical of the Court's decision on this point. The Court's view that 'the reservation is incapable of application at a jurisdictional stage of the proceedings' constituted an 'unacceptable' interpretation of the reservation, because it was 'a result

ever, the Court did make clear that there was nothing self-judging about the reservation, even if the United States had purported to designate Nicaragua's neighbours as 'affected' States. In the view of the Court, 'the determination of the States "affected" could not be left to the parties but must be made by the Court'.[374]

In its decision on the merits,[375] however, the Court did not examine the circumstances of all three States nominated by the United States as being affected by the decision, but limited itself to the position of El Salvador, explaining that, 'even if only one of these States is found to be "affected", the United States reservation takes full effect'.[376] Given El Salvador's complaint that it had been 'the victim of an armed attack by Nicaragua' and assertion 'that it had asked the United States to exercise for its benefit the right of collective self-defence',[377] the position seemed straightforward enough:[378]

> In order to rule upon Nicaragua's complaint against the United States, the Court would have to decide whether any justification for certain United States activities in and against Nicaragua can be found in the right of collective self-defence which may, it is alleged, be exercised in response to an armed attack by Nicaragua on El Salvador. Furthermore, reserving for the present the question of the content of the applicable customary international law, the right of self-defence is of course enshrined in the United Nations Charter, so that the dispute is, to this extent, a dispute 'arising under a multilateral treaty' to which the United States, Nicaragua and El Salvador are parties.

The determination of these issues in relation to the United States was inevitably going to affect the position of El Salvador, as the Court went on to specify:[379]

> The Court has to consider the consequences of a rejection of the United States justification of its actions as the exercise of the right of collective self-defence for the sake of El Salvador, in accordance with the United Nations Charter. A judgment to that effect would declare contrary to treaty-law the indirect aid which the United States Government considers itself entitled to give the Government of El Salvador in the form of activities in and against Nicaragua. The Court would of course refrain from any finding on whether El Salvador could lawfully exercise the right of

which denies a reservation its obvious object' (*ICJ Reports*, 1984, at p. 604). The Court had not experienced the same difficulty in determining at a preliminary stage whether a State should be allowed to intervene under Article 62 of the Court's Statute on the ground that it was a State having 'an interest of a legal nature which might be affected by the decision in a case' (see at p. 605).

374 Ibid.

375 El Salvador, Honduras and Costa Rica.

376 *ICJ Reports*, 1986, at p. 34.

377 At p. 35.

378 Ibid.

379 At p. 36. For the part of the judgment dealing with the somewhat curious argument 'that the Court, if it found that the situation does not permit the exercise by El Salvador of its right of self-defence, would not be "affecting" that right itself but the application of it by El Salvador', see ibid.; for the part dealing with the proposition that the 'multilateral treaty reservation does not require, as a condition for the exclusion of a dispute from the jurisdiction of the Court, that a State party to the relevant treaty be "adversely" or "prejudicially" affected by the decision', see at p. 37.

individual self-defence; but El Salvador would still be affected by the Court's decision on the lawfulness of resort by the United States to collective self-defence. If the Court found that no armed attack had occurred, then not only would action by the United States in purported exercise of the right of collective self-defence prove to be unjustified, but so also would any action which El Salvador might take or might have taken on the asserted ground of individual self-defence.

(c) *Scope of the Reservation*

1. *The Court's view*

Having decided that El Salvador was a State that would be affected by a decision based upon a breach by the United States of the provisions of the two Charters, the Court had subsequently to decide whether it was possible for Nicaragua to establish its claim from sources of international law apart from those instruments. To a large extent the Court had already settled the issue. In the course of its judgment on the preliminary objections, it had said:[380]

> Nicaragua invokes a number of principles of customary and general international law that, according to the Application, have been violated by the United States. The Court cannot dismiss the claims of Nicaragua under principles of customary and general international law, simply because such principles have been enshrined in the texts of the conventions relied upon by Nicaragua. The fact that the above-mentioned principles, recognized as such, have been codified or embodied in multilateral conventions does not mean that they cease to exist and to apply as principles of customary law, even as regards countries that are parties to such conventions. Principles such as those of the non-use of force, non-intervention, respect for the independence and territorial integrity of States, and the freedom of navigation, continue to be binding as part of customary international law, despite the operation of provisions of conventional law in which they have been incorporated. Therefore, since the claim before the Court in this case is not confined to violation of the multilateral conventional provisions invoked, it would not in any event be barred by the multilateral treaty reservation in the United States 1946 Declaration.

All that was left for the Court to do on this issue in its judgment on the merits was to 'develop and refine upon these initial remarks'.[381] In response to the United States' 'view that the existence of principles in the United Nations Charter precludes the possibility that similar rules might exist independently in customary international law, either because existing customary rules had been incorporated into the Charter, or because the Charter influenced the later adoption of customary rules with a corresponding content',[382] the Court had this to say:[383]

> The Court does not consider that, in the areas of law relevant to the present dis-

[380] *ICJ Reports*, 1984, at pp. 424–5.
[381] *ICJ Reports*, 1986, at p. 93.
[382] Ibid.
[383] At pp. 93–4.

pute, it can be claimed that all the customary rules which may be invoked have a content exactly identical to that of the rules contained in the treaties which cannot be applied by virtue of the United States reservation. On a number of points, the areas governed by the two sources of law do not exactly overlap, and the substantive rules in which they are framed are not identical in content. But in addition, even if a treaty norm and a customary norm relevant to the present dispute were to have exactly the same content, this would not be a reason for the Court to take the view that the operation of the treaty process must necessarily deprive the customary norm of its separate applicability. Nor can the multilateral treaty reservation be interpreted as meaning that, once applicable to a given dispute, it would exclude the application of any rule of customary international law the content of which was the same as, or analogous to, that of the treaty-law which had caused the reservation to become effective.

In fact, of course, the conventional and customary rules were not identical. As the example of Article 51 of the United Nations Charter[384] illustrated, the conventional rules were to an extent dependent upon the customary rules. The reference to an 'inherent' right of self-defence was only explicable if self-defence was regarded as 'of a customary nature', while the meaning to be attributed to an 'armed attack' was dependent upon sources outside the Charter itself.[385] In the Court's opinion:[386]

It cannot therefore be held that Article 51 is a provision which 'subsumes and supervenes' customary international law. It rather demonstrates that in the field in question, the importance of which for the present dispute need hardly be stressed, customary international law continues to exist alongside treaty law. The areas governed by the two sources of law thus do not overlap exactly, and the rules do not have the same content. This could also be demonstrated for other subjects, in particular for the principle of non-intervention.

The Court also pointed to a 'number of reasons for considering that, even if two norms belonging to two sources of international law appear identical in content, and even if the States in question are bound by these rules both on the level of treaty law and that of customary international law, those norms retain their separate existence'.[387] The principal example given was that of the consequences of termination of a treaty by one State for a material breach of that treaty by another State.[388] While this might absolve the innocent party from further compliance with the treaty obligation, that State would still be subject to norms of customary international law

[384] According to Article 51:

'Nothing in the present Charter shall impair the inherent right of individual or collective self-defence if an armed attack occurs against a Member of the United Nations, until the Security Council has taken measures necessary to maintain international peace and security. Measures taken by Members in the exercise of this right of self-defence shall be immediately reported to the Security Council and shall not in any way affect the authority and responsibility of the Security Council under the present Charter to take at any time such action as it deems necessary in order to maintain or restore international peace and security.'

[385] *ICJ Reports*, 1986, at p. 94.

[386] Ibid.

[387] At p. 95.

[388] Ibid.

encompassed by the treaty. The Court also mentioned the additional possibility that:[389]

> A State may accept a rule contained in a treaty not simply because it favours the application of the rule itself, but also because the treaty establishes what that State regards as desirable institutions or mechanisms to ensure implementation of the rule. Thus, if that rule parallels a rule of customary international law, two rules of the same content are subject to separate treatment as regards the organs competent to verify their implementation, depending on whether they are customary rules or treaty rules. The present dispute illustrates this point.

The Court's view of the relationship between conventional and customary international law was hardly surprising, though the same could not be said of its subsequent treatment of the content of the rules of customary international law with regard to the use of force by States[390] and how those rules should be identified.[391]

As to the Court's interpretation of the Vandenberg reservation, it is difficult to express any firm opinion. Its approach hardly gave adequate expression to the section from the Dulles Memorandum relating to 'reciprocity' quoted above,[392] but the text of the reservation was not an accurate reflection of the purpose envisaged for it in that document. It should not have been difficult for the Senate Committee, which formulated that text, also to have given an example of a reservation that would have prevented a State bringing any claim against the United States to the Court, with regard to a dispute involving other States, unless those other States all became parties to the proceedings. The Committee chose to limit its suggestion to multilateral treaties, presumably because it was not seeking to promote any such limitation, let alone a broader version.

It cannot be said that the Committee was unaware of problems arising in relation to the United Nations Charter. Mention has already been made of the discussion about how to limit the scope of any such reservation to States 'affected' by a particular decision. From this point of view the drafting of the reservation would seem to have achieved its objective. It was not all members of the United Nations which had to be parties, but only those 'affected', in the sense that their rights were involved in the issues being litigated.

[389] At pp. 95–6.

[390] Amongst examples that might be quoted are the Court's insistence upon the existence of an armed attack for the right of self-defence to arise, even under customary international law; its rather vague distinction between a situation where an armed attack has occurred and that in which the victim might be entitled to take counter-measures, though not in conjunction with another State acting 'collectively' (see *ICJ Reports*, 1986, at pp. 103–4, 110–11); and the extraordinary proposition that, for a right of collective self-defence to arise at all, the State subject to an attack must both have declared itself to be the victim of an armed attack (at p. 104) and have requested the assistance of the State purporting to act 'collectively' on its behalf (at p. 105).

[391] Perhaps the most remarkable feature in the Court's approach was the elasticity with which it treated the requirements of *opinio juris* and State practice in the creation of customary international law (see *ICJ Reports*, 1986, at pp. 97 ff.), and the role of General Assembly resolutions in relation thereto (at pp. 101 ff.).

[392] At p. 214.

It is somewhat curious therefore that the issue of overlapping obligations under the Charter and customary international law was not also dealt with. It was a matter that was then of current concern in the context of the Nuremberg trials with regard to the operation of various rules of the law of war which, though contained in international conventions, were given a wider operation as part of customary law.[393] In addition the International Military Tribunal employed conventional proscriptions on the use of force to establish 'crimes against peace', with which major war criminals were charged.[394]

2. *The dissenting opinions*

The Vandenberg reservation was far from explicit as to its scope. There was thus uncertainty as to whether there was a basis for the independent application of rules of customary international law substantially similar to those contained in conventions the operation of which was excluded by the reservation. Dissenting members of the International Court admitted that a State which is not a member of the United Nations, or which withdraws from the organization, is not free of the obligations contained in Article 2(4) of the Charter, nor from the restrictions upon the right of self-defence imposed by Article 51.[395] In their view, however, this factor was irrelevant to the ambit of the reservation. As Judge Schwebel pointed out, the fact could not be ignored that Nicaragua and the United States were members of the United Nations (and of the Organization of American States as well). As the two States (and indeed Nicaragua's neighbours) were bound by both Charters, 'it would be an artificial application of the law to treat them as if

[393] Article 6(*b*) of the Charter of the International Military Tribunal (the Nuremberg Tribunal) 1946 described war crimes as 'violations of the laws and customs of war'. The Tribunal pointed out (*IMT Judgment*, vol. 22, p. 411 at p. 497) that the crimes referred to in that provision 'were already recognized as war crimes under international law'. They were covered *inter alia* by the Hague Convention respecting the Laws and Customs of War on Land 1907. Several of the belligerents in the 1939–45 war were not parties to that Convention, so that the Convention did not apply to the conflict by virtue of the so-called 'general participation clause' (Article II) whereby:

> 'The provisions contained in the regulations (Rules of Land Warfare) referred to in Article I, as well as in the present Convention, do not apply except between contracting powers, and then only if all the Belligerents are parties to the Convention'.

The Tribunal did not regard this factor as precluding the operation of the provisions as part of customary international law. As the Tribunal explained:

> 'The rules of land warfare expressed in the Convention undoubtedly represented an advance over existing International Law at the time of their adoption. But the Convention expressly stated that it was an attempt "to revise the general laws and customs of war", which it thus recognized to be then existing, but by 1939 these rules laid down in the Convention were recognized by all civilized nations, and were regarded as being declaratory of the laws and customs of war which are referred to in Article 6(*b*) of the Charter.'

[394] For the International Military Tribunal's discussion of the General Treaty for the Renunciation of War (the Kellogg-Briand Pact) 1928 in connection with its view that Article 6(*a*) of the Charter of the Tribunal made the planning or waging of a war of aggression, or a war in violation of international treaties, a crime, see *IMT Judgment*, vol. 22, at pp. 462 ff.

[395] At the jurisdictional stage, Judge Schwebel admitted that the fact that 'Switzerland, which has not yet joined the United Nations, or Indonesia, which for a time withdrew from the United Nations, were and are so bound by the prescriptions of Article 2, paragraph 4, as are the States members of the United Nations' was 'a powerful and probably correct argument' (*ICJ Reports*, 1984, at p. 615).

they were not bound, but bound only by customary international law'. Accordingly, since Article 2(4) and Article 51 of the United Nations Charter (and equivalent provisions in the Charter of the Organization of American States) 'are the specific and governing legal standards to which the Parties in this case have agreed, and since the multilateral treaty reservation debars the Court from applying to the dispute those standards as expressed in those treaties, I conclude that the Court lacks jurisdiction to apply both those treaties and their standards to this dispute'.[396]

Like Judge Schwebel, at the jurisdiction stage, Judge Jennings left open the question whether Nicaragua could rely upon customary international law.[397] On the merits, however, Judge Jennings expressed his conviction that the reservation was effective, giving a number of reasons why the customary international law argument failed. In the first place, in 1945, the principle contained in Article 2(4) was an innovation, and thus Article 51, though speaking of an 'inherent right', introduced a 'novel concept' in the form of collective self-defence.[398]

Secondly, it could not be said that 'a general customary law, replicating the Charter provisions, has developed as a result of the influence of the Charter provisions, coupled presumably with subsequent and consonant States' practice'.[399] The reason suggested by the Judge as to why this had not occurred was because all States had regarded themselves as bound by the Charter provisions. This hypothesis was supported by the fact that there were 'obvious difficulties about extracting even a scintilla of relevant "practice" on these matters from the behaviour of those few States which are not parties to the Charter'.[400] Moreover, Article 2(6) 'contemplates obligations for non-members arising immediately upon the coming into operation of the Charter, which obligations could at that time only be derived, like those for Members, directly from the Charter itself. . . . There is, therefore, no room and no need for the very artificial postulate of a customary law paralleling these Charter provisions.'[401]

Thirdly, in Judge Jennings' opinion, 'Although the multilateral treaty reservation qualifies the jurisdiction of the Court, it does not qualify the substantive law governing the behaviour of the parties at the material

[396] *ICJ Reports*, 1986, at p. 304.

[397] *ICJ Reports*, 1984, at p. 555.

[398] *ICJ Reports*, 1986, at pp. 530–1.

[399] At p. 531.

[400] Ibid. As is pointed out below, p. 235, there is not the space to consider in detail various aspects of the Court's judgment dealing with customary international law. Suffice it to say that, despite the Court's apparent acceptance (see at pp. 97–8) of the same traditional benchmarks for the creation of customary law as Judge Jennings, the difference in the conclusions reached can probably be best ascribed to a fundamental difference in the two approaches. In fact, the Court's judgment seemed to come close to accepting the proposition that the statement of rules in international fora by States, individually or collectively, can have the effect of consolidating rules of 'customary' law. For an elaboration of this thesis, see the present writer's 'Reflections on the Role of Consent', soon to be published in the *Australian Year Book of International Law*.

[401] *ICJ Reports*, 1986, at p. 531, citing Kelsen, *The Law of the United Nations* (1950), pp. 108, 110.

times'.[402] Viewed from this perspective, it could hardly be denied that the two Charters 'have at all material times been principal elements of the applicable law governing the conduct, rights and obligations of the Parties. It seems, therefore, eccentric, if not perverse, to attempt to determine the central issues of the present case, after having first abstracted these principal elements of the law applicable to the case, and which still obligate both the Parties.'[403]

The final point made by the Judge was that, even supposing that a residuary customary law could be 'disentangled from treaty and separately identified as to its content', the 'multilateral treaty reservation does not merely reserve jurisdiction over a multilateral treaty, where there is an "affected" party not a party to the case before the Court; it reserves jurisdiction over "disputes arising under a multilateral treaty" '.[404] While this part of his opinion is logical enough, Judge Jennings backed it up by a less acceptable proposition. He expressed the view that 'the legal nature of a dispute is determined by the attitude of the parties between which the dispute is joined'. This might be justifiable in some contexts, but in the present situation the Judge relied for support upon the fact that the United States had based its 'response to the charge of the unlawful use of force . . . firmly on the terms of Article 51 of the Charter. One party cannot in effect redefine the response of the other party. If the Respondent relies on Article 51, there is a dispute arising under a multilateral treaty.'[405] This explanation is hardly conclusive. When one of the issues in dispute is whether the United States' view of the situation was the correct one, the mere fact that it is making the assertion is not definitive of the matter. It is still for the Court to decide whether, as a matter of law, the assertion is justified.

Even if one were to accept the persuasiveness of the last of Judge Jennings' contentions, it would not necessarily prove decisive. There were other members of the Court who were able to reach a contrary interpretation of the reservation without referring at all to arguments about the role of customary international law. Judge Ruda, for example, interpreted the reservation as having the following meaning:[406]

> the United States will accept the jurisdiction of the Court in a dispute arising under a multilateral treaty, when all other parties to the treaty involved in the dispute have previously accepted the jurisdiction of the Court. In other words, the United States wishes to avoid a situation under a multilateral treaty, in which it would be obliged to apply the treaty in a certain way because of the Court's decision and the other parties to the treaty would remain juridically free to apply it in another form, because of the effects of Article 59 of the Statute.

The Judge did not deny that there was a dispute arising under a multilateral

[402] *ICJ Reports*, 1986, at p. 533.
[403] Ibid.
[404] Ibid.
[405] Ibid.
[406] *ICJ Reports*, 1984, at p. 456.

treaty, but in his view the dispute could be regarded as limited to Nicaragua and the United States:[407]

It is true that there is a complex and generalized conflict among Central American countries, but not the whole conflict, with all its economic, social, political and security aspects, is submitted to the Court, only the claims of Nicaragua against the United States. . . . In my analysis there are two disputes: the first, Nicaragua *v.* United States, and the second, involving the grievances of El Salvador, Honduras and Costa Rica against Nicaragua. A decision of the Court in the first dispute will not affect the reciprocal rights, duties and obligations of these Central American countries. Whatever conduct, if any, that the Court would impose on the United States, such a decision would not debar the rights of these three countries vis-à-vis Nicaragua.

A similar view was expressed on the merits by Judge Sette-Camara.[408] However, he went on to point out that the consequence of adopting this approach would have been to let in a proper consideration of the Charter of the United Nations and the Charter of the Organization of American States 'as sources of the law violated by the Respondent'.[409] Not that they were entirely ruled out upon the approach adopted by the Court. In Judge Sette-Camara's opinion:[410]

the non-use of force as well as non-intervention—the latter as a corollary of equality of States and self-determination—are not only cardinal principles of customary international law but could in addition be recognized as peremptory rules of customary international law which impose obligations on all States.

(d) *Concern for Third Party Rights*

The Vandenberg reservation was in some respects an aberration. If one refers to the Dulles Memorandum,[411] the problem with multilateral treaties was used as a specific aspect of a much wider problem, the possibility of the determination by the Court of disputes between the United States and another State where the dispute also concerned third parties. It is not at all clear why the Senate Foreign Relations Committee, and the Senate itself, singled out the issue of multilateral treaties for specific reservation. It seemed to run counter to the whole trend in United States practice to that date which had been directed almost totally towards the exclusion from international jurisdiction of disputes involving the interests of third

[407] At pp. 457–8. There are difficulties with this analysis. Even if one is prepared to overlook the fact that the complaints by its neighbours against Nicaragua were patently three distinct disputes, the very nature of collective self-defence, especially in the way it was interpreted by the Court, involved a third party in the dispute.

[408] *ICJ Reports*, 1986, at p. 198.

[409] Ibid.

[410] At p. 199.

[411] Above, p. 214.

States.[412] Moreover, when the United States sought to explain the objectives behind the reservation to the Court, the emphasis was upon the position of third parties in general:[413]

(1) the United States does not wish to have its legal rights and obligations under multilateral treaties adjudicated with respect to a multilateral dispute when the rights and obligations of *all* the treaty parties involved in that dispute will also be adjudicated; (2) adjudication of bilateral aspects of a multilateral dispute is potentially unjust insofar as absent States may have sole possession of facts and documents directly relevant to the rights of the parties to the adjudication *inter se*; and (3) adjudication of bilateral aspects of a multilateral dispute will invariably affect the legal rights and practical interests of the absent States.

It is not altogether clear what the United States was inferring by assertions (2) and (3). They are only of relevance to specifically treaty disputes if read subject to (1). In other words, as far as (2) is concerned, because it might be unjust in any situation involving a third party for the Court to determine the issues involved, the United States had reserved for itself the power either of invoking the limitation on the Court's jurisdiction with regard to multilateral treaties, or of consenting to the exercise of that jurisdiction. With regard to (3), the United States seemed to be concerned to provide its own understanding of the extent to which the Court might, as a matter of propriety, adjudicate upon rights attaching to a third party under a multilateral treaty.

Despite this apparent flirtation with the notion that the Vandenberg reservation was a means whereby the United States could impose upon the Court a definition of the role which the Court was entitled to play with regard to disputes concerning third party rights, the reservation has not

[412] See Damrosch, 'Multilateral Disputes', in Damrosch (ed.), *The International Court of Justice at a Crossroads* (1987), p. 376 at pp. 396–7:

'The U.S. Counter-Memorial's lengthy discussion of historical analogues to the Vandenberg Reservation in U.S. practice demonstrates that all other U.S efforts to deal with the problem of multilateral disputes have focused on the interests of third states in the dispute and not on whether a multilateral treaty was involved. A group of twenty two U.S. arbitration treaties concluded in 1908–09 drew on the Anglo-French treaty of general arbitration of 1903 to exclude from arbitration matters that "concern the interests of third parties". The U.S. strongly objected to a 1917 decision of the Central American Court of Justice in claims brought by Costa Rica and El Salvador against Nicaragua, in which the Court found that Nicaragua had breached its legal obligations to the claimant states by entering into a bilateral treaty with the United States. In the aftermath of this decision, the United States insisted upon a provision in twenty-eight arbitration treaties concluded in the 1920s, to the effect that the undertaking to arbitrate would not apply "in respect of any dispute the subject matter of which involves the interests of third parties". Similarly, the United States required an exclusion of matters "which affect the interest or refer to the action of a state not a party to this treaty" in the General Treaty of Inter-American Arbitration concluded in 1929. This U.S. position differed from that of most other states in the same period: the European states had moved from the 1903 Anglo-French model to the model of the Locarno treaties of 1925, under which disputes could be submitted to arbitration or adjudication "even when other powers are also interested in the dispute".

This historical review shows that the U.S. multilateral treaty reservation in the 1946 declaration was an aberration in its focus on multilateral treaties rather than multilateral disputes and that even the traditional U.S. approach to multilateral disputes was abandoned by most other states in the generation of treaties beginning in 1925.'

[413] The counter-memorial, p. 195, as quoted by Damrosch, op. cit. (previous note), at p. 395.

been treated as anything unusual. In the *Nicaragua* case, the Court dealt with it as raising ordinary matters of interpretation. In so far as it perceived that the reservation might have given rise to an issue of automatic application (the question of whether the United States was purporting to determine which States were 'affected' by the division), the Court was adamant that such an issue was for it to decide, not for the State invoking the reservation.[414]

The scope of the Court's jurisdiction is for it to determine on the basis of the relevant titles to jurisdiction: this is made explicit in Article 36(6) of the Statute. On the other hand, issues of competence are, for the most part,[415] not specifically provided for in the Statute: whether the Court has a discretion to decline to exercise its contentious jurisdiction in a matter otherwise falling within its jurisdiction, and the extent of any such discretion, are matters left for the Court to decide. However, as long as these principles are not interfered with, there is no reason why a State should not define its acceptance of the Court's jurisdiction in order to emphasize what role it believes the Court is entitled to play. A domestic jurisdiction reservation in which the determination of what is within that jurisdiction is not arrogated to the reserving State, but is left in the hands of the Court, has been a common, and valid, reservation in declarations under Article 36(2) of the Court's Statute. In fact, the dividing line between what is within a State's jurisdiction, and what is a matter of international concern, and not subject to international jurisdiction, has moved so far in the latter direction[416] that there seems little point in including such a reservation in a declaration.[417]

In the case of third party rights, the Court's attitude has been erratic.[418]

[414] See above, p. 217.

[415] The restriction on the Court to deciding 'legal disputes' being perhaps an exception. This limitation is placed on the Court's jurisdiction in relation to Article 36(2) of the Statute, but not under Article 36(1). See also Article 65(1) with regard to the Court's advisory jurisdiction, discussed in Greig, 'The Advisory Jurisdiction of the International Court and the Settlement of Disputes between States', *International and Comparative Law Quarterly*, 15 (1966), p. 325.

[416] Above, pp. 207–8.

[417] The United Kingdom declaration of 1 January 1969 (text in International Court of Justice *Yearbook*, 1987–8, p. 96) omitted any reference to domestic jurisdiction. The previous declaration of 27 November 1963 excluded 'disputes with regard to questions which by international law fell exclusively within the jurisdiction of the United Kingdom' (see *Yearbook*, 1963–4. p. 239).

[418] The Court's judgment in the *Monetary Gold* case, *ICJ Reports*, 1954, p. 19, is open to differing interpretations. At its narrowest it precluded the Court, in a case joined between Italy on the one hand and the United Kingdom, the United States and France on the other, from deciding an issue which arose solely between Italy and another State, Albania. As the Court said (at p. 32):

> 'In the determination of these questions — questions which relate to the lawful or unlawful character of certain actions of Albania vis-à-vis Italy — only two States, Italy and Albania, are directly interested. To go into the merits of such questions would be to decide a dispute between Italy and Albania.'

In contrast, the Court also stated (ibid.) that, where the legal rights of a third party 'would not only be affected by a decision, but would form the very subject matter of a decision . . . the Statute cannot be regarded as authorizing proceedings to be continued in the absence' of that party. As this statement was quoted with approval in the *Libya/Malta (Application of Italy)* case, *ICJ Reports*, 1984, p. 3 at p. 25, it would seem that the principle is applicable even in a situation where the third-party rights might, but do not necessarily, exist in opposition to the claims of the litigating States. In the *Nicaragua* case, *ICJ*

As a consequence there would seem to be some justification for a State attempting to define, in its declaration, the scope of the Court's authority over disputes concerning that State when a third State, also involved in the substance of the dispute, was not before the Court.

As to why a State should wish to place such a limit upon the Court's jurisdiction, it is unlikely that it would take such a step for totally altruistic motives. Protection of the interests of others, unless the interests of self are also involved,[419] is not a noticeable feature of international relations. What is true of the political stage in general is equally true of the decision to become a party to international litigation, whether by making application to the Court or by refraining from objecting to the exercise of the Court's jurisdiction. It is doubtful therefore whether a State in the position of the United States would set up the exercise of third party rights as a reason for excluding international jurisdiction solely as a matter of principle. After all, if one considers the circumstances of the Court's decision in the *Nicaragua* case, the findings in relation to the right, claimed by the United States, to act in collective self-defence in conjunction with El Salvador arguably impinged upon El Salvador's position. They could only have constituted an infringement of the rights of the United States in so far as the exercise of jurisdiction by the Court was in excess of the jurisdiction bestowed upon it by the United States declaration. However, the principal reason for advancing the excess of jurisdiction, based upon the alleged interference with El Salvador's rights, was the desire of the United States to avoid the embarrassment that would accrue if the action proceeded and an adverse verdict were pronounced against the United States itself.

Not that the motive for invoking a reservation is necessarily a relevant issue. It should not make any difference to the Court's assessment of the scope of a State's declaration if a reservation is invoked wholly or partly for the protection of a third party, or entirely for the benefit of the invoking State. The intention of the party concerned in making the reservation might be relevant in connection with the question of the extent to which the Court feels that it is under a duty to give a degree of protection to third party

Reports, 1984, at p. 431, the Court confined the scope of the *Monetary Gold* limitation on its jurisdiction to the narrowest version when it said:

> 'The circumstances of the *Monetary Gold* case probably represent the limit of the power of the Court to refuse to exercise its jurisdiction, and none of the States referred to can be regarded as in the same position as Albania in that case, so as to be truly indispensable to the pursuance of the proceedings'.

Even more surprising is that, having rejected Italy's application to intervene in the *Libya/Malta* case, on the ground that Italy did not have 'an interest of a legal nature which may be affected by the decision in the case' as required by Article 62(1) of the Statute, the Court subsequently, in its decision on the merits, *ICJ Reports*, 1985, p. 13, excluded from consideration all those areas of continental shelf to which Italy had claimed it had an interest in its application to intervene.

419 As in a collective security agreement like the Act of Chapultepec 1945, Section 5 (J), text in *American Journal of International Law*, 39 (1945), documents section, p. 109, which led to the incorporation of Article 51 into the United Nations Charter (see the comments of Judge Schwebel in the *Nicaragua* case, *ICJ Reports*, 1986, p. 3 at pp. 357–60); or the North Atlantic Treaty 1949, Article 5, text in *American Journal of International Law*, 43 (1949), documents section, p. 159 at p. 160.

rights. It could make a difference whether the reserving State was intending simply to remind the Court of its duty in this regard (which would seem to be the only possible explanation of a normal type of domestic jurisdiction reservation), or was seeking to express its own view on the scope of the Court's competence to deal with third party rights.

With regard to those States which have incorporated in their declarations multilateral treaty reservations without the limitation relating to parties to the treaty affected by the decision, it would appear that their intention is to go far beyond any protection of third party rights that the Court would provide. For example, if the attempt was made to bring a dispute before the Court relating to the continental shelf rights of such a State, and that State was a party to the Geneva Convention on the Continental Shelf 1958, the application of which was in issue in the proceedings, it could be argued that the case could not proceed in the absence of all other parties to the Convention being before the Court in the instant case. To provide an interpretation of such a reservation which avoids this absurdity would surely be the role of any interpreter. Otherwise, given the enormous and increasing range of conventional rules which makes it likely that some issue of treaty law will be germane to most disputes, the reservation could bar almost any case being heard.

There are a number of possible avenues of escape from such a conclusion. In the first place, it is for the declarant State to define the necessary connection between the dispute and the relevant multilateral treaty. In the case of the United States, the dispute must arise out of the treaty in question. On the other hand, the declaration of India[420] excludes from its ambit:

> disputes concerning the interpretation or application of a multilateral treaty unless all the parties to the treaty are also parties to the case before the Court.

As far as a reservation of the former kind is concerned, a dispute where the interpretation or effect of a treaty is peripheral to the substance of a dispute can hardly be said to arise out of the treaty. Nor, in relation to the latter, is there any reason to give the word 'concern' a broader interpretation.

Secondly, it is at least arguable that the declarant State did not intend to require the participation in the litigation of States which had no interest in the subject matter of the dispute. All States have a general interest in the development of rules of international law, be they customary or conventional, but that does not give them a sufficient interest to intervene in an existing case.[421] Nor should the general interest that a party to a treaty has in its interpretation and application be sufficient to make that State an indispensable party in any litigation concerning the treaty in question. Not only is there good reason for supporting the Court's approach in the *Nicaragua* case that a party to the treaty must have its rights affected by the

[420] Text in International Court of Justice *Yearbook*, 1987–8, p. 75 at p. 76.

[421] See the *Tunisia/Libya (Application of Malta)* case, *ICJ Reports*, 1981, p. 3; *Libya/Malta (Application of Italy)* case, *ICJ Reports*, 1984, p. 3.

decision before a reservation in the American form operates. There is also every reason for supposing that, by implication, a similar interpretation should be placed upon reservations in the more restrictive form adopted by India and others.

In the *Nicaragua* case, the Court preferred to base its rejection of the Vandenberg reservation as a ground for excluding the Court's jurisdiction upon the applicability of rules of customary international law, independently of their application as part of the Charters of the United Nations and the Organization of American States. This led Judge Jennings to voice the criticism that the Court had ignored the obvious fact that the reservation related to the ambit of the Court's jurisdiction and not to the rules which the Court was entitled to apply.[422] Even if one were to accept the validity of this observation, it would not follow that the Court's jurisdiction would have been ousted. As the discussion of the Vandenberg reservation has demonstrated, there were alternative grounds upon which the Court could have avoided the limiting effect of that reservation.

(e) *The Relationship between Customary and Conventional Rules*

The final aspect of the multilateral treaty reservation which needs to be considered concerns the relationship between customary law and treaty rules of similar content.

1. *Reservations to treaties compared with reservations to jurisdictional texts*

Some light may be thrown upon this problem by examining a little further the significance of the distinction between the applicability of rules of international law and the scope of the Court's jurisdiction, a matter to which Judge Jennings called attention.

Take the example given earlier with regard to States parties to the Continental Shelf Convention 1958. If one of them had made a reservation to that instrument, its object in doing so would have been to affect the rules of international law to be applied to any dispute in which it was involved concerning the application of the Convention. For example, in the *Anglo-French Continental Shelf* arbitration,[423] France had made a reservation to Article 6 of the 1958 Continental Shelf Convention which read in part:[424]

In the absence of a specific agreement the Government of the French Republic

[422] *ICJ Reports*, 1986, p. 3 at p. 533, above, pp. 222–3.

[423] (1977), 54 ILR 6.

[424] At p. 40. Article 6 provides:

'1. Where the same continental shelf is adjacent to the territories of two or more States whose coasts are opposite each other, the boundary of the continental shelf appertaining to such States shall be determined by agreement between them. In the absence of agreement, and unless another boundary line is justified by special circumstances, the boundary is the median line, every point of which is

will not accept that any boundary of the continental shelf determined by the application of the principle of equidistance shall be invoked against it . . . if it lies in areas where, in the Government's opinion, there are 'special circumstances' within the meaning of Article 6, paragraphs 1 and 2, that is to say: the Bay of Biscay, the Bay of Granville, and the sea areas of the Straits of Dover and of the North Sea off the French coast.

The United Kingdom's reaction was to notify the Secretary-General of the United Nations, as depositary of the Convention, that, *inter alia*, it was 'unable to accept the reservations made by the Government of the French Republic' to Article 6.[425] As a consequence, the tribunal had to decide upon the law to be applied in the light of the fact that Article 6 could only operate to the extent envisaged by Article 21(3) of the Vienna Convention on the Law of Treaties 1969:

When a State objecting to a reservation agrees to consider the treaty in force between itself and the reserving State, the provisions to which the reservation relates do not apply as between the two States to the extent of the reservation.

In this case, as the reference to the Bay of Granville had the effect of excluding that area from the operation of Article 6, the consequence was that the tribunal was obliged to base the award upon the rules of customary international law. However, as the tribunal emphasized with regard to all the areas covered by the award, because of a coincidence in the two sources of norms, the course of the boundary was 'the same whether the delimitation is made on the basis of Article 6 or the rules of customary law'.[426]

If the reservation concerns only the scope of a tribunal's jurisdiction, the exclusion of the conventional rule is not total, and different factors operate. In the Anglo-French dispute, it would have made no difference to the tribunal (though it might well have done to the decision it reached) whether or not the rules of customary international law were substantially those contained in Article 6. It would have been for the tribunal to ascertain the appropriate rules operating between the parties and to apply those rules to the facts. On the other hand, in a case where a reservation to the jurisdiction of the International Court excludes the operation of a multilateral treaty, it becomes a crucial matter whether the conventional rules and the customary rules do coincide. It would reduce the decision in the case to an absurdity if the Court were to admit that it had reached the conclusion on

equidistant from the nearest points of the baselines from which the breadth of the territorial sea of each State is measured.
2. Where the same continental shelf is adjacent to the territories of two adjacent States, the boundary of the continental shelf shall be determined by agreement between them. In the absence of agreement, and unless another boundary line is justified by special circumstances, the boundary shall be determined by application of the principle of equidistance from the nearest points of the baselines from which the breadth of the territorial sea of each State is measured.'

[425] At p. 41.

[426] At p. 57. As the Court also pointed out (at pp. 57–8):

'In the present case, whether discussing the application of Article 6 or the position under customary law, both parties have had free recourse to pronouncements of the International Court of Justice regarding the rules of customary law applicable in the matter'.

the basis of customary rules, but that, if it could have had recourse to the conventional rules, by which the parties were legally bound, it would have come to a different decision.

This point had been made by the United States in the *Nicaragua* case in a form explained by the Court as follows:[427]

> The United States observed that the multilateral treaties in question contain legal standards specifically agreed between the parties to govern their mutual rights and obligations, and that the conduct of the Parties will continue to be governed by these treaties, irrespective of what the Court may decide on the customary law issue, because of the principle of *pacta sunt servanda*. Accordingly, in the contention of the United States, the Court cannot properly adjudicate the mutual rights and obligations of the two States when reference to their treaty rights and obligations is barred; the Court would be adjudicating those rights and obligations by standards other than those to which the Parties have agreed to conduct themselves in their actual international relations.

Or, as the Court went on to interpret this contention:[428]

> The question raised by this argument is whether the provisions of the multilateral treaties in question, particularly the United Nations Charter, diverge from the relevant rules of customary international law to such an extent that a judgment of the Court as to the rights and obligations of the parties under customary law, disregarding the content of the multilateral treaties binding on the parties, would be a wholly academic exercise, and not 'susceptible of any compliance or execution whatever' (*Northern Cameroons, I.C.J. Reports 1963*, p. 37).

While the thrust of the last part of this statement might be obvious enough in general terms, it is open to question if subjected to more careful analysis. The reason why any decision in the *Northern Cameroons* case[429] would have been academic was that the action concerned past breaches of a treaty which had already come to an end, and all that the applicant State was seeking was a pronouncement on the law, not any specific relief. It was for this reason that the Court expressed the view that:[430]

> It may also be agreed, as Counsel for the applicant suggested, that after a judgment is rendered, the use which the successful party makes of the judgment is a matter which lies on the political and not on the judicial plane. But it is not the function of a court merely to provide a basis for political action if no question of actual legal rights is involved. Whenever the Court adjudicates on the merits of a dispute, one or the other party, or both parties, as a factual matter, are in a position to take some retroactive or prospective action or avoidance of action, which would constitute a compliance with the Court's judgment or a defiance thereof. That is not the situation here.

In the context of the *Nicaragua* case, if there had been a significant divergence between the conventional rules and 'the relevant rules of

[427] *ICJ Reports*, 1986, p. 3 at p. 96.
[428] Ibid.
[429] *ICJ Reports*, 1963, p. 15.
[430] At pp. 37–8.

customary international law', a decision reached on the basis of the latter in disregard of the former would hardly have been 'academic'. Formally, the judgment would have been binding on the parties.[431] The only sense in which it could have been described as 'academic' was the unlikelihood of the State against which judgment was given abiding by the decision. Moreover, if the convention, which had to be disregarded, was, as in this case, the United Nations Charter, it is hardly likely that the successful litigant could have resorted to the procedures for the enforcement of decisions of the Court referred to in Article 94(2) of the Charter:

> If any party to a case fails to perform the obligations incumbent upon it under a judgment rendered by the Court, the other party may have recourse to the Security Council, which may, if it deems necessary, make recommendations or decide upon measures to be taken to give effect to the judgment.

The problem is, of course, that some measures of enforcement of a decision might be within the power of the successful litigant to carry out, such as the seizure of the assets of the other party which are situated within the jurisdiction of the litigant State. If this should have occurred, it would not have been regarded as an 'academic' exercise by either party.

The important point is that the consequence of the Court deciding a case by reference to one source of law, to the exclusion of the other, and thereby reaching a different conclusion, would be bizarre. Indeed, such a possibility would seem to be excluded by the specific wording of Article 38(1) of the Statute of the Court whereby the Court is enjoined to apply all the sources enumerated therein.[432] Certainly Judge Lauterpacht regarded any attempt to restrict the Court's choice of sources in disputes submitted to it as involving a conflict with the Statute and a necessary finding of invalidity. In his separate opinion in the *Norwegian Loans* case, in answer to the question 'what is the result of the fact that a reservation or part of it [is] contrary to the provisions of the Statute', he said that the 'reservation or that part of

[431] The binding force of a judgment is implicit in Article 59 of the Statute of the Court:

> 'The decision of the Court has no binding force except between the parties and in respect of that particular case'.

It is explicit in Article 94(1) of the United Nations Charter:

> 'Each Member of the United Nations undertakes to comply with the decision of the International Court of Justice in any case to which it is a party'.

Moreover, by Article 94(2) of the Rules of Court:

> 'The judgment shall be read at a public sitting of the Court and shall become binding on the Parties on the day of the reading'.

[432] By that provision:

> 'The Court, whose function is to decide in accordance with international law such disputes as are submitted to it, shall apply:
>
> a. international conventions, whether general or particular, establishing rules expressly recognized by the contesting States;
> b. international custom, as evidence of a general practice accepted as law;
> c. the general principles of law recognized by civilized nations;
> d. subject to the provisions of Article 59, judicial decisions and the teachings of the most highly qualified publicists of the various nations, as subsidiary means for the determination of rules of law'.

it is invalid'.[433] The axiomatic nature of this conclusion he illustrated by reference to a number of examples of which one was as follows:[434]

> What would be the position if the Declaration were to make it a condition . . . that, contrary to what is said in Article 38 of its Statute, the Court shall apply only treaties and custom in the sense that it shall not be authorized to apply general principles of law as recognized by civilized States and that if it is unable to base its decision on treaty or custom it shall pronounce a *non liquet*?

Admittedly, in the *Nicaragua* case, Judge Jennings saw no problem with a State making a declaration which excluded from the Court's jurisdiction 'any case whatsoever involving a treaty to which it is party'.[435] This was, however, because of the distinction he drew between jurisdiction over a dispute and the relevant sources of law. 'Although the multilateral treaty reservation qualifies the jurisdiction of this Court, it does not qualify the substantive law governing the behaviour of the Parties at the material times.'[436] In Judge Jennings' view, given the prescription contained in Article 38 of the Statute, it would have been 'eccentric, if not perverse, to attempt to determine the central issues of the present case', having first removed the principal elements of the relevant law contained in the treaties concerned.[437]

This criticism would be valid if there were marked differences between the rules of customary international law and those contained in the two Charters. Where, however, the two sources of law are identical in all significant respects, there is no reason why the International Court should not proceed to decide the case on the basis of the customary rules (as in the hypothetical case of a dispute relating to the extent of the continental shelf of neighbouring States). While the Court's pronouncements may be relevant to the interpretation of the conventional provisions, the dispute does not in essence concern or arise out of the Convention itself.

If this approach is justifiable in the case of an unrestricted multilateral treaty reservation, there is no reason why the same approach should not be adopted with regard to the restricted version of the American type. Although there is not the need to attempt to avoid the absurdity which the unrestricted version creates, the two types of reservation are otherwise so similar that the same approach to their interpretation is entirely justified.

2. *The similarity of the relevant rules*

The question which was rightly asked by the Court in the *Nicaragua* case was whether the two legal sources were sufficiently similar for the exclusive application of one of them alone to produce a result that was not in conflict with the rules prescribed by the other. Despite the Court's

433 *ICJ Reports*, 1957, p. 9 at p. 44.
434 At p. 45.
435 *ICJ Reports*, 1984, at p. 554.
436 *ICJ Reports*, 1986, at p. 533; above, pp. 222–3.
437 Ibid.

identification of this issue, the acknowledgment that this requirement had been satisfied was as much a matter of inference as of explicit statement. Although it must be assumed that it had been, the position was obscured by the fact that the United States also sought to argue that even the identity of the two sets of rules precluded the Court from giving judgment on the basis of customary international law:[438]

> the United States apparently takes the view that the existence of principles in the United Nations Charter precludes the possibility that similar rules might exist independently in customary international law either because existing customary rules had been incorporated into the Charter, or because the Charter influenced the later adoption of customary rules with a corresponding content.

In the Court's view,[439]

> even if a treaty norm and a customary norm relevant to the present dispute were to have exactly the same content, this would not be a reason for the Court to take the view that the operation of the treaty process must necessarily deprive the customary norm of its separate applicability. Nor can the multilateral treaty reservation be interpreted as meaning that, once applicable to a given dispute, it would exclude the application of any rule of customary international law the content of which was the same as, or analogous to, that of the treaty-law rule which had caused the reservation to become effective.

However, the main thrust of the Court's judgment in this context was directed to showing that on 'a number of points, the areas governed by the two sources of law do not overlap and the substantive rules in which they are framed are not identical in content'.[440] Transposed to the issue being considered here (whether there is sufficient coincidence in the rules defined by the two legal orders for a decision in accordance with one set of rules not to conflict with the outcome designated by the other), this assertion could have created a critical problem. The former factor (i.e. the non-overlapping) would not constitute a reason for holding that the multilateral treaty reservation should have applied; but the same might not hold true of the latter (i.e. the fact that the rules are not identical).

As far as the first factor was concerned, the Court was only acknowledging that the United Nations Charter 'by no means covers the whole area of the regulation of the use of force in international relations'.[441] In particular, the right of self-defence in Article 51 could only be interpreted against a background of pre-existing customary law (the 'inherent right' to which Article 51 refers).[442] Among other illustrations given by the Court of this point were that the definition of an 'armed attack' was not contained in any

[438] At p. 93.
[439] At p. 94.
[440] Ibid.
[441] Ibid.
[442] In the Court's words (ibid.):
'The Court . . . finds that Article 51 of the Charter is only meaningful on the basis that there is a "natural" or "inherent" right of self-defence, and it is hard to see how this can be other than of a customary nature, even if its present content has been confirmed and influenced by the Charter'.

treaty, but was dependent upon customary rules, while the requirements imposed upon the right of self-defence, that it warranted 'only measures which are proportional to the armed attack and necessary to respond to it', constituted 'a rule well established in customary international law'.[443]

However, the fact that the relevant law is to be found in a range of customary rules, overlaid in part by a patchwork of conventional rules, is not destructive of the Court's approach. The crucial matter was therefore the second referred to above, the fact that the substantive rules 'are not identical in content'.[444] If there is a significant degree of divergence, then it could hardly have been proper for the Court to have reached a decision by applying one set of legal norms to the exclusion of overriding Charter provisions. In the Court's view, however, there was sufficient identity between the two for it to decide the relevant issues by reference to the customary rules alone:[445]

> so far from having constituted a marked departure from a customary international law which still exists unmodified, the Charter gave expression in this field to principles already present in customary international law, and that law has in the subsequent four decades developed under the influence of the Charter to such an extent that a number of rules contained in the Charter have acquired a status independent of it. The essential consideration is that both the Charter and the customary international law flow from a common fundamental principle outlawing the use of force in international relations. The differences which may exist between the specific content of each are not, in the Court's view, such as to cause a judgment confined to the field of customary international law to be ineffective or inappropriate, or a judgment not susceptible of compliance or execution.

3. *International law and the use of force*

This article is hardly the appropriate medium for a detailed analysis of the differences between the rules of customary law and the conventional provisions with regard to the use of force. Nor is there occasion to consider in any depth the correctness of the 'rules' which the Court regarded as representing contemporary international law relating to the use of force by States. However, with regard to certain aspects of that law, there was a degree of ambiguity that might give rise to uncertainties in this context.

On the one hand, the Court adopted a cautious approach to the requirement in Article 51 of the United Nations Charter that measures taken by States in the purported exercise of the right of self-defence 'shall be immediately reported to the Security Council'.[446] In the Court's view, it did not constitute a condition of the continuing validity under customary international law of an action taken in self-defence that it should have been reported in accordance with that provision, though the making or absence

[443] Ibid.

[444] Text at n. 440, above.

[445] At pp. 96–7.

[446] The material in this section is based upon Greig, 'Self-Defence and the Security Council: What does Article 51 Require?', *International and Comparative Law Quarterly*, 40 (1991), p. 366.

of such a report would constitute evidence of the State's own convictions in the matter. As the Court explained:[447]

Whatever influence the Charter may have had on customary international law in these matters, it is clear that in customary international law it is not a condition of the lawfulness of the use of force in self-defence that a procedure so closely dependent on the content of a treaty commitment and of the institutions established by it, should have been followed. On the other hand, if self-defence is advanced as a justification for measures which would otherwise be in breach both of the principle of customary international law and of that contained in the Charter, it is to be expected that the conditions of the Charter should be respected. Thus for the purpose of enquiry into the customary law position, the absence of a report may be one of the factors indicating whether the State in question was itself convinced that it was acting in self-defence.

Translated into the terminology of municipal law, the reporting requirement, as far as customary international law was concerned, would be designated as directory rather than mandatory.[448] However, the Court did not make explicit which of those roles it regarded the reporting requirement as playing under the Charter.

Akin to this were two other factors which the Court regarded as significant to the proper exercise of the right of self-defence. The first was the Court's insistence that 'the State which is the victim of an armed attack . . . must form and declare the view that it has been so attacked'. The second of the Court's assertions was that, in the case of collective self-defence, there was no rule permitting its exercise 'in the absence of a request by the State which regards itself as the victim of an armed attack'. In short, the Court concluded, 'the requirement of a request by the State which is the victim of the alleged attack is additional to the requirement that such a State should have declared itself to have been attacked'.[449] The way in which these requirements were stated initially, and were juxtaposed in relation to the reporting issue in Article 51, suggested that the Court regarded the former two as essential to the validity of the exercise of the right of collective self-defence (mandatory), rather than of evidential significance (directory).

There are, however, a number of difficulties with this assessment of the relevant law. For example, it is understandable enough[450] that a request to the ultimate defender might be a matter of importance in a case of collective

[447] At p. 105.

[448] Only in the case of a breach of a mandatory requirement would an act in pursuance of a power granted by legislation be rendered invalid, and, for this reason, the courts would lean against concluding that a particular condition for the exercise of the power was mandatory: see *Montreal Street Rly. Co.* v. *Normandia*, [1917] AC 170 at pp. 174–5. In more recent times the distinction has become further blurred by the emergence of the doctrine of 'substantial compliance': see *London Clydesdale Estates Ltd.* v. *Aberdeen District Council*, [1980] 1 WLR 182 at p. 189.

[449] *ICJ Reports*, 1986, at p. 105.

[450] Though not necessarily correct as it is possible to suggest that this proposition demonstrates a misunderstanding of the concept of collective self-defence in which it is the right of the State itself acting collectively which gives it the power to act in defence of the victim: see Judge Jennings at p. 545.

self-defence. It is less obvious why there must be a declaration by the victim that it has been subject to an armed attack before any right of collective (but not necessarily, it would seem, individual) self-defence is available. Ultimately, whether the necessary circumstances for action in individual or collective self-defence exist is a matter for objective assessment by the international community and not for subjective determination by the victim or its allies. On this basis it is possible to support the Court's assertion that:[451]

> There is no rule in customary international law permitting another State to exercise the right of collective self-defence on the basis of its own assessment of the situation.

However, as this proposition was advanced by the Court immediately after it stated the two criteria referred to above, it would seem that the Court was simply restating them in composite form. The problem is that, despite a degree of ambiguity created by the negative formulation of the composite version, the Court appeared to be stating the effect of the two requirements as mandatory rather than directory.

This is more a matter of inference than explicit statement by the Court. In contrast, more in keeping with a directory approach to these requirements were a number of later passages in the Court's judgment which appeared to treat the conduct of the alleged victim as more evidentiary than substantive. At one stage the Court said:[452]

> The exercise of the right of collective self-defence presupposes that an armed attack has occurred; and it is evident that it is the victim State, being the most directly aware of that fact, which is likely to draw general attention to its plight. It is also evident that if the victim State wishes another State to come to its help in the exercise of the right of collective self-defence, it will normally make an express request to that effect. Thus in the present instance, the Court is entitled to take account, in judging the asserted justification of the exercise of collective self-defence by the United States, of the actual conduct of El Salvador, Honduras and Costa Rica at the relevant time, as indicative of a belief by the State in question that it was the victim of an armed attack by Nicaragua, and of the making of a request by the victim State to the United States for help in the exercise of collective self-defence.

More specifically, when the Court came to consider the conduct of El Salvador in this regard, it treated that State's declaration of intervention to the Court of 15 August 1984 as the only public indication by El Salvador that it had been the victim of an armed attack. Although the declaration gave imprecise information as to when the alleged aggression by Nicaragua had taken place, the Court treated the accusation as relating primarily to contemporaneous, or at least very recent, events, and as signifying that no such concern had existed on El Salvador's part at an earlier date. In the Court's explanation, the events of 1984 provided a basis for rejecting 'the conten-

[451] At p. 104.
[452] At p. 120.

tion that in 1981 there was an armed attack capable of serving as a legal foundation for United States activities which began in the second half of that year'.[453]

The question of whether the declaration of being a victim of an attack and the request to the collective defender exist as mandatory requirements under customary international law is obviously of considerable significance as far as the law relating to the use of force is concerned. However, as the two requirements would operate in an area not covered by the Charter provisions, no question could arise of a conflict between the customary and conventional rules. It would make no difference from this point of view whether the Court intended them to be mandatory or purely evidentiary and directory. In the context of the present debate, therefore, the issue is of less importance.

It should be said, however, that principle and rationality would suggest that they should be regarded as falling into the latter category. It would be strange indeed if they were regarded as of such significance that they should be classified as mandatory, not least because there are the strongest reasons for supposing that the reporting requirement in Article 51 does not have that status.[454]

First, if this requirement did play a mandatory role in the Charter, the fact that 'in customary international law it is not a condition of the lawfulness of the use of force in self-defence that a procedure so closely dependent on the content of a treaty commitment and of the institutions established by it, should have been followed'[455] would have created a dramatic divergence between the customary and conventional rules. Such a possibility would be totally inconsistent with the premiss upon which the Court's decision on this point was based, namely that the rules of customary law and those of conventional law were substantially identical.[456]

Secondly, and perhaps more importantly, it would not be possible to

[453] At p. 122. The Court continued by saying (ibid.):

'The States concerned did not behave as though there were an armed attack at the time when the activities attributed by the United States to Nicaragua, without actually constituting such an attack, were nevertheless the most accentuated; they did so behave only at a time when these facts fell furthest short of what would be required for the Court to take the view that an armed attack existed on the part of Nicaragua against El Salvador'.

In the Court's view, therefore,

'the condition *sine qua non* required for the right of collective self defence by the United States [i.e. an armed attack by Nicaragua against one of its neighbours] is not fulfilled in this case'.

[454] As has already been pointed out in the text, the Court's judgment was far from clear on this point. The words it used were limited to the position under customary international law which was 'unencumbered with the conditions and modalities surrounding it in the treaty' (including the reporting requirement) (at p. 105). The Court's caution as to the position under the Charter in this regard was remarked upon by President Nagendra Singh who said (at pp. 152–3):

'In this context the Court's approach has indeed been cautious. For example, the requirement "to report" under Article 51 of the Charter is not insisted upon as an essential condition of the concept of self-defence but mentioned by the Court as an indication of the attitude of the State which is invoking the right of self-defence but certainly not closely following the treaty.'

[455] At p. 105.

[456] See above, p. 234.

treat the reporting requirement as mandatory under the Charter, while holding that such a report was not essential under customary international law, because of the primacy of the provisions of the Charter. Article 103 only speaks of the obligations under the Charter prevailing in 'the event of a conflict between the obligations of the Members of the United Nations under the present Charter and their obligations under any other international agreement'.[457] The same must be equally true with regard to rules derived from the practice of States,[458] except in so far as such practice has brought about a modification of the prescriptions contained in the Charter.[459]

The only member of the Court who considered the issue of the status of the reporting requirement was Judge Schwebel. His main concern was to demonstrate why, particularly in a case of alleged covert aggression, the victim or its allies might wish to conduct their counter-operations in an equally secretive manner.[460] As the aggressor could hardly complain at the failure to report,[461] the only substantive wrong arises out of the breach of the duty owed to the international community to report the matter to the Security Council. Judge Schwebel expressed the position as follows:[462]

> there is nevertheless a violation of an important provision which is designed to permit the Security Council to exert its supervening authority in a timely way. Even if Nicaragua, by reason of its prior and continuing acts of covert intervention and aggression, may reasonably be deemed to be debarred from complaining of responsive covert measures of the United States, the international community at large, as represented by the Security Council, has an interest in the maintenance of international peace and security which should not be pre-empted by the failure of a State to report its defensive measures to the Security Council.

[457] For some of the obvious difficulties with this provison, see Kelsen, *The Law of the United Nations* (1951), pp. 111–21.

[458] Certainly decisions taken by the Security Council which fall within Article 25 of the Charter have priority over contrary State practice. By that provision:

> 'The Members of the United Nations agree to accept and carry out decisions of the Security Council in accordance with the present Charter'.

For example, if the Council acting under the powers conferred by Article 24, paragraph 1 of which opens with the words: 'In order to ensure prompt and effective action by the United Nations, its Members confer on the Security Council primary responsibility for the maintenance of international peace and security', were to declare that a certain situation or course of conduct was contrary to law, it would be 'untenable to maintain' that members of the organization 'would be free to act in disregard of such illegality or even to recognize violations of law resulting from it . . . Thus when the Security Council adopts a decision under Article 25 in accordance with the Charter, it is for member States to comply with that decision' (*Namibia* case, *ICJ Reports*, 1971, p. 16 at pp. 52, 54). See Greig, *International Law* (2nd edn., 1976), pp. 744–51.

[459] As may have been the situation with regard to the interpretation and application of Article 27(3) of the Charter: see the *Namibia* case, *ICJ Reports*, 1971, at p. 22; and comment thereon in Greig, 'The Interpretation of Treaties and Article IV. 2 of the Nuclear Non-Proliferation Treaty', *Australian Year Book of International Law*, 6 (1978), p. 77 at pp. 97–8.

[460] *ICJ Reports*, 1986, at p. 373.

[461] As the Judge said (ibid): 'where a State commits aggression, a profound violation of its international legal obligations, and where it commits that aggression covertly, it cannot be heard to complain if a State or States acting in self-defence to that aggression respond covertly. *Ex injuria jus non oritur*: no legal right can spring from a wrong.'

[462] At p. 376.

However this requirement was approached, the term in question was 'a procedural term'. Judge Schwebel continued:[463]

> of itself it does not, and by the terms of Article 51, cannot, impair the substantive, inherent right of self-defence, individual or collective. The measures of the United States in assisting El Salvador by, among other means, applying force against Nicaragua, are not transformed from defensive into aggressive measures by the failure to report those measures to the Security Council.

The view that the reporting requirement is directory and not mandatory would also seem to be borne out by the practice of States. It would seem that the attitude towards the reporting requirement has been neglectful. According to one writer, there has been 'very little trace' of any reference to Article 51 in the records of the Security Council,[464] partly because of the reluctance of the Council to determine that one of the sides involved in international armed conflict is the aggressor (or to determine which party was entitled to rely upon a plea of self-defence).[465]

Even as a matter of treaty interpretation it is difficult to establish that the reporting requirement should be regarded as mandatory. It is true that the use of such words as 'shall' and 'immediately' suggests such an interpretation. However, this part of Article 51 lacks the precision expected of a provision intended to have such a dramatic consequence if not complied with. The issue of the beneficiary of the duty has already been mentioned (i.e. the international community rather than the alleged aggressor).

Within the framework of the Charter, it is a matter for the Security Council, as the executive arm of the world community, to determine whether there has been a threat to the peace, breach of the peace, or act of aggression within Article 39, and to decide what measures should be taken to resolve the conflict. In carrying out this task, there is no evidence to sug-

[463] Ibid.

[464] Combacau, 'The Exception of Self-Defence in UN Practice', in Cassese (ed.), *The Current Regulation of the Use of Force* (1986), p. 9 at p. 19.

[465] For various political reasons, the usual procedure adopted by the Council has been to call upon the parties to cease hostilities and, in the same or a subsequent resolution, to require them to withdraw to their positions before the hostilities commenced. Dinstein ascribed this approach to the 'profound rift between the super-powers' (Dinstein, *War, Aggression and Self-Defence* (1988), p. 196). While this may have been true in most cases, even where the interests of those two States did not appear to clash, there might well have been a reluctance on the part of the Council as a whole to designate one of the parties the aggressor. Thus, as Dinstein went on to say (ibid.):

> 'Even when faced with an obvious case of an armed attack, political considerations may prevent the Council from taking a concerted stand. In the absence of an authoritative determination as to who actually attacked whom, both opposing parties can pretend that they are acting in legitimate self-defence, and the hostilities are likely to go on. To avert further carnage, the Council tends to bring about at least a cease-fire.'

In the Iran-Iraq war, despite the obvious fact that it was the armed forces of the latter which were the first to cross the frontier into the territory of the other State, the Council refrained from determining that there had been an act of aggression by Iraq against Iran. See David, 'La Guerre du golfe et le droit international', *Revue belge de droit international*, 20 (1987), p. 153 at 156; and for the background to the war, Amin, *International and Legal Problems of the Gulf* (1981); 'The Iran-Iraq Conflict: Legal Implications', *International and Comparative Law Quarterly*, 31 (1982), 167; Khadduri, *The Gulf War* (1988).

gest that the issues are in any way predetermined by a failure to report actions that might reasonably or even conceivably be regarded as having been taken in self-defence.

It is also possible to question who is under the duty. The words used in Article 51 require the measures to be reported without specifying any particular party as being under the obligation to report. It is only an assumption that, because the right to act in self-defence lasts until the Security Council takes over the task of dealing with the situation, the acting State would be responsible for the reporting. It is equally arguable that the failure to identify the acting State as being under the duty creates an ambiguity which the subsequent practice of States may resolve. Apart from the difficulty in this regard created by the dearth of evidence concerning the employment of Article 51, which has already been referred to, the attitude of States points to the fact that the target State of the action claimed to have been taken by the victim State in self-defence is at least as likely as the victim State to refer the matter to the Council.[466] The lack of concern over compliance with this requirement reflects the fact that the decision to involve the Security Council in a particular situation or dispute is a political matter for the various members of the United Nations. It also suggests that those States do not regard the reporting requirement as mandatory or that a claim to be acting in self-defence can be rendered nugatory by a failure to make the report referred to in Article 51.

If that is the true position with regard to reporting, it would be unlikely that States would regard the two conditions attaching, in the Court's view, to collective self-defence as mandatory in effect. Whether a victim of an attack has declared its status as such, or has requested publicly the assistance of the collective defender, are questions which hardly go to the substance of the right of the latter to act. According to Judge Schwebel, a State 'cannot be deprived, and cannot deprive itself, of its inherent right of individual or collective self-defence because of its failure to report measures taken in the exercise of that right to the Security Council'.[467] Nor should a State be deprived of its right of collective self-defence (i.e., a right pertaining to itself)[468] by the facts that the victim State has neither publicly declared that it has been attacked, nor requested the assistance.

Despite the ambiguities present in the Court's judgment, there seem to be good reasons for accepting the Court's conclusion that the rules of conventional law and those of customary law are sufficiently similar, if not in most respects identical, to justify deciding the case by reference to the customary rules alone. This would seem to be a permissible way of limiting the scope of a multilateral treaties type of reservation, which would otherwise have extreme, even absurd, consequences for international litigation.

[466] Combacau, loc. cit. above (n. 464), at p. 16.
[467] *ICJ Reports*, 1986, at p. 377.
[468] As explained by Judge Jennings at p. 545: see above, p. 236 n. 450.

4. *Were the issues primarily matters of customary law?*

It has already been mentioned that Article 51 assumes the existence of a background of rules of customary international law. In the *Nicaragua* case, the Court held that those rules continued to operate in so far as they were not dealt with in Article 51. Thus the requirements of necessity and proportionality, which are not mentioned in that provision, retained their relevance,[469] while responses to a lesser use of force, which is not within the compass of the 'armed attack' referred to in Article 51, can only be justified on some ground other than self-defence.[470]

The Court's underlying philosophy was that these rules of customary law, in so far as they were not contained in the relevant conventions, simply supplemented those instruments, so that the two together constituted a coherent whole. Moreover, in those areas where the customary and the conventional rules covered the same ground, the former were a reflection of the latter, so that a decision in accordance with the customary rules would be in harmony with any decision reached by the application of the conventional rules. Nevertheless, as has already been mentioned, the view persisted that it was eccentric or even perverse to purport to decide the case by reference to one order of legal norms to the exclusion of the other merely to circumvent the effect of the Vandenberg reservation.[471]

(i) *Approaches to the interpretation of Article 51*. There are at least three alternative ways of viewing Article 51, and it is possible to make a case in support of the proposition that the decision in the *Nicaragua* case was (or should have been) primarily a matter of customary international law. One approach to Article 51 is based upon an interpretation of its text which gives much wider scope for a customary right of self-defence alongside what is specifically referred to in that provision (a textual approach). The second, which can either stand independently, or can be employed to reinforce the first, is based upon the hypothesis that Article 51 was designed, not to restrict or limit the inherent right of self-defence, but both to preserve it and to link it into the other provisions of the Charter (the object and purpose approach). The third has been a response to the inclination in many quarters (politically inspired recriminations against the conduct of certain States in the organs of the United Nations; and a particular view of Article 51 by some academic writers) to read Article 51 as restrictive of the customary right of self-defence. It takes as its starting point the failure of the Security Council to function effectively in maintaining international peace and security. This has necessitated States reasserting greater freedom of action than that envisaged by Article 51 (the effectiveness approach).

[469] Above, p. 235.

[470] *ICJ Reports*, 1986, at pp. 110–11.

[471] Examples include the arbitrary requirements that, in a case of collective self-defence, there must be both a public declaration by the victim State and a request by that State to the States acting collectively on its behalf, for assistance (see above, p. 236); and, of primary relevance in this context, the striking contrast between the right of reaction by a victim State and its allies, depending upon whether or not the use of force which has to be confronted amounted to the armed attack (see above n. 470).

Without embarking upon a detailed survey of these various possibilities for redefining the scope of Article 51, a number of points are nevertheless worth making in the present context. At the outset, however, it should be recognized that the Court's approach in the *Nicaragua* case was based upon a limited view of that provision and is therefore difficult to reconcile with any attempt to give a more extended role for self-defence under customary international law. As, in a number of respects,[472] the Court's judgment creates an aura of unreality in the law, it is doubtful whether the decision will for long remain the last word on the legal parameters to the use of force by States. Accordingly, alternative approaches to the interpretation and application of Article 51 are likely to retain their attraction to a number of States for which self-defence is a matter of immediate and vital concern.

(ii) *The relevance of an armed attack*. The most crucial aspect of Article 51 and the role it plays has been the significance of the words 'if an armed attack occurs'. Obviously the scope of the right of self-defence would be extremely narrow if it were accepted that (i) the right was limited solely within the parameters of Article 51 and (ii) the right could only arise therefore if such an attack had taken place.

One particular aspect of the law which has given rise to controversy in this context concerns the legitimacy or otherwise of so-called anticipatory self-defence. Is a State, threatened by what appears to be an imminent attack, entitled to strike first, or does it have to wait until an armed attack actually occurs before taking action against the aggressor? Although various attempts have been made to justify anticipatory self-defence by reference to the textual or object and purpose approaches (or even on the basis that an armed attack within Article 51 includes the deployment of troops in preparation for an invasion of the victim's territory[473]), the main justification for the legality of such action in an appropriate situation would be the effectiveness principle. The Security Council has so often in the past proved to be ineffective in dealing with threats to the peace of this nature that individual States have found it necessary to regard a right of pre-emptive action as essential for their own security.[474] Interestingly enough, in the *Nicaragua*

[472] See Judge Jennings at p. 543.

[473] Dinstein, op. cit. above (n. 465), pp. 178–81; this also appears to have been the view of Waldock, 'The Regulation of the Use of Force by Individual States in International Law', *Recueil des cours*, 81 (1952-II), p. 451 at p. 498.

[474] This would be because, as some writers maintain, on a literal interpretation of Article 51, there is no scope at all for a right of anticipatory self-defence: see Brownlie, *International Law and the Use of Force by States* (1963), p. 278; 'The United Nations Charter and the Use of Force, 1945–1985', in Cassese (ed.), op. cit. above (n. 464), p. 491 at pp. 498–9; Skubiszewski, 'Use of Force by States. Collective Security, Law of War and Neutrality', in Sorensen (ed.), *Manual of Public International Law* (1968), p. 739 at p. 767; Ago, 'Addendum to the Eighth Report on State Responsibility', *Yearbook of the International Law Commission*, 1980, vol. 2, pt. 1, p. 13 at pp. 67–8. The main exponents of the doctrine have tended to be apologists for Israel in the so-called six-day war of 1967, though there is a wide range of literature on the subject: see Forward, Jay, Koslowe, Linsider and Mezan, 'The Arab-Israeli War and International Law', *Harvard International Law Journal*, 9(1968), p. 232; Wright, 'The Middle East Crisis Working Paper', in Shapiro (ed.), *The Middle East: Prospects for Peace* (1969), p. 34; Lapidoth, 'The Security Council in the May 1967 Crisis: A Study in Frustration', *Israel Law*

case, the International Court refrained from indicating any view on the issue, merely commenting that:[475]

In view of the circumstances in which the dispute has arisen, reliance is placed by the Parties only on the right of self-defence in the case of an armed attack which has already occurred, and the issue of the lawfulness of a response to the imminent threat of armed attack has not been raised. Accordingly the Court expressed no view on that issue.

The first of the alternative views of the scope of Article 51, based upon the textual approach, takes its lead from the words actually used in Article 51: 'Nothing in the present Charter shall impair the inherent right of individual or collective self-defence if an armed attack occurs'. There is no clear statement that the right of self-defence only exists if an armed attack occurs. All that Article 51 says is that, if there is such an attack, the right of self-defence takes precedence over (it is not impaired by) the other provisions of the Charter. If there is not such an attack, then the right of self-defence is subordinated to the other provisions of the Charter.

The distinction between a case where an armed attack has occurred, when therefore the security and existence of the victim State is at stake, and the situation where a less serious use of force has been directed against that State, makes sense in the setting of the Charter. In the former circumstance, a State retains the right to respond to force with force; it is necessary but it must also be proportional to the extent of the threat with which the victim is faced. In the latter situation, as the consequences are less serious, it is, initially, for the States concerned and for the international community to deal with.

Translated into the provisions of the Charter, this means that, before a State can take action in circumstances where the force to which it is responding falls short of an armed attack, it is subject to the obligation contained in Article 2(3) to attempt to settle the dispute by peaceful means.[476] In addition, Article 39 of the Charter empowers the Security Council to deal with 'any threat to the peace' or 'breach of the peace' with a view to maintaining or restoring international peace and security.[477] But (and here there is an obvious link with the effectiveness principle), if there appears no likelihood of the various procedures proving adequate to deal with the situ-

Review, 4(1969), p. 534; Dinstein, 'The Legal Issues of "Para-War" and Peace in the Middle East', *St John's Law Review*, 44(1970), p. 466; Falk, 'Reply to Professor Julius Stone', *American Journal of International Law*, 64(1970), p. 161; Shapira, 'The Six-Day War and the Right of Self-Defence', *Israel Law Review*, 6(1971), p. 65; O'Brien, *The Conduct of Just and Limited War* (1981), p. 132; Miller, 'Self-Defence, International Law and the Six Day War', *Israel Law Review*, 20(1985), p. 49.

[475] *ICJ Reports*, 1986, at p. 103.

[476] By Article 2(3):

'All Members shall settle their international disputes by peaceful means in such a manner that international peace and security, and justice, are not endangered'.

[477] By Article 39:

'The Security Council shall determine the existence of any threat to the peace, breach of the peace, or act of aggression and shall make recommendations or decide upon what measures shall be taken . . . to maintain or restore international peace and security'.

The Council could of course also have recourse to the powers granted to it under Chapter VI of the Charter.

ation, or *a fortiori* if they have been tried and found wanting, States retain a residual power to act in self-defence even if no armed attack has taken place.

The political inevitability of this approach was reluctantly acknowledged in the *Nicaragua* case, although the Court was careful to deny the use of the expression self-defence in such circumstances. The reason for this chariness was that it wished to draw a distinction between the case of an armed attack, which gave rise to a right of self-defence, both individual and collective,[478] and a case of armed intervention falling short in extent of an armed attack, which gave rise to a right to take counter-measures on the part of the victim,[479] but not to any right, on the part of its allies, to take collective action[480] (at least beyond the territorial limits of the victim[481]).

A restrictive approach to the interpretation of Article 51 also creates problems for the victim of a series of incursions on to its territory which individually fall below the level of intensity of an armed attack.[482] Reference has been made to such reactive measures as 'reprisals',[483] but that

[478] *ICJ Reports*, 1986, at p. 110:

'for one State to use force against another, on the ground that that State has committed a wrongful act of force against a third State, is regarded as lawful, by way of exception, only when the lawful act provoking the response was an armed attack'.

[479] The Court evaded this issue in the following passage (ibid.):

'Since the Court is bound to confine its decision to those points of law which are essential to the settlement of the dispute before it, it is not for the Court here to determine what direct reactions are lawfully open to a State which considers itself the victim of another State's act of intervention, possibly involving the use of force. Hence it has not to determine whether, in the event of Nicaragua's having committed any such acts against El Salvador, the latter was lawfully entitled to take any particular counter-measure.'

However, it cannot be supposed that a victim State has no right of reaction with regard to, for example, an intrusion into its territory, falling short of an armed attack.

[480] In the Court's words (ibid.):

'The lawfulness of the use of force by a State in response to a wrongful act of which it has not itself been the victim is not admitted when this wrongful act is not an armed attack. In the view of the Court, under international law in force today—whether customary international law or that of the United Nations system—States do not have a right of "collective" armed response to acts which do not constitute an "armed attack".'

[481] That the Court was dealing with the use of force on the territory of another State is apparent from the following passage (ibid.):

'Since the Court is here dealing with a dispute in which a wrongful use of force is alleged, it has primarily to consider whether a State has a right to respond to intervention with intervention going so far as to justify a use of force in reaction to measures which do not constitute an armed attack but may nevertheless involve a use of force'.

[482] The seriousness of the problem has been identified in the literature. See the comment of Franck, 'Who Killed Article 2(4)? or Changing Norms Governing the Use of Force by States', *American Journal of International Law*, 64 (1970), p. 809 at p. 812:

'The great wars of the past, up to the time of the San Francisco Conference, were generally initiated by organized incursions of large military formations of one State on to the territory of another . . . Modern warfare, however, has inconveniently by-passed these Queensberry-like practices.'

See also Feder, 'Reading the UN Charter Connotatively: Toward a New Definition of Armed Attack', *New York University Journal of International Law and Politics*, 19(1987), p. 395 at pp. 396–7.

[483] A reprisal is an action taken by one State against another which would otherwise be wrongful. Its legitimacy depends upon its satisfying three requirements:

1. A prior wrongful act committed by the State against which the measure is directed in breach of an obligation owed to the State taking the action;

expression has fallen into disfavour in diplomatic parlance on the ground that reprisals involving the use of force are illegal.[484] The position of the victim State is not assisted by the fact that it is retaliating against a hostile action that has already been completed, and is also seeking to discourage similar future activities. The appearance of over-reaction militates against both the concept of reprisals (assuming their coercive use could be justified) and the right of self-defence. However, the restrictive interpretation of exceptions to the proscription on the use of force places a State which is the victim of acts falling short of an armed attack in a difficult position, and it is hardly surprising that the practice of such States has not coincided with that view of the law. One writer pointed to four reasons why the restrictive approach is so unsatisfactory:[485]

> The first reason is that a fundamental predicate for the restricted right of self-defence—a reasonably operational Security Council—has never come to pass . . .
> Second, there is no logic to the limitation of the right of self-defence to armed attack . . .
> Third, adoption of the restricted interpretation gives rise to the anomalous situation in which members of the United Nations may be left remediless . . .
> Fourth, the interpretation of restricted self-defense ignores the special problems inherent in counter-insurgency self-defense.

The strength of this case is undeniable in terms of the effectiveness approach. It is true that the further the situation differs from a classic invasion of the territory of one State by another, the more difficult it is to argue that the original definition or concept of an armed attack has been satisfied. Yet it would be a mistaken, and altogether unreasonable, view of the United Nations Charter to regard the original meaning as having been retained in the changing patterns of State conduct in the years since 1945.

2. an unsuccessful attempt by the acting State to obtain redress through normal diplomatic or other procedures (unless, exceptionally, such procedures are unavailable); and
3. the action taken by way of counter-measures must be proportionate to the original wrongful act.

See *Naulilaa* incident (1928), *Reports of International Arbitral Awards*, vol. 2 p. 1013 at pp. 1026–8; *Yearbook of the International Law Commission*, 1979, vol. 2, pt. 1, p. 43, fn. 191; Bowett, 'Reprisals Involving Recourse to Armed Force', *American Journal of International Law*, 66 (1972), p. 1 at p. 3; case concerning the *Air Services Agreement of 27 March 1946* (1978), 53 ILR 303 at pp. 338–9;Malanczuk, 'Countermeasures and Self-Defence as Circumstances precluding Wrongfulness in the International Law Commission's Draft Articles on State Responsibility', in Spineda and Simma (eds.), *United Nations Codification of State Responsibility* (1987), p. 197 at pp. 212–16.

[484] According to the Declaration on Principles of International Law concerning Friendly Relations and Co-operation among States in accordance with the Charter of the United Nations of 24 October 1970 (text in *International Legal Materials*, 9 (1970), p. 1292 at p. 1294), 'States have a duty to refrain from acts of reprisal involving the use of force'. There have been repeated condemnations of forcible reprisals as illegal under contemporary international law: see the examples given by Bowett, loc. cit. (previous note), at pp. 33–6. Zoller, *Peacetime Unilateral Remedies: An Analysis of Countermeasures* (1984), pp. xv-xvii, 40 ff., explained her preference for the last mentioned term by reference to the fact that words like 'reprisal' and 'retaliation' had largely disappeared from the international legal vocabulary because of their association with the impermissible use of force.

[485] Levenfeld, 'Israel's Counter-Fedayeen Tactics in Lebanon: Self-Defense and Reprisal under Modern International Law', *Columbia Journal of Transnational Law*, 21 (1982), p. 1 at pp. 20–1. It remains to be seen how enduring is the fragile unity amongst the permanent members of the Security

(iii) *The priorities for, rather than a definition of, self-defence*. The above analysis can also support the view that, even in 1945, States would not have been so sanguine about the prospects of leaving the protection of their integrity and independence totally to the obligations of the Charter enforced by the Security Council. It is therefore arguable that States deliberately retained an inherent, and not too restrictive, right of self-defence in Article 51.

This was apparent from the fact that the original proposals for the Charter contained nothing akin to Article 51. All that the incorporation of such a provision did was to establish a sequence of priorities. In the case of an armed attack, a State could respond with force in advance of any measures being taken by the Security Council. In other circumstances in which that inherent right existed, the order of priorities was reversed and a victim State was under a duty to allow the United Nations the opportunity first to fulfil its primary task of dealing with the situation posing a threat to international peace and security. If the United Nations did not, or demonstrated that it was unable to, deal with the situation, the victim State was then entitled to exercise its underlying right to act in self-defence on its own account.

The implications of this approach for the interpretation of the Charter are significant. First and foremost, it is apparent that Article 51 could no longer be regarded as definitional in effect. That is to say, the reference to an armed attack in that provision would not constitute a *sine qua non* of the valid exercise of the right of self-defence in all circumstances. Article 51 would simply determine the relationship between the powers of the Council on the one hand and the area within which individual States would retain freedom of action on the other. In other words, the provision would be complementary to the Council's primary responsibility for the maintenance of international peace and security bestowed upon it by Article 24 of the Charter, in contrast to the rights reserved to individual States to act on their own behalf.

There are a number of aspects of the relevant provisions which point in this direction. According to Article 24(1), the Security Council is to act on behalf of members of the United Nations in performing the tasks allocated to the Organization:

> In order to ensure prompt and effective action by the United Nations, its Members confer on the Security Council primary responsibility for the maintenance of international peace and security, and agree that in carrying out its duties under this responsibility the Security Council acts on their behalf.

Council arising out of Iraq's invasion of Kuwait, which enabled the Council to pass a series of resolutions condemning the invasion (see esp. Resolutions 660 and 661 (1990) of 2 and 6 August 1990), and to authorize by Resolution 678 of 29 November 1990:

'Member States co-operating with the Government of Kuwait, unless Iraq on or before 15 January 1991 fully implements, as set forth in paragraph 1 above, the foregoing resolutions, to use all necessary means to uphold and implement Security Council resolution 660 (1990) and all subsequent relevant resolutions and to restore international peace and security in the area'.

It would seem, therefore, that, if the Council is unable to act, the secondary responsibility for the taking of 'prompt and effective action' must be vested elsewhere. At times, and to an extent, the General Assembly has attempted to assume this role,[486] a step which is only possible, in accordance with Article 18 of the Charter, if two-thirds of the members of the Assembly present and voting recommend the taking of the appropriate measures. In the field of international peace and security, the Assembly is limited to recommending measures under Article 14, while Article 11(2) states that any question relating to international peace and security 'on which action is necessary shall be referred to the Security Council by the General Assembly either before or after discussion'. It is clear, therefore, that the Assembly has no authority to take coercive action.

While the primary responsibility for international peace and security is, as between the two principal political organs of the United Nations, vested in the Council rather than the Assembly, Article 24(1) also signifies the priority between the Organization and individual States. Members have transferred their individual and community interests to the Council acting on behalf of them, the United Nations. Article 51 is a specific instance of these priorities, but Article 51 does not, any more than Article 24, transfer to the Organization all rights formerly belonging to individual States in relation to international peace and security and the right to respond to the illegal use of force, at whatever level of intensity. All that Article 51 does is to set the priorities by reference to the level of intensity of the threat to the victim State. After all, if it had been the intention of the framers of the Charter, and those who initially subscribed to that instrument, to exclude any right of self-defence, except in a case of an armed attack, it would have been a simple matter to have made this intention clear. It could have been stated that no member could resort to force in self-defence except in response to an armed attack.

If this had been the intention, there would have been no need to refer to self-defence as an inherent right, with the implication of such an expression that it is otherwise of general application or availability. It is not obvious where such a provision would have been placed in the Charter. The siting

[486] For a discussion of the scope of its powers and their relationship to the role of the Security Council, see the *Expenses* case, *ICJ Reports*, 1962, p. 151 at pp. 162 ff. As the Court said of Article 24 (at p. 163):

> 'The responsibility conferred is "primary", not exclusive. This primary responsibility is conferred upon the Security Council, as stated in Article 24, "in order to ensure prompt and effective action". To this end, it is the Security Council which is given a power to impose an explicit obligation of compliance if for example it issues an order or command to an aggressor under Chapter VII. It is only the Security Council which can require enforcement by coercive action against an aggressor.
>
> The Charter makes it abundantly clear, however, that the General Assembly is also to be concerned with international peace and security. Article 14 authorizes the General Assembly to "recommend measures for the peaceful adjustment of any situation, regardless of origin, which it deems likely to impair the general welfare or friendly relations among nations, including situations resulting from a violation of the provisions of the present Charter setting forth the purposes and principles of the United Nations".'

of a provision in its present form in Chapter VII, dealing with 'Action with Respect to Threats to the Peace, Breaches of the Peace, and Acts of Aggression' conducted by the Security Council, would seem to be more concerned with the relationship between the legitimate activities of a State in the exercise of this inherent right and the powers of the Council to take action in such circumstances. As has already been pointed out, the more obvious interpretation of the text of Article 51 is that, in the case of an armed attack, the rights of the victim State take priority (i.e., nothing is to impair that inherent right) until the Council has taken the measures necessary to restore international peace and security. If the threat or use of force to which Chapter VII (including Article 51) applies is less than an armed attack, the inherent right is made subject to the Charter provision and in particular to the authority of the Council to attempt to deal with the situation from which the threat emanates.

If this is indeed the correct view of the Charter, the right of self-defence would be almost entirely a matter of customary international law. Article 51 would not be definitional in effect, because its purpose would be to deal with the allocation of responsibility and authority between the United Nations and its members. Viewed in this light, it would be difficult to contend that the dispute before the Court in the *Nicaragua* case arose 'under a multilateral treaty'. The dispute would primarily have concerned the rules of customary international law. Moreover, even if, in light of the Court's finding that no armed attack had occurred, the situation was one in which, by Article 51, the primary responsibility and power to act lay with the Security Council, rather than with individual States, the State or States, facing a use of force of lesser intensity than an armed attack, would not be deprived of all right of response. In the absence of adequate action by the Council, the inherent right of the State concerned would revive. In the context of the *Nicaragua* case, the validity or otherwise of United States' conduct would therefore be assessed by reference to the rules of customary international law. On this analysis, the Vandenberg reservation would have been irrelevant.

VII. The Treaty of Friendship, Commerce and Navigation 1956

By a very large majority,[487] the Court held[488] that it had jurisdiction in the *Nicaragua* case under Article XXIV of the 1956 Treaty between the United States and Nicaragua.[489]

[487] By 14 to 2, Judges Ruda and Schwebel dissenting.
[488] *ICJ Reports*, 1984, p. 396 at p. 426 ff.
[489] The text of Article XXIV(2) is given above, p. 122.

(a) *Should the Alternative Basis of Jurisdiction have been Pleaded Earlier?*

Although there thus appeared to be a large measure of agreement as to the Treaty's application, there were a number of matters upon which opinions could differ. For example, the United States had raised as an issue the fact that Nicaragua had not sought to rely upon this title of jurisdiction until the submission of its memorial in the proceedings. The Court saw no merit in this objection:[490]

> it is certainly desirable that 'the legal grounds upon which the jurisdiction of the Court is said to be based' should be indicated at an early stage in the proceedings, and Article 38 of the Rules of Court therefore provides for these to be specified 'as far as possible' in the application. An additional ground of jurisdiction may however be brought to the Court's attention later, and the Court may take it into account provided the Applicant makes it clear that it intends to proceed upon that basis . . . and provided also that the result is not to transform the dispute brought before the Court by the application into another dispute which is different in character . . . Both these conditions are satisfied in the present case.

(b) *Did there have to be Prior Negotiations?*

A further preliminary matter raised by the United States was the contention that Nicaragua had failed to satisfy the *sine qua non* of international adjudication contained in Article XXIV(2) of the Treaty whereby:

> Any dispute between the Parties as to the interpretation or application of the present Treaty, not satisfactorily adjusted by diplomacy, shall be submitted to the International Court of Justice, unless the Parties agree to settlement by some other specific means.

Indeed, it was doubtful whether there was even a dispute arising out of that Treaty for, as Judge Schwebel said:[491]

> Nicaragua does not allege that it has ever claimed, before or during these negotiations or otherwise, that there is any dispute between it and the United States over the interpretation or application of the Treaty. Such claims for the first time appear in the Nicaraguan Memorial. For its part, the United States denies that there has been any effort to adjust by diplomacy any dispute with Nicaragua over the interpretation and application of the Treaty, particularly because Nicaragua has not even made representations under the Treaty that could give rise to a dispute.

[490] At p. 427. As the Court went on to point out (at pp. 428–9):

> 'The United States was well aware that Nicaragua alleged that its conduct was a breach of international obligations before the present case was instituted; and it is now aware that specific articles of the 1956 Treaty are alleged to have been violated. It would make no sense to require Nicaragua now to institute fresh proceedings based on the Treaty, which it would be fully entitled to do.'

For a contrary option, see Judge Schwebel at pp. 628–9. It should also be mentioned, in support of the Court's view, that Nicaragua, in its application of 9 April 1984, expressly reserved 'the right to supplement and amend this Application': see *ICJ Reports*, 1986, p. 3 at p. 18.

[491] *ICJ Reports*, 1984, at pp. 629–30.

Accordingly, in Judge Schwebel's view, Nicaragua had 'not discharged the procedural prerequisites for invocation' of the Treaty.[492]

The Court rejected this argument, though the reason for doing so may not provide a clear principle for later use. As the Court expressed it:[493]

> In the view of the Court, it does not necessarily follow that, because a State has not expressly referred in negotiations with another State to a particular treaty as having been violated by conduct of that other State, it is debarred from invoking a compromissory clause in that treaty. The United States was well aware that Nicaragua alleged that its conduct was a breach of international obligations before the present case was instituted: and it is now aware that specific articles of the 1956 Treaty are alleged to have been violated. It would make no sense to require Nicaragua now to institute fresh proceedings based on the Treaty, as it would be fully entitled to do.

It will readily be appreciated that the last sentence, if it qualifies the entire passage, greatly limits its potential scope. If, for example, the respondent State validly exercised a right of termination of a treaty containing a compromissory clause, after the case was commenced, but before the violations were spelt out in the course of the litigation, it would seem that it would follow that the applicant State was 'debarred from invoking the compromissory clause in that treaty'.

On the other hand, if the last sentence of the quoted passage were only an alternative justification for the Court's decision on the issue, an applicant State would not necessarily be debarred in a situation where a respondent had validly terminated a treaty at that time. The passage can plausibly be read as offering an alternative situation for the exercise of jurisdiction. This would be on the basis that, as long as the respondent State was aware of allegations that it was in breach of its international obligations, the subsequent attachment of those allegations to specific treaty provisions was permissible. On the face of it, this proposition is extremely broad, and might need to be limited in some way. For example, it might be said that subsequent specification of the relevant treaty provisions is only possible where the earlier allegations had not been directed exclusively to some other source of obligation, thus in effect excluding the possibility of recourse to the treaty as the basis for the allegations of wrongful conduct.

There is, however, a preferable basis for the Court's decision on the operation of the 1956 Treaty. The wording of Article XXIV(2) did not expressly require prior identification of the substance of the dispute in terms of the Treaty, nor a prior period of negotiation before submission to the Court. Accordingly, in the words of Judge Nagendra Singh, 'the allegation made by the United States that Nicaragua in its negotiations has never raised the application or interpretation of the Treaty would appear to have no relevance to the jurisdiction of the Court because negotiations have

[492] At p. 630.
[493] At pp. 428–9.

not been specifically prescribed as a *sine qua non* for the Parties to proceed to the Court'.[494]

Under the local remedies rule, an applicant State cannot bring a case to an international tribunal with respect to a wrong caused to its national by the respondent State unless local remedies have first been exhausted. There is, however, no equivalent obligation, with regard to the general rights and duties operating directly between States on the international plane, as long as a dispute can be seen to exist between them, to try to negotiate a resolution prior to seising an international tribunal of the matter. Nor is there any reason for imposing such a requirement unless the jurisdictional text upon which the applicant relies makes such a requirement clear and explicit. Indeed, the ease with which a potential respondent State might withdraw from the Court's jurisdiction makes it more likely (and necessary) that an applicant State should come to the Court sooner rather than later.[495]

(c) *Had the United States committed Breaches of such a Treaty?*

A more fundamental issue was whether or how far a treaty which was essentially commercial in nature could legitimately cover the 'grave and sweeping charges'[496] made by Nicaragua in its application against the United States. In Judge Schwebel's view, the Treaty could not be extended to such weighty matters. In the view of other members of the Court,[497] the scope for jurisdiction on this basis was restricted, particularly as Article XXI(1)(*d*) expressly excluded from the prohibitions on the various commercial freedoms granted by the Treaty measures 'necessary to fulfil the obligations of a party for the maintenance or restoration of international peace and security, or necessary to protect its essential security interests'.

The Court had no doubt that, in two significant respects, the United States was in breach of specific obligations of the 1956 Treaty. With regard to the mining of access to Nicaraguan ports by the United States, this was 'in manifest contradiction with the freedom of navigation and commerce guaranteed by Article XIX, paragraph 1'.[498] With regard to the Presidential Order of 1 May 1985 whereby vessels of Nicaraguan registry were prohibited from entering United States ports and related transactions also

[494] At pp. 445–6.

[495] Where negotiations are made a condition precedent to submission of a dispute to an international tribunal, it is arguable that the situation should be treated as akin to that arising under the local remedies rule. In that situation there is no need to have recourse to such remedies when there are none available. With regard to prior negotiations, such a requirement did not have to be satisfied, according to Judge Ago, 'when the hopelessness of expecting any negotiations to succeed is clear from the state of relations between the parties, and . . . there is no warrant for using it as a ground for delaying the opening of arbitral or judicial proceedings when provision for recourse to them exists' (at p. 516).

[496] The words used by Judge Schwebel at p. 631.

[497] See Judge Oda, *ICJ Reports*, 1986, at pp. 252–3; cp. Judge Jennings at p. 541.

[498] At p. 139. By Article XIX(1) it was provided: 'Between the territories of the two Parties there shall be freedom of commerce and navigation'.

proscribed, and to the notice of twelve months given the same day to terminate the Treaty, the Court held:[499]

The freedom of Nicaraguan vessels, under Article XIX, paragraph 3, 'to come with their cargoes to all ports, places and waters' of the United States could not . . . be interfered with during that period of notice, let alone terminated abruptly by the declaration of an embargo.

Of the provisos to Article XXI(1), the only one dealt with was (*d*).[500] By this paragraph, the Treaty was not to 'preclude the application of' measures:

necessary to fulfil the obligations of a Party for the maintenance or restoration of international peace and security, or necessary to protect its essential security interests.

With regard to the actions by the United States involving the use of force in potential breach of the Treaty, the Court decided:[501]

that the mining of Nicaraguan ports, and the direct attacks on ports and oil installations, cannot possibly be justified as 'necessary' to protect the essential security interests of the United States.

Nor could the trade embargo be justified on such a ground:[502]

by the terms of the Treaty itself, whether a measure is necessary to protect the essential security interests of a party is not . . . purely a question for the subjective judgment of the party; the text does not refer to what the party 'considers necessary' for that purpose. Since no evidence at all is available to show how Nicaraguan policies had in fact become a threat to 'essential security interests' in May 1985, when those policies had been consistent, and consistently criticized by the United States, for four years previously, the Court is unable to find that the embargo was 'necessary' to protect those interests.

There was some disquiet expressed about these conclusions. The principal objection seemed to be based upon the Court's approach in first deciding whether the conduct was in breach of the Treaty, and then considering whether that conduct could be excused (the exculpatory view of the Treaty's interpretation). In the opinion of some members of the Court, a different conclusion would have followed from a more correct (exclusionary) approach to the interpretation of Article XXI. According to them, the

[499] At p. 140. Article XIX(3) provided in part:

'Vessels of either Party shall have liberty, on equal terms with vessels of the other Party and on equal terms with vessels of any third country, to come with their cargoes to all ports, places and waters of such other Party open to foreign commerce and navigation'.

[500] The exclusion from the Treaty's obligations of matters relating to traffic in arms by Article XXI(1)(*c*) was held by the Court not to be pertinent to the merits of the case. The Court said (at p. 141):

'This paragraph appears . . . to be relevant only in respect of the complaint of supply of arms to the *contras*, and since the Court does not find that arms supply to be a breach of the Treaty . . . paragraph 9(1)(*c*) does not need to be considered further'.

[501] At p. 141.

[502] Ibid.

Treaty did not apply to such measures at all so that it was impermissible to treat them as prima facie constituting breaches of the Treaty. This argument was expressed most clearly in the dissenting opinion of Judge Schwebel:[503]

> The application of such measures is not regulated by the Treaty: the preclusion clause is an exclusion clause. In my view, where a treaty excludes from its regulated reach certain areas, those areas do not fall within the jurisdictional scope of the Treaty . . . That this Treaty's preclusion clause is indeed an exclusion clause is indicated not only by its terms but by the quoted *travaux préparatoires*. Thus . . . I remain of the view that the Treaty fails to provide a basis of jurisdiction for the Court in this case, certainly for the central questions posed by it, unless, at any rate, United States reliance upon Article XXI.1(*d*) is, on its face, without basis.

The result of this view of interpretation, taken to its extreme conclusion, was dramatic indeed. It would have been for the applicant State to have shown that reliance upon the exclusion was 'without basis', suggesting that as long as some credible or plausible reason could be adduced in satisfaction of paragraph (*d*), the Court would be without jurisdiction. This must surely be a departure from normal processes of judicial reasoning where the fact that the applicant can show that an activity appears to fall within the provisions of the Treaty places some onus upon the respondent to show why its conduct is excused in the particular circumstances, or exempted from the Court's jurisdiction. If one considers the opinion of Judge Jennings, one of the Judges who, along with Judge Schwebel, was least satisfied with this aspect of the Court's judgment, he also employed language consonant with the Court's sequence of reasoning when he said:[504]

> it must be emphasized that the issue here is not simply the lawfulness or unlawfulness of the act in general international law, but whether it was also in breach of the terms of the Treaty? Certainly it is prima facie a breach of Article XIX, providing for freedom of navigation; but is it a 'measure' excepted by the proviso clause of Article XXI?

(d) *The Nature of the Obligation not to Defeat the Object and Purpose of a Treaty*

The Court accepted that its jurisdiction under the Treaty was narrower in scope than it was by virtue of the declarations made under Article 36 of the Statute. Jurisdiction under the former instrument existed only 'to the extent that claims in Nicaragua's Application constitute a dispute as to the interpretation or the application of the Articles of the Treaty' as provided for in Article XXIV.[505] This limitation was regarded by the Court as being

[503] At pp. 310–11.
[504] At p. 541. For the view of Judge Oda, see at p. 252.
[505] *ICJ Reports*, 1984, at p. 429.

of particular significance in connection with Nicaragua's argument that 'the United States, by its conduct in relation to Nicaragua, has deprived the Treaty of its object and purpose, and emptied it of real content. For this purpose, Nicaragua has relied on the existence of a legal obligation of States to refrain from acts which would impede the due performance of any treaties entered into by them.'[506]

If there were such an obligation, it would have been a matter of importance for the scope of the Court's jurisdiction whether the obligation arose separately from, or as part of, the treaty. In the latter case, breach of the obligation would seem to involve a breach of the treaty. In the former view, it might be more difficult to establish that its breach had such an effect. Perhaps surprisingly, therefore, Nicaragua presented the issue on the basis that the duty did not arise out of the Treaty itself, but from some principle of 'customary international law . . . that is implicit in the rule of *pacta sunt servanda*'.[507]

The Court accepted Nicaragua's classification of the obligation as arising under the general law, but drew an unexplained distinction between matters relating to the interpretation and application of the Treaty and jurisdiction which it regarded as limited solely to breaches of specific provisions of the Treaty:[508]

> if there is a duty of a State not to impede the due performance of a treaty to which it is a party, that is not a duty imposed by the treaty itself . . . This claim therefore does not in fact fall under the heading of a possible breach by the United States of the provisions of the 1956 Treaty, though it may involve the interpretation or application thereof.

It was the Court's view that Article XXIV(2), though conferring jurisdiction with respect to any dispute 'as to the interpretation or application of the present Treaty', did not operate except with regard to breaches of the obligations specified in its provisions. In so far as the allegations of conduct depriving the Treaty of its object and purpose were not related to any such breaches, the Court could only entertain a claim with regard to such matters by virtue of the jurisdiction bestowed upon the Court by the parties' declarations under Article 36 of the Court's Statute.[509]

On the face of it, it would seem to be a curious proposition that a State could act in a way that deprived a treaty of its object and purpose without breaking that treaty and without being subject to any obligation to answer for such conduct under the treaty's compromissory clause. This section will therefore examine this conclusion in the light of various analogies that can be drawn with municipal law and with similar rules of international law.

[506] *ICJ Reports*, 1986, at p. 135.
[507] Ibid.
[508] Ibid.
[509] At p. 136.

1. *The implication of terms*

As a starting point, it is worth considering whether it is correct to assume that the obligation not to impede the achievement of the object and purpose of a treaty should be regarded as arising *dehors* that treaty.

This would not necessarily be the situation under municipal law with regard to contracts. The courts in England and Australia have been prepared to imply as one of the terms of an actual contract various undertakings designed to promote the due performance of that contract. This is particularly the case 'where in a written contract it appears that both parties have agreed that something shall be done, which cannot effectively be done unless both concur in doing it'.[510] The inference in such a situation would, in the absence of anything indicating the contrary, be 'that each agrees to do all that is necessary to be done on his part for the carrying out of that thing, though there may be no express words to that effect'.[511]

Of more direct relevance to the *Nicaragua* case is the issue of whether the general duty to co-operate involves an obligation not to interfere in the fulfilment of the purpose of a contract. So much depends upon the particular circumstances that, even under municipal law, no general answer, that holds good in all cases, can be given to the question.[512] The point is that, in municipal law, the implication of terms is a valuable means of promoting a particular view of consensual relationships. There is some evidence to suggest that the same may be true of international law. After all, it is recognized that a State is under some sort of obligation 'to refrain from acts which would defeat the object and purpose of a treaty' before it enters into force.[513] Such a principle cannot arise from the implication of a term in the treaty itself as, at the relevant time, the instrument had not yet come into force for the States concerned. There is no reason, however, why the

[510] *Mackay* v. *Dick* (1881), 6 App. Cas. 251 at p. 263 *per* Lord Blackburn.

[511] Ibid. The principle was stated as a rule of construction, though that can hardly be the case. As Mason J pointed out in *Secured Income Real Estate (Australia) Ltd.* v. *St Martin's Investments Pty. Ltd.* (1979), 144 CLR 596 at p. 607, ultimately, 'the correct interpretation of the contract depends . . . not so much on the application of the general rule of construction as on the intention of the parties as manifested by the contract itself'.

[512] As Gibbs CJ said in *Hospital Products Ltd.* v. *United States Surgical Corp.* (1984), 156 CLR 41 at p. 65, referring to American illustrations of one example of such a situation:

> 'An undertaking to use best endeavours or best efforts to promote the sale of one product does not necessarily impose an obligation not to sell a competing product (see *Van Valkensburgh Nooger and Neville Inc.* v. *Hayden Publishing Co.* 330 NYS (2d) 329 (1972) at 333, and cases there cited), although it may do so in some circumstances, as was held to be the case in *Randall* v. *Peerless Motor Car Co.* 99 NE 221 (1912)'.

See generally, Greig and Davis, op. cit. above (n. 42), pp. 532 ff.

[513] According to Article 18 of the Vienna Convention on the Law of Treaties 1969:

> 'A State is obliged to refrain from acts which would defeat the object and purpose of a treaty when:
> (*a*) it has signed the treaty or has exchanged instruments constituting the treaty subject to ratification, acceptance or approval, until it shall have made its intention clear not to become a party to the treaty; or
> (*b*) it has expressed its consent to be bound by the treaty, pending the entry into force of the treaty and provided that such entry into force is not unduly delayed'.

general duty upon States to act in good faith in their dealings with each other should not be regarded as giving rise to such an obligation, arising from implied unilateral promises by the parties who have negotiated the treaty to so conduct themselves, and binding upon them.

When the treaty comes into force for the parties concerned, it is possible to adopt alternative explanations for the basis of an obligation not to impede the achievement of the object and purpose of the treaty. As with the situation where the treaty does not come into force, it can plausibly be posited that the promises of the parties are collateral to the treaty itself. If a State has undertaken a duty not to defeat the object and purpose of a treaty prior to its entry into force as an obligation implicit in its participation in the negotiating process up to and including the moment of adoption of the text of the treaty, then *a fortiori* that obligation should carry over into the post-entry into force phase. To cover the situation of a State which did not participate in the negotiations but which subsequently accedes to the treaty, the same obligation can be said to arise by virtue of the act of accession.

If this concept is adopted, it has to be recognized that there is a difference in the extent of the obligation with regard to the parties once the treaty comes into force. In the case of the pre-entry into force stage, the obligation is of limited duration. Once a party which negotiated the treaty, after the lapse of a reasonable time, makes clear its intention not to become a party to the treaty, it ceases to be bound by the obligation in question. Indeed, after such a period has passed, conduct inconsistent with the treaty's object and purpose would itself signify the existence of such an intention. Once the treaty has entered into force, the collateral undertaking would be coterminous with a party's obligations under the treaty itself.

The alternative possibility once the treaty comes into force is to employ the concept of an implied obligation as if it represented a term written into the treaty itself. It differs from the collateral obligation arising from participation in drawing up the text of the treaty in that it is designed to promote the effectiveness of the treaty throughout the period during which the State remains a party to that instrument. The implication of a term for such a purpose has been recognized in international jurisprudence.

In the *Polish Upper Silesia* case,[514] the Permanent Court had to consider the effects *inter alia* of Article 256 of the Treaty of Versailles 1919, paragraph 1 of which provided in part:

> Powers to which German territory is ceded shall acquire all property and possessions situated therein belonging to the German Empire or to the German States.

Poland had passed a law purporting to nullify certain transactions with

As the International Law Commission asserted in its Report to the General Assembly on the work of the Commission's eighteenth session (*Yearbook of the International Law Commission*, 1966, vol. 2, p. 172 at p. 202):

> 'That an obligation of good faith to refrain from acts calculated to frustrate the object of the treaty attaches to a State which has signed a treaty subject to ratification appears to be generally accepted'.

[514] (1926), *PCIJ*, Series A, No. 7.

regard to German State property, situated in territory subsequently transferred to Poland, in the period between the making of the Treaty of Versailles and effect being given to Article 256 as far as Poland was concerned in Article 4 of the Geneva Convention of 1920.[515] The Court was of the opinion that there was no provision in the two treaties which could be 'construed as annulling or rendering liable to annulment any alienation of public property'.[516] However, the Court went on to suggest that there might still be a limitation upon the freedom of Germany to deal with such property and that such dealing could involve a breach of a *treaty* obligation. In the Court's words:[517]

> Germany undoubtedly retained until the actual transfer of sovereignty the right to dispose of her property, and only a misuse of this right could endow an act of alienation with the character of a breach of the Treaty; such misuse cannot be presumed, and it rests with the party who states that there has been such misuse to prove his statement.

The significance of this pronouncement is obvious. As there was no express prohibition of, or limitation on, the power of alienation, the limitation, to give rise to a breach of the Treaty, must have been implicit in the Treaty, and not arising by virtue of some obligation of customary law external to the Treaty. In other words, whatever the content of the limitation might be, the means of enforcing the duty to act in good faith (a feature of civil law systems), or to act reasonably in all the circumstances (the hallmark of the common law), was through the medium of an implied obligation.

2. *The example of fundamental change of circumstances*

Reverting to the analogy of municipal law, or more particularly the common law, the implication of terms has been both a vehicle of judicial policy and a means of disguising innovation by ascribing it to the intentions of the parties to a contract.[518]

Such an approach was, until comparatively recent times, employed as a justification for the doctrine of frustration in the common law.[519] By virtue of this doctrine, a contract comes to an end when, during the course of performance, and without the fault of either of the parties, there is a radical

[515] As the Court said of Article 4 (at p. 29):

'This article lays down that the date of transfer of sovereignty over the portion of Upper Silesia allotted to Poland is the decisive date for the purposes of the recognition of vested rights'.

[516] At p. 30.

[517] Ibid.

[518] As Stephen J said in *Helicopter Sales (Australia) Pty. Ltd.* v. *Rotor-Work Pty. Ltd.* (1974), 132 CLR 1 at p. 13:

'Terms are implied so as the better to give effect to the bargain arrived at between the parties, thus carrying out their presumed intention'.

[519] *Taylor* v. *Caldwell* (1863), 3 B & S 826; 122 ER 309; and see the words of Viscount Simon LC in *Constantine (Joseph) Steamship Line Ltd.* v. *Imperial Smelting Corp. Ltd.*, [1942] AC 154 at p. 164: 'Every case in this branch of the law can be stated as turning on the question whether from the express terms of the particular contract a further term should be implied which, when its conditions are fulfilled, puts an end to the contract'.

change in the situation envisaged by the contract so as to render further performance of the contract impossible. This impossibility extends not just to physical impossibility, but also to impossibility in a legal or commercial sense.[520] Today, however, the courts in England and Australia have abandoned the notion of an implied term and prefer to base their decision as to whether a contract has been frustrated upon whether, on a fair and reasonable assessment of the circumstances in the light of the terms of the contract, the contract should come to an end.[521]

There is an obvious parallel in international law, where the idea that a treaty should come to an end following a radical change of circumstances owed its original existence to a similar implied term theory, known as *clausula rebus sic stantibus*. As one commentator explained:[522]

> One explanation given of this name is that it was at one period customary to insert in treaties an express term or *clausula* that the generality of their stipulations should have force only so long as certain stated conditions should continue to obtain. But such clauses, if ever employed, are not now generally employed and the modern doctrine of *clausula* requires that such a term shall be implied to be contained in treaties.

Given the reliance placed upon private law concepts in the early development of international law, it is not surprising that this particular doctrine was taken from the civil law of obligations and applied to international agreements.[523] A further similarity with municipal law of this tendency 'to attach the clause to the will of the parties' has been the attempt to convert the problem 'into one of treaty interpretation'.[524]

It was of course widely recognized that the notion of an implied term was a fiction and it was also acknowledged that ascribing the doctrine to the parties' intentions as a matter of interpretation of the treaty was not necessarily very much different.[525] In a further development akin to what has

[520] For example, if the circumstances show that a particular means of performance is contemplated by the parties as the basis of their relationship and that means becomes unavailable, the contract will come to an end: *Codelfa Construction Pty. Ltd.* v. *State Rail Authority of New South Wales* (1982), 149 CLR 337; or where delay in performance is likely to be a significant proportion of the time for which a contract still has to run: see *Pioneer Shipping Ltd.* v. *BTP Tioxide Ltd.*, [1982] AC 724; cp. *National Carriers Ltd.* v. *Panalpina (Northern) Ltd.*, [1981] AC 675.

[521] See *Davis Contractors Ltd.* v. *Fareham Urban District Council*, [1956] AC 696 esp. at p. 728 *per* Lord Radcliffe; *National Carriers Ltd.* v. *Panalpina (Northern) Ltd.* (above); *Pioneer Shipping Ltd.* v. *BTP Tioxide Ltd.* (above); *Brisbane City Council* v. *Group Projects Pty. Ltd.* (1979), 145 CLR 143; *Codelfa Construction Pty. Ltd.* v. *State Rail Authority of New South Wales* (above).

[522] Parry, 'The Law of Treaties', in Sorensen (ed.), *Manual of Public International Law* (1968), p. 175 at p. 234.

[523] See Haraszti, 'Treaties and the Fundamental Change of Circumstances', *Recueil des cours*, 146 (1975-III), p. 1 at pp. 10 ff.

[524] Ibid., at p. 46. See also Lissitzyn, 'Treaties and Changed Circumstances (*Rebus Sic Stantibus*)', *American Journal of International law*, 61 (1967), p. 895 at p. 896:

> 'Thus viewed, the problem of the effect of a change of circumstances on treaty relationships becomes in principle one of interpretation—establishing the shared intentions and expectations of the parties. This approach is consistent with the goal of stability in treaty relationships and with the principle of *Pacta sunt servanda*.'

[525] Haraszti, loc. cit. above (n. 523), at p. 46. See also Lissitzyn, loc. cit. (previous note).

happened in municipal law (certainly, as has already been explained, in Anglo–Australian law), the International Law Commission rejected the traditional basis of *rebus sic stantibus*, preferring instead the principle's formulation 'as an objective rule of law by which, on grounds of equity and justice, a fundamental change of circumstances may, under certain conditions, be invoked by a party as a ground for terminating the treaty'.[526] As finally adopted, Article 62(1) of the Vienna Convention on the Law of Treaties 1969 reads:[527]

> A fundamental change of circumstances which has occurred with regard to those existing at the time of the conclusion of a treaty, and which was not foreseen by the parties, may not be invoked as a ground for terminating or withdrawing from the treaty unless:
>
> (*a*) the existence of those circumstances constituted an essential basis of the consent of the parties to be bound by the treaty; and
> (*b*) the effect of the change is radically to transform the extent of obligations still to be performed under the treaty.

3. *Attitudes within the International Law Commission*

Much of the uncertainty apparent in the *Nicaragua* case about the existence and status of an obligation upon States not to defeat the object and purpose of treaties to which they are parties can be traced to the outcome of the work of the International Law Commission. In his third Report on the Law of Treaties, Waldock as Special Rapporteur proposed a Draft Article 55 which read in part as follows:[528]

> 1. A treaty in force is binding upon the parties and must be applied by them in

[526] Report of the International Law Commission on the Work of its Eighteenth Session, *Yearbook of the International Law Commission*, 1966, vol. 2, at p. 258. The full text of the passage was as follows:

'In the past the principle has almost always been presented in the guise of a tacit condition implied in every "perpetual" Treaty that would dissolve it in the event of a fundamental change of circumstances. The Commission noted, however, that the tendency to-day was to regard the implied term as only a fiction by which it was attempted to reconcile the principle of the dissolution of treaties in consequence of a fundamental change of circumstances with the rule *pacta sunt servanda*. In most cases the parties gave no thought to the possibility of a change of circumstances and, if they had done so, would probably have provided for it in a different manner. Furthermore, the Commission considered the fiction to be an undesirable one since it increased the risk of subjective interpretations and abuse. For this reason, the Commission was agreed that the theory of an implied term must be rejected and the doctrine formulated as an objective rule of law by which, on grounds of equity and justice, a fundamental change of circumstances may, under certain conditions, be invoked by a party as a ground for terminating the treaty. It further decided that, in order to emphasize the objective character of the rule, it would be better not to use the term "rebus sic stantibus" either in the text of the article or even in the title, and so avoid the doctrinal implication of that term.'

[527] By Article 62(2):

'A fundamental change of circumstances may not be invoked as a ground for terminating or withdrawing from a treaty:
(*a*) if the treaty establishes a boundary; or
(*b*) if the fundamental change is the result of a breach by the party invoking it either of an obligation under the treaty or of any other international obligation owed to any other party to the treaty'.

Physical impossibility of performance is dealt with in Article 61 of the Convention.

[528] *Yearbook of the International Law Commission*, 1964, vol. 2, p. 7.

good faith in accordance with its terms and in the light of the general rules of international law governing the interpretation of treaties.
2. Good faith, *inter alia*, requires that a party to a treaty shall refrain from any acts calculated to prevent the due execution of the treaty or otherwise to frustrate its objects.

In the attached Commentary, Waldock equated the principle of good faith with a requirement that States should not seek to avoid their treaty obligations by employing 'a merely literal application of its clauses'.[529] As far as paragraph 2 was concerned, the Special Rapporteur saw the conduct proscribed as contrary not only 'to good faith but also to the undertaking to perform the treaty according to its terms which is implied in the treaty itself'.[530] Such a provision was necessary, in his opinion, to achieve consistency with the obligation imposed upon potential parties 'to refrain from acts calculated to frustrate the objects of the treaty'.[531]

Opinion within the Commission was divided between those who supported the Special Rapporteur,[532] those who wanted all but paragraph 1 deleted,[533] and those who wished to have paragraph 2 incorporated as part of paragraph 1.[534] In the event, the matter was referred to a drafting committee which attempted to rewrite paragraphs 1 and 2 as follows:[535]

A treaty in force is binding upon the parties to it and must be performed by them in good faith. [Every party shall abstain from any act incompatible with the object and purpose of the treaty.]

This combination did not prove to be acceptable to a majority of the Commission and the second sentence was subsequently dropped, a step which did not receive unanimous approval.[536] Indeed, a number of governments had expressed concern at the omission of any such provision.[537]

The link with the view later propounded by Nicaragua is thus apparent. The obligation not to defeat the object and purpose of a treaty was said to

[529] Ibid., p. 8, para. (2).
[530] Ibid., para. (4).
[531] *Yearbook of the International Law Commission*, 1964, vol. 1, p. 23, para. 42.
[532] Briggs, ibid., p. 24, para. 46; Castrén, para. 51; Verdross, para. 58; Reuter, p. 26, para. 77; for suggestions that the draft did not go far enough, see Paredes, p. 25, para. 62; El-Erian, p. 30, para. 40.
[533] Elias, ibid., paras. 53, 54; Yasseen, p. 26, para. 80; Amado, para. 84; Pal, p. 27, para, 7; Tunkin, para. 14.
[534] Rosenne, ibid., p. 25, para. 72; Tabibi, p. 27, para. 12.
[535] Ibid., p. 162, para. 52.
[536] Ibid., p. 232.
[537] As Castrén observed at a later meeting of the Commission, *Yearbook of the International Law Commission*, 1966, vol. 1, pt. 2, pp. 33–4, para. 24.

'The Finnish and Turkish Governments wished article 55 to include a provision requiring the parties to refrain from acts calculated to frustrate the object and purpose of the treaty; that had been part of the Special Rapporteur's original intention, and two delegations to the General Assembly, those of Greece and the United Arab Republic, had proposed an amendment to that effect. The Government of Israel also seemed favourable to the idea, though it had stated that it would be satisfied if the matter were dealt with in the commentary. Since the Commission had reached the conclusion, after long discussion in 1964, that the obligation which the governments in question wished to emphasize was implicit in the existing text and since there were strong reasons in favour of that concise and simple formulation, he was willing to accept it.'

See also the comment by Ago. ibid., pp. 34–5, para. 38.

be implicit in the notion of *pacta sunt servanda*. The concern of the Commission seemed to be to avoid weakening that notion by specifying any particular consequences stemming from it. However, it does not follow from what members of the Commission said that the result of taking this view of the obligation in question was that it should be regarded as external to the treaty. It was essentially bound up with proper performance of the treaty and good faith in the interpretation of its terms.[538]

There is certainly no suggestion that the result of adopting this approach might be to take certain aspects of due performance of the treaty as a whole outside the scope of any compromissory clause in the treaty. Nor should a contrary inference be drawn from Waldock's earlier references to cases where a treaty obligation had been broadly interpreted in order to give effect to the instrument's object and purpose.[539] Admittedly, the Special Rapporteur only identified the 'undertaking to perform the treaty according to its terms' as 'implied in the treaty itself', but this proposition must surely have included a negative covenant to refrain from conduct undermining the object and purpose of the treaty. Ultimately, however, the message to be drawn from the deliberations of the Commission is that it should make no difference to its consequences whether the obligation is classified as arising directly from the principle of *pacta sunt servanda*, or indirectly through some implied term in each individual treaty.

4. *Relevance to the* Nicaragua *Case*

(i) *The Court's view*. It would seem that the Court was faced with an initial problem that Nicaragua's argument that the United States had 'deprived the Treaty of its object and purpose' had 'a scope which is not very clearly defined'.[540] It was Nicaragua's view that 'the Court could on this ground make a blanket condemnation of the United States for all the activities of which Nicaragua complains on more specific grounds'.[541]

The Court was justifiably sceptical of such a contention, particularly when it was translated into a more specific obligation upon the parties, arising out of the fact that this was a Treaty of Friendship, to conduct amicable relations with each other:[542]

In other words, the Court is asked to rule that a State which enters into a treaty of

[538] See Lachs' observation, ibid., p. 3, para. 17:

'What was essential was clarity in the rule. The principle of good faith stood on its own feet and needed no explanation: any attempt to provide one would lead to casuistry. It meant fidelity and the conscientious fulfilment of promises by acts, or by refraining from acts that could frustrate the purpose of the contract. It meant honesty, not evasion—the obligation not to do anything that might prevent the execution of the treaty. Any enumeration might be deceptive for lack of completeness.'

[539] Commentary to the Third Report, *Yearbook of the International Law Commission*, 1964, vol. 2, p. 8, para. 2, referring to the *Admissions* case, *ICJ Reports*, 1948, p. 57 at p. 63; *United States Nationals in Morocco* case, *ICJ Reports*, 1952, p. 176 at p. 212; *North Atlantic Fisheries* arbitration (1910), *Reports of International Arbitral Awards*, vol. 11, p. 167 at p. 188.

[540] *ICJ Reports*, 1986, p. 3 at p. 136.

[541] Ibid.

[542] At pp. 136–7.

friendship binds itself, for so long as the Treaty is in force, to abstain from any act toward the other party which could be classified as an unfriendly act, even if such an act is not in itself the breach of an international obligation.

The Court then pointed out:[543]

Such a duty might . . . be expressly stipulated in a treaty, or might even emerge as a necessary implication from the text; but as a matter of customary international law, it is not clear that the existence of such a far-reaching rule is evidenced in the practice of States. There must be a distinction, even in the case of a treaty of friendship, between the broad category of unfriendly acts, and the narrower category of acts tending to defeat the object and purpose of the Treaty. That object and purpose is the effective implementation of friendship in the specific fields provided for in the Treaty, not friendship in a vague general sense.

As to where the line should be drawn between the two categories of acts, those directly contrary to friendship in 'specific fields', and those not in accordance with 'friendship in a vague general sense', the Court went on to say:[544]

In respect of the claim that the United States activities have been such as to deprive the 1956 FCN Treaty of its object and purpose, the Court has to make a distinction. It is unable to regard all the acts complained of in that light; but it does consider that there are certain activities of the United States which are such as to undermine the whole spirit of a bilateral agreement directed to sponsoring friendship between the two States parties to it. These are: the direct attacks on ports, oil installations etc. . . . ; and the mining of Nicaraguan ports . . . Any action less calculated to serve the purpose of 'strengthening the bonds of peace and friendship traditionally existing between' the Parties, stated in the Preamble of the Treaty, could hardly be imagined.

While the acts of economic pressure . . . are less flagrantly in contradiction with the purpose of the Treaty, the Court reaches a similar conclusion in respect of some of them. A State is not bound to continue particular trade relations longer than it sees fit to do so, in the absence of a treaty commitment or other specific legal obligation; but where there exists such a commitment, of the kind implied in a treaty of friendship and commerce, such an abrupt act of termination of commercial intercourse as the general trade embargo of 1 May 1985 will normally constitute a violation of the obligation not to defeat the object and purpose of the treaty.

It is possible to draw from this part of the Court's judgment recognition that such an obligation could be implied into the 1956 Treaty rather than be regarded as arising from some principle operating under the general law. The first step in this line of reasoning lies in the Court's acceptance that a broader duty to promote friendship could have arisen from the express terms of the 1956 Treaty, or by 'necessary implication' from those express terms. There was, however, no evidence for the existence of such a far reaching obligation stemming from such a treaty in State practice. When it

[543] At p. 137.
[544] At p. 138.

came to recognizing the narrower duty limited to 'specific fields provided for in the Treaty', the Court did not at this stage stipulate the source of this obligation. It had of course earlier apparently adopted Nicaragua's view that the duty in question arose 'under customary international law independently of the treaty'.[545] However, given that the Court imposed only a duty tied to the express terms of the treaty, it would be an easy matter to regard the duty as arising by implication out of those terms. If, as posited by the Court, there was an 'implied commitment' to continue trade relations, arising from the nature of the Treaty, it is difficult to see why an obligation not to defeat the specific objects and purposes of the Treaty should not equally be implied. Indeed, when it came to dealing with Nicaragua's contention that the cessation of voluntary aid was also an act impeding the operation of the Treaty, the Court had recourse to an argument that was akin to that of refusing to imply a term because such was not the intention of the parties when it said:[546]

> The Court has also to note that, by the very terms of the legislation authorizing such aid (the Special Central American Assistance Act, 1979), of which the Government of Nicaragua must have been aware, the continuance of aid was made subject to the appreciation of Nicaragua's conduct by the President of the United States.

A term would hardly be implied to augment the terms of a treaty that was in conflict with the understanding of one of the parties as to the extent of the obligation which it was entering into, if that understanding was known to, and accepted or acquiesced in by, the other party to the treaty.

In the circumstances, therefore, the Court's adoption of the proposition that, though the matter concerned the interpretation and application of the 1956 Treaty, it was not covered by the compromissory clause in the Treaty, appears especially curious. The obligation only arose by virtue of entering into the Treaty, and it is very much a matter of theoretical choice whether the obligation is implied, as if it were a term in the Treaty, or arises by virtue of some extraneous rule of law. Had the case been less contentious, and had such a treaty been the only basis of obligations, including jurisdiction over the dispute, it might be that a tribunal would have been less inclined to draw such a distinction.

(ii) *The existence of such an obligation*. Two questions have to be addressed: whether there does exist any such obligation as that accepted by the Court whereby the parties are under an obligation not to deprive a treaty of its object and purpose; and, if there is, what is its nature and scope. As has already been explained, the work of the International Law Commission was ambivalent. There was some obligation inherent in the

[545] At p. 135: see above, p. 255.
[546] At p. 138.

concept of *pacta sunt servanda*, but its status as part of a treaty or at any rate as implicit in it was not spelt out. This was in contrast to the Commission's view of the position prior to the entry into force of a treaty.

In its Report to the General Assembly in which it recommended that the Assembly convene an international conference to conclude a convention on the law of treaties,[547] the International Law Commission referred to the fact that, in the *Polish Upper Silesia* case,[548] the Permanent Court appeared 'to have recognized that, if ratification takes place, a signatory State's misuse of its rights in the interval preceding ratification may amount to a violation of its obligations in respect of the treaty'.[549] On this foundation, the Commission was of the opinion that the obligation must exist, at least temporarily, even for a State that does not become bound by a treaty.[550]

While there are obvious reasons why a State which becomes a party to a treaty should be bound by an obligation in appropriate circumstances not to act in a way inimical to the treaty after it signifies its assent to the text of the treaty, but before ratification, it does not necessarily follow that a similar obligation exists for a State which never becomes a party. In the first situation, it is possible to regard the treaty as operating retrospectively by reference to what the parties presumably intended. In the second case, the inimical conduct would by implication denote the intention not to become bound by the terms of the treaty. It amounts to the exercise of a right of unilateral denunciation of what is no more than an intention to consider whether to ratify the treaty.[551] The acceptance of the existence of an obligation not to act in derogation of the treaty for a State which does not become a party to the treaty in question until it makes that intention clear is therefore an extension of the *Polish Upper Silesia* principle.

In the case of a State which does become a party to a treaty, there is no conclusive need to regard the situation after the treaty has come into force as including an obligation of the sort that applies in the twilight period between signature and ratification or ratification and entry into force. In theoretical terms it could be argued that the general obligation designed to preserve the integrity of the treaty pending its likely entry into force is replaced by the specific obligations contained in the express terms of the treaty.

This is an inadequate thesis. It is no consolation to the party deprived of performance of the treaty by the conduct of the other party which

[547] *Yearbook of the International Law Commission*, 1966, vol. 2, p. 169 at p. 177.

[548] Above, n. 514.

[549] *Yearbook of the International Law Commission*, 1966, vol. 2, at p. 202.

[550] The Commission proposed that the obligation should extend to a party which 'has agreed to enter into negotiations for the conclusion of the treaty, while these negotiations are in progress' (Draft Article 15(*a*): ibid.). The Vienna Conference rejected this formulation, restricting the obligation to States which had signified their acceptance of the text of the treaty by signature or by ratification prior to entry into force: see the text of Article 18, above, p. 256 n. 513.

[551] From this point of view, the original Draft Article 15(*a*) requiring a State to refrain from acts tending to frustrate the object of a proposed treaty for as long as negotiations were in progress made more sense.

undermines the object and purpose of the instrument that no breach of its specific terms has occurred. The acceptance of such a contention would have a deleterious effect on the operation of Article 62(2)(*b*) of the Vienna Convention whereby a fundamental change of circumstances may not be invoked as a ground for terminating a treaty 'if the fundamental change is the result of a breach by the party invoking it either of an obligation under the treaty or of any other international obligation owed to any other party to the treaty'.

Suppose, as a result of a sequence of events, there is a fundamental change of circumstances with regard to a treaty between States A and B. A wishes to terminate; B does not. If A has not contributed to the events, so that A could not be in breach of any obligation, A is entitled to rely upon Article 62. If, without breaking any of the express obligations of the treaty, A's conduct does contribute to undermining its object and purpose (thus radically transforming the extent of the obligations still to be performed under the treaty[552]), A would still be able to withdraw from the treaty in reliance upon Article 62, unless its conduct could be classified either as a breach of the treaty, or of some obligation arising outside the treaty. It would seem to be implicit in, or inevitably to follow from, Article 62 that a party's conduct, having such a consequence, will normally involve a breach of an obligation arising out of the treaty. For the purposes of protecting the non-acting party from the inequitable operation of Article 62, it would not matter of course whether the obligation existed directly as an implied term in the treaty, or indirectly by virtue of some international obligation arising under the general law by virtue of the existence of the treaty.

This conclusion is at least reconcilable with the Court's view as outlined above, when it seemed to accept the stance taken by Nicaragua that the obligation arose under customary international law and not by anything implied into the 1956 Treaty. As has already been pointed out, this is not necessarily the better theoretical construct for the obligation, in particular because it could result in breach of such an obligation not being covered by a compromissory clause which is limited (expressly or by interpretation) to breaches of the actual terms of the treaty.

It was this matter which formed the substance of Judge Oda's criticism of the Court's judgment. Having referred to various provisions of the Vienna Convention on the Law of Treaties which did mention the object and/or purpose of a treaty as an element in the operation of the particular provision,[553] the Judge went on to say, in the context of Article 60(3)(*b*), that there was 'no suggestion that the undermining of the object and/or purpose, *independently* of any breach of a provision, would be tantamount in itself to

552 Thus satisfying the requirement for a fundamental change of circumstances under Article 62(1)(*b*) of the Vienna Convention.

553 By Article 19(*c*) a State may formulate a reservation to a treaty unless 'the reservation is incompatible with the object and purpose of the treaty'.

By Article 41(1)(*b*)(ii), two or more parties to a multilateral treaty may conclude an agreement to modify the treaty as between themselves alone if the modification is not prohibited by the treaty and it

a violation of the Treaty'.[554] He then concluded his opinion on this matter as follows:[555]

> Thus the Court appears to have misinterpreted the words 'the object and purpose' of a treaty, as introduced by the 1969 Convention on the Law of Treaties in a completely different context. Independently of that Convention, it is noted that the Court attributes to Nicaragua an argument to the effect that abstention from conduct likely to defeat the object and purpose of a treaty is an obligation implicit in the principle *pacta sunt servanda*. However, the Judgment does not make it clear whether it is espousing this point of view. In any case, I would like to take this opportunity of indicating my own understanding of this principle, which to my mind requires compliance with the letter of obligations subscribed to, and not necessarily the avoidance of conduct not expressly precluded by the terms of the given treaty. It may furthermore be asked where the jurisdiction granted by a treaty clause would ever end if it were held to entitle the Court to scrutinize any act remotely describable as inimical to the object and purpose of the treaty in question. The ultimate result of so sweeping an assumption could only be an increasing reluctance on the part of States to support the inclusion of such clauses in their treaties.

It cannot be said that Judge Oda was convincing. No mention was made of Article 18 which, as has already been discussed, does create an obligation not to defeat the object and purpose of a treaty prior to its entry into force. This would seem to provide a much closer analogy for the principle being advanced by Nicaragua than the provisions referred to by the judge. Nor did he attempt to deal with the possible implications for the issue of Article 62. As to the suggestion that such an approach would 'entitle the Court to scrutinize any act remotely describable as inimical to the object and purpose of the treaty', two points can be made. First, even if the Court might examine such evidence, the conduct called in question must, in order to constitute a breach of the obligation, be such as to undermine (not just be 'remotely describable as inimical' to) the object and purpose of the treaty. In this respect, it places no greater obligation upon a State than does Article 18, although of course that obligation would not fall within the compromissory clause of the treaty concerned. Secondly, the Court itself did not suggest that the similar obligation for a State which does become a party to the treaty was subject to the treaty's compromissory clause (at least not one in the form of the 1956 Treaty). Even if one accepts the thrust of this article that such a conclusion does not seem sustainable, it does not follow that Judge Oda's criticism is correct. The object and purpose of the treaty are ascertainable by examining the instrument as a whole, so that conduct

'does not relate to a provision, derogation from which is incompatible with the effective execution of the object and purpose of the treaty as a whole'.

By Article 60(1), a material breach of a treaty is a ground for the party or parties not in breach to terminate the treaty. According to Article 60(3)(*b*), a material breach for this purpose consists, *inter alia*, in 'the violation of a provision essential to the accomplishment of the object or purpose of the treaty'.

554 *ICJ Reports*, 1986, at p. 250 (original emphasis).

555 Ibid.

which undermines that object and purpose must be both sufficiently grave and linked in a causative sense to achieving that objective (i.e. the undermining of the treaty).

In Judge Jennings' dissenting opinion, the potentially extensive nature of what he called this 'roving jurisdiction'[556] was related to a general denial of the concept of 'object and purpose' as extending the obligations of the specific provisions of a treaty. He said:[557]

> The jurisdiction clause of such a treaty could not be regarded as conferring a jurisdiction to pass upon matters external to the actual provisions of the treaty, even though such matters may affect the operation of the treaty. Suppose hostilities, or even war, should arise between parties to an FCN treaty, then the Court under a jurisdiction clause surely does not have jurisdiction to pass upon the general question of the lawfulness or otherwise of the outbreak of hostilities or of war, on the ground only that this defeated the object and purpose of the treaty.

These observations reflect the uncertainties which arise with regard to the effect of war upon treaty relations. The traditional view was that 'the outbreak of war *ipso facto* cancels all treaties previously concluded between the belligerents, excepting only those concluded especially for the war'.[558] This view changed in the period after the First World War,[559] although State practice was far from uniform. In a number of cases, United States courts upheld the continuing validity of provisions of the Treaty of Friendship, Commerce and Consular Rights of 1923 between that country and Germany with regard to the ownership of property, specifically in the context of rights of inheritance.[560]

The effects of war upon the treaty rights of belligerents *inter se* was not covered in the International Law Commission's Draft Articles on the Law of Treaties. Following criticism at the Vienna Conference, the Convention included a provision reflecting the uncertain position under customary law. According to Article 73, the provisions of the Convention were not to 'prejudge any question that may arise in regard to a treaty . . . from the outbreak of hostilities between States'.[561]

556 At p. 539.

557 Ibid.

558 Oppenheim, *International Law*, vol. 2 (7th edn., 1952), p. 302.

559 See the letter of US Secretary of State Green of 21 May 1945 (Whiteman, *Digest of International Law*, vol. 14, p. 496) in which he wrote:

> 'There appears to be a trend towards recognizing greater continuing effectiveness of treaty provisions during war than in earlier times'.

560 *Clark* v. *Allen*, 331 US 503 (1947); *Blank* v. *Clark*, 79 F Supp. 373 (1948); applying a case on a similar provision in the convention between the United States and Austria of 1848, *Techt* v. *Hughes*, 128 NE 185 (1920); cert. denied 254 US 643 (1920), in which Cardozo J said that, although political treaties and those which were related to the cause of the war were dissolved, 'the general principle' was that 'treaties which it is reasonably practicable to execute after the outbreak of hostilities must be observed' (128 NE at 191).

561 See Nahlik, 'The Grounds of Invalidity and Termination of Treaties', *American Journal of International Law*, 65 (1971), p. 736 at p. 753.

In so far as it is possible to describe the present legal position, the trend has been towards the diminution of the importance of the nature of a treaty (for example, the earlier assumption that no treaty of a political nature can survive the outbreak of hostilities), and the shift towards attempting to assess the parties' intentions. The point was made by Hurst:[562]

> the true test as to whether or not a treaty survives an outbreak of war between the parties is to be found in the intention of the parties at the time when the treaty was concluded . . . [J]ust as the duration of contracts between private persons depends on the intentions of the parties, so also the duration of treaties between States must depend on the intention of the parties, and . . . the treaties will survive the outbreak of war or will then disappear, according as the parties intended when they made the treaty.

It is of course possible that the intentions of the parties might change and that, from their conduct, it might be inferred that, though their original intention might have been for the treaty to remain in force, following the outbreak of hostilities their wishes might have changed in this regard. Abrogation of the treaty might therefore be assumed.

In assessing the attitude of the parties at the time of making the treaty, all factors could be taken into account, including the nature of the treaty. While the last-mentioned would not be a conclusive factor, it might nevertheless raise a presumption that treaties of a particular type are normally terminated by an outbreak of hostilities. Nevertheless, much would also depend upon the form which the hostilities took. The traditional rules arose under an international order in which the use of force was regarded as legitimate and in which a state of war depended upon its overt recognition by the participants. These considerations no longer apply in the former case, and may not apply in the latter. The scope of the hostilities, and the attitude of the parties towards them, could also be of importance.

There are however limits to the municipal law analogy of taking account of the parties' intentions as objectively assessed from all the relevant circumstances. This approach is possible in a system which is essentially court-based, where an independent tribunal can play the role of an 'objective bystander'. However, where the law-makers and (in this situation) the intention assessors are the States themselves, the equivalent criteria are less likely to be applied objectively. To some extent, Judge Jennings' opinion in the *Nicaragua* case accepts the subjectivity of the situation. The rhetorical, 'the Court under a jurisdiction clause surely does not have jurisdiction to pass upon the general question of the lawfulness or otherwise of

[562] 'The Effect of War on Treaties', this *Year Book*, 2 (1921–2), p. 37 at p. 40. In this passage, there is no reference to the treaty merely being suspended for the duration of the hostilities, but that alternative possibility is not germane to the present discussion and so will not be pursued. The important issue is the continued enforceability of the treaty at the time of the hostilities. See also Carpenter, 'Recent Decisions—Treaties', in *Virginia Journal of International Law*, 16(1976), p. 951 at pp. 954–5.

the outbreak of hostilities or of war',[563] was really an identification of the view of the State(s) concerned at the time of the hostilities. The objective issue would (equally surely) be whether a party to a treaty of friendship should, without becoming subject to the treaty's dispute settlement provisions, including the jurisdiction of the International Court, be able to act in a generally hostile manner (without necessarily breaching particular provisions of the treaty) to such an extent as to undermine those specific obligations.

The Jennings view could also be supported from a different standpoint. If there is an outbreak of hostilities between the parties to a treaty, the question of whether the treaty survives this event is dependent upon a number of factors, including an assessment of the political nature of the treaty in question. It is at least arguable that a treaty of friendship has hybrid characteristics. To the extent that it has commercial clauses, certainly those relating to the rights of nationals of the other party, these might well survive the outbreak of hostilities, at least to the extent that they are compatible with the conduct of those hostilities.[564] Indeed, as Judge Jennings pointed out in relation to the United States–Nicaragua Treaty of 1956:[565]

> If one looks accordingly at the actual provisions of the Treaty, perhaps one is struck first by the extent to which many of the terms of the Treaty have been faithfully observed by both Parties. There is much, for example, concerning the treatment of the nationals of one Party in the territory of the other . . . and United

[563] *ICJ Reports*, 1986, at p. 539: above, p. 268.

[564] In *Clark* v. *Allen*, 331 US 503 (1947), the Supreme Court upheld the inheritance provisions of Article IV of the Treaty of Friendship, Commerce and Consular Rights 1923 between the United States and Germany. The Court endorsed (at pp. 509–10) the principles stated by Cardozo J in *Techt* v. *Hughes*, 128 NE 185 (1920) at p. 192, that, if the President or Congress had not made the position clear on the outbreak of war by denouncing the treaty or by passing inconsistent legislation, the court's role was to examine 'whether, alone, or by force of connection with an inseparable scheme, the provision is inconsistent with the policy or safety of the nation in the emergency of war, and hence presumably intended to be limited to times of peace. The mere fact that other parts of the treaty are suspended or even abrogated is not conclusive. The treaty does not fall in its entirety unless it has the character of an indivisible act.'

The Supreme Court went on to apply these principles as follows (331 US at 510–11):

> 'We do not think that the national policy expressed in the Trading with the Enemy Act, as amended, is incompatible with the right of inheritance granted German aliens under Article IV of the treaty. It is true that since the declaration of war on December 11, 1941, the Act and the Executive Orders issued thereunder have prohibited the entry of German nationals into this country, have outlawed communications or transactions of a commercial character with them, and have precluded the removal of money or property from this country for their use or account. We assume that these provisions abrogate the parts of Article IV of the treaty dealing with the liquidation of the inheritance and the withdrawal of the proceeds, even though the Act provides that the prohibited activities and transactions may be licensed. But the Act and the Executive Orders do not evince such hostility to ownership of property by alien enemies as to imply that its acquisition conflicts with the national policy. There is, indeed, tacit recognition that acquisition of property by inheritance is compatible with the scheme of the Act. For the custodian is expressly empowered to represent the alien enemy heir in all legal proceedings, including those incident to succession.'

[565] *ICJ Reports*, 1986, at p. 540.

States citizens seem to be able to travel freely to Nicaragua. As to Nicaraguans in the United States, it was striking that Mr Chamorro, whose affidavit is much relied upon by the Court excuses himself from travelling to The Hague to give oral testimony, because travel outside the United States could possibly, he had been advised, prejudice his application for leave to establish himself and his family as permanent residents in the United States.

On the other hand, it could plausibly be argued that 'political' provisions would not survive an outbreak of hostilities, and this perception would include any obligation for the parties to remain at amity on the political level. It would seem to follow from the above premiss that a gradual breakdown in a relatively amicable relationship should not be regarded as involving any breach of the treaty. After all, the notion of friendship has little part to play in international relations in the sense that many States enter into such treaties and remain bound by their specific provisions despite an absence of any but the most limited degree of formal, and scarcely amicable, co-operation at an intergovernmental level.

The conclusion reached by Judge Jennings on the basis of what appears to be a similar line of reasoning was that 'such a potentially roving jurisdiction could not have been within the intention of the parties when they agreed the jurisdiction clause'.[566] It may be, however, that the emphasis upon the jurisdictional aspect is misplaced. The jurisdiction bestowed was clearly related to the obligations contained in the Treaty of 1956. The important issue of the parties' intentions should therefore have been directed towards the scope of those obligations.

Viewed from this perspective, there is value in the implied term or obligation approach. This can take into account both the nature and tenor of the treaty and the parties' attitudes towards the treaty. It may be that there are certain types of treaty or parts of a treaty of a particular nature to which no obligation would attach requiring the parties not to defeat the object and purpose of the treaty or part of the treaty in question. As far as the tenor of a treaty is concerned, there is a parallel with municipal law in which a term would not be implied into a contract if it conflicted with either the express terms of the agreement or with its tenor.[567] In the case of the 1956 Treaty, it could be argued that, given the commercial thrust of its principal terms, and the exception of matters 'necessary to protect [the] essential security interests' of a party, it would be inappropriate to import into the Treaty any obligation treating a use of force as inconsistent with its object and purpose. If such an undertaking could not legitimately be implied as one of its terms, there would be no basis for imposing such an obligation *dehors* the Treaty. The difference in theoretical basis for the imposition of a collateral

566 At p. 539.

567 As Lord Campbell CJ said in *Humphrey* v. *Dale* (1857), 7 E & B 266 at p. 274, an additional term will only be implied if it is not 'repugnant to or inconsistent with the tenor of the written instrument'. See also *Tamplin (F.A.) Steamship Co. Ltd.* v. *Anglo-Mexican Petroleum Products Ltd.*, [1916] 2 AC 397 at pp. 422–3 *per* Lord Parker; and Greig and Davis, op. cit. above (n. 42), pp. 520–3.

undertaking should not affect the outcome of the application of the law to the facts of the case.

This line of argument is not conclusive against the implication of such an obligation into the 1956 Treaty. The view of the majority might still be justifiable even on the implied term approach. It is possible to argue that, by including the proviso contained in Article XXI(1)(*d*) in their Treaty, the parties themselves must be taken to have defined the political parameters of their obligations. In a sense, therefore, as the obligation not to defeat the object and purpose of the Treaty represents the common intention of parties at the inception of their treaty relations, it is for them to limit its scope by provisions which they regard as appropriate. The majority of the Court was of the opinion that this limitation upon the parties' obligations did not extend to any aspects of the conduct of the United States.

The implied term concept would seem to have the advantage of emphasizing the parties' intentions in defining the scope of their obligations in relation to the express terms of the agreement. The Court's approach (or at least that put forward by Nicaragua, and apparently accepted or adopted by the Court[568]) suggests the imposition of an external and possibly arbitrary standard which pays little regard to the presumed intentions of the parties.

The implication of a term forming part of a party's obligations under the treaty has an obvious advantage in that it brings the undertaking in question within the scope of the treaty's dispute settlement procedures, which might include submission of any dispute to the International Court. This at least avoids the absurdity inherent in the Court's position that the conduct of a party might involve the breach of an obligation arising by virtue of the treaty, and concern the interpretation and application of the treaty, but nevertheless not be covered by the treaty's compromissory clause. Provided the scope of the treaty's obligations, including those implied to protect its object and purpose, coincides with an objective assessment of the parties' intentions, this situation would be preferable to that envisaged by the Court.

It follows from the adoption of the implied term theory that the Court's conclusion on the facts of the *Nicaragua* case would be less acceptable. It is doubtful whether the term contended for by Nicaragua would have been implied. If it had been implied in accordance with a proper appreciation of the parties' intentions when they entered into the Treaty, then of course the obligation would have been subject to the Court's jurisdiction by virtue of the terms of the Treaty.

In conclusion, it can be said that, even if the implication of such a term and the imposition of such an obligation were less likely in light of the nature of the 1956 Treaty and its terms, it would not mean that a term

[568] See above, p. 255.

might not be implied into other treaties requiring conduct consistent with the object and purpose of the instrument in question. All would depend upon the circumstances of that particular case. Moreover, conduct in breach of such an obligation would be subject to any compromissory clause in the treaty so that submission to a tribunal would not be dependent, as in the *Nicaragua* case, upon the existence of some other title of jurisdiction.

VIII. Conclusions

The assertion of jurisdiction by the International Court in the *Nicaragua* case led to the United States withdrawing from further participation in the proceedings,[569] and terminating its declaration accepting the compulsory jurisdiction of the Court.[570] Although dissatisfaction with the Court's handling of the dispute at the preliminary stages was the underlying cause,[571] the reasons given by the United States differed in the two situations.

In justification of its withdrawal, the United States alleged that the Court's decision over jurisdiction was in effect a nullity as it was 'contrary to law and fact'.[572] As far as the termination of its acceptance of the Court's compulsory jurisdiction was concerned, no legal excuse was necessary as the right to terminate on six months' notice was expressly reserved by the terms of the declaration.[573] However, when it took this step, the United States issued a press statement of reasons in which it sought to justify the termination in political terms.[574]

The statement pointed out that few States had accepted the Court's compulsory jurisdiction, contrary to the hopes that had existed in 1946. In particular, in the United States' view, Nicaragua was one of the States which had not made such a commitment. The United States also said:[575]

> Our experience with compulsory jurisdiction has been deeply disappointing. We have never been able to use our acceptance of compulsory jurisdiction to bring other States before the Court, but have ourselves been sued three times.

As for the political elements that had impinged upon the judicial process, the American statement first pointed to the assumptions upon which its acceptance of the Court's jurisdiction had been based:[576]

569 Statement of 18 January 1985: text in *International Legal Materials*, 24 (1985), p. 246.

570 Notice of termination of 7 October 1985 giving 6 months' notice as required by the declaration itself: text in ibid, p. 1742.

571 In addition to objections to the assertion of jurisdiction, the United States was resentful at the court's dismissal of El Salvador's request to intervene without allowing the latter a hearing. The Court's order appears in *ICJ Reports*, 1984, p. 215. For comment on this aspect of the Court's actions, see the statement by the United States of 18 January 1985, *International Legal Materials*, 24 (1985), at pp. 247–8.

572 Ibid. at p. 246.

573 See above, p. 122.

574 *International Legal Materials*, 24 (1985), at p. 1743.

575 At p. 1744.

576 Ibid.

In 1946 we accepted the risks of our submitting to the Court's compulsory jurisdiction because we believed that the respect owed to the Court by other States and the Court's own appreciation of the need to adhere scrupulously to its proper judicial role, would prevent the Court's process from being abused for political ends.

Having claimed that these assumptions had been proved wrong, the statement continued as follows:[577]

The objectives of the ICJ to which we subscribe—the peaceful adjudication of international disputes—were being subverted to the effort of Nicaragua and its Cuban and Soviet sponsors to use the Court as a political weapon. Indeed, the Court itself has never seen fit to accept jurisdiction over any other political conflict involving ongoing hostilities.

The complaints made by the United States fell broadly into three categories, relating to

(i) the reasons why Nicaragua submitted the case to the Court;
(ii) the exceeding of its jurisdictional competence by the Court; and
(iii) the admissibility of a dispute of this nature to judicial determination.

The third category falls outside the scope of the present article. The same is to an extent true of the first category. Nevertheless some comment is necessary on the matters which it raises, although the substance of this article has been directed primarily to the second category.

(a) *The Decision to go to the Court*

If one accepts the verity of the accusations levelled by the United States against Nicaragua, it is easier to understand the course of action taken by the United States against the Sandinista regime. However, it is clear that those actions, involving the mining of access to Nicaraguan ports, direct attacks on oil installations and promoting the armed intervention in Nicaraguan territory by the *contras*, were political choices.

Inevitably, the existence of an ongoing conflict on this scale would be raised before various international fora. The selection of time and place would be a matter for political judgment for the party raising the matter. Amongst the fora that might be chosen for the settlement of disputes would be the International Court or some arbitral tribunal. As far as international claims are concerned, it is trite to point out that the decision to press a claim or to submit it for judicial settlement, if that avenue is available, is a political decision reflecting a number of factors including the state of relations between the parties to the dispute.[578]

577 Ibid.

578 The International Court asserted this principle in the context of the diplomatic protection of nationals in the *Barcelona Traction* case, *ICJ Reports*, 1970, p. 3 at p. 44:

'The Court would here observe that, within the limits prescribed by international law, a State may exercise diplomatic protection by whatever means and to whatever extent it thinks fit, for it is its own right that the State is asserting. . . . The State must be viewed as the sole judge to decide whether its

Given the discretion vested in a State whether or not to prosecute a claim, it is hardly surprising that the decision to do so may be taken for some political motive, even to embarrass or put pressure on the respondent State. Moreover, as Article 33 of the United Nations Charter enjoins States to seek a solution of their disputes by peaceful means, including judicial settlement, it is scarcely to be expected that the selection of such a procedure should be regarded by the Court, or indeed by the international community, as tainted by bad faith because of the motives behind the submission.

(b) *The Assumption of Jurisdiction by the Court*

With regard to the allegations of political bias against the Court, the Court's less than satisfactory handling of the intervention request by El Salvador was open to criticism,[579] not least because it raised American suspicions as to the Court's impartiality.[580] After those events, it is less surprising that the United States regarded the Court's judgment on the jurisdictional issues as flawed because of what it regarded as the Court's prejudging of those issues.

Attached to the American statement of withdrawal from the proceedings were a set of observations on the Court's judgment,[581] covering in turn the effectiveness of the Nicaraguan declaration, the position under the United States declaration and the relevance of the 1956 Treaty.[582]

protection will be granted, to what extent it is granted, and when it will cease. It retains in this respect a discretionary power the exercise of which may be determined by considerations of a political or other nature, unrelated to the particular case.'

The reason for this principle is that the claim is regarded as belonging to the State, not to the injured national. *A fortiori*, where the claim relates to a breach of an obligation owed directly to the claimant State, its discretion whether and how to pursue the claim is fettered only by the rules of international law. See also *Restatement of the Law, Third, Foreign Relations Law of the United States* (1987), vol. 2, p. 347, section 902, Comments *g.* and *i.*

579 See the comments of Judge Schwebel in the *Nicaragua (Application of El Salvador)* case, *ICJ Reports*, 1984, p. 215 at pp. 230–2.

580 As the United States put it in its statement of 18 January 1985 on its withdrawal from the proceedings (*International Legal Materials*, 24 (1985), at pp. 247–8):

'El Salvador sought to participate in the suit to argue that the Court was not the appropriate forum to address the Central American conflict. El Salvador declared that it was under attack by Nicaragua and, in the exercise of its inherent right of self-defense, had requested assistance from the United States. The Court rejected El Salvador's application summarily—without givng reasons and without even granting El Salvador a hearing, in violation of El Salvador's right and in disregard of the Court's own rules.'

The statement then referred to this factor and the United States' view that Nicaragua had never accepted the Court's compulsory jurisdiction and continued (at p. 248):

'The Court's decision is a marked departure from its past, cautious approach to jurisdictional questions. The haste with which the Court proceeded to a judgment on these issues—noted in several of the separate and dissenting opinions—only adds to the impression that the Court is determined to find in favour of Nicaragua in the case.'

581 Text in ibid., p. 249.

582 The final part dealing with issues of admissibility will not be discussed here.

1. *The Nicaraguan declaration*

While legitimate doubts could be raised as to the effectiveness of the Nicaraguan declaration, the criticisms are nowhere near as damaging to the Court's decision as the observations suggest. The view that the 'Court's theory is impossible to reconcile with the plain, consistent texts of four of the five authentic languages of the Charter, which state that only declarations "still in force" in 1945 would have legal effect for the present Court'[583] is exaggerated. It is possible to take the Court's line and, as their paper earlier pointed out, the *travaux* do not necessarily support the American case.[584]

The United States also advanced the proposition that the 'Court's theory is flatly inconsistent with two prior decisions of the Court (the *Aerial Incident* and *Barcelona Traction* cases)'.[585] The Court did not in fact pay much attention to the decisions in question. However, as has already been explained, it is possible to mount an argument from them that is more favourable to the Nicaraguan, than to the United States', position.[586]

The same can also be said of the *Yearbooks* of the Court as evidence of Nicaragua as a State which had accepted the jurisdiction of the Court. Some of the objections from members of the Court seemed to misunderstand the significance of the 1957 caveat.[587] The United States observations as to what passed between the two States at the diplomatic level[588] are less easy to assess. However, there are certainly grounds for rejecting the Court's conclusion that the *Yearbook* entries and the conduct of the two States towards them established not just an estoppel against Nicaragua,[589] but the implied agreement of the parties to the exercise of jurisdiction under Article 36(2) of the Court's Statute.[590]

2. *The United States' declaration*

The principal objection to the assumption of jurisdiction by the Court centred upon its refusal, at the jurisdictional stage, to determine the effect of the multilateral treaty reservation in the United States' declaration, but rather to join the issue to the merits. This step was taken notwithstanding the fact that other Central American States would be affected by any decision of the Court, as was clear from explicit representation by the States concerned and from Nicaragua's own pleadings.[591]

The real issue, addressed principally at the merits stage, was whether it was possible to decide the matter on the basis of customary international

583 Ibid., at p. 252.
584 Above, p. 130.
585 *International Legal Materials*, 24 (1985), at p. 253.
586 See above, p. 138.
587 See above, pp. 143–4.
588 *International Legal Materials*, 24 (1985), at pp. 253–4.
589 Above, p. 162.
590 *International Legal Materials*, 24 (1985), at pp. 255–6.
591 At p. 257.

law, or whether the relevant law was so bound up with the provisions of the United Nations Charter and the Charter of the Organization of American States that it was an absurdity to regard the reservation as inapplicable.[592]

There were difficulties with the reservation given the (equal) absurdity inherent in its potential scope. Nor was the proposition that a decision could be reached on the basis of customary rules so very surprising. There are a number of areas of international law where treaty provisions are intertwined with State practice to establish customary norms. Moreover, if some rules proscribing the use of force do constitute part of the *jus cogens*, the reason for this being so is ultimately a matter of customary law. This does not mean that criticisms of the Court's judgment can be lightly dismissed. What is important is that it is equally not possible to dismiss the majority view as politically inspired and without any legal foundation.

Less persuasive are the United States' views on the effect of the Shultz letter purporting to modify the United States' declaration. The first prong of the United States' attack on the holding that the United States was bound to give notice of its amendment was that it ignored 'intervening State practice and hence customary international law'.[593] As has been suggested, the practice seems to have established a right of withdrawal in the case of declarations containing no requirement of notice (though the practice is not totally unambiguous as the issue has not been put before the Court), but this is not necessarily the case with regard to declarations requiring a specific period of notice.[594] In light of the Court's previous attitude to the nature of such declarations as creating consensual or a series of bilateral relationships,[595] its conclusion on this point would seem to have been inevitable.

The other prong of the United States' attack was the claim that to require a period of notice in the case of the United States, in view of the fact that no such period would have applied to Nicaragua,[596] was to assert a broader application of the concept of reciprocity than had hitherto been the case.[597] At most the United States' argument presented a choice to the Court of whether or not to extend the ambit of reciprocity. It could hardly be regarded as irrational or perverse for the Court to have adopted the conclusion it did. After all, it is a matter of choice in the first place for a declarant State whether it proclaims the requirement of a period of notice of withdrawal as part of its acceptance of the Court's compulsory jurisdiction.

3. *The 1956 Treaty*

The arguments presented by the United States in criticism of the assumption of jurisdiction on this basis were predictable enough: Nicaragua's failure to rely upon the Treaty originally or, even subsequently, to

592 Above, pp. 221–3.
593 *International Legal Materials*, 24 (1985). at p. 258.
594 Above, pp. 167–8.
595 Above, p. 166.
596 *International Legal Materials*, 24 (1985), at p. 259.
597 Except perhaps in the *Norwegian Loans* case: above, p. 170.

any significant extent;[598] the failure of Nicaragua to attempt to adjust the dispute by diplomacy before taking the matter to the Court;[599] and the exclusion of security matters from the provision of the Treaty.[600]

While the first of these contentions may have signified hesitation as to the existence of jurisdiction under the Treaty, there are alternative explanations, including the obvious one that there were no doubts as to the applicability of the treaty, only a realization that the scope of such jurisdiction would be more limited. The second objection hardly seems to counter the Court's view that recourse to diplomacy was not a *sine qua non* of submission of a dispute to the Court.[601] Indeed, Article 33 of the United Nations Charter refers to negotiation and judicial settlement as alternative (and not consecutive) methods of peaceful settlement. The only crucial requirement is that a dispute should already exist.

As for the scope of the Treaty, the treatment of this issue, particularly in relation to the obligation not to act in a manner destructive of the object and purpose of the Treaty, was less than adequate and far from clear.[602] Nevertheless, the finding by the Court that there had been breaches of express terms of the Treaty would appear to justify the exercise of jurisdiction over the parties.

It has to be admitted that, weighing the totality of findings, the result was overwhelmingly against the case presented by the United States. Not so long before, the United States had been as successful in its claim against Iran in the *Tehran Hostages* case[603] as Nicaragua had been to date in the present case. Admittedly the basis of jurisdiction (and the applicable law) was uncontrovertible in that case, but it could plausibly be suggested that there was a degree of similarity between the two in the view of some of the judges towards the conduct complained of by the applicant State. Both involved the use of force by an armed group, acting with the support or encouragement of the respondent government, against the territory in one case and the diplomatic and consular premises in the other of the applicant State. Such conduct was likely to and did in fact meet with widespread disapproval by most members of the international community of States, a view equally likely to be shared by members of the Court given the breaches of international law allegedly arising from the conduct in question.

While this perception would support the United States' complaints about the intrusion of political elements into what should have been a matter of purely legal judgment, such a phenomenon is not without precedent in the history of the Court. As has already been explained,[604] the *Hearings of Petitioners* case sanctioned a qualitative change in the degree of supervision

598 *International Legal Materials*, 24 (1985), at p. 260.
599 Ibid.
600 At pp. 261–2.
601 Above, pp. 251–2.
602 Above, pp. 254 ff.
603 *ICJ Reports*, 1980, p. 3.
604 Above, p. 154.

exercisable by the General Assembly over the mandate for South West Africa. The step was taken for the express purpose of increasing the control exercisable over South Africa as mandatory in light of its lack of co-operation with the United Nations.

It is true that the *Petitioners* case did not concern the jurisdiction of the International Court, but there is otherwise a level of similarity. The Court regarded the sanctioned control mechanism as an important element in advancing the interests of the international community. It is possible to explain the *Nicaragua* case in similar terms, although in this instance the control was to be exercised by the Court itself.

The circumstances illustrate vividly the tensions inherent in the attitude of most States to acceptance of the Court's compulsory jurisdiction. The United States was critical of Nicaragua's ambivalence over whether or not it was subject to that jurisdiction by virtue of its 1929 declaration. At the time of the Permanent Court, Nicaragua had taken all steps necessary at the municipal level to ratify the Statute, but could not show that it committed itself by a formal act of ratification at the international level. In the period since 1945, it had neither confirmed nor denied the validity of that declaration and had preferred to continue with the air of uncertainty arising from the entries in the *Yearbooks* of the Court.

Nor was the United States' position so significantly different. In its case, there was a formal act of acceptance of the jurisdiction of the Court by the deposit of its 1946 declaration. However, behind the apparent intention to become subject to the Court's jurisdiction, there were indications of a reluctance to do so in the form of the Connally and Vandenberg reservations. Moreover, if the attitude at times expressed towards the former is any guide,[605] the reservation could be regarded as being as extensive as the declaration itself. In light of this fact, the United States' bemoaning of its lack of success as applicant before the Court[606] is not something with which one can sympathize.

The question for the Court to face was whether, both States having created the appearance of being subject to the Court's compulsory jurisdiction, their position should be assessed at face value. It may be that the Court was departing from its earlier 'cautious' attitude towards interpreting the jurisdictional links between States and the Court.[607] However, it was dealing with arguments which would have destroyed altogether the Nicaraguan declaration, or significantly undermined the American declaration through the operation of the Vandenberg reservation. From this perspective, the Court's attitude, in keeping with that which it might well have applied to the Connally reservation if the need had arisen, is less open to objection.

Similar considerations apply to the 1956 Treaty. The tension there was

[605] Above, p. 85.
[606] Above, p. 273.
[607] Above, p. 275 n. 580.

between the general scope of that instrument and Article XXI(1)(*d*).[608] If, as the United States contended, the Treaty was entirely limited to commercial relations (and not to a concept of amicable relations as suggested by the title), there would have been no need for that provision. Its inclusion suggested that the scope of the Treaty was limited by that provision and not by some notion of commercial relations as the Treaty's object and purpose to which the specific terms had to relate. On this hypothesis, it was by no means *objectively* certain that the actions of the United States fell outside the ambit of the Treaty and of its compromissory clause.

One final point may perhaps be made. If it is indeed true that the Court's approach to the jurisdictional issues in the *Nicaragua* case does mark a departure from its earlier caution, the question arises as to what it has to lose. The demand for judicial restraint in the assumption of jurisdiction may appear to members of the Court to be as destructive of its jurisdiction as a more assertive approach, even if it does lead to the denunciation of declarations under Article 36(2). As far as jurisdiction based upon instruments similar to the 1956 Treaty between the United States and Nicaragua is concerned, the Court's decision was inconclusive. It advanced a principle of treaty-related liability without including it within the treaty's compromissory clause. With regard to allegations as to the politicization of the Court, this has undoubtedly led to the employment of chambers of the Court in an attempt to ensure the political acceptability of the bench. In this development, however, the United States has been a prime mover.[609] Could not the accusation made by the United States against the Court that the course it had embarked upon 'could do enormous harm to it as an institution and to the cause of international law'[610] be reversed to apply to the United States itself?

The establishment of chambers of the Court at the behest of the United States (and Canada in one case, Italy in the other) created a tension between the wishes of the parties to the arrangement in being able to select acceptable judges, and the integrity of the Court represented by Article 26(2) of its Statute which appears to place the decision-making authority in the formation of a chamber in the hands of the Court. According to that provision:

> The Court may at any time form a chamber for dealing with a particular case. The number of judges to constitute such a chamber shall be determined by the Court with the approval of the parties.

There is of course a further tension between the role of the Court in providing a ready forum for the peaceful settlement of disputes available to particular parties, and the role of the Court in declaring rules of international

[608] Above, p. 253.
[609] *Gulf of Maine* case, *ICJ Reports*, 1982, p. 3; *Elettronica Sicula SpA* case, *ICJ Reports*, 1987, p. 3.
[610] Statement of withdrawal from the proceedings, *International Legal Materials*, 24 (1985), at p. 249.

law on the basis of its representative character as prescribed in Article 9 of the Statute:

> At every election, the electors shall bear in mind not only that the persons to be elected should individually possess the qualifications required, but also that in the body as a whole the representation of the main forms of civilization and the principal legal systems of the world should be assured.

The decisions of the Court to accept the membership of the chambers nominated by the parties could be regarded as a triumph of pragmatism over principles, of flexibility over formalism, of individual circumstances over possible longer-term considerations. The factors involved may have been in a sense 'political'. It could be argued that the course adopted was unwise, but not conclusively wrong. So, too, with the decision of the Court on its jurisdiction in the *Nicaragua* case. At that level, it does not necessarily follow that the majority of the Court were any the less wise than the minority (some of whom would in any case have exercised some jurisdiction over the United States and its activities), or than the United States, which can hardly be regarded as less partial than the majority of judges whose analytical skills or even judicial impartiality it had so openly brought into question.

COMPLIANCE WITH JUDGMENTS OF THE EUROPEAN COURT OF HUMAN RIGHTS AND DECISIONS OF THE COMMITTEE OF MINISTERS: THE EXPERIENCE OF THE UNITED KINGDOM, 1975–1987*

By R. R. CHURCHILL AND J. R. YOUNG‡

I. Introduction

The European Convention on Human Rights requires States parties to secure to all within their jurisdiction certain listed rights and freedoms. Under the international machinery established by the Convention an allegation that a State party has failed to secure these rights and freedoms may be made by another State party or by an individual by means of an application to the European Commission of Human Rights. If the Commission decides that the application is admissible, and fails to obtain a friendly settlement between the applicant and the defendant State, it draws up a report in which it gives its opinion as to whether the Convention has been violated. This report is then sent to the Committee of Ministers of the Council of Europe. The case may be referred to the European Court of Human Rights (hereafter referred to as 'the Court') either by the Commission or by an interested State party. The Court hearing takes place in public; the applicant, the defendant State and the Commission are represented; the Court gives reasoned judgments and makes its determinations by a simple majority. If the case has not been referred to the Court within three months of the Committee of Ministers receiving the Commission's report, a decision as to whether the Convention has been violated is taken by the Committee of Ministers. Thus a definitive determination as to whether a State has violated the Convention is made by either the Court or the Committee of Ministers. In this connection it should be noted that the Committee of Ministers, which is a political body, falls a long way short of the ideal as an organ for making such determinations. In contrast to the Court the Committee deliberates in private, with the defendant State being present, but in the absence of the applicant (unless a State) or the Commission; it takes its decision (in which the defendant State may participate) by a two-thirds majority. There is no re-hearing of the case before the

* © R.R. Churchill and J. R. Young, 1992.

‡ Senior Lecturer and Lecturer in Law, respectively, Cardiff Law School.

Committee, which simply reviews the Commission's report and agrees or disagrees with the Commission's opinion as to whether the Convention has been breached, giving no reasons for its decision.

Under Articles 32(2) and 53 of the Convention a State party found by the Court or the Committee to have violated the Convention 'must take the necessary measures required by the decision of the Committee of Ministers' finding a violation or 'abide by the decision of the Court', respectively. Neither the Court nor the Committee has the power to specify what measures should be taken, although the Committee may make suggestions in this regard.[1] Nor, even in those States parties which take a monist approach to the relationship of international law to municipal law and where therefore the self-executing provisions of the Convention are part of domestic law, are judgments of the Court or decisions of the Committee of Ministers regarded as being part of domestic law and therefore directly enforceable.[2]

While a certain amount has been written about the way in which States parties have complied with judgments of the Court and decisions of the Committee of Ministers in individual cases, little appears to have been attempted in the way of more comprehensive surveys. This is rather surprising, given that the degree to which States comply with judgments of the Court and decisions of the Committee of Ministers is one of the tests of the effectiveness of the Convention (although of course by no means the only test). To undertake a truly comprehensive examination of compliance by States would, however, be difficult, since it would require considerable knowledge of a variety of legal systems and considerable linguistic skills. Because of these difficulties the authors of this article have not attempted a comprehensive survey. Instead, the aim of this article is a more modest one, to see whether the United Kingdom has complied with those judgments of the Court and decisions of the Committee of Ministers, adopted up to mid-1987, finding it to have violated the Convention, and if so, to see in what way and how quickly this has been done. Such an exercise, while obviously of interest in the United Kingdom, also has a broader significance in assessing the effectiveness of the Convention, for of the 95 cases decided by the Court and Committee of Ministers up to 30 June 1987 in which a violation of the Convention was found, the United Kingdom was the defendant State in no less than 29 of them, i.e. about 31 per cent.[3]

Even an examination of compliance limited to the United Kingdom is not an easy or straightforward task because of the difficulty of determining what constitutes compliance with a judgment of the Court or a decision of the Committee of Ministers. Except in inter-State cases, applications are brought in respect of the way in which the Convention has been applied to a

[1] Higgins, 'The Execution of the Decisions of Organs under the European Convention on Human Rights', *Revue hellénique de droit international*, 31 (1978), p. 1 at pp. 31–4.

[2] Ibid., at pp. 30–1.

[3] These figures exclude inter-State cases.

particular individual or particular individuals, rather than being concerned with some part of a State's legal system in the abstract. Thus compliance with a ruling of the Court or Committee of Ministers may require no more than the payment of compensation or a change in administrative practice. However, usually, this 'individual compliance' is not sufficient to prevent the commission of future breaches of the Convention against other individuals, since the individual violation is symptomatic of a more general and systematic failure of the State concerned to comply with the Convention. Thus compliance in its broader sense includes the remedial action, legislative or administrative, taken to prevent future breaches.

It is also clear that there is a spectrum of this 'general compliance'. At one end, literal compliance may occur when a State takes the narrowest interpretation of the decision against it. Extended compliance takes place when a State considers the broader implications of the decision and the reasons given for it. It could be said that it looks to the spirit of the decision, thereby forestalling future complaints and adverse decisions.

Of course, the determination of whether there has been extended compliance may be particularly problematic. It is for the State which is in breach to determine what more general remedial action should be taken, not for the Court or Committee to direct it. In the case of the Committee, assessment of the quality of compliance is particularly difficult, since the Committee does not give reasoned decisions, and although the Commission's report forms the basis on which the Committee acts it may not necessarily adopt all the Commission's reasoning, even though it may agree with the Commission's opinion that there has been a violation. With judgments of the European Court there are the same problems of interpretation as with national courts. There may be disagreement in identifying the *ratio decidendi* of a case. In some cases this may be clear enough, in others the European Court may give unclear or confusing signals.

A further complication with the United Kingdom is that, with respect to the Convention, it is responsible for a number of legal systems. The United Kingdom itself contains three separate legal systems (those of England and Wales, Scotland and Northern Ireland). Furthermore, under Article 63 it has extended its acceptance of the Convention to include a number of dependent territories for whose international relations it is responsible. While an adverse decision of the Court or Committee will relate to a breach within one of the jurisdictions of the United Kingdom or its dependent territories, broad compliance would require corrective action in other jurisdictions where the law is the same or similar. Accordingly, this article looks at compliance in all three jurisdictions of the United Kingdom, but for reasons of space and accessibility of information is more selective when dealing with compliance in dependent territories.

The 30 cases to be considered (all those decided up to 30 June 1987 in which the Court or Committee found the United Kingdom to have violated the Convention) are arranged in order of the Convention article (or principal article) at issue in each case. Cases concerning a common subject (such as corporal punishment or prisoners) are grouped together.

The Convention contains its own machinery (in Articles 32 and 54), through the Committee of Ministers, for overseeing compliance by a State party with a ruling of the Court or Committee of Ministers. However, this does not involve a close scrutiny of the State's corrective action, and is thus not always a sound indication of the extent of compliance. This article is not concerned with this machinery or its effectiveness in further detail.

II. Corporal Punishment

The first two cases to be considered, both decided by the Court, concern corporal punishment. The first case, *Tyrer*,[4] concerned judicial corporal punishment on the Isle of Man. Tyrer was a 15-year old boy who had been convicted by a Manx court of unlawful assault and who had been subsequently punished by three strokes of the birch on the bare bottom. The Court, in a judgment given on 25 April 1978, held that this punishment was 'degrading treatment' and therefore a breach of Article 3 of the Convention. It should be noted that there were no unusual circumstances in Tyrer's case: furthermore, the fact that he was birched on the bare bottom, though aggravating the degrading nature of the treatment, was not decisive of the issue. Thus, although the Court was concerned only with Tyrer's individual case, its judgment was effectively a condemnation of the judicial birching of adolescents generally, and probably a condemnation of all forms of judicial corporal punishment.

The Court's judgment placed the defendant in this case, the UK Government, in something of a quandary when it came to complying with the judgment. Although the UK authorities have the competence to legislate for the Isle of Man, because of the special constitutional status of the Isle of Man (which as a British Crown dependency enjoys self rule in domestic matters), they do not normally legislate contrary to the wishes of Tynwald, the Manx Parliament.[5] It was clear from the reaction to the Court's judgment in the Isle of Man that Tynwald would be opposed to abolishing judicial corporal punishment (and in fact it has made no move towards legislating for abolition). Thus, because of the UK authorities' traditional reluctance to legislate contrary to the wishes of Tynwald, it appears that no suggestion was made for UK legislation to abolish judicial corporal punishment in the Isle of Man. Instead, the UK Government wrote to the Lieutenant Governor of the Isle of Man on 13 June 1978 informing him that in the light of the Court's judgment it was of the view that judicial corporal punishment on the Isle of Man was contrary to the

[4] Series A, No. 26 (1978); *European Human Rights Reports* (hereinafter *EHRR*), vol. 2, p. 1.

[5] Wade and Bradley, *Constitutional and Administrative Law* (10th edn., 1985), p. 45.

Convention. Subsequently, the Chief Justice of the Isle of Man (the First Deemster) informed the High Court, the High Bailiffs and magistrates (i.e. all those who were legally entitled to pass a sentence of birching) that the effect of the Court's judgment was that judicial corporal punishment was contrary to the Convention.[6]

In spite of the First Deemster's announcement referred to above, in the subsequent case of *Teare* v. *O'Callaghan*[7] magistrates imposed a sentence of birching on a youth convicted of unlawful and malicious wounding. On appeal, however, the Isle of Man High Court quashed the sentence on the ground that it was contrary to the Isle of Man's international obligations. The Court did not say, however, that a Manx court could never impose birching as a punishment: to have done so would have been to have usurped the function of the legislature. But the Court suggested that birching should only be used if all other forms of punishment were unsuitable.

The record of compliance with the European Court's judgment in *Tyrer* is rather unsatisfactory. No legislation has been passed to give effect to the judgment and to abolish judicial corporal punishment in the Isle of Man. Even if Tynwald were unwilling to legislate, it is not unknown for the United Kingdom to legislate for the Isle of Man contrary to Tynwald's wishes, especially if the matter concerns an international obligation.[8] Furthermore, while in practice, as far as the writers have been able to ascertain, there has been no judicial corporal punishment on the Isle of Man since the European Court's judgment, the Isle of Man High Court's judgment in *Teare* v. *O'Callaghan* does not completely exclude the possibility that there might in some future case be such punishment. And if there were, the victim of such punishment, unlike Tyrer, would not be able to bring a case before the organs of the Convention because the right of individual petition from the Isle of Man lapsed in 1976 and has not been renewed subsequently (though an inter-State case would always be possible, if unlikely). Overall, as far as compliance (in the broader sense used in the introduction) with the Court's judgment in the *Tyrer* case is concerned, it is difficult to resist the conclusion that concern for Manx sensibilities has weighed more with the UK Government than a full-hearted commitment to its international obligations.

The second case to be considered, *Campbell and Cosans* v. *UK*,[9] concerns corporal punishment in schools. Mrs Campbell and Mrs Cosans were the mothers of children at State schools in Scotland where corporal punishment was used. Neither of their children was actually subjected to such punishment, although Mrs Cosans' son was suspended from school when

[6] HC Debs., vol. 958, Written Answers, cols. *518–19*: 21 November 1978.

[7] *EHRR*, vol. 4, p. 232.

[8] e.g. the Marine etc. Broadcasting Offences Act 1967 was extended to the Isle of Man against Tynwald's wishes: Wade and Bradley, op cit. above (n. 5).

[9] Series A, No. 48 (1982); *EHRR*, vol. 4, p. 293.

he refused to accept such punishment. The two mothers alleged two violations of the Convention. First, they argued that Article 3 (which prohibits inhuman and degrading treatment) had been violated by reason of their sons' fear, and the threat to them, of corporal punishment. Secondly, they claimed a breach of Article 2 of Protocol 1[10] as their sons' education was not in conformity with their philosophical convictions. In a judgment given on 25 February 1982 the Court upheld the latter contention, but held that there had been no breach of Article 3. It is important to note that the Court did not rule on the question of whether the actual application of corporal punishment might be inhuman and degrading treatment contrary to Article 3.

Before turning to see whether the Court's judgment has been complied with, it is worth briefly examining a number of other cases concerning corporal punishment in schools brought against the United Kingdom. In *X* v. *UK*[11] a complaint that the caning of a child in an English school was a violation of Article 3 was found to be admissible by the Commission, which subsequently effected a friendly settlement (in December 1981) without the case going on to the Court or Committee of Ministers. Part of the terms of the settlement were that the UK Government undertook to send a circular to all local education authorities informing them that the use of corporal punishment might in certain circumstances amount to treatment contrary to Article 3. Secondly, in four cases where a breach of Article 3 and/or Article 2 of Protocol 1 was alleged, the Commission found all the cases admissible as regards the latter article but not as regards the former. In 1987 all the cases were resolved by friendly settlements.[12] Finally, in *Warwick* v. *UK* complaints of a violation of both Article 3 and Article 2 of Protocol 1 were made by a mother and her daughter. The Commission not only found both complaints admissible but also was of the opinion that both articles had been violated. The case went to the Committee of Ministers, which in March 1989 found that there had been a violation of Article 2, but did not obtain the requisite two-thirds majority to establish that there had been a breach of Article 3.[13]

Turning now to the question of compliance, it is obvious from the cases just quoted that *Campbell and Cosans* was not an isolated violation, but was symptomatic of a general problem, and one that was not confined to Scotland. To comply, in the broader sense, with the Court's judgment therefore required legislation. Theoretically, such legislation could involve

[10] Article 2 reads (in part): 'In the exercise of any functions which it assumes in relation to education and to teaching, the State shall respect the right of parents to ensure such education and teaching in conformity with their own religious and philosophical convictions'.

[11] Application 7907/77, *Yearbook of the European Convention on Human Rights*, 24 (1981), p. 403.

[12] Application 9114/80, *Durairaj*; Application 9119/80, *Townend and Townend*; Application 9303/81, *B*; and Application 10,592/83, *S, J and A*: Council of Europe, *Human Rights Information Sheet*, No. 21 (1987), pp. 70–2.

[13] Committee of Ministers Res. DH(89)5, Application 9471/81, *Warwick* v. *United Kingdom*.

one of two possible solutions. More narrowly, it could allow parents to request that their children be exempted from corporal punishment, either by having separate schools (which would be very expensive) or by having dual forms of punishment in the same schools (which would be administratively awkward and might be perceived to be unfair). Such an approach, moreover, while complying with the Court's judgment in *Campbell and Cosans*, would be undone if the Court or Committee of Ministers were ever to rule that corporal punishment was contrary to Article 3. In the light of the friendly settlement in *X* discussed above, and the Court's emphasis in *Tyrer* that the degrading nature of the punishment lay in its being a form of institutional violence, such a ruling was a distinct possibility. A more radical and straightforward form of compliance, therefore, would be to abolish corporal punishment altogether.

In fact, it was over a year after the Court's judgment before the Government gave any public indication of its intention. In July 1983 the Secretary of State for Education, Sir Keith Joseph, announced that the Government intended to give effect to the Court's judgment by putting forward legislation which would allow parents who objected to corporal punishment to have their children exempted from such punishment. Before putting forward such legislation, the Government would consult widely.[14] The reason why the Government chose the narrower form of compliance was probably because the main teachers' unions at that time generally favoured corporal punishment and because the Education Ministers, particularly the junior minister, Dr Rhodes Boyson, themselves personally favoured such punishment. Although the closing date for the consultation exercise referred to was the end of November 1983, it was not until January 1985 that the Government published the promised Bill—the Education (Corporal Punishment) Bill.

The Bill would have allowed parents whose children would otherwise have been liable to corporal punishment in school to exempt them from such punishment. Although criticized by MPs on all sides and defended by Sir Keith Joseph with a marked lack of enthusiasm, the Bill nevertheless successfully completed all its stages in the House of Commons. In the House of Lords, however, an amendment was made to the Bill at the Report stage which effectively would have banned corporal punishment.[15] Faced with this defeat and being unprepared to accept the amendment, the Government withdrew the Bill, influenced no doubt by the opposition of many Conservative backbench MPs both to the abolition of corporal punishment and to the Bill.[16]

[14] HC Debs., vol. 46, Written Answers col. *545*: 28 July 1983. But note that in Scotland the Secretary of State had recommended all Scottish local education authorities to abolish corporal punishment by the summer of 1984: ibid., col. *608*: 28 July 1983.

[15] HL Debs., vol. 465, cols. 1314–33: 4 July 1985.

[16] HC Debs., vol. 83, col. 865: 23 July 1985; HL Debs., vol. 466, cols. 1097–8: 23 July 1985.

There matters rested for several months. The next development in this lengthy saga occurred in early 1986, when the Government published an Education Bill. Though wide-ranging in its provisions, the Bill as published did not deal with the question of corporal punishment at all. In the House of Lords, where the Bill was introduced, an amendment was put forward at the Committee stage by Lord McIntosh which would abolish corporal punishment. In spite of opposition from the Government, the amendment was carried by 94 votes to 92.[17] At the Report stage in the House of Commons a Conservative backbench amendment to delete the Lords amendment and restore the status quo was put forward. In spite of having the support of Education Ministers, the amendment was defeated by the smallest possible margin, by 230 votes to 231.[18] The Bill, with the House of Lords amendment having precariously survived intact, received the Royal Assent on 7 November 1986 as the Education (No. 2) Act 1986.

Section 47 of the Act applies to England and Wales and abolishes corporal punishment in State schools, in certain other schools for which the State provides financial assistance, and in respect of pupils at private schools any of whose fees are paid out of public funds. Section 48 makes similar provision for Scotland, and similar provision has been made for Northern Ireland by order.[19]

Sections 47 and 48 came into force on 15 August 1987, some five and a half years after the judgment in *Campbell and Cosans*. Clearly the Act amounts to the fullest possible compliance with the judgment as far as the State sector of education is concerned.[20] As far as the private sector is concerned, because it seems very unlikely that a parent would send a child to a private school which employed corporal punishment if the parent held strong convictions opposed to corporal punishment, it is unlikely that there would be any breach of Article 2 of Protocol 1 in practice—even if the article applies to the private sector (which is perhaps doubtful since it refers to respect for convictions by the *State* where the *State* exercises functions related to education and teaching). There still remains the possibility that corporal punishment could be degrading (or even inhuman) treatment contrary to Article 3, but in practice a parent who favoured corporal punishment would hardly be likely to bring an application before the Convention organs on this ground.

As a study in compliance with judgments of the European Court by the United Kingdom, this case is noteworthy in two respects. First, the time taken to comply—five and a half years—is by far the longest in cases involving the United Kingdom. Secondly, and unusually, compliance in this case

[17] HL Debs., vol. 473, cols. 788–801: 17 April 1986.

[18] HC Debs., vol. 102, cols. 226–77: 22 July 1986. Conservative MPs had a free vote; there was a three-line Labour whip against the amendment.

[19] Education (Corporal Punishment) (Northern Ireland) Order 1987, SI 1987, No. 461.

[20] And also allowed friendly settlements to be achieved in the four cases referred to in n. 12.

was the result of a backbench initiative in Parliament, and the form of compliance was one that was contrary to the Government's wishes.[21]

III. Cases arising from the Political Situation in Northern Ireland

(a) *Ill-treatment of Detainees*

The case of *Ireland* v. *UK*[22] arose from the exercise of emergency powers in Northern Ireland from August 1971 to June 1974 against the background of escalating terrorist violence. Emergency legislation gave power to the security forces to arrest and detain persons for interrogation and the power of indefinite detention without trial.[23] These powers were used extensively and predominantly against persons suspected of involvement with IRA terrorism. On 16 December 1971 the Republic of Ireland lodged an application with the Commission alleging that the policy of detention without trial and the ill-treatment of certain detainees were in breach of the Convention.

In a judgment given in January 1978 the Court held, as regards the question of detention without trial, that while the powers of arrest and detention were inconsistent with Article 5, which safeguards liberty and security of the person, there was no breach because a valid derogation had been made under Article 15.[24] In relation to the question of whether there had been a breach of Article 3, the Court agreed with the Commission that in order to impute a breach of this article to the United Kingdom it had to be shown not only that there had been some ill-treatment by members of the police or army, but that this constituted an administrative practice involving a pattern of activity and official tolerance for which the authorities of the State should be held liable.[25]

One practice was not contested by the United Kingdom. It was admitted that it had been authorized at 'high level' and had been taught as a technique of interrogation. This was the practice of 'interrogation in depth',

[21] A final point of interest is that in February 1988 the United Kingdom made a declaration extending Protocol 1 of the Convention to 10 territories for whose international relations it is responsible (including Guernsey and Jersey, but not the Isle of Man). In respect of all these territories except Gibraltar, Guernsey and Jersey, the United Kingdom accepts the provisions of Article 2 of the Protocol only in so far as it does not affect the existing law permitting corporal punishment in those territories. See *UK Treaty Series*, No. 78 (1988).

[22] Series A, No. 25 (1978); *EHRR*, vol. 2, p. 25.

[23] Initially these powers were exercised under the Civil Authorities (Special Powers) Act (Northern Ireland) 1922. After the UK Government assumed responsibility for the government of Northern Ireland, similar powers were continued under a series of legislative measures and are still available under the Northern Ireland (Emergency Provisions) Act 1978 and the Prevention of Terrorism Act 1989.

[24] Loc. cit. above (n. 22), paras. 188–224.

[25] Ibid., paras. 156–9. On the concept of an administrative practice see also the Commission report, 25 January 1976, Series B, No. 23–1, pp. 369–72 and 467–70.

using what came to be known as 'the five techniques', designed to disorientate the detainee and make him more disposed to give information during interrogation. The techniques consisted of forcing detainees to stand spreadeagled against a wall for some hours in a most uncomfortable posture; covering their heads with a dark hood except during interrogation; subjecting them to continuous hissing noises; depriving them of sleep; and putting them on an extremely restricted diet. This practice, which was only proved to have been used against fourteen of the detainees, was held by the Court to be 'inhuman and degrading treatment' and therefore contrary to Article 3 of the Convention: unlike the Commission, however, the Court did not find that the practice amounted to torture. It was inhuman because it caused 'if not actual bodily injury, at least intense physical and mental suffering to the persons subjected thereto and also led to acute psychiatric disturbances during interrogation'; it was degrading since the techniques were 'such as to arouse in their victims feelings of fear, anguish and inferiority capable of humiliating and debasing them and possibly breaking their physical or moral resistance'.[26]

In addition, the Court also found that at one of the detention centres there had been a number of instances of assault, sometimes very serious and violent, by police against detainees over a period of months and that senior officers could not have been ignorant of them. These were not occasional beatings, but 'a sort of scheme in order to make [the victims] speak'. The failure of these officers or of any higher authorities to take any action in relation to this violence led the Court to conclude that this was an administrative practice constituting inhuman treatment and a breach of Article 3 for which the United Kingdom must be held responsible.[27]

The British Government had already taken steps towards compliance with the Convention by the time the Court gave its judgment in January 1978. In November 1971, a committee[28] set up by the Government to enquire into allegations of ill-treatment following the exercise of the emergency powers exonerated the security forces of most of the allegations against them. While it held that the five techniques amounted to 'ill-treatment', it did not condemn them and held that they did not amount to 'brutality'. It was shortly after the publication of this report that the Irish Government lodged its application with the Commission, by which time the United Kingdom had announced the establishment of another committee under the chairmanship of Lord Parker CJ 'to consider authorized procedures for the interrogation of persons suspected of terrorism'. Although two of the three-man committee[29] expressed themselves satisfied that the five techniques might sometimes be morally justified, Lord Gar-

[26] Loc. cit. above (n. 22), paras. 167–8.

[27] Ibid., para. 173. Three judges thought that it did amount to torture and two that further breaches had occurred in other places.

[28] Under the chairmanship of Sir Edmund Compton: Cmnd. 4823 (1971).

[29] The other members were Lord Gardiner and Mr J.A. Boyd-Carpenter: Cmnd. 4901 (1972).

diner wrote a strong dissent denouncing both the illegality and immorality of the practices. In March 1972 the Prime Minister, Edward Heath, confirmed that the techniques had not been used since October 1971 and that they would not be used in future.[30] This renunciation was reinforced by an unqualified undertaking to the European Court during the proceedings that the five techniques would not in any circumstances be reintroduced as an aid to interrogation. In addition to this renunciation, the victims of the five techniques had received compensation by the time the Commission reported in 1976,[31] and other victims of ill-treatment had also won compensation.

Measures were also taken to make these declarations of intent effective. From November 1971 medical inspections of terrorist suspects after arrest and before release were introduced. In April 1972 the Attorney-General issued a directive to the police and the army emphasizing that interrogation must be carried out in accordance with the law and warning of 'immediate prosecution' in the event of assault on a person in custody.[32] The United Kingdom also pointed to directives addressed to the security forces in 1972 forbidding the use of the five techniques and other forms of physical maltreatment. These were incorporated into existing army and police regulations.[33] Members of the security forces were prosecuted for and convicted of assault.[34] Furthermore, in 1977, as a result of the Gardiner Report,[35] the Police Complaints Board for Northern Ireland, composed of persons who had at no time been members of any police force, was established to supervise the investigation of complaints against police.[36] Responsibility for investigating serious complaints against the army had been taken from the army authorities and placed in the hands of a joint army and police investigation team.[37]

However, the Irish Government was not satisfied that sufficient steps had been taken to prevent the repetition of systematic ill-treatment, pointing to the apparent failure to take disciplinary or criminal proceedings against members of the security forces who had been guilty of breaches of the Convention established by the Court and Commission.[38] Such action was apparently limited to only one case,[39] and according to one writer two police officers in command at Palace Barracks 'were later believed to have

[30] HC Debs., vol. 832, col. 744: 2 March 1972.

[31] Compensation ranged from £12,000–£25,000.

[32] Commission report, 25 January 1976, Series B, No. 23–1, p. 28.

[33] Ibid., pp. 286–7.

[34] From April 1972 to January 1977, 218 members of the security forces were prosecuted for assault, and 155 of them were convicted: judgment of the Court, para. 140.

[35] *Report of a Committee to consider, in the context of civil liberties and human rights, measures to deal with terrorism in Northern Ireland*, Cmnd. 5847 (1975).

[36] Police (Northern Ireland) Order, SI 1977, No. 53.

[37] Judgment of the Court, para. 139.

[38] The Court ruled itself incompetent to make an order directing the UK Government to take such action: paras. 186–7.

[39] Ibid., para. 141.

been promoted'.[40] It was also further claimed that mere directives to the security forces were of little use in themselves, since army and police regulations had forbidden ill-treatment of detainees when the breaches of Article 3 had been committed.[41]

There had also been a change in the rules governing the admissibility of confessions as evidence in criminal trials. Section 6 of the Northern Ireland (Temporary Provisions) Act 1973 provided that a confession was admissible unless obtained as a result of the accused being subject to 'torture or to inhuman or degrading treatment'.[42] This of course quotes Article 3 of the Convention and appears therefore to be an implementation of its provisions.[43] However, since it was intended to narrow down judicial discretion to exclude confessions, it has been suggested that the provision sent ambiguous signals to the security forces, suggesting that some form of physical ill-treatment might be condoned if it fell short of torture or inhuman or degrading treatment.[44] If then interrogators felt that some violence was condoned, they might sometimes stray beyond the boundaries of what was permissible under the Convention.[45]

Whatever the view of the Irish Government, the Committee of Ministers in considering the case under Article 54 was satisfied that the United Kingdom's action was sufficient to comply with the Court's judgment.[46] However, the rather optimistic view which the United Kingdom presented to the Court of its successful elimination of widespread physical violence against terrorist suspects in detention seemed less justified in the light of events unfolding even as proceedings continued before the Court. Concern was being expressed about the number of allegations of police ill-treatment of terrorist suspects, which had risen substantially in 1976 and 1977.[47] As early as March 1977, the Forensic Medical Officers' Association was making representations to the Police Authority.[48] Thereafter medical officers expressed mounting anxiety and the Police Authority and concerned third parties made representations to the Chief Constable, but these

[40] Taylor, *Beating the Terrorists* (1980), p. 26.

[41] Commission Report, p. 278.

[42] Enacted following a recommendation of the *Report of the Commission to consider legal procedures to deal with terrorist activities in Northern Ireland*, Cmnd. 5185 (1972), para. 89.

[43] In *R* v. *McCormick*, [1977] NILR 105, the section was interpreted in the light of the Convention, although McGonigal LJ's view that the Convention permitted 'a moderate degree of physical maltreatment for the purpose of inducing a person to make a statement' is, to say the least, questionable.

[44] Boyle, Hadden and Hillyard, *Ten Years on in Northern Ireland: The Legal Control of Political Violence* (1980), p. 48. It should be added that the courts continued to exercise their common-law discretion to exclude involuntary confessions. The provision was subsequently amended by the Northern Ireland (Emergency Provisions) Act 1987, s. 5, to add the words 'any violence or threat of violence (whether or not amounting to torture)'.

[45] Indeed, any ill-treatment or threat of it intended to obtain a confession would, if successful, probably be inhuman and degrading treatment within Article 3.

[46] Res. DH(78)35.

[47] From 180 in 1975 to 384 in 1976 and 671 in 1977: *Report of a Committee of Inquiry into police interrogation procedures in Northern Ireland*, Cmnd. 7497 (1979) ('The Bennett Committee Report').

[48] Taylor, op. cit. above (n. 40), pp. 177–8.

seemed to have produced little effective response.[49] At the beginning of May 1978, less than four months after the judgment of the Court was published, Amnesty International published a report calling for a public inquiry into widespread allegations of police violence against detainees.[50] The Bennett Committee[51] was set up to consider interrogation procedures and it reported in February 1979. Although its terms of reference did not include the investigation of individual complaints of ill-treatment, the Committee did find that 'whatever the precise explanation' there could be 'no doubt that some of the injuries . . . were not self-inflicted and were sustained during the period of detention at a police office'.[52]

Given the seriousness of some of the injuries sustained there can be little doubt that if they were deliberately inflicted, as is cautiously implied by the Bennett Report, there was inhuman and degrading treatment within Article 3 of the Convention, as interpreted by the Court.[53] Less easy to determine is whether the ill-treatment amounted to an administrative practice as defined by the Court, and thus engaged the responsibility of the United Kingdom under the Convention. However, the apparent delay in any official response to the medical officers' serious disquiet gives this view some credibility and substantiates the Irish Government's doubts about the efficacy of simply issuing directives.

As a result of the Bennett Committee's recommendations, steps were taken to monitor interrogations more closely.[54] Supervision of interrogating officers was increased; medical officers were to visit detainees every twenty-four hours; changes were made to the complaints system; the duties of police officers were rotated so that interrogating officers were not solely and continuously involved in such duties. While some doubt has been cast on the extent of the implementation of some of the recommendations by police officers themselves, the number of complaints dropped and the measures seem to have been a serious attempt to prevent widespread abuse by introducing institutional changes rather than relying largely on exhortation.[55]

There must then be grave doubts as to whether the action taken by the United Kingdom prior to the Bennett Committee Report was sufficient to ensure broad compliance with the Court's judgment. However, the difficulty in evaluating compliance in this case was that a change in the law was not necessary, since the powers conferred on the security forces by law did not require amendment. What required amendment was official tolerance of, or complicity in, behaviour which was already unlawful under the law of

[49] Ibid., chs. 9–16.

[50] *Report of an Amnesty International Mission to Northern Ireland* (1978).

[51] Loc. cit. above (n. 47).

[52] Ibid., para. 163.

[53] The Government's acceptance that, on the basis of the Bennett Committee Report, ill-treatment was not widespread (HC Debs., vol. 967, col. 1211 : 24 May 1979) must be regarded with scepticism, since the Committee kept within its terms of reference and did not investigate individual cases of alleged assault.

[54] HC Debs., vol. 988, cols. 749–50: 10 July 1980.

[55] Walsh, 'Arrest and Interrogation in Northern Ireland', *Journal of Law and Society*, 9 (1981), p. 37.

Northern Ireland and was in breach of existing disciplinary regulations. This was a matter of evidence which would probably only have been determined as a result of an application to the Commission alleging continuing breaches of Article 3.

(b) *Refusing Detainees Permission to Notify their Families of their Detention*

In the case of *McVeigh, O'Neill and Evans*[56] the applicants had been arrested in Liverpool in February 1977 after arriving on a boat from Ireland, and were held in custody for 45 hours in accordance with anti-terrorism legislation. The applicants' claim that the legislation was in breach of the Convention failed.[57]

However, the Commission found that the failure to allow two of the applicants to contact their wives was in breach of Article 8, which guarantees the right to respect for private and family life. While accepting that there might be circumstances where it would be justified to delay contacting a spouse, where for example this might alert an accomplice of the detainee, the Commission held that there was no evidence to justify delay in the cases under consideration. At the time of the applicants' arrest the Judges' Rules provided that generally a detainee should be given access to a solicitor, but they gave no legal right, being only relevant to the question of whether evidence obtained in breach of the rules might be held admissible. In order to achieve general compliance, legislation was required to give a legal right to communicate with a spouse.

The Commission reported in March 1981 and the Committee of Ministers endorsed its findings. However, on the day that the application to the Commission was introduced, section 62 of the Criminal Law Act 1977 was enacted, giving a person arrested and held in custody the right to 'have intimation of his arrest and of the place where he is held sent to one person reasonably named by him, without delay, or where some delay is necessary in the interests of the investigation or prevention of crime or the apprehension of offenders, with no more delay than is necessary'. This satisfied the Committee of Ministers and seems to be adequate compliance with the requirements of the Convention, although the lack of any obvious redress for breach of this right might be questioned. However, it is ironic that the Government should demonstrate its compliance with Article 8 by reference to this statutory provision, since it had not planned such anticipatory compliance. Section 62 was introduced by a backbench amendment to the Criminal Law Bill on third reading in the House of Commons, and the

[56] Res. DH(82)1; Report of the Commission, *Decisions and Reports of the European Commission of Human Rights* (hereinafter *Decisions and Reports*), vol. 25, p. 15.

[57] The applicants also claimed unsuccessfully that Article 5(2) had been breached in that they had not been informed 'promptly' of the reason for their arrest.

amendment was carried by a narrow vote against the advice of the Home Secretary,[58] who wished to await the report of the Royal Commission on Criminal Procedure.[59] Even then compliance was confined to England and Wales, and it was not until some time later that legislation was passed introducing similar rights in the rest of the United Kingdom.[60]

(c) *Delay in Criminal Proceedings*

In *Orchin*[61] the applicant had been arrested in December 1972 in Northern Ireland and charged with possession of a firearm and ammunition in suspicious circumstances. In March 1973 he was committed for trial on a charge of murder and other charges including the firearms charge. He was acquitted of murder in February 1974 and at the end of February he was released on bail pending trial for the other offences. The charges against him remained outstanding until March 1978 when the Attorney-General entered a *nolle prosequi*. Orchin alleged that the firearms charge had not been determined 'within a reasonable time', as required by Article 6.

The Commission accepted that the authorities had decided not to proceed with that charge by February 1975 and that the delay of one year from his acquittal on the murder charge was due to an administrative oversight in implementing the decision, and not, as the applicant alleged, to official malice. The Commission held that it was reasonable for these proceedings to be delayed until the disposal of the murder charge, but that the subsequent three years' delay prior to the *nolle prosequi* exceeded what was reasonable, and thus breached Article 6.[62]

The Committee of Ministers adopted the Commission's findings, but decided that no further action was necessary since the United Kingdom Government had taken action designed to prevent a recurrence of such a delay. The DPP for Northern Ireland had instructed his staff to expedite trials and had instituted procedures to monitor the progress of cases. Secondly, after the reorganization of the Northern Ireland court system in 1978, an officer of the court had the duty to list cases committed for trial and to have them brought forward for disposal, so that the prosecuting authorities no longer had sole responsibility for the expedition of proceedings between committal and trial. In this case it can hardly be said that the

58 HC Debs., vol. 935, cols. 469–565: 13 July 1977.

59 Cmnd. 8092, eventually published in 1981.

60 In England and Wales the Police and Criminal Evidence Act 1984, s. 56, replaced s. 62 of the 1977 Act, with separate provisions for persons held under anti-terrorism legislation, rather more detail on the circumstances justifying interference with the right, and a time limit after which no interference with the right is justifiable. For Scotland, see the Criminal Justice (Scotland) Act 1980, s. 33. For Northern Ireland, see the Northern Ireland (Emergency Provisions) Act 1987, s. 14, which applies only to arrest under the provisions of the Prevention of Terrorism (Temporary Provisions) Act 1989.

61 Res. DH(83)14.

62 Commission report, para. 47, *Decisions and Reports*, vol. 34, p. 5.

decision of the Committee placed a heavy onus on the United Kingdom as regards general compliance, since the delay appears to have been an aberration and did not require significant reform of procedure to reduce delays in criminal cases generally.

IV. Mental Patients

Four of the cases in which the United Kingdom has been found to have violated the Convention concern mental patients, and all four cases involve much the same point. The first and most important of these cases, decided by the Court, is *X* v. *UK*.[63] X had been committed to Broadmoor following his conviction for causing grievous bodily harm and had been ordered to be detained for an indefinite period because of his mental ill-health. After a time his condition improved and he was conditionally discharged. Later, following complaints from his wife, the Home Secretary ordered his recall and X was returned to Broadmoor. X complained that there was no procedure by which he could have had the lawfulness of his renewed detention in Broadmoor speedily decided by a court, as required by Article 5(4) of the Convention, and that consequently the Convention had been violated. In fact there were two procedures which potentially satisfied Article 5(4)—habeas corpus (which X had unsuccessfully invoked) and proceedings before a Mental Health Review Tribunal. The Court, however, in a judgment given on 5 November 1981, held that neither of these procedures satisfied Article 5(4). First, habeas corpus proceedings were inadequate to satisfy the requirements of Article 5(4) because in such proceedings the court lacked jurisdiction to carry out a sufficient review of the merits, in particular to see whether a patient's disorder still persisted and whether his continued compulsory confinement was necessary in the interests of public safety. Secondly, in the case of Mental Health Review Tribunals, Article 5(4) was not satisfied because such bodies lacked the competence to decide the lawfulness of detention and order a patient's release. The Court emphasized that anyone detained in a psychiatric institution for an indefinite or lengthy period should be entitled to take proceedings at reasonable intervals before a court to test the lawfulness of his detention.

To comply with the Court's judgment the United Kingdom could either alter the scope of judicial review in habeas corpus proceedings or enlarge the powers of Mental Health Review Tribunals. Not surprisingly, the latter course was chosen.[64] By coincidence, the Government was in the process of preparing a major reform of mental health legislation at the time of the

[63] Series A, No. 46 (1981); *EHRR*, vol. 4, p. 188.

[64] For the Government's reasons for thinking this the better course, see HL Debs., vol. 426, cols. 760–1: 25 January 1982.

judgment. The Mental Health (Amendment) Bill was published a few days after the Court gave its judgment. Although at that stage the Bill did not reflect the Court's judgment, amendments were made to the Bill during its committee stage in the House of Lords (where it had been introduced) to take account of the judgment.[65] The Bill received the Royal Assent on 28 October 1982 and came into force on 30 September 1983—nearly two years after the judgment in *X*.

Section 28(4) and Schedule 1 of the Act (now to be found in Part V of the consolidating Mental Health Act 1983) change the Mental Health Review Tribunals' functions in respect of restricted patients like X to confer a power of discharge. A patient can apply to a Tribunal once a year for release. Recalled patients like X have their cases automatically reviewed within one month of recall. A Tribunal must direct the discharge of a patient if continued detention is not necessary in the interests of the patient's health or safety or for the protection of other people.

In applying for just satisfaction under Article 50 of the Convention, X (or rather the representatives of his estate, X being by this time dead) agreed that the above provisions remedied the deficiencies in the previous law found by the Court in its judgment on the merits.[66] With that conclusion the writers of this article would concur.[67]

The other three cases on mental patients referred to at the beginning of this section, all of which were decided by the Committee of Ministers, raise essentially the same issue as *X*. In *B* v. *UK*[68] and *C, Medway and Ball* v. *UK*[69] the European Commission of Human Rights had given its opinion, following the reasoning of the Court in *X*, that there had been a breach of Article 5(4).[70] The Committee of Ministers endorsed this opinion but held that in the light of the Mental Health (Amendment) Act no further action was necessary.[71] The third case, *Gordon* v. *UK*,[72] is slightly different in that it concerns the law in Scotland. As in the other two cases, the Commission had found a violation of Article 5(4). The Committee of Ministers again endorsed this opinion but held that in the light of the Mental Health

[65] Ibid., cols. 759–66.

[66] *X* v. *United Kingdom*, judgment on Article 50, Series A, No. 55 (1982), p. 12 at p. 15.

[67] It should be noted that some writers have taken a rather more critical view of the UK's record of compliance in this case. See, e.g., Hoggett, 'The Mental Health Act 1983', *Public Law*, 1983, p. 172 at p. 185 (who suggests the Tribunals' powers have been carefully limited to the minimum required under the Convention); and Peay, 'Mental Health Review Tribunals and the Mental Health (Amendment) Act', *Criminal Law Review*, 1982, p. 794 at pp. 798–808 (who casts doubt on whether the Tribunals are sufficiently independent for the purposes of Art. 5(4)). Contrast Gostin, 'Human Rights, Judicial Review and the Mentally Disordered Offender', ibid., p. 776 at p. 785 (who suggests that the UK has gone further than necessary).

[68] Application 6780/75.

[69] Applications 7099/75, 7699/76 and 9292/81.

[70] For the Commission's opinion in *B*, see *Decisions and Reports*, vol. 32, p. 5; for its opinion in *C*, see ibid., vol. 40, p. 5.

[71] Res. DH(83)8 of 22 April 1983 (*B*); Res. DH(85)1 of 25 January 1985 (*C, Medway and Ball*).

[72] Application 10213/82.

(Amendment) (Scotland) Act 1983, which introduced an appeal procedure for restricted patients,[73] no further action was necessary.[74]

V. Prisoners

(a) *Access to Legal Advice*

One of the more persistent problems under the Convention has been the extent to which the rights of prisoners are affected by their lawful detention. The first such case to be pursued successfully against the United Kingdom Government was that of a prisoner's access to legal advice, refusal of which was held to be in breach of Article 6. Article 6(1) provides:

> In the determination of his civil rights and obligations or of any criminal charge against him, everyone is entitled to a fair and public hearing within a reasonable time by an independent and impartial tribunal established by law.

In *Golder*,[75] an inmate of Parkhurst prison was refused permission to consult a solicitor with a view to bringing libel proceedings against a prison officer who had made false allegations about Golder's participation in a prison riot and assault on a prison officer in 1969.

By statute the administration of prisons is entrusted in England and Wales to the Home Secretary, and in Scotland and Northern Ireland to the respective Secretaries of State.[76] Under the authority of these statutory provisions further regulation is made by statutory instruments known as the Prison Rules.[77] The application of these rules is further regulated by standing orders, only some of which have been officially published, and by circular instructions issued by the relevant Secretary of State to Prison Governors, none of which have been officially published.

At the time of the events giving rise to Golder's complaint, the entitlement to consult a solicitor was confined to cases where the prisoner was already a party to legal proceedings, and then only in the form of an interview within the sight, but out of the hearing, of a prison officer, although, after a friendly settlement of *Knechtl* v. *UK*,[78] it was the practice to allow

[73] See s. 21 of the Act. Appeals are heard by a Sheriff, whose powers and functions are broadly comparable to those of Mental Health Review Tribunals in England and Wales. The law in Northern Ireland has been reformed along lines similar to that in Great Britain: see the Mental Health (Northern Ireland) Order 1986, SI 1986, No. 595, Part V. On the other hand, the law in Jersey has not and is contrary to the Convention: reform, however, is currently underway.

[74] Res. DH(86)9 of 16 September 1986.

[75] Series A, No. 18 (1975); *EHRR* , vol. 1, p. 524. Subsequently to the Court's judgment the Committee of Ministers held that there had been a similar breach in *Kiss* v. *UK*: Res. DH(78)3. For an account of the prisoners' cases up to 1983, including unsuccessful applications to the Commission, see Douglas and Jones, 'Prisoners and the European Convention on Human Rights', in Furmston, Kerridge and Sufrin (eds.), *The Effect on English Domestic Law of Membership of the European Communities and of Ratification of the European Convention on Human Rights* (1983), p. 352.

[76] Prison Act 1952; Prisons (Scotland) Act 1989; Prison (Northern Ireland) Act 1952.

[77] In England and Wales, SI 1964, No. 388, as amended.

[78] *Yearbook of the European Convention on Human Rights*, 13 (1970), p. 730.

access to a solicitor in medical negligence cases.[79] Furthermore, while the *Golder* proceedings were before the Commission, the Prison Rules were altered to entitle a prisoner to correspond with a legal adviser, but still only regarding proceedings to which he was already a party.[80] In the absence of any specific entitlement, Rule 33 of the English Prison Rules 1964 gave a general power to the Home Secretary to impose restrictions on communication between a prisoner and other persons 'with a view to securing discipline and good order or the prevention of crime or in the interests of any persons'. In particular, Rule 34(8) specifically provided that there should be:

> no communication with any person in connection with any legal or other business, or with any person other than a relative or friend, except with the leave of the Secretary of State.

Golder's petition to the Home Secretary to be allowed access to a solicitor was rejected in April 1970, apparently on the basis that his prospects of success in a libel action were slim. The Court, giving judgment in February 1975, held that there had been a breach of Article 6(1), since this provision not only protected the right to a fair hearing once proceedings were instituted, but also protected the right of access to the courts. The effective exercise of this right required that a person should not be denied access to legal advice in contemplation of court proceedings.

In considering the British Government's response to this ruling, three features of the judgment should be borne in mind. First, the Court stressed that Article 6(1) was breached when access to the courts was impeded, as well as when there was a complete prevention of such access. Secondly, the Court conceded that there might be some 'implied limitations' on the right conferred by Article 6, though it was not prepared to indicate their nature or extent, being satisfied that no such limitations could justify the refusal of access to Golder. Thirdly, the Court emphasized that, since Golder was seeking to exculpate himself from a serious charge, concerning an incident within the prison against an officer under the control of the Home Secretary, it was quite wrong for the Home Secretary to appraise the prospects of a successful legal action.

A month after the judgment Mr Jenkins, the Home Secretary, indicated that a review was in progress in the light of the *Golder* decision[81] and four months later he announced the Government's intention to give effect to the *Golder* judgment.[82] On 5 August 1975, five and a half months after the Court's judgment, he made public the Government's response.[83] This was

[79] *Legal Advice to Prisoners*, Cmnd. 4846 (1971).

[80] Rule 37A(1), added by SI 1972, No. 1860, which came into force on 1 January 1973.

[81] HC Debs., vol. 888, Written Answers, col. *147*: 12 March 1975.

[82] HC Debs., vol. 895, Written Answers, cols. *1703–4*: 7 July 1975.

[83] HC Debs., vol. 897, Written Answers, cols. *147–8*: 5 August 1975. Equivalent changes were made in Scotland and Northern Ireland at the same time.

effected immediately by circular instruction to prison governors,[84] and subsequently formalized by an amendment to the Prison Rules:

37A(4). Subject to any directions of the Secretary of State, a prisoner may correspond with a solicitor for the purpose of obtaining legal advice concerning any cause of action in relation to which the prisoner may become a party to civil proceedings or for the purpose of instructing the solicitor to issue such proceedings.[85]

Under the directions qualifying this rule a prisoner was to apply to the Governor for leave to seek legal advice. This would be granted unless the proposed proceedings arose 'out of or in connection with his imprisonment', in which case the 'prior ventilation rule' applied, i.e. access to legal advice was only to be granted if the prison complaints procedure had first been exhausted.[86]

After five months of review, this was a niggardly response to the *Golder* decision and at the time doubt was expressed as to its adequacy, since the revised rule could still be regarded as imposing conditions impeding or hindering access to the courts, particularly as exhaustion of the prison complaints procedure might take up to a year.[87] There is little doubt that the Government was aware of this criticism, for the circular instruction justified the new role as allowing steps to be taken 'in the interests both of prisoners and of prison order'.[88]

The criticism was borne out by subsequent developments. In *Reed* v. *UK*,[89] the applicant challenged the validity of the prior ventilation rule and, after the Commission had held the application to be admissible, a friendly settlement was reached. As part of the settlement the British Government undertook to abolish the prior ventilation rule, a change effected by a revision of the relevant standing order.[90] The prior ventilation rule was subsequently declared by the European Court to have been in breach of Article 6 in *Campbell and Fell*,[91] which related to events occurring before the abolition of that rule. Under the new regime, access to legal advice was permitted in respect of matters arising from imprisonment, provided that an internal complaint had first been lodged (the 'simultaneous ventilation rule'). This rule in turn was held by the Committee of Ministers to be in breach of Article 6 in *Byrne* v. *UK*.[92] However, by the time of this decision,

[84] Circular Instruction 45/1975 of 6 August 1975, parts of which are reproduced in Cohen and Taylor, *Prison Secrets* (1976), pp. 42–3.
[85] SI 1976, No. 503.
[86] CI 45/1975, para. 3(11), loc. cit. above (n. 84).
[87] Cohen and Taylor, op. cit. above (n. 84), p. 46.
[88] This echoes Article 8 of the Convention, discussed below, which permits interference with correspondence *inter alia* 'for the prevention of disorder' and 'for the protection of the rights and freedoms of others'.
[89] *Decisions and Reports*, vol. 25, p. 5.
[90] This was part of an overhaul of Standing Order 5 following *Silver* v. *UK*, discussed below.
[91] Series A, No. 80 (1984); *EHRR*, vol. 7, p. 165.
[92] Res. DH(87)7 of 20 March 1987.

the English High Court in *R* v. *Secretary of State for the Home Department, ex parte Anderson*[93] had already declared that the simultaneous ventilation rule was *ultra vires* since it was an interference with access to the courts which had not been authorized by the Prison Act.[94]

(b) *Conduct of Interviews with Legal Advisers*

In *Campbell and Fell* Article 6(1) was invoked to challenge the rules regulating consultations between prisoners and their solicitors visiting them in prison. The general rule was, and is, that all prison visits should be held within sight and hearing of a prison officer, unless the Home Secretary directs otherwise.[95] Rule 37(1) of the Prison Rules provided that a prisoner's interview with his legal adviser 'in any legal proceedings' might be conducted 'out of hearing but in sight of an officer', but, under Rule 37(2) as it then stood, any other legal business might only be discussed within both sight and hearing of an officer.[96]

In 1977 Fell was denied the right to consult his solicitor out of hearing of a prison officer *with a view* to bringing civil proceedings against prison officers in respect of personal injuries suffered, since he was not then a party to proceedings. In 1984 the Court held that this constituted a breach of Article 6, but by this time the prison standing orders had been changed so that such consultations might be allowed out of the hearing, but in the sight, of a prison officer, provided that the subject to be discussed was disclosed in advance and did not offend against the restrictions on correspondence with legal advisers.[97]

The piecemeal nature of the response following an adverse decision is characteristic of the approach of the British Government to reform in this area of the law. In this case it was not the effect of the reform which was dubious, but the way it was achieved. Rule 37 itself was unaltered, creating the impression that nothing had changed, and the modification of practice was achieved by standing order, made in exercise of the Home Secretary's power to direct how visits should be controlled. This was a convoluted and obfuscating way of achieving the change, which offended against the notion embodied in the Convention that laws should be clear and accessible. Not

[93] [1984] QB 778.

[94] This decision was implemented by Circular Instruction 48/1984.

[95] Rule 33(5).

[96] This may be contrasted with the position in Scotland, where the Prison Rules provided that an interview with a legal adviser 'on any legal business' should take place in the sight but not in the hearing of a prison officer: SI 1952, No. 565, reg. 18.25.

[97] Standing Order 5A 34, introduced in 1981. Subsequently the Committee of Ministers held that there had been similar breaches of Article 6 in preventing confidential consultations in the further cases of *Byrne, McFadden, McCluskey and McLarnon* v. *UK*: Res. DH(87)7, *Decisions and Reports*, vol. 51, p. 5. The changes already effected by the UK were sufficient to satisfy the Committee of Ministers that no further action was required.

until 1989 was a change made to the Prison Rules themselves in England and Wales to reflect the change of practice.[98]

(c) *Prisoners' Correspondence*

Closely related to prisoners' access to legal advice has been the issue of regulation of correspondence sent and received by prisoners. Under Article 8:

> Everyone has the right to respect for . . . his correspondence.

Interference with this right is only permissible if it is:

> . . . in accordance with the law and is necessary in a democratic society in the interests of national security, public safety or the economic well-being of the country, for the prevention of disorder or crime, for the protection of health or morals, or for the protection of the rights and freedoms of others.

In *Golder* the Court found that the refusal of permission to correspond with a solicitor was a breach not only of Article 6(1), but also of Article 8. The exceptions contained in Article 8(2) were exhaustive of the justifications for limiting the right protected, and the factors which had weighed with the Court in rejecting any implied limitation on Article 6(1) led them to reject the British Government's attempt to justify the stopping of correspondence with a legal adviser relating to legal proceedings. The introduction of the prior ventilation rule was intended to repair the breach of Article 8 as well as that of Article 6. However, Golder had also complained of the stopping of a letter to a Chief Constable and to a Member of Parliament, and although these complaints were held inadmissible by the Commission (on the ground that he had failed to exhaust domestic remedies), after 1975 prisoners were permitted to correspond with Members of Parliament and foreign nationals with the relevant diplomatic representatives.[99] In *Silver v. UK*[100] seven applicants challenged the system of regulation, and a number of its features were held to be in breach of Article 8.

At the time of Silver's application to the Commission the regulation of correspondence was contained, as now, in the Prison Rules, standing orders and circular instructions. In addition to the specific regulations

[98] SI 1989, No. 30, amending Rule 37(2) to allow interviews on legal business other than that relating to existing proceedings out of hearing of an officer 'subject to the direction of the Secretary of State'. Under the revised Standing Order 5 of 1989 the fact that the purpose of the visit is contemplated legal proceedings must be disclosed, but not what these proceedings are about (Standing Order 5A 34).

[99] Subject of course to the prior ventilation rule: HC Debs., vol. 901, cols. 378–9: 1 December 1975.

[100] Judgment of 25 March 1983, Series A, No. 64; *EHRR*, vol. 5, p. 347. The seven applicants were taken as a representative sample of some fifty applicants. Subsequently the Committee of Ministers decided that there had been breaches of Article 8 in respect of 24 other applicants. All applications related to interference with correspondence before the revision of the Rules effected as a result of *Silver*, and so established no new point of principle nor required further action: *Brady et al.*, Res. DH(86)5, *Marritt et al.*, Res. DH(86)6, *Jenkinson et al.*, Res DH(86)8, *Farrant et al.*, Res. DH(87)3, *Byrne et al.*, Res. DH(87)7.

relating to communications with legal advisers, already considered, provision was made in the Prison Rules regarding the identity of correspondents and the frequency and contents of correspondence. Under the rules unconvicted prisoners might send and receive as many letters as they wished, subject to conditions imposed by the Home Secretary,[101] but convicted prisoners were entitled to send and receive only one letter a week, except in special circumstances.[102] A prisoner was not entitled to correspond with any person other than a relative or friend except with the leave of the Secretary of State.[103] The rules prohibited correspondence in connection with any business, other than legal business, except with the leave of the Home Secretary,[104] who also had a general discretion to impose restrictions on communication by and with prisoners 'with a view to securing discipline and good order or the prevention of crime or in the interests of any persons'.[105] The rules further provided that letters to and from a prisoner might be read or examined and, at the discretion of the governor, stopped on the grounds that their contents were 'objectionable' or of 'inordinate length'.[106]

Exercising his discretion under the Prison Rules, the Home Secretary had issued Standing Order 5, which amplified the rules. It is extraordinary, and a matter of significance in the case, that this was not published nor made available to the prisoners, and that its contents only became widely known as a result of the proceedings under the Convention. Under this order, in addition to the entitlement to send a weekly letter, convicted prisoners were allowed to send at least one additional letter at their own expense and to receive a reply. Prisoners would normally be allowed to correspond with relatives or existing friends, subject to the discretion of the Governor to prohibit this in the interests of security, good order and discipline or the prevention or discouragement of crime. They were also permitted to write to their Members of Parliament and to specified organizations concerned with the welfare and rights of prisoners. Governors had a discretion to allow correspondence with other persons, but not normally with, *inter alia*, prisoners, ex-prisoners and marriage bureaux. There were extensive restrictions on the permissible contents of correspondence. Some of these were closely connected with the prevention of crime and disorder, others were less obviously or directly related to such purposes. For example, it was forbidden to make objectionable references to persons in public life or to hold up the courts, the police or the prison authorities to contempt.

In *Silver et al.* letters of the applicants were stopped on the grounds both of the identity of correspondents and the content of the correspondence.

101 Rule 34(1).
102 Rule 34(3) and (6)–(8).
103 Rule 34(8).
104 Ibid.
105 Rule 33(1).
106 Rule 33(3).

The complaints related to the particular restrictions on the contents and quantity of correspondence and the identity of correspondents, rather than to the general practice of censorship.[107] The British Government's defence lay in the limitations on the right to respect for correspondence permitted by Article 8. The Commission reported in October 1980, holding that there had been breaches of Articles 6, 8 and 13. After discussions with the Commission, the Home Office published a revised version of Standing Order 5 intended to accommodate most of the Commission's findings, and this came into force in December 1981.[108] The United Kingdom referred the matter to the Court and in doing so contested some of the Commission's findings, and asked the Court to confirm that the revised standing order remedied those breaches in respect of which the United Kingdom had admitted responsibility.

The Court upheld the Commission's view, not contested by the Government, that a number of the interferences with correspondence were not 'in accordance with the law' as required by Article 8, because the Prison Rules were insufficiently precise to enable a person to foresee many of the interferences permitted by standing order, and the unpublished standing order itself was not adequately accessible to make good this failing. But the Court did not accept the applicants' contention that the procedures and conditions for interference with correspondence must be contained in the law, rather than in administrative directives, in order to be sufficiently accessible to satisfy the criterion of foreseeability. Interferences with correspondence based on the prior ventilation rule were thus in accordance with the law, since prisoners had been informed of the rule before writing their letters.

There remained the question of whether even those interferences which were in accordance with the law were legitimate under Article 8(2). The Government did not contest the Commission's finding that certain of the interferences were not necessary, and the Court concurred. The Court did, however, support the United Kingdom Government's challenge to some of the Commission's adverse findings, recognizing that some measure of control over prisoners is called for and not in itself incompatible with the Convention.

Although the complaints before the European Court resulted in the condemnation of a number of rules on correspondence, by the time the Court heard the case, new rules were in force. First, the standing order relating to correspondence was published, so that the question of whether future interferences were in accordance with the law could be determined on the basis of the standing orders as well as the Act and the rules. The UK Govern-

[107] Following the publication of *Prison Disturbances April 1990. Report of an Inquiry by The Right Honourable Lord Justice Woolf* ('The Woolf Report'), Cm. 1456 (1991), the Home Secretary has announced that routine censorship will end in all but dispersal prisons: HC Debs., vol. 186, col. 660: 25 February 1991.

[108] Memorial of the UK Government to the European Court, Series B, No. 51, para. 124. The Standing Order is obtainable from the Home Office and is made available in all Prison Department establishments.

ment also declared its intention to revise all other standing orders and thereafter to publish them.[109] Secondly, the simultaneous ventilation rule was introduced, apparently with the blessing of the Commission. Thirdly, the restrictions on the quantity of correspondence were changed. The basic entitlement in the Prison Rules remained, but additional letters were now to be allowed 'to the extent that is practicable taking into account the staff resources available and the need to examine and read correspondence'.[110] Finally, the restrictions on the identity of correspondents were liberalized,[111] and the categories of objectionable content more narrowly defined,[112] in both cases to serve more closely the purposes of preventing behaviour which is criminal or prejudicial to prison order.

While it is strongly arguable that, after *Golder*, the United Kingdom should have anticipated that aspects of the regulation of correspondence were in breach of the Convention, the speed of the United Kingdom's response to the *Silver* decision can hardly be criticized, at least as regards England and Wales and Scotland,[113] and, generally speaking, these changes seem to have anticipated the particular findings of the European Court sufficiently to preclude the need for any further action by the British Government. However, some reservations should be entered.

First, the reform of the restrictions on the contents of correspondence satisfied the requirements of Article 8, with some exceptions. Initially, the restriction on the institution of private prosecutions,[114] which survived after *Golder*, remained untouched. It was the intervention of the English courts, applying the common law principle against interference with access to the courts, which led to the lifting of this prohibition in 1983.[115] Subsequently, in the cases of *Farrant et al.*,[116] the Committee of Ministers confirmed that this rule had been in breach of Article 8. The continuing restriction on any form of conducting business may be too broad to be regarded as a necessary restriction under Article 8. This was left open by the European Court in *Silver*, where the applicant failed on the narrow ground that the ambiguous nature of the letter justified its being stopped 'for the prevention of disorder or crime', but the extensive restriction on

[109] HC Debs., vol. 26, Written Answers, col. *101*: 23 June 1982. By May 1991 the whole of ten standing orders and parts of three others for England and Wales had been published. In Scotland, however, only one has been published, and in Northern Ireland only two.

[110] Standing Order 5B 7.

[111] Standing Order 5B 21–30.

[112] Standing Order 5B 34–37.

[113] The Scottish standing orders were amended in substantially the same form as the English on 1 August 1983: Prison (Scotland) Standing Orders Section M. Two judgments of the European Court holding the Scottish Standing Order to be in breach of Article 8 relate to events preceding the amendment: see *Boyle and Rice* v. *UK*, 27 April 1988, Series A, No. 131; *EHRR*, vol. 10, p. 425; *McCallum* v. *UK*, 30 August 1990, Series A, No. 183. However, reform in Northern Ireland was delayed until 1 February 1985: Standing Orders, Section 5.

[114] Standing Order 5B 34.

[115] See *R* v. *Honey*, [1983] 1 AC 1, actually not a private prosecution, but a case of application to the court for the committal of a prison governor for contempt.

[116] Res. DH(87)3, *Decisions and Reports*, vol. 50, p. 5.

any business activity, for example, sending material for publication or broadcast for payment, is less obviously justifiable.

A second reservation concerns the replacement of the prior ventilation rule by the simultaneous ventilation rule. Perhaps nothing exemplifies the reluctant and piecemeal approach to reform better than this. It is no surprise that in *Byrne*[117] the Committee of Ministers held that the simultaneous ventilation rule was contrary to Articles 6 and 8 as regards communications with lawyers, although, by the time of the Committee's decision, this aspect of the rule had already been abolished. Nevertheless, the rules remained, qualified only by being inapplicable to communications with lawyers, the European Commission of Human Rights and, in the case of a foreign prisoner, the representative of his country of nationality. It is doubtful whether its continued application to most other communications, including letters to MPs and the Ombudsman, could have been justified as necessary under Article 8 once it became permissible to air them through the initiation of legal proceedings or an application to the European Commission of Human Rights.[118] In 1989, six years after the Court's judgment in *Silver*, following a review by HM Inspector of Prisons,[119] the simultaneous ventilation rule was finally abolished in England and Wales.[120] However, in Scotland and Northern Ireland the rule continues to apply to all communications except those with legal advisers and applications to the European Commission of Human Rights or the Court.

Finally, while the Court's judgment allowed for the regulations to be contained in administrative directions, the relationship between the Prison Rules and Standing Order 5 was not simplified, and it might be thought that in the interests of accessibility of the law, which is regarded as important under the Convention, they should all be contained in a single piece of primary or secondary legislation.[121]

(d) *Access to Reading Matter and Writing Materials*

In *T* v. *UK*[122] the applicant was refused access to the writing paper of his choice for the book he was writing, and the notebooks in which he wrote his book were stopped when he attempted to send them out of the prison. Further he was refused access to newspapers and periodicals, in particular as part of a disciplinary penalty. The Commission found that, while the authorities were entitled to read the materials which he sent out, stopping them completely was a breach of the right to freedom of expression under Article 10. It further held that there had been a breach of Article 10 in

[117] Res. DH(87)7. See also *Grace* v. *UK*, Res DH(89)21.

[118] *Report of Her Majesty's Inspector of Prisons on a Review of Prisoners' Complaints* (1987), para. 8.12.

[119] Ibid.

[120] Revised Standing Order 5, effective from 1 April 1989.

[121] See also the report by Justice, *Justice in Prisons* (1983), paras. 21–2.

[122] Res. DH(86)12.

refusing access to writing paper of his choice and in the withholding of newspapers. The Committee of Ministers agreed with the Commission in finding these actions to be in breach of Article 10. However, no action was necessary because of an earlier change in the standing orders. Under Standing Order 4, revised and published in May 1985, certain privileges are permitted at the discretion of the governor, 'whose decision will be based on the availability of resources and the management requirements of his establishment'. On application, an inmate may receive a daily, weekly and Sunday newspaper, together with two further periodicals.[123] He may also be issued with a 'general notebook and a drawing book'.[124] A prisoner may send out a completed book or 'any other artistic or written material which is not correspondence',[125] subject only to the restrictions on contents under Standing Order 5 already discussed. While these privileges may be withdrawn as a punishment, a prisoner may not be 'deprived for a substantial period of time of access to newspapers altogether'.[126] By this revision of the standing order the United Kingdom complied with the requirements of the Convention.

(e) *Disciplinary Proceedings in Prison*

In the case of *Campbell and Fell*,[127] the prison disciplinary system, and in particular its compatibility with Article 6, came under scrutiny. Article 6 provides for 'a fair and public hearing . . . by an independent and impartial tribunal' in respect of any criminal charges and of the determination of a person's civil rights. It also specifies minimum rights for everyone charged with a criminal offence, including the right to be informed promptly of the charge (Article 6(3)(*a*)); adequate time and facilities for the preparation of a defence (Article 6(3)(*b*)); 'the right to defend himself in person or through legal assistance of his own choosing or, if he has not sufficient means to pay for legal assistance, to be given it free when the interests of justice so require' (Article 6(3)(*c*)).

The Prison Rules created three categories of disciplinary offences.[128] Less serious offences were dealt with by the Prison Governor;[129] more serious offences, categorized as 'graver'[130] or 'especially grave',[131] were

[123] Standing Order 4A 5. Similar changes were made in Scotland in July 1985 (unpublished), and in Northern Ireland in July 1986: Standing Orders, section 4, published in 1987.

[124] Standing Order 4A 17.

[125] Standing Order 4A 19.

[126] Standing Order 4A 11.

[127] Series A, No. 80 (1984); *EHRR*, vol. 7, p. 165. See also Livingstone, 'Prisoners' Rights in Northern Ireland', *Northern Ireland Legal Quarterly*, 37 (1986), p. 75, and 'Prisoners and Boards of Visitors Hearings: A Right to Representation After All?', ibid. 38 (1987), p. 144.

[128] The offences are set out in Prison Rule 47, SI 1964, No. 388, prior to 1989 amendment.

[129] Rule 50.

[130] Rule 51.

[131] Rule 52.

referred to the Board of Visitors, a body consisting of appointees of the Home Secretary having both a supervisory function regarding the running of the prison and a judicial function in hearing disciplinary charges.

In 1976 Campbell had been charged with mutiny or incitement to mutiny and with gross personal violence to an officer, both categorized as 'especially grave offences'. He was convicted by the Board of Visitors of Albany Prison and awarded a total of 570 days' loss of remission together with 91 days' loss of privileges and a further 35 days' loss of certain privileges, exclusion from associated work, stoppage of earnings and confinement to his cell.

The Court held that Article 6 did apply to the proceedings against Campbell, rejecting the submission that they were not concerned with criminal charges. Following its earlier decision in *Engel*,[132] the European Court held that the definition of a 'criminal charge' in Article 6 was independent of any definition under national law. Whether a charge was criminal depended upon the gravity of the offence, whether the alleged act also constituted a criminal offence under English law, and the nature and degree of the possible penalty. Since Campbell's offences might also have been prosecuted as offences under English criminal law, the Prison Rules described them as especially grave and the maximum penalties were severe,[133] the Court had little difficulty in finding that the charges were 'criminal' within Article 6.[134]

The Court rejected the claim that the Board was not 'independent and impartial'. It also rejected the submission that the proceedings should have been held in public, recognizing that it was in the interests of order and security that the case be heard in the prison and without public access. However, it did hold that as no steps had been taken to make the decision public, Article 6 had been violated in that the judgment had not been 'pronounced publicly'.

Campbell further alleged that he had been denied other procedural protections. The procedural protections for the prisoner are contained in the Prison Rules. He has a right to be informed of the charge 'as soon as possible' and is entitled to be 'given a full opportunity of hearing what is alleged against him and of presenting his own case'.[135]

A number of Campbell's claims failed on the facts, but it was held that, in breach of Article 6(3), he had been denied the right to legal advice and representation, and 'adequate facilities for the preparation of his defence'. The Board of Visitors had refused his application for legal representation

[132] Series A, No. 22 (1976); *EHRR*, vol. 1, p. 647. See Kidd, 'Disciplinary Proceedings and the Right to a Fair Trial under the European Convention on Human Rights', *International and Comparative Law Quarterly*, 36 (1987), p. 856.

[133] In Campbell's case loss of remission could have been almost three years.

[134] Loc. cit. above (n. 127), paras. 71–3. There was therefore no need for the Court to determine whether the proceedings involved the determination of Campbell's civil rights: ibid., para. 74.

[135] Prison Rule 49.

following existing English case law according to which there was no entitlement to such representation.[136]

The Government's response to the publicity point took the form of a letter of 12 July 1984 to chairmen of Boards of Visitors informing them that, in proceedings involving especially grave charges, arrangements should be made to communicate to the local press the prisoner's name, the finding and any award,[137] but this guidance has been omitted from the most recent Home Office *Manual*.[138]

By the time that the European Court gave judgment, English law on the right to legal representation had been changed by a decision of the Divisional Court. In *R* v. *Secretary of State for the Home Department, ex parte Tarrant*[139] it was held that while there was no *entitlement* to legal representation, a Board of Visitors had a discretion to grant legal representation in the interests of natural justice. In exercising that discretion it must take into account all the relevant factors, including the seriousness of the charge and potential penalty, the likelihood of any points of law arising, the capacity of the prisoner to present his own case, procedural difficulties which a prisoner might face in cross-examining witnesses, the need for 'reasonable speed' in the making of the adjudication, and the need for fairness as between prisoner and prison officers. The Divisional Court added that 'in most, if not all, charges of mutiny', points of law were likely to arise such that no Board could reasonably refuse representation.[140]

The Home Office informed chairmen of Boards of Visitors that legal representation should be permitted in all cases involving especially grave offences, and seems to have taken the view that in other cases no action was necessary beyond drawing attention to the implications of *Tarrant*.[141]

Since legal representation had not been available to Campbell, the issue of free legal assistance provided for by Article 6(3)(*c*) did not arise. However, by the time of the European Court's judgment, steps had already been taken after *Tarrant* to provide 'legal assistance by way of representation' where a Board of Visitors had granted legal representation in a case before it.[142]

As a further response to *Campbell and Fell* and *Tarrant*, the Home Secretary established a committee to review the disciplinary regime in prisons[143] and implemented a number of its recommendations, relevant to

[136] *Fraser* v. *Mudge*, [1975] 1 WLR 1132.

[137] Subsequently incorporated into the *Manual on the Conduct of Adjudications in Prison Department Establishments* (1984), para. 76.

[138] *Manual on the Conduct of Adjudications in Prison Department Establishments* (1989).

[139] [1985] QB 251.

[140] At p. 287.

[141] Letter of 12 July 1984, subsequently incorporated into *Manual on the Conduct of Adjudications in Prison Department Establishments* (1984), para. 27.

[142] SI 1984, No. 241, amending SI 1980, No. 1898, reg. 17(3). See now SI 1989, No. 550, reg. 9(6).

[143] Set up under the chairmanship of Mr Peter Prior in October 1983, it reported in October 1985: Cmnd. 9641.

the decision in *Campbell and Fell*, by amendment to the Prison Rules.[144] First, mutiny and incitement to mutiny have been abolished as disciplinary offences.[145] Secondly, the classification of offences according to their gravity has been abolished. Instead, charges are to be referred to the Board of Visitors where the Governor decides that the penalties which he is empowered to impose would, 'having regard to the nature and circumstances of the offence', be inadequate.[146] Penalties have also been altered, so that the maximum loss of remission imposable in respect of offences arising from the same incident is 180 days.

The guidance on the granting of legal representation has not changed significantly. No guidance is given as to the meaning of a criminal charge under the Convention, beyond pointing out that the offences under the old rules of mutiny and gross personal violence to a prison officer were criminal charges, and that legal representation must be granted in cases which are considered to be especially grave.[147] Apart from this the guidance concentrates on explaining the *Tarrant* criteria.

While the Home Office response was prompt and sufficient to deal with the particular facts of *Campbell and Fell*, it lacks clarity and to that extent its consistency with the Convention is uncertain, and general compliance is perhaps only partial. Since the category of especially grave offences has been abolished, it does not give much assistance to Boards of Visitors to be informed that these are cases in which legal representation should be granted. In any event the reasoning of the European Court did not confine the right to legal representation to cases which might be described as especially grave. Furthermore, the *Tarrant* criteria and the European Court's approach will not necessarily lead to the same result in every case.[148] For example, in *Tarrant* a key factor was the complexity of the legal points likely to be raised by a charge,[149] a factor not mentioned as relevant in *Campbell and Fell*. In *Tarrant* it was held that it was quite conceivable that legal representation might be refused on a charge of assaulting a prison officer,[150] presumably because the nature of the allegations might raise no points of difficulty and the prisoner might be quite able to defend himself. However, following the reasoning of the European Court in *Campbell and Fell*, there are grounds for thinking that such a charge might be characterized as criminal under Article 6, since the charge of assaulting a prison officer may be regarded as serious, it can be prosecuted as a criminal offence, and the maximum penalty is 120 days' loss of remission. Once such

[144] SI 1989, No. 330.

[145] Prison mutiny is to be made a criminal offence punishable with ten years' imprisonment. See the statement of the Home Secretary, HC Debs., vol. 186, col. 659: 25 February 1991.

[146] Rule 51, substituted by SI 1989, No. 330, rule 2(*b*).

[147] *Manual on the Conduct of Adjudications in Prison Department Establishments* (1989), para. 3.11.

[148] Cf. Lord Goff in *R* v. *Board of Visitors of Maze Prison, ex parte Hone*, [1988] AC 379.

[149] At p. 285.

[150] At p. 293. To the same effect *R* v. *Board of Visitors of Blunderston Prison, ex parte Norley* (1984) (gross personal violence).

a characterization is made, there is a right to legal representation under Article 6, and there is no room for the exercise of discretion in the light of further criteria.

(f) *Release on Licence*

Weeks v. *UK*[151] concerned the compatibility of the review arrangements for the continued imprisonment of a prisoner sentenced to life imprisonment with the right to liberty and security of the person protected by Article 5. In 1966 Weeks, then aged 17, robbed a pet shop with a starting pistol loaded with a blank cartridge and stole 35 pence. The court accepted a probation officer's evidence of his aggressive and unstable nature and sentenced him to life imprisonment. This meant that the Home Secretary might release him, but he would always be liable to be recalled.[152] This extraordinary decision, upheld on appeal, was justified on the grounds that the Home Secretary would be able to release Weeks when he was no longer a danger to the public, a date which might be earlier than release after a long determinate sentence of imprisonment.

Weeks was released on licence in March 1976. In June 1977 he was recalled after being charged with offences committed while on licence. He was released again in October 1982, but after breaking the conditions of his licence he was again recalled in November 1984 and rearrested in April 1985. Later that year he was released again on licence but this was once again revoked when he failed to keep appointments with his probation officer. At the time of the Court hearing he was still at liberty.

Before the Court, the original sentence was not at issue and the case was only concerned with events up until his release on licence in 1982. Weeks complained that his recall offended against Article 5(1):

> . . . No one shall be deprived of his liberty save in the following cases and in accordance with a procedure prescribed by law:
> (*a*) the lawful detention of a person after conviction by a competent court . . .

The British Government argued that once it was conceded that the original sentence was in accordance with Article 5 then the article did not apply to subsequent events. Release on licence was not a restoration of liberty, therefore the revocation of the licence and recall of a prisoner was not a new deprivation of liberty. The Court held that the article did apply, but that the circumstances of Weeks' detention until his release in 1976, his recall in 1977 and his continued detention until 1982 had not breached Article 5(1). In order to satisfy the requirement that Weeks' deprivation of liberty was in accordance with Article 5(1)(*a*) his recall and his continued imprisonment had to be in accordance with the court's original reason for imposing a life sentence. While it might be extremely difficult or impossible in many cases

[151] Series A, No. 114 (1987); *EHRR*, vol. 10, p. 293.
[152] Criminal Justice Act 1967, s. 61.

to determine the reasons for the sentence and their relative importance, in this case the clearly expressed reasoning of the English courts put the case in a special category, particularly since the life sentence was imposed precisely so that it could be reviewed in the light of the change in circumstances. In the case of the recall in 1977 the Court was satisfied that, within the margin of appreciation allowed to States under the Convention, there were grounds for the Home Secretary to consider that Weeks' continued liberty was a threat to the public and himself, and that these constituted grounds for his continued detention until 1982.

However, the Court held that there had been a breach of Article 5(4), whereby:

> Everyone who is deprived of his liberty . . . shall be entitled to take proceedings by which the lawfulness of his detention shall be decided speedily by a court . . .

Since the reason for Weeks' continued detention might change and cease to be in accordance with the original court's reason for imposing a life sentence, he should have been entitled to apply to a court which was empowered to decide speedily on the lawfulness of his imprisonment on the occasion of any recall and at reasonable intervals during his imprisonment.

There were two avenues of review open to Weeks—the Parole Board and the courts. The Parole Board was empowered to recommend to the Home Secretary that a prisoner be released on licence or recalled.[153] In the event of the Home Secretary exercising his power to recall a prisoner without consulting the Board, as he did with Weeks in 1977, he was obliged thereafter to refer the matter to the Board. In the event of his recall on the recommendation of the Board the prisoner was to be informed of the reason for his recall and of his right to make representations. Any representations were to be referred to the Board, and if it recommended immediate release then the Home Secretary was bound to comply.[154]

The applicant argued that the Parole Board was not an independent and impartial court, that it had not sufficient powers to satisfy Article 5(4), that there were insufficient procedural guarantees, and that the hearing was not speedy. The Court held that the Parole Board was sufficiently independent of the Home Secretary, despite the fact that he appointed its members, provided its staff and laid down its rules of procedure. However, following an interpretation similar to that applied in the mental health cases,[155] it held that the Board did not generally have the power of decision which a court must have to satisfy Article 5(4). Except in cases referred to it after recall, the Board's role was purely advisory. The Court further held that judicial review did not remedy the deficiencies of the Parole Board, since the courts could not review the consistency of Weeks' continued detention with the original objectives of the sentence.

[153] Criminal Justice Act 1967, s. 61(1).

[154] Ibid., s. 62(1)–(5).

[155] See above, p. 298.

Even in those cases of referral where the Board's recommendation was binding on the Home Secretary, the Court held that there were insufficient procedural guarantees. The Home Office had consistently denied the right of a prisoner to have access to material upon which decisions were based, and this practice had been upheld in the English courts. Although the latter had held that the prisoner was entitled to be sufficiently informed of the reasons for his recall to enable him to make written representations, he was not entitled to full disclosure of material held by the Parole Board and adverse to his case.[156] This, held the European Court, prevented the prisoner from participating properly in the hearing. Regrettably perhaps, the Court did not rule on whether, in accordance with 5(4), Weeks should have been entitled to an oral hearing, or whether the proceedings were sufficiently speedy.

The Government's response to the European Court's judgment has been limited. Almost two months after the judgment the Home Secretary announced his decision to remit Weeks' life sentence.[157] Welcome, if belated, this was not required by the Court's decision. The exercise of mercy did not extend to exercising the prerogative discretion to award compensation to Weeks.[158] However, the European Court awarded him £8,000 for loss of opportunities and for feelings of frustration and helplessness engendered by the breach of the Convention.[159]

On the general question of reform the Home Secretary announced that the implications of the judgment for domestic law and practice were being considered, but that the kind of case covered by the judgment 'is in any view very limited'.[160] The British Government's attempt to limit the implications of *Weeks* by treating it as a special case failed to take account of the reasoning of the Court. Although it was unusual for a person to be sentenced to life imprisonment for such a minor offence, Mr Weeks was typical in that discretionary life sentences are imposed to protect the public from mentally unstable persons.[161] There must come a point during the detention of all discretionary life prisoners when they have served the punitive part of their sentence, and the only reason for continued imprisonment is that they are still a danger to the public. Although there has not always been a clear way of identifying when this period has expired, there will

[156] *Gunnell* v. *Chairman of the Parole Board*, *The Times*, 7 November 1984; *R* v. *Parole Board, ex parte Wilson*, *The Times*, 20 March 1985.

[157] HC Debs., vol. 115, Written Answers, cols. *152–3*: 29 April 1987.

[158] *R* v. *Secretary of State for the Home Department, ex parte Weeks*, *The Independent*, 18 February 1988.

[159] Series A, No. 145 (1988), paras. 14–15. A further application by Weeks resulted in a friendly settlement and the payment of a further £5,000.

[160] HC Debs., vol. 115, Written Answers, col. *152*: 29 April 1987.

[161] *R* v. *Wilkinson* (1983), 5 Cr.App.Rep.(S) 105. In *R* v. *Secretary of State for the Home Department, ex parte Benson*, *The Times*, 21 November 1988, the Divisional Court quashed a decision of the Home Secretary to ignore the recommendation of the Parole Board to release a discretionary life prisoner, on the ground that he had taken into account irrelevant considerations. However, this does not repair the breach of the Convention, since the European Court held that this degree of judicial review was not enough to satisfy Article 5(4).

come a point when it is no longer arguable that the prisoner is still serving the punitive part of the sentence. At this point the requirements of the *Weeks* judgment must be satisfied. In the case of *Thynne, Wilson and Gunnell* v. *UK*[162] the Government resisted this conclusion before the Court. All three applicants had been sentenced to life imprisonment for serious sex offences. It was clear that in all three cases the time during which they could be regarded as serving a punitive sentence had long passed. The Court, giving judgment on 25 October 1990, found no reason to distinguish the case from *Weeks*.

After *Weeks* it had seemed clear that some reform was necessary. First, the Secretary of State had to be relieved of the decision whether to release a prisoner on licence; secondly, some measures had to be taken to ensure periodic review of a discretionary life prisoner's continued imprisonment; and finally prisoners had to be given reasons for the refusal of release or recall and be given access to the materials upon which a decision was based. However, the Government only acknowledged the need for any reform after *Thynne, Wilson and Gunnell*, nearly four and a half years after the *Weeks* judgment. Its response is contained in section 34 of the Criminal Justice Act 1991. Indeed, the Government was reluctant to include this provision in the Act, preferring to defer legislation until after more consideration had been given to the appropriate response, but it bowed to parliamentary pressure especially from the House of Lords.[163]

Under section 34 (1) and (2), a court sentencing a discretionary life prisoner may specify that part of the sentence which reflects the severity of the offence. Section 34(4) provides that once that part of the sentence has been served the prisoner may require the Home Secretary to refer the case to the Parole Board, which is empowered to direct the Home Secretary to release the defendant if it 'is satisfied that it is no longer necessary for the protection of the public that the prisoner should be imprisoned'. Thereafter, the prisoner may require further review two years after the previous adverse decision.

On the question of prisoners' access to materials upon which a decision is based, a Home Office Minister has indicated that it is the Government's intention to introduce more openness and, in particular, to enable prisoners 'to see what is written about them and [be] advised why parole has not been granted', and that the Government intends to start to implement this policy early in 1992.[164]

Section 34 of the Criminal Justice Act broadly satisfies the requirements of the decision in *Weeks* in taking the decision-making on release out of the Home Secretary's hands. It is probable that the new government policy of openness in the Parole Board's decision-making will allow the prisoner

[162] Series A, No. 190 (1990), discussed by Richardson, 'Discretionary Life Sentences and the European Convention on Human Rights', *Public Law*, 1991, p. 34.

[163] HC Debs., vol. 193, col. *903*: 25 June 1991.

[164] HC Debs., Standing Committee A, 15 January 1991, cols. 324–5.

adequate access to relevant materials, although this may depend on the detailed implementation of the policy.

(g) *Prisoners Marrying*

In two cases the right of prisoners in English prisons to marry has been considered. In both cases the refusal of facilities to marry was held by the Committee of Ministers to be in breach of Article 12:

> Men and women of marriageable age have the right to marry and found a family, according to the national laws governing the exercise of this right.

Under English law, there was no provision for the celebration of a marriage in a prison, marriage outside a registry office or 'place of religious worship'[165] generally being confined to cases of serious illness. It was thus necessary for a prisoner to be allowed temporary absence.[166] Under the Prison Rules a prisoner might be granted temporary release 'for any special purpose or to enable him to engage in employment, to receive instruction or training or to assist him in his transition from prison life to freedom'.[167] The practice was only to grant temporary release to marry so that a child of the prisoner might be legitimized or possibly in exceptional compassionate circumstances. Hamer was on remand when he first requested and was refused permission to marry in 1974. Later that year he was sentenced to five years' imprisonment and he unsuccessfully renewed his request.

Hearing Hamer's application, the Commission rejected the United Kingdom Government's ingenious argument that it was Hamer who had prevented himself from marrying since his own actions had put him in his predicament.[168] Following the approach of the Court in *Golder*, the Commission held that the 'substantial delay' resulting from the failure to provide facilities for marriage was a breach of the right to marry. The Committee of Ministers adopted the Commission's report by its decision of April 1981.[169]

In 1977 the practice had been changed so that prisoners could be granted temporary release to marry if they had more than twelve months to serve before the earliest date for release, and this was later reduced to more than six months before that date.[170] This was enough to avoid future breaches of the Convention in relation to prisoners in Hamer's position, but it did nothing for prisoners serving a life sentence. This problem, unresolved after *Hamer*, was the subject of an application to the Commission by Draper, sentenced to life imprisonment for robbery. In 1977 he applied for permission to marry and, since he had neither a child to legitimize nor a

[165] Prison chapels are apparently excluded, since the place should be a place of 'public religious worship': Marriage Act 1949, s. 41(2).

[166] Marriage (Registrar General's Licence) Act 1970, s. 1.

[167] Prison Rule 6.

[168] Commission Report, paras. 64–9, *Decisions and Reports*, vol. 24, p. 5.

[169] Res. DH(81)5.

[170] Commission Report in *Draper* v. *UK*, *Decisions and Reports*, vol. 24, p. 72, para. 25.

provisional date for release, his request was refused. The Government argued before the Commission that special considerations applied to prisoners serving life terms of imprisonment, since there might be types of case 'notably involving prisoners convicted of crime in a family context (such as murder of a spouse) or offences against women or children, where marriage or remarriage of the prisoner could give rise to public outrage or difficulties concerning release'. The Commission, whilst not excluding the possibility of such exceptional cases, held that this could not justify the practice when applied to persons such as the applicant who did not fall within any of the Government's preferred categories. On 2 April 1981 the Committee of Ministers adopted the Commission's report, finding that the United Kingdom had been in breach of Article 12.[171] By this time the Government had offered facilities to Draper to marry, and had informed the Committee of its intention to bring forward legislation to enable marriages to take place in prisons. Indeed, the Government had already changed its practice, allowing prisoners to marry 'in so far as this is practicable'.[172] This of course still meant that some prisoners might be denied the right to marry if the prison authorities felt that they did not have the resources to provide adequate security.

In December 1982 the Marriage Bill had its first reading in the House of Lords; it received the Royal Assent in May 1983 and was brought into force on 1 May 1984.[173] The Act allows prisoners in England and Wales and in Northern Ireland[174] to be married in prison, and also gives the right to long-stay patients detained in hospital under the Mental Health Act 1983 to be married in hospital. The Act therefore goes further than the Committee's decision required in bringing the law of the United Kingdom into line with the Convention.[175]

(h) *Conclusion*

While the cases on prisoners cover a variety of topics, some general reflections are possible about the nature of British compliance in these cases. In relation to any particular subject of complaint the response to the initial adverse finding has often been limited compliance. Thus in relation to *Weeks* there was individual compliance only until the Court's judgment in *Thynne, Wilson and Gunnell*, and in relation to *Golder* compliance was with the letter of the decision and ignored the underlying reasoning. More-

[171] Res. DH(81)4.

[172] HC Debs., vol. 1, Written Answers, col. *283*: 23 March 1981.

[173] SI 1984, No. 413.

[174] The Act does not extend to Scotland since the law governing formalities of marriage was already sufficiently unrestrictive to enable the celebration of marriages in such cases.

[175] Even in this context, the Government's reluctance to fetter the Prison Governor's discretion is to be seen in the rejection of proposals to prevent the Act being used when temporary release might be appropriate, the Government preferring to rely on administrative advice to Governors on the exercise of their discretion: HL Debs., vol. 440, cols. 886–9: 17 March 1983; HC Debs., Standing Committee E, col. 506: 3 May 1983.

over, grouping the cases according to subject-matter should not obscure the fact that from *Golder* onwards every decision had implications for the prison system as a whole. One feature common to all the cases is that they show a clash of approaches to the status of prisoners. The traditional British approach treated them as the recipients of privileges granted on the basis of executive discretion, and in principle stripped of rights, whereas the approach under the Convention has been to treat them as bearers of rights. The broadest of compliance might have led to an early recognition of this and an overhaul of prison regulations which would have forestalled most of the adverse decisions. Instead the approach was piecemeal and often half-hearted and inadequate, and, if there is to be a more radical change in the attitude towards prisoners' rights, it is likely to come not from the Convention, but from the pressures of national politics. Thus the Woolf Report,[176] commissioned after a number of prison disturbances in 1990, advocates a more open approach to prison administration and a movement away from a system based upon the bestowal of privileges. If the approach of the Report is adopted, then it is likely that the steady stream of successful applications to the Commission concerning prisoners in the United Kingdom will begin to dry up.

VI. Homosexuality

Article 8, paragraph 1, of the Convention provides that 'Everyone has the right to respect for his private and family life, his home and his correspondence'. Paragraph 2 of Article 8 goes on to provide that there shall be no interference with this right except such 'as is in accordance with the law and is necessary in a democratic society in the interests of national security, public safety or the economic well-being of the country, for the prevention of disorder or crime, for the protection of health or morals, or for the protection of the rights and freedoms of others'. The applicability of Article 8 to legislation relating to homosexuality in Northern Ireland was the issue in *Dudgeon*.[177]

Dudgeon argued that Northern Irish legislation which made certain homosexual acts between consenting adult males (buggery and gross indecency) criminal offences was a breach of Article 8. The Court, in a judgment given on 22 October 1981, agreed with him. The legislation in question was an interference with Dudgeon's private life, and although it was clearly 'in accordance with the law' and served one of the listed purposes (the protection of morals), it went beyond what was 'necessary in a democratic society'. It was unnecessary, and therefore contrary to Article 8, to make private homosexual acts between consenting adult males criminal offences.

[176] See n. 107, above.

[177] Series A, No. 45 (1971); *EHRR*, vol. 4, p. 149.

Before turning to the action taken by the UK Government to comply with the Court's judgment, it is worth briefly recalling attempts to reform the law on homosexuality in Northern Ireland made well before the Court's judgment in *Dudgeon*. In April 1977 the Northern Ireland Standing Advisory Commission on Human Rights, after having been asked by the UK Government to look at the law in Northern Ireland relating to homosexuality, published a report in which it recommended that the law in Northern Ireland should be brought into line with that in England and Wales.[178] The then Labour Government published draft legislation to give effect to the Committee's recommendations in July 1978, but this attempt at reform was abandoned in the last weeks of the Labour Government because of vociferous opposition from Ulster Unionist MPs, on whose support the Government was dependent for its existence. After the fall of the Labour Government and the subsequent general election, the new Conservative Government announced that it had no intention of re-introducing the previous Government's draft legislation because of political and religious opposition in Northern Ireland.[179]

Following the Court's judgment in the *Dudgeon* case in October 1981, however, the Government was forced to reconsider its position. In February 1982 it announced that legislation would be introduced to bring the law in Northern Ireland into line with that in the rest of the United Kingdom.[180] Subsequently, in July 1982, the Homosexual Offences (Northern Ireland) Order was laid before Parliament; it was approved by large majorities in each House in October, and came into force on 9 December 1982.[181] The Order brings the law in Northern Ireland into conformity with that in England and Wales (the law in Scotland differs in some detail) : in particular, the Order provides that, subject to certain exceptions relating to mental patients, members of the armed forces and merchant seamen, homosexual acts committed in private between consenting males over the age of 21 are no longer criminal offences.[182]

Thus, as a result of the Order, the United Kingdom authorities complied with the Court's judgment in *Dudgeon* a little over a year after it was given, in spite of encountering vociferous objection in Northern Ireland. It can be

[178] Northern Ireland Standing Advisory Commission on Human Rights, *Report on the Law in Northern Ireland relating to Divorce and Homosexuality* (1977).

[179] HC Debs, vol. 969, Written Answers, col. *466*: 2 July 1979. It should also be noted that in March 1981, following the opinion on the merits of the European Commission of Human Rights in the *Dudgeon* case (which upheld the applicant's submissions), the Northern Ireland Standing Advisory Commission on Human Rights urged that legislation should be introduced without waiting for the judgment of the Court: HC 143 (1980–1), pp. 22–3.

[180] HC Debs, vol. 18, Written Answers, cols. *387–8*: 24 February 1982. Note that the law in Scotland was brought into line with that of England and Wales in 1980 by the Criminal Justice (Scotland) Act 1980.

[181] SI 1982, No. 1536.

[182] As regards the exceptions mentioned, it may be noted that the European Commission of Human Rights has held that restrictions on homosexual acts between members of the armed forces are justifiable under paragraph 2 of Article 8: see Application 9237/81, *B* v. *UK, Decisions and Reports*, vol. 24, p. 68.

argued, however, that to have complied fully with the spirit of the Court's judgment, the UK authorities should have done more to reform the law in the Isle of Man and Jersey, where homosexual acts between adult males remain illegal. While the Manx and Jersey authorities have been informed of the Court's judgment,[183] it is arguable that the UK authorities should have gone further and legislated for the Isle of Man and Jersey in this regard.[184]

VII. Telephone Tapping

A different aspect of Article 8 of the Convention (whose provisions were quoted at the beginning of the previous section) was at issue in *Malone* v. *UK*.[185] Malone's telephone had been tapped under a warrant obtained by the police from the Home Secretary (Malone was suspected of handling stolen goods). He brought an action claiming that this telephone tapping was a breach of his rights under Article 8 of the Convention. Malone also claimed a breach of Article 8 by reason of the alleged interception of his mail (unlike the telephone tapping, the Government denied this had occurred) and by the 'metering' of his telephone (i.e. British Telecom noting all his calls and passing the information on to the police). In a judgment given on 2 August 1984, the Court found for Malone on all three points. There was no doubt that in each case the acts complained of amounted to an interference contrary to paragraph 1 of Article 8. The question then was whether these interferences were justified by paragraph 2. Here the first point to be considered was whether the interferences were 'in accordance with the law'. The Court stressed that this phrase refers not only to the existence of some domestic law (including the common law), but also 'to the quality of the law, requiring it to be compatible with the rule of law'.[186] This includes the idea that the law must be adequately accessible (by which the Court means that a person must be able to have an adequate indication of the legal rules applicable in a given case) and the law must be sufficiently precise to enable a person to regulate his conduct. In particular, it must be sufficiently clear to give individuals an adequate indication of the circumstances in which and conditions on which public authorities can resort to telephone tapping : any discretion given to the executive must not be unfettered and its scope must be indicated.

In the case of both telephone tapping and the interception of mail, the

[183] HC Debs., vol. 142, Written Answers, col. *396*: 1 December 1988.

[184] Cf. the discussion on the *Tyrer* case, above. Note that in Guernsey homosexual acts were decriminalized in 1983 (*The Guardian*, 31 March 1983). In March 1991 the Manx Parliament approved the recommendation of a select committee not to decriminalize homosexual acts. The British Government has apparently warned the Manx authorities that it will impose its own legislation (*The Guardian*, 28 March 1991). Legislation to decriminalize homosexual acts is currently being considered in Jersey.

[185] Series A, No. 82 (1984); *EHRR*, vol. 7, p. 14.

[186] Court's judgment, para. 67. Cf. the discussion in relation to prisoners' correspondence at p. 306, above.

Court found that these activities, while lawful in English law, did not meet the broader test of being 'in accordance with the law'. The English law in this area was 'somewhat obscure'; it was not clear what elements of these activities were incorporated in legal rules and what elements remained within the discretion of the executive; the scope and manner of the exercise of such discretion were not indicated with 'reasonable clarity'.[187] The Court reached a similar conclusion as regards the question of metering, noting that there were no legal rules governing the discretion of British Telecom to pass the information obtained from metering on to the police. Because the Court found the three activities complained of were not 'in accordance with the law', it did not find it necessary to consider the other elements of paragraph 2 of Article 8, in particular whether the interferences were 'necessary in a democratic society'.

Before turning to see whether the UK authorities have complied with this judgment, it is worth observing that attempts to reform the law on telephone tapping had been made before the Court's judgment. In the case Malone brought in the English courts, prior to invoking the Convention machinery, to challenge the legality of his telephone being tapped, Megarry V-C found that the telephone tapping was not contrary to English law. He nevertheless observed that the subject 'cries out for legislation' and expressed strong doubts as to whether the position of telephone tapping in English law was in accordance with the Convention.[188] After Megarry's judgment in April 1980, the Government resisted backbench MPs'attempts to put telephone tapping on a statutory basis, and did not accept such a recommendation by the Royal Commission on Criminal Procedure.[189] However, in 1984, during the passage of the Telecommunications Bill privatizing British Telecom, concern was expressed that tapping would be controlled by a private body, and the Government undertook to bring forward separate legislation on telephone tapping in the next session of Parliament, regardless of the Court's judgment, then pending, in *Malone*.[190]

Under the twin pressures of this undertaking and the Court's judgment, the Government announced in the Queen's Speech in November 1984 that legislation would be introduced to 'establish a new and comprehensive framework governing the interception of communications'.[191] In February 1985 the Government published a White Paper in which it said that legislation would shortly be introduced along the lines foreshadowed in the Queen's Speech which would 'ensure that, having regard to the decisions of the European Court of Human Rights, United Kingdom law is in compliance with the European Convention'.[192] The White Paper was followed shortly afterwards by the publication of the Interception of Communica-

[187] Ibid., para. 79.
[188] *Malone* v. *Metropolitan Police Commissioner*, [1979] 2 All ER 620.
[189] Cmnd. 8092 (1981), paras. 3.56–60.
[190] HL Debs., vol. 449, cols. 1032–6: 19 March 1984.
[191] HL Debs., vol. 457, col. 3: 6 November 1984.
[192] *The Interception of Communications in the United Kingdom*, Cmnd. 9438 (1985), p. 4.

tions Bill, which passed through Parliament and received the Royal Assent on 25 July 1985. The Act, which applies to the whole of the United Kingdom, came into force on 10 April 1986, some 20 months after the European Court's judgment.

Very briefly the Act provides that mail or telephone calls may not be intercepted unless this is done pursuant to a warrant issued only for a limited range of purposes (discussed below). The Act establishes a Tribunal to investigate complaints of telephone tapping or interception of mail. The Act also provides for the appointment of a Commissioner whose general function is to review the operation of the Act. Do these provisions amount to compliance with the Court's judgment?

It will be recalled that the Court's finding in relation to telephone tapping and the interception of mail was that the law was not clear, in particular as to the way and circumstances in which the authorities can intercept telephone calls and mail. At first sight the Act appears to meet this objection. It provides that interception may only be made under a warrant issued by the Secretary of State. Such warrants may be issued only on the following grounds: (1) the interests of national security; (2) for the purpose of preventing or detecting serious crime; (3) for the purpose of safeguarding the economic well-being of the United Kingdom (provided that the information which it is thought necessary to acquire relates to acts or intentions of persons outside the United Kingdom).

Superficially, each of these three grounds seems reasonably clear. Further examination, however, suggests the opposite. The first ground, national security, may be taken first. The Government, in debates on the Bill, defined national security as 'concerned with espionage, terrorism and subversion and also with the acquisition of intelligence in support of the Government's defence and overseas policies'.[193] While the first half of this definition seems reasonably clear, it must be doubted whether the second half is sufficiently precise to meet the requirements of the Convention.[194] Turning to the next ground, preventing or detecting serious crimes, 'serious crime' is defined in section 10(3). Again, while much of the definition is acceptably clear, there are some elements which are very vague and which seem insufficiently precise to meet the requirements of the Convention. Thus, 'serious crime' includes offences which result in 'substantial financial gain' (substantial by what criteria?) and offences involving 'conduct by a large number of persons in pursuit of a common purpose'. The final ground for issue of a warrant is safeguarding the economic well-being of the United Kingdom. This is again a vague provision, although it must be admitted that this ground is found in paragraph 2 of Article 8 of the Convention. Of this ground the Government said that it is 'concerned with

[193] HL Debs., vol. 463, col. 1257: 16 May 1985.

[194] The term 'subversion' can also be regarded as too broad and vague. For an exploration of what the term means to the Government, see Cameron, 'Telephone Tapping and the Interception of Communications Act 1985', *Northern Ireland Legal Quarterly*, 37 (1986), p. 126 at pp. 136–8.

interception that is necessary for the effective protection of the country's economic interests at the international level', although the Government spokesman, Lord Whitelaw, felt unable to give even hypothetical examples of what this might cover because to do so would in itself be damaging.[195] This extraordinary example of Whitehall's concern for secrecy is hardly calculated to promote the accessibility and precision of the law which the European Court requires.

Turning now to the other matter where the Court found the United Kingdom at fault in *Malone*—telephone 'metering'—it will be recalled that the fault lay in the fact that there were no legal rules governing the circumstances in which information about calls could be passed on. Again, at first sight the Act appears to meet this objection. Schedule 2 provides that metering may only be done in the following circumstances: (1) the prevention and detection of crime; (2) further to a warrant issued for telephone tapping; (3) in the interests of national security, of which a ministerial certificate shall be conclusive evidence; and (4) pursuant to a court order. In the light of the earlier discussion, it may be questioned whether all of these circumstances, particularly the second and third, meet the tests of accessibility and precision laid down by the Court.

If the Act hardly appears to fulfil the letter of the Court's judgment, even less does it comply with the spirit of the Court's judgment. Although the Court did not find it necessary to consider the requirement that, to be valid under the Convention, telephone tapping must be 'necessary in a democratic society', the Court did comment, referring to its earlier judgment in *Klass* v. *Federal Republic of Germany*,[196] that an acceptable system of telephone tapping must contain 'adequate guarantees against abuse'.[197] There must be serious doubts as to whether the Interception of Communications Act does provide such guarantees. The main potential guarantee is the Tribunal. There are a number of features about its role and powers which cast doubt on its adequacy as a guarantee against abuse. The Tribunal may investigate complaints of telephone tapping, but can only take action (in the form of notifying the complainant and, if it thinks fit, ordering corrective measures) where the complainant's telephone has been tapped under a warrant which in the Tribunal's view was wrongfully issued by the Minister. Thus, if the Tribunal finds there was an interception which was not authorized by a warrant, it cannot investigate further or inform the complainant of this fact: presumably it is intended that the Tribunal should inform the police (since prima facie an offence has been committed), but the Act does not require it to do so. Secondly, where tapping has been done under a warrant, the Tribunal can review the legality of its exercise only in accordance with the principles of judicial review. This may be too narrow to provide an

195 HL Debs., vol. 464, col. 879: 6 June 1985.
196 Series A, No. 28 (1978); *EHRR*, vol. 2, p. 214.
197 Court's judgment in *Malone*, para. 81.

effective safeguard against abuse.[198] Thirdly, if a person's telephone has been legally tapped, he cannot be told this. All he can be told is that there has been no breach of sections 2–5. From this he might deduce that his phone has been lawfully tapped; or that his telephone has not been tapped at all; or that the Tribunal has been unable to discover what has happened. On the other hand, on the positive side, if the Tribunal finds a warrant has been wrongly issued, it shall inform the complainant and may, if it thinks fit, quash the warrant, order the intercepted material to be destroyed and require the Home Secretary to pay the complainant compensation. A final flaw in the Tribunal procedure is that its decisions are not reviewable in the courts.

If the Tribunal has a number of defects as a guarantee against abuse, the Commissioner provided for under the Act is even less of a guarantor. He cannot receive complaints; he cannot look at telephone taps where there has been no warrant. He reports to the Prime Minister; and his published reports may be an expurgated version of his reports to the Prime Minister, as indeed his first three reports[199] have been[200]. Other aspects of the Act which create doubts as to whether it offers sufficient guarantees against abuse are the rules on exclusion of evidence in section 9, which would make it impossible for an individual to bring civil proceedings against a Minister or any one else based on breach of the Act. Thus a future complainant in the position of Malone would be unable to get his case off the ground. Nor could he bring a private prosecution, because under the Act the consent of the DPP is necessary.

It is instructive to compare the safeguards against abuse in German law which were in issue in the *Klass* case. These safeguards include: an independent Commission to review the Minister's decisions to permit telephone tapping and if appropriate reverse them (in practice the Commission is normally consulted before a decision is made); a Parliamentary Board keeping the system under overall review; a requirement that a person whose telephone has been tapped be informed once tapping has ceased, provided national security allows; and the possibility of challenging the legality of a telephone tap before the Constitutional Court (though not the ordinary courts). In finding that these safeguards met the requirements of the Convention, the European Court in the *Klass* case stressed the fact that the Commission and Board were independent of the authorities carrying out the surveillance and were vested with sufficient powers to exercise an effective and continuous control; the democratic character of the Board, which included opposition MPs; and the fact that in many cases the individual concerned was notified of the tapping.

In conclusion, there must be real doubt as to whether the Interception of Communications Act complies with the stipulation in the Court's judgment

[198] Further on this point, see Cameron, loc. cit. above (n. 194), pp. 146–7.

[199] Cm. 108 (1987); Cm. 351 (1988); and Cm. 652 (1989).

[200] For further criticisms, see Cameron, loc. cit. above (n. 194), p. 148.

in *Malone* that telephone tapping be 'in accordance with the law'. There is even more doubt as to whether the Act complies with the other requirements of the Convention as interpreted by the Court in *Klass*. The minimalist nature of the Act is probably due to the traditional reluctance of British Governments to open surveillance by the State to public scrutiny.

VIII. Immigration

(a) *Delay in Proceedings*

In *Zamir*[201] the applicant was arrested and held in custody with a view to his removal from the United Kingdom as an illegal immigrant. His application for habeas corpus failed. In his application to the Commission Zamir alleged breaches of the Convention owing to the uncertainty of the law, the presumption of guilt involved in the decision to deport, and the inadequacy of the habeas corpus proceedings as a review of the legality of his detention. None of these claims was successful before the Commission, which, however, did hold that there had been a breach of Article 5(4), entitling everyone deprived of liberty to have the lawfulness of his detention decided speedily by a court, the breach consisting in the delay in the hearing of the habeas corpus proceedings.

The history of the proceedings is involved and the precise cause of the delay not always clear from the Commission's account. Zamir had been arrested on 2 October 1978. He applied for habeas corpus on 24 October 1978 and was released on bail about eleven weeks after his arrest on 19 December. His application was heard on 14 March 1979 and his appeal to the House of Lords was dismissed on 17 July 1980. The most important delay was held to be the seven weeks spent by the applicant in detention after he had applied for habeas corpus.[202] Apart from some initial tardiness on the part of Zamir's advisers, the delay seems to have been attributable to three factors.

First and most significant was the delay in the grant of legal aid. It was over seven weeks between the first application for and the grant of an emergency certificate. The rules provided for the grant of emergency legal aid if it was 'in the interests of justice that an applicant should as a matter of urgency be granted legal aid',[203] but contained no provision requiring that an application be dealt with within a particular time-limit. The second factor was the delay on the part of the Treasury Solicitor in filing the Home Office evidence against Zamir. Finally, there was a delay in having an application for bail determined and in fixing a date for hearing. The delay in granting bail was also bound up with the legal aid question, since the bail

[201] Committee of Ministers, Res. DH(85)3, 25 January 1985.
[202] Commission's report, 11 October 1983, *Decisions and Reports*, vol. 40, p. 42, para. 110.
[203] Legal Aid (General) Regulations, SI 1971, No. 62, reg. 11(5)(*b*).

application was adjourned together with that for habeas corpus. The Commission pointed out that the Home Office itself had refused to grant temporary admission to Zamir pending the outcome of the habeas corpus application. It was the duty of the State so to organize its procedures that proceedings could be conducted with minimum delay.

After bail was granted it is unclear how much, if any, of the delay in fixing a hearing was due to the administrative problems of court lists. It is also unclear whether the Commission regarded this delay as a breach of Article 5(4), and if so how serious it was. Certainly some of the delay seems to have been due to less urgency on the part of Zamir's advisers once bail had been granted.

The case was not referred to the European Court and the Committee of Ministers adopted a resolution agreeing with the findings of the Commission. There is no evidence of a response to the adverse findings in the *Zamir* case. The legal aid rules were not changed,[204] nor were the *Notes of Guidance* issued by the Law Society.[205] It must be assumed that the reason for this was the Government's view that it was not the rules, but rather their application in the instant case that was at fault, and that the delay was, as was submitted to the Commission, 'unusual among cases concerned with habeas corpus'.[206] Since the delay in the Treasury Solicitor's filing of evidence was related to the delay in legal aid, presumably no formal action was believed to be necessary in that regard.

The Government did claim to have made a relevant alteration to the law prior to the hearing of the application by the Commission:

> [T]he hearing of the habeas corpus application would have taken place more quickly had the applicant been detained subsequent to a change in 1980 in the Rules of the Supreme Court dealing with habeas corpus applications.[207]

Prior to 1980 an application had first to be made to the Divisional Court of the Queen's Bench, and only if it was not sitting, to a single judge,[208] whereas under the revised rule the application is generally to be made first to a judge in court.[209] This may prevent the delay involved in obtaining a date for hearing before the two or three judges normally sitting in the Divisional Court. It was not explained how this would have accelerated the hearing of the *Zamir* case, and it is difficult to see how it would have had much bearing on the speed of the proceedings prior to the granting of bail or would have accelerated the granting of bail. No change was made in the law regarding the granting of bail.

In any event, the Committee of Ministers took the view that no further action was required. The Government's view seems to have been that

[204] See now SI 1980, No. 1894, reg. 19(2)(*b*).
[205] See now *Notes of Guidance* (1989), n. 8, in substantially similar terms.
[206] Loc. cit. above (n. 202), para. 75.
[207] Ibid., para. 76.
[208] RSC 1965, Ord. 54, r. 1(1).
[209] Ibid., as amended by RSC (Amendment No. 4) 1980, SI 1980, No. 2000.

Zamir was a case where the applicant lost on the main issue, and the subsidiary issue was due to poor application of the law in the particular case, rather than inherently inadequate law. While it may be true that the extensive delay in *Zamir* was unusual, the Government did not respond to the claim that the present rules do not require a sufficiently expedited hearing.[210]

(b) *Sex Discrimination*

In *Abdulaziz, Cabales and Balkandali*[211] the United Kingdom was held to be in breach of Article 14 in failing to secure without discrimination on the grounds of sex the right to respect for family life protected by Article 8.

The United Kingdom's immigration policy had already come under the scrutiny of the European Commission on a number of occasions, most notably in the *East African Asians* case,[212] where the Commission found, *inter alia*, that the Commonwealth Immigrants Act 1962, as amended by the Commonwealth Immigrants Act 1968, breached Article 14 taken together with Article 8 in giving the right of admission to wives of Commonwealth citizens resident in the United Kingdom, while denying that right to husbands. That case ended indecisively when the Committee of Ministers did not adopt the Commission's report because it failed to obtain the necessary two-thirds majority.[213]

The Immigration Act 1971, which was the legislation in force when the applicants in the *Abdulaziz* case complained, had continued this kind of discrimination. A person qualifying as a 'patrial' had the right to enter and remain in the United Kingdom free from immigration controls. The statutory discrimination lay in the fact that only a woman could become a patrial by marriage.[214] In 1974 the Immigration Rules made under the authority of the Act eliminated this discrimination by providing that a spouse or person affianced of either sex might be allowed to enter and remain if the partner were settled in the UK.[215] In 1977 the rules were changed by a Labour Home Secretary and a discriminatory bias was reintroduced in an attempt to prevent marriage being used to gain entry to and settlement in the UK. These provisions only applied to male applicants. An application for entry clearance or leave to remain in the United Kingdom which was based on marriage or betrothal to a woman settled in the United Kingdom might be refused if there was reason to believe that the marriage was entered into primarily to obtain admission or that one of the parties no longer intended to live with the other. If the marriage had been entered into within 12 months

210 See, e.g., HC Debs., vol. 988, col. 1252: 15 July 1980; Gifford and O'Connor, *Legal Action Group Bulletin*, 1979, p. 182.

211 Series A, No. 94 (1985); *EHRR*, vol. 7, p. 471.

212 A summary of this and other complaints brought against the United Kingdom's immigration law prior to *Abdulaziz* is to be found in *Memorandum of the Home Office—Background Note on the European Convention of Human Rights*, Minutes of Evidence, pp. 2–6, HC 434 (1979–80).

213 Res. DH(77)2.

214 S. 2(2).

215 Cmnd. 5115–18 (1974).

of the application then admission or leave to remain was granted for an initial period of 12 months, after which the marriage might be reviewed again before indefinite leave was granted.[216]

This remained the position until 1980 when the newly elected Conservative Government made further discriminatory amendment to the rules,[217] and it was in this form that they were challenged in *Abdulaziz*. A husband would not be given entry clearance if the parties had not already met; he would only be given clearance or leave to remain if the wife were a citizen of the UK and Colonies who had herself been born in the UK or one of whose parents had been born there. The changes in rules for fiancés and fiancées followed those for husbands and wives respectively.

Even before these rules had been approved by the House of Commons their compatibility with the European Convention had come under public scrutiny. The House of Commons Home Affairs Committee prepared a report on the subject, and although it put forward no conclusion, much of the evidence showed that the compatibility of the rules with the Convention was, at best, dubious.[218] The Government admitted, as it was bound to, that there were differences of treatment on the grounds of sex, but claimed that there were arguments which could be used against an application under the Convention.[219] It was also argued that the rules were radically discriminatory in that they were designed to keep out immigrants from the Indian sub-continent in particular, while not excluding citizens from the old Commonwealth. In pressing ahead with its proposals the Government was clearly prepared to risk an adverse adjudication under the European Convention in order to redeem its election pledge and respond to pressure for stricter immigration control from some of its supporters.[220]

However, the Court decided unanimously that there had been a breach of Article 14 taken together with Article 8 on the grounds of sexual discrimination. The British Government's case was that the discrimination was justifiable under Article 8(2) as 'necessary in a democratic society' in the interests of 'economic well-being of the country', 'for the prevention of disorder' and 'for the protection of the rights and freedoms of others'. The arguments were those which are by now familiar in immigration debates. At a time of high unemployment it was necessary to control immigration to protect the job market. Women, tending not to be as economically active as men, had less of an impact on the job market. Strict immigration controls promoted public tranquillity and were for the benefit of immigrant communities since they promoted harmonious relations between different communities living in the UK.

While the Court accepted that the protection of the job market was the

[216] HC 238–41 (1976–7).

[217] HC 394 (1979–80).

[218] Loc. cit. above (n. 212).

[219] HC Debs., vol. 980, cols. 1029–30: 10 March 1980.

[220] The election manifesto declared: 'We shall end the concession introduced by the Labour Government in 1974 to husbands and male fiancés'.

aim of the rules, it was not convinced by the British Government's evidence in support of its case. In any event, it held that sexual equality was so important that 'very weighty reasons' were required to justify any discrimination. The British Government had not shown that the impact of male immigration on the job market was sufficient to justify the difference in treatment between the sexes. Similarly, it did not accept that public tranquillity was advanced by the discriminatory rules.

After the case had reached the Commission, but before it had come before the Court, changes had taken place in the Immigration Rules following the entry into force of the British Nationality Act 1981.[221] These were consequent upon the abolition of the concept of patriality and the creation of new categories of citizenship. The purpose of these rules was to make British citizenship coterminous with the right to enter and remain in the UK free from immigration controls (the 'right of abode'). The rules on fiancées and wives remained the same, i.e. they might enter provided that the husband was settled in the UK. The discrimination against the admission and settlement of husbands and fiancés remained. In one respect, however, inequality of treatment had been diminished, for male applicants could be admitted for settlement if the wife or fiancée was a British citizen, regardless of whether she or one of her parents had been born in the UK. This only resolved the case of Mrs Balkandali, who alone of the three applicants was a British citizen. Even this change was the cause of substantial opposition from the Government's own backbenchers, and it was only with the support of the Opposition that these rules were approved by the House of Commons. The rules on sham marriages remained, although now the onus was on the husband to show that the marriage was within the rules.

The Government's response to the judgment was not difficult to forecast. Judgment was given on 28 May 1985. In August 1985 the Government amended the Immigration Rules[222] by removing the privileges of wives and fiancées of men settled in the United Kingdom, thus assimilating their status to that of husbands and fiancés of women who, like the applicants in *Abdulaziz*, were settled in the United Kingdom. From the Government's viewpoint this removed the discretion, while not undermining the Government's immigration policy nor further alienating its own supporters.

However, while this amendment dealt with the law as it applied to persons in the position of the applicants in *Abdulaziz*, it fell short of full compliance with the clear principle of non-discrimination enunciated by the Court, since it did not remove all discrimination as to the admission of spouses of persons settled in the United Kingdom. First, an anomaly remained in relation to Commonwealth citizens settled in the United Kingdom at the time that the Immigration Act 1971 had come into force on 1

[221] HC 169 (1982–3).

[222] HC 503 (1984–5), amending HC 169 (1982–3). Now consolidated with further amendments in HC 388 (1988–9).

January 1971. Section 1(5) of that Act had preserved the pre-existing freedom from immigration controls of the wives and children of such Commonwealth citizens[223] and provided that this could not be restricted by the Immigration Rules. Thus primary legislation was required to remove this element of sex discrimination. This was not achieved until the repeal of section 1(5) by the Immigration Act 1988, some three years after the decision of the European Court.[224]

Secondly, some discrimination on grounds of sex still remained under the Immigration Rules. Whereas the wives of men admitted as students or for business purposes were to be given leave to enter, the husbands of women admitted for such purposes were not entitled to enter.[225] It seems difficult to argue that this could be justified after the decision in *Abdulaziz*, since it seems implausible that discrimination which was not 'necessary in a democratic society' with regard to persons settled in the United Kingdom could be justified as regards these other persons entering the United Kingdom. In 1989 the Immigration Rules were amended to remove the discrimination between husbands and wives of persons entering for business or employment purposes, allowing both to enter on the same conditions.[226] However, the discrimination remains for students.[227] It therefore appears that the United Kingdom was tardy in its general compliance with the Convention and at the present time remains in breach of Article 8, taken together with Article 14, as regards students.

IX Guernsey's Housing Laws

A further case involving breach of Article 8 by the United Kingdom concerned Guernsey's housing laws. A British couple, Mr and Mrs Gillow, moved to Guernsey in 1956, bought a plot of land and built themselves a house. Between 1960 and 1978 they lived and worked outside Guernsey and the house was let. In 1979 Mr Gillow retired, and he and his wife sought to reoccupy their house with the intention of spending their retirement there. To reoccupy their house, the Gillows were required by the Guernsey housing laws to obtain a licence. Their application for such a licence was, however, rejected by the Guernsey Housing Authority. As a result the Gillows were forced to sell their house.

The Gillows alleged that their treatment by the Guernsey authorities breached various articles of the Convention, of which only Article 8 is relevant here, as no breach of the other articles was found. The case eventually came before the Court, which gave judgment on 24 November

[223] Under the Commonwealth Immigrants Act 1962, s. 2.
[224] S. 1, which was brought into force on 1 August 1988 by SI 1988, No. 1133.
[225] HC 169 (1982–3), paras. 25 and 40.
[226] HC 388 (1988–9), para. 46, effective from 8 July 1989.
[227] Ibid., para. 31.

1986.[228] The Court held, first of all, that there had been an interference with the Gillows' 'right to respect for [their] . . . home' contrary to paragraph 1 of Article 8. The next question was whether this interference was justified by paragraph 2 of the article. The Court found that the licensing system laid down by the Guernsey housing laws was so justified because the system was 'necessary in a democratic society' for the 'economic well-being' of Guernsey. However, the way in which the licensing system had been applied in the case of the Gillows did not meet the Convention's requirements of being 'necessary in a democratic society': the Housing Authority had given insufficient weight to the Gillows' particular circumstances, seen against a background of a marginally declining population on Guernsey and adequate housing stock. There was therefore a breach of Article 8 as far as the application of the housing laws to the Gillows was concerned.

Turning to the question of compliance with the Court's judgment, it is clear that no legislative changes were needed, as the Court had specifically ruled that Guernsey's housing laws were not contrary to the Convention. What would seem to have been required for compliance was the grant of a licence to the Gillows and/or the payment of compensation. In practice the former would appear not to have been a realistic option because, as mentioned, the Gillows had already sold their house. As regards the latter, the Court, in proceedings under Article 50 of the Convention, awarded the Gillows £10,000 as compensation for the 'moral damage' they had suffered.[229] Given that this compensation has been paid,[230] the Court's judgment on the merits in *Gillow* would appear to have been fully complied with.

X. Contempt of Court

In the case of the *Sunday Times* v. *UK*[231] it was claimed that an injunction restraining the publication of an article infringed the right to freedom of expression guaranteed by Article 10. The article was part of a campaign conducted by the *Sunday Times* to obtain a more favourable settlement for children born physically handicapped as a result of their mothers having taken the drug thalidomide during pregnancy. The avowed purpose of the campaign was to pressurize the drug's manufacturer, Distillers, into a more favourable offer, and the article in question marshalled the evidence with a view to demonstrating that there were strong grounds for supposing that Distillers had been legally negligent. The Attorney-General obtained an injunction in the Divisional Court on the grounds that its publication would be a contempt of court. This was overturned in the Court of

[228] *Gillow* v. *UK*, Series A, No. 109 (1986).
[229] Series A, No. 124 (1987).
[230] HC Debs., vol. 132, Written Answers, col. *532*: 5 May 1988.
[231] Series A, No. 30 (1979); *EHRR*, vol. 2, p. 245. For a fuller analysis of the judgment see Rosen, *The Sunday Times Thalidomide Case: Contempt of Court and the Freedom of the Press* (1979).

Appeal,[232] but the injunction was restored by the House of Lords.[233] In upholding unanimously the grant of an injunction, the Law Lords were not unanimous in their reasons.[234] There were two basic approaches, the 'prejudgment principle' and the 'pressure principle'.

Only Lord Simon unequivocally applied the pressure principle. In his view, any attempt to pressurize a litigant not to seek to resolve a dispute through due process of law was a contempt, since it undermined society's established procedures for the resolution of disputes. Lords Cross and Reid, while accepting that public pressure might amount to contempt, rejected the breadth of Lord Simon's pressure principle. For them the pressure principle did not apply to public criticism of a litigant which was fair, accurate and temperate, and the *Sunday Times* article satisfied these criteria. However, in their view, any publication which prejudged the outcome of legal proceedings was unacceptable because it encouraged the public rehearsal of the merits of a case, usurping the proper role of the courts and undermining public confidence in the established machinery of justice for the adjudication of the merits of disputes. The remaining two Law Lords, Lords Diplock and Morris, tended to blur the distinction between the two principles.

The House of Lords gave judgment on 18 July 1973. The *Sunday Times* complained to the Commission that there had been a breach of Article 10, protecting freedom of expression, that there had been discrimination contrary to Article 14 in not taking contempt proceedings against other newspapers in respect of similar publications, and that there had been a breach of Article 18.[235] The case eventually came before the Court, which delivered its judgment on 26 April 1979.[236]

The Court agreed that there had been no breach of Article 14 and did not consider the question of Article 18. However, it held by a narrow majority of 11 to 9 that there had been a breach of Article 10. There was of course no doubt that there had been a restriction on freedom of expression, and it was its justification which was at issue. Article 10 provides that the right to freedom of expression may be subject to restrictions provided that they are 'prescribed by law and are necessary in a democratic society' for, *inter alia*, 'maintaining the authority and impartiality of the judiciary'.

The Court held that the principles of contempt as applied by the House of Lords were sufficiently certain and foreseeable to satisfy the requirement that they be 'prescribed by law'. It further held that the aims of the law of contempt as enunciated by each of the Law Lords were concerned with maintaining the authority of the judiciary, and were thus, in general principle, within the restrictions allowed by Article 10. However, the particular

[232] *Attorney-General* v. *Times Newspapers*, [1973] QB 710.

[233] [1974] AC 273.

[234] For more detailed analysis of the case see Miller, *Criminal Law Review*, 1975, p. 132.

[235] Article 18 provides that restrictions which the Convention permits to be placed on rights and freedoms 'shall not be applied for any purposes other than those for which they have been prescribed'.

[236] Loc. cit. above (n. 231).

application of the principles of contempt to the *Sunday Times* article was not 'necessary in a democratic society'. In so deciding, the Court applied the tests earlier enunciated in the *Handyside* case, considering whether the interference corresponded to a 'pressing social need', whether it was 'proportionate to the legitimate aim pursued', and whether the reasons given by the national authorities to justify it were 'relevant and sufficient' under Article 10(2).[237]

It was a feature of both approaches in the House of Lords that they precluded the balancing of freedom of expression against the protection of the administration of justice in the individual case. This was partly because their Lordships were concerned with the cumulative effect of conduct like that of the *Sunday Times* on the administration of justice generally, rather than the effect of that conduct taken in isolation. The European Court held that in order to determine whether there was a pressing social need for any interference with freedom of expression, the individual circumstances of each case had to be considered. Article 10 protected the right of the public, and in this case the right of the families of the victims of thalidomide in particular, to be informed. Since the information in the article was important to the families, the terms of the article were moderate, and since the case had been in a 'legal cocoon' for several years with no prospect of an imminent trial, the injunction was not necessary to maintain the authority of the judiciary.

The British Government's response to the judgment was contained in the Contempt of Court Act 1981, given its first reading in the House of Lords in December 1980, the provisions of which came into force two years and four months after the Court's judgment. Most of the Act does not bear directly upon the *Sunday Times* case, but implements proposals resulting from a broader review of the law of contempt. The delay between the European Court's judgment and the enactment of the 1981 Act is readily explicable. Although much of the groundwork for the more general reform of the law of contempt had already been done,[238] the date of the judgment fell during a general election campaign in the United Kingdom. That election was won by the Conservative Party, which had been out of government for five years and thus had a busy legislative programme in which a reform of the law of contempt could not have been regarded as having priority.

The Government's view was that all that was necessary to ensure compliance with the European judgment was the abolition of the prejudgment principle. This was to be effected by giving a statutory definition of the principle according to which a person might be held liable for non-intentional contempt (referred to in the Act as the 'strict liability rule'). This is defined in section 2(1) as the rule 'whereby conduct may be treated as a contempt of court as tending to interfere with the course of justice in

[237] Series A, No. 24 (1976), paras. 48–50; *EHRR*, vol. 1, p. 737.

[238] *Report of the Committee on Contempt of Court* ('The Phillimore Committee Report'), Cmnd. 5794 (1974).

particular legal proceedings regardless of intent to do so'. By section 2(2) conduct is only punishable under the rule if 'it creates a substantial risk that the course of justice in the proceedings will be seriously impeded or prejudiced'. Thus in each case the court must weigh up the impact of any publication upon the particular proceedings and may not treat a prejudgment as contempt *per se*. It is arguable that the formulation of this test does not satisfy the requirements of the *Sunday Times* judgment, since the strict liability rule does not even mention freedom of expression, far less give it the pre-eminence required by the Court's judgment. Against this it may be argued that, since the strict liability test does require that there should be a '*substantial* risk that the course of justice . . . will be *seriously* impeded or prejudiced', interference with freedom of expression is limited to those cases where there is a 'pressing social need' and such interference is proportionate to the aim of protecting the administration of justice. Much may depend upon the approach of the Attorney-General in bringing contempt proceedings and the judges in applying the law to the particular facts,[239] but it seems likely that the evaluation of the substantial risk of serious interference with the course of justice is likely to fall within the margin of appreciation allowed to States under the Convention.

At a more fundamental level it has been suggested that the strict liability rule defined in section 2(1) leaves the prejudgment principle as applied in the *Sunday Times* case untouched.[240] The House of Lords was concerned with the cumulative effect of the prejudgment of particular proceedings when taken together with other prejudgments of other proceedings to undermine the administration of justice generally, and of this the Act says nothing. This is not a far-fetched interpretation, and it appears to have some judicial support.[241] However, there is no reported case in which this form of the prejudgment test has been revived and such an interpretation would represent a significant distortion of the intended effect of the Act.

On the assumption that the prejudgment test has been effectively abolished, this is enough to ensure minimum compliance with the decision of the European Court. Furthermore, two other provisions of the Act make it less likely that there will be a repetition of the *Sunday Times* case in the English courts. First, the strict liability rule now only applies when proceedings are 'active', and in civil proceedings this will normally mean the time when the case is set down for trial,[242] a stage which had not been

[239] Since the *Sunday Times* case there seem to have been no reported cases where the strict liability rule has been applied to prevent or punish the publication of material affecting civil proceedings. Furthermore, on a number of occasions judges have stressed the importance of both the terms 'substantial' and 'seriously' in section 2(2). See, e.g., *Attorney-General* v. *BBC*, [1981] AC 303 at 362, where Lord Scarman specifically equated the provisions of the Act and the Convention requirement of 'pressing social need'; *Attorney-General* v. *News Group Newspapers Ltd.*, [1987] QB 1; *Barnet* v. *Crozier*, [1987] 1 WLR 272.

[240] Tettenborn, 'The Contempt of Court Bill: Some Problems', *Solicitors Journal*, 125 (1981), p. 123.

[241] See the comments of Sir John Donaldson MR in *Attorney-General* v. *Newspaper Publishing plc*, [1988] Ch. 333, 374.

[242] S. 2(4) and Schedule 1, although this date may still be some time before the hearing.

reached in the proceedings against Distillers with which the *Sunday Times* case was concerned. Secondly, a publication which is part of a discussion 'in good faith of public affairs or other matters of general public interest is not to be treated as a contempt of court under the strict liability rule if the risk of prejudice to particular proceedings is merely incidental to the discussion'.[243] While this falls short of a defence of public interest, since it is not concerned with the discussion of proceedings, but rather with discussion which impinges upon proceedings, it does represent a recognition that freedom of public discussion may in some cases take priority over a risk of prejudice to 'active' proceedings.[244]

Despite these provisions it is still arguable that the British Government's response fails to recognize the wider implications of the *Sunday Times* judgment. The Government successfully resisted a proposal to enact a recommendation of the Phillimore Committee[245] to abolish the pressure principle unless the conduct amounted to 'intimidation or unlawful threats to person, property or reputation'.[246] However, given the uncertainty about the precise *ratio* of the House of Lords judgment,[247] this refusal to legislate specifically on the pressure principle suggests a less than whole-hearted acceptance of the European Court's judgment.

Intentional contempts also remain a potential problem. The Act preserves unchanged the common law relating to contempts intended to impede or prejudice the administration of justice.[248] In order to commit such a contempt it is only necessary to do a voluntary act in the knowledge that it is virtually certain that it will have a consequence which the courts characterize as an interference with the administration of justice.[249] There appears to be no room here for the defence that the importance of freedom of expression outweighs the maintenance and impartiality of the judiciary. Indeed, it is possible to see how the conduct of the *Sunday Times* could have been characterized as intentional, since it consisted of a voluntary act in the knowledge that it prejudged the issue.[250]

The criticism that the reform of the law fails to demonstrate a whole-hearted response to the spirit of the Court's judgment results from the failure to restate the law of contempt in a form which gives a specific priority to

[243] S. 5.

[244] Applied in *Attorney-General* v. *English*, [1983] AC 116.

[245] Loc. cit. above (n. 238), para. 62.

[246] HL Debs., vol. 416, cols. 194–302: 15 January 1981. See in particular the views quoted there of the Law Society and the Outer Circle Policy Unit, which took the view that legislation was needed to clarify the position on the pressure principle.

[247] Manifested, for example, by the fact that the Divisional Court discharged the injunction against the *Sunday Times* on the basis of the absence of continued pressure on Distillers, rather than on the basis that it no longer prejudged issues yet to be tried: *The Times*, 23 June 1976. See also the *dicta* of Lord Diplock in *Attorney-General* v. *English*, [1983] AC 116, at p. 143.

[248] S. 6(*c*).

[249] *Attorney-General* v. *Newspaper Publishing plc*, [1988] Ch. 333; *Attorney-General* v. *News Group Newspapers Ltd.*, [1989] QB 110; *Attorney-General* v. *Newspaper Publishing plc*, *The Times*, 28 February 1990.

[250] See Tettenborn, loc. cit. above (n. 240).

freedom of expression. Such an approach would have required a more radical restructuring of the long-established common law of contempt than the Government was prepared to countenance. Nevertheless, as a result, there are other areas of the law of criminal contempt which have been or are likely to be challenged under the Convention.[251]

XI The Closed Shop

In *Young, James and Webster*[252] the issue was the compatibility of the Labour Government's legislation on the closed shop with the right to freedom of association guaranteed by Article 11:

> Everyone has the right to freedom of peaceful assembly and to freedom of association with others, including the right to form and to join trade unions for the protection of his interests.

Young, James and Webster were employed by British Rail when the corporation concluded a closed shop agreement with the railway unions. Under the agreement every employee, future and existing alike, was required to join a union. None of the applicants was a trade union member and all refused to join for reasons ranging from objection in principle to compulsory membership to objections to the existing trade union movement and objections to a particular union. They were all dismissed on account of their refusal to join. They had no legal remedy against their dismissal because the agreement was within the provisions of the Trade Union and Labour Relations Act 1974. This provided that if a 'union membership agreement' existed, as in this case, dismissal for refusal to join a union was fair unless the refusal was based on a genuine religious objection to trade union membership.[253] The applicants argued that their dismissal was a breach of Article 11. The Court gave judgment in August 1981, ruling that the United Kingdom was in breach of Article 11.

The Court refused to go so far as to say that there was a symmetrical negative right not to belong to a trade union protected by Article 11, and refrained from any general review of the closed shop. However, the Court did hold that the particular factors present in the case before it meant that

[251] See on this Lowe, in Furmston *et al.*, op. cit. above (n. 75), pp. 344–5; *Harman* v. *UK* regarding the publication of documents, application declared admissible, *Decisions and Reports*, vol. 38, p. 53, resulting in friendly settlement; see further Miller, *Contempt of Court* (2nd edn., 1983), pp. 338–42. See also Criminal Justice Act 1988, s. 159, giving a right of appeal against a Crown Court decision to restrict reporting under the Contempt of Court Act, in the light of applications made to the European Commission: see HC Debs., vol. 135, col. 608: 16 June 1988. The applications ended in a friendly settlement: *Hodgson* v. *UK* (Application No. 11553/85) and *Channel Four Television Co. Ltd.* v. *UK* (Application No. 11658/85), *Information Sheet*, No. 23 (1989). However, it seems likely that this will not be enough to forestall further applications: see *The Independent*, 11 November 1989.

[252] Series A, No. 44 (1980); *EHRR*, vol. 4, p. 38. For an analysis of the implications of the Convention for the closed shop, see Dugdale and Rawlings, 'The Closed Shop and the European Convention on Human Rights' in Furmston *et al.*, op. cit. above (n. 75), p. 283.

[253] Schedule 1, para. 6(5).

the closed shop as it affected the applicants breached Article 11. First, the fact that the 1974 Act allowed the dismissal of existing employees meant that the form of compulsion, namely loss of livelihood, was particularly serious. Secondly, there was no free choice as to the trade union which the applicants could join. Thirdly, part of the purpose of Article 11 was the protection of freedom of thought, conscience, religion and expression, freedoms also protected by other articles of the Convention. Since the applicants had principled and political objections to joining a trade union or to a particular trade union it was contrary to Article 11 to bring to bear this kind of pressure to force them to associate contrary to their convictions.

The Court considered whether the restriction on the applicants' freedom was justified within the terms of Article 11(2) as being 'necessary in democratic society . . . for the protection of the rights of others'. In rejecting the argument it emphasized that 'necessity' must be interpreted strictly and is not synonymous with 'useful' or 'desirable'. Emphasizing the importance of tolerance in a democratic society, it concluded that the loss of employment of the applicants was not proportionate to the aims pursued by the closed shop agreement. Trade union membership was already high among British Rail employees, and it was a common feature of closed shop agreements to exclude from their operation existing non-union employees.

The applications to the Commission had been filed and declared admissible when the Labour Government was in power. By the time of the proceedings before the Commission in 1979, a Conservative Government had been elected with the avowed intention of reforming the closed shop legislation. Indeed, it is a matter of some interest as to why the proceedings continued rather than ending in a friendly settlement.[254] Before the European Court the British Government restricted the grounds of its argument to the question whether Article 11 was applicable and did not seek to justify the infringement under Article 11(2).[255] By the time the Commission had reported, the Government felt able to express confidence that its legislative proposals would satisfy the requirements of the Convention.[256] When the European Court gave judgment in August 1981 the relevant provisions of the Employment Act 1980 had already come into force.[257]

There is no basis for seeing this legislation as a response to the Court's decision. The change in government happened to coincide with the hearings in the case and the possibility of an adverse judgement can have had little effect on the Conservative Government's legislation. The new Act did not outlaw the closed shop, but it aimed to make it more difficult for the

[254] Rule 52 of the then Rules of the European Court provided that particulars relating to the attempt to reach a friendly settlement should not be published.

[255] Series B, No. 39, pp. 77 ff. In the House of Commons in the debate on the Second Reading of the Employment Bill (1982) Mr Waddington, Under-Secretary of State for Employment, stated that the desirability of a ruling on these matters was the reason for the Government arguing the case before the European Court: HC Debs., vol. 17, col. 818: 8 February 1982.

[256] HC Debs., vol. 987, col. 236: 26 June 1980.

[257] The relevant provisions were brought into force on 15 August 1980.

closed shop to be imposed upon unwilling employees, by requiring union membership agreements to be approved by a ballot of the relevant employees.[258] Of more relevance to the *Young, James and Webster* case, it broadened the class of persons entitled to opt out of a closed shop agreement.

The Act provided that the dismissal of an employee for not belonging to a union would be unfair if, prior to the implementation of the closed shop agreement, he was already one of the class of employees to which the agreement applied.[259] This would have been sufficient to comply strictly with the European Court's judgment, but the Act went further, by extending the protection of the law of unfair dismissal to any employee who objected 'on grounds of conscience or other deeply-held personal conviction to being a member of any trade union whatsoever or of a particular trade union'.[260] This met the argument that the imposition of the closed shop by threat of dismissal might have been in breach of the Convention by infringing freedoms of thought, conscience and expression.

The European Court had emphasized the seriousness of dismissal as the sanction for refusal to join a union, leaving open the question whether lesser coercive measures would be permissible. The Employment Act 1980 provided that existing employees and conscientious objectors afforded protection by the law of unfair dismissal under the Act also had the right not to have action short of dismissal taken against them to compel them to join a trade union.[261]

Subsequent legislation has further inhibited the operation of closed shops. First, the Employment Act 1982 strengthened the provisions on ballots approving union membership agreements,[262] and made it automatically unfair to dismiss an employee for not belonging to a trade union irrespective of the existence of a closed shop agreement, thus strengthening the right not to associate.[263] Furthermore, if an employee were dismissed for non-membership, the industrial tribunal to which he applied was empowered to make a special award to all victims of unfair dismissal.[264] One of the practices often to be found in industries covered by a closed shop was a provision that employees not belonging to a trade union should still pay the equivalent of the union membership fee, usually to some charity. The 1982 Act made it unfair to dismiss a person for failing to agree to such a

[258] S. 7(3), inserting s. 58(A) into the Employment Protection (Consolidation) Act 1978.

[259] S. 7(2), inserting s. 58(3B) and (3C), subsequently s. 58(3)–(6), into the 1978 Act. The qualifying period of employment normally necessary before an employee can avail himself of the unfair dismissal provisions does not apply in cases of dismissal relating to membership or non-membership of a trade union, nor does the exclusion of employees over retiring age (1978 Act, ss. 64 and 65).

[260] S. 7(2), inserting s. 58(3A) into the 1978 Act.

[261] S. 15(1), amending s. 23(1)(*c*) of the 1978 Act.

[262] S. 3, amending s. 58A of the 1978 Act.

[263] S. 3, amending s. 58 of the 1978 Act. A remedy was also provided if action was taken short of dismissal: s. 10, amending s. 23.

[264] S. 10, amending s. 23 of the 1978 Act.

requirement in the event of non-membership of a trade union.[265] A remedy was also granted to employees in respect of coercive action short of dismissal.[266]

The 1980 legislation alone was more than enough to bring the law of the United Kingdom into line with the narrow basis of the reasoning of the majority of the European Court, and resolved in favour of the individual employee some of the questions left unanswered by the Court. The law as it then stood might still have been held to have infringed a freedom not to associate, first in giving no protection to a person whose choice of union was circumscribed by a closed shop agreement, and secondly, by requiring him to give a reason for not joining, or ceasing to be a member of, a union.[267] However, the Employment Act 1988 removed such concerns by abolishing the provisions giving protection to closed shop agreements approved by ballot, and thus making any dismissal for failing to be a union member unfair.[268] Furthermore, it removed the immunity of trades unions in tort in respect of industrial action to enforce a closed shop. The Employment Act 1990 is intended to abolish the last vestiges of the closed shop—the pre-entry closed shop—whereby membership of a trade union is made a condition of engagement by an employer.

After the Court's judgment the Employment Protection Act 1982[269] introduced, *inter alia*, a compensation scheme for employees whose dismissal in accordance with a union membership agreement had been fair under the provisions of the Trade Union and Labour Relations Act 1974, but whose dismissal would have been unfair under the provisions of the Employment Act 1980. At the time the question of compensation to Young, James and Webster had not been resolved, but there could be no obligation to pay compensation to those who had made no application to the Commission.[270] The Government did not present this measure as a response to the European Court's decision. Shortly afterwards the European Court awarded compensation to the applicants for pecuniary and non-pecuniary loss suffered as a result of their dismissal. These awards were substantially greater than the maximum compensation available under the British legislative scheme.[271].

In conclusion then, *Young, James and Webster* was a case where as a result of the change in the political colour of the Government of the United Kingdom, the European Court's decision did not conflict with the Conservative Government's policy. Indeed, apart from the compensation paid

[265] S. 3, adding s. 58(13) to the 1978 Act. A remedy was also provided in respect of coercive action to compel membership short of dismissal (s. 10).

[266] S. 5, adding s. 75A to the Act of 1978.

[267] See the concurring opinion of eight of the majority in *Young, James and Webster*.

[268] Ss. 10 and 11.

[269] S. 2 and Sch. 1.

[270] In most, if not all cases, time would have run out under Article 26. Following the Court's judgment, a friendly settlement was reached in *Reid*, Application 9520/81.

[271] The totals excluding the award for costs were £45,215, £17,626, and £8,076. Under the legislative scheme the award was calculated on the basis of the basic award for unfair dismissal plus interest, which in 1982 was £7,500.

to the three complainants, and perhaps the introduction of the retrospective statutory compensation scheme, the employment legislation would have been enacted in the same form, even had there been no attempt to seek redress under the Convention.

XII. Article 13

Article 13 of the Convention provides as follows:

Everyone whose rights and freedoms as set forth in this Convention are violated shall have an effective remedy before a national authority notwithstanding that the violation has been committed by persons acting in an official capacity.

This article is one of the more obscurely drafted provisions of the Convention and the views of the Convention organs as to its meaning have varied significantly since the Convention was adopted.[272] Before 1978 the Commission, where it was seised of a complaint alleging violation of Article 13 because the applicant had no effective remedy in domestic law for an alleged violation of one of the Convention's rights, generally took the approach of asking whether the Convention right in question had in fact been violated. If it had, a violation of the Convention had been established without its being necessary to consider Article 13. If the Convention right had been violated, then Article 13 did not apply. Under this approach Article 13 was largely tautologous; its only significance might be in providing a remedy at the domestic level after a breach of a Convention right had been found by the Convention organs.

A major change in approach came in the Court's judgment in the *Klass* case,[273] where the Court for the first time considered Article 13 in detail. The Court observed that it was not a prerequisite for the application of Article 13 that the Convention had in fact been violated. What Article 13 requires is that 'where an individual considers himself to have been prejudiced by a measure allegedly in breach of the Convention he should have a remedy before a national authority in order both to have his claim decided and, if appropriate, to obtain redress'.[274] The Court also said that the requirement in Article 13 for the remedy to be 'effective' would vary according to the circumstances, and added that a 'national authority' need not necessarily be a judicial authority in the strict sense. This view of Article 13 has been followed by both the Court and the Commission since the *Klass* case, although it has been made clear that Article 13 does not

[272] See Robertson, *Human Rights in Europe* (2nd edn., 1977), p. 107; Raymond, 'A Contribution to the Interpretation of Article 13 of the European Convention on Human Rights', *Human Rights Review*, 5 (1980), p. 161 at pp. 162–4; and Hampson, 'The Concept of an "Arguable Claim" under Article 13 of the European Convention on Human Rights', *International and Comparative Law Quarterly*, 39 (1990), p. 891 at pp. 892–3.

[273] Loc. cit. above (n. 196).

[274] Court's judgment, para. 64.

apply where the alleged violation stems from the primary legislation of the State concerned.[275]

A violation of Article 13 has been found in four cases involving the United Kingdom—*Silver*,[276] *Campbell and Fell*,[277] *Farrant*,[278] and *Abdulaziz, Cabales and Balkandali*.[279] In *Silver*, *Campbell and Fell* and *Farrant* the violations were virtually identical. In each case the applicants complained that Article 13 had been violated in that they had had no remedy to challenge the interference with their correspondence as being contrary to their rights under the Convention. There were four potential remedies open to the applicants: application to the Board of Prison Visitors; application to the Parliamentary Commissioner for Administration; a petition to the Home Secretary; and the institution of proceedings before the courts. The Court examined each of these and found that none of them amounted to 'an effective remedy before a national authority' as required by Article 13. The Board of Prison Visitors and the Parliamentary Commissioner for Administration were not 'effective' because they could not take binding decisions. The Home Secretary was not sufficiently independent (at least in this context) to satisfy the requirements of Article 13. Finally, as far as the courts were concerned, while they could consider the validity of the Prison Rules and orders made thereunder (which authorized the interference with correspondence complained of) under English law, they lacked the competence to decide whether the Rules were compatible with the Convention.

To comply with the Court's judgments in *Silver* and *Campbell and Fell* and the Committee of Ministers' decision in *Farrant*, it was not necessary to incorporate the Convention. In *Silver* the Court, confirming its earlier case law, said that Article 13 did not require incorporation of the Convention. It therefore followed that the application of Article 13 in a given case would depend on the way in which the State concerned had chosen to discharge its obligation under Article 1 directly to secure to everyone within its jurisdiction the rights set out in the Convention. In the light of this ruling, a number of ways to comply would seem possible. Either the roles of the Board of Prison Visitors and/or the Parliamentary Commissioner for Administration might be radically altered or, more realistically, the Prison Act 1952 (under which the Prison Rules are made) could be amended by adding a section incorporating Article 8 of the Convention either verbatim or in substance, which would then allow the courts to judge the compatibility of the rules with the Convention. In fact, the UK authorities have taken none of these steps. It would seem, from the information supplied by the UK Government to the Committee of Ministers when the latter was exer-

[275] *James et al.* v. *UK*, Series A, No. 98 (1986); *EHRR*, vol. 8, p. 123; *Lithgow et al.* v. *UK*, Series A, No. 102 (1986); *EHRR*, vol. 8, p. 328.

[276] Loc. cit. above (n. 100).

[277] Loc. cit. above (n. 91).

[278] Res. DH(87)3, and see n. 100, above.

[279] Loc. cit. above (n. 211).

cising its functions under Article 54 in respect of the Court's judgments in *Silver* and *Campbell and Fell*, that the Government appears to take the view that by terminating the violation of Article 8 by means of amendments to the Prison Rules and orders in 1981, it has thereby terminated the violation of Article 13. There is some support for the Government's view in a passage of the Court's judgment in *Silver*,[280] where the Court said that to the extent that the Prison Rules were contrary to the Convention, there could be no effective remedy as required by Article 13 and consequently there was a breach of Article 13. On the other hand, said the Court, to the extent that the rules were compatible, there were remedies in the shape, first, of the Home Secretary, who could ensure compliance with the rules, and, secondly, the courts, which could see if interference with correspondence was in conformity with the rules.

This passage of the Court's judgment harks back to the position before *Klass*, and is neither very satisfactory nor very logical. It makes compliance with Article 13 dependent on whether the substantive articles of the Convention have been complied with. This seems to contradict the approach in *Klass*, according to which Article 13 is an autonomous right, which requires that there must be a means whereby at the domestic level it can be ascertained whether an alleged breach of the Convention by the national authorities has occurred: it is irrelevant whether the allegation is substantiated or not. That this is the correct interpretation of Article 13 is supported by a passage from the Court's judgment in the later case of *Boyle and Rice* v. *United Kingdom*,[281] where the Court says:

> Notwithstanding the terms of Article 13 read literally, the existence of an actual breach of another provision of the Convention (a 'substantive' provision) is not a prerequisite for the application of the Article (see the Klass and Others judgment . . .). Article 13 guarantees the availability of a remedy at national level to enforce—and hence to allege non-compliance with—the substance of the Convention rights and freedoms in whatever form they may happen to be secured in the domestic legal order.[282]

On the reading of one passage in the *Silver* case, the United Kingdom has complied with the Court's judgment in relation to Article 13 in that case and in *Campbell and Fell*. On a broader reading of *Silver*, in the light of the approach of the Court exemplified in *Klass*, and reiterated in *Boyle and Rice*, the United Kingdom has not complied with the two judgments of the Court. This inconclusive and unsatisfactory situation reflects the problematic nature of Article 13 and its varying treatment by the Convention organs.

The other case involving the United Kingdom where a violation of Article 13 has been found is *Abdulaziz, Cabales and Balkandali* (hereafter

280 Paragraph 118 of the Court's judgment.
281 Series A, No. 131 (1988).
282 Paragraph 52 of the Court's judgment.

referred to simply as *Abdulaziz*). In this case the three applicants argued that Article 13 had been violated in that they had been unable to challenge the compatibility of the Immigration Rules with the Convention at the domestic level. The Court agreed with this submission. In rather tortuous language, which deserves quotation at length, it said:

> The Court has found that the discrimination on the ground of sex of which [the applicants] were victims was the result of norms that were in this respect incompatible with the Convention. In this regard, since the United Kingdom has not incorporated the Convention into its domestic law, there could be no 'effective remedy' as required by Article 13. Recourse to the available channels of complaint (the immigration appeals system, representations to the Home Secretary, application for judicial review) could have been effective only if the complainant alleged that the discrimination resulted from a misapplication of the 1980 Rules. Yet no such allegation was made nor was it suggested that discrimination in any other way contravened domestic law. The Court accordingly concludes that there has been a violation of Article 13.[283]

The reasoning in this passage was criticized by Judge Bernhardt in a separate opinion (with which Judges Gersing and Pettiti concurred). The effect of the Court's judgment was that Article 13 was always and automatically violated if (1) the Convention had not been incorporated in the law of the State concerned and (2) one of the substantive rights of the Convention had been violated. This, said Judge Bernhardt, was contrary to the object and purpose of Article 13. What the article required was that whenever a person complains that the Convention has been violated, some remedy should be available. This view, which was also taken by the Commission in its opinion in the case, accords with what was suggested earlier, on the basis of *Klass* and *Boyle and Rice*, is the correct interpretation of Article 13.

When asked in the House of Commons how the Government intended to comply with the Court's judgment as far as the breach of Article 13 was concerned, the junior Home Office minister, Mr Waddington, replied:

> The decision in the present case means no more than that, as there was a breach of [a] substantive provision, there was also a breach of Article 13 because we had not incorporated. If there had not been a breach of a substantive provision, there would not have been a breach of Article 13. When we remedy the breach of the substantive article, we shall no longer be in breach of Article 13.[284]

Earlier he had said: 'We do not accept that lack of incorporation puts us in automatic and continuing breach of the Convention'.[285]

There is some support for the Government's view in the tortuous language of the Court's judgment and the gloss put on it by Judge Bernhardt. On the other hand it appears that the Court was also suggesting that compliance with its judgment required the Convention to be incorporated. There may be some doubt as to whether the Court really meant this,

283 Paragraph 93 of the Court's judgment (references omitted).
284 HC Debs., vol. 83, col. 954: 23 July 1985.
285 Ibid.

because in earlier cases it has made it very clear that Article 13 does not require the Convention to be incorporated.[286] If the Court had intended to depart from its earlier case law, one would have expected it to say so more clearly. As with the prisoners' correspondence cases, no very firm conclusion can be reached as to whether the United Kingdom has complied with the Court's judgment in *Abdulaziz*.

XIII. Conclusions

The United Kingdom's record of compliance with the judgments and decisions of the Court and the Committee of Ministers finding it to have violated the Convention has been mixed. In a considerable number of cases there seems little doubt, even when bearing in mind the difficulties involved in ascertaining compliance (referred to in the introduction), that the United Kingdom has complied. These cases include: *Campbell and Cosans* (though compliance was not the result of Government action); *Ireland* v. *UK* (though effective compliance was delayed and was the result of further political pressure, especially from Amnesty International); *McVeigh et al.* (though compliance was fortuitous because of an earlier backbench amendment to the Criminal Law Act 1977); *Orchin*; *X* and the other mental health cases; most aspects of the prisoners' cases, although reform of the law has been piecemeal and in some cases delayed, or the result of further application under the Convention, and then there is doubt whether there is full compliance in relation to prisoners' correspondence and legal representation in disciplinary proceedings (furthermore, reform has been slower in Northern Ireland and Scotland); *Dudgeon* (though there has been no reform yet of the law relating to homosexuality in the Isle of Man and Jersey, which is in breach of the Convention); *Abdulaziz et al.* (though compliance was narrow and in some respects delayed, and it is probable that, as regards students, the Immigration Rules are still in breach of Article 8 taken together with Article 14); *Gillow*; and *Young, James and Webster*. In most of these cases, the most notable exception being *Campbell and Cosans*, compliance was achieved in a reasonably speedy time.

The cases where it has been doubtful that there has been proper compliance or where there clearly has been no compliance are *Tyrer*; *Malone*; *The Sunday Times*; and the Article 13 cases. The explanation for non-compliance in *Tyrer*, and the failure to secure homosexual law reform in the Isle of Man following *Dudgeon*, can possibly be explained by the British Government's desire not to offend Manx sensibilities. In the other cases a general reason for defective compliance seems to be because successive United Kingdom Governments have been reluctant to face the possibility that their obligations under the European Convention may sometimes

[286] *Swedish Engine Drivers' Union* v. *Sweden*, Series A, No. 20 (1976); *EHRR*, vol. 1, p. 617; and cf. the discussion on the *Silver* case, above.

require something more drastic than a minor readjustment or reform. The response to *Malone* has been inadequate because the Government has been reluctant to face the challenge to its habits of thought and preferred way of governing, especially where national security may be involved. In the face of the *Sunday Times* case, there was no sign of any attempt to review the reform of the law of contempt against the touchstone of the European Convention, with the result that the extent of compliance remains uncertain. A similar explanation may be offered for some of the cases where compliance has been piecemeal and half-hearted or unnecessarily delayed. The laborious process of reforming some aspects of the prison system could have been avoided if it had been recognized that the thinking behind the early decisions was simply incompatible with the traditional way in which British prisons were being run. This reluctance continues with the compliance with *Weeks* only being achieved after *Thynne, Wilson and Gunnell*. After the case brought by the Irish Government about the ill-treatment of detainees, the action taken fell short of a recognition that changes in interrogation practices were required rather than the profession of a change of heart. The response to the Article 13 cases is probably because a full-hearted compliance could hardly be achieved without incorporation of the Convention into United Kingdom law—something to which the present Government remains opposed.

This paper also demonstrates some of the problems involved in carrying out a study of compliance with judgments of the Court and decisions of the Committee of Ministers. Considerable knowledge in detail of the relevant law is necessary, a matter complicated in the United Kingdom by the existence of three separate legal systems. The relevant law is not always very accessible (e.g. in relation to prisoners), nor is it always easy to ascertain how the law applies in practice (e.g. in relation to the treatment of detainees in Northern Ireland). A further complication, as explained at the beginning of this article, is that it is not always easy to see what the Court's judgment requires in the way of compliance, especially where a case based on the individual circumstances of the applicant may have wider implications (e.g. *Tyrer*, cf. *Zamir*), or where a case is decided on narrow grounds but patently could have involved broader considerations (e.g. *Malone*). For these reasons there may not infrequently be room for genuine differences of view as to whether a judgment of the Court has been complied with.

DIPLOMATIC RELATIONS AND CONTACTS*

By ALAN JAMES‡

'Diplomatic relations' may be presumed to have a specialized meaning and to refer to a matter of some importance. The Vienna Convention of 1961 is 'on Diplomatic Relations', and States commonly speak of the establishment of diplomatic relations, of their existence, and not all that infrequently of their breach. It might therefore be supposed that the meaning of the phrase is explained in relevant documentation and writing, and that the significance of the condition of being in diplomatic relations is explored in analyses of diplomacy.

No so! The Vienna Convention's Preamble makes no mention of the stated subject-matter of the instrument, and while its first article defines nine phrases which are used in the Convention, 'diplomatic relations' does not figure among them. Only in two articles is the phrase used. Article 2 says that 'The establishment of diplomatic relations between States, and of permanent diplomatic missions, takes place by consent'—suggesting that there is a distinction between the two matters. And Article 45 speaks of certain consequences 'If diplomatic relations are broken off between two States, or if a mission is permanently or temporarily recalled . . . '—again pointing to the same distinction. But while the Convention has a lot to say about diplomatic missions, it gives no further hint—indeed, one might say no specific hint at all—as to what might be meant by diplomatic relations. Moreover, it appears from Denza's *Commentary*[1] on the Convention that this matter was not discussed during its preparation and negotiation.[2]

* © Professor Alan James, 1992.

‡ Research Professor of International Relations, University of Keele. This article is based on a paper prepared for a meeting of the International Studies Association (International Law Section) held at Vancouver, Canada, in March 1991. The writer is indebted to Ambassador Fred Hadsel and Mr Colin Warbrick for having read it in draft and suggesting a number of improvements; to Ambassador David Newsom for his numerous and very helpful comments; to Mrs Eileen Denza, Counsel, European Communities Committee, House of Lords, for the same service; and, in particular, to assistance received from the staff of the Foreign and Commonwealth Office Legal Adviser.

In view of the current spate of developments regarding diplomatic relations, it should be noted that the information given is, to the writer's best knowledge, correct as at 31 August 1991.

[1] Eileen Denza, *Diplomatic Law. Commentary on the Vienna Convention on Diplomatic Relations* (Dobbs Ferry, NY: Oceana, 1976).

[2] Mr Richard Langhorne, of the Centre of International Studies at the University of Cambridge, has told the writer that the term 'diplomatic relations' was only used very late in the day to describe the contents of the 1961 Convention—indeed, only at the Vienna Conference itself and not in any of the preparatory meetings. He suspects it was introduced by the newer States. Previously, the phrase in use to describe the discussions which were in progress throughout much of the 1950s was 'diplomatic privileges and immunities', or, occasionally, 'diplomatic practice'. This goes a long way towards explaining why the substance of the concept of diplomatic relations finds virtually no reflection in the Convention.

If one turns to writers on diplomatic law, as represented by four well-known books on the subject, one finds that they are in this respect of singularly little help. Sen's chapter on 'Establishment and Conduct of Diplomatic Relations'[3] is wholly about diplomatic missions and agents. Nothing is said about a separate concept of diplomatic relations; indeed, and contrary to the Convention, Sen more or less equates diplomatic relations with diplomatic representation. Hardy's brief section on 'Establishment of Diplomatic Relations and of Diplomatic Missions'[4] does distinguish between the two matters, but gives no indication of the nature and significance of the former. The treatment of the subject in the current (Gore-Booth) edition of *Satow*—which is widely regarded as a, if not the, leading work on diplomacy—consists almost entirely of a short chapter on 'Breach of Diplomatic Relations'[5] and a few other illustrative references to the same issue. Dembinski's page and a half on 'Diplomatic and Consular Relations'[6] is simply a historical sketch of the law relating to diplomacy.

So far as writers on international relations are concerned, it would appear that the concept of diplomatic relations might as well not exist. Nicolson,[7] for example, appears not to mention it. Neither does Watson,[8] nor Barston.[9] This may have something to do with the view that 'diplomatic relations' has a formal and therefore a legal content, and to a widespread tendency on the part of the international relations fraternity to avoid, as Nicolson puts it, 'the marshes of international law'.[10] Be that as it may, one might have expected such scholars to have had something to say on the implications, for the relations of States, of the concept of diplomatic relations. Correspondingly, it may be that legal writers do not feel it within their brief to speculate on what they might deem to be political issues. But it is surely reasonable to look in their writings for some elaboration of the key phrase in the title of the most notable legal instrument on diplomacy.

One can imagine two responses to the last point. The first is that the concept of diplomatic relations is so well understood that there is no need to say anything specific about it. The second, which is not necessarily separate from the first, is that 'diplomatic relations' is a portmanteau phrase which encompasses all the matters which are dealt with in the Vienna Convention.

For the historical background to the Vienna Convention, see Richard Langhorne, 'The Regulation of Diplomatic Practice: the Beginnings to the Vienna Convention on Diplomatic Relations, 1961', *Review of International Studies*, 18 (1992), no. 1.

[3] B. Sen, *A Diplomat's Handbook of Diplomatic Law and Practice* (The Hague: Nijhoff, 2nd edn., 1979), pp. 15–45.

[4] Michael Hardy, *Modern Diplomatic Law* (Manchester University Press, 1968), pp. 13–15.

[5] Lord Gore-Booth, *Satow's Guide to Diplomatic Practice* (London: Longman, 5th edn., 1979) (hereafter referred to as *Satow*), pp. 187–91.

[6] Ludwik Dembinski, *The Modern Law of Diplomacy* (Dordrecht: Nijhoff and UNITAR, 1988), pp. 8–9.

[7] Sir Harold Nicolson, *Diplomacy* (London: Oxford University Press, 3rd edn., 1963).

[8] Adam Watson, *Diplomacy. The Dialogue between States* (London: Eyre Methuen, 1982).

[9] R. P. Barston, *Modern Diplomacy* (London: Longman, 1988).

[10] Nicolson, op. cit. above (n. 7), p. 15.

Neither, however, carries conviction. The Convention itself, notwithstanding its title, would appear to deny the second claim by distinguishing between diplomatic relations and other associated matters. And as one of the eminent legal writers referred to above fails to make one of these distinctions—that between diplomatic relations and diplomatic missions—there is some prima facie ground for supposing that the first response is also faulty. Furthermore, even if the concept of diplomatic relations is perfectly well understood by most international lawyers and diplomats, there would still be a case for explaining it to others who are interested in international relations.

In *Satow's* chapter on 'The Diplomatic Body (*corps diplomatique*)', the section on 'Communication in the absence of diplomatic relations' begins: 'Between the representatives of States, one of which does not accord the other diplomatic recognition, there can be no official communication; and calling is excluded'.[11] In this negative way, one is given the essential clue to the nature of diplomatic relations. What it connotes is a mutual willingness on the part of the two States concerned (for diplomatic relations refers to a bilateral situation) to engage in direct communication, the medium for such communication being their official representatives—or diplomats. When two States have this kind of relationship, there is no formal obstacle to their getting in touch with each other, to one expressing a view to the other about this or that, and to the two of them entering into bilateral legal agreements. As the *Encyclopedia of Public International Law* puts it, at the start of a two-page article on both the establishment and the severance of diplomatic relations, 'Diplomatic relations are the customary form of permanent contact between sovereign States'.[12]

If they are not in this relationship, it does not follow that they cannot communicate with each other. Outside the diplomatic realm, signalling may take place,[13] or officially unofficial meetings may occur. But even within the diplomatic context it is possible for States not in diplomatic relations to make contacts of various kinds. (In this article, 'contacts' is the term used to refer to the diplomatic links which may exist in the absence of diplomatic relations.) In these circumstances, however, the diplomatic process is neither straightforward nor unencumbered. And certain complications arise when the representatives of two States not in diplomatic relations come across each other in the capitals of third States or in multilateral gatherings.

In the rest of this article an attempt is made to outline the various forms

[11] *Satow*, op. cit. above (n. 5), p. 166.

[12] Horst Blomeyer-Bartenstein, 'Diplomatic Relations, Establishment and Severance', *Encyclopedia of Public International Law*, vol. 9: *International Relations and Legal Co-operation in General, Diplomacy and Consular Relations* (Amsterdam: North-Holland, under the auspices of the Max Planck Institute for Comparative Law, and under the general direction of Rudolf Bernhardt, 1986), p. 99.

[13] See, generally, Raymond Cohen, *Theatre of Power: The Art of Diplomatic Signalling* (London: Longman, 1987).

which diplomatic relations can take, and the ways in which States can retain diplomatic contact with those of their fellows with whom they are not in diplomatic relations.

To assist in distinguishing between the various ways in which States can make contact with each other, and the forms in which they can enjoy diplomatic relations, a chart has been drawn up (see p. 351). It is not suggested that it is exhaustive. Other 'stages' could be identified. All that has been attempted in this respect is to identify the main possibilities which exist for States. It must also be emphasized that the chart is not meant to imply that States do, or should, go through each of the named stages in the course of developing or diminishing their diplomatic relations and contacts. In practice some stages may be 'jumped', and others conflated.

Nor is it suggested that there is anything sacrosanct about the order in which the stages have been given. To assist in the presentation of the chart, the stages have been set out in ascending and descending 'ladders', and there is some empirical justification for so depicting them. But while there is a certain logic about the bottom and perhaps the top end of the chart, any two States may proceed in this matter entirely as they wish. It could be that political developments will result in the stages being adopted in a different order from that in which they have been depicted here. And of course there is no suggestion that in reality there is always a smooth directional progression up and down the ladders. Fluctuating political relations could well result in States shuttling about within and between each of the four main sections of the chart—that is to say, above and below the 'diplomatic relations line' on each of the two ladders.

For convenience, in the rest of this article each of the numbered stages will be considered separately, and in the order which has been imposed upon them.

1. Emergence of Sovereign State

On the scene which is generally characterized as 'international', more than one type of actor is to be found. Intergovernmental organizations, multinational corporations, sub-State entities and groups, and terrorist bodies all come easily to mind, quite apart from States. Moreover, the external delegations of the European Communities are now coming more and more to resemble embassies, albeit functioning in limited areas of substance. But 'diplomatic' relations, in the formal sense of that term, exist only between States. Thus, a spokesman of the British Government has said that 'We cannot establish diplomatic relations with Lithuania, which is not a sovereign independent State'—adding, for good measure, 'It was unlawfully incorporated into the Soviet Union in 1940'.[14]

[14] HC Debs., vol. 166, Written Answers, col. *697* : 7 February 1990. Eighteen months later, the United Kingdom, together with the other States of the European Community, recognized Lithuania, and also Latvia and Estonia, as independent sovereign States. This was a consequence not just of the dramatic events within the Soviet Union and the international reaction thereto, but also of the fact that the UK had never accorded *de jure* recognitition to the incorporation of the three Baltic States within the Soviet Union. It also appeared—the Foreign Secretary's reported statement was less than entirely clear—that the UK had at the same time established diplomatic relations with the three States. See *The Independent*, 28 August 1991.

Diplomatic Relations and Contacts: Schematic Depiction of Possible Stages in their Development and Diminution

8. Resident Ambassadorial Mission

7. Resident Mission at less than Ambassadorial Level

9. Temporary Withdrawal of Head of Mission

6. Special Missions

10. Downgrading of Level of Head of Mission

5. Non-Resident Mission

11. Withdrawal of Mission, temporary or permanent

4. Diplomatic Relations -- 12. Breach of Diplomatic Relations

13. Protecting Power/Interests Section

3. Consular Relations

14. Diplomatic Functions by Consular Officer

15. Intermittent Diplomatic Contacts, direct and indirect

2. Recognition

1. Emergence of Sovereign State

16. Absence of Diplomatic Contacts

It is a consequence of that situation that the Vienna Convention on Diplomatic Relations was made by and in its application is limited to States. This is the orthodox position—and is totally unrelated to the different, and analytical, issue of whether States are the pre-eminent international actors. (The evaluative issue of whether States should be the chief international actors is separate again from the two already-mentioned matters.)

Accordingly, the existence of a State is a logical pre-condition for the establishment of diplomatic relations. And by 'State' is meant the type of territorial entity which, in official international parlance, is termed 'sovereign'.[15] At this level, sovereignty connotes constitutional independence—the existence of a domestic constitution which is not a formal part of any wider constitutional arrangement.[16] Thus, Australia is a sovereign State, and as such is eligible to establish diplomatic relations with other such States. But the constituent Australian State of New South Wales is not sovereign (in the officially-accepted international sense), and therefore cannot establish the sort of relations which are termed diplomatic. It may establish offices abroad, as it has done, for example, in London. And it may be that, as there, the host State will as a matter of courtesy accord the office limited privileges and immunities. But such offices will not have the status of diplomatic missions, and will therefore not benefit from the provisions of the Vienna Convention on Diplomatic Relations.

2. Recognition

A further pre-condition for the establishment of diplomatic relations is recognition. Each of the parties to a diplomatic relationship must, in the formal sense in which the term is used in international law, 'recognize' the other as a State. Thus, on behalf of the British Government it has been stated that 'We have no plans to establish diplomatic relations with North Korea, which we do not recognize as a 'State'.[17] Additionally, to the extent to which States still practice the recognition of governments,[18] it is also necessary that the government of each State is recognized by the other, governments being the entities which act on behalf of States. In the absence

[15] There may, however, be exceptions to this generalization, for States may sometimes have good political reasons for identifying a different sort of entity as a State. A notable current example is the recognition by a number of States of the Palestine Liberation Organization as a State, and their establishment of diplomatic relations with it. A rather different type of anomaly consists of the maintenance of diplomatic relations with States under occupation, diplomats being accredited to their governments-in-exile. A number of such governments were to be found in London during the Second World War.

[16] See Alan James, *Sovereign Statehood. The Basis of International Society* (London: Allen and Unwin, 1986), Part One, pp. 13–95.

[17] HL Debs., vol. 525, Written Answers, col. *49*: 6 February 1991. The admission, in September 1991, of North Korea to the United Nations may, however, change this position.

[18] The United Kingdom gave up this practice in 1980. See HC Debs., vol. 983, Written Answers, cols. *277–9*: 25 April 1980; also HL Debs., vol. 408, cols. 1121–2: 28 April 1980. See also Colin Warbrick, 'The New British Policy on Recognition of Governments', *International and Comparative Law Quarterly*, 30 (1981), p. 568.

of recognition, there is an obstacle to direct communication. For example, at the Geneva Conference of 1954 on Indochina, 'the Canadian and Chinese delegations sat side by side, but, given the state of non-recognition between their governments, each delegation pretended the other didn't exist'.[19] However, this did not prevent China's Foreign Minister from paying a courtesy call on Canada's Minister of External Affairs shortly before the latter was due to leave Geneva.[20]

In distinguishing in this way between the existence of a sovereign State and its recognition, favour is being given to the 'declaratory' rather than the 'constitutive' school of thought regarding recognition. The recognition of a State indicates that the recognizing State formally acknowledges that the entity concerned possesses the characteristics of sovereign statehood, and hence exists as such, rather than helps to bring it into existence. Once that has been done, the recognizing State is logically able to have diplomatic dealings with the now-recognized State, including those which are summed up by the phrase 'diplomatic relations'. Logic, however, is no more the ruling faculty at the international than it is at any other political level. Accordingly, if interest points in that direction, a State which does not recognize another may none the less be willing to communicate with it. This perhaps suggests that some questions might be asked about the utility of recognition—provided it is assumed that the rights and duties of international law apply to all sovereign States without reference to the extent to which such States have been recognized.[21]

A different type of distinction which may be noted here is that between the recognition of an entity as a State and communication with the representatives of that entity. The United Kingdom, for example, has made use of this distinction in receiving the elected representatives of the Lithuanian people, emphasizing that they are not seen as the representatives of a sovereign State.[22] On a presumably-comparable basis, the United States has been reported as having agreed to establish a 'permanent presence' in the Estonian capital, Tallinn, the other side to this bargain being an Estonian undertaking not to 'embarrass the West with a demand for formal diplomatic recognition'.[23]

Implicit in the designation of recognition as a separate stage on the 'route'

[19] George Ignatieff, *The Making of a Peacemonger* (Markham, Ontario: Penguin Books, 1987), p. 193.

[20] See ibid., p. 194.

[21] However, while recognition may be of reduced utility in international relations, it has important domestic legal consequences. For a discussion of the legal problems which have arisen in the UK in consequence of the abandonment of the recognition of governments, see M. J. Dixon, 'Recent Developments in United Kingdom Practice Concerning the Recognition of States and Governments', *The International Lawyer*, 22 (1988), p. 555.

[22] This situation is to be distinguished from the extension of certain diplomatic courtesies, on a personal basis, to the surviving representatives in London of the Baltic States which were forcibly incorporated into the USSR in 1940. For a more general discussion of the representation of these States when they were constituent republics of the USSR, see *The New York Times*, 6 June 1989, Section B, p. 7.

[23] *The Independent*, 30 March 1991.

to diplomatic relations is the distinction between recognition and the establishment of such relations. However, it is probably unusual for a State to recognize another without subsequently establishing diplomatic relations with it. Indeed, it seems that in practice States sometimes combine these two matters, the immediate establishment of diplomatic relations with a new State carrying with it an implicit recognition of that State. This would be in accord with one of the two well-established ways in which States recognize others—impliedly (the other being expressly). Moreover, it appears, on a highly impressionistic basis, that nowadays the former process is the usual one. In this connection it is interesting to note *Satow's* use (quoted above) of the phrase 'diplomatic recognition'. It would therefore appear to be a distinct anomaly that the United Kingdom, although she recognizes the Kingdom of Bhutan, and 'maintains friendly contacts and conducts official business with its embassy in New Delhi', 'does not have diplomatic relations'[24] with that State. The conduct of official business in a friendly way would normally be regarded as indicative of the existence of diplomatic relations. Perhaps this unusual situation has something to do with India's sensitivity about her own rather special relationship with Bhutan.

But while, as a practical matter, there may often be little or no distinction on the 'up' diplomatic relations ladder between recognition and the establishment of diplomatic relations, in principle it seems clear that recognition is distinguishable from, and a prerequisite of, diplomatic relations—not least because recognition is a unilateral act, whereas diplomatic relations can only be established on a bilateral basis. (The phrase 'diplomatic recognition', notwithstanding its increasing use in the media, is therefore best avoided.) Moreover, on the 'down' ladder the distinction between recognition and diplomatic relations is a very real one. For a breach of diplomatic relations does not imply a withdrawal of recognition. Indeed, it is generally accepted that if the facts remain the same, recognition cannot be withdrawn.

3. Consular Relations

Formally speaking, consular relations are distinct from diplomatic relations.[25] Accordingly, two States may be in consular relations but not in diplomatic relations, and vice versa. In part this is a reflection of the historical fact that the functions of consuls were quite different from those of diplomats. The consul was 'an administrator and an observer', having 'no representative character'.[26] It is also the case that the general legal regimes

[24] HC Debs., vol. 152, Written Answers, col. *275*: 5 May 1989.

[25] See, generally, on this subject, Luke T. Lee, *Consular Law and Practice* (Oxford: Clarendon Press, 2nd edn., 1991).

[26] John R. Wood and Jean Serres, *Diplomatic Ceremonial and Protocol. Principles, Procedures, and Practices* (London: Macmillan, 1970), p. 64.

which apply to the two offices are different, a separate Convention on Consular Relations having been signed at Vienna in 1963. But there is, of course, no obstacle to the two States agreeing on a special regime for their consuls, as, for example, the United Kingdom and China have done.[27] In consequence, a consul may enjoy a legal position almost identical to that of a diplomat. Moreover, the functional distinction between the two offices has latterly become much less clear cut. Chiefly this manifests itself in some matters of a traditionally consular kind—those concerned with the advancement of commerce—now being performed by diplomatic missions. Furthermore, in capital cities it appears that bread-and-butter consular duties, such as the rendering of assistance to one's nationals and dealing with applications for visas, are nowadays almost always dealt with by the consular section of an embassy rather than by a separate consulate. In this connection it should be noted that in accordance with Article 70, paragraph 4, of the Vienna Convention on Consular Relations of 1963,[28] the members of a diplomatic mission assigned to an embassy's consular section receive the privileges and immunities which are accorded to diplomats rather than the lesser privileges of consuls.

On the other hand, in consequence of the heightened interplay between international and domestic politics, consular missions outside capital cities tend now to have some political responsibilities of a very general kind—mainly the task of reporting on local conditions. It is also possible that, in the absence of a diplomatic mission and of representation by a third State, a sending State's consular mission may, with the consent of the receiving State, be empowered to perform diplomatic acts[29]—principally those which relate to the transmission of official communications between the two States. This opens the way to the use of consular relations as a stage on the 'upward' diplomatic relations route. It is one which is likely to be utilized only when the States concerned have had poor relations but are cautiously anxious to improve them. As a move in the direction of the establishment or resumption of diplomatic relations, they may establish or resume consular relations (and entrust the consular missions with diplomatic functions). Such a development assumes the character of a testing of the diplomatic water, a symbol of the intention of the two States to increase the warmth of their relationship and to progress towards what in this context are likely to be called 'full' diplomatic relations.

A recent example of this device concerns Israel and the Soviet Union. The latter was one of the first States to recognize Israel following that State's proclamation in May 1948, and in the ensuing Arab-Israeli war gave her military assistance which was both massive and crucial.[30] However, the

[27] See C. A. Whomersley, 'The United Kingdom-China Consular Agreement', *International and Comparative Law Quarterly*, 34 (1985), p. 621.

[28] See *UK Treaty Series*, No. 14 (1973), Cmnd. 5219.

[29] This is provided for by Article 17(1) of the Vienna Convention on Consular Relations.

[30] See Amitzur Ilan, *Bernadotte in Palestine, 1948* (London: Macmillan, 1989), pp. 115 and 254.

Soviet Union broke off diplomatic relations during the Six Day War of 1967. Twenty-three years later, an agreement was reached to establish consular relations, the Israeli Consulate-General in Moscow being opened on 3 January 1991. At that time its head observed: 'We have a gentleman's agreement with the Soviet Union that we will meet at the diplomatic level in spite of the fact that we are just a consulate'.[31] In a further move towards the resumption of diplomatic relations, the Soviet Foreign Minister visited Israel in May 1991.[32]

This case also provides a reminder that there are stages within stages. It was as long ago as July 1987 that a low-level Soviet delegation went to Jerusalem for the stated purpose of overseeing property owned by the Russian Orthodox Church. In the following January the Soviet Union agreed to allow an Israeli consular delegation to visit Moscow—the first official Israeli visit to the Soviet capital since 1967. The delegation was, a Soviet spokesman said, to be 'small' and concerned with 'technical' matters.[33] Negotiations proceeded slowly. But in the weeks before the agreement on consular relations was reached, tentative agreements were announced on certain economic and scientific matters, and it was then agreed that air flights would be resumed between the two countries.[34]

In a rather similar way, China and Israel held talks (at the United Nations) during the late 1980s about a possible resumption of diplomatic relations. These resulted, in February 1990, in China setting up a 'liaison office in Israel under the guise of a travel agency'. And in June of that year Israel opened a liaison office of her Academy of Sciences and Humanities in Beijing. It was headed by a scientist, but his assistant 'worked previously for the Israeli Foreign Ministry'.[35] The device of a 'liaison office' as a move in the direction of orthodox relations, whether of a consular or of a diplomatic kind, was also used by Israel in connection with her attempt to regularize her relations with Lebanon. For the Peace Treaty between the two States of May 1983 provided for such offices in each other's capitals, and were 'viewed by most observers as embryonic embassies'.[36] However, Israel had gone too fast, and before long, under Syrian pressure, Lebanon had denounced the Treaty.

The need for caution in this sort of matter is well understood by China, one instance of her approach having just been given. Another is apparent in her gradually-developing relations with South Africa. For when it was revealed in May 1991 that she had sent a secret mission there to 'discuss trade and other links', a government spokesman in Beijing responded by admitting only that 'non-governmental exchanges'[37] had begun. One other

[31] See *The Independent*, 1 October 1990 and 4 January 1991.
[32] See *The Independent*, 11 May 1991.
[33] *The Times*, 20 January 1988.
[34] *The Independent*, 1 October 1990.
[35] *The Independent*, 16 June 1990.
[36] Larry Pintak, *Beirut Outtakes* (Lexington, Mass.: Lexington Books, 1988) p. 106.
[37] *The Independent*, 30 and 31 May 1991.

example of this sort of procedure concerns Hungary and South Africa. In January 1990 talks were held in Budapest between the foreign ministers of the two States about the possibility of formalizing their trade relations. This was said to be the beginning of 'a gradual process of establishing official diplomatic relations'.[38]

It should be noted here that one aspect of the historical evolution of the (former British) Commonwealth was that its sovereign members did not use, among themselves, the device of consular relations. But the need remained for the execution of what elsewhere would be called consular functions. Accordingly, deputy high commissions (a high commission being the Commonwealth equivalent of an embassy) were established outside capital cities for this purpose. About two decades ago, however, a number of the older Commonwealth States said that they would like, in this respect, to adopt the more usual terminology, and its associated arrangements. In consequence, a number of deputy high commissions disappeared, to be replaced by consulates. However, United Kingdom deputy high commissions are still to be found in, for example, India and Nigeria. And in such Commonwealth States as adhere to the old practice, those persons who elsewhere would be known as honorary consuls are called honorary British representatives.

4. Diplomatic Relations

The condition of being in diplomatic relations may be referred to as the 'normal' bilateral relationship. The pair of States concerned may engage directly in any kind of peaceful official contact, and may do so without first having to make a special check as to the acceptability of such a contact or a special arrangement for its transmission. The two States can freely relate to each other, and do so through their diplomats. For this purpose, 'diplomats' include not just all those who have been officially accredited by a State to represent the State abroad, but also political office-holders at such times as they are engaged on inter-State activity. The latter may on such occasions be termed (or at least conceived as) '*ad hoc* diplomats'; the phrase 'temporary diplomats' may be used to categorize those who are seconded or recruited from a domestic department or position to serve abroad in a diplomatic capacity; while members of the diplomatic service, on service abroad, may simply be called diplomats—with the British-favoured term 'diplomatist' being reserved for the professional description of career members of a foreign ministry.

The establishment of diplomatic relations is, unlike recognition, a bilateral act. Thus a spokesman of the British Government has said, in respect of Albania, that 'we renewed on 20 April [1990] our 1980 offer to establish

[38] *The Star* (Johannesburg), 5 January 1990.

diplomatic relations without pre-conditions'.[39] (An agreement, in principle, to restore relations was announced in May 1991.)[40] Communications regarding this matter may be made through the good offices of a third party, but it appears more usual for the two States concerned to engage in direct diplomatic contacts. Here, on at least one occasion, there has been scope for some confusion. Following the United Kingdom's recognition of the new (Communist) Government of China in 1950, some of the diplomats who had been in the Embassy in Nanking, under an ambassador accredited to the Nationalist Government, were transferred to Beijing (then known as Peking), to form the nucleus of what the United Kingdom conceived as a diplomatic mission. But China insisted that the establishment of diplomatic relations could only follow the settlement of a number of issues in dispute between the two countries, and insisted on calling the mission a 'negotiating mission'. (Rather contradictorily, however, the mission was included in China's diplomatic list, albeit as a separate category, and its members were treated as diplomats.) Owing to the intervention of the Korean War it was not until 1954 that agreement was reached on the establishment of a diplomatic mission.[41]

The more usual practice, however, seems to be that diplomatic relations are established by way of a specific agreement to that effect. This may be done through an exchange of notes between foreign ministers, or between ambassadors stationed in a third State or at an international organization such as, to take the most likely instance, the United Nations. Or there may be a simultaneous announcement in the capitals of the two States. Or a joint communiqué may be issued following a meeting of foreign ministers—as, for example, happened at Namibia's independence celebrations when the new State established diplomatic relations with the Soviet Union,[42] and probably with a number of other States as well. In respect of new States, an existing State may announce its recognition of the State and its willingness to establish diplomatic relations: this has certainly been Soviet practice.[43] In that event it is up to the newly-recognized State to respond if it wishes to take up the offer, or for either State to return to the matter at a later date. Exceptionally, the State to whom such an offer is made may expressly reject it, which was how Malawi responded in 1968 to a Soviet announcement (made in 1964, but perhaps followed up by further enquiries) that she was prepared to establish diplomatic relations with Malawi.[44,45]

In most cases, therefore, a precise date can be given to the establishment

[39] HL Debs., vol. 521, Written Answers, col. *1108*: 19 July 1990.

[40] See *The Independent*, 23 May 1991.

[41] The writer is indebted to Sir Richard Evans, a retired member of the British Foreign and Commonwealth Diplomatic Service, for this information.

[42] See *Vestnik* (Moscow), May 1990, p. 34.

[43] See *USSR Diplomatic Relations* (London: Foreign and Commonwealth Office, Foreign Policy Documents, No. 67, August 1981).

[44] Ibid.

[45] The writer is indebted to the late Mr Patrick Bannerman, of the UK Foreign and Commonwealth Office, for advice on certain of the matters discussed in this paragraph.

of diplomatic relations. This is unlikely to be possible, however, in respect of very old States—the United Kingdom and France, for example. One also wonders about the position in this respect of smaller and newer States. It could be that with regard to some other States of the same kind and with which they have little to do, diplomatic relations have not been formally established—yet when such States come across each other at the United Nations it seems that they behave normally towards each other. The writer has been told, for example, in the context of an enquiry about relations between Namibian diplomats and others in third States and at international organizations, that normal diplomatic intercourse is taken for granted unless Namibia has explicitly decided not to have diplomatic relations with a particular country. This would appear to give rise to the category of implied diplomatic relations. Some States, however—Malawi, for example—may wish to insist on the formal nature of diplomatic relations, with the consequence that the free mixing of its diplomats with those of other States must not be taken to imply the existence of diplomatic relations between the States concerned.[46]

5. Non-Resident Mission

It sometimes seems to be thought that the establishment of diplomatic relations is synonymous with the exchange of residential missions (the reference above to Sen is illustrative of this view). But this is inaccurate. The condition of being in diplomatic relations signifies that there is no let or hindrance to normal contacts between the two States, which will be executed by their officially-accredited representatives—that is to say, by diplomats. Towards this end, if one such State wishes to establish a resident diplomatic mission in the other, it is customary for that other to agree. Indeed, in 1976 it was possible to say that there 'appears to be no precedent'[47] for the second State withholding its (necessary) consent. However, in the early 1980s, although the United Kingdom and Iran were in diplomatic relations, Iran refused to allow the United Kingdom to re-establish a permanent diplomatic mission in Tehran, notwithstanding the fact that there was an Iranian Embassy in London.[48] (The United Kingdom Embassy had earlier been closed for security reasons, and a United Kingdom Interests Section had been established in the Swedish Embassy.) It may also be that some of the States with which the former Soviet Union was in diplomatic relations but in which she had no resident diplomatic missions (26 in

[46] The writer is indebted to Mrs Nandi Ndaitwah, Namibia's Deputy Minister of Foreign Affairs, and Mrs Annie Sajiwa, a member of Malawi's Ministry of External Affairs, for information and comment on this matter.

[47] Denza, op. cit. above (n. 1), p. 18.

[48] The writer is indebted for this information to a member of the UK Foreign and Commonwealth Office.

April 1990)[49] may on security grounds, have refused to permit the establishment of a Soviet embassy. Or there may, in some cases, have been a mutual understanding that no missions were to be established. But it remains the customary position that a State in diplomatic relations with another does not refuse permission for the establishment by that other State of a diplomatic mission.

It must be emphasized, however, that there is no requirement that diplomatic relations be accompanied by the establishment of resident diplomatic missions. It may be that both sides to a diplomatic relationship will establish missions in each other's capitals; but it may be that only one side will do so; and there is no necessity for either State to take this step. The Maldives, for example, has resident diplomatic missions only in Sri Lanka and at the United Nations,[50] while enjoying wide diplomatic relations. Given that its population is only in the region of 200,000, this is entirely explicable. An instance of the mutual non-establishment of diplomatic missions which is notable on account of the close bilateral relationship of the States concerned is that of Lebanon and Syria. Lebanon, represented by the Christian element in the country, would have liked to exchange embassies, but Syria has always refused. Syria said that the ties of the two States are so close that nothing so formal as embassies is required. But it is more likely that her attitude reflects her dissatisfaction with the way the boundaries of Lebanon were drawn by France in the early 1920s. In 1970 it was agreed that offices, without diplomatic status, should be opened in each other's capitals, and Lebanon opened one in Damascus. But Syria did not reciprocate.[51] The presence since 1976 of about 30,000 Syrian troops in Lebanon—albeit early on and latterly with the consent of the Lebanese Government—is perhaps indicative of Syria's attitude to the proper relationship of the two entities.

Where a State, having established diplomatic relations with another State, does not establish a resident mission in that State's capital (or has withdrawn such a mission), it may designate someone as the person through whom official communication should be channelled. This can be the State's ambassador to a geographically-convenient State—provided there is no objection to this on the part of either of the receiving States—or an official of appropriate seniority in the sending State's foreign ministry. (It has, for example, for at least two decades been the United Kingdom's practice to accredit the Head of the West African Department in the Foreign and Commonwealth Office as the non-resident Ambassador to

[49] See *Vestnik*, May 1990, p. 78. This figure is calculated on the assumption that the 17 countries with which the Soviet Union maintained diplomatic relations but in which she had 'no diplomatic missions' did not include the nine countries to which '[n]on-resident Soviet ambassadors [were] accredited'.

[50] The writer is indebted to Ms Farah Faizal, a Maldivian national formerly at the University of Keele, for this information.

[51] The material contained in the last five sentences is based on Sam Younger, 'The Syrian Stake in Lebanon', *The World Today*, 32 (1976), p. 403, and on information kindly supplied to the writer by a member of the Embassy of Lebanon in London.

Chad.) Another possibility is the use of an ambassador to an international organization as a non-resident ambassador to a nearby capital. A number of small States have accredited their New York-based ambassadors to the UN also as their ambassadors to the United States. This has not been much liked by the State Department in Washington, but the United States has not thought it politic to object formally to the practice.

Furthermore, and again provided the receiving State does not object, some or all of the lesser members of the sending State's diplomatic mission in a third capital or to an international organization can also be designated as members of the first State's diplomatic mission to the second State. It is, for example, not uncommon for the African States who were once French colonies to be represented in London by their ambassadors in Paris, together with other members of these States' Paris embassies. Their diplomatic missions to the UK are not resident, but are no less diplomatic missions than any others. Accordingly, their members, when in the UK, receive immunities and privileges which are identical to those of resident diplomats.

The appointment of non-resident missions is well within the diplomatic capability of larger States: they have the resources, in terms of both numbers and seniority, to do this, and seem always to make such arrangements. But smaller and poorer States do not invariably go through this procedure in respect of all States with which they have expressly established diplomatic relations. Where a State does not have many interests to advance and protect in another State, no geographically convenient diplomatic mission, and few senior officials in its home foreign ministry, it is not too surprising that even a non-resident mission is not always appointed to that State. Malawi, for example, although in diplomatic relations with India (which has a resident mission in Lilongwe), has neither a resident nor a non-resident mission in New Delhi. This is not too surprising, given that Malawi's diplomatic representation in the whole of Asia consists of honorary consuls in China and the Republic of Korea.[52]

From one point of view the non-appointment of a non-resident mission might be seen as undesirable, on the grounds that it is somewhat inconsistent with the idea of being in diplomatic relations, and perhaps also with the principle of comity, although, in principle, States may by mutual agreement come to any arrangement they like. From another point of view it could be seen as a desirable development, for it would prevent a handful of ambassadors and officials accumulating offices which they were likely to exercise only with the greatest rarity. It might be added that the appointment of numerous non-resident missions could also be seen as superfluous in the light of the growth of the United Nations. For that organization's almost-universal membership, together with the presence in New York of permanent missions to the UN from—in September 1990—all 160 members

[52] See *Diplomatic and Consular Directory No. 29* (Lilongwe: Ministry of External Affairs, 1 April 1991). This Directory was kindly sent to the writer by Mrs Annie Sajiwa.

(plus observer missions from six non-member States),[53] provides an easy and a legitimate means for States in diplomatic relations to make contact with each other. It is not always the most advantageous way of doing bilateral diplomatic business. But for those States with little business in a particular capital, it could be a sufficient means.

There is, however, one further way, short of the despatch of a special mission (see stage 6, below), in which a State may make diplomatic contact with a State in which it is not represented. For in 1961 the Vienna Convention endorsed a 'recent innovation'[54] in diplomatic practice by providing, in Article 46, that a State 'not represented in' a particular State might, with the prior consent of that State, arrange for the 'temporary protection' of its interests there by a third State. Denza, writing in 1976, says that this procedure 'is frequently used by small and new States who find it difficult to justify maintaining diplomatic missions in a large number of countries'.[55] Namibia, for example, at the time of its independence in 1990, asked for the assistance of Zambia's diplomatic missions in connection with the issue of visas.[56] Some new States have also used this procedure 'until they could organize their own diplomatic services'.[57] The extent of its current use is unclear, and there is also a question about the word 'temporary': does it imply that the procedure is meant to be used on an *ad hoc* rather than a long term basis, or does it mean pending the (possibly unlikely) appointment of a representative? One assumes that both possibilities are open.

It should be noted, however, that it is not just new States which avail themselves of this type of device, and that it is not entirely new. 'For many years The Netherlands has acted in behalf of Luxembourg on political matters in certain countries, as has Belgium on commercial and consular matters in the same countries'.[58] Luxembourg's Convention with Belgium to this effect was made in 1965, and her Treaty with the Netherlands in 1964. But the last-mentioned agreement refers to an arrangement along the same lines having been concluded by an exchange of notes as long ago as 1880.[59]

The possibility opened up by Article 46 of the Vienna Convention would appear not to be available to States which have appointed a non-resident mission to the State in question. For in that circumstance there is representation, albeit of a non-resident kind, and therefore an established channel for the protection of the State's interests. As, however, such a channel may

[53] See *Permanent Missions to the United Nations*, No. 267 (New York: United Nations, September 1990).

[54] Denza, op. cit. above (n. 1), p. 278.

[55] Ibid., p. 279.

[56] The writer is indebted to Mrs Nandi Ndaitwah, Namibia's Deputy Minister of Foreign Affairs, for this information.

[57] James J. Blake, 'Pragmatic Diplomacy. The Origins and Use of the Protecting Power', in David D. Newsom (ed.), *Diplomacy under a Foreign Flag* (Washington, DC: Institute for the Study of Diplomacy, Georgetown University, 1990), p. 6.

[58] Ibid.

[59] Luxembourg's Ministry of Foreign Affairs kindly sent the writer copies of these agreements.

have very little utility for a State with a distant non-resident ambassador, some States, especially smaller ones, may prefer to protect their interests via the Article 46 route. This would also avoid what could be the rather empty process of appointing non-resident missions to each of the States with which a State is in diplomatic relations. In turn, that offers a way of avoiding the assignment of a large number of ambassadorships to one individual.

On the other hand, it is understandable that States may sometimes prefer to maintain a rarely-used non-resident link rather than seek a formal arrangement with a third State. It should be noted, however, that it is always open to one State to ask another to protect its interests in a third State in the temporary absence, from that State, of its accredited representative. Provision is in fact made for this in the Treaty between Luxembourg and the Netherlands mentioned above. The Vienna Convention offers no discouragement to such an arrangement.

A corollary of the appointment of non-resident ambassadors is that one diplomat can at the same time be ambassador to two or more States. This can give rise to a difficulty in relation to the position of doyen (or dean) of the diplomatic body. The doyen speaks, on appropriate occasions and matters, for the whole diplomatic body in a particular capital. In most capitals he (or she) is the longest-serving ambassador (exceptions to this practice occurring in most Roman Catholic countries—where the Papal Nuncio[60] is traditionally the doyen—and in some others where different arrangements have been specially made). The question arises whether a non-resident ambassador can or should serve as doyen. The function of the office would suggest not; but the traditional understanding about the filling of the post says nothing about residence.

This question arose in the United States in 1989. On the departure of the existing doyen, the next in line for the office was the non-resident Ambassador of Western Samoa (also known as Samoa), a small Pacific State with a population of about 160,000. He was also his country's Foreign Minister and Ambassador to the United Nations, and in response to its enquiry the United States was informed that he would not be taking up the position of doyen. Next in seniority was the Ambassador of Tuvalu (a State of 8,000 people), but he, too, was not resident in Washington, was rarely seen there, and proved (to the surprise of the United States) to have had his ambassadorial appointment terminated some years before. The post therefore passed to the (resident) Cypriot Ambassador. Almost immediately, however, he was recalled to Cyprus. Next in seniority was the Ambassador of

[60] The Nuncio (or, more fully, the Apostolic Nuncio) is to be distinguished from the Pro-Nuncio. The latter has the status of ambassador, but does not lay claim to the doyenship of the diplomatic body in the capital to which he is accredited. It is an office which was invented in 1965 to get over the problem for the Vatican City of establishing diplomatic relations with States which did not want to send less than an ambassador to the Vatican City but which were not prepared to accept a Nuncio in return. See *The Times*, 18 February 1966. For the history of the Roman Catholic Church in international relations, see Robert A. Graham, *Vatican Diplomacy* (Princeton University Press, 1959).

Nauru (another State of 8,000 people). He had never taken up residence in Washington, and reportedly lived in Melbourne, Australia. The State Department had great difficulty in tracking him down, and eventually learned from his Government that here was another case of an ambassadorial appointment which had been terminated without notification. Accordingly, the (resident) Ambassador of Cape Verde eventually became doyen.[61] Although it was not spelt out in so many words, what was being said by the State Department in these exchanges was that a non-resident ambassador was entitled to assume the office of doyen, but that the execution of his duties would require his residence in Washington.[62] This position is entirely reasonable.

Although it is not a case of a non-resident mission, it is perhaps appropriate to mention at this juncture the possibility, referred to in Article 6 of the Vienna Convention, of two or more States accrediting the same person as head of mission to another State—provided that no objection is offered by the receiving State. Manifestly, this is not an ideal course for a sending State, and it could give rise to situations of some delicacy. But it could be a convenient resort for a State which would like to be represented on a residential basis in another State but does not have either the interests or the money, or both, to justify a normal residential mission. In August 1981 two very small east Caribbean States—Saint Lucia and Saint Vincent and the Grenadines—were sharing the same High Commissioner in London.[63] Two years later, the same High Commissioner was also representing the State of Antigua and Barbuda.[64] The last-mentioned State then dropped out of the arrangement, but the other two, together with Saint Christopher and Nevis, went on to set up an integrated diplomatic mission in London, with the same set of officials representing all three Eastern Caribbean States. This arrangement was still in force at the end of 1990.[65]

A rather different situation which might result in the establishment of integrated diplomatic missions is where the States concerned are moving towards integration. Thus the States of the European Community are currently exploring the possibility of joint embassies. It could be, however, that some time will elapse before this discussion bears fruit.

6. Special Missions

At the beginning of the modern international system, in the fifteenth and sixteenth centuries, special missions were the usual means through which diplomatic business was done. But gradually they were edged out by the

[61] For assistance with this matter, the writer is indebted to Mr Richard Gookin, Associate Chief of Protocol, United States Department of State.

[62] See previous footnote, and also *The Washington Post*, 20 June 1989. The writer is indebted to his Departmental colleague, Professor Alex Danchev, for drawing his attention to this reference.

[63] See *The London Diplomatic List* (London: Her Majesty's Stationery Office, August 1981).

[64] See ibid., July 1983.

[65] See ibid., December 1990.

growth of residential diplomatic missions, being used only for occasions of special ceremonial or substantive significance, such as important weddings and funerals, and the signing of some peace treaties. In the present century, however, and especially in its second half, they have increased greatly. Occasionally the States concerned may not be in diplomatic relations—as, for example, in the case of Namibia and South Africa; sometimes the sending State may not have a resident mission in the State to which a special mission may be sent; but usually special missions are sent as a supplement to residential diplomacy.[66]

The pre-condition for the widespread use of special missions is the development of air travel. The reasons why considerable advantage has been taken of the device are perhaps fivefold. The first is the almost universal orthodoxy of democratic theory (which does not mean that its detailed implementation is equally universal). As presidents, prime ministers and other governmental ministers are deemed to be acting in a representative capacity, they, and the people they represent, consider it appropriate that matters of some importance should be directly dealt with, and be seen to be so dealt with, by the people's representatives. Thus 'summits' of heads of government abound (relatively speaking), as do meetings of foreign, finance and trade ministers, and so on.

Secondly, there are political and personal factors which help to account for the growth of such *ad hoc* diplomacy. Heads of government are not unaware of the political advantage which may accrue domestically from reports and pictures of their presence and activity at high-level international meetings. It is also the case that the foreign travel which such meetings involve and the privileged context in which it takes place may have some personal appeal, pandering to the sense of importance and dignity which the individuals concerned could perhaps have of themselves.

Thirdly, the greatly increased complexity of international relations encourages special missions. Much international discussion of co-operative activity deals with highly technical matters, and it is therefore extremely desirable that national officials with the appropriate expertise participate directly in it. Delegations of such people sent to other States may be led by a career diplomat, but the experts who form the backbone of such delegations will, of course, be temporary diplomats only.

Fourthly, special missions frequently appear because of the poverty and smallness of many members of the present international society. Such States have neither the resources nor the interests to justify permanent representation in more than a fairly small number of foreign capitals, and they may not have gone far in the direction of non-resident representation. But from time to time 'ordinary' diplomatic matters will arise in respect of States in which they have no representation. These will require bilateral

[66] For a general discussion of this subject, see, Milan Bartos, 'Fourth report on special missions', *Yearbook of the International Law Commission*, 1967, vol. 2, p. 1, UN Doc. A/CN.4/SER.A/1967/Add.1.

attention, and the preferred way of dealing with them may be on a face to face basis in the foreign capital (rather than at the UN). In these circumstances, a special mission is the answer. It may also be used where a State has a non-resident mission in the capital concerned, or even a resident mission, especially if the latter consists of just one or two members. Thus, as *Satow* has put it, 'to a certain extent special missions [are] the typical form of diplomacy for the poorer countries'.[67]

Finally, the use of special missions may reflect a poor relationship between the two States concerned. This may result in their not being in diplomatic relations, and perhaps in their not even having recognized each other. But this does not prevent certain political or practical issues arising which require joint discussion, particularly if the two States are contiguous. If they can bring themselves to it (and the obstacles will be political, not formal or logical), special missions may be used to consider such matters. Alternatively, such a relationship may give rise to a special mission in the shape of the representative of a mediating third State, in the manner of Dr Henry Kissinger's 'shuttle diplomacy' in the Arab-Israeli context in the 1970s. Yet another possibility is that a special mission may be used to discuss the opening of diplomatic relations, or to make a move in that direction.

This is a reminder that special missions may be used 'below' the diplomatic relations line as well as, much more usually, above it. Even, however, when such missions are used 'above' the line, they are distinguishable from resident missions in two important respects. One is that, notwithstanding the existence of diplomatic relations between two States, the consent of the receiving State is necessary for every special mission. The other is that there is no universally agreed legal regime applicable to special missions. The General Assembly of the United Nations did adopt a Convention on Special Missions in 1969 (generally known as the New York Convention). But this masked a substantial disagreement among the member States of the UN about the extent of the legal privileges and immunities which should attach to such missions. No doubt in consequence of this, the Convention has been little ratified. Accordingly, agreement should, in principle, be reached with the receiving State not just for the despatch and agenda of a special mission but also on the legal position of its members—although it appears that in practice this is rarely done.

7. Resident Mission at less than Ambassadorial Level

If a State has substantial interests in another, the absence of a resident mission entails considerable inconvenience, for which special missions offer

[67] *Satow*, op. cit. above (n. 5), p. 157. In the case of one such State—Malawi—special missions have often been used for what might be called normal diplomatic business. The writer is indebted to Mrs Annie Sajiwa, a member of Malawi's Ministry of External Affairs, for this information.

inadequate compensation. A graphic illustration of the problems which can arise if one does not have one's own diplomats in a foreign capital is provided in a Parliamentary defence of Canada's establishment, in the late 1920s, of a legation in Washington. After referring to 'the difficulty of carrying on negotiations on various important Canadian matters' through the British Embassy, the governmental spokesman went on to say that for 25 years a Deputy Minister (Sir Joseph Pope)

> had been obliged to go to the British Embassy at Washington to discuss Canadian affairs. He could not entrust most of his mandates to the Ambassador himself. The Ambassador appointed one of his attachés from London to represent Canada, and Sir Joseph had to give him a few lessons in geography and explain to him the details of the record. While the attaché was a brilliant young man and did his best, he knew little of Canada, never having set foot in this country. After corresponding with him for a time, and before the mandate was carried out, Sir Joseph would find that that young attaché had been transferred to another embassy, and the correspondence would cease. Then Sir Joseph would have to journey again to Washington and begin over again to post another young attaché on Canadian affairs, giving him a few lessons in geography, handing him a brief and sending him along with it.[68]

Correspondingly, following the recognition by the Imperial Conference of 1926 that the King's representative in the Dominions—the governor-general—could no longer also be seen as the representative of the British Government, senior members of the Government considered how best to respond to this new situation. They judged it a 'serious weakness in our system of inter-Imperial contact'[69] that the Dominions were 'the only countries in the world where there was no one with real authority charged with the duty of protecting the general interests of Great Britain or championing the special interests and claims of British traders, investors or immigrants'.[70]

Strictly speaking, a resident mission at less than ambassadorial level offers just two possibilities, but for practical purposes it may be extended to cover a third. The third case is that of a resident mission headed by a non-resident ambassador—a situation envisaged by Article 5(2) of the Vienna Convention, and of which a 1991 illustration is the United Kingdom Mission to Nicaragua. By reason of its headship, such a mission is properly classed as an ambassadorial one. But as its day-to-day leadership has been placed, on a permanent basis, in the hands of a chargé d'affaires *ad interim*, it may not be seen locally as having exactly the same standing as a mission headed by a resident ambassador. Correspondingly, the establishment of such a mission probably indicates that the sending State sees the receiving

[68] Dominion of Canada, Senate, *Debates*, 31 January 1928, p. 10. The writer is indebted to his Departmental colleague, Dr Lorna Lloyd, for drawing his attention to this debate.

[69] Quoted in Norman Hillmer, 'A British High Commissioner for Canada, 1927–28', *Journal of Imperial and Commonwealth History*, 1 (1979), p. 341.

[70] Ibid.—but here Hillmer is not quoting. In footnote 14 (p. 353) he observes that 'The governor-general had retained his political functions in New Zealand and Newfoundland'.

State as of less importance than those States to whom it sends a resident ambassador. Of course, if there is a serious business to be done, the non-resident ambassador will come to do it. But that is not quite the same thing as having such a representative permanently on hand.

The second possibility is that of a free-standing diplomatic mission headed by a chargé d'affaires *en titre*—the lowest of the three classes into which heads of mission are divided. Such a chargé would have his (or her) own letter of accreditation (unlike the chargé *ad interim*), but it would be addressed and therefore presented not to the head of State (as would be the case with heads of mission of the two senior classes) but to the Minister of Foreign Affairs of the receiving State. In terms of the order of precedence, chargés *en titre* rank ahead of chargés *ad interim*.

It might be assumed that a mission headed by a chargé d'affaires *en titre* would be called something other than an embassy or a legation. One such instance arose as part of the resumption of contacts between Egypt and the United Kingdom following the Suez affair of 1956. First a British Trade Mission was established in Cairo; subsequently it was upgraded to a 'Diplomatic Mission', headed by a chargé d'affaires *en titre*; and only later, with the accreditation of an ambassador, was it further promoted to an 'Embassy'.[71] In a rather similar way, the United Kingdom mission to the People's Republic of China, which, for political reasons, was for almost two decades headed by a chargé d'affaires, was called the Office of the British Chargé d'Affaires. China's mission in London was correspondingly termed. It might be noted, however, that in Britain's view her mission in Beijing was an 'embassy', notwithstanding the fact that it was led by a chargé d'affaires *en titre*. It was the host State which, with some reason, insisted on the less-imposing terminology. This had the consequence that, on occasion, letters addressed to the 'British Embassy' were returned to the sender, marked 'unknown'. The two missions were upgraded to embassies, headed by ambassadors, in 1972.[72]

However, perhaps because States are now reluctant to accept such a semantic downgrading, and perhaps because of the (probably associated) rarity of chargés d'affaires *en titre*, diplomatic missions seem now hardly ever to be called anything other than embassies. Thus, on the re-establishment of a United Kingdom mission in Tehran in 1990, it was called an embassy, notwithstanding the fact that it was headed by a chargé d'affaires. This could be justified on the ground that the chargé was a chargé *ad*

[71] See Anthony Parsons, *They Say the Lion* (London: Cape, 1986), p. 56; the writer has also corresponded with Sir Anthony Parsons on the matter.

[72] See the various issues of *The Diplomatic Service List* and the *London Diplomatic List* (which, during the earlier years of this period, was called *Alphabetical List of the Representatives of Foreign States and Commonwealth Countries in London with the Names and Designations of the Persons Returned as Comprising the Establishment of their Respective Offices*), both published in London by Her Majesty's Stationery Office. They also reveal that for one period the British Mission in Beijing was headed by a chargé d'affaires *ad interim*. The writer is much indebted to Sir Richard Evans for assistance with this matter, and also to the staff of the Library of the Foreign and Commonwealth Office in Cornwall House.

interim, and it even might be that he was so designated to facilitate his mission being termed an embassy. But it was entirely clear that he was not standing in for anyone else. Accordingly, in logic he should have been a chargé *en titre*. But in diplomatic matters, as in other spheres, logic does not always hold sway.

The accreditation of a mission headed by a chargé d'affaires was presumably once a favoured course when a new State had emerged somewhat uncertainly, leading to its *de facto* rather than its *de jure* recognition. Any diplomatic mission appointed in these circumstances would consequentially have been of the lowest class. Another circumstance in which such an appointment was deemed appropriate was where it reflected diplomatic caution or disapproval. The re-opening of diplomatic relations between the United Kingdom and Egypt following the Suez affair was indicative of the toe-in-the-water approach. Disapproval was exemplified, at least during the mid-1960s, by Turkey's diplomatic missions in Cyprus, which were headed by chargés d'affaires. For Turkey 'objected in principle to the disregard of the constitution, and in practice to sending an Ambassador to present credentials to Makarios'.[73]

Latterly, however, such politically tepid measures appear to have gone out of fashion—and thus the appearance in diplomatic lists of chargés *en titre* is rare. This, at least, seems certainly to be so on the 'up' side of the diplomatic relations ladder, where a diplomatic appointment at such a level might even be seen as in the nature of a less than friendly act. One piece of evidence in support of this supposition is derived from the manner in which Britain and Iran restored diplomatic relations in 1990, referred to in the previous paragraph but one. On the 'down' side there would appear, in theory, to be more scope for the use of chargés d'affaires *en titre*, by way of the downgrading of the level of the head of mission. But it may be conjectured that in practice this does not take place more than very occasionally, if that.

The general sense of these remarks is also applicable to the other possible type of resident mission at less than ambassadorial level—one headed by an 'envoy extraordinary and minister plenipotentiary', that is, by a head of mission of the second class. In shorter terms, the mission would be one headed by a minister (or, in respect of papal missions, an internuncio), and would be referred to as a legation (or internunciature) rather than an embassy (or nunciature). In the nineteenth century it is probable that most resident missions were of this type, embassies being reserved for the missions exchanged between States which saw themselves, and were generally so seen, as the leading powers of the day.[74] Thus, out of thirty diplomatic missions in London in 1877, eighteen were of the second rank, with just

[73] David Hunt, *On the Spot* (London: Davies, 1975), p. 162.

[74] See Eileen Young, 'The Development of the Law of Diplomatic Relations', this *Year Book*, 40 (1964), pp. 166–8.

five missions headed by ambassadors and the remaining seven by a chargé d'affaires.[75]

The growth of egalitarianism in the middle years of the twentieth century, however, has resulted in an abrupt rejection of the hierarchical implications of the previous practice. Thus free-standing diplomatic missions seem now almost invariably to be of the first class, and therefore headed by an ambassador. Correspondingly, missions headed by ministers appear to be a virtually extinct category. In the last two decades the United Kingdom has had only one legation—to the Vatican City—and in 1982 this solitary diplomatic post of the second rank disappeared through being raised to an embassy.[76,77] Even when the Vienna Convention was being negotiated in the late 1950s attention could be given to the possible amalgamation of the classes of diplomatic agents to two—ambassadors and chargés d'affaires. It did not happen, but this was due to a lack of enthusiasm for the change rather than objection to it.[78] However, legations have not totally disappeared. South Africa, doubtless owing to the special circumstances of her case, had two in 1988,[79] and three years later still had one—in Sweden.[80] It has also been stated that early in 1990 'Israel and the Soviet Union agreed to upgrade Soviet representation in Israel from a consular delegation to a legation, a step closer to full embassy status'.[81] This would be a rather surprising development—but, twenty months later, had not taken place. (Consular relations had, however, by then been established.)[82]

A residential mission can expect to be situated in the capital city of the receiving State, so that it can have immediate access to its government, and vice versa. (In South Africa, embassies shuttle, with the government, between the administrative and legislative capitals.) Moreover, there can only be one diplomatic mission to a State. Thus, if two States merge, third States previously represented in both can retain an embassy only in the new

[75] See J. D. Frodsham, *The First Chinese Embassy to the West* (Oxford: Clarendon Press, 1974), p. 79.

[76] See *The Diplomatic Service List 1989* (London: Her Majesty's Stationery Office, 1989), Part III.

[77] This followed the grant in 1979, for the first time, of diplomatic status to the Pope's official representative in London. Previously he had been known as the Apostolic Delegate, and while certain diplomatic courtesies were accorded him he did not have the status of a diplomatic agent. The British reluctance to change this situation was connected with the sixteenth-century break with Rome by King Henry VIII and the Papal excommunication of Queen Elizabeth I. Even in 1979 the change was made very quietly and, partly with an eye to the situation in Northern Ireland, with 'considerable nervousness' (*The Times*, 13 November 1979). Although it may not have been a formal prerequisite, no doubt in political terms this development opened the way to the British Legation in the Vatican City subsequently being raised to an embassy. At this time it was the only remaining such diplomatic mission to the Holy See, Monte Carlo, the Knights of Malta and San Marino all having apparently abandoned this status, which latterly they had been alone in sharing with the United Kingdom: see nn. 60 and 76 above.

[78] See Denza, op. cit. above (n. 1), p. 61.

[79] See Deon Geldenhuys, *Isolated States: A Comparative Analysis* (Cambridge University Press, 1990), p. 161.

[80] Communication to the writer from a member of the South African Embassy in London.

[81] 'Diplomatic Chronology', in David D. Newsom (ed.), *The Diplomatic Record 1989–1990* (Boulder: Westview, 1991), p. 197.

[82] See n. 31, above.

capital. The other mission may perhaps continue as a consulate. There may, for special reasons, occasionally be exceptions to these arrangements. In the nineteenth century, for example, China kept foreign missions at a distance from Beijing, in Canton. But the difficulties to which this was deemed to give rise resulted in pressure being put on China for the opening of the Forbidden City to diplomatic representation, which was granted following the Arrow War of 1856.[83] In a not wholly dissimilar way, embassies to Saudi Arabia used to be kept in Jedda, away from the capital city. It was only in the mid-1980s that the British Embassy, for example, moved to Riyadh. A twentieth-century example of a rather different sort is the siting of most embassies to Israel in greater Tel Aviv because of the internationally-disputed status of Israel's capital, Jerusalem.[84] But generally, both convenience and logic point powerfully, for both sides to a diplomatic relationship, in the direction indicated in the first sentence of this paragraph.

8. Resident Ambassadorial Mission

Resident diplomatic missions headed by an ambassador (who, formally speaking, is always an 'ambassador extraordinary and plenipotentiary') represent the highest level of diplomatic relations. The ambassador is accredited by his (or her) head of State to the head of the receiving State, and ambassadors make up the first of the classes into which heads of mission are divided. Nuncios (that is, diplomatic representatives of the Papacy) also fall within this class, as do high commissioners (a terminology employed by Commonwealth States for the heads of the diplomatic missions exchanged between themselves). A resident embassy can include only one ambassador, in the sense of being head of the mission. However, at least in respect of missions to the United Nations, it sometimes happens that more than one member of the mission bears the title of ambassador—although here, too, there can be only one permanent representative to the organization. This may be related to the fact that in some States, notably the United States, those who have served as an ambassador retain the title thereafter—even after their retirement—by way of courtesy. It appears that the Spanish-speaking States also make appreciable use of the courtesy title of ambassador. In current British practice only one member of the Diplomatic Service is given, and just for the period of his office, the personal rank of ambassador—the Vice-Marshal of the Diplomatic Corps (the senior official responsible for relations with the London Diplomatic Corps).

When an ambassador is temporarily unavailable to serve in that capacity, because he is out of the receiving State (or, in the practice of some States,

[83] See Samuel S. Kim, *China, the United Nations, and World Order* (Princeton University Press, 1979), pp. 31–6.

[84] In 1991, only two States had their embassies in Jerusalem—Costa Rica and El Salvador: communication to the writer from a member of the Israeli Embassy in London.

out of its capital), or when the post is vacant, a chargé d'affaires *ad interim* is appointed to head the mission. The name of this person must be notified to the Ministry of Foreign Affairs of the receiving State by the (permanent) head of mission or by the sending State's Foreign Ministry.

9. Temporary Withdrawal of Head of Mission

Now the 'down' side of the diplomatic relations ladder has been reached. This does not mean that the stages to be examined refer to developments which can only occur in the context of deteriorating or poor relations. But that is the predominant background to the stages which will be discussed in the rest of the article.

One way in which some dissatisfaction with the receiving State may be signified by the sending State is through the temporary withdrawal of the head of its resident diplomatic mission. In practice, nowadays, this almost always means the withdrawal of an ambassador. In 1958, for example, the Soviet Union withdrew her ambassador to Helsinki following the formation of a Finnish Government of which the Soviets disapproved.[85] In 1989 the European Community States agreed on the simultaneous withdrawal of their heads of mission from Tehran, following the Ayatollah Khomeini's pronouncement of a death sentence on Mr Salman Rushdie, who had published a controversial novel in Britain.[86] (The United Kingdom went further, and withdrew its entire diplomatic staff—see stage 11 below.) The expressed purpose of such a recall seems usually to be 'for consultations', and the consultative period can become quite extensive. However, the sending State will presumably wish for the return, in due course, of the same ambassador, so as not to suggest that its own head of mission might in any way have been responsible for the deterioration in relations.

The receiving State may take a different view. It may have been upset by the personal behaviour of the ambassador, or wish to hold him responsible for some particularly offensive action by members of his embassy. In that event it will make it known that the return of the temporarily recalled ambassador would not be welcome—effectively ending his tour of duty. This was the response of the British Government to the recall of the High Commissioner of Nigeria following the attempted abduction of Mr Umaru Dikko in 1984.[87] Alternatively, in respect of an ambassador still on duty in the receiving State, the same result can be achieved by declaring him *persona non grata*—as Sri Lanka did in respect of the British High Commissioner in May 1991, charging him with having interfered in the country's domestic affairs.[88]

[85] See E. Karsh, *Neutrality and Small States* (London: Routledge, 1988), p. 142.
[86] See *Keesing's Record of World Events*, 1989, pp. 36450–1.
[87] See House of Commons Foreign Affairs Committee, 1984–5, *The Abuse of Diplomatic Privileges and Immunities* (London: Her Majesty's Stationery Office, 1984), p. xxxiii.
[88] See *The Independent*, 31 May 1991 and 10 June 1991.

10. Downgrading of Level of Head of Mission

There is one circumstance in which the permanent withdrawal of a head of mission (in effect, an ambassador) by the sending State would, in theory, be acceptable to that State. It is where, as a way of expressing dissatisfaction with the receiving State, the sending State decides to downgrade the level of its head of mission. Nowadays, however, this is an unpopular option, as (for the reasons given under stage 7) States are firmly of the opinion that residential diplomatic relations should be at the highest—ambassadorial—level. They certainly have no desire to reintroduce the second class of relations—legations headed by ministers—and seem in most cases not much less reluctant to downgrade an embassy to a mission headed, permanently, by a chargé d'affaires. After a period during which diplomatic relations have been broken or a mission withdrawn, relations might be first repaired by the re-establishment of relations at chargé d'affaires level, as happened between the United Kingdom and Iran in 1988.[89] But that is better seen as an event on the 'up' side of the diplomatic relations ladder rather than one on the 'down' side.

11. Withdrawal of Mission, temporary or permanent

The withdrawal of a diplomatic mission has no necessary bearing on the existence of diplomatic relations between the two States concerned. A mission might be permanently withdrawn because there is no real work to be done. This was the ostensible reason for the closure, in 1938, by the Soviet Union and Saudi Arabia of their missions in Jedda and Moscow. In this case both sides made it clear that diplomatic relations were not being ruptured and that such bilateral contact as was necessary would be conducted through their respective missions in London.[90] Another reason for a mission's withdrawal might be the need for economy: Britain has pursued this course on a number of occasions during the last two decades, as have other States. In these cases diplomatic relations are maintained, but on a non-resident basis.

Embassies might also be withdrawn, without a breach of diplomatic relations, in the interests of the security of the staff of the mission—but in this kind of case the withdrawal is almost always meant to be temporary. For example, a number of embassies have been withdrawn from Beirut for this reason in recent years; after the withdrawal of Soviet forces from Afghanistan in February 1989 a number of Western States withdrew their embassies from Kabul in mistaken anticipation of an early and violent overthrow of

[89] See *The Times*, 5 December 1988.

[90] A former member of the Foreign and Commonwealth Office and the late Mr Patrick Bannerman, in communications to the writer. *USSR Diplomatic Relations* (see n. 43 above) is somewhat imprecise in saying that relations between the two States 'have lapsed'.

the regime; and early in 1991 some coalition States withdrew their embassies from Baghdad on the approach of the 15 January deadline set by the UN for Iraq's departure from Kuwait. (A month later Iraq broke diplomatic relations with the main members of the coalition.) An earlier example of the same phenomenon occurred during the German siege of Paris in 1870. And then, as sometimes now, it was liable to attract criticism. In 1870 '[t]he "bolting" of the British diplomats provoked considerable anger, both among the British in Paris and at home'.[91]

Another, and associated, circumstance in which a mission might be withdrawn arises when the host, or perhaps the occupying, State interferes with the functioning of the mission to such an extent that, as a practical matter, its maintenance becomes virtually impossible. The withdrawal of coalition embassies from Kuwait following the Iraqi invasion of 1990 is a case in point. And, to underline the impropriety of the invasion, the departing States went out of their way to emphasize that their missions were being closed only temporarily.[92]

Additionally, however, or in association with a security threat, a mission might be withdrawn, either temporarily or permanently, as a mark of a deterioration in relations. The 1991 closure of Western embassies in Baghdad was in part an instance of this. Two years earlier the United Kingdom withdrew its mission from Tehran in consequence of Iran's behaviour in the Rushdie affair. (Iran responded by breaking diplomatic relations with the United Kingdom a month later.) However, in the absence of a problem over security, or of a political situation which is deemed to justify a breach of diplomatic relations, this is a rather drastic and perhaps not a very fruitful step. For it means that the sending State is depriving itself of the opportunity to make direct representations in the capital of the receiving State, not to mention what might be termed 'propaganda'. It is by no means clear that the need for this facility is lessened by a worsening of relations. Moreover, because the closure of a mission (unlike the breach of diplomatic relations) has no reciprocal implications, the State from which a mission is withdrawn will be free to maintain such representation as it has in the other State.

In the event of the permanent or temporary withdrawal of a mission, it is open to the sending (and now departing) State to entrust the protection of its interests to a third State acceptable to the receiving State, and also to set up an 'interests section' within the embassy of that third State. This is what the United Kingdom did in Iran after the closure of its embassy there in 1980, a British interests section operating within the Swedish Embassy. However, as these devices are probably more used after a breach of diplomatic relations than in connection with the mere closure of a mission, they

[91] Alistair Horne, *The Fall of Paris* (London: The Reprint Society, 1967), p. 169.

[92] For the statement made in this connection by the United Kingdom, see *Security Council Official Records*, UN Doc. S/22020, 19 December 1990.

will be considered in this article once the 'diplomatic relations line' has been crossed (see stage 13, below).

12. Breach of Diplomatic Relations

Whereas the establishment of diplomatic relations is dependent on the agreement of the two States concerned, a break in diplomatic relations may be, and usually is, the result of a decision to this effect by one side only. However, it has consequences for both. For diplomatic relations is a bilateral relationship, and if one party withdraws from it the other must do likewise. Thus a breach of diplomatic relations involves the withdrawal of each side's residential missions to the other and the cancellation of any non-resident representation which may have been established. In principle, the two States concerned are now in a condition of 'not speaking' to, or boycotting, each other.

It follows that in third States normal contacts between the missions of two States not in diplomatic relations would not occur. In general, the members of the two missions would not communicate or do direct business with each other, or invite their opposite numbers to social occasions. Equally, hosts would not knowingly invite the representatives of States not in diplomatic relations to relatively intimate social events—unless, perhaps, consciously trying to provide an opportunity for the two States concerned to talk to each other—nor to larger ones at which a representative of one such State was the guest of honour. Should, none the less, two such representatives find themselves together at a small event, or seated near or next to each other at a larger one, it appears that they do not necessarily feel themselves under an obligation to object or leave, but instead, as a matter of courtesy, might just treat each other as colleagues. On other occasions when the representatives of two such States happen to come across each other, a formal bow might be thought to suffice.

A somewhat different situation arises in a third State when the doyen of the diplomatic corps represents a State with which one or more of the other States represented there are not in diplomatic relations. In this circumstance a distinction is drawn between the role of the ambassador in question as doyen and as the representative of his State. Ambassadors of States having no relations with the doyen's State may none the less speak to and attend meetings called by the doyen when he is acting in that capacity. Equally, the doyen, in that capacity, may have dealings with such ambassadors. It is not unknown, however, when relations between the two States concerned are very difficult, for normal diplomatic courtesies to be omitted. (What is not known, and would be very interesting to know, is whether such discourtesy is sometimes offered on instructions.)

At international organizations the understandings which prevail in third States regarding contacts between the representatives of States not in diplomatic relations with each other inevitably undergo some relaxation. Thus there is no objection to the representatives of two such States being present at the same plenary meeting, sitting on the same committee or subcommittee, addressing each other on such occasions (through the chairman), and working with each other in their common capacity as members of the same body. The actual degree of effective co-operation which so develops in such contexts will, of course, depend to a large extent on the actual state of relations between the two States concerned, and to a lesser extent on the personalities of the relevant individuals.[93] But they do well to take care. The removal from office in the 1980s of one Foreign Minister followed, in point of time, some informal contacts he had had at the United Nations with the Israeli Ambassador, notwithstanding the fact that the two States concerned were not in diplomatic relations. The reasons for his downfall were extensive and complicated. But his incautious behaviour seems to have been a pretext for his sacking, and was believed by some to have been a substantive factor in the case.[94] The episode is a reminder that diplomatic contacts in the absence of diplomatic relations are not normally straightforward.

The circumstances in which diplomatic relations are broken (and also in which they are not broken) have changed a good deal during the present century. Before the First World War a breach of such relations was a very serious matter indeed, and often presaged or accompanied the outbreak of war. In the immediate events leading to that War, for example, only half an hour elapsed between the announcement by the Austro-Hungarian Minister to Serbia that his country was breaking off diplomatic relations, and the departure of the entire staff of the Legation (by train) from Belgrade. Three days later Austria-Hungary declared war on Serbia.[95] As late as 1949 the British Foreign Office pointed out that the 'removal of a diplomatic representative without sufficient cause was tantamount to an act of war'.[96]

Since about 1960, however, diplomatic relations have been broken off for a variety of lesser reasons, not excluding, sometimes, behaviour which has no direct impact on the State breaking relations. In 1965, for example, seven African States broke off relations with the United Kingdom as a way of objecting to that State's response to the unilateral declaration of independence by the white regime in Rhodesia.[97] On the other hand, it seems that armed conflict is not now seen as a situation which necessarily requires a

[93] The material contained prior to this point in the present paragraph and in the previous two paragraphs is based on the writer's correspondence with the late Mr Patrick Bannerman and conversations with Dame Anne Warburton, Sir Richard Evans and Sir John Thomson, all of whom served in the United Kingdom Foreign and Commonwealth Office.

[94] These remarks are based on private conversations.

[95] See John G. Stoessinger, *Why Nations Go to War* (New York: St. Martin's Press, 5th edn., 1990), p. 8.

[96] G. H. Kelling, *Countdown to Rebellion. British Policy in Cyprus 1939–1955* (New York: Greenwood, 1990), p. 99. The diplomatic representative in question was in fact a consul, but the observation is no less good an illustration of the point being made—indeed, it is a better one.

[97] See *Satow*, op. cit. above (n. 5), p. 188.

breach of relations. It appears, for example, that Iraq maintained a diplomatic mission in Iran for much of the (Gulf) War between the two of them (1980–1988), and that Pakistan was represented in Afghanistan throughout the civil war in which she was helping those who were trying to unseat the Soviet-supported Afghan Government. Similarly, Nicaragua maintained diplomatic relations with the United States, and a diplomatic mission in Washington, throughout the 1980s, notwithstanding the fact that that State was overtly giving considerable aid to the group which was seeking to overthrow the Nicaraguan Government.

When diplomatic relations have been broken, the formal initiative for their re-institution is expected to come from the State which was responsible for the breach. In political terms this may be less easy than it sounds. A State might look, or be made to look, rather silly if it broke relations one day and re-opened them after only a brief interval of time. Saudi Arabia, for example, having broken relations with France and the United Kingdom on the day before they called off their assault on Egypt in 1956, found it necessary to wait six years before re-opening them.[98] Statements may have been heatedly made on the occasion of the breach which then stand in the way of a resumption of relations, on account of the continuation of the situation which gave rise to the initial action. Most of the African States which broke off relations with Britain in 1965 over the Rhodesian affair, for example, took between two and three years to re-institute them.

Once a breach has taken place, further problems in the relationship may make a resumption difficult—as has happened between Cuba and the United States,[99] who have not been in diplomatic relations for 30 years—whereas such problems might not themselves have caused a break in relations. And generally, a resumption of relations has to take account of the symbolism which will probably be read into that act, and which the actual state of relations might be judged unable to bear. The domestic political scene in a State contemplating a resumption of relations may also exert an important inhibitory influence. One reason why the United States, for example, hesitates over restoring diplomatic relations with Cuba is because of the internal outcry which that would provoke, not least from the community of Cuban exiles. This situation, however, has not prevented the two States from concluding an Agreement on Maritime Delimitation.[100]

As this last point indicates, and as will be seen in the remainder of this article, there is a variety of ways in which States not in diplomatic relations are able to maintain diplomatic contact. But there are usually some disadvantages attaching to such situations, which are not present in a normal diplomatic relationship. One comment which such a situation has attracted

[98] Ibid.

[99] See Wayne S. Smith, 'The Protecting Power and the US Interests Section in Cuba', in Newsom, op. cit. above (n. 57), pp. 106–7.

[100] See *International Legal Materials*, 17 (1978), p. 110. I am indebted to Professor Ian Brownlie for this information.

is that the absence of 'direct official relations was a great handicap in ironing out differences and misunderstandings', which was very little alleviated by the 'exchange of diplomatic correspondence'[101] between ambassadors in the capital of a third State. Moreover, the sort of difficulty which can give rise to a breach of diplomatic relations is often also the sort which would benefit greatly from a straightforward diplomatic relationship. As Winston Churchill said, 'The reason for having diplomatic relations is not to confer a compliment but to secure a convenience'.[102] Perhaps this is being increasingly realized by States. Certainly, in the wake of the 'Gorbachev revolution' there have been numerous instances of States re-establishing diplomatic relations, often after a long breach. It could be that in future this convenience will be more highly valued than it sometimes appears to have been in the past.

13. Protecting Power/Interests Section

It has been noted above (under stage 5) that the concept of a protecting power is applicable to States which are in diplomatic relations but have no resident representation. Historically, however, and to a considerable extent still, its use is associated with the absence of diplomatic relations.[103] And this is wholly so in respect of the relatively recent development of interests sections within the embassies of protecting powers.

A protecting power is a State which, with the consent of the receiving State, acts within that State on behalf of an absent State ('protected State' has other connotations in British constitutional practice, and perhaps also more generally, and is therefore a phrase which is best avoided). The extent of the activity which is to be undertaken by the protecting power is governed by what is agreed between it and the State whose interests are being protected, and perhaps also by what the receiving State is willing to accept. The tasks undertaken by the protecting power can vary a good deal, from a limited to a wide range of services. The protecting power would certainly take any vacated property under its wing, and might also provide such essential help as was needed by nationals of the absent State. Additionally, the protecting power could be expected to pass messages between the absent State and the receiving State, and might also report on conditions there to the absent State and provide it with such general advice as was required. The actual extent of its role would to a large extent depend on the

[101] Arthur Marder, *Operation 'Menace': The Dakar Expedition and the Dudley North Affair* (Oxford University Press, 1976), p. 4. The reference is to the lack of diplomatic relations between the United Kingdom and the (French) Vichy regime in the summer of 1940. It was a very unusual and difficult situation, but this does not detract from the general validity of the point which is made.

[102] Quoted in Brian Porter, *Britain and the Rise of Communist China. A Study of British Attitudes 1945–1954* (London: Oxford University Press, 1967), p. 25.

[103] See Charles Henn, *The Origins and Early Development of the Idea of Protecting Power* (Cambridge University, unpublished doctoral thesis, 1986), *passim*.

amount of protection required by the absent State, which in turn would be influenced by whether the absent State had, and had retained, a consular service in the receiving State.

The protecting State can expect its additional costs to be reimbursed by the absent State, and arrangements on this matter would form a part of their initial agreement. It might be that the protecting State would need to expand its diplomatic staff in the receiving State to cope with the additional work involved. In 1967, for example, when Belgium took over the protection of United States' interests in Iraq, a diplomat was sent from Belgium to Baghdad for this purpose.[104] And when, in 1961, United States' interests in Cuba came under Swiss protection, Switzerland needed 'to fly in an entire diplomatic team . . . [of] nine diplomats headed by an officer of ambassadorial rank'.[105] Because of her traditional policy of neutrality, Switzerland has often been asked, and agreed, to perform the office of protecting power. At one point during the Second World War she had about 200 obligations of this kind, no fewer than 35 States having asked her to protect their interests, generally in more than one country. At the end of 1988 she was responsible for 14 such undertakings.[106]

Neither party to a traditional protecting power relationship, however, finds it particularly satisfactory. Some of its roles have become increasingly onerous for the protecting power. Commissioning States, on the other hand, often wish for a less remote relationship with the States with whom they are not in diplomatic relations—one which would enable them, in effect, to have a measure of direct representation in the receiving State, and so to protect at least some of their interests themselves. This concern assumed increasing weight in the post-Second World War period, when breaches of diplomatic relations often involved States with a continuing bilateral relationship which was of considerable political, economic, and sometimes cultural importance to both of them. Clearly, what was ideally being looked for from the protecting power went beyond the traditional protecting role of placing a vacated embassy under its flag, literally as well as metaphorically, making its 'good offices' available as a channel of communication, and perhaps also providing consular-type services for nationals of the State no longer represented in the receiving State. Moreover, the ideal sort of help was, even with the best will in the world, not the kind which a protecting power was particularly well placed to provide.

These factors help to account for the emergence, since the end of the Second World War, of the concept and actuality of the interests section. It involves the presence in the receiving State of diplomatic staff from what might now be called, instead of the absent State, the sending State—but as

[104] See Grant V. McClanahan, 'Evacuation and Hand-over to a Protecting Power. The Baghdad Embassy in 1967', in Newsom, op. cit. above (n. 57), p. 60.

[105] Wayne S. Smith, 'The Protecting Power and the US Interests Section in Cuba', in Newsom, op. cit. above (n. 57), p. 100.

[106] See Raymond Probst, 'The "Good Offices" of Switzerland and her Role as Protecting Power', in Newsom, op. cit. above (n. 57), pp. 25–6.

part of the diplomatic mission of the protecting power. They might be based in the existing embassy of the protecting State or in their own State's ex-embassy—but the latter would now be a sub-division of the embassy of the protecting power, would be so described on its name-plate (albeit with the addition of 'Ruritanian Interests Section'), and would fly the protecting power's flag. The diplomats making up the interests section would appear in the local diplomatic list as members of the protecting power's mission, in a sub-section dealing with the Ruritanian Interests Section: they would, as it were, have become honorary Ruritanian diplomats. Very often they would be the same people who had previously been in the capital in question as diplomats, in their own right, of the sending State. But, formally speaking at least, they would now have a less senior head, for the embassy of the protecting power, like any other, can have only one ambassador. Accordingly, Ruritania's ambassador will certainly have departed, and its interests section will be headed by a diplomat of (at least ostensibly) lower rank who in formal terms will be under the authority of the protecting power's ambassador.

This kind of arrangement first appeared in a formal way in 1965, when it was employed by the United Kingdom and the Federal Republic of Germany to get over the difficulties which arose following the decision of a number of States to break diplomatic relations with them.[107] In Britain's case the States concerned were African, and were protesting about her inaction following Rhodesia's unilateral declaration of independence; in West Germany's case they were Arab States reacting to the recognition of Israel. Other instances soon followed, so that it quickly became an accepted device of the diplomatic system.

Initially, it seems to have been assumed that interests sections would deal largely with 'non-political' matters of a consular, commercial, and cultural kind;[108] that such political issues as were discussed by members of the interests section would be dealt with at a relatively junior level—with, for example, the relevant country officer in the receiving State's foreign ministry;[109] that these and any other such meetings would be arranged through the protocol office of the receiving State's foreign ministry, with a member of that office always in attendance;[110] and that any representations which the sending State wished to make at a high political level would have to be

[107] See 'The Protecting Power', Introduction to Part I, Newsom, op. cit. above (n. 57), p. 4. However, it seems that the device was used informally, in the sense of a diplomat from the protected State being attached to the embassy of the protecting power, at least some time before 1965. The writer is indebted to Ambassador Fred Hadsel, formerly of the United States Foreign Service, for this information.

[108] See Denza, op. cit. above (n. 1), p. 280.

[109] See Ashraf Ghorbal, 'The Interests Section as a Practical System of Diplomatic Contact. Egyptian-US Relations at the Time of No Relations, 1967–1974', in Newsom, op. cit. above (n. 57), p. 82.

[110] See ibid., and William Eagleton, 'Evolution of the US Interests Section in Algiers and Baghdad', in Newsom, op. cit. above (n. 57), p. 92.

made through the ambassador of the protecting power or a senior member of his embassy—not, in other words, through the head of the interests section.[111]

However, in a number of instances the perceived need, on both sides, for a more intimate political dialogue resulted in these expectations quickly being put on one side. The United States' interests section (of the Spanish embassy) in Cairo, for example, which opened in 1967, was permitted to have its own cypher communications with Washington and to have access to the bank account of the American ex-embassy; and before long it was holding direct meetings, at a high level, with Egyptian officials.[112] The head of the Egyptian interests section in Washington was equally privileged.[113] The United States' interests section (of the Swiss Embassy) in Algiers between 1969 and 1974 also gradually developed a diplomatic relationship which was 'virtually normal in everything but name'.[114] And the arrangements made (directly) between Cuba and the United States for the establishment of interests sections in each other's capitals (the respective protecting powers being Czechoslovakia and Switzerland) provided for 'everything embassies would have done—everything, that is, except fly their colors and call their chiefs "ambassador" '.[115] By 1979, two years after the establishment of the United States' interests section, it had become 'the largest non-Communist diplomatic mission in Havana, dwarfing its parent entity, the Swiss embassy'. And it was operating so much as an independent diplomatic mission that the Swiss Ambassador had to accept that the Head of the section might walk out of an occasion on which the United States was insulted, notwithstanding the fact that Head's technical superior, the Swiss Ambassador, remained seated.[116]

It is important to emphasize, however, that conceptually there is a very significant difference between even the most imposing interests section and a regular diplomatic mission. An interests section is indicative of the absence of diplomatic relations between the States concerned. A diplomatic mission indicates their presence. And the condition of being in diplomatic relations is the prerequisite for unhindered and normal communication between sovereign States. It is still, overwhelmingly, the typical basis for inter-State relations, and almost universally seen as a desirable condition. It is therefore a matter of some regret that in a recent statement a member of the British Government distinguished between States with whom 'the United Kingdom does not have diplomatic relations', and States where there are 'British interest sections with United Kingdom staff in the

[111] See Denza, op. cit. above (n. 1), p. 280.

[112] See Donald C. Bergus, 'US Diplomacy under the Flag of Spain. Cairo, 1967–1974', in Newsom, op. cit. above (n. 57), pp. 71–4.

[113] See Ghorbal, loc. cit. above (n. 109), p. 83.

[114] Eagleton, loc. cit. above (n. 110), p. 96.

[115] Smith, loc. cit. above (n. 105), p. 104.

[116] Ibid., pp. 107 and 106.

embassies of protecting powers'[117]—rather as if the latter situation might be seen as a form of diplomatic relations. Admittedly, the questioner wanted to know in which countries there was no United Kingdom embassy. But even so, an opportunity to distinguish clearly between the existence and lack of diplomatic relations was lost.

It should not be assumed that the development of the interests section employing career officials of the commissioning State has resulted in the disappearance of the older type of protecting power role—where the State assuming this responsibility has to arrange for its discharge by members of its own foreign service. In some circumstances it might be undesirable, on security grounds, for officials of the departed State to remain in the capital of the State concerned. This may have been the reason for the fact that, when Sweden assumed the protection of British interests in Iran in 1989 (following the breach of relations over the Rushdie affair), no United Kingdom staff were employed for this purpose in the Swedish Embassy in Tehran.[118] It is also possible that, in the case of the closure of a small embassy, or where a consulate is retained, the requirements of the protecting role might be thought not to necessitate the full-time employment of an official of the departed State. It is perhaps noteworthy, however, that the Agreement between the United Kingdom and Sweden formalizing the latter's assumption of the protecting power role provided for the establishment of an 'Interests Section',[119] despite the fact that when the Agreement was signed no British personnel were in Sweden's Tehran Embassy. The Agreement also envisaged the possible continuation of this situation. It would therefore appear that the concept of an interests section is now integral to that of a protecting power.

What is shown by this stage in inter-State relations is that if two States find it desirable, they will overcome the impediments which are a usual consequence of a breach of diplomatic relations. In this rather paradoxical way, therefore, the value of a normal diplomatic relationship is boldly underlined—as is, more generally, the importance of the diplomatic system as a means of international communication.

14. Diplomatic Functions by Consular Officer

In an earlier part of this article (stage 3, above), note was taken of the fact that in the absence of a diplomatic mission and of representation by a third State, a member of a sending State's consular mission may, with the con-

[117] HC Debs., vol. 152, Written Answers, col. *275*: 5 May 1989. The answer is reprinted in Geoffrey Marston (ed.), 'United Kingdom Materials on International Law 1989', this *Year Book*, 60 (1989), pp. 615–26.

[118] See HC Debs., vol. 152, Written Answers, col. *275*: 5 May 1989.

[119] *Treaty Series*, No. 45 (1989), Cm. 809, Article 2. The text of this Agreement is reproduced in Vaughan Lowe, 'Diplomatic Law: Protecting Powers', *International and Comparative Law Quarterly*, 39 (1990), p. 471.

sent of the receiving State, perform diplomatic acts. It was suggested that this provision might be particularly useful on the 'up' diplomatic ladder, as an approach to the opening of diplomatic relations. Use might also be made of it by a State which is in diplomatic relations with another State but has no diplomatic representation there. And it might also be employed on the 'down' diplomatic ladder after diplomatic relations have been broken but where consular relations remain intact. (The Vienna Convention on Consular Relations provides, in Article 2, paragraph 3, that the severance of diplomatic relations does not automatically involve the severance of consular relations.) This would, in effect, be an instance of the downgrading of relations from the diplomatic to the consular level.

One imagines that until the mid-1960s this could, in appropriate circumstances, have been seen as a possibly desirable alternative to the appointment of a protecting power, for it would have resulted in the protection of a State's interests by its own personnel. Moreover, although there is a distinction between the functions of and the legal regimes applicable to diplomatic and consular work, since the Second World War diplomatic and consular services have generally been integrated. Thus a consular official would almost certainly have had diplomatic experience and in consequence be well aware of his State's diplomatic needs. He (or she) could therefore confidently be entrusted with diplomatic tasks.

Instances of the maintenance of consular relations after a breach of diplomatic relations certainly occurred in the century prior to specific provision being made for it in the Vienna Convention on Consular Relations.[120] But the extent of the practice was perhaps not great, for breaches of diplomatic relations were often regarded as *ipso facto* involving a breach of consular relations. The contrary position only became clearly established with the Vienna Convention.[121]

More or less contemporaneously with the Vienna Convention on Consular Relations, however, the concept of the interests section emerged. This made it possible for a State which had been involved in a breach of diplomatic relations none the less to retain a measure of (formally indirect) diplomatic representation in the other State, and sometimes this has come to differ very little from the representation which was enjoyed before the breach (see stage 13, above). In view of this it is probable that very little use has been made of consular officers on the down side of the diplomatic ladder (unlike on the up side). But in the absence of diplomatic relations it remains a possible means of keeping in regular diplomatic touch, and has the advantage of direct representation. For example, following Guatemala's breach of diplomatic relations with the United Kingdom in 1963 in connection with her claim to British Honduras, consular relations remained intact until independence was granted to the colony (by then known as Belize) in

[120] See *Satow*, op. cit. above (n. 5), p. 213.

[121] The writer is indebted to a member of the Foreign and Commonwealth Office for this information.

1981.[122] (Consular relations were resumed in August 1986, and diplomatic relations four months later.)

However, the maintenance of diplomatic contacts in this way has two possible disadvantages. The first is that, unlike the interests section, it necessarily involves the presence in the receiving State of a mission whose senior staff will be nationals of the sending State. This may be inadvisable on security grounds. It may be observed, for example, that when the United Kingdom and Iran were not in diplomatic relations in the 1980s, advantage was not taken of the possibility of consular relations. Secondly, it may be that the circumstances which have given rise to the breach of diplomatic relations are deemed to be of such political magnitude as to prevent the continuation of any form of direct relations. It may be noted, for example, that after the shooting of a woman police constable from Libya's London Embassy in 1984, there was a complete breach of formal relations between the two States, contacts being maintained through the establishment of interests sections in the embassies of third States.

One interesting anomaly which is best mentioned at this point concerns relations between the United States and Afghanistan during the presence of Soviet forces in that country from 1979 to 1989. The United States refused to conduct formal diplomatic business with the Soviet-supported regime, but nevertheless kept her Kabul embassy open and used its consular section as a channel for communication with Afghanistan. Through this means considerable diplomatic business was in fact conducted.[123]

15. Intermittent Diplomatic Contacts, Direct and Indirect

There are four main ways in which intermittent diplomatic contacts may be made between two States which have broken diplomatic relations. It may be that these are their sole such contacts. But they can also be a supplement to the standing representation of one or both in the other by a protecting power, perhaps in the shape of an interests section within that power's embassy, or by their own consular personnel. It is also the case that intermittent contacts of this kind may be made by States which have never been in diplomatic relations. But it is probable that most pairs of States move fairly quickly and easily towards the initial establishment of diplomatic relations, reducing the necessity for other communicative devices in the pre-establishment period. After a breach, however, the re-establishment of relations is rarely a straightforward process, creating a need for alternative arrangements.

The first type of intermittent contact, however, usually offers an excep-

[122] See *Keesing's Contemporary Archives*, 1982, p. 31335.

[123] The writer is indebted to Ambassador David Newsom, formerly of the United States Foreign Service, for this information.

tion to these last remarks, inasmuch as it chiefly relates to a situation where diplomatic relations have never been established and where the two States concerned cannot be seen as moving in the direction of the establishment of such relations. For this reason it seems appropriate to include it on the 'down' rather than the 'up' side of the diplomatic relations ladder. The situation which is being particularly thought of is that of territorially-contiguous States which do not recognize each other, let alone contemplate the establishment of diplomatic relations. However, their very contiguity probably gives rise to issues which call for bilateral handling. In consequence they may develop well-understood ways (short of full-blown special missions) of getting in touch with each other to conduct necessary business. The two Germanies in the 1950s and 1960s provide one such case. Israel and Jordan, particularly since 1967, provide another.[124] Since the ending of the Korean War in 1953, North and South Korea have been able to keep in touch with each other through the meetings of the Military Armistice Commission. The Republic of Cyprus and the Turkish Republic of Northern Cyprus provide a fourth instance of this kind of arrangement, co-operating in the solution of problems regarding the supply of electricity and water from one part of the island to the other.[125] As in this last instance, much of the business so transacted may be of a technical rather than a recognizably 'political' kind—although that does not make it non-diplomatic—but these connections also offer the opportunity for contacts on political matters.

Secondly, States which have broken diplomatic relations may from time to time deal with particular items of joint business through the use of special missions, in the same way as States not yet or already in diplomatic relations (see stage 6, above).

Thirdly, there are rich opportunities at international organizations, especially the United Nations, for States which have broken diplomatic relations to get in touch with each other. They may do so directly, or, perhaps more likely, through the good offices of a third State. These good offices may be restricted to the setting up of a meeting, even on so limited a basis as sitting the ambassadors of two States not in diplomatic relations next to each other at lunch. In the normal way this would not consciously be done, but it has been known for one such ambassador to let certain friendly States know that there would be no objection to such a happening. Or, if more of an arms-length relationship is sought, the good offices of a third State may be used for the regular transmission of substantial

[124] The writer is indebted to his Departmental colleague, Mr Noam Livne, for the information that there are several well-documented sources in Hebrew which give details of these sorts of relationship. Cf. a report referring to an Israeli brigade commander's statement that 'there was liaison between the Israelis and the Jordanians at low-ranking level to prevent misunderstandings and to avoid unwanted incidents': *The Independent*, 11 January 1991.

[125] In this case they are able to use the good offices of the United Nations Peace-Keeping Force in Cyprus: see *Report of the Secretary-General on the United Nations Operation in Cyprus*, UN Doc. S/21340, 13 May 1990, para. 19 (p. 5). Presumably, however, in the absence of this Force they would, willy nilly, co-operate directly.

messages. In these ways the atmosphere between two States may be improved; particular problems may be disposed of; and it may even be that such contacts could herald a move sideways from the down side of the diplomatic relations ladder to a rung on the lower part of the up side.

A variant of this third method of intermittent diplomatic contact is the use as intermediaries not of representatives to the organization, but of members of the organization's secretariat. The organization itself may have formally asked for the appointment of such a mediator, or its executive head may have taken it upon himself to act in this way, either personally or through a special representative. In those circumstances where an international peace-keeping force or observer group endeavours to maintain calm between two States, the States concerned may use the individual in charge of the peace-keeping body to act as a go-between. Or that person, who in the case of UN peace-keeping missions will have been given the status of a senior member of the UN Secretariat, may initiate (direct or indirect) talks with a view to increasing the likelihood of calm.[126]

Finally, it is always possible for two States which have broken off diplomatic relations to make contact through their diplomatic representatives in the capital of a third State. This may be done directly or indirectly. The events leading to the resumption of diplomatic relations between the United Kingdom and Argentina in 1990, for example, included discussions between the two States in Berne. In the case of indirect contacts, varying degrees of use may be made of the diplomats of third States or, perhaps more likely, the members of the foreign ministry of the receiving State. The co-operation so received could be quite considerable, as in the case of Poland's provision, in the 1950s and 1960s, of a suitable venue for the numerous talks held in Warsaw between the ambassadors of the People's Republic of China and the United States.

16. Absence of Diplomatic Contacts

On the up side of the diplomatic relations ladder recognition was included as a separate stage. As was then pointed out, there is no equivalent stage on the down side. Recognition of a State cannot be withdrawn in the absence of a change in the facts. It is the case that when a State undergoes some substantial physical change, other States may have to decide whether to recognize the expanded or truncated State. But that process is more in the nature of the recognition of a new State than the withdrawal of recognition from an existing one.

It doubtless sometimes happens that where two States have broken dip-

[126] For two instances of the last phenomenon, see Alan James, *Peacekeeping in International Politics* (London: Macmillan in association with the International Institute for Strategic Studies, 1990), pp. 156 and 234.

lomatic relations they also, over a long period of time, have no diplomatic contacts with each other of any kind. Such an absence of contacts may also occur in relation to two States which have never been in diplomatic relations. Accordingly, this situation is justifiably included as the final stage on the down side of the diplomatic relations ladder.

However, it is necessary to distinguish between specific bilateral instances of this phenomenon and the case of a particular State being in total diplomatic isolation. The latter is an exceedingly unlikely condition. Most States are clearly in or probably regard themselves as in diplomatic relations with most other States, even if they have virtually no direct dealings with certain of them. And where breaches of diplomatic relations occur, it is highly probable that they relate to bilateral relationships which have some substance to them—which gives rise to the necessity of continuing diplomatic contact, the varying nature of which has been discussed in the three previous stages. References are indeed sometimes made to 'hermit States', such as Burma in the 1970s, North Korea in the earlier 1980s, and Albania for much of the last few decades. But it is improbable that a close examination of these or any other like instances would reveal a condition which could strictly be described as 'hermitry'.

****

Diplomatic relations and contacts are ubiquitous. The reason for this is that States conduct their business with each other largely by communicating with each other, and such communications are chiefly channelled through the diplomatic system. This system is therefore of overwhelming international importance. Its significance may be more fully examined on another occasion.[127]

****

[127] For the writer's preliminary foray into this question, see Alan James, 'Diplomacy and International Society', *International Relations*, vol. 6, no. 6 (November 1980); and 'International Society', *British Journal of International Studies*, vol. 4, no. 2 (July 1978).

REVIEWS OF BOOKS

Surrender, Occupation, and Private Property in International Law. By NISUKE ANDO. Oxford: Clarendon Press, 1991. xvi + 208 pp. £30.

Professor Nisuke Ando seeks in this work, based upon his Ph.D thesis, to evaluate the international legality of Allied, meaning US, occupation policies designed to demilitarize and democratize post-war Japanese society in the particular context of their impact upon private property rights in Japan. This is an important question and relatively under-studied in comparison with the post-war settlement in Germany. It has also gained in contemporary significance in the light of the debate on the meaning and implementation of the 'new world order' claimed after the 1990 Gulf conflict. In Japan, unlike Germany, there was a degree of continuity between the wartime and post-war regimes—notwithstanding the trial of some prominent members as war criminals. To a considerable extent therefore the US occupation functioned through the network of the Imperial Government, although the latter had, of course, very little independence of action during this time.

The book commences with an historical account of the occupation regime and its measures 'purporting to transform Japan from a militant despotic state into a peaceful, democratic one' (p 11). These included in particular the purge of militarists and ultra-nationalists, the dissolution of the *Zaibatsu* (the pre-1945 monopolistic industrial conglomerates), and land reform with particular emphasis upon the abolition of 'feudal' structures.

Ando raises the basic question, referring also to the case of *Kakyu Saiban-sho Minji Saiban-Rei-Shu*, of the applicability of the Regulations respecting the Laws and Customs of War on Land annexed to 1907 Hague Convention IV and in particular the prohibition of property confiscation by Article 46. It is pointed out that the Hague Regulations in general were incorporated in the relevant US Army Field Manual, but also that President Truman on 6 September 1945 expressly stated that the power of the Supreme Commander for the Allied Powers rested upon the *unconditional surrender* and the Potsdam Declaration. The interaction of the Hague Regulations, the instrument of surrender and the Potsdam Declaration forms the main substance of the work.

Assuming that the 'occupation' provisions of the *jus in bello* apply throughout a hostile military occupation (the point is mildly arguable but common sense suggests this), the main question is then of the effect of 'unconditional surrender'. Ando suggests that the concept is singularly vague and submits that 'the legal nature of an unconditional surrender is purely military . . . [political] terms are binding [only] . . . because they are a result of mutual consent' (p. 65). The military/political distinction has an obvious degree of practical validity, but the degree of 'consent' upon the 'political' side at the end of the Second World War must be thought somewhat notional. It is concluded that, in the light of occupation experiences, post-surrender occupations may in practice be based upon a variation of the prima facie demands of the Hague Regulations.

Ando draws an important distinction between Allied practice in Germany and Japan in so far as the assumption of Allied authority in Germany was unilateral; the effective collapse of the Reich Government rendered this perhaps inevitable. In Japan political terms were reached constituting 'the Allies' as well as Japan's advance commitment regarding post-surrender treatment of Japan and the Japanese people' (p. 86). These are represented as a 'contractual' basis for occupation and, since the occupation was patently not an annexation, it is argued that in fact the Hague Regulations did remain applicable.

Upon this basis it is argued that the continuation of the Japanese Government precluded the occupation authorities from relying upon the powers of government under Article 43 of the Hague Regulations, presupposing 'The authority of the legitimate power having in fact passed into the hands of the occupant . . . '. The exercise of economic power, e.g. in the dissolution of the *Zaibatsu*, is argued to have exceeded occupation powers in so far as they went beyond the immediate necessities of the occupation. Ando's final conclusion is that 'The principle of self-determination of peoples, . . . will certainly reject the concept of social change, under a post-surrender occupation, imposed against the will of local populations' (p. 124). The analysis is scholarly and makes a number of important points about the legal authority of Occupying Powers in post-surrender situations. It must however be remarked that little emphasis is placed upon the somewhat *sui generis* nature of the Second World War in its closing stages. Thus, without for a moment denying the importance of 'self-determination', the doctrine might reasonably be held not to extend to the maintenance of a regime committed to continuing policies of 'unlawful' aggression which has been defeated in the consequent armed conflict. Equally the preservation of the Imperial Japanese Government for a variety of political reasons, whilst not legally insignificant, did not mean that it actually had any significant range of choice. This of course raises the interesting question of whether such settlements are ever 'voluntary' in any meaningful sense—perhaps an irresolvable dilemma. These historical quibbles do not however detract from the scholarly claims of the general discussion and Professor Ando is to be congratulated upon a useful contribution to the literature.

H. McCoubrey

Competition Policy and Merger Control in the Single European Market. By Sir Leon Brittan. Cambridge: Grotius Publications Ltd., 1991. 70 pp. Paperback, £15. *New Directions in European Community Law*. By F. Snyder. London: Weidenfeld, 1990. xviii + 176 pp. £25.

The lectures which form the substance of the first of these books were delivered by Sir Leon Brittan in Cambridge in February 1990, as part of a series of memorial lectures in honour of Sir Hersch Lauterpacht. The subjects, covering aspects of EEC competition law, are matters on which Sir Leon, as an international lawyer and Vice President of the European Commission and EC Commissioner for Competition, is eminently qualified to speak.

Part I, entitled 'Jurisdictional Issues of EEC Competition Law', considers the question of the jurisdictional reach of EEC competition law: to what extent, and on what principles, should EEC competition law be applied to companies, persons and activities outside its territory? Acknowledging that 'the key to the jurisdictional reach of competition rules is the precise extent and qualification of the territorial principle', he traces the course of the Court of Justice's interpretation of that principle via *Béguelin* and *ICI* v. *Commission*, culminating in the *Wood Pulp* case, in which the Court failed to endorse the full 'effects' doctrine advocated by the Commission, and concluded that the appropriate test is the place where the agreement is *implemented*.

As Sir Leon points out, however, the real problem is not the legal problem of definition but the practical one of enforcement. This is a matter of politics and diplomacy. Citing Lord Wilberforce's dictum that 'in anti-trust matters the policy of one State is to defend what it is the policy of another State to attack' he acknowledges the need to respect the principles of non-interference and comity, and to exercise jurisdiction in the light of reasonableness and proportionality. But the increase in international trade resulting from the completion of the internal market, and the growth of world trade in general, demand that existing consultation and dispute-solving procedures with our major trading partners be improved and extended if problems of enforcement of EEC competition law are to be overcome.

The second lecture is a straightforward account of the development of merger control in the EEC, from its modest beginnings with the Commission's Memorandum in 1966, which suggested that Article 86 might be applied to mergers, via the Court's judgments in *Continental Can* and *Philip Morris*, which laid the foundations for a Community merger policy, to the final passing of the Merger Regulation, 4064/89. Uncertainty concerning the scope of Articles 85 and 86, the 1992 single market programme, bringing with it increased merger activity, and the great variation in national competition laws, some States having no merger policy at all, had combined finally to convince member States of the need for a Community mergers policy.

Sir Leon outlines the scope of Regulation 4064/89 and the likely approach of the Commission in interpreting and applying its provisions. Its main advantage, he suggests, is the clear demarcation line between Community and national jurisdiction, the 'one-stop shopping' principle, which, he suggests, will greatly increase security for businessmen. He provides welcome reassurance that the Commission 'does not intend' to enforce Articles 85 and 86 below the Regulation's threshold levels. Whilst he alludes to the problems involved in the application of the Regulation, the problem of assessing the relevant product market and geographical market, of whether 'effective competition will be significantly impeded' by a proposed merger, or whether it will bring about 'technical and economic progress', he has no doubts that they can be satisfactorily resolved.

As might be expected, Sir Leon writes clearly and confidently, as a lawyer concerned with practical legal issues, speaking to lawyers and business men and women. For those with little or no knowledge of EEC competition law, or of international law, the lectures provide, as the publishers suggest, an excellent 'simple introduction' to the legal and practical problems involved. For those engaged in the practice of competition law, there are insights into the Commission's thinking in this area and indications of likely future developments. The writer does not attempt in these lectures to dig beneath the surface, to explore the deeper policy issues involved, or to cast doubts on the rightness of the Commission's competition policy; nor could he be expected to do so. As a result the lectures are informative, interesting, and thought-provoking, but they do not touch on the larger issues.

Professor Snyder's essays on *New Directions in European Community Law*, on the other hand, set out with quite a different aim. The essays are critical, academic, analytical. They look beyond the practical 'legal' issues of Community law to their political, economic and social causes and consequences. The writer is more interested in the policy behind the law and the forces that shape that policy than its content or interpretation. He is concerned with the hidden agenda.

The book consists of five chapters, all previously published as separate articles between 1987 and 1989, revised and updated, and in some cases substantially rewritten. They focus on a number of recurring and interconnected themes and ideas, some of a highly abstract nature, illustrated by concrete examples drawn from the Community's common agricultural policy.

Chapter 1, 'New Directions', which is largely introductory, calls for a new 'contextual' approach to the study of Community law. The law must be studied and understood in its theoretical framework, in the light of the forces, political, economic and social, which shape it. Taking as his model one particular area of the Community activity, the disposal of surpluses of skimmed milk powder under the Common Agricultural Policy, he demonstrates the interaction between different groups, national and international, public and private, in the law and policy-making process. He shows how the thinking of the EC institutions is based on accepted western capitalist notions and economic philosophies and how the ramifications of these policies extend not only throughout the Community but around the world.

Chapter 2, entitled 'Interests and the Legislative Process', explores the concept of interests and their role in the Community law-making process. He points out the paradox of a process which is highly visible in the formal sense, with negotiations conducted in Brussels 'in the full glare of publicity', but in which the nature and role of specific interests 'remains generally opaque'. He suggests that the most important interests in the legislative process may not be represented directly or indirectly at all.

He explores the meaning of 'interest' and the complex interaction between 'interests', 'structures' and 'outcomes', demonstrating how past interests 'become embodied in institutions' and how 'structures themselves define, delimit and shape objective interests'.

'Structures are the representations of previous outcomes as well as frameworks, influences and sometimes determinants of continuing conflicts and compromises.' There is 'no clean slate'. Nor is there any clear conception of a 'national' or a 'public interest'. 'The standard proposition that States acts in their self interest' begs two basic questions: 'What self'? and 'which interest'?

In similar vein, Chapter 3, 'Ideologies of Competition', begins with the observation that 'the distortion of competition does not have any single, clear, generally accepted meaning'. He considers two contrasting ideologies of competition embodied in the British and the French attitudes towards the Community's sheepmeat regime during the 'Lamb War' of the 1980s. On one analysis, the British view, distortion of competition is seen as a 'reduction of free trade'; on another, espoused by the French, as an 'undue moderation of market structure'. The former assumes formal equality between individuals and places almost exclusive reliance on the regulation of the market. It presupposes that the operation of market forces alone, both in the production of goods and their distribution, tends necessarily to result only in beneficial effects. The latter, recognizing the fact of inequality but deploring its inequities, considers the market to be only one of several means of governing society. The sympathies of the writer are clearly with the latter.

Chapter 4 raises questions about another matter which lawyers may take for granted, namely the distinction and difference in treatment in EEC law between agriculture and industry. He examines the reasons, historical, social and political, for this difference and reveals the gap between theory and reality. Agriculture has become industrialized; measures which were designed to protect the small farmer have in fact benefited the large producers and first-stage processors. He questions whether agriculture *should* have a special legal status and concludes, convincingly, that the Community should not treat agriculture differently but should 'focus on improving the basic conditions of life and the decision-making powers of disadvantaged individuals, groups and classes'.

Finally, Chapter 5, on the European Community's food aid legislation, charts the changes in the Community's food aid policy as expressed through its landmark legislation. Starting as a means whereby the Community could dispose of its agricultural surpluses, it has developed over the years into an instrument of development policy. Applauding this move, he questions whether a food aid policy might not run counter to long-term, self-sustaining rural development. As he comments, a system whereby financial transfers take place under the guise of 'food aid' lacks transparency.

These essays are undoubtedly stimulating and thought-provoking. They cast fresh light on the Community policy-making process, as well as on some of the policies themselves. For those who need persuading, they demonstrate the utility as well as the attraction of the 'contextual' approach to the study of law. Despite being written as separate units, they form a coherent whole. Nor do they date, since the approach can be applied equally to other policies, as to other areas of the law. Although the transition from theory to practical example is occasionally abrupt, generally the use of concrete illustration serves to leaven and clarify the more abstract ideas. This book will, or should, be read by teachers of EEC law and their students, particularly postgraduate students. Notwithstanding the competing demands of a three-year undergraduate course and the ever-increasing range of Community activity, this book is a timely reminder of the need for teachers and students to find time to pursue new directions in Community law.

J. STEINER

Principles of Public International Law. By IAN BROWNLIE. 4th edition. Oxford: Clarendon Press, 1990. xlviii + 735 pp. + index. Hardback £55; paper £25.

The outstretched hand—of whatever hue—searching for guidance on any matter of international law usually first reaches for this textbook. It has a powerful reputation and broad acceptance. Eleven years had elapsed since the third edition and a new edition was eagerly awaited by scholars worldwide.

This edition has generally updated the earlier work, although the same format and presentation has been maintained, with some modification of the subjects considered. In particular, the developments in the law of the sea, as influenced by the 1982 Convention and decisions of international tribunals, are expounded; the present law on immunity from jurisdiction is clarified; and the recent complex cases involving expropriation of foreign-owned property are dealt with. However, as with many later editions of textbooks, it could have had the benefit of some small pruning, particularly in the areas of territorial sovereignty and diplomatic and consular relations.

It is the extensive research and detailed footnotes which have made this textbook so valuable for practitioners in international law and for graduates—but it can cause some undergraduates to blanch. Yet this edition does have some gaps in its coverage of the developments in international law in the past decade. It is surprising how little comment is made in the chapter on sources about the very important decision by the International Court of Justice on the merits in the *Nicaragua* v. *United States* case. The interaction there between customary international law and treaty law is all too briefly alluded to by the author and no real criticism of the Court's judgment is given. Also, the decision of the House of Lords in the *International Tin Council* case has had wide impact on a number of areas of international law, as seen from the British perspective (which is the author's standpoint), from the relationship between international law and national law to immunity of international organizations. Nevertheless, the author refrains from discussing it in any detail.

The maintenance of the format and presentation of the earlier edition has also meant that the scope for the author to bring his scholarship to bear on contemporary issues in international law is unfortunately limited. Self-determination, probably one of the main concerns affecting territorial sovereignty today, warrants only a few pages overall, and the vibrant field of international environmental law is not indexed and is only obliquely referred to. Also the impact of terrorism on questions of jurisdictional sovereignty could have been considered more closely and the chapter on human rights has little mention of the rapidly expanding recent case law, particularly of the European Court of Human Rights, or of the comments by the Human Rights Committee. Some acknowledgement of the different theoretical approaches to international law would also have been of assistance.

Despite these criticisms, the author covers the subjects dealt with in considerable depth for a one-volume textbook on international law. The structure is clear and the analysis firmly and strongly made. The wealth of footnotes is evidence of the research involved.

It is, therefore, disappointing that this textbook does not more fully reflect some of the growth in thought, values and priorities in international law in the past decade. Nevertheless, because of its impressive reputation and scholarship, it will continue to be read widely and used as a complete authority by many who reach for it.

ROBERT McCORQUODALE

Law After Revolution. Edited by W. E. BUTLER, P. B. MAGGS and J. B. QUIGLEY, JR. New York, London, Rome: Oceana Publications Inc., 1988. xiii + 247 pp. $40.

The title of this collection of essays, written to commemorate the 70th birthday of Professor Joseph Berman, a distinguished American scholar of Soviet law and socialist legal systems, is rich in irony. The volume, which was published in 1988, only months before the collapse of Soviet-backed regimes in central and eastern Europe, treats certain aspects of 'modern socialist law' from a variety of perspectives.

Of course, the 'revolution' of the title, the Bolshevik seizure of power in what became the Soviet Union, has been overtaken by at least two further upheavals which can justly be characterized as 'revolutions'. The first, initiated by President Gorbachev, represented an attempt to reform and revitalize the politico-economic system from within. At the time of writing, a further 'revolution' has commenced, with the disintegration of the Soviet Union into its various constituent parts, and an abandonment of Marxist-Leninism. This second, potentially darker, revolution has barely begun. Fuelled by the incipient nationalism of the diverse peoples brought together in the former Soviet Union, and a resentment born of protracted and worsening economic privation, its consequences can only be guessed.

What then of 'modern socialist law'? Inevitably, 'socialist law' is of diminishing significance, especially in the newly-constituted democracies of Poland, Czechoslovakia and Hungary, which are rapidly transforming their legal systems, particularly in the areas of constitutional law, economic law, foreign investment law, company, banking and commercial law. The same fate awaits 'socialist law' in at least some parts of what was the Soviet Union.

Nevertheless, these essays, by a distinguished group of legal specialists, remain of considerable importance, both as a historical record of one of the major socio-political movements of the twentieth century, and for their insights into matters of contemporary relevance. In particular, a chapter by two Paris-based lawyers, D. Hascher and J. M. Hertzfeld, on 'East-West Countertrade and the International Legal and Business Environment', is especially pertinent to current business practices. After all, 'countertrade', as a species of international trade, is generally a product of economic necessity rather than of political ideology. Indeed, the incidence of countertrade has increased recently on an East-East as well as on an East-West basis, particularly on the inter-business level, as a result of the financial difficulties of most of the former socialist States.

The authors offer a detailed description of the different types of countertrade currently practised, ranging from simple barter deals to sophisticated 'buy back' arrangements. The chapter assesses the impact of countertrade on the obligations of States parties to the GATT, presents a detailed and informed discussion of the process of negotiating and structuring the contract(s), and comments on the phenomenon of 'triangular countertrade'. In addition, the authors consider the antitrust implications of countertrade under EC and US law, and offer judicious and balanced conclusions concerning the economic and business implications of countertrade transactions.

In an interesting chapter, Professor J. B. Quigley considers the impact of Soviet law in the West. Regrettably, his analysis does not extend to the impact of Soviet doctrines on the development of public international law, which would have been of particular interest to readers of this *Year Book*. Instead, his examples are drawn from areas of municipal law such as labour law, social welfare law, sex discrimination law and general economic law.

In addition, the book contains generally interesting contributions on 'Necessary Defence, Judge-Made Law and Soviet Man' (W.E. Butler); 'Seizure of Power and War Communism (1917–21) in Soviet Legal Historiography' (Z. L. Zile); 'Choice and Compulsion in Soviet Labour Law: Labour Conscription 1917–21' (P. B. Maggs); '"Non-Labour" Income and Individual Labor Activity in the USSR' (O. S. Ioffe); 'More Equal Than Others: The Legal Basis for Awarding Medals in the USSR' (D. D. Barry); 'A China-Watcher's Impressions of the Soviet Joint Enterprise Legislation' (J. A. Cohen), as well as a list of Professor Berman's published and unpublished writings on Soviet law and related topics.

STEPHEN I. POGANY

Répertoire des documents de la Cour de la Haye, série 1 (1922–45), Volume 5: *La Responsabilité internationale, la guerre et la neutralité.* Publication No. 54 of L'Institut des Hautes Etudes (Geneva), under the direction of LUCIUS CAFLISCH. Geneva: 1989. 1637 pp. (including index). No price stated.

This is another volume which will take its place in every library as an essential tool of research.

The first topic covered, international responsibility, is perhaps likely to prove more interesting, if only because of the frequency with which issues of responsibility still arise, and perhaps also because the topic is under current—seemingly interminable—study by the ILC. The case law of the Permanent Court is surprisingly rich in this field, and there is a very useful guide to this law in the introduction to the volume.

The selection of texts is excellent, and prompts only two comments. The first is that the *Chorzów* case, so far as it concerns damages, cannot properly be understood without reference to the questions posed by the Court to the experts in that case, and these are not reproduced. Certainly in the *Amoco International Finance Co.* case (US/Iran Claims Tribunal, 14 July 1987) Virally's analysis of what the Court meant in *Chorzów* turned on those questions posed to the experts. The second is that, in order to provide the maximum assistance to the researcher, a little more editorial guidance—even in footnotes—might be welcome. Thus, in the section on nationality, in relation to diplomatic protection, a brief cross-reference to ICJ decisions like *Nottebohm* and *Barcelona Traction*, or to Case A.18 before the US/Iran Claims Tribunal, might prevent the researcher from falling into error, by assuming that the PCIJ decisions represent the current law.

The part on war and neutrality is of less direct interest today, but is restricted to fewer cases.

The quality of production is excellent and adds to the welcome this volume is bound to receive.

D. W. BOWETT

'East-West' Diplomacy for Environment in the United Nations. By E. M. CHOSSUDOVSKY. New York: UNITAR, 1990. 247 pp. No price stated.

The development of international environmental law since the Stockholm Conference on the Human Environment in 1972 is one of the more striking examples of international law-making in the past twenty-five years. Where, formerly, much had to be derived from principles of reasonableness, equity and responsibility for damage in customary law, today the international lawyer is confronted by an ever-growing body of treaty law and international institutions dedicated to the control of environmental problems. These treaties can be seen as law-making in several different senses. Some, like the 1982 UNCLOS, codify and develop rules of general application. They are perhaps different in scope, but not in kind, from earlier codification treaties. The legal principles proposed by the World Commission on Environment and Development represent an extension of this approach to the global protection of the environment.

This is not the typical model of international law-making for the environment however. Much more significant are the many treaties, some global, but many regional, which establish detailed rules and rule-making structures for specific environmental problems. Examples of this category are the Ozone Convention, the London Dumping Convention, regional agreements concerned with land-based pollution of the marine environment, international watercourse treaties, and the Basel Convention on Transboundary Transport of Hazardous Waste. What characterizes each of these treaties is the creation of intergovernmental institutions, which act as a continuing diplomatic forum for negotiation of the measures, including protocols, amendments and annexes, necessary to respond effectively to the particular issue in question. These bodies additionally perform a general supervisory role in monitoring treaty implementation and assessing its impact and effectiveness.

Framework agreements of this kind are thus an essential feature of modern environmental law and represent both a means of law-making and law-enforcement which has very largely supplanted earlier reliance on customary law. Since they presuppose co-operation between States, such agreements require diplomatic consensus if they are to be adopted and to operate successfully. Chossudovsky has chosen for his study one of the better examples of this genre, which displays both the strengths and the typical weaknesses of such a fiduciary approach to environmental management. His book explores the interplay of a UN agency, the Economic Commission for Europe, and a diplomatic forum, the Conference on Security and Co-operation in Europe, in developing agreements and measures to tackle environmental problems affecting both Eastern and Western Europe. He shows how the former body became in effect the instrument of the CSCE for implementing and supervising the environmental policies agreed by participating States as part of the process of broadening their co-operation on security matters. The most concrete expression of this co-operation between East and West is the Geneva Convention on Long-Range Transboundary Air Pollution, concluded in 1979. Although itself rather weak and of limited value, this treaty has eventually led to the adoption of much stronger protocols dealing with monitoring, and the control of sulphur dioxide and nitrogen oxide emissions. Its dynamic character very much reflects the pattern of development in many other environmental treaties, where the continuing process of negotiation and scrutiny have, in some cases, such as the London Dumping Convention, resulted in the adoption of measures very much stronger than initially indicated by the original treaty.

The value of this book lies in its detailed examination of the evolution of an environmental role for the ECE and CSCE, and of the process leading to negotiation of the 1979 Convention. It does not explore the more recent attempts to involve the CSCE in promoting protection of the Mediterranean environment, nor does it examine the rather pertinent question why after so long both bodies have failed to come up with any more substantial policies and measures of environmental protection in Europe. In this respect both institutions compare rather unfavourably with the OECD, the EEC, and even the International North Sea Conference, whose impact on national policy has been very much greater. Chossudovsky has not set out to write a broad-ranging examination of the role of multilateral diplomacy and international institutions in protecting the environment, and he offers only limited insights into this central issue. But his book does represent a useful case-study of a neglected area of European co-operation.

Quite correctly, he concludes with the observation that institutions alone cannot generate co-operation, and that more attention needs to be devoted to the interaction of institutional arrangements and governments. An annex sets out some useful documentation.

Alan E. Boyle

Straits Used for International Navigation: A Spanish Perspective. By José A. de Yturriaga. Dordrecht/Boston/London: Martinus Nijhoff, 1991. xvi + 372 pp. (including index). £69.50.

The subtitle of this volume puts the author's cards on the table, but in some respects it is nevertheless misleading.

Spain was a (perhaps the) leader of the 'straits States' group at the Third United Nations Conference on the Law of the Sea, and Sr de Yturriaga (now Spanish Ambassador to Ireland) was one of its delegates. There is no pretence here of detachment: in the author's view his country's resistance to attempts to transform the right of innocent passage in straits into the much broader right of transit passage was wholly justified, and failed only because the other members of the group lacked the diplomatic adroitness needed to stop the US-Soviet juggernaut. (This is not to say, however, that the tone is one of heated accusation or self-exculpation: it remains measured and dignified throughout.) In places the book offers a first-hand account of the negotiations, and the fact that it is in this respect more of a memoir than the traditional law book does not make it the less interesting. To this extent, then, the subtitle reflects the contents.

On the other hand, the reader who is drawn to the book in the hope of finding a detailed account of Spanish law, practice and preoccupations regarding straits, and particularly those Spain borders, is due for a disappointment. There is, in particular, no in-depth discussion of the implications for navigation and aviation of the dispute between Spain and the United Kingdom over Gibraltar.

Part I concerns the definition of straits used for international navigation. Part II is entitled 'Historical Development'; but by far the largest part of it is devoted to an account of the evolution of the relevant provisions of the 1982 Law of the Sea Convention, and there is very little earlier history. The third Part, of roughly equal length, contains a detailed analysis of the articles adopted. This is competently and in general accurately carried out, but does not add much to what has already been done by Reisman, Moore and others. The author identifies the manifold drafting deficiencies of the Convention and explains how they came about. Perhaps inevitably, there is a good deal of duplication of what was dealt with in the previous Parts. The final Part is entitled 'Critical Appraisal and Conclusions', but this is not wholly accurate: most of the critical appraisal comes earlier on, and the bulk of this section concerns the attitude of various States to the question whether countries which do not accept the Convention, such as the United States, can avail themselves of the transit passage regime.

It is perhaps in this area that the book is at its weakest. Given the limited acceptance of both the 1958 Geneva Convention on the Territorial Sea and the 1982 Convention, it is very important to assess the customary law on the subject of passage through straits, both as it stood before 1958 and as it has evolved subsequently (even post-1982). Ambassador de Yturriaga does not deal with this very thoroughly. For example, he evidently disagrees with O'Connell's views on the legal character of straits, but does not offer a detailed refutation.

This feature, above all, prevents the work from being the definitive account of the law on straits or even, one suspects, of the Spanish position. On the other hand, the clear and even lively writing makes it very readable; and, rejecting as it does the predominant doctrinal view that the new regime is progressive and beneficial to the world community, it constitutes a useful and stimulating addition to the literature.

M. H. Mendelson

The North Sea: Basic Legal Documents on Regional Environmental Co-operation. Edited by D. Freestone and T. Ijlstra. Dordrecht: Graham and Trotman/Martinus Nijhoff, 1991. xx + 450 pp. £89.50.

This is best seen as a companion book to the book of essays edited by the same editors and published by the same publishers in 1990, *The North Sea: Perspectives on Regional Environmental Cooperation*. Indeed, the original plan had been to include a documentary annex in that book, and only when the large volume of the relevant legal documentation became apparent was it decided to produce a separate book of documents.

The book contains only a selection, but a fairly comprehensive one, of the documents relevant to regional environmental co-operation concerning avoidance or reduction of pollution of the North Sea and the protection of marine wildlife and conservation of fisheries there.

Its brief introduction aims to do little more than illustrate the great variety of these documents, which are separated into twelve chapters on, respectively: North Sea Conference Declarations; ocean dumping; land-based pollution; joint statements of the regional bodies primarily concerned with ocean dumping and land-based pollution, the Oslo and Paris Commissions; the Bonn Agreement of 1983; EC instruments; fisheries; the Wadden Sea; nature protection; navigation; oil and gas exploitation; and delimitation agreements. It is valuable to have in one volume so many pertinent and up to date instruments concerning one of the most advanced regional sea areas in terms of international environmental co-operation, although this reviewer has doubts that the average reader would be prepared to pay such a high price for the convenience.

Treaty references are given in a table of treaties, and there is a table of ratifications by littoral States covering ten of the major treaties and protocols (at pp. 427–9). Eight useful, but not always clearly annotated, maps follow this.

The book has adopted a uniform format for each document, which must have entailed a great deal of work. It has allowed the documents, some of them lengthy, to be set out in chronological sequence within each chapter in a manner which, if not aesthetically pleasing, avoids waste of space.

The choice of documents involved balanced judgments, which on the whole strike this reviewer as correctly made. He would, however, have preferred to see inclusion of more international conventions with relevant regional implications, such as the Ramsar and Berne Conventions and even additional regional conventions, such as the Rhine Convention. These could have appeared instead of one or two of those fisheries documents which are not primarily concerned with conservation, the Frigg and Murchison Field Agreements on joint oil and gas exploitation and the delimitation agreements, as the latter documents are relevant to questions of jurisdiction over fisheries or offshore exploration and exploitation, but not necessarily central to an understanding of environmental co-operation. Nevertheless, the book is not unduly lengthened as a result, and their inclusion makes it a useful reference book for more general law of the sea interests. It might also have been possible to include some relevant case reports.

I would recommend this book as a valuable resource, albeit recognizing that it is probably beyond the pocket of most readers.

G. Plant

Titoli Storici e Linee di Base del Mare Territoriale. By Andrea Gioia. Padua: Cedam—Casa Editrice Dott. Antonio Milani, 1990. xv + 971 pp. No price stated.

This book represents a formidable undertaking. It begins with a survey of the doctrine on historic waters and then follows this with a series of chapters devoted to State practice. Successive chapters deal with the practice of Great Britain, the USA, Canada, Scandinavia, the USSR, Portugal and the Mediterranean, and then, finally, 'Others'. The final chapter concludes with an assessment of the role of the concept of historic waters in the evolving law of the sea.

The US practice is particularly rich, and Chapter III contains a very detailed analysis of the recent Supreme Court judgments in the cases dealing with the Gulf of California, Long Island Sound, Mississippi Sound, and Alaska.

The chapter on Soviet practice is less detailed, but it is concluded by a useful analysis of the Soviet position. There is a very detailed examination of the Soviet claim over Peter the Great Bay, which brings out the heavy reliance of the USSR on geographical, economic and strategic factors, as much as the historical proof of acquiescence by other States (p. 566). The other, Baltic, claims are also discussed, as are the claims over the Sea of Azov.

Chapter VII deals with the Portuguese claims relating to the estuary of the Tagus and the Sado rivers. It also deals with the Tunisian claim over the Gulf of Gabes and the Libyan claim over the Gulf of Sirte. This last claim is of interest for two reasons: first, because of the military incidents it gave rise to in 1986, and, second, because it emphasizes how States tend to base their claims on their perceived strategic interests rather than the historical evidence. This is, in essence, the notion of 'vital' bays. The comparison with the Gulf of Taranto (pp. 685–701) is an interesting one, for, as the author points out, Italy, too, has favoured the 'vital' bay theory, and a new acquiescence in the claim, rather than evidence of a historical acquiescence in the claim, becomes the crucial test. But it seems Malta has protested, and the UK and the USA have entered reservations on this claim (pp. 696–7).

Chapter VIII deals with a miscellany of other bays or waters, claimed to be 'historic', certain Australian bays, the Gulf of Fonseca, some European bays (including, surprisingly, Granville Bay on the French coast), the Zuider Zee, and Pohai Bay, in China. This last is, for China, very much a 'vital' bay, for there is little real historical evidence of general acquiescence. The Thai claim over the Gulf of Thailand is somewhat similar (p. 761).

The author, in a final chapter, looks to the future of the concept of historic waters in the evolution of the law of the sea. He correctly concludes that codification of a 'regime' of historic waters, or bays, is not the answer, for each case turns on the specific claim and the degree of acquiescence in that claim.

It has to be said that this book reveals an enormous amount of research, and it really has no counterpart elsewhere. The conclusions are sound, and we now have a monograph which will deservedly become a standard source of reference.

D. W. BOWETT

Collective Responses to Illegal Acts in International Law: UN Action in the Question of Southern Rhodesia. By VERA GOWLLAND-DEBBAS. Dordrecht: Martinus Nijhoff, 1990. 663 pp. + appendices. £129.

This exceedingly thorough examination of the treatment of the Rhodesian question in the United Nations enables the reader to re-assess—with a detachment which the passage of time has brought—one of the most impressive collective responses ever made by the UN to an illegal situation. But, as the author makes clear, the illegality arose on the international plane, not on the constitutional plane. The illegality arose from a violation of human rights and fundamental freedoms, and of the right of self-determination, for the declaration of independence was aimed at 'the extension of colonialism in another form' (p. 227). The argument that Rhodesia was not recognized as a State, and therefore could not commit an international delict, is dismissed summarily (and correctly), on the ground that such delicts can be committed by entities other than States.

But how does one move from reparation to nullity, as the consequence of such a delict? The author justifies this by reference to the concepts of *jus cogens*, obligations *erga omnes*, and international crimes (all concepts without mention in the UN resolutions on Rhodesia). The argument is well-made and basically convincing, especially when based on the violation of the right of self-determination. The only unease felt by this reviewer relates to the reliance on Article 19 of the ILC Draft on State Responsibility, and the notion of an international crime. The application of that notion to a denial of self-determination remains a highly controversial matter and seems, in the present context, unnecessary if all one needs to support it is the proposition that UDI was not only a delict but a nullity.

But non-recognition is a different matter, and Chapter 4 emphasizes that non-recognition did not spring from doubts over whether Rhodesia met the criteria for statehood: it was conceived as an obligation designed to refuse all validity to an illegal act, the principle *ex factis jus oritur* notwithstanding. The author supports the view that the duty of non-recognition, as a collective sanction for internationally illegal acts, is not simply a duty arising from the UN Charter, but is a customary law duty. There remains the question of which delicts trigger this sanction. The unlawful resort to force, certainly: but violation of the right of self-determination? The *Namibia* opinion suggests an affirmative answer.

The quite separate question of whether the United Kingdom either could, or should, use the different sanction of the use of force against the white, minority regime always had an air of unreality, and this is highlighted by the discussion at pp. 331–6. The Charter does not forbid States to use force to suppress a rebellion (assuming the rebellion is not itself an expression of the right to self-determination). But, equally, the Charter does not impose a duty to use force, in the absence of agreements under Article 43 and a decision by the Security Council.

Of course the General Assembly upheld the legitimacy of the use of force by 'the people of Zimbabwe' as an expression of their right to self-determination. But the General Assembly's view that the United Kingdom had the *duty* to ensure compliance by Rhodesia with the POW Convention had the double defect of impracticality and unsoundness.

The coercive measures undertaken against Rhodesia are examined in detail in Part III. This is meticulous, detailed analysis and, as regards SC Resolution 331, the author is surely right to conclude that a Council *authorization* to a Member to use force legitimates what would otherwise be a breach of Article 2(4). The contrary view by Fitzmaurice (this *Year Book*, 34 (1958)) was wrong. There follows a detailed account of the other mandatory measures—all in all, an impressive array—and the question which naturally arises is 'Why were they not effective?'

This leads to an examination of the legal basis for the positions adopted by States declining to co-operate in these mandatory sanctions. The author rightly dismisses the Portuguese and South African positions as untenable. But the plea of 'necessity' by States like Malawi, Botswana and Lesotho is more difficult. The author is unsympathetic to this plea, absent a dispensation under Article 48 of the Charter, but here, unusually, the analysis lacks penetration.

In contrast, the rejection of the pleas of the USA and of the 'permanent neutrals' is much more convincing, and is closely reasoned. The obligations of Articles 25 and 103 must override pleas based on domestic law or 'neutrality' treaties.

However, the weakness of the sanctions had other causes: inadequacy of information, inadequacy of implementation, ineffective control (the author gives a very detailed account of the working of the Sanctions Committee), defective enforcement machinery within the Member States, and perhaps failure to compensate States seriously damaged by having to apply sanctions. This detailed analysis is important for the future—although the author has no easy solutions to offer. The work will be one to which UN member States will wish to refer in the future before allowing optimism to dictate policy.

D. W. Bowett

The Return of Cultural Treasures. By Jeanette Greenfield. Cambridge: Cambridge University Press, 1989. xviii + 361 pp. + annexes on microfiche. £35.

The international art market is one of the purest manifestations of market capitalism in existence. Consumer knowledge approaches perfect levels, and prices—with which value is equated—are determined by the interaction of supply with a pure demand, flowing from the desire for an object and undistorted by necessity or utility. Art objects are intrinsically practically useless: desire for them is generated by the significance attached to them. Objects which derive their particular significance from their place in the life of a people or culture come to be regarded as cultural treasures.

Almost every nation has or has had some of its cultural treasures in 'foreign' custody: the Parthenon marbles, the Benin bronzes, and the Icelandic *Flateyjarbok* and *Codex Regius* are among the better known. Demands for the return of such treasures to their 'proper home' are frequently made, and much effort has been invested in the drafting of international conventions, national laws and specific agreements on the subject. But, as Dr Greenfield is careful to point out, the issues involved are anything but simple.

The concept of a 'home' for an object is elusive. Some works were made for foreign clients abroad: the Bayeux tapestry may fall into this category. Others were made by itinerant foreign artists, often working for a succession of noble patrons. Some objects, such as the Koh-i-Noor diamond, have significance in the culture of more than one nation. Some nations have been divided into two or more modern States; others have become parts of larger States in which they may seek to preserve, and sometimes to regain, their autonomy. Where then is 'home'? The problem is compounded by questions of the manner in which objects were acquired by their present custodians. Many, plainly, were simply stolen. Some were smuggled out of their country of origin and illegally sold. On the other hand, although the facts are often controversial (as they are in the case of Elgin's acquisition of the Parthenon marbles), it is clear that many acquisitions were, according to the law in force at the time of the transfer, lawful, no matter how ill-advised or how much regretted the transfer might have been. How far should such issues influence the resolution of claims for the return of cultural property? And how far should considerations of the accessibility of objects to the general public and to scholars, and of their optimal conservation and presentation, bear on the question?

In this beautifully illustrated book Dr Greenfield raises these issues through a review of international practice on the return of cultural treasures. She charts the successes, such as the amicable restoration of the *Flateyjarbok* by Denmark to Iceland in 1971, and the unresolved disputes, such as the often acrimonious debate over the return of the Parthenon marbles to Greece. By examining a number of cases in detail, she illustrates the complexity of the issues of private and public international law which arise, and the difficulties standing in the way of securing international agreement on a comprehensive policy concerning cultural treasures. Few of the main protagonists emerge well from her study. Western curators and governments can display a Scrooge-like retentiveness bolstered by intemperate language and reasoning that often seems to depart from dogmatism only in the direction of crassness. In other cases, one suspects that objects of relatively little note have acquired cultural significance for the requesting government primarily by virtue of the fact that they are located outside the country. And yet there is more than a glimmer of light in the considerable number of *ad hoc* arrangements which Dr Greenfield reviews under which objects have been returned to more appropriate settings.

The book is written for the intelligent general reader rather than the specialist lawyer, and it succeeds. Inevitably, it is already becoming dated: for instance, the Council of Europe Convention on Offences against Cultural Property, noted in its 1983 draft form, was adopted in 1985, as was the Granada Convention for the Protection of the Architectural Heritage of Europe. Similarly, in explaining for the general reader the unfolding of the often complex litigation over cultural treasures and the drafting of international agreements Dr Greenfield has necessarily had to proceed by generalization and exemplification, rather than by way of a comprehensive legal analysis. But this is the book's strength. It is a fine introduction to the legal aspects of the topic, both readable and, with its one hundred excellent illustrations, a delight to browse through.

VAUGHAN LOWE

Droits de l'homme et droit au développement. Edited by SILVIO MARCUS HELMONS. Louvain-la-Neuve and Brussels: Academia and Bruylant, 1989. 92 pp. BF 480.

This short collection of essays is based on a number of papers delivered at a colloquy organized by the Centre for Human Rights of the Catholic University of Louvain, in October 1985, on the theme of 'The Rights of Man and the Right to Development'.

The notion of a right to development has already generated a considerable literature (see, e.g., the bibliography in Bernhardt (ed.), *Encyclopaedia of Public International Law*, vol. 9, pp. 201–2). This book offers a lucid exposition of the principal arguments favouring the existence of such a right, as well as a discussion of some related matters. However, the central defect of the book is a certain lack of balance. In particular, the volume might have benefited from the inclusion of a chapter by a sceptic, who might have subjected the notion of a right to development to rigorous legal analysis.

In the longest contribution to the book, Judge M'Baye discusses the nature, sources and content of the right to development. As the originator of the term, if not the concept, of a right to development, Judge M'Baye argues eloquently for recognition of the right as a matter of positive law. However, despite his references to diverse legal texts, including the Covenant of the League of Nations, the UN Charter, the Constitutions of the ILO and of the World Health Organization, as well as to treaties concerned with the protection of human rights and to resolutions of the UN General Assembly and other international organs, this reviewer remains unconvinced. A *right* to development, if it is to mean anything, must entail specific and legally identifiable duties on the part of States. It is far from clear that these can be inferred from the vague, hortatory and often politically-inspired formulations of such an alleged right in some of the above-mentioned texts. Moreover, State practice scarcely recognizes any tangible duties on the part of developed States, in terms of their treatment of developing countries and peoples, amounting to confirmation of a right to development under general international law. Of course, specific treaty regimes, such as the GATT, incorporate notions of preferential treatment for developing countries. However, such provisions do not stem from the recognition of a general right to development.

In a thoughtful contribution, Peter Leuprecht, Director of Human Rights at the Council of Europe, alerts us to the totalitarian dangers implicit in certain applications of the right to development. In particular, he warns that peoples' rights, such as the right to development, should not be equated with the rights of the State. Moreover, he argues that in the event of a conflict between the collective right to development and certain individual rights, the latter must prevail. This clearly accords with the dominant Western ethos.

In a chapter on the contribution of the European Community to the right to development, Claude Cheysson, formerly Foreign Minister of France and currently an EC Commissioner, argues that the Community's relations with developing countries have been informed by a sense of political equality and mutual respect. M. Cheysson tactfully refrains from commenting on the disastrous effects on the fragile economies of many developing countries of the Community's wasteful and selfish Common Agricultural Policy. A balanced and perceptive review of the principal contributions, by Professor Helmons of the University of Louvain, concludes the book.

STEPHEN I. POGANY

Federalism and Decentralization: Constitutional Problems of Territorial Decentralization in Federal and Centralized States, Volume 2. INTERNATIONAL ASSOCIATION OF CONSTITUTIONAL LAW. Fribourg, Switzerland: Éditions Universitaires, 1987. 488 pp. SF 80.

This is the second volume of essays originating in papers delivered at a Round Table Conference, in December 1984, held to mark the opening of the Swiss Institute of Federalism. The book is divided into six sections dealing, successively, with 'Decision of Decentralization' (a more felicitous translation from the original French would probably be 'The Decision to Decentralize'), 'Structure of Decentralized Units', 'Autonomy of Decentralized Units', 'External Power of Decentralized Units', 'Financial Autonomy' and 'Decentralization and the Protection of Basic Rights'. The book concludes with a number of general reports.

Each of the six principal sections is introduced by a 'general report', which is generally followed by a series of 'national reports'. Each section concludes with a summary of the discussion and, occasionally, an excerpt from the discussion. Papers appear in either English or French.

The book contains much that will be of enduring interest. For example, the contributions of Professor Louis Henkin, on 'Federalism, Decentralization and Human Rights', are characteristically thoughtful, lucid and rewarding. Mention may also be made of Professor Antoine Messarra's essay, 'Principe de territorialité et principe de personnalité en fédéralisme comparé'. Professor Messarra, a Lebanese Maronite, raises the interesting question of whether federalism necessarily entails constitutional divisions between units defined geographically. Lebanon, since Ottoman times, has provided an example (not always encouraging) of divisions defined on the basis of personal identity—essentially that of religious affiliation. This system, as the author points out, may be more appropriate than the traditional federal model, where the disparate elements of a multi-confessional society are not clearly separated geographically.

Inevitably, some of the contributions have been eclipsed by recent events. In particular, the papers on the Yugoslav federal model, by Lidija Basta and Professor Pavle Nikolic, are now of mainly historic interest. In addition, the contribution by Poland's then Minister of Justice, on 'Decentralization and the Optimalization of the Local Decision-Making Process', could probably have benefited from a balancing contribution from a representative of Solidarity.

More fundamentally, however, the very theme of the book, 'Territorial Decentralization in Federal and Centralized States', appears to be no longer in step with contemporary developments, at least in Central and Eastern Europe. Thus, the disintegration of the Soviet and Yugoslav federations, and the emergence (or re-emergence) of sovereign States with a distinct national and cultural identity, are indicative of a reversion to a robust and uncompromising nationalism. It is to be hoped that the less palatable consequences of this phenomenon can be contained by international mechanisms, such as the European Convention on Human Rights and by eventual membership, for some, of the European Economic Community.

STEPHEN I. POGANY

Pacific Ocean Boundary Problems—Status and Solutions. By D. M. JOHNSTON and M. J. VALENCIA. *Publications on Ocean Development*, Volume 16. Dordrecht: Martinus Nijhoff, 1991. 214 pp. £49.50.

It has been estimated that by the middle of 1989 fewer than half of the ocean boundary delimitation problems around the globe had been solved. Of the one hundred and fifty or so agreements which did exist, many had been the result of the legally liberated diplomacy in the wake of the lengthy negotiations and final agreement of the 1982 Law of the Sea Convention. It is, of course, not always essential that such ocean boundaries be determined and it is only where failure to do so would increase the risk of conflict or deny one of the party States an essential share in the resources that the matter achieves high priority in the diplomatic programme. Human beings, like many other animals, are by instinct territorial, and the desire to draw lines around areas to indicate superior rights has spread into the sea. Land boundaries, however, serve a multi-purpose jurisdictional end, whereas allocation of rights and obligations within the maritime area are dictated more by the predominant sea-use to which the waters or the sea-bed are to be put. As a result, the authors make out a case for a 'functionalist' approach in solving maritime boundary disputes. Such boundaries, they urge, should be seen as operational not symbolic. Delimitation can be determined in a relatively rational manner in the light of the uses of the area, and the resulting boundaries should be characterized as administrative and negotiated in the context of long-term opportunities for ocean development and management.

The book divides the Pacific into five geographical areas and considers functionalist solutions to some thirteen complex boundary problems. The authors point out that although there are difficult geographical, technical, political, diplomatic and legal questions to be addressed, there are many examples of imaginative, innovative and sophisticated agreements already negotiated which give rise to optimism for the future, particularly in the light of the present shifting nature of international affairs. Nevertheless, many of the regions considered are characterized by high level military or political tension and by the co-existence of geographic congestion and high resource productivity. However, this means, the authors suggest, that any agreements, although they may be difficult to achieve in the first place, may well be strenuously maintained.

In several of the problems considered it can be seen that earlier agreements, often made by former colonial powers, have the effect of impeding attempts at present solution. Few of these agreements were made, of course, with any reference to sea-use; they were merely intended to be jurisdictional lines drawn on charts. For instance, the treaty of 1867 whereby Alaska was ceded to the United States by Russia laid down an ocean boundary in the Bering Sea. This line did not in fact represent the median line between the two territories, but neither does it provide an 'equitable solution' to delimitation in respect of the oil, gas and fish resources which have since been found there. Similarly, the 1887 Sino-French Convention on the delimitation of the frontier between China and Tonkin (Vietnam) has not aided the settlement of a boundary in the Gulf of Tonkin, although it has, in this case, had a restraining influence by discouraging actual exploitation in the disputed area. It is pointed out that while a legalistic approach to diplomacy in this region is likely to be harmful to effective negotiations, many Pacific States were prolific contributors to UNCLOS III. This apparent inconsistency, the authors maintain, is explained by the 'liberated' approach of the Law of the Sea Convention which advocates boundary delimitation diplomacy free from artificial constraints in the form of binding rules, principles, criteria or methods. This 'free-for-all' diplomacy may well be suited to boundary delimitation where the geographic and resource factors can be relatively easily identified. It would seem to be important, however, to preserve some principles or criteria where there is evidence of superpower involvement, or where third party rights of passage or high seas usage may be compromised.

The core of the book, which exemplifies the need for flexible diplomacy, is Chapter 4, an examination of thirteen complex ocean boundary problems. Here Johnston and Valencia reveal an impressive knowledge of the entire area, its geography and geology and the associated political tensions. Interesting and fascinating as their survey is, it is not altogether successful. The problems, although of the same genre, have a particular life and involvement of their own which fit uneasily into a comparative survey of this kind. The Bering sea boundary question has little in common with the Spratly Islands disputes, or with the maritime boundaries within the Singapore and Malacca Straits, except in so far as any solution will involve a large number of States and that some kind of joint administration might be a preferable outcome. This, although easily and often well illustrated, does not, it is submitted, take us very far when the authors themselves are able to enumerate fifty-one factors which should be taken into account. Does this broad analysis help? It is questionable whether the Pacific area can be considered as a whole. The table which takes up much of the final chapter and rates each of the fifty-one factors in relation to each problem considered on a facultative or obstructive scale of -5 to $+5$ must surely be taken as an amusing pastime and little more.

The main pleasure which the present commentator received from the book was the description of the varied problems which exist and the proposals for their solution. The authors reveal an exciting optimism and no little expertise in selecting them. The problems are, necessarily, illustrated by maps, but it is a pity that these are from other sources and often contain unnecessary detail which prevents clarification of the discussion. Similarly there is some inconsistency in the use of names, and this too can be confusing.

RALPH BEDDARD

Aspects of the Administration of International Justice. By E. LAUTERPACHT. Hersch Lauterpacht Memorial Lectures. Cambridge: Grotius Publications Ltd., 1991. 166 pp. £35.

This volume is a revised and enlarged version of three lectures given in the Hersch Lauterpacht Memorial Lecture series at Cambridge by Lauterpacht *fils* in November 1990, the thirtieth year following Sir Hersch's death in May 1960. The book relates to a central concern of the latter's work as academic and practitioner. The author anticipates heightened interest in all aspects of dispute settlement in the United Nations Decade of International Law, and hopes to deliver a larger work in due course on the various facets of international litigation. The three lectures have been expanded into seven chapters comprising some 150 pages of substantive text. There are useful tables of treaties and cases and an extensive index. Footnotes are few but interesting and to the point. The author (at p. xiv) acknowledges that ' . . . there are many more contributions to the literature than I have been able to recognize in the footnotes', adding, however, that he has limited the references ' . . . to items of which I have actually made use'. Authors might take this to heart.

The introductory chapter reviews some contributions of Hersch Lauterpacht to thinking on international dispute settlement, and defines the scope of the work. The problems of international justice under consideration are not the broad questions of right and wrong and the best ordering of society, but ' . . . justice on a different plane, namely, the methods and institutions that States use in the litigious settlement of disputes' (p. 6). In case this appears unduly narrow, it is later (p. 8) explained that ' . . . our concern is not simply with tribunals that apply law and reach binding judgments . . . [but also with] . . . the identification and consideration of a range of contentious situations characterized by the fact that one party is enabled to present a case to a third person in order to obtain a conclusion, whether it be a judgment or merely a view or a recommendation . . . '. There follow chapters on (II) 'The Range of International Judicial and Quasi-Judicial Machinery', (III) 'Consent', (IV) 'Access', (V) 'The Composition of Tribunals', (VI) 'Appeals', and (VII) 'Equality'. While the work will be of interest to practitioners, it addresses a broader audience and deserves a wide readership.

The author offers some trenchant opinions. Chapter II notes the great proliferation of international tribunals of all kinds and suggests historical and functional reasons why the International Court of Justice is only one among many such institutions. He has little time for the Law of the Sea Tribunal which is ' . . . essentially concerned with traditional maritime matters of a kind which the ICJ is perfectly competent to handle . . . ', and suggests that the Law of the Sea Treaty be amended to delete the Tribunal provisions (p. 20). Earlier in the chapter, he outlines an appreciation of claims commissions: ' . . . the case for a specialist tribunal is strong where it is foreseen that there will be many cases with similar issues . . . ' (p. 18). Could this not be applied in defence of the targeted Tribunal? He does not offer an assessment of the practical possibilities of such deletion.

The substantial chapter on consent of the parties to international proceedings is also strongly argued. The general theme is the etiolation of State consent in practice, contrasted with the strenuous insistence upon it in the theory of international law. The section 'The Quasi-judicial Activity of the Security Council' asks searching questions about the creeping extension of Security Council jurisdiction into 'judicial' areas, highly pertinent to recent resolutions on Iraq: 'It would be a strange reversal of positions if the fundamental right to due process of law and fair trial, at long last internationally acknowledged as belonging to the individual, should now come to be denied by the Security Council to States or other entities affected by its decisions!' (p. 48). Security Council resolution 662 (1990) is quoted (p. 41); what would the author make of resolution 687, the cease-fire resolution, with its full complement of 'judicial' elements (*International Legal Materials*, 30 (1991), p. 846)?

In general, the author favours extension of the role of international organizations in litigation, especially in the field of human rights, but is pessimistic about an enhanced role for individuals—consideration of Protocol No. 9 to the European Convention on Human Rights was not possible for reasons of time. The review of the institution of the *ad hoc* judge draws forth the suggestion that he/she should be regarded rather as an 'arbitrator/advocate' (p. 81) and swear a different oath from the titular judges—perhaps wisely, no formula is offered for this new declaration. The developing use of chambers in the administration of international justice is welcomed and legally defended. Forms of appeal in the system are distinguished and clarified, and the possibility of a system of recourse to an international tribunal for municipal cases with an international element is mooted. The over-use of equity and equitable principles by a range of tribunals is given a fair drubbing: 'Attractive though the concept of equity may be in many situations, and perhaps as much beyond criticism as is mother love, it is not a concept that can be sprinkled like salt on every part of the law. There are many situations in which the law prescribes absolute rules' (p. 135).

At the beginning of the book, the author purports to eschew grand theory or writing 'on a highly generalized plane', preferring specifics (p. 6). The problem with specifics is that they may be thematically unconnected and of little interest except to those directly confronted with them. But although the author does not define it, there is a coherence about the whole book in that it consistently addresses key interfaces between the State and international law and growing pressures of 'internationalization' in many spheres. Any new international order will not arrive as a revolutionary whole but will be the resolution of a multiplicity of practical problems, many of which the author skilfully identifies and explains.

PATRICK THORNBERRY

The Kuwait Crisis: Basic Documents. Volume 1. Edited by E. LAUTERPACT, C. J. GREENWOOD, MARC WELLER and DANIEL BETHLEHEM. Cambridge: Grotius Publications Ltd., 1991. xvi + 330 pp. £35; $70.

One of the problems with teaching, researching or studying international law is the need to have access to a wide variety of primary sources—treaties, governmental statements, records of international, regional and non-governmental organizations, and basic factual information about situations or conflicts. Even a well-stocked library is bound to have significant gaps. A step towards solving this problem has been taken by the University of Cambridge's Research Centre for International Law in its *Cambridge International Document Series*. Volume 1 covers the Kuwait crisis until the beginning of December 1990 and therefore includes the debates surrounding the adoption of the Security Council's resolutions aimed at combatting the Iraqi aggression and occupation of Kuwait and culminating in the authorization to use force in resolution 678 of 29 November 1990. The speed of production of this volume is also important to note, enabling teacher, researcher and student to discuss a current crisis using accurate and well-organized information, rather than relying on newspaper or television accounts. It is hoped that this series will continue to provide such excellent service to cover all major future crises and perhaps also those situations of a long-standing nature, such as Cyprus, the Occupied Territories, Western Sahara, etc.

Chapter 1 contains a large collection of documents covering the history of the emergence of the States of Iraq and Kuwait. These reveal that Iraq has no supportable claim to Kuwait (see 1963 agreement, p. 56), and indeed it could be argued that the large number of historical documents is unnecessary in that they add nothing to the determination that Iraq unlawfully committed armed aggression against Kuwait in August 1990. This point is reinforced if one bears in mind the post-1945 norm that force cannot be used to settle territorial disputes no matter how valid the claim. Having said that, the documents do highlight some of the problems forgotten in the euphoria of the allied victory. For instance, the section on the 1961 crisis (pp. 50–6) reveals that it is worthwhile taking threats of force as seriously as actual uses of force, a fact that appears to have been forgotten by Kuwait and the rest of the world in the days leading up to the Iraqi invasion.

In addition, the historical documents are useful in a variety of general ways. For example, they not only set the crisis of 1990–91 in context, they also are a useful foundation for a discussion of problems which later became heightened. For instance, the documents show the 'artificial' nature of States created by colonialism. The documents can then be used as a foundation for a discussion of aspects of the crisis not thought central at the time of compilation, such as the Kurdish issue, which became 'internationalized' in March and April 1991, after the volume had been produced. Inevitably, this has resulted in an incomplete picture of such issues. For instance, the extract of the unratified 1920 Treaty of Sèvres (p. 30) excludes the proposal to create an independent State of Kurdistan. This is not meant as a criticism, only as an indication of the need for updating.

Chapters 2–5, which document the United Nations' involvement in the crisis, appear, at first sight, to lack any depth. A casual reader may be tempted to criticize the editors for creating this impression by substantial editing, but the reason in fact was that publicly the Security Council, while producing a plethora of wide ranging resolutions, did not debate them to any great extent. Most of the hard bargaining occurred behind closed doors, mainly between the permanent members. The end result was that the legal issues, while being raised, were not resolved because the Council as a whole was presented with a series of *faits accomplis*. This is somewhat disappointing in that one hoped for a greater legal emphasis at the UN with the removal of Cold War posturing and with the statements made portraying the response to the Iraqi invasion as part of a new world order in which the rule of law is paramount. The brief statements on the legal problems of whether Article 51 permits the right of collective self-defence to survive the adoption of a resolution imposing sanctions under Article 41 (examples—p. 113, p. 120, p. 170), and on the issue of whether the Military Staff Committee needed to be formally convened in order to control the military action (examples—p. 106, p. 117, p. 118), were, in themselves, inconclusive. The Article 51 question remains undecided, whilst the question of Security Council control over a military action seems to have been decided to allow in practice for the total delegation of authority to a State or States. Although the Cold War spectre of Korea was not raised, it now seems confirmed as a 'precedent' for UN action rather than as an historical aberration as previously thought.

The period up to and including the authorization to use force in resolution 678 was essentially concerned with aspects of the *jus ad bellum* and to this extent the volume can be seen as self-contained, although *jus in bello* aspects such as the brutal Iraqi occupation of Kuwait are also in issue and are covered to a limited extent in chapter 6. A further volume is needed to cover the outbreak of hostilities and accompanying *jus in bello* issues (while not forgetting the question of war aims), the cease-fire resolutions, the internal developments in Iraq and the question of non-intervention. The other chapters in the present volume on the unsuccessful attempts at settlement (chapter 7), and the response of regional bodies to the invasion (chapter 8), are also in need of updating. With hindsight it might have been advisable to wait so that all aspects of the crisis could have been addressed at once, but on balance the value of having these documents in an accessible form so quickly outweighs any criticism based on incompleteness. The need for updating is an inherent problem in any work or collection which deals with current issues. It is therefore not something which should deter the Centre from producing further collections, the importance of which cannot be overemphasized, particularly at a time when issues of international law are being discussed so widely.

N. D. White

Consular Law and Practice. By Luke T. Lee. 2nd edition. Oxford: Clarendon Press, 1991. 700 pp. £77.

The publication of the first edition of this text, thirty years ago, predated by two years the adoption of the United Nations Vienna Convention on Consular Relations. Consequently, although the Convention itself is examined in the current text, the time lapse is such that the author is in a position to articulate the impact of the Convention on State practice, and he consistently illustrates issues by reference to relevant treaties, State practice, regulations and judicial decisions. Although almost twice the length of the initial text, the original format of the book is retained. The book is divided into seven parts each containing clearly defined sections so facilitating easy consultation.

In the introduction, the author *inter alia* charts the historical evolution of consular relations. Part II deals with consular relations in general, viz. consular relations and consular posts and the acquisition and termination of consular status. Part III identifies fourteen consular functions as meriting separate treatment. This serves to demonstrate both the new type of problems which may be encountered by a consul and the growth in the frequency of certain problems in today's internationalized community—for example, civil aviation, child abduction and refugees. In respect of refugees the author has drawn on his own experience as Director of Plans and Programmes, Office of the US Coordinator for Refugees Affairs. Privileges and immunities, honorary consuls and consuls, diplomats and the United Nations are dealt with in parts IV, V and VI respectively. The author concludes by observing that the Vienna Convention has contributed to international relations by serving as a catalyst to bring about bilateral treaties between States long distrustful of each other, allaying the distrust and suspicions held by developing countries towards developed or former colonial powers, and the standardization and streamlining of domestic legislation. Certain deficiencies of the Vienna Convention are also identified viz. the limited role of consuls in regard to dual nationals and consular status under unrecognized regimes. Neither issue was addressed by the Convention.

This is a work of considerable academic standing. It is a scholarly contribution which has been extensively researched, and much attention has been paid to detail. It provides insight into consular activity and demonstrates the relationship between convention and customary international law. The text will serve as an invaluable reference tool to those engaged in consular activity, as well as serving the needs of those with either a developed or passing interest in what is one of the oldest forms of international activity.

REBECCA M. M. WALLACE

Droit de la mer, Tome I: *La Mer et son droit, les espaces maritimes.* By LAURENT LUCCHINI and MICHEL VOELCKEL. Paris: Pedone, 1990. x + 640 pp. (including appendices and index). F 390.

This is the first of a two-volume treatment of the law of the sea by a leading French academic and the French contrôleur général de la Marine. The present volume is divided into two sections which address 'La Mer et son droit' and 'Les Espaces marins: une pluralité de régimes juridiques'. The second volume will examine delimitation of maritime spaces, marine activities such as economic exploitation and research, and conflicts at sea and their peaceful and non-peaceful resolution. Both volumes are addressed to students and 'professionals of the sea'—practitioners, administrators and navigators.

The focus of Lucchini and Voelckel's work is geographic and functional. This approach is reflected in the organization of the volume, three-quarters of which is devoted to an analysis of maritime spaces, starting with internal waters and concluding with the deep sea-bed. This section includes a discussion of 'les situations spéciales'—islands, archipelagos, straits and canals, closed and semi-enclosed seas, the Arctic and Antarctic (the authors noting that whilst there is no decisive reason for including the latter, the French Ministry of Foreign Affairs' department on the law of the sea is officially 'le droit de la mer *et* de l'Antarctique'), land-locked and geographically disadvantaged States, and historic waters—all instances where '[l]e droit ajoute à la nature'. This reflects the importance the authors attach to the influence of geographic as well as economic and political factors on the development of the law of the sea.

Their focus is stated to derive from the methodology of Guy Ladreit de Lacharrière which the authors have taken as their touchstone in examining 'tout le tissu normatif qui enveloppe les activitiés dont la mer est l'objet'. Lucchini and Voelckel seek to set in historical, geographical and legal context the development of the law of the sea, particularly the 1982 Law of the Sea Convention. From the perspective of 1 December 1989, to which date the volume is current, the 1982 Law of the Sea Convention is viewed not as an end in itself but as a further stage in the development of the law of the sea. It is not surprising therefore that the authors have rejected 'new' for the title of their work. Theirs is a salutory reminder that the law of the sea is not reducible to a single instrument—as they state in one of many emphasized passages in the text, 'l'importance de la C.M.B. [Convention de Montego Bay] doit être relativisée'.

Perhaps one of the most valuable assets of this volume is its emphasis on State practice, reflecting both the methodology of the authors and the particular practical expertise of M. Voelckel as contrôleur général de la Marine. Thus, for example, the discussion of archipelagos begins with an analysis of their geographic features and navigational importance, notes the attempts by Indonesia and the Philippines in particular to obtain recognition for their national archipelagic legislation, and then describes the juridical nature of archipelagic States under the 1982 Convention. Reference is made throughout to negotiations at UNCLOS III and to the nature of the compromise solution reached, and the consistency of subsequent State practice with this solution. Here and throughout the volume the authors, whilst emphasizing the 'package deal' approach of UNCLOS III (the compromise over transit passage being pithily described as 'no strait, no fish'), point to the acute particularization evident in the law of the sea and witnessed in the strenuous efforts by States to gain recognition for their own particular interests at the Conference—the example of Indonesia and the Philippines above, or Canada with respect to Article 234 and ice-covered areas. There is frequent use of diagrams and tables, sadly occasionally rather poorly reproduced, which will assist the reader in conceptualizing issues, whilst also serving to underscore the importance of geography and of State practice.

This is a fascinating and comprehensively researched book which will bring to teachers and students alike a greater awareness of the historical and geographical factors which continue to shape the developing law of the sea. It manifestly succeeds in its aim of conveying a sense of the relative importance of the 1982 Convention in this process.

CATHERINE REDGWELL

The Human Rights Committee: Its Role in the Development of the International Covenant on Civil and Political Rights. By DOMINIC MCGOLDRICK. Oxford: Clarendon Press, 1991. xliii + 576 pp. £60.

The arrival of Dominic McGoldrick's book has been eagerly awaited by those who have a special interest in the work of the Human Rights Committee of the International Covenant on Civil and Political Rights. It is without doubt a very important piece of research and a substantial contribution to the learning on the role of the Committee in the interpretation of the Covenant. The book is a revised and updated version of a doctoral thesis submitted in 1988.

The layout of the work is logical and clear. There are the usual tables including a catalogue of States parties to the Covenant but not, oddly enough, to the Optional Protocol. There are chapters dealing with the 'Origins, Drafting, and Significance' of the Covenant, the Committee itself and various institutional aspects and the two main implementation provisions—periodic reporting and the right of individual communication. There follows a series of chapters on various substantive provisions of the Covenant which all adopt the same pattern. Each of these chapters deals with one particular article (except in the case of Article 7 where the treatment is rightly linked with Article 10) both under the reporting process and under the Optional Protocol, with assessments offered as conclusions. The final chapter of the book is an overall general assessment of the work of the Committee. It concludes with a variety of appendices and an extremely wide-ranging bibliography, in which the reviewer failed, however, to unearth a reference to Yogesh Tyagi's book, which was frequently cited in the text. Shorn of all its accessories, the actual text is some 508 pages long of which no fewer than 185 pages are in the form of end-notes. There is obviously a colossal wealth of material here which is extremely detailed and wide-ranging in its effort to place the work of the Committee in the context of general international law and the practice of other regional human rights organs. Although, no doubt for practical purposes, end-notes are becoming more and more the norm in this type of work, this reviewer retains his preference for the more user-friendly footnote.

The opening chapter contains a detailed drafting history including the decision to split into two Covenants, one on Civil and Political Rights and the other on Economic, Social and Cultural Rights, and the reasons therefor, including the need to adjust the measures of implementation to fit the rights stipulated. The origins of the right of individual communication (or petition) are examined and the reasons for the emergence of a separate Optional Protocol are made clear. The issue of the nature of the rights under the Covenant is considered. Does the Covenant impose immediately binding obligations or is the duty one of progressive realization only? Although, as the author remarks, the correct view is one of immediacy of obligation (and this is supported by the Committee), there may be room for some exceptions to the general rule as Professor Capotorti has explained. In a final section on the significance of the Covenant in contemporary international law, McGoldrick stresses, *inter alia*, the importance of the Covenant in developing further than general international law the protection offered to aliens.

The chapter on the nature and function of the Committee contains a wealth of detail. It stresses the importance of Committee members' status as independent experts and of the general thrust of consensus decision-making and examines the Committee's relations with the Secretariat. The Committee is not strictly speaking a UN organ, but in practice it is, in effect, in the position of a UN organ. The author notes a number of other features which underline the link between the Committee and the UN by listing the Secretary-General's involvement in the Covenant, but does not mention his role in relation to derogation notices. The functions of the Committee as an implementation authority are spelt out, though nowhere in the book is the inter-State procedure examined in any detail because, as the author remarks, it 'has not been invoked'. It is a pity that in a book of this length and detail this procedure could not at least have been examined and criticized, albeit at a theoretical level only. The experience of the Strasbourg human rights institutions has, of course, by contrast, been markedly different with respect to inter-State proceedings, with some of the most notorious cases such as the *Greek* cases, *Ireland* v. *UK* and the cases against Turkey falling within this category. Finally, in this chapter the author submits that the nature of the Committee is multi-faceted depending on what role it is performing. He concludes (rightly in the estimation of the reviewer) that it includes 'elements of judicial, quasi-judicial, administrative, investigative, inquisitorial, supervisory, and conciliatory functions'.

The examination of the reporting procedure is most comprehensive. In the course of the chapter on this implementation measure, several important issues are addressed. To what extent may Committee members use other sources of information 'outside' the State reports when conducting their examination under Article 40? McGoldrick concludes that the 'majority of members of the HRC . . . accepted that the ICCPR places no restriction on the sources of information that the Committee is entitled to use', and indeed, concludes quite properly that outside sources are 'no longer an issue in the HRC'. The section on the Committee's jurisdiction under Article 40 focuses on the tension between the two schools of thought (liberal and conservative) on the Committee's powers under Article 40: ' . . . [S]hort of adopting country specific reports, in practice it appears that it is the liberal view of the HRC's role which is now accepted and applied by all members of the HRC including the Eastern European members'. The nub of the jurisdictional question is, of course, whether the Committee will move towards adoption of *country specific* reports and general comments addressed to one *specific* State party. The author's prognosis here is that such a development is not at present likely. The judgment on the reporting procedure is positive and great stress is laid on the Committee's objective of securing a constructive dialogue with States parties under this procedure.

The treatment of the Optional Protocol and the jurisprudence thereunder is once again extremely detailed and thorough. All the important cases are examined and analysed; the unsatisfactory nature of a system which lacks an oral procedure is highlighted and linked to the problem of resources; a plea is entered for the Committee's views under Article 5(4) of the Optional Protocol to be made legally binding, and the appointment of Janos Fodor as Special Rapporteur for Follow-Up is singled out as a highly desirable development. However, the potentially very important power to take interim measures, although discussed in relation, for example, to the Jamaican death penalty cases, is insufficiently stressed. As far as the interpretation of the Optional Protocol is concerned, the detail is compendious and authoritative; the 'autonomous meaning' of the terms (*Van Duzen* v. *Canada*) is remarked on; the function of the Committee is discussed and all the grounds of inadmissibility covered. What a pity it is that the author shrinks from expressing a view on the controversial decisions in *Broeks*, *Zwaan de Vries* and *Danning* on the interrelationship of the two Covenants. The appraisal suggests that the Committee could develop practices and procedures directed to the securing of friendly settlements: this is sound and sensible. The author rightly bemoans the lack of publicity for and availability of the publications of the Committee.

The final section of the book on the substantive rights may be remarked on in one respect in particular. The whole catalogue of rights is not examined; the articles analysed are very selective—most are obviously very important; some, like Article 20 (prohibition of propaganda for war etc.), less obviously so when contrasted with the complete omission of any consideration of the very important Article 9. The author offers little explanation for this selection of articles discussed save to say that he had 'hoped to consider each of the articles on which the Human Rights Committee had seen fit to express a General Comment under Article 40(4) of the Covenant. In the event that proved to be impossible.' Why it was so is not stated. The treatment given to the articles is generally very good and particularly good on Articles 7 and 10(1)—with criticisms thereon that the reviewer has himself expressed elsewhere. The analysis of the derogation Article 4 could perhaps have been more developed—there is no discussion of the propriety of a derogations clause in a human rights treaty and little in the way of the background of general international law including the concept of *jus cogens*.

The monograph makes a significant and extremely detailed contribution to the literature on the Human Rights Committee. It is a monumental achievement. Its imperfections are few and minor; perhaps the reviewer may be permitted to single out a few too many typographical errors in the spelling of case names and names of authors in a book of otherwise such high quality. This work will never reach the reviewer's bookshelf—it will be on his desk permanently for constant reference.

P. R. GHANDHI

International Dispute Settlement. By J. G. MERRILLS. 2nd edition. Cambridge: Grotius Publications Ltd., 1991. 288 pp. Paperback, £19.50.

This is the second edition of a little book which first appeared in 1984 in the *Modern Legal Studies Series*. It has a new publisher, which has had one entirely beneficial consequence: the footnotes appear at the foot of the page instead of at the end of each chapter. Fortunately, the text has only expanded from 180 to 254 pages, thus avoiding the regrettable elephantiasis which so often seems nowadays to set in with second editions of works which, when they first came out, were the more useful because they were then of a manageable size.

To some extent, of course, such expansion as there is has resulted from the need to include material which has appeared since 1984, in particular important decisions of the ICJ, several arbitrations, notably the *Taba* and *Rainbow Warrior* awards, the work of the US–Iran Claims Tribunal and the events of the 1980s in Central America.

But some sections are new, or almost entirely new. Thus, the author includes a few pages on private international arbitration. As to this matter, one wonders what he considers the jurisprudence such cases, as, say, *Liamco* v. *Libya* and *Aminoil* v. *Kuwait*, or some of the decisions of the *US–Iran* Tribunal, contributed to general international law; it is rather a pity he did not give his views.

There is some expansion of the chapter on regional organizations, especially as regards their relationship with adjudication of disputes. But the two sections which have been very significantly re-cast and filled out concern the International Court (which the author, to the reviewer's slight distaste, calls the 'World Court') and what formerly were the work's conclusions.

The first edition's rather peremptory account of the Court was only 24 pages long and left many important matters unconsidered. There are now two chapters instead of one. The first is concerned with the Court's organization and procedure, and there are now much longer and fuller analyses of the Court's incidental jurisdiction, that is, interim measures, and intervention under its Statute, Article 62. There is a balanced account of the new phenomenon, the resort to Chambers, a matter to which the author later returns. In the other chapter he considers the work of the Court. One agrees with all the author has to say about this, in particular his accounting for the Court's relative lack of business (though things have bucked up recently). It is curious, however, that the fact that the Court has so few prospective litigants (at the time of writing this review membership of the United Nations has risen to 166) is not emphasized. Even a comparatively small State like New Zealand has three and a half million. However, the cogent comments (on pp. 250–1) on the bizarre proposal to give the Court the power to hear preliminary references must command agreement: how often do real questions of international law come before domestic courts?

The three-page conclusion has been replaced by a twenty-five page chapter on trends and prospects from both political and legal perspectives and discussion of possible improvements in methods of international dispute settlement. This is a typically judicious and moderate piece of writing and is redolent with the common sense which permeates the entire book.

There is one puzzling matter. This concerns the date of completion. The preface is dated April 1991. But there is no mention of the Kuwait crisis, which is highly relevant to chapter 9, on the United Nations. This episode began on 2 August 1990. However, there is, at p. 281 note 20, a brief reference to the judgment on Nicaragua's application to intervene in the *Land, Island and Maritime Frontier* case (*ICJ Reports*, 1990, p. 192). This was handed down in September 1990. It is rather a pity that, if it was possible to mention that judgment, it is not discussed at pp. 118–21 where intervention and the possible requirement of a jurisdictional link is fully considered. Indeed, the footnote would have been more suitably placed on p. 121 than where it is.

Still, that conundrum apart, it has to be said that this is an excellent introduction to the subject, even better than the first edition. It is not weighted down with technicalities. It is highly readable and is characterized by brevity, clarity and a sense of reality.

J. G. COLLIER

International Business and National Jurisdiction. By A. D. NEALE and M. L. STEPHENS. Oxford: Clarendon Press, 1988. xix + 216 pp. £25.

Controversial areas of international law tend to go through a succession of stages. First, the broad issues of principle arise in litigation or diplomatic exchanges. Next, the principles are applied in circumstances which are at one level similar but which on closer inspection reveal particular characteristics which suggest that the broad principles need refinement or modification. Thereafter, agreement may be reached on a set of rules or principles governing the controversy in question, or the controversy may remain unresolved, but with the opposing views clarified and articulated with greater precision than in the initial stages. In the past two decades jurisdictional disputes have passed from the initial stage, represented by the *Alcoa* case and what appear, in retrospect, to be the relatively crude responses of blocking statutes such as Britain's Shipping Contracts and Commercial Documents Act 1964, into the area of refinement and articulation of the underlying issues of principle. This monograph provides an excellent survey of this transition.

As might be expected from Sir Alan Neale, past chairman of the Monopolies and Mergers Commission and co-author (with D.G. Goyder) of an outstanding study of US antitrust law, the focus of the volume is on the tension generated in the transatlantic community by the attempts of the US courts and regulatory authorities to apply US law to business activities outside the USA. The history of these attempts is charted with great elegance and clarity from the conservative jurisdictional claims of the *American Banana* case in 1909, through the *Alcoa* decision in 1945, which is commonly regarded as the *fons et origo* of the 'effects' doctrine, into the fog of *Timberlane*, *Mannington Mills*, the *Uranium* and *Laker* litigation, and other recent cases. The authors acknowledge the fragmentation of the broad issues of principle by devoting separate chapters to accounts of the development of the act of State and foreign sovereign compulsion defences, the handling of problems involving transnational mergers and international transportation, and procedural questions such as demands for the production of evidence located abroad and the extra-territorial enforcement of remedies awarded in civil litigation.

There are two levels on which this text might be judged. The first is as a survey of the recent history of the topic. Here reviewers must tread with great caution. An obvious criticism is the lack of attention to major episodes such as the 1982 *Siberian Pipeline* dispute and the 1985 *Achille Lauro* affair. The authors' choice of a narrower focus is defended on the ground that 'the issues of extraterritorial application of domestic law have been analyzed and explored most fully and over the longest time-span in the field of US antitrust law' (p. 9). This is not wholly convincing. There is at least an argument to be made out for the view that an account of the development of the international law concerning jurisdiction is seriously flawed by the omission of detailed consideration of these episodes. However, the authors have not written a book on jurisdiction as such, but rather on international business and national jurisdiction; and if the omission of detailed consideration of the extra-territorial impact of export controls on international contracts of sale and licensing agreements (both as a matter of public and of private international law) may yet appear as idiosyncratic, the text certainly deals admirably with the core of regulatory problems facing international business. There is, quite simply, no better account of these matters.

There is, perhaps, room for a better defence of the scope of the work on a second level of analysis. The focus in this book may indicate that there is a need—or at least that there is room—for greater subtlety in approaching jurisdictional conflicts than by treating jurisdictional issues as a homogenous unit. It may be that we are witnessing the evolution of a body of law concerning the extra-territorial regulation of commercial activities, distinct from that regulating the more traditionally 'criminal' activities and even the acutely political category of export controls, which may itself be taken as an instrument of high political policy rather than routine regulation of commerce. There are signs of this development in several areas. One is the increasingly pragmatic stance taken by the British Government towards the US extra-territorial claims. The outright opposition of the UK to the export controls at the heart of the *Pipeline* dispute can be seen with increasing clarity to contrast with the cautious attempts to modify US claims according to the criteria of comity laid down in *Timberlane* and *Mannington Mills*. There are clear indications of a willingness to meet the US half way: the British *amicus curiae* brief in *Aérospatiale* is a case in point. Another example, reaching even into the lion's den of the export controls themselves, is the fact that the British Government has declared that it is prepared (on undisclosed terms) to allow US officials to make visits in the UK to monitor compliance with US export laws. Such practical accommodations may in time be seen to signal the beginnings of a kind of jurisdictional *lex mercatoria*, according to which deviations from general jurisdictional principles are tolerated in order to facilitate the development of a workable system for the regulation of international commerce.

On this second level the present text succeeds very well indeed. The case-by-case analysis of the most important recent developments teases out the subtle variations in the basic principles from which the fabric of this new approach may be woven. The account would have even greater value had the question of the relevance of private international law, and the relationship between its rules and those of public international law, been tackled more directly; but such an extension of the text might well have blurred the lines of the argument and diminished the clarity which is one of the book's most praiseworthy characteristics. The same cannot be said of the lack of an index, which is an unmitigated defect.

Scholars will prize the book for its account of what has happened. Judges and policy-makers should prize it for the trenchancy of the discussion of what should happen next. The final pages contain one of the most effective arguments against the utility of the 'balancing of interests' approach espoused by the US courts which has yet appeared. Criticizing the *ad hoc* nature of the balancing approach, in which the existence (or the exercise) of jurisdiction, and with it the obligation to obey the laws in question, is made to turn on the particular combination of governmental and private interests and other factors which happens to arise in any case thrown up by the vagaries of commercial life, the authors remark that 'If we want a rule of law, we should opt for principles of jurisdiction which tell us, over the widest possible range of practical situations, where we stand and to whom we are answerable'. Quite so.

VAUGHAN LOWE

Friends but no Allies: Economic Liberalism and the Law of Nations. By STEPHEN NEFF. New York: Columbia University Press, 1990. $37.50.

Stephen Neff has written a lucid and wide-ranging study of the conflict between nationalist and cosmopolitan conceptions of the international economic system. He identifies two core positions which recur throughout the debate, ones he traces back to classical antiquity, and which have been particularly evident since the eighteenth century: the first argues for a defence of national economic strength, on both economic and political grounds, while the other argues that the world economy is constituted as a single unit and that the good of the whole should transcend individual national and State interests.

There have been three great attempts to construct an economic system based on this latter, cosmopolitan, position: the nineteenth century liberal free trade system, the international order of the 1920s, and the post-1945 financial and trading system. If the first two succumbed to economic crisis and nationalist pressures, the last has survived and developed: yet, as Neff points out, this has been at the cost of allowing a division to prevail between a political realm that rests upon the survival of separate States and an economic one, which aims to promote a single international system.

Neff is, by his own admission, an idealist, and would like to see the cosmopolitan principle prevail through law. All the more interesting, therefore, is his exploration of how the positivist mainstream of international law, far from promoting the cosmopolitan ideal, has, by resting upon the powers and legitimacy of States, reinforced that of nationalism. The claim of such early modern writers as Vitoria, that there is a 'natural right' to trade, has been supplanted, in the main, by the intervention of States.

To the non-legal reader this argument underlines a particular difficulty: while international law is the law of States and hence reinforces their powers, the alternative aspiration, well articulated by Neff, that law itself can guarantee an alternative, cosmopolitan, order is presented out of context. It is no disrespect to the efficacy of law to stress that most of the factors that could sustain such an order are themselves extra-legal, lying in the political, economic and indeed military realms, and that the postulation of a cosmopolitan order requires examination of these factors. Not the least of these extra-legal issues is that of the inequalities of wealth and power in the contemporary international system; these are one of the major stimulants to economic and other nationalism, and can only be overcome by purposive action. Yet such action can come only from States: EEC integration into a single market is possible because, and in so far as, it involves the merging of relatively equal economies and societies. Hence, as Neff's treatment of third world demands for a reformed international system shows, reforms designed to promote greater equality can themselves run counter to cosmopolitan and international principles.

It is easy to overstate the extent to which contemporary processes of internationalisation are unique. As is well demonstrated in Neff's account, the issue of how to constitute a truly international system, be it at the political, economic or cultural levels, has been with us for hundreds of years. Plato or the physiocrats would find much that is familiar in current debates. In some respects, the degree of economic interdependence, measured in terms of trade, movement of capital and population, was greater in the pre-1914 period than it is today. Yet the expansion of economic and communications links between societies, and the growing political interdependence of much of the world, following upon the end of the cold war, make the late twentieth century an especially important moment in this history. If the arguments themselves are long familiar, the conflict in the real world between the forces of fusion and those of fragmentation is especially clear today. In this contest, international law, in both its statist and cosmopolitan forms, has a distinct, if somewhat contingent, role to play.

FRED HALLIDAY

World of Our Making. By NICHOLAS GREENWOOD ONUF. Columbia, South Carolina: University of South Carolina Press, 1989. x + 341 pp. No price stated.

International relations scholars are the primary audience of Nicholas Onuf's new study: but it is one of the small but growing number of texts, sitting alongside the recent works of David Kennedy, Martti Koskenniemi and Philip Allot, which no one concerned with the theoretical development of international law can afford to ignore.

The task which Onuf sets himself is the reconstruction of the field of study or discipline of international relations. As that description implies, he attempts this from a constructivist standpoint, in which 'reality' is neither a *datum* passively apprehended by the individual nor an order generated by some inner logic immanent in human consciousness. Seeking to overcome the dualism of self and world, which he regards as one of many false dualities characteristic of Western thought, Onuf argues that the individual actively participates in the construction of his or her own social reality. This takes him into a subtle and complex discussion of the nature of rules.

Through the ordering of the social institution of language, rules both construct reality and direct behaviour: they are both constitutive and regulative. Rules, in Onuf's scheme, are of three kinds, whose types are derived from speech act theory:

> ' . . . all rules are either assertives of the form, I state that X counts as Y, or directives of the form, I state that X person (should, must, may) do Y, or commissives of the form, I state that I (can, will, should) do Y. While each is a distinctive category, all three play on each other in the production of rules. People make assertions about each other's promises, respond to assertives with directives, and so on.' (p. 90)

With this foundation Onuf proceeds to discuss the manner in which reasoning, in the sense not simply of acquiring propositional knowledge but also of knowing how to use that knowledge, including knowledge of rules, is learned. In some of the most stimulating passages of the book he charts the stages of the emergence of this skill in individuals, through a critique of the work of Piaget, Kohlberg and others.

Onuf associates the three types of rule with three characteristic modes of reasoning, according to what he calls the 'directional fit' of speech acts:

> 'In the case of assertives, one state of affairs is held to count for another. With directives, the intent is to alter some circumscribed part of an initial, larger state of affairs. With commissives, the intent is to take a circumscribed state of affairs and have it alter a resulting, larger state of affairs. Assertives relate wholes to wholes, whether spatially or temporally. Directives relate wholes to parts, and commissive parts to wholes. . . . To proceed from a whole to its parts is what one normally describes as deductive reasoning. To proceed from parts to wholes is inductive. [C.S.] Pierces's abduction is a matter of leaping from one whole to another without having to proceed down to the parts and up to the next whole'. (pp. 98–99)

Reflection on the relationship between modes of reasoning and the nature of rules, and on its relevance to the processes by which, for instance, customary international law is constituted, gives some sense of the richness and compass of Onuf's scheme.

From this point Onuf's argument advances rapidly into an account of the manner in which concepts of order are constructed, and of the ways in which uses of rules are reinforced by the roles of guilt, shame, sanctions and so on. Consideration of the critical process of the internalization of rules leads him to a compelling defence of a proposition of immediate concern to international lawyers: that the (often tacit) adoption of the State as the paradigm of order in international society is wrong, and a distortion of the notion of what a State properly is. What is often taken for anarchy in the international arena is no more than the absence of one particular and a typical form of social ordering of which the sovereign State is the clearest example. But there can be, and is, order without State structures. Onuf develops this proposition into a critique of existing models of international relations, and presents his own conception of the subject.

While the sections of the book defending the international order against charges of anarchy are probably the most immediately accessible to international lawyers, in the longer term Onuf's work on the nature of rules and reasoning may prove more influential. As a lawyer operating at the edges of his known world, I cannot judge how original other social scientists would find this work: but for me the richness of the insights which Onuf offers amply repay the perseverance sometimes needed to follow the details of his argument.

Many of the casual references to the writings of other social scientists presuppose a knowledge of a body of literature unlikely to be familiar to international lawyers, who will probably share my feeling of exclusion from a clever and important conversation at various stages in the work. Even those who can tell their Aron from their Foucault are likely to be defeated by some of the more arcane allusions. But if international lawyers want to develop a coherent account of international law as a normative system, they must be prepared to go at least half way towards meeting other social scientists who share their concerns. This is a provocative, stimulating text, and a most valuable contribution to the recent wave of writing on the theoretical underpinnings of international law. If its assimilation into the way international lawyers traditionally think and teach requires some effort, that effort needs to be made for the sake of the vitality of international law.

VAUGHAN LOWE

The Age of the Arctic. Hot Conflicts and Cold Realities. By GAIL OSHERENKO and ORAN R. YOUNG. Cambridge: Cambridge University Press, 1989. xvi + 316 pp. £37.50.

In recent years the Arctic has become an area of great military and strategic significance and the scene of substantial economic activity as the region's rich natural resources (fish, oil and gas, coal and minerals) are increasingly exploited. These uses of the Arctic cause friction with its native peoples as well as posing threats to its delicate environment. It is these conflicts and their possible resolution which are the subject of this book. After a brief first part setting the scene, Part II (entitled 'Players and Interests') examines successively the militarization of the Arctic, its industrialization, the interests of native peoples and environmental issues. The third part of the book ('Handling Arctic Conflicts') opens (in Chapter 6) with a general review of the types of conflict in the Arctic and the various techniques available for resolving them. The three remaining chapters focus on three particular conflict resolution techniques. Chapter 7 examines private initiatives, looking in particular at two interesting, but as yet not notably successful, Alternative Dispute Resolution techniques in the North American Arctic, negotiation with the assistance of third parties and problem solving activities. Chapter 8 discusses public (i.e. government) initiatives, concentrating almost exclusively on the position in the USA, while Chapter 9 examines international initiatives and the prospects for the creation of international regimes in the Arctic.

The authors are concerned as much, if not more, with conflicts within States as with conflicts between States. Partly for this reason, and partly because the book is not written specifically for lawyers (although one of the authors is a lawyer) but rather for political scientists, the book is of rather limited interest to international lawyers. Their main interest is likely to be in some of the background material in Part II and the discussion of international initiatives in Chapter 9. Although the latter contains a good deal of interesting and sensible discussion about the prospects for international regimes in the Arctic—with the likeliest candidates for such regimes being the interests of native peoples and environmental issues—a weakness with this discussion (particularly with that concerning environmental issues) is the failure to take into account (or even enumerate) the various specialized treaty regimes that already apply to the Arctic (such as the 1973 Polar Bears Agreement and various bilateral pollution agreements), as well as more general treaty regimes that are relevant to the Arctic (such as the International Whaling Convention and various multilateral and regional pollution treaties). Without a consideration of such existing regimes, it is difficult to see what gaps in environmental protection remain to be plugged.

The book is well written, in a lively and informative style. There are occasions when it is over-allusive, so that those who are not already fairly familiar with Arctic issues may have difficulty understanding the point of particular incidents and examples referred to. There is more emphasis on practice and policy in the North American Arctic (which is perhaps not surprising given that both authors work in the USA) than in the Eurasian Arctic, where the discussion is less detailed, accurate and up to date. Finally, it must be said that the authors have adopted a rather odd definition of the Arctic—the area north of 60° North. It will come as a surprise to the inhabitants of Lerwick, Bergen and Helsinki to learn that they live in the Arctic. In fact, the authors do not stick very rigidly to their definition, most areas between 60° and the Arctic Circle in Eurasia being ignored.

R. R. CHURCHILL

Federal Courts and the International Human Rights Paradigm. By KENNETH C. RANDALL. Durham, North Carolina: Duke University Press, 1990. vii + 282 pp. $45.

Professor Randall has presented a treatment of two distinct, though related, topics, each of which could readily stand as a short monograph (or a long article) on its own. The first part, comprising some three-quarters of the text, is on the subject of jurisdictional competence within the American federal system concerning two classes of cases: torture and terrorism. This portion of the book is quite consciously modelled on, and indeed is presented as an updating of, Richard Falk's *The Role of Domestic Courts in the International Legal Order* (1964). The topicality of the two categories of cases arises from two key American Court of Appeal cases of the 1980s: *Filartiga* v. *Peña-Irala*, 630 F 2d 876 (2d Cir. 1980); and *Tel Oren* v. *Arab Republic of Libya*, 726 F 2d 774 (DC Cir. 1984).

This first section entails an extended exploration of some of the most tangled thickets of American federalism. Persons whose interest in the subject is merely casual might well be daunted by the welter of domestic American legal technicalities. Fortunately, Professor Randall is among the surest (if not the most exciting) of guides. He is indeed a guide in the truest sense, in that he has a firm and precise idea of where he wishes his readers to go; and he is determined to take them there. He makes no pretence of being above the intellectual battle. The book is therefore, in essence, a legal brief—and a relentlessly thorough one at that—for its author's thesis.

The basic thesis is that the two heinous acts of torture and terrorism are very much the proper business of American federal courts and of individual claimants in them. En route to this conclusion, the determined reader will receive enlightening discussions of many aspects of American federal court jurisdiction, some of them highly technical. Notable items on the agenda include: the nature of the federal-question jurisdiction of federal courts (concerning, of course, both the statutory and the constitutional avatars of this wily beast); the foreign act of State doctrine; the history and meaning of the Alien Tort Statute of 1789 (the basis of both the *Filartiga* and the *Tel Oren* cases); the constitutional political-question principle; aspects of the diversity jurisdiction of federal courts; State immunity in American courts; and principles determining the presence or absence of private rights of action for acts forbidden either by statute or by international law. This venture is not for the intellectually faint-hearted; but the material is clearly and succinctly presented, and bolstered by extensive and valuable citation.

In the second part of the book, the focus shifts to public international law *per se*. The principal attention is devoted to universal jurisdiction (i.e., to the principle that certain acts are threats to the whole of the international community and that consequently any State can take action on a kind of *actio popularis* basis). Here too, the author has a conclusion firmly in mind, and he is resolved to steer his readers towards it. His thesis is that torture and terrorism belong in the category of offences covered by the universality principle, along with such traditional acts as piracy and slave-trading.

In the final chapter, the author embarks on something of a speculative spree, presenting the thesis that international human rights law and international criminal law represent a paradigmatic shift (in the sense made famous by Thomas Kuhn) in the very nature of international law: from a State-centred system to a humanity-centred one. Even here, though, the tone is more that of the lawyer than the evangelist.

The book is characterized throughout by clarity of purpose and thoroughness and fair-mindedness of argument. At the same time, there is never any mistaking that this author is out to convince us that his views are correct and that rival ones are wrong. Resolute doubters of his conclusions will probably not be swayed by his arguments. But there can be no doubt he has presented an outstanding brief for his views.

STEPHEN C. NEFF

Developments in the Law of Treaties 1945–1986. By SHABTAI ROSENNE. Cambridge: Cambridge University Press, 1989. xxxv + 447 pp. + appendices and indices. £60.

During the academic year 1985–6 Shabtai Rosenne held the position of Arthur Goodhart Professor of Legal Science at the University of Cambridge, devoting his time principally to continued research into the international law of treaties. *Developments in the Law of Treaties* comprises a series of studies which represent expanded versions of lectures, talks and seminars given during that year. It is accordingly not intended as a comprehensive treatment of the law of treaties, nor even of the way in which that regime has developed during the post-war period, but rather as an exploration of particular issues against the backcloth of the process of codification of treaty law embodied in the three Vienna Conventions of 1969, 1978 and 1986.

The topics covered include the role of the written arrangement in international relations and international law, the significance of good faith in the codified law, the question whether the constituent instrument of an international organization is to be regarded as an international treaty, the settlement of treaty disputes under the Vienna Conventions and the contribution of the United Nations to the development of the law of treaties. By way of introduction, the first chapter concerns itself with certain issues unaddressed in the codified law: that is, matters which the International Law Commission or the Vienna Conferences decided for one reason or another not to include in their work. The most-favoured-nation clause, the effect of hostilities upon treaties and the State responsibility dimension of the law of treaties are amongst those referred to.

These diverse questions are all discussed in the meticulous and scholarly fashion that is to be expected of one of the author's great experience and expertise. The volume concludes with two valuable appendices which incorporate the text of the 1969 Vienna Convention and of certain documents deriving from the General Assembly's Review of the Multilateral Treaty-Making Process.

No doubt inevitably, the author does on occasion embrace arguments which cannot command unreserved approval, at least in the absence of further explanation. A notable example occurs at p. 51 in the context of a discussion of the relationship between 'the treaty-obligation' and the draft articles on State responsibility elaborated by the International Law Commission. The author refers to Article 29 of the latter, which the Commission included under the heading 'Circumstances precluding wrongfulness' and which would broadly incorporate into international law the principle *volenti non fit iniuria*. In his view, this represents 'little more than a new formulation of article 45 of the Vienna Convention' (the provision establishing that a State may lose the right to invalidate, terminate or suspend the operation of a treaty on appropriate grounds if, after becoming aware of the facts, it expressly or impliedly agrees that the treaty remains valid). It is submitted, however, that the two principles are quite distinct, since Article 45 is not concerned with the legitimization by consent of conduct which would otherwise be wrongful, but only with the exclusion by acquiescence of a particular legal remedy or response in circumstances which may or may not have involved the commission of a wrongful act. It is consequently difficult to agree that confusion has been introduced into the law by the mere co-existence of these two principles.

A more general observation regarding this work, however, relates to the author's overall perspective upon his subject. This perspective, in keeping admittedly with much of the codified law of treaties itself, might be judged by some to be a little too firmly rooted in the diplomatic and jurisprudential traditions of the past. Heavy emphasis is placed, for example, upon the sovereignty of States and upon the mutuality of inter-State relations as the foundation of treaty law. A restrictive view is taken regarding the justiciability of certain kinds of international dispute. It is firmly denied that the treaty might serve any legislative or quasi-legislative function.

It must be regarded as extremely doubtful whether such an approach can adequately serve the needs of contemporary international society, which it is no longer realistic to regard simply as a community of sovereign States. Whatever the formal position regarding legal personality, it is clear that modern social, political, commercial and technological realities require the recognition of multinational corporations, non-governmental organizations and individual human beings as significant actors upon the international stage. Indeed, many evolving legal principles have little to do with the rights or interests of States as such. Owing to the paucity of legal mechanisms available, the primitive and cumbersome device of the treaty has had to be pressed into service and adapted to meet the ever-changing needs of this expanded community, much as an arquebus might have been modified in order to deliver a tactical nuclear weapon. Even more remarkable than that such an enterprise has been essayed, however, is the fact that a substantial degree of success has arguably been achieved. The prospects for the future will nevertheless depend crucially upon the degree of flexibility and inventiveness displayed with regard to such processes as the adoption, interpretation, implementation and enforcement of treaties, particularly of the multilateral standard-setting variety. The conservatism inherent in traditional perspectives upon the international legal system in general and the international law of treaties in particular is likely to prove a major impediment in this regard.

It is interesting to note, therefore, that the author brings his opening chapter to a reflective conclusion, in a section significantly entitled 'Afterthoughts', in which he recognizes that a survey of the codification process as a whole suggests that 'no attempt has been made to get to grips with the real nature and function of the multilateral treaty today'. He concedes that this is a question which 'is seen to impinge on the very structure of international law as it now exists' and argues that it is incumbent upon international lawyers, whether of diplomatic or of academic orientation, 'to take a new look at received doctrines, and to search for a way to adapt them to the new pluricultural conditions now existing in the world generally'. It is encouraging that one who has played so eminent a role in the exposition and analysis of the law of treaties in the past should ultimately perceive so clearly the urgent need for its continued development in order to meet the challenges of the future. Professor Rosenne himself will doubtless have a significant part to play in this process.

M. J. Bowman

Common Heritage or Common Burden? The United States Position on the Development of a Regime for Deep Sea-Bed Mining in the Law of the Sea Convention. By Markus G. Schmidt. Oxford: Clarendon Press, 1989. 365 + xiv pp. £40.

The scope of Dr. Schmidt's study is identified in the book's sub-title. Based on his Oxford doctoral thesis, it comprises a full and illuminating account, for the outsider, of the US role in the controversial diplomatic history of Part XI of the 1982 Law of the Sea

Convention (LOSC) and of US 'sea-bed politics' (p. vii) from 1973, when the UN Conference opened, to 1988. The author emphasizes that his work should be classified as a study in international relations and politics. None the less, it has much to offer international lawyers, particularly the careful exposition and analysis of the US position in Committee One at UNCLOS, which occupy three chapters: negotiation of the system of exploitation (Chapter 4); negotiation of the financial terms of mining contracts, technology transfer, preparatory investment protection and the structure of the International Sea-Bed Authority (Chapter 5); and the production policy debate (Chapter 6).

In the first four years of the Conference the US priorities were the achievement of provisions satisfactory to its interests on straits passage and on the exclusive economic zone. Deep sea-bed mining occupied a lower place on the agenda of US delegation leaders. When this issue moved nearer to centre-stage, that gap between the US position (and that of several other industrialized countries with the technological capacity to engage in sea-bed mining) and the negotiating stance of the G77 developing countries became starkly apparent. In 1975 and 1976 Kissinger offered compromises—the parallel system of exploitation, and various proposals on production policy, technology transfer and financing of the Enterprise. Schmidt demonstrates the vagueness and insufficiency of these proposals, and the growing opposition within the United States, among industry and conservative groups, to the UNCLOS sea-bed texts. However, the Carter Administration persisted with the multilateral, Conference-based approach, eschewing unilateral legislative and bilateral treaty options.

With the advent of the Reagan Administration and the major policy review of the draft LOSC, ideological considerations came to the fore. Schmidt unravels the somewhat tangled skein of domestic political events, personnel changes, the Strategic Mineral Task Force report and the 1981 and 1982 sessions of UNCLOS with dexterity and objectivity (Chapter 7). Eleventh hour efforts by the Group of 11 (Australia, Austria, Canada, the Netherlands and the Scandinavian countries) to negotiate some improvements in Part XI following the end of the Conference in April 1982 were aborted by President Reagan's decision of 29 June to reject the Convention (p. 257).

Schmidt then analyses the Reagan Administration's law of the sea policy 1982–1987, the EEZ Proclamation and the Ocean Policy Statement. On the legal debate as to the permissibility of 'picking and choosing' sections of the LOSC, which was intended as a 'package-deal', he offers some general hypotheses: that by express or tacit agreement plus consistent practice the United States, and States in general, have accepted most LOSC provisions as statements of customary international law; that in some instances there is substantial disagreement on whether a Convention provision reflects customary law, and that the deep sea-bed mining regime is such a case, as is transit passage and the provisions on archipelagic sea-lanes. On transit passage through straits, one cannot quarrel with his assessment that in the near or medium-term future it is unlikely that LOSC parties will deny the US Navy the exercise of such rights, and 'as the US regularly uses these rights, they will be transformed into customary international law', but that the test will come if and when the need arises for interpretation of the ambiguities in the transit passage regime (p. 272). He cautions that it may be difficult for the navigational rights of maritime States within extended coastal State zones to become accepted as customary law, and that the United States' inability to assert these rights through LOSC compulsory dispute settlement processes may modify or weaken the rights (p. 274).

The book ends with an account of the 1982 and 1984 agreements—the Reciprocating States Agreement and the Provisional Understanding regarding Deep Sea-Bed Matters—and of developments in PrepCom. to the end of 1987. Schmidt canvasses the possibility that the LOSC may secure sufficient ratifications to enter into force (an outcome that now appears less likely than when he wrote) but 'perhaps in a leaner form' (p. 314). If the sea-bed regime were to be implemented 'on a more modest scale' this would not necessarily be disastrous for the UN or the future of 'international regime-building' (ibid.) PrepCom. has to draft rules and regulations with flexibility and which are compatible with the legitimate economic interests of States whose nationals possess the technology to mine the sea-bed. It remains to be seen whether there is sufficient commercial impetus for any mining operations to be undertaken this century.

Schmidt's research has been enriched by numerous interviews with officials, delegates, legislators, academics and members of relevant industrial companies or professional bodies (all these people are identified in an annex). The text is fully referenced and indexed, and there is a lengthy bibliography. The book should find a place in any collection on international law of the sea which purports to be comprehensive.

GILLIAN WHITE

Basic Documents on United Nations and Related Peace-Keeping Forces. By ROBERT C.R. SIEKMANN. 2nd enlarged edition. Dordrecht: Martinus Nijhoff, 1989. 415 pp. (including Appendix on Observer Missions, bibliography and index). £68.

This now represents a very complete, and extremely useful, collection of documents on peace-keeping. As compared with the first edition in 1984, it contains additional materials on UNEF, ONUC, UNEF II, UNIFIL, UNTAG, MFO and MFN. In addition, there is now a useful appendix on observer missions, and a bibliography.

For the reviewer, however, it is a matter of some regret that the editor—who clearly knows a great deal about the subject—has not been more ambitious. A collection of documents to accompany a textbook is one thing. But a collection of documents without any accompanying text is quite another, and many students using these documents may easily miss significant points emerging from these texts because there is not a word of commentary from the editor to guide them.

For example, we now see the almost standard formula used by the Assembly for the allocation of peace-keeping expenses in relation to UNEF II, UNIFIL, UNTAG, etc. But how useful it would have been to have given the student a short note on the formulae mooted in the work of the Special Committee in the 1960s, which came to nought; or a brief word on how the sums allocated between the various classes of contributors (permanent members, developed, developing, least developed States) are arrived at. Or take the rather novel power of arrest conceded to the host government in Paragraph 49 of the UNTAG Status of Forces Agreement: might not the novelty of this be pointed out with advantage? It certainly differs from Paragraph 16 of the UNEF Agreement. And the difficulties experienced by UNIFIL, and referred to rather obliquely in the 1980 Communiqué of the contributing States, do they not need some explanation? Many students will not readily comprehend that UNIFIL was dealing with what were virtually private armies, not responsible to member governments.

D. W. BOWETT

International Commercial Arbitration. By M. SORNARAJAH. Singapore: Longman Singapore Publishers Ltd., 1990. ix + 306 pp. $69.95; £44.95.

This is a useful book because of its scope. It covers all the fundamental problems, from the nature of State contracts through to the enforcement of arbitral awards, but it is about *State* contracts and it might have been better if the title had reflected this perspective.

A first chapter affords an overview. Entitled 'The Climate of International Arbitration', it attacks the theory of 'internationalization' of State contracts, demonstrating the weakness of the theoretical underpinnings of this theory. It then surveys what are described as 'competing norms', such as the universalization of the Calvo clause, the evolution of the international law of development, principles of consumer protection and merchantability. These are conceded to be 'weak sources of law' (p. 40), but preferred by the author as better suited to the evolving needs of international society.

In a sense, this discussion comes too early in the book. What one needs, first, is a discussion of choice of law problems—which is in chapter four—or at least a discussion of *why* these international law problems arise at all. For if State contracts are not treaties, and are governed not by international law but by the national law of the State party, as the author earlier maintains, why does international law become relevant? The answer is that rules of international law may be relevant *either* as the chosen proper law (in which case they become relevant to the question of contractual breach) *or* as part of the law of State responsibility governing the State's treatment of the property rights of aliens.

The second chapter on 'The Nature and Characteristics of State Contracts' argues, correctly, that such contracts cannot be assimilated to ordinary commercial contracts: the domain of State contracts is characterized by the dominance of the State's obligation to promote the national interest, and therefore to require such changes to the contractual relationship as public interest requires. The corollary of this, of course, is that with a State contract the exceptional prerogatives attaching to the State—prerogatives of adjustment, amendment or even termination in the public interest—have to be recognized.

A third chapter on dispute resolution is perhaps spoilt by its political overtones: it abounds with statements about anti-colonialism which are not really necessary to the thesis. The author's strictures on the ICSID nullification and appeal system, citing *Klockner* v. *Cameroon*, are well justified, but to depict arbitration as a sort of Western conspiracy, with sub-heads such as 'European domination of the arbitral system' or 'exclusive use of Western concepts', is going too far. There are in fact quite sensible, practical reasons why these arbitrations take place in localities such as Geneva, Paris or Washington, and why developing States brief law firms from Western countries. No doubt things will change over time, as expertise in arbitration spreads, but the dominance of Western jurists and practitioners, such as it is, derives from the wish of the parties—including Third-World Governments—to use the best available legal skills.

Chapter 4 tackles the choice of law issue. This is an excellent chapter which expresses some reservations about the acceptance of autonomy of choice in absolute terms, and then turns to a rejection of, first, the *lex mercatoria*, then transnational law, and finally general principles of law, as systems of 'proper law'. They are all, in truth, guises for arbitral discretion (or subjectivity) and none of these sources provides a coherent, developed set of rules capable of application to contractual disputes. The author reminds us that McNair saw general principles as performing an essentially subsidiary function, i.e. to fill a gap where the national law contained no specific rules on the problem to hand. He cautions against too liberal an approach to Article 42 of the ICSID Convention, showing by reference to the *travaux* that many delegates saw 'international law' as having a similar subsidiary role, supplementing but not displacing national law.

In Chapter 5 he turns to jurisdictional issues. In examining the rather delicate issues posed when the *lex arbitri* excludes certain categories of disputes from the scope of arbitration, it is perhaps useful to emphasize that these issues will tend to arise more in contracts between private parties. For a State party will normally not commit itself to arbitration over matters excluded from arbitration by its own law. As to corporate nationality—highly relevant in situations like ICSID which presuppose either a foreign nationality or an agreement to treat as such—the author is highly critical of the rather lax approach in cases like *Amco Asia*, or *Klockner* v. *Cameroon*.

Chapter 6 considers 'The Award' and, as to remedies, casts doubt on the value of orders for specific performance or declarations, largely because they cannot be enforced against a State. Thus, for the author, damages become the primary remedy and he is sceptical about the standard of 'full compensation', pointing to the latest US *Restatement* and to the case law of the US/Iran Claims Tribunal. It is perhaps a pity that the author was unable to take account of the late Judge Virally's award in the *Amoco International Finance Co.* case, for that award examines closely the distinction between a lawful and an unlawful taking and its effect on the level of compensation. As to the finality of the award, the recent ICSID cases, showing free use of the nullification procedure, escape with surprisingly little criticism.

Chapter 7 on 'Enforcement of Arbitral Awards' is in many ways the best chapter of all, for it analyses extremely thoroughly some of the most difficult questions posed in contemporary arbitration. Does acceptance of the theory of restrictive immunity increase the chances of enforcement, by excluding a plea of sovereign immunity? Is the test of 'commercial nature' applied to the original transaction or contract, or to the act of the State in varying or terminating the contract? How are the pleas of sovereign immunity and act of State related? Is an arbitration clause a waiver of immunity for purposes of execution of an award and, if so, is this effective only for execution in the courts of the *situs* of the arbitration or for courts anywhere? Is execution under the New York Convention different? Or under ICSID? The author's treatment is an excellent introduction into this legal morass.

Finally, the author essays a glance at the future ('Towards a New Beginning'). He argues strongly in favour of a duty to re-negotiate contracts, and favours re-negotiation clauses rather than stabilization clauses. If negotiation fails, arbitration takes over, but guided not by 'transnational law' but by 'the emerging principles of the international law of development'. It is a bold thesis, likely to appeal to emerging States rather than businessmen, and, of course, until the 'law of development' is clearer than 'transnational law' we are not much better off. But, whether one agrees or disagrees, this is a worthwhile book.

D. W. Bowett

Survey of International Arbitrations 1794–1990. By A. M. Stuyt. Dordrecht: Martinus Nijhoff, 1990. xix + 653 pp. £97.

This is essentially the third edition of this book (following a first edition in 1939 and a second in 1972) and it is sufficiently well-known, and appreciated, to require little introduction to those engaged in research in international law.

The general format remains the same. For each arbitration we have a statement of the issue to be decided, the composition of the tribunal, the date of the *compromis* and the award, the result, information as to its implementation, and references to literature concerning the case. And, of course, there are useful appendices on the various 'political' means of settlement, and also on such matters as administrative tribunals, regional tribunals, and military tribunals.

What one tends to ignore, when using the book as a reference source, is the extremely well-written Introduction which would serve any student well. It surveys the history, and problems, of arbitrations (including 'transnational' arbitrations between States and private entities) in a quite masterly way.

D. W. Bowett

Mixed International Arbitration. By Stephen J. Toope. Cambridge: Grotius Publications Ltd., 1990. 436 pp. £58.

It is a remarkable feature of the process of mixed international arbitration that, notwithstanding the substantial and increasing number of arbitrations between States and foreign private persons in recent years, many fundamental issues as to the nature of that system remain the subject of great uncertainty. Is arbitration between a State and a foreign private entity merely a procedure for the adjustment of private law rights and duties, or must the sovereign policy objectives of the State party also be recognized? What systems of law govern the procedure and substantive issues in the arbitration? To what extent is it possible to delocalize the procedural and substantive law of the arbitration? Are the awards of mixed arbitral tribunals enforceable under international law and, if so, by whom? The unsettled status of this category of international arbitration, a matter of considerable practical importance, makes Dr Toope's study particularly timely and valuable.

The work falls into two sections. The first addresses the central problems of mixed international arbitration, commencing with the immensely complicated problem of the delocalization of procedural and substantive law and providing a critical survey of the delocalization debate as it has developed in academic writings and arbitral decisions. Dr Toope contends that there is no compelling reason for the mandatory application of the *lex loci arbitri* to procedural issues and that the principle of party autonomy and the goals of practicality and efficiency all point towards flexibility as the preferred approach to procedural law. In reaching this conclusion he attaches great weight to the power of a prospective enforcement jurisdiction to evaluate the fairness of the arbitration procedure. The title of the chapter on delocalization of substantive law refers to 'the illusion of stabilization'. Here, Dr Toope argues that the concept of a *lex mercatoria* is largely fictitious and that neither the invocation of general principles of law, nor of international law *per se*, can effectively accomplish the stabilization of a contractual relationship so as to prevent unilateral modification or termination of the contract by the State party.

There follows a chapter on recognition and enforcement of arbitral awards in which the author takes issue with the concentration on the concept of 'foreign' awards and contends that awards involving a State and a foreign private person are now enforceable even when they are not 'foreign' in the traditional sense. Whatever may be the position under the New York Convention, a matter considered at length by Dr Toope, there is considerable force in his conclusion that, given the fact that in arbitrations involving States and foreign private parties the situs of an arbitration will often be entirely fortuitous, chosen simply for the sake of neutrality or for the convenience of the parties or the arbitrators and with no intention that the local law should govern, it would seem that enforcement in other States should in no way depend upon the peculiarities of the local law. In this chapter the author also deals in detail with public policy, State immunity and act of State as possible defences to enforcement of international arbitral awards. This is followed by a chapter on remedies before mixed arbitral tribunals.

The second section of the book is devoted to the principal examples of institutional mixed arbitration and considers ICC arbitration, ICSID arbitration, and the Iran-United States Claims Tribunal. Two lengthy chapters are devoted to the last of these and that tribunal's nature, jurisdiction, procedure and decisions are considered in detail. The precise nature and functions of the Iran-US Claims Tribunal remain obscure. It was brought into being in extraordinary circumstances in response to an unprecedented emergency and accordingly it is not entirely surprising that its constituent instruments do not provide a clear statement of its role. At the heart of the controversy is the question whether the Tribunal is an alternative forum created by international agreement for the adjudication of private law rights and duties, an international tribunal charged with ruling on the responsibility of States in international law, or a hybrid. This is not merely an academic controversy; it has a vital bearing on such issues as choice of law, remedies and the status before municipal courts of awards of the Tribunal and, as Dr Toope points out, the persuasive value of the Tribunal's practice and jurisprudence. The Tribunal's decisions show that it appears to be performing these different functions at different times. Indeed it has expressly acknowledged as much. Dr Toope is undoubtedly correct in his conclusion that the existence of the security account, a fund controlled by the Tribunal from which awards may be met, has made it possible for the Tribunal 'to hold to the comfortable if ill-defined notion that the Tribunal is a mixed creature of public and private law'.

However, enforcement is not the only context in which a municipal court might be called upon to consider the status of an award of the Tribunal as *Dallal* v. *Bank Mellat*, [1986] QB 441, a decision considered in detail by Dr Toope, demonstrates. He argues that the Tribunal is probably incapable of a clear division of function and warns that the price of a rigorous differentiation of function would be a corresponding loss of flexibility. This accords with his general thesis that arbitrations between States and foreign private parties are of a mixed nature and that the issues that must be addressed concern both private law rights and public law actions. Drawing a balance between the competing demands of certainty and flexibility in the system of mixed international arbitration is a recurring theme in this book. Opinions will inevitably differ as to where a satisfactory balance is drawn. Those who have to advise parties or present cases in proceedings before a tribunal such as the Iran-US Claims Tribunal might consider that Dr Toope under-estimates the difficulties created by the flexibility for which he contends.

Few would dissent from Dr Toope's conclusion that the arbitral system as it applies to States and foreign private parties does not fit very neatly within existing international structures and that a continuing and expanding debate concerning its role and status is essential to the development of a system still in its infancy. In this admirable study Dr Toope has made a most distinguished contribution to the debate.

David Lloyd Jones

The Oxford Encyclopaedia of European Community Law, Volume I: *Institutional Law*. By A. G. Toth. Oxford: Clarendon Press, 1990. xcviii + 547 pp. £75.

The justification given for this book is essentially that the advent of this new legal system has brought with it a host of new legal terms and concepts upon which the ordinary practitioner, or even the researcher, may need guidance.

In a sense, this states the aims of the book too modestly. It is not so much a terminological novelty as a *conceptual* novelty which is apt to create difficulties for the newcomer. There is, for example, no particular novelty about the term 'External Relations'. But the concept is new in its application, and so an excellent and clearly-written 12 pages of text describes the way in which certain external relationships, previously the exclusive domain of the sovereign State, now fall within the competence of the Communities.

The same is true of headings such as Human Rights, Treaty-Making Power, Treaty-Making Procedure. It is true, but in a rather different sense, of terms with which any English lawyer is familiar: Equity, Costs, Retroactive Effect, Plea of Illegality, Equality, Confidentiality, etc. What the English lawyer may not be familiar with is the way these quite familiar concepts have assumed a special role in Community Law.

Certainly there are novel terms: Direct Effect, Reference Proceedings, Preliminary Ruling, Individual Concern and so forth. But here again the value of the book lies more in its clear exposition of the operation of legal concepts or procedures, rather than in its explanation of terms.

There are also very useful features in the Table of Cases, Table of Community Treaties, Table of Community Acts, and Table of International Agreements.

It needs to be added that there will be two further volumes, covering Substantive Law and Community Policies. These, one suspects, will be much more difficult to write. But if they are of the same quality as this first volume, the entire work will, in due course, represent a major contribution.

D. W. Bowett

Land-Locked and Geographically Disadvantaged States in the International Law of the Sea. By Stephen C. Vasciannie. Oxford: Oxford University Press, 1990. 237 pp. £30.

The inclusion of provisions relating to land-locked and geographically disadvantaged States in the 1982 Law of the Sea Convention was, as Brownlie says in his Preface to this work, one of the 'more radical and difficult' aspects of the Third UN LOS Conference and the Convention. Prior to UNCLOS III international law attached very little significance to the views of land-locked States on the law of the sea, and the term 'geographically disadvantaged State' still has no generally agreed and precise definition. It was no doubt a considerable achievement for the Group of Land-Locked and Geographically Disadvantaged States (LLGDS) to have raised their concerns so effectively at UNCLOS, but also perhaps no surprise that at the end of the day their interests were largely subordinated to those of others. A book which attempts to analyse the role of the LLGDS Group at UNCLOS and to place it within an historical context is therefore most welcome, and it is a credit to Vasciannie that he has accomplished this task with rigour and elegance.

As the author demonstrates, the LLGDS Group were always strange bedfellows. Although there was a core of twenty-nine States with no sea coasts, they were a particularly diverse group ranging from Switzerland to Chad, Nepal to Bolivia. Vatican City left the group during the course of the Conference and Zimbabwe joined on independence in 1980. The Geographically Disadvantaged States were even more diverse. Vasciannie lists twenty-six GD States, including Bulgaria, the two Germanies, Greece, Iraq, Sweden, Zaire and Jamaica (of which the author is a national). The LLGDS Group adopted a very liberal policy on membership in order to reach the fifty members needed to constitute a 'blocking third' under the rules of procedure. This was, as he points out, not only the source of its strength but also the source of its ultimate weakness. Thirty-five members were also members of the Group of 77 but the developing State members of the LLGDS Group, by forging alliances with developed LLGDS, divided the Group of 77 along geographical lines, putting their interests in conflict with those of certain developing coastal States. This meant they were unable to rely on the Group of 77 for support, and indeed damaged the unity of that Group. With the advantage of hindsight Vasciannie regards this alliance as 'politically misguided'. He takes the view that if the developing LLGDS had remained loyal to their coastal counterparts it is likely that they could have reached compromise positions before entering into negotiations with developed States. The hundred or so members of the Group of 77 would then have ensured that all participants treated these positions with respect. It is a persuasive argument which he develops skilfully, but it is ultimately unverifiable. Although there was strong initial support for LLGDS positions from coastal States, as the framework of the Convention, and particularly the EEZ regime, emerged more clearly then any alliance between groups with such fundamentally conflicting interests was likely to run into difficulties. There has been little evidence since the conclusion of the 1982 Convention that even the little achieved by the LLGDS Group has been embraced by coastal States. Nevertheless his argument that the LLGDS position damaged Group of 77 unity is clearly true, and reinforces a singular merit of this book, which is that although the author has a clear analytical framework, he presents the wealth of detail he has collated in such a way as to open rather than close discussion.

After this initial scene-setting Vasciannie then critically examines the whole question of preferential treatment for LLGDS. In a most useful chapter he examines general arguments for preferential treatment which will be familiar to those involved in work on international law and development, including that of justice and equity derived from the dissenting judgment of Judge Tanaka in the *South West Africa* case (*Second Phase*) (1966), interdependence, as elaborated by Judge Bedjaoui, and the moral responsibility of colonial States to compensate for past exploitation (1970 Lusaka Seminar on Economic and Social Rights Report). Applying these concepts to LLGDS, the author detects clear problems with an argument for preferential treatment for land-locked States, while that for GDS he regards as 'even less cogent'. He concludes that 'given the complexities of geography in various parts of the world, it may be unfair to single out some features for special attention'.

The main original contribution of the work then follows in chapters on access to the living resources of the exclusive economic zone for LLGDS (Chapter 3), the question of access to the non-living resources of the continental shelf for LLGDS (Chapter 4), LLGDS and the question of the outer limit of the continental shelf (Chapter 5) and the rights and interests of LLGDS with respect to the sea-bed beyond national jurisdiction (Chapter 6). These chapters are very worthwhile indeed, well structured and clearly analysed. In relation to EEZ resources there is an initial review of access to living resources prior to UNLCLOS III including the early emergence of the EEZ concept itself through the 1972 Lagos Meeting and the Caribbean Santo Domingo Declaration on the 'patrimononial sea'. There follows an assessment of the rationale for LLGDS claims to EEZ resources and a detailed analysis of the way that arguments for these fared at UNCLOS III. With the finalization of the texts of Articles 69 and 79 (as mere shadows of their earlier substance) the author then assesses whether these rules constitute customary law in the light of the emergence of the EEZ itself into custom. The result of his survey is a depressing lack of State practice to support LLGDS' rights of access to living resources, leading him to the view that it does not at present represent *lex lata*, although accepting that an alternative 'package deal' argument would run counter to the view that selective implementation of the EEZ regime by coastal States has legitimized a 'pick-and-mix' approach to EEZ rights and duties.

A similar approach is taken to LLGDS' access to non-living continental shelf resources. The survival of the continental shelf as a concept discrete from the EEZ in the 1982 Convention severely damaged the arguments of land-locked States for access to the mineral resources of the continental shelf, and although Vasciannie assesses the arguments advanced for shelf entitlement for land-locked States, these must remain *de lege ferenda*. GDS' access, by contrast, must be argued in terms of maritime boundary delimitation, and the emergence of the single maritime boundary may well assist such arguments. In relation to rights and interests of LLGDS with respect to areas beyond national jurisdiction, the narrative links in with the broad spread of literature on Part XI of the 1982 Convention, but the author manages to maintain his brief well, teasing out those issues from the general debate which are of particular concern for LLGDS. Under the Convention—if not perhaps under customary law—LLGDS rights have been recognized and the author, in sanguine mood, suggests that Article 161 could result in twelve LLGDS being elected to the Council of the Sea Bed Authority 'if the international community adheres to the spirit of the provisions on membership'—enough to form a blocking third.

The book concludes with a brief historical evaluation of treaties governing rights of access to the sea for land-locked States—the main issue in the literature prior to UNCLOS—and the question of access in general international law. Again the 1982 Convention makes advances, but not enough to meet LLS aspirations. Transit States felt obliged to accept obligations, but the author must be correct to suggest that these were 'close to the minimum required to bring the right of access into operation'. The general right of transit is accepted by Article 125 but the means and modalities still have, as before, to be negotiated. Under general international law the issue of a right of transit still involves a very delicate assessment of evidence, through which Vasciannie briefly but deftly guides the reader.

The conclusion by this time is all too obvious and well known to those who work in the law of the sea. LLGDS played an active and prominent role in the UNCLOS negotiations. Major advances were made in the recognition of their rights of access to, and interests in, marine resources, but most often subject to important qualifications which deprived them of much of their utility. The very size of the LLGDS Group itself, while ensuring it an audience, contained the seeds of its own weakness by splitting its unity of aspiration. Vasciannie's brief conclusion draws the threads together with some hope for the future, that the passing of time will consolidate still further, as customary law, the mandatory nature of the right of access to the sea.

Vasciannie is to be warmly congratulated for this work. It is well written in a careful but lively style and the diverse and often difficult source materials are handled in a sensitive and scholarly way. This is a most welcome addition to the *Oxford Monographs in International Law* and to the literature on the law of the sea.

DAVID FREESTONE

Resolutions and Statements of the United Nations Security Council (1946–1989): A Thematic Guide. Edited by KAREL C. WELLENS. Dordrecht: Martinus Nijhoff, 1990. xxxiv + 691 pp. £130.

There can be few researchers who have not been daunted by the sheer mass of the materials on Security Council practice. To these researchers, this volume will be of considerable help.

As the editor's Introduction explains, classification was no easy matter. What has been done is to have two Parts, the first dealing with matters involving international peace and security, and the second with other matters. Within that broad division, the classification is a geographical one, that is to say by region. Thus, in Part I we have: General, Western Europe and other States, Eastern Europe, Africa, Asia, Latin America, the Palestine Question, the Middle East.

Within each region, each topic is given a heading to denote its subject-matter, and this is followed by an introductory note reciting the basic facts, followed by a list of meetings, the texts of resolutions, and any Presidential statements. Obviously, a researcher can still be in difficulty, but there is further help in an Analytical Table of Contents and, as Annex I, a chronological list of the 635 resolutions covered and a page reference to locate them within the book.

The topics in Part II are of rather a disparate character, ranging from admission of new members to hijacking and disarmament.

The volume thus represents a considerable amount of work, and of its utility there can be no doubt.

D. W. Bowett

International Law and World Order. A Problem-Oriented Coursebook. 2nd edition, and Documents Volume and Teachers' Manual. By Burns H. Weston, Richard A. Falk and Anthony A. D'Amato. St. Paul: West Publishing Co., 1990. 1,335 pp. No price stated.

As in the first edition of this work, the authors offer a challenging approach to the teaching and learning of international law. Their brief is avowedly wider than a conventional textbook and aims to attract a readership of liberal arts students as well as those in law. They examine international law as part of the study of international relations, and specifically in the context of the world order movement. They encourage readers to discover and use not just legal precedent but any norms and policies that seem relevant; their purpose is to influence, directly or indirectly, decision-makers and policy-makers.

The coursebook is divided into three sections. Part I deals with the international legal process and uses the Nuremberg Trials as a vehicle for exploration. As an introduction to the operation and context of the international law system, it could hardly be bettered. Part II contains problems set in the four areas which the authors perceive to be in most urgent need of examination and resolution. They concern environmental protection, economic well-being, sociopolitical justice and war prevention. The problems are well-constructed and the teachers' manual suggests helpful outline arguments for each. In Part III, the authors are more explicit about their vision of world order and the intellectual framework in which threats to it should be resolved. The challenge they pose to conventional doctrinal treatments of international law and the assumptions they make within that challenge provide a stimulating debate not just for students but also for those more familiar with international legal jurisprudence. The materials as a whole are wide-ranging and accompanied by excellent bibliographic references and searching questions. The separate collection of documents comprises 157 items. Many of them are available in mainstream sources, but the width and relevance of the selections make this an invaluable collection in its own right.

The emphasis of the work is on American legal traditions and concerns, but these in themselves add a richness to British perspectives; the detailed examination of US Government delinquencies and the professional responsibilities of international lawyers raises questions for us all. More pertinent is the concern that students working from these materials will derive only a partial knowledge of the doctrines and principles of international law. The authors acknowledge that they emphasize precisely those areas where the law is uncertain and most in need of formulation. In addition, the problem-oriented approach can lead to some surprising arrangements, for instance, finding material on military retorsion and reprisals in the section on environmental protection but none on self-defence anywhere. The index, although described as comprehensive, is too linked to the authors' conceptions and terminology to make it easy to use for the student working with an orthodox doctrinal textbook. These reservations apart, the coursebook and documents collection will make an invaluable contribution to any library and a stimulating source of new ideas.

ILONA C. CHEYNE

Treatment of Detainees: Examination of Issues Relevant to Detention by the United Nations Human Rights Committee. By PAUL R. WILLIAMS. Geneva: Henry Dunant Institute, 1990. xvii + 267 pp. SF 28; US $23.

This is a short but useful work on the issues relevant to detention that have been considered by the Human Rights Committee. However, the purpose of the work is not so much to provide a legal analysis as 'to assist penitentiary officials in their efforts to ensure the protection of detainees' human rights' (p. 3). Indeed, there are a number of legal and factual errors. Although the Human Rights Committee (HRC) is very closely connected with the United Nations, it is not a United Nations body as the title suggests. The geographical representation of members is not fixed in terms of the precise numbers indicated on page 6. State reports are not usually considered 'at the next regular session' (p. 15) after their submission because the HRC has a backlog of reports. The annual report of the HRC is not sent to the General Assembly for 'approval' in any meaningful sense (p. 16). It is misleading to state that the HRC has taken the view that 'the term torture as used in the article [7] includes: corporal punishment, which itself includes excessive chastisement' (p. 19). The relevant General Comment by the HRC was in terms of the prohibition in Article 7 rather than specifically on the term 'torture'. It was also phrased in an ambiguous way in as much as it was not clear whether corporal punishment *per se* was a violation of Article 7 or only if it constituted 'excessive chastisement as an educational or disciplinary measure'. The Human Rights Commission never accepted the proposals for a right of individual petition as is suggested (p. 22). The Human Rights Commission is not comprised of political representatives for 'each member State to the United Nations' (p. 97, n. 1). To state simply that a State has a 'right to make reservations to articles or sections which it believes are inapplicable to the State's particular circumstances' (p. 118, n. 681) is misleading if it is not accompanied by some reference to the governing rules on the validity of reservations.

These comments are enough to indicate that this work will not be relied upon for an authoritative legal perspective on the HRC. However, the chapter which specifically deals with the 'Detention Issues Addressed by the HRC' is very helpful. It draws out those issues from an examination of the work of the HRC under its reporting and individual petition procedures. The issues addressed are helpfully broken down into a series of categories and subcategories. There are also various suggestions as to other issues which the HRC should raise. The final chapter of the work contains a number of sensible and practical suggestions for improving the efficiency and effectiveness of the HRC. A number of them already occur in the practices of the HRC, for example, the use of a special rapporteur in difficult cases under the first Optional Protocol. A less welcome suggestion is that the HRC could decide that if the State takes appropriate remedies then a decision under the first Optional Protocol which found a violation of the Covenant could remain confidential. This fails to take account of the wider public interest involved in human rights cases and the important effect of publicity both on States and in demonstrating the practical successes that human rights systems can achieve.

Over half of the text of this work consists of documentary appendices of international instruments concerning the treatment of detainees. Finally, there is a short bibliography.

DOMINIC MCGOLDRICK

Fontes Juris Gentium, Series A, Sectio 1, Tomus 7 (1976–1985). Berlin: Springer-Verlag, 1990. xxxviii + 386 pp. DM 390.

This series, as a source of reference, is quite invaluable and the present volume brings it reasonably up-to-date. As with previous volumes, the subject index is in three languages so as to maximize its utility. The format remains the same as in previous volumes, but the increasing tendency towards separate and dissenting judgments (often of considerable length) has imposed the need for a certain selectivity.

The summaries of the cases, at the back of the volume, are exceedingly useful, and very accurate. The need to give students a concise statement of a case often arises, for the full reports are often so prolix as to daunt a beginner. These summaries meet the need admirably.

A perusal of this volume demonstrates how much questions of maritime delimitation and, to a lesser extent, of international responsibility have dominated the work of the Court during this period. On present evidence, this pattern is likely to remain.

D. W. Bowett

Pax—Ius—Libertas: Miscellanea in honorem Demitrii S. Constantopouli. Thessalonicae: Aristotelea Universitas Studiorum Thessalonicensis, 1990. 2 volumes. lxiv + 1313 pp. Paperback. No price stated.

The two volumes under review form a very substantial tribute to Professor Dimitri Constantopoulos. There are sixty-five essays in four languages, over a variety of disciplines, among which international law predominates. The essays range in length from a few pages to sixty or so. They form an eclectic collection which has no common theme but which does give some idea of the wide interests of Professor Constantopoulos, whose accomplishments occupy many pages of the introduction. It is likely that he is most widely known as the inspiration of the summer courses on international law and relations at Thessalonika. It is a tribute to the quality of the lecturers and participants in those seminars that it has been possible to assemble from among them so distinguished a panel of contributors.

Those essays which carry an indication of when they were completed show that they were done by 1987. It is a measure of how far and how fast they world has moved since then that some, by reason of their perspective (Terz, 'For a Modern Theory of the Creation of Norms in the Nuclear-Cosmic Era') or their subject-matter (Schmidt, 'The Two German States and European Security'), seem to belong to legal history. One hardly expected to see again President Ceausescu being the principal authority relied on in an academic article (Marim, 'Pour une nouvelle approche des problèmes de l'édification d'un nouvel ordre économique international'). Blischenko's 'Concept of an Act of Terrorism' is a reminder of how difficult it has been to reach any degree of international consensus about terrorism if attention is given to the reasons for violent acts, rather than isolating particular activities, like hostage-taking, regardless of the motivation of their perpetrators.

If some essays are about a time which has gone, the time has come for others, notably Wolfe's 'Cyprus: The Proposal for an International Conference'. The concluding stages of the Iran-Iraq war and the early stages of the action against Iraq after its invasion of Kuwait have underlined the importance of Lowe's 'The Gulf Conflict and the Law of War at Sea'. Bello's 'Border Disputes and Boundary Problems in Africa' is one of the longest essays and deals with a subject of increasing interest and difficulty. It is unsatisfactory. There are surprising omissions, no reference, not even prospective, to the Burkina Faso-Mali and Chad-Libya disputes nor to Shaw's book, *Title to Territory in Africa*; the Balkans and the Baltic States are confused; the treatment of *uti possidetis*, a crucial matter, is unhelpful. Of course, there are drawbacks to relying on old colonial boundaries in Africa but the States themselves obviously thought that the alternatives were worse. Bello seems reluctant to concede that the OAU resolution has provided some stability which might yet allow for peaceful adjustment for boundaries in the future.

There are several essays on aspects of the law of armed conflict, including one on the legality of nuclear weapons and testing as considered by national courts (McWhinney) and a group on human rights, among which are ones on capital punishment (Grahl-Madsen), the interpretation of the European Convention (Andrews), and friendly settlements (Ermacora). Others stand by themselves, for example, Nafziger, 'A Prologue to the Study of International Sports Law'. The range of subjects shows that these volumes contain something for practically every international lawyer. The distinction of the writers speaks to the success of the schools at Thessalonika, their enthusiasm no doubt bolstered, as one of them admits, by the 'hedonistic' as well as the academic environment there established.

COLIN WARBRICK

La Réparation des dommages catastrophiques. Travaux des XIII journées de'études juridiques Jean Dabin. Brussels: Bruylant, 1990. 580 pp. BF 4,325.

This book is a collection of papers presented at a conference in 1988; as is usual with such a collection, the standard of contributions varies very substantially. But a much more serious weakness is the apparent absence of any attempt to edit the conference papers. The book is 580 pages long and much of this—about a third of the total—is taken up by repetition of the same material by different contributors. This unnecessary repetition of basic information about the occurrence and aftermath of catastrophes such as Chernobyl, Bhopal, Sandoz and Seveso and about the relevant legal instruments reduces the opportunity for analysis and discourages even the most enthusiastic reader.

Almost all the contributors discuss the meaning of catastrophe and agree that it is a man-made, accidental, sudden disaster that causes serious damage. Many of them regret the limitations imposed by the topic: it excludes gradual harm such as damage to the ozone layer, the greenhouse effect, acid rain, and river and sea pollution. Also the preface by Rigaux makes it clear that the programme of the conference did not include the question of prevention of harm or of damage to the environment, as opposed to harm to individual victims.

The book is divided into three main sections: public international law, private international law and European Community law. Each section begins with a general report (by Ballarino, Dupuy and Zuleeg respectively) that is followed by more specific papers and some extracts from the discussion at the conference (the last generally not worth the reproduction). There is also a series of useful annexes on the chemical, nuclear and oil sectors and on transport. The main value of the book lies in its bringing together these different areas of the law. A clear theme is that on this question of reparation of damage resulting from catastrophes, no strict distinctions can be made between the different areas of the law, particularly not between public and private international law.

Questions such as how far the activities of private enterprises are imputable to the State and how far government action is necessary to secure adequate reparation for victims are central to this work. Catastrophes are a subject for international law when an activity in one State causes harm in others (as with Chernobyl) or when multinational corporations export risks by investment in hazardous activities in other States (as with Seveso and Bhopal). Treaties laying down special regimes for hazardous activities may provide for civil liability in municipal courts. All these factors, and others, blur the traditional distinction between public and private international law. Dupuy is alone in his insistence on such a distinction, and his sneer at 'Anglo-Saxon jurists' who fail to observe it is puzzling, given the overwhelming rejection of the distinction by his fellow contributors (with not an Anglo-Saxon among them).

International law on reparation for victims of catastrophes has developed in a piecemeal fashion in response to particular disasters. The second and third sections of the book on private and public international law discuss the different mechanisms that have been used or proposed: the establishments of funds by those involved in hazardous activities, the use of insurance, the role of civil liability and State responsibility. What emerges very strongly is the limited role played by traditional inter-State reparation. As Dupuy describes, none of the major catastrophes discussed in this work have led to claims for or payment of compensation on the basis of State responsibility. Another theme is the problems yet to be overcome in the use of municipal courts to establish civil liability. Smets in his paper on the costs of accidental pollution establishes that full compensation is rarely, if ever, obtained. Tenière-Buchot, Clave and Hetzel (in their paper on the different methods of indemnification) express doubts about the use of courts to provide reparation. Questions of group actions, access to information and how to deal with long-term damage remain.

These issues also face the European Communities. Zuleeg, Gautier and Krämer all cover much the same ground in their accounts of Community action on the environment since the 1970s, of the rather limited legal basis for action provided by the Treaty of Rome, and of the increased emphasis on the prevention of pollution in the Single European Act. It is clear that except in the area of product liability little provision has been made for reparation. One of the most interesting questions to arise in this section is on the meaning of the 'polluter pays' principle espoused in the Single European Act; the contributors disagree on whether this includes a duty to make reparation.

It will be apparent that important and interesting issues, well-summarized by Verhoeven in his conclusions, do emerge from this book, although the form of the book makes it hard work for the reader to concentrate on them. Inside this fat, repetitive book is a thin, interesting book trying to get out.

CHRISTINE GRAY

* * * * *

In September 1985 Oxford University Press published a book entitled *Termination of Treaties in International Law: The Doctrines of Rebus Sic Stantibus and Desuetude* by Athanassios Vamvoukos. The book was reviewed in this *Year Book*, 58 (1987), p. 393.

The script of the above-mentioned book was accepted for publication in good faith and on the understanding that it was an original piece of work. A Tribunal established by the University of Oxford has recently found that the thesis on which the book was based plagiarized an earlier Ph.D thesis written by Dr A. Toth (now Professor of Law at the University of Strathclyde) and a series of three articles based on that Ph.D thesis and published in the *Juridical Review*, 1974, pp. 56, 147 and 263 under the title 'The Doctrine of Rebus Sic Stantibus in International Law'. The publisher has now destroyed all unsold copies of the book and apologizes for any distress and embarrassment inadvertently caused to Professor Toth.

DECISIONS OF BRITISH COURTS DURING 1991 INVOLVING QUESTIONS OF PUBLIC OR PRIVATE INTERNATIONAL LAW

A. Public International Law*

International organization—personality in international law—personality not recognized by domestic legislation—capacity to sue and be sued in England—Arab Monetary Fund Agreement 1976

Case No. 1. Arab Monetary Fund v. *Hashim and others (No. 3)*, [1991] 2 AC 114, [1991] 2 WLR 729, [1991] 1 All ER 871, HL. The common law of England *will* recognize the juridical personality of an international organization of which the United Kingdom is not a member, provided that it has had legal personality conferred on it under the municipal law of at least one of its member States. It is not necessary that such organizations have legal personality conferred on them by United Kingdom legislation in order for them to be able to bring or defend proceedings in the English courts. This proposition can now be considered settled following the decision of the House of Lords in this case,[1] notwithstanding the dissenting opinion of Lord Lowry. It appears to be irrelevant whether the organization has had legal personality conferred on it under the law of a member State by legislation of that State, or whether it enjoys legal personality in that system of law by virtue of the fact that, under the constitutional law of that State, the treaty establishing the organization is considered to be self-executing and binding in domestic law.[2]

The House of Lords has thereby confirmed what was generally considered to be the position at common law prior to the commencement of proceedings in this case. Numerous international organizations of which the United Kingdom is not a member and whose existence has never been acknowledged by legislation in this country have over the last decade been borrowing and placing on deposit large sums of money in the City of London,[3] and have always dealt and been dealt with on the basis that they could, if necessary, sue and be made liable on these transactions. Indeed, in 1978 the Foreign and Commonwealth Office had advised the Bank of England that this was the case, and that the executive would be willing officially to acknowledge that such entities enjoyed legal personality and capacity.[4] Writers had

* © Christopher Staker, 1992.

[1] Proceedings in this case at first instance and before the Court of Appeal have been noted in earlier volumes of this *Year Book*: 60 (1989), pp. 475–6, and 61 (1990), pp. 380–3. See also pp. 447 ff., below.

[2] See [1991] 2 AC at 163G–164B.

[3] See Carver, 'International Organisations After Arab Monetary Fund', *Butterworths Journal of International Banking and Financial Law*, 1991, p. 215.

[4] See this *Year Book*, 49 (1978), at pp. 346–8. This statement by the FCO was referred to at all stages in the proceedings in this case.

supported this view.[5] This was also the practical result of the decision of Hoffmann J at first instance in this case.

The decision of the Court of Appeal that this was not so, and that an international organization could not be recognized as having legal capacity under English law unless such personality had been conferred by legislation, understandably was the cause of much consternation to all of these organizations and their creditors.[6] The judgment of the House of Lords will thus come as a great relief to many.

There is, of course, every reason why the legal personality of such organizations *should* be recognized by common law. They exist in fact—they are, as Lord Donaldson had put it,[7] 'as much a fact as a tree, a road or a hill'. Evidence had been given that the Arab Monetary Fund

> holds assets and has incurred liabilities in its own name in every part of the world. The fund has in its own name deposits in the London market which at 30 June 1989 exceeded US $235m. The fund has brought proceedings in different parts of the world.[8]

To Lord Templeman, for the courts of England to decide simply to ignore this reality would be 'perverse' and 'unthinkable',[9] 'profoundly unsatisfactory',[10] and 'would cause great dismay and uncertainty . . . The enactment of legislation could not repair the damage caused by the decision'.[11] Lord Templeman (with whose judgment Lord Bridge, Lord Griffiths and Lord Ackner agreed) was able to avoid this result, but with respect, it is unfortunate that he, like Hoffmann J at first instance, felt it necessary to employ such circuitous reasoning to do so.

It will be recalled that the Arab Monetary Fund is an international organization with its seat in Abu Dhabi in the United Arab Emirates (UAE). The Arab Monetary Fund Agreement of 1976 which established the organization provides that it has 'independent juridical personality and . . . in particular, the right to own, contract and litigate'.[12] The United Kingdom is not a member of the organization and its legal personality has never been recognized by legislation in this country.[13] The Fund brought proceedings in the Chancery Division against its former director-general, Dr Hashim, and several other defendants, alleging that while in office Dr Hashim had stolen about US $50 million of the organization's assets. The issue was whether the Fund had capacity to bring these proceedings.

Before Hoffmann J, it was initially argued that English law recognizes the existence of legal entities constituted under international law just as it recognizes those

[5] See Jenks, 'The Legal Personality of International Organizations', this *Year Book*, 22 (1945), pp. 267–75, esp, at pp. 273–4; Mann, 'International Corporations and National Law', this *Year Book*, 42 (1967), pp. 145–74 (provided the organization has been recognized by the Executive); Collier, 'The Status of an International Corporation', in *Multum non Multa: Festschrift für Kurt Lipstein* (Karlsruhe, 1980), pp. 21–9. These writers were referred to by Hoffmann J: [1991] 2 AC at 119. See also, e.g., *Halsbury's Laws of England*, vol. 9 (4th edn., 1974), p. 743, para 1248.

[6] See Carver, loc.cit. above (n. 3).

[7] [1991] 2 AC at 133.

[8] Ibid., at 162 (*per* Lord Templeman).

[9] Ibid., at 163.

[10] Ibid., at 167.

[11] Ibid.

[12] Article 2 of the Agreement. Other relevant provisions of the Agreement are set out in the judgment of Lord Templeman, ibid., at pp. 158–9.

[13] The organization could not have the legal capacities of a body corporate conferred on it by an Order in Council under the International Organizations Act 1968, since the United Kingdom was not a member of the organization, nor did it maintain or propose to maintain an establishment in the United Kingdom: see ss. 1(2)(*a*) and 4(*a*) of that Act.

constituted under foreign systems of domestic law. However, once the House of Lords had given judgment in the *Tin Council* case,[14] it was assumed by everyone, including counsel for the Fund, that this argument had become untenable. In the *Tin Council* case, Lord Oliver, referring to the principle of constitutional law that 'a treaty is not part of English law unless and until it has been incorporated into the law by legislation',[15] had said that in the absence of legislation, the International Tin Council 'had no legal existence in the law of the United Kingdom and no significance save as the name of an international body created by a treaty between sovereign states which was not justiciable by municipal courts'.[16] In the present case, both Lord Templeman and Lord Lowry had no doubt that an international organization created by treaty with separate juridical personality under international law cannot as such be recognized as a juridical person by English law.[17]

The case therefore hinged on an alternative argument. The treaty establishing the Fund had been ratified by a Decree of the Supreme Council of the UAE, a result of which was that the Fund enjoyed legal personality under the municipal law of that State. It was argued on behalf of the Fund that it could thus be recognized as a domestic UAE corporation under principles of English private international law.[18] Lord Templeman had no difficulty at all with this argument:

> The *Tin Council* case reaffirmed that the English courts cannot identify and allow actions by international organisations which sovereign states by treaty agree to bring into existence. The *Tin Council* case decided, however, that the international organisation called the ITC had been created a corporate body by the English Order in Council. No one disputed the right of the ITC based on the English Order in Council to bring an action. In the present case the English courts cannot identify and accept the right to sue of an international organisation which sovereign states by the AMF agreement agreed to create. But the English courts can identify and accept the right to sue of a corporate body created by a sovereign state pursuant to the obligations accepted by that state in the agreement. In the *Tin Council* case there was the ITC treaty, followed by the Order in Council which created the ITC a corporate body. In the present case there is the AMF agreement, followed by Federal Decree No 35 which created the fund a corporate body.[19]

Yet the reality clearly is that UAE law did not *create* the Fund, but merely conferred on an existing organization legal capacity under the law of that State.[20] If

[14] *J.H. Rayner (Mincing Lane) Ltd.* v. *Department of Trade and Industry*, [1990] 2 AC 418, [1989] 3 WLR 969, [1989] 3 All ER 523, this *Year Book*, 60 (1989), pp. 461–73.

[15] [1990] 2 AC at 500.

[16] Ibid., at 510.

[17] '. . . the courts of the United Kingdom cannot enforce treaty rights . . . A treaty cannot create a corporation': [1991] 2 AC at 163, *per* Lord Templeman. 'At common law . . . international organisations set up by treaty are not recognised as having legal status in our courts': ibid., at 173, *per* Lord Lowry.

[18] Reference was made to Dicey and Morris, *Conflict of Laws* (11th edn., 1987), vol. 2, p. 28 ('Rule 171: The existence or dissolution of a foreign corporation duly created or dissolved under the law of a foreign country is recognised in England'); and to *Lazard Brothers & Co.* v. *Midland Bank Ltd.*, [1933] AC 289, 297 ('English courts have long since recognised as juristic persons corporations established by foreign law in virtue of the fact of their creation and continuance under and by that law').

[19] [1991] 2 AC at 165.

[20] Cf. the quotations at n. 18 above. This was the essence of Lord Lowry's dissenting judgment. He said that English private international law will recognize a separate juridical persona which has been *created* under the law of a foreign State, but not one which has merely been *recognized* under the law of a foreign State: see esp. [1991] 2 AC at 176. He referred to *Banque Internationale de Commerce de Petrograd* v. *Goukassow*, [1923] 2 KB 682 (reversed on other grounds [1925] AC 150), in which the Court

English law treats UAE law as having *created* a corporate body, then (as counsel for the respondents had argued) there must be as many separate entities called the Arab Monetary Fund as there are States which have recognized its legal personality in domestic law. Lord Templeman dismissed this argument as 'fanciful'.[21] He said:

> But there is only one fund to which each of the member states accorded legal personality. No one can bring an action to recover the money of the fund in any part of the world except the one duly authorised director-general. The articles of agreement which were annexed to the federal decree of the UAE and which thus became part of the law of the UAE are no different from the memorandum and articles of a limited liability company established under the law of England . . . It may safely be assumed that no one except Dr Hashim and the other respondents has doubted that the fund is a separate corporate entity or has conceived the fanciful notion of the existence of more than one fund.[22]

Yet it seems impossible to reconcile the view that there is only one Fund, governed by the terms of the AMF Agreement, with the principle also affirmed by Lord Templeman that an international organization cannot be recognized as such, without legislation. This seems tantamount to saying that the treaty establishing the organization could be given effect in English law by the municipal legislation of another State. Moreover, the notion of multiple juridical personalities is not entirely fanciful, and could raise problems in practice, since the one organization could have different capacities under the law of different States.[23] To the law of which State would English law then refer to determine whether the organization had legal capacity to enter into a particular transaction?[24]

If it is desirable that the personality of international organizations be recognized by common law (at least where they have legal personality under the municipal law of one member State), could the court not have found a direct rule to that effect? True, there is the well established rule that a treaty cannot alter domestic law unless given effect by legislation. But this rule has always been subject to certain qualifications. Most pertinently, the legal personality of a foreign State is recognized by common law (provided that the State has been recognized by the executive),[25] even if that State was established by a treaty. Could not this rule have been extended by analogy to an international organization which has been recognized by the executive? If recognized in this way, the capacity of the organization presumably would be governed by English substantive law, rather than the substantive law of one or more other States in which its juridical personality has been recognized. Such an approach might have been difficult to reconcile with some of the pronounce-

of Appeal held that the existence of a Russian company that had been dissolved by a decree of the Soviet government (which government was recognized by the United Kingdom) could not be recognized in English law, even though it still existed in French law, where the Soviet measure had been refused recognition, and even though the plaintiff sought to sue the company on a contract entered into in France.

[21] [1991] 2 AC at 162. Even Lord Lowry was admittedly 'not much impressed' by it: ibid., at 180.

[22] Ibid., at 162.

[23] Treaties establishing some international organizations leave it to each member State to determine the precise extent of their juridical pesonality under municipal law. See, by way of example, United Nations Charter, Art. 104 ('The Organization shall enjoy in the territory of each of its Members such legal capacity as may be necessary for the exercise of its functions and the fulfilment of its purposes'); and EEC Treaty, Art. 211 ('In each of the Member States, the Community shall enjoy the most extensive legal capacity accorded to legal persons under their laws').

[24] Cf. Dicey and Morris, op.cit. above (n. 18), at p. 1134, Rule 174(2): 'All matters concerning the constitution of a corporation are governed by the law of the place of incorporation'.

[25] *United States of America* v. *Wagner* (1867), LR 2 Ch.App. 582.

ments made in the *Tin Council* case, though not necessarily impossible, and the House of Lords is in any case not precluded from departing from its own previous decisions. It is disappointing that this possibility was not even explored.

One question that was not addressed directly was whether the position of the Arab Monetary Fund would have been any different if it had been an organization in respect of which an Order in Council might potentially have been made under the International Organizations Act 1968. If, for instance, the United Kingdom had been a member of the organization but no Order in Council had been made, could it still be recognized in English law as a UAE corporation? The generality of the language used by Lord Templeman suggests that this would be so, yet the Act could be interpreted as making the legal personality of such organizations dependent on the making of an Order in Council.[26]

In view of these unresolved questions, and in view of their practical importance, the enactment of legislation in this area would still appear to be most desirable.

Judicial review—unimplemented treaty—statutory interpretation—whether legislation presumed consistent with treaty obligations—human rights—European Convention for the Protection of Human Rights and Fundamental Freedoms 1950

Blasphemy—common law offence—human rights—freedom of religion—relevance of European Convention for the Protection of Human Rights and Fundamental Freedoms 1950

Case No. 2. R v. *Secretary of State for the Home Department, ex parte Brind*, [1991] 1 AC 696, [1991] 2 WLR 588, [1991] 1 All ER 720, HL. *Case No. 3. R* v. *Chief Metropolitan Stipendiary Magistrate, ex parte Choudhury*, [1991] 1 QB 429, [1990] 3 WLR 986, [1991] 1 All ER 306, 91 Cr.App.R 363, QBD DC. In both of these cases the court had occasion once again to consider the effect in English law of the 1950 European Convention for the Protection of Human Rights and Fundamental Freedoms (the European Convention).[27] In *Brind* the House of Lords affirmed the judgment of the Court of Appeal, which was noted in the previous volume of this *Year Book*.[28] It concerned the legality of directives given by the Secretary of State to the Independent Broadcasting Authority (IBA) and the British Broadcasting Corporation (BBC), requiring them to refrain from broadcasting the voices (but not the reported speech) of persons representing or supporting certain specified organizations.[29] In the case of the IBA, the directive had been given pursuant to section 29(3) of the Broadcasting Act 1981, which provides that:

> [T]he Secretary of State may at any time by notice in writing require the [IBA] to refrain from broadcasting any matter or classes of matter specified in the notice; and it shall be the duty of the [IBA] to comply with the notice.[30]

The appellants, several members and an employee of the National Union of

[26] Cf. the argument of counsel for the banks: [1991] 2 AC at 151.

[27] *United Nations Treaty Series*, vol. 213, p. 221, TS 71 (1953), Cmd. 8969.

[28] This *Year Book*, 61 (1991), at pp. 383–7.

[29] The directives applied to any proscribed organization under the Prevention of Terrorism (Temporary Provisions) Act 1984 or the Northern Ireland (Emergency Provisions) Act 1978, Sinn Fein, Republican Sinn Fein and the Ulster Defence Association.

[30] The directive to the BBC was given pursuant to clause 13(4) of the licence and agreement between the Secretary of State and the BBC (Cmnd. 8233), which is substantially similar to this provision. The arguments in relation to the directive given to the IBA were considered by the appellants to apply by parity of reasoning to that given to the BBC.

Journalists, maintained that the directive to the IBA was *ultra vires* the powers under that section, *inter alia* because it was inconsistent with the right to freedom of expression guaranteed by Article 10 of the European Convention.

The appellants did not challenge the settled view that the courts cannot enforce treaty rights directly[31] and that, if legislation is inconsistent with the United Kingdom's treaty obligations, the courts must nevertheless apply it.[32] However, as Lord Bridge pointed out, it is also well settled that:

> in construing any provision in domestic legislation which is ambiguous in the sense that it is capable of a meaning which either conforms to or conflicts with the Convention, the courts will presume that Parliament intended to legislate in conformity with the Convention, not in conflict with it.[33]

The appellants argued that section 29(3) of the Broadcasting Act was ambiguous in the sense that it purported to confer an unfettered discretion on the Secretary of State, when clearly it was subject to some limits, including the requirement that it not be exercised for an improper purpose,[34] and that it not be exercised unreasonably.[35] Hence, it was submitted that:

> when a statute confers upon an administrative authority a discretion capable of being exercised in a way which infringes any basic human right protected by the Convention, it may similarly be presumed that the legislative intention was that the discretion should be exercised within the limitations which the Convention imposes.[36]

None of the judges was prepared to accept this argument (although Lord Bridge found that it had 'considerable persuasive force'[37]), for the same reasons as the Court of Appeal. As Lord Bridge put it, this argument if accepted would go far beyond the resolution of an ambiguity.

> It would be to impute to Parliament an intention not only that the executive should exercise the discretion in conformity with the Convention, but also that the domestic courts should enforce that conformity by the importation into domestic administrative law of the text of the Convention and the jurisprudence of the European Court of Human Rights in the interpretation and application of it. If such a presumption is to apply . . . in the instant case, it must also apply to any other statutory discretion exercised by the executive which is capable of involving an infringement of Convention rights. When Parliament has been content for so long to leave those who complain that their Convention rights have been infringed to seek their remedy in Strasbourg, it would be surprising suddenly to find that the judiciary had, without Parliament's aid, the means to incorporate the Convention into such an important area of domestic law and I cannot escape the conclusion that this would be a judicial usurpation of the legislative function.[38]

Or as Lord Ackner put it, accepting the appellants' argument 'inevitably would result in incorporating the Convention into English domestic law by the back door'.[39]

[31] Above, text to n. 15.

[32] See *Salomon* v. *Commissioners of Customs and Excise*, [1967] 2 QB 116, 143.

[33] [1991] 1 AC at 747–78. See, e.g., *Garland* v. *British Rail Engineering Ltd.*, [1983] 2 AC 751, 771; and the *Tin Council* case, above, n. 14, at [1990] 2 AC 418, 500 (*per* Lord Oliver).

[34] *Padfield* v. *Minister of Agiculture, Fisheries and Food*, [1968] AC 997.

[35] *Associated Provincial Picture Houses Ltd.* v. *Wednesbury Corporation*, [1948] 1 KB 223.

[36] [1991] 1 AC at 748 (as paraphrased by Lord Bridge).

[37] Ibid.

[38] Ibid.

[39] Ibid., at 761–2.

Nevertheless, the decision of the House of Lords is significant for a number of reasons. First, Lord Bridge appears to confirm that in appropriate circumstances, reference may be made to *any* treaty obligation of the United Kingdom for the purposes of resolving a genuine ambiguity in *any* statute,[40] and that it is not necessary for the statutory provision to have been enacted for the purpose of giving effect to the treaty to which reference is made.[41] Given the enormous number of treaties to which the United Kingdom is a party and the range of subject matters with which they deal, this is of some importance.

Secondly, although Lord Ackner considered that there is never a duty to have regard to the European Convention in exercising a statutory discretion unless the statute imposes such an obligation,[42] the speeches of three other members of the House of Lords suggest that the European Convention still has a role to play in English administrative law. Lord Bridge said that in cases in which judicial review of executive action is sought on grounds of unreasonableness, although the English courts could not be bound by the European Convention, they were nonetheless 'perfectly entitled to start from the premise that any restriction of the right to freedom of expression requires to be justified and that nothing less than an important competing public interest will be sufficient to justify it'.[43] He noted further that such competing public interests were spelled out in Article 10(2) of the Convention. This leaves open the possibility that, in future, some regard may be had to the Convention in determining what is reasonable.[44]

Of even greater interest was the discussion whether the principle of 'proportionality' may emerge as a new ground of judicial review in English administrative law.[45] This principle already exists in the administrative law of several other member States of the European Communities, as well as in that of the European Communities itself.[46] Its future adoption in England was considered a possibility by Lord Diplock in *Council of Civil Service Unions* v. *Minister for the Civil Service*,[47] and has been supported in some legal literature.[48] In this case, Lord Ackner and Lord Lowry were clearly opposed to any such development.[49] However, Lord Roskill (with whom Lord Bridge agreed on this point), while not willing to apply such a

[40] See text to n. 33. Also ibid., at 760G (*per* Lord Ackner).

[41] See the discussion above, n. 28, at 385–6.

[42] [1991] 1 AC at 760–2, referring to *R* v. *Chief Immigration Officer, Heathrow Airport, ex parte Salamat Bibi*, [1976] 1 WLR 979; *Fernandes* v. *Secretary of State for the Home Department*, [1981] Imm. AR 1; *Chundawadra* v. *Immigration Appeal Tribunal*, [1988] Imm. AR 161, in which a similar conclusion was reached. Lord Lowry appeared to agree on this point: [1991] 1 AC at 763C.

[43] [1991] 1 AC at 748–9.

[44] See below, text to nn. 53–4.

[45] Judicial review on the existing grounds of *Wednesbury* unreasonableness requires a finding that the decision is 'so absurd that no sensible person could ever dream that it lay within the powers of the authority' (*Wednesbury*, above, n. 35, at 229, *per* Lord Greene MR). Such decisions are sometimes described as 'irrational' or 'perverse'. A decision which failed a test of proportionality would not necessarily be unreasonable in this sense.

[46] See, e.g., *Johnston* v. *Chief Constable of the Royal Ulster Constabulary*, (Case 222/84) [1987] ECR 83, [1987] 1 QB 129, at para. 38.

[47] [1985] AC 374, 410. For a list of other cases in which the principle of proportionality has been referred to, see *Halsbury's Laws of England*, vol. 1(1) (4th edn. reissue, 1989), para. 78, which was referred to in the speech of Lord Lowry.

[48] Jowell and Lester, 'Beyond *Wednesbury*: Substantive Principles of Administrative Law', *Public Law*, 1987, p. 368, esp. pp. 375–6. Cf. *Halsbury*, above, n. 47 (the doctrine is 'still at a stage of development in English law').

[49] [1991] 1 AC at 762–3 (*per* Lord Ackner) and 766–7 (*per* Lord Lowry).

principle in the instant case, expressly refused to exclude its possible future development.[50] Lord Templeman, on the other hand, went so far as to say that the principle is an existing part of English law:

> The subject matter and date of the *Wednesbury* principles cannot in my opinion make it either necessary or appropriate for the courts to judge the validity of an interference with human rights by asking themselves whether the Home Secretary has acted irrationally or perversely. It seems to me that the courts cannot escape from asking themselves whether a reasonable Secretary of State, on the material before him, could reasonably conclude that the interference with freedom of expression which he determined to impose was justifiable. In terms of the Convention, as construed by the European Court, the interference with freedom of expression must be necessary and proportionate to the damage which the restriction is designed to prevent.[51]

However, Lord Templeman did not consider that the Secretary of State's action in this case could be considered disproportionate.[52] None of the members of the House of Lords considered that it was unreasonable.

The extent to which the doctrine of proportionality may become established in English administrative law in future remains to be seen. Clearly, there is a division in the House of Lords. The adoption of such a doctrine would not, of course, necessarily result in the incorporation of European Convention standards into domestic administrative law. However, as the speech of Lord Templeman indicates, many of the provisions of that Convention are concerned with striking what may be described as a 'proportionate' balance between the rights of individuals and competing public interests.[53] The courts have in the past referred to the European Convention in ascertaining common law standards of justice,[54] and it could be expected that they would continue to do so in applying a common law principle of proportionality. If the proportionality doctrine does become an accepted part of administrative law, the provisions of the European Convention (as well as the case law of the European Court of Human Rights) may be expected to achieve a much higher degree of prominence.[55] This may prove to be the most significant aspect of this case.

In the second case concerning the European Convention, *Choudhury*, the applicant was seeking judicial review of the refusal of the magistrate to issue summonses against the author and publisher of the novel *The Satanic Verses* alleging the common law offence of blasphemous libel.[56] The magistrate's decision was based on

[50] Ibid., at 749H (*per* Lord Bridge) and 750 (*per* Lord Roskill).

[51] Ibid., at 751.

[52] Ibid.

[53] See esp. Articles 8 (right to respect for private and family life), 9 (right to freedom of thought, conscience and religion), 10 (right to freedom of expression) and 11 (right to freedom of assembly and association), in which the rights conferred are expressed to be subject to such restrictions or limitations as are 'necessary in a democratic society'.

[54] See, e.g., *Cheall* v. *APEX*, [1983] 1 QB 126, 136–7; *Trawnik* v. *Lennox*, [1985] 1 WLR 532, 541.

[55] See in particular the earlier passage in the speech of Lord Templeman: 'On an application for judicial review, the courts must not substitute their own views for the informed views of the Home Secretary. *In terms of the Convention, as construed by the European Court*, a margin of appreciation must be afforded to the Home Secretary to decide whether and in what terms a restriction on freedom of expression is justified' ([1991] 1 AC at 751, emphasis added). Lord Ackner also appeared to assume that this would be the case if the doctrine were accepted (see [1991] 1 AC at 762–3).

[56] For background on reaction to this novel and the 'Rushdie affair', see *Keesing's Record of World Events*, February 1989, pp. 36450–1, March 1989, pp. 36537–8, September 1990, p. 37727.

the view that the offence of blasphemy protects only the Christian religion (whereas this book was alleged to be blasphemous of the religion of Islam). After a consideration of the history of the law of blasphemy, Watkins LJ concluded that the magistrate had been correct.[57] The court then considered a submission by the applicant that the magistrate had failed to take into account the United Kingdom's obligations under the European Convention.

On this, Watkins LJ was persuaded by the arguments of counsel for the publishers.[58] He had argued first that although 'the obligations imposed on the United Kingdom by the Convention are relevant sources of public policy where the common law is uncertain . . . the common law of blasphemy is, without doubt, certain'.[59] Moreover, Watkins LJ found that there were policy reasons against extending the law of blasphemy in this case,[60] and it was argued that to do so would violate the rights of the defendants under Article 7 of the European Convention,[61] as well as Article 10 (freedom of expression).[62] Secondly, counsel for the publishers had argued that by protecting the Christian religion alone, the common law was not in any case inconsistent with the provisions of the European Convention.[63] There was already a decision of the European Commission of Human Rights to this effect.[64]

Extradition—fugitive convicted in another State—whether extradition an abuse of process—whether prosecution barred by lapse of time—jurisdiction of police magistrate—Extradition Act 1870

Case No. 4. R v. *Governor of Pentonville Prison, ex parte Sinclair*, [1991] 2 AC 64, [1991] 2 WLR 1028, [1991] 2 All ER 366, HL. The House of Lords dismissed this appeal against the decision of the Divisional Court, which was noted in the previous volume of this *Year Book*.[65] The Divisional Court had dismissed the appellant's application for a writ of habeas corpus directed to the Governor of Pentonville Prison, where he had been committed to await extradition to the United States of America. The appellant, a national of Trinidad and Tobago, had in 1976 been convicted of various offences by a United States court, and sentenced to four years' imprisonment. However, before he had begun to serve the sentence, he left the United States (apparently with the consent of the United States authorities), and claimed he had been denied a visa when he sought to return to the United States to serve the sentence. Attempts to extradite him from Trinidad and Tobago

57 [1991] 1 QB at 440–7.

58 Ibid., at 452B.

59 Ibid., at 449G. Cf. n. 54, above, and accompanying text.

60 Ibid., at 447–8. Watkins LJ noted also that in 1985 a majority of the Law Commission recommended the abolition of the offence of blasphemy altogether.

61 'No one shall be held guilty of any criminal offence on account of any act or omission which did not constitute a criminal offence . . . at the time when it was committed.'

62 [1991] 1 QB at 449–50.

63 It had been argued that there was a breach of Article 9 (freedom of religion), read together with Article 14 (requiring that the enjoyment of rights and freedoms under the Convention be secured without discrimination).

64 *Gay News Ltd.* v. *United Kingdom* (1982), 5 EHRR 123, 131 (para. 14). See also *Church of X* v. *United Kingdom* (1968), *Collection of Decisions of the European Commission of Human Rights*, vol. 29, p. 70.

65 This *Year Book*, 61 (1990), at pp. 387–9.

were not pursued. He subsequently moved to the United Kingdom, from where the United States Justice Department decided to seek his extradition in 1983, although no formal request for extradition was made to the United Kingdom Government until 1987.

The appellant sought to challenge the committal order on two grounds. First, he argued that the magistrate had failed to consider whether in view of the delay in the bringing of the extradition proceedings, they amounted to an abuse of the process of the court. The question was whether the magistrate had any inherent jurisdiction to prevent an abuse of the process of the court under the Extradition Act 1870. In *Atkinson* v. *United States of America Government*[66] the House of Lords had answered this question negatively, on the grounds that, under section 9 of the Extradition Act 1870, the magistrate shall 'hear the case in the same manner, and have the same jurisdiction and powers, as near as may be, as if the prisoner were brought before him charged with an indictable offence committed in England'. In that case, it was observed that in domestic criminal proceedings the magistrate had no power 'to refuse to commit an accused for trial on the ground that it would be unjust or oppressive to require him to be tried', and that the Extradition Act 1870 did not give magistrate 'any wider power in extradition proceedings than he has when he is committing for trial in England'.[67] Since *Atkinson's* case there have, however, been a number of decisions of lower courts to the effect that in domestic criminal proceedings the magistrate does have power to stay proceedings where there has been an abuse of the process of the court.[68] When this case was argued before the Divisional Court, Watkins LJ was prepared to accept that this discretion was likewise applicable in proceedings under the 1870 Act where the extradition of an *accused* person is sought,[69] but thought that there was no precedent for applying it in *conviction* cases. So far, the House of Lords itself has not expressed any opinion on the power of the magistrate to stop proceedings on grounds of an abuse of process in domestic litigation, and did not take the opportunity to do so in this case. Lord Ackner (with whom Lords Bridge, Templeman, Griffiths and Goff agreed) confined himself to finding that no such discretion existed in any proceedings under the Extradition Act 1870. In so doing, he adopted the reasons advanced in *Atkinson's* case:

> There can be cases where it would clearly be contrary to natural justice to surrender a man although there is sufficient evidence to justify committal . . . It is not unknown for convictions to be obtained in a few foreign countries by improper means, and it would be intolerable if a man so convicted had to be surrendered. Parliament can never have so intended when the Act of 1870 was passed.
>
> But the Act does provide a safeguard. The Secretary of State always has power [under section 11 of the Act] to refuse to surrender a man committed to prison by the magistrate. It appears that Parliament must have intended the Secretary of State to use that power whenever in his view it would be wrong, unjust or oppressive to surrender the man . . .
>
> If I had thought that Parliament did not intend this safeguard to be used in this way, then I would think it necessary to infer that the magistrate has power to refuse to commit if he

[66] [1971] AC 197.

[67] Ibid., at 232.

[68] See the cases referred to by counsel, [1991] 2 AC at 67.

[69] Cf. *R* v. *Bow Street Magistrates Court, ex parte Van der Holst* (1985), 83 Cr.App.R 114, and *In re Brij Parekh* (unreported), 17 May 1988, in which this question was left open.

finds that it would be contrary to natural justice to surrender the man. But in my judgment Parliament by providing this safeguard has excluded the jurisdiction of the courts.[70]

Lord Ackner noted further that, under section 11(3) of the new Extradition Act 1889,[71] the *High Court* may, in habeas corpus proceedings, order the applicant's discharge if it appears to the court that 'it would, having regard to all the circumstances, be unjust or oppressive to return him'. Lord Ackner considered this 'the clearest possible recognition by the legislature that hitherto no such discretion existed in the courts and in particular in the magistrate's court'.[72] The implication is that under the 1989 Act, the *magistrate* still lacks this power.

The appellant's second argument was that extradition in this case was barred by Article V(1)(*b*)of the Extradition Treaty between the United Kingdom and the United States,[73] which provides that extradition shall not be granted if 'the offence for which extradition is requested has become barred by lapse of time according to the law of the requesting or requested party'. It was argued that under United States law, prosecution of an offence is not completed until the defendant begins to serve his sentence. However, Lord Ackner thought it clear that a 'prosecution' within the meaning of that provision of the Treaty encompassed only the initiation of criminal proceedings, and not the commencement of the service of any sentence imposed.[74]

Lord Ackner also made some further observations on the powers of the magistrate under the 1870 Act. He outlined at some length the submissions of counsel for the respondents, to the effect that the powers of the magistrate are confined to those conferred by sections 3(1), 8, 9 and 10 of the Act,[75] and that the magistrate has no wider power to ensure that the provisions of the extradition treaty have been complied with. It was submitted that this was a matter for the Secretary of State to determine (who can refuse to surrender the person if he considers the requirements of the treaty have not been met), but that a decision by the Secretary of State to surrender a person could be challenged by a writ of habeas corpus or judicial review.[76] Lord Ackner appeared to agree, saying:

Your Lordships are concerned with the construction of an Act passed over a hundred

[70] [1971] AC at 232–3 (*per* Lord Reid). To the same effect, Lord Ackner also quoted Lord Morris (ibid., at 238–9), and Lord Guest (ibid., at 247), as well as Lord Morris in *R* v. *Governor of Brixton Prison, ex parte Kotronis*, [1971] AC 250, 279–80.

[71] This Act consolidates the Extradition Acts 1870–1935, the Fugitive Offenders Act 1967 and provisions relating to extradition in the Criminal Justice Act 1988. This last Act introduced a new regime of extradition law (for background, see Warbrick, 'The Criminal Justice Act 1988: (1) The New Law on Extradition', *Criminal Law Review*, 1989, p. 4). Orders in Council made under the 1870 Act will continue in force under the old regime, until replaced by Orders in Council under the 1989 Act: see ss. 1(3), 4 and Schedule 1 of the 1989 Act.

[72] [1991] 2 AC at 81.

[73] The text of the treaty is contained in the United States of America (Extradition) Order 1976, SI 1976, No. 2144.

[74] He noted that some extradition treaties, unlike the present one, expressly referred to both 'prosecution' and 'punishment' having become barred by lapse of time, and that the present treaty could have included such a reference if this had been intended: [1991] 2 AC at 92.

[75] Essentially, these provisions require the magistrate to do no more than (1) determine the identity of the accused; (2) determine (in an accusation case) whether the evidence would establish a prima facie case under English law or (in a conviction case) whether the conviction has been properly proved; (3) determine whether the relevant crime is an extradition crime; and (4) determine in relevant cases whether the crime is a political offfence (see [1991] 2 AC at 81–2).

[76] Ibid., and see the cases described at 82–9.

years ago. I cannot accept that the legislature intended that it was to be part of the function of the police magistrate to preside over lengthy proceedings occupying weeks, and on occasions months, of his time hearing heavily contested evidence of foreign law directed to whether there had been due compliance with the many and varied obligations of the relevant Treaty . . . Had the challenges which the applicant wished to make been ventilated initially before the Divisional Court in habeas corpus proceedings, it is unlikely that the court would have permitted the lengthy oral evidence which the magistrate, as matters stood, felt himself obliged to hear. Certainly for the future, if your Lordships concur that the magistrate has no jurisdiction to decide either whether there has been an abuse of the process of the court, or whether the requirements of the Treaty have been satisfied, his powers being limited to those specified in sections 3(1), 8, 9 and 10, much time should be saved both in the magistrates' and in the Divisional Court.[77]

If this is so, it would seem that under the 1989 Act, the magistrate also lacks jurisdiction to decide whether the requirements of the treaty have been satisfied,[78] and that this question must be raised in the Divisional Court in proceedings challenging a decision of the Secretary of State.

Citizenship of the United Kingdom and Colonies—whether acquired by British subject on 1 January 1949—whether person potentially a citizen of South Africa—British Nationality Act 1948, sections 12(4)(b) and 32(7)

Citizen of the United Kingdom and Colonies—British protected person—whether possible to hold both statuses simultaneously—British Nationality Act 1948—Zambia Independence Act 1963, section 3(3)

Case No 5. R v. *Secretary of State for Foreign and Commonwealth Affairs, ex parte Ross-Clunis*, [1991] 2 AC 439, [1991] 3 WLR 146, [1991] 3 All ER 353, HL. *Case No. 6. Motala and others* v. *Attorney-General*, [1991] 2 All ER 312, [1991] Fam. Law 425, CA. Both of these cases highlight the difficulties in nationality law which continue to arise from the transition of former British possessions to independence.

In *Ross-Clunis*, the question whether the respondent was a British citizen under the British Nationality Act 1981 depended on whether he had been a citizen of the United Kingdom and Colonies under the British Nationality Act 1948. As Lord Bridge observed, the 1948 Act (which only came into effect on 1 January 1949) 'introduced a new nationality regime the broad effect of which was that all British subjects were to become citizens either of the United Kingdom and Colonies or of one of the fully independent countries within the Commonwealth which are named in section 1(3) and which had then already introduced or were about to introduce their own separate citizenship laws'.[79]

The respondent was born in 1948 in Athens. His father was born in 1905 in Cape Town, in the then colony of the Cape of Good Hope. His father's father was born in England. Prior to the commencement of the 1948 Act, the respondent was a British subject, by virtue of the fact that his father was a British subject born 'within His Majesty's allegiance'.[80] On the commencement of the 1948 Act, he would become a citizen of the United Kingdom and Colonies by virtue of section 12(4) of that Act unless he was at that time 'potentially a citizen' of South Africa,

[77] Ibid., at 91–2.
[78] Compare ss. 9 and 10 of the 1870 Act with s. 9 of the 1989 Act.
[79] [1991] 2 AC at 444.
[80] See British Nationality and Status of Aliens Act 1914, s. 1(1)(*a*) and (*b*).

one of the countries mentioned in section 1(3) of the Act.[81] South Africa's citizenship law had not yet taken effect at that point in time, but he was for the purposes of the Act deemed by section 32(7) to be 'potentially a citizen' of that country, *inter alia*:

if he, or his nearest ancestor in the male line who acquired British nationality otherwise than by reason of his parentage, acquired British nationality by any of the following means, that is to say—(*a*) by birth within the territory comprised at the date of the commencement of this Act in that country . . .

Thus, the respondent was 'potentially a citizen' of South Africa if his father acquired British nationality by virtue of his birth in the colony of the Cape of Good Hope, but not if his father acquired British nationality by virtue of his 'parentage'. Under the law as it stood *prior* to the commencement of the 1948 Act, the respondent's father acquired British nationality by virtue of his birth in South Africa.[82] However, under the 1948 Act itself his father became a citizen of the United Kingdom and Colonies by virtue of the fact that his father (the respondent's grandfather) was a British subject born in the United Kingdom.[83] The respondent argued (and the Court of Appeal agreed) that the method by which his father 'acquired British nationality' for the purposes of this provision had to be determined by reference to the law as it stood on the date of commencement of the 1948 Act. In the House of Lords, Lord Bridge disagreed. He noted that 'Each of the relevant subsections of section 12 [of the 1948 Act] begins with the words "A person who was a British subject immediately before the date of commencement of this Act", and is looking at past circumstances as determinative of future status'.[84] Furthermore, he said, the language of section 32(7) necessarily refers to past events and not to 1 January 1949. In particular, he considered that the words 'acquired British nationality' which appear twice in that provision must bear the same meaning in each case. The second time they appear, they could only refer to the acquisition of British nationality by the respondent's father at the time of his birth, under the previous law.[85]

As a matter of statutory interpretation, this clearly must be correct, but it leads to a rather bizarre result. Immediately prior to the commencement of the 1948 Act, both the respondent's father and the respondent were British subjects. On commencement of that Act, the respondent's father became a citizen of the United Kingdom and Colonies, but the respondent (who was then less than a year old) did not. This was so, notwithstanding that the respondent had no practical connection at all with South Africa.[86] The respondent argued that this could not have been the intention of Parliament. Lord Bridge said that the short answer to this submission was afforded by section 7(1) of the 1948 Act.[87]

In *Motala*, the question was whether the two respondents had lost their citizenship

[81] See s. 12(4)(*b*) of the 1948 Act.

[82] British Nationality and Status of Aliens Act 1914, s. 1(1)(*a*).

[83] British Nationality Act 1948, s. 12(1)(*a*) and (2).

[84] [1991] 2 AC at 445.

[85] [1991] 2 AC, at pp. 445–6. Lords Brandon, Templeman, Griffiths and Jauncey agreed with Lord Bridge.

[86] See [1991] 3 All ER at 357.

[87] Section 7(1) provides: 'The Secretary of State may cause the minor child of any citizen of the United Kingdom and Colonies to be registered as a citizen of the United Kingdom and Colonies upon application made in the prescribed manner by a parent or guardian of the child.' No such application was made in respect of the respondent.

of the United Kingdom and Colonies when Northern Rhodesia became the independent Republic of Zambia in 1964 (and hence were not now British citizens under the British Nationality Act 1981). Section 3(3) of the Zambia Independence Act 1964 provided that:

Except as provided by section 4 of this Act, any person who immediately before the appointed day [24 October 1964] is a citizen of the United Kingdom and Colonies shall on that day cease to be such a citizen if he becomes on that day a citizen of Zambia.

Section 3(1) of the Constitution of Zambia (as contained in Schedule 2 of the Zambia Independence Order 1964[88]) provided that:

Every person who, having been born in the former Protectorate of Northern Rhodesia, is on 23rd October 1964, a British protected person shall become a citizen of Zambia on 24th October 1964.

It was not disputed that the respondents, who were born in Northern Rhodesia, were citizens of the United Kingdom and Colonies immediately before the appointed day. Whether they had lost that status under section 3(3) of the Zambia Independence Act depended on whether they were also British protected persons, so that they acquired Zambian citizenship on the appointed day.

Although the respondents appeared to fall within the class of persons described as British protected persons,[89] and although nothing in the British Nationality Act 1948 provided that a citizen of the United Kingdom and Colonies could not have this status, the court held that the former status was incompatible with the latter. Beldam LJ said that:

Which persons belong to or come within a particular status or class as defined in the Act and regulations made under it depends on the proper construction of the Act and regulations; whether a person so given one status was intended at the same time to be able to possess another or to retain membership of a different class can, in my judgment, only be decided by looking at the scheme of the Act, its historical context and the attributes conferred on each status or class.

Under Part II of the 1948 Act citizenship of the United Kingdom and Colonies is acquired by birth, descent or registration, and may be acquired by naturalisation or incorporation of territory . . . A British protected person, like an alien, must apply for citizenship by naturalisation . . . The grant of a certificate of naturalisation, as in the case of an alien is discretionary . . . [90]

He observed that under the 1948 Act, a citizen of the United Kingdom and Colonies acquired no additional right or privilege by virtue of a connection with a protectorate. Thus, he concluded:

The clear implication from the form of the Act is that the status of British protected person is different from and inconsistent with status as a citizen of the United Kingdom and Colonies, to which it adds nothing. The Act was drafted against the background of the common law which traditionally regarded protected persons as aliens who were in practice exempted from

[88] SI 1964, No. 1652, which was made under the Zambia Independence Act 1964.

[89] See the British Protectorates, Protected States and Protected Persons Order in Council 1949, SI 1949, No. 140, which was made under the British Nationality Act 1948. Section 5(1) and Schedule 1 of the Order in Council made Northern Rhodesia a protectorate for the purposes of the Act, and s. 9(1)(*a*) of the Order in Council provided that a person shall be a British protected person if he was born in a protectorate.

[90] [1991] 2 All ER, at 315. See also Lord Donaldson MR at 317–18 (saying that the two statuses were as mutually inconsistent as the statuses of citizen and alien).

some of an alien's attendant disabilities . . . Against the background of the common law it must have appeared to the draftsman of the British Nationality Act 1948 unnecessary to state that a citizen of the United Kingdom and Colonies was not and could not at the same time be a British protected person.[91]

Both Beldam LJ and Lord Donaldson MR also noted that where other former colonies had attained independence, legislation had expressly provided that citizens of the United Kingdom and Colonies as well as British protected persons should lose that status and should become citizens of the newly independent State, where this was intended.[92] Accordingly, the Court found that the respondents were now British citizens under the British Nationality Act 1981.

The points decided in both of these cases seem straightforward and fundamental. What is surprising is that there appeared to be no judicial authority on either point,[93] and that, in *Ross-Clunis*, so basic a question as to the operation of the 1948 Act could be the subject of disagreement between the Court of Appeal and the House of Lords over 40 years later.[94, 95]

CHRISTOPHER STAKER

B. PRIVATE INTERNATIONAL LAW*

Recognition of foreign juridical personality

Case No. 1. The legal issue in the case of *Arab Monetary Fund* v. *Hashim (No. 3)*[1] when it reached the House of Lords was single and susceptible to simple formulation, namely as to the circumstances in which a foreign organization will be recognized as having juridical personality for the purpose of capacity to sue in an English court. The trial judge, Hoffmann J, had held that the Arab Monetary Fund, an international banking organization with its headquarters in Abu Dhabi, did qualify for such recognition. The Court of Appeal by a majority (Lord Donaldson MR and Nourse LJ) reversed this holding, Bingham LJ dissenting. The House of

[91] Ibid. See also Lord Donaldson, at 317.

[92] Reference was made to the cases of Botswana, Kenya, Malawi, Mauritius and Nigeria.

[93] As to the point raised in *Motala*, see however Parry, *Nationality and Citizenship Laws of the Commonwealth and of the Republic of Ireland* (London, 1957), p. 355, who said that it was possible under the 1948 Act for a person to have simultaneously the status of citizen of the United Kingdom and Colonies and British protected person. Cf. the British Protectorates, Protected States and Protected Persons Order 1982, SI 1982, No. 1070, Article 10, which provides that the status of British protected person is lost if the person at any time becomes a British citizen, a British dependent territories citizen or a British overseas citizen or acquires another nationality.

[94] Another case decided during the period under review involved a short point of interpretation of the 1980 Hague Convention on the Civil Aspects of International Child Abduction (TS 66 (1986)), which is given the force of law in the United Kingdom by the Child Abduction and Custody Act 1985. In *Re H (Minors) (Abduction: Custody Rights); Re S (Minors) (Abduction: Custody Rights)*, [1991] 3 WLR 68, [1991] 3 All ER 230, [1991] 2 FLR 262, [1991] Fam.Law 427, the House of Lords held that the concepts of 'wrongful removal' and 'wrongful retention' under the Convention were mutually exclusive, so that where a child was wrongfully removed from a country prior to the coming into force of the Convention between the United Kingdom and that country, the Convention did not apply. It could not be argued that after the coming into force of the Convention, the child continued to be wrongfully retained. Cf. *C* v. *S (Minor: Abduction: Illegitimate Child)*, [1990] 3 WLR 492, noted in this *Year Book* 61 (1990), pp. 389–91.

[95] The decision in *Motala* has now been reversed on appeal by the House of Lords ([1991] 3 WLR 903, [1991] 4 All ER 682). This appeal will be noted in the next volume of this *Year Book*.

* © P.B Carter, 1992.

[1] [1991] 2 AC 114. See also pp. 433 ff., above.

Lords with only one dissent (that of Lord Lowry) allowed the Fund's further appeal and restored the order of Hoffmann J.

The Fund had its origin in an agreement entered into by twenty Arab States and Palestine in 1976. By its terms the agreement conferred on the Fund an 'independent juridical personality and . . . in particular the right to own, contract and litigate' and required ratification by the signatory States in accordance with their particular constitutional arrangements. By a federal decree promulgated in the following year the United Arab Emirates (UAE), including Abu Dhabi, complied with this latter requirement.

In 1985 the Fund instituted criminal proceedings in Switzerland against Jawad Mahmoud Hashim, its former director-general, claiming that large sums of the Fund's money had been paid into his account and that of his wife at the Geneva branch of the Fund's bankers. In 1988 these proceedings were dismissed for lack of jurisdiction. Then, in proceedings brought in England against *inter alios* Hashim, members of his family and a number of banks, the Fund sought to recover the sums allegedly misappropriated by Hashim, and damages for alleged negligence on the part of the bankers. Some of the defendants applied to strike out the action, contending that the Fund was not an entity recognized under English law and therefore could not bring suit in England. Hoffmann J rejected this contention, holding that, without regard to the 1976 agreement as such, the Fund was 'plainly a legal entity under the law of Abu Dhabi'[2] and was, therefore, entitled to recognition under the rules of the English conflict of laws. At the same time his Lordship felt obliged, in the light of the judgment of the House of Lords in *J.H. Rayner (Mincing Lane) Ltd.* v. *Department of Trade and Industry* (the *Tin* case),[3] to reject an alternative argument to the effect that the Fund, an international organization, was entitled to recognition as such. His Lordship did this with considerable (and in the instant circumstances understandable) reluctance. He said:

> Extending our conflicts rule to international organizations seems to me sensible and practicable. The rule as it applies to entities created by foreign domestic laws is based on the inconvenience of having legal entities which exist in one country but not in another. International organizations set up by foreign States do exist in fairly substantial numbers, trade with this country and bank in the City of London. They are invariably recognized as juridical entities by the domestic systems of the parties to the treaty as well as by many other countries. . . . It is difficult to see why an entity created by treaty between two or more foreign States should be less entitled to recognition than an entity created under the sovereign authority of a single foreign State within its domestic system.[4]

It is perhaps ironic that in the Court of Appeal it was apparently this inelegance (or inconsistency) which largely influenced Nourse LJ in concluding that the appeal should be allowed. His Lordship said:

> It would be inconsistent with what the House of Lords [in the *Tin* case] has held to be the policy of our law if we were to recognize an international organization constituted as a *persona ficta* under some other municipal law when, without such a constitution, we cannot recognize it for itself.[5]

So, too, Lord Donaldson MR, the other member of the majority, said:

[2] Ibid. 124.
[3] [1990] 2 AC 418.
[4] [1991] 2 AC 114, 119–20.
[5] Ibid. 136.

> . . . legislation conferring personality under the law of a member state should as a matter of English private international law, be regarded as purely territorial in scope . . . I can see no escape from this conclusion, given the attitude of English law to international organizations as explained in the *Tin* case.[6]

Bingham LJ, however, took the traditional high ground in his dissent. His Lordship said:

> But in suing as a juridical person the A.M.F. does not depend on a status derived from a non-justiciable treaty but on a status conferred by the law of a friendly foreign sovereign. Comity would seem to require that the United Kingdom recognise the A.M.F. by virtue of the decree, as the United Kingdom would doubtless wish the U.A.E. [United Arab Emirates] to recognize the I.T.C. [International Tin Council] by virtue of the Order in Council . . . .[7]

His Lordship supplemented this invocation of comity with reference to strong and more specific practical considerations:

> Given the importance of the City of London as a financial and commercial centre, I would regret it if I were obliged to hold that the A.M.F. as a juridical person could not sue and be sued in respect of transactions into which it had entered as such.[8]

In the House of Lords the leading judgment (in which Lords Bridge, Griffiths and Ackner concurred) was that of Lord Templeman. His Lordship, having reviewed the position of the Fund under the law of the United Emirates ('an independent sovereign federal State'), found that 'the fund was created a corporate body by the U.A.E. and corresponds roughly to an English company limited by shares with the member states as the shareholders, a board of governors which represents the shareholders, a board of executive directors and a director-general corresponding to a managing director'.[9] Later in his judgment Lord Templeman again referred to the circumstance that 'the articles of agreement which are annexed to the federal decree of the U.A.E. and which thus become part of the law of the U.A.E. are no different from the memorandum and articles of a limited liability company established under the law of England'.[10] His Lordship then restated the established principle that:

> Although a treaty cannot become part of the law of the United Kingdom without the intervention of Parliament, the recognition of foreign States is a matter for the Crown to decide and by comity the courts of the United Kingdom recognize a corporate body created by the law of a foreign state recognized by the Crown.[11]

Lord Templeman cited English authority going back to 1728[12] and including the holding of Lord Wright in 1933 that 'English courts have long since recognized as juristic persons corporations established by foreign law in virtue of the fact of their creation and continuance under and by that law. Such recognition is said to be by the comity of nations';[13] he also cited the succinct *dictum* of McTiernan J in the High Court of Australia in 1947 to the effect that 'courts of one country give

[6] Ibid. 135.
[7] Ibid. 141.
[8] Ibid. 142.
[9] Ibid. 160.
[10] Ibid. 162.
[11] Ibid. 161.
[12] *Henriques* v. *Dutch West India Co.* (1728), Ld. Raym. 1532.
[13] *Lazard Brothers & Co.* v. *Midland Bank Ltd.*, [1933] AC 289, 297.

recognition, by comity of nations, to a legal personality created by the law of another country'.[14]

Lord Templeman then referred to the difficulties which, it had been argued, could arise in the case of multiple incorporation: 'It was argued that the fund, as incorporated in Iraq, for example, might be different from the fund as incorporated in the U.A.E. and that the Iraqi fund might even sue the U.A.E. fund'.[15] But his Lordship had merely to point out that there was here only one fund to which each of the member States had accorded legal personality.

His Lordship also invoked advice, concerning 'banks and other financial entities set up by a group of foreign sovereign States by a treaty (to which the United Kingdom is not a party)', given by the Foreign and Commonwealth Office in 1978[16] to the effect that,

> on the assumption that the entity enjoys, under its constitutive instrument or instruments and under the law of one or more member States or the State wherein it has its seat or permanent location, legal personality and capacity to engage in transactions of the type concerned governed by the law of a non-member State, the Foreign and Commonwealth Office, as the branch of the executive responsible for the conduct of foreign relations, would be willing officially to acknowledge that the entity concerned enjoyed such legal personality and capacity, and to state this.

Of this advice Lord Templeman said: 'It seems to me that it would be unthinkable for the courts of the United Kingdom applying the principles of comity to reach any other conclusion'.[17] His Lordship re-affirmed:

> A treaty cannot create a corporation but a sovereign state which is a party to a treaty can, in pursuance of its obligations accepted under the treaty, create a corporation which will be recognized in the United Kingdom.[18]

Finally his Lordship considered the 'inhibitions' seemingly felt by the majority of the Court of Appeal deriving from observations made in the House of Lords in the *Tin* case. His Lordship pointed out that there the particular international organization, the ITC, was recognized as a legal person in English law only because it had been so created by Order in Council. Regarding the position of international organizations more generally he said:

> There is no uniform practice with regard to international organizations in this country. In some cases, as in the *Tin Council* case, the organization is given corporate capacity by means of an Order in Council issued under the Act of 1968 or its predecessors. In other cases provisions of the treaty agreeing to the establishment of the international organization are declared by Parliament to have the force of the law. This was done, for example, by the Bretton Woods Agreements Act 1945 and the Bretton Woods Agreements Order in Council 1946 (SR and O 1946 No. 36). In other cases, principally but not exclusively, cases where the United Kingdom is not a party to the treaty, no legislative steps are taken in the United Kingdom but this does not debar Her Majesty's Government from recognizing the international organization and does not debar the courts of the United Kingdom from recognizing the international organization as a separate entity by comity *provided that the separate*

[14] *Chaff and Hay Acquisition Committee* v. *J.A. Hemphill and Sons Pty. Ltd.* (1947), 74 CLR 375, 390.

[15] [1991] 2 AC 114, 162.

[16] See this *Year Book*, 49 (1978), pp. 346–8.

[17] [1991] 2 AC 114, 163.

[18] Ibid.

entity is created not by the treaty but by one or more of the member States. This is the position of the fund.[19]

Lord Lowry's lone dissent would seem to be largely on a question of foreign law, i.e., fact, the issue being as to the legal position of the Fund under the law of the United Arab Emirates. His Lordship took the view that, although recognized as a juridical entity under that law, the Fund had not been created as such by that law. He said:

> I think it is clear that both the I.T.C. and the fund, having started as international organizations created by agreements made under international law, continue as such with the addition of legal personality and capacity which have been conferred on them by one or more member States. Like the I.T.C. the fund is not a new creation under the law of the headquarters State; it is still an international organization with a conferred capacity in that State.[20]

Lord Templeman, speaking for the majority, took a different view of the evidence on the matter. He said:

> The expert evidence which I have quoted states that Federal Decree No.35 conferred legal personality on the fund and in the face of that evidence I cannot agree with Lord Lowry that the effect of the decree was only to recognize an international organization.[21]

At the doctrinal level *Arab Monetary Fund* v. *Hashim (No. 3)* exemplifies adherence to a 'dualist' rather than a 'monist' approach. To have allowed the Fund to sue simply because it was a body recognized under public international law would clearly have smacked of 'monism'.

It would appear, too, although not specifically decided, that with regard to recognition of international organizations as such controlling, and perhaps exclusive, effect is to be given to legislation and particularly the International Organizations Act 1968.

Again, it may be noted that the actual outcome of the instant case was seemingly acknowledged, even by the three judges who thought that Hoffmann J had erred, to be benign. In the Court of Appeal Lord Donaldson MR concluded his judgment thus:

> I would allow the appeal and strike out this action. I do so with the greatest possible reluctance, because I regard the result as wholly without merit from the point of view of doing justice between the parties. However, I can see no escape from this conclusion, given the attitude of English law to international organizations as explained in the *Tin* case.[22]

Nourse LJ reached the same conclusion 'without enthusiasm'.[23] In the House of Lords Lord Lowry conceded that it might be regrettable (although not surprising) that 'our legislation has not moved far enough or fast enough to embrace every international organization'. But he, of course, saw the only remedy as being 'by way of legislation to amend the Act of 1968'.[24]

There is, however, certainly room for the view that to allow suit by an unduly wide range of international organizations (or partially international organizations,

[19] Ibid. 166–7 (italics supplied).
[20] Ibid. 180.
[21] Ibid. 160.
[22] Ibid. 135.
[23] Ibid. 136.
[24] Ibid. 181.

international quasi-organizations, or partially international quasi-organizations) as such would not be without its dangers. At the same time it must be acknowledged that limitation for practical purposes by insistence upon 'creation' of a separate justistic entity under a system of national law is not without its defects. First, it is a form of control that could operate somewhat arbitrarily in particular circumstances. Secondly, the problem of characterizing the position of the entity under the relevant national law may give rise to difficulty and uncertainty. The fact of, and the principal reason for, Lord Lowry's dissent is symptomatic of this latter. However the cynic may see advantage in this. Characterization is a well-trodden escape route in a different and more general conflict of laws context.

Suit by an inanimate foreign juristic entity; proof of foreign law.

Case No. 2. In the recent Court of Appeal case of *Bumper Development Corporation* v. *Commissioner of Police of the Metropolis and others*[25] the appellant company had brought an action against the respondent police officers to recover a twelfth-century bronze idol, representing the Hindu god Siva, which the company had purchased in good faith in England from a dealer in antiques, but which had subsequently been seized by the police as part of their policy of returning stolen artefacts to their rightful owners. The idol was alleged to have been stolen from the site of a ruined twelfth-century temple in the Indian state of Tamil Nadu. Several claimants, including the temple itself (suing through its representative), also sought to recover the idol. The police interpleaded between the company and the claimants. On the trial of a preliminary issue Ian Kennedy J held, *inter alia*, that the temple, being recognized as a juristic entity under the law of Tamil Nadu, could sue in the English courts for the recovery of the idol, and could do so notwithstanding that it was not capable of having legal personality under domestic English law; and further that on the merits the temple's title to the idol was superior to that of the plaintiff company. The company's appeal was dismissed. Purchas LJ handed down the judgment of the Court of Appeal. Several issues fell to be considered.

The first was as to the legal status of the temple under the law of Tamil Nadu. As Purchas LJ observed,

> It is trite law that foreign law in our courts is treated as a question of fact which must be proved by evidence. In the absence of evidence to the contrary, it must be assumed to be the same as English law. It is however the duty of the judge when faced with conflicting evidence from witnesses about a foreign law to resolve these differences in the same way as he must in the case of other conflicting evidence as to facts.[26]

His Lordship then referred to the fact that the trial judge, Ian Kennedy J, had rejected evidence upon a particular matter concerning which both expert witnesses were in fact agreed and had substituted his own opinion based upon his own researches. In doing this Purchas LJ indicated that Ian Kennedy J had erred. His Lordship said:

> . . . we have come to the conclusion that the judge was not entitled to reject the evidence of the experts to the effect that Sadogopan did not have a sufficient continuity of association with the temple to qualify as a 'de facto' trustee. Furthermore, we have also come to the conclusion that . . . Ian Kennedy J was not entitled to rely upon his own researches based on

[25] [1991] 1 WLR 1362.
[26] Ibid. 1368.

passages from *B.K. Mukherjea on The Hindu Law of Religious and Charitable Trust*, 5th. ed. (1983) without having the assistance of the expert witnesses and the submissions of counsel.[27]

Ian Kennedy J had, of course, crossed the divide separating proof of facts from taking judicial notice of facts. In the face of uncontradicted evidence this was not permissible. A more difficult situation is presented in cases in which the experts on foreign law disagree. The principle as stated by Purchas LJ may be clear: it is 'the duty of the judge . . . to resolve those differences in the same way as he must in the case of other conflicting evidence as to facts'.[28] But in practice difficulties peculiar to the context of evidence of foreign law may appear to be presented. This is implicitly acknowledged in *Dicey and Morris*: 'If the evidence of several expert witnesses conflicts as to the effect of foreign sources, the court is entitled, and indeed bound, to look at those sources in order itself to decide between the conflicting testimony'.[29] Indeed, as Purchas LJ pointed out,[30] this was expressly acknowledged by Lord Langdale MR as long ago as 1845 when in *Nelson* v. *Bridport*[31] he said:

> . . . I am not disposed to say, that there may not be cases, in which the judge may without impropriety, take upon himself to construe the words of a foreign law, and determine their application to the case in question, especially, if there should be a variance or want of clearness in the testimony.

Viewing the matter in a wider modern perspective, it is to be noted that—although not of significance in the particular circumstances of the instant case—explicit inroads are being made into the dogma that foreign law must be proved as fact. For example, most States of the United States now have statutes which authorize (but usually do not require) courts to take judicial notice of the law of other States in a range of circumstances.[32] Similarly in Canada there is federal[33] and provincial legislation which provides for the taking of judicial notice of the law of other Provinces and certain other countries in certain circumstances.[34] Moreover, the European Convention on Information on Foreign Law, which came into force in 1969 and which has been ratified by most of the Member States of the Council of Europe, has obvious potentiality as an alternative source of means by which foreign law may be ascertained in civil and commercial matters in the European context.

Having held in *Bumper Development Corporation* v. *Commissioner of Police of the Metropolis and others* that in the court's judgment there had been sufficient evidence before Ian Kennedy J to justify his finding that under the law of Tamil Nadu the temple was a juristic entity and that its representative had the right to sue (and be sued) on its behalf, Purchas LJ turned to a second issue: 'The novel question which arises is whether a foreign legal person by our own law can sue in the English courts'.[35] Here, as his Lordship pointed out,

> The particular difficulty arises out of English law's restriction of legal personality to

27 Ibid. 1371.
28 Ibid. 1368; see n. 26, above.
29 *The Conflict of Laws* (11th edn., 1987), p. 223, cited with approval by Purchas LJ at p. 1369.
30 [1991] 1 WLR 1362, 1370.
31 (1845) 8 Beav. 527, 537.
32 See *Restatement of the Law, Conflict of Laws 2nd*, § 136, Comment on Subsection (2).
33 RSC 1970, c. E–10.
34 See, generally, Castel, *Canadian Conflict of Laws* (2nd edn., 1986), pp. 139–41.
35 [1991] 1 WLR 1362, 1371.

> corporations or the like, that is to say to personified groups or series of individuals. This insistence on an essentially animate content in a legal person leads to a formidable conceptual difficulty in recognizing as a party entitled to sue in our courts something which on one view is little more than a pile of stones.[36]

However his Lordship seems to have rightly seen this conceptual difficulty (even if formidable) as not being insuperable. He proceeded to cite *Salmond on Jurisprudence* to the effect that: 'Legal persons, being the arbitrary creations of the law, may be of as many kinds as the law pleases'.[37] The circumstance that under English domestic law legal personality is not accorded to non-human animals, let alone inanimate objects, does not present any logical bar to recognition in a private international law context of any legal personality so accorded under relevant foreign law. The matter is one of policy, and Purchas LJ saw no objection on this score in the instant case. Citing the hypothetical example of a Catholic cathedral having legal personality under the *lex situs* he said: 'It would, we think, be a strange thing for the English court to refuse the cathedral access simply on the ground that our own law would not recognize a similarly constituted entity as a legal person'. To differentiate between that case and the temple of another major religion would obviously by unwarranted. The court accordingly held that the temple was acceptable as a party to the proceedings and, as such, was entitled to sue for the recovery of the idol.

This decision is important in the sense that it can be seen as involving a novel determination of principle. At the same time it has limitations. The first relates to procedure. Purchas LJ was at pains to emphasize

> that it is essential to our decision that the third claimant [the temple's representative], although not himself a competent party, is empowered by the constitution of the temple to take all necessary steps in the proceedings on its behalf, very much as they would be taken by the next friend or guardian ad litem of a minor or a patient. Steps for which the third claimant is responsible will therefore include giving security for costs, affording discovery and doing other acts at interlocutory stages and in course of the trial itself.[38]

Secondly, and more generally, the scale of operation of the new doctrine is in practice likely to be small. Although any public policy inhibitions were rightly held to be misconceived on the facts of the instant case, it could well be that public policy would have a controlling effect in a range of other circumstances. A significant amount of litigation involving (or between) inanimate objects (or non-human animals) is unlikely to ensue. Finally, it is to be remembered that, realistically speaking, every valid exercise of jurisdiction ultimately affects the interests of human beings. There are various well-established procedural doctrines and devices designed to achieve fairness in this regard. A procedural readiness to allow certain non-human entities to bring suit will in a limited number of sets of circumstances make its contribution. As Purchas LJ said of the holding in *Bumper Development Corporation* v. *Commissioner of Police of the Metroplis and others*, 'it avoids the danger of there being any fetter of an artificial procedural nature imported from the lex fori which might otherwise stand between a right recognized by and enforceable under the lex causae'.[39]

[36] Ibid.
[37] *Salmond on Jurisprudence* (12th edn., 1966), p. 306.
[38] [1991] 1 WLR 1362, 1373.
[39] Ibid.

Finally and dealing with the substantive merits, the Court of Appeal affirmed the holding of the trial judge that the claimant temple had a superior title to that enjoyed by the Bumper Development Corporation.

The Brussels Convention 1968: lis pendens and related actions

Case No. 3. Article 21 of the Brussels Convention[40] provides:

> Where proceedings involving the same cause of action and between the same parties are brought in the courts of different Contracting States, any court other than the court first seised shall of its own motion decline jurisdiction in favour of that court.
>
> A court which would be required to decline jurisdiction may stay its proceedings if the jurisdiction of the other court is contested.[41]

Article 22 provides:

> Where related actions are brought in the courts of different Contracting States, any court other than the court first seised may, while actions are pending at first instance, stay its proceedings.
>
> A court other than the court first seised may also, on the application of one of the parties, decline jurisdiction if the law of that court permits the consolidation of related actions and the court first seised has jurisdiction over both actions.
>
> For the purposes of this Article, actions are deemed to be related when they are so closely connected that it is expedient to hear and determine them together to avoid the risk of irreconcilable judgments resulting from separate proceedings.

It is to be seen that whereas Article 21 is concerned with 'proceedings involving the same cause of action' and is essentially mandatory in its terms, Article 22 is concerned with 'related actions' and is merely permissive. The two principal issues with which Sheen J had to deal in the recent case of *The Maciej Rataj*[42] were as to the respective meanings of the phrase 'proceedings involving the same cause of action' and the phrase 'related actions'.

The facts giving rise to the case may be summarized as follows. In September 1988 the defendants' ship *Tairy* loaded a cargo of soya bean oil in Brazil for delivery at Rotterdam and at Hamburg. All the cargo owners complained that on delivery their cargo was contaminated with diesel oil. In September 1989 the owners of the cargo discharged at Hamburg issued a writ *in rem* (1989 Folio 2006) against the carrying ship and another ship in the same ownership, *Maciej Rataj*. The writ was served and the vessel was arrested. In October 1989 the owners of the cargo discharged at Rotterdam issued a writ *in rem* (1989 Folio 2007) against the ship *Maciej Rataj*. The writ was served and the vessel was arrested.

The defendants in Folio 2006 and in Folio 2007 challenged the jurisdiction of the courts and/or its exercise, by notices of motion given to the plaintiffs on 2 October 1989. In the case of Folio 2006 the grounds were that at the date of the writ a court in Rotterdam was already seised of proceedings involving the same cause of action and between the same parties, or that the Rotterdam court was already seised of related proceedings. It was contended in the alternative that the Rotterdam court was the most appropriate forum. In the case of Folio 2007 the grounds were that at the date of the writ the Rotterdam court was already seised of related proceedings.

[40] For text, see the Civil Jurisdiction and Judgments Act 1982, Sched. 1.

[41] In the Lugano and San Sebastian Conventions the wording of Article 21 is modified so as to provide that the second court must always stay proceedings until the jurisdiction of the first is established.

[42] [1991] 2 Lloyd's Rep. 458.

Again it was contended in the alternative that the Rotterdam court was the most appropriate forum.

The Dutch proceedings had been instituted by the shipowners, the present defendants. The likely advantage to them (assessed by Sheen J at about $ 3,000,000) in having the extent of their liability, if any, decided in the Netherlands, lay in the difference between the limit of that liability in the Netherlands and the limit of their liability in England. What the defendant shipowners had sought in Rotterdam was a declaration that the plaintiff cargo owners were not entitled to damages against them.

Sheen J rejected any applicability of Article 21. He held that the Rotterdam proceedings did not involve the same cause of action as Folio 2006. In the English proceedings the plaintiffs were claiming damages from the shipowners for compensation. The defendants could, of course, resist this. They might deny liability and/or plead limitation of liability as a defence. However, they had no counterclaim because, said Sheen J, 'they do not have a "cause of action" in the sense in which those words are used in English law'.[43] His Lordship then invoked the words of Diplock LJ in *Letang* v. *Cooper*:[44] 'A cause of action is simply a factual situation the existence of which entitles one person to obtain from the Court a remedy against another person'. Sheen J continued: 'In Rotterdam the shipowners are not claiming a "remedy" against any of the owners of cargo; they merely ask the Court to say that the owners of the cargo are not entitled to the remedy of damages against them'.[45] It was, of course, conceded that the phrase 'cause of action' is not to be construed simply by reference to English law but is to be given the meaning attributed to it in the context of the Convention. Sheen J noted that the French text expresses 'the concept of "the same cause of action" in a double form: "Le même objet et la même cause" '.[46] It is clearly of the essence of Sheen J's holding that 'cause of action' is not to be seen as meaning simply 'subject matter'.

More than once in the course of his judgment Sheen J did refer to the defendants' motivation in bringing the Rotterdam proceedings. They were, he said, 'solely a pre-emptive strike designed to give the shipowners the choice of forum by a misuse of the Convention and contrary to the spirit of the Convention'.[47] In making an assessment of the scope of the decision as an authority, it is not altogether clear how much weight was attached to this factor as such. It is perhaps not without significance that the learned judge cited the words of Kerr LJ in *The Volvox Hollandia*:[48] 'Claims for declarations, and in particular negative declarations, must be viewed with great caution in all situations involving possible conflicts of jurisdictions, since they obviously lend themselves to improper attempts at forum shopping'.

Also, Sheen J emphasized that 'it is clear that the shipowners would not in England be entitled to claim the declaration which they seek in Rotterdam'.[49] Again there is no indication as to how much weight was attached to this circumstance.

His Lordship gave a careful review of earlier cases. He was able to distinguish

[43] Ibid. 463.
[44] [1965] 1 QB 232, 242.
[45] [1991] 2 Lloyd's Rep. 458, 463.
[46] Ibid. 463–4.
[47] Ibid. 463.
[48] [1988] 2 Lloyd's Rep. 361, 371.
[49] [1991] 2 Lloyd's Rep. 458, 463.

Gubisch Maschinenfabrik KG v. *Giulio Palumbo*,[50] *Overseas Union Insurance Ltd.* v. *New Hampshire Insurance Ltd.*[51] and *Kloeckner & Co. AG* v. *Gatoil Overseas Inc.*[52] on the ground that

> In each of these three cases there was a useful purpose in seeking declaratory relief, which was to disclose or define the existence or extent of the substantive legal right vested in, or obligations assumed by, the party seeking the declaration. That is very different from the declaration sought by the shipowners in the Rotterdam proceedings, which is no more than a declaration that they are not liable in damages to the cargo owners.[53]

Again one wonders whether, if it had been shown that, although the shipowners were not seeking a 'remedy' in the Rotterdam proceedings, they had a 'useful purpose' in bringing them, this would have sufficed to bring the case within Article 21.

As an alternative ground of the application in Folio 2006, and as the principal ground in Folio 2007, the defendants contended that the actions should be stayed because the Rotterdam court was already seised of 'related' proceedings. Here reliance was being placed upon Article 22. Counsel for the plaintiff did concede that Folio 2006 was related to the Rotterdam proceedings. The judge therefore had a discretion to stay the English action. Sheen J noted that, as is explicitly stated in the third paragraph of the Article, the object of granting such a stay is the avoidance of the risk of irreconcilable judgments. But the risk here was not very great. Moreover, there were other factors to be considered. No substantive relief was being claimed in the Rotterdam proceedings. The issue in that action would depend upon the cargo owners' defence and not upon the assertions of the shipowners, because, if their assertions were valid, they would have no cause of action. Moreover, if a stay were granted pending the outcome of the Rotterdam proceedings, the real claim made by the cargo owners would be 'unnecessarily and indefinitely delayed'.[54] His Lordship, therefore, in the exercise of his discretion declined to stay Folio 2006. Counsel did contend that Folio 2007 was not related to the Rotterdam proceedings. However, after referring to the wording of the third paragraph of Article 22, Sheen J said: 'As a matter of good sense Folio 2007 is related to Folio 2006'.[55] His Lordship concluded:

> If, as is admitted, Folio 2006 is an action related to the Rotterdam proceedings, it seems to me that it would be flying in the face of good sense and the whole spirit of the Convention to hold that action Folio 2007 is not a related action. That being so, it would also lack good sense if the court were not to exercise its discretion whether or not to stay that action or to decline jurisdiction in precisely the same way as Folio 2006. I propose to exercise my discretion in the same way in both actions.[56]

In construing Article 22 there must sensibly be a correlation between the scope ascribed to it and the fact that its impact is discretionary. The notion of 'related action' can be safely seen as a broad one in the light of this latter fact. Indeed, there is room for the view that, had the 'relationship' between the English and Dutch proceedings been more tenuous than it in fact was, it would still have been appropriate for a judge to have a discretion to stay. In some sets of circumstances

50 [1989] ECC 420.
51 See *Current Law Year Book*, 1988, p. 397; and see now [1992] 2 WLR 586.
52 [1990] 1 Lloyd's Rep. 177.
53 [1991] 2 Lloyd's Rep. 458, 464.
54 Ibid. 466.
55 Ibid. 467.
56 Ibid. 467.

significantly different from those existing in *The Maciej Rataj* this could be of considerable value.

In both actions before Sheen J the defendants supported their applications for a stay on the alternative ground of *forum non conveniens*. Dealing with this, Sheen J referred to the 'definitive speech' of Lord Goff in *Spiliada Maritime Corporation* v. *Cansulex Ltd.*[57] He noted that in the instant case the defendants were Polish, and that of the four plaintiffs two had their registered offices in London and two had them in Germany. Not one of the parties was Dutch. The bills of lading were in English. His Lordship said that, although there was no natural forum, 'the plaintiffs have established English jurisdiction as of right in accordance with international convention. In those circumstances the burden resting on the defendant is to show that there is another available forum which is clearly or distinctly more appropriate than the English forum.'[58] Sheen J concluded:

> The defendants have not been able to establish that Rotterdam is a distinctly more appropriate forum than this Court. Indeed it appears to me to be distinctly less appropriate.[59]

Foreign judgments: merger of the cause of action

Case No. 4. At common law an unsatisfied foreign judgment was seen as being in effect a simple contract debt in that there was no merger of the original cause of action. It was, therefore, open to the successful foreign plaintiff, as an alternative to suing in England on the foreign judgment, to sue in England on the original cause of action. This position was fundamentally changed by section 34 of the Civil Jurisdiction and Judgments Act 1982, which provides that no proceedings may be brought by a person in the United Kingdom 'on a cause of action in respect of which a judgment has been given in his favour in proceedings between the same parties, or their privies, in a court in another part of the United Kingdom or in a court in an overseas country, unless the judgment is not enforceable or entitled to recognition in the relevant part of the United Kingdom'. The abrogation of the non-merger rule was thus achieved by making the foreign judgment a bar to further proceedings on the original cause of action.

In the recent case of *Black* v. *Yates*[60] Potter J had to consider various aspects of the scope and meaning of section 34. The facts giving rise to English proceedings in that case may be summarized as follows. The plaintiff's husband was killed in a motor-cycle accident in Spain whilst riding as the defendant's passenger. In Spanish criminal proceedings guilt and liability were in effect admitted by the defendant, so that only the extent of compensation remained to be determined. Under Spanish law the plaintiff, if she intended to seek damages elsewhere, had to reserve her right of civil action expressly. She did not do so, and the Spanish court proceeded to award compensation of 4 million pesetas to the 'successors of the deceased'. The plaintiff had appointed a Spanish lawyer to exercise power of attorney and he accepted this compensation on her behalf.

The plaintiff subsequently brought actions in England on behalf of herself and her two children as dependants of the deceased under the Fatal Accidents Act 1976, and for the benefit of the deceased's estate under the Law Reform (Miscel-

57 [1987] AC 460.
58 [1991] 2 Lloyd's Rep. 458, 467.
59 Ibid.
60 [1991] 3 WLR 90.

laneous Provisions) Act 1934. The defendant relied on section 34 of the Civil Jurisdiction and Judgments Act 1982. Reliance was also placed upon the fact of payment pursuant to a foreign judgment, res judicata and issue estoppel. On a preliminary issue as to the effect of the Spanish judgment, Potter J dismissed the plaintiff's claims on her own behalf under the Fatal Accidents Act 1976, but he upheld both her right to pursue claims on behalf of her children under that Act and her claims on behalf of the deceased's estate under the Law Reform (Miscellaneous Provisions) Act 1934.

The learned judge indicated[61] that with regard to section 34 it was incumbent upon the defendant to show that three requirements of that section were satisfied, namely, (1) that the proceedings were being brought on the same cause of action as were the Spanish proceedings; (2) that the proceedings were between the same parties (or their privies) as were the Spanish proceedings; and (3) that the Spanish judgment was enforceable or entitled to recognition in England and Wales.

His Lordship had no doubt that there had been compliance with the first of these requirements. Having referred to Diplock LJ's definition of a 'cause of action' in *Letang* v. *Cooper*[62] as being 'simply a factual situation the existence of which entitles one person to obtain from the court a remedy against another person', Potter J said:

> It seems to me clear that the facts which give rise to a remedy in England gave rise to a comparable civil remedy in Spain, albeit such remedy fails to be pursued in essentially criminal proceedings by intervention of the aggrieved party: see article 109 of the Civil Code and articles 19 and 101 of the Penal Code. So far as damages are concerned, articles 101 to 104 of the Penal Code and the evidence which I have heard satisfy me that the heads of damage in civil proceedings dealt with under those articles correspond with the heads of damage recoverable under English law.[63]

With regard to the second of the above mentioned requirements, counsel for the plaintiff had submitted first that she had not been a party to the Spanish proceedings 'in any real sense of the word', in that she did not initiate those proceedings although she did subsequently participate in them. Potter J rejected the interpretation of section 34 underlying this submission. His Lordship said:

> It seems to me unnecessary and inappropriate to read into the section any requirement that the English plaintiff should have been the original party in the overseas proceedings or that such proceedings be exclusively civil in character. What is aimed at by the section, in my view, is an extension of the English doctrine of merger to the judgments of all overseas courts of competent jurisdiction which are enforceable and entitled to recognition in this country.[64]

His Lordship also rejected a second argument put forward by counsel for the plaintiff, namely that, as at common law the plaintiff (now suing *not only* in a personal capacity) would not be estopped from re-opening her, and her children's, claims for compensation by reason of any matter decided in the Spanish proceedings in which she had appeared *only* in a personal capacity, so, too, she should not be precluded by section 34. In rejecting this argument Potter J expressed the opinion that what 'may be a good working rule for the purposes of the law of estoppel . . . should not

61 Ibid. 102.
62 [1965] 1 QB 232 at p. 242.
63 [1991] 3 WLR 90, 103.
64 Ibid. 103.

be applied willy-nilly in the construction of section 34 . . . ' and concluded that he did not think that

> it can have been the intention of Parliament that the English form of action in such cases, i.e. a claim brought by the executor or administrator of the deceased, although in fact brought for the benefit of the defendants, should limit the application of section 34 to previous proceedings in those countries which have an identical form of action.[65]

Satisfaction of the third requirement, namely that it be shown that the Spanish judgment was enforceable and/or entitled to recognition in England and Wales, was challenged on two grounds. First, it was contended that the judgment was not final and conclusive. This was, of course, a matter for Spanish law, and Potter J preferred the evidence of the defendant's expert witness to the effect that the judgment had this effect in Spain. Secondly, it was argued that the Spanish court had not been a court of competent jurisdiction in respect of the claims of the children. On this issue, too, the evidence of the defendant's expert was accepted by the learned judge.

Thus, so far as the plaintiff's claims on her own behalf and in respect of her own dependency under the Fatal Accidents Act 1976 were concerned, a defence based on section 34 was made out.

Although Potter J indicated that the defence of actual payment pursuant to the Spanish judgment would also have been available as a defence to the plaintiff's claim in a personal capacity, he recoiled from unnecessary investigation of the problems surrounding defences based upon the doctrines of res judicata and/or issue estoppel.

In support of the plaintiff's claim in a representative capacity under the Law Reform (Miscellaneous Provisions) Act 1934, counsel had contended that Spanish law recognizes no claim by a representative on behalf of 'an estate', and furthermore that the plaintiff had not appeared in any such guise in the Spanish proceedings. Potter J, accepting at least the latter of these contentions, held that section 34 provided no defence to the plaintiff's claim under the 1934 Act.

A multiplicity of arguments was put by counsel with regard to the position of the plaintiff's children as infant dependants under the Fatal Accidents Act 1976. The argument that in substance prevailed was that section 34 was neither designed nor intended to affect the ordinary law of infancy. The actions taken on behalf of the children in the Spanish proceedings, were, on the evidence, contrary to their interests, and, furthermore, there was no evidence that they had been able to give any informed consent to the power of attorney. His Lordship said

> . . . it is true that in considering the interests of the children, the court is going behind the foreign judgment to look at the position at the time of the grant of the original power of attorney; however, that is what the court should do, if necessary in order to protect the interests of an infant. If the power of attorney was no power, then there can be no injustice in permitting the children to repudiate it. Even if it was a power, the English law of infancy recognises that its benefits vis-à-vis the children should be considered . . . Accordingly, I hold that the matters pleaded in the defence do not amount to a defence against the plaintiff's claims in so far as they relate to the dependence of the children . . . [66]

Section 34 of the 1982 Act is formulated in general terms. It embodies principle. No attempt was made by Parliament to deal with specifics. Given the diverse

[65] Ibid. 107–8.
[66] Ibid. 114.

variety of problems that can arise when assessing foreign judicative procedures this forbearance was prudent. Its consequence is that judges in the United Kingdom are free to construe the section in accord with underlying policy. It is a matter for regret that legislative intervention in other areas of private international law has not always taken this form. The sequence of legislation relating to matrimonial causes and the resulting pattern of case law provide a sombre illustration of this.

The generality of the formulation of section 34 enabled Potter J to approach all the various issues concerning its construction which fell to be considered in *Black* v. *Yates* in a way which stands in benign contrast. Perhaps the most striking examples of this are to be seen in the learned judge's refusal to be deterred by technicalities from holding that the Spanish and the English proceedings were between the same parties, and by his holding that section 34 [despite its unqualified terms] was not 'designed or intended to set aside the ordinary provisions of English law in relation to infancy'.[67]

Foreign judgment inconsistent with prior English judgment—public policy; extra-territorial injunctive relief.

Case No. 5. Neill LJ prefaced his judgment in the recent Court of Appeal case of *E.D. and F. Man (Sugar) Ltd.* v. *Yani Haryanto (No. 2)*[68] with the observation that 'The history of this matter is a little complicated'. This understatement notwithstanding, the legal issues in the case, although several, interesting and not free from difficulty, were relatively clear-cut.

In 1982 the plaintiffs (Man), major international sugar traders, had entered into two agreements (or disputed contracts) for the sale of substantial quantities of sugar to the defendant (Haryanto), an Indonesian citizen. Each contract provided that English law should govern and that any disputes were to be referred to arbitration in London. In 1984 a dispute was so referred. Haryanto then applied to the English Commercial Court for a declaration that he was not bound by the disputed contracts and for an injunction restraining Man from pursuing the arbitration. This application was unsuccessful, as was his appeal to the Court of Appeal. In 1986 Haryanto began a second English action seeking a declaration that the disputed contracts were unenforceable and/or void as being illegal and/or contrary to English public policy. Man in turn commenced a third English action seeking a declaration that Haryanto was estopped from contending that the contracts were unenforceable on the grounds alleged. Later in 1986 a settlement agreement of the English arbitration and the English legal proceedings was reached, and Haryanto agreed thereunder to pay Man specified amounts on specified days. In the event Haryanto failed to pay the second and third instalments.

In 1988 Haryanto commenced an action in Indonesia claiming an annulment of the contracts and a declaration that they were null and void. A few months later Man brought an action also in Indonesia seeking enforcement of the debt which had become due under the settlement agreement. In the following year the Indonesian court delivered judgment in both proceedings. It held in Haryanto's action that the disputed contracts were illegal as having been entered into for a purpose illegal under Indonesian law and as being subversive to Indonesian public policy, and moreover that the decision of the English Court of Appeal was not binding on

[67] Ibid.
[68] [1991] 1 Lloyd's Rep. 429.

the Indonesian court. In the Man action the Indonesian court held that, as the settlement agreement arose from the tainted contracts, it was itself illegal as being contrary to Indonesian public policy and that the acknowledgment of debt and an associated share pledge were similarly illegal.

In the present English proceedings Man sought a declaration that the settlement agreement, the acknowledgement of debt and the additional security given by Haryanto pursuant to that agreement, were all valid and binding on Haryanto. Man further sought an injunction having extra-territorial effect and designed to restrain Haryanto from repeating anywhere in the world the assertions which he had put forward in the Indonesian proceedings. Haryanto contended that Man was bound by the decision of the Indonesian court and that the issues of the validity of the settlement agreement and the acknowledgement of the debt were res judicata, the decision of the Indonesian court being entitled to recognition. Man argued that the English court should not recognize the Indonesian court's decision because (1) it was inconsistent with the earlier English decisions, and (2) to recognize it would be contrary to English public policy. The trial judge, Steyn J, accepted these two last-mentioned contentions, and held that Man was entitled to the declaratory relief sought. However, his Lordship held that it would be an affront to the Indonesian courts and an illegitimate interference (even if indirect) with the process of courts worldwide to grant extra-territorial injunctive relief, which was designed to prohibit Haryanto from relying on the Indonesian judgment. Man's application for such relief was accordingly refused. Man appealed against this discharge of the injunction, and Haryanto cross-appealed against the grant of the declaration.

The Court of Appeal was unanimous in dismissing both the appeal and the cross-appeal. In dealing with the former, Neill LJ (with whose judgment Balcombe and Mann LJJ concurred) said that it was clear that, although the Indonesian court's declaration was in form directed to the settlement agreement, the real issue was as to the validity of the contracts, and this had already been the subject of decision by the English Court of Appeal. His Lordship said:

> It follows therefore that, at any rate prima facie, Mr Haryanto is faced with an issue estoppel as to the validity of the disputed contracts and that this estoppel will cover defences which might have been raised but were not raised in the English proceedings. Furthermore, it is to be emphasized that an English court will not recognize a foreign judgment, even if otherwise unimpeachable, if it is inconsistent with a previous decision of a competent English Court: see *Vervaeke* v. *Smith* [1983] 1 AC 145.[69]

Neill LJ then considered the relevance (if any) of public policy His Lordship differentiated between the role of English public policy and the role of Indonesian public policy. The public policy invoked in fact derived from Indonesian law. As Neill LJ indicated, a defence based on this ground could have been raised by Haryanto in the previous English proceedings as going to the merits, but it was irrelevant in the present context, this being the recognition of the Indonesian judgment. Of course, recognition of a foreign judgment can be withheld on the grounds of the public policy of the forum (here England) in which recognition is being sought, but to take account of the public policy of the forum of rendition at that stage would involve re-opening the merits. In the present case, therefore, as Neill LJ emphasized, ' . . . the crucial question . . . is whether *as a matter of Eng-*

[69] Ibid. 436.

lish law, the public policy in favour of finality is overridden by some more important policy based upon the unenforceability of illegal contracts'.[70] There was in the instant case no such overriding policy. It may perhaps be noted that to accord to public policy the *positive* role of being instrumental in according recognition to a foreign judgment (otherwise not so entitled) would be unusual, although not in all circumstances unwarranted.

Neill LJ examined the application for injunctive relief under three headings, two of which gave rise to little difficulty. An injunction to prevent reliance on the Indonesian judgment either to bring or to defend proceedings in England was unnecessary in view of the fact that the declaration was being upheld: the remedies of striking out would suffice. To grant an injunction aimed at preventing reliance on the Indonesian judgment in proceedings in Indonesia would be wrong in that it would interfere, or purport to interfere, with the judgment of a court of competent jurisdiction inside that country. More difficult was the question of granting an injunction designed to prevent reliance on the Indonesian judgment in proceedings in third countries throughout the world. His Lordship had relatively little difficulty in coming to the conclusion

> that there can be no satisfactory basis in this case for restraining Mr Haryanto from relying on the Indonesian judgment *as a matter of defence* in any enforcement proceedings brought against him in third countries. It is true that unconscionability has to be judged by reference to English law, but I do not consider that an English Court would be right to prevent Mr Haryanto relying on the Indonesian judgment *as a shield* in a country where he was permitted to do so by the local law.[71]

With regard to restraint from *instituting* proceedings in third countries in order to enforce or obtain other recognition of the Indonesian judgment, Neill LJ felt considerable hesitation but in the end came to the 'conclusion that it would not be right *on the facts of this case* to grant *any* injunction which would have an extra-territorial effect on proceedings abroad'.[72]

Mann LJ presented his concurrence with this result within a doctrinal framework. His Lordship, citing from the speech of Lord Brandon in *South Carolina Insurance Co.* v. *Assurantie Maatschappij 'De Zeven Provincien' NV*,[73] identified the two situations[74] in which an injunction with regard to the institution or conduct of foreign legal proceedings can be granted as being (1) where one party can show that the other party has invaded, or threatens to invade, a legal or equitable right of the former, for the enforcement of which the latter is amenable to the jurisdiction of the court; and (2) where one party to an action has behaved, or threatens to behave, in an unconscionable manner. Man had argued that its case fell within either or both of these categories. Mann LJ had little difficulty in holding that Haryanto had not invaded any identifiable legal or equitable right enjoyed by Man by securing the Indonesian judgment. Accordingly, it was impossible to hold that prospective reliance on that judgment could constitute a threatened invasion of a legal or equitable right. But what of unconscionable behaviour actual or threatened?

[70] Ibid. (original italics).

[71] Ibid. 438 (original italics).

[72] Ibid. (italics supplied).

[73] [1987] AC 24, 40.

[74] Mann LJ also mentioned a third situation which was not relevant in the instant case, namely that in which proceedings in respect of the same subject-matter have been commenced in England (see, e.g., *Société Nationale Industrielle Aérospatiale* v. *Lee Kui Jak*, [1987] AC 871).

Here his Lordship was willing to concede that perhaps obtaining the Indonesian judgment and relying upon it by way of offence (as distinct from merely defence) somewhere in the future was, and would be, unconscionable. However, even if jurisdiction to grant an injunction did therefore exist, it was to be exercised with caution: 'the reason for caution is that an exercise of jurisdiction does involve an indirect interference with extant or future proceedings before a foreign court . . . '.[75] Mann LJ concluded by noting that it was as a matter of discretion that the trial judge had dismissed the claim for an injunction. In doing so he had been right and his discretion had been properly exercised in that he had balanced the interests of each party and considerations of comity. The learned Lord Justice cited with approval what Steyn J had said in this regard:

> In all the circumstances it seems to me that it would be an affront to the Indonesian Court, and an illegitimate interference (albeit indirectly) with the process of Courts worldwide to grant an injunction, the expressed objective of which is to prohibit Mr Haryanto from relying on the Indonesian judgment. Balancing the competing private and public interests as best I can, I conclude that Man will have to be content with declaratory relief, leaving it to Courts in foreign jurisdictions to choose (if the matter arises) whether to recognize the judgments of the English or Indonesian Courts.[76]

Inconsistent judgments by courts of different countries concerning the same subject-matter are obviously liable to give rise to difficulty. The availability of injunctive relief presents opportunities for enhancement of such difficulty. Matters could be further exacerbated by indulgence in counter-injunctive relief. This, indeed, occurred in the United States case of *James* v. *Grand Track Western Railroad Co.*[77] There the defendant had previously obtained an injunction in Michigan restraining the plaintiff from proceeding in Illinois. The plaintiff then obtained an injunction in Illinois to restrain the defendant from enforcing the Michigan injunction. Justice Schaefer in his dissent in the Supreme Court of Illinois said: 'The place to stop this unseemly kind of judicial disorder is where it begins'. The approach taken by their Lordships in *E.D. and F. Man (Sugar) Ltd.* v. *Yani Haryanto (No. 2)* is clearly consistent with respect for this prudent admonition. Recognition will not be given to a foreign judgment which is inconsistent with *previous* resolution of the issue in the present forum. Nor, exceptional circumstances apart, will a forum *initiate* injunctive interference or attempted interference in foreign proceedings actual or potential.

P. B. CARTER

[75] [1991] 1 Lloyd's Rep. 429, *per* Mann LJ at p. 440.
[76] Ibid.
[77] 14 Ill. 2d 356; 152 NE 2d 858.

DECISIONS ON THE EUROPEAN CONVENTION ON HUMAN RIGHTS DURING 1991*

Right to have the lawfulness of detention determined 'speedily' (Article 5(4))—just satisfaction (Article 50)

Case No. 1. E v. *Norway.*[1] The Court held unanimously that there had been a violation of Article 5(4) of the Convention because proceedings instituted by the applicant to determine the lawfulness of his detention had not been conducted speedily. Two other complaints involving the same provision were rejected. The applicant's claim for just satisfaction under Article 50 was also dismissed.

In 1965 the applicant, E, was involved in a traffic accident which caused him serious brain damage. As a result of the injury he developed a tendency to become aggressive and was convicted of assaults on several occasions. He has therefore been in prison or in another correctional facility almost constantly since 1978. Most of the time he has not been serving an actual prison sentence, but has been held in preventive detention which has been authorized by the Norwegian courts and implemented by the prosecuting authority. Such detention can be terminated, resumed or varied by the Ministry of Justice in accordance with the Penal Code which allows preventive detention where a punishable act has been committed 'by someone with an underdeveloped or permanently impaired mental capacity' and there is a danger that the offender, because of his condition, will repeat the act.

On 3 August 1988 E applied to the Oslo City Court for judicial review of one of the detention decisions. He alleged that the Ministry had not observed the necessary procedural requirements; that the decision was unfair because it was an unreasonably harsh response to his behaviour; and finally that it was unconstitutional because the Ministry had used preventive measures instead of the normal criminal procedure. After holding a hearing on 7 September the City Court dismissed E's application on the 27th of the month. The applicant did not appeal.

In April 1990 E was set free when the prosecuting authorities withdrew their application for an extension of the authorization to implement security measures.

In his application to the Commission in May 1985 E complained of violations of Article 3 (inhuman or degrading treatment or punishment) and Article 5(4) of the Convention. The complaint relating to Article 3 was found to be inadmissible, but in its report in March 1989 the Commission unanimously expressed the opinion that there had been a breach of Article 5(4). The Commission and the Government then referred the case to the Court.

Article 5(4) of the Convention provides:

Everyone who is deprived of his liberty by arrest or detention shall be entitled to take

* © Professor J. G. Merrills, 1992. I should like to express my gratitude to the Registrar of the Court for his co-operation in the preparation of these notes. Cases decided in the latter part of 1991, which appeared too late for inclusion in the present survey, will be covered in the next issue of the *Year Book*.

[1] European Court of Human Rights (ECHR), judgment of 29 August 1990, Series A, No. 181. The Court consisted of the following Chamber of Judges: Cremona (President); Ryssdal, Thór Vilhjálmsson, Matscher, Sir Vincent Evans, Russo, Spielmann (Judges).

proceedings by which the lawfulness of his detention shall be decided speedily by a court and his release ordered if the detention is not lawful.

The applicant put forward three arguments in support of his submission that this provision had been violated. First, he maintained that the domestic court's power to review the Ministry's detention decisions was too limited. It is clear from the Court's case law that:

> Article 5(4) does not guarantee a right to judicial review of such a scope as to empower the court, on all aspects of the case including questions of pure expediency, to substitute its own discretion for that of the decision-making authority. The review should, however, be wide enough to bear on those conditions which are essential for the 'lawful' detention of a person according to Article 5(1). This applies equally whether the detention at issue is covered by sub-paragraph (*a*) of paragraph 1—'the lawful detention of a person after conviction by a competent court' . . . or by sub-paragraph (*e*)—'the lawful detention . . . of persons of unsound mind . . . [2]

However, having examined the relevant domestic law, the Court found that the judicial review available was wide enough to satisfy the Convention's requirements. It therefore rejected this argument.

The applicant's second argument was that Article 5(4) had been violated because the domestic courts lacked the power to order his release. This argument too was rejected because the Court found that the material before it indicated that the Norwegian courts had this power where an administrative decision to detain a person was found to be invalid. In the Court's view, therefore, the Oslo City Court had refused to order E's release because it had rejected his argument on the merits, not because it lacked the power to do so.

The applicant's third argument was that the proceedings before the national court had not been conducted 'speedily'. There is now a considerable body of case law on this requirement[3] and, applying the principles laid down by its previous decisions, the Court had no difficulty in concluding that a period of almost eight weeks from the filing of the summons to the final judgment was difficult to reconcile with the Convention. The Court pointed out that there were no special circumstances to justify such a long period and that part of the delay appeared to be attributable to the lack of a procedure for dealing with applications filed during the court's vacation period. The Court therefore concluded that on this point there had been a breach of Article 5(4).

Having identified a violation of the Convention, the Court's final task was to consider the question of 'just satisfaction' for the applicant under Article 50. According to that provision:

> If the Court finds that a decision or a measure taken by a legal authority or any other authority of a High Contracting Party, is completely or partially in conflict with the obligations arising from the present Convention, and if the internal law of the said Party allows only partial reparation to be made for the consequences of this decision or measure, the decision of the Court shall, if necessary, afford just satisfaction to the injured party.

The applicant, who had received free legal aid in Norway for his representation

[2] Judgment, para. 50. As regards Article 5(1)(*a*), see the *Weeks* case, Series A, No. 114, and this *Year Book*, 58 (1987), p. 470; as regards Article 5(1)(*e*), see the *Ashingdane* case, Series A, No. 93, and this *Year Book*, 56 (1985), p. 348.

[3] See, for example, the *Sanchez-Reisse* case, Series A, No. 107, and this *Year Book*, 57 (1986), p. 471.

at Strasbourg, sought only compensation for pecuniary and non-pecuniary damage. The Court, however, observed that these claims were based on circumstances which were unrelated to the violation identified in the judgment. If the applicant had suffered any non-pecuniary damage as a result of the delay in the domestic proceedings, the Court considered that the present judgment provided him with sufficient just satisfaction. It therefore made no award under Article 50.

Other cases which raised issues under Article 5(4) in the period covered by this review were the *Wassink* case (Case No. 3), the *Thynne, Wilson and Gunnell* case (Case No. 8), the *Koendjbiharie* case (Case No. 9) and the *Keus* case (Case No. 10).

Right to respect for private life (Article 8)—application to civil status of transsexual—right to marry (Article 12)—distinguishing and departing from previous decisions

Case No. 2. Cossey case.[4] In this case, which concerned the United Kingdom, the Court held by 10 votes to 8 that the fact that a male-to-female transsexual was unable to obtain a birth certificate showing her sex as female did not constitute a violation of Article 8 of the Convention. It also held by 14 votes to 4 that the applicant's inability to contract a marriage with a man which would be valid under English law did not constitute a violation of Article 12.

The applicant was a transsexual who, having been born in 1952 with all the physical and biological characteristics of a male and registered as such, in adolescence came to regard herself as psychologically a female. In 1972 she assumed a female name and role and in 1974 underwent gender reassignment surgery which enabled her to live a full life as a female, both psychologically and physically, and between 1979 and 1986 to pursue a career as a fashion model.

In 1983 Miss Cossey and Mr L, an Italian, wished to marry, but the British authorities informed her that such a marriage would be void because English law would regard her as male. She had been issued with a passport as a female, but was told that she could not be issued with a birth certificate showing her sex as female. In 1989 Miss Cossey purported to marry a Mr X at a ceremony conducted at a London synagogue. However, their relationship terminated shortly afterwards. In 1990, following a petition filed by Miss Cossey, the marriage was declared void by the High Court on the ground that the parties were not respectively male and female.

In her application to the Commission in 1984 Miss Cossey complained that she was the victim of a violation of her right to respect for her private life under Article 8 of the Convention and of her right to marry under Article 12. In its report in May 1989 the Commission expressed the opinion by 10 votes to 6 that there had been a violation of Article 12, but not of Article 8. The Government and the Commission then referred the case to the Court.

The rights of transsexuals have already been considered by the Court on one previous occasion, in the *Rees* case[5] in 1986. That case, which also involved the

[4] ECHR, judgment of 27 September 1990, Series A, No. 184. This case was decided by the plenary Court.

[5] ECHR, judgment of 17 October 1986, Series A, No. 106, and this *Year Book*, 57 (1986), p. 469. The rights of transsexuals under Article 8 were also in issue in the *Van Oosterwijck* case, Series A, No. 40, and this *Year Book*, 51 (1980), p. 339, but in that case the Court was able to avoid deciding the point by holding that the applicant had failed to exhaust domestic remedies, as required by Article 26.

United Kingdom, raised similar issues under Articles 8 and 12, and the Court there decided that neither provision had been violated. In the present case the Court began by ruling that the situation before it was not materially distinguishable from that in *Rees* and deciding that, as a consequence, the broad issue was whether it should depart from its previous decision. On this question, which is likely to arise with increasing frequency as points are relitigated, the Court said:

> It is true that . . . the Court is not bound by its previous judgments; . . . However, it usually follows and applies its own precedents, such a course being in the interests of legal certainty and the orderly development of the Convention case-law. Nevertheless, this would not prevent the Court from departing from an earlier decision if it was persuaded that there were cogent reasons for doing so. Such a departure might, for example, be warranted in order to ensure that the interpretation of the Convention reflects societal changes and remains in line with present-day conditions.[6]

The relevant part of Article 8(1) of the Convention provides:

> Everyone has the right to respect for his private . . . life . . .

The applicant complained that she was obliged to reveal intimate personal details whenever she had to produce a birth certificate, since she could not obtain one showing her sex as female. The Court said that the question was therefore whether an effective respect for her private life imposed a positive obligation on the United Kingdom to modify its birth registration system. In answering this type of question, as the Court has frequently pointed out, 'regard must be had to the fair balance that has to be struck between the general interest of the community, and the interests of the individual, the search for which balance is inherent in the whole of the Convention'.[7]

In the *Rees* case the Court had concluded that there was no such obligation. In doing so it had taken into account matters such as access by the public to the register of births and its function as an historical record, which it regarded as no less cogent in the present case. It observed in particular that arrangements for supplying the applicant with a new certificate showing her present sex, while maintaining the old record in its present form, would not be practicable if the public character of the register was to be maintained.

The Court ruled that there had been no significant scientific developments since the date of the *Rees* case. Gender reassignment surgery still did not result in the acquisition of all the biological characteristics of the other sex. Whilst there had been 'certain developments' in the laws of some Council of Europe States, there was still little common ground between them. Accordingly they continued to enjoy a wide margin of appreciation in this area and departure from the *Rees* judgment could not be said to be needed in order to reflect present-day conditions. Thus the Court by a narrow majority concluded that there had been no violation of Article 8.

The issue under Article 12 was less controversial and treated more briefly. Article 12 provides:

> Men and women of marriageable age have the right to marry and to found a family, according to the national laws governing the exercise of this right.

In her submission the applicant emphasized that as a result of her situation she

[6] Judgment, para. 35.

[7] Ibid., para. 37. On the Court's approach to positive obligations in general see Merrills, *The Development of International Law by the European Court of Human Rights* (1988), pp. 94–7.

could not marry at all. As a woman she could not realistically marry another woman, while English law prevented her from marrying a man. In addressing this point the Court recalled that in its case law on Article 12 it has always maintained that limitations on the right to marry introduced by national laws must not have the effect of impairing the very essence of the right.[8] However, the Court pointed out that the applicant's inability to marry a woman did not stem from any legal impediment. As regards her inability to marry a man, on the other hand, the criteria of English law were in conformity with the concept of marriage to which Article 12 referred, namely the traditional marriage of persons of opposite biological sex.

The Court acknowledged that some States would now regard a marriage between a person in Miss Cossey's situation and a man as valid. However, it considered that these developments 'cannot be said to evidence any general abandonment of the traditional concept of marriage'.[9] It followed that it was not open to the Court to take a new approach to the interpretation of this aspect of Article 12. Moreover, in a significant final sentence it added that in its view:

> . . . attachment to the traditional concept of marriage provides sufficient reason for the continued adoption of biological criteria for determining a person's sex for the purposes of marriage, this being a matter encompassed within the power of the Contracting States to regulate by national law the exercise of the right to marry.[10]

The Court therefore concluded that there was no violation of Article 12.

Eight judges delivered dissenting or partly dissenting opinions. Four dissented only on the issue of Article 8. For Judges Bindschedler-Robert and Russo this was because they had dissented on this point in the *Rees* case; for Judges Macdonald and Spielmann, on the other hand, it was because since 1986 there had been 'clear developments' in the laws of many member States which made a wide margin of appreciation on this matter no longer appropriate. Of the judges who disagreed with the majority on both Articles 8 and 12, Judges Palm, Foighel and Pekkanen in a joint dissenting opinion held that 'social and moral developments' called for a reinterpretation of the right to marry, while Judge Martens in a long and forcefully argued individual dissenting opinion reviewed both the phenomenon of transsexualism and the role of the Court, with particular criticism of its reliance on the margin of appreciation.[11]

This was the first of three cases involving the United Kingdom in the period under review[12] and, in terms of the Court's jurisprudence, by far the most important. Few will disagree with Judge Martens' observation that:

> . . . the Court, at least as far as family law and sexuality are concerned, moves extremely cautiously when confronted with an evolution which has reached completion in some member States, is still in progress in others but has seemingly left yet others untouched. In such cases the Court's policy seems to be to adapt its interpretation to the relevant societal change only if almost all member States have adopted the new ideas.[13]

[8] In addition to the *Rees* case, the Court has previously discussed the right to marry in the *Johnston* case, Series A, No. 112, and this *Year Book*, 58 (1987), p. 463, and the case of *F* v. *Switzerland*, Series A, No. 128, and this *Year Book*, 59 (1988), p. 375.

[9] Judgment, para. 46.

[10] Ibid.

[11] For discussion of the increasingly important role of this concept in the Court's case law, see Merrills, op. cit. above (n. 7), Chapter 7.

[12] See also Cases No. 8 and 38, below.

[13] Dissenting opinion of Judge Martens, para. 5.6.3.

But whether, as he went on to suggest, 'this caution is in principle not consistent with the Court's mission to protect the individual against the collectivity and to do so by elaborating common standards'[14] is more contentious. The fact that four members of the Court dissented on Article 8, but not on Article 12, indicates that there are degrees of judicial caution and that an incremental development of the Court's case law can be an alternative to a complete repudiation of a previous decision.

Right to liberty (Article 5(1))—the meaning of 'in accordance with a procedure prescribed by law' in Article 5(1)—right to have the lawfulness of detention determined by a court (Article 5(4))—right to compensation for unlawful arrest or detention (Article 5(5))—just satisfaction (Article 50)

Case No. 3. Wassink case.[15] In this case, which concerned the detention of a patient in a psychiatric hospital in the Netherlands, the Court held by 6 votes to 1 that there had been a violation of Article 5(1) of the Convention. Other complaints based on Articles 5(4) and 5(5) were rejected. As just satisfaction for the violation of Article 5(1) the Government was ordered to pay the applicant 11,897.40 guilders, less 8,657.50 French francs in respect of his costs and expenses.

On 11 November 1985 the applicant, Mr Wassink, was committed to a psychiatric establishment by order of the Burgomaster of Emmen acting under the Mentally Ill Persons Act. A psychiatrist had earlier certified that there were serious grounds for supposing that the applicant suffered from a mental disorder which presented an immediate danger to himself, to others or to public order. On 25 November the President of the local District Court ordered the applicant's confinement to be continued. Before doing this he had heard the applicant in person and interviewed four other people, three of them by telephone. He had telephoned the applicant's 'confidential counsellor' to inform him briefly of the statements made by the latter three, but had not sent him his written notes of the conversations. Mr Wassink left the psychiatric hospital on 20 December 1985. On 18 April 1986 the Supreme Court declared an appeal on points of law from the President's order inadmissible, on the ground that the applicant no longer had any interest in challenging the order, since the maximum period for an emergency confinement had expired.

In his application to the Commission in October 1986 Mr Wassink claimed that the circumstances of his confinement had violated several of his rights under Article 5, as well as his right to a fair trial under Article 6(1). In its report in July 1989 the Commission expressed the opinion that there had been violations of Articles 5(1), 5(4) and 5(5), but no violation of Article 6(1). The Commission then referred the case to the Court.

The relevant part of Article 5(1) of the Convention provides:

> 1. Everyone has the right to liberty and security of person. No one shall be deprived of his liberty save in the following cases and in accordance with a procedure prescribed by law;
>
> . . .
>
> (*e*) the lawful detention . . . of persons of unsound mind . . .

[14] Ibid.

[15] ECHR, judgment of 27 September 1990, Series A, No. 185. The Court consisted of the following Chamber of Judges: Ryssdal (President); Thór Vilhjálmsson, Gölcüklü, Pettiti, Walsh, De Meyer, Roelvink (Judges).

Mr Wassink claimed that the order authorizing his confinement had not been made 'in accordance with a procedure prescribed by law', with the result that his detention had been unlawful. The arguments put forward in support of this submission were: first, that the President of the District Court had not properly established that the applicant was mentally ill; secondly, that the President had failed to comply with the conditions laid down by the Supreme Court for the use of information obtained by telephone; and thirdly, that no registrar was present at the hearing as required by the relevant legislation. The Court rejected the first and second submissions on the facts,[16] but agreed that the absence of a registrar had rendered the decision unlawful. It therefore held by 6 votes to 1 that there had been a violation of Article 5(1).

It will be recalled from *E* v. *Norway* (Case No. 1) that Article 5(4) lays down that those who are deprived of their liberty by arrest or detention have a right to take proceedings by which the lawfulness of the detention can be decided speedily by a court. Mr Wassink's complaint here was that he had been deprived of an opportunity to comment on the information which the President had obtained by telephone and on which he was proposing to base his decision. He also maintained that the Supreme Court had deprived him of his sole remedy against the contested order by ruling that his appeal on points of law was inadmissible for lack of interest.

The Court, however, found the applicant's argument unpersuasive. Whilst recognizing the risks inherent in the procedure adopted by the President, the Court noted that the questioning 'took place on the initiative and under the responsibility of an independent judicial officer acting under an emergency procedure whose effects were moreover limited as to their duration'.[17] In addition, the President had given the applicant's 'confidential counsellor' a summary of the interviews and an opportunity to comment on them. Thus, although when dealing with the complaint under Article 5(1) the Court had already decided that the 'procedure prescribed by law' was not strictly followed, it held that 'the judge nevertheless reviewed at the outset the lawfulness of the detention as such to an extent consistent with the requirement of paragraph 4'.[18] The Court therefore dismissed this complaint.

Article 5(5) of the Convention, which formed the subject of the applicant's final complaint,[19] provides:

> Everyone who has been the victim of arrest or detention in contravention of the provisions of this Article shall have an enforceable right to compensation.

The applicant maintained that the law of the Netherlands made no provision for compensating him because in his view the relevant article of the Civil Code applied only where damage could be shown and in his case this would have been almost impossible to prove. The Court, however, held that Article 5(5) is complied with so long as it is possible to apply for compensation in respect of an unlawful deprivation of liberty, and that there is nothing in the Convention to prevent a Contracting

[16] On the scope of the Court's power to review the authorities' decision when someone has been detained as a 'person of unsound mind', see the *Winterwerp* case, Series A, No. 33, and this *Year Book*, 50 (1979), p. 267, and the *Luberti* case, Series A, No. 75, and this *Year Book*, 55 (1984), p. 374.

[17] Judgment, para. 33.

[18] Ibid., para. 34.

[19] The applicant withdrew the complaint relating to Article 6(1), which had been rejected by the Commission.

State from making the award of compensation dependent upon the ability of the claimant to show damage. Consequently, 'the status of "victim" may exist, even where there is no damage, but there can be no question of "compensation" where there is no pecuniary or non-pecuniary damage to compensate'.[20] More generally, the Court found that the evidence did not suggest that an action based on the relevant article of the Civil Code would have failed to satisfy the requirements of Article 5(5). The Court therefore dismissed this complaint.

As just satisfaction under Article 50 Mr Wassink claimed a substantial sum as compensation for damage. But the Court decided that as the only violation which had been established related to the absence of a registrar at the hearing in the District Court, the judgment itself constituted just satisfaction. The applicant's claim in respect of his costs and expenses at Strasbourg was allowed in full, however, less the sum already paid as legal aid.

Two members of the Chamber delivered dissenting opinions. Judge Ryssdal held that since a violation of Article 5(1) had been established in the proceedings before the District Court, it should have been possible to appeal against that Court's decision to obtain redress. As no such appeal appeared to be possible, he accepted the applicant's argument that there had also been a violation of Article 5(4). Judge Walsh, on the other hand, considered that as the sole function of a registrar is to record decisions, 'The procedural omission in question did not go to the substance of the matter and did not touch upon any matter fundamental to the adjudication of the President of the District Court'.[21] In his view, therefore, there had been no violation of Article 5(1).

Article 5(5) of the Convention was also in issue in the case of *Thynne, Wilson and Gunnell* (Case No. 8, below).

Right to a fair trial (Article 6(1))—right to examine witnesses (Article 6(3)(d))—just satisfaction (Article 50)

Case No. 4. Windisch case.[22] The Court held unanimously that the applicant's conviction in Austria, on the basis of statements made by two anonymous witnesses, had given rise to a violation of Article 6(3)(*d*) of the Convention, taken together with Article 6(1). The Court also ordered the Government to pay the applicant 86,526 Austrian schillings, less 5,290 French francs, in respect of his costs before the Commission and the Court.

In May 1985 a burglary was committed at a café in the Tyrol. On the following day two women, who wished to remain anonymous for fear of reprisals, reported to the police that they had seen two men in a minibus in the vicinity of the café. The applicant was arrested in June and in a 'covert confrontation' the women indicated that they recognized him as one of the two men. In November 1985 the applicant was convicted of the burglary and sentenced to 3 years' imprisonment. In its judgment the court referred to statements made to the police by the two unidentified witnesses. Although the court examined the police officers who had interrogated the witnesses, it refused the applicant's request to have the women summoned on the ground that the police had undertaken not to reveal their identities. An appeal

[20] Judgment, para. 38.

[21] Dissenting opinion of Judge Walsh.

[22] ECHR, judgment of 27 September 1990, Series A, No. 186. The Court consisted of the following Chamber of Judges: Ryssdal (President); Cremona, Matscher, Macdonald, Bernhardt, De Meyer, Foighel (Judges).

against the verdict and sentence was rejected. However, in July 1990 the Government informed the Court that the Attorney-General had recently begun proceedings to annul the judgment in the Supreme Court.

In his application to the Commission in July 1986 Mr Windisch relied on Articles 6(1) and 6(3)(*d*) of the Convention. In its report in July 1989 the Commission expressed the unanimous opinion that there had been a violation of Article 6(3)(*d*), read in conjunction with Article 6(1). The Commission then referred the case to the Court.

The parts of Article 6 with which the Court was concerned in this case provide:

> 1. In the determination of . . . any criminal charge against him, everyone is entitled to a fair . . . hearing . . . by [a] . . . tribunal . . .
>
> 3. Everyone charged with a criminal offence has the following minimum rights:
>
> . . .
>
> (*d*) to examine or have examined witnesses against him and to obtain the attendance and examination of witnesses on his behalf under the same conditions as witnesses against him.

The applicant complained that he had been convicted on the basis of statements made by the two anonymous witnesses which were of decisive importance for the assessment of the other evidence. The plenary Court examined an argument of this kind in the *Kostovski* case[23] in 1989, and in the present case the Chamber adopted a similar approach. Observing that although the two people in question did not give direct evidence in court, they must be considered as witnesses, the Court recalled that its task was not to see whether their evidence had been correctly admitted and assessed, but rather whether the proceedings as a whole had been fair. In principle, the Court stated, all the evidence must be produced in the presence of the accused at a public hearing with a view to adversarial argument. This does not exclude the use of statements obtained at the pre-trial stage, so long as the rights of the defence are respected. However, here this requirement was not satisfied as neither the applicant nor his counsel ever had an opportunity to examine the witnesses.

The possibility of questioning the police officers or putting written questions to the witnesses could not, in the Court's view, replace the right to examine prosecution witnesses before the trial court directly. Moreover, the nature and scope of the questions had been restricted by the decision to preserve the witnesses' anonymity, and the trial court had no way of seeing and assessing the reliability of the anonymous witnesses for itself. As in the *Kostovski* case, the Court emphasized that it recognized the importance of securing public co-operation in the suppression of crime, but explained that the right to the fair administration of justice cannot be sacrificed. While the use of anonymous informants at the investigation stage was permissible, the use of anonymous statements to found a conviction, as here, was a different matter.

The Court therefore concluded that in the circumstances of the case the use of this evidence by the trial court involved such limitations on the rights of the defence that Mr Windisch could not be said to have received a fair trial. It therefore agreed with the Commission that there had been a violation of Articles 6(3)(*d*) and 6(1) taken together.

As just satisfaction the applicant claimed a large sum as compensation for loss of earnings and unjustified detention. However, the Court considered that this

[23] ECHR, judgment of 20 November 1989, Series A, No. 166, and this *Year Book*, 60 (1989), p. 564.

question was not ready for decision and reserved it. As regards costs and expenses, the Court rejected a claim for the costs incurred by the applicant in Austria, but awarded the sum mentioned earlier, less the sum already received in legal aid, for the cost of the proceedings at Strasbourg.

Five other cases involving Article 6(3)(*d*) were decided by the Court in the period under review: the *Delta* case (Case No. 11), the *Isgrò* case (Case No. 15), the *Cardot* case (Case No. 36), the *Asch* case (Case No. 40) and the *Brandstetter* case (Case No. 50).

Discrimination on grounds of residence (Article 14)—right to the peaceful enjoyment of possessions (Article 1 of Protocol No. 1)—application to religious tax—just satisfaction (Article 50)

Case No. 5. Darby case.[24] In this case, which involved the payment of a special tax to the Church of Sweden, the Court held unanimously that there had been a violation of Article 14 of the Convention, taken together with Article 1 of Protocol No. 1. As just satisfaction under Article 50, the Court ordered the Government to pay the applicant 8,000 Swedish kronor for pecuniary damage and 90,000 kronor in respect of his costs and expenses.

The applicant was a doctor whose home was in Finland. Between 1977 and 1986 he worked in Sweden and for three of those years had to pay a special tax imposed by the Church of Sweden. He was not a member of that church and, had he been a Swedish resident, he would have been entitled to exemption from the part of the tax which finances its religious activities. Dr Darby had, however, maintained his Finnish domicile throughout the relevant period. Consequently, he was liable to pay the full tax and was unsuccessful when he sought to challenge it before the local courts.

In his application to the Commission in 1984 Dr Darby claimed that the fact that he was compelled to pay the tax violated his freedom of religion as guaranteed by Article 9 of the Convention[25] and was also discriminatory contrary to Article 14 taken in conjunction with Article 9 and Article 1 of Protocol No. 1. In its report in May 1989 the Commission upheld the allegations in respect of Article 9 and did not find it necessary to examine the Protocol. The Commission and the Government then referred the case to the Court.

As the applicant's grievances were mainly concerned with the allegedly discriminatory effects of the tax legislation, the Court adopted a different approach from the Commission and examined the case under Article 14 taken together with Article 1 of Protocol No. 1. The latter reads:

> Every natural or legal person is entitled to the peaceful enjoyment of his possessions. No one shall be deprived of his possessions except in the public interest and subject to the conditions provided for by law and by the general principles of international law.
>
> The preceding provisions shall not, however, in any way impair the right of a State to enforce such laws as it deems necessary to control the use of property in accordance with the general interest or to secure the payment of taxes or other contributions or penalties.

[24] ECHR, judgment of 23 October 1990, Series A, No. 187. The Court consisted of the following Chamber of Judges: Ryssdal (President); Pettiti, Russo, Spielmann, Valticos, Palm, Foighel (Judges).

[25] Article 9(1) of the Convention provides:

'Everyone has the right to freedom of thought, conscience and religion; this right includes freedom to change his religion or belief, and freedom, either alone or in community with others and in public or private, to manifest his religion or belief, in worship, teaching, practice and observance.'

And Article 14 provides:

> The enjoyment of the rights and freedoms set forth in this Convention shall be secured without discrimination on any ground such as sex, race, colour, language, religion, political or other opinion, national or social origin, association with a national minority, property, birth or other status.

Article 1 of the Protocol establishes that the duty to pay tax falls within its field of application. Accordingly, although Article 14 has no independent existence, but complements the substantive provisions, the applicant would succeed if he could show that his obligation to pay church tax was discriminatory. Convention jurisprudence establishes that Article 14 protects individuals in similar situations from discrimination in their enjoyment of their rights under the Convention and its Protocols.[26] However, a difference of treatment will only be discriminatory if it 'has no objective and reasonable justification', that is if it does not pursue a legitimate aim, or if there is no 'reasonable relationship of proportionality between the means employed and the aim sought to be realised'.[27]

Examining the facts in the light of these principles, the Court found that, as regards the right to a reduction of the church tax, Dr Darby's situation was similar to that of other non-members of the Church of Sweden. On the issue of justification the Court found that the distinction between residents and non-residents was based largely on administrative convenience and that the Government had not sought to argue that it had a legitimate aim. The Court therefore concluded that there had been a violation of Article 14 in conjunction with Article 1 of Protocol No. 1.

As the Court also decided that it was unnecessary to examine the complaints under Article 9, the only remaining issue was just satisfaction under Article 50. As regards pecuniary damage, the applicant claimed repayment of the disputed tax, together with interest, and this sum was awarded. He claimed a much larger sum as compensation for non-pecuniary damage, but here the Court concluded that the judgment itself provided just satisfaction. The claim in respect of costs and expenses was challenged by the Government and, making an equitable assessment, the Court awarded a reduced sum under this head.

If the Court had approached this case in the same way as the Commission, this would have been its first case on Article 9. However Article 1 of Protocol No. 1, which was also in issue in the *Fredin* case (Case No. 13), is much more familiar and it is not surprising that the Court preferred to examine Dr Darby's complaint on this basis. In 1987, following a proposal made by the Parliamentary Ombudsman, Sweden amended its legislation on the church tax. As a result, individuals in the applicant's position are now treated in the same way as residents.

Right to be brought before an 'officer authorized by law to exercise judicial power' (Article 5(3))—just satisfaction (Article 50)

Case No. 6. Huber case.[28] The Court held by 21 votes to 1 that Switzerland had committed a violation of Article 5(3) of the Convention because a Zürich District

[26] For an illustration of the importance of this requirement, see the *Fredin* case (Case No. 13, below).

[27] See the *Inze* case, Series A, No. 126, at para. 41.

[28] ECHR, judgment of 23 October 1990, Series A, No. 188. This case was decided by the plenary Court.

Attorney acted as the prosecuting authority in a case in which in earlier proceedings he had charged the applicant and ordered her detention on remand. As just satisfaction under Article 50, the Government was unanimously ordered to pay the applicant 4,492 Swiss francs in respect of her costs and expenses.

On 11 August 1983 a Zürich District Attorney, J, issued a warrant for the arrest of the applicant, Mrs Huber, on the grounds that she was suspected of involvement in a prostitution ring and of having given false evidence. She was released from detention on 19 August. In October 1984 an indictment signed by J was drawn up against Mrs Huber, alleging *inter alia* that she had given false evidence in judicial proceedings. At the trial before the Zürich District Court J did not assume the role of prosecuting counsel, although he would have been entitled to do so because, under the Cantonal Code of Criminal Procedure, as the prosecuting authority he was a party to the trial proceedings. Mrs Huber was acquitted by the District Court, but was subsequently convicted in the Court of Appeal of attempting to commit the same offence and fined a substantial sum. Appeals by the applicant against this decision were unsuccessful.

In her application to the Commission in February 1987 Mrs Huber relied on Article 5(3) of the Convention, complaining that J had both ruled on her detention and indicted her. In its report in April 1989 the Commission expressed the opinion that there had been a violation of Article 5(3). The Commission and the Government then referred the case to the Court.

Article 5(1)(*c*) of the Convention authorizes 'the lawful arrest or detention of a person effected for the purpose of bringing him before the competent legal authority on reasonable suspicion of having committed an offence . . . '. And Article 5(3) provides:

> Everyone arrested or detained in accordance with the provisions of paragraph 1(*c*) of this Article shall be brought promptly before a judge or other officer authorized by law to exercise judicial power and shall be entitled to trial within a reasonable time or to release pending trial. Release may be conditioned by guarantees to appear for trial.

The case law on this provision establishes that, in order to qualify as 'a judge or other officer authorized by law to exercise judicial power', the person who deals with an applicant's detention on remand must be independent of the executive and of the parties. In a number of recent cases concerning the detention of military personnel, the Court has held that an official known as the *auditeur-militair* did not satisfy this requirement because, *inter alia*, after dealing with the issue of detention he could also be called upon to assume the role of prosecuting authority in the Military Court.[29] On the other hand, in the *Schiesser* case[30] in 1979 the Court held that the Zürich District Attorney did so qualify, the only difference from the present case being that in *Schiesser* he had not actually acted as the prosecuting authority and drawn up the indictment. The question in *Huber* was thus whether the more stringent test of independence and impartiality laid down in the Court's recent case law had effectively overruled the earlier decision, or whether, as the Government argued, the decision in the *Schiesser* case should be followed.

Dealing first with the facts, the Court noted that J intervened initially at the

[29] See the cases of *de Jong, Baljet and van den Brink*, *van der Sluijs, Zuiderveld and Klappe* and *Duinhof and Duijf*, Series A, Nos. 77–9, and this *Year Book*, 55 (1984), p. 377, and the *Pauwels* case, Series A, No. 135, and this *Year Book*, 59 (1988), p. 394.

[30] ECHR, judgment of 4 December 1979, Series A, No. 34, and this *Year Book*, 50 (1979), p. 270.

stage of investigation. He considered whether it was necessary to charge the applicant and ordered her detention on remand, then conducted the investigation. Subsequently, fourteen months after the arrest, he acted as prosecuting authority in drawing up the indictment, although he did not assume the role of prosecuting counsel at the trial. As regards the law, the Court referred to its decisions in cases involving the *auditeur-militair* and stated that the same principles must apply in relation to justice under the ordinary law. While recognizing that 'the Convention does not rule out the possibility of the judicial officer who orders the detention carrying out other duties', it held that 'his impartiality is capable of appearing open to doubt . . . if he is entitled to intervene in the subsequent criminal proceedings as a representative of the prosecuting authority'.[31] Thus, without expressly overruling the decision in the *Schiesser* case, the Court rejected the Government's argument that it should be followed and decided that there had been a violation of Article 5(3).

As regards the issue of just satisfaction, the Court rejected Mrs Huber's claim for a large sum of compensation for alleged pecuniary damage on the ground that no damage resulting from the breach had been established. The Court also decided that no award was required in respect of non-pecuniary damage. The claim for costs and expenses was more successful, although the award in respect of costs at Strasbourg was much less than the sum claimed.

Judge Matscher dissented on the ground that a complete separation of functions between prosecution, investigation and judgment, though desirable in principle, was an impractical objective, and because he considered that the issue of independence and impartiality should be determined in the light of the situation at the time of the remand proceedings without reference to possible subsequent events. He also maintained that the decision in the *Schiesser* case should have been followed, and regarded the decisions on the *auditeur-militair* to be distinguishable.

Another aspect of Article 5(3) was examined in the *Letellier* case (Case No. 46).

Trial within a reasonable time (Article 6(1))—application to criminal proceedings with a civil component—the meaning of 'contestation' *in Article 6(1)*

Case No. 7. Moreira de Azevedo case.[32] The Court held unanimously that Portugal had violated Article 6(1) of the Convention on account of the length of criminal proceedings.

In 1977 the applicant, who was a bus driver, was shot in the head by G, one of his brothers-in-law. Criminal proceedings were instituted against G in which the applicant intervened as an assistant (*assistente*) of the prosecuting authority. The applicant did not submit a formal claim for damages in connection with these proceedings. In February 1985 a first instance court convicted G of assault and ordered him to pay the applicant damages in an amount to be determined in proceedings for the enforcement of the judgment. However, in October 1985 the Oporto Court of Appeal allowed G's appeal and declared the criminal proceedings to be out of time. An appeal from this decision by the applicant on a point of law was dismissed by the Supreme Court in May 1986.

In his application to the Commission in November 1984 Mr Moreira de Azevedo

[31] Judgment, para. 43.

[32] ECHR, judgment of 23 October 1990, Series A, No. 189. The Court consisted of the following Chamber of Judges: Ryssdal (President); Cremona, Pinheiro Farinha, Spielmann, De Meyer, Martens, Palm (Judges).

invoked Article 6(1) of the Convention on account of the length of the proceedings. In its report in July 1989 the Commission expressed the opinion by a narrow majority that there had been no violation of this provision. The Commission then referred the case to the Court.

The relevant part of Article 6(1) provides:

> In the determination of his civil rights and obligations . . . everyone is entitled to a . . . hearing within a reasonable time by [a] . . . tribunal . . .

Having rejected a preliminary objection from the Government based on an alleged failure to exhaust domestic remedies, the Court addressed a more substantial argument concerning the applicability of the Convention. According to the Government there was no sign in the contested proceedings of any '*contestation*' (dispute) relating to the applicant's 'civil rights and obligations'. He had never claimed compensation for the injury suffered and the status of *assistente* was not equivalent to such a claim. It followed that there were no proceedings relevant to Mr Moreira de Azevedo's claim and consequently Article 6(1) was inapplicable to the case.

The above argument had persuaded a majority of the Commission, but was rejected by the Court. Observing that the right to a fair trial is so important that there can be no justification for interpreting Article 6(1) narrowly, the Court went on to say that 'Conformity with the spirit of the Convention requires that the word "contestation" should not be construed too technically and that it should be given a substantive rather than a formal meaning.'[33] It then decided that the facts of the case showed that there had been a dispute and that the case concerned the determination of a right. The impact on civil proceedings of the status of *assistente* was admittedly the subject of controversy among Portuguese legal writers, but in the light of the principles laid down by the Supreme Court in a case in 1976, the European Court considered that to intervene as an *assistente* was equivalent to filing a claim for compensation in civil proceedings. In view of this finding it ruled that Article 6(1) was applicable.

The period to be taken into consideration did not begin on the date of the incident in question (1977), but only when the Convention entered into force with regard to Portugal (9 November 1978). It ended in May 1986 with the Supreme Court's judgment. To decide whether this period of more than seven years was acceptable, the Court applied the criteria laid down in its case law. The case was not complex and the Court observed that the applicant was not obliged to take various steps which the Government suggested would have expedited the proceedings. Part of the delay was attributable to the inefficiency of the medical authorities, but the Court recalled that 'the State is responsible for all its authorities and not merely its judicial organs'.[34] As the Government had failed to show what practical and effective measures Portuguese law provided to accelerate the progress of the criminal proceedings in the present case, the Court decided that a 'reasonable time' had been exceeded and that there was a violation of Article 6(1).

The question of just satisfaction under Article 50, which the Court found was not yet ready for decision, was reserved and as Case No. 52 is described below.

This was the first of a large number of cases on this aspect of Article 6(1) which

[33] Judgment, para. 66.
[34] Ibid., para. 73.

were decided in the period under review.[35] Here, as in the later cases, the Court's determination of the reasonable time issue involved an application of well-established standards, but the difference of opinion with the Commission over the applicability of the Convention raises an important general point. Cases in which issues of criminal and civil liability become so intertwined are relatively rare in this context and there is little guidance from previous case law as to how they should be approached. By adopting a broad interpretation of the Convention and disregarding technical considerations, the Court has now made a further contribution to its effectiveness.

Right to take proceedings to contest the lawfulness of detention (Article 5(4))—application to prisoners serving a discretionary life sentence—right to compensation for unlawful arrest or detention (Article 5(5))—just satisfaction (Article 50)

Case No. 8. Thynne, Wilson and Gunnell case.[36] In these cases, which concerned three men who were serving discretionary life sentences of imprisonment in the United Kingdom, the Court held by 18 votes to 1 that the absence of a judicial procedure to determine the continued lawfulness of their detention, and, in the case of two of the applicants, the lawfulness of their redetention after they had been released, constituted a violation of Article 5(4) of the Convention. Since the above violation did not give rise to an enforceable right to compensation before the courts in the United Kingdom, it held that in the case of one applicant there had also been a violation of Article 5(5). As just satisfaction the Court awarded the first applicant £4,500, less 7,845 French francs, and the second and third applicants jointly £18,000, less 24,849.98 French francs, in respect of their costs and expenses.

Each of the applicants was convicted of several serious sexual offences and sentenced to a discretionary life sentence of imprisonment. In so doing the national courts recognized the need to punish each applicant for the gravity of their offences, but also had regard to their mental instability and the likelihood of their committing further offences which made them a danger to the public.

The first applicant, Mr Thynne, was sentenced in 1975 and has been in custody ever since, although he has twice absconded from prison. A Local Review Committee recommended that he should be released in May 1989, but the Parole Board subsequently recommended that he should remain in custody with a further review one year after his transfer to an open prison. It is accepted that he has served the punitive stage of his sentence and that his continued detention now rests on an assessment of the risk to the public.

The second applicant, Mr Wilson, was sentenced in 1972 and released on conditional licence in 1982. However, five months after his release he was recalled to prison following a recommendation from the Parole Board because his conduct was causing concern. In June 1989 the Local Review Committee recommended a further review in two years' time, with a proviso that if his health so deteriorated that he no longer posed a threat, the case should be reviewed earlier. In normal circumstances the next review would be in October 1991.

The third applicant, Mr Gunnell, was sentenced in 1965. Like Mr Wilson, he was released on conditional licence in 1982, but recalled to prison within a year

[35] See Cases Nos. 16 to 18, 19 to 33, 34 and 43 to 45, below.

[36] ECHR, judgment of 25 October 1990, Series A, No. 190. This case was decided by the plenary Court.

following two incidents at the beginning of 1983. His case was then reviewed by the Parole Board which recommended his release a month later, subject to arrangements being made relating to housing and psychiatric supervision. However, the Home Secretary, after consulting with the Lord Chief Justice and the trial judge in accordance with section 67(1) of the Criminal Justice Act 1967, decided not to accept the Board's recommendation. In November 1983 the Court of Appeal dismissed applications from Mr Gunnell for judicial review of the decisions of the Parole Board and the Home Secretary, and for discovery of the documents relating to their determination of his case. In September 1988 he was again released on licence. However, in September 1990 the applicant pleaded guilty to one charge of attempted rape, five charges of indecent assault and three charges of robbery. He was sentenced again to life imprisonment, the life sentence for his original offences having already been revoked.

In their applications to the Commission on various dates in 1985 the applicants each relied on Article 5(4) of the Convention and Mr Wilson also invoked Article 5(5). The Commission then joined the applications and in its report in September 1989 expressed the opinion that there had been a violation of Article 5(4) in each case and that Mr Wilson had also been the victim of a violation of Article 5(5). The Commission then referred the case to the Court.

Article 5(4), which was quoted in Case No. 1, lays down that a person who is deprived of his liberty by arrest or detention shall be entitled 'to take proceedings by which the lawfulness of his detention shall be decided speedily by a court . . . '. The Court's case law indicates that the review required by this provision may or may not be a once and for all affair depending upon the particular circumstances. Thus in the case of a criminal conviction and detention under Article 5(1)(*a*) review is normally deemed to be incorporated in the original conviction and nothing further is required. In the case of a person who is detained as a person 'of unsound mind' under Article 5(1)(*e*), on the other hand, regular reviews will usually be regarded as necessary to confirm that the detention is still justified. In the *Weeks* case[37] in 1987 the Court held that a procedure for subsequent review was also required where a person had been given an indeterminate life sentence. The central question in the present case was whether the same principle applied here.

The applicants maintained that it did on the ground that a discretionary life sentence consists of a punitive element (the 'tariff' period) and a security element, and that as the latter depends on factors which are susceptible to change, a right to judicial review at reasonable intervals is required. The Government, however, maintained that the *Weeks* case was not in point because there the offence itself was not particularly serious and the security element predominated. In the present cases, in contrast, the offences were very serious and the sentencing courts had emphasized the punitive element. Although this argument was developed at some length, it did not convince the Court.

In the Court's view each of the applicants was given a life sentence because, in addition to the need for punishment, they were considered to be suffering from a mental or personality disorder and to be dangerous and in need of treatment. In English law the discretionary life sentence had been developed to deal with such cases, and although the punitive element here was admittedly much more promi-

[37] ECHR, judgment of 2 March 1987, Series A, No. 114, and this *Year Book*, 58 (1987), p. 470.

nent than in the *Weeks* case, that case offered a relevant parallel. In the case of each applicant the tariff element of the sentence had now expired; consequently the grounds justifying their continued detention were essentially similar to those in the *Weeks* case and the earlier *Van Droogenbroeck* case.[38] Observing that 'the factors of mental instability and dangerousness are susceptible to change over the passage of time and new issues of lawfulness may thus arise in the course of detention',[39] the Court held that it followed that the applicants were entitled to take proceedings to have the lawfulness of their continued detention decided by a court at reasonable intervals and to have the lawfulness of any redetention decided by a court.

Having established that Article 5(4) was applicable, the Court then had to decide whether its requirements had been satisfied. This was a relatively simple matter. It will be recalled from Case No. 1 that the 'court' referred to in Article 5(4) does not have to be able to substitute its own discretion for that of the decision-making authority, but does have to possess a wide power of review. As in the *Weeks* case, the Court decided that neither the Parole Board nor the judicial review proceedings satisfied these requirements. It therefore concluded that in the case of each applicant there had been a breach of this provision.

Mr Wilson had also put forward a claim under Article 5(5). This provision, which was quoted in the *Wassink* case (Case No. 3), guarantees a right to compensation for unlawful arrest or detention. As the breach of Article 5(4) could not give rise to an enforceable claim for compensation in the English courts, the Court held that in Mr Wilson's case this article too had been violated.

As just satisfaction the applicants claimed various sums in respect of the feelings of 'helplessness and frustration' they had allegedly suffered on account of the breach of Article 5(4), but the Court, considering that its judgment constituted adequate satisfaction, dismissed these claims. The applicants' claims in respect of their costs and expenses, however, were unanimously allowed.

Only one member of the Court voted against the decisions on Articles 5(4) and 5(5). In a characteristically forthright dissenting opinion, Judge Thór Vilhjálmsson reiterated the objections to the Court's approach which he had originally put forward in the *Weeks* case[40] and endorsed the Government's argument that splitting sentences into their 'punitive' and 'security' elements presents considerable practical difficulties. This would certainly be a powerful objection if it were sought to introduce Article 5(4) into the area of sentencing generally. In the present cases, however, indeterminate sentences were clearly being used in part for security purposes and so, as in the *Weeks* case, there was a close parallel between the position of a convicted person and that of a mental patient. A procedure to ensure that the need for continued detention is examined regularly would thus appear to be indispensable.

Right to liberty (Article 5(1))—right to have the lawfulness of detention decided 'speedily' (Article 5(4))—just satisfaction (Article 50)

[38] ECHR, judgment of 24 June 1982, Series A, No. 50, and this *Year Book*, 53 (1982), p. 314.

[39] Judgment, para. 76.

[40] In the *Weeks* case the Court arrived at its decision by 13 votes to 4. Sir Vincent Evans, who dissented on this point with Judge Thór Vilhjálmsson in that case, was also a member of the Court in the present case, but on this occasion voted with the majority.

Case No. 9. Koendjbiharie case.[41] In this case, which concerned detention in a psychiatric hospital in the Netherlands, the Court held unanimously that there had been a violation of Article 5(4) of the Convention. As just satisfaction under Article 50 the Government was ordered to pay the applicant 18,989.62 guilders, less 12,397.50 French francs, in respect of his costs and expenses.

In 1979 the applicant, who lived in the Netherlands, was convicted of rape, aggravated by a previous conviction for a similar offence. The District Court ordered that when he had served his prison sentence he should be held 'at the Government's disposal' and, as a result, he was subsequently interned in a psychiatric hospital. On 17 May 1984 the applicant, who considered that his detention in hospital had become unlawful, requested his immediate release. On the same day the Crown Prosecutor sought a one year extension of the placement, which in his view was due to terminate on 8 July 1984. On 21 September 1984 this application was granted.

Mr Koendjbiharie applied to the Commission in March 1985 alleging that he was the victim of a violation of numerous articles of the Convention. In its report in October 1989 the Commission expressed the unanimous opinion that there had been a violation of Articles 5(1) and 5(4), but no violation of Articles 6(1) and 6(3) or of Articles 3 and 14. The Commission then referred the case to the Court.

Although the main issue in this case concerned Article 5(4), before considering that provision the Court dealt with the applicant's claim that the order extending his confinement had not been made 'in accordance with a procedure prescribed by law', as required by Article 5(1). On this point the applicant drew attention to a number of alleged procedural deficiencies: the application for an extension of the confinement was lodged after the statutory time limit had expired; when the extension was ordered no record had been drawn up of the hearing and the decision had not been given within the required two month time limit; and, finally, the decision had never been served on the applicant, as only his lawyer had received a copy of it a month later. One member of the Court considered that in view of these allegations it was necessary for the Court to examine the applicant's rights under Article 5(1).[42] The majority, however, held that as the complaints in question all related to the proceedings for the extension of the confinement, it was appropriate to examine them, if necessary, under Article 5(4). The Court therefore decided not to consider the complaint under Article 5(1).

Article 5(4), which was quoted in Case No. 1, guarantees a 'speedy' review by a court of the lawfulness of arrest or detention. In the Court's view the contested proceedings in the present case amounted to an 'automatic periodic review of a judicial character', which was prescribed for situations of this type in the case of *X v. United Kingdom*.[43] Furthermore, the Court observed, the case law on Articles 5(1) and 5(4) establishes that:

> . . . in order to satisfy the requirements of the Convention, such review must comply with both the substantive and procedural rules of the national legislation and moreover be con-

[41] ECHR, judgment of 25 October 1990, Series A, No. 185 B. The Court consisted of the following Chamber of Judges: Ryssdal (President); Thór Vilhjálmsson, Pettiti, Walsh, Bernhardt, Spielmann, Valticos, Martens, Foighel (Judges).

[42] See the dissenting opinion of Judge Bernhardt.

[43] ECHR, judgment of 5 November 1981, Series A, No. 46, and this *Year Book*, 52 (1981), p. 347.

ducted in conformity with the aim of Article 5: to protect the individual against arbitrariness, in particular with regard to the time taken to give a decision.[44]

In the present case the Court of Appeal had allowed the application for extension more that four months after it was lodged. Since no justification for this delay had been put forward, the European Court decided that there had been a failure to decide the issue 'speedily' and consequently a violation of Article 5(4).

As the complaints regarding Articles 3, 6 and 14 were withdrawn, the only remaining issue was the applicant's just satisfaction. Mr Koendjbiharie claimed compensation of 100 guilders for each day of 'unlawful' detention, but the Court considered that the judgment itself constituted sufficient just satisfaction for any frustration which the applicant might have felt over the length of the proceedings. It therefore awarded him nothing under this head. He was, however, awarded a sum representing his costs and expenses before the Strasbourg organs, less what he had already received by way of legal aid.

Right to liberty (Article 5(1))—right to be informed of the reasons for arrest (Article 5(2))—right to have the lawfulness of detention determined by a court (Article 5(4))—right to compensation for unlawful arrest or detention (Article 5(5))

Case No. 10. Keus case.[45] In this case, which concerned the detention of a person in a psychiatric hospital in the Netherlands after he had completed a prison sentence, the Court held unanimously that there had been no violation of Article 5(2) of the Convention and by 5 votes to 4 that there had been no violation of Article 5(4).

In 1981 the applicant was convicted by a court in the Netherlands of murder and attempted armed robbery. The District Court ordered that, after he had served his prison sentence, he should be held 'at the Government's disposal', and as a result he was subsequently confined in a psychiatric hospital for treatment. On 4 December 1985 the Crown Prosecutor applied for a two-year extension of his placement; neither the applicant, who had absconded from the hospital, nor his lawyer were informed of this application. The District Court granted the application on 7 January 1986, following a hearing attended by the Crown Prosecutor and a member of the hospital staff, but not by the applicant or a person representing him. Mr Keus later returned to the hospital where he was again confined, in accordance with the above-mentioned decision.

In his application to the Commission in June 1986 Mr Keus relied on various parts of Articles 5 and 6. In its report in October 1989 the Commission expressed the unanimous opinion that there had been a violation of Articles 5(4) and 5(5), but not of Articles 5(1), 6(1) and 6(3), and that it was unnecessary to examine separately whether there had been a violation of Article 5(2). The Commission then referred the case to the Court.

The facts in this case were rather similar to those of the *Koendjbiharie* case (Case No. 9) and, as in those proceedings, the applicant's first complaint was that the order extending his confinement had not been made 'in accordance with a procedure prescribed by law', and thus violated his right to liberty as guaranteed by

[44] Judgment, para. 27.

[45] ECHR, judgment of 25 October 1990, Series A, No. 185 C. The Court consisted of the following Chamber of Judges: Ryssdal (President); Thór Viljhálmsson, Pettiti, Walsh, Bernhardt, Spielmann, Valticos, Martens, Foighel (Judges).

Article 5(1). It will be recalled that in the *Koendjbiharie* case the Court held that a similar complaint related to the proceedings for the extension of the confinement and consequently should be examined under Article 5(4). In the present case it adopted the same approach.

The applicant's complaint under Article 5(4) was that the lack of any information concerning the proceedings to extend the confinement had prevented him from taking part in the hearing before the District Court and that there was no other remedy satisfying the Convention's requirements. The Court noted that, as in the *Koendjbiharie* case, the contested proceedings amounted to an 'automatic periodic review of a judicial character', and reiterated the conditions which, according to its jurisprudence, such a review must satisfy. It observed that in ordering the extension of the placement the District Court had infringed neither national law nor the Convention. It pointed out, however, that 'a measure depriving a person of his liberty does not afford the fundamental guarantees against arbitrariness if it is taken following proceedings in which neither the person concerned himself nor a person representing him has participated . . . '.[46] From this it followed that the applicant retained the right protected by Article 5(4) and on his return to the clinic was entitled to institute proceedings to test the lawfulness of his detention.

The Court decided, however, that at that time a remedy satisfying the requirements of Article 5(4) had been available to Mr Keus in the form of an interlocutory application to the President of the District Court. It was true that the applicant had chosen not to use it, but, said the Court, whether or not Mr Keus considered it advisable to make such an application, the remedy in question had been available to him. It therefore concluded that there had been no violation of Article 5(4).

Two other claims put forward by the applicant were also rejected. The first concerned Article 5(2), which provides:

> Everyone who is arrested shall be informed promptly, in a language which he understands, of the reasons for his arrest and of any charge against him.

The applicant maintained that this provision placed the authorities under a duty to notify him of the application to extend his confinement and the order extending it, and that as he himself had absconded, they should have alerted his lawyer. Not surprisingly, this argument was summarily dismissed. The applicant also complained of a violation of Article 5(5) which, it will be recalled, provides a right to compensation for unlawful arrest or detention. Since, however, no breach of any other provision of Article 5 had been identified, this claim automatically failed.

Four judges dissented on the issue of Article 5(4).[47] In their view the possibility of an interlocutory application to the President of the District Court had been mentioned by the Government so late in the proceedings that the existence of this remedy could not be regarded as sufficiently certain. As they pointed out, if the issue had been one of non-exhaustion of domestic remedies, the Government would not have been permitted, almost at the end of the proceedings, to put forward a remedy that had never been previously mentioned. Although in the present case the question of a remedy arose in the context of Article 5(4) rather than Article 26, there was, as the dissenting judges indicated, a strong case for treating it in the same way.

[46] Judgment, para. 27.

[47] See the joint dissenting opinion of Judges Ryssdal, Pettiti, Bernhardt and Spielmann.

Right to a fair trial (Article 6(1))—right to examine witnesses (Article 6(3)(d))—just satisfaction (Article 50)

Case No. 11. Delta case.[48] In this case, which concerned France, the Court held unanimously that there had been a violation of Article 6(3)(*d*) of the Convention, taken in conjunction with Article 6(1). The applicant had not received a fair trial because his conviction on a criminal charge had been based to a decisive degree on statements by the complainant and a friend, who were interviewed by the police, but not examined as witnesses at the trial. As just satisfaction the Government was ordered to pay the applicant 100,000 French francs in respect of damage suffered.

In May 1983 the applicant, who was born in Guadeloupe, was convicted of robbery in the Paris underground and sentenced to 3 years' imprisonment. The French court's decision was based on evidence given at the trial by a policeman who had not witnessed the attack but who, while accompanied by the 16-year-old victim and her friend, had arrested the applicant. Mr Delta was not formally confronted with the two girls and they did not attend the trial, despite having been summoned by the prosecution. In September 1983 the Paris Court of Appeal dismissed an appeal by the applicant alleging mistaken identification. In doing so it refused Mr Delta's application to have the victim, her friend and two defence witnesses called. In October 1984 the Court of Cassation dismissed the applicant's appeal on points of law.

In his application to the Commission in August 1984 Mr Delta relied *inter alia* on Article 6(3)(*d*) of the Convention, taken in conjunction with Article 6(1). In its report in October 1989 the Commission expressed the unanimous opinion that there had been a violation of these provisions. The Commission then referred the case to the Court.

It will be recalled from the *Windisch* case (Case No. 4) that Article 6(3)(*d*) provides for the right of an accused to examine and to have examined witnesses, both for and against him, as a specific aspect of the right to a fair trial which is guaranteed by Article 6(1). It will also be recalled that these rights require that the accused should normally have an adequate and proper opportunity to challenge and question an adverse witness, either at the time the witness makes her statement or at some later stage of the proceedings. In the present case the Court, after reiterating the above principles, pointed out that the victim of the attack and her friend were interviewed by the police, but not by an investigating judge owing to the use of a direct committal procedure. Before the criminal court the defence had not asked for any witnesses to be called; nevertheless the prosecution had summoned the two girls and, as they did not appear, could have compelled them to attend. In the Court of Appeal, on the other hand, the applicant had expressly asked for the two girls and two other witnesses to be summoned, but this request had been refused.

In the light of the facts the Court decided that neither the applicant nor his counsel ever had an adequate opportunity to examine the two girls, whose testimony had been crucial because the file on Mr Delta's case contained no other evidence. Thus the applicant had been unable to test the witnesses' reliability or cast doubt on their credibility. The Court therefore concluded that the rights of the defence

48 ECHR, judgment of 19 December 1990, Series A, No. 191. The Court consisted of the following Chamber of Judges: Ryssdal (President); Cremona, Thór Vilhjálmsson, Gölcüklü, Pettiti, Sir Vincent Evans, Macdonald, Russo, De Meyer (Judges).

had been subject to such restrictions that the applicant had not received a fair trial. Accordingly, it agreed with the Commission that there had been a violation of Article 6(3)(*d*), taken together with Article 6(1).

As the Court considered that it was unnecessary to examine various other complaints arising out of the same facts, the only other issue was the applicant's just satisfaction under Article 50. As regards compensation for damage, the Court observed that it could not speculate as to the outcome of Mr Delta's trial if he had received all the guarantees of Article 6, but that it was not unreasonable to regard him as having suffered a loss of real opportunities. It therefore awarded him a sum under this head. As regards costs and expenses, the applicant had foregone legal aid in the domestic proceedings, but had received it for the proceedings at Strasbourg. His counsel, on the other hand, sought compensation for the loss of earnings he had sustained in defending Mr Delta free of charge. The Court, however, pointed out that according to its case law[49] an applicant's lawyer cannot rely on Article 50 to claim just satisfaction on his own account. It therefore dismissed this part of the claim.

Right to respect for private and family life (Article 8)—freedom from inhuman or degrading treatment (Article 3)—friendly settlement (Rule 49(2))

Case No. 12. Djeroud case.[50] The Court decided to strike this case, which concerned France, out of the list. It reached this decision unanimously, following the conclusion of a friendly settlement between the Government and the applicant.

The applicant, who was born in Algeria in 1958 and had Algerian nationality, moved to France in 1959 with his family who set up home there. His mother and his six brothers and sisters, four of whom have French nationality, live in France. In 1977 and 1978 the applicant was convicted *inter alia* on theft charges and ordered to be deported. He went to Algeria of his own accord in 1980 but returned to France in 1982 and, while living under a provisional residence permit, committed further offences. He was deported in 1985 and 1987 in accordance with the 1979 order but on each occasion returned to France. In December 1987 he refused to board a flight to Algeria, as a result of which he was sentenced to a term of imprisonment. Since 1988 he had been subject to a compulsory residence order confining him to a municipality near Paris until such time as he chose to comply with the deportation order. An application for political asylum in 1987 was unsuccessful.

The applicant took his case to the European Commission in September 1987 alleging that his deportation constituted an interference with his right to respect for his private and family life contrary to Article 8 and also constituted inhuman and degrading treatment in breach of Article 3. In its report in March 1990 the Commission upheld the first of these complaints, but rejected the other. The Commission then referred the case to the Court.

The Registrar of the Court was subsequently notified of a settlement concluded between Mr Djeroud and the French Government. Under its terms the applicant obtained a revocation of the deportation order against him, a residence certificate

[49] See, for example, the *Artico* case, Series A, No. 37, para. 40.

[50] ECHR, judgment of 23 January 1991, Series A, No. 191 B. The Court consisted of the following Chamber of Judges: Ryssdal (President); Matscher, Pettiti, Sir Vincent Evans, Russo, De Meyer, Valticos, Martens, Morenilla (Judges).

valid for ten years and the payment of 150,000 French francs as compensation. In return Mr Djeroud agreed to discontinue the proceedings.

In view of the settlement the Government asked the Court to strike the case off its list in accordance with Rule 49(2) of the Rules of the Court which provides:

> Where the Chamber is informed of a friendly settlement, arrangement or other fact of a kind to provide a solution of the matter, it may, after consulting, if necessary, the Parties, the Delegates of the Commission and the applicant, strike the case out of the list.

The Commission had no objection. Thus the only question was whether reasons of public policy called for a continuation of the proceedings under Rule 49(4) which provides:

> The Chamber may, having regard to the responsibilities of the Court under Article 19 of the Convention, decide that, notwithstanding the notice of discontinuance, friendly settlement, arrangement or other fact referred to in paragraphs 1 and 2 of this Rule, it should proceed with the consideration of the case.

The Court ruled that there were no such reasons in the present case and so decided to strike it out of the list.

Right to the peaceful enjoyment of possessions (Article 1 of Protocol No. 1)—non-discrimination (Article 14)—right to a court (Article 6(1))—just satisfaction (Article 50)

Case No. 13. Fredin case.[51] The Court held unanimously that the revocation of a permit to exploit gravel on the applicants' property did not amount to a breach of either Article 1 of Protocol No. 1 or of Article 14 taken together with Article 1. However, it also held that the lack of any provision for judicial review of the revocation decision constituted a violation of Article 6(1). As just satisfaction under Article 50 Sweden was ordered to pay the applicant 10,000 Swedish kronor in respect of non-pecuniary damage and 75,000 kronor in respect of costs and expenses.

In 1963 Mr Fredin's parents were granted a permit to exploit an old gravel pit by a local administrative board. The permit provided for exploitation in three stages, each of which would not exceed ten years. However, no work was actually started. In 1977 Mr and Mrs Fredin became owners of the land and, after making a considerable investment in equipment, began to work the pit in 1980. In 1983 the exploitation permit was transferred to them, but the administrative board indicated that it intended to reconsider the issue of exploitation. In 1984 the board, acting under legislation passed in 1973 which permitted the revocation of permits, ordered exploitation to cease. The applicants appealed against the decision to the Government but were unsuccessful. The Government did, however, extend the validity of the permit until the end of 1988, on which date the extraction of gravel ceased. The Government's decisions were not, at that time,[52] subject to judicial review.

In their application to the Commission in March 1986 Mr and Mrs Fredin relied

[51] ECHR, judgment of 18 February 1991, Series A, No. 192. The Court consisted of the following Chamber of Judges: Ryssdal (President); Thór Vilhjálmsson, Pettiti, Walsh, Macdonald, Russo, De Meyer, Martens, Palm (Judges).

[52] This was subsequently changed by legislation providing for judicial review of certain administrative decisions which came into force in 1988.

on Article 6(1), Article 1 of Protocol No. 1 and Article 14. In its report in September 1989 the Commission expressed the unanimous opinion that there had been a violation of Article 6(1), but no violation of Article 1 of the Protocol taken either alone or in conjunction with Article 14. The Commission then referred the case to the Court.

The first provision considered by the Court was Article 1 of Protocol No. 1, which was quoted in Case No. 5. This article deals with both deprivation of possessions by the State and control of the use of property, which are distinct, but closely related, concepts. According to the applicants the revocation of their permit amounted to a deprivation of possessions. The Court, however, disagreed. Noting that there had been no formal or *de facto* expropriation and that exploitation had been at risk since the 1973 legislation, it decided that the measure constituted a control of the use of property, with the result that it fell under the second paragraph of Article 1.

To be permissible under the Protocol a control of the use of property must be lawful and have a legitimate aim, and the interference in question 'must achieve a "fair balance" between the demands of the general interest of the community and the requirements of the protection of the individual's fundamental rights'.[53] The first and second requirements were clearly satisfied—the revocation was lawful in Swedish law and met the Convention's own standards of legality,[54] while the aim of the legislation was the protection of the environment, 'an increasingly important consideration'[55] in today's society. The main question was thus the issue of proportionality.

On this point the Court observed that the effects of the revocation had to be assessed not simply in the light of the applicant's loss of their investment, but also in the context of the situation when they took over the land. Pointing out that the applicants must have been aware that they risked losing their permit as a result of the 1973 legislation, the Court held that they could not have had any legitimate expectation of being allowed to work the pit for an extended period. At no time had the authorities misled them or falsely raised their hopes, and a closing down period of almost four years was eventually granted. In the light of these considerations the Court concluded that the revocation decision was not disproportionate to the legitimate aim, with the result that there had been no violation of the Protocol.

The next provision to be considered was Article 14, which was also quoted in Case No. 5. It will be recalled that this provision provides a guarantee against discrimination in relation to the rights protected by the Convention and the Protocol, and that 'discrimination' means *inter alia* treating differently persons who are in similar situations. This requirement, which has not hitherto received much attention in the case law, assumed significance in the present case when the Commission concluded that the applicants had failed to show that their situation was similar to that of other gravel businesses whose permits had not been revoked, and on this account rejected their claim. Before the Court the applicants did not seek to refute this view, but argued instead that it was for the Government to explain how their business was different from others. The Court, however, rejected this argument

[53] Judgment, para. 51.

[54] The Court was urged to hold that the absence of judicial review in itself amounted to a violation of the principle of legality, but rejected the argument.

[55] Judgment, para. 48.

and, holding that there was no reason to assess the evidence differently from the Commission, decided that no issue of discrimination contrary to Article 14 arose.

The third and final substantive issue concerned Article 6(1), the relevant part of which provides:

> In the determination of his civil rights and obligation . . . everyone is entitled to a . . . hearing by [a] . . . tribunal . . .

The Court found that the applicants' right to develop their property in accordance with the applicable laws and regulations was a 'civil' right. It also found that there was a 'genuine and serious' dispute over the lawfulness of the impugned decisions. Thus Article 6 was applicable. However, at the time in question the dispute could be determined only by the Government as the final instance and there was no right of access to the courts as this provision requires. The Court therefore agreed with the Commission that there had been a violation of Article 6(1).

The issue of just satisfaction under Article 50 was soon dealt with. The applicants claimed an enormous sum as compensation for pecuniary damage, but the Court disallowed this on the ground that no causal link between the violation of Article 6(1) and the alleged damage had been shown. On the other hand, in respect of non-pecuniary damage and their costs and expenses the applicants were awarded reduced sums on an equitable basis.

Right to respect for family life (Article 8)—application to an alien subject to deportation for offences committed as an adolescent—the meaning of 'necessary in a democratic society' in Article 8(2)—non-discrimination (Article 14)—just satisfaction (Article 50)

Case No. 14. Moustaquim case.[56] In this case, which concerned Belgium, the Court held by 7 votes to 2 that there had been a violation of Article 8 of the Convention because the applicant's deportation had infringed his right to respect for his family life. As just satisfaction the Court ordered the Government to pay the applicant 100,000 Belgian francs in respect of non-pecuniary damage and 340,000 francs, less 10,730 French francs, in respect of his costs and expenses.

The applicant was born in Morocco in 1963 but had lived in Belgium since he was two with his parents and seven brothers and sisters. In November 1982 he was found guilty by the Liège Court of Appeal of 22 offences, committed in 1980 while he was still a minor, and sentenced to 26 months' imprisonment. The offences included aggravated theft and assault, and the applicant's conviction followed earlier proceedings before the juvenile courts at which no less than 147 charges of a similar nature had been considered. In February 1984 the applicant's deportation was ordered on the ground that he was a danger to society and had seriously prejudiced public order. In March the applicant was released and, having been unsuccessful in his attempts to challenge the order, was deported, going first to Spain, and then to Greece and Sweden. In 1989, however, permission was given to Mr Moustaquim to reside in Belgium for a trial period of two years and he returned there in January 1990.

In his application to the Commission in May 1986 Mr Moustaquim complained

[56] ECHR, judgment of 18 February 1991, Series A, No. 193. The Court consisted of the following Chamber of Judges: Ryssdal (President); Bindschedler-Robert, Matscher, Sir Vincent Evans, Bernhardt, De Meyer, Valticos, Palm, Foighel (Judges).

that his deportation had involved violations of several articles of the Convention. In its report in October 1989 the Commission expressed the opinion that there had been a breach of Article 8, but not of Article 14 taken together with Article 8, nor of Articles 3 and 7. The Commission then referred the case to the Court.

Article 8 of the Convention provides:

1. Everyone has the right to respect for his private and family life, his home and his correspondence.
2. There shall be no interference by a public authority with the exercise of this right except such as is in accordance with the law and is necessary in a democratic society in the interests of national security, public safety or the economic well-being of the country, for the prevention of disorder or crime, for the protection of health or morals, or for the protection of the rights and freedoms of others.

Having established that the order allowing the applicant to return to Belgium had not rendered the case devoid of purpose, the Court had to determine whether the applicant's deportation constituted an interference with his right to respect for his family life as guaranteed by Article 8(1) and, if so, whether the interference could be justified under Article 8(2). On the first point the Court found that the applicant had been living in Belgium, where his family also resided, and had never broken off relations with them. The deportation had, of course, resulted in their becoming separated, although the applicant had tried to remain in touch by correspondence. The Court therefore concluded that, despite certain doubts expressed by the Government, there had been an interference with the right to respect for family life.

The question of justification was more difficult. The Court was satisfied that the deportation was 'in accordance with the law' and had a legitimate aim, namely 'the prevention of disorder'. The crucial issue, then, as in so many cases involving the scope of the Convention's limitations, was whether the applicant's deportation could be regarded as 'necessary in a democratic society' to achieve its aim.

The Court began by observing that it did not underestimate the concern of the Contracting States to maintain public order 'in particular in exercising their right, as a matter of well-established international law and subject to their treaty obligations to control the entry, residence and expulsion of aliens'.[57] It noted, however, that the applicant's alleged offences had a number of special features. They all went back to when he had been an adolescent; criminal proceedings had been brought only in respect of 26 offences which had been spread over less than a year; and there had been a relatively long interval between the last offence in December 1980 and the deportation order in February 1984.

Turning to the applicant's personal situation, the Court pointed out that at the time of the deportation order all his close relatives were living in Belgium, with which they and the applicant had become closely connected. His family life had thus been seriously disrupted by the deportation, which the Advisory Board on Aliens had judged to be 'inappropriate'. In all the circumstances therefore the Court concluded that the means employed had been disproportionate to the legitimate aim pursued, with the result that there had been a violation of Article 8.

The only other claim to be considered[58] concerned Article 14, which was quoted

[57] Judgment, para. 43.

[58] As the applicant's complaints under Articles 3 and 7 had not been reiterated before the Court, it decided that it was unnecessary to deal with them.

earlier in Case No. 5. The applicant, uncertain perhaps whether a complaint based upon Article 8 alone would succeed, had argued that he was the victim of discrimination on the ground of nationality as regards respect for his family life, contrary to Article 14 taken together with Article 8. However, the Court agreed with the Commission that this complaint could not be sustained. This was because Article 14 safeguards individuals placed in similar situations and Mr Moustaquim's position could not be compared to that of juvenile delinquents who were Belgian nationals, or nationals of one of the other members of the European Communities. The former had a right to live in their own country, while preferential treatment of the latter had an objective and reasonable justification 'as Belgium belongs, together with those States, to a special legal order'.[59] There was therefore no violation of Article 14.

As just satisfaction for the violation of Article 8 the applicant claimed a large sum of compensation for pecuniary damage, based on a loss of possible earnings. This was, however, unanimously dismissed, as the Court could perceive no causal link between the breach of the Convention and the alleged damage. A claim for compensation for non-pecuniary damage, on the other hand, was allowed, though on a much reduced basis. A claim in respect of costs and expenses was also allowed, although as the applicant had failed to provide adequate particulars, the sum awarded was again reduced, with a further deduction of the amount already paid by the Council of Europe as legal aid.

Judges Bindschedler-Robert and Valticos dissented from the decision on Article 8 because they considered that the applicant's appalling record, when viewed alongside his somewhat tenuous family life, meant that the authorities were fully within their rights to deport him. There is room for this uncompromising view, although emphasizing, as the majority did, the applicant's youth and personal ties with Belgium may be thought conducive to a more sensitive decision. The conclusion that it is not contrary to the Convention to give preferential treatment to the nationals of members of the European Communities was not unexpected. The point has, however, not previously been made by the Court and adds a significant ruling to the case law on Article 14.

Right to a fair trial (Article 6(1))—right to examine witnesses (Article 6(3)(d))

Case No. 15. Isgrò case.[60] The Court held unanimously that the applicant's conviction on a criminal charge in Italy had not infringed Article 6(3)(*d*) of the Convention, taken in conjunction with Article 6(1).

In November 1978 criminal proceedings were begun against the applicant in connection with a kidnapping which resulted in the victim's death. In March 1980 the applicant was found guilty and sentenced to 30 years' imprisonment. On appeal the conviction was upheld but the sentence was reduced by 10 years. A further appeal on points of law to the Court of Cassation was unsuccessful.

The conviction of Mr Isgrò was based partly on records of statements made by a witness, D, in the absence of the applicant and his lawyer at the investigation stage, and on the results of a confrontation between D and the applicant at which the applicant's lawyer had not been present. D did not give evidence in court at any

[59] Judgment, para. 49.

[60] ECHR, judgment of 19 February 1991, Series A, No. 194 A. The Court consisted of the following Chamber of Judges: Ryssdal (President); Cremona, Gölcüklü, Pettiti, Russo, De Meyer, Palm, Foighel, Loizou (Judges).

stage because, although he had been summoned to appear, he proved to be untraceable.

In his application to the Commission in September 1984 Mr Isgrò relied on Article 6(3)(*d*) of the Convention in conjunction with Article 6(1). In its report in December 1989 the Commission expressed the opinion by 10 votes to 3 that these provisions had been violated. The Commission then referred the case to the Court.

After dismissing certain preliminary objections from the Government,[61] the Court considered the main issue. The principles governing the right to examine witnesses, as they have developed in the Court's case law, have been set out in Case No. 4 and will not be reiterated. In the present case the Court noted that D was not an anonymous witness and that the investigating judge had questioned him several times. The judge had also organized a confrontation at which the applicant had an opportunity to put questions directly to D and to discuss his allegations. Other factors which distinguished the case from *Windisch* (Case No. 4) and *Delta* (Case No. 11) were that the domestic courts had not based their decisions solely on the testimony of D, but had also taken into account other evidence, and that during the trial the applicant's lawyer had been able to challenge the accuracy of D's allegations and his credibility.

In the Court's view the way in which D's evidence had been taken and used indicated that any limitation which might have been imposed on the rights of the defence had not been such as to deprive the applicant of a fair trial. It therefore concluded that there had been no violation of the Convention.

Trial within a reasonable time (Article 6(1))—just satisfaction (Article 50)

Cases Nos. 16, 17 and 18. Brigandì case. *Zanghì* case. *Santilli* case.[62] In these cases, which concerned Italy, the Court held unanimously that there had been a violation of Article 6(1) of the Convention on account of the length of civil proceedings. As just satisfaction the Government was ordered to pay Mr Brigandì 15,000,000 lire in respect of damage and Mr Santilli 10,000,000 lire in respect of non-pecuniary damage, together with 4,000,000 lire for his costs and expenses.

The applicants in these cases had all been involved in civil litigation in Italy over extended periods of time. Mr Brigandì's action was for an injunction requiring the defendant to rebuild a demolished warehouse and had lasted for more than 17 years; Mr Zanghì's for an injunction and damages over the height of a party wall and had lasted more than 8 years; and Mr Santilli's against a bank over a loan and had lasted nearly 7 years. The action brought by Mr Santilli had now terminated, but those brought by the other two applicants were still unresolved.

In their applications to the Commission in 1985 the three applicants complained of a violation of Article 6(1) of the Convention in view of the length of the proceedings, and also of Article 1 of Protocol No. 1 (the right to the peaceful enjoyment of possessions). In its reports in November and December 1989 the Commission expressed the opinion that in all three cases there had been a violation of Article 6(1), but no violation of Article 1 of Protocol No. 1. The Commission then referred the cases to the Court.

[61] The objections in question concerned the applicant's status as a 'victim' for the purposes of Article 25 and the exhaustion of domestic remedies under Article 26. Neither received detailed discussion.

[62] ECHR, judgments of 19 February 1991, Series A, Nos. 194 B–D. The Court consisted of the following Chamber of Judges: Ryssdal (President); Cremona, Thór Vilhjálmsson, Bindschedler-Robert, Gölcüklü, Russo, Valticos, Martens, Morenilla (Judges).

Article 6(1) of the Convention, which has been quoted in Case No. 7, guarantees *inter alia* a hearing within a reasonable time in the determination of civil rights and obligations. The Court's first task in cases involving this right is to determine the period to be taken into account. In the present cases the Court determined these to be as follows: in the *Brigandì* case from 1 August 1973, when Italy's declaration recognizing the right of individual petition took effect, to 8 October 1990, when a judgment of the Messina Court of Appeal was filed; in the *Zanghì* case from 3 April 1982 to the present time; and in the *Santilli* case from 27 September 1979 to 18 June 1986. The question was therefore whether in the circumstances of each case these periods exceeded the Convention's standard.

Holding that in each case it was appropriate to make an overall assessment, the Court decided that in all three the lapses of time were unreasonable. In reaching its decision it took into account that the cases of Mr Brigandì and Mr Zanghì were not complex, although Mr Brigandì's action had involved several levels of jurisdiction. Mr Santilli's case, on the other hand, was complex and one of the adjournments had been due to the parties. However, in this case between the hearings the first instance court had allowed periods to elapse that were too long, and for nearly two years had been totally inactive. The Court therefore concluded that in each of the three cases there had been a violation of Article 6(1).

As the Court decided that it was unnecessary to investigate the complaints based upon Article 1 of Protocol No. 1, there only remained the question of just satisfaction. Here the Court applied the criteria laid down in its case law and, making an assessment on an equitable basis, awarded Mr Brigandì and Mr Santilli the sums mentioned earlier. Mr Zanghì had claimed only compensation for the alleged violation of Article 1 of Protocol No. 1, and the Court considered that it was still possible for the national courts to make reparation for the financial consequences of their failure to try the case within a reasonable time. That being so the Court decided that it was 'appropriate, as matters stand, to dismiss the claim'.[63]

These cases, each concerned with civil proceedings, were referred to the Court at the same time as fifteen others concerned with the length of criminal proceedings. The latter were also against Italy and as Cases Nos. 19 to 33 are examined below.

Trial within a reasonable time (Article 6(1))—right to legal assistance (Article 6(3)(c))—just satisfaction (Article 50)

Cases Nos. 19 to 33. Cases of *Motta, Manzoni, Pugliese (I), Alimena, Frau, Ficara, Viezzer, Angelucci, Maj, Girolami, Ferraro, Triggiani, Mori, Colacioppo* and *Adiletta and others*.[64] The Court held unanimously that in all of these cases there had been a violation of Article 6(1) of the Convention on account of the length of criminal or civil proceedings in Italy. In the *Alimena* case (Case No. 22) it also found that there had been an infringement of Article 6(3)(*c*) because the applicant had been denied effective legal representation. In each case the Government was ordered to pay specified sums to the applicant, or applicants, by way of just satisfaction.

[63] *Zanghì* judgment, para. 25.

[64] ECHR, judgments of 19 February 1991, Series A, Nos. 195 A–E (*Motta* to *Frau*), Nos. 196 A–E (*Ficara* to *Girolami*) and Nos. 197 A–E (*Ferraro* to *Adiletta*). These cases were all decided by the same Chamber which consisted of: Ryssdal (President); Matscher, Pettiti, Sir Vincent Evans, Russo, De Meyer, Valticos, Loizou and Morenilla (Judges).

The applicants in these cases were all involved in criminal proceedings in Italy on charges ranging from insulting a judge to extortion, forgery and political espionage. One applicant, Mr Motta, was also involved in civil proceedings there. In all cases the proceedings were prolonged. Furthermore in Mr Alimena's case the Court of Cassation held a hearing and dismissed his appeal without notifying his lawyer of the proceedings.

In their applications to the Commission on various dates between December 1982 and March 1988 the applicants all relied on Article 6(1) of the Convention. Mr Alimena also relied on Article 6(3)(*c*). In its reports in November and December 1989 the Commission expressed the opinion that there had been a violation of Article 6(1) on account of the length of the proceedings in each case and also in the case of Mr Alimena an infringement of Article 6(3)(*c*). The Commission then referred all the cases, together with those of *Brigandì*, *Zanghì* and *Santilli* (Cases Nos. 16, 17 and 18, above) to the Court.

To decide whether these cases had been concluded within a reasonable time the Court first established the period to be taken into account in each set of proceedings. These ranged from five years and two months in the *Pugliese (I)* case to thirteen years and five months in the case of *Adiletta and others*. It then noted that Article 6(1) of the Convention guarantees everyone the right to a final decision within a reasonable time in the determination of any criminal charge against him and, with reference to the *Motta* case, also of his civil rights and obligations. As noted earlier, the reasonableness of the length of proceedings must be assessed in the light of the specific circumstances, and the Court observed that in each of the present cases this called for an overall assessment. After commenting upon various aspects of the proceedings in question, which it is unnecessary to describe here, the Court decided that in each case the proceedings had exceeded a reasonable time. It therefore agreed with the Commission that in all fifteen cases there had been a violation of Article 6(1).

Article 6(3)(*c*) of the Convention provides that everyone charged with a criminal offence has the right:

> to defend himself in person or through legal assistance of his own choosing or, if he has not sufficient means to pay for legal assistance, to be given it free when the interests of justice so require . . .

In its decision in the *Artico* case[65] in 1980 the Court held that the Convention requires the provision of legal aid which is effective and also that the failure to provide such assistance is actionable even without proof that an applicant has been prejudiced thereby. As regards Mr Alimena's complaint, the Court had no difficulty in concluding that by holding a hearing without notifying the applicant's lawyer the Court of Cassation had deprived the applicant of effective legal assistance and that the Government's argument that the appeal had no prospects of success was irrelevant. It therefore agreed with the Commission that in Mr Alimena's case there had also been a violation of Article 6(3)(*c*).

The issue of just satisfaction under Article 50 called for the Court to apply its established criteria to the various claims for compensation for damage and the applicants' costs and expenses. Again it is unnecessary to examine these assessments in detail except to note that the sums awarded for damage ranged from nothing in the *Pugliese (I)* and *Girolami* cases, to 150,000,000 lire in the *Triggiani*

[65] ECHR, judgment of 13 May 1980, Series A, No. 37, and this *Year Book*, 51 (1980), p. 332.

case, and the reimbursement of costs and expenses from nothing in the *Pugliese (I)* case, to 6,008,600 lire and 743 French francs in the *Ferraro* case.

The decision to refer so many cases to the Court simultaneously, though unprecedented, has yet to be officially explained. It was not based on the need to develop the Convention's jurisprudence, for there have been numerous cases on this aspect of Article 6(1) and the present applications raised no new points of interpretation. Nor, as is sometimes the case, can the explanation be that the Commission was divided, because its opinions in the present cases were unanimous on virtually all points. What then is the explanation? In the light of the deplorable situation revealed by these cases it is tempting to conclude that they were referred to the Court as a way of highlighting the problem and encouraging the respondent to do something about it. This would no doubt be a legitimate exercise of the Commission's powers, but is not something that can be done very often. The Court is already very busy and should not have to spend large amounts of time on routine cases when others of greater importance are waiting to be decided. If therefore the Commission's aim was to speed up the administration of justice in Italy, it is to be hoped that the tactic will prove to have been successful and that this curious exercise will not need to be repeated.

Trial within a reasonable time (Article 6(1))—exhaustion of domestic remedies (Article 26)

Case No. 34. Vernillo case.[66] In this case, which concerned France, the Court held unanimously that the length of civil proceedings had not exceeded the 'reasonable time' laid down in Article 6(1) of the Convention.

In October 1967 the applicants, Mr and Mrs Vernillo, bought a flat in Nice from Mr and Mrs T for a down payment of 10,000 French francs, to be followed by monthly payments of 100 francs. In July 1977 they were given a formal notice to pay arrears and service charges on the flat but failed to act on it. In December 1977 Mr and Mrs T began proceedings seeking a declaration that the contract of sale was automatically rescinded through the applicants' fault. In June 1981 their action was dismissed, but in June 1983 the decision was reversed on appeal. In June 1985 the Court of Cassation dismissed an appeal on points of law by the applicants against this judgment. The contract of sale was therefore finally rescinded.

In their applications to the Commission in November 1985 Mr and Mrs Vernillo claimed that the length of the civil proceedings had violated Article 6(1) of the Convention. In its report in February 1990 the Commission expressed the unanimous opinion that this provision had been violated. The Commission then referred the case to the Court.

Before it could examine the merits of the case the Court first had to deal with a preliminary objection from the Government, based on Article 26 of the Convention. That provision concerns the admissibility of complaints and lays down that:

> The Commission may only deal with the matter after all domestic remedies have been exhausted, according to the generally recognized rules of international law . . .

The Government maintained that the applicants had not exhausted domestic

[66] ECHR, judgment of 20 February 1991, Series A, No. 198. The Court consisted of the following Chamber of Judges: Ryssdal (President); Cremona, Bindschedler-Robert, Pettiti, Sir Vincent Evans, Spielmann, Valticos, Foighel, Loizou (Judges).

remedies, since they had not brought an action against the State under the Code of Judicial Organization, seeking compensation for the delay in hearing their case. The Commission had rejected this submission and the Court agreed. While recognizing that an action for damages may be relevant for the purposes of Article 26, the Court recalled that according to its case law:

> . . . the only remedies which that Article requires to be exhausted are those that relate to the breaches alleged and at the same time are available and sufficient. The existence of such remedies must be sufficiently certain not only in theory but also in practice, failing which they will lack the requisite accessibility and effectiveness; it falls to the respondent State to establish that these various conditions are satisfied.[67]

In the present case the Code of Judicial Organization circumscribed the State's liability very narrowly and the applicants had not claimed to be the victims of either gross negligence or a denial of justice as the Code required. The Court therefore concluded that the applicants' claim was admissible.

On the substantive issue the period to be considered ran from December 1977, when the applicants were summoned before the court of first instance, to June 1985, when the final appeal was dismissed. To decide whether this period of $7\frac{1}{2}$ years was excessive the Court employed the same criteria as in the *Moreira de Azevedo* case (Case No. 7) and the other cases already considered. It found that the case had not been a very complex one, but that the parties themselves had done much to prolong the proceedings. Moreover, delays which appeared to be abnormal and which were attributable to the judicial authorities were 'not so long as to warrant the conclusion that the total duration of the proceedings was excessive'.[68] The Court therefore decided that there had been no violation of Article 6(1).

This was the only case in the period under review in which the Court and the Commission disagreed on the question whether proceedings had been unreasonably prolonged. Exhaustion of domestic remedies was also an issue in the *Cardot* case (Case No. 36, below).

Right to liberty (Article 5(1))—right to a fair hearing (Article 6(1))—application to an alleged governmental kidnapping—the Court's approach to disputed facts

Case No. 35. Stocké case.[69] In this case, which concerned an alleged kidnapping by the Federal German police, the Court held unanimously that there had been no breach of Articles 5 and 6 of the Convention.

The applicant in this unusual case was a German whose building firm went bankrupt in 1975. He was then the subject of a criminal investigation in the Federal Republic, where he was suspected of fraud and tax offences. While the investigation was in progress he fled abroad, taking up residence across the border at Strasbourg in France. In 1978 a Mr Köster (K), a German police informer, who was himself the subject of criminal proceedings, had a meeting with certain German officials at which ways of finding Mr Stocké and securing his return to Germany were discussed. It was emphasized at this meeting that only lawful methods were to be used, but K was told that any assistance he could provide might be taken

[67] Judgment, para. 27.

[68] Ibid., para. 39.

[69] ECHR, judgment of 19 March 1991, Series A, No. 199. The Court consisted of the following Chamber of Judges: Ryssdal (President); Cremona, Gölcüklü, Matscher, Sir Vincent Evans, Russo, Bernhardt, De Meyer, Martens (Judges).

into account at his own trial. K then went to Strasbourg and, after contacting Mr Stocké, on 7 November 1978 induced him to board a chartered aircraft in the belief that he was about to fly to Luxembourg to discuss a business deal. Before take-off, however, K secretly instructed one of the two pilots to land at Saarbrücken in Germany and informed the authorities there by telephone that Mr Stocké would be arriving shortly. When the aircraft landed in Saarbrücken the police were waiting and the applicant was arrested. K, together with the policemen and the two pilots, celebrated this event with champagne and K was later reimbursed for the cost of hiring the aircraft. In 1982 Mr Stocké was convicted by a German court on charges of fraud and tax evasion, and appeals against this decision were unsuccessful. K, for his part, was convicted in 1988 on charges of fraud and forgery, unconnected with this episode, and sentenced to nine years' imprisonment.

In his application to the Commission in September 1985, Mr Stocké claimed that he had been lured into a trap set up by the German authorities and that as a consequence his trial had involved violations of his right to liberty, as guaranteed by Article 5(1), and his right to a fair trial, as guaranteed by Article 6(1). After examining a mass of evidence relating to the events complained of, obtained during investigations of the alleged kidnapping in France and Germany, and in proceedings before the Commission involving numerous witnesses, the Commission declared the application admissible in July 1989. However, in its report in October it expressed the opinion that the collusion of the German authorities had not been established, with the result that there could be no violation of Articles 5(1) and 6(1). The Commission then referred the case to the Court.

Unusually for a case before the Court, the applicant's claim rested wholly on the view to be taken of the facts. Mr Stocké alleged that the German authorities had been acquainted in minute detail with the plan to kidnap him in Strasbourg. Notwithstanding doubts about the lawfulness of K's methods, they had responded to his telephone call by arranging for the applicant to be arrested and had thus endorsed the kidnapping. This complicity was, the applicant suggested, supported by the circumstantial evidence, notably the reimbursement of K's expenses and the fact that proceedings brought by Mr Stocké against K for false imprisonment had come to nothing. The Government, on the other hand, categorically denied these allegations. In their submission not only had they had no warning of K's intentions, but they had subsequently undertaken strenuous investigations in an attempt to clarify the situation. As to K, the Government maintained that he had been neither shielded nor dealt with leniently; on the contrary he had been proceeded against for false imprisonment in relation to the incident and subsequently convicted and punished for other offences.

While the proceedings were pending before the Court, Mr Stocké made an application to it for five witnesses to be called, four of whom had not been heard by the Commission. The Court decided, however, that this application should not be granted. Recalling that 'under the Convention system, the establishment and verification of the facts is primarily a matter for the Commission',[70] the Court explained that it was only in exceptional circumstances that it would use its powers in this area. Having regard to the conclusions reached by the French and German authorities and to the investigations of the Commission, which had not deemed it necessary to hear further evidence, the Court decided that in the present case there

[70] Judgment, para. 53.

was no reason to entertain the applicant's request. Agreeing with the Commission that the evidence before it did not establish collusion between K and the German authorities in unlawful activities abroad, the Court held that it was unnecessary to examine whether, if the facts had been otherwise, the applicant's arrest would have violated the Convention. The Court therefore concluded that no violation of Article 5 or Article 6 had been established.

The judgment in this case can be summed up by saying that as there was no proof that the applicant's abduction had been arranged by the German Government, the question of a violation of the Convention did not arise. On the evidence considered by the Court this conclusion appears to have been well founded. There were, nevertheless, as Judge Matscher delicately put it, 'doubts about the unfolding of certain events',[71] and what really happened was far from clear. In view of this uncertainty it would perhaps have been more satisfactory if the Court had treated this as an exceptional case and heard the witnesses put forward by Mr Stocké.

Right to a fair trial (Article 6(1))—right to call witnesses (Article 6(3)(d))—exhaustion of domestic remedies (Article 26)

Case No. 36. Cardot case.[72] In this case, which concerned a dispute over the need to call witnesses at a criminal trial in France, the Court held by 6 votes to 3 that as the applicant had failed to exhaust his domestic remedies, it was unable to consider the merits of the case.

The applicant in this case was a road haulier. In 1979, together with fourteen others, he was charged with committing or attempting to commit drugs offences by using trucks fitted with false compartments to bring large quantities of hashish to Europe from Iran. The proceedings against the fourteen ended in February 1982 with the conviction of the majority of the accused. The trial of the applicant, on the other hand, was postponed because he was in custody in Italy.

Mr Cardot was subsequently extradited to France from Italy and in September 1982 was convicted of the same offences and sentenced to six years' imprisonment. The applicant's conviction was based partly on evidence gathered for the proceedings against his former co-defendants, and in particular on statements which they had made implicating him. A confrontation between Mr Cardot and his former co-defendants took place before an investigating judge, but they were not examined before the criminal court and neither the applicant, nor the prosecution, applied for them to be heard as witnesses. The applicant then appealed against his conviction, but the Court of Appeal upheld the judgment and increased the sentence to seven years. A further appeal on points of law was made to the Court of Cassation; in it the applicant claimed *inter alia* that his conviction on the basis of evidence given at the earlier trial violated the rights of the defence. However, this appeal was also dismissed.

In his application to the Commission in December 1983 Mr Cardot claimed that the circumstances in which he had been convicted violated his rights under Articles 6(1) and 6(3)(*d*) of the Convention. In its report in April 1990 the Commission

[71] Concurring opinion of Judge Matscher.

[72] ECHR, judgment of 19 March 1991, Series A, No. 200. The Court consisted of the following Chamber of Judges: Ryssdal (President); Thór Vilhjálmsson, Gölcüklü, Pettiti, Walsh, Macdonald, Russo, Martens, Morenilla (Judges).

expressed the unanimous opinion that these provisions had been violated. The Commission then referred the case to the Court.

Before the Commission the French Government's main submission had been that the application was inadmissible because Mr Cardot had failed to raise his complaint concerning the evidence of witnesses in the French courts, so transgressing Article 26 of the Convention which was quoted in Case No. 34. Although this preliminary objection had been rejected by the Commission, it was raised again before the Court which, in accordance with its decision in the *Vagrancy* cases,[73] has jurisdiction to reconsider such issues. Consequently, before it could examine the applicant's substantive complaint, the Court first had to establish that the issue of the witnesses' evidence had been sufficiently aired in the domestic courts.

There is, of course, much more case law on Article 26 in the jurisprudence of the Commission than of the Court, but the approach which should be adopted to cases which raise this issue is, as the Court indicated, not controversial. Thus it is clear that:

> . . . Article 26 must be applied with some degree of flexibility and without excessive formalism . . . , but it does not require merely that applications should be made to the appropriate domestic courts and that use should be made of remedies designed to challenge decisions already given. It normally requires also that the complaints intended to be made subsequently at Strasbourg should have been made to those same courts, at least in substance and in compliance with the formal requirements and time-limits laid down in domestic law . . . , and, further, that any procedural means which might prevent a breach of the Convention should have been used . . . [74]

In the present case the applicant had not expressed any wish that evidence should be heard from his former co-defendants in the court of first instance, although they had implicated him and three of them had confirmed their earlier statements at the confrontation. Nor had he made any application to the Court of Appeal for such evidence to be heard, although the case file disclosed 'no special reason which could have excused him from calling those witnesses or applying to have them called'.[75] As to the appeal on points of law, the applicant had not relied on Article 6(3)(*d*), or even on the general principle of Article 6(1), and had not referred to the statements that the former co-defendants had made to the investigating judge. Consequently, the appeal was 'too vague to draw the Court of Cassation's attention to the issue subsequently submitted to the Convention institutions, namely the failure to hear prosecution witnesses at any stage of the court proceedings . . . '.[76] The Court therefore concluded that the applicant had not provided the French courts with the opportunity to prevent or put right the alleged violation which it is the function of Article 26 to provide. The Court thus held that the Government's objection that domestic remedies had not been exhausted was well founded, and decided that it could not take cognizance of the merits of the case.

Three judges disagreed with this conclusion and delivered dissenting opinions.[77]

[73] ECHR, judgment of 18 June 1971, Series A, No. 12, and this *Year Book*, 46 (1972–3), p. 463. For discussion of the significance of the Court's ruling in this case see Merrills, *The Development of International Law by the European Court of Human Rights* (1988), p. 44.

[74] Judgment, para. 34.

[75] Ibid., para. 35.

[76] Ibid.

[77] See the dissenting opinion of Judge Macdonald, and those of Judges Martens and Morenilla who made the same point in their concurring opinions in the *Oberschlick* case (Case No. 41).

They all considered that although the applicant had not raised the issue of his rights under the Convention specifically, he had provided the Court of Cassation with a sufficient opportunity to consider the point. In the light of the more lenient application of Article 26 in previous cases such as *Guzzardi*,[78] this is a persuasive position. Judge Martens and Judge Morenilla put forward a second reason for considering the case on the merits, which was that the Court should adopt an entirely new approach to this and other issues of admissibility and leave all such questions to the Commission. Judge Martens first put this radical view forward in his separate opinion in the *Brozicek* case,[79] and now evidently has an ally. As 'the continuing and rather alarming increase in the Court's case-load'[80] which he then identified shows no sign of abating, it will be interesting to see whether the proposal for a change of course will receive further support.

Freedom from inhuman or degrading treatment (Article 3)—application to expulsion to a non-European State—right to respect for family life (Article 8)—scope of the obligation not to hinder the right of individual petition (Article 25(1))—effect of interim measures (Rule 36 of the Commission's Rules)

Case No. 37. Cruz Varas case.[81] In this case, which concerned a decision to expel a Chilean family from Sweden, the Court held by 18 votes to 1 that there had been no violation of Article 3 of the Convention and unanimously that there had been no violation of Article 8. It also held by 10 votes to 9 that the failure to comply with an indication from the Commission that one of the applicants should not be expelled until his case had been examined at Strasbourg did not constitute a violation of Sweden's obligations under Article 25(1).

This case arose out of a decision to deport three Chilean nationals, a husband (H), his wife (W) and their son (S), from Sweden to Chile.

In April 1988 the National Immigration Board decided to expel the three applicants and refused their request for refugee status. In September an appeal against this decision was rejected by the Government. H subsequently told the police that while in Sweden he had worked for a radical organization which had tried to kill General Pinochet and that he ran the risk of political persecution if he returned to Chile. He also claimed to have been tortured on several occasions by the Chilean authorities. The police referred the case back to the National Immigration Board which in turn referred the case to the Government, at the same time expressing the opinion that the expulsion order should be enforced. H then submitted two medical certificates to the Government concerning his allegations of torture. However, on 5 October 1989 the Government found that there was no impediment to the enforcement of the expulsion order. On the same day H, W and S made an application to Strasbourg.

On 6 October the National Immigration Board decided not to stop the expulsion. However, at 9.10 a.m. on that day the Swedish Government was informed that the Commission had decided, in accordance with Rule 36 of its Rules of Procedure, to indicate to the Government that in the interests of the parties and the

[78] ECHR, judgment of 6 November 1980, Series A, No. 39, and this *Year Book*, 51 (1980), p. 335.

[79] ECHR, judgment of 19 December 1989, Series A, No. 167, and this *Year Book*, 61 (1990), p. 413.

[80] *Brozicek* case, separate opinion of Judge Martens, para. 4.4.

[81] ECHR, judgment of 20 March 1991, Series A, No. 201. This case was decided by the plenary Court.

proper conduct of proceedings before the Commission, it was desirable not to deport the applicants to Chile until the Commission had had an opportunity to examine their application further. Notwithstanding this communication, H was expelled to Chile at 4.40 p.m. on the same day. His wife and son, who had gone into hiding, remained in Sweden.

In their application to the Commission H, W and S relied on Articles 3, 8 and 25(1) of the Convention. In its report in June 1990 the Commission expressed the opinion that there had been no violation of Article 3 (8 votes to 5); that there had also been no violation of Article 8 (unanimously); but that Sweden had failed to comply with its obligation not to hinder the right of individual petition under Article 25(1) (12 votes to 1). The Commission and the Government then referred the case to the Court.

Article 3 of the Convention provides:

> No one shall be subjected to torture or to inhuman or degrading treatment or punishment.

In the *Soering* case[82] in 1989 the Court held that a decision to extradite a fugitive can raise an issue under this provision 'where substantial grounds have been shown for believing that the person concerned, if extradited, faces a real risk of being subjected to inhuman or degrading treatment or punishment in the requesting country'.[83] Liability in such a case is not, of course, based upon the responsibility of the receiving State, but rather upon that of the Contracting State for having taken action which, as one of its consequences, exposes an individual to possible ill-treatment. The present case concerned expulsion, not extradition, but the Court decided that the same principle applies to expulsion decisions 'and *a fortiori* to cases of actual expulsion'.[84] It followed from this that Article 3 was applicable.

On the question of Article 3, the nub of the present case was the risk which the applicant H faced in returning to Chile. This was a matter of dispute, H's submissions on this point having been rejected by the Government and the Commission. The Court recalled that 'under the Convention system, the establishment and verification of the facts is primarily a matter for the Commission'.[85] However, in exceptional cases the Court may use its powers in this area and is not bound by the Commission's finding. When assessing whether there was a risk, the Court stated that the facts which were known or ought to have been known to the State at the time of the expulsion were the primary source of reference, although information which came to light subsequently could be of value in confirming or refuting the State's assessment.

Having studied the evidence, the Court rejected the applicant's argument. While the medical evidence supported his allegations of ill-treatment, his delay in bringing this to light cast doubt on his credibility. This was further undermined by continual changes in his story and the lack of evidence of political activity. In addition, the improvement in the political situation in Chile, the voluntary return of refugees, the particular knowledge and experience of the Swedish authorities and the fact that the final decision was taken only after a thorough examination of his case, were all relevant factors. In the light of this review the Court concluded that no

[82] ECHR, judgment of 7 July 1989, Series A, No. 161, and this *Year Book*, 60 (1989), p. 552.

[83] Judgment, para. 69.

[84] Ibid., para. 70.

[85] Ibid., para. 74.

substantial basis had been shown for H's fears, and so decided that there had been no violation of Article 3.

All three applicants claimed that the expulsion of H led to a splitting of the family and so violated their right to respect for their family life which is protected by Article 8. However, the Court, like the Commission, rejected this claim also. Pointing out that W and S went into hiding to avoid the expulsion order, the Court found that the evidence, including that already considered in relation to Article 3, did not show that there were obstacles to establishing family life in their own country. In these circumstances the Court ruled that responsibility for separating the family could not be imputed to Sweden. It therefore decided that there had been no lack of respect for the applicants' family life contrary to Article 8.

The final issue, and the one which caused greatest difficulty, concerned Sweden's expulsion of the applicant H and its defiance of the Commission's request that he should be permitted to stay. This raised two questions: firstly, the status of interim measures which are provided for in Rule 36 of the Commission's Rules; and secondly, the scope of the obligation not to hinder the right of individual petition under Article 25(1).

Rule 36 provides:

> The Commission, or where it is not in session, the President may indicate to the parties any interim measure the adoption of which seems desirable in the interest of the parties or the proper conduct of the proceedings before it.

And Article 25(1) provides:

> The Commission may receive petitions addressed to the Secretary General of the Council of Europe from any person, non-governmental organisation or group of individuals claiming to be the victim of a violation by one of the High Contracting Parties of the rights set forth in this Convention, provided that the High Contracting Party against which the complaint has been lodged has declared that it recognizes the competence of the Commission to receive such petitions. Those of the High Contracting Parties who have made such a declaration undertake not to hinder in any way the effective exercise of this right.

The Court began by surveying the legal background. Unlike other international instruments, the Convention contains no provision specifically empowering its organs to order interim measures. The *travaux préparatoires* are silent on this issue, and while the Consultative Assembly called on the Committee of Ministers to draft an additional protocol on this matter in 1971, the Ministers decided not to do so. Recommendations were subsequently made by the Assembly in 1977 and by the Committee of Ministers in 1980, asking member States to suspend extradition or expulsion to a Non-Contracting State where complaints involving Article 3 were pending before the Commission or the Court.

The Court decided that in the absence of a specific power in the Convention a Rule 36 indication could not give rise to a binding obligation. Furthermore, it decided that such an obligation could not be derived from the obligation which States assume under Article 25(1) because although individuals can complain of infringements of this provision, in the absence of a specific interim measure provision it would 'strain the language of Article 25'[86] to infer an obligation to comply with a Rule 36 indication. The Court recognized that in practice there was almost total compliance with Rule 36 indications, but held that while subsequent practice was relevant on issues of interpretation, it could not 'create new rights and obli-

[86] Ibid., para. 99.

gations which were not included in the Convention at the outset'. The practice was thus 'a matter of good faith co-operation with the Commission in cases where this was considered reasonable and practicable'.[87]

Finding that no assistance could be derived from general principles of international law, the Court concluded that a power to order binding interim measures could not be inferred either from Article 25(1) or from other sources. Observing that 'it lies within the appreciation of the Contracting Parties to decide whether it is expedient to remedy this situation',[88] the Court added that a State which decided not to comply with a Rule 36 indication 'knowingly assumes the risk of being found in breach of Article 3 following adjudication of the dispute by the Convention organs'.[89] Moreover, in the Court's view any such finding would have to be regarded as aggravated by the failure to comply with the indication.

Having rejected the view that compliance with Rule 36 was mandatory, the Court had only one further issue to resolve, which was whether H's expulsion hindered the effective exercise of his right of petition and so violated Article 25(1). Its decision was that it did not because although allowing H to remain would have facilitated the presentation of the case before the Commission, the Court was satisfied that there was no evidence of hindrance to a significant degree. Following his return to Chile, H was at liberty and counsel was able to represent the applicants fully before the Commission. Nor was the Court satisfied that H's inability to confer with his lawyer hampered the gathering of additional evidence. The Court therefore concluded by 10 votes to 9 that there had been no breach of Article 25(1).

The judges who dissented delivered a joint dissenting opinion in which they maintained that Article 25(1) had been violated because it was in their view 'implicit in the Convention that in cases such as the present the Convention organs have the power to require the parties to abstain from a measure which might not only give rise to serious harm but which might also nullify the result of the entire procedure under the Convention'.[90] They were not saying that every complaint under Article 25 should inhibit extradition or expulsion; rather, their argument was that in cases where the possibility of irreparable harm leads to a request by the Commission under Rule 36, the State should be required to comply. As they pointed out, the Court has repeatedly emphasized that 'the object and purpose of the Convention as an instrument for the protection of individual human beings required that its provisions be interpreted and applied so as to make its safeguards practical and effective'.[91] The argument that the majority construed the Convention too narrowly in the present case is therefore a very persuasive one.

Just satisfaction (Article 50)—costs and expenses—pecuniary and non-pecuniary loss

Case No. 38. Fox, Campbell and Hartley case (Application of Article 50).[92] The

[87] Ibid., para. 100.
[88] Ibid., para. 102.
[89] Ibid., para. 103.
[90] See the dissenting opinion of Judges Cremona, Thór Vilhjálmsson, Walsh, Macdonald, Bernhardt, De Meyer, Martens, Foighel and Morenilla, para. 3.
[91] Ibid., para. 1.
[92] ECHR, judgment of 27 March 1991, Series A, No. 202. The Court consisted of the following Chamber of Judges: Ryssdal (President); Cremona, Pinheiro Farinha, Sir Vincent Evans, Bernhardt, Martens, Palm (Judges).

Court held unanimously that the United Kingdom must pay the applicants jointly, in respect of their costs and expenses, the sum of £11,000 together with any value-added tax that may be chargeable. It also decided by 6 votes to 1 that in respect of non-pecuniary damage the judgment itself constituted sufficient just satisfaction, and unanimously dismissed the remainder of the claim.

In its judgment on the merits in 1990[93] the Court held *inter alia* that the arrest and detention of the applicants as suspected terrorists in Northern Ireland had involved violations of Articles 5(1) and 5(5) of the Convention. The issue of just satisfaction under Article 50 was reserved.

In the present proceedings the first of the applicants' claims was for £70,001 by way of costs and expenses. The Government submitted that this claim was 'wholly excessive' and also pointed out that several of the applicants' substantive complaints had been rejected. The Court agreed and, for the reasons suggested by the Government, reduced the award to the sum indicated above.

As compensation for pecuniary damage the applicants claimed the difference between the costs and expenses awarded under Article 50 and the amount they were legally obliged to pay. Not surprisingly, the Court rejected this claim on the ground that the issue of costs and expenses had already been dealt with.

By way of non-pecuniary damage the applicants sought compensation for the prejudice allegedly sustained as a result of the breaches of Article 5. The Court was not prepared to exclude the possibility of non-pecuniary damage, but having regard to the circumstances of the case, decided that the judgment constituted adequate satisfaction.[94]

Freedom of peaceful assembly (Article 11)—relation to freedom of expression in Article 10—responsibilities of a lawyer participating in a demonstration—just satisfaction (Article 50)

Case No. 39. Ezelin case.[95] The Court held by 6 votes to 3 that France had committed a violation of Article 11 of the Convention when a disciplinary sanction was imposed on a lawyer for taking part in a demonstration. The Court also held unanimously that the Government should pay the applicant 40,000 French francs in respect of his costs and expenses.

The applicant lived on the French island of Guadeloupe where he practised as a lawyer (*avocat*). In February 1983 he took part in a demonstration to protest over three recent criminal cases in which activists who supported independence for Guadeloupe were found guilty of causing criminal damage to public buildings. During the demonstration, at which the applicant carried a placard indicating that he was an *avocat*, insults were hurled at the police and graffiti, directed mainly at the judiciary, were daubed on public buildings. On a complaint by the Public Prosecutor disciplinary proceedings were brought against the applicant. The Guadeloupe Bar Council which heard the case considered that as the evidence merely indicated that the applicant had been present at the demonstration, there was no reason to impose a disciplinary sanction. However, on appeal by the prosecutor the Court of Appeal set aside the decision and imposed a reprimand as a sanc-

[93] ECHR, judgment of 30 August 1990, Series A, No. 182, and this *Year Book*, 61 (1990), p. 444.

[94] Judge Pinheiro Farinha delivered a short dissenting opinion on this point.

[95] ECHR, judgment of 26 April 1991, Series A, No. 202. The Court consisted of the following Chamber of Judges: Ryssdal (President); Cremona, Gölcüklü, Matscher, Pettiti, Walsh, Spielmann, De Meyer, Pekkanen (Judges).

tion for the applicant's failure to exercise 'discretion', as required by legislation relating to the professional responsibilities of *avocats*. An appeal to the Court of Cassation against this decision was unsuccessful.

In his application to the Commission in October 1985 Mr Ezelin relied on Article 10 of the Convention, which guarantees freedom of expression, and Article 11, which guarantees freedom of peaceful assembly. In its report in December 1989 the Commission expressed the opinion that there had been a breach of Article 11 and that no separate issue arose under Article 10. The Commission then referred the case to the Court.

The decision in this case centred on Article 11, but before the Court could address that issue it had to deal with two preliminary matters relating to the scope of the case. The first concerned the basis for the Court of Appeal's decision. The European Court noted that Mr Ezelin had been punished for refusing to give evidence to an investigating judge, as well as for having neither shown his disapproval of the demonstrators' 'offensive and insulting acts', nor left the procession in order to dissociate himself from them. It found, however, that he had been summoned before the investigating judge as a result of having taken part in the demonstration. That being so, the Court decided that the question of the applicant's refusal to give evidence, which did not fall within the ambit of Articles 10 or 11, was a secondary one which need not be further considered.

The other matter was the relation between Articles 10 and 11, both of which were relied on in Mr Ezelin's application. Here the Court decided that in the circumstances of the case Article 10 was to be regarded 'as a *lex generalis* in relation to Article 11, a *lex specialis*',[96] and in view of this agreed unanimously with the Commission that it was unnecessary to take the right to freedom of expression into consideration separately.[97]

Article 11 of the Convention provides:

1. Everyone has the right to freedom of peaceful assembly and to freedom of association with others, including the right to form and to join trade unions for the protection of his interests.
2. No restrictions shall be placed on the exercise of these rights other than such as are prescribed by law and are necessary in a democratic society in the interests of national security or public safety, for the prevention of disorder or crime, for the protection of health or morals or for the protection of the rights and freedoms of others. This Article shall not prevent the imposition of lawful restrictions on the exercise of these rights by members of the armed forces, of the police or of the administration of the State.

The Government began by arguing that as the applicant had not actually been prevented from taking part in the demonstration, there had been no 'restrictions' placed on his freedom of peaceful assembly. This weak point was quickly rejected. The Court stated that the term 'restrictions' in Article 11(2) could not be interpreted as excluding subsequent measures. It added that in joining the demonstration the applicant had availed himself of his freedom of peaceful assembly, and pointed out that he had not himself made threats or daubed graffiti. Accordingly there had been an interference with his freedom of peaceful assembly and the only question was whether it could be justified.

The legal basis of the sanction complained of lay in the special rules governing

[96] Judgment, para. 35.

[97] For comment on this point see the concurring opinion of Judge De Meyer.

the profession of *avocat*. The Court was therefore satisfied that the interference had been 'prescribed by law'. Similarly, it agreed with the Government that the interference had a legitimate aim, namely the 'prevention of disorder'. It disagreed, however, with the Government's argument that the punishment of Mr Ezelin was 'necessary in a democratic society' for achieving that aim. On this issue the Court said:

> The proportionality principle demands that a balance be struck between the requirements of the purposes listed in Article 11(2) and those of the free expression of opinion by word, gesture or even silence by persons assembled on the streets or in other public places. The pursuit of a just balance must not result in *avocats* being discouraged, for fear of disciplinary sanctions, from making clear their beliefs on such occasions.[98]

The Court recognized that the penalty imposed on the applicant was at the lower end of the scale and did not prevent him from practising. It considered, however, that the freedom to take part in a peaceful assembly 'is of such importance that it cannot be restricted in any way, even for an *avocat*, so long as the person concerned does not himself commit any reprehensible act on such an occasion'.[99] It therefore agreed with the Commission that there had been a violation of Article 11.

As just satisfaction under Article 50 Mr Ezelin claimed a substantial sum in respect of alleged non-pecuniary damage, but the Court, having upheld his complaint, decided that its judgment constituted adequate satisfaction. His claim in respect of costs and expenses, which was not contested, was allowed in full.

Three judges dissented from the decision on Article 11,[100] essentially on the ground that, as Judge Matscher put it, 'Attitudes towards the conduct of members of the Bar differ from country to country', with the result that the decision here lay within the respondent's margin of appreciation. The sanction imposed on Mr Ezelin was relatively slight and, as Judge Pettiti pointed out, there have certainly been cases involving other rights in which the margin of appreciation has been interpreted more broadly.[101] This is, however, the first case in which the Court has been concerned directly with freedom of peaceful assembly,[102] and the majority were surely right to support the Commission and emphasize its importance.

Right to a fair trial (Article 6(1))—right to examine witnesses (Article 6(3)(d))

Case No. 40. Asch case.[103] In this case, which concerned the rights of the defence in a criminal trial in Austria, the Court held by 7 votes to 2 that there had been no violation of Article 6(3)(*d*) of the Convention, taken in conjunction with Article 6(1).

In July 1985 there was a dispute between the applicant, Mr Asch, and Mrs L, the woman he lived with at their home. Mrs L subsequently informed the police

[98] Judgment, para. 52.

[99] Ibid., para. 53.

[100] See the dissenting opinions of Judges Matscher and Pettiti and the partly dissenting opinion of Judge Ryssdal.

[101] See, for example, the *Markt intern* case, Series A, No. 165, and this *Year Book*, 60 (1989), p. 562.

[102] Note, however, that in the *Plattform 'Ärzte für das Leben'* case, Series A, No. 139, and this *Year Book*, 59 (1988), p. 401, the scope of this freedom was examined in the context of Article 13.

[103] ECHR, judgment of 26 April 1991, Series A, No. 203. The Court consisted of the following Chamber of Judges: Ryssdal (President); Matscher, Sir Vincent Evans, Macdonald, Russo, Bernhardt, Spielmann, De Meyer, Valticos (Judges).

that the applicant had beaten and threatened to kill her. As a result, criminal proceedings were begun against the applicant on charges of intimidation and causing actual bodily harm. Shortly afterwards Mr Asch and Mrs L were reconciled and the latter asked for her complaint to be withdrawn. The prosecution, however, was continued. At the applicant's trial in November 1985 Mrs L exercised her right under Austrian law and declined to give evidence against the applicant. The original statement which Mrs L had made to the police was then read out. The court heard evidence from the officer who had taken down the statement and also had before it two medical reports, indicating that at the time in question Mrs L had bruises on her head and body. The applicant, who had pleaded not guilty, was convicted and fined. In March 1986 an appeal by Mr Asch against his conviction was dismissed.

In his application to the Commission in August 1986 Mr Asch complained of a violation of Article 6(3)(*d*) taken in conjunction with Article 6(1) of the Convention. In its report in April 1990 the Commission expressed the opinion by 12 votes to 5 that there had been a violation of these provisions. The Commission and the Government then referred the case to the Court.

Article 6(3)(*d*), which concerns the rights of the defence with regard to witnesses, has been quoted in *Windisch* (Case No. 4) and, as already noted, the scope of a State's obligations under this provision has been thoroughly explored in the case law. As with other parts of the Convention, however, the application of these well-established principles to the facts can sometimes be contentious. In *Isgrò* (Case No. 15) the Court and the Commission disagreed on whether the rights of the defence had been violated and there was a similar disagreement, and a division of opinion in the Court itself, in the present case.

It will be recalled that a basic requirement of Article 6(3)(*d*) is that the defendant should have an adequate and proper opportunity to challenge and question a witness against him, either when she is making her statements, or at a later stage of the proceedings. The crucial issue in the present case was whether this requirement had been complied with. When reviewing the proceedings against Mr Asch the Court found that only the police officer had recounted the relevant facts at the trial, but ruled that provided the rights of the defence were respected, it was open to the trial court to take the officer's statement into account, especially as it appeared to be corroborated by the medical evidence. Furthermore, the Court noted that the applicant had had the opportunity to discuss Mrs L's version of events and to put his own, first to the police and later to the court. Moreover, the applicant had chosen not to question the police officer, or to call other witnesses. Finally, the Court found that it was clear from the file that Mrs L's statements were not the only evidence on which the trial court based its decision. Thus in all the circumstances the fact that it had been impossible to question Mrs L at the hearing had not, in the Court's view, violated the rights of the defence, or deprived the applicant of a fair trial. The Court therefore concluded that there had been no violation of the Convention.

Two judges dissented from this decision because in their view the rights of the defence had not been respected.[104] While in no way questioning the propriety of the law which had enabled Mrs L to avoid giving evidence, they considered that, as

[104] See the joint dissenting opinion of Judges Sir Vincent Evans and Bernhardt.

in the *Unterpertinger* case,[105] where the same law was involved, Article 6(3)(*d*) had been violated. Their colleagues, however, clearly saw the present case as closer to the situation in *Isgrò* (Case No. 15) than *Delta* (Case No. 11) and distinguished *Unterpertinger* on the ground that in that case there was little other evidence against the accused. Another difference is that in *Unterpertinger* the accused was denied an opportunity to challenge the credibility of the incriminating statements, whereas here he was able to do so.

Right to a 'fair' hearing before an 'impartial' tribunal (Article 6(1))—freedom of expression (Article 10)—application to alleged defamation of a politician in the press—just satisfaction (Article 50)

Case No. 41. Oberschlick case.[106] In this case, which concerned the conviction of an Austrian journalist for defamation, the Court held unanimously that there had been a violation of Article 6(1) of the Convention as regards the impartiality of one of the courts which dealt with the case, and by 16 votes to 3 that there had also been a violation of Article 10. As just satisfaction the Court ordered the Government to pay the applicant 18,123.84 Austrian schillings as compensation for pecuniary damage and 85,285 schillings in respect of his costs and expenses.

In April 1983 the applicant and a number of other people laid a criminal information against an Austrian politician, G, who had suggested that Austrian women and immigrant mothers should be treated differently as regards the payment of family allowances. The criminal information referred to the crimes of incitement to hatred and of activities contrary to the National Socialism Prohibition Act, and its full text was published by the applicant on the same day in the periodical *Forum*, for which he worked as a journalist.

G thereupon instituted a private prosecution for defamation. Initially the proceedings were discontinued by the Vienna Regional Criminal Court, but in May 1983, on appeal by G, the Vienna Court of Appeal quashed this decision and referred the case back. In May 1984 the Regional Court convicted the applicant and fined him. It also ordered the seizure of the relevant issue of *Forum* and the publication of its judgment in the review. In December 1984 an appeal by the applicant against this decision was dismissed by the Court of Appeal, which was made up of the same judges who had dealt with the case in the previous year. The Court of Appeal found that the applicant had insinuated, without a sufficient basis in the facts, that G held National Socialist attitudes.

In his application to the Commission in June 1985 Mr Oberschlick complained of violations of Article 6(1) and Article 10 of the Convention. In its report in December 1989 the Commission expressed the opinion that there had been a violation of Article 6(1) as regards the proceedings before the Court of Appeal, but not as regards those before the Regional Court, and that there had also been a violation of Article 10. The Commission then referred the case to the Court.

After rejecting a preliminary objection from the Government relating to the tim-

[105] ECHR, judgment of 24 November 1986, Series A, No. 110, and this *Year Book*, 58 (1987), p. 458.

[106] ECHR, judgment of 23 May 1991, Series A, No. 204. This case was decided by the plenary Court.

ing of Mr Oberschlick's application,[107] the Court turned to the first substantive issue. This concerned the proceedings in the two domestic courts and was based on Article 6(1), the relevant part of which provides:

> In the determination of . . . any criminal charge . . . everyone is entitled to a fair . . . hearing . . . by an independent and impartial tribunal established by law . . .

As regards the Regional Court the Court agreed with the Commission that this provision had been complied with. The Regional Court had found that it was bound by the Court of Appeal's decision of May 1983 which was in fact an erroneous view of domestic law. However, since the Regional Court had considered the evidence before it and reached a fully-reasoned conclusion as to guilt, which was upheld on appeal, there had been no violation of the applicant's right to a fair trial. As regards the subsequent proceedings, on the other hand, the applicant alleged that when hearing his appeal in December 1984 the Court of Appeal was neither 'impartial', nor 'established by law' because, contrary to Austrian law, it had the same composition as in May 1983. Noting that these complaints coincided in substance, the European Court observed that the relevant domestic law demonstrated a concern to remove any doubts on the issue of impartiality. Consequently, the Court of Appeal's failure to observe this provision meant that the applicant's appeal had been heard by a tribunal whose impartiality the legislature regarded as questionable. Moreover, there was no evidence that the applicant had waived his right to an impartial tribunal, as neither he nor his counsel were aware at the time that all three appeal judges had taken part in both decisions. The Court therefore concluded that in relation to the proceedings in the Court of Appeal, Article 6(1) had been violated.

The applicant's other complaint related to Article 10 of the Convention, which provides:

> 1. Everyone has the right to freedom of expression. This right shall include freedom to hold opinions and to receive and impart information and ideas without interference by public authority and regardless of frontiers. . . .
> 2. The exercise of these freedoms, since it carries with it duties and responsibilities, may be subject to such formalities, conditions, restrictions or penalties as are prescribed by law and are necessary in a democratic society, . . . for the protection of the reputation or rights of others . . .

It was not disputed that the applicant's conviction constituted an interference with his right to freedom of expression which was both 'prescribed by law' and had the legitimate aim of protecting the reputation or rights of others. The crucial question therefore was whether the interference was necessary in a democratic society to achieve this aim. In its case law on Article 10, which is now quite extensive,[108] the Court has consistently emphasized the fundamental importance of freedom of expression, its particular value to the press, and the relation between the right to criticize and democracy which has specific implications for politicians. Recalling these principles, which were previously adumbrated in its decision in the *Lingens*

[107] The objection was that the applicant had not lodged his application within 6 months of the date of the final national decision as Article 26 of the Convention requires. It was rejected, however, when the Court examined the facts.

[108] In addition to the cases referred to below, see the *Handyside* case, Series A, No. 24, and this *Year Book*, 48 (1975–6), p. 381; the *Sunday Times* case, Series A, No. 30, and this *Year Book*, 50 (1979), p. 257, and the *Barthold* case, Series A, No. 90, and this *Year Book*, 56 (1985), p. 341.

case,[109] it observed that what was at stake in the present case was the limits of acceptable criticism in the context of public debate on a political question of general interest.

Turning to the particular facts, the Court noted that the applicant had been convicted for having published in a review the text of a criminal information which he and others had lodged against a politician. In it they had expressed the opinion that G had made a proposal which corresponded to the philosophy and aims of National Socialism. In the Court's view this publication contributed to a public debate on a political question of general importance, namely the differential treatment of nationals and foreigners in the social field. The applicant was seeking, in a provocative manner, to draw public attention to a proposal which many were likely to find shocking.

After examining the impugned court decisions, the Court found that the applicant had been convicted because he was unable to prove the truth of his allegations. In the Court's view, however, the publication in question contained a true statement of facts, namely G's proposal, followed by a statement of the authors' opinion. This opinion constituted a value-judgment, the truth of which by definition could not be proved, with the result that imposing this requirement infringed freedom of opinion. Moreover, in the light of the importance of the issue at stake, the applicant could not be said to have exceeded the limits of freedom of expression by choosing that particular form of publication. The Court therefore concluded that there had been a violation of Article 10.

As just satisfaction, Mr Oberschlick claimed a large sum as compensation for non-pecuniary damage and the reimbursement of the fine and the costs which he had been ordered to pay by the Austrian courts. He also requested the Court to order the Government to set aside his conviction and annul the seizure of the relevant issue of *Forum*. The Court accepted the claim for pecuniary damage, but rejected the other claims, as either unsubstantiated or beyond its powers. A further claim in respect of the applicant's costs and expenses was allowed in its entirety.

This was the Court's only case on Article 10 in the period under review, and although three judges dissented from its decision on this point,[110] the judgment is a straightforward application of the principles of the *Lingens* case. Not all decisions on the right to freedom of expression in recent years have been so liberal, however.[111] It is therefore reassuring to find the propositions that politicians must learn to take criticism and that material which constitutes fair comment does not need to be justified so firmly emphasized in the present case.

Right to legal assistance (Article 6(3)(c))—just satisfaction (Article 50)

Case No. 42. Quaranta case.[112] The Court held unanimously that there had been a violation of Article 6(3)(*c*) of the Convention because the applicant had not

[109] ECHR, judgment of 8 July 1986, Series A, No. 103, and this *Year Book*, 57 (1986), p. 463.

[110] See the partly dissenting opinion of Judge Thór Vilhjálmsson and the partly dissenting opinion of Judge Matscher, approved by Judge Bindschedler-Robert; Judges Martens and Morenilla delivered concurring opinions.

[111] See the *Barfod* case, Series A, No. 149, and this *Year Book*, 60 (1989), p. 523, and the *Markt intern* case, Series A, No. 165, and ibid., p. 562.

[112] ECHR, judgment of 24 May 1991, Series A, No. 205. The Court consisted of the following Chamber of Judges: Ryssdal (President); Bindschedler-Robert, Matscher, Pettiti, Russo, Bernhardt, Palm, Loizou, Morenilla (Judges).

received the free assistance of a lawyer during a criminal investigation and subsequently at his trial in Switzerland. As just satisfaction the Government was ordered to pay the applicant 3,000 Swiss francs as compensation for damage and 7,000 francs in respect of his costs and expenses.

The applicant, who was born in 1962, was an Italian who lived in Switzerland. In 1985 a district investigating judge opened an investigation concerning drugs offences which it was suspected the applicant had committed. Mr Quaranta applied on several occasions for free legal assistance for the investigation and subsequently for the trial, but his applications were dismissed. At the trial he was convicted and sentenced to 6 months' imprisonment. The court also activated a suspended sentence which had been imposed on the applicant for another offence in 1982. Appeals against the decision were unsuccessful.

In his application to the Commission in December 1986 Mr Quaranta claimed to be the victim of a violation of the right to free legal assistance as guaranteed by Article 6(3)(*c*) of the Convention. In its report in February 1990 the Commission expressed the unanimous opinion that this provision had been violated. The Commission and the Government then referred the case to the Court.

Article 6(3)(*c*) of the Convention provides:

3. Everyone charged with a criminal offence has the following minimum rights:

. . .

(*c*) to defend himself in person or through legal assistance of his own choosing or, if he has not sufficient means to pay for legal assistance, to be given it free when the interests of justice so require;

. . .

In previous cases on this provision the Court has held that, like the other rights of the defence, the right to free legal assistance is a specific aspect of the right to a fair trial guaranteed by Article 6(1) and should be applied with this in mind.[113] It is also clear that Article 6(3)(*c*) attaches two conditions to the right. The first, 'lack of sufficient means to pay for legal assistance', was not in dispute in the present case. The question was therefore whether the second condition, that 'the interests of justice' required such assistance, was fulfilled.

To determine this point the Court applied the various criteria laid down in its case law. These in fact largely corresponded to the criteria applied by the Swiss authorities in rejecting Mr Quaranta's application, but, as the Court explained, the way in which they had applied them might differ, and in this case did differ, from the Court's approach.

The first factor, to which the Court appeared to attach particular significance, was the seriousness of the alleged offence and the corresponding severity of the possible sentence. The applicant was charged with drugs offences and faced a sentence of up to three years' imprisonment. In these circumstances, said the Court, 'free legal assistance should have been afforded by reason of the mere fact that so much was at stake'.[114]

A second factor was the complexity of the case. The applicant had admitted the offence, and consequently establishing the facts had not been difficult; nevertheless, the outcome of the trial was of considerable importance to him. The alleged offence had occurred while he was on probation and a wide range of options had

[113] See the *Artico* case, Series A, No. 37, and this *Year Book*, 51 (1980), p. 332.

[114] Judgment, para. 33.

been available to the court. Accordingly, the participation of a lawyer would have created the best conditions for the accused's defence.

A final factor was the applicant's personal situation. He was a young adult of foreign origin from an underprivileged background; moreover, he had had no real occupational training, had accumulated a long criminal record and was an habitual drug user. In this situation the Court, perhaps not surprisingly, considered that his appearances, first before the investigating judge and then before the criminal court, in each case without a lawyer, had not enabled him to present his case in an adequate manner. This defect had not been cured by the subsequent proceedings on appeal because the higher courts' powers of review were limited. The Court therefore concluded that there had been a violation of Article 6(3)(*c*).

As just satisfaction the applicant sought compensation for alleged pecuniary damage, but the Court rejected this part of the claim for lack of a causal connection. It did, however, make an award on an equitable basis in respect of non-pecuniary damage and reimbursed the relevant part of the applicant's costs and expenses, less the sum already received by way of legal aid.

In the period under review, Article 6(3)(*c*) was also considered in the *Brandstetter* case (Case No. 50) and the case of *FCB* v. *Italy* (Case No. 51), which involved other aspects of this provision.

Trial within a reasonable time (Article 6(1))—just satisfaction (Article 50)

Cases Nos. 43, 44 and 45. Pugliese (II) case. *Caleffi* case. *Vocaturo* case.[115] The Court held unanimously that there had been a breach of Article 6(1) of the Convention because of the length of civil proceedings in Italy. As just satisfaction Mr Caleffi was awarded 10,000,000 lire for damage suffered and 3,000,000 lire in respect of his costs and expenses, and Mr Vocaturo 10,500,000 lire for damage suffered and 3,000,000 lire for costs and expenses.

Like Cases Nos. 16, 17 and 18, these complaints were based upon the delays in dealing with civil claims in Italy. Mr Pugliese's claim concerned an action by a company for revocation of an order to reimburse the applicant for expenses which he had incurred as one of its directors; Mr Caleffi's was a claim against his employer in respect of upgrading; and Mr Vocaturo's claim was also against his employer, in this case for alleged underpayment of remuneration. All three claims had taken some time to determine. Mr Pugliese's was the shortest at nearly $4\frac{1}{2}$ years; Mr Caleffi's had taken more than $7\frac{1}{2}$ years; and Mr Vocaturo's had taken more than 12 years.

In their complaints to the Commission in 1985 the applicants relied on Article 6(1) of the Convention. In its reports in March 1990 the Commission upheld the three complaints. The Commission then referred the cases to the Court.

Having identified the periods to be taken into consideration, as indicated above, the Court examined whether in the circumstances of each case the proceedings had exceeded a reasonable time. It agreed with the Commission that they had. In the *Pugliese (II)* case it acknowledged that a third party, Mrs F, had intervened in the proceedings, but decided that even so it was not an especially complex case. In the *Caleffi* and *Vocaturo* cases, on the other hand, the

[115] ECHR, judgments of 24 May 1991, Series A, Nos. 206 A–C. The Court consisted of the following Chamber of Judges: Ryssdal (President); Cremona, Thór Vilhjálmsson, Bindschedler-Robert, Gölcüklü, Sir Vincent Evans, Russo, Martens, Morenilla (Judges).

distinctive feature was that the time limits applicable to employment cases under Italian law had not been complied with, the proceedings before the Court of Cassation in both cases being particularly open to criticism in this respect. The Court therefore decided that in each case there had been a violation of Article 6(1).

The issue of just satisfaction presented no special difficulties. Mr Caleffi's award was for non-pecuniary damage and Mr Vocaturo's for both pecuniary and non-pecuniary damage. In the *Pugliese (II)* case, however, the Court considered that the judgment itself constituted adequate satisfaction. In the *Caleffi* and *Vocaturo* cases the applicants asked the Court, when applying Article 50, to order the Government to publish the judgments, but the Court, in accordance with its established practice, held that it had no jurisdiction to do so.

Pre-trial detention (Article 5(3))—right to have the lawfulness of detention decided 'speedily' (Article 5(4))—just satisfaction (Article 50)

Case No. 46. Letellier case.[116] The Court held unanimously that France had violated Article 5(3) of the Convention on account of the excessive length of the applicant's pre-trial detention. As just satisfaction the Government was ordered to pay the applicant 21,433 French francs in respect of her costs and expenses.

The applicant, Mrs Letellier, owned a bar-restaurant which she ran single-handed. She was the mother of eight children from two marriages and was separated from her second husband, M. Some of her children were grown up but others were still dependent. In July 1985 M was killed by a shot fired from a car and Mrs Letellier was arrested on suspicion of being an accessory to his murder. In December 1985 the investigating judge ordered her provisional release from detention, but in January 1986 this order was rescinded by the indictments division of the Paris Court of Appeal. In February the same court dismissed a further application for release. In May that decision was set aside by the Court of Cassation, but in September the indictments division again dismissed the application. In December the decision was again overturned on appeal. The case was then remitted to the indictments division of the Amiens Court of Appeal, which dismissed the application for release in a judgment which was upheld by the Court of Cassation in June 1987. Six further applications for release were also dismissed by the indictments division of the Paris Court of Appeal in 1986 and 1987. Mrs Letellier therefore remained in detention on remand until May 1988, when she was convicted of being an accessory to murder and sentenced to three years' imprisonment. However, as the period of pre-trial detention was automatically deducted from the sentence, she was released immediately.

In her application to the Commission in August 1986 Mrs Letellier relied on Articles 5(3) and 5(4) of the Convention. In its report in March 1990 the Commission expressed the opinion that there had been a violation of both provisions. The Commission then referred the case to the Court.

It will be recalled from Case No. 6 that Article 5(3) provides that everyone arrested or detained in accordance with Article 5(1)(*c*) 'shall be entitled to trial within a reasonable time or to release pending trial. Release may be conditioned by

[116] ECHR, judgment of 26 June 1991, Series A, No. 207. The Court consisted of the following Chamber of Judges: Ryssdal (President); Thór Vilhjálmsson, Matscher, Pettiti, Macdonald, Bernhardt, Spielmann, De Meyer, Martens (Judges).

guarantees to appear for trial.' The main question in the present case was whether the length of Mrs Letellier's detention on remand had exceeded a reasonable time.

The period to be taken into consideration began in July 1985, when the applicant was remanded in custody, and ended in May 1988, when she was convicted, less one month following the investigating judge's order, when she was at liberty. It therefore lasted two years and nine months. There is a considerable amount of case law on the issue of pre-trial detention which establishes that it falls in the first place to the national authorities to ensure that pre-trial detention does not exceed a reasonable time and:

> To this end they must examine all the facts arguing for or against the existence of a genuine requirement of public interest justifying, with due regard to the principle of the presumption of innocence, a departure from the rule of respect for individual liberty and set them out in their decisions on the applications for release. It is essentially on the basis of the reasons given in these decisions and of the true facts mentioned by the applicant in his appeals, that the Court is called upon to decide whether or not there has been a violation of Article 5(3) of the Convention . . . [117]

It is also established that the persistence of a reasonable suspicion that the person arrested has committed an offence is a necessary condition for the validity of continued detention, but that after a certain time it is not in itself sufficient. The Court must at that point establish whether the other grounds relied on by the authorities continued to justify the deprivation of liberty. Where the grounds were 'relevant' and 'sufficient', the Court also has to ascertain whether the authorities displayed the necessary 'special diligence' in the conduct of the proceedings.

The national courts had put forward four reasons to justify their refusal to release Mrs Letellier, which the Court accordingly examined individually.

First, there was the risk of pressure being brought to bear on the witnesses. The Court accepted that this might have been a genuine risk initially, but considered that with the passage of time it had diminished and eventually disappeared. Indeed, after December 1986 the courts no longer referred to such a risk. Consequently, after that date the continued detention on remand could no longer be justified on this basis.

Secondly, there was the danger of Mrs Letellier absconding. The Court pointed out that the danger of this could not be gauged only on the basis of the severity of the sentence if she was convicted. While this was relevant, other factors had to be taken into account which might add to the risk or decrease it. In the present case the French courts had not explained why they regarded the risk of the applicant absconding to be decisive, notwithstanding arguments put forward by the applicant relating to her family and business, which suggested that in fact the risk was slight.

A third reason was the alleged inadequacy of court supervision. Here the Court noted that when the only remaining reason for continued detention was the fear that the accused would abscond, he or she had to be released if adequate guarantees to ensure appearance could be given. In the present case, however, the Court found that the French courts had failed to establish that this could not be done.

The fourth and final reason was the preservation of public order. The Court gave this point particular attention, and as it has not previously been discussed in

[117] Judgment, para. 35. On this point see *inter alia* the *Neumeister* case, Series A, No. 8.

such detail, this aspect of the judgment is of particular interest. The Court said that it accepted that:

> . . . by reason of their particular gravity and public reaction to them, certain offences may give rise to a social disturbance capable of justifying pre-trial detention, at least for a time. In exceptional circumstances this factor may therefore be taken into account for the purposes of the Convention, in any event in so far as domestic law recognizes . . . the notion of disturbance to public order caused by an offence.[118]

But it then qualified this by adding:

> However, this ground can be regarded as relevant and sufficient only provided that it is based on facts capable of showing that the accused's release would actually disturb public order. In addition detention will continue to be legitimate only if public order remains actually threatened; its continuation cannot be used to anticipate a custodial sentence.[119]

In the present case the Court found that these conditions had not been satisfied. The courts had assessed the need to continue the detention 'from a purely abstract point of view, taking into consideration only the gravity of the offence',[120] rather than, as the Convention required, studying the facts. This was therefore not an adequate ground for the continued detention.

In the light of the above review of the reasons for Mrs Letellier's detention, the Court concluded that at least from December 1986 the contested detention had ceased to be based on sufficient and relevant grounds. It therefore decided that there had been a violation of Article 5(3).

As the Court briefly rejected a further complaint based on Article 5(4), the only remaining issue was just satisfaction. Mrs Letellier's claim in respect of pecuniary damage, which was based on the loss to her business, was rejected because the period of detention had been deducted from her sentence. Similarly, no award was made in respect of non-pecuniary damage. The applicant's claim for her costs and expenses was, however, allowed in its entirety.

This was clearly a case in which detention on remand was initially justifiable but became increasingly hard to defend as time passed and circumstances changed. Article 5(3) does not require the authorities to release an individual where to do so would present a genuine risk; however, as this case shows, it does not follow that someone can continue to be detained merely on the basis of a repetition of previous justifications and as a matter of official convenience. As the object of Article 5 is to protect the right to liberty, pre-trial detention must be continually justified. Accordingly, if the reasons for it become tenuous or disappear, then even when the charge is very serious, the accused is entitled to her freedom.

Trial within a reasonable time (Article 6(1))—discontinuation of proceedings (Rule 49(2))

Case No. 47. Owner's Services Ltd. case.[121] The Court decided to strike this case, which concerned Italy, out of the list. It reached this decision unanimously, following the applicant's decision not to pursue its claim.

[118] Judgment, para. 51.
[119] Ibid.
[120] Ibid.
[121] ECHR, judgment of 28 June 1991, Series A, No. 208. The Court consisted of the following Chamber of Judges: Ryssdal (President); Walsh, Pinheiro Farinha, Bernhardt, Russo, Spielmann, Foighel, Morenilla, Bigi (Judges).

The applicant was a company which in March 1982 began civil proceedings in Italy to recover a large sum of money which it had paid in error and the defendant refused to refund. The proceedings were protracted and the case was not concluded at first instance until March 1987. In June of that year the applicant and the defendant settled the case.

The applicant's complaint to the Commission in March 1986 relied on Article 6(1) of the Convention. In its report in January 1991 the Commission expressed the opinion that that provision had been violated on account of the excessive length of the proceedings. The Commission then referred the case to the Court.

In a letter to the Registrar in May 1991 the applicant informed the Court that it wished to 'withdraw' and had decided not to seek just satisfaction. The Government then suggested that the case should be struck out in accordance with Rule 49(2) of the Rules of the Court.

Rule 49(2), which has been quoted in Case No. 12, provides *inter alia* for the striking out of cases when the Chamber is informed of a 'fact of a kind to provide a solution of the matter'. In the present case the applicant's decision was not technically a withdrawal since individuals do not currently have the status of parties to cases before the Court.[122] The Court decided, however, that it was a 'fact of a kind to provide a solution of the matter' for the purposes of the Rule. As the Commission had no objection and the Court found that there was nothing to justify retaining the case under Rule 49(4), it decided to strike the case out of the list.

Access to the courts (Article 6(1))—just satisfaction (Article 50)

Case No. 48. Philis case.[123] The Court held by 8 votes to 1 that there had been a violation of Article 6(1) of the Convention because the applicant was denied access to a court in Greece to claim monies due to him for a number of projects he had designed. As just satisfaction the Government was ordered to pay the applicant 1,000,000 drachmas in respect of non-pecuniary damage and 6,800,000 drachmas in respect of his costs and expenses.

The applicant was a consultant engineer in Athens. Between 1971 and 1978 he carried out a series of projects for installation of central heating and other equipment for two public institutions and a private individual. As the applicant did not receive the payment due, he began several actions in the Athens Court of First Instance either via the Technical Chamber of Greece (TEE), acting on his behalf, or in one case directly. In the latter case the action was dismissed on the ground that by virtue of a Royal Decree making regulations for the payment of engineers, only the TEE had capacity to bring proceedings for recovery of the fees.

In three applications to the Commission which he brought in January 1987 and April and June 1988, Mr Philis relied on several articles of the Convention including Article 6(1) and Article 13 (the right to a domestic remedy). In its report in March 1990 the Commission expressed the opinion that there had been a violation of Article 6(1) because the applicant had been deprived of access to a court for his civil claims and because his civil rights had not been determined within a reason-

[122] This situation will change when Protocol No. 9, which permits individuals to refer cases to the Court, comes into force.

[123] ECHR, judgment of 27 August 1991, Series A, No. 209. The Court consisted of the following Chamber of Judges: Ryssdal (President); Bindschedler-Robert, Gölcüklü, Pettiti, Walsh, Russo, Valticos, Palm, Foighel (Judges).

able time; it also considered that no separate question arose with regard to Article 13. The Commission then referred the case to the Court.

It has been clear since the *Golder* case[124] that Article 6(1), which has been quoted earlier, guarantees the 'right to a court', one aspect of which is the right of access, that is to say, the right to bring civil proceedings before a court. While this right may be subject to limitations, it is also established that these must not restrict the access available to the individual in such a way, or to such an extent, that the very essence of the right is impaired. The main question in the present case was whether the arrangements governing the civil claims of engineers in Greek law had this effect.

The applicant claimed that he had been deprived of his right of access to a court because the Royal Decree gave the TEE sole capacity to bring claims for the recovery of fees. The Government, on the other hand, maintained that the Decree did not expressly preclude engineers from themselves instituting proceedings and, further, that even if it did, the aim and effect of such an arrangement were such that it did not violate Article 6. The Court acknowledged that the system of subrogation did indeed have certain advantages, but noted that the legislation in question was worded ambiguously. Taken literally it had the effect of precluding individual actions, and this was confirmed by judicial practice in applying the legislation and the applicant's experience when he had attempted to sue in his own capacity.

The Government also submitted that, despite the effect of subrogation, the applicant had other means of redress available under Greek law. However, the Court rejected this argument on the ground that these could not be regarded as a substitute for an action to recover fees which were owing. As the applicant was unable to institute proceedings directly and independently to seek payment from his clients, the Court held that 'the very essence of his "right to a court" was impaired, and this could not be redressed by any remedy available under Greek law'.[125] The Court therefore concluded that on this point there had been a violation of Article 6(1).

In view of the above finding the Court ruled that it was unnecessary to consider whether the proceedings in which Mr Philis had been involved were concluded within a reasonable time. It came to the same conclusion as regards alleged violations of Articles 13 and 14 and so needed only to deal finally with the issue of just satisfaction. The applicant's claim for a very large sum as compensation for alleged pecuniary damage was rejected on the ground that no causal connection had been shown between the loss and the violation of Article 6(1). However, a claim in respect of non-pecuniary damage was allowed, though on a reduced basis, and the same approach was taken to the applicant's claim for reimbursement of his costs and expenses. As regards the latter, the applicant asked for the judgment to specify that the sums awarded under Article 50 should be exempt from attachment, but the Court held that it was not in a position to accede to this request.

Judge Pettiti voted against the decision on Article 6(1) and delivered a separate opinion in which he suggested that as the position in domestic law was still somewhat uncertain, it was premature to hold that the Convention had been violated.

[124] ECHR, judgment of 21 February 1975, Series A, No. 18, and this *Year Book*, 47 (1973–4), p. 391.

[125] Judgment, para. 65.

Right to a hearing before an 'impartial' tribunal (Article 6(1))—application to proceedings for breach of privilege before a legislative organ—just satisfaction (Article 50)

Case No. 49. Demicoli case.[126] In this case, which concerned proceedings for breach of privilege before the House of Representatives in Malta, the Court held unanimously that there had been a violation of Article 6(1) of the Convention because the applicant's case had not been heard by an impartial tribunal. As just satisfaction the Government was ordered to pay the applicant 5,000 Maltese liri for his costs and expenses.

The applicant was the editor of a satirical periodical in Malta. In January 1986 two Members of the House of Representatives brought an article that had recently appeared in the periodical to the attention of the House as an alleged breach of privilege. The article in question concerned a parliamentary debate which had been broadcast live on television, and included what the Members regarded as offensive references to them. In February the House passed a resolution which deemed the article to be a breach of privilege in accordance with legislation relating to the publication of any defamatory libel on a Member of the House. A further resolution on 4 March recited the previous resolution and summoned the applicant before the House to state why he should not be declared guilty of a breach of privilege. The applicant duly appeared and, after a sitting over three days at which the two Members made statements, he was found guilty by a resolution on 19 March, but the question of punishment was postponed.

In the meantime, the applicant had challenged the proceedings against him in the courts on the grounds that they violated his constitutional right to a fair hearing by an independent and impartial court. He was initially successful, but in October 1986 the Constitutional Court rejected the claim on the ground that the House of Representatives had been given authority to determine its own procedures. In December 1986 the House summoned Mr Demicoli again in order to decide the penalty and ruled that he should be fined 250 liri and must publish the resolution of 19 March in his periodical.

In his application to the Commission in May 1987 Mr Demicoli complained of a violation of Article 6(1) of the Convention and also of Article 6(2) (the presumption of innocence). In its report in March 1990 the Commission expressed the unanimous opinion that there had been a violation of Article 6(1) and that no separate issue arose under Article 6(2). The Commission then referred the case to the Court.

After rejecting a preliminary objection based on the six months' rule,[127] the Court examined the main issue in the case, the applicant's claim under Article 6(1), the relevant part of which has already been quoted in Case No. 41. The main issue here was whether that provision was applicable to the proceedings against Mr Demicoli. The Government submitted that the proceedings for breach of privilege were not 'criminal' but disciplinary in character, with the result that they lay outside the Convention. This case is by no means the first to raise the question of the scope of Article 6(1) in this regard, and in rejecting the Government's submission

[126] ECHR, judgment of 27 August 1991, Series A, No. 210. The Court consisted of the following Chamber of Judges: Ryssdal (President); Cremona, Thór Vilhjálmsson, Pinheiro Farinha, Sir Vincent Evans, Bernhardt, Spielmann, Valticos, Foighel (Judges).

[127] For an earlier case on a similar point see the *Oberschlick* case (Case No. 41, above).

the Court applied the three criteria which were originally laid down in the *Engel* case[128] and which have been consistently applied in its subsequent case law. These criteria are: the classification of the offence in domestic law (though as an indicator only); the nature of the offence itself; and the severity of the possible penalty. In the present case the classification of the offence under the law of Malta was unsettled; the offence itself was not a matter of internal regulation, but akin to a criminal offence; and the penalty, which could be imprisonment, was severe. The Court therefore concluded that Article 6(1) was applicable.

The issue of compliance was straightforward. In the Court's view 'the House of Representatives undoubtedly exercised a judicial function in determining the applicant's guilt',[129] but the two Members whose conduct had been criticized participated throughout the proceedings. This was enough for the impartiality of the adjudicating body to appear to be open to doubt. Without, therefore, finding it necessary to go into other aspects of Article 6(1), or into Article 6(2), the Court held that by reason of the House of Representatives' lack of impartiality, there had been a violation of the Convention.

As just satisfaction the applicant was awarded his costs and expenses in Malta and before the Strasbourg institutions. However, a claim in respect of non-pecuniary damage was rejected on the ground that the judgment itself constituted adequate satisfaction. The applicant also sought an order rescinding the resolutions relating to the proceedings for contempt and modifying the law of Malta. But, in accordance with its established jurisprudence, the Court held that these remedies were beyond its powers.

Malta accepted the right of individual application under Article 25 on 1 May 1987, and this is the first case involving a claim against that State. It is also the first case in which the Court has had to deal with proceedings for breach of privilege. The decision that such proceedings are covered by Article 6(1), in so far as they go beyond the regulation of internal matters, is in line with previous case law and is to be welcomed. With that point established, the question becomes when, and indeed whether, a trial before Parliament conforms to the Convention's requirements. On that point, however, as the Court confined itself to the issue of impartiality, the judgment affords only limited guidance.

Right to a fair trial (Article 6(1))—rights of the defence (Article 6(3)(c))—right to examine witnesses (Article 6(3)(d))—equality of arms—just satisfaction (Article 50)

Case No. 50. Brandstetter case.[130] In this case, which concerned Austria, the Court held by 6 votes to 3 that there had been a violation of Article 6(1) of the Convention at the appeal stage of proceedings against the applicant for defamation. A number of other complaints based on Article 6 were rejected. As just satisfaction for the violation of Article 6(1), the Government was ordered to pay the applicant 60,000 Austrian Schillings in respect of his costs and expenses.

The applicant in this rather complicated case was a wine merchant. His

[128] ECHR, judgment of 8 June 1976, Series A, No. 22, and this *Year Book*, 48 (1976–7), p. 386.

[129] Judgment, para. 40.

[130] ECHR, judgment of 28 August 1991, Series A, No. 211. The Court consisted of the following Chamber of Judges: Ryssdal (President); Thór Vilhjálmsson, Bindschedler-Robert, Gölcüklü, Matscher, Macdonald, Russo, Spielmann, Martens (Judges).

complaints related to three successive sets of criminal proceedings against him, each of which was the subject of a separate application to Strasbourg.

In the first proceedings ('the wine case') the applicant was convicted in the District Court of the offence of adulterating wine. He was fined, two tanks of his wine were forfeited and the court ordered its judgment to be published. For the proceedings against Mr Brandstetter the court had appointed an official expert who was a member of the staff of the Federal Agricultural Chemical Research Institute. The Institute was also the body which had drawn up the report that provided the basis for the criminal proceedings. However, the court had refused a request from the applicant to appoint other experts.

In the second proceedings ('the evidence case') the applicant was convicted by a Regional Court of tampering with the evidence relevant to the wine case and sentenced to 3 months' imprisonment. The Regional Court had appointed an expert who was also a member of the above mentioned Institute and who, moreover, had raised the initial suspicions against Mr Brandstetter. In these proceedings the applicant had commissioned his own expert to give evidence, but the latter was heard only as a witness.

In the third proceedings ('the defamation case') the applicant was convicted by the Regional Court of criminal defamation on account of allegations of incompetence he had made against the official cellar inspector in the wine case. For this offence he received a conditional prison sentence of 3 months. During appeal proceedings following the applicant's conviction, the Public Prosecutor had filed observations which were not communicated to the applicant's lawyer and which he was allegedly unaware of.

Mr Brandstetter's applications to the Commission were lodged in September 1984, and in March and October 1987. In them he complained of various violations of Article 6 of the Convention. The three applications were subsequently joined and in its report in May 1990 the Commission expressed the opinion that in the wine case and the evidence case there had been a violation of Article 6(1), read in conjunction with Article 6(3)(*d*), and that in the defamation case there had been a violation of Article 6(3)(*c*). Various other complaints were dismissed. The Commission and the Government then referred the case to the Court.

Articles 6(3)(*c*) and 6(3)(*d*), which, together with Article 6(1), were in issue in this case, have already been quoted in Case No. 42 and Case No. 4 respectively. To ascertain whether their requirements had been satisfied in the present case the Court, like the Commission, examined the three sets of criminal proceedings separately.

As regards the wine case the applicant maintained that the District Court had violated the principle of equality of arms by its appointment of a member of the Agricultural Institute as expert and its refusal to appoint other experts and to call a witness. The Court considered this complaint under Article 6(1), but with regard to the specific position of witnesses under Article 6(3)(*d*). In this connection it took into account the position occupied by the expert throughout the proceedings and the manner in which he performed his duties. It pointed out that the court's expert had not prepared the original report and it did not regard the mere fact that he was employed by the Institute as significant. The defence had not objected to the expert's appointment until he filed an unfavourable report, and in the Court's view there was no reason to regard him as a witness for the prosecution. The Court therefore concluded that the refusal to appoint other experts and to call a witness was not a breach of the principle of equality of arms and had not rendered the proceedings unfair. It therefore decided that there was no violation of Article 6(1), read in conjunction with Article 6(3)(*d*).

Having rejected a subsidiary argument relating to other witnesses,[131] the only other point to be considered in relation to the wine case concerned Article 6(3)(*c*). The applicant argued that the rights of the defence had been violated because his subsequent conviction for defamation had been based on allegations he had made relating to the cellar inspector's competence during the wine case. The Court, however, rejected the argument. Observing that this provision does not provide for an unlimited right to use any defence arguments, the Court pointed out that it would be absurd if the concept of the rights of the defence extended so far as to prevent a person from subsequently being charged with perjury or an equivalent offence. In this case it was not for the European Court to say whether the national courts had been correct in convicting the applicant of defamation. Moreover, although the Regional Court regarded the applicant's allegations as an aggravating circumstance when they determined his sentence for the wine offence, there was no evidence that he had been in any way inhibited or restrained from making his allegations. The Court therefore decided that in the wine case and the defamation case there had been no violations of Article 6(3)(*c*).

In relation to the evidence case the applicant's complaint was that the principle of equality of arms had been violated because, unlike the court-appointed expert, his own expert had been heard only as a witness. In order to determine this issue the Court took into account both the position of the officially appointed expert and the manner in which he performed his functions. It noted that the charge of tampering with the evidence had originated in a report which the expert had prepared. In these circumstances the applicant's apprehension as to the expert's neutrality and objectivity were justified and so, in accordance with the principle of equality of arms, 'persons who were or could be called, in whatever capacity by the defence . . . should have been examined under the same conditions as he was'.[132] The Court noted, however, that the official expert had not played a dominant role. Furthermore, although the applicant's expert was not heard under the same conditions, the refusal to appoint him as a second official expert did not, having regard to the line of argument taken by the defence and the evidence, breach the requirements of a fair trial. The Court therefore decided that on this point too there had been no violation of Article 6(1) in conjunction with Article 6(3)(*d*).

The applicant's complaint as regards the defamation proceedings also relied on the principle of equality of arms, because the Court of Appeal had relied on submissions from the Prosecutor which the applicant had not had communicated to him, or been told about. On this issue the Court pointed out that the right to an adversarial argument, which is part of the wider concept of a fair trial, implies that both prosecution and defence have to be given the opportunity to know and comment on each other's observations and evidence. In the present case, although the defence could have inquired to see what action, if any, the Prosecutor had taken, the Court did not consider this sufficient protection. It also rejected an argument that the Court of Appeal had reproduced the Prosecutor's points in its judgment, with the result that they were available to the applicant when he brought a second

[131] This concerned the report of an anonymous wine tasting panel which played some part in the proceedings against Mr Brandstetter, but which the Court decided had not infringed Article 6(3)(*d*).

[132] Judgment, para. 61.

appeal. Although this argument had been accepted by the Commission, the Court held that 'An indirect and purely hypothetical possibility for an accused to comment on prosecution arguments included in the text of a judgment can scarcely be regarded as a proper substitute for the right to examine and reply directly to submissions made by the prosecution'.[133] The Court therefore concluded that in the appeal proceedings concerning the defamation case, there was a violation of Article 6(1).

Since the majority of the applicant's complaints had been rejected, the issue of just satisfaction was not a difficult one. The Court dismissed the applicant's claims in respect of damage and costs in the wine case and the evidence case, since no violation had been found. It also rejected the claim for costs and expenses in the defamation proceedings, as they were not a direct consequence of the violation. On the other hand, the Court, after taking into account the fact that only one of the applicant's claims had succeeded and that he had already received legal aid, awarded him a sum on an equitable basis for his costs and expenses at Strasbourg.

The bearing of Article 6(3)(*d*) on the role of expert witnesses, which was a prominent issue in this case, is a matter which was previously considered in the *Bönisch* case.[134] In that case, which also concerned Austria, the decision was that the Convention had been violated. Although in the present case the Court came to the opposite conclusion, the facts were somewhat different. This latest decision can thus be regarded as an application of the principles to be found in its earlier jurisprudence.

Right to a fair trial (Article 6(1))—right to defend oneself in person (Article 6(3)(c))—just satisfaction (Article 50)

Case No. 51. FCB v. *Italy*.[135] The Court held unanimously that a decision to try the applicant on a criminal charge in his absence had violated Article 6(1) of the Convention, in conjunction with Article 6(3)(*c*). The Italian Government was ordered to pay the applicant 5,000,000 lire in respect of his costs and expenses.

In 1977 the applicant, Mr FCB, was sentenced to 24 years' imprisonment for armed robbery, murder and attempted murder. In March 1980 he was acquitted on appeal for lack of evidence and released. However, in April 1983 the Court of Cassation set aside that judgment and remitted the case to the Court of Appeal. In the meantime the applicant, who had left Italy without notifying the authorities of his change of address, had been detained in the Netherlands. He therefore failed to appear at the Court of Appeal's hearing. Despite various statements by the applicant's lawyer to the effect that the applicant was unable to appear, the Court of Appeal decided to try him in his absence and again sentenced him to 24 years' imprisonment.

In November 1985 the Court of Cassation dismissed the applicant's appeal, holding that it was for the trial court to rule on the issue of non-appearance and that its decision was not open to review. The court also refused to take account of written evidence relating to the applicant's non-appearance, ruling that it had been submitted out of time. According to information available to the European Court, the

133 Ibid., para. 68.

134 ECHR, judgment of 6 May 1985, Series A, No. 92, and this *Year Book*, 56 (1985), p. 347.

135 ECHR, judgment of 28 August 1991, Series A, No. 208 B. The Court consisted of the following Chamber of Judges: Ryssdal (President); Bindschedler-Robert, Gölcüklü, Matscher, Pinheiro Farinha, Walsh, Russo, Bernhardt, Spielmann (Judges).

latest position was that Mr FCB was currently in custody in Belgium and would have to return to the Netherlands to serve a one year prison sentence there. If the Italian authorities succeeded in obtaining his extradition, he would then have to serve there 6 years and 6 months of the prison sentence imposed on him by the Court of Appeal.

In his application to the Commission in 1986 Mr FCB complained of a violation of the rights of the defence as guaranteed by Article 6(3)(*c*) in conjunction with Article 6(1) of the Convention. In its report in May 1990 the Commission expressed the unanimous opinion that these provisions had been violated. The Commission then referred the case to the Court.

It will be recalled from the *Quaranta* case (Case No. 42) that Article 6(3)(*c*) provides that everyone charged with a criminal offence 'has the right to defend himself in person or through legal assistance of his own choosing . . . '. The present case was unusual because it concerned not the right to free legal assistance, which is the basis of most claims, but the opportunity for a person to attend his trial alongside his counsel. As such, it could be regarded as a particular aspect of the right to a fair trial guaranteed by Article 6(1), and so the Court considered the two provisions together.

The Court's starting point was that Mr FCB, though not present at the hearing in the Court of Appeal, had not expressed a wish to waive attendance. Indeed, the Italian court had learned that he was apparently in custody in the Netherlands, but instead of adjourning the trial, had merely said that he had failed to produce evidence of his inability to attend. In choosing to deal with the case in this way, the Court said that the behaviour of the Italian authorities 'was scarcely compatible with the diligence which the Contracting States must exercise in order to ensure that the rights guaranteed by Article 6 are enjoyed in an effective manner . . . '.[136]

Turning to consider the applicant's conduct, the Court said that even supposing indirect knowledge of the trial date was enough to allow the applicant to participate in the trial and that such knowledge was sufficient for the purposes of Article 6, it did not appear from the case-file that Mr FCB intended in an unequivocal manner to waive his right to appear at the trial and defend himself. It was thus unnecessary for the Court to decide 'whether and under what conditions an accused can waive exercise of his right to appear at the hearing . . . '.[137] The Court therefore concluded that there was a violation here of Article 6(1) in conjunction with Article 6(3)(*c*) of the Convention.

As just satisfaction under Article 50 the applicant sought compensation for damage and reimbursement of his lawyer's fees and costs relating to the national and the European proceedings. The Court rejected the claim for compensation on the ground that the judgment itself constituted sufficient just satisfaction. As regards the other part of the claim, it awarded a sum on an equitable basis to cover the costs incurred at Strasbourg, but decided that there was no causal link between the violation and the costs incurred in the domestic proceedings and so made no award under that head.

This is not the first case to consider the circumstances in which someone can be

[136] Judgment, para. 33.

[137] Ibid., para. 35. On the treatment of waiver in the Court's jurisprudence, see Merrills, *The Development of International Law by the European Court of Human Rights* (1988), pp. 160–6.

tried *in absentia*,[138] but it is the first case in which the accused's counsel was present at the trial, but the accused himself was not. As the right to defend oneself is in issue in such a case, technically the situation falls within Article 6(3)(*c*). However, as the substantive point relates to the question of a fair trial, the Court was right to treat the present complaint in the same way as its earlier cases and to consider it in the light of Article 6(1).

Just satisfaction (Article 50)—costs and expenses—pecuniary and non-pecuniary loss

Case No. 52. Moreira de Azevedo case (Application of Article 50).[139] The Court held unanimously that Portugal must pay the applicant 4,000,000 escudos for damage and 946,800 escudos in respect of costs and expenses, less 20,153.90 French francs.

In its judgment in October 1990 (Case No. 7) the Court found that there had been a violation of Article 6(1) of the Convention occasioned by the excessive length of criminal proceedings. The question of just satisfaction under Article 50 was reserved.

In the present proceedings the applicant claimed a total of 10,000,000 escudos in respect of pecuniary and non-pecuniary damage, together with his costs and expenses. The Court noted that there was still some uncertainty as to the outcome of an action for damages brought by the applicant in Portugal. Regardless of that outcome, however, it considered that the excessive length of the criminal proceedings must have caused the applicant pecuniary damage and certainly caused him non-pecuniary damage. It therefore awarded him the sum indicated above under these heads. As regards costs and expenses the Court did not regard the amount claimed by the applicant as excessive, but in accordance with its normal practice decided that the sum paid by the Council of Europe as legal aid should be deducted therefrom.

J. G. MERRILLS

[138] See, for example, the *Goddi* case, Series A, No. 76, and this *Year Book*, 55 (1984), p. 376; the *Colozza* case, Series A, No. 89, and this *Year Book*, 56 (1985), p. 339, and most recently the *Brozicek* case, Series A, No. 167, and this *Year Book*, 61 (1990), p. 413.

[139] ECHR, judgment of 28 August 1991, Series A, No. 208 C. The Court consisted of the following Chamber of Judges: Ryssdal (President); Cremona, Pinheiro Farinha, Speilmann, De Meyer, Martens, Palm (Judges).

DECISIONS OF THE COURT OF JUSTICE OF THE EUROPEAN COMMUNITIES DURING 1991

I. *Rights derived from provisions of Community Law—protection by national courts—relationship between rights under Community law and remedies under national law—national time limits—Member States' liability for failure to implement Directives*

I.1 *Case C–208/90, T. Emmot* v. *Minister for Social Welfare*, 25 July 1991. In proceedings before the High Court of Ireland the applicant claimed the benefit of a provision of Community law producing direct effects, namely Article 4(1) of Council Directive 79/9 of 19 December 1978 on the Equal Treatment of Men and Women in Matters of Social Security, *Official Journal*, 1979, No. L 6/24. It was contended by the respondent that she was precluded from doing so since she had not complied with time limits laid down by national law. The High Court therefore referred to the European Court for preliminary ruling a question on the relationship between national time limits and provisions of Community law producing direct effects. The European Court reasoned that where provisions in a Directive had not been properly transposed into national law, individuals were unable to ascertain the full extent of their rights. That state of uncertainty subsisted even if the provisions of the Directive were sufficiently precise and unconditional to produce direct effects and even where the European Court had ruled that in failing to implement the Directive the Member State had infringed the EEC Treaty. Accordingly, in proceedings brought against a Member State by an individual before a national court, Community law precludes that State from relying on national time limits so as to relieve itself of liability arising from directly-effective provisions of a Directive on which the individual relies.

I.2 *Joined Cases 6 and 9/90, Francovich* v. *Italy and Bonifaci and others* v. *Italy*, 19 November 1991. Italy failed to implement Council Directive 80/987 of 20 October 1980 on the Approximation of the Laws of the Member States relating to the Protection of Employees in the Event of the Insolvency of their Employer, *Official Journal*, 1980, No. L 283/23. That Directive imposed on Member States the obligation to establish guarantee institutions to secure the payment of salaries owed to employees in the event of the insolvency of their employers. The applicants were former employees of insolvent employers who claimed to be owed salaries by those employers. They sought to be reimbursed by the Italian Republic the minimum sums that they would have received from a guarantee institution, pursuant to the Directive, had Italy complied with its obligation to implement it. The Commission contended that the provisions of the Directive on which the Applicants relied were sufficiently precise and unconditional to produce direct effects; that the Directive presupposed that the guarantee institutions established thereby should be State institutions; and that it was not open to a Member State to rely on its own failure to implement a Directive so as to relieve itself of an obligation thereunder to fulfil a duty to an individual. The United Kingdom (intervening) and Italy contended that the terms of the Directive were insufficiently precise to produce direct effects. The Court accepted that the Directive did not produce direct effects; it ruled nevertheless that an obligation to make reparation arose. In the Court's ruling, the obligation on Member States to compensate those who suffer in consequence of their failure to comply with obligations imposed by the Treaty may be deduced from Article 5 thereof, which requires Member States to take all appropriate measures to ensure fulfilment of the obligations incumbent on them. Where an individual claims to have suffered damage in consequence of a Member State's failure to implement a Directive, he is entitled to be compensated by the Member State provided that three conditions are fulfilled. First, the aim of the Directive must be to give rise to rights for individuals. Second, the content of these rights must be capable of being ascertained on the basis of the provisions of the Directive. Third, there must be a causal link between the obligation incumbent on the Member State and the loss suffered by the individual.

II. *Nationality of vessels—right of Member States under public international law to lay down conditions—exercise of right under international law subject to Community Law—duty to refrain from discrimination between nationals of Member States seeking to exercise EEC Treaty rights—territorial sea—baselines—Member States' right to determine baselines in conformity with international law is subject to Community law*

II.1. *Case C–221/89, R* v. *Secretary of State for Transport, ex parte Factortame Ltd. and others*, 25 July 1991. The Merchant Shipping Act 1988 and the Merchant Shipping (Registration of Fishing Vessels) Regulations 1988, SI No. 1926, imposed certain conditions for registration of fishing vessels as British. Among these was the requirement that the owners or charterers (or shareholders and directors of corporate owners or charterers) should have specified connections with the United Kingdom by nationality, residence or domicile and that the vessel should be managed and its operations directed and controlled from within the United Kingdom. The purpose of the imposition of these conditions was to put an end to the practice of 'quota-hopping' whereby the fishing quotas attributed to the United Kingdom under Community law were consumed by vessels flying the British flag but having no effective link with the United Kingdom. Pursuant to that legislation the Secretary of State refused to register 95 vessels owned by the applicant companies, which were formed in England and Wales but controlled by Spanish interests. The applicants sought judicial review of that decision and interim relief pending determination of their claims. (On the question of interim relief, see the European Court's ruling dated 19 June 1990 in *Case C–213/89, R* v. *Secretary of State for Transport, ex parte Factortame Ltd. and others*, this *Year Book*, 61 (1990), p. 451.) The Divisional Court decided, by Order dated 10 March 1989, to refer to the European Court certain questions designed to ascertain whether the right of Member States to determine the conditions for registration of fishing vessels in their registers is subject to limitations imposed by Community law; and in particular, whether such limitations are imposed by Article 52 of the EEC Treaty (which governs the right of establishment); Article 7 thereof (which prohibits discrimination on grounds of nationality in matters falling within the scope of the Treaty); or the general principles of proportionality and non-discrimination. The British, Belgian, Danish, German, Greek, Irish and Spanish Governments and the Commission appeared before the Court, together with the applicants. The Court reasoned that where a vessel constituted an instrument for pursuing an economic activity which involved a fixed establishment in the Member State concerned, the registration of that vessel could not be dissociated from the exercise of freedom of establishment. Accordingly, in exercising their powers for the purpose of defining the conditions for the attribution of nationality to a ship, Member States must refrain from discriminating on grounds of nationality between nationals of Member States. On the other hand, a national rule requiring a vessel to be managed from within the Member State in which it was to be registered did not detract from the exercise of freedom of establishment; for that freedom presupposed the established presence in one Member State of a natural or legal person having the nationality of another Member State. The Court therefore ruled:

1. As Community Law stands at present, it is for the Member States to determine, in accordance with the general rules of international law, the conditions which must be fulfilled in order for a vessel to be registered in their registers and granted the right to fly their flag, but, in exercising that power, the Member States must comply with the rules of Community Law.

2. It is contrary to the provisions of Community Law and, in particular, to Article 52 of the EEC Treaty, for a Member State to stipulate as conditions for the registration of a fishing vessel in its national register (*a*) that the legal owners and beneficial owners and the charterers, managers and operators of the vessel must be nationals of that Member State or companies incorporated in that Member State, and that, in the latter case, at least 75% of the shares in the company must be owned by nationals of that Member State or by companies fulfilling the same requirements and 75% of the directors of the company must be nationals of that Member State; and (*b*) that the said legal owners and beneficial owners, charterers, managers, operators shareholders and directors, as the case may be, must be resident and domiciled in that Member State.

3. It is not contrary to Community Law for a Member State to stipulate as a condition for the registration of a fishing vessel in its national register that the vessel in question must be managed and its operations directed and controlled from within that Member State . . .

II.2. *Case C–246/89, Commission* v. *United Kingdom*, 4 October 1991. The Commission, supported by Spain, instituted proceedings on the basis of Article 169 of the EEC Treaty for a declaration that in adopting and maintaining the Merchant Shipping Act 1988 and the Merchant Shipping (Registration of Vessels) Regulations, the United Kingdom had failed to fulfil its obligations under the Treaty. The Court duly made that declaration, the corollary of its ruling in *Case C–221/89, R* v. *Secretary of State, ex parte Factortame Ltd. and others*.

II.3. *Case C–93/89, Commission* v. *Ireland*, 4 October 1991. Section 2 of the (Irish) Fisheries (Amendment) Act 1983 amended the Fisheries (Consolidation) Act 1959 by inserting therein section 222B. This provided in subsection (2) that a fishing vessel registered in Ireland cannot be used for sea fishing, whether in the Irish exclusive fishing zone or elsewhere, unless covered by a licence issued by the responsible Minister. Subsection (4) provided that the Minister would not issue such a licence unless the vessel is owned by an Irish citizen or a legal person formed under Irish law and having its principal place of business in Ireland. The Commission instituted proceedings against Ireland seeking a declaration that by adopting and maintaining these provisions Ireland had failed to fulfil its obligations under the EEC Treaty. To that end the Commission contended that the provisions in issue entailed discrimination on grounds of nationality in respect of a matter falling within the scope of the Treaty. Ireland, supported by the United Kingdom, contended that the provisions in question did not discriminate on grounds of nationality: they applied only to fishing vessels registered in Ireland and did not prevent fishing vessel owners established in other Member States from establishing themselves in Ireland. The Court reasoned that the Commission's complaint did not refer to discrimination between vessels registered in the various Member States but to different treatment of Irish nationals owning fishing vessels registered in Ireland and nationals of other Member States owning fishing vessels registered in Ireland. That difference in treatment constituted discrimination contrary to Article 52 of the EEC Treaty. The Court therefore granted the Commission the declaration it had sought.

II.4. *Case C–146/89, Commission* v. *United Kingdom*, 9 July 1991. The Commission brought proceedings against the United Kingdom seeking a declaration that the latter had failed to fulfil her obligations under the EEC Treaty by applying in certain areas new baselines for the demarcation of the territorial sea, thereby shifting the limits of territorial sea further from the land mass than the limits in force on the entry into force of Council Regulation 170/83 of 25 January 1983, *Official Journal*, 1983, No. L 24/1. That Regulation determines the areas within the twelve-mile limit in which fishermen from other Member States may engage in certain fishing activities. The Commission, supported by France, took the view that the zones indicated in Annex I to that Regulation in accordance with Article 6 thereof (particularly those located in United Kingdom territorial waters between the six- and twelve-mile limits) must be measured from the baselines as they existed on 25 January 1983. The United Kingdom contended that the baselines to be taken into account are those which exist from time to time, as drawn in accordance with principles of public international law by the Member State concerned. The European Court noted that the essential point of dispute was not over the rules of international law governing the determination of baselines but over the interpretation of Article 6 of Council Regulation 170/83 and Annex I thereto. The relevant rules of international law were consolidated, in particular, by Articles 3, 4 and 11 of the Geneva Convention on the Territorial Sea and Contiguous Zone, 29 April 1958, *UN Treaty Series*, vol. 516, p. 205, and Articles 5, 7 and 13 of the United Nations Convention on the Law of the Sea, signed at Montego Bay on 10 December 1982, UN Doc. A/CONF. 62/122. The Commission did not contend that the baselines designated by the United Kingdom entailed contravention of those principles. However, in the Court's view, Council Regulation 170/83 represented a carefully achieved balance between exclusive access for local fishermen and the principle of equal access. This balance could be compromised if Member States could vary it unilaterally by altering national baselines. Moreover a Joint Declaration of the Council and Commission, recorded in the Council minutes at the time of the adoption of the Annex, specified that it would be capable of being amended by a further Regulation; and this implied that it could not be varied by unilateral action.

III. *Treaties with non-Member States—capacity of European Court to interpret treaties between EEC and non-Member States—direct effects—treaties between Member States inter se or between Member States and non-Member States—rights created by Community law not to be made subject to such treaties—interpretation of treaties by reference to objects—proposed EEC–EFTA Agreement—incompatibility with EEC Treaty*

III.1 *Case C–18/90, Office National de l'Emploi (ONEM)* v. *Bahia Kziber*, 31 January 1991. Mrs Kziber was an unemployed person dependent on her father, a retired man who had worked and who continued to live in Belgium. In proceedings before the *Cour du Travail de Liège* she claimed an unemployment benefit available under Belgian legislation to young persons seeking work and dependent on retired persons resident in Belgium. The ONEM refused to grant her that benefit on the ground that Mrs Kziber (like her father) was a Moroccan national. Mrs Kziber relied on Article 4(1) of a treaty between the EEC and Morocco signed in Rabat on 27 April 1976 and concluded on behalf of the Community by Council Regulation 2211/78 of 26 September 1978, *Official Journal*, 1978, No. L 264/1. That article prohibits discrimination on grounds of nationality in the field of social security. The *Tribunal du Travail* referred to the European Court for a preliminary ruling a question on the interpretation of that article. The European Court reiterated its previous rulings whereby it has jurisdiction to interpret a provision in such a treaty, which forms an integral part of Community law. (See *Case 181/73, Haegemann*, [1974] ECR 449.) It also reiterated previous rulings holding that a provision in an agreement concluded with a non-Member State must be regarded as directly applicable when, having regard to its wording and to the purpose of the agreement itself, the provision contained a clear and precise obligation which was not subject, in its implementation or effects, to the adoption of any subsequent measure. (See *Case C–192, Sevince* v. *Staatssecretaris van Justitie*, 20 September 1990, this *Year Book*, 61 (1990), p. 458.) In the light of this jurisprudence and on the interpretation of the contested provision, read in its context and in view of the purpose of the treaty as a whole, the Court concluded that:

> Article 4(1) of the Cooperation Agreement between the European Economic Community and the Kingdom of Morocco, signed in Rabat on 27 April 1976 . . . must be interpreted as meaning that it precludes a Member State from refusing to grant an unemployment benefit, which its legislation makes available to young persons seeking work, to a member of the family of a worker of Moroccan nationality residing with him, on the ground that the person seeking work is a Moroccan national.

III.2. *Case C–307/89, Commission* v. *France*, 11 June 1991. Articles L 815.82 and L 815.83 of the new French Social Security Code made entitlement to certain social security benefits subject to two conditions: the conclusion of reciprocal international agreements and prior residence on French territory. The Commission took the view that the application of these provisions to Community nationals was incompatible with Council Regulation 1408/71 of 14 June 1971 on the Application of Social Security Schemes, *Official Journal*, Special Edition 1971, p. 416. It called upon the French authorities to modify the legislation accordingly. Although the legislation was not amended, a Ministerial Circular (number 1370 of 5 November 1987) provided in effect that the contested legislative provisions would not be applied to French nationals. The Commission instituted proceedings against France pursuant to Article 169 of the EEC Treaty, seeking a declaration that it had failed to fulfil its obligations under the EEC Treaty. The Court recalled its decision in *Case 167/73, Commission* v. *France, 'French Merchant Seamen'*, [1974] ECR 359, in which it had held that a breach of the Treaty arises where a Member State maintains in force inconsistent legislative provisions, even if it does not apply them in practice. Accordingly, it held that France had failed to fulfil its obligations under the EEC Treaty by maintaining in force legislative provisions authorizing the competent French authorities to make access to rights created by Community law contingent on the the conclusion of reciprocal treaty arrangements.

III.3. *Opinion 1/91, Draft Agreement between the European Economic Community and the States belonging to the European Free Trade Association, relating to the Creation of the European Economic Area*, 16 December 1991. Pursuant to Article 228(1) of the EEC Treaty, the Commission asked the European Court for its opinion on the compatibility with the EEC Treaty of certain terms of the draft EEA Agreement, establishing a system for judicial supervision. The declared purpose of the draft EEA Agreement was to create a European Economic Area covering the territories of the EEC and the EFTA States. It envisaged the establishment of an EEA Court for settlement of disputes between contracting parties. That Court would consist of eight judges including five from the European Court and three from EFTA States. Attached to the EEA Court would be an EEA Court of First Instance composed of five judges including two judges of the European Court of First Instance and three from EFTA States. The provisions of the draft EEA Agreement were to be interpreted in conformity with rulings of the European Court on the corresponding provisions of the EEC Treaty. The European Court stated in part:

The fact that the provisions of the Agreement and the corresponding Community provisions are identically worded does not mean that they must necessarily be interpreted identically. An international treaty is to be interpreted not only on the basis of its wording but also in the light of its objectives. Article 31 of the Vienna Convention on the Law of Treaties stipulates in this respect that a treaty is to be interpreted in good faith in accordance with the ordinary meaning to be given to its terms in their context and in the light of its object and purpose . . .

Whereas the draft EEA Agreement

is concerned with the application of rules on free trade and competition in economic and commercial relations between the Contracting Parties . . . the EEC Treaty . . . aims to achieve economic integration leading to the establishment of an internal market and economic and monetary union . . . The EEA is to be established on the basis of an international treaty which, essentially, merely creates rights and obligations as between the Contracting Parties . . . In contrast, the EEC Treaty, although concluded in the form of an international agreement, none the less constitutes the constitutional charter of a Community based on the rule of law.

In view of this fundamental difference, the European Court concluded that the proposed system of judicial supervision of the draft EEA Agreement would give rise to insuperable difficulties for judges of the European Court required to participate in the EEA Court. The first difficulty arose from the jurisdiction of the EEA Court. That Court would have jurisdiction with regard to the settlement of disputes between the contracting parties. As far as the EEC and its Member States were concerned, the term 'contracting parties' meant the Community and the Member States, or the Community, or the Member States, depending on the attribution of competence as between the Community and the Member States under Community law. Hence the jurisdiction conferred on the EEA Court was likely to affect the allocation of responsibilities defined by the Treaties. Moreover, although the proposed EEA Court would be under a duty to interpret the provisions of the Agreement in the light of the relevant rulings of the Court of Justice given prior to its conclusion, the EEA Court would not be subject to a like obligation in the case of subsequent decisions of the European Court.

Consequently, depending on whether they are sitting on the Court of Justice or on the EEA

Court, the judges of the Court of Justice who are members of the EEA Court will have to apply and interpret the same provisions but using different approaches, methods and concepts in order to take account of the nature of each treaty and its particular objectives. In those circumstances it will be very difficult, if not impossible, for those judges, when sitting in the Court of Justice, to tackle questions with completely open minds where they have taken part in determining those questions as members of the EEA Court.

The second area of difficulty identified by the European Court occurred in the event of references from courts in EFTA States. Protocol 34 to the draft EEA Agreement envisaged that EFTA States would be free to authorize their courts to refer questions to the European Court for preliminary ruling where an identical question on interpretation arises under the EEA Agreement and the EEC Treaty. The European Court objected that there would be no obligation to refer, in the case of courts of last instance, and no guarantee that rulings given by the European Court would be binding on the courts making the reference.

[I]t is unacceptable that the answers which the Court of Justice gives to the courts and tribunals in the EFTA States are purely advisory and without any binding effects. Such a situation would change the nature and function of the Court of Justice as it is conceived by the EEC Treaty . . .

The third difficulty arose from Article 238 of the EEC Treaty which deals with the conclusion of association agreements between the Community and non-Member States.

Article 238 of the EEC Treaty does not provide any basis for setting up a system of courts which conflicts with Article 164 of the EEC Treaty and, more generally, with the very foundations of the Community.

An amendment of Article 238, as proposed by the Commission, could not cure the incompatibility with Community law of the system of courts envisaged by the draft EEA Agreement.

IV. *Recognition—unrecognized 'State'—Turkish Republic of Northern Cyprus—whether a 'person' capable of intervening before the European Court—whether certificates issued by that body to be treated as authentic by Member States*

Case C–50/90, Sunzest (Europe) BV and Sunzest (Netherlands) BV v. *Commission*, 13 June 1991. The applicant companies challenged a 'decision' of the Commission said to be contained in a letter dated 5 December 1989 whereby the Director General of DG VI (Directorate General for Agriculture) notified the Permanent Representative of Belgium to the EEC that any imports from Cyprus must be accompanied by phytosanitary certificates issued in accordance with Council Directive 77/93 of 21 December 1976 on the Introduction of Harmful Organisms in Plants, *Official Journal*, 1977, No. L 26/20; and that only certificates issued by the Government of the Republic of Cyprus are authentic (i.e. those issued by the Turkish Republic of Northern Cyprus were not authentic). The applicants sought the annulment of the 'decision' and damages, contending that the letter omitted to take account of the fact that in refusing to issue such certificates for products originating in the northern part of Cyprus, the Government of the Republic of Cyprus was itself acting in breach of Article 5 of the Association Agreement between the EEC and Cyprus of 19 December 1972, *Official Journal*, 1973, No. L 133/1, which provides that the rules governing trade between the contracting parties may not give rise to any 'discrimination between . . . nationals or companies of Cyprus'.

Greece intervened in support of the Commission, exercising its rights under Article 37 of the Statute of the Court to do so as a Member State. The Republic of Cyprus and the Turkish Republic of Northern Cyprus applied to intervene, claiming the right to do so as 'any other person establishing an interest in the result of any case submitted to the court' within the meaning of the second paragraph of Article 37. (Non-Member States are 'persons' capable of intervening pursuant to Article 37: see *Joined Cases 91 and 200/82, Chris International Foods* v. *Commission*, [1983] ECR 417.) The Court deferred consideration of these applications and considered the admissibility of the main action. It concluded that the contested 'decision' was not an act capable of being challenged since it was merely advisory and produced no legal effects; and for the same reason the contested 'decision' could not give rise to an action for damages. The main action was therefore inadmissible and it was unnecessary to rule on the applications of the prospective interveners.

V. *European Convention on Human Rights—jurisdiction of Court of Justice of European Communities to interpret and apply Convention when considering national legislation subject to Community Law—absence of such jurisdiction where national legislation not subject to Community law*

V.1. *Case C–290/89, Elliniki Radiophonia Tileorassi–Anonimi Etairia* v. *Dimotiki Etiaira Pliroforissis and Kouvelas*, 18 June 1991. The applicant was a Greek radio and television undertaking to which the Greek State, by Law No. 1730/1987, granted exclusive rights. The respondents were a municipal information company in Thessaloniki and the mayor of that city. The applicants instituted proceedings before the *Monomeles Protodikeio Thessolonikis* (court of first instance) seeking a declaration that in setting up a television station in Thessaloniki the respondents had infringed exclusive rights conferred upon them by Greek law. The applicants sought interim relief including a temporary injunction to restrain the respondents from broadcasting and the seizure of technical equipment. The respondents relied on provisions of European Community Law governing the progressive adjustment of monopolies, the free movement of goods, freedom to provide services and national monopolies, together with Article 2 of the EEC Treaty (which describes the Community's tasks) and Article 10 of the European Convention on Human Rights (which protects freedom of expression). Although it ruled against the respondents' submissions on other points, the Court held that

> Article 59 of the EEC Treaty prohibits national rules which create a monopoly comprising exclusive rights to transmit the broadcasts of the holder of the monopoly and to retransmit broadcasts from other Member States, where such a monopoly gives rise to discriminatory effects detrimental to broadcasts from other Member States, unless such rules are justified by any of the reasons indicated in Article 56 of the EEC Treaty [viz. public policy, public security or public health] to which Article 66 thereof refers . . . The limitations imposed on the power of the Member States to apply the provisions referred to in Articles 66 and 56 of the Treaty on grounds of public policy, public security and public health must be appraised in the light of the general principle of freedom of expression embodied in Article 10 of the European Convention of Human Rights.

V.2. *Case 159/90, Society for the Protection of Unborn Children* v. *Grogan*, 4 October 1991. Legislation in force in Ireland prohibited a students' organization from distributing information designed to assist persons in Ireland to obtain abortions in other Member States of the EEC. In proceedings instituted before the

High Court of Ireland for an injunction it was contended on behalf of the respondents that the national prohibition amounted to an infringement of provisions of Community law governing freedom to supply services and Article 10 of the European Convention on Human Rights, governing freedom of expression. The European Court ruled that a restriction on the advertising in a Member State of a service which could not lawfully be supplied there is non-discriminatory and consequently not incompatible with Community rules governing the supply of services. On the question arising under the European Convention on Human Rights the Court held that it was without jurisdiction. It acknowledged that where (as in Case 260/89) national legislation fell within the field of application of Community law, the European Court, when requested to give a preliminary ruling, must supply the national court with all the elements necessary to assess the compatibility of that legislation with the European Convention on Human Rights. It added however that it has no such jurisdiction with regard to national legislation lying outside Community law, as was true of the prohibition in this case.

VI. *Brussels Convention on Jurisdiction and the Enforcement of Judgments in Civil and Commercial Matters—lis alibi pendens—domicile of parties—jurisdiction in matters of insurance and reinsurance—exclusion of arbitration—extent of exclusion*

VI.1. *Case C–351/89, Overseas Union Insurance Ltd., Deutsche Ruck UK, Pine Top Insurance Company* v. *New Hampshire Insurance Company*, 27 June 1991. The New Hampshire Insurance Company, formed in New Hampshire in the United States, was registered in France as a foreign company and in England as an oversea company under the Companies Act 1985. It issued a policy of insurance covering the repair or replacement of electrical appliances sold in France with a five year guarantee. It reinsured part of the risk with the appellants, companies incorporated in England with their registered offices in London. The appellants sought to avoid the contracts of reinsurance alleging non-disclosure of material particulars. New Hampshire issued proceedings against the appellants before the *Tribunal du commerce* in Paris. The appellants challenged the jurisdiction of the French courts and instituted proceedings against New Hampshire in the Commercial Court in London seeking a declaration of non-liability. The Commercial Court stayed proceedings pending the decision of the French court, in accordance with Article 21 of the Brussels Convention, which governs *lis pendens*. The appellants contended that Article 21 did not apply where the proposed defendant was domiciled in a contracting State and, by Article 2, could be sued only there. The Court of Appeal referred questions to the European Court, which ruled that Article 21 applies irrespective of the domicile of the parties to the two sets of proceedings. It added, without prejudice to the case where the court second seised has exclusive jurisdiction under Article 16, that where the jurisdiction of the court first seised is contested, the court second seised may, if it does not decline jurisdiction, only stay the proceedings and may not itself examine the jurisdiction of the court first seised.

VI.2. *Case C–190/89, Marc Rich & Co. AG* v. *Società Italiana Impianti*, 25 July 1991. By telex dated 23 January 1987 Marc Rich offered to purchase a quantity of Iranian crude from the respondents, Società Italiana Impianti. On 25 January the respondents replied, accepting the offer subject to certain conditions. These were apparently accepted by Marc Rich on 26 January, when the respondents considered the contract concluded. Marc Rich then sent a further telex setting out terms including a clause selecting English governing law and providing for arbitration in London. There was no reply. The oil was loaded on board *The Atlantic Emperor*. On the completion of the loading Marc Rich complained that the oil was seriously contaminated and claimed damages exceeding $7,000,000. On 18 February the respondents initiated proceedings in Italy claiming a declaration of non-liability. The writ was served on Marc Rich on 29 February, on which date that party commenced arbitration proceedings in London. Marc Rich also sought a declaration from the *Corte Suprema di Cassazione* that the Italian courts were without jurisdiction. Since the respondents failed to appoint an arbitrator, Marc Rich applied to the High Court to appoint one. That court gave leave to serve the notice of the writ in Italy. The respondents applied for that leave to be withdrawn, contending that the real dispute was whether the contract contained an arbitration clause: this fell within the Brussels Convention and should be determined in Italy. According to Marc Rich, the dispute fell outside the Brussels Convention by Article 1(4), which excludes 'arbitration'. Hirst J held that the Convention did not apply to the dispute and that the contract was subject to English law. On appeal the Court of Appeal referred to the European Court a question on the interpretation of Article 1(4). The European Court ruled that the exclusion created by Article 1(4) extends to litigation pending before a national court concerning the appointment of an arbitrator, even if the existence or validity of an arbitration agreement is a preliminary issue in that litigation.

RICHARD PLENDER

UNITED KINGDOM MATERIALS ON INTERNATIONAL LAW 1991*

Edited by GEOFFREY MARSTON[1]

[*Editorial note*: Attention is drawn to the editorial note in UKMIL 1983, p. 361. The publication schedule of the present edition of UKMIL has permitted the citation of the definitive column references in the bound volumes of the Parliamentary Debates.]

INDEX[2]

* Editorial arrangement and comments © Geoffrey Marston, 1992. Copyright in the materials cited is in the original copyright holders.

[1] LL M, Ph.D (Lond.): Lecturer in Law, University of Cambridge; Fellow of Sidney Sussex College. The assistance of Mr M.C. Wood and Mr C.A. Whomersley, Legal Counsellors, Mr J.J. Rankin, Assistant Legal Adviser, and the News Department, Foreign and Commonwealth Office, and the staff of the Official Publications Department, University Library, Cambridge, is gratefully acknowledged.

[2] Based on the *Model Plan for the Classification of Documents concerning State Practice in the field of Public International Law* adopted by the Committee of Ministers of the Council of Europe in Resolution (68) 17 of 28 June 1968. For a more detailed index of subject-matter, readers are referred to the general index to this volume.

Abbreviations

HC Debs *Hansard*, House of Commons Debates (6th series)
HL Debs *Hansard*, House of Lords Debates (5th series)
Cmnd. Command Paper (5th series)
Cm. Command Paper (6th series)
UKMIL *United Kingdom Materials on International Law*
TS *United Kingdom Treaty Series*
EC European Community
FCO Foreign and Commonwealth Office
WA Written Answers

Part One: I. *International law in general—nature, basis, purpose*

In the course of a debate on the subject of the UN Decade of International Law, the Parliamentary Under-Secretary of State, FCO, Mr Mark Lennox-Boyd, stated:

By a resolution in 1989, the General Assembly of the United Nations declared the period from 1990 to 1999 the United Nations decade of international law. That same resolution stated that the main purposes of the decade were

'to promote acceptance of and respect for the principles of international law;

to promote means and methods for the peaceful settlement of disputes between States, including resort to and full respect for the International Court of Justice;

to encourage the progressive development of international law and its codification;

to encourage the teaching, study, dissemination and wider appreciation of international law.'

. . . The Government strongly support all those objectives.

In 1990, the General Assembly adopted a programme for the first two-year period of the decade. The programme, which is rather detailed, envisages full co-operation with other international and regional organisations, and with such eminent private institutions as the International Law Association, the Institute of International Law and national societies.

It is too early to predict what concrete results will emerge, but I can say that work on the decade has started well. It began as an initiative by the non-aligned countries—welcome evidence of the importance that those countries attach to international law. I am happy to say that the days are past when some developing countries regarded international law and its institutions with suspicion, as something imposed on them by the west. There is also a welcome new emphasis in Soviet policy on the primacy of law and there has been a radical and welcome change in the approach of many eastern European countries as they free themselves from stale communist dogma.

The General Assembly has acted by consensus in declaring the decade and in drawing up the programme of activities. Let me stress the importance that we attach to consensus. If the decade is to contribute to the healthy development of international law, it is essential for that consensus to be maintained in every area.

(HC Debs., vol. 188, cols. 1116–7: 28 March 1991)

Mr Lennox-Boyd continued:

The United Kingdom has always played a full role in the discussions on the decade. We co-sponsored the General Assembly resolutions of 1989 and 1990, and we participated actively in the work of the legal committee of the General Assembly and its working group on the subject. We shall continue to do so. That contribution to the decade reflects our contribution to international law more generally. The Government are committed to upholding the rule of law in international affairs and fostering good government and a respect for human rights. I recall the document 'Human Rights in Foreign Policy' that the Foreign Office made public a week or so ago. . . .

The United Kingdom has always made a major contribution to the development of international law, both through its practice—now well recorded each year in the 'British Year Book of International Law'—and by its role in the elaboration of treaties and as a depositary of many important treaties. It is not only in relation to questions of war and peace that international law is important. In today's world it plays an increasing part in everyday life. In the past year or so we have made an important contribution to the elaboration of worldwide conventions on drug trafficking and the marking of explosives and to treaties relating to the environment and disarmament. If we look back over a longer period, we see that we have played, and that we continue to play, a major role in the Antarctic treaty system and in the law of the sea. Much international law is already of a positive nature—for example, on the environment, drugs and crime prevention. However, I agree that much more could be done. For example, the Government are working very hard on the climate convention.

. . .

The United Kingdom's contribution to international law goes well beyond the Government. The British Institute of International and Comparative Law, the British branch of the International Law Association, and the many universities which teach international law play an important role and have influence well beyond this country. We are particularly pleased that in February the British judge on the International Court of Justice, Sir Robert Jennings, formerly professor of international law at Cambridge University, was elected president of the court for a three-year term. He is, in fact, the third British president of the court since 1946.

Successive British members of the United Nations International Law Commission have been influential. The commission has the potential to make further important contributions to the codification and development of international law.

. . .

Public awareness of international law has, I believe never been higher than it is at present. Public awareness is important, for it is ultimately for the people of the various states to ensure, through their elected representatives and through public opinion, that Governments comply with international law. International law will be respected fully only when public opinion in all countries demands that Governments comply not only with the rule of law at home but with the rule of law in international affairs. Debates like this one, stimulated by the United Nations decade of international law, contribute to that end.

(Ibid., cols. 1167–9)

Speaking on 13 November 1991 in the Sixth Committee of the UN General Assembly considering the subject of the UN Decade of International Law, the representative of the Netherlands, on behalf of the EC and its Twelve Member States, observed:

The Member States of the European Community would like to reiterate their endorsement of Resolution 45/40, which they co-sponsored. They remain convinced, as the distinguished representative of Italy stated on behalf of the Twelve last year, that 'the time is ripe for co-ordinated initiatives, whose overall impact will be the strengthening of international law in various fields: from questions concerning increasing the number of parties to important multilateral treaties and improving their application; to assistance to developing countries in the treaty-making process; to the maintenance of international peace and security; to the strengthening of the International Court of Justice and of procedures for the peaceful settlement of disputes; to taking stock of the achievements obtained and of work still to be done as regards the codification and progressive development of international law; to initiatives for the teaching, study, dissemination and wider appreciation of international law'.

(Text provided by the FCO; see also A/C.6/46/SR. 37, p. 12)

Part One: II. D. 1. *International law in general—relationship between international law and municipal law—implementation of international law in municipal law—treaties*

(See also Part Ten: III., below)

In moving the approval in the House of Lords of the European Communities (Definition of Treaties) (Fourth ACP-EEC Convention of Lomé) Order 1991, the Government spokesman, Lord Reay, stated in part:

. . . the Fourth ACP-EEC Convention, or Lomé IV as it is commonly known, governs development and trade relations between the Community and the 69 countries described as the African Caribbean and Pacific (or ACP) group. The convention was signed on 15 December 1989 in Lomé. . . .

The draft Order in Council to which the Motion refers was approved in another place on 26 February. It will allow the convention's provisions to be effected in United Kingdom law, which opens the way for ratification of the convention by the United Kingdom. The convention takes force when ratified by all EC member states and two thirds of the ACP countries and concluded by the Community.

(HL Debs., vol. 526, col. 1173: 28 February 1991; see also HC Debs., vol. 186, cols. 932–3: 26 February 1991)

Speaking on 1 April 1991 in the UN Human Rights Committee deliberating upon the third periodic report of the UK, the UK representative, Mr Halliday, stated of the International Covenant on Civil and Political Rights, 1966:

34. Incorporation of the Covenant would be a highly complex exercise, and would involve an essentially political decision based on a close examination of the ways in which existing United Kingdom law, both common law and statute law, in fact fulfilled the country's obligations under the Covenant. Debate on the issue was continuing and it was unlikely that any decision would be taken in the immediate future.
35. In reply to Mr Myullerson, who had asked whether the norms in the Covenant, as part of customary international law, were to be considered as already having some special status in United Kingdom law, he said that he was unaware of any ruling by the courts to that effect.

(CCPR/C/SR. 1046, p. 8)

Later in the same discussion, Mr Beamish, also in the UK delegation, stated on 2 April 1991:

15. A question had been raised regarding apparent inconsistencies in the Constitution of the Cayman Islands. Under the Cayman Islands Royal Instructions, the

Governor could not assent to any bill the provisions of which appeared to be inconsistent with obligations imposed by treaty without the prior instructions of Her Majesty through a Secretary of State. It followed that, if the Governor deemed a bill to be inconsistent with a treaty, he was obliged, under section 39(2) of the Constitution, to seek instructions on the matter from London. The question of consistency of the bill with the treaty would be examined and, if the bill was found to be inconsistent with treaty obligations, assent would not be given.

16. The disallowance procedure, set forth in section 41 of the Constitution of the Cayman Islands, provided that any law to which the Governor had given his consent could be disallowed by Her Majesty through a Secretary of State. Once the law had been disallowed, notice to that effect was published and the law was annulled with effect from the date of publication. One ground on which a law might be disallowed would be that it was inconsistent with a treaty obligation. Those formal procedures were applied very rarely, since the greatest care was taken to ensure that bills were compatible with treaty obligations.

(CCPR/C/SR. 1047, p. 5)

In moving the Second Reading in the House of Lords of the Arms Control and Disarmament Bill, the Government spokesman, Lord Reay, stated:

The Bill will enable effect to be given in the law of the United Kingdom to the protocol on inspection of the Treaty on Conventional Armed Forces in Europe. The purpose of the Bill is twofold: first, to create rights of access, entry and inspection for the purposes of conducting challenge inspections under the protocol on inspection; secondly, to confer certain privileges and immunities on inspectors and transport crew members in connection with all inspections under the protocol.

The CFE treaty was signed at Paris on 19th November 1990 by 22 states, all 16 members of the North Atlantic Alliance (including of course the United Kingdom) and six states which were members of the Warsaw Pact (including the Soviet Union). It is a fundamental stage in the negotiations on conventional armed forces in Europe. It is to be followed by negotiations to limit manpower and by further measures which will enhance stability and openness in military affairs in Europe.

. . .

The Bill will be brought into force only when all 22 parties have ratified the treaty. However, we need the Bill in the present Session so that the United Kingdom will be in a position to ratify the treaty swiftly when circumstances permit. Without the Bill we could find ourselves holding up entry into force of the treaty and I am sure that none of your Lordships would wish that to happen.

(HL Debs., vol. 527, cols. 1695–8, *passim*: 19 April 1991; see also HC Debs., vol. 194, cols. 872–4: 9 July 1991)

In reply to a question, the Parliamentary Under-Secretary of State, Home Office, wrote:

We have made clear to the Isle of Man authorities that, in order to enable the United Kingdom to conform with its obligations under the [European Convention on Human Rights], the island's legislation on homosexuality should be amended;

that it is desirable that the Isle of Man should itself amend the legislation; but that, if necessary, the United Kingdom will legislate on the island's behalf.

(HC Debs., vol. 189, WA, col. *560*: 26 April 1991)

In announcing the UK's ratification on 3 May 1991 of the Convention for the Suppression of Unlawful Acts against Maritime Navigation, with the Protocol for the Suppression of Unlawful Acts against the Safety of Fixed Platforms located on the Continental Shelf, done at Rome on 10 March 1988, the FCO stated:

The United Kingdom was unable to ratify the Convention and Protocol until appropriate domestic legislation had been put in place. The Aviation and Maritime Security Act 1990 provided the necessary legislation for ratification. The UK's Dependent Territories, the Sovereign Base Areas in Cyprus, the Channel Islands and Isle of Man would not be included in the ratification at this stage because local legislation had not yet been effected. Ratification in respect of these territories would follow in due course.

(Text provided by the FCO)

In moving the consideration in HC Standing Committee of the draft Drug Trafficking Offences Act 1986 (Designated Countries and Territories) (Amendment) Order 1991 and the draft Criminal Justice (International Co-operation) Act 1990 (Enforcement of Overseas Forfeiture Orders) Order 1991, the Minister of State, Home Office, Mr John Patten, stated:

The purpose of the orders is twofold. First, they will enable us to comply with obligations that arise out of our ratification of the United Nations convention against illicit traffic in narcotic drugs and psychotropic substances. That will take place towards the end of June or at the beginning of July. Secondly, the orders will enable us to implement further agreements and arrangements of a practical sort, which we have negotiated with specific countries to confiscate the proceeds of drug trafficking and to order the forfeiture of materials used. Therefore, I commend the orders to the Committee.

(HC Debs., 1990–91, Fifth Standing Committee on Statutory Instruments, etc.: 19 June 1991, col. 3; see also Statutory Instruments 1991, Nos. 1463 and 1465)

In moving the consideration in HC Standing Committee of the draft Criminal Justice (International Co-operation) Act 1990 (Enforcement of Overseas Forfeiture Orders) (Scotland) Order 1991, the Parliamentary Under-Secretary of State for Scotland, Lord James Douglas-Hamilton, stated:

For simplicity's sake, I shall refer to the United Nations convention on illicit traffic in narcotic drugs and illicit substances as the Vienna convention. The United Kingdom signed the convention on 20 December 1988. In order to comply with obligations arising out of our ratification of the Vienna Convention on 1 July [1990], we have to ensure that the necessary legal and procedural frameworks are in place to enable action to be taken across international boundaries, to forfeit property, and to confiscate proceeds related to drug trafficking.

(HC Debs., 1990–91, Third Standing Committee on Statutory Instruments, etc., 20 June 1991, cols. 4–5; see also Statutory Instruments 1991, No. 1468)

In moving the consideration in HC Standing Committee of the draft Criminal Justice Act 1988 (Designated Countries and Territories) Order 1991, the Minister of State, Home Office, Mr John Patten, stated:

In practical terms, the order has two purposes. It will enable us to implement agreements which we have negotiated with Italy, Nigeria and Sweden to co-operate in freezing and confiscating the proceeds of crime. It paves the way for us to ratify in the new year the Council of Europe convention on laundering, search, seizure and confiscation of the proceeds from crime.

(HC Debs., 1991–92, Third Standing Committee on Statutory Instruments, etc., 5 December 1991, cols. 3–4; see now Statutory Instruments 1991, No. 2873)

Later in his statement, Mr Patten remarked:

Needless to say, the United Kingdom has signed the convention, and we plan to ratify it early next year, as soon as the necessary subsidiary legislation—including this order—is in place.

(Ibid., col. 9)

He went on to state:

. . . it was not until we passed the Criminal Justice Act 1988 that we could modify our extradition legislation—which dated back to 1870—to allow us to sign bilateral and multilateral extradition conventions.

(Ibid., col. 10)

In reply to the question what progress has been made on the implementation of Annex II of MARPOL 1973/78, the Parliamentary Under-Secretary of State, Department of Transport, wrote:

The Merchant Shipping (Control of Pollution by Noxious Liquid Substances in Bulk) Regulations 1987 came into force on 6 April 1987. They apply to United Kingdom ships wherever they may be and to other ships while they are in the United Kingdom or its territorial waters.

The regulations were updated with effect from 1 January 1991 to take into account additional noxious substances.

(HC Debs., vol. 200, WA, col. *306* : 9 December 1991)

Part Two: I. *Sources of international law—treaties*

Speaking on 1 April 1991 in the UN Human Rights Committee considering the third periodic report of the UK, the UK representative, Mr Halliday, referred to the UK's relations with China over Hong Kong and continued:

The Joint Declaration was a legally binding treaty which provided that all the provisions of the [International Covenant on Civil and Political Rights], including reporting obligations, would remain in force after 1997. . . . It also provided for action to be taken by China and the United Kingdom to ensure continued application of international rights and obligations affecting Hong Kong, including the Covenant. On the question of possible breaches, the status of the Joint Declaration as an international treaty ensured that any breaches would be regarded as a very serious matter.

(CCPR/C/SR. 1046, p. 10)

The speaker later remarked:

The Anglo-Irish Agreement of 1985 remained an important foundation for action, although the Governments of both the United Kingdom and the Republic of Ireland were prepared to contemplate changes in it. The Agreement was a binding treaty which stipulated that the status of Northern Ireland was to be determined by the democratic choice of the people of Northern Ireland.

(Ibid., p. 13)

Part Two: II. *Sources of international law—custom*

(See Part One: II. D. 1. (item of 1 April 1991), above and Part Three: I. A. 3. (paragraph 32 of document of January 1991), and Part Four: VII. (document of January 1991), below)

Part Two: VIII. *Sources of international law—restatement by formal processes of codification and progressive development*

(See also Part One: I., above)

Speaking on 13 November 1991 in the Sixth Committee of the UN General Assembly considering the future work of the International Law Commission, the UK representative, Sir Arthur Watts, stated:

The progress being made by the international community is taking us beyond old-fashioned concepts of the codification of international law. We now have a multi-structured international community, with overlapping legal competences and a proliferation of treaty networks. There is a need for coordination, and for a certain weeding out of instruments which have now become irrelevant or have been superseded. This calls for work to be done somewhere, by someone, and we should consider whether the appropriate body to undertake some at least of the work would be the Commission.

(Text provided by the FCO; see also A/C.6/46/SR. 36, pp. 14–15)

Part Two: X. *Sources of international law—acquisition, retention and loss of rights*

A joint press statement was issued on 6 December 1991 by the UK and Argentine delegations to the second meeting of the South Atlantic Fisheries Commission which took place in London on 4 and 5 December 1991. The following paragraph appeared in the statement:

The two delegations agreed that there applied to this meeting the formula on sovereignty over the Falkland Islands, South Georgia and the South Sandwich Islands and the surrounding maritime areas agreed by the British and Argentine

Governments in paragraph 2 of the Joint Statement issued in Madrid on 19 October 1989 and included in paragraph 1 of the Joint Statement on the Conservation of Fisheries of 28 November 1990.

(Text provided by the FCO: for the document of 19 October 1989, see UKMIL 1989, p. 583; for the document of 28 November 1990, see UKMIL 1990, p. 483)

The following statement was issued to the press by the FCO on 9 December 1991:

Officials from the British and Argentine Governments met in London on 4 and 5 December to explore the implications of the legislative measures both Governments announced on 22 November 1991 regarding the Continental Shelf in the South West Atlantic and the scope for co-operation.

Officials agreed that the following formula agreed by both Governments and recorded in paragraph 2 of the Joint Statement issued by the British and Argentine delegations in Madrid on 19 October 1989 applied to the present meeting and to any similar subsequent meetings:

(1) Nothing in the conduct or content of the present meeting or of any similar subsequent meetings shall be interpreted as:

(a) A change in the position of the United Kingdom with regard to sovereignty or territorial and maritime jurisdiction over the Falkland Islands, South Georgia and the South Sandwich Islands and the surrounding maritime areas;

(b) A change in the position of the Argentine Republic with regard to sovereignty or territorial and maritime jurisdiction over the Falkland Islands, South Georgia and the South Sandwich Islands and the surrounding maritime areas;

(c) Recognition of or support for the position of the United Kingdom or the Argentine Republic with regard to sovereignty or territorial and maritime jurisdiction over the Falkland Islands, South Georgia and the South Sandwich Islands and the surrounding maritime areas.

(2) No act or activity carried out by the United Kingdom, the Argentine Republic or third parties as a consequence and in implementation of anything agreed to in the present meeting or in any similar subsequent meetings shall constitute a basis for affirming, supporting, or denying the position of the United Kingdom or the Argentine Republic regarding the sovereignty or territorial and maritime jurisdiction over the Falkland Islands, South Georgia, and the South Sandwich Islands and the surrounding maritime areas.

(Text provided by the FCO)

Part Three: I. A. 1. *Subjects of international law—States—international status—sovereignty and independence*

(See also Part Three: I. B. 1. (material concerning the Baltic States), Part Three: I. B. 5. (items of 26 February and 26 March 1991), and Part Five: IV. (items of 1 and 5 September 1991), below)

In moving the Second Reading of the Namibia Bill in the House of Commons, the Minister for Overseas Development, Mrs Lynda Chalker, made a speech in terms similar to that made in the House of Lords by the Minister of State, FCO, on 27 November 1990.

(HC Debs., vol. 185, cols. 228–9: 5 February 1991; see UKMIL 1990, pp. 485–6)

The Twelve Member States of the EC issued the following statement on 19 February 1991 with regard to the situation in the Gulf:

They reaffirm the commitment of the Community and its Member States to contribute actively, once international legality is re-established, to security, stability and development for all the countries in the region, in an appropriate framework which also takes into account the need for a global, flexible and gradual approach to the various problems of the area. In this connection, they reaffirm their commitment to the sovereignty, unity, independence and territorial integrity of all the countries of the region. They will continue their consultations with the United States and other concerned countries, notably the Soviet Union.

(Text provided by the FCO)

Part Three: I. A. 2. *Subjects of international law—States—international status—non-intervention and non-use of force*

(See also Part Five: IV. (items of 1 and 5 September 1991), below)

On 11 January 1991, an FCO spokesman made the following statement:

. . . in the absence abroad of the Secretary of State and Mr Hogg, Mr John Weston, FCO Political Director, had called in Soviet Chargé, Mr Vladimir Ivanov, this morning. Mr Weston recalled the Foreign Secretary's meeting with the Soviet Ambassador on 8 January at which Mr Hurd had expressed our serious concern at the situation in Lithuania. This morning the Twelve had made a démarche through the Presidency in Moscow.

Mr Weston said that our concern had been heightened by news in the past few hours of increased pressure on the elected Lithuanian authorities, and of reported action by Soviet troops in Vilnius.

He made clear that the British Government could see no justification for the present action against Lithuania. Repression of democracy in the Baltic States would contradict Soviet obligations under the Paris Charter for a new Europe and would provide no long-term solution to the problem of the Baltic States.

Mr Weston therefore strongly urged the Soviet Government to withdraw its troops from the streets of Lithuania, refrain from further military action there, allow the elected republican bodies to exercise their democratic authority, and resume a process of peaceful negotiation with them.

(Text provided by the FCO)

The Twelve Member States of the EC made the following statement on 14 January 1991:

The Community and its member states are convinced that the use of force, [as] happened in Lithuania, is unacceptable. They deeply regret that this repression has caused innocent victims. A solution can only be found through a dialogue between the Soviet authorities and the elected representatives of the Baltic peoples, with a view to satisfying the legitimate aspirations of these peoples.

They address an urgent appeal to the Soviet authorities to refrain from the use of force, resume the path of dialogue and end the military intervention.

. . .

The CSCE process, from the Helsinki Final Act to the Charter of Paris, has as guiding ideas that democratic Government is based on the will of the people and that the use of force constitutes among the thirty-four states participating in the CSCE an unacceptable means of resolving differences. The architecture of the new Europe can only be based on the principles of the rule of law.

(Text provided by the FCO)

On 18 January 1991, the Twelve Members States of the EC issued the following statement:

By launching a non-provoked and entirely unjustified missile attack on Israeli territory last night, Saddam Hussein is aiming, through a cynical and deliberate provocation, to draw Israel into the Gulf conflict.

The Community and its member states strongly condemn this attack which represents a further violation of international law by the Iraqi authorities.

(Ibid.)

Speaking on 31 January 1991 in the UN Human Rights Commission, the Minister for Foreign Affairs of Luxembourg and President of the Council of Ministers of the EC, Mr Jacques Poos, stated on behalf of the EC and its Twelve Member States:

The Communities had made an urgent appeal to the Soviet authorities to refrain from the use of force, put an end to their military intervention and resume a dialogue with the elected representatives of the Baltic peoples.

(E/CN.4/1991/SR. 5, p. 10)

On 29 August 1991, a spokesman for the FCO issued a statement which read in part as follows:

The landing by a large group of Iraqi military personnel on Bubiyan island on 28 August is the most serious Iraqi violation yet of the border with Kuwait, in direct contravention of the terms of the ceasefire contained in SCR 687. We condemn this further example of the Iraqi government's continuing refusal to meet its international obligations and congratulate the Kuwaiti armed forces on their prompt response.

(Text provided by the FCO)

In its written observations, dated October 1991, on the Third Report of the HC Foreign Affairs Committee, dealing with the Middle East after the Gulf War, Her Majesty's Government stated:

Iraq's invasion of Kuwait on 2 August 1990 was a blatant act of aggression. It violated the basic tenets of the United Nations and Arab League Charters and international law.

(Cm. 1682, p. 3)

In the preamble to the Agreement concerning the Sovereignty, Independence, Territorial Integrity and Inviolability, Neutrality and National Unity of Cambodia, concluded on 23 October 1991 by, *inter alia*, the UK, the parties, 'recalling their obligations under the Charter of the United Nations and other rules of international law', considered

that full observance of the principles of non-interference and non-intervention in the internal and external affairs of States is of the greatest importance for the maintenance of international peace and security.

Article 2 of the Agreement reads as follows:

1. The other parties to this Agreement [i.e. excluding Cambodia] hereby solemnly undertake to recognize and to respect in every way the sovereignty, independence, territorial integrity and inviolability, neutrality and national unity of Cambodia.
2. To this end, they undertake:
(a) To refrain from entering into any military alliances or other military agreements with Cambodia that would be inconsistent with Cambodia's neutrality, without prejudice to Cambodia's right to acquire the necessary military equipment, arms, munitions and assistance to enable it to exercise its inherent right of self-defence and to maintain law and order;
(b) To refrain from interference in any form whatsoever, whether direct or indirect, in the internal affairs of Cambodia;
(c) To refrain from the threat or use of force against the territorial integrity or political independence of Cambodia, or in any other manner inconsistent with the purposes of the United Nations;
(d) To settle all disputes with Cambodia by peaceful means;
(e) To refrain from using their territories or the territories of other States to impair the sovereignty, independence, territorial integrity and inviolability, neutrality and national unity of Cambodia;
(f) To refrain from using the territory of Cambodia to impair the sovereignty, independence and territorial integrity and inviolability of other States;
(g) To refrain from the introduction or stationing of foreign forces, including military personnel, in any form whatsoever, in Cambodia and from establishing or maintaining military bases, strong points or facilities in Cambodia, except pursuant to United Nations authorization for the implementation of the comprehensive political settlement.

(TS No. 111 (1991); Cm. 1786)

In reply to the question

whether in [the view of Her Majesty's Government], international law allows for the use of military force to secure the persons of those charged in relation to the Lockerbie disaster, the Minister of State, FCO, wrote:

It would be a violation of the territorial sovereignty of a state for another state to send military forces into it without its consent, for the purposes of apprehending a fugitive criminal.

(HL Debs., vol. 533, *WA 27* : 10 December 1991)

Part Three: I. A. 3. *Subjects of international law—States—international status—domestic jurisdiction*

In a statement made on 31 January 1991 to the UN Commission on Human Rights, the Minister for Foreign Affairs of Luxembourg and President of the Council of Ministers of the EC, Mr Jacques Poos, observed on behalf of the EC and its Twelve Member States:

43. In the opinion of the Twelve, the implementation of the principles of the Charter of the United Nations, particularly Articles 55 and 56, did not constitute unwarranted interference in the domestic affairs of a given country, but a moral right and duty of the international community. Intervention was all the more justified because respect for human rights was one of the essential factors in maintaining peace in the world.

(E/CN.4/1991/SR.5, p. 11)

The following passages appear in Foreign Policy Document No. 215, 'Human Rights in Foreign Policy', issued by the FCO in January 1991:

HMG'S STANDING TO RAISE HUMAN RIGHTS

10. The duty not to intervene in matters within the domestic jurisdiction of other States is a recognised principle of international law, reflected in Article 2(7) of the United Nations Charter. However, Articles 55 and 56 of the Charter set out the obligation of all Members of the United Nations to promote universal respect for, and observance of, human rights . . . . This obligation, reinforced over the years by the creation of a framework for international promotion and discussion of human rights and by the elaboration of international human rights law, means that human rights violations are no longer insulated from external criticism or expressions of concern on the grounds that the matter is exclusively a domestic one.
11. We do not accept that expressions of concern at violations of human rights can be considered as interference in the internal affairs of a state. In 1989 alone we participated with our EC partners in about 70 démarches to a wide range of countries where human rights had been violated (in addition to joint statements and declarations). We also made numerous bilateral representations. Third World Governments increasingly acknowledge that human rights are a matter of legitimate international concern and even those which argue to the contrary often implicitly accept the legitimacy of human rights criticism by themselves criticising others. As a corollary, we must be prepared to discuss human rights issues in the United Kingdom when these are raised with us.
12. It follows from the above that, if asked whether we will take up a human rights violation with another State on behalf of one or more of its nationals, it is wrong to take the line that this is an internal affair in which we have no standing.

13. Where British nationals are directly involved, we of course also have an additional consular standing to raise a human rights issue.

WAYS IN WHICH HMG RAISES HUMAN RIGHTS

Bilateral Action

14. We frequently raise human rights issues with other Governments. We have made representations in every region of the world and to all forms of government from military (e.g. Chile 1973–1990) to democratic (e.g. Sri Lanka). Whether to express concern, and how best to do so, are questions that we address carefully in each case, taking account of the whole range of interests involved. We do not consider it necessary to react to every infringement of human rights that is brought to our notice. The level at which we make a representation (Ministerial, senior official, etc.) will depend on the seriousness of the violation, the extent of British public and Parliamentary concern, whether our influence with the particular Government is great or small, the receptivity of our chosen target, etc.

15. We take a wide range of bilateral action. For example:

- confidential representations (Prime Ministerial, Ministerial and at all levels of official) about a general problem (such as torture, disappearances or detention without trial) or about individual cases;
- public statements (e.g. on China in June 1989);
- curtailment or reduction of aid (e.g. to Burma and Somalia in 1988);
- enquiries about individual cases of concern to the British public or Parliament;
- attending trials (e.g. in Cameroon in 1989);
- sending observers to elections (e.g. Nicaragua and Romania in 1990);
- arranging sponsored visits for people whose work relates to human rights;
- maintaining contacts with local human rights organisations.

Joint Action with the Twelve

16. Joint action on human rights has grown rapidly in recent years and now is fairly commonplace. The European Parliament takes an active interest in human rights questions. The Twelve's policy on human rights was set out in 1986 in a Declaration by Foreign Ministers. The implications for the rest of the world of developments in Eastern Europe were spelt out by the Twelve in a statement by the Irish Minister of Foreign Affairs at the 1990 session of the UN's most important human rights forum, the Commission on Human Rights . . . There is an advantage to joint action by the Twelve: it carries greater weight than bilateral action (particularly important where we have little influence).

17. Action taken by the Twelve takes a number of forms:

- *declarations*, both general (e.g. on Sudan in March and November 1989) and specific (e.g. in November 1989 on the murder of six Jesuit priests in El Salvador);
- *démarches* (around 70 in 1989 in all regions of the world) by the Presidency, the Troika or by all Ambassadors of the Twelve resident in a capital. These démarches are usually confidential though we are able to refer to them in correspondence with MPs, NGOs, etc;
- *multilateral* (the Twelve take joint and separate action on human rights at relevant UN and CSCE meetings—see section on multilateral action below);

– *decisions* (in a limited number of cases, concern among the Twelve at human rights abuses has led to decisions on common action. This usually takes the form of coordinated diplomatic measures, for example against Burma, China and Noriega's Panama, but can extend to actual measures taken by the Council, e.g. the decision to rescind Romania's GSP benefits before Ceausescu's fall in 1989 and the Council decision in April 1989 to suspend negotiations on an EC/Romanian agreement).

18. Action by the Twelve often follows from recommendations made by Heads of Mission in joint reports on human rights. . . . Guidelines for the preparation of these reports were drawn up in 1987 by the EC Working Group on Human Rights.

. . .

32. If representations are rejected on the grounds of interference in internal affairs, it will be necessary to explain why we (and the international community as a whole) regard human rights as a matter of legitimate international concern (see paragraphs 10–13). If the country has ratified relevant international human rights conventions (e.g. the International Covenant on Civil and Political Rights), it will be possible to refer to its obligations under these conventions. If not, we would still consider the country to be bound to respect the rights and freedoms in the Universal Declaration of Human Rights . . . by virtue of the fact that the obligation to respect these rights and freedoms forms part of customary international law. In making representations in ACP countries we can use the entrée provided by the Fourth Lomé Convention in which the ACP and EC States 'reiterate our deep attachment to human dignity and human rights which are legitimate aspirations of individuals and peoples'.

Speaking on behalf of the EC and its Member States at a meeting of the UN Commission on Human Rights on 27 February 1991, the representative of Luxembourg stated:

The Twelve reiterate their profound conviction that the protection of human rights and fundamental freedoms can in no way be considered as interference in a State's internal affairs. The United Nations Charter, in particular Articles 55 and 56, confers on us the moral right to intervene whenever human rights are violated.

(Text provided by the FCO; see also E/CN. 4/1991/SR. 43, p. 8)

Speaking on 5 April 1991 in the UN Security Council after the adoption of Resolution 688, the UK Permanent Representative, Sir David Hannay, stated:

It has been argued in our debates that this action is in some way outside the scope of the Security Council, that it is an entirely internal matter. My delegation cannot accept that, and I am glad the resolution makes clear that it is not so. For one thing, Article 2, paragraph 7, an essential part of the Charter, does not apply to matters which, under the Charter, are not essentially domestic, and we have often seen human rights—for example in South Africa—defined in that category.

(S/PV. 2982, pp. 64–5)

Speaking on 12 November 1991 in the Third Committee of the UN General Assembly, the representative of the Netherlands, on behalf of the EC and its Twelve Member States, stated:

Implementation of human rights instruments is in the first place the responsibility of individual Governments. However, all Governments are accountable to the international community and cannot use the argument that supervision of the implementation of these instruments constitutes interference in their internal affairs. By adhering to the human rights instruments they have committed themselves to being supervised by international Treaty Bodies.

(Text provided by the FCO; see also A/C.3/46/SR. 39, pp. 17–21)

Part Three: I. B. 1. *Subjects of international law—States—recognition—recognition of States*

(See also Part Three: I.B.5., below)

In reply to a question, the Minister of State, FCO, wrote:

The United Kingdom recognises many states whose borders are not fully agreed with their neighbours. This is normally a bilateral matter for the states concerned.

(HC Debs., vol. 185, WA, col. *84*: 5 February 1991)

In his opening statement at the South Pacific Forum Dialogue at Pohnpei, Micronesia, on 1 August 1991, the Minister of State, FCO, the Earl of Caithness, declared:

I would like to use the occasion, amongst other things, to perform two agreeable tasks:

- To congratulate the Forum on its 20th Anniversary and offer it my best wishes for the next two decades; and
- To announce the British Government's recognition of the Federated States of Micronesia and the Republic of the Marshall Islands and our support for their applications to join the United Nations and other international organisations. My Government looks forward to enjoying with these two countries the friendly and constructive relations which it enjoys with the other members of the Forum.

(Text provided by the FCO)

At a press conference given by the FCO on 20 August 1991, the following item appeared in the report:

Asked about Britain's position on recognition, Spokesman drew attention to Mr Hurd's comments in an interview on Radio 4's Today programme this morning: 'We do not actually recognise governments, we recognise states, we recognise the Soviet Union and certainly our view is that legality should be restored. That President Gorbachev was illegally deposed, and that it is highly desirable that he should be back in place.

(Text provided by the FCO)

Speaking in a radio interview on 27 August 1991, the Secretary of State for Foreign and Commonwealth Affairs, Mr Douglas Hurd, stated:

We are ready to recognise the three Baltic Republics and argue that case this afternoon in Brussels . . . .We never accepted that Stalin was justified in swallowing them up in 1940, and we believe that they have now established a degree of effective independence which justifies their being recognised.

(Text provided by the FCO)

The following declaration was made on 27 August 1991 in Brussels at an EC Extraordinary Ministerial Meeting:

The Community and its member States warmly welcome the restoration of the sovereignty and independence of the Baltic States which they lost in 1940. They have consistently regarded the democratically elected parliaments and governments of these states as the legitimate representatives of the Baltic peoples. They call for open and constructive negotiations between the Baltic States and the Soviet Union to settle outstanding issues between them.

It is now time, after more than fifty years, that these States resume their rightful place among the Nations of Europe. Therefore, the Community and its member States confirm their decision to establish diplomatic relations with the Baltic States without delay. Implementing measures will be taken by member States individually.

The Community and its member States look forward to the early membership and participation of the Baltic States in all relevant international organisations, such as the United Nations, CSCE and the Council of Europe.

. . .

(Text provided by the FCO)

The Secretary of State for Foreign and Commonwealth Affairs, Mr Douglas Hurd, addressed the following letter, dated 30 August 1991, to the Minister of Foreign Affairs of Estonia. At the same time he sent similar letters to the Ministers of Foreign Affairs of Latvia and Lithuania:

I am delighted that after fifty-one years the Baltic states at last have regained their independence. It gives me particular pleasure that Douglas Hogg is visiting Estonia so soon after our recognition of your independent statehood to start discussions about the re-establishment of diplomatic relations. I am sure that relations between our two countries will flourish as they did in the past.

I also look forward to welcoming you soon as a colleague in international bodies in which the Baltic states may now take their rightful place. As you know, membership of the United Nations is agreed by the General Assembly on the recommendation of the UN Security Council. Roland Dumas and I have agreed, as the two European Permanent Members of the Security Council, to offer our help if you decide to apply for United Nations membership.

. . .

(Text provided by the FCO)

In reply to a question, the Minister of State, FCO, wrote:

Her Majesty's Government, in common with our partners in the European Community, recognised the Republics of Lithuania, Latvia and Estonia on 27 August

1991. Permanent diplomatic missions arrived in Tallinn on 4 October 1991, in Riga on 5 October 1991 and Vilnius on 6 October 1991. Accredited ambassadors were appointed to each republic on 8 October and have been in post since. They are now identifying suitable premises for our embassies.

(HC Debs., vol. 196, WA, col. *60*: 14 October 1991)

In reply to a question, the Parliamentary Under-Secretary of State, FCO, wrote:

I warmly welcome the entry of Estonia, Latvia, Lithuania, the Republic of Korea, the Democratic People's Republic of Korea, the Republic of the Marshall Islands, and the Federated States of Micronesia to the United Nations.

We have long had diplomatic relations with the Republic of Korea and now have diplomatic relations with each of the Baltic states. We hope to establish diplomatic relations with the Marshall Islands and the Federated States of Micronesia shortly. Our support for the admission of the Democratic People's Republic of Korea to the United Nations has meant that we also now recognise the Democratic People's Republic of Korea as a state, but have no plans to establish diplomatic relations.

(Ibid., WA, col. *156*: 16 October 1991)

In the course of a debate, the Minister of State, FCO, Mr Douglas Hogg, stated:

The traditional criteria that we adopt for the recognition of states probably apply to Slovenia. They do not apply in the case of Croatia in the same way, but I accept . . . that one of the reasons why the criteria do not apply to Croatia is that Croatian territory has been invaded by the [Jugoslav National Army] and Serbian irregulars.

Rather than argue whether the traditional criteria apply, I would like to take a slightly broader perspective on the issue. My right honourable Friend the Foreign Secretary has made it plain in the House and elsewhere that we accept the principle of recognition of the Republics of Yugoslavia which wish it.

(HC Debs., vol. 200, col. 1166: 12 December 1991)

The following Declaration was issued by the EC and its Twelve Member States on 16 December 1991:

Guidelines on the Recognition of New States in Eastern Europe and in the Soviet Union

In compliance with the European Council's request, Ministers have assessed developments in Eastern Europe and in the Soviet Union with a view to elaborating an approach regarding relations with new States.

In this connection they adopted the following guidelines on the formal recognition of new States in Eastern Europe and in the Soviet Union:

'The Community and its Member States confirm their attachment to the principles of the Helsinki Final Act and the Charter of Paris, in particular the principle of self-determination. They affirm their readiness to recognise, subject to the normal standards of international practice and the political realities in each case, those new States which, following the historic changes in the region, have constituted themselves on a democratic basis, have accepted the appropriate international obligations and have committed themselves in good faith to a peaceful process and to negotiations.

Therefore, they adopt a common position on the process of recognition of these new States, which requires:

- respect for the provisions of the Charter of the United Nations and the commitments subscribed to in the Final Act of Helsinki and in the Charter of Paris, especially with regard to the rule of law, democracy and human rights;
- guarantees for the rights of ethnic and national groups and minorities in accordance with the commitments subscribed to in the framework of the CSCE:
- respect for the inviolability of all frontiers which can only be changed by peaceful means and by common agreement:
- acceptance of all relevant commitments with regard to disarmament and nuclear non-proliferation as well as to security and regional stability:
- commitment to settle by agreement, including where appropriate by recourse to arbitration, all questions concerning state succession and regional disputes.

The Community and its Member States will not recognise entities which are the result of aggression. They would take account of the effects of recognition on neighbouring States.

The commitment to these principles opens the way to recognition by the Community and its Member States and to the establishment of diplomatic relations. It could be laid down in agreements.'

(Text provided by the FCO)

The following Declaration was also issued by the EC and its Twelve Member States on the same day:

Declaration on Yugoslavia

The European Community and its Member States discussed the situation in Yugoslavia in the light of their guidelines on the recognition of new States in Eastern Europe and in the Soviet Union. They adopted a common position with regard to the recognition of Yugoslav Republics. In this connection they concluded the following:

'The Community and its Member States agree to recognise the independence of all the Yugoslav Republics fulfilling all the conditions set out below. The implementation of this decision will take place on January 15, 1992.

They are therefore inviting all Yugoslav Republics to state by 23 December whether:

- they wish to be recognised as independent
- they accept the commitments contained in the above-mentioned guidelines.
- they accept the provisions laid down in the draft convention—especially those in Chapter II on human rights and rights of national or ethnic groups—under consideration by the Conference on Yugoslavia.
- they continue to support the efforts of the Secretary General and the Security Council of the United Nations, and the continuation of the Conference on Yugoslavia.

The application of those Republics which reply positively will be submitted through the chair of the Conference to the Arbitration Commission for advice before the implementation date.

In the meantime, the Community and its Member States request the UN Secretary General and the UN Security Council to continue their efforts to establish an effective cease-fire and promote a peaceful and negotiated outcome to the conflict. They continue to attach the greatest importance to the early deployment of a UN peace-keeping force referred to in UN Security Council Resolution 724.

The Community and its Member States also require a Yugoslav Republic to commit itself, prior to recognition, to adopt constitutional and political guarantees ensuring that it has no territorial claims towards a neighbouring Community State and that it will conduct no hostile propaganda activities versus a neighbouring Community State, including the use of a denomination which implies territorial claims.'

(Text provided by the FCO)

The following statement was issued in Brussels by the EC on 31 December 1991:

The Community and its member States welcome the assurances received from Armenia, Azerbaijan, Belarus, Kazakhstan, Moldova, Turkmenistan, Ukraine and Uzbekistan that they are prepared to fulfil the requirements contained in the 'Guidelines on the recognition of new States in Eastern Europe and the Soviet Union'. Consequently, they are ready to proceed with the recognition of these Republics.

They reiterate their readiness also to recognise Kyrghyzstan and Tadzhikistan once similar assurances will have been received.

Recognition shall not be taken to imply acceptance by the European Community and its member States of the position of any of the Republics concerning territory which is the subject of a dispute between two or more Republics.

Recognition will furthermore be extended on the understanding that all Republics participating with Russia in the Commonwealth of Independent States on whose territory nuclear weapons are stationed, will adhere shortly to the Nuclear Non-Proliferation Treaty as non-nuclear weapon States.

(Text provided by the FCO)

In referring to the above statement, a spokesman for the FCO stated that the Prime Minister would now send messages to the Presidents of the eight Republics about UK recognition.

Part Three: I. B. 2. *Subjects of international law—States—recognition—recognition of governments*

(See also Part Three: I.B.5 (item of 18 October 1991), below)

In reply to an oral question on the subject of relations with Afghanistan, the Parliamentary Under-Secretary of State, FCO, Mr Mark Lennox-Boyd, stated:

We do not have substantive dealings with the Najibullah regime, which is not supported by the majority of Afghans. We would welcome its replacement by a

Government truly acceptable to the Afghan people with whom normal relations would be possible.

. . .

We have not broken off diplomatic relations with Afghanistan but the Najibullah regime is only there with the support of the Soviet Union. It remains unrepresentative and unacceptable to a majority of the Afghans and controls only some 20 per cent. of the territory.

(HC Debs., vol. 185, cols. 848–9: 13 February 1991)

In reply to an oral question, the Secretary of State for Foreign and Commonwealth Affairs, Mr Douglas Hurd, stated:

We recognise the Government of the Republic of Cyprus as the Government of the whole of Cyprus.

(HC Debs., vol. 199, col. 259: 20 November 1991)

Part Three: I. B. 5. *Subjects of international law—States—recognition—non-recognition*

The following text was issued by a FCO spokesman on 8 January 1991:

Spokesman said that during a call by the Soviet Ambassador (arranged some days ago) on other business, the Foreign Secretary took the opportunity to seek clarification of the Soviet Defence Ministry's decision to deploy paratroopers to certain Republics.

He said that the Foreign Secretary reminded Ambassador Zamyatin of the special status of the Baltic States, whose annexation by the Soviet Union in 1940 had never been recognised by the British Government. Mr Hurd urged the Soviet Government to use negotiation to resolve the problems of the Baltic and he stressed the importance the British Government attached to due process of law and to the Soviet Union's CSCE commitments.

(Text provided by the FCO)

In the course of a debate on the subject of the Baltic States, the Secretary of State for Foreign and Commonwealth Affairs, Mr Douglas Hurd, was asked the following question:

Would my right hon. Friend unambiguously reiterate Her Majesty's Government's position, which is that the United Kingdom does not recognise the present authority of the Soviet Union within the three Baltic states and that, *de jure*, the Soviet Union has no locus? Therefore would it not be better for the people of the three Baltic states if their right to self-determination were to be recognised forthwith?

In reply, Mr Hurd stated:

My hon. Friend states the legal position exactly.

(HC Debs., vol. 183, col. 853: 16 January 1991)

In the course of a debate on the same subject in the House of Lords, the Minister of State, FCO, the Earl of Caithness, stated:

Perhaps I may make the legal position absolutely clear. We have never recognised the incorporation of the Baltic states into the USSR. Therefore, we fully support the right of the Baltic people to determine their own future.

(HL Debs., vol. 524, col. 1177; 16 January 1991)

In reply to a question on the subject of the legal status of Turkey's relations with northern Cyprus, the Minister of State, FCO, wrote:

I refer the hon. Member to United Nations Security Council resolution 541 of 18 November 1983 which calls upon all states not to recognise any Cypriot state other than the Republic of Cyprus. The Turkish Government are well aware of our position in full support of that resolution, and of all the Security Council resolutions on Cyprus.

(HC Debs., vol. 185, WA, col. *3*: 4 February 1991)

In reply to a question on the subject of representations to be made to the Taiwanese authorities regarding drift-net fishing, the Parliamentary Under-Secretary of State, FCO, wrote in part:

We have no dealings with the authorities in Taiwan.

(HC Debs., vol. 184, WA, col. *692*: 1 February 1991; see also ibid., vol. 191, WA, col. *342*: 20 May 1991)

In the course of a debate on the subject of the Baltic States, the Minister of State, FCO, the Earl of Caithness, stated:

As this House knows well, the British Government believe the Baltic states to be a special case and have never recognised *de jure* the forcible incorporation of the Baltic states into the Soviet Union.

(HL Debs., vol. 525, col. 1264: 6 February 1991)

In reply to a question, the Minister of State, FCO, wrote in part:

We have no plans to establish diplomatic relations with North Korea, which we do not recognise as a State.

(HL Debs., vol. 525, *WA 49*: 6 February 1991)

In the course of a debate on the subject of the visit to London of the Dalai Lama, the Government Minister in the House of Lords, Lord Reay, stated:

. . . the Dalai Lama remains a political figure as well as a spiritual leader, regarded by many of his followers as the leader of a government-in-exile. It is important for everyone to be clear that no government recognises this political body and we like others have no dealings with them. Often meetings with the Dalai Lama organised in his spiritual capacity have later been portrayed by his supporters in a political manner. In these circumstances we have concluded that it would not be right for the Prime Minister or Foreign and Commonwealth Office Minister to meet the Dalai Lama during his visit.

(HL Debs., vol. 526, col. 963: 26 February 1991)

The Minister continued:

So far as the status of Tibet is concerned, successive British Governments have consistently regarded Tibet as autonomous while recognising the special position of the Chinese there. That continues to be the Government's view. Tibet was declared an autonomous region of China in 1965.

(Ibid., col. 964)

He later stated:

. . . the noble Lord . . . observed that Tibet had enjoyed *de facto* independence after 1911, but Tibet never enjoyed *de jure* independence. Tibet was never internationally recognised as independent. That is why there is no parallel with Kuwait. Kuwait is a sovereign independent state recognised internationally as such, and is a member of the United Nations.

. . .

. . . it remains the case that successive British governments have regarded Tibet as autonomous, while always recognising the special position of China. That continues to be our view. Similarly, we do not regard the situation of the Baltic States as a comparable parallel. Her Majesty's Government never recognised the legality of the incorporation of the Baltic States into the Soviet Union, whereas we have always recognised the special position of the Chinese in Tibet.

(Ibid., col. 966; see also HL Debs., vol. 528, cols. 1861–3: 17 May 1991)

In reply to questions, the Parliamentary Under-Secretary of State, FCO, wrote:

The Baltic states have no diplomatic representatives accredited to the Court of St. James's though one individual continues to enjoy certain privileges as a matter of courtesy.

. . .

. . . The Baltic states do not fulfil the conditions for recognition as independent sovereign states. The question of diplomatic accreditation for their representatives therefore does not arise. We continue, however, to extend certain diplomatic courtesies on a personal basis to the sole surviving member of the pre-war Baltic legations.

(HC Debs., vol. 186, WA, col. *457*: 26 February 1991)

In reply to a question, the Minister of State, FCO, wrote:

We do not recognise the individual Soviet republics as states. The question of diplomatic relations, therefore, does not arise.

(HC Debs., vol. 188, WA, col. *1*: 18 March 1991)

In the course of a debate on the subject of the Baltic States, the Minister of State, FCO, Mr Douglas Hogg, stated:

I should like to take advantage of the debate to outline in general terms the Government's policy towards the Baltic states, as well as to respond to the specific questions that have been posed. It would be helpful if I summarised the Government's policy towards those states and our policy towards the Soviet Union's own policy to the Baltic states.

I should make it clear that the United Kingdom Government have never accepted the legality of the incorporation of the three Baltic states into the Soviet

Union. . . . that was a clear act of aggression, and the three republics were sovereign, independent states at the time of their incorporation.

Although we never recognised as lawful the incorporation of the Baltic republics into the Union, one must accept as a matter of de facto law that the republics are part of the Soviet Union. Although we have recognised that fact, we also assert their right to self-determination. But, if we are realistic about this, we must accept that the right to self-determination can only be effectively achieved through genuine and free negotiation between the Soviet Union and the republics. The outcome will necessarily depend upon those negotiations.

(HC Debs., vol. 188, cols. 935–6: 26 March 1991; see also ibid., vol. 193, col. 988: 26 June 1991)

In moving the Second Reading in the House of Lords of the Foreign Corporations Bill, the Lord Advocate, Lord Fraser of Carmyllie, stated:

This is a short, straightforward Bill which seeks to deal with a problem in the international commercial field. The matters at issue are ones of private international law, which deals with ordinary legal relationships involving different legal systems. The problem is that these matters have, quite unnecessarily, been linked with public international law, which deals with relationships between states. In particular, this has affected the law relating to foreign corporations. The object of the Bill is to sever those two matters and to give primacy to commercial reality where the question at issue is one of commercial law.

There are indications that the courts are prepared to adopt a realistic attitude and to look not at whether a territory is a recognised state but at what actually happens in the territory and at the law that is in fact applied there. As an example I might mention the comments of the noble and learned Lord, Lord Wilberforce, in a case involving the optical instrument manufacturers Carl Zeiss. The opposing view has been that a foreign corporation has no legal personality under our laws unless it is incorporated under the laws of a territory which the United Kingdom recognises as a state. If the Government do not recognise the state, it is argued, the law should not recognise the corporation. That is not a view that the Government share.

Whichever view is the better as a matter of policy the law cannot be said to be certain, and some doubts and problems have recently been raised on behalf of City interests and institutions. This Bill will dispel the aura of doubt that has appeared. The Bill will enable the legal capacity of foreign corporations incorporated under the laws of territories which the United Kingdom does not recognise as states to be accepted in this country. The question which the courts and others will have to consider is whether there is a corporation established by laws which are recognised by the courts of a settled legal system in the territory in question.

I stress that the Bill does not affect by one iota the Government's policy on the recognition of states, still less their policies in relation to particular cases. It is a Bill dealing with private international law, not with foreign relations. We shall continue to recognise states in accordance with common international doctrine; at the same time, like many other countries, we do not accord recognition to governments. We believe that where questions arise as to the law governing the incorporation of commercial bodies, they should be for the courts to answer, looking at any relevant evidence as to that law. They should not be treated as matters which are to be decided by reference to the Government's foreign policy. The Bill leaves commercial law to the courts and to businessmen and their legal advisers.

As I have said, this is a straightforward Bill. It provides a pointer for the courts and others to follow and enables them to work out the consequences of adopting this approach. Clause 1(1) applies where a question arises whether a corporation incorporated under the laws of a territory which is not a recognised state should be regarded as having legal personality in the United Kingdom. It provides that if the laws of that territory are applied by a settled court system there, that question, together with other material questions, is to be determined without regard to whether the territory is or is not a recognised state. That does not of course accord any sort of recognition to the non-state; all that the clause does is to ask the courts to approach questions relating to the status of corporations from non-states in the same way, whether or not the corporation comes from a recognised state.

It is a requirement of the Bill that there must be a settled court system in the non-state concerned. The corollary of that requirement is that there may be transitional situations in which the law cannot provide a simple solution. There may be a case, for example, where part of a state is seeking to break away from the rest of the state; until it has clearly succeeded and, as a sign of its stability, has a settled court system, or has clearly failed, so that the structures of the original state are re-established, one cannot be sure what laws apply. The Bill does not attempt to solve that problem. Nor does it attempt to deal with the case of two factions fighting for power within a state.

Because subsection (1) uses the case of a recognised state as a point of reference, subsection (2) defines that phrase. It also deals with the territories of recognised federal states which would fall within subsection (1) if no other provision were made. However, our existing law on the recognition of companies incorporated under the laws of, say, California, is settled and needs no amendment, and it is unnecessary for subsection (1) to include federal states.

(HL Debs., vol. 528, cols. 67–9: 22 April 1991)

In reply to the question

Whether, following the announcement by the Eritrean People's Liberation Front of the formation of a provisional government in Eritrea at the press conference held in London, they will be the first to recognise the independence of Eritrea,

the Minister of State, FCO, wrote:

The statement by the EPLF did not constitute a declaration of independence. The question of recognition of independence therefore does not arise.

(HL Debs., vol. 529, *WA* 77: 14 June 1991)

During the Third Reading debate in the House of Lords of the Foreign Corporations Bill, the Lord Chancellor, Lord Mackay of Clashfern, stated:

I should like to say a few words about the question of the recognition of states, which was raised in Committee by the noble Lord, Lord Kennet. He suggested that because the Bill, explicitly or implicitly, requires a territory to have a legislature, an executive and a judicature, that is tantamount to the recognition of that territory as a state. However, the accepted international criteria in accordance with which Her Majesty's Government recognise states also include a settled population and a defined territory, as well as some prospect of permanence of all these indices. The territories to which the Bill applies are not recognised states, because not all of these criteria are met, and the Bill does not alter that.

In cases where recognition as a state is withheld, the rule traditionally followed by our courts—although the law cannot be said to be clear—is that, because of that withholding of recognition, they will not give effect to the creation or dissolution of corporations in the unrecognised territory. What the Bill does is to enable our courts to determine the status of corporations in accordance with commercial realities, instead of making them dependent upon unconnected issues of foreign policy.

Our foreign policy is unaffected by the Bill. I must make it quite clear that the Bill does not accord any form of recognition of any territory as a state and should not be read as doing so. It is simply concerned with the legal personality of corporations which come here and how we are to regard them under our law. We need to determine that and to clarify the present position.

(HL Debs., vol. 530, col. 988: 3 July 1991)

In moving the Second Reading of the above Bill in the House of Commons, the Solicitor-General, Sir Nicholas Lyell, stated:

This is a short but important Bill. Its object is to ensure that corporations incorporated under the laws of territories that the United Kingdom does not recognise as states can be treated here as having legal personality. A decision by the Court of Appeal last year on the legal personality of an international organisation, since reversed by the House of Lords, led to consideration being given to other questions of legal personality. It was agreed that the law relating to the status of corporations from non-states should be clarified by legislation.

If the Government do not recognise the territory of another part of the world as a state, it has been argued that our courts should not recognise its laws either, including those on the incorporation of companies. The result is that a company, although perhaps doing business here and well accepted as doing so, might not be able to sue or be sued in our courts. On the other hand, there are signs that the court will seek to avoid such a strict approach and will look at the commercial realities of such a case rather than at the political relations between the territory and this country from time to time. That is, of course, the view that the Government prefer.

In the Government's view, such basic legal questions as, 'Is this body a corporation?' and, 'What does its constitution permit?' should not depend on questions of foreign policy. All that the Bill seeks to do is to say that companies are not to be denied legal personality here simply because the territories in which they are incorporated are not recognised as states.

I should make it clear that the Bill does not change our policy or practice on the recognition of states in any way. The internationally accepted criteria according to which the Government do or do not recognise territories as states remain the same. The Bill will reassure not only foreign corporations that already operate in this country or which may wish to do so, but companies and individuals who do business with them. It will not be possible for either party to try to avoid its obligations, as happened in a recent case, by claiming that the corporation has no legal personality here because it comes from a non-state.

. . .

Legislation in this area has been called for by City firms of solicitors, and the content of the Bill has been discussed with them. Similar legislation has recently been introduced in Australia. The Bill does not accord any recognition of any territory as a state, and should not be interpreted as doing so. It clarifies, in accordance with commercial reality, the law on the legal personality of corporations from non-states which come to this country. I commend it to the House.

(HC Debs., vol. 195, cols. 413–14: 17 July 1991)

The following extract appeared in a report of a press conference held by the FCO on 31 July 1991 in which the alleged death of Lithuanian border guards following an attack from within Byelorussia was mentioned:

Spokesman added that we believed that the only way to reach a solution satisfying the legitimate aspirations of the Baltic peoples was through negotiation. Incidents such as that reported today would harm this process and the Soviet Union's international credibility. Spokesman recalled that the United Kingdom had never recognised the forcible incorporation of the Baltic States into the Soviet Union.

(Text provided by the FCO)

In the course of a debate on the subject of events in Yugoslavia, the Minister of State, FCO, Mr. Douglas Hogg, stated:

The hon. Gentleman is right when he talks about the problems of minorities . . . The hon. Gentleman is right to emphasise the position of the Albanians, most particular in the Kosovo. There are also many Albanians in Macedonia, for example. He is also right to emphasise the position of Bosnia. All those points underline the importance of not prematurely recognising Croatia and Solvenia.

(HC Debs., vol. 196, col. 45: 14 October 1991)

In reply to a question, the Parliamentary Under-Secretary of State, FCO, wrote:

As was set out in the 1972 Joint Communiqué with the People's Republic of China, the British Government recognise the Government of the People's Republic of China as the sole legal government of China, and acknowledges the position of the Chinese Government that Taiwan is a province of the People's Republic of China.

(HC Debs., vol. 196, WA, col. *293*: 18 October 1991)

In the course of a debate on the subject of human rights in Azerbaijan, the Government spokesman, Lord Cavendish of Furness, stated:

My noble friends . . . raised specific questions on whether recognition and aid are dependent on human rights performance. Recognition of the independence of republics depends on whether they meet well-established criteria for recognition. We will consider recognition on a case-by-case basis. However, it would be premature to recognise either Armenia or Azerbaijan as independent while they are still discussing with the centre and other republics the form of their future relationships.

Not to recognise a republic's independence solely on the grounds of its human rights record would deny us an opportunity to press for improvements. But republics should be in no doubt that our relations will depend on their respect for democratic principles, including their human rights performance: independence does not give them a blank cheque.

(HL Debs., vol. 532, col. 1137: 21 November 1991)

In reply to an oral question, the Parliamentary Under-Secretary of State, FCO, Mr Mark Lennox-Boyd, stated:

Her Majesty's Government most certainly do not recognise the incorporation of East Timor into Indonesia.

(HC Debs., vol. 199, col. 267: 20 November 1991)

In reply to an oral question, the Prime Minister, Mr John Major, stated:

Tibet has never been internationally recognised as an independent country. No country in the world regards Tibet as independent now. Having said that, we have taken every opportunity, including my recent visit to China, to set out our concerns about the way in which Tibetans are treated and to urge that they have proper human rights.

(HC Debs., vol. 199, col. 418: 21 November 1991)

In reply to the question

what is the position of Her Majesty's Government on the question of state immunity being used in the case of *Polly Peck* in connection with the unrecognised state of the Turkish Republic of Northern Cyprus,

the Minister of State, FCO, wrote:

The Government do not recognise the 'Turkish Republic of Northern Cyprus' as a state. It would not be appropriate for me to comment on the matter raised by the hon. Gentleman, which is *sub judice*.

(HC Debs., vol. 199, WA, col. *243*: 21 November 1991; see also ibid., vol. 200, WA, col. *262*: 6 December 1991)

In reply to an oral question, the Minister of State, FCO, the Earl of Caithness, stated:

. . . I confirm that we have not recognised the incorporation of East Timor into Indonesia, *de jure*. But I must point out to the House that, among others, the United States, Canada, Australia and New Zealand have done so.

(HL Debs., vol. 532, col. 1146: 25 November 1991; see also ibid., col. 1316: 27 November 1991)

In reply to oral questions on the subject of Croatia, the Government spokesman in the House of Lords, Lord Cavendish, stated:

. . . Croatia's wish for independence cannot in the end be denied. But recognition would not stop the fighting. We have to judge whether recognition of Croatia now would increase the danger of civil war in the other republics. That question is constantly being reviewed.

. . . we believe that recognition should come as part of a negotiated general settlement involving all the Yugoslav parties. That is the only way of guaranteeing the rights of minorities.

(HL Debs., vol. 533, col. 731: 11 December 1991; see also HC Debs., vol. 200, WA, col. *594*: 13 December 1991)

In reply to a question about the situation in Somalia, the Minister of State, FCO, wrote in part:

We have not recognised the north's purported secession.

(HC Debs., vol. 200, WA, col. *391*: 10 December 1991; see also HC Debs., vol. 193, WA, col. *32*: 17 June 1991, and ibid., vol. 200, WA, cols. *421–2*: 11 December 1991)

In the course of a debate on the subject of the future of the Western Sahara, the Minister of State, FCO, Mr Douglas Hogg, stated:

We do not recognise the Polisario or the Sahrawi Arab Democratic Republic. Nor do we accept Moroccan claims to the territory.

(HC Debs., vol. 200, col. 1174: 12 December 1991)

In reply to a question, the Parliamentary Under-Secretary of State, FCO, wrote:

The Indonesian authorities are well aware that we do not recognise their annexation of East Timor.

(HC Debs., vol. 201, WA, col. *181*: 18 December 1991)

Part Three I. C. 4. *Subjects of international law—States—types of States—dependent States and territories*

(See also Part One: II. D. 1. (items of 2 and 26 April 1991), above, and Part Three: I. E. (items of 2 April and 15 July 1991), Part Eight: I. A. (item of 3 July 1991), Part Nine: I. A., Part Nine: VIII. (items of 31 January 1991 and those concerning the Falkland Islands), and Part Nine: IX., below)

The following letter, dated 16 December 1990, was sent by the Secretary of State for Foreign and Commonwealth Affairs to the Governor of Hong Kong:

I have the honour to refer to the draft Agreement for the purpose of providing the framework for air services between Hong Kong and New Zealand, the text of which was negotiated during the period from May 1987 to March 1989.

The United Kingdom Government remains responsible for the external relations of Hong Kong until 30 June 1997. However, the United Kingdom Government hereby entrusts to you authority:

(a) to conclude the said Agreement;
(b) in accordance with prior specific authorisations in that behalf from the United Kingdom Government, to agree and confirm amendments to the said Agreement;
(c) to carry into effect and to exercise the other powers conferred upon a Contracting Party by the said Agreement.

Further, with the prior agreement of the United Kingdom Government, you may terminate the said Agreement in accordance with its terms.

If action is required to be taken relating to the international conventions referred to in the said Agreement it shall be taken either by the United Kingdom Government or, as appropriate, by the Hong Kong Government acting under the authority of the United Kingdom Government.

Following the coming into force of the said Agreement, the United Kingdom Government will register it on behalf of the Hong Kong Government.

(Special Supplement No. 5 to the *Hong Kong Government Gazette*, vol. 133 (1990), p. E 19. See also letters in similar terms in respect of air services agreements between Hong Kong and France (undated, Special Supplement No. 5 to the *Hong Kong Government Gazette*, vol. 132 (1989), p. E 171); Hong Kong and Malaysia (16 December 1990, ibid., vol. 133 (1990), p. E 54); Hong Kong and Brazil (24 June 1991, ibid., p. E 234); see also UKMIL 1987, pp. 515–16 and UKMIL 1988, pp. 593–4)

Speaking on 2 April 1991 in the UN Human Rights Committee considering the third periodic report of the UK, the UK representative, Mr Beamish, stated:

11. A question had been asked regarding that part of the territory of Hong Kong which was not subject to the lease which expired in 1997. Under the Treaty of Nanking of 1842 and the Convention of Peking of 1860, Hong Kong Island, the southern part of the Kowloon Peninsula and Stonecutter's Island had been leased to the British Government in perpetuity. The rest of the territory of Hong Kong, comprising 92 per cent of the total land area, had been leased to Britain for 99 years, from 1 July 1898, under a further convention signed at Peking in that year. The leased area, consisting of the areas north of Kowloon up to the Shenzhen River, and 235 adjacent islands, was known as the New Territories.

(CCPR/C/SR. 1047, p. 4)

In the course of a press release dated 1 August 1991 in respect of the extension to 12 nautical miles of the territorial sea of the Isle of Man, the Home Office stated:

The Island is not part of the UK but is [an] internally self-governing dependency of the Crown. The UK Government is directly responsible for the Island's defence and international relations and ultimately for [its] good government. All Island primary legislation requires the approval of the Privy Council to which it is submitted on the recommendation of the Home Secretary.

(Text provided by the Home Office)

In August 1991, the UK Central Authority for Mutual Legal Assistance in Criminal Matters issued through the Home Office a document entitled 'United Kingdom Guidelines'. This contained the following passage:

The Channel Islands and Isle of Man, which are Crown Dependencies, are not part of the United Kingdom. Whilst the Home Office is responsible for the Islands' international relations and is therefore in a position to make representations to the Islands in respect of mutual assistance relations with other States, the Islands themselves are wholly responsible for executing requests within their jurisdictions and will shortly have their own separate legislation for doing so.

In reply to a question, the Parliamentary Under-Secretary of State, FCO, wrote:

Constitutions of dependent territories are periodically reviewed, normally at the request of the elected representatives of the territory. This ad hoc process is appropriate and flexible and fully discharges our international obligations under article 73 of the UN charter. It is implicit in article 73 that the constitutional arrangements must be tailored to the particular circumstances of each territory.

(HC Debs., vol. 199, WA, cols. *197–8*: 20 November 1991)

In reply to a question, the Minister of State, FCO, wrote:

Under the constitution of Gibraltar the assent of the Governor of Gibraltar is required before any Bill passed by the legislature of Gibraltar can become law. The governor, who is responsible to, and appointed by, my right hon. Friend the Secretary of State for Foreign and Commonwealth Affairs considers all such legislation carefully with advice from the Attorney-General of Gibraltar and the Foreign and Commonwealth Office and other Government Departments as appropriate. My right hon. Friend the Secretary of State has the power to disallow any legislation to which the Governor has given his assent. I am not aware that there are any laws in Gibraltar with conflict with decisions of the European Court [of Human Rights].

(HC Debs., vol. 200, WA, col. *155*: 4 December 1991)

Part Three: I. D. 2. *Subjects of international law—States—formation, continuity and succession of States—identity, continuity and succession*

The following passages appeared in the report of a press conference given by the FCO on 13 December 1991:

Asked about Mr Pankin's appointment as Ambassador of the Soviet Union, Spokesman said that for the time being, the USSR retained an identity in international law and international relations. The country was represented around the world and at the United Nations by Ambassadors and representatives of the 'USSR'. No alternative identity, such as the 'Commonwealth of Independent States', has yet been established internationally in its place.

Spokesman said that neither the 'Commonwealth' nor the Russian Republic had yet sought recognition from us. In practical terms, it was important at this critically difficult time to keep communications channels functioning; and to have a senior and effective Ambassador here. Mr Pankin's appointment followed consultation between the All-Union and Republican authorities. The role of the Soviet Embassy would doubtless adapt in the future to meet changing circumstances.

(Text provided by the FCO)

Part Three: I. E. *Subjects of international law—States—self-determination*

(See also Part Three: I. B. 1. (declarations of 16 December 1991) and Part Three: I. B. 5. (items of 16 January and 26 March 1991), above, and Part Six: I. B. (item of 5 April 1991) and Part Fourteen: I. B. 7. (item of 29 November 1991), below)

The following statement was made by the Twelve Member States of the EC on 9 January 1991:

The European Community and its member states unreservedly condemn the violent seizure of power in Haiti by Mr Roger Lafontant during the night of 6 to 7 January 1991. This constituted a flagrant violation of the popular will, freely expressed in the Presidential elections of last December.

The European Community and its member states are glad that democratic legality has prevailed, and the position of the elected president been upheld, with the help of the country's civil and military authorities.

(Text provided by the FCO)

In reply to a question, the Minister of State, FCO, wrote in part:

We fully support the right of the Baltic peoples to determine their own future, and welcome the progress made in the last two years towards this goal.

(HC Debs., vol. 184, WA, col. *51*: 21 January 1991)

In reply to the question,

Whether in international law the USSR has any right to impose military conscription on the three Baltic States, which it had previously seized and occupied; and whether they have made or will make representations to the Soviet Government on this matter,

the Minister of State, FCO, wrote:

The imposition of military conscription cannot be held to be unlawful under international law provided that international human rights standards are respected. However, the British Government has never recognised *de jure* the annexation of the Baltic States by the Soviet Union. *De facto* we acknowledge that the Baltic States at present lie under Soviet control and that the laws and constitution applied to other parts of the USSR have been extended to them. We support the right of the Baltic peoples to self-determination, and to resolve their future status through free negotiation with the Soviet authorities in a way which takes proper account of the legitimate rights and interests of the parties concerned. We have urged the Soviet authorities to enter into such negotiations and to refrain from any further coercion of the Baltic peoples.

(HL Debs., vol. 525, *WA 9*: 23 January 1991)

In reply to a question, the Minister of State, FCO, Mr Douglas Hogg, stated in part:

. . . we believe that the peoples of the three Baltic republics have a right to self-determination and we hope that they and the Soviet Union will be able to negotiate the outcome that is wished by the people of those republics.

(HC Debs., vol. 185, col. 841: 13 February 1991)

In reply to an oral question, the Minister of State, FCO, Mr Tristan Garel-Jones, stated:

The United Kingdom is obliged under the CSCE Final Act to continue to support the unity and integrity of Yugoslavia and also the right of individual peoples to national self-determination. We would deplore the use or the threat of force against any democratically-elected Government.

(HC Debs., vol. 185, cols. 849–50: 13 February 1991)

In the course of a debate on the subject of the visit to London of the Dalai Lama, the Minister of State in the House of Lords, Lord Reay, stated:

We believe that all peoples have a right to self-determination, but that right can be exercised in several different ways. We do not believe that independence for Tibet is a realistic proposal and consider that it would be no service to the Tibetans to encourage them to seek independence. We continue to believe that the most promising solution to the problem of Tibet is through dialogue between the Chinese Government and the Tibetan people, including the Dalai Lama. The Chinese authorities have recently reiterated their willingness to open such a dialogue and we welcome this commitment.

(HL Debs., vol. 526, col. 964: 26 February 1991)

Later in the debate, the Minister stated:

The noble Lord, Lord Avebury, asked whether we saw the Tibetans as a people with a right to self-determination. The United Nations has not determined the criteria for establishing who are a people. We are not in a position to make a definite decision on that.

(Ibid., col. 968)

In reply to a question, the Parliamentary Under-Secretary of State, FCO, wrote:

United Nations Security Council resolution 384 of 22 December 1975 deplored the armed Indonesian intervention in East Timor. United Nations Security Council resolution 389 of 22 April 1976 confirmed the right of the East Timorese to self-determination and called on the Indonesians to withdraw. The United Kingdom supported both resolutions.

With most European Community partners, the United Kingdom abstained on resolutions in the fourth committee on East Timor between 1976 and 1982.

United Nations General Assembly resolution No. 37/30 of 1982 invited the United Nations Secretary General to encourage a bilateral settlement and initiate discussions with the parties concerned.

The United Kingdom has welcomed the United Nations Secretary-General's initiative, which began in 1982, to promote contacts between Indonesia and Portugal to achieve a just settlement.

(HC Debs., vol. 188, WA, cols. *94–5*: 19 March 1991; see also ibid., vol. 189, WA, cols. *205–6* : 18 April 1991)

Speaking on 2 April 1991 in the UN Human Rights Committee considering the third periodic report of the UK, the UK representative, Mr Beamish, stated:

13. The United Kingdom's views on self-determination were contained in its report. The extent to which and the manner in which self-determination was exer-

cised in any particular territory depended on the particular circumstances and conditions in that territory. The people of the Falkland Islands, for example, expressed their views in regular elections and there was no doubt that their wish was to remain under British sovereignty.

(CCPR/C/SR. 1047, p. 4; see also UKMIL 1990, p. 506)

The Presidency Conclusions of the European Council representing also the views of the UK Government, issued on 29 June 1991, contained the following paragraph in its Annex II:

Besides a settlement of the Palestinian question through the exercise of the Palestinian people's right to self-determination, lasting peace and the stability of the region should involve the end of the state of belligerence among all States in the region, the commitment not to resort to force and to the peaceful settlement of disputes and respect for the territorial integrity of all States including Israel.

(Text provided by the FCO)

In the course of a debate on the subject of Gibraltar, the Minister of State, FCO, Mr Tristan Garel-Jones, stated:

There are two basic pillars on which our relationship rests. The first . . . is the Gibraltar Constitution Order 1969. That sets out the constitutional provisions for the dependent territory and specifically states in the preamble that

> 'Her Majesty's Government will never enter into arrangements under which the people of Gibraltar would pass under the sovereignty of another state against their freely and democratically expressed wishes'.

That undertaking remains, and it means what it says. The Government stand by it and this Minister of all people—and the House will understand why—has no intention of presiding over any hedging on that undertaking.

(HC Debs., vol. 195, col. 199: 15 July 1991)

Speaking in the UN General Assembly on 11 October 1991 on the subject of democracy and human rights in Haiti, the Permanent Representative of the Netherlands, on behalf of the EC and its Twelve Member States, observed:

It is the longstanding position of the European Community and its Member States that all peoples have an inalienable right freely to determine, in accordance with the rules of international law, their political status and to pursue their economic, social and cultural development. The people have the right to vote and to be elected at genuine periodic elections which shall be by universal and equal suffrage.

(Text provided by the FCO: see also A/46/PV. 31, p. 35)

Speaking at the concluding session on 23 October 1991 of the Paris Conference on Cambodia, the Minister of State, FCO, the Earl of Caithness, stated:

We had throughout pursued two basic principles: A comprehensive settlement; and the right of the Cambodian people to self determination through free and fair elections.

(Text provided by the FCO)

In the Agreement concerning the Sovereignty, Independence, Territorial Integrity and Inviolability, Neutrality and National Unity of Cambodia, also concluded on 23 October 1991 by, *inter alia*, the UK, the parties in the preamble, 'recalling their obligations under the Charter of the United Nations and other rules of international law', reaffirm

> the inalienable right of States freely to determine their own political, economic, cultural and social systems in accordance with the will of their peoples, without outside interference, subversion, coercion or threat in any form whatsoever.

(TS No. 111 (1991); Cm. 1786)

In the course of a debate on the subject of the future of the Western Sahara, the Minister of State, FCO, Mr Douglas Hogg, remarked:

> We have consistently reaffirmed our belief in the principle of self-determination, and that has governed our policies in this matter in the United Nations and elsewhere.

(HC Debs., vol. 200, col. 1174: 12 December 1991)

Part Three: II. A. 1. (a). *Subjects of international law—international organizations—in general—legal status—personality*

The Headquarters Agreement, signed on 15 April 1991 between the UK Government and the European Bank for Reconstruction and Development, contains the following provisions:

ARTICLE 3

Judicial Personality

The Bank shall possess full legal personality and, in particular, the full legal capacity:
(a) to contract;
(b) to acquire, and dispose of, immovable and movable property; and
(c) to institute legal proceedings.

ARTICLE 7

Protection of the Premises of the Bank

1. The Government is under a special duty to take all appropriate measures to protect the Premises of the Bank against any intrusion or damage and to prevent any disturbance of the peace of the Bank or impairment of its dignity.
2. If so requested by the Bank, the Government shall, in consultation with the Commissioner of Metropolitan Police and the Bank, develop policies and procedures so that unauthorized entry of any person shall be prevented, order on the Premises of the Bank shall be preserved, and uninvited persons shall be removed from those Premises.

. . .

(TS No. 45 (1991); Cm. 1615)

Part Three: II. A. 1. (c). *Subjects of international law—international organizations—in general—legal status—privileges and immunities*

In February 1991, a draft Headquarters Agreement between the UK Government and the European Bank for Reconstruction and Development was presented to Parliament by the Secretary of State for Foreign and Commonwealth Affairs. Article 6 of the draft Agreement read as follows:

ARTICLE 6

Inviolability of the Premises of the Bank

1. The Premises of the Bank shall be inviolable, and shall be under the control and authority of the Bank which may establish any regulations necessary for the exercise of its functions therein.
2. No official of the Government or person exercising any public authority, whether administrative, judicial, military, or police, shall enter the Premises of the Bank except with the consent of and under conditions approved by the President. Such consent may be assumed in the case of fire or other disasters requiring prompt protective action. The Bank and the Government shall agree under what circumstances and in what manner any such official may enter the Premises of the Bank without the prior consent of the Bank in connection with fire prevention, sanitary regulations or emergencies.
3. The Bank shall allow duly authorised representatives of public utilities to inspect, repair, maintain, reconstruct, and relocate utilities, conduits, mains and sewers within the Premises of the Bank and its facilities.
4. No service (other than service by post) or execution of any legal process or any ancillary act such as the seizure of private property shall be permitted by the Government to take place within the Premises of the Bank except with the express consent of and under conditions approved by the President.
5. Without prejudice to the terms of this Agreement, the Bank shall prevent the Premises of the Bank from becoming a refuge from justice for persons subject to extradition or deportation, or who are avoiding arrest or service of legal process under the law of the United Kingdom.

(Cm. 1440, p. 5)

A draft European Bank for Reconstruction and Development (Immunities and Privileges) Order 1991 was then prepared. The Parliamentary Joint Committee on Statutory Instruments raised a question about the formulation of Article 6 of the draft Order. In response, the FCO furnished the Joint Committee with the following memorandum dated March 1991:

DRAFT EUROPEAN BANK FOR RECONSTRUCTION AND DEVELOPMENT (IMMUNITIES AND PRIVILEGES) ORDER 1991

1. The Joint Committee has requested a Memorandum indicating the justification for omitting from Article 6 of the draft Order the limitations on inviolability of premises embodied in the last sentence of Article 6.2 and in Article 6.3 of the Headquarters Agreement, given that under s.1(6)(a) of the International Organisations Act 1968, the privileges and immunities granted by an Order under the Act

are not to be greater in extent than those required by the relevant international agreement.

2. As regards Article 6.2, the Department accept that words reflecting the last sentence of this provision might appropriately be inserted in the draft Order. The Order has therefore been withdrawn and will be relaid with a second paragraph to its Article 6 as follows:

> '(2) The Premises of the Bank may be entered in connection with fire prevention, sanitary regulations or emergencies without the prior consent of the Bank in such circumstances and in such a manner as may have been determined by any agreement for that purpose entered into between the Government and the Bank.'

The Department would regard the effect of such an addition as being consistent with the respective rights of both the Bank and the Government under Article 6 of the Headquarters Agreement.

3. Article 6.3 of the Headquarters Agreement is however regarded as being a somewhat different case. That provision places an obligation on the Bank to allow entry to its premises for the specified purposes. It was understood in the negotiation of the Headquarters Agreement that this was one of a class of provisions that imposed obligations on the Bank exclusively under international law. Although Article 6.3 breaks new ground in headquarters agreements between the Government and international organisations the Department do not anticipate practical difficulties in its operation. If any such were to occur it would be for the Government to insist upon compliance by the Bank with its obligation under the Headquarters Agreement.

(*Parliamentary Papers*, 1990–91, HC, Paper 26–xiv, pp. 8–9)

In moving the approval by the House of Lords of the draft European Bank for Reconstruction and Development (Immunities and Privileges) Order 1991, the Government spokesman, Lord Reay, stated:

Your Lordships will remember that the House approved the European Bank for Reconstruction and Development (Immunities and Privileges) Order 1990 on 25th July 1990. That order gave effect to the immunities and privileges set out in Chapter VIII of the agreement establishing the bank. The order before the House today will revoke the 1990 order and replace it with fresh provisions. The immunities and privileges set out in the agreement establishing the bank, previously given effect to by the 1990 order, and the new privileges and immunities accorded in the headquarters agreement negotiated between the bank and Her Majesty's Government, are now consolidated in the draft order before us. The order, when made, will enable the United Kingdom to grant to the bank, its officers and employees, experts performing missions for the bank and representatives of members of the bank these privileges and immunities.

I informed the House on 25th July last year when privileges and immunities for the bank were first debated in the House that the Government would be presenting the order now before us for approval once the negotiations for a headquarters agreement for the bank were completed. The headquarters agreement was laid before the House in draft on 7th February as Command Paper 1440. The order requires the approval of each House under Section 10 of the International Organisations Act 1968 before it can be submitted to Her Majesty in Council.

The order needs to be formally made at the meeting of the Privy Council tomorrow so that the headquarters agreement may be signed at the inaugural meeting of the bank on 15th April—a most important occasion, which will be attended by my right honourable friend the Prime Minister, by President Mitterrand and by several other heads of state or government. The agreement will enter into force on signature. It is for this reason that the order is before the House today.

When presenting the 1990 privileges and immunities order last July, I explained that the privileges and immunities set out therein had been accepted by all the prospective members of the bank as necessary to enable the bank to fulfil its purpose and function. All member countries of the EBRD will grant the bank these immunities and privileges. The House approved the 1990 order and the privileges and immunities set out therein. Those privileges and immunities are now reproduced in the draft order and include certain exemptions from duties and taxation for the bank and certain immunities from seizure for its property. The officers and employees of the bank are exempted from taxation on the salaries paid to them by the bank (although they will pay an internal tax for the benefit of the bank) and they will be immune from suit and legal process in respect of their official acts. Legal status is conferred on the bank by the order.

In a number of respects the draft headquarters agreement goes beyond the agreement establishing the bank; this is because there are certain matters which are obviously not especially relevant to the membership of the bank as a whole but are of particular concern to the bank and to the United Kingdom as the host state, in their mutual relations. The headquarters agreement gives immunity to the bank within the scope of its official activities from legal proceedings, subject to specified exceptions, and inviolability for the bank's premises. Persons connected with the bank (which includes officers and employees, experts performing missions for the bank and representatives of members of the bank) are granted varying privileges and immunities according to their status. Those who are British citizens or permanent residents of the United Kingdom receive, however, only the essential minimum privileges and immunities to enable them to perform their official functions.

I should explain that the original of the draft order before us was withdrawn and relaid on 11th March to take account of a point raised by the Joint Committee on Statutory Instruments. A second paragraph has been added to Article 6 of the draft order to reflect the last sentence of Article 6.2 of the draft headquarters agreement negotiated between the Government and the bank. This article regulates the inviolability of the bank's premises. A second point concerning this article raised by the joint committee was addressed by the department in a further memorandum sent to the committee. The joint committee completed its consideration of the draft order on 12th March.

In conclusion, we are satisfied that the privileges and immunities accorded under the draft order are necessary to fulfil our obligations under the agreement establishing the bank and the headquarters agreement. The House may rest assured that the privileges and immunities accorded are no more than are necessary for the effective operation of the bank in London and that they are granted in accordance with the limitation imposed by the International Organisations Act 1968, as amended, under whose provisions the order is made.

(HL Debs., vol. 527, cols. 594–5: 19 March 1991; see also UKMIL 1990, pp. 511–12)

The Order (Statutory Instruments 1991, No. 757) was made on 20 March 1991, revoking the Order (Statutory Instruments 1990, No. 2142) of the same title. The most significant relevant parts of the Order read as follows:

Interpretation

2. In this Order:

(a) 'the 1961 Convention Articles' means the Articles (being certain Articles of the Vienna Convention on Diplomatic Relations signed in 1961) which are set out in Schedule 1 to the Diplomatic Privileges Act 1964:

. . .

PART II

THE BANK

3. The Bank is an organisation of which the United Kingdom and other sovereign Powers are members.

4. The Bank shall have the legal capacities of a body corporate.

5.—(1) Except to the extent that the Board of Directors of the Bank shall have waived immunity, the Bank shall have immunity from suit and legal process—

(a) where the Bank has no office in the United Kingdom, nor has appointed an agent in the United Kingdom for the purpose of accepting service or notice of process, nor has issued or guaranteed securities in the United Kingdom; or

(b) where actions are brought by any member of the Bank or by any person acting for or deriving claims from any member of the Bank; or

(c) in respect of any form of seizure of, or restraint, attachment or execution on, the property or assets of the Bank, wheresoever located or by whomsoever held, before the delivery of final judgment against the Bank; or

(d) in respect of the search, requisition, confiscation or expropriation of, or any other form of interference with, or taking of or foreclosure on, the property or assets of the Bank, wheresoever located and by whomsoever held.

(2) Without prejudice to paragraph (1), the Bank shall, within the scope of its Official Activities, have immunity from suit and legal process, except that the immunity of the Bank shall not apply—

(a) to the extent that the Bank shall have expressly waived any such immunity in any particular case or in any written document;

(b) in respect of a civil action arising out of the exercise of its powers to borrow money, to guarantee obligations and to buy or sell or underwrite the sale of any securities;

(c) in respect of a civil action by a third party for damage arising from a road traffic accident caused by an Officer or an Employee of the Bank acting on behalf of the Bank;

(d) in respect of a civil action relating to death or personal injury caused by an act or omission in the United Kingdom;

(e) in respect of the enforcement of an arbitration award made against the Bank as a result of an express submission to arbitration by or on behalf of the Bank; or

(f) in respect of any counter-claim directly connected with court proceedings initiated by the Bank.

6.—(1) The Premises of the Bank and the Archives of the Bank shall have the like inviolability as, in accordance with the 1961 Convention Articles, is accorded in respect of the official archives and premises of a diplomatic mission, except that the Premises of the Bank may be entered with the consent of and under conditions approved by the President; such consent may be assumed in the case of fire or other disasters requiring prompt action.

(2) The Premises of the Bank may be entered in connection with fire prevention, sanitary regulations or emergencies without the prior consent of the Bank in such circumstances and in such a manner as may have been determined by any agreement for that purpose entered into between the Government and the Bank.

7. Within the scope of its Official Activities the Bank, its property, assets, income and profits shall have exemption from income tax, capital gains tax and corporation tax.

8. The Bank shall have the like relief from rates on the Premises of the Bank as in accordance with Article 23 of the 1961 Convention Articles is accorded in respect of the premises of a diplomatic mission.

9. The Bank shall have exemption from duties (whether of customs or excise) and taxes on the importation by it or on its behalf of goods necessary for the exercise of the Official Activities of the Bank and on the importation of any publications of the Bank imported by it or on its behalf, such exemption to be subject to compliance with such conditions as the Commissioners of Customs and Excise may prescribe for the protection of the Revenue.

10. The Bank shall have exemption from prohibitions and restrictions on importation or exportation in the case of goods imported or exported by the Bank and necessary for the exercise of its Official Activities and in the case of any publications of the Bank imported or exported by it.

11. The Bank shall have relief, under arrangements made by the Commissioners of Customs and Excise, by way of refund of duty (whether of customs or excise) paid on imported hydrocarbon oil (within the meaning of the Hydrocarbon Oil Duties Act 1979) or value added tax paid on the importation of such oil which is bought in the United Kingdom and is necessary for the exercise of its Official Activities, such relief to be subject to compliance with such conditions as may be imposed in accordance with the arrangements.

12. The Bank shall have relief, under arrangements made by Secretary of State, by way of refund of car tax and value added tax paid on any official vehicle and value added tax paid on the supply of any goods or services which are supplied for the Official Activities of the Bank, such relief to be subject to compliance with such conditions as may be imposed in accordance with the arrangements.

PART III

PERSONS CONNECTED WITH THE BANK

13.—(1) A Person Connected with the Bank shall enjoy—

(a) immunity from suit and legal process, even after the termination of his mission or service, in respect of acts performed by him in his official capacity including words written or spoken by him, except in respect of civil liability in the case of damage arising from a road traffic accident caused by him;

(b) such immunity from suit and legal process as is necessary to ensure that all their official papers and documents have the like inviolability as, in accordance with the 1961 Convention Articles, is accorded in respect of official archives of a diplomatic mission.

(2) In addition to the immunities set out in paragraph (1), Directors, Alternate Directors, Officers and Employees, and experts performing missions for the Bank under contract longer than 18 months shall, at the time of first taking up their post in the United Kingdom, be exempt from duties (whether of customs or excise) and taxes on the importation of articles (except payments for services) in respect of import of their furniture and personal effects (including one motor car each), and the furniture and personal effects of members of their family forming part of their household, which are in their ownership or possession or already ordered by them and intended for their personal use or for their establishment.

(3) In addition to the privileges and immunities set out in paragraph (1), Governors, Alternate Governors, and Representatives of Members shall enjoy—

(i) the like exemption from duties (whether of customs or excise) and taxes on the importation of their personal baggage, and the like privilege as to the importation of such articles, as in accordance with paragraph 1 of Article 36 of the 1961 Convention Articles is accorded to a diplomatic agent;

(ii) the like exemption and privileges in respect of their personal baggage as in accordance with paragraph 2 of Article 36 of the 1961 Convention Articles are accorded to a diplomatic agent;

(iii) such immunity from suit and legal process as is necessary to ensure that their personal baggage cannot be seized;

(iv) immunity from arrest or detention.

(4) In addition to the immunities set out in paragraph (1), the President and five Vice-Presidents, as nominated by the President, shall enjoy—

(a) the like immunity from suit and legal process, the like inviolability of residence and the like exemption or relief from taxes (other than income tax in respect of their emoluments and duties and taxes on the importation of goods) as are accorded to or in respect of a diplomatic agent;

(b) the like exemption or relief from being subject to a community charge, or being liable to pay anything in respect of a community charge or anything by way of contribution in respect of a collective community charge, as is accorded to or in respect of a diplomatic agent;

(c) the like exemption from duties and taxes on the importation of articles imported for their personal use, including articles intended for their establishment, as in accordance with paragraph 1 of Article 36 of the 1961 Convention Articles is accorded to a diplomatic agent;

(d) the like exemption and privileges in respect of their personal baggage as in accordance with paragraph 2 of Article 36 of the 1961 Convention Articles are accorded to a diplomatic agent;

(e) relief, under arrangements made by the Commissioners of Customs and Excise, by way of refund of duty (whether of customs or excise) or value added tax paid on any hydrocarbon oil (within the meaning of the Hydrocarbon Oil Duties Act 1979) which is bought in the United Kingdom by them or on their behalf and which is for their personal use or for that of members of their family forming part of their household, such relief to be subject to compliance with such conditions as may be imposed in accordance with the arrangements.

(5) Paragraphs (2), (3) and (4) of this Article shall not apply to any person who is a British citizen, a British Dependent Territories citizen, a British Overseas citizen, or a British National (Overseas), or who is a permanent resident of the United Kingdom.

(6) Part IV of Schedule 1 to the Act shall not operate so as to confer any privilege or immunity on the official staff of representatives other than Members of Delegations, nor so as to confer any privilege or immunity on the family of any person to whom this Article applies.

(7) Neither the provisions of the preceding paragraphs of this Article, nor those of Part IV of Schedule 1 to the Act, shall operate so as to confer any privilege or immunity on any persons as the representative of the United Kingdom or as a member of the delegation of such a representative.

(8) Any privilege or immunity conferred by the preceding paragraphs of this Article may be waived as follows:—

(i) in the case of any privilege or immunity conferred on any officer or employee of the Bank (other than the President or a Vice-President), or on an expert performing a mission for the Bank, by the President;

(ii) in the case of any privilege or immunity conferred on the President or a Vice-President, by the Board of Directors;

(iii) in the case of any privilege or immunity conferred on a Representative of a Member or a member of his delegation, by the Member concerned.

The above draft Headquarters Agreement came into force on its signature on 15 April 1991. In addition to Article 6 set out above, the following provisions deal with privileges and immunities:

ARTICLE 4

Immunity from judicial proceedings

1. Within the scope of its official activities the Bank shall enjoy immunity from jurisdiction, except that the immunity of the Bank shall not apply:

(a) to the extent that the bank shall have expressly waived any such immunity in any particular case or in any written document;

(b) in respect of civil action arising out of the exercise of its powers to borrow money, to guarantee obligations and to buy or sell or underwrite the sale of any securities;

(c) in respect of a civil action by a third party for damage arising from a road traffic accident caused by an Officer or an Employee of the Bank acting on behalf of the Bank;

(d) in respect of a civil action relating to death or personal injury caused by an act or omission in the United Kingdom;

(e) in respect of the enforcement of an arbitration award made against the Bank as a result of an express submission to arbitration by or on behalf of the Bank; or

(f) in respect of any counter-claim directly connected with court proceedings initiated by the Bank.

2. The property and assets of the Bank shall, wheresoever located and by

whomsoever held, be immune from all forms of restraint, seizure, attachment or execution except upon the delivery of final judgment against the Bank.

ARTICLE 10

Immunity of property and inviolability of Archives of the Bank

1. The property and assets of the Bank, wheresoever located and by whomsoever held, shall be immune from search, requisition, confiscation, expropriation and any other form of interference or taking or foreclosure by executive or legislative action.
2. The Archives of the Bank shall be inviolable.

ARTICLE 12

Exemption from taxation

1. Within the scope of its Official Activities the Bank, its property, assets, income and profits shall be exempt from all present and future direct taxes including income tax, capital gains tax and corporation tax.
2. The Bank shall be granted relief from rates, or any other local taxes or duties or rates in substitution therefor or in addition thereto, levied on the Premises of the Bank with the exception of the proportion which, as in the case of diplomatic missions, represents a charge for public services. The rates, or any other local taxes or duties or rates levied in substitution therefor or in addition thereto, referred to in this paragraph shall in the first instance be paid by the Government, which shall recover from the Bank the proportion which represents a charge for public services.

ARTICLE 13

Exemption from Customs and Indirect Taxes

1. The Bank shall have exemption from duties (whether of customs or excise) and taxes on importation and exportation of goods which are imported and exported by or on behalf of the Bank and are necessary for its Official Activities, or on the importation or exportation of any publications of the Bank imported and exported by it or on its behalf. Documentation signed by or on behalf of the President shall be conclusive evidence as to the necessity of any such goods for the Official Activities of the Bank.
2. The Bank shall have exemption from prohibitions and restrictions on importation or exportation in the case of goods which are imported or exported by the Bank and are necessary for its Official Activities and in the case of any publications of the Bank imported or exported by it.
3. The Bank shall be exempt from car tax and Value Added Tax on any official vehicles and shall be accorded a refund of Value Added Tax paid on any other goods and services which are supplied for the Official Activities of the Bank.
4. The Bank shall be accorded a refund of duty (whether of customs or excise) and Value Added Tax paid on the importation of hydrocarbon oils (as defined in Section 1 of the Hydrocarbon Oil Duties Act 1979) purchased by it and necessary for the exercise of its Official Activities.
5. The Bank shall have exemption from excise duty on spirits of United Kingdom origin purchased in the United Kingdom for the purpose of official entertainment

to the extent that such exemption is accorded to diplomatic missions. Documentation signed by or on behalf of the President shall be conclusive evidence that any purchase is for the purpose of official entertainment.

6. The Bank shall also be exempt from any indirect taxes which may be introduced in the future in the United Kingdom where the Agreement Establishing the Bank provides for such an exemption. The Bank and the Government shall consult as to the method for implementing such exemption.

ARTICLE 15

Privileges and Immunities for Persons Connected with the Bank

1. The Government undertakes to authorise the entry into the United Kingdom without delay, and without charge for visas, of Persons Connected with the Bank, and members of their families forming part of their households.

2. Persons Connected with the Bank shall:

(a) be immune from jurisdiction and legal process, including arrest and detention, even after termination of their mission or service, in respect of acts performed by them in their official capacity, including words written or spoken by them; this immunity shall not apply, however, to civil liability in the case of damage arising from a road traffic accident caused by any such person;

(b) be exempt, together with members of their family forming part of their households, from immigration restrictions and alien registration and from registration formalities for the purposes of immigration control;

(c) be exempt, together with members of their families forming part of their households, from national service obligations;

(d) have the same freedom of movement in the territory of the United Kingdom (subject to its laws and regulations concerning zones entry into which is prohibited or regulated for reasons of national security), and the same treatment in respect of travelling facilities, as is generally accorded to officials of comparable rank of diplomatic missions;

(e) be given, together with members of their families forming part of their households, the same repatriation facilities in time of international crises as officials of comparable rank of diplomatic missions; and

(f) be accorded inviolability for all their official papers and documents.

3. In addition to the privileges and immunities set out in paragraph 2, Directors, Alternate Directors, Officers and Employees of the Bank, and experts under contract longer than 18 months shall, at the time of first taking up their post in the United Kingdom, be exempt from duties (whether of customs or excise) and other such taxes and charges (except payments for services) in respect of import of their furniture and personal effects (including one motor car each), and the furniture and personal effects of members of their family forming part of their household, which are in their ownership or possession or already ordered by them and intended for their personal use or for their establishment. Such goods shall normally be imported within six months of the first entry of such person into the United Kingdom; an extension of this period will however be granted where justified. If such persons on the termination of their functions export goods to which this paragraph applies, they shall be exempt from any duty or other charge which may be imposed by reason of such export (except payment for services). The privileges referred to in this paragraph shall be subject to the conditions governing the

disposal of goods imported into the United Kingdom free of duty and to the general restrictions applied in the United Kingdom to all imports and exports.

4. (a) In addition to the privileges and immunities set out in paragraph 2, Governors, Alternate Governors, and Representatives of Members shall:

(i) have the right to use codes and to receive documents or correspondence by special courier or diplomatic bag;

(ii) have the same customs facilities as regards their personal baggage as are accorded to diplomatic agents; and

(iii) be immune from arrest and detention, and from seizure of their personal baggage.

(b) The provisions of this Article in respect of Governors, Alternate Governors, Temporary Alternate Governors, Directors, Alternate Directors, Temporary Alternate Directors and Representatives of Members shall be applicable irrespective of the relations existing between the Governments which those persons represent and the Government of the United Kingdom, and are without prejudice to any special immunities to which such persons may otherwise be entitled.

5. In addition to the privileges and immunities set out in paragraph 2, the President and five (5) Vice-Presidents shall enjoy the same privileges and immunities as are accorded to diplomatic agents, in accordance with international law supplemented by practice in the United Kingdom.

6. The privileges and immunities set out in paragraphs 2(b), 2(c), 2(e), 3, 4 and 5 shall not apply to Persons Connected with the Bank who are nationals of the United Kingdom and the privileges and immunities set out in paragraphs 2(e), 3, 4 and 5 shall not apply to Persons Connected with the Bank who are permanent residents of the United Kingdom.

7. The privileges and immunities in this Article shall not apply to Representatives of the United Kingdom nor the members of their delegations.

ARTICLE 16

Income Tax

1. The Directors, Alternate Directors, Officers and Employees of the Bank shall be subject to an internal effective tax imposed by the Bank for its benefit on salaries and emoluments paid by the Bank. From the date on which this tax is applied such salaries and emoluments shall be exempt from United Kingdom income tax, but the Government shall retain the right to take these salaries and emoluments into account for the purpose of assessing the amount of taxation to be applied to income from other sources.

2. In the event that the Bank operates a system for the payment of pensions or annuities to former Officers and Employees of the Bank, the provisions of paragraph 1 of this Article shall not apply to such pensions or annuities.

ARTICLE 17

Social Security

From the date on which the Bank establishes or joins a social security scheme, the Directors, Alternate Directors, Officers and Employees of the bank shall with respect to services rendered for the Bank be exempt from the provisions of any social security scheme established by the United Kingdom.

ARTICLE 19

Object of immunities, privileges and exemptions; Waiver

1. The immunities, privileges and exemptions conferred under this Agreement are granted in the interests of the Bank. The Board of Directors may waive to such extent and upon such conditions as it may determine any of the immunities, privileges and exemptions conferred under this Agreement in cases where such action would, in its opinion, be appropriate in the best interests of the Bank. The President shall have the right and duty to waive any immunity, privilege or exemption in respect of any Officer or Employee of the Bank or expert performing services for the Bank, other than the President or a Vice-President, where, in his or her opinion, the immunity, privilege or exemption would impede the course of justice and can be waived without prejudice to the interests of the Bank. In similar circumstances and under the same conditions, the Board of Directors shall have the right and the duty to waive any immunity, privilege or exemption in respect of the President and each Vice-President.
2. Privileges and immunities accorded to Representatives of Members and Members of Delegations under Article 15 are provided in order to assure complete independence in the exercise of their functions, and may be waived by the Member concerned.

(TS No. 45 (1991); Cm. 1615)

Speaking on 31 October 1991 in the Fifth Committee of the UN General Assembly, the representative of the Netherlands, on behalf of the Twelve Member States of the EC, stated:

J'ai l'honneur de prendre la parole au nom des Douze Etats de la Communauté Européenne, au titre du sous-point 115 b) de l'ordre du jour, relatif au respect des privilèges et immunités des fonctionnaires de l'Organisation des Nations Unies et des institutions spécialisées et organismes apparantés.

. . .

Nous notons avec une vive inquiétude que ce cas n'est pas le seul et que les atteintes aux privilèges et immunités des fonctionnaires ont pris des formes multiples et variées, comme l'adoption de législations contraires au statut des fonctionnaires internationaux. Le rapport du Secrétaire Général en donne de nombreux et regrettables exemples.

Les Douze rappellent que d'après l'article 105 de la Charte, l'Organisation, les représentants de ses Etats Membres et ses fonctionnaires doivent jouir des privilèges et immunités nécessaires pour atteindre ses buts et exercer leurs fonctions en toute indépendance. D'après la résolution 76 (I) de l'Assemblée générale les privilèges et immunités mentionnés aux articles 5 et 7 de la Convention sur les privilèges et immunités des Nations Unies s'appliquent (citation) 'a tous les membres du personnel des Nations Unies à l'exception de ceux recrutés sur place et payés à l'heure' (fin citation).

Bien entendu, ces privilèges et immunités sont accordés non pas à titre personnel, mais dans l'intérêt des organisations. Il revient au Secretaire General de décider quels actes liés à leurs fonctions doivent etre accomplis par les membres du Sécretariat. La résolution 45/240, qui a été adoptée sans vote par la 45e session de l'Assemblée générale, affirme que les entraves persistantes à l'exercice des attributions des fonctionnaires des Nations Unies constituent un obstacle à l'accomplissement de la mission confiée par les Etats Membres aux organismes des Nations Unies et risquent, les Douze le soulignent, de compromettre l'exécution des programmes.

. . .

Les Douze renouvellent leur appel aux gouvernements concernés afin que soit mis fin rapidement aux violations des privilèges et immunités des fonctionnaires des Nations Unies, et que les fonctionnaires internationaux puissent exercer leurs fonctions sans contraintes d'aucune sorte. Nous appuyons les efforts constants du Secrétaire Général en vue de faire appliquer les accords internationaux relatifs aux privilèges et immunités des organisations internationales et de leur personnel. Nous l'assurons de notre entière coopération et nous encourageons les Etats membres à faire de même.

(Text provided by the FCO; see also A/C.5/46/SR. 18, pp. 8–9)

Speaking on 13 November 1991 in the Sixth Committee of the UN General Assembly considering the work of the International Law Commission on the subject of relations between States and international organizations, the UK representative, Sir Arthur Watts, stated:

My delegation still, however, finds itself faced with a problem with this topic. It is essentially this. Functional requirements must be one of the main criteria for determining the extent of the privileges and immunities to be accorded to a given organisation. Yet each international organisation has its own characteristics and requirements, different from those of other international organisations with different aims and functions. Consequently, each has a different need for privileges and immunities.

We thus see some difficulty in preparing binding, uniform rules to apply generally to international organisations of a universal character. It might be better if the Commission's work on this topic were to be directed towards developing guidelines and recommendations to be adopted by States and international organizations as they see fit.

(Text provided by the FCO; see also A/C. 6/46/SR. 36, p. 13)

Speaking in the UN Special Political Committee on 15 November 1991, the representative of the Netherlands, on behalf of the EC and its Twelve Member States, stated:

Other reasons for grave concern to the Community and its Member States have been the continual disregard by Israeli authorities of privileges of UNRWA staff and immunities of UNRWA-premises, thus hampering an effective discharge of its work. Throughout the period from 1 July 1990 until the end of June this year infringements were committed by Israeli authorities in schools, health centres and clinics and other Agency installations in Gaza and on the West Bank including almost permanent occupations of parts of two Agency schools in the West Bank territory. Entry by Israeli military personnel into the Agency's clinics to question Palestinian patients is an unacceptable infringement of UN privileges and immunities, not to mention a violation of the Fourth Geneva Convention.

Moreover, the Agency's work is still encountering frequent administrative obstacles on the part of the Israeli authorities in the form of red tape and time consuming clearance procedures for activities that used to be carried out within the Agency's authority.

(Text provided by the FCO; see also A/SPC/46/SR. 22, p. 11)

In a statement made on 26 November 1991 in the Sixth Committee of the UN General Assembly considering the report of the Committee on Relations with the Host State, the representative of the Netherlands, on behalf of the Twelve Member States of the EC, observed:

En ce qui concerne plus particulièrement les questions de transport et d'application du code de la route, les douze Etats membres de la Communauté Européenne souhaitent rappeler à nouveau l'importance qu'ils attachent à l'application des articles IV et V de l'accord de siège de 1947 et des articles 29 à 31 de la Convention de Vienne de 1961 portant sur l'inviolabilité et l'immunité de juridiction pénale, civile et administrative vis-à-vis de l'Etat accréditaire. Ils attendent du pays hôte qu'il prenne les mesures appropriées pour s'acquitter complètement des obligations auxquelles il est, à cet égard, tenu.

Le règlement des questions souvent délicates touchant à l'application de l'accord de siège exige aussi bien de la vigilance que de la courtoisie. Ces questions, qu'elles soient de principe ou d'ordre pratique, doivent en outre être traitées dans le plein respect du droit international.

(Text provided by the FCO; see also A/C.6/46/SR. 44, p. 2)

Part Three: II. A. 2. (a). *Subjects of international law—international organizations—in general—participation of States in international organizations—admission*

In reply to the question

Whether [Her Majesty's Government] will sponsor the former Baltic States as members of the General Agreement on Tariffs and Trade and other international bodies,

the Minister of State, Department of Trade and Industry, wrote:

We do not believe that the current governments of the Baltic States are able to exercise the rights of independent states in international bodies such as the General Agreement on Tariffs and Trade.

(HL Debs., vol. 525, *WA 53–4*: 6 February 1991)

In reply to a question, the Parliamentary Under-Secretary of State, Department of Trade and Industry, wrote:

Her Majesty's Government are sympathetic to applications from Estonia, Latvia and Lithuania for readmission to the Universal Postal Union. However, we are not able to support their membership until they fulfil the Universal Postal Union's criteria for membership, which is open only to members of the United Nations or other sovereign countries.

(HL Debs., vol. 531, *WA 74*: 25 July 1991)

Part Three: III. D. *Subjects of international law—subjects of international law other than States and organizations—mandated and trust territories, Namibia*

(See Part Three: I. A. 1. (item of 5 February 1991) and Part Three: I. B. 1. (item of 1 August 1991), above)

Part Four: V. *The individual (including the corporation) in international law—statelessness, refugees*

In reply to a question, the Parliamentary Under-Secretary of State, FCO, wrote in part:

The criteria applied by the Hong Kong immigration authorities to determine refugee status are those laid down in the 1951 convention and the 1967 protocol relating to the status of refugees. Their procedures follow UNHCR guidelines.

(HC Debs., vol. 184, WA, col. *213*: 23 January 1991)

In reply to the question what is Her Majesty's Government's policy towards South Africans who refuse to answer army call-ups or who desert, the Government Minister in the House of Lords wrote:

All applications for asylum are considered under the terms of the 1951 United Nations Convention on Refugees. The outcome of such consideration depends on the merits of each individual's case. Evasion of military service is not in itself grounds for asylum but may be so in individual cases of conscientious objection. There are no plans to change this policy.

(HL Debs., vol. 525, *WA 18*: 28 January 1991)

In reply to a question, the Permanent Under-Secretary of State, Home Office, wrote:

The Government's current review of asylum arrangements is taking full account of our obligations under relevant human rights instruments. I am satisfied that current procedures are wholly consistent with our obligations to refugees under the 1951 United Nations convention.

(HC Debs., vol. 185, WA, col. *236*: 7 February 1991)

In the course of a debate in the House of Lords on the subject of refugees, the Government spokesman, Lord Reay, stated:

The 1951 United Nations convention relating to the status of refugees, and its 1967 protocol, provide the main international framework for the recognition and treatment of refugees. Indeed these instruments give the accepted definition of a refugee as a person outside his or her country of nationality who has a: 'well founded fear of being persecuted for reasons of race, religion, nationality, membership of a particular social group or political opinion and is unable, or owing to such fear, is unwilling to avail himself of the protection of that country'. The United Kingdom has ratified both these international instruments. The 1951 United Nations convention and its 1967 protocol form the basis of the United Kingdom's policy on refugees. We uphold the rule of international law, both at home and abroad, as laid out in these instruments.

(HL Debs., vol. 526, col. 1459: 6 March 1991)

Lord Reay later observed:

The Government's policy is carefully and correctly to apply the criteria of the 1951 convention in every case. There is no question of denying refugee status to those entitled to it.

(Ibid., col. 1464)

Speaking on 3 April 1991 in the UN Human Rights Committee considering the third periodic report of the UK, the UK representative, Mr Stock, stated:

The question of Vietnamese boat people had posed mammoth problems for Hong Kong, and the territory had made a genuine effort to deal fairly with them. It should, however, be noted that articles 13 and 14 of the Covenant related to those lawfully present in the territory of a State party, which was not true of the boat people in Hong Kong.

(CCPR/C/SR. 1050, p. 8)

In reply to a question, the Minister of State, FCO, wrote:

Our frequent discussions with our partners about Yugoslavia cover the likely humanitarian consequences of civil unrest. The arrangements for the reception of refugees would be a matter for the individual countries concerned. The 1951 UN Convention of Refugees obliges signatory governments not to return genuine refugees to their country of origin.

(HL Debs., vol. 528, *WA* 77 : 17 May 1991)

In reply to the question what criteria are used for determining political refugee status for Vietnamese boat people in Hong Kong, the Parliamentary Under-Secretary of State, FCO, wrote in part:

The criterion used is that contained in the 1951 United Nations convention and the 1967 protocol relating to the status of refugees which states that a person is a refugee if he has a well-founded fear of being persecuted for reasons of race, religion, nationality, membership of a particular social group or political opinion and who, owing to such fear, is unwilling to avail himself of the protection of his country of nationality.

(HC Debs., vol. 192, WA, col. 727 : 14 June 1991; see also ibid., vol. 195, cols. 1286–7: 25 July 1991)

Part Four: VI. *The individual (including the corporation) in international law—immigration and emigration, extradition, expulsion and asylum*

(See also Part Four: V. (items of 28 January and 7 February 1991), above)

In reply to a question, the Minister of State, FCO, wrote:

The UK and the Soviet Union, as states party to the International Covenant on Civil and Political Rights, and through their CSCE commitments, recognise the freedom of individuals to leave their own country. We have therefore encouraged the Soviet Union to fulfil such obligations and commitments through reform of its emigration legislation. The new Soviet emigration law, passed in May, is a positive step in this direction.

(HL Debs., vol. 529, *WA 61*: 12 June 1991)

Part Four: VII. *The individual (including the corporation) in international law—protection of human rights and fundamental freedoms*

(See also Part Three: I. A. 3., above, and Part Fourteen: I. B. 6. and Part Fourteen: I. B. 7., below)

Foreign Policy Document No. 215, 'Human Rights in Foreign Policy', issued by the FCO in January 1991, mentions the Universal Declaration of Human Rights, 1948, and continues:

Four decades after its proclamation, the Declaration is widely accepted as a gauge by which Governments can measure their progress in the protection of human rights. Although it is not in itself legally binding, much of its content can now be said to form part of customary international law. It is quoted in many international legal instruments, including the Council of Europe's Convention for the Protection of Human Rights and Fundamental Freedoms and the Constitution of the OAU. It is also referred to in the Helsinki Final Act of the Conference on Security and Co-operation in Europe and it has inspired many national constitutions.

(Text provided by the FCO)

In reply to a question on the legality in international law of conscription in the Baltic States, the Minister of State, FCO, wrote in part:

The imposition of military conscription cannot be held to be unlawful under international law provided that international human rights standards are respected.

(HL Debs., vol. 525, *WA 9*: 23 January 1991)

On 31 January 1991 in the UN Commission on Human Rights the Minister for Foreign Affairs of Luxembourg and President of the Council of Ministers of the EC, Mr Jacques Poos,

. . . speaking first on the subject of respect for human rights in international relations, reiterated the condemnation of the 12 members of the European Communities of Iraq's invasion of Kuwait and the violations committed by the Iraqi authorities against their own population and the population of Kuwait. He recalled that the Twelve had also condemned Iraq's unacceptable violations of the standards laid down in the Geneva Convention relative to the Treatment of Prisoners of War and had categorically demanded that, during the hostilities in the Gulf, Iraq should comply fully with all the principles of humanitarian law applicable in wartime.

40. Following the tragic events which had occurred during the night of 12/13 January in Vilnius, and the night of 20/21 January in Riga, the Communities and their member States had condemned the acts of repression committed by the USSR, which were in flagrant violation, in particular, of the Charter of Paris, for-

mally adopted on 21 November 1990 at the summit held by the Conference on Security and Co-operation in Europe (CSCE) in that city.

. . .

42. In the opinion of the European Communities and their member States, civil and political rights, on the one hand, and economic, social and cultural rights, on the other hand, were indivisible. A policy designed to implement one category of rights should not be used as a pretext for denying or neglecting other fundamental rights. That principle had been clearly reiterated at the latest ministerial conference held under the Lomé Convention. A declaration issued by the Twelve on 21 July 1986 stated that neither a lack of social and economic development nor any persuasion or ideology could justify a denial of civil and political rights. The Twelve acted and reacted jointly in situations where fundamental rights were flouted, whoever was responsible for the violations.

(E/CN.4/1991/SR.5, pp. 10–11)

Speaking on 5 February 1991 in the UN Commission on Human Rights, the Parliamentary Under-Secretary of State, FCO, Mr Mark Lennox-Boyd, stated:

Let me ask for Iraq to respect human life and dignity. To respect in particular the Third and Fourth Geneva Conventions. And at all times to apply in good faith the international standards to which Iraq has committed itself.

. . .

The United Kingdom has consistently recognised the rights of the Baltic peoples to determine their own future through free negotiation based on democratic principles. We urge the Soviet authorities to negotiate peacefully; not to threaten or use force; and to stand by their commitments, which they accepted at the highest level, in the Paris Charter and other instruments.

. . .

The Commission has just concluded its debate on the violation of human rights in the Occupied Territories. The representative of Luxembourg has already outlined my Government's views in speaking on behalf of the European Community last week. I wish simply to take this opportunity to reiterate those views, and to recall Israel's obligations under the Fourth Geneva Convention, and to the importance of full respect for the human rights of the Palestinian population.

(Text provided by the FCO; see also E/CN.4/1991/SR. 11)

In reply to a question, the Minister of State, FCO, wrote:

We have made repeated representations, both bilaterally and in company with our EC partners and other like-minded States, to the Burmese military authorities to urge them to release political prisoners immediately, including Aung San Suu Kyi. We will continue to urge the Burmese military authorities to adhere to internationally accepted standards of behaviour and to respect human rights.

(HL Debs., vol. 525, *WA 47*: 6 February 1991)

Speaking to the UN Commission on Human Rights on 11 February 1991, the UK representative, Mr D. Campbell, stated:

Respect for human rights, individually and as a group, as enshrined in the United Nations Charter and the Universal Declaration of Human Rights, constitutes a universal obligation and stimulates the creativity, innovation and initiative necessary for socio-economic development. Its fulfilment, along with democratization and observance of the rule of law, is a part of the process of development.

(Text provided by the FCO)

In reply to a question, the Parliamentary Under-Secretary of State, FCO, wrote in part:

. . . we have repeatedly urged the Turkish authorities, at ministerial level, to respect their obligations under international human rights conventions.

(HC Debs., vol. 185, WA, col. *388*: 12 February 1991)

In reply to the question what is Her Majesty's Government's policy on the United Nations optional protocol on civil and political rights, the Parliamentary Under-Secretary of State, FCO, wrote:

As we have accepted the right of individual petition under the European convention on human rights and the compulsory jurisdiction of the European Court, we have accepted the strongest available mechanism for individual petition available to us and therefore need not accept that offered by the optional protocol.

(HC Debs., vol. 186, WA, col. *51*: 18 February 1991)

Speaking on 27 February 1991 at a meeting of the UN Commission on Human Rights, the representative of Luxembourg, on behalf of the EC and its Member States, declared:

The Community and its Member States have on a number of occasions both in this forum and elsewhere, denounced and condemned the perpetration of serious acts of violence in the Baltic countries. The Twelve have taken a number of specific measures. Among these we should emphasise the triggering of the machinery existing in the framework of the human dimension of the CSCE. This procedure ought to make it possible to get a full picture of these events. In addition, further to the commitments which the Soviet Union has entered into within the United Nations, the international community has the right to require that those guilty of these unlawful acts should be identified and punished and that the Soviet authorities should henceforth refrain from any recourse to force and encourage the establishment of a dialogue, as they have undertaken to do. The Twelve have noted with satisfaction the assurances given in this regard by the Representative of the Soviet Union to the Commission on Human Rights early yesterday evening and the important statement on this subject then read by the Chairman of the Commission. It should be noted that the Twelve are demanding the full implementation of human rights and fundamental freedoms in the Baltic countries as in all the Soviet Republics and autonomous regions.

. . .

Throughout the past year, the European Community has strongly reiterated its total rejection of apartheid. Its aim remains the abolition of this hateful system of racial discrimination which is an affront to human dignity, a violation of the United Nations Charter and contrary to the Universal Declaration of Human Rights.

. . .

The Community and its Member States remain concerned at the human rights situation in China. The Twelve can only express their reprobation of the severe sentences passed following summary trials, most recently on 12 February last, on Chinese citizens committed to democracy. They renew their appeal to the Chinese authorities to guarantee respect for human rights throughout the country, including Tibet, in accordance with their international obligations. Meanwhile, the Twelve will continue their dialogue with the Chinese authorities, in a constructive spirit, in order to obtain the release of all political prisoners and respect for the citizens' right to peaceful assembly and freedom of speech.

. . .

The Twelve are still concerned at the continued violations of human rights in Vietnam. A number of political detainees are still in prison, contrary to the international obligations which Vietnam has entered into. The Twelve hope that the Vietnamese authorities will take swift measures to free them. At the same time, they note that the Vietnamese authorities have kept to their obligations towards repatriated citizens.

The Community and its Member States are gravely concerned at the deterioration in the human rights situation in the Union of Myanmar over the past few months; they note that the country features in the report on torture compiled by the Special Rapporteur, Mr Kooijmans. In breach of Article 25 of the Covenant on Civil and Political Rights, the Myanmar authorities have failed to act on the elections held on 27 May 1990, in which victory went to the opposition.

. . .

With regard to the human rights situation in the Territories occupied by Israel since 1967, the Community and its Member States were able to express their attitude in their statement on item 4 of our agenda, entitled 'Question of the violation of human rights in the occupied Arab territories, including Palestine'. The Twelve deplore Israel's attacks on the fundamental freedoms and rights of the populations of the Occupied Territories. Accordingly, the European Community and its Member States urgently call upon Israel to act in accordance with its obligations under Article 49 of the Fourth Geneva Convention. The Twelve are concerned at the fact that the situation in the Arab territories occupied by Israel has deteriorated considerably. The Twelve believe that violence breeds violence and they condemn its use by anyone at all.

(Text provided by the FCO; see also E/CN.4/1991/SR.43, pp. 8–14)

In reply to a question asking about Lithuanian laws said to discriminate against the Russian and Polish minorities, the Government Minister wrote:

We do not have full details of Lithuanian legislation, but we are aware that anxieties have been expressed by some members of the Russian and Polish minorities over some items of legislation passed by the Lithuanian parliament. We have encouraged the Lithuanian authorities to ensure that the rights of minorities in Lithuania are fully protected and that all their legislation is in line with internationally recognised human rights standards.

(HL Debs., vol. 526, *WA 60*: 28 February 1991)

In reply to questions, the Minister of State, FCO, wrote:

At the 47th Session of the UN Commission on Human Rights, which ended in Geneva on 7th March, the Presidency, on behalf of the European Community, made a statement calling upon the Chinese authorities to guarantee respect for human rights throughout China, including Tibet.

. . .

We have taken steps both before and after liberation to make clear to the Kuwaiti Government our concern that human rights should be respected. They have assured us that Kuwait will be administered in strict accordance with law.

(HL Debs., vol. 257, *WA 9* and *10 passim*: 14 March 1991)

In a statement issued on 26 March 1991, the Twelve Members States of the EC remarked:

The Community and its Member States follow with the greatest concern the situation in Yugoslavia. They encourage the efforts underway to resolve the constitutional crisis in the country by way of dialogue and appeal to all parties concerned to refrain from the use of force and to respect fully human rights and democratic principles in conformity with the charter of Paris on the new Europe.

(Text provided by the FCO)

Speaking on 1 April 1991 in the UN Human Rights Committee considering the third periodic report of the UK, the UK representative, Mr Beamish, referred to the European Convention on Human Rights. He continued:

45. Replying to questions relating to the Optional Protocol, he said that his Government had noted the growing number of Parties to that instrument, including some of the States members of the Council of Europe which also accepted the right of individual petition under the European Convention. Most of the Territories to which the Covenant applied were within the Council of Europe system. The European Convention and the First Protocol thereto extended to Guernsey, Jersey, the Isle of Man, Bermuda, the British Virgin Islands, the Cayman Islands, the Falkland Islands, Gibraltar, Montserrat, St. Helena and the Turks and Caicos Islands. Of those, all but the British Virgin Islands, the Cayman Islands and the Isle of Man accepted the right of petition under article 25 of the European Convention and the jurisdiction of the European Court under article 46. The acceptance of the right of petition had recently been renewed for a further five-year period in respect of the United Kingdom itself and also the Territories concerned. Those territories which were not so far included did not wish the right of petition to apply to them and the United Kingdom respected their position. The only territories in which the Covenant, but not the European Convention, applied were Pitcairn and Hong Kong. The Government was concentrating, in regard to the latter, on implementation of the Joint Declaration and the Bill of Rights.

(CCPR/C/SR. 1046, p. 10)

In reply to a question asking about religious freedom in Hong Kong after 1997, the Minister of State, FCO, wrote in part:

The Sino-British joint declaration and the Basic Law both make provision for the continuation of freedom of religious belief and practice in Hong Kong after 1997. In addition, the international covenant on civil and political rights, article 18 of which covers religious freedom, will, under the joint declaration and Basic Law, continue to apply to Hong Kong after 1997.

(HC Debs., vol. 189, WA. cols. *187–8*: 17 April 1991)

In the *Annual Report on Hong Kong, 1990*, presented to Parliament in April 1991 by the Secretary of State for Foreign and Commonwealth Affairs, it was stated:

VII. Human Rights

28. The people of Hong Kong have been assured of their basic human rights through the application of the International Covenant on Civil and Political Rights (ICCPR) and International Covenant on Economic, Social and Cultural Rights (ICESCR) to Hong Kong since 1976. At present the Covenants are implemented in Hong Kong, as in the United Kingdom, through a combination of common law, legislation and administrative rules. The continued application of the two Covenants after 1997 is provided for in the Sino-British Joint Declaration.

(Cm. 1527, pp. 7–8)

In reply to a question, the Minister of State, FCO, wrote:

We expect Iraq to live up to its international obligations under the Geneva conventions, the international convention on civil and political rights and the genocide convention. In addition, SCR 688, adopted on 5 April, demands that the Iraqi Government stop their repression of their own people.

(HC Debs., vol. 189, WA, col. *288*: 19 April 1991)

In reply to the question 'what international treaties and conventions exist providing for the protection of the rights of minority groups, as opposed to the rights of individuals', the Parliamentary Under-Secretary of State, FCO, wrote:

There are no multilateral United Nations or Council of Europe treaties and conventions which protect minority groups as such. Individuals belonging to minorities are given particular mention in article 27 of the International Covenant on Civil and Political Rights.

(HC Debs., vol. 192, WA, col. *559*: 12 June 1991)

In reply to a question about the refusal of the Soviet authorities to permit Mrs Gordievsky and family to join Mr Oleg Gordievsky in the UK, the Parliamentary Under-Secretary of State, FCO, wrote in part:

Mrs. Leila Gordievsky and her two small daughters, Mariya and Anna, are entirely innocent of any wrong-doing. We believe that there can be no justification for the Soviet authorities' refusal to them of permission to come to Britain to be reunited with Mr. Oleg Gordievsky, in accordance with their clearly expressed wish. The Soviet Government's denial to them of the right to travel stands in clear contravention of the detailed provisions relating to family reunification and freedom of travel in the documents of the conference on security and co-operation in Europe, to which the Soviet Union is a party. We will continue to press this human rights case strongly until the family are granted their right to travel.

(HC Debs., vol. 192, WA, col. *637*, 13 June 1991)

In reply to the question what response had been made by Her Majesty's Government to the violations of human rights in Azerbaijan and Armenia, the Minister of State, FCO, the Earl of Caithness, wrote:

. . . we have made our anxieties about recent events known to the Soviet authorities. We look to them to preserve law and order in an even-handed way. We continue to urge all concerned to refrain from intimidation and violence and to act in accordance with the principles of the CSCE.

. . .

I confirm that in calling on the Soviet authorities to live up to their undertakings made in the Paris Charter and the CSCE documents we have made it perfectly clear that assistance will depend on continued commitment to reform.

(HL Debs., vol. 529, col. 1277: 14 June 1991)

The following declaration comprised Annex V of the Presidency Conclusions of the European Council, representing also the views of the UK Government, issued on 29 June 1991:

DECLARATION ON HUMAN RIGHTS

Recalling the 1986 declaration of Foreign Ministers of the Community on Human Rights (21 July 1986), the European Council reaffirms that respecting, promoting and safeguarding human rights is an essential part of international relations and one of the cornerstones of European cooperation as well as of relations between the Community and its member States and other countries. In this regard the European Council stresses its attachment to the principles of parliamentary democracy and the primacy of law.

The European Council welcomes the considerable progress made in recent years in the field of human rights, and the advances in democracy in Europe and throughout the world, particularly in certain developing countries. It welcomes the growing prominence of demands of peoples for freedom and democracy throughout the world.

They deplore, however, the persistence of flagrant violations of human rights in many countries. The Community and its member States undertake to pursue their policy of promoting and safeguarding human rights and fundamental freedoms throughout the world. This is the legitimate and permanent duty of the world community and of all States acting individually or collectively. They recall that the different ways of expressing concern about violations of rights, as well as requests designed to secure those rights, cannot be considered as interference in the internal affairs of a State and constitute an important and legitimate part of their dialogue with third countries. For their part, the Community and its member States will continue to take up violations wherever they occur.

The European Community and its member States seek universal respect for human rights. Many international instruments have been elaborated in the last decades, first among which rank the Universal Declaration of Human Rights and the Covenants on civil and political rights and on economic, social and cultural rights. No specific provision based on national, cultural or religious factors can validly be invoked to detract from the principles established by these instruments. The European Council calls on all States to become a party to the international instruments in force.

. . .

The Council of Europe plays a leading role in the field of human rights with its expertise, its numerous projects in this field, training and educational activities, and programmes of cooperation with the countries of Central and Eastern Europe which possess or are seeking to possess democratic institutions. Under its aegis, the European Convention on the Protection of Human Rights and Fundamental Freedoms, given the binding character of its norms and the strictness and reliability of its provisions of control, is both an advanced, effective system of protection and a point of reference for other regions of the world. The European Council welcomes the readiness of the Council of Europe to put its experience at the service of the CSCE.

(Text provided by the FCO)

In its written observations, presented in October 1991, on the Third Report of the HC Foreign Affairs Committee concerning the Middle East after the Gulf War, Her Majesty's Government stated:

The Government have made regular representations . . . to the Israeli authorities about human rights abuses in the Occupied Territories. We favour joint démarches by the Twelve where this is possible. We have repeatedly reminded the Israelis of their responsibilities under the Fourth Geneva Convention, which we believe applies to the Occupied Territories including East Jerusalem. We voted in favour of [Security Council Resolution] 681 of 20 December 1990 which focused on this issue.

(Cm. 1682, p. 5)

Speaking on 12 November 1991 in the Third Committee of the UN General Assembly, the representative of the Netherlands, on behalf of the EC and its Member States, stated:

The European Community and its Member States have on many occasions expressed their firm commitment to furthering the cause of human rights as well as the importance they attach to the role of the United Nations in this respect. It is therefore an honour to speak on behalf of the European Community and its Member States on agenda item 98 a: Implementation of Human Rights Instruments.

The promotion and protection of human rights is one of the highest priorities of the United Nations. This priority can only be fully achieved when States abide their international obligations and effectively implement the human rights instruments to which they have adhered. In this respect, the European Community and its Member States note with satisfaction the increasing number of ratifications or accessions to the International Covenant on Civil and Political Rights and its Optional Protocols, the Covenant on Economic, Social and Cultural Rights, the Convention on the Elimination of all Forms of Racial Discrimination, the Convention against Torture and Other Cruel, Inhuman or Degrading Treatment or Punishment and the Convention on the Rights of the Child. We call on all States who have not already done so to ratify, or to accede to, the international human rights instruments. We believe that in future particular attention must be given to securing universal adherence to, and monitoring compliance with, these existing instruments. A new development is the International Convention on the Protection of the Rights of all Migrant Workers and Their Families which was adopted last year by consensus.

(Text provided by the FCO; see also A/C.3/46/SR. 39, p. 17)

In the course of a debate on the Second Reading of the Asylum Bill, the Secretary of State for the Home Department, Mr Kenneth Baker, stated:

The category of 'refugee' is defined in the 1951 United Nations convention. It is important to recognise the philosophical background to that definition. There is a basic assumption in international law—and in common sense—that a state will protect its citizens. That is the very reason for the existence of states. The 1951 convention is about citizens whom a state is actively seeking to harm.

(HC Debs., vol. 198, col. 1087: 13 November 1991)

In the course of a debate on the subject of human rights in Azerbaijan, the Government spokesman, Lord Cavendish of Furness, stated:

In September at the CSCE Conference on the Human Dimension in Moscow, the leader of the British delegation raised in plenary session the issue of human rights violations in the Transcaucasus. He called for CSCE principles to be upheld, and for the conflict over Nagorno-Karabakh to be resolved through dialogue, not violence.

In his speech at the opening of the conference, the Foreign Secretary went out of his way to make clear that the West's dealings with each Soviet republic would depend heavily on their respect for human rights and the rule of law. He referred to the need to ensure the rights of minorities in accordance with the Paris Charter.

(HL Debs., vol. 532, col. 1136: 21 November 1991)

In reply to a question, the Minister of State, FCO, wrote:

The European convention on human rights applies in full to Gibraltar and provides Gibraltarians with the right of individual petition in relation to the rights covered by the convention. Furthermore, Gibraltar's constitution contains a chapter setting out the fundamental rights and freedoms of Gibraltarians and provides for their enforcement through the courts.

(HC Debs., vol. 199, WA, col. *460*: 26 November 1991)

Part Five: I. *Organs of the State—the head of the State*

In reply to a question on the subject of the functions and role of the Privy Council, the Lord President of the Council wrote:

The functions of the Privy Council are legislative, judicial and executive. In its legislative role the Privy Council provides the machinery for the exercise of certain powers of the royal prerogative now confined almost entirely to the fields of the dependent territories, Crown servants, and the grant of legal personality by the approval of royal charters of incorporation. Much the larger part of the Council's legislative role is in the exercise of the wide range of powers conferred by statute on the sovereign in Council or directly on the Council itself.

The judicial functions of the Privy Council are exercised by the Council's judicial committee which acts as the supreme court of appeal from courts of some Commonwealth countries which have retained this right of appeal, from courts of dependent territories and from those of the Channel Islands and the Isle of Man. The judicial committee also exercises an appellate jurisdiction in respect of disciplinary proceedings in certain professions and certain decisions made by authorities of the Church of England.

The executive functions of the Privy Council also derive from both the royal prerogative of which the most important are the sovereign's powers to prorogue and dissolve Parliament, and statute. The rest largely comprise responsibility for a wide variety of appointments including the formalities of appointment of various Cabinet and other Ministers, high sheriffs, members of various statutory bodies, Her Majesty's inspector of schools, and members of university courts and councils.

(HC Debs., vol. 184, WA, col. *366*: 25 January 1991)

Part Five: II. *Organs of the State—ministers*

In reply to a question, the Attorney-General, Sir Patrick Mayhew, stated:

As the Government's principal legal adviser, I give advice to Ministers on any matter involving domestic or international legal issues.

(HC Debs., vol. 189, col. 766: 22 April 1991)

Part Five: IV. *Organs of the State—diplomatic agents and missions*

(See also Part Five: VIII. B. (item of 15 November 1991), below)

In the course of criminal proceedings in a London magistrates' court against a number of persons who on 5 April 1991 had occupied premises at 22 Queen's Gate, London, in an attempt to draw attention to the plight of Kurdish refugees in Iraq, the following certificate was issued by the FCO on 7 May 1991:

Under the authority of Her Majesty's Principal Secretary of State for Foreign and Commonwealth Affairs conferred on me in accordance with the provisions of Section 9(4) of the Criminal Law Act 1977, I, David Colin Baskcomb Beaumont, Head of Protocol Department at the Foreign and Commonwealth Office, hereby certify that on 5 April 1991, the premises at 22 Queen's Gate, London, SE7 5JG formed part of the premises of a closed diplomatic mission as mentioned in paragraph (aa) of Section 9(2) of the Criminal Law Act 1977.

(Text provided by the FCO. See also the material in Part Five: IX., below which indicates that the premises were those occupied by the Iraqi Embassy)

On 1 September 1991, the following joint declaration was issued in Vilnius, Lithuania:

The Government of the Republic of Lithuania and the Government of the United Kingdom of Great Britain and Northern Ireland, being desirous of further promoting relations of friendship and cooperation, have agreed to re-establish diplomatic relations between the two countries on the basis of international law, contained in the UN Charter, including the principles of mutual respect for sovereignty, equality and non-interference in each other's internal affairs, in accordance with the Vienna Convention of 18 April 1961 on Diplomatic Relations.

(Text provided by the FCO)

On 5 September 1991, the following joint declaration was issued in Tallinn, Estonia:

The Government of the Republic of Estonia and the Government of the United Kingdom of Great Britain and Northern Ireland, being desirous of further promoting relations of friendship and cooperation, have agreed to re-establish diplomatic relations between the two countries on the basis of international law, contained in the UN Charter, including the principles of mutual respect for sovereignty, equality and non-interference in each other's internal affairs, in accordance with the Vienna Convention on Diplomatic Relations of April 18, 1961.

(Text provided by the FCO)

Part Five: V. *Organs of the State—consular agents and consulates*

A Joint Communiqué concerning the establishment of consular relations between Ukraine and the UK was issued on 14 December 1991 in the following terms:

Ukraine and the United Kingdom of Great Britain and Northern Ireland,

Inspired by the desire to establish and develop comprehensive cooperation in the fields of political, economic, trade, scientific and technological, cultural and humanitarian relations,

Confident that the establishment of consular relations will favour the development of friendly relations between Ukraine and the United Kingdom,

Have decided to establish consular relations with immediate effect, and to base their relations in this respect on the Vienna Convention on Consular Relations adopted on 24 April 1963 and on the principle of reciprocity, subject to the provisions relating to consular relations which are implemented in their respective laws.

(Text provided by the FCO)

Part Five: VIII. A. *Organs of the State—immunity of organs of the State—diplomatic and consular immunity*

In reply to a question, the Parliamentary Under-Secretary of State, FCO, wrote in part:

All members of the staff of diplomatic missions in London who are not United Kingdom nationals nor permanently resident here enjoy a degree of diplomatic immunity under the Diplomatic Privileges Act 1964. Those who are diplomatic agents enjoy personal inviolability including freedom from arrest or detention. They are immune from the criminal jurisdiction of the receiving state, and except in relation to certain private matters, from its civil and administrative jurisdiction. Members of the administrative and technical staff also enjoy personal inviolability and the same immunities except that their immunity from civil and administrative jurisdiction does not extend to acts performed outside the course of their duties. Members of the service staff have immunity only in respect of acts performed in the course of their duties. The immunity of consular officers is governed by the Consular Relations Act 1968.

(HC Debs., vol. 184, WA, col. *456*: 29 January 1991)

In reply to a later question on the subject of criminal offences committed by foreign diplomats in the UK, the same Minister wrote:

Our policy on diplomatic immunities and privileges is set out in the 1985 White

Paper. In the most serious cases we require the withdrawal of the diplomat concerned. The figures requested for the past five years are shown in the table. . . .

	1986	*1987*	*1988*	*1989*	*1990*
Traffic offences[1]					
(a) Drink/Driving	24	25	28	27	24
(b) Minor offences	71	86	103	75	52
Serious offences					
Includes (a) above	41	40	44	40	33
Parking					
Unpaid fines	22,331	14,437	10,079	7,831	[2]6,282
Diplomats withdrawn at FCO request	17	18	14	14	6

[1] Technically all traffic offences are 'criminal' offences.
[2] Provisional to 31 October 1990—latest figures processed.

(Ibid.; see also UKMIL 1985, pp. 437–53)

In reply to the question 'what provisions control the circumstances in which entry to a diplomatic mission in the UK can be authorized in order to check for the presence of illegal arms or ammunition', the Parliamentary Under-Secretary of State, FCO, wrote:

Article 22 of the Vienna convention on diplomatic relations provides that the premises of the mission shall be inviolable, and that the agents of the receiving state may not enter them except with consent of the head of mission.

The same article provides that the receiving state is under a special duty to take all appropriate steps to protect the premises of the mission against any intrusion or damage.

(HC Debs., vol. 185, WA, col. *609*: 15 February 1991)

In reply to the question whether the Minister 'will list the limitations on the powers of the police to apprehend and search for arms and ammunition foreign diplomats leaving their foreign missions in the UK', the same Minister wrote:

Article 29 of the Vienna convention on diplomatic relations provides that the person of a diplomatic agent shall be inviolable and that he shall not be liable to any form of arrest or detention. Article 41 of the convention provides that it is the duty of all persons enjoying such privileges and immunities to respect the laws and regulations of the receiving state.

We have made clear to all missions in London that it is the duty of the police to prevent the unauthorised carriage of firearms, and that persons suspected of carrying firearms are likely to be questioned.

(Ibid.)

In reply to the question 'whether it is the practice when diplomatic relations have been terminated with a foreign country for Her Majesty's Government to accept the nomination of any other foreign country with a recognised mission in the United Kingdom as protector of the interests of the first country; and what freedom to decline to accept such arrangements is available to Her Majesty's Government', the same Minister wrote:

> In accordance with articles 45 and 46 of the Vienna convention on diplomatic relations, when diplomatic relations have been broken off with a foreign country, Her Majesty's Government as the receiving state, will consider the nomination by the sending state, of a third state to assume the role of a protecting power. It is for Her Majesty's Government alone to decide whether or not the nomination is acceptable.

(Ibid., col. *610*)

In reply to a question, the Parliamentary Under-Secretary of State, FCO, wrote that the Government had no plans to seek amendment of the Vienna Convention on Diplomatic Relations in order to end the practice of granting diplomatic immunity for driving and parking offences.

(HC Debs., vol. 186, WA, col. *580*: 28 February 1991)

In moving the Second Reading in the House of Lords of the Arms Control and Disarmament Bill, the Government spokesman, Lord Reay, stated:

> Clause 5 confers specified privileges and immunities on inspectors and transport crew members. These are the same as those conferred in 1988 on inspectors under the INF treaty. It is necessary that our own inspectors enjoy such immunities and privileges operating in other countries (for example, in the Soviet Union) and we therefore have to accord them on a reciprocal basis. The number of persons involved will not be large and they will be present in the United Kingdom for short periods only.

(HL Debs., vol. 527, col. 1697: 19 April 1991)

In reply to a question, the Government Minister in the House of Lords wrote:

> Thirty-three alleged serious offences by persons entitled to diplomatic immunity were drawn to the attention of the Foreign and Commonwealth Office in 1990 (seven fewer than in 1989). 'Serious offences' are defined in accordance with the Report to the Foreign Affairs Committee, *The Abuse of Diplomatic Immunities and Privileges (1985)*, as offences falling into a category which would in certain circumstances attract a maximum penalty of six months' or more imprisonment; we are advised that none of the alleged offences would have been likely to attract a custodial sentence. The majority involved drinking and driving and shoplifting.
>
> Six diplomats were withdrawn from their posts in Britain in 1990 following alleged offences, as against 14 in the previous year.

(HL Debs., vol. 528, *WA 40–1*: 7 May 1991)

The following explanatory note, dated May 1991, was prepared by the FCO for the Parliamentary Joint Committee on Statutory Instruments considering the draft Vienna Document (Privileges and Immunities) Order 1991:

It is proposed that this Order should be made under section 1(2) of the Arms Control and Disarmament (Privileges and Immunities) Act 1988. That section provides that no such Order shall be made unless a draft of it has been laid before and approved by a resolution of each House of Parliament.

The Vienna Document 1990 on the Negotiations on Confidence- and Security-Building Measures convened in accordance with the relevant provisions of the Concluding Document of the Vienna Meeting of the Conference on Security and Coordination in Europe (Cm.1466) integrates a set of new confidence- and security-building measures with measures adopted in the Document of the Stockholm Conference (Cm.26) which have been further developed in the light of experience gained. The Vienna Document is an arrangement superseding most provisions of the Stockholm Document and is also an arrangement otherwise making provision for furthering arms control and disarmament within the meaning of section 1(2) of the 1988 Act.

The present Order is required to implement in the law of the United Kingdom paragraph 58 of the Vienna Document, under which observers of military activities are to be granted, during their mission, the privileges and immunities of diplomatic agents under the Vienna Convention on Diplomatic Relations; paragraph 97, under which inspectors and, if applicable, auxiliary personnel are to be granted during their mission privileges and immunities in accordance with the Vienna Convention; and paragraph 130, under which members of evaluation teams and, if applicable, auxiliary personnel are to be granted during their mission privileges and immunities in accordance with the Vienna Convention. The scheme of the 1988 Act, under which observers and inspectors under the Stockholm Document were granted the privileges and immunities of diplomatic agents, and auxiliary personnel were granted the privileges and immunities of the administrative and technical staff or the service staff of a mission, has been followed in the proposed Order.

In accordance with section 1(2) of the 1988 Act, the privileges and immunities granted by this Order do not exceed those conferred by the Diplomatic Privileges Act 1964 and are no greater in extent than is required to give effect to the relevant provisions of the Vienna Document.

(Text provided by the FCO)

In moving the approval by the House of Lords of the draft Vienna Document (Privileges and Immunities) Order 1991, the Government Minister, Lord Cavendish of Furness, stated:

. . . the purpose of this order is to confer privileges and immunities on observers, inspectors, evaluators and auxiliary personnel, in accordance with the provisions of the 1990 Vienna document of the negotiations on confidence and security-building measures.

The order is necessary for the United Kingdom to give effect in domestic law to those provisions on privileges and immunities. The order is being made under Section 1(2) of the Arms Control and Disarmament (Privileges and Immunities) Act 1988. The privileges and immunities it confers follow the pattern of Section 1(1) of the 1988 Act under which observers and inspectors visiting the UK under the

Stockholm document were granted the privileges and immunities of diplomatic agents and auxiliary personnel were granted the privileges and immunities of the administrative and technical staff or the service staff of a mission.

Those privileges and immunities will in practice be enjoyed only rarely by visitors to the UK. The Vienna document sets limits on what each participating state is obliged to accept. For the United Kingdom this amounts to three inspections and one evaluation visit per year. Observations are linked to the size of military exercises. The United Kingdom has been obliged to host only one since the adoption of the 1986 Stockholm document.

(HL Debs., vol. 530, col. 744: 27 June 1991)

On 24 July 1991, the Vienna Document (Privileges and Immunities) Order 1991 (Statutory Instruments 1991, No. 1704) was made under powers in section 1(2) of the Arms Control and Disarmament (Privileges and Immunities) Act 1988. An explanatory note accompanying the Order reads:

This Order confers privileges and immunities on observers, inspectors and evaluators, and auxiliary personnel, as required for giving effect in the United Kingdom to paragraphs 58, 97 and 130 of the Vienna Document 1990 of the Negotiations on Confidence- and Security-Building Measures convened in accordance with the relevant provisions of the Concluding Document of the Vienna Meeting of the Conference on Security and Co-operation in Europe (Cm 1466).

The Arms Control and Disarmament (Inspections) Act 1991 was enacted on 25 July 1991. Its relevant provisions read:

Privileges and immunities

5.—(1) Inspectors and transport crew members shall enjoy the same privileges and immunities as are enjoyed by diplomatic agents in accordance with the following provisions of the 1961 Articles, namely—

(a) Article 29,
(b) paragraph 2 of Article 30,
(c) paragraphs 1, 2 and 3 of Article 31, and
(d) Articles 34 and 35.

(2) Such persons shall, in addition, enjoy the same privileges as are enjoyed by diplomatic agents in accordance with paragraph 1(b) of Article 36 of the 1961 Articles, except in relation to articles the importing or exporting of which is prohibited by law or controlled by the enactments relating to quarantine.

(3) Subject to subsection (4), the privileges and immunities accorded to inspectors and transport crew members by virtue of this section—

(a) shall be enjoyed by them at any time when they are in the United Kingdom—

(i) in connection with the carrying out of an inspection there pursuant to any provision of the Protocol, or

(ii) while in transit to or from the territory of another State Party in connection with the carrying out of such an inspection there; and

(b) shall also be enjoyed by them at any time with respect to acts previously performed in the exercise of official functions as an inspector or a transport crew member.

(4) The immunity from jurisdiction enjoyed by an inspector or a transport crew member by virtue of subsection (1)(c) shall cease to be so enjoyed if expressly waived by the State Party of which he is a national.

(5) Any means of transport—

(a) used by inspectors to travel to or from the United Kingdom in connection with the carrying out of an inspection pursuant to any provision of the Protocol (whether in the United Kingdom or elsewhere), and

(b) specifically provided for such use by, or by arrangement with, any State Party,

shall be inviolable.

(6) If in any proceedings any question arises whether a person is or is not entitled to any privilege or immunity by virtue of this section, a certificate issued by or under the authority of the Secretary of State stating any fact relating to that question shall be conclusive evidence of that fact.

(7) In this section—

'the 1961 Articles' means the Articles which are set out in Schedule 1 to the Diplomatic Privileges Act 1964 (Articles of Vienna Convention on Diplomatic Relations of 1961 having force of law in United Kingdom) . . .

Part Five: VIII. B. *Organs of the State—immunity of organs of the State—immunity other than diplomatic and consular*

The Parliamentary Joint Committee on Statutory Instruments considered the Quick-Frozen Foodstuffs Regulations 1990 (Statutory Instruments 1990, No. 2615) which was designed to implement EEC Council Directive 89/108/EEC. Regulation 2(2) lists the kinds of food to which the Regulations do not apply. These include food: '(*b*) which is supplied under government contracts for consumption by Her Majesty's Forces or supplied for consumption by a visiting force; or (*c*) which is supplied by the service authorities of a visiting force and to a headquarters or to members of such a force or headquarters or to property held or used by such force or headquarters.' The Committee asked the Ministry of Agriculture, Fisheries and Food how it was established that these sub-paragraphs were consistent with the Directive. In a memorandum dated 1 February 1991 the Ministry replied in part as follows:

First, the Ministry accepts that Crown immunity is not recognised in Community law as such; construction rules relating to UK legislation do not apply to Community instruments. The position in relation to visiting forces is more doubtful, since the Treaty takes its place within the context of international law, and the extent to which international law requires recipient states to exempt visiting forces from domestic legislation is open to debate.

(*Parliamentary Papers*, 1990–91, HC, Paper 26–x, p. 7)

Speaking on 30 October 1991 in the Sixth Committee of the UN General Assembly considering the draft articles drawn up by the International Law

Commission on the subject of jurisdictional immunities of States and their property, the UK representative, Professor D. W. Bowett, stated:

In previous years the British delegation has set out the basic position of the United Kingdom on this matter. It is that, in the light of contemporary State practice, the old rule of absolute immunity is obsolete, and that persons dealing with a foreign State in a non-sovereign capacity, and who find themselves in dispute with that State, should be able to have their dispute determined by the ordinary processes of law. The draft articles now before us, in general, accept that position and so the Commission's approach is welcomed by the British delegation.

But there remain certain difficulties in the implementation of that approach—and I will refer to some of them in a moment. And we have yet to see whether the approach is acceptable to Member States generally. Certainly the United Kingdom hopes to be able to give sympathetic consideration to the Commission's recommendation that a plenipotentiary conference be convened, with a view to adopting a Convention. But the practicability of that proposal must depend upon the views of other States, for there needs to be a fair measure of support for the Commission's approach to the topic before a reasonable prospect of success can be assured. For this reason, the British delegation will follow the views expressed here with the greatest of interest.

Mr Chairman, I referred a moment ago to certain difficulties in the implementation of the Commission's basic approach. Let me illustrate this by making three specific points.

The first is the definition of a 'commercial transaction'. Article 2, para. 2 adopts the primary test of the nature of the contract or transaction. We agree with that: a contract for the purchase of goods, for example, is by its nature a commercial transaction. But the Commission has adopted a secondary test, that of the *purpose* of the transaction, which a State can invoke to rebut the apparent commercial nature of the transaction if, in the practice of that State, the test of purpose would be relevant.

I believe this secondary test to be mistaken, and likely to lead to great uncertainty. First, the *purpose* of the transaction may not be clear to the private party. When a private party sells denim cloth to a foreign State how will he know whether the State intends to use it to make uniforms for its armed forces, or to make it available for private distribution for making ordinary work-clothes? If a State purchases computer hardware, how is the supplier to know whether the state intends to use it for organising the logistics of its Army, or the bus and railway time-tables of the various private enterprises who provide the country's transport system?

Of course the State will know the purpose for which it entered into the transaction. And one can share the Commission's concern to 'provide an adequate safeguard and protection for developing countries' (Commentary, A/CN.4/L.462/Add.1 p. 22). We have no quarrel with that. But isn't it easier for the State to specify, in the contract, or as part of the transaction, that it is acting for a sovereign rather than a commercial purpose? Otherwise, how will the foreign, private party know what the purpose is? Nor does it very much help to say that this secondary test will apply only when it is the practice of the particular State to apply it. As we all know, evidence of State practice is often extremely difficult to come by.

So, Mr Chairman, let us by all means ensure that developing States have all the powers they need to protect their economic development. But if they exercise their powers openly, by stating that they are transacting in a sovereign capacity, we avoid the risk of causing prejudice to a private party who may otherwise be unaware of the State's purposes.

My second point concerns immunity from measures of constraint, now covered in draft Article 18. In principle, if a State has no immunity from jurisdiction it ought to have no immunity from measures of execution to give effect to a judgment against it. Put in another way, we have to ask the question: if the private party has a right to bring an action, do we not frustrate that right if we deny him a right of execution?

Of course it can be argued that certain types of property ought to be immune—bank accounts of embassies used to meet the costs of the functioning of the Mission, military property, property belonging to a central bank, property forming part of an exhibition etc. But this special case for immunity is met by Article 19.

So the question remains, why, in Article 18, is the State not treated like a private party for purposes of execution as a general rule—the special cases of Article 19 apart?

My concern relates specifically to Article 18, para. 1(*c*) which allows State property in use, or intended for use, for commercial purposes to be attached. But then comes a phrase which introduces a quite remarkable restriction on the power of attachment. The property must have 'a connection with the claim which is the object of the proceeding or with the agency or instrumentality against which the proceeding was directed.' Mr Chairman, that does seem excessively restrictive. I note that the Special Rapporteur proposed its deletion (A/CN.4/431, p. 40) and that views in the Commission were divided. But its deletion was opposed by some Members, for reasons which are not apparent. I believe the Special Rapporteur's proposal was the right one.

My third and last point concerns the retention of the concept of 'segregated State property' in Article 10, para. 3. True, the term is not used, as such, and the original proposal—former Article 11 *bis*—has disappeared. But the basic idea remains, namely that a State's immunity is not affected by proceedings relating to a commercial transaction entered into by a State enterprise or other entity with separate legal personality and capable of bringing suit and owning property in its own name. Implicit in this there seems to be the idea that, for purposes of execution, it is only the property of such a State enterprise or entity that can be attached—and not the property of the State in general.

If this is right, then I feel the point could have been expressed in the Draft Articles rather more clearly. Moreover, if this is right, there is a major cause for concern. It was this same concern which was expressed so well by the distinguished Representative of the Federal Republic of Germany on Tuesday. What would prevent a State from organising its commercial activities through such separate Agencies or entities, but making sure that in fact they own very little property which could be used to satisfy a judgment? Given that the State's own property cannot be attached, the judgment creditor is left with an unenforceable judgment.

In principle, either the Agency operates as a separate entity: in which case no issue of State immunity arises, and, naturally, attachment could only be against the Agency's own property. But in such a case the private Party is entitled to be told, in clear terms, that he is *not* contracting with the State, and perhaps also to have some means of knowing what are the capital resources of the State entity. Or, alternatively, the Agency operates on behalf of the State: in which case immunity attaches in principle, but is forfeited because of the commercial nature of the transaction. But in that event it is difficult to see why only the property of the Agency, and not that of the State, can be attached. I confess to being somewhat puzzled by the logic of Article 10, para. 3, but I would welcome clarification by those members of the Committee with a longer experience of this draft than I have.

(Text provided by the FCO; see also A/C.6/46/SR.25, pp. 4–6)

The following letter, dated 15 November 1991, was addressed by the FCO (Legal Advisers) to the Assistant Secretary of Tribunals (Regional Office of the Industrial Tribunals London (South)), in London:

MRS E PEREZ V. AMERICAN EMBASSY EMPLOYEES' ASSOCIATION

I am writing to you as a result of a letter of 30 October from the Ambassador of the United States of America in London to the Secretary of State for Foreign and Commonwealth Affairs concerning the above matter. That letter stated that the Embassy has been informed orally by ACAS of a hearing scheduled for December 6, 1991 regarding the status of the American Embassy Employees' Association. The Embassy then found out through telephoning the Industrial Tribunal that an Order had been made for further particulars on 25 September 1991. Protocol Department of the Foreign and Commonwealth Office received copies of both the Order for further particulars and the Notice of Preliminary Hearing. However, the Foreign and Commonwealth Office were at no time requested to forward these documents to the American Embassy. On those documents the respondent was named as the American Embassy Employees' Association and the view was taken here that the documents were copied to us for information. I have now spoken to one of your staff at the Regional Office who informed me that a decision had been taken by the President of the Industrial Tribunal that documents should be sent to the American Embassy via the Foreign and Commonwealth Office. Unfortunately we were not told of that and the documents were not therefore forwarded.

The Ambassador has informed the Foreign and Commonwealth Office that the American Embassy Employees' Association is an integral part of the American Embassy. As you may know, diplomatic missions do not have legal personality; they are an extension of the Government of the sending State. They are in fact a mission of the Government itself. It would seem therefore that the proper person against whom proceedings should be brought in the Industrial Tribunal is the United States Government. A decision to take such a step is of course for Mrs Perez with the advice of her legal representative.

For your information section 12 of the State Immunity Act 1978 provides that any writ or other document required to be served for instituting proceedings against a State shall be served by being transmitted through the Foreign and Commonwealth Office to the Ministry of Foreign Affairs of the State concerned and service shall be deemed to have been effected when the writ or document is received at the Ministry. The relevant department dealing with such service abroad is the Legal Procedures Section of the Nationality, Treaty & Claims Department of the Foreign and Commonwealth Office. The address is Clive House, Petty France, SW1H 9HD.

On the basis of the above information you may feel it is appropriate to cancel the preliminary hearing scheduled for Friday, 6 December.

(Text provided by the FCO)

Part Five: IX. *Organs of the State—protecting powers*

The FCO addressed a note, dated 28 March 1991, to the Embassy in London of the Kingdom of Jordan which read in part as follows:

The Foreign and Commonwealth Office present their compliments to the Embassy of the Hashemite Kingdom of Jordan and have the honour to refer to the Embassy's Note No. MK/1 of 18 March requesting agreement to act as protecting power for the interests of the Republic of Iraq in this country under Articles 45(b) and (c) of the Vienna Convention on Diplomatic Relations.

The Foreign and Commonwealth Office accept this proposal. The Iraqi Interests Section of the Jordanian Embassy should remain at the premises of the former Iraqi Embassy. The Jordanian Embassy should now make an application to the Secretary of State for this consent to the premises of the former Iraqi Embassy being part of the premises of the Jordanian Mission, as required under the Diplomatic and Consular Premises Act 1987.

The Iraqi Interests Section may only employ the following personnel:

(i) [name] (Head of Section)
(ii) [name] (Clerk)
(iii) [name] (Clerk)
(iv) A driver/caretaker, subject to Foreign and Commonwealth Office approval
(v) [name] (Secretary)
(vi) [name] (Secretary)
(vii) [name] (cleaner).

The Iraqi Interests Section should employ no other personnel either at their premises or elsewhere. The Iraqi Cultural Centre must be closed.

The FCO addressed a further note, dated 1 May 1991, to the same Embassy which read in part as follows:

Protocol Department present their compliments to the Embassy of the Hashemite Kingdom of Jordan and have the honour to acknowledge receipt of the Embassy's Note No. MK/1 of 13 April seeking the Secretary of State's consent for the premises of the Iraqi Interest Section of 20–22 Queen's Gate, London SW7 5JG to be regarded as forming part of the premises of the Mission of the Embassy of the Hashemite Kingdom of Jordan.

Protocol Department would like to state, for and on behalf of the Secretary of State for Foreign and Commonwealth Affairs, that, under Section 1 of the Diplomatic and Consular Premises Act 1987, this consent is granted.

Protocol Department request that the necessary application for rating relief is submitted in due course.

(Texts provided by the FCO)

Part Six: I. A. *Treaties—conclusion and entry into force—conclusion, signature, ratification and accession*

(See Part One: II. D. 1., above, and Part Eight: I. A. (item of 5 February 1991), below)

In reply to a question, the Parliamentary Under-Secretary of State, FCO, wrote:

Before ratifying a treaty Her Majesty's Government must ensure that they have the necessary statutory powers to enable them to give effect to its provisions and, if not, that the necessary enabling legislation is made. The text of the treaty is then laid before Parliament for a minimum of 21 parliamentary sitting days before it is ratified in order to give Parliament the opportunity to debate its provisions.

(HC Debs., vol. 194, WA, col. *354*: 10 July 1991)

In moving the consideration by HC Standing Committee of the draft Double Taxation Relief (Taxes on Income) (Isle of Man) Order 1991, the Financial Secretary to the Treasury, Mr Francis Maude, stated:

I am confident that there is no conflict with the Treaty of Rome—obviously we would not sign international agreements that we believed were in conflict with another international treaty to which we were signatories.

(HC Debs., 1991–2, First Standing Committee on Statutory Instruments, etc.: 4 December 1991, col. 5)

Part Six: I. B. *Treaties—conclusion and entry into force—reservations and declarations to multilateral treaties*

(See also Part Eight: II. A. (item of 2 August 1990) and Part Fourteen: I. B. 8. (items of 27 September and 16 October 1991), below)

Speaking on 5 April 1991 in the UN Human Rights Committee considering the third periodic report of the UK, the UK representative, Mr Halliday, referred to the International Covenant on Civil and Political Rights, 1966. He went on:

In connection with his Government's reservations to the Covenant, he said that he would convey the views expressed in the Committee, but wished to point out that he could not accept the claim that the reservations had the effect of consigning human rights in the United Kingdom to a kind of limbo: if anything, the Government tended to err on the side of caution in its approach, going to great pains to elucidate any possible incompatibilities between the provisions of the Covenant and those of domestic legislation.

Mr Beamish, also of the UK delegation, then continued:

. . . his Government's Declaration in connection with article 1 of the Covenant did not constitute a reservation. It had been made in 1968 when the Government signed the Covenant and had been maintained in 1976 when the Covenant was ratified. It did not purport to limit the right of self-determination, and merely stated his Government's understanding that, in the event of a conflict between its obligations under article 1 and its obligations under the Charter, the latter would prevail. The Declaration had been made at a time when the right of self-determination was less clearly defined than was now the case. It referred in part to Articles 1 and 2 of the Charter, and to Article 73 which, *inter alia*, affirmed basic obligations in respect of Non-Self-Governing Territories, and the Declaration was thus a correct statement of the legal position, although opinions might differ as to the need to retain it.

(CCPR/C/SR. 1046, p. 9)

Upon accession in April 1990 to the International Covenant on Civil and Political Rights adopted by the General Assembly of the UN on 16 December 1966, the Government of the Republic of Korea declared 'that the provisions of paragraphs 5 and 7 of Article 14, Article 22 and paragraph 4 of Article 23 of the Covenant shall be so applied as to be in conformity with the provisions of the local laws including the Constitution of the Republic of Korea'. On 23 May 1991, the UK Permanent Representative to the UN in New York addressed the following letter to the UN Secretary-General:

I have the honour to refer to circular letter No. C.N.113.1990.Treaties–2/5/3 (Depositary Notification) of 4 June 1990 concerning the instrument of accession to the International Covenant on Civil and Political Rights adopted by the General Assembly of the United Nations on 16 December 1966, deposited by the Government of the Republic of Korea on 10 April 1990.

The Government of the United Kingdom have noted the statement formulated by the Government of the Republic of Korea on accession, under the title 'RESERVATIONS'. They are not however able to take a position on these purported reservations in the absence of a sufficient indication of their intended effect, in accordance with the terms of the Vienna Convention on the Law of Treaties and the practice of the Parties to the Covenant. Pending receipt of such an indication, the Government of the United Kingdom reserve their rights under the Covenant in their entirety.

(Text provided by the FCO)

By a letter dated 5 December 1991, the Secretary of State for Foreign and Commonwealth Affairs notified the Secretary-General of the UN as follows:

I have the honour to refer to the Instrument of Ratification by the United Kingdom of the Convention on the Rights of the Child adopted by the General Assembly of the United Nations on 20 November 1989, and to make the following reservations and declarations on behalf of the United Kingdom:

(*a*) The United Kingdom interprets the Convention as applicable only following a live birth.

(*b*) The United Kingdom interprets the references in the Convention to 'parents' to mean only those persons who, as a matter of national law, are treated as parents. This includes cases where the law regards a child as having only one parent, for example where a child has been adopted by one person only and in certain cases where a child is conceived other than as a result of sexual intercourse by the woman who gives birth to it and she is treated as the only parent.

(*c*) The United Kingdom reserves the right to apply such legislation, in so far as it relates to the entry into, stay in and departure from the United Kingdom of those who do not have the right under the law of the United Kingdom to enter and remain in the United Kingdom, and to the acquisition and possession of citizenship, as it may deem necessary from time to time.

(*d*) Employment legislation in the United Kingdom does not treat persons under 18, but over the school-leaving age as children, but as 'young people'. Accordingly the United Kingdom reserves the right to continue to apply Article 32 subject to such employment legislation.

(*e*) Where at any time there is a lack of suitable accommodation or adequate facilities for a particular individual in any institution in which young offenders are detained, or where the mixing of adults and children is deemed to be mutually beneficial, the United Kingdom reserves the right not to apply Article 37(*c*) in so far as those provisions require children who are detained to be accommodated separately from adults.

(*f*) In Scotland there are tribunals (known as 'children's hearings') which consider the welfare of the child and deal with the majority of offences which a child is alleged to have committed. In some cases, mainly of a welfare nature, the child is temporarily deprived of its liberty for up to seven days prior to attending the hearing. The child and its family are, however, allowed access to a lawyer during this period. Although the decisions of the hearings are subject to appeal to the courts, legal representation is not permitted at the proceedings of the children's hearings themselves. Children's hearings have proved over the years to be a very effective way of dealing with the problems of children in a less formal, non-adversarial manner. Accordingly, the United Kingdom, in respect of Article 37(d), reserves its right to continue the present operation of children's hearings.

(Text provided by the FCO)

Part Six: I. C. *Treaties—conclusion and entry into force—entry into force, provisional application*

(See Part Six: II. B. (item of 30 October 1991), and Part Eight: I. A. (item of 5 February 1991), below)

Part Six: II. B. *Treaties—observance, application and interpretation—application*

Article 1 of the Agreement between the Governments of the UK and the Republic of Burundi for the Promotion and Protection of Investments, which was signed and entered into force on 13 September 1990, reads in part as follows:

ARTICLE 1

Definitions

For the purposes of this Agreement:

(e) 'territory' means:

(i) in respect of the Republic of Burundi: the area of land, including waters, delimited by the Rwandese Republic to the North, the United Republic of Tanzania to the East and the Republic of Zaire to the West, the area of which is 28,734 sq. km;

(ii) in respect of the United Kingdom: Great Britain and Northern Ireland, and any territory to which this Agreement is extended in accordance with the provisions of Article 12.

(TS No. 11 (1991); Cm. 1420)

The corresponding provision in a similar agreement between the Governments of the UK and the Republic of Argentina, signed on 11 December 1990, reads:

(d) 'territory' means the territory of the United Kingdom of Great Britain and Northern Ireland or of the Republic of Argentina, as well as the territorial sea and any maritime area situated beyond the territorial sea of the State concerned which has been or might in the future be designated under the national law of the State concerned in accordance with international law as an area within which the State concerned may exercise rights with regard to the sea-bed and subsoil and the natural resources; and any territory to which this Agreement may be extended in accordance with the provisions of Article 12. (Cm. 1449)

The corresponding provision in a similar agreement between the Governments of the UK and the Republic of Turkey, signed on 15 March 1991, reads:

(e) 'territory' means:
- (i) in respect of the Republic of Turkey: the Republic of Turkey and the maritime areas adjacent to the coast of the Republic of Turkey to the extent to which the Republic of Turkey may exercise sovereign rights or jurisdiction in those areas according to international law;
- (ii) in respect of the United Kingdom: Great Britain and Northern Ireland and any territory to which this Agreement is extended in accordance with the provisions of Article 12 together with the adjacent maritime areas to the extent to which sovereign rights or jurisdiction in these areas is exercised in accordance with international law.

(Cm. 1600)

The corresponding provision in a similar agreement between the Governments of the UK and the Kingdom of Morocco, which was signed and entered into force provisionally on 30 October 1990, reads:

(d) 'territory' means:
- (i) in respect of the United Kingdom: Great Britain and Northern Ireland, including any maritime area situated beyond the territorial waters of the United Kingdom which has been or might in the future be designated under the national law of the United Kingdom in accordance with international law as an area within which the United Kingdom may exercise rights with regard to the sea-bed and subsoil and the natural resources; and any territory to which this Agreement is extended in accordance with the provisions of Article 12;
- (ii) in respect of the Kingdom of Morocco: the territory of the Kingdom of Morocco, including any maritime area situated beyond the territorial waters of the Kingdom of Morocco and which has been or might in the future be designated by the laws of the Kingdom of Morocco in accordance with international law as an area within which the Kingdom of Morocco may exercise rights with regard to the sea-bed and subsoil and the natural resources.

(Cm. 1603)

The following provision, taken from the agreement with Burundi, is typical of similar provisions in other agreements of this kind made during the period:

ARTICLE 12

Territorial Extension

At the time of signature of this Agreement, or at any time thereafter, the provisions of this Agreement may be extended to such territories for whose international relations the Government of the United Kingdom are responsible, as may be agreed between the Contracting Parties in an Exchange of Notes.

(TS No. 11 (1991); Cm. 1420)

Part Six: II. D. *Treaties—observance, application and interpretation—treaties and third States*

The following item was announced by the FCO on 7 November 1991:

BALTIC GOLD

Spokesman confirmed that senior British and Estonian officials would be meeting in the FCO on 7 November for discussions on financial questions. The issues would include the gold deposited with the Bank of England by the Bank of Estonia in the 1930s and the question of British assets held in and with Baltic states prior to the events of 1939/40.

Spokesman said that the UK had always made clear that the 1968 agreement with USSR did not preclude any future independent Baltic Republic from submitting a claim. The UK wanted to see a mutually acceptable settlement as soon as possible, which was why we had proposed these talks.

(Text provided by the FCO)

Part Six: IV. C. *Treaties—invalidity, termination and suspension of operation—termination, suspension of operation, denunciation and withdrawal*

In reply to a question, the Minister of State, FCO, wrote:

A large number of bilateral treaties and agreements were signed by Her Majesty's Government and the Baltic governments before 1941. These included agreements with all three Baltic states on the extradition of fugitive criminals, on legal procedures and on commerce. Because we recognise de facto, although not de jure, the incorporation of the Baltic states into the Soviet Union, none of these pre-1941 agreements is currently operative.

(HC Debs., vol. 195, WA, col. *363*: 22 July 1991)

In introducing a debate on the subject of the European Coal and Steel Community, the Parliamentary Under-Secretary of State for Industry and Consumer Affairs, Mr Edward Leigh, stated:

The treaty establishing the European Coal and Steel Community expires in 2002. The European Commission has produced a document which identifies three principal options. The first is to extend the treaty beyond 2002, either as it stands or in an amended form. The second is early termination of the treaty, with the coal and steel industries then becoming subject, like other industries, to the provisions of the EEC treaty. The third option is to allow the treaty to expire in 2002. In that case, the interim period could be used to repeal or modify certain ECSC provisions and to incorporate others into the EEC treaty if that should prove to be necessary.

Early termination of the ECSC treaty is the Government's preferred option. But we recognise that such a solution may not be attainable. It would require unanimous acceptance by the Council and ratification by the national Parliaments of all member states; and that seems unlikely. We would, therefore, be prepared to allow the treaty to continue until it lapses in 2002, provided that the interim period is used to bring about a less interventionist approach and to reduce burdens on business.

(HC Debs., vol. 196, col. 257: 15 October 1991)

By a decision of 11 November 1991 of the Council of the EC and the representatives of the Governments of the Member States, meeting within the Council, the Agreements between the EC, its Member States and the Socialist Federal Republic of Yugoslavia were suspended.
(*Official Journal of the EC*, L 315/47)

By a decision of the representatives of the Governments of the Member States of the EC, meeting with the Council, the Agreement of 1983 between the Member States of the European Coal and Steel Community and the Socialist Federal Republic of Yugoslavia was denounced.
(Ibid., L 315/48)

Part Six: VII. *Treaties—consensual arrangements in other than treaty form*

The following statement was made at a FCO Press Conference held on 7 February 1990:

Spokesman announced that a Memorandum of Understanding on co-operation in the field of maritime narcotics interdiction operations ('Shiprider' Memorandum) between the United Kingdom (on behalf of the Government of the British Virgin Islands), and the United States of America, was signed on 6 February [1990] in Tortola, British Virgin Islands.

(Text provided by the FCO)

The following statement was made at a FCO Press Conference held on 12 July 1990:

Spokesman announced that a Memorandum of Understanding on co-operation in the field of narcotics interdiction operations between the United Kingdom (on behalf of the Government of the Turks and Caicos Islands), the United States of America and the Commonwealth of the Bahamas would be signed on 12 July [1990] in Grand Turk, Turks and Caicos Islands.

(Text provided by the FCO)

On 22 February 1991, the Government of the UK, together with the Governments of Belgium, Canada, the Federal Republic of Germany, Italy, the Netherlands, the USA, and the People's Republic of China, concluded a Memorandum of Understanding on the Avoidance of Overlaps and Conflicts relating to Deep Seabed Areas.
[*Editorial note*: This document, which states that the parties 'have agreed

as follows', has been included in the UK Treaty Series (TS No. 52 (1991); Cm. 1628).]

On 13 July 1991, the European Community and its Member States, including the UK, signed with the Federal Authorities of Yugoslavia and the Republics of Croatia and Slovenia a Memorandum of Understanding on the Monitor Mission to Yugoslavia.
(Text provided by the FCO)

On 25 September 1991, a Memorandum of Understanding on Mutual Assistance and the Exchange of Information was signed between, on the one hand, the United States Securities and Exchange Commission and the Commodity Futures Trading Commission, and, on the other hand, the United Kingdom Department of Trade and Industry and the Securities and Investments Board.
(Text provided by the FCO)

Part Seven: II. C. *Personal jurisdiction—exercise—miscellaneous*

(See Part Eight: II. D., below)

Part Eight: I. A. *State territory and territorial jurisdiction—parts of territory, delimitation—frontiers, boundaries*

(See Part Three: I. B. 1. (items of 5 February and 16 December 1991), above)

In response to the question whether Her Majesty's Government will seek EC and UN support for a homeland and State for the Kurdish people, the Prime Minister wrote:

No. The United Kingdom is a signatory to the treaty of Lausanne of 1923 which established the present-day frontiers in the region bounded by Iran, Iraq and Turkey. There can be no question of our seeking support for the establishment of a separate Kurdish state within these boundaries.

(HC Debs., vol. 184, WA, col. *285*: 24 January 1991)

In reply to the question whether since 1945 a valid peace treaty exists between the USSR and Romania, the Government Minister in the House of Lords wrote in part:

The Soviet Union and Romania signed a peace treaty in 1947 which inter alia defined the present Soviet/Romanian border. The United Kingdom, United States and other countries were parties to the treaty which came into force on 15th September 1947.

(HL Debs. vol. 525, *WA 34–5*: 31 January 1991)

In reply to a question asking about 'the status of the Treaty of Sèvres and the joint declaration of 1922 between the United Kingdom and Iraq', the Minister of State, FCO, wrote:

Our records show that the treaty of Sèvres was never ratified and, consequently, never came into force. It was overtaken by the treaty of Lausanne of 1923 which established the present-day frontiers of the region bounded by Iran, Iraq and Turkey.

(HC Debs., vol. 185, WA, col. *84*: 5 February 1991)

In reply to a question, the Parliamentary Under-Secretary of State, FCO, wrote:

We believe that the Kurdish people should enjoy proper representation and respect for human rights in all of the countries in which they live. But as a signatory to the treaty of Lausanne of 1923, which established the present boundaries in the area, we cannot seek support for the establishment of a separate Kurdish state within these boundaries.

(HC Debs., vol. 187, WA, col. *433*: 12 March 1991; see also ibid., vol. 198, WA, col. *286*: 19 April 1991)

Speaking on 3 April 1991 in the UN Security Council, the UK Permanent Representative to the UN in New York, Sir Richard Hannay, stated:

. . . there is the question of the boundary between Iraq and Kuwait and of the future security of that small country, living always next door, as it is bound to do, to its larger and more powerful neighbour. The resolution is not attempting to settle the boundary between these two countries; that was done by the 1963 Agreement between them, which was registered with the United Nations. But the failure to demarcate that boundary and the determination of Iraq to raise territorial claims that are incompatible with the 1963 Agreement are at the roots of this dispute, and they must be addressed. Rapid demarcation of the boundary, the setting up of a United Nations unit to monitor a demilitarized zone along the frontier and a guarantee by the Security Council to step in if ever it is violated again are a carefully integrated package designed to ensure that there is no repetition of the events of last August. My Government is well aware of the great sensitivity to many Members of the Organization of the question of defining boundaries. We have no desire and no intention of overturning the principle that it is for the parties in question to negotiate and reach agreement, as was done in this case in 1932 and 1963. But, naturally, the Security Council has a duty to respond when disputes over boundaries arise and come to threaten international peace and security.

(S/PV. 2981, pp. 113–14)

In reply to a question, the Minister of State, FCO, wrote:

Gibraltar is part of the Community by virtue of article 227(4). Gibraltar's frontier with Spain is therefore an internal EC frontier for all purposes except as regards free trade in goods where Community rules do not apply because Gibraltar is not part of the Community customs territory.

(HC Debs., vol. 193, WA, col. *29*: 17 June 1991)

In reply to a question, the Minister of State, FCO, wrote:

Security Council Resolution 687 (1991) called on the UN Secretary General to lend his assistance to make arrangements with Iraq and Kuwait to demarcate the boundary between them. The Council also demanded that Iraq and Kuwait respect the inviolability of the international boundary set out in the Agreed Minutes of 1963 between Iraq and Kuwait, which were registered with the United Nations.

The Foreign Ministers of Iraq and Kuwait have notified the Secretary General of their acceptance of the relevant provisions of this resolution. After further consultations with the Governments of Kuwait and Iraq, the Secretary General established a boundary commission to carry out the demarcation of the border on the ground. He had our full support in doing so.

(HL Debs., vol. 530, *WA 71*: 3 July 1991)

In the course of a debate on the subject of Croatia, the Minister of State, FCO, Mr Douglas Hogg, stated:

I agree . . . about the importance of frontiers. They should not be changed by unilateral action, nor by force. An important presumption to which we should all adhere is that existing frontiers, however inconvenient and however arbitrarily they may have been drawn, are the lines from which we start. They can be changed only by agreement or by the adjudication of a lawful authority such as an international court.

(HC Debs., vol. 198, col. 1206: 13 November 1991)

In reply to an oral question, the Secretary of State for Foreign and Commonwealth Affairs, Mr Douglas Hurd, stated:

We and our EC partners have repeatedly made it clear that we will not recognise changes in Yugoslavia's internal borders unless they are brought about by peaceful negotiation. They cannot be brought about by force.

(HC Debs., vol. 199, col. 262: 20 November 1991)

In reply to a question, the Minister of State, FCO, wrote:

We will continue to uphold the principles and provisions of the Helsinki final act and other CSCE documents which include respect for the territorial integrity of states and the recognition that frontiers can be changed in accordance with international law, by peaceful means and agreement.

(HC Debs., vol. 199, WA, col. *196*: 20 November 1991)

In reply to an oral question on the subject of Yugoslavia, the Minister of State, FCO, Mr Douglas Hogg, stated:

. . . we and our partners—and, I believe, the whole world—made it clear that we are not prepared to recognise the alteration of boundaries by force.

(HC Debs., vol. 201, col. 265: 18 December 1991)

Part Eight: II. A. *State territory and territorial jurisdiction—territorial jurisdiction—territorial sovereignty*

In the course of a debate on the subject of human rights in Kashmir, the Parliamentary Under-Secretary of State, FCO, Mr Mark Lennox-Boyd, stated:

We share concern about the violence in Kashmir, the tension it has caused between India and Pakistan—both good friends of Britain—and the need for human rights to be respected. It is, however, important to understand something of the historical background to the problem before considering the present situation.

At the time of Indian independence in 1947, there were some 560 princely states, of which Jammu and Kashmir was one of the largest. A majority of its population was Muslim, but there was a large Hindu community, and also significant Buddhist and tribal minorities. The maharaja was Hindu.

The rulers of all the princely states were advised to accede to either India or Pakistan. Most did, opting for the country in which their state was situated. At independence, the Maharaja of Jammu and Kashmir had still not opted for either country. However, an uprising among the Muslims of his western territories, supported by irregular forces from the new state of Pakistan, led the maharaja to sign an instrument of accession to India in October 1947. Pakistan did not accept the decision and the first war broke out between the two newly independent countries. It continued throughout 1948 until a ceasefire came into effect on 1 January 1949. In July 1949 India and Pakistan agreed a ceasefire line which passed through the territory of the former princely states. That line was subsequently redefined as the 'line of control' after the 1971 war.

At the heart of the present disturbances in Kashmir is the longstanding dispute over its status. As the hon. Gentleman reminded the House, India and Pakistan originally agreed to a plebiscite covering the entire princely state, as set out in United Nations resolutions in the late 1940s and early 1950s. The issue was whether Kashmir should accede to India or to Pakistan, not independence. But apart from that, much has happened since then. There have been two wars over Kashmir. The territory of the former princely state has in practice been divided between India and Pakistan by the line of control. In 1972 India and Pakistan reached a fresh agreement at Simla. Under the Simla agreement both countries agreed 'to settle their differences by peaceful means through bilateral negotiations or by any other peaceful means mutually agreed on between them'. Those are words with which many hon. Members will be familiar. Both sides also committed themselves to a 'final settlement of Jammu and Kashmir'. So the earlier agreement to which the hon. Gentleman referred was superseded by the 1972 agreement.

That brief synopsis shows some of the complex background to the Kashmir problem.

(HC Debs., vol. 185, cols. 1101–2: 14 February 1991)

In the course of a statement on the subject of the relief of suffering in Iraq, the Secretary of State for Foreign and Commonwealth Affairs, Mr Douglas Hurd, stated:

We are vigorously pursuing this proposal for safe havens. Our aim is to create places and conditions in which the refugees can feel secure. We are not talking of a territorial enclave, a separate Kurdistan or a permanent UN presence. We support the territorial integrity of Iraq.

(HC Debs., vol. 189, col. 21: 15 April 1991)

In reply to the question 'what measures Her Majesty's Government undertake to maintain a visible demonstration of United Kingdom sovereignty and presence in the South Atlantic', the Parliamentary Under-Secretary of State, FCO, wrote:

The Government's administration of its South Atlantic dependent territories and the British Antarctic Territory is backed by Her Majesty's forces, including military garrisons on the Falkland Islands and South Georgia, and a presence on Ascension Island, together with naval patrols in the area.

(HC Debs., vol. 193, WA, col. *111*: 18 June 1991)

In the course of a debate on the subject of Gibraltar, the Minister of State, FCO, Mr Tristan Garel-Jones, stated:

. . . the House will know that Spain has a territorial claim over Gibraltar. The fact that we reject that claim does not make it go away.

I shall try to sum up for the House the nature of the Spanish claim. Spain accepts—acquiesces to might be a more accurate word—the terms of the treaty of Utrecht, which ceded the town and castle of Gibraltar to the British Crown in 1713. She does not accept our sovereignty over the isthmus which Spain regards as having been usurped over the years. I make no comment on the Spanish claim other than to say that it does not change our right to administer Gibraltar, that it exists as a claim, and that it will not go away. Equally, we accept that independence for Gibraltar is not an option.

(HC Debs., vol. 195, col. 199: 15 July 1991)

In reply to a question, the Minister of State, FCO, wrote in part:

The sovereign base areas are sovereign British territory under section 2 of the Cyprus Act 1960 and article 1 of the Treaty of Establishment, to which the Republic of Cyprus is a party.

(HC Debs., vol. 196, WA, col. *55*: 14 October 1991)

Part Eight: II. C. *State territory and territorial jurisdiction—territorial jurisdiction—concurrent territorial jurisdiction*

The UK Permanent Representative to the UN in New York addressed the following letter, dated 5 April 1991, to the UN Secretary-General. Similar letters were sent by the Permanent Representatives of the USA, USSR and France.

I have the honour to refer to my predecessor's letter of 16 June 1973 addressed to the Secretary-General (S/10954) transmitting the text of a declaration of the French Republic, the Union of Soviet Socialist Republics, the United Kingdom of Great Britain and Northern Ireland, and the United States of America, issued on 9 November 1972, and to inform you that, with the entry into force on 15 March 1991 of the Treaty on the Final Settlement with respect to Germany, the rights and responsibilities of the Four Powers relating to Berlin and to Germany as a whole are terminated. As a result, the corresponding related quadripartite agreements, decisions and practices are terminated and all related Four Power institutions are dissolved.

(A/45/993; S/22449, p. 4)

Part Eight: II. D. *State territory and territorial jurisdiction—territorial jurisdiction—extra-territoriality*

On 18 April 1990, the US District Court for the Southern District of New York gave judgment in *Transnor (Bermuda) Ltd.* v. *BP North American Petroleum et al.*, in which the Court asserted jurisdiction under the US antitrust laws in a case concerning futures traded at the London branch of the North Sea Brent crude oil market. Following the judgment, the Department of Trade and Industry sent a letter to the US Commodity Futures Trading Commission, which read in part as follows:

My Department received on Tuesday 24 April a copy of the 18 April 1990 Opinion and Order denying summary judgment in this case.

It will take Government Departments here some time to assess the implications of the Opinion for United Kingdom interests. However, preliminary considerations suggests that there are elements of the Opinion that, on one interpretation, would assert U.S. jurisdiction to an extent objectionable to the U.K.

The Opinion states (page 7) that 'Where the market in question has even slight ties to U.S. commerce, that market is not an exclusively foreign market and is therefore deemed a U.S. market.' This could be interpreted to mean that all trading in Brent oil contracts, including such trading between U.K. persons within the U.K. is subject to U.S. commodities law at large. Under this interpretation of the Opinion the jurisdictional reach asserted is, in the British Government's view, contrary to international law and damaging to the British national interest. We would be most concerned at the possibility that such trades might be held in the U.S. to be illegal and/or void, with potential damage to trading in Brent contracts in the U.K.

(Attachment to Department of Trade and Industry Press Notice 90/253 of 1 May 1990; see also [1991] 2 *International Litigation Procedure* 322, 330. This is the item mentioned in UKMIL 1990, p. 569)

The War Crimes Act 1991, enacted on 9 May 1991, contains the following provision:

1.—(1) Subject to the provisions of this section, proceedings for murder, manslaughter or culpable homicide may be brought against a person in the United Kingdom irrespective of his nationality at the time of the alleged offence if that offence—

(a) was committed during the period beginning with 1st September 1939 and ending with 5th June 1945 in a place which at the time was part of Germany or under German occupation; and

(b) constituted a violation of the laws and customs of war.

(2) No proceedings shall by virtue of this section be brought against any person unless he was on 8th March 1990, or has subsequently become, a British citizen or resident in the United Kingdom, the Isle of Man or any of the Channel Islands.

. . .

The Protocol concerning Frontier Controls and Policing, Co-operation in Criminal Justice, Public Safety and Mutual Assistance relating to the Channel Fixed Link, signed by the Governments of the UK and France on

25 November 1991, contains provisions permitting the jurisdiction of one State to be exercised within the territory of the other. The main such provisions are as follows:

ARTICLE 1

Definitions

. . .

(*g*) 'control zone' means the part of the territory of the host State determined by mutual agreement between the two Governments within which the officers of the adjoining State are empowered to effect controls.

ARTICLE 9

The laws and regulations relating to frontier controls of the adjoining State shall be applicable in the control zone situated in the host State and shall be put into effect by the officers of the adjoining State in the same way as in their own territory.

ARTICLE 10

(1) The officers of the adjoining State shall, in exercise of their national powers, be permitted in the control zone situated in the host State to detain or arrest persons in accordance with the laws and regulations relating to frontier controls of the adjoining State or persons sought by the authorities of the adjoining State. These officers shall also be permitted to conduct such persons to the territory of the adjoining State.

. . .

ARTICLE 11

Breaches of the laws and regulations relating to frontier controls of the adjoining State which are detected in the control zone situated in the host State shall be subject to the laws and regulations of the adjoining State, as if the breaches had occurred in the latter's own territory.

. . .

ARTICLE 28

(1) Officers of the adjoining State may wear their national uniform or visible distinctive insignia in the host State.

(2) In accordance with the laws, regulations and procedures governing the carriage and use of firearms in the host State, the competent authorities of the State will issue permanent licences to carry arms:

(a) to officers of the adjoining State exercising their official functions on board trains within the Fixed Link; and

(b) to an agreed number of specified officers of the adjoining State exercising their functions within the control zone of the host State.

. . .

ARTICLE 38

(1) Without prejudice to the provisions of Articles [11] and 30(2), when an offence is committed in the territory of one of the two States, including that lying within the Fixed Link up to its frontier, that State shall have jurisdiction.

(2) (a) Within the Fixed Link, each State shall have jurisdiction and shall apply its own law:
(i) when it cannot be ascertained with certainty where an offence has been committed; or
(ii) when an offence committed in the territory of one State is related to an offence committed on the territory of the other State; or
(iii) when an offence has begun in or has been continued into its own territory;
(b) however, the State which first receives the person suspected of having committed such an offence (in this Article referred to as 'the receiving State') shall have priority in exercising jurisdiction.

(3) When the receiving State decides not to exercise its priority jurisdiction under paragraph (2) of this Article it shall inform the other State without delay. If the latter decides not to exercise its jurisdiction, the receiving State shall be obliged to exercise its jurisdiction in accordance with its own national law.

ARTICLE 39

Where an arrest has been made for an offence in respect of which a State has jurisdiction under Article 38, that arrest shall not be affected by the fact that it continues in the territory of the other State.

ARTICLE 40

Without prejudice to the application of Article 3 of the Treaty and of Part II of this Protocol, the police and customs officers of one State may in accordance with their own national laws make arrests on the territory of the other State in cases where a person is found committing, attempting to commit, or just having committed an offence:
(a) on board any train which has commenced its journey from one State to the other and is within the Fixed Link; or
(b) within any tunnel described in Article 1(2) of the Treaty.

ARTICLE 41

In the case of arrests covered by Articles 39 and 40:
(a) the person arrested shall be presented without delay to the competent authorities of the State of arrival for that State to be responsible for determining the exercise of jurisdiction as required by Article 38; and
(b) where jurisdiction shall be exercised by the other State in accordance with Article 38, the person arrested may be transferred to the territory of that State. However, any such transfer shall take place within 48 hours of the presentation under paragraph (a) of this Article. Moreover, each State reserves the right not to transfer its nationals.

(Cm. 1802)

Part Eight: III. A. *State territory and territorial jurisdiction—acquisition and transfer of territory—acquisition*

(See Part Fourteen: I. B. 7. (item of 22 November 1991 concerning acquisition of land by force), below)

Part Eight: IV. *State territory and territorial jurisdiction—regime under the Antarctic Treaty*

(See also Part Eight: II. A. (item of 18 June 1990), above)

In reply to the question

What matters relating to Antarctica are within the competence of the European Community; and when such competence was agreed by them and by Parliament,

the Minister of State, FCO, wrote:

The EC's competence relating to Antarctica is confined to fisheries matters. The EC is a party to the Convention on the Conservation of Antarctic Marine Living Resources (CCAMLR), which was laid before Parliament in the usual way prior to ratification by the United Kingdom in 1981. EC competence in relation to fisheries derives from the Treaty of Rome.

Within the context of CCAMLR the UK retains responsibility regarding the resources within and adjacent to the territorial waters of the Dependent Territories of South Georgia, the South Sandwich Islands and the British Antarctic Territory.

(HL Debs., vol. 525, *WA 44*: 5 February 1991)

In reply to a question, the Minister of State, FCO, wrote:

The United Kingdom will take no unilateral action concerning mineral activities in Antarctica. We believe that decisions on such activities must be agreed by consensus amongst the Antarctic treaty consultative parties before they are implemented. A consensus on mineral activity has yet to be achieved. However, at the XIth special consultative meeting in Chile in November, the Antarctic treaty parties renewed their agreement to a voluntary restraint on mineral activity in the absence of any formal agreement. The United Kingdom will abide by this voluntary restraint.

(HC Debs., vol. 186, WA, col. *98*: 19 February 1991)

Part Nine: I. A. *Seas, waterways, ships—territorial sea—delimitation, baselines*

On 24 July 1991, the Territorial Sea Act (Isle of Man) Order 1991 (1991 No. 1722) was promulgated pursuant to section 4(4) of the Territorial Sea Act 1987. Section 2 of the Order, which came into force on 2 September 1991, reads:

The Territorial Sea Act 1987 shall extend to the Isle of Man with the exceptions, adaptations and modifications specified in the Schedule to this Order.

The Order, which extends the breadth of the territorial sea adjacent to the Isle of Man to 12 nautical miles from the baselines, provides in its schedule that there shall be added to section 1(1) of the 1987 Act the following provision:

Provided that where the baselines from which the breadth of the territorial sea adjacent to the Isle of Man is measured are less than 24 nautical miles from the baselines from which the breadth of the territorial sea adjacent to the United Kingdom is measured the seaward limit of the territorial sea adjacent to the Isle of Man shall be the median line.

The Order provides that section 1(7) of the 1987 Act be adapted to read:

median line is a line every point of which is equidistant from the nearest points of the baselines from which the breadth of the territorial sea adjacent to the Isle of Man and the United Kingdom respectively is measured.

In a press release dated 1 August 1991, the Home Office stated in part:

An extension of the territorial sea around the Isle of Man from 3 to 12 miles was the subject of an Order published today by the Privy Council.

The agreement to extend the provisions of the Territorial Sea Act 1987 to the Isle of Man follows negotiations between Her Majesty's Government and the Isle of Man Government on the precise terms and conditions for extension.

The effect of the Order will be to extend the territorial sea around the Island to 12 miles except where the distance between the United Kingdom and the Isle of Man is less than 24 miles, where the Manx territorial sea will extend to the median line only. The Order will come into effect on 2 September 1991.

(Text provided by the Home Office: see now Territorial Sea Act 1987 (Isle of Man) Order 1991 (Statutory Instruments 1991, No. 1722))

The following notice was issued by the Hydrographic Division of the Navy on 1 January 1992:

ADMIRALTY NOTICES TO MARINERS

12. NATIONAL CLAIMS TO MARITIME JURISDICTION.

Former Notice 1919/91 is cancelled.

The following list shows the breadth of sea (measured from the appropriate baselines) claimed respectively as territorial sea (TS), contiguous zone (CZ), exclusive economic zone (EEZ) and fishery zone (FZ), where no EEZ is claimed, as being under the state's jurisdiction. The information is compiled from various, sometimes unofficial, sources; the absence of a limit from this list indicates that the information is not held.

The claims are published for information only. Her Majesty's Government does not recognise claims to territorial seas exceeding twelve nautical miles, to contiguous zones exceeding twenty four nautical miles or to exclusive economic zones and fisheries zones exceeding two hundred nautical miles.

Country	*TS*	*CZ*	*EEZ*	*FZ*
Albania[1]	12**	—	—	15
Algeria[1 8]	12**	—	—	12

Country	*TS*	*CZ*	*EEZ*	*FZ*
Angola	20	—	—	200
Antigua and Barbuda[2]*	12**	24	200	—
Argentina	200[14]	—	200	—
Australia[1]	12[13]	—	—	200
Australian Antarctica	3	—	—	12
Bahamas*	3	—	—	200
Bahrain*	3	—	—	—
Bangladesh[4]	12**	18	200	—
Barbados	12**	—	200	—
Belgium	12	—	—	200
Belize*	3	—	—	3
Benin	200	—	—	200
Brazil*	200**	—	—	200
Brunei	12	—	—	200
Bulgaria	12**	24	200	—
Burma[1]	12**	24	200	—
Cambodia[1]	12	24	200	—
Cameroon*	50	—	—	—
Canada[1]	12	—	—	200
Cape Verde Islands[2]*	12	24	200	—
Chile[1]	12	24	200	—
Chinese People's Republic[1]	12**	—	—	—
Colombia[1]	12	—	200	—
Comoros[2]	12	—	200	—
Congo	200	—	—	200
Costa Rica	12	—	200	—
Cuba[1]*	12	—	200	—
Cyprus*	12	—	—	12
Denmark[1]	3**	—	—	200
Djibouti[1]	12	24	200	—
Dominica	12	24	200	—
Dominican Republic[1]	6	24	200	—
Ecuador[1]	200	—	—	200
Egypt[1]*	12**	24	200	—
El Salvador	200	—	—	200
Equatorial Guinea	12**	—	200	—
Ethiopia[1]	12[15]	—	—	—
Fiji[2]*	12	24	200	—
Finland[1]	4**[16]	6	—	12
France[1]	12	12	200[17]	12[17]
French Antarctica	12	—	—	—
Gabon	12	24	200	—

Country	*TS*	*CZ*	*EEZ*	*FZ*
Gambia*	12	18	200	—
Germany[1 10 11]	12	—	—	200
Ghana*	12	24	200	—
Greece	6	—	—	6
Grenada*	12**	—	200	—
Guatemala	12	—	—	200
Guinea[1]*	12	—	200	—
Guineau Bissau[1]*	12	—	200	—
Guyana	12**	—	—	200
Haiti	12	24	200	—
Honduras	12	24	200	—
Iceland[1]*	12	—	200	—
India	12**	24	200	—
Indonesia[2]*	12	—	200	—
Iran[1]	12**	—	—	50
Iraq*	12	—	—	—
Irish Republic[1]	12	—	—	200
Israel	12	—	—	12
Italy[1]	12	—	—	12
Ivory Coast*	12	—	200	—
Jamaica*	12	—	—	12
Japan[11]	12	—	—	200
Jordan	3	—	—	3
Kenya[1]*	12	—	200	—
Kiribati[2]	12	—	200	—
Korea (North)	12**	—	200	—
Korea (South)[1]	12[6]**	—	—	—
Kuwait*	12	—	—	—
Lebanon	12	—	—	—
Liberia	200	—	—	200
Libya[5]	12**	—	—	20
Madagascar[1]	12	24	200	—
Malaysia[1]	12	—	200	—
Maldives[3]	12[3]**	—	200[3]	—
Malta[1]	12**	24	—	25
Mauritania[1]	12	24	200	—
Mauritius[1]	12**	—	200	—
Mexico[1]*	12	24	200	—
Monaco[3]	12	—	—	12
Morocco[1]	12	24	200	—
Mozambique[1]	12	—	200	—

Country	*TS*	*CZ*	*EEZ*	*FZ*
Namibia*	12	—	200	—
Nauru	12	—	200	—
Netherlands[1]	12	—	—	200
Netherlands Antilles	12	—	—	12
New Zealand	12	—	200	—
Ross Dependency	12	—	—	—
Nicaragua	200**	—	—	200
Nigeria*	30**	—	200	—
Norway[1]	4	—	200	—
Oman[1]*	12	24	200	—
Pakistan	12**	24	200	—
Panama	200	—	—	200
Papua New Guinea[2]	12[18]	—	200	—
Peru	200	—	—	200
Philippines[2,3]*	12	—	200	—
Poland[8]	12**	—	—	12
Portugal[1]	12	—	200	—
Qatar	3	—	—	to median lines
Romania	12**	—	200	—
St. Kitts-Nevis	12	24	200	—
St. Lucia*	12	24	200	—
St. Vincent and the Grenadines[2]	12**	24	200	—
Sao Tome and Principe[2]*	12	—	200	—
Saudi Arabia[1]	12	18	—	—
Senegal[1]*	12	24	200	—
Seychelles	12	24	200	—
Sierra Leone	200	—	—	200
Singapore	3	—	—	3
Solomon Islands[2]	12	—	200	—
Somalia*	200**	—	—	200
South Africa	12	—	—	200
Spain[1]	12	—	200[17]	12[17]
Sri Lanka	12**	24	200	—
Sudan*	12**	24	—	—
Suriname	12	—	200	—
Sweden[1,11]	12**	—	—	200
Syria	35**	41	—	—
Taiwan	12	—	—	200
Tanzania[1]*	12	—	200	—
Thailand[1]	12	—	200	—
Togo*	30	—	200	—
Tonga[3]	12	—	200	—

Country	*TS*	*CZ*	*EEZ*	*FZ*
Trinidad and Tobago[2]*	12	24	200	—
Tunisia[1]*	12	—	—	12[9]
Turkey[1]	12[7]**	—	—	12[7]
Tuvalu	12	24	200	—
UAE	—	—	—	up to 73
Abu Zabi	3	—	—	—
Ajman	3	—	—	—
Dubayy	3	—	—	—
Fujayrah	12	—	—	—
Ra's al Khaymah	3	—	—	—
Ash Shariqah	12	—	—	—
Umm al Qaywayn	3	—	—	—
UK[1]	12	—	—	200
Anguilla	3	—	—	200
Bailiwick of Guernsey	3	—	—	12
Bailiwick of Jersey	3	—	—	3
Bermuda	12	—	—	200
British Antarctic Territory	3	—	—	3
British Indian Ocean Territory	3	—	—	200
British Virgin Islands	3	—	—	200
Cayman Islands	12	—	—	200
Cyprus (Sovereign Base Areas)	3	—	—	3
Falkland Islands[1]	12	—	—	200[12]
Gibraltar	3	—	—	3
Hong Kong	3	—	—	3
Isle of Man	12	—	—	12
Montserrat	3	—	—	200
Pitcairn	3	—	—	200
St. Helena and Dependencies	12	—	—	200
South Georgia[1]	12	—	—	12
South Sandwich Islands	12	—	—	12
Turks and Caicos Islands[1]	12	—	—	200
Uruguay	200[14]	—	—	200
USA	12	12	200	—
Federated States of Micronesia*	12	12	200	—
USSR[1]	12	—	200	—
Vanuatu[2]	12	24	200	—
Venezuela[1]	12	15	200	—
Vietnam[1]	12**	24	200	—
Western Samoa	12	—	200	—
Yemen*	12**	24	200	—
Yugoslavia[1]*	12	—	—	12
Zaire*	12	—	—	200

Limits of dependent territories have not been listed unless they differ from those of the metropolitan state.

[1] Employs straight baseline systems along all or a part of the coast.
[2] Claims archipelago status.
[3] Claims waters within limits defined by geographic co-ordinates not related to distance from the coastline.
[4] Claims straight baseline system between points along the 18 metre isobath.
[5] Claims all water south of 32° 30′ N in the Gulf of Sirte as internal waters.
[6] Claims 3 nm in Korea Strait.
[7] Claims 6 nm in Aegean Sea.
[8] Fishery limit extends beyond 12 nm to limits to be agreed.
[9] Fishery limit extends to 50 metre isobath off the Gulf of Gabes.
[10] Special claim extends limit to include the deep water anchorage west of Helgoland.
[11] Reduced limits in some straits and in the former Federal Republic (but see Note 10).
[12] 150 nm in west with a rhumb line between 52° 30′·00 S, 63° 19′·25 W and 54° 08′·68 S, 60° 00′·00 W.
[13] Certain islands in the Torres Strait retain 3 nm territorial sea limit.
[14] Freedom of navigation and overflight is not curtailed beyond 12 nm.
[15] Jurisdiction claimed to the limit of the pearl and sedentary fishery grounds.
[16] Aland Islands have a 3 nm territorial sea limit.
[17] Does not claim an EEZ in the Mediterranean, only a 12 nm fishery limit.
[18] Reduced to 3 nm in the Torres Strait area.
* Indicates a state which has ratified the 1982 U.N. Convention of the Law of the Sea. The Convention does not come into force until one year after 60 instruments of ratification or accession have been deposited.
** Indicates a state which requires prior permission or notification for entry of foreign warships into territorial sea. The United Kingdom government does not recognise this requirement.

Hydrographic Department. (*HH. 085/012/01*).

(Published in *Annual Summary of Admiralty Notices to Mariners in Force on 1 January 1992*, pp. 101–5).

Part Nine: I. B. 1. *Seas, waterways, ships—territorial sea—legal status—right of innocent passage*

Article 4(12) of the Basel Convention on the Control of Transboundary Movements of Hazardous Wastes and their Disposal, 1989, reads as follows:

12. Nothing in this Convention shall affect in any way the sovereignty of States over their territorial sea established in accordance with international law, and the sovereign rights and the jurisdiction which States have in their exclusive economic zones and their continental shelves in accordance with international law, and the exercise by ships and aircraft of all States of navigational rights and freedoms as provided for in international law and as reflected in relevant international instruments.

On its signature of the Convention on 6 October 1989, the UK Government made the following declaration:

The Government of the United Kingdom of Great Britain and Northern Ireland declare that, in accordance with article 4(12), the provisions of the Convention do not affect in any way the exercise of navigational rights and freedoms as provided for in international law. Accordingly, nothing in this Convention requires notice to or consent of any state for the passage of hazardous wastes on a vessel under the flag of a party, exercising rights of passage through the territorial sea or freedom of navigation in an exclusive economic zone under international law.

(UN Doc. ST/LEG/SER. E/9, p. 850)

On 22 July 1991, the Department of Transport addressed the following letter to the owners of three vessels anchored in Lyme Bay:

Lyme Bay is regularly used for lightening operations, or temporary anchorage for a few days. But it has become evident in the past few months that the number of tankers anchoring there has greatly increased, as has the length of stay of individual vessels. From our inquiries it would appear that laden tankers are being held there sometimes for periods of up to 30 days while a port of discharge is selected.

The almost continuous presence in this sea area of so many laden tankers presents a high risk of major pollution to the United Kingdom and this is causing some concern. There is no doubt that vessels anchored in our territorial waters in these circumstances cannot claim to be exercising the right of innocent passage. We are justified under international law in asking you to move them on.

One of the tankers presently anchored in Lyme Bay is the [name of vessel] and I must ask if you will take urgent action to remove the vessel from the area.

(Text provided by the FCO: see also HC Debs., vol. 199, WA, col. *237*: 21 November 1991)

Part Nine: I. B. 2. *Seas, waterways, ships—territorial sea—legal status—regime of merchant ships*

(See Part Nine: III. (item of 21 November 1991), below)

Part Nine: I. B. 5. *Seas, waterways, ships—territorial sea—legal status—bed and subsoil*

The *Daily Telegraph* published on 2 December 1991 a report that fishermen's associations in Kent, Essex and Suffolk had launched a protest campaign after dredging companies had secured licences from the Crown Estate Commissioners to prospect for gravel on inshore fishing grounds. A spokesman for the Crown Estate Commissioners was reported to have stated:

We own the seabed up to the 12-mile limit and we have granted these licences to prospect for gravel.

Part Nine: III. *Seas, waterways, ships—internal waters, including ports*

The Embassy of the USSR sought from the FCO permission for the Soviet research vessel *Academician B. Petrov* to visit UK waters, particularly internal waters and territorial sea off the coast of south-west Scotland. In a note dated 10 June 1991, the FCO replied:

The Aviation and Maritime Department of the Foreign and Commonwealth Office present their compliments to the Embassy of the Union of Soviet Socialist Republics, and have the honour to refer to the Embassy's Note No 139/KO of 6 May 1991 with regard to the proposed research cruise of the 'Academician B Petrov' from 12 to 28 June 1991.

Permission for this cruise and related port calls is not granted on the grounds that inadequate information has been given about the research programme and itinerary of the vessel. From the little information available it appears that elements of this programme are unacceptable, particularly regarding research in UK internal waters, and in areas where UK defence and security interests may be affected.

It is noted that in 1989 the Soviet Authorities refused the proposed research cruise of the British Government research ship Cirolana on the following grounds:

a. less than six months notice had been given;
b. the application did not include a full crew list;
c. there was no specific provision that data be shared with the coastal state authorities.

The current application also fails to meet these criteria.

(Text provided by the FCO)

In reply to a question on the subject of this refusal of permission, the Parliamentary Under-Secretary of State, FCO, wrote:

An application was received from the Soviet embassy for permission to conduct research in Scottish waters from Leith around to Port Glasgow. Such permission was not granted.

(HC Debs., vol. 193, WA, col. *217*: 19 June 1991)

In reply to a further question, the same Minister wrote:

Certain elements of the research programme were unacceptable, particularly regarding research in United Kingdom internal waters and in areas where our defence and security interests may be affected.

(Ibid., col. *444*: 25 June 1991)

In reply to a question, the Parliamentary Under-Secretary of State, Northern Ireland Office, wrote in part:

The Crown Estate does not require the approval of the Secretary of State for Northern Ireland to impose mooring charges in Strangford lough. As the largest owner of the foreshore and seabed it would seem reasonable that the Crown Estate should be invited to play a role in the proposed management structure for the lough.

(HC Debs., vol. 196, WA, col. *538*: 22 October 1991)

In reply to a question on the subject of the proposed Hook Island, Poole Harbour, development, the Parliamentary Under-Secretary of State, Department of the Environment, wrote in part:

Following successful appraisal drilling to determine the extent of the Wytch Farm oilfield, B[ritish] P[etroleum] consulted widely on various development concepts. Its preferred option is the construction of an artificial island large enough to accommodate a well site and drilling facilities on which a conventional land-type drilling rig could be operated. Because the island would be in navigable waters, it is necessary for the construction of the island and the works associated with it to have the authority of Parliament. However, the Bill provides that the area of the sea bed on which BP proposes to construct the island will become part of Dorset for planning purposes. This means that, if the Bill is granted consent, no development will take place unless planning approval is obtained from Dorset county council, or the Secretary of State on appeal.

(HC Debs., vol. 199, WA, col. *164*: 20 November 1991)

[*Editorial note*: This reply has reference to the Hook Island (Poole Bay) Bill 1991, a private Bill introduced by BP Exploration Operating Company Limited for the purpose of empowering the company to construct in Poole Bay an island of an area of not greater than 12.15 hectares to be used to get petroleum from undersea strata. The Bill was subsequently withdrawn.]

In moving the consideration in HC Standing Committee of the draft Merchant Shipping (Prevention of Oil Pollution) (Amendment) Order 1991, the Minister for Shipping, Mr Patrick McLoughlin, stated:

The order paves the way for foreign owners to be prosecuted in our courts for oil pollution offences committed by their ships in United Kingdom waters. Before the enactment of the Environmental Protection Act 1990, a summons arising from an oil incident could not usually be served on the owner of a foreign ship because he was outside the jurisdiction of our courts. It was thus not possible to prosecute him, and court proceedings have almost invariably been limited to action against the master. That was not satisfactory and, last year, my hon. Friend the Member for Stroud (Mr. Knapman), with all party support, tabled a successful amendment to the Environmental Protection Bill which enabled foreign owners to be properly punished for oil pollution offences.

The enactment of section 148 of the Environmental Protection Act 1990 deals with this objective in two parts: first, by treating pollution incidents in ports and harbours by amendment of the Oil Pollution Act 1971; and, secondly, by treating pollution incidents in territorial waters by amendment of the Merchant Shipping (Prevention of Oil Pollution) Regulations 1983.

Under these amendments, a ship that has discharged oil into the waters of a port, harbour or the territorial seas of the United Kingdom can be detained. It may be released in advance of the hearing only on the security of a £55,000 bond. A summons would be deemed to have been properly served on the foreign owner if it is served on the master of the ship. The courts are already empowered to impose fines on an owner which is a company, even if it chooses not to appear in court to answer the charge, provided it has been properly served with a summons.

If any fine, costs or compensation ordered are not paid, the ship may be sold to defray those charges. There are, of course, safeguards for the owner so that, for instance, a ship must be released from bond and detention if proceedings are not started within seven days; and there is provision for the repayment of any moneys held in excess of any penalties imposed.

The legislation to deal with pollution incidents in ports and harbours has already come into force. It now remains to deal with territorial waters in the same way. The powers sought in the order will allow the amendment of the Merchant Shipping (Prevention of Oil Pollution) Regulations 1983 to include those important provisions.

(HC Debs., 1991–92, Fifth Standing Committee on Statutory Instruments, etc.: 21 November 1991, col. 3)

Part Nine: IV. *Seas, waterways, ships—straits*

In reply to the question

Whether they consider that the Soviet aircraft carrier, 'Admiral Flota SSSR Kuznetsov', may lawfully pass through the straits from the Black Sea to the Mediterranean, in view of the prohibitions in the Montreux Convention,

the Government Minister in the House of Lords wrote:

It is the view of the British Government that the Montreux Convention prohibits the passage of aircraft carriers through the Turkish Straits, and that the 'Admiral Flota SSSR Kuznetsov' meets the definition of aircraft carriers annexed to that convention. However, these views are not shared by all of the other parties to the convention.

(HL Debs., vol. 528, col. *WA 17* : 30 April 1991)

Part Nine: VII. A. 2. *Seas, waterways, ships—the high seas—freedoms of the high seas—fishery*

In reply to a question on the subject of reports of salmon fishing in international waters, the Minister of State, Ministry of Agriculture, Fisheries and Food, wrote:

We are fully aware and concerned about both these reports from the North Atlantic Salmon Conservation Organisation (NASCO) which suggest (but do not confirm) fishing for salmon by certain vessels in international waters.

We deplore those activities as contrary to the objectives of the NASCO convention and that organisation's efforts to conserve and rationally manage stocks. When these events first came to light last year, we discussed the issue with the Commission of the European Communities (which represents the interests of all Member States within NASCO); we communicated all available information on sightings; and we took an active part in discussions at the annual meeting of NASCO held in Helsinki last June. Her Majesty's Government fully support the resolution passed by NASCO as a result of these discussions and the action it called for in making formal representations to the states of registration of those vessels believed to be involved. Action was duly taken by the Commission on behalf of the European Community in notes to the Governments of Poland and Panama drawing attention to the potential impact of unregulated high seas fishing on the conservation of North Atlantic stocks. These were received sympathetically. UK enforcement agencies have been briefed and will take such action as is appropriate.

(HL Debs., vol. 526, WA *3–4*: 12 February 1991)

Part Nine: VII. H. *Seas, waterways, ships—the high seas—jurisdiction over ships*

The Marine, &c, Broadcasting (Offences) (Prescribed Areas of the High Seas) Order 1990 (Statutory Instruments 1990, No. 2503), which came into force on 1 January 1991, provides in its Article 3:

The areas of the high seas prescribed for the purposes of section 2A of the Marine, &c, Broadcasting (Offences) Act 1967 shall be the areas described in the Schedule hereto.

An Explanatory Note accompanying the Order reads in part:

Under section 2A of the Marine, &c, Broadcasting (Offences) Act 1967 (inserted by paragraph 2 of Schedule 16 to the Broadcasting Act 1990), it is an offence to make a broadcast from a ship (other than one registered in the United Kingdom, the Isle of Man or any of the Channel Islands) while the ship is within any area of the high seas prescribed for the purposes of that section. This Order (Article 3 and the Schedule) prescribes the areas of the high seas in which it is an offence to make such a broadcast.

The owner or master of the ship, and any person who operates, or participates in the operation of, the apparatus by means of which such a broadcast is made, may be convicted (section 2A(2)). An offence under section 2A may, pursuant to section 6(3) of the 1967 Act, be taken to have been committed in any place in the United Kingdom. The enforcement powers provided for in section 7A of the 1967 Act (inserted by paragraph 8 of Schedule 16 to the 1990 Act) apply to the offence under section 2A.

. . .

A broadcast made from a ship in one of the areas prescribed by this Order does not contravene section 2A of the 1967 Act if it is authorised under the law of a country or territory outside the United Kingdom (subsection (4)).

The areas prescribed by this Order cover areas of the high seas, that is to say, areas outside the territorial waters of the United Kingdom (which presently extend to a distance of 12 nautical miles pursuant to the Territorial Sea Act 1987 (c.49)). It remains an offence to broadcast from a ship or structure within the territorial sea (sections 1 and 2 of the 1967 Act respectively), or from a ship registered in the United Kingdom, Isle of Man or any of the Channel Islands wherever it may be (section 1), or for a British subject to make a broadcast from a place on the high seas outside the areas prescribed in this Order (section 3).

Part Nine: VIII. *Seas, waterways, ships—continental shelf*

(See also Admiralty Notice in Part Nine: I. A., above)

[*Editorial note*: The following item should be regarded as part of UKMIL 1986:]

On 31 January 1986, the following proclamation was made in Montserrat by the Governor of Montserrat:

CLAIM TO MONTSERRAT'S CONTINENTAL SHELF
BY THE GOVERNOR
A PROCLAMATION

A. C. WATSON,
Governor.

I ARTHUR CHRISTOPHER WATSON C.M.G. Governor in and over Montserrat, acting on the advice of Executive Council and in pursuance of instructions from Her Majesty through a Secretary of State, do hereby proclaim and declare as follows:—

1. The rights of a coastal state with respect to the adjacent seabed and subsoil and their natural resources outside territorial waters are vested, in respect of Montserrat, in the Crown in the right of the Government of Montserrat.

2. (a) The area within which grants in respect of such rights may be made by the Crown and activities may in connection with such grants be regulated may be designated by further Proclamations.

(b) The area defined in sub-paragraph (a) may be varied, and additional areas may be designated as areas within which such grants may be made, by further Proclamations.

3. Every such grant shall be made and activities in connection with it shall be regulated in accordance with the laws made in that behalf for Montserrat.

GIVEN at Government House, Plymouth, Montserrat, this 31st day of January, 1986.

(Montserrat: Statutory Rules and Orders, No. 2 of 1986)

On 21 and 27 March 1990, an Exchange of Notes took place between the Governments of the UK and the French Republic. The substance of the exchange appears in the following note dated 27 March 1990 from the British Embassy, Paris, to the French Ministry of Foreign Affairs:

Note No. 58

The British Embassy presents its compliments to the Ministry of Foreign Affairs and has the honour to refer to the latter's Note No. 725/DJ/BG/CD of 21 March 1990 worded as follows:

'The Ministry of Foreign Affairs presents its compliments to the Embassy of the United Kingdom of Great Britain and Northern Ireland and with reference to the Anglo-French Agreement relating to the Delimitation of the Continental Shelf in the area East of 30 minutes West of the Greenwich Meridian, which was signed in London on 24 June 1982 and entered into force on 4 February 1983, has the honour to inform it of the following.

As a result of a clerical error in the list of coordinates of the Breedt Bank used to define points 13 and 14 in the table in Article 1 of the Agreement, British and French hydrographic experts have agreed to amend the coordinates of those points as follows:

Position	Latitude	Longitude
13	51° 20′ 11″ N	2° 02′ 18″ E
14	51° 30′ 14″ N	2° 07′ 18″ E

If this amendment meets with the approval of the British authorities, the Ministry of Foreign Affairs has the honour to propose to the Embassy of the United Kingdom of Great Britain and Northern Ireland that this note verbale and the note verbale sent in reply by your Embassy should constitute an amendment to the Agreement signed by our two Governments on 24 June 1982 relating to the Delimitation of the Continental Shelf in the area East of 30 minutes West of the Greenwich Meridian, which will enter into force on the date of receipt of the Embassy's reply.

The Ministry of Foreign Affairs avails itself of this opportunity to renew to the Embassy of the United Kingdom of Great Britain and Northern Ireland the assurances of its highest consideration.'

In reply, the Embassy has been instructed to inform the Ministry that the above proposal meets with the approval of the Government of the United Kingdom of Great Britain and Northern Ireland and that the note from the Ministry together with this note verbale therefore constitute an amendment to the Agreement signed by the two Governments on 24 June 1972 relating to the Delimitation of the Continental Shelf in the area East of 30 minutes West of the Greenwich Meridian. This amendment will come into force on the date of this note.

(Cm. 1732, p. 8)

On 23 July 1991, the two Governments signed an Agreement relating to the completion of the Delimitation of the Continental Shelf in the Southern North Sea. This reads in material part as follows:

The Government of the United Kingdom of Great Britain and Northern Ireland and the Government of the French Republic,

Recalling Article 2(2) of their Agreement of 24 June 1982 relating to the Delimitation of the Continental Shelf in the area East of 30 minutes West of the Greenwich Meridian, according to which the delimitation from Point 14 to the tripoint between the boundaries of the continental shelf appertaining respectively to the parties and to the Kingdom of Belgium is to be completed at the appropriate time by application of the same methods as were utilised for the definition of the boundary line between Points 1 and 14;

Noting that, following the discovery of a material error in the coordinates used for the Banc Breedt in 1982, the coordinates of Points 13 and 14 were corrected by the Note from the Ministry of Foreign Affairs to the British Embassy in Paris dated 21 March 1990 and the Embassy's Note in reply dated 27 March 1990;

Desiring to complete the definition of the boundary beyond Point 14;

Have agreed as follows:

Article 1

1. The tripoint between the boundaries of the continental shelf appertaining respectively to the Parties and to the Kingdom of Belgium shall be defined on European Datum (1st Adjustment 1950), as follows:

Point 15:	Lat. 51° 33′ 28″ N	Long. 2° 14′ 18″ E

2. The boundary between the parts of the continental shelf which appertain to the United Kingdom and the French Republic respectively in the area of the Southern North Sea shall be a loxodrome joining Points 14 and 15.
3. The boundary defined in paragraph 2 is illustrated on the chart annexed to this Agreement.

Article 2

It is hereby recorded that the corrected coordinates for Points 13 and 14 are as follows:

Point 13:	Lat. 51° 20′ 11″ N	Long. 2° 02′ 18″ E
Point 14:	Lat. 51° 30′ 14″ N	Long. 2° 07′ 18″ E

ARTICLE 3

1 Each Contracting Party shall notify the other of the completion of the constitutional procedures required for the entry into force of the Agreement.
2. The Agreement shall enter into force on the date when the last notification is received.

(Cm. 1732, p. 3)

The following chart was annexed to the agreement:

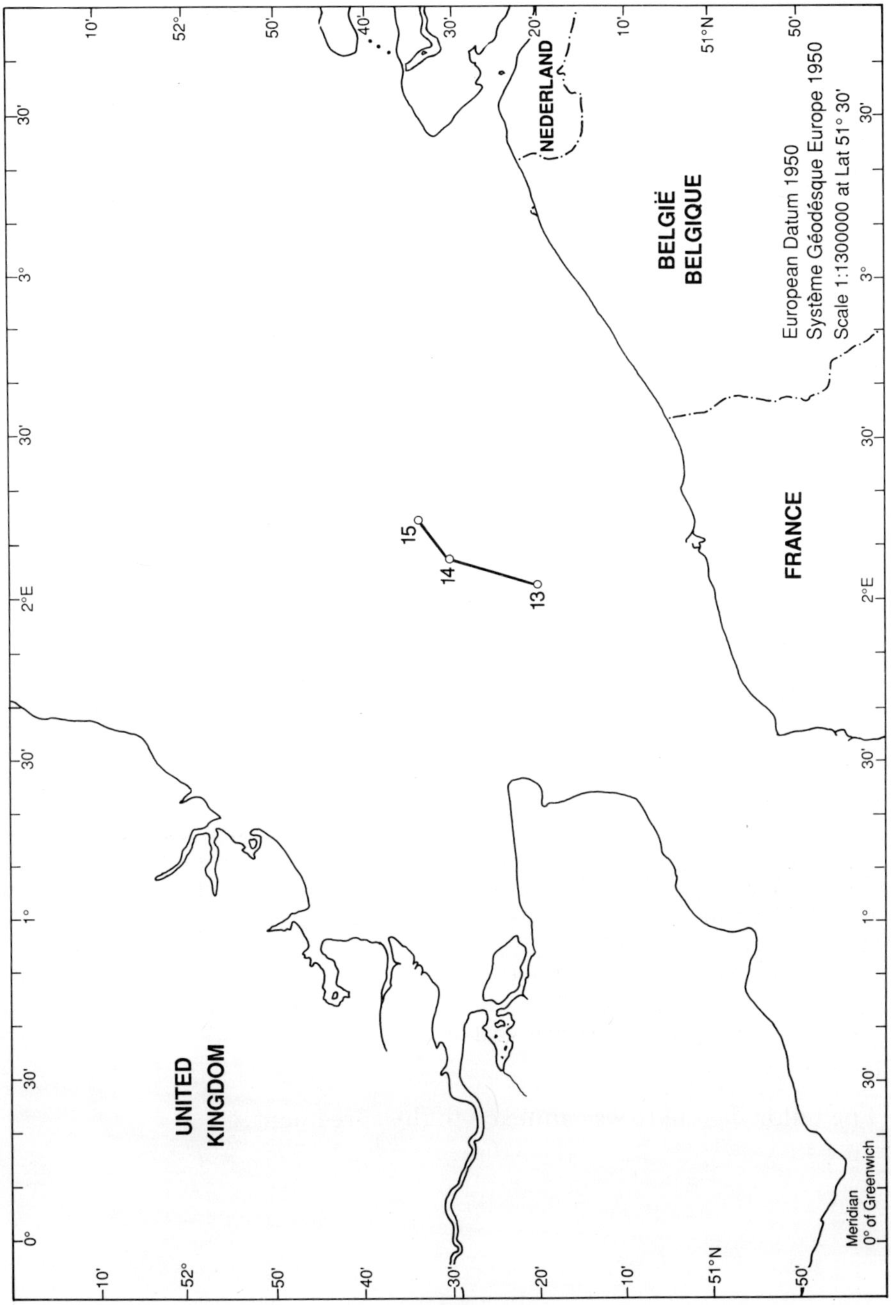
UNITED KINGDOM
FRANCE
BELGIË
BELGIQUE
NEDERLAND
European Datum 1950
Système Géodésque Europe 1950
Scale 1:1300000 at Lat 51° 30'
Meridian 0° of Greenwich
13
14
15
0°
30'
1°
30'
2°E
30'
3°
30'
10'
52°
50'
40'
30'
20'
10'
51°N
50'

On 29 May 1991 the Governments of the UK and the Kingdom of Belgium signed an Agreement relating to the Delimitation of the Continental Shelf between the two countries. The agreement reads in material part as follows:

The Government of the United Kingdom of Great Britain and Northern Ireland and the Government of the Kingdom of Belgium,

Desiring to establish the common boundary between their respective parts of the continental shelf, taking full account of the current rules of international law on international boundaries in order to achieve an equitable solution,

Have agreed as follows:

ARTICLE 1

(1) The boundary between that part of the continental shelf which appertains to the United Kingdom of Great Britain and Northern Ireland and that part which appertains to the Kingdom of Belgium shall be a line composed of loxodromes joining in the sequence given the points defined as follows by their co-ordinates:

1.	51° 33′ 28″ N	02° 14′ 18″ E
2.	51° 36′ 47″ N	02° 15′ 12″ E
3.	51° 48′ 18″ N	02° 28′ 54″ E

The positions of the points in this Article are defined by latitude and longitude on European Datum (1st Adjustment 1950).

(2) The dividing line has been drawn by way of illustration on the chart annexed to this Agreement.

ARTICLE 2

(1) If any single geological mineral oil or natural gas structure or field, or any single geological structure or field of any other mineral deposit extends across the boundary and the part of such structure or field which is situated on one side of the boundary is exploitable, wholly or in part, from the other side of the boundary, the Contracting Parties shall seek to reach agreement as to the exploitation of such structure or field.

(2) In this Article the term 'mineral' is used in its most general, extensive and comprehensive sense and includes all non-living substances occurring on, in or under the ground, irrespective of chemical or physical state.

(Cm. 1735)

The following chart was annexed to the agreement:

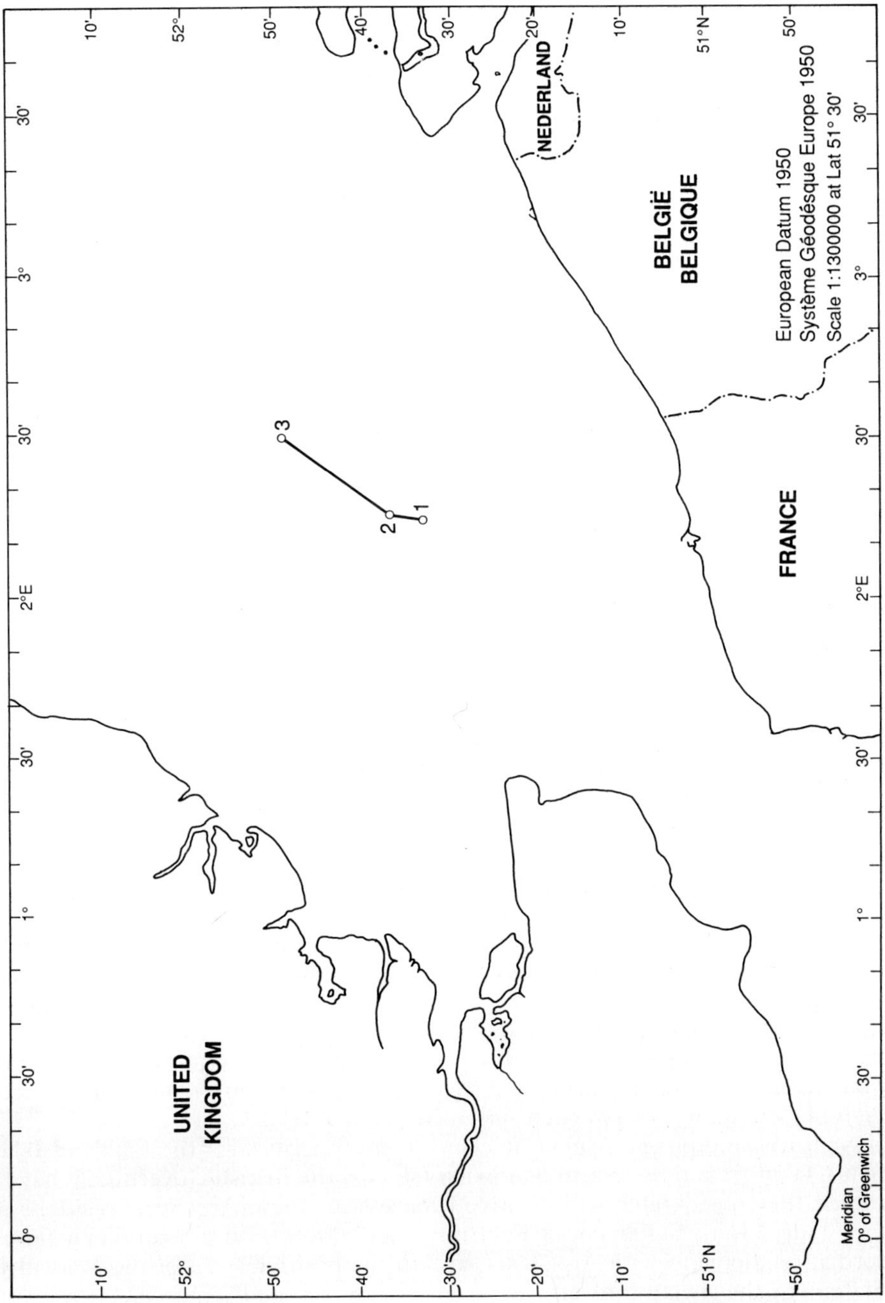
UNITED
KINGDOM
FRANCE
BELGIË
BELGIQUE
NEDERLAND
European Datum 1950
Système Géodésque Europe 1950
Scale 1:1300000 at Lat 51° 30'
Meridian
0° of Greenwich
1
2
3

In reply to a question, the Minister of State, FCO, wrote:

The question of oil in the south Atlantic, specifically in the continental shelf off Patagonia and around the Falkland Islands, has been receiving increasing attention in recent years. Her Majesty's Government have been in contact with the Falkland Islands Government on the matter.

Having considered proposals by the Falkland Islands Government, [the Secretary of State for Foreign and Commonwealth Affairs] has instructed the Governor of the Falkland Islands to take the necessary legislative measures to provide for the exercise of the Crown's rights over the sea bed and the sub-soil of the continental shelf around the Falkland Islands.

In addition, an ordinance known as the Continental Shelf Bill 1991, will be laid before the Legislative Council of the Falkland Islands. Upon entry into force, this would allow seismic surveying to take place under licence in designated areas of the continental shelf.

Officials from the British and Argentine Governments will meet shortly to explore the scope for co-operation.

(HC Debs., vol. 199, WA, col. *318*: 22 November 1991; see also HL Debs., vol. 532, *WA 78*: 25 November 1991)

After setting out the above reply, an FCO press release issued on 22 November 1991 went on:

This action on the continental shelf follows the declaration by the government of 29 October 1986 concerning the continental shelf around the Falkland Islands. On that occasion, Her Majesty's Government declared for the avoidance of doubt that:

'The continental shelf around the Falkland Islands extends to a distance of 200 nautical miles from the baselines from which the breadth of the territorial sea of the Falkland Islands is measured or to such other limits as are prescribed by the rules of international law, including those concerning the delimitation of maritime jurisdiction between neighbours.

It will be for the authorities of the Falkland Islands to take legislative measures in order to implement this declaration.'

The latest action will have the effect of bringing up to date the Falkland Islands (Continental Shelf) Order in Council of 1950 by taking into account developments in international law since that time. HMG are aware that the Government of the Republic of Argentina will be enacting legislation to re-define baselines from which maritime jurisdiction is measured, and purporting to claim jurisdiction over maritime areas over which HMG have sovereign rights in international law. Accordingly, HMG do not accept such Argentine claims.

Notwithstanding the Argentine claim to sovereignty over the Falkland Islands, South Georgia and the South Sandwich Islands, the British Government have welcomed the considerable and positive progress in Anglo-Argentine relations since the Madrid Joint Statement of February 1990. They wish to maintain a close and cordial relationship with Argentina, and in the positive spirit of the Madrid Joint Statement the meeting of officials from the British and Argentine Governments referred to in the Parliamentary reply will explore the implications of their respective legislative measures and the scope for cooperation.

(FCO Press Release No. 200 of 1991)

On the same day, 22 November 1991, the following Proclamation was made by the Governor of the Falkland Islands:

IN THE NAME OF HER MAJESTY ELIZABETH II, by the Grace of God of the United Kingdom of Great Britain and Northern Ireland and of Her other Realms and Territories Queen, Head of the Commonwealth, Defender of the Faith,

By HIS EXCELLENCY WILLIAM HUGH FULLERTON ESQUIRE, COMPANION OF THE ORDER OF SAINT MICHAEL AND SAINT GEORGE, Governor of the Falkland Islands,

WHEREAS for the purposes of international law the continental shelf around the Falkland Islands extends beyond the outer limit of the territorial sea of the Falkland Islands to a distance of 200 nautical miles from the baselines from which the breadth of the territorial sea is measured or to such other limit as prescribed by the rules of international law, including rules for the delimitation of maritime jurisdiction between neighbours,

WHEREAS the Falkland Islands (Continental Shelf) Order 1950 applies to the inner part of the continental shelf as prescribed by the rules of international law,

AND WHEREAS there is a need to regulate activity on the entire continental shelf around the Falkland Islands, subject to the rules of international law,

NOW THEREFORE I, WILLIAM HUGH FULLERTON, acting in pursuance of instructions given by Her Majesty through a Secretary of State, do HEREBY PROCLAIM as follows:

1. Any rights exercisable over the seabed and subsoil of the continental shelf, including the natural resources thereof, beyond and adjacent to the territorial sea around the Falkland Islands are hereby vested in Her Majesty.

2. In addition to that area of the continental shelf described in Article 2 of the Falkland Islands (Continental Shelf) Order 1950, the areas of the continental shelf around the Falkland Islands within which the rights mentioned in section 1 above are exercisable comprise:

(a) the area defined in section 2 of Proclamation No. 4 of 1986;

(b) the area defined in section 2 of and the schedule to Proclamation No. 2 of 1990; and

(c) any such area designated by a further Proclamation as an area within which any such rights are exercisable.

All such areas are hereafter referred to as designated areas.

3. Her Majesty will exercise the same jurisdiction in respect of the exploration and exploitation of designated areas, including the natural resources thereof, as She has in respect of those matters in the territorial sea of the Falkland Islands subject to such provision as may hereafter be made by law for the exploration and exploitation of the designated areas, including the natural resources thereof.

4. This Proclamation becomes effective forthwith.

GIVEN under my hand and the Public Seal of the Falkland Islands at Government House, Stanley, Falkland Islands, this 22nd day of November in the year of Our Lord One Thousand Fine Hundred and Ninety One.

W H FULLERTON,
Governor

(Falkland Islands: Proclamation No. 1 of 1991)

The following map was issued by the FCO at the same time:

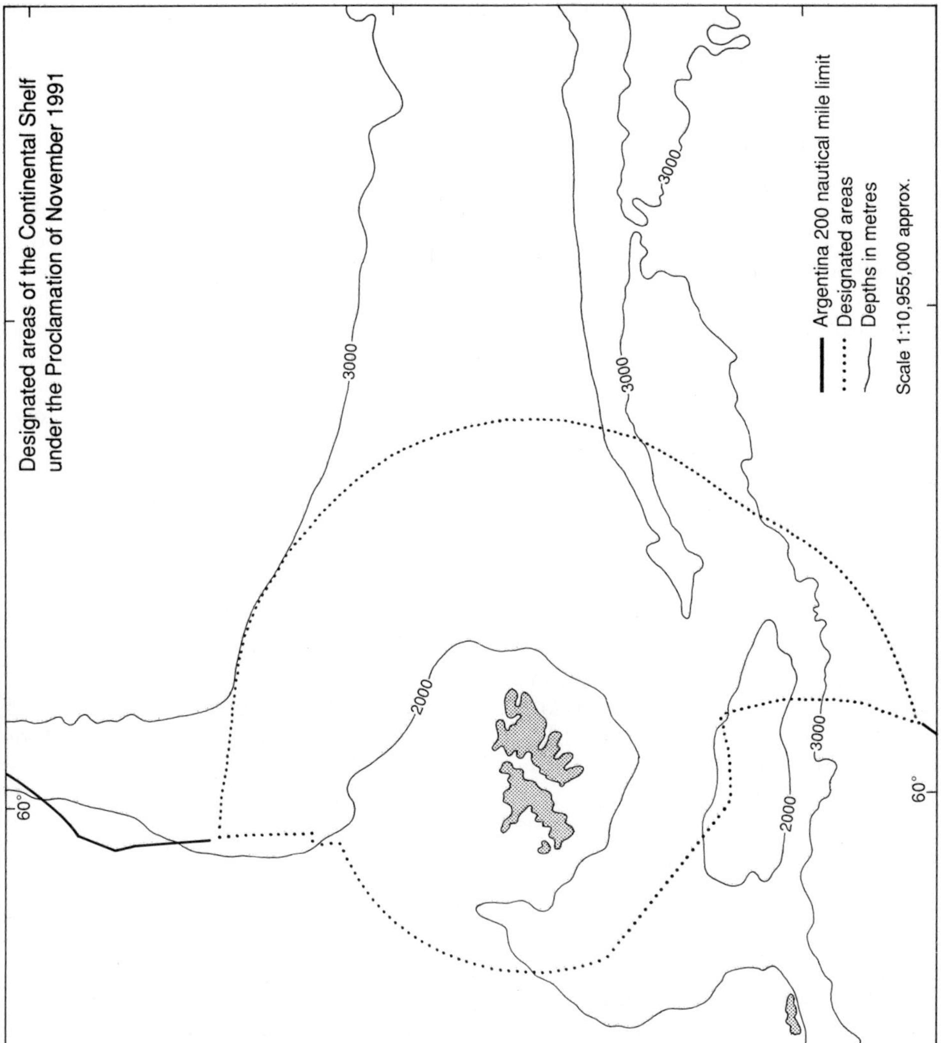
Designated areas of the Continental Shelf
under the Proclamation of November 1991
Argentina 200 nautical mile limit
Designated areas
Depths in metres
Scale 1:10,955,000 approx.
3000
3000
3000
3000
2000
2000
2000
45°
50°
55°
60°
60°

[*Editorial note*: Article 2 of the Falkland Islands (Continental Shelf) Order 1950 reads as follows:

The boundaries of the Colony of the Falkland Islands are hereby extended to include the area of the continental shelf being the sea-bed and its subsoil contiguous to the coasts of the Falkland Islands. The boundary of such area shall be from a position on the 100 fathom line 110 nautical miles 023 degrees true from Jason West Cay (the Westernmost of the Jason Islands, latitude 50 degrees 58 minutes South, longitude 61 degrees 27 minutes West approximately), following the 100 fathom line as shown on Admiralty Chart No. 2202B round the northern, eastern, southern and western sides of the Falkland Islands to a position 20 nautical miles 278 degrees true from Jason West Cay, thence by a straight line crossing in its narrowest part the area where the depths are less than 100 fathoms, in a 032 degree true direction for 115 nautical miles to the starting point.

(Statutory Instruments 1950, No. 2100)

The text of section 2 of Proclamation No. 4 of 1986 is reproduced in UKMIL 1986, pp. 588–9.
The text of section 2 of Proclamation No. 2 of 1990 is reproduced in the present volume at p. 648, below.]

Part Nine: IX. *Seas, waterways, ships—exclusive fishery zone*

(See also Admiralty Notice in Part Nine: I. A., above)

The following Proclamation was made on 20 December 1990 by the Acting Governor of the Falkland Islands:

IN THE NAME OF HER MAJESTY ELIZABETH II, by the Grace of God of the United Kingdom of Great Britain and Northern Ireland and of Her other Realms and Territories Queen, Head of the Commonwealth, Defender of the Faith;
By HIS HONOUR RONALD SAMPSON ESQUIRE, the person designated in accordance with law to perform the functions of the office of Governor of the Falkland Islands during the present absence therefrom of HIS EXCELLENCY WILLIAM HUGH FULLERTON ESQUIRE, Governor of the Falkland Islands
WHEREAS a Joint Statement on the Conservation of Fisheries was issued by the Governments of the United Kingdom and Argentina on 28 November 1990 according to which the two Governments are to cooperate over the conservation of fish stocks in the South Atlantic between Latitude 45 degrees South and Latitude 60 degrees South and fishing is to be controlled in certain waters around the Falkland Islands,
AND WHEREAS there is a need to make further provision for the conservation of living resources and for the regulation of fishing in the seas around the Falkland Islands,
NOW THEREFORE I, RONALD SAMPSON, acting in pursuance of instructions given by Her Majesty through a Secretary of State, do HEREBY PROCLAIM as follows:
1. There is established for the Falkland Islands an outer fishery conservation zone, hereinafter referred to as 'the outer zone'.

2. The outer zone has as its limits the lines defined in the schedule to this Proclamation.
3. The outer limits of the outer zone may be varied by means of a further Proclamation for the purpose of implementing any agreement or arrangements with another state or states or an international organisation or otherwise.
4. Her Majesty will exercise the same jurisdiction in respect of fisheries in the outer zone as she has in respect of fisheries in the territorial sea of the Falkland Islands subject to such provision as is in force or may hereafter be made by law for those matters within the territorial sea and the outer zone.
5. This Proclamation will become effective on the twenty-sixth day of December 1990.

GIVEN under my hand and the Public Seal of the Falkland Islands at Government House, Stanley, Falkland Islands, this twentieth day of December in the year of our Lord One Thousand Nine Hundred and Ninety.

R SAMPSON,
Acting Governor.

(Falkland Islands: Proclamation No. 2 of 1990 (Schedule not reproduced))

In reply to the question to which States have licences been granted for fishing operations in the exclusive economic zones of British dependent territories, the Minister of State, FCO, wrote:

Dependent territories of the United Kingdom do not have exclusive economic zones, but a number of them have fisheries jurisdictions. Licences have been issued to vessels and associations from a number of countries; it is not normal practice to enter into licence agreements with foreign Governments.

(HC Debs., vol. 184, WA, col. *693*: 1 February 1991)

On 20 September 1991, the captain and the owner of the Spanish fishing vessel *Fragana* were found guilty in the Magistrates' Court in Stanley, Falkland Islands, of fishing illegally in the Falklands Outer Conservation Zone and fines were imposed upon each of them. The *Fragana* was intercepted in the zone by a fisheries patrol vessel, boarded, arrested and brought to Stanley. (Information provided by the FCO)

The following Proclamation was made on 1 October 1991 by the Commissioner for the British Indian Ocean Territory:

IN THE NAME of Her Majesty ELIZABETH the Second, by the Grace of God, of the United Kingdom of Great Britain and Northern Ireland and of Her other Realms and Territories, Queen, Head of the Commonwealth, Defender of the Faith.

By Richard John Smale Edis, Commissioner for the British Indian Ocean Territory.

I, Richard John Smale Edis, Commissioner for the British Indian Ocean Territory, acting in pursuance of instructions given by Her Majesty through a Secretary of State do hereby proclaim and declare that—
1. There is established for the British Indian Ocean Territory a fisheries zone, to

be known as the Fisheries Conservation and Management Zone, contiguous to the territorial sea of the British Indian Ocean Territory.
2. The said fisheries zone has as its inner boundary the outer limits of the territorial sea of the British Indian Ocean Territory and as its seaward boundary a line drawn so that each point on the line is two hundred nautical miles from the nearest point on the low-water line on the coast or other baseline from which the territorial sea is measured or unless another line is declared by Proclamation, the median line where this is less than two hundred nautical miles from the baseline. The median line is a line every point of which is equidistant from the nearest points of the baseline of the British Indian Ocean Territory and the corresponding points on the coasts of the Republic of the Maldives.
3. Her Majesty will exercise the same jurisdiction in respect of fisheries in the said fisheries zone as She has in respect of fisheries in the territorial sea of the British Indian Ocean Territory, subject to such provisions as may hereafter be made by law for the control and regulation of fishing within the said zone.
4. In this Proclamation 'the British Indian Ocean Territory' means the islands of the British Indian Ocean Territory set out in the Schedule to this Proclamation.
5. Proclamation No. 8 of 1984 is hereby revoked.

SCHEDULE

The Islands of the British Indian Ocean Territory

The Chagos Archipelago consisting of:

Diego Garcia	The Brothers Islands
Egmont or the Six Islands	Nelson or Legom Island
Peros Banhos	Eagle Islands
Salomon Islands	Danger Island

(British Indian Ocean Territory: Proclamation No. 1 of 1991)

[*Editorial note*: Proclamation No. 8 of 1984 had created a 12-mile fisheries zone]

In reply to a question, the Minister of State, FCO, wrote:

We have been examining the fishing regimes of our dependent territories. We are about to approach other Governments in the Caribbean with a view to delimiting zones of maritime jurisdiction by agreement for our dependent territories. On 1 October we introduced a 200 mile fisheries zone around the British Indian Ocean Territory.

(HC Debs., vol. 196, WA, col. *125*: 15 October 1991)

Part Nine: X. *Seas, waterways, ships—exclusive economic zone*

(See Admiralty Notice in Part Nine: I. A., above)

Part Nine: XII. *Seas, waterways, ships—bed of the sea beyond national jurisdiction*

On 22 February 1991, the Government of the UK, together with other Governments, entered into a Memorandum of Understanding with the

Government of the People's Republic of China on the avoidance of overlaps and conflicts relating to deep sea-bed areas.

(TS No. 52 (1991); Cm. 1628)

In reply to a question on the subject of the United Kingdom's attitude towards the 1982 Convention on the Law of the Sea, the Minister of State, FCO, wrote:

The provisions of this convention are in the main helpful, but there are serious objections to Part XI. This provides for an over-regulatory and unworkable regime governing mining from the deep sea-bed. We are actively involved in discussions on this issue chaired by the UN Secretary-General.

(HL Debs., vol. 528, *WA 58*: 10 May 1991)

In a speech on 12 December 1991 in the UN General Assembly in explanation of vote on the Law of the Sea Resolution, the UK representative stated of the UN Convention on the Law of the Sea, 1982:

I would stress that the UK Government sees this as a valuable Convention, which could become one of the significant achievements of the United Nations. Unfortunately, as is now clear, Part XI is fatally flawed. A market-based approach to deep sea-bed mining is required.

(Text provided by the FCO)

Part Nine: XV. B. *Seas, waterways, ships—ships—nationality*

In the course of oral evidence given on 11 July 1990 to the House of Lords Select Committee on the European Communities examining the subject of Community Shipping Measures, the following question was put to Mr R. Jones, Assistant Secretary, Shipping Policy and Foreign Relations Department, Department of Transport:

To what extent do States Parties now observe the requirement in Article 5 of the 1958 Geneva Convention on the High Seas that there must be a 'genuine link' between ship and flag State to guarantee property enforcement of international maritime and national social rules?

Mr Jones replied in part:

. . . there is no internationally agreed convention concerning registration policy. The UK is party to the 1958 Geneva Convention on the High Seas which contains the provision that you mentioned. There was in 1986 a further UN convention on the registration of ships which has not been implemented which attempted to define how this genuine link should be put to the test by countries. The practical point is that most countries, certainly those in Europe, see this in terms of either ownership or effective control.

(*Parliamentary Papers*, 1989–90, HL, Paper 90 (Minutes of Evidence, p. 65))

In the course of his argument before the Appellate Committee of the House of Lords in July 1990, the Solicitor-General, Sir Nicholas Lyell, appearing on behalf of the Secretary of State for Transport, stated:

The United Kingdom's arguments in the main proceedings still pending before the European Court included the following. Community law does not affect the sovereign right of a member state to lay down the conditions for the grant of its flag to ships. The requirements laid down in the Act of 1988 govern access to the British flag. The purpose of Part II of the Act was to ensure that (i) British fishing vessels had a real economic link with the United Kingdom; (ii) the United Kingdom was able to exercise effective jurisdiction over vessels flying its flag; (iii) the United Kingdom quotas granted under the common fisheries policy enured to the benefit of the genuine British fishing fleet.

The grant of the flag gives rise to legal and international obligations. It (a) engages the state in question in real and far-reaching international obligations and (b) asserts the jurisdiction of that state over the ship and those on board in civil, criminal, operational and employment matters: see article 94 of the 1982 Convention on the Law of the Sea. Similar provisions apply, mutatis mutandis, to aircraft. The grant of the flag is intrinsically an act of sovereignty, and, in the absence of any express provision in the Treaty and any power for the Community to assume direct legal and international responsibility for vessels registered in the member states, it is not to be presumed that the Treaty interferes with the exercise of a state's sovereign power.

Customary international law, as expressed in article 5(1) of the 1958 Geneva Convention on the High Seas, requires a genuine link between a vessel and the state whose flag it flies. The nationality of owner criterion is a means of ensuring a genuine link between the vessel and the state whose flag it flies. Such a criterion is recognised in international law: article 5(1) of the 1958 Geneva Convention on the High Seas and the commentary thereon by the International Law Commission, the corresponding provision in the 1982 United Nations Convention on the Law of the Sea and article 8 of the 1986 Convention on Conditions for Registration of Ships. The other requirements, e.g. as to residence, of the Act of 1988 seek to reinforce the genuine link. Community law does not take precedence over customary international law (cf. article 234 of the Treaty); rather, customary international law is a source of Community law: *van Duyn v. Home Office* (Case 41/74) [1974] E.C.R. 1337, 1350–1351.

(*R v. Secretary of State for Transport, ex parte Factortame Ltd.*, [1991] 1 AC 603, 654–5)

Part Ten: III. *Air space, outer space—outer space*

In reply to the question which government department is responsible for space safety, the Parliamentary Under-Secretary of State, Department of Trade and Industry, wrote:

The United Kingdom is party to a number of UN Conventions regulating space activities. Signatories to these conventions accept liability for damage caused by the space activities of their nationals. To give effect to United Kingdom obligations under the relevant conventions, licences are issued under the Outer Space Act 1986 by the British National Space Centre on behalf of the Secretary of State for Trade and Industry. The Secretary of State has to be satisfied that a licensed activity will not jeopardise public health and the safety of persons and property.

(HL Debs., vol. 530, *WA 89*: 10 July 1991)

Part Eleven: II. A. 1. *Responsibility—responsible entities—States—elements of responsibility*

Speaking on 7 November 1991 in the Sixth Committee of the UN General Assembly considering the International Law Commission's work on international liability for injurious consequences arising out of acts not prohibited by international law, the UK representative, Sir Arthur Watts, stated:

On substance, this topic seems in practice to fall naturally into two distinct parts: prevention of transboundary harm and compensation for such harm. These two aspects raise quite different issues.

I shall now turn to the second part of this topic, namely, compensation. It is the view of the United Kingdom that where transboundary harm occurs which cannot be attributed to any breach on the part of the State of origin of its legal obligations, liability should rest with the operator. It is surely unrealistic for States to assume financial liability vis-a-vis non-nationals for all acts by private entities and individuals under their jurisdiction. That would not accord with the 'polluter pays principle' to which the United Kingdom attaches importance, and would undermine the deterrent effect of a civil liability system. What States could realistically undertake to do is to institute effective liability systems in their domestic law, and ensure that where transboundary harm is caused by activities within their jurisdiction, recourse against the operator is available to non-nationals and other States on a non-discriminatory basis. State responsibility should be engaged for failure by the State to provide adequate civil remedies. The Commission might usefully provide assistance to States in this respect, by, for example, drafting model clauses dealing with civil liability which they could consider adopting in their domestic law. States should also be encouraged to strengthen their international arrangements for reciprocal recognition of civil jurisdiction and enforcement of civil judgments, so as to give practical assistance to those affected by transboundary harm. It is the view of the United Kingdom that any imposition of strict or residual liability on States, in the absence of any breach of obligations on their part, should be left to other instruments especially designed to deal with specific problems taking into account all their own distinctive and particular characteristics.

More generally, Mr Chairman, after considering the overall development of this topic, my delegation is unconvinced that there is any sound basis for treating it as a subject outside the application of the normal rules of State responsibility. On the contrary, it will undoubtedly require the elaboration of and the specific application of those rules. It seems to my delegation that this question of the essential relationship of this topic to the general rules of State responsibility is still not satisfactorily resolved in the Commission's work on this topic. Yet it is one of the most important of the fundamental issues which needs to be resolved before detailed drafting work can usefully resume.

(Text provided by the FCO; see also A/C.6/46/SR.32, pp. 16–17)

Part Eleven: II. A. 2. *Responsibility—responsible entities—States—executive acts*

In a speech in the UN Security Council on 14 February 1991 on the subject of the Gulf conflict, the UK Permanent Representative to the UN in New York, Sir David Hannay, stated:

Since 2 August Iraq has broken any number of its international obligations. It has invaded and annexed its neighbour by force; it has pillaged and tortured Kuwait's population; it has taken hostages; since 15 January it has fired missiles at a country not a party to the dispute; it has defied its obligations towards prisoners-of-war under the Geneva Conventions; and it has resorted to unprecedented environmental terrorism. Now it is threatening further actions against international law.

(S/PV. 2977, p. 78)

In reply to a question, the Secretary of State for the Environment wrote in part:

Iraqi action has already led to damage to the environment as indicated by the deliberate release of oil into the Gulf. The Government together with the countries of the OECD has condemned this action as a violation of international law and a crime against the environment.

(HC Debs., vol. 186, WA, col. *283*: 22 February 1991)

In reply to a question, the Minister of State, FCO, wrote:

Iraq has accepted that it is liable under international law for loss, damage and injury arising out of its invasion of Kuwait. Under Security Council Resolution 687, the Security Council has decided to create a fund from which claims for compensation may be paid, and has directed the Secretary General to make detailed recommendations for such a fund, taking into account Iraq's ability to pay and the needs of the Iraqi people. It is for individual governments and their nationals to decide what claims to put forward.

(HL Debs., vol. 527, *WA 80*: 15 April 1991)

Speaking on 24 October 1991 in the Sixth Committee of the UN General Assembly on the subject of the exploitation of the environment as a weapon in times of armed conflict, the representative of the Netherlands, on behalf of the EC and its Twelve Member States, stated:

The twelve Member States of the European Community attach great importance to the protection of the environment both in times of peace and of armed conflict, and to the observance of international humanitarian law. Therefore they welcome the decision to place on the agenda of the Sixth Committee the subject 'Exploitation of the environment as a weapon in times of armed conflict and the taking of practical measures to prevent such exploitation'. When speaking about the use of the environment as a weapon in times of conflict we of course cannot ignore the unprecedented environmental damage caused by Iraq in Kuwait. In this context I would like to draw your attention to what was recently stated in a report to the Secretary-General of the United Nations based on a United Nations mission, namely that the deliberate torching of the oilfields represents Kuwait's most pressing environmental problem of today, besides which all else pales into insignificance. As this report rightly points out there has never been anything like it in history before.

There cannot be any doubt that these Iraqi activities were in flagrant contravention of existing international law.

It is clear that international law limits the rights of belligerents to cause suffering and injury to people and to wreak destruction on objects. Massive ecological damage as a consequence of armed conflict—be it of international or non international character—can endanger the very basis of life on this planet for a long period of time.

(Text provided by the FCO; see also A/C.6/46/SR. 20, pp. 2–3)

In a statement made in the House of Commons, the Secretary of State for Foreign and Commonwealth Affairs, Mr Douglas Hurd, described the conclusion of the investigation into the destruction of a US commercial aircraft, flight PA 103, over Lockerbie, Scotland, on 21 December 1988. He stated:

The accusations levelled at Libyan officials are of the gravest possible kind. As the warrants which the Lord Advocate will be making public make clear, the charges allege that the individuals acted as part of a conspiracy to further the purposes of the Libyan Intelligence Services by criminal means, and that those means were acts of terrorism. This was a mass murder, which is alleged to involve the organs of government of a State.

(HC Debs., vol. 198, col. 1229: 14 November 1991)

On 27 November 1991, Her Majesty's Government issued a statement in the UN Security Council which read in part as follows:

The British and American Governments today declare that the Government of Libya must:

. . .

—Pay appropriate compensation.

(S/23307)

By a letter dated 20 December 1991 addressed to the UN Secretary-General, the Permanent Representatives to the UN in New York of the UK, USA and France made the following statement:

We have the honour to circulate herewith the text of a tripartite declaration on terrorism issued by our three Governments on 27 November following the investigation into the bombings of flights Pan Am 103 and UTA 772.

Declaration of the United States of America, France and Great Britain on terrorism

The three States reaffirm their complete condemnation of terrorism in all its forms and denounce any complicity of States in terrorism acts. The three States reaffirm their commitment to put an end to terrorism.

They consider that the responsibility of States begins whenever they take part directly in terrorist actions, or indirectly through harbouring, training, providing facilities, arming or providing financial support, or any form of protection, and that they are responsible for their actions before the individual States and the United Nations.

In this connection, following the investigation carried out into the bombings of Pan Am 103 and UTA 772 the three States have presented specific demands to the Libyan authorities related to the judicial procedures that are under way. They require that Libya comply with all these demands, and, in addition, that Libya commit itself concretely and definitively to cease all forms of terrorist action and all assistance to terrorist groups. Libya must promptly, by concrete actions, prove its renunciation of terrorism.

(S/23309)

Part Eleven: II. A. 6. *Responsibility—responsible entities—States—reparation*

(See also Part Eleven: II. A. 2. (items of 15 April and 27 November 1991), above)

The following provisions appear in the Agreement between the Governments of the UK and the Republic of Burundi for the Promotion and Protection of Investments, which was signed and entered into force on 13 September 1990. Similar provisions appear in other such agreements made during the period.

ARTICLE 5

Expropriation

(1) Investments of nationals or companies of either Contracting Party shall not be nationalised, expropriated or subjected to measures having effect equivalent to nationalisation or expropriation (hereinafter referred to as 'expropriation') in the territory of the other Contracting Party except for a public purpose related to the internal needs of that Party on a non-discriminatory basis and against prompt, adequate and effective compensation. Such compensation shall amount to the genuine value of the investment expropriated immediately before the expropriation or before the impending expropriation became public knowledge, whichever is the earlier, shall include interest at a normal commercial rate until the date of payment, shall be made without delay, be effectively realisable and be freely transferable. The national or company affected shall have a right, under the law of the Contracting Party making the expropriation, to prompt review, by a judicial or other independent authority of that Party, of his or its case and of the valuation of his or its investment in accordance with the principles set out in this paragraph.
(2) Where a Contracting Party expropriates the assets of a company which is incorporated or constituted under the law in force in any part of its own territory, and in which nationals or companies of the other Contracting Party own shares, it shall ensure that the provisions of paragraph (1) of this Article are applied to the extent necessary to guarantee prompt, adequate and effective compensation in respect of their investment to such nationals or companies of the other Contracting Party who are owners of those shares.

ARTICLE 6

Repatriation of Investment and Returns

Each Contracting Party shall in respect of investments guarantee to nationals or companies of the other Contracting Party the unrestricted transfer of their investments and returns. Transfers shall be effected without delay in the convertible currency in which the capital was originally invested or in any other convertible currency agreed by the investor and the Contracting Party concerned. Unless otherwise agreed by the investor transfers shall be made at the rate of exchange applicable on the date of transfer pursuant to the exchange regulations in force.

(TS No. 11 (1991); Cm. 1420)

The following provisions appear in the Agreement between the Governments of the UK and the Kingdom of Morocco for the Promotion and Protection of Investments, which was signed and entered into force provisionally on 30 October 1990:

ARTICLE 6

Expropriation

(1) Measures of nationalisation, expropriation or any other measures having an equivalent effect, that might be taken by one of the Contracting Parties against the investments of nationals of the other Contracting Parties shall be neither discriminatory nor taken other than for a public purpose. The Contracting Party that takes such measures shall, in return, give fair and equitable compensation which shall amount to the real value of the investment immediately before the said measures were taken or before they became public. The amount of the said compensation shall be effectively realizable, transferable and shall be paid promptly and at the latest within three months of the date of implementation of the said measures. The national concerned shall have a right, under the law of the Contracting Party that has taken such measures, to prompt review of his case and of the valuation of his investments by the competent courts of the said Party, in accordance with the principles set out in this paragraph.

(2) Where a Contracting Party expropriates the assets of one of its nationals which is a legal person referred to in Article 1(c)(i) or Article 1(c)(ii), whichever is applicable, and in which nationals of the other Contracting Party own shares, it shall ensure that the provisions of paragraph (1) of this Article are applied to the extent necessary to guarantee fair and equitable compensation in respect of their investments to such nationals of the other Contracting Party who are the owners of those shares.

ARTICLE 7

Repatriation of Investment and Returns

Each Contracting Party shall guarantee to nationals of the other Contracting Party the transfer of their investments and returns, subject to the right of each Contracting Party in exceptional financial or economic circumstances including exceptional balance of payment difficulties and for a limited period to exercise equitably and in good faith powers conferred by its laws. Such powers shall not however be used to impede the transfer of returns: as regards the proceeds of the sale or the liquidation of the investment, each Contracting Party shall guarantee the transfer of a minimum of 20 per cent a year. Transfers shall be effected promptly in convertible currency at the rate of exchange applicable on the date of transfer, pursuant to the exchange regulations in force.

(Cm. 1603)

In the course of a debate on the subject of the Gulf conflict, the Prime Minister, Mr John Major, stated:

We shall also insist on a public and authoritative statement from the highest levels of Iraq's leadership of its intention to comply fully with all the relevant Security Council resolutions. This must include renunciation of Iraq's claim to Kuwait and acceptance of Iraq's responsibility to pay reparations for the damage that its aggression has caused.

(HC Debs., vol. 186, col. 1117: 28 February 1991)

In reply to a question, the Secretary of State for Foreign and Commonwealth Affairs wrote in part:

Security Council resolution 674, which has now been accepted by the Government of Iraq, reminded Iraq of its liability for any loss, damage or injury ensuing in regard to Kuwait and third states and their nationals as a result of its invasion and illegal occupation of Kuwait.

(HC Debs., vol. 187, WA, cols. *252–3*: 7 March 1991)

On 28 March 1991, the FCO issued the following press release:

Mr Mark Lennox-Boyd, the Parliamentary Under Secretary for Foreign and Commonwealth Affairs, has informed the House of Commons on 28 March 1991 . . . that the Foreign Compensation Commission will start making payments from the China Compensation Fund to successful claimants on 2 April 1991.

The payments will amount to approximately £25 million, representing 62.25% of the value assigned by the Commission to successful claims. Successful bond holders were awarded an interim payment of 5% in 1989 and will now receive the remainder of the monies due to them.

The British claims being compensated are those arising from bonds, company property and assets, and privately owned property. Altogether 2,037 bond claims and 1,064 property claims were received. The bond claims were made in fifteen different currencies and cover the period 1898–1938. Most of the claims by private individuals and companies, for the loss of bank accounts and possessions, including houses, hotels, clubs, machinery, shares, investments and pensions, date from the period after 1949.

The compensation was made available as the result of a Claims Agreement between the United Kingdom and the People's Republic of China signed in Peking on 5 June 1987. An Order in Council, which came into effect on 1 March 1988, set out the arrangements for the determination of claims from British bond holders and property owners by the Foreign Compensation Commission and for the distribution of monies to successful claimants.

(Text provided by the FCO; see also HC Debs., vol. 188, WA, col. *502*: 28 March 1991)

In reply to a question, the Prime Minister wrote:

No compensation has been paid to the United Kingdom for damage suffered following the Chernobyl accident. The Soviet Union is not a party to the international conventions on third party liability for nuclear damage.

(HC Debs., vol. 189, WA, col. *520*: 25 April 1991)

In the course of a debate on the subject of compensation for Allied prisoners of war in the hands of Japan during the Second World War, the Parliamentary Under-Secretary of State, FCO, Mr Mark Lennox-Boyd, stated:

I shall set out again the settlement reached in 1951 in the peace treaty with Japan. I do not suggest that it is a tidy bureaucratic solution to the problem and brooks no opposition, but simply set out the historical facts of the matter . . . [T]he peace treaty signed in San Francisco on 8 September 1951 contained a specific provision for compensation for former prisoners of war. We had insisted on that provision, which had not been included in the original treaty, because we thought it important that the treaty should recognise the cruel and barbaric treatment to which allied service men in the far east had been subjected.

The negotiations leading to the treaty were heavily influenced by the moving debate in the House in May 1951 . . . That debate helped to develop the Government's policy and negotiating position as the treaty was drawn up. No one could dispute that the issue of compensation was crucial and it was the only aspect of the treaty on which a debate was held prior to its signing. The 1951 treaty ended the state of war between the United Kingdom and Japan.

I shall briefly outline the provisions that are relevant to the debate. I know that I am repeating some of the words of . . . the Chief Secretary to the Treasury when he replied to the 1988 debate on this subject. Article 14 of the treaty recognised 'that Japanese should pay reparations to the Allied Powers for the damage and suffering caused by it during the war'.

The treaty gave the allied powers the right to seize and dispose of Japanese property within their jurisdiction. Article 14(b) concluded:

'Except as otherwise provided in the present Treaty, the Allied Powers waive all reparations claims of the Allied Powers, other claims of the Allied Powers and their nationals arising out of any actions taken by Japan and its nationals in the course of the prosecution of the War'.

Article 16 is central to the matter, because it provided specifically for the compensation of prisoners. It states:

'As an expression of its desire to indemnify those members of the armed forces of the Allied Powers who suffered undue hardships while Prisoners of War of Japan, Japan will transfer its assets and those of its nationals in countries which were neutral during the war, or which were at war with any of the Allied Powers or, at its option, the equivalent of such assets, to the International Committee of the Red Cross which shall liquidate such assets and distribute the resultant fund to appropriate national agencies for the benefit of former Prisoners of War and their families on such basis as it may determine to be equitable.'

From the disposal of Japanese property within its jurisdiction, the United Kingdom received just over £3 million. The United Kingdom's share of the £4.5 million that the Japanese Government placed at the disposal of the International Red Cross in accordance with article 16 of the treaty was just over £1.6 million.

It was agreed in a minute between the Japanese and the allied powers that the payment of the £4.5 million would be recognised as a full discharge by the Japanese Government of their obligations under article 16 of the peace treaty. As is well known, and as my right hon. Friend has said, the sums of £76 paid to service men or to their dependants was unbelievably small. No British Government have ever denied that. In the debate on the peace treaty before its ratification, a Government spokesman said that he would have preferred to be able to offer greater compensation. I am sure that all members of the Government and the Opposition at that time shared that wish. As my right hon. Friend knows, the treaty was signed by a Labour Government and ratified by their Conservative successors.

I sympathise with my right hon. Friend's contention that the settlement was unsatisfactory but, as my predecessors have said, the provisions of the treaty remove any possibility of the British Government claiming further compensation or reparations from the Japanese Government. That is our best understanding of our legal obligations, although I hear with respect my right hon. Friend's different views.

We are not alone in that understanding. We have been in touch with our missions in the countries that my right hon. Friend mentioned to ascertain the position of their Governments. Other allied powers share our view that the question of compensation was settled by the 1951 peace treaty. However inadequate the terms may appear now or appeared at the time, it was accepted that the Japanese had fully discharged their obligations.

. . .

I should not give my right hon. Friend any reason to believe that the chances of success of claims for further compensation are likely to be good, but I shall touch upon a recent development to the claim lodged with the United Nations Commission for Human Rights by the Japanese Labour Camp Survivors Association. It was lodged under a procedure known as resolution 1503, to which my right hon. Friend made comment.

I shall go into a little detail about the procedure. It is a confidential system that is designed to establish, on the basis of personal petition, whether there has occurred a consistent pattern of gross violations of human rights by states rather than to adjudicate on individual complaints. There is no obligation on the Japanese Government to pay compensation to complainants under the procedure.

(HC Debs., vol. 192, cols. 479–82: 6 June 1991)

In reply to a question, the Minister of State, FCO, wrote:

In recommending that the level of Iraq's contributions to the UN Compensation Fund should not exceed 30 per cent. of the annual value of the exports of petroleum and petroleum products from Iraq, the UN Secretary General drew on data from various sources, including the IMF. The final decision on this matter will be taken by the Security Council. Neither SCR 687 nor SCR 692, nor the Secretary

General's report on arrangements for the fund, envisages any role for the International Court of Justice.

(HL Debs., vol. 529, *WA 65*: 13 June 1991)

Part Eleven: II. A. 7. (a). *Responsibility—responsible entities—States—procedure—diplomatic and consular protection*

(See Part Fourteen; I. B. 6. (item of 31 May 1991), below)

Part Eleven: II. A. 7. (a). (i). *Responsibility—responsible entities—States—procedure—diplomatic and consular protection—nationality of claims*

The following provision appears in the Agreement between the Governments of the UK and the Republic of Burundi for the Promotion and Protection of Investments, which was signed and entered into force on 13 September 1990, and is typical of other provisions in similar agreements made during the period:

ARTICLE 1

Definitions

For the purposes of this Agreement:

. . .

(c) 'nationals' means:

   (i) in respect of the Republic of Burundi: citizens of Burundi within the meaning of the law in force;

   (ii) in respect of the United Kingdom: physical persons deriving their status as United Kingdom nationals from the law in force in the United Kingdom;

(d) 'companies' means:

   (i) in respect of the Republic of Burundi: any corporation and any civil commercial company or any other company, association or co-operative with or without legal personality which has its registered place of business within the Burundi scope of application of this Agreement and which is legally established in accordance with the law, regardless of whether the liability of its partners, shareholders or members is limited or unlimited and whether its activity is profit-making or not;

   (ii) in respect of the United Kingdom: corporations, firms and associations incorporated or constituted under the law in force in any part of the United Kingdom or in any territory to which this Agreement is extended in accordance with the provisions of Article 12; . . .

(TS No. 11 (1991); Cm. 1420)

In reply to the question whether enquiries would be made with the authorities in the Republic of Ireland to ascertain why entry visas were not given to two Pakistani and one Bangla Deshi national, settled in the UK, the Minister of State, FCO, wrote:

It is not the practice of Her Majesty's Government to intervene on behalf of foreign nationals who have been refused visas by independent sovereign states.

(HC Debs., vol. 194, WA, col. *164*: 3 July 1991)

Part Eleven: II. D. *Responsibility—responsible entities—individuals, including corporations*

(See also Part Fourteen: I. B. 6. (FCO statement of 21 January 1991), below)

In giving oral evidence to the Foreign Affairs Committee of the House of Commons considering events in the Middle East, the Minister of State, FCO, Mr Douglas Hogg, stated:

We believe people are held or can be held personally liable for gross breaches of relevant conventions and there are here a range of conventions which naturally are material. There is the Geneva Convention in so far as it applies to the treatment of prisoners of war and we do believe there is a lot of evidence that there have been gross breaches of certainly Article 19, Article 23 and other Articles of the Geneva Convention. Where you have a gross breach of a convention you then, of course, have personal liability.

(*Parliamentary Papers*, 1990–91, HC, Paper 143–iii, p. 91: 30 January 1991)

In reply to a question about the treatment of British prisoners of war working for I.G. Farben during the Second World War, the Minister of State, FCO, wrote:

We have received a number of representations. Some cases of mistreatment by individuals were investigated after the War with a view to war crimes proceedings, but, as a general matter, we do not consider that treatment of prisoners of war who worked for I.G. Farben can be shown to have been contrary to the 1929 Geneva convention. There is no basis to raise this matter with the German authorities.

(HC Debs., vol. 185, WA, col. *303*: 11 February 1991)

In the course of replying to an oral question, the Minister of State, FCO, Mr Douglas Hogg, stated that he had summoned the Iraqi Ambassador to the Foreign and Commonwealth Office on 29 January 1991. He continued:

I made it plain to the ambassador that where there was a gross breach of international obligations, those responsible could be held personally liable.

Mr Hogg was then asked what were the penalties for a reckless breach of the third Geneva Convention, and who is responsible for enforcing them. He replied:

There are a variety of ways in which individuals can be made accountable for their individual action. Of course, the consequences depend upon the precise nature of the breach alleged.

(HC Debs., vol. 185, cols. 847–8: 13 February 1991)

In the course of a debate on the subject of the Gulf conflict, the Secretary of State for Defence, Mr Tom King, stated:

We have already warned every Iraqi by leaflets and other methods of the personal responsibility that he bears under international law.

(HC Debs., vol. 186, col. 799: 26 February 1991)

In the course of a later debate on the same subject, the Prime Minister, Mr John Major, stated:

We have made it clear from the outset of the conflict that anyone who breaks the provisions of the Geneva convention may be held liable, and that remains the case.

(HC Debs., vol. 186, col. 1124: 28 February 1991)

In moving the Second Reading in the House of Commons of the War Crimes Bill, the Secretary of State for the Home Department, Mr Kenneth Baker, stated:

The House will be familiar with the heart of the Bill, in clause 1(1), which establishes jurisdiction in respect of offences of murder, manslaughter or culpable homicide. It is important that those offences are covered in the Bill. This is not a Bill concerning crimes against humanity. Those who have studied and debated the matter previously will know that there is a big distinction between the position post-1957 and the position pre-1957 in these matters. The Bill is limited to the crimes of murder, manslaughter and culpable homicide committed in violation of the laws and customs of war in German-held territory during the second world war.

The Bill is concerned with the specific wrongdoing uncovered by the Hetherington inquiry and is intended precisely to deal with that. The Bill refers to 'war crimes' for the very reason to which I alluded—to keep the Bill within the terms of international law as it stood at the relevant time and not to bring in any other form of atrocity of which international law had not then taken cognisance.

(HC Debs., vol. 188, col. 27: 18 March 1991)

Speaking later in the same debate, the Minister of State, Home Office, Mr John Patten, stated:

. . . in the Bill before the House we are not inventing any new offence. Murder was an offence in Germany and in German-occupied territory between 1939 and 1945. As many right hon. and hon. Members will be aware, international law finds its fountainhead back in the fourth Hague convention of 1907. That made it absolutely clear that activities involving murder, manslaughter or culpable homicide were against international law. That was recognised in the manuals of both the British and German armies. There is no doubt that murder, manslaughter and culpable homicide were crimes then, as they are now. It is rather a matter for the judgment of the House and the other place: we must decide whether to extend our jurisdiction and provide the laws, which the courts may then interpret.

. . .

My right hon. Friend . . . asked about the present state of international law on any alleged incidents connected with the Gulf conflict. All the states involved in the Gulf conflict are parties to the Geneva convention of 1949. We took that convention into our own law in 1957. So we have a wide jurisdiction over war crimes committed anywhere in the world after 1957 under international law.

(Ibid., cols. 111–12)

In reply to a question, the Parliamentary Under-Secretary of State, FCO, wrote:

We have consistently stated that individuals bear personal responsibility for crimes under international law. This position is reflected in Security Council resolution 674.

(HC Debs., vol. 186, WA, col. *583*: 28 February 1991)

In the course of a debate in the House of Lords on the subject of peace and security in the Middle East, the Government spokesman, Lord Reay, stated:

My noble friend raised the question of war crimes. We have made it clear that anyone who breaks the provisions of the Geneva Convention may be held liable, and that remains the case. That will not be a decision for the United Kingdom alone. Machinery already exists under the Geneva Conventions [Act 1957] for prosecuting grave breaches. The Kuwaiti Government intends to establish a commission to catalogue war crimes, which we welcome.

(HL Debs., vol. 526, cols. 1484–5: 6 March 1991; see also HC Debs., vol. 188, WA, col. *2*: 18 March 1991)

In the course of a debate on the subject of the UN Decade of International Law, the Parliamentary Under-Secretary of State, FCO, Mr Mark Lennox-Boyd, was asked about the possibility of an international criminal court. He replied:

We have welcomed the discussion of that issue in the General Assembly, especially in connection with the proposed code of crimes. It would be a major undertaking, and would raise political and practical questions as well as legal and financial ones. Although we are interested in the idea of such a court, we firmly believe that its existence would be justified only if some crimes could not be dealt with effectively by established means.

(HC Debs., vol. 188, col. 1167: 28 March 1991)

In the course of a debate on the subject of the Middle East, the Parliamentary Under-Secretary of State, FCO, Mr Mark Lennox-Boyd, stated:

Anyone who breaks the provisions of the Geneva conventions may be held liable. Thus, individual Iraqis now bear personal responsibility for breaches of them. That position was reaffirmed in Security Council resolutions 670 and 674. The superior orders defence will not be accepted as an excuse. Machinery already exists under [the Geneva Conventions Act of 1957] for prosecuting grave breaches of them. The three avenues are: first, a trial before Iraqi courts: secondly, extradition for trial before courts of another party to the conventions, including other Arab states; and, thirdly, the possibility of special international tribunals. There are obvious difficulties with all those approaches, and it is too early to say what mechanisms might be applied in this case.

(HC Debs., vol. 188, col. 1100: 28 March 1991)

In the course of a debate on the subject of Kurdish refugees from Iraq, the Minister of State, FCO, the Earl of Caithness, stated:

. . . it is true that genocide is a crime under international law. The noble Lord referred to the Genocide Convention 1948 under which the contracting parties have agreed to prevent and to punish the offence. Persons charged with genocide can be tried before national courts.

(HL Debs., vol. 527, cols. 1274–5: 15 April 1991; see also ibid., col. 1348: 16 April 1991)

In the course of a debate on the subject of the relief of suffering in Iraq, the Secretary of State for Foreign and Commonwealth Affairs, Mr Douglas Hurd, observed:

. . . the right hon. Gentleman correctly said that genocide is a crime under international law—the convention of 1948—and that the contracting parties have agreed to prevent and punish that crime. People charged with genocide can be tried before national courts. Proof is required of the intention to destroy in whole or in part one of the groups defined in the convention by carrying out certain acts.

(HC Debs., vol. 189, col. 23: 15 April 1991)

In reply to a question, the Minister of State, FCO, in the House of Lords, the Earl of Caithness, stated in part:

. . . while neither the Geneva Convention of 1949 nor the Genocide Convention of 1948 precludes setting up an international tribunal, they specifically provide for suspected war criminals to be tried before national courts. The noble Lord the Leader of the Opposition raises an important point because it is difficult to see an international tribunal having the power to bring Saddam Hussein to trial against his will. That is one of the many difficulties.

(HL Debs., vol. 527, cols. 1659–60: 19 April 1991)

In reply to a question, the Minister of State, FCO, wrote

Individual Iraqis bear personal responsibility under international law for any grave breaches of the Geneva conventions they order or commit. This principle is reiterated in United Nations Security Council resolution 674.

We are already in regular contact with coalition allies in connection with the collation of evidence which might support criminal charges against Iraqis or others who are in their custody as a result of the conflict. We understand that the Kuwait authorities intend to start such trials in the near future.

(HC Debs., vol. 189, WA, cols. *412–13*: 23 April 1991)

In a letter dated 25 April 1991 addressed to Sir Michael Marshall MP, the Attorney-General, Sir Patrick Mayhew, wrote in part:

We have consistently stated that individual Iraqis are personally responsible if they order or commit 'grave breaches' as defined in the four Geneva Conventions of 1949. This position was affirmed by the UN Security Council in Resolutions 670 of 25 September and 674 of 29 October 1990.

As you are aware, both the Geneva Conventions of 1949 and the Genocide Convention of 1948, adopted in the aftermath of the events of the Second World War, provide for trial before national courts (though they do not exclude the establishment of an international tribunal).

This question of establishing a standing international criminal court has for some time been under consideration at the United Nations in connection with a draft Code of Crimes against the Peace and Security of Mankind. Creating such a court would be a major undertaking which raises many important and difficult issues: political and practical as well as legal and financial. These issues were well set out by the International Law Commission (ILC) in its 1990 report. The question of setting up an ad hoc international criminal tribunal would raise many of the same issues. We have followed the work of the ILC closely, but we are of the view that an international criminal court would only be useful if there were offences for which the existing procedures, and in particular, national courts, were ineffective.

(Text provided by the FCO)

In moving the Second Reading in the House of Lords of the War Crimes Bill, the Lord Privy Seal, Lord Waddington, stated:

As to more recent war crimes, including, for instance, war crimes committed in Iraq, the position as I understand is that ever since the passing of the Geneva Conventions Act in 1957 our courts have had jurisdiction to try grave breaches of the convention, including killing and torture, wherever in the world they have been committed and whatever the nationality of the suspect. So there is no need for us to legislate to cover events in Iraq. Of course whether Iraqi war crimes trials will be held is another matter entirely and not for our Government alone.

(HL Debs., vol. 528, col. 621: 30 April 1991)

In reply to a question, the Attorney-General wrote:

Ministers have stated on a number of occasions that Iraqis bear individual responsibility for grave breaches of the Geneva conventions of 1949. The question of a prosecution within the United Kingdom would arise in practice only if a person against whom sufficient evidence were available should be within the jurisdiction of the United Kingdom courts.

(HC Debs., vol. 192, WA, col. *1*: 3 June 1991)

In reply to the question what is Her Majesty's Government's policy on bringing Saddam Hussein to justice for crimes against humanity, the Parliamentary Under-Secretary of State, FCO, wrote:

. . . Iraqi leaders bear personal responsibility under international law for their actions. This principle was reiterated in United Nations Security Council resolution 674. In the case of both the Geneva conventions of 1949 and the genocide convention of 1948, Iraqi leaders can, in law, be brought to national court or international tribunal. We and our EC partners have asked the United Nations Secretary-General to investigate how this might be achieved.

(HC Debs., vol. 192, WA, col. *416*: 10 June 1991)

In a statement made on 6 November 1991 in the Sixth Committee of the UN General Assembly considering the draft articles of the Code of Crimes against the Peace and Security of Mankind, adopted by the International Law Commission, the UK representative, Sir Arthur Watts, observed:

In Resolution 45/41 the General Assembly refrained from choosing between a system whereby States should exercise universal jurisdiction over international crimes and, on the other hand, the establishment of an international criminal court. The Special Rapporteur therefore put to the Commission this year draft provisions on two major issues on which he needed views in order to give him the necessary guidance in drafting a possible statute. The first of these major issues concerned the jurisdiction of an international criminal court; the second concerned the question of who should institute proceedings before the court.

The summary of the discussion of these two major issues in the Commission shows—if we did not know it already—just how difficult they are. Given that difficulty, the question does need to be addressed whether the establishment of an international criminal court would mark any significant practical improvement upon the situation which prevails at present. For many international crimes there is already an elaborate system of universal jurisdiction. One of the most all-embracing is that in the Geneva Conventions of 1949 and their Additional Protocols of 1977. This most complete system is nevertheless largely ineffective. I do not have to quote the numerous cases where grave breaches have occurred but where those responsible have not been brought to justice by any High Contracting Party. Most often the alleged offenders are protected by their own authorities, which may well indeed have ordered the commission of the offences; any request for their extradition would be refused. There is at least a question whether we have reasonable grounds for believing that having an international criminal court would in practice improve matters.

Of course, we do not necessarily have to envisage a system in which all the crimes identified in the draft Code have to be referred to an international criminal court. There could perhaps be a mix of States exercising universal jurisdiction for some crimes, and an international criminal court to deal with such crimes as acts or threats of aggression. Limiting the jurisdiction of such a court to a narrow range of crimes may make it somewhat easier to deal with the complex problems which were discussed this year by the Commission. At the same time, the Commission might consider it worth examining ways in which the system of universal jurisdiction, which is well-established and uncontroversial, might be made more effective in practice.

The debate in the Commission this year has shown graphically the enormous task faced by the Commission in its work on the international criminal court. Indeed some members thought that the Commission should wait until it had a clear and specific request from the General Assembly before embarking on further work. The subject is certainly at the outer edge of the Commission's mandate to promote 'the progressive development of international law and its codification'.

The problems are, in the view of the United Kingdom delegation, as much problems of policy as of law. We think that this committee owes it to the new Commission to give it clearer policy guidance before it goes any further.

(Text provided by the FCO; see also A/C.6/46/SR.30, pp. 2–4)

Part Twelve: II. A. *Pacific settlement of disputes—modes of settlement—negotiation*

(See also Part Three: I. B. 5. (item of 31 July 1991), above)

Speaking in Valletta, Malta, on 15 January 1991 on behalf of the EC and its Member States, the President of the EC Council of Ministers, Mr Jacques Poos, stated:

Dans l'optique de l'élaboration à La Valette d'une méthode de règlement pacifique des différends les Douze partent de l'idée que tous les Etats participants à la CSCE—entretenant des relations diplomatiques mutuelles—considèrent par la même la négociation comme la forme initiale normale de tout règlement pacifique des différends. Dans ce contexte il échet [sic] de rappeler les principes de droit international public qui s'appliquent en la matière, à savoir le délai raisonnable et la bonne foi.

(Text provided by the FCO)

In reply to a question, the Government Minister in the House of Lords wrote:

Our policy has not changed. Our position remains that the dispute over the status of Kashmir should be settled peacefully between the governments of India and Pakistan, by whatever means are mutually agreed between them. We have offered to help in this if both sides would like us to do so.

(HL Debs., vol. 526, *WA 60*: 28 February 1991)

In reply to a question on the subject of East Timor, the Prime Minister wrote:

The United Kingdom abstained on United Nations resolution 35/27 of 1980. We took the view that by so doing, in company with most European Community partners and others, we could help to promote reconciliation and the search for a diplomatic solution by Indonesia and Portugal. Since 1982, the United Kingdom has supported the efforts of the United Nations Secretary-General to find a solution to the problem which is acceptable to all parties.

(HC Debs., vol. 189, WA, col. *206*: 18 April 1991)

In the course of a debate on the subject of Pakistan and Kashmir, the Parliamentary Under-Secretary of State, FCO, Mr Mark Lennox-Boyd, stated:

Our position on the status of Kashmir remains that this should be settled by peaceful agreement between India and Pakistan, in accordance with their agreement in 1972 at Simla, under which both countries 'resolved to settle their differences through bilateral negotiations or by any other peaceful means mutually agreed between them.' This agreement also looked forward to a 'final settlement of Jammu and Kashmir.'

(HC Debs., vol. 195, col. 1355: 25 July 1991)

Part Twelve: II. D. *Pacific settlement of disputes—modes of settlement—good offices*

In the course of a speech in the UN Security Council on 15 February 1991, the UK Permanent Representative to the UN in New York, Sir David Hannay, stated:

The good offices of the Secretary-General are set out very clearly in the Charter and they are encouraged to be used in Security Council resolution 674 (1990). I have no doubt whatsoever that if there were any opening for the use of those good offices, the Secretary-General would seize it with both hands.

(S/PV. 2977, p. 203)

Part Twelve: II. G. 1. *Pacific settlement of disputes—modes of settlement—arbitration—arbitral tribunals and commissions*

(See also Part Three: I. B. 1. (item of 16 December 1991), above)

The following provisions appear in the Agreement between the Government of the UK and the Republic of Burundi for the Promotion and Protection of Investments, which was signed and entered into force on 13 September 1990, and are typical of provisions in other similar agreements made during the period:

ARTICLE 8

Reference to International Centre for Settlement of Investment Disputes

(1) Each Contracting Party hereby consents to submit to the International Centre for the Settlement of Investment Disputes (hereinafter referred to as 'the Centre') for settlement by conciliation or arbitration under the Convention on the Settlement of Investment Disputes between States and Nationals of Other States opened for signature at Washington on 18 March 1965 any legal dispute arising between the Contracting Party and a national or company of the other Contracting Party concerning an investment of the latter in the territory of the former.
(2) A company which is incorporated or constituted under the law in force in the territory of one Contracting Party and in which before such a dispute arises the majority of shares are owned by nationals or companies of the other Contracting Party shall in accordance with Article 25(2)(b) of the Convention be treated for the purposes of the Convention as a company of the other Contracting Party.
(3) If any such dispute should arise and agreement cannot be reached within three months between the parties to this dispute through pursuit of local remedies or otherwise, then, if the national or company affected also consents in writing to submit the dispute to the Centre for settlement by conciliation or arbitration under the Convention, either party may institute proceedings by addressing a request to that effect to the Secretary-General of the Centre as provided in Articles 28 and 36 of the Convention. In the event of disagreement as to whether conciliation or arbitration is the more appropriate procedure the national or company affected shall have the right to choose. The Contracting Party which is a party to the dispute shall not raise as an objection at any stage of the proceedings or enforcement of an award the fact that the national or company which is the other party to the dispute has received in pursuance of an insurance contract an indemnity in respect of some or all of his or its losses.
(4) Neither Contracting Party shall pursue through the diplomatic channel any dispute referred to the Centre unless
(a) the Secretary-General of the Centre, or a conciliation commission or an arbitral tribunal constituted by it, decides that the dispute is not within the jurisdiction of the Centre, or
(b) the other Contracting Party should fail to abide by or to comply with any award rendered by an arbitral tribunal.

ARTICLE 9

Disputes between the Contracting Parties

(1) Disputes between the Contracting Parties concerning the interpretation or application of this Agreement should, if possible, be settled through the diplomatic channel.
(2) If a dispute between the Contracting Parties cannot thus be settled, it shall upon the request of either Contracting Party be submitted to an arbitral tribunal.
(3) Such an arbitral tribunal shall be constituted for each individual case in the following way. Within two months of the receipt of the request for arbitration, each Contracting Party shall appoint one member of the tribunal. Those two members shall then select a national of a third State who on approval by the two Contracting Parties shall be appointed Chairman of the tribunal. The Chairman shall be appointed within two months from the date of appointment of the other two members.
(4) If within the periods specified in paragraph (3) of this Article the necessary appointments have not been made, either Contracting Party may, in the absence of any other agreement, invite the President of the International Court of Justice to make any necessary appointments. If the President is a national of either Contracting Party or if he is otherwise prevented from discharging the said function, the Vice-President shall be invited to make the necessary appointments. If the Vice-President is a national of either Contracting Party or if he too is prevented from discharging the said function, the Member of the International Court of Justice next in seniority who is not a national of either Contracting Party shall be invited to made the necessary appointments.
(5) The arbitral tribunal shall reach its decision by a majority of votes. Such decision shall be binding on both Contracting Parties. Each Contracting Party shall bear the cost of its own member of the tribunal and of its representation in the arbitral proceedings: the cost of the Chairman and the remaining costs shall be borne in equal parts by the Contracting Parties. The tribunal may, however, in its decision direct that a higher proportion of costs shall be borne by one of the two Contracting Parties, and this award shall be binding on both Contracting Parties. The tribunal shall determine its own procedure.

(TS No. 11 (1991); Cm. 1420)

The following provision appears in a similar agreement between the Governments of the UK and the Republic of Argentina which was signed on 11 December 1990:

ARTICLE 8

Settlement of Disputes Between an Investor and the Host State

(1) Disputes with regard to an investment which arise within the terms of this Agreement between an investor of one Contracting Party and the other Contracting Party, which have not been amicably settled shall be submitted, at the request of one of the Parties to the dispute, to the decision of the competent tribunal of the Contracting Party in whose territory the investment was made.
(2) The aforementioned disputes shall be submitted to international arbitration in the following cases:
(a) if one of the Parties so requests, in any of the following circumstances:

(i) where, after a period of eighteen months has elapsed from the moment when the dispute was submitted to the competent tribunal of the Contracting Party in whose territory the investment was made, the said tribunal has not given its final decision;

(ii) where the final decision of the aforementioned tribunal has been made but the Parties are still in dispute;

(b) where the Contracting Party and the investor of the other Contracting Party have so agreed.

(3) Where the dispute is referred to international arbitration, the investor and the Contracting Party concerned in the dispute may agree to refer the dispute either to:

(a) the International Centre for the Settlement of Investment Disputes (having regard to the provisions, where applicable, of the Convention on the Settlement of Investment Disputes between States and Nationals of other States, opened for signature at Washington DC on 18 March 1965 (provided that both Contracting Parties are Parties to the said Convention) and the Additional Facility for the Administration of Conciliation, Arbitration and Fact-Finding Proceedings); or

(b) an international arbitrator or *ad hoc* arbitration tribunal to be appointed by a special agreement or established under the Arbitration Rules of the United Nations Commission on International Trade Law.

If after a period of three months from written notification of the claim there is no agreement to one of the above alternative procedures, the Parties to the dispute shall be bound to submit it to arbitration under the Arbitration Rules of the United Nations Commission on International Trade Law as then in force. The Parties to the dispute may agree in writing to modify these Rules.

(4) The arbitral tribunal shall decide the dispute in accordance with the provisions of this Agreement, the laws of the Contracting Party involved in the dispute, including its rules on conflict of laws, the terms of any specific agreement concluded in relation to such an investment and the applicable principles of international law. The arbitration decision shall be final and binding on both Parties.

(5) The provisions of this Article shall not apply where an investor of one Contracting Party is a natural person who has been ordinarily resident in the territory of the other Contracting Party for a period of more than two years before the original investment was made and the original investment was not admitted into that territory from abroad. But, if a dispute should arise between such an investor and the other Contracting Party, the Contracting Parties agree to consult together as soon as possible so that they can reach a mutually acceptable solution.

(Cm. 1449)

Article 23 of the Headquarters Agreement signed on 15 April 1991 between the UK Government and the European Bank for Reconstruction and Development, reads as follows:

Settlement of Disputes

1. Any dispute between the Government and the Bank concerning the interpretation or application of this Agreement, which is not settled by negotiation or other agreed mode of settlement, shall be referred for final decision to an arbitral tribunal of three arbitrators, to be constituted for each individual case in the following way. Within two months of the receipt of the request for arbitration, the Bank and the

Government each shall appoint one member of the tribunal. The two members so appointed shall then select a third arbitrator who is not a national of the United Kingdom. That third arbitrator shall be President of the tribunal.
2. If within three months from the date of notification of the request for arbitration, the necessary appointments have not been made, either the Government or the Bank may, in the absence of any other agreement, invite the President of the International Court of Justice to make the necessary appointments. If the President is a national of the United Kingdom or if he is otherwise prevented from discharging the said function, the Vice-President shall be invited to make the necessary appointments. If the Vice-President is a national of the United Kingdom or if he too is prevented from discharging the said function, the Member of the International Court of Justice next in seniority who is not a national of the United Kingdom shall be invited to make the necessary appointments.
3. The decisions of the tribunal shall be final and binding. The tribunal shall adopt its own rules of procedure, and in this respect shall be guided by the Rules of Procedure for Arbitration Proceedings of the International Centre of Settlement of Investment Disputes established by the Convention on the Settlement of Investment Disputes between the States and Nationals of Other States, done at Washington D.C. on 18th March 1965.
4. The costs of the tribunal shall be shared equally between the Bank and the Government, unless the tribunal decides otherwise.

(TS No. 45 (1991); Cm. 1615)

Part Twelve: II. H. 1. *Pacific settlement of disputes—modes of settlement—judicial settlement—the International Court of Justice*

(See also Part One: I., above)

In reply to the question whether, and if so by what procedures, the future status of Lithuania, Latvia and Estonia could be brought before the International Court of Justice, the Minister of State, FCO, wrote:

These issues could only be brought before the International Court of Justice with the agreement of the Soviet Government.

(HL Debs., vol. 525, *WA 47*: 6 February 1991)

In the course of a debate on the subject of the UN Decade of International Law, the Parliamentary Under-Secretary of State, FCO, Mr Mark Lennox-Boyd, stated:

The United Kingdom is committed to the peaceful settlement of international disputes. Within the conference on security and co-operation in Europe process—a political rather than a legal process—the conciliation proposals that we put forward last autumn formed the core of the mechanism for settling disputes, agreed by officials at the recent meeting in Valletta. On the legal side, we are encouraged by the increasing number of states that accept the compulsory jurisdiction of the International Court of Justice. In the last couple of years a significant number of additional states have made the necessary declaration. Some of them were developing countries. That is a most welcome trend. As the right hon. and learned Gentleman will know, we are the only permanent member of the Security Council that currently accepts the compulsory jurisdiction of the International Court of Justice.

We have always accepted its jurisdiction. Therefore, we are well placed to urge all states that have not yet accepted the court's jurisdiction to consider doing so.

Last year, the Secretary-General of the United Nations established a trust fund to assist developing countries to bring cases before the International Court of Justice by agreement—for example, territorial disputes. The United Kingdom was the first to announce a contribution to the fund. That is a very practical way of encouraging recourse to the court and the rule of law.

(HC Debs., vol. 188, col. 1168: 28 March 1991)

In reply to the question whether it would help the peaceful solution of disputes if the UN Secretary-General were given the power to seek advisory opinions of the International Court of Justice, the Parliamentary Under-Secretary of State, FCO, Mr Mark Lennox-Boyd, replied in part:

. . . the United Nations bodies which need legal advice are those bodies which make the decisions—the General Assembly, the Security Council, and other bodies composed of member states. Those are the bodies that need advice from the International Court of Justice. Although we very much welcome all the hard work of the Secretary-General and the success that he has had, it would not be appropriate to press in the direction that the hon. Gentleman suggests.

(HC Debs., vol. 191, col. 925: 22 May 1991)

Part Thirteen: I. D. *Coercion and counter-measures short of the use of force—unilateral acts—other unilateral acts, including self-defence*

In reply to an oral question concerning the sales of arms from the UK to Indonesia, the Minister of State, FCO, the Earl of Caithness, stated:

. . . all countries have a sovereign right under the United Nations Charter to secure the means of their own defence. Applications to export British defence equipment are carefully scrutinised on a case by case basis. It is important to remember that we do not allow the export of arms and equipment likely to be used for repressive purposes against civil populations.

(HL Debs., vol. 532, col. 1147: 25 November 1991; see also ibid., cols. 1315–16: 27 November 1991)

Part Thirteen: II. A. *Coercion and counter-measures short of the use of force—collective measures—regime of the UN*

In reply to the question

Whether [Her Majesty's Government] will seek international agreement on an embargo on the export of arms and ammunition by South Africa,

the Minister of State, FCO, wrote:

There is already an international agreement to which the British Government adhere—UN Security Council Resolution 558 of 1984 banning imports of arms, ammunition and military vehicles from South Africa.

(HL Debs., vol. 527, *WA 1*: 11 March 1991)

In the course of a reply, the Secretary of State for Trade and Industry wrote:

The Government fully share the determination of the United States administration to enforce United Nations sanctions against Iraq, and in particular to prevent the export of arms to Iraq. We have taken the following key measures.

First, we are continuing to prevent the supply of goods to persons in Iraq, including companies controlled by Iraqi residents or Iraqi incorporated companies, or imports from Iraq in compliance with Security Council resolution 661. The legislation giving effect to the resolution applies to all persons and companies in the United Kingdom and to United Kingdom nationals and companies abroad. Compliance is carefully monitored. Very few breaches of this embargo have come to light, and these few cases are being pursued vigorously. The United States authorities have not alleged that the firms on this list have broken sanctions.

Secondly, we are continuing to maintain controls which have the effect of freezing the assets in the United Kingdom of persons and companies normally resident in Iraq on or after 4 August 1990, also in compliance with Security Council resolution 661. This embargo, too, is rigorously enforced.

Third, for many years before Iraq's invasion of Kuwait exports of lethal military equipment to Iraq were prohibited by the Export of Goods (Control) Order. These controls, which apply to all persons and companies in the United Kingdom, remain in place, though they are in practice overtaken for the time being by the wider trade embargo introduced last August.

(HC Debs., vol. 189, WA, cols. *30–1* : 15 April 1991)

In reply to a question, the Minister of State, FCO, the Earl of Caithness, stated:

Britain has had strict controls on arms sales to Iraq since 1980. United Nations Security Council Resolution 661 established a world-wide trade embargo against Iraq, reaffirmed by United Nations Security Council Resolution 687. We are in close touch with the United States and our EC partners on its enforcement.

(HL Debs., vol. 529, col. 7: 20 May 1991)

The following letter, dated 25 July 1991, was addressed to the UN Secretary-General by the UK Permanent Representative to the UN in New York, Sir David Hannay:

In response to your Note SCPC/7/91(4–1) of 3 July 1991, I am writing to inform you about the measures undertaken by the United Kingdom to implement Security Council resolution 700 (1991).

Current United Kingdom laws and regulations already meet the obligations and requirements of resolution 687 (1991) as regards the sale, supply, or the promotion or facilitation of the sale or supply of goods to Iraq, including those items specified in paragraph 24 of resolution 687 (1991). The Guidelines adopted by Security Council resolution 700 (1991) fall largely within the scope of existing United Kingdom legislation. This includes the following Orders in Council:

— The Hong Kong (Control of Gold, Securities, Payments and Credits: Kuwait and Republic of Iraq) Order 1990 (6 August 1990);
— The Caribbean Territories (Control of Gold, Securities, Payments and Credits: Kuwait and Republic of Iraq) Order 1990: SI No. 1625 (6 August 1990);

— The Iraq and Kuwait (United Nations Sanctions) Order 1990: SI No. 1651 (8 August 1990);
— The Iraq and Kuwait (United Nations Sanctions) (Dependent Territories) Order 1990: SI No. 1652 (8 August 1990);
— The Export of Goods (Control) (Iraq and Kuwait Sanctions) Order 1990: SI No. 1640 (8 August 1990);
— The Iraq and Kuwait (United Nations Sanctions) (Amendment) Order 1990: SI No. 1768 (29 August 1990);
— The Iraq and Kuwait (United Nations Sanctions) (Bermuda) Order 1990: SI No. 1769 (29 August 1990);
— The Iraq and Kuwait (United Nations Sanctions) (Dependent Territories) (Amendment) Order 1990: SI No. 1770 (29 August 1990);
— The Iraq and Kuwait (United Nations Sanctions) (Channel Islands) Order 1990: SI No. 1771 (29 August 1990);
— The Iraq and Kuwait (United Nations Sanctions) (No. 2) Order 1990 (5 October 1990);
— The Iraq and Kuwait (United Nations Sanctions) (Dependent Territories) (No. 2) Order 1990 (5 October 1990);
— The Iraq and Kuwait (United Nations Sanctions) (Second Amendment) Order 1990: SI No. 2144 (31 October 1990).

Her Majesty's Treasury issued a separate legal direction—the Control of Gold, Securities, Payments and Credits (Republic of Iraq) Directions 1990: SI No. 1616—on 4 August 1990. The Bank of England issued a notice—Emergency Laws (Re-enactments and Appeals) Act 1964: Iraq—on 7 August 1990.

In addition, the European Community has enacted the following legislation preventing trade by Community members with Iraq:
— EEC regulation 2340/90 extended and amended by EEC regulation 3155/90.
— ECSC decision 90/414.

These regulations and decisions have direct effect in the United Kingdom.

The controls on the sale or supply of technology and personnel or materials referred to in subparagraphs (c) and (d) of paragraph 24 of resolution 687 (1991) will be reinforced by a new Order in Council. This will be self-contained and will fully implement all the requirements of paragraph 24, and the Guidelines adopted by Security Council resolution 700 (1991). A copy of the new Order in Council will be made available to the United Nations when it has been promulgated. The legislation will provide for criminal sanctions in the form of imprisonment or fines. Responsibilities for enforcement of the new legislation will fall largely to the Department of Trade and Industry and Her Majesty's Customs and Excise.

(S/22841)

Part Fourteen: I. A. 1. *Use of force—international war and armed conflict—resort to war—definition of war*

(See Part Fourteen: IV. A. (item of 28 January 1991), below)

Part Fourteen: I. A. 4. *Use of force—international war and armed conflict—resort to war—limitation and reduction of armaments*

The Final Document of an Extraordinary Conference pursuant to Article XXI of the Treaty of Conventional Armed Forces in Europe, 1990, issued on 14 June 1991 in Vienna, contained a statement by the Government of the USSR and identical statements by twenty-one States parties attending including the UK. The UK's statement read as follows:

The Government of the United Kingdom of Great Britain and Northern Ireland hereby agrees that the Statement of the Government of the Union of Soviet Socialist Republics of today's date provides a satisfactory basis for proceeding toward ratification and implementation of the Treaty on Conventional Armed Forces in Europe of 19 November 1990 (the Treaty).

The aforementioned Statement of the Government of the Union of Soviet Socialist Republics and this Statement of the Government of the United Kingdom of Great Britain and Northern Ireland shall be equally legally binding; they shall enter into force simultaneously with the Treaty, and shall have the same duration as the Treaty.

(Cm. 1684)

Part Fourteen: I. B. 2. *Use of force—international war and armed conflict—the laws of war and armed conflict—land warfare*

In reply to the question

What is the position in international law relating to the use of 'conventional' weapons against

(a) nuclear facilities;
(b) chemical weapons plants and dumps, and
(c) petrochemical enterprises situated in towns or cities,

when such use may release radioactivity, toxic chemicals, or firestorms, on a scale comparable to the use of nuclear, chemical, and other weapons deemed to be weapons of mass destruction,

the Minister of State, FCO, wrote in part:

International law requires that, in planning an attack on any military objective, account is taken of certain principles. These include the principles that civilian losses, whether of life or property, should be avoided or minimised so far as practicable, and that an attack should not be launched if it can be expected to cause civilian losses which would be disproportionate to the military advantage expected from the attack as a whole.

(HL Debs., vol. 525, *WA 37*: 4 February 1991)

In reply to the question whether there were any prior consultations between US and UK officials about the legality of allied bombing of Iraqi nuclear facilities, the Minister of State for the Armed Forces wrote in part:

I am satisfied that the allied policy of attacking only targets which could pose a threat to allied forces and facilities which support Iraq's illegal occupation of Kuwait is entirely within international law.

(HC Debs., vol. 186, WA, col. *611*: 28 February 1991)

In reply to the question

Whether during hostilities against Iraq [Her Majesty's Government] interpreted the relevant United Nations Security Council Resolution as allowing unlimited damage and destruction to the Iraqi civil economy,

the Parliamentary Under-Secretary of State, Ministry of Defence, wrote:

United Nations Security Council Resolution 678 of 29th November 1990 authorised member states co-operating with the Government of Kuwait to use all necessary means to uphold and implement Security Council Resolution 660 and all other resolutions and to restore international peace and security in the area. It was the common understanding, reflected at all times in the practice of coalition forces, that member states acting under that authorisation remained bound by the principles and rules of international law regulating the conduct of armed conflict. As to those principles and rules, I refer the noble Lord to the Answer given to him . . . on 4th February, at col. *WA 37*.

(HL Debs., vol. 531, *WA 43–4*: 22 July 1991)

Part Fourteen: I. B. 5. *Use of force—international war and armed conflict—the laws of war and armed conflict—distinction between combatants and non-combatants*

In reply to the question

Whether [Her Majesty's Government] agree with the interpretation of the Geneva Conventions that holds that, while Iraqi civilians might not be targeted, their means of livelihood and health might be targeted; whether this was the interpretation of the convention adopted by those engaged in planning the bombing of Iraq; and whether they agree with the United States Secretary of Defense [Mr Cheney], who is reported as saying that every Iraqi target was 'perfectly legitimate',

the Parliamentary Under-Secretary of State, Ministry of Defence, wrote:

The Geneva Conventions contain no provisions expressly regulating targeting in armed conflict. The Hague Regulations of 1907 and customary international law do, however, incorporate the twin principles of distinction between military and civilian objects, and of proportionality so far as the risk of collateral civilian damage from an attack on a military objective is concerned.

These principles and associated rules of international law were observed at all times by coalition forces in the planning and execution of attacks against Iraq. I understand that Mr. Cheney has made clear his belief that every Iraqi target selected by the coalition forces was perfectly legitimate.

(HL Debs., vol. 531, *WA 43*: 22 July 1991)

Part Fourteen: I. B. 6. *Use of force—international war and armed conflict—the laws of war and armed conflict—humanitarian law*

The following passages are taken from a Briefing Note on the Gulf Crisis issued by the FCO in November 1990:

FOREIGN HOSTAGES IN IRAQ AND KUWAIT

Iraq is holding several hundred foreign nationals, of whom about 350 are British, as hostages in Iraq and Kuwait. The Iraqi Government persists in referring to these people as their 'guests', an offensive perversion of the term since they are being detained against their will as human shields at a number of strategic military and civilian sites. There are thousands more foreign workers in the two countries, who are not being allowed to leave because they are needed to maintain certain essential services. Hundreds more foreigners, including about 500 Britons, are in hiding in Kuwait.

The detention of foreign nationals is a moral and humanitarian outrage, and a gross violation of international law. Iraq is a party to the Fourth Geneva Convention (the Civilian Convention), which lays down minimum standards for the treatment of foreign nationals who find themselves caught up in a conflict or an occupation. Such persons are 'protected persons'. The main relevant provisions of the Convention are:

— the taking of hostages is prohibited;
— protected persons may not be used to render areas immune from military operations;
— all persons have the right to humane treatment and protection from violence;
— they are protected from reprisals;
— they have the right to leave an occupied territory;
— individual or mass forcible transfers, as well as deportation of protected persons from occupied territory to the territory of the occupying power, are prohibited, regardless of motive.

Many hostages have been moved from Kuwait to Iraq. In both countries people are being held at such strategic sites as power stations and dams, military and oil installations, chemical or biological research plants, and factories. The hostages are frequently moved from site to site, so as to add to the uncertainty surrounding their fate. The exact numbers involved are not known, but of the thousands of Western and Japanese nationals being prevented from leaving Iraq and Kuwait, 600 are being held as hostages.

Many of the hostages suffer from poor sanitation, inadequate food and clothing, crowded accommodation and limited facilities for exercise. Many of them are exposed to health hazards as a result of being locked inside industrial plants at night, as well as being exposed to industrial pollution during the day. The Iraqis claim that the hostages 'enjoy full treatment in terms of residence, food and medical care' and that 'their situation is natural and that they are well treated'. They have allowed a limited number of Western journalists to visit some of the hostages at carefully selected sites in Iraq (but not in Kuwait). Reports from Western hostages who have been released, as well as letters from those still held, make it clear that the picture Iraq shows to the media is highly selective.

Not only are the hostages unable to leave, they are also being denied visits from their consular representatives. This is in direct contravention of the Vienna Convention on Consular Relations to which Iraq is also a party.

. . .

The UN Security Council adopted Resolution 674 on 29 October, which reminded Iraq of her obligations under international law and in particular under the Fourth Geneva Convention. This Resolution is further evidence of the vigorous and unremitting efforts which the British Government and others have made bilaterally and multilaterally to secure the release of their nationals, both through their diplomatic representatives in Baghdad and through contacts in their own capitals.

(Text provided by the FCO)

In January 1991, the FCO issued a further Briefing Note on the Gulf Crisis which read in part as follows:

AN OFFENCE AGAINST INTERNATIONAL LAW

On 20 January, Iraqi television showed recorded interviews with captured allied pilots, as well as pictures of American prisoners being paraded blindfold through streets in Baghdad. Further video footage of interviews with captured aircrew have since been shown on Iraqi television. This parading of prisoners of war (PWs) has aroused feelings of revulsion and anger around the world. On every score such treatment is abhorrent, not least because by abusing prisoners in this way Iraq is in flagrant violation of the 1949 Geneva Prisoners of War Convention, to which it has been a party since 1956. This was the latest evidence of Saddam Hussein's willingness to flout international law.

The parading of captured allied airmen on Iraqi television is contrary to the provisions of Article 13 of the Convention, which requires the detaining forces to protect PWs not only against 'violence or intimidation' but against 'insults and public curiosity'. Coercing prisoners, eg into making statements condemning their own side, is also prohibited. Article 17 states that a PW may give his name, rank, date of birth and service number. His captors are free to ask any further questions they wish, but Article 17 provides that 'no physical or mental torture, nor any other form of coercion' may be inflicted to secure an answer. Nor may any penalty be imposed on those who refuse to give more than the basic details required by the Convention. The recent Iraqi television pictures of the bruised and dazed faces of captured airmen, together with their robotic delivery of denunciations of the coalition and its use of force against Iraq, indicate that the Iraqi authorities are violating the Convention on this point also.

Despite Saddam Hussein's recent broadcast pledge that he would comply with the Geneva Convention, the Iraqi Ambassador to Paris is quoted as saying that only those servicemen whom the multinational forces officially acknowledge as captured will be treated in accordance with the Convention. This has no foundation in international law. The duty to provide humane treatment for PWs is unconditional and cannot be made to depend upon allied reaction to grossly inflated Iraqi claims about the number of allied aircraft shot down and the number of prisoners taken. Nor can a new duty be imposed on the multinational forces to declare the name of every serviceman who may be taken prisoner. Iraq has an obligation under Article 122 of the Convention to inform the Central Tracing Agency of the International Committee of the Red Cross (ICRC) immediately of any PWs captured. This they have not done yet.

Iraq's Ambassador to London has said that Iraq will abide by the Convention only if the allied aircrews avoid civilian targets—again contrary to Iraq's duty to protect PWs unconditionally. (Nevertheless it is worth underlining that the allies have made it clear that only objectives of military value are to be targeted, every effort is to be made to keep civilian casualties to a minimum, and religious and cultural sites are to be avoided. This contrasts with Iraq's policy of launching Scud missiles against Israel and Saudi Arabia, since these missiles are not precision weapons and are clearly intended to hit civilian targets.)

Baghdad Radio has announced that the recently captured airmen would be assigned as 'human shields' in target areas. Article 23 of the Geneva Convention is categorical on this point: 'No prisoner of war may at any time be sent to, or detained in areas where he may be exposed to the fire of the combat zone, nor may his presence be used to render certain points or areas immune from military operations'.

Iraq has announced that PWs have now been moved to strategic sites (presumed to be chemical and biological weapons plants). Saddam Hussein adopted a policy of using 'human shields' following the invasion of Kuwait, when several hundred civilian foreign nationals were detained against their will at a number of strategic military and civilian sites. He abandoned the policy when it became clear that it was bringing shame on him and strengthening rather than weakening the resolve of his adversaries. Similar treatment of PWs is equally shameful to Iraq—a country which has ratified the Geneva Convention and which has in the past made claims to be a modern and civilised State.

Iraq's behaviour has met with widespread condemnation. The UN Secretary-General said on 22 January, about the appearance of captured aircrew on Iraqi television, 'I am extremely concerned because it is something which goes against the Geneva Convention in a very clear manner . . . it is a practice which cannot be supported at the United Nations'.

(Text provided by the FCO)

The following letter, dated 21 January 1991, was sent to the President of the UN Security Council by the Permanent Representative of the UK to the UN in New York:

Further to my earlier letter of 21 January (S/22115) I have the honour to inform you on behalf of my Government that the Government of the United Kingdom of Great Britain and Northern Ireland has been obliged to make clear to the Iraqi authorities its concern about Iraq's compliance with the Third and Fourth Geneva Conventions in its response to the military action undertaken by the United Kingdom and other States pursuant to SCR 678. Two separate demarches have been made to the Iraqi Ambassador in London on 19 January and 21 January.

On 19 January the Iraqi Ambassador was asked whether the Iraqi Government was holding any British prisoners of war and reminded of Iraq's obligations under the Third Geneva Convention to notify the names of any prisoners held and to arrange access by the ICRC. The Iraqi Ambassador gave an assurance that any British prisoners of war would be treated in accordance with the Geneva Conventions and that their names would be given to the ICRC. He drew attention to the first military communiqué of the Iraqi Government which contained such assurances and called on the civilian population to treat any servicemen humanely.

In the light of television and news agency reports on 21 January indicating that captured British airmen had been displayed on Iraqi television, the Iraqi Ambassador was summoned again. He was told of the British Government's acute concern. Article 13 of the Geneva Convention provides that 'Prisoners of war must at all times be protected particularly against acts of violence or intimidation and against insults and public curiosity'. There had also been news agency reports that the Iraqi authorities were considering sending the captured POWs to strategic sites in Iraq. This would be a serious breach of Iraq's obligations under the Conventions.

We expected scrupulous compliance with the Conventions in respect of all British prisoners of war including British servicemen. The Iraqi Ambassador was reminded of the responsibility of his Government and of individual Iraqis for any grave breach of the Conventions.

The Iraqi Ambassador was also reminded on 21 January of Iraq's obligations under the 1925 Geneva Protocol in respect of chemical and biological weapons. The United Kingdom would take the severest view of any use of these weapons by Iraq.

The United Kingdom sought an assurance that Iraq had no intention of using chemical or biological weapons. The Ambassador responded that he had no military authority to give such an assurance.

The British Government has made clear to the Iraqi Ambassador and to the International Committee of the Red Cross that for its part it will be complying scrupulously with its obligations under international humanitarian law, including the Third and Fourth Geneva Conventions. The British Government will be allowing full access by the ICRC both to Iraqi prisoners of war and to Iraqi citizens detained in the United Kingdom. The ICRC have already been provided with details of and access to all Iraqi nationals held in the United Kingdom.

(S/22117)

On 21 January 1991, an FCO spokesman made the following statement:

Spokesman announced that Mr Hogg [Minister of State, FCO] had summoned the Iraqi Ambassador on 21 January to discuss Iraq's obligation under international law. The meeting had lasted for 25 minutes and had been conducted in a businesslike atmosphere.

Mr Hogg had told the Ambassador that he had just seen the representative of the International Committee of the Red Cross, Mr Francis Amar, and had made it clear that Britain would abide by the Geneva Conventions and facilitate ICRC activities in the UK. Mr Hogg had asked the ICRC to make representations in Baghdad to ensure Iraqi compliance with the Conventions.

Mr Hogg had made clear to the Ambassador our concern for the proper treatment of all prisoners of war, particularly our own. He had said that he understood that the ICRC had already raised the breach of Article 13 with the Iraqis. He had also raised press reports concerning the detention of POWs at strategic sites. Mr Hogg had made it clear that if Iraq did this it would be an outrageous breach of the Geneva Conventions. The British Government would take the gravest view of any such breach. He also reminded the Iraqi Ambassador of the personal liability of those individuals who broke the Conventions in this way.

The Ambassador said that Iraq would abide by the Conventions and treat POWs well if the Allies avoided civilian targets. Mr Hogg said that we expected unconditional observance of the requirements of the Convention.

Mr Hogg also reminded the Ambassador of the 1925 Geneva Protocols relating to chemical and biological weapons and said that we would take the severest view of any use of these weapons by the Iraqis wherever used. He again reminded the Ambassador of the personal liability of those who authorised their use and asked for assurances that Iraq would not use them.

Mr Hogg expressed concern at the indiscriminate targeting of civilian sites by Iraqi SCUD missiles. He also raised the cases of two British citizens, Mr Douglas

Brand and Mr Bruce Cheesman, and asked that details of their whereabouts be provided as soon as possible.

The Ambassador undertook to transmit all of the points made by Mr Hogg to Baghdad and report further.

(Text provided by the FCO)

In the course of a debate on the subject of the hostilities in the Gulf, the Prime Minister, Mr John Major, stated:

Today, there has been a reported threat to use captured airmen as human shields. Such action would be inhuman, illegal and totally contrary to the third Geneva convention. The convention expressly provides that prisoners of war shall be evacuated as soon as possible after their capture to camps situated far enough from the combat zone for them to be out of danger. It expressly prohibits the sending of a prisoner of war to an area where he may be exposed to fire, or his detention there, and forbids the use of the presence of prisoners of war to render points or areas immune from military operations.

There is no doubt about Iraq's obligations under the Geneva convention. I can assure the House that we have reminded Iraq very forcefully indeed of its obligations under that convention. . . . the Minister of State, Foreign and Commonwealth Office, summoned the Iraqi ambassador once again this morning to register beyond doubt what our views are in this matter. I remind the Iraqis that they are bound to give us the names of any prisoners that they take and to notify the International Red Cross and provide it with access. They are also bound to grant those taken prisoner all their rights under the convention. We shall hold them to that completely.

(HC Debs., vol. 184, col. 27: 21 January 1991)

In the course of a later debate on the same subject, the Secretary of State for Defence, Mr Tom King, stated in reply to a previous speaker:

He is absolute right to say that Iraq is a party to the Geneva convention, and it cannot pick and choose which bits of the convention it applies. We demand without qualification that, just as we shall extend to any Iraqi prisoners of war the rights to which they are entitled under the convention because we are a party to it, those rights must be extended to our prisoners of war.

(Ibid., col. 149: 22 January 1991)

The following statement was issued in Brussels on 22 January 1991 on behalf of the EC and its Twelve Member States:

La Communauté et ses Etats membres expriment leur profonde préoccupation devant l'utilisation sans scrupules des prisonniers de guerre ainsi que l'intention annoncée par l'Irak de les concentrer à proximité des bases et des objectifs militaires. Ils considèrent ces actes comme particulièrement odieux car contraires au respect élémentaire du Droit international et des principes humanitaires. Ils les condamnent sans réserve. Ils demandent aux autorités irakiennes le respect rigoureux de toutes les Conventions de Genève relatives à des faits de guerre et notamment à la Convention du 12 août 1949 relative au traitement des prisonniers de guerre. Cette dernière stipule notamment dans son article 13 que 'les prisonniers de guerre doivent être protégés en tout temps, notamment contre toute acte de violence ou d'intimidation, contre les insultes et la curiosité publique' et dans son article 23 qu' 'aucun prisonnier de guerre ne pourra, à quelque moment que ce soit, être envoyé ou retenu dans une région où il serait exposé au feu de la zone de combat, ni être utilisé pour mettre par sa présence certains points ou certaines régions à l'abri des opérations militaires.'

En application de l'article 125 de cette même Convention, la situation particulière du Comité international de la Croix-Rouge dans ce domaine devrait être en tout temps reconnue et respectée. La Communauté et ses Etats membres saluent l'action de la Croix-Rouge et soutiennent toute démarche visant à renforcer son intervention.

La Communauté et ses Etats membres tiennent les autorités irakiennes responsables, conformément au Droit international—y compris à titre personnel—de toutes actions illégales mettant en péril l'intégrité de la personne et la vie des prisonniers de guerre et qui constituent clairement un crime de guerre.

(Text provided by the FCO)

In the course of a letter, dated 28 January 1991, addressed to the President of the Security Council, the UK Permanent Representative to the UN in New York wrote:

As the Secretary of State for Defence said in the House of Commons on [22] January, we have made the strongest representations again to the International Committee of the Red Cross, the representatives of which have been here seeking access to Iraqis who have been detained to ensure that they are receiving proper treatment. They were naturally granted access and we gave them every opportunity, to which they are entitled, to visit Iraqis to see whether they are receiving proper treatment. We have insisted that similar facilities must be available to representatives of the International Red Cross in Baghdad.

The ICRC team confirmed at the end of their visit that the United Kingdom in the UK was complying with the Geneva Conventions as regards Prisoners of War and civilian detainees.

There was also an ICRC visit to facilities for prisoners of war in Riyadh. They were able to see there the provision made for the sick and wounded, and the arrangements to discharge our obligations under the Geneva Conventions.

(S/22156)

On 29 January 1991, a FCO spokesman made the following statement:

Spokesman said that the Iraqi Ambassador, Dr Azmi Al-Salihi called on Mr Hogg [Minister of State, FCO] at the latter's request. The meeting was very formal and lasted 15 minutes. The Minister expressed the gravest concern at reports that allied POWs had been injured as a result of their having been detained at strategic sites in contravention of the terms of the Geneva Convention.

The Ambassador replied that POWs were being held at scientific and economic rather than strategic installations. Mr Hogg rejected this explanation and said that anything short of full compliance with the Convention was unacceptable. The UK would not overlook such a serious breach and would hold those responsible personally liable.

The Minister pointed out that Britain had observed its obligations under the Geneva Convention scrupulously. He expressed concern at the lack of access to

POWs given by the Iraqi Government to the ICRC and the lack of information about their personal details.

Mr Hogg pressed for access by the ICRC and for an assurance that POWs would be held in camps away from the conflict or other danger areas.

The Minister asked the Ambassador, in view of his imminent departure, to report personally to his Government on the UK's concerns and representations.

(Text provided by the FCO)

On 31 January 1991, the Commander in Chief, US Central Command, and the Commander, British Forces, Middle East, signed at Riyadh, Saudi Arabia, the following instrument:

AN ARRANGEMENT FOR THE TRANSFER OF ENEMY PRISONERS OF WAR AND CIVILIAN INTERNEES FROM THE CUSTODY OF THE BRITISH FORCES TO THE CUSTODY OF THE AMERICAN FORCES

This arrangement establishes procedures for the transfer from the custody of the British Forces to the custody of the Armed Forces of the United States of Enemy Prisoners of War and Civilian Internees taken during the combined effort to liberate Kuwait. The parties undertake as follows:

1. The American Forces and the British Forces will treat all prisoners of war and civilian internees in accordance with the relevant provisions of the Geneva Conventions of 1949.

2. The American Forces shall accept prisoners of war and civilian internees taken by the British Forces, and shall be responsible for maintaining and safeguarding all such individuals whose custody has been transferred to them by the British Forces.

3. The British Forces shall initially process and classify enemy prisoners of war under Articles 4 and 5 of the Geneva Convention Relative to the Treatment of Prisoners of War.

4. The American Forces will be responsible for the accurate accountability of all persons turned over to the American Forces by the British Forces. Such records will be made available for inspection by the British Forces upon request.

5. Any prisoner of war or civilian internee transferred by the British Forces shall be returned upon the request of the British Forces to their control.

6. The British Forces will retain a right of access to prisoners of war and civilian internees transferred from British custody while such persons are in the custody of the American Forces.

7. The release or repatriation of enemy prisoners of war transferred under this arrangement shall be made upon mutual agreement by the military authorities of both parties or when otherwise required under the terms of the 1949 Geneva Conventions.

8. The British Forces will reimburse the United States for the costs involved in maintaining enemy prisoners of war and civilian internees transferred by the British Forces to the custody of the American Forces pursuant to this arrangement.

9. The British Forces shall assign a liaison officer to the American Forces to facilitate the implementation of this arrangement.

10. The British Forces expressly acknowledge and agree that the American Forces may transfer enemy prisoners of war and civilian internees transferred to them by the British Forces to the power of the Kingdom of Saudi Arabia upon such terms and conditions as are required by the 1949 Geneva Conventions.

Done at Riyadh, Saudi Arabia on this 31 of January, 1991.
(Text provided by the FCO)

In the course of a statement on the subject of the hostilities in the Gulf, the Secretary of State for Defence, Mr Tom King, stated:

The House will be aware that we are now starting to hold a number of Iraqi prisoners of war. I reaffirm that they will be held in strict conformity with the requirements of the Geneva convention. That is our absolute commitment and we insist on those requirements being observed by the Government of Iraq as well. The parade of captured aircrew on television is in total breach of the convention—as would be any detention of them at strategic sites. I regret to inform the House that the International Committee of the Red Cross has still not even been informed of the names of any prisoners, let alone been granted the access to which it is entitled. That inhuman treatment of the prisoners is causing great distress and the thoughts of us all are with their families—as is our admiration for their courage and steadfastness at such a difficult time. I confirm that we are making the strongest representations to the Red Cross and the Iraqi authorities for our concerns to be met.

(HC Debs., vol. 184, col. 1108: 31 January 1991)

In reply to a question, the Minister of State, FCO, wrote:

We need no representations to express our disgust at the Iraqi treatment of allied POWs in Iraq. Iraq has been in breach of her obligations under the third Geneva convention. It has paraded and interrogated captured allied airmen before the television cameras, has announced they would be sent to strategic sites, that some had been wounded and that one was now dead. Specifically, Iraq has breached article 13 which says that POWs must at all times be protected against acts of violence or intimidation and against insults and public curiosity, article 17, as regards interrogation, and article 19 as regards evacuation out of danger. Finally, article 23 states that no POW may at any time be sent or detained in areas where he may be exposed to the fire of the combat zone, nor may his presence be used to render certain points immune for military operations. Using the POWs as a human shield as Iraq claims to have done would be seen as a serious breach under the terms of article 23.

We have been in very close touch with the International Committee of the Red Cross. Our mission in Geneva has drawn each successive report to their attention immediately and asked for verification. Specifically on 29 January, we immediately informed it of Iraq media reports on the wounding and possible death of an allied POW and asked that it seek confirmation as rapidly as possible. So far Iraq has refused to give access to the ICRC and has not notified it of the capture of any POWs. Representations have been made to the ICRC by other allied countries and by the presidency on behalf of the EC. We have also asked some governments who may have good contacts with the Iraqis to press them to comply with their obligation. In addition, I have summoned the Iraqi ambassador twice, most recently on 29 January, to whom I made clear Iraq's obligations under the convention. The ambassador in Geneva made representations on humanitarian grounds to his Iraqi counterpart who undertook to pass the demarche to Baghdad. We are exploring what other avenues may be open.

(Ibid., WA, col. *602*: 31 January 1991)

In reply to a question, the Minister of State for the Armed Forces wrote:

Thirty-five Iraqis known or suspected to be military personnel have been detained in this country as prisoners of war under the provisions of the third Geneva convention. All had entered the United Kingdom to study at various colleges.

(HC Debs., vol. 184, WA, col. *637* : 31 January 1991)

In reply to the question whether there were any areas in Iraq sufficiently far from military action to constitute safe areas for prisoners of war under Article 14 of the third Geneva Convention, the same Minister of State wrote:

The targets being attacked by the coalition are sites which could pose a threat to allied forces or facilities supporting Iraq's occupation of Kuwait. Article 23 of the third Geneva convention states that no prisoner of war may at any time be sent to, or detained in areas where he may be exposed to the fire of the combat zone, nor may his presence be used to render certain points or areas immune from military operations. Iraq has not yet provided any information to the International Committee of the Red Cross on the personnel being held or their location, nor permitted the ICRC to satisfy itself that they are being held in accordance with Iraq's obligations.

(Ibid., col. *688*: 1 February 1991)

In a statement made on 4 February 1991 in the UN Commission on Human Rights, the UK observer, Mr H. Steel, remarked:

84. As from the outbreak of hostilities, all Iraqi citizens in the United Kingdom, whether or not they were being held in custody, had become protected persons under the relevant Geneva Conventions: civilians were protected under the Fourth Convention, and the military as prisoners of war under the Third Convention. Two military personnel were among those in custody at that time. The United Kingdom Government had promptly notified the International Committee of the Red Cross (ICRC). The latter had immediately requested access to the detainees and, on the same day as the request had been made, the United Kingdom Government had authorized access and offered ICRC its collaboration. An ICRC team had interviewed individually and in private all the Iraqis held in custody—namely, two prisoners of war and 63 civilians. The United Kingdom authorities had received the ICRC delegation at the beginning and at the end of its mission and had made clear the United Kingdom Government's determination to comply with its obligations under the Third and Fourth Geneva Conventions.
85. On 25 January a further 35 persons of Iraqi nationality had been placed in custody. They had been studying at British universities with the financial support of the Iraqi military attaché's department in London. All had been identified as Iraqi army officers, a fact which they had actually acknowledged. They were therefore being treated as prisoners of war. All prisoners of war had been placed in military custody and were now at a prisoner-of-war camp. ICRC had been promptly informed when the persons concerned had been placed in military custody and at the time of their transfer. Capture cards would be forwarded to the ICRC.

. . .

187. British nationals and nationals of other countries in Iraq were being treated in quite a different way. Iraq had not given the ICRC access to captive allied servicemen.

Iraq had not notified ICRC of their names. No Red Cross capture card had been sent to ICRC. No Red Cross form had been received. As far as was known, Iraq had not established a body equivalent to the British Prisoner of War Information Bureau.

88. If Iraq set any store by its legal obligations and by humanitarian requirements, it must discharge to the letter, without any reservation or condition, all its obligations under the Geneva Conventions.

(E/CN.4/1991/SR. 9, pp. 19–20)

Later on the same day, the UK observer stated:

As to the status of [Iraqi] former students who were treated as prisoners of war in his country, those persons had all admitted to being serving officers of the Iraqi armed forces. Thus, the United Kingdom was justified in treating them as prisoners of war. That status had not been forced upon them, but was theirs in accordance with international law, and the International Committee of the Red Cross recognized it. As such, they were also entitled to the protection guaranteed under international law.

(E/CN.4/1991/SR. 10; see also HC Debs., vol. 186, WA, col. *136*: 19 February 1991)

In reply to a question, the Attorney-General, Sir Patrick Mayhew, stated:

. . . any advice that I give and any advice I receive as a Law Officer is, for good reasons, confidential. Throughout this affair, Britain has committed itself to acting strictly in accordance with international law. In that context, the principles of international law require that account be taken of two factors when planning attacks on military objectives. First, civilian losses, whether of life or property, should be avoided or minimised as far as practicable. Secondly, we should not cause civilian losses that are disproportionate to the military advantage expected from the attack as a whole. The hon. Gentleman will know, because it has been frequently stated by the Prime Minister and others, that British military commanders have been instructed to comply with those principles.

(HC Debs., vol. 185, cols. 14–15: 4 February 1991)

In the course of a letter, dated 13 February 1991, addressed to the President of the Security Council, the UK Permanent Representative to the UN in New York wrote:

The British Government has notified the International Committee of the Red Cross (ICRC) of 10 missing British airmen believed to be POWs in Iraqi hands. As yet, no notification as to their capture and whereabouts have been received by ICRC. As stated in my letter of 21 January, the British Government is complying scrupulously with its obligations under the Geneva Conventions and has given ICRC full and immediate access to Iraqi POWs and civilian detainees both in the United Kingdom and in the Gulf theatre. We look to see Iraq act similarly in keeping with its international humanitarian obligations.

We note statements made by the Iraqi Government as regards the conditions under which ICRC access would be granted to allied POWs. My authorities consider it a breach of Iraq's obligations under the Geneva Conventions that it is attempting to create extraneous linkages rather than simply comply with its legal obligations under the Conventions as the United Kingdom is doing.

(S/22218)

In reply to an oral question, the Minister of State, FCO, Mr Douglas Hogg, stated in part:

I summoned the Iraqi ambassador on 21 January to protest about Iraqi threats to use allied prisoners of war as human shields. I summoned him again on 29 January, following Iraqi news reports that prisoners of war had been wounded and that one perhaps had been killed. I told the ambassador that the Iraqi Government were in breach of their international obligations under articles 19 and 23 of the third Geneva Convention.

(HC Debs., vol. 185, cols. 847–8: 13 February 1991)

In the course of a speech to the UN Security Council on 16 February 1991, the UK Permanent Representative to the UN in New York, Sir David Hannay, made reference to a statement by the Iraqi Revolutionary Command Council. He continued:

I am grateful for the answers he gave to the very serious humanitarian issue I raised about prisoners of war, although I must say that the answers were in most respects inadequate and unsatisfactory. But I note that he stated categorically and without any ambiguity that Iraq applied the Geneva Conventions in respect of prisoners of war. My Government will certainly expect that in future dealings between the International Committee of the Red Cross and the Government of Iraq that undertaking will be validated. If it is not, I am afraid the representative of Iraq will be left looking very foolish indeed. But I express the hope now that it will be validated and not invalidated, and that the Government of Iraq will now fulfil all its obligations, which include the notification of names and giving the International Committee of the Red Cross access to the prisoners, without any further delay and without any attempt to make conditions or to make linkages with other supposed parts of the Geneva Conventions. But I noted that the representative of Iraq did not make such linkages, did not make such conditions, and my Government will now wait to see whether the Government of Iraq does not indeed make such conditions. We will be very glad if that is so.

I am afraid I have to say that I think the explanation given about the presentation of prisoners of war on television by the Iraqi Government was a quite unsatisfactory one and an unconvincing one. There was absolutely no case for showing them on television; that this is permissible is specifically contradicted in the Geneva Conventions. And of course the Geneva Conventions provide for a perfectly good way of ensuring that the next of kin are aware that their relations are prisoners of war, that is to say by communicating their names and details through the International Committee of the Red Cross. So there was no need whatsoever to use television for that purpose, and I find that explanation unconvincing.

(S/PV. 2977, p. 258)

In reply to a question, the Parliamentary Under-Secretary of State, Ministry of Defence, wrote:

It is Allied policy only to attack military targets and facilities which support

Iraq's illegal occupation of Kuwait, and to make every possible effort to minimise civilian casualties. This is entirely in accordance with the rules of war and the Geneva Conventions. The extraordinary measures that Allied air forces have taken to avoid causing civilian casualties demonstrate clearly that Allied military commanders are working strictly within this policy.

(HL Debs., vol. 526, *WA 52*: 27 February 1991)

In reply to a question about the bombing of Iraqi nuclear facilities, the Parliamentary Under-Secretary of State, FCO, wrote:

Due consideration was given to all relevant rules of international law, including those reflected in protocol 1 of 1977 additional to the Geneva conventions, which is not however applicable to the conflict in the Gulf.

(HC Debs., vol. 186, WA, col. *582*: 28 February 1991)

In reply to a question during a debate in the House of Lords on the subject of Middle East peace and security, the Government spokesman, Lord Reay, stated:

The noble Lord asked if the bombing of civilians was not contrary to the Geneva Convention. The answer to that is no. We attacked targets accepted as legitimate in international law. Iraq's stationing of military targets in civilian areas was contrary to the rules of war.

(HL Debs., vol. 526, col. 1485: 6 March 1991)

In reply to an oral question, the Secretary of State for the Home Department, Mr Kenneth Baker, stated in part:

I am satisfied that the action taken against Iraqi nationals is in accordance with domestic law and our international obligations. The International Committee of the Red Cross has visited all Iraqis detained and has stated that they are being treated in accordance with the Geneva conventions.

(HC Debs., vol. 187, col. 446: 7 March 1991)

In reply to an oral question, the Minister of State, FCO, the Earl of Caithness, observed:

. . . we do not believe that prisoners of war should be used as bargaining chips. We have a unilateral obligation under the third Geneva Convention to repatriate Iraqi prisoners of war without delay.

(HL Debs., vol. 527, col. 517: 19 March 1991)

In reply to a question, the Minister of State, FCO, wrote in part:

The provisions of the fourth Geneva convention, such as article 15 which provides for the setting up of neutralised zones in regions where fighting is taking place, are applicable only to international conflicts. During non-international armed conflict, article 3 of the fourth Geneva convention sets out the minimum humanitarian standards which are to be applied.

(HC Debs., vol. 189, WA, col. *412*: 23 April 1991)

In the course of a letter, dated 23 April 1991, addressed to the President of the UN Security Council, the UK Permanent Representative to the UN in New York, Sir David Hannay, wrote:

The number of prisoners of war taken by British Forces during the ground campaign was some 8,000. All were treated in accordance with the United Kingdom's obligations under the Geneva conventions.

(S/22522)

In reply to the question

Whether the forced internal deportations from their homes and land in 1988 to 1990 of Iraqi Kurds, constitute a breach of the Fourth Geneva Convention, especially Articles 45, 49 and 147,

the Minister of State, FCO, wrote:

The Fourth Geneva Convention covers the case of those who find themselves in the hands of a party to a conflict or occupying power of which they are not nationals. The treatment of Iraqi Kurds by their own government contravenes international humanitarian obligations accepted by the Government of Iraq.

(HL Debs., vol. 528, *WA 11*: 25 April 1991)

In reply to the question

What steps [is Her Majesty's Government] seeking, in conjunction with the International Committee of the Red Cross and other signatories of the four International Conventions of 1949, to which Iraq is a party, to activate these conventions in respect of the Kurds and Shias, including the fourth convention concerning the protection of civilians in conflicts not of an international nature, thus involving the international community in the intended creation of neutral and safety zones,

the Minister of State, FCO, wrote in part:

The provisions of the Fourth Geneva Convention, such as Article 15, which provides for the setting up of neutralised zones in regions where fighting is taking place, are applicable only to international conflicts. During non-international armed conflict, Article 3 of the Fourth Geneva Convention sets out the minimum humanitarian standards which are to be applied.

(Ibid., *WA 12*)

In reply to the question

Whether the Kurdish National Front is eligible to become a party, as distinct from a High Contracting Party, to the 1949 Red Cross international conventions to which Iraq is a party; and whether it has sought to do so,

the Minister of State, FCO, wrote:

The Geneva Conventions of 12th August 1949 do not provide for any status other than that of High Contracting Party. They do however, in Article 3 common to all four conventions, lay down certain minimum provisions which must be complied with in the case of an armed conflict not of an international character occurring in the territory of a High Contracting Party. This provision applies to the present situation in Iraq.

(HL Debs., vol. 528, WA *61*: 13 May 1991)

In reply to the question

Whether Article 3 of the Fourth Geneva Convention relative to the protection of civilian persons in time of war applies specifically to armed conflict not of an international character; whether it requires each party to the conflict to be bound to apply minimum humanitarian standards; whether it provides for the International Committee of the Red Cross to offer its services to the parties; and whether it requires the parties to endeavour to bring into force by special agreement all or part of the other provisions of the present convention, including those which are not mandatory such as the creation of safety zones and localities,

the Minister of State, FCO, wrote:

Article 3, common to all four of the Geneva Conventions, lays down certain minimum standards which each party to a non-international armed conflict occurring in the territory of a High Contracting Party was bound to apply. In addition, it allows the ICRC to offer its services to the parties to the conflict and encourages the parties to the conflict to endeavour to bring into force, by means of special agreements, all or part of the other provisions of the convention in question.

(Ibid.)

The UK Permanent Representative to the UN in New York, Sir David Hannay, addressed the following letter, dated 31 May 1991, to the President of the UN Security Council:

The Security Council is soon to conduct its first review of the provisions of Security Council resolution 687 on imports by Iraq. The resolution requires it to do so in the light of the policies and practices of the Government of Iraq. In advance of this review I am writing on instructions from my Government to inform you of our deep concern over Iraq's treatment of two British nationals, Mr. Douglas Brand and Mr. Ian Richter, both held in Iraq.

Mr. Douglas Brand has recently been sentenced to life imprisonment for espionage. He was detained in September while trying to flee Iraq, where he was being held as a hostage under Iraq's illegal human shield policy. The British Government was not informed of his detention nor given consular access to him until April this year. His trial before an Iraqi revolutionary court was wholly inadequate.

Iraq is in clear contravention of Security Council resolutions 664, 674 and 686, which were reaffirmed by Security Council resolution 687, in respect of Mr. Brand. These resolutions call for the release of third country nationals detained after 2 August 1990. Iraq is also in flagrant violation of its obligations under international law in its treatment of Mr. Brand.

Mr. Ian Ritcher was sentenced in 1987 to life imprisonment on corruption charges which he has always denied. The British Government has protested many times about the inadequate nature of his trial, which did not meet the requirements of Iraq's international obligations, including those under the International Covenant on Civil and Political Rights and the Vienna Convention on Consular Relations. We believe that he should also be set free.

(S/22664)

On 27 November 1991, a spokesman for the FCO referred with regret to the indefinite postponement of the 26th International Conference of the Red Cross and Red Crescent, which was to have taken place in Budapest. He concluded:

I should like to take this opportunity to reassert the United Kingdom's support for the ICRC and the Red Cross Movement as a whole and express our appreciation of their unwavering dedication to the principles of international humanitarian law as enshrined in the Geneva Conventions.

(Text provided by the FCO)

Part Fourteen: I. B. 7. *Use of force—international war and armed conflict—the laws of war and armed conflict—belligerent occupation*

(See also Part Three: II. A. 1. (c). (item of 15 November 1991), Part Four: VII. (item of 27 February 1991), and Part Fourteen: I. B. 6. (materials concerning Iraq's occupation of Kuwait), above)

In the course of a debate on the subject of Israel, the Minister of State, FCO, Mr Douglas Hogg, stated:

Our attitude towards Israeli policy in the occupied territories is wholly plain. I have taken the opportunity to stress our policy both to the Israeli ambassador and Deputy Foreign Minister and they know well that we regard the Israelis' occupation of the territories as unlawful and believe that they should withdraw.

(HC Debs., vol. 183, cols. 842–3: 16 January 1991)

In reply to questions, the Minister of State, FCO, wrote in part:

[UN Security Council Resolution] 672 requires a continuing commitment by the Israeli government to apply the provisions of the Fourth Geneva convention in its administration of the occupied territories. We continue to press for this.

(HC Debs., vol. 184, WA, col. *523*: 30 January 1991; see also HL Debs., vol. 527, *WA 9*: 14 March 1991)

We regularly take up with the Israelis incidents in which we believe that their security forces have acted in breach of the fourth Geneva convention.

(HC Debs., vol. 185, WA, col. *1*: 4 February 1991)

Speaking in the UN Commission on Human Rights on 27 February 1991, the representative of Luxembourg, on behalf of the EC and its Member States, observed:

With regard to the human rights situation in the Territories occupied by Israel since 1967, the Community and its Member States were able to express their attitude in their statement on item 4 of our agenda, entitled 'Question of the violation of human rights in the occupied Arab territories, including Palestine'. The Twelve deplore Israel's attacks on the fundamental freedoms and rights of the populations of the Occupied Territories. Accordingly, the European Community and its Member States urgently call upon Israel to act in accordance with its obligations under Article 49 of the Fourth Geneva Convention. The Twelve are concerned at the fact that the situation in the Arab territories occupied by Israel has deteriorated considerably. The Twelve believe that violence breeds violence and they condemn its use by anyone at all.

(Text provided by the FCO; see also E/CN.4/1991/SR.43, p. 13)

In reply to a question, the Parliamentary Under-Secretary of State, FCO, wrote:

Israel is obliged under the fourth Geneva convention to provide the same degree of protection for the inhabitants of the occupied territories as she does for her own citizens. It follows that the Israeli Government have the right to deploy Patriot missile launchers in Israel and in the occupied territories.

(HC Debs., vol. 186, WA, col. *583*: 28 February 1991)

In reply to a question on the subject of Mr Taher Shriteh, journalist of Gaza, alleged to have been imprisoned by the Israeli authorities, the Minister of State, FCO, wrote:

According to our information Mr. Shriteh was arrested on 28th January and released on bail on 7th March. He has made allegations of ill-treatment which we have taken up with the Israelis. We regularly remind the Israelis of their duty to administer the Occupied Territories in accordance with the provisions of the Fourth Geneva Convention.

(HL Debs., vol. 527, *WA 1*: 11 March 1991)

In the course of a debate on the subject of the Middle East, the Parliamentary Under-Secretary of State, FCO, Mr Mark Lennox-Boyd, stated:

We welcome unreservedly the liberalisation of Soviet emigration controls, including the freedom of Soviet Jews to go to Israel. But Jewish settlements in the occupied territories, including east Jerusalem, are illegal. Allowing Soviet Jews to settle there would set back further the search for peace.

(HC Debs., vol. 188, col. 1101: 28 March 1991; see also ibid., vol. 189, WA, cols. *186–7*: 17 April 1991)

In the course of a debate on the subject of the living conditions of Palestinians in the West Bank and Gaza, the Minister of State, FCO, the Earl of Caithness, stated:

We have long been working for a just and lasting settlement of the Arab/Israel dispute, based on UN Security Council Resolution 242 which calls for Israel to withdraw from territories occupied during the 1967 war, and recognition of the right of all states in the region, including Israel, to a secure existence. . . .

Until a settlement is reached, Israel should administer the territories in accordance with international law and human rights obligations. Civilians in occupied territory are protected by the Fourth Geneva Convention which prohibits forcible deportation, detention without trial, destruction of property and denial of access to food, health and education. I am happy to confirm . . . that we have made that clear to the Israeli Government. We have also made clear that we are concerned by the failure of the Israelis to live up to their obligations under the convention. We regularly raise human rights issues both with the Israeli Government and with the Israeli ambassador in London.

The noble Lord . . . has drawn particular attention to Israeli settlement policy. I take this opportunity to reiterate our firm conviction that the settlement by the occupying power of its own civilians in occupied territory is illegal under the Fourth Geneva Convention. It creates further obstacles to peace. We estimate that over 200,000 settlers are now living in approximately 200 settlements in the occupied territories. Jewish settlers now make up about 13 per cent. of the total population of the occupied territories. About one-half of the West Bank and one-third of the Gaza Strip have been allocated to Israeli use. Most of the settlers live in the West Bank but 3,000 live in Gaza and 120,000 in Jewish settlements in East Jerusalem. A further 12,000 live in settlements on the Golan. The continuing expansion of these settlements is a cause of deep and continuing concern to us . . .

We have regularly stated our opposition to the Israeli settlement policy. While we welcome the liberalisation of Soviet emigration controls and the new freedom of Soviet Jews to go to Israel, all Jewish settlements in the occupied territories, including East Jerusalem, are illegal. We therefore agree with the noble Lord . . . that to allow Soviet Jews to settle there will further set back and search for peace.

(HL Debs., vol. 527, cols. 1506–7: 17 April 1991)

Later in his speech the Minister remarked:

. . . the Israelis are obliged to administer the occupied territories in accordance with provisions of the Fourth Geneva Convention. We deplore their continuing failure to do so. We are particularly concerned by their continuing use of deportations and collective punishments, such as the sealing and demolition of Palestinian homes. We deplore the continuing closure of four of the six Palestinian universities in the occupied territories.

(Ibid., col. 1508)

In reply to the question

Whether [Her Majesty's Government] will prosecute under Article 146 of the Fourth Geneva Convention all Israelis within their jurisdiction suspected of having deported Palestinians from the Occupied Territories and Gaza, and ask all signatories of the convention to do likewise,

the Minister of State, FCO, wrote:

We have consistently opposed deportations from the Occupied Territories as being inconsistent with Israel's obligations under the Fourth Geneva Convention. But we do not believe that the action proposed would influence Israeli policies in the Occupied Territories—including the deportation policy—or that it would advance the search for peace.

(HL Debs., vol. 528, *WA 11*: 25 April 1991)

The Twelve Member States of the EC issued the following statement on 3 May 1991:

The Community and its member States are gravely concerned at the recent establishment of two new Israeli settlements in the Occupied Territories, at Revava on 15 and 16 April and at Talmon Keva on 22 April.

They deplore the fact that the Israeli government has given permission for these new settlements.

The Community and its member States reaffirm their long-standing position that Jewish settlements in the territories occupied by Israel since 1967, including East Jerusalem, are illegal under international law and under the 4th Geneva Convention in particular.

The Community and its member States consider that the initiative of the American Secretary of State, Mr Baker, now offers genuine prospects of progress towards peace in the region. They fully support this initiative and the process envisaged, which should enable the necessary dialogue between the parties concerned to get underway. They also consider that any establishment of new settlements in the Occupied Territories, which is in any case illegal, is especially harmful at a time when all parties should show flexibility and realism so as to bring about a climate of confidence favourable to the starting of negotiations.

The Community and its member States strongly urge the Israeli government neither to allow nor encourage the establishment of settlements in the Occupied Territories.

(Text provided by the FCO)

A joint communiqué, issued on 11 May 1991 by the Joint Council established under the Co-operation Agreement between the European Community and the countries parties to the Charter of the Co-operation Council for the Arab States of the Gulf, GCC, contained the following passage:

The Ministers of the EC and of the GCC remain deeply concerned about the deteriorating situation in the Occupied Territories, including East Jerusalem. In particular, they referred to the need for the occupying power to comply with its obligations under the 4th Geneva Convention and abide by the relevant principles of international law. They deplored the Israeli policy of settlement in the Occupied Territories and stressed that they regarded all such settlements as illegal under international law. They also considered that any further Israeli settlement in the Occupied Territories would be especially prejudicial at a time when all parties should be adopting a flexible and realistic approach so as to bring about a climate of confidence favourable to the launching of negotiations.

(Reproduced in *Parliamentary Papers*, 1990–91, HC, Paper 143–II, p. 293)

In reply to questions, the Minister of State, FCO, wrote in part:

The Israeli Government is in no doubt about our attitude to recent settlement activity in the Occupied Territories: this is illegal and particularly damaging to prospects for peace at a time when we are working to begin a negotiating process . . . The best way of preventing the establishment of new illegal settlements is by securing an Israeli withdrawal from territories occupied in 1967 as part of a settlement of the Arab/Israel dispute. We are continuing to work hard for this.

We deplore the deportation on 18th May of four Gazans, as we have deplored earlier deportations from the Occupied Territories. It is a clear breach of the Fourth Geneva Convention. It does not help efforts to promote peace talks. We urge Israel to desist from further deportations and ensure the safe return of those already deported.

(HL Debs., vol. 529, *WA 22*: 23 May 1991; see also HC Debs., vol. 201, col. 256: 18 December 1991)

In the Presidency Conclusions of the European Council on 29 June 1991, representing also the views of the UK Government, the following paragraph appeared in Annex II dealing with the peace process in the Middle East:

The European Council once again underlines the need for all parties to adopt reciprocal and balanced measures to establish a climate of confidence to get the negotiations going, and to avoid all measures that might hinder the process. It believes specifically that the policy of establishing settlements in the territories occupied by Israel, which is in any case illegal, is incompatible with the will expressed to make progress with the peace process.

(Text provided by the FCO)

In the course of a debate in the House of Lords on the subject of Israel's non-compliance with Security Council Resolutions 242 and 338, the Government Minister, Lord Cavendish of Furness, stated:

. . . we and our European partners are firmly opposed to Israel's settlement activity. As the European Council made clear in its declaration in Luxembourg on 29th June, we believe that a policy of establishing settlements in the Occupied Territories is not only illegal, . . . but incompatible with Israel's expressed desire to make progress in the peace process.

(HL Debs., vol. 531, col. 932: 25 July 1991)

Lord Cavendish later observed in the same debate:

The Israelis' continued failure to administer the Occupied Territories according to international law and human rights standards is well known to us all. We have never hesitated to make clear our rejection of Israel's policies of repression in the occupied Territories and our worries about deteriorating conditions there.

We take the view that the Fourth Geneva Convention applies to the Occupied Territories, and we regularly remind the Israelis of their obligation to abide by it.

(Ibid., col. 933)

The following statement was issued by the FCO on 7 August 1991:

We are deeply concerned by reports that yet another Israeli settlement has been opened in the Occupied Territories. This is illegal and provocative. It runs directly counter to the calls made by heads of government of the Group of 7 at the London Summit and by foreign ministers of the European Community at their meeting on 29 July for settlement activity to be suspended. Those responsible for continuing this activity can be in no doubt of the damage they are causing to prospects for peace in the region.

(Text provided by the FCO)

In its written observations, presented in October 1991, on the Third Report of the HC Foreign Affairs Committee concerning the Middle East after the Gulf War, Her Majesty's Government stated:

The Government . . . condemn continuing Israeli settlement activity, which is illegal under Article 49 of the Fourth Geneva Convention. We have made our views clear to Israel. The recent establishment of a further new settlement at Eshkolot is illegal and provocative.

(Cm. 1682, p. 5)

Speaking in the UN Special Political Committee on 21 November 1991, the representative of the Netherlands, on behalf of the EC and its Twelve Member States, stated:

The Community and its Member States wish to reiterate their position that the Fourth Geneva Convention of 1949 relating to the protection of civilians in time of war is fully applicable to the territories occupied by Israel since 1967, including East Jerusalem. The Security Council has repeatedly confirmed the applicability of the Fourth Geneva Convention, most recently in its resolutions 672, 681 and 694. Following a request of the Security Council in res. 681, the Secretary-General has put forward some ideas and ways to enhance the protection of Palestinians in the occupied territories, which the Twelve in general support.

The Twelve call upon Israel to recognize the applicability of the Fourth Geneva Convention to the occupied territories and to abide by its provisions.

The European Community and its Member States have repeatedly stated that the settlement policy is illegal, being a clear violation of the provisions of the Fourth Geneva Convention, and is an obstacle to peace. The Twelve also believe that the establishment of new settlements, or the enlargement of existing ones, in the Occupied Territories threatens to change their demographic structure. Hence the Twelve once again call on Israel to halt its settlement activity in the Occupied Territories. . . . Finally, the Twelve wish to restate that the United Nations Charter rules out the acquisition of territory by force which in relation to the Arab-Israeli conflict was recalled by Security Council resolution 242, one of the basic tenets for the peace process.

The Twelve reaffirm the right of the freedom of movement in accordance with the provisions of the International Covenant on Civil and Political Rights. In this regard, they support the right of Jews, who wish to do so, to emigrate. However, they reiterate their view that this right must not be implemented at the expense of the right of the Palestinians in the Occupied Territories.

The Twelve consider null and void, any unilateral decisions taken by Israel to modify the status of Jerusalem and to impose its law, jurisdiction and administration on the occupied Syrian Golan. They reaffirm the particular importance of Jerusalem, holy city of three religions, and state that the freedom for everyone to have access to places of worship must be safeguarded in any future agreement on Jerusalem. The Twelve have noted in this respect the positive decision of last June by the Israeli authorities to terminate the taxation of the religious communities.

. . .

Although abstention from violence on both sides would be an important step to confidence-building between Israelis and Palestinians, we think that more is needed. The repeal by the Israeli Government of its policies in the field of security as well as in the economic and fiscal fields would be significant in this connection. Measures of collective punishment such as economic sanctions, demolition and sealing-up of houses, curfews and restrictions of freedom are still applied. The Twelve regret this. Furthermore, arbitrary arrests, detention without charge or trial and house arrests inflicted upon the Palestinian civilian population are unacceptable under the rules of the 4th Geneva Convention.

. . .

Furthermore, the holding of Palestinian detainees on Israeli territory cannot be accepted in the light of Article 76 of the Fourth Geneva Convention. This also applies to the special permit introduced by the Israeli civil administration in March this year and requested from each visitor wishing to cross the green line. The Twelve also deplore the continued application of high taxes and fiscal sanctions in the occupied territories.

(Text provided by the FCO; see also A/SPC/46/SR.26, pp. 5–6)

Speaking in the same Committee on 21 November 1991 on the subject of Palestine, the Netherlands' representative, on behalf of the EC and its Twelve Member States, observed:

The acquisition of land by force is not acceptable under international law and creates new political and humanitarian problems.

. . .

As long as a peaceful settlement has not yet been reached and the territories continue to be occupied, the Fourth Geneva Convention of 12 August 1949 applies to the occupied territories. Since one of the main objectives of the Fourth Geneva Convention is the protection of civilians under occupation, the Twelve remain of the opinion that measures to provide for the safety and protection of Palestinian civilians living under Israeli occupation could be considered. The Twelve call on Israel to recognize the applicability of the Fourth Geneva Convention to the occupied territories and to abide by its provisions. The lack of security and the unstable educational conditions will affect more than one generation of Palestinians and jeopardize the social and economic future of the Palestinian population. In this respect the Twelve welcome the decision of the Israeli Government to reopen educational institutions in the occupied territories and hope that the University of Bir Zeit will also be included in this positive gesture. They urge the Israeli government to cooperate with the United Nations by allowing the civilian population in the occupied territories to take full advantage of economic and social support provided by the UN and other organizations.

The establishment of settlements in the occupied territories including East Jerusalem is illegal and contrary to the provisions of the Fourth Geneva Convention. The settlement policy in particular affects the demographic structure of the occupied territories. It is clearly an obstacle to the ongoing international peace efforts.

The Twelve are aware of the particular importance of Jerusalem as a holy city for three religions. The freedom of everyone to have access to the places of worship must be safeguarded. We consider the status of Jerusalem a fundamental issue that can not be prejudged by any unilateral decision.

(Text provided by the FCO; see also A/SPC/46/SR.26, p. 5)

The following passages are extracted from a press release dated 29 November 1991 issued on behalf of the EC and its Twelve Member States to mark the International Day of Solidarity with the Palestinian People:

The European Community and its Member States, convinced that the peace conference offers real prospects for peace in the region, are prepared to continue—as a participant in the conference—to make a full contribution notably to the multilateral negotiations. They urge all parties concerned to show the flexibility needed to make the negotiations a success and to refrain from actions that could jeopardize the process. In this respect they emphasize that the establishment of new settlements and the extension of existing ones in the occupied territories, including East Jerusalem, is illegal and incompatible with the stated will to make progress with the peace process.

Furthermore and apart from a settlement of the Palestinian question through the exercise of the Palestinian people's right to self-determination, endeavours for lasting peace and stability in the region should at the same time involve the end of the state of belligerence amoung all states in the region, the commitment not to resort to force and to the peaceful settlement of disputes, and respect for the right of all the states of the region, including Israel, to exist within safe, recognized and guaranteed borders.

The European Community and its Member States remain seriously concerned about the situation in the occupied territories which adversely affects the living conditions of the Palestinian people and hampers the economic and social development of the occupied territories. The breach of human rights obligations by the Israeli authorities in the occupied territories has led the European Community and its Member States to repeatedly state their concern. They call once more upon Israel to meet fully its obligations under the Fourth Geneva Convention relative to the Protection of Civilian Persons in Time of War and to cooperate with the United Nations.

(Text provided by the FCO)

Part Fourteen: I. B. 9. *Use of force—international war and armed conflict—the laws of war and armed conflict—nuclear, bacteriological and chemical weapons*

(See also Part Fourteen: I. B. 6. (FCO statements of January 1991), above)

In the course of a debate on the subject of the Gulf conflict, the Prime Minister, Mr John Major, stated:

Chemical weapons, already used by Saddam Hussein against his own people, have been deployed. Contrary to international agreements, Iraq has produced and threatened to use both chemical and biological weapons, the use of which would be wholly contrary to international agreements.

(HC Debs., vol. 183, col. 735: 15 January 1991)

In reply to a question, the Minister of State, FCO, wrote in part:

Each non-nuclear-weapon State Party to the Non Proliferation Treaty undertakes to conclude a safeguards agreement with the International Atomic Energy Authority in accordance with Article III of the Non Proliferation Treaty, to enter into force not later than 18 months after the Non Proliferation Treaty enters into force for the state concerned. This obligation is unqualified.

(HL Debs., vol. 525, *WA 64*: 7 February 1991)

In reply to a question, the Parliamentary Under-Secretary of State, Ministry of Defence, wrote:

The UK Government, in common with the US Government, have made it clear that they regard CS gas, and other such gases, as outside the scope of the 1925 Geneva Protocol. They are not chemical weapons, and any use of chemical weapons, allegedly in response, would be wholly unjustified. We have always made it clear that we would take a very grave view of any Iraqi use of chemical weapons.

(HL Debs., vol. 526, *WA 45*: 26 February 1991)

In the course of a debate on the subject of the Gulf conflict, the Minister of State, FCO, Mr Douglas Hogg, stated:

We have always recognised that Saddam Hussein possesses chemical weapons and judging from his track record, he may well use them. To do so would be a breach of the 1925 convention. It would be a gross crime, and it would be contrary to morality and the interests of Iraq.

(HC Debs., vol. 186, col. 576: 22 February 1991)

In reply to a question, the Attorney-General, Sir Patrick Mayhew, stated in part:

There is no convention or instrument of international law bearing on the use of napalm.

(HC Debs., vol. 186, col. 640: 25 February 1991)

In reply to a question, the Minister of State, FCO, wrote:

Peace and security in the Middle East depend primarily on the establishment of security arrangements worked out by the states of the region and underpinned by mutual economic co-operation. Other countries could have a role in underpinning these arrangements. We stand ready to play our part if asked. We have made clear that our ground forces will not be stationed permanently in the region. US deployments are a matter for the US authorities to decide.

(HL Debs., vol. 527, *WA 80*: 15 April 1991)

In the course of an oral reply, the Prime Minister, Mr John Major, stated:

Iraq has now admitted to having a secret uranium enrichment programme. That is a clear violation of the nuclear safeguards agreement and of Iraq's non-proliferation treaty obligations.

(HC Debs., vol. 194, col. 775: 9 July 1991)

In reply to a question on the subject of the South Pacific Nuclear Free Zone Treaty of 1986, the Government Minister in the House of Lords wrote:

Australia, the Cook Islands, Fiji, Kiribati, Nauru, New Zealand, Niue, Papua New Guinea, Solomon Islands, Tuvalu and Western Samoa have signed and ratified the treaty. It is open to South Pacific forum members only, although it also has three protocols: the first for states with territories in the region; the second and third for nuclear weapons states. We decided not to become party to the protocols in 1987, when a full statement of our policy was made in another place [HC Debs., vol. 112, WA, col. *639*: 20 March 1991]. That remains our position.

(HL Debs., vol. 531, *WA 47*: 23 July 1991; see also UKMIL 1987, p. 635)

At a press conference given by the FCO on 9 September 1991, the following statement was issued:

Spokesman said that on 5 September the Governments of Argentina, Chile and Brazil had signed a tri-partite declaration, the 'Mendoza commitment', renouncing the development, production, acquisition and use of chemical and biological weapons.

The very real threat of the large-scale use of chemical and biological weapons had been demonstrated during the Gulf War. The United Kingdom Government believed that the most effective long-term answer to preventing the proliferation of chemical and biological weapons would be the early conclusion of a multi-lateral Chemical Weapons Convention, currently under negotiation at the Conference on Disarmament (CD) in Geneva and agreement, at the Third Review Conference of the 1972 Biological Weapons Convention which started today in Geneva, on measures to strengthen the effectiveness of the Convention.

We welcomed the joint declaration by the Governments of Argentina, Chile and Brazil which reaffirmed their continuing commitment to work towards the early conclusion of the Chemical Weapons Convention and to contribute to achieving a successful outcome to the Third Review Conference of the Biological Weapons Convention.

(Text provided by the FCO)

The UK representative to the Biological Weapons Convention Review Conference made the following statement on 27 September 1991:

I should like to make an announcement on instructions from my Government.

When the British Government acceded to the 1925 Geneva Protocol they made a reservation which inter alia maintained our right to retaliate in kind if biological weapons were used against the United Kingdom.

In the 1950s we abandoned offensive research in biological weapons. Since then our research has been entirely defence orientated. On acceding to the Biological Weapons Convention the United Kingdom gave legislative effect to its provisions by the Biological Weapons Act of 1974.

HMG has now decided to withdraw that part of its reservation to the Protocol for the Prohibition of the Use in War of Asphyxiating, Poisonous or other Gases and of Bacteriological Methods of Warfare signed at Geneva in 1925 which maintained our right to retaliate in kind if biological weapons were used against the United Kingdom.

This decision reflects the continued determination of the British Government to exclude completely the possibility of the use of biological agents and toxins as weapons. It also demonstrates HMG's commitment to the two key international instruments for this purpose, the 1925 Geneva Protocol and the Biological Weapons Convention.

My Government has chosen to instruct me to make the announcement of this withdrawal in this Review Conference. This choice underlines our commitment to the Convention and the importance we attach to the work of the Review Conference to ensure its effective implementation.

(Text provided by the FCO)

In reply to a question, the Minister of State, FCO, wrote:

I am pleased to say that on 27 September the ambassador of the United Kingdom delegation to the conference on disarmament in Geneva announced at the third review conference of the biological and toxin weapons convention that Her Majesty's Government had decided to withdraw that part of our reservation to the 1925 Geneva protocol which maintained our right to retaliate in kind if biological weapons were used against us. The protocol prohibits the use in war of asphyxiating, poisonous or other gases, and of bacteriological methods of warfare.

(HC Debs., vol. 196, WA col. *156*: 16 October 1991)

In reply to a question, the Minister of State, FCO, wrote in part:

North Korea acceded to the [Non-Proliferation Treaty] in 1985. Her subsequent failure to sign a safeguards agreement, as she is obliged to do, with the IAEA is a clear breach of the NPT and has been the subject of international criticism. We expect North Korea to abide by her international commitments and take every appropriate opportunity to remind her of our concern.

(HL Debs., vol. 532, *WA 59*: 19 November 1991)

Part Fourteen: I. B. 11. *Use of force—international war and armed conflict—the laws of war and armed conflict—termination of hostilities*

In reply to the question

How a decision to conclude the present Gulf war will be taken and by whom in the event that Iraqi forces are removed from Kuwait,

the Government Minister in the House of Lords wrote:

[Security Council Resolution] 678 authorises UN member states co-operating with the Government of Kuwait to use all necessary means to uphold and implement its Resolution 660 and all subsequent relevant resolutions and to restore international peace and security in the region. Hostilities will cease when their contribution to achieving these objectives has been completed.

Any modification of the UN sanctions currently on Iraq would be a matter for the Security Council.

(HL Debs., vol. 525, *WA 31*: 30 January 1991)

Part Fourteen: III. *Use of force—self-defence*

(See also Part Fourteen: I. B. 7. (item of 28 February 1991), above, and Part Fourteen: IV. A. (item of 6 February 1991), below)

In the course of a debate in the House of Lords on the subject of the hostilities in the Gulf, the Lord Privy Seal, Lord Waddington, referred to Scud missile attacks by Iraq on Israel. He continued:

Since the first of the Scud attacks we have of course been in consultation with the Israeli Government along with the Americans. We can well understand the sense of outrage which must have been felt in Israel, and the Israelis would have been perfectly entitled to respond, exercising their right of self-defence. We welcome the restraint they have shown. As the House knows, it has been possible to send to Israel additional Patriot missiles to meet the threat within its own borders while allied operations have continued to eliminate the Scud sites.

(HL Debs., vol. 525, col. 11: 21 January 1991)

In reply to an oral question, the Minister of State for Defence Procurement, Mr Alan Clark, stated in part:

The basis of Britain's role in defence sales is the right to self-defence as enshrined in article 51 of the United Nations Charter . . .

(HC Debs., vol. 186, col. 140: 19 February 1991)

In reply to the oral question

. . . is it not the case that every country is entitled to the right of self defence and that that is enshrined in the United Nations Charter and ought to be preserved,

the Minister of State, FCO, the Earl of Caithness, stated:

. . . my noble friend is absolutely right. I agree with him.

(HL Debs., vol. 527, col. 391: 18 March 1991)

Speaking on 2 April 1991 in the UN Human Rights Committee considering the third periodic report of the UK, the UK representative, Mr Beamish, stated:

17. The United Kingdom rejected most firmly any suggestion that the use of force by the allied coalition in the Persian Gulf conflict had been excessive. The allied side had endeavoured to keep civilian casualties to a minimum and to stay strictly within the confines of the laws and customs of war. The United Kingdom's forces had been deployed alongside those of other members of the international coalition in response to an appeal made by countries of the region for assistance in the defence of their territory following Iraq's invasion of Kuwait. Such assistance had been rendered in accordance with the Charter of the United Nations.

(CCPR/C/SR.1047, p. 5)

Part Fourteen: IV. A. *Use of force—use of force under collective measures—regime of the UN*

The UK Mission to the UN in New York addressed the following letter, dated 9 January 1991, to the Chairman of the Security Council Committee established by Security Council Resolution 661:

You will recall that at the last meeting of the Sanctions Committee it was decided to postpone discussion of the Iraqi ship 'Ibn Khaldoun' until the Committee next met, pending further information on the vessel's cargo.

I would like to inform you that on the morning of 26 December 1990, naval units from the Royal Navy, the United States Navy and the Royal Australian Navy intercepted the 'Ibn Khaldoun' in the North Arabian Sea after it had failed to respond to repeated requests to stop in order that its cargo could be verified and inspected in accordance with UN SCRs 661 and 665.

A multinational boarding party, including Royal Navy and Royal Marines personnel, subsequently discovered cargo including 600 tons of sugar, 200 tons of powdered milk, and a quantity of other foodstuffs. Under the terms of UN SCRs 661 and 666 the delivery of foodstuffs to Iraq and Kuwait is prohibited unless the

Security Council or the Sanctions Committee determines that humanitarian circumstances warrant an exception. Neither has done so. The vessel's cargo had not therefore been authorised by the Committee.

The interception and subsequent boarding themselves were conducted in accordance with UN SCR 665, paragraph 1 of which calls on Member States deploying maritime forces to the region to use such measures as may be necessary to halt all inward and outward maritime shipping in order to inspect and verify their cargoes and to ensure strict implementation of the provisions related to such shipping laid down in UN SCR 661.

I should add that the whole operation was conducted with a minimum use of force, on the part of the intercepting ship and the multinational boarding party. There were attempts by some of the passengers and crew to obstruct the inspection and one of the inspecting team was assaulted. I understand that a US doctor conducted a medical examination of the passengers and crew, and discovered no cases of injury resulting from the interception which required medical treatment.

It was made clear to the Master of the 'Ibn Khaldoun' that the prohibited cargo found on board his ship would have to be off-loaded before the vessel could proceed either to Iraq or Kuwait. The Royal Navy vessels involved in the interception have now deployed elsewhere in the Gulf.

(Text provided by the FCO)

The following letter, dated 17 January 1991, was sent to the President of the Security Council by the UK Permanent Representative to the UN in New York:

I have the honour to inform you on behalf of my Government that the Armed Forces of the United Kingdom in association with those of other States co-operating with the Government of Kuwait commenced action on the evening of 16 January 1991 pursuant to operative paragraph 2 of resolution 678.

Military action initiated by the United States, United Kingdom, Saudi Arabia, Kuwait and France on 16 and 17 January is designed to achieve the liberation of Kuwait called for in the resolutions, and not the destruction, occupation or dismemberment of Iraq. The United Kingdom hopes these actions will be concluded as soon as possible consistent with the full implementation of resolution 660 and all subsequent relevant resolutions and with the restoration of international peace and security in the area.

(S/22097)

A further letter, dated 21 January 1991, read as follows:

Further to my letter of 17 January (S/22097) and in accordance with paragraph 4 of resolution 678 (1990), I have the honour to inform you on behalf of my Government that the armed forces of the United Kingdom in association with those of other States co-operating with the Government of Kuwait have continued their military action pursuant to operative paragraph 2 of resolution 678 (1990).

The United Kingdom's objectives are as before to bring about Iraq's full and unconditional withdrawal from Kuwait and the restoration of the legitimate Government of Kuwait, and re-establish international peace and security in the area, and to uphold the authority of the United Nations.

Operations by United Kingdom forces have involved aerial attacks on Iraqi installations supporting Iraq's capacity to sustain its illegal occupation of Kuwait. The instructions issued to our pilots are to avoid causing civilian casualties so far as possible. British commanders have also been briefed on the locations and significance of sites of religious and cultural importance in Iraq, and operations will take account of this.

(S/22115)

The Prime Minister, Mr John Major, made a statement at the start of hostilities against Iraq. He stated in part:

Aircraft of the multinational force began attacks on military targets in Iraq from around midnight Greenwich mean time. Several hundred aircraft were involved in the action, including a substantial number of RAF aircraft. The action was taken under the authority of United Nations Security Council resolution 678 which authorises use of all necessary means, including force, after 15 January to bring about Iraq's withdrawal from Kuwait.

(HC Debs., vol. 183, col. 979: 17 January 1991)

He later observed:

There is no need to reconvene the United Nations Security Council. The resolutions and the authority are clear. The United Nations is not directly involved in the conflict; its member states are, but under the authority of the United Nations.

(Ibid., col. 987)

The Prime Minister was asked the following questions:

(1) what would be the effects of an official declaration of war on the maintenance of an Iraqi diplomatic capability in the United Kingdom;

(2) whether the United Kingdom is at war with Iraq;

(3) what representations he has received concerning parliamentary consideration of the declaration of war.

In reply, the Prime Minister wrote:

The United Kingdom is not in a state of war with Iraq. British forces are engaged, together with the armed forces of Kuwait and other coalition partners, in hostilities against Iraq under the authority of the United Nations Security Council. The rules of international law applying in cases of armed conflict apply to these hostilities, notably the Geneva protocol of 1925 and the four Geneva conventions of 1949. We will observe our obligations under those treaties scrupulously and expect the Government of Iraq to do the same.

(Ibid., vol. 184, WA col. *375*: 28 January 1991)

In reply to a question, the Minister of State, FCO, wrote:

British forces are engaged under the express authority of the Security Council in resolution 678. The action has the support and approval of the Government of Kuwait, whose forces are also in action alongside those of their allies.

(Ibid., cols. *522–3*: 30 January 1991)

In the course of evidence given on 30 January 1991 by Mr P. Fairweather, Deputy Under-Secretary of State, FCO, to the HC Foreign

Affairs Committee investigating events in the Gulf, the following passage appeared:

> . . . it is a United Nations' operation in the sense that it takes place under the authority of the Security Council but it is a rather special kind of United Nations' operation in the sense that it is not a blue beret type of operation with the United Nations' command.
>
> You will recall, Chairman, the operative paragraph 2 of Resolution 678 says 'authorises Member States co-operating with the Government of Kuwait . . . ': that is the phrase. It is a slightly special United Nations' operation.
>
> [Question:] Under Article 52 presumably?
>
> Under Chapter 7.

(*Parliamentary Papers*, 1990–91, HC, Paper 143–iii, p. 94)

During a debate in the House of Lords on the subject of collective security, the Minister of State, FCO, the Earl of Caithness, stated:

> The preamble of the UN Charter begins by noting the determination of the people of the United Nations: 'to save succeeding generations from the scourge of war'. The question of how to do this is the specific subject of the 13 articles of Chapter VII. They therefore form a cornerstone of the Charter as a whole.
>
> As the Motion states, Chapter VII deals with: 'action with respect to threats to the peace, breaches of the peace, and acts of aggression'. Together with Chapter VI, dealing with the 'Pacific Settlement of Disputes', it sets out the special powers accorded to the Security Council so that the council may exercise the: 'primary responsibility for the maintenance of international peace and security' conferred on it by the members of the United Nations under Article 24 of the Charter.
>
> The provisions of Chapter VII reflect the concerns of the drafters of the Charter, at the San Francisco conference in 1945, to set up a system for the maintenance of international peace and security which would be more effective than that of the League of Nations. The League's provisions in this area had shown themselves to be inadequate. Under the League's covenant, each member state had been allowed to reserve the right to determine for itself whether the hostile actions of another state amounted to a breach of the covenant, and whether or not to comply with the League's recommendations—for they were no more than that—on how to respond. The events of the 1930s had demonstrated all too clearly the fatal shortcomings of such a system.
>
> With the drafting of Chapter VII of the UN Charter, these shortcomings were tackled by explicitly concentrating the power to take decisive action on the Security Council. The council was given the power to determine the existence of any threat to the peace, breach of the peace or act of aggression and what should be done about it. Moreover, under Article 25 of the Charter, all members of the United Nations are bound to accept and carry out the council's decisions. Under Article 103, obligations arising under the Charter prevail over a member's obligations under other international agreements.
>
> Action may only be taken by the Security Council under Chapter VII where there is a threat to the peace, a breach of the peace or an act of aggression. All decisions of the Security Council on non-procedural matters require the concurring votes of the five permanent members. It is chiefly for this reason that the coun-

cil has so rarely determined that such a situation exists. Through the long decades of the cold war, occasions when the five permanent members—in particular the United States and the Soviet Union—took a common view were rare. Before the present crisis in the Gulf erupted on 2nd August last year, the council had only done so explicitly in six cases: Palestine in 1948, Korea in 1950 (in the absence of the Soviet Union), Southern Rhodesia in the late 1960s and 1970s; South Africa in 1977; the Falklands in 1982; and the Iran/Iraq war in 1987.

Where a threat to the peace, a breach of the peace or an act of aggression exists, the Security Council has the choice of either making recommendations for action or deciding on mandatory measures. These mandatory measures can be ordered under Article 41, which covers measures not involving the use of armed force, such as complete or partial interruption of economic, transport and communication links, and the breaking of diplomatic relations. The economic sanctions against Rhodesia and the arms embargo against South Africa are examples of this.

If non-forcible measures are insufficient, Article 42 provides for the Security Council to take such action by air, sea or land forces as may be necessary to maintain or restore international peace and security. However, the five permanent members have never been able to agree which forces should be put at the council's disposal and what they should do. Articles 43 to 45, relating to agreements between member states and the Security Council for the provision of forces and other assistance, have never been implemented.

Perhaps it may be opportune to pause and consider a quotation from the then Sir Gladwyn Jebb, now the noble Lord, Lord Gladwyn, one of the founding fathers of the Charter, which he made in the Security Council on 7th July 1950 in connection with the Korean war. He said: 'Had the Charter come fully into force and had the agreement provided for in Article 43 of the Charter been concluded, we should, of course, have proceeded differently, and the action to be taken by the Security Council would no doubt have been founded on Article 42. As it is, however, the Council can naturally act only under Article 39, which enables the Security Council to recommend what measures should be taken to restore international peace and security'.

Subsequent articles of Chapter VII also remain unfulfilled. Articles 46 and 47 deal with the Military Staff Committee, consisting of the chiefs of staff of the permanent five members or their representatives, and tasked according to Article 47 with: 'advising and assisting the Security Council on all questions relating to the Security Council's military requirements for the maintenance of international peace and security, the employment and command of forces placed at its disposal, the regulation of armaments, and possible disarmament'.

The Military Staff Committee was duly established in 1945, and has continued to this day to meet roughly twice a month. However, in the absence of any forces placed at the council's disposal on the basis of the special agreements referred to in these articles, it has never exercised the responsibilities originally envisaged for it.

. . .

Articles 48 and 49 concern implementation of Security Council decisions by the members of the United Nations. Article 50 deals with the question of assistance to states which find themselves confronted with special economic problems arising from the carrying out of measures taken by the Security Council. This article was invoked by various front line states when sanctions were placed on Rhodesia. Finally, Article 51, the chapter's concluding article, records the important principle that the inherent right of individual or collective self-defence remains unimpaired by the other provisions of the Charter, until the Security Council has taken measures necessary to maintain international peace and security.

I turn now to the present. The application of Chapter VII during the Gulf crisis has shown that it has sufficient versatility to cope with circumstances that might not have been directly anticipated by its drafters in 1945.

The present crisis in the Gulf represents the seventh occasion when the Security Council has made an explicit formal determination that there exists a breach of international peace and security under Article 39 of the Charter. It was undoubtedly right to do so. A more unequivocal breach of the Charter than Saddam Hussein's aggression against Kuwait is hard to imagine. It is also the third occasion when the Council has proceeded to call for mandatory measures under Chapter VII, imposing comprehensive economic sanctions on Iraq and occupied Kuwait under Security Council Resolution 661. These were subsequently reinforced by maritime enforcement measures under Resolution 665 and an air embargo under Resolution 670. Resolution 665 also provided for the use of mechanisms of the Military Staff Committee. On five occasions in the second half of 1990 ad hoc meetings of the Military Staff Committee provided a forum for the exchange of information on the measures taken by maritime forces to enforce the embargo.

Other articles of Chapter VII have also been invoked as part of the council's response to the Iraqi invasion. Resolution 669 led to the establishment of a special working group of the council's Sanctions Committee, to consider requests for economic assistance under Article 50, from states suffering economic disruption as a result of applying sanctions. The working group dealt with applications from 19 countries in the last quarter of the year.

Article 51 of Chapter VII was invoked in Resolution 661, affirming the inherent right of individual or collective self-defence in response to Iraq's armed attack on Kuwait. This inherent right provided a firm legal basis for the government of Kuwait, Saudi Arabia and other Gulf states to request the assistance of the armed forces of other states following the Iraqi invasion.

The comprehensive economic sanctions imposed by Resolution 661 represent only one form of the mandatory measures under Chapter VII called for by the council in response to the Gulf crisis. Since 15th January the member states co-operating with Kuwait have been authorised to use all necessary means to that end in the face of persistent Iraqi intransigence. They have resorted to military force in order to see the council's resolutions implemented and upheld.

The council has not invoked Article 42 explicitly and the command and control arrangements of the forces continue to be handled by host nations and contributing countries for reasons of military efficacy. Nevertheless . . . it is because of Resolution 678 that the forces are operating just as much on the basis of UN authority as if they were under UN command.

(HL Debs., vol. 525, cols. 1192–5: 6 February 1991)

In the course of a debate on the subject of hostilities in the Gulf, the Parliamentary Under-Secretary of State, FCO, Mr Mark Lennox-Boyd, stated:

Our objectives and the objectives of the alliance, and our actions in the hostilities, are all conducted under the authority of United Nations Security Council resolutions. Hon. Members who have waxed strong and indignant have failed to recognise the import and meaning of resolution 678, which authorises the use of all necessary means to seek the objectives of resolution 660.

(HC Debs., vol. 185, col. 830: 12 February 1991)

In a speech in the UN Security Council on 25 February 1991, the UK Permanent Representative to the UN in New York, Sir David Hannay, made reference to a preceding speech by the representative of Iraq. He continued:

I note that he mentions only [Security Council] resolution 660 (1990), as if that resolution were somehow different in nature from all the other resolutions that the Council has adopted on the dispute between Iraq and Kuwait. But, frankly, that is not so. Those resolutions are a single corpus of international law adopted under Chapter VII of the Charter of the United Nations, and they are a single whole. They cannot be taken to pieces and dealt with one by one as a process of negotiation. If anybody in this room doubts it, I would recommend that he turn to resolution 678 (1990), which is the basis on which the current action by my country and others cooperating with the Government of Kuwait is being taken, and there he will see that it is stated quite categorically that the Council is determined to secure full compliance with its decisions, all of which are referred to above, that it demands that Iraq comply with resolution 660 (1990) and all subsequent relevant resolutions, and that it authorizes the Member States cooperating with the Government of Kuwait to use all necessary means to implement Security Council resolution 660 (1990) and all subsequent resolutions.

So this division between resolution 660 (1990) and the other resolutions does not exist in the jurisprudence of the Council and is not a basis for the taking of decisions by it.

(S/PV. 2977, p. 377)

In a memorandum dated 29 April 1991 submitted by the FCO to the HC Foreign Affairs Committee considering events in the Gulf, it was stated:

At the end of November 1990 the United Nations Security Council gave Iraq a clear message to consider its position. If by 15 January 1991 Iraq had not complied with all United Nations Resolutions concerning its illegal invasion of Kuwait, Security Council Resolution 678 authorized the use of all necessary means to uphold the resolutions and to restore international peace to the area.

(*Parliamentary Papers*, 1990–91, HC, Paper 143–xi, p. 226)

Part Fourteen: IV. B. *Use of force—use of force under collective measures—outside the UN*

In reply to the question

Whether [Her Majesty's Government] will confirm that the North Atlantic Treaty would not allow an Iraqi response to air attacks launched from Turkey by United States aircraft to be interpreted as an attack on a member state,

the Government Minister in the House of Lords wrote:

Article 5 of the North Atlantic Treaty states that, 'The parties agree that an armed attack against one or more of them in Europe or North America shall be considered an attack against them all'. This is not qualified by any reference to the circumstances of such an attack.

(HL Debs., vol. 526, *WA 34*: 21 February 1991)

Part Fifteen: I. *Neutrality, non-belligerency—legal nature of neutrality*

In the course of a debate on the subject of the future of the Western Sahara, the Minister of State, FCO, Mr Douglas Hogg, stated:

We have been neutral throughout this dispute.

(HC Debs., vol. 200, col. 1174: 12 December 1991)

APPENDICES

I. Multilateral Agreements Signed by the United Kingdom in 1991[1]

Title	*Place and Date*	*UK Signature*	*Text*[2]
European Convention on Mutual Assistance in Criminal Matters	Strasbourg, 20.4.1959	21.6.1991	TS No. 24 (1992) (Cm 1928)
Additional Protocol to the European Convention on Mutual Assistance in Criminal Matters of 20.4.1959	Strasbourg, 17.3.1978	21.6.1991	Misc. No. 13 (1991) (Cm 1577)
Convention against Torture and Other Cruel, Inhuman or Degrading Treatment or Punishment	New York, 4.2.1985	7.1.1989 (entry into force)	TS No. 107 (1991) (Cm 1775)
Amendments to the Convention on the International Regulations for Prevention of Collisions at Sea, 1972	London, 19.11.1987	19.11.1989 (entry into force)	
Unidroit Convention on International Factoring	Ottawa, 28.5.1988	31.12.1990	Misc. No. 5 (1991) (Cm. 1487)
Amendment of the Convention relating to International Exhibitions signed at Paris on 22.11.1928, amended and supplemented by the Protocols of 1948, 1966 and 1972 and by the Amendment of 24.6.1982	Paris, 31.5.1988	26.10.1988	
Amendments to the International Convention for the Safety of Life at Sea, 1974 (October Ro-Ro Amendments)	London, 28.10.1988	29.4.1990 (entry into force)	

[1] Information supplied by the Foreign and Commonwealth Office. The table includes some agreements signed by the United Kingdom before 1991, where information was not previously available. The information is correct as at January 1992, although in some cases information available since that time has been included.

[2] Publication is in various series of UK Command Papers, namely: DTI = Department of Trade and Industry; EC = European Communities Series; Misc. = Miscellaneous Series; TS = Treaty Series; Cm = Command Paper number.

Title	*Place and Date*	*UK Signature*	*Text*
Decision concerning Amendments to the Agreement for Co-operation in dealing with Pollution of the North Sea by Oil and other Harmful Substances, 1983	Bonn, 22.9.1989	13.7.1990 (approval)	
1989 Amendments to the Annex of the Protocol of 1978 relating to the International Convention for the Prevention of Pollution from Ships, 1973	London, 17.10.1989	18.2.1991 (entry into force)	
Protocol of Decisions amending the Convention concerning International Carriage by Rail (COTIF) signed at Berne, 9.5.1980	Berne, 14.12.1989		Misc. No. 20 (1991) (Cm 1690)
General Regulations of the Universal Postal Union	Washington, 14.12.1989	14.12.1989	DTI
Universal Postal Convention	Washington, 14.12.1989	14.12.1989	DTI (Cm 1369)
Cash on Delivery Agreement	Washington, 14.12.1989	14.12.1989	DTI
Giro Agreement	Washington, 14.12.1989	14.12.1989	DTI (Cm 1373)
Postal Parcels Agreement	Washington, 14.12.1989	14.12.1989	DTI (Cm 1371)
Fourth Additional Protocol to the Constitution of the Universal Postal Union	Washington, 14.12.1989	14.12.1989	DTI (Cm 1374)
International Agreement on Jute and Jute Products, 1989	Geneva, 3.11.1989/New York 1.1.1990	20.12.1991	Misc. No. 7 (1991) (Cm 1494)
1990 Amendments to the Annex of the Protocol of 1978 relating to the International Convention for the Prevention of Pollution from Ships, 1973	London, 16.3.1990		
Amendments to the Commonwealth Telecommunications Organization Financial Agreement, 1983	Nicosia, 3.5.1990	1.4.1990 (entry into force)	TS No. 29 (1991) (Cm 1533)
1990 Amendments to the International Code for the Construction and Equipment of Ships Carrying Dangerous Chemicals in Bulk (IBC Code)	London, 24.5.1990		

Title	*Place and Date*	*UK Signature*	*Text*
1990 Amendments to the International Code for the Construction and Equipment of Ships Carrying Liquefied Gases in Bulk (IGC Code)	London, 24.5.1990		
Amendments to the International Convention for the Safety of Life at Sea, 1974	London, 25.5.1990	1.2.1992 (entry into force)	
Protocol of Decisions amending the Convention concerning International Carriage by Rail (COTIF) signed at Berne, 9.5.1980	Berne, 28.5.1990	Misc. No. 21 (1991) (Cm 1689)	
Convention on Temporary Admission, with Annexes	Instanbul/ Brussels, 26.6.1990	28.6.1990	Misc. No. 18 (1991) (Cm 1669)
Adjustments to the Montreal Protocol on Substances that Deplete the Ozone Layer, done at Montreal, 16.9.1987	London, 27.6.1990	7.3.1991 (entry into force)	TS No. 32 (1991) (Cm 1545)
Amendment to the Montreal Protocol on Substances that Deplete the Ozone Layer, done at Montreal, 16.9.1987	London, 29.6.1990		Misc. No. 12 (1991) (Cm 1567)
Convention on the Elimination of Double Taxation in Connection with the Adjustments of Profits of Associated Enterprises, with Final Act	Brussels, 23.7.1990	23.7.1990	EC No. 27 (1991) (Cm 1524)
Resolution to further extend the International Coffee Agreement, 1983 (Resolution No. 352 of the International Coffee Council)	London, 28.9.1990		Misc. No. 11 (1991) (Cm 1566)
Convention between the Member States of the European Communities on the Simplification of Procedures for the Recovery of Maintenance Payments	Rome, 6.11.1990	6.11.1990	EC No. 37 (1991) (Cm 1604)
1990 Amendments to the Annex of the Protocol of 1978 relating to the International Convention for the Prevention of Pollution from Ships, 1973	London, 16.11.1990		
Treaty on Conventional Armed Forces in Europe, and Declarations	Paris, 19.11.1990	19.11.1990	Misc. No. 4 (1991) (Cm 1477)

Title	*Place and Date*	*UK Signature*	*Text*
Protocol of Decisions to amend the Convention concerning International Carriage by Rail (COTIF) done at Berne, 9.5.1980	Berne, 20.12.1990	20.12.1990	
Amended Appendix I to the Convention on the Conservation of European Wildlife and Natural Habitats done at Berne, 19.9.1979	Berne, 11.1.1991	11.1.1991 (acceptance)	TS No. 106 (1991) (Cm 1774)
Proposed Amendments to the European Agreement concerning the Work of Crews of Vehicles Engaged in International Road Transport (AETR), done at Geneva on 1.7.1970	New York, 1.2.1991		Misc. No. 22 (1991) (Cm. 1776)
Amendment to Article 26 of the Statute of the Council of Europe	Madrid, 21.2.1991	21.2.1991 (entry into force)	
Convention on Environmental Impact Assessment in a Transboundary Context	Espo, 25.2.1991	26.2.1991	Misc. No. 15 (1991) (Cm. 1645)
Convention on the Marking of Plastic Explosives for the Purpose of Detection	Montreal, 1.3.1991	1.3.1991	Misc. No. 9 (1991) (Cm 1558)
Resolution on Amendments to the Convention for the Establishment of a European Organization for the Exploitation of Meteorological Satellites ('EUMTSAT') done at Geneva on 24.5.1983	Geneva, 4/5.6.1991		Misc. No. 16 (1991) (Cm 1665)
1991 Amendments to the Annex to the Protocol relating to Intervention on the High Seas in Cases of Marine Pollution by Substances other than Oil, 1973	London, 4.7.1991		
1991 Amendments to Annexes I and II to the International Convention for Safe Containers (CSC), 1972	London, 25.9.1991		
Protocol amending the European Social Charter	Turin, 21.10.1991	21.10.1991	
Agreement on a Comprehensive Political Settlement of the Cambodia Conflict: Agreement concerning the Sovereignty, Independence, Territorial Integrity and Inviolability, Neutrality and National Unity of Cambodia, with a	Paris, 23.10.1991	23.10.1991	TS No. 111 (1991) (Cm 1786)

Title	*Place and Date*	*UK Signature*	*Text*
Declaration on the Rehabilitation and Reconstruction of Cambodia and the Final Act of the Paris Conference on Cambodia			
Amendment to Article 26 of the Statute of the Council of Europe	Strasbourg, 26.11.1991	26.11.1991 (entry into force)	
Agreement on the Conservation of Bats in Europe	London, 4.12.1991	4.12.1991	

II. Bilateral Agreements Signed by the United Kingdom in 1991[1]

Country and Title	*Place and Date*	*Text*[2]
ARGENTINA		
Agreement concerning Mutual Judicial Assistance against Illicit Drug Trafficking	Buenos Aires, 27.8.1991	
BAHRAIN		
Agreement for the Promotion and Protection of Investments	Manama, 30.10.1991	TS No. 21 (1992) (Cm 1841)
BARBADOS		
Agreement concerning Mutual Assistance in relation to Drug Trafficking	Bridgetown, 19.4.1991	
BELGIUM		
Agreement relating to the Delimitation of the Continental Shelf between the two Countries, with Exchange of Letters	Brussels, 29.5.1991	Belgium No. 1 (1991) (Cm 1735)
BOLIVIA		
Exchange of Notes concerning Certain Commercial Debts (The UK/Bolivia Debt Agreement No. 3 (1990))	La Paz, 19.3.1991	TS No. 12 (1992) (Cm 1817)
BULGARIA		
Agreement on the Establishment and Activities of Cultural Centres	London, 18.2.1991	TS No. 64 (1991) (Cm 1654)
Agreement on Co-operation in the Fields of Education, Science and Culture	London, 18.2.1991	TS No. 63 (1991) (Cm 1653)
CAMEROON		
Exchange of Notes concerning Certain Commercial Debts (The UK/Cameroon Debt Agreement (1989))	Yaoundé, 5/29.11.1990	TS No. 29 (1992) (Cm 1933)

[1] Information supplied by the Foreign and Commonwealth Office. The table includes some agreements signed by the United Kingdom before 1991, where information was not previously available. The information is correct as at January 1991, although in some cases information available since that time has been included.

[2] Publication is in various series of UK Command Papers, including Treaty Series (TS). Cm. = Command Paper number.

Country and Title	*Place and Date*	*Text*
Exchange of Notes concerning the Extension of the UK/Cameroon Investment Promotion and Protection Agreement, signed at Yaoundé on 4.6.1982, to the Channel Islands and the Isle of Man	Yaoundé, 7.12.1990/ 17.1.1991	TS No. 43 (1991) (Cm 1619), p.3
CANADA		
Exchange of Letters concerning the Training of British Armed Forces in Canada	London, 4.9.1991	TS No. 109 (1991) (Cm 1783)
CENTRAL AFRICAN REPUBLIC		
Exchange of Notes concerning Certain Commercial Debts (The UK/Central African Republic Debt Agreement No. 4 (1988))	Yaoundé/Bangui, 10.4.1990/28.6.1991	TS No. 102 (1991) (Cm 1738)
COSTA RICA		
Exchange of Notes concerning Certain Commercial Debts (The UK/Costa Rica Debt Rescheduling Agreement (1989))	San José, 5.7.1991	
Exchange of Notes concerning Certain Commercial Debts (The UK/Costa Rica Debt Agreement No. 4 (1991))	San José, 12.11.1991	TS No. 11 (1992) (Cm 1814)
COTE D'IVOIRE		
Exchange of Notes constituting the UK/ Côte d'Ivoire Debt Rescheduling Agreement 1989	Abidjan, 18.2.1991	
CZECHOSLOVAKIA		
Agreement on the Establishment and Activities of Cultural Centres	London, 12.12.1991	TS No. 31 (1992) (Cm 1938)
DENMARK		
Protocol amending the Convention for the Avoidance of Double Taxation and the Prevention of Fiscal Evasion with respect to Taxes on Income and Capital Gains signed at Copenhagen on 11.11.1980	London, 1.7.1991	TS No. 33 (1992) (Cm 1951)
Exchange of Notes amending the Protocol to the Double Taxation Convention signed in London on 1.7.1991	Copenhagen, 4.11.1991	
EGYPT		
Exchange of Notes amending the UK/ Egypt Loan (No. 1) 1982 (The UK/Egypt Retrospective Terms Agreement (1991))	London, 25.7.1991	TS No. 108 (1991) (Cm 1781)
FINLAND		
Exchange of Notes abrogating Articles 5, 7, 9 and 21 of the Treaty of Commerce and Navigation signed at Helsinki on 14.12.1923	Helsinki, 15.9.1989	TS No. 38 (1990) (Cm 1074)

Country and Title	*Place and Date*	*Text*
Protocol to amend the Convention for the Avoidance of Double Taxation and the Prevention of Fiscal Evasion with respect to Taxes on Income and Capital signed at London on 17.7.1969, as amended by the Protocols signed at London on 17.5.1973, 16.11.1979 and 1.10.1985	London, 26.9.1991	TS No. 25 (1992) (Cm 1929)
FRANCE		
Exchange of Notes concerning Article 3, paragraph 3, of the Treaty concerning the Construction and Operation by Private Concessionaires of a Channel Fixed Link	Paris, 11.10.1990/ 9.11.1990	TS No. 25 (1991) (Cm 1495)
Agreement relating to the Completion of the Delimitation of the Continental Shelf in the Southern North Sea	London, 23.7.1991	
Protocol concerning Frontier Controls and Policing, Co-operation in Criminal Justice, Public Safety and Mutual Assistance relating to the Channel Fixed Link	Sangatte, 25.11.1991	France No. 1 (1992) (Cm 1802)
GABON		
Exchange of Notes concerning Certain Commercial Debts (The UK/Gabon Debt Agreement No. 3 (1989))	Libreville, 13.11.1990/ 12.3.1991	TS No. 76 (1991) (Cm 1740)
GERMANY		
Exchange of Notes concerning contracts between British Nuclear Fuels plc and the Deutsche Gesellschaft für Wiederaufbauarbeitung von Kernbrennstoffen for the Reprocessing by British Nuclear Fuels plc of certain quantities of Irradiated Nuclear Fuel Elements	Bonn, 21.3.1991	TS No. 59 (1991) (Cm 1639)
GUINEA		
Exchange of Notes concerning Certain Commercial Debts (The UK/Guinea Debt Agreement No. 3 (1989))	Dakar/Conakry, 25/27.2.1991	TS No. 74 (1991) (Cm 1677)
GUYANA		
Agreement concerning Co-operation in the Investigation of Drug Trafficking Offences, the Forfeiture of Instruments used for or in connection with such Offences and the Deprivation of Drug Traffickers of Financial Benefits from their Criminal Activities	Georgetown, 17.7.1991	
HONDURAS		
Exchange of Notes concerning Certain Commercial Debts (The UK/Honduras Debt Rescheduling Agreement (1991))	Tegucigalpa, 1.7.1991	

Country and Title	*Place and Date*	*Text*
HUNGARY		
Agreement concerning the Establishment of the International Peto Institute in Budapest	Budapest, 12.2.1991	TS No. 35 (1991) (Cm 1548)
Exchange of Notes amending the Agreement concerning the Establishment of the International Peto Institute in Budapest signed at Budapest on 12.2.1991	Budapest, 22/25.3.1991	TS No. 89 (1991) (Cm 1755)
ICELAND		
Convention for the Avoidance of Double Taxation and Fiscal Evasion with respect to Taxes on Income and Capital Gains	Reykjavik, 30.9.1991	TS No. 19 (1992) (Cm 1836)
JORDAN		
Exchange of Notes further amending the UK/Jordan Loan 1982 done at Amman on 14.3.1982	Amman, 4/11.12.1990	TS No. 92 (1990) (Cm 1596), p. 12
Exchange of Notes amending the UK/Jordan Loan Agreement 1987 done at Amman on 6.1.1988	Amman, 19.2.1991/12.3.1991	TS No. 50 (1991) (Cm 1816), p. 18
Exchange of Notes concerning Certain Commercial Debts (The UK/Jordan Debt Agreement No. 1 (1989))	Amman, 29.8.1991	TS No. 105 (1991) (Cm 1777)
MADAGASCAR		
Exchange of Notes concerning Certain Commercial Debts (The UK/Madagascar Debt Agreement No. 6 (1988))	Antananarivo, 25.10.1990	TS No. 46 (1991) (Cm 1616)
Exchange of Notes concerning Certain Commercial Debts (The UK/Madagascar Debt Agreement No. 7 (1990))	Antananarivo, 11.3.1991	TS No. 104 (1991) (Cm 1768)
MEXICO		
Exchange of Notes concerning Certain Commercial Debts (The UK/Mexico Debt Agreement No. 3 (1989))	Mexico City, 22.3.1991	TS No. 51 (1991) (Cm 1626)
MISCELLANEOUS		
Headquarters Agreement between the Government of the UK and the European Bank for Reconstruction and Development	London, 15.4.1991	TS No. 45 (1991) (Cm 1615)
MONGOLIA		
Agreement concerning the Development of Economic, Industrial, Scientific and Technical Co-operation	London, 20.6.1991	TS No. 82 (1991) (Cm 1749)
Agreement for the Promotion and Protection of Investments	Ulan Bator, 4.10.1991	TS No. 22 (1992) (Cm 1840)
MOROCCO		
Exchange of Notes concerning Certain Commercial Debts (The UK/Morocco Debt Agreement No. 5 (1990))	Rabat, 25/28.3.1991	TS No. 60 (1991) (Cm 1643)

Country and Title	*Place and Date*	*Text*
MOZAMBIQUE		
Exchange of Notes concerning an Interest Free Loan (UK/Mozambique Programme Loan (1977))	Maputo, 1/28.5.1990	TS No. 43 (1991) (Cm 1619), p. 12
Exchange of Notes concerning Certain Commercial Debts (The UK/Mozambique Debt Agreement No. 3 (1990))	Maputo, 25/29.3.1991	TS No. 78 (1991) (Cm 1745)
NETHERLANDS		
Exchange of Notes concerning the Implementation of the Treaty for the Mutual Surrender of Fugitive Criminals signed at London on 26.9.1898, with respect to Hong Kong	The Hague, 20.8/13.9.1991	TS No. 6 (1992) (Cm 1801)
NEW ZEALAND		
Exchange of Notes amending the Agreement concerning Air Services signed at London on 4.10.1982	Wellington, 12.2.1991	TS No. 87 (1991) (Cm 1754)
NIGERIA		
Exchange of Notes concerning Certain Commercial Debts (The UK/Nigeria Debt Agreement No. 3 (1991))	Lagos, 10.6.1991	TS No. 86 (1991) (Cm 1753)
NORWAY		
Exchange of Notes concerning the Export from the UK to the Kingdom of Norway of 36 Irradiated Fuel Pins	Oslo, 10.6.1991	
PAPUA NEW GUINEA		
Convention for the Avoidance of Double Taxation and the Prevention of Fiscal Evasion with respect to Taxes	London, 17.9.1991	TS No. 18 (1992) (Cm 1835)
PHILIPPINES		
Exchange of Notes concerning Certain Commercial Debts (The UK/Philippines Debt Agreement No. 4 (1991))	London, 13.11.1991	TS No. 23 (1992) (Cm 1925)
POLAND		
Exchange of Notes concerning Certain Commercial Debts (The UK/Poland Debt Agreement No. 5 (1990))	Warsaw, 4.10.1991	TS No. 30 (1992) (Cm 1939)
ROMANIA		
Agreement on the Establishment and Activities of Cultural Centres	Bucharest, 22.2.1991	
SIERRA LEONE		
Exchange of Notes concerning Certain Commercial Debts (The UK/Sierra Leone Debt Agreement No. 4 (1986))	Freetown, 22.5.1987/6.3.1991	TS No. 69 (1991) (Cm 1671)

Country and Title	*Place and Date*	*Text*
SOVIET UNION		
Exchange of Notes concerning the Residences of the Ambassadors of the two Countries	London, 22.11.1991	TS No. 27 (1992) (Cm 1930)
SPAIN		
Exchange of Notes concerning the Extension to Certain Dependent Territories of the Extradition Treaty signed at London on 22.7.1985	Madrid, 1.2.1991	
Exchange of Notes constituting an Agreement to extend the Extradition Treaty of 22.7.1985 to Gibraltar	Madrid, 1.2.1991	TS No. 101 (1991) (Cm 1739)
Convention on Social Security, with Protocol on Health Care and Supplementary Protocol concerning Medical Treatment for Residents of Jersey and Spain	Madrid, 5.2.1991	Spain No. 1 (1991) (Cm 1618)
Exchange of Notes concerning the Extension to Gibraltar of the Agreement concerning the Prevention and Suppression of Drug Trafficking and the Misuse of Drugs signed at Madrid on 26.6.1989	Madrid, 3.4.1991	
SWEDEN		
Exchange of Notes concerning the Termination of Sweden's Commission as Protecting Power for the UK in the Islamic Republic of Iran	London, 25.1.1991/ 4.2.1991	TS No. 33 (1991) (Cm 1544)
TANZANIA		
Exchange of Notes concerning Certain Commercial Debts	Dar es Salaam, 4.3.1991	TS No. 61 (1991) (Cm 1649)
TURKEY		
Agreement for the Promotion and Protection of Investments	London, 15.3.1991	
UNITED STATES OF AMERICA		
Exchange of Notes further extending the Narcotics Co-operation Agreement with respect to the British Virgin Islands which entered into force on 12.8.1987	Washington, 9.5.1990	
Exchange of Notes further extending the Narcotics Co-operation Agreement with respect to the British Virgin Islands which entered into force on 12.8.1987	Washington, 9.8.1990	
Exchange of Notes further extending the Narcotics Co-operation Agreement with respect to Montserrat signed at London on 14.5.1987	Washington, 29.11.1990	TS No. 43 (1991) (Cm 1619), p. 18

Country and Title	Place and Date	Text
Exchange of Notes further extending the Narcotics Co-operation Agreement with respect to Montserrat signed at London on 14.5.1987	Washington, 26.2.1991	TS No. 50 (1991) (Cm 1816), p. 28
Exchange of Notes extending the Treaty concerning the Cayman Islands relating to Mutual Assistance in Criminal Matters, signed at Grand Cayman on 3.7.1986, to Montserrat	Washington, 26.4.1991	TS No. 50 (1991) (Cm 1816), p. 28
URUGUAY		
Agreement for the Promotion and Protection of Investments	London, 21.10.1991	
ZAMBIA		
Exchange of Notes concerning Certain Commercial Debts (The UK/Zambia Debt Agreement No. 4 (1990))	Lusaka, 5.3/20.5.1991	TS No. 34 (1992) (Cm 1952)

III. United Kingdom Legislation during 1991 Concerning Matters of International Law[1]

The Arms Control and Disarmament (Inspections) Act (1991 c. 41) makes provision for the carrying out in the United Kingdom of inspections under the Protocol on Inspection incorporated in the Treaty on Conventional Armed Forces in Europe of 19 November 1990. It creates rights of entry for the purpose of conducting challenge inspections pursuant to the Protocol, and confers privileges and immunities on inspectors and transport crew members. (See Parts One: II. D. 1. and Five: VIII. A., above.)

The Civil Jurisdiction and Judgments Act (1991 c. 12) gives effect to the Convention on Jurisdiction and Enforcement of Judgments in Civil and Commercial Matters, and the Protocols annexed thereto, opened for signature at Lugano on 16 September 1988.

The Foreign Corporations Act (1991 c. 44) enables foreign corporations incorporated under the laws of territories which the United Kingdom does not recognize as States to be treated for the purposes of United Kingdom law as having legal personality, and validates acts which would have been valid when done if the Act had then been in force. (See Part Three: I. B. 5., above.)

The Namibia Act (1991 c. 4) makes provision in connection with the admission of Namibia as a member of the Commonwealth on 21 March 1990. It modifies certain enactments relating to the Commonwealth Institute, the services, visiting forces and shipping. (See Part Three: I. A. 1., above.)

The War Crimes Act (1991 c. 13) confers jurisdiction on United Kingdom courts in respect of certain grave violations of the laws and customs of war committed in German-held territory during the Second World War. (See Parts Eight: II. D. and Eleven: II. D., above.)

[1] Compiled by C. A. Hopkins.

TABLE OF CASES[1]

[1] The figures in heavier type indicate the pages on which cases are reviewed.

INDEX